Worldmark Encyclopedia of Cultures and Daily Life

Worldmark Encyclopedia of
Cultures and Daily Life

VOLUME 1 Africa
Second Edition

Editors

Timothy L. Gall and Jeneen Hobby

GALE
CENGAGE Learning

Detroit • New York • San Francisco • New Haven, Conn • Waterville, Maine • London

Worldmark Encyclopedia of Cultures and Daily Life, Second Edition

Editors: Timothy L. Gall and Jeneen Hobby

Product Management: Julia Furtaw and Carol Nagel

Manufacturing: Rita Wimberley

Gale
27500 Drake Rd.
Farmington Hills, MI 48331-3535

ISBN 978-1-4144-4882-4 (set)
ISBN 978-1-4144-4883-1 (vol. 1)
ISBN 978-1-4144-4890-9 (vol. 2)
ISBN 978-1-4144-4891-6 (vol. 3)
ISBN 978-1-4144-4892-3 (vol. 4)
ISBN 978-1-4144-6430-5 (vol. 5)

ISSN 0196-2809

For product information and technology assistance, contact us at Gale Customer Support, 1-800-877-4253.
For permission to use material from this text or product, submit all requests online at www.cengage.com/permissions.
Further permissions questions can be emailed to permissionrequest@cengage.com

This publication is a creative work fully protected by all applicable copyright laws, as well as by misappropriation, trade secret, unfair competition, and other applicable laws. The authors and editors of this work have added value to the underlying factual material herein through one or more of the following: unique and original selection, coordination, expression, arrangement, and classification of the information.

While every effort has been made to ensure the reliability of the information presented in this publication, Gale, a part of Cengage Learning, does not guarantee the accuracy of the data contained herein. Gale accepts no payment for listing; and inclusion in the publication of any organization, agency, institution, publication, service, or individual does not imply endorsement of the editors or publisher. Errors brought to the attention of the publisher and verified to the satisfaction of the publisher will be corrected in future editions.

EDITORIAL DATA PRIVACY POLICY: Does this product contain information about you as an individual? If so, for more information about our editorial data privacy policies, please see our Privacy Statement at www.gale.cengage.com.

Library of Congress Cataloging-in-Publication Data

Worldmark encyclopedia of cultures and daily life / Timothy L. Gall, editor. -- 2nd ed.
    p. cm.
  Includes bibliographical references and index.
  ISBN 978-1-4144-4882-4 (set) -- ISBN 978-1-4144-4883-1 (vol. 1) -- ISBN 978-1-4144-4890-9 (vol. 2) -- ISBN 978-1-4144-4891-6 (vol. 3) -- ISBN 978-1-4144-4892-3 (vol. 4) -- ISBN 978-1-4144-6430-5 (vol. 5)
  1. Ethnology--Encyclopedias, Juvenile. 2. Manners and customs--Encyclopedias, Juvenile. [1. Ethnology--Encyclopedias. 2. Manners and customs--Encyclopedias.] I. Gall, Timothy L. II. Title: Encyclopedia of cultures and daily life.
  GN333.W67 2009
  305.8003--dc22
                                           2009004744

This title is also available as an e-book.
ISBN: 978-1-4144-4893-0
Contact your Gale sales representative for ordering information.

Printed in Mexico
4 5 6 7 13 12 11

CONTENTS

Contents

JUSTIN CORFIELD. Department of History, Geelong Grammar School.

DIANNE K. DAEG DE MOTT. Researcher/Writer, Tucson, Arizona.

CATHARIN DALPINO. Department of Asian Studies, Georgetown University

MICHAEL DE JONGH. Professor, Department of Anthropology, University of South Africa.

GEORGI DERLUGUIAN. Senior Fellow, Ph.D., U. S. Institute of Peace.

CHRISTINE DRAKE. Department of Political Science and Geography, Old Dominion University.

ARTURO DUARTE. Guatemalan Mission to the OAS.

CALEB DUBE. Department of Anthropology, Northwestern University.

BRIAN DU TOIT. Professor, Department of Anthropology, University of Florida.

LEAH ERMARTH. Worldspace Foundation, Washington, DC.

NANCY J. FAIRLEY. Associate Professor of Anthropology, Department of Anthropology/Sociology, Davidson College.

GREGORY A. FINNEGAN, Ph.D. Tozzer Library, Harvard University.

ALLEN J. FRANK, Ph.D.

DAVID P. GAMBLE. Professor Emeritus, Department of Anthropology, San Francisco State University.

FREDERICK GAMST. Professor Emeritus, Department of Anthropology, University of Massachusetts, Harbor Campus.

PAULA GARB. Associate Director of Global Peace and Conflict Studies and Adjunct Professor of Social Ecology, University of California, Irvine.

HAROLD GASKI. Associate Professor of Sami Literature, School of Languages and Literature, University of Tromsø.

STEPHEN J. GENDZIER.

FLORENCE GERDEL.

ANTHONY P. GLASCOCK. Professor of Anthropology; Department of Anthropology, Psychology, and Sociology; Drexel University.

LUIS GONZALEZ. Researcher/Writer, River Edge, New Jersey.

JENNIFER GRAHAM. Researcher/Writer, Sydney, Australia.

MARIE-CÉCILE GROELSEMA. Doctoral candidate, Comparative Literature, Indiana University.

ROBERT GROELSEMA. MPIA and doctoral candidate, Political Science, Indiana University.

MARIA GROSZ-NGATÉ. Visiting Assistant Professor, Department of Anthropology, Northwestern University.

ELLEN GRUENBAUM. Professor, School of Social Sciences, California State University, Fresno.

N. THOMAS HAKANSSON. University of Kentucky.

ROBERT HALASZ. Researcher/Writer, New York, New York.

MARC HANREZ. Professor, Department of French and Italian, University of Wisconsin-Madison.

ANWAR UL HAQ. Central Asian Studies Department, Indiana University.

LIAM HARTE. Department of Philosophy, Loyola University, Chicago.

FR. VASILE HATEGAN. Author, Romanian Culture in America.

BRUCE HEILMAN. Doctoral candidate, Department of Political Science, Indiana University.

JIM HENRY. Researcher/Writer, Cleveland, Ohio.

BARRY HEWLETT. Department of Anthropology, Washington State University.

SUSAN F. HIRSCH. Department of Anthropology, Wesleyan University.

MARIDA HOLLOS. Department of Anthropology, Brown University.

HALYNA HOLUBEC. Researcher/Writer, Cleveland, Ohio.

YVONNE HOOSAVA. Legal Researcher and Cultural Preservation Officer, Hopi Tribal Council.

HUIQIN HUANG, Ph.D. Center for East Asia Studies, University of Montreal.

MARCEL IONESCU-HEROIU. Teaching Assistant, Cornell University

ASAFA JALATA. Assistant Professor of Sociology and African and African American Studies, Department of Sociology, The University of Tennessee, Knoxville.

STEPHEN F. JONES. Russian Department, Mount Holyoke College.

THOMAS JOVANOVSKI, PH.D. Lorain County Community College.

A. KEN JULES. Minister Plenipotentiary and Deputy Head of Mission, Embassy of St. Kitts and Nevis.

GENEROSA KAGARUKI-KAKOTI. Economist, Department of Urban and Rural Planning, College of Lands and Architectural Studies, Dar es Salaam, Tanzania.

EZEKIEL KALIPENI. Department of Geography, University of Illinois at Urbana-Champaign.

DON KAVANAUGH. Program Director, Lake of the Woods Ojibwa Cultural Centre.

SUSAN M. KENYON. Associate Professor of Anthropology, Department of History and Anthropology, Butler University.

ALLA GOLOVINA KHADKA. PhD Candidate, University of Pittsburgh

MARIA GROSZ-NGATÉ. Visiting Associate Director of the African Studies Program, Indiana University.

ADEL ISKANDAR. Center for Contemporary Arab Studies, Georgetown University

ASAFA JALATA. Professor of Sociology, The University of Tennessee, Knoxville.

THOMAS JOVANOVSKI, Ph.D. Lorain County Community College.

EZEKIEL KALIPENI. Associate Professor of Geography, University of Illinois at Urbana-Champaign.

SUSAN M. KENYON. Associate Professor of Anthropology, Butler University.

WELILE KHUZWAYO. Department of Anthropology, University of South Africa.

PHILIP L. KILBRIDE. Professor of Anthropology, Mary Hale Chase Chair in the Social Sciences, Department of Anthropology, Bryn Mawr College.

RICHARD O. KISIARA. Doctoral candidate, Department of Anthropology, Washington University in St. Louis.

SARAH KLUMP. Center for Eurasian, Russian and East European Studies, Edmund A. Walsh School of Foreign Service, Georgetown University .

KAREN KNOWLES. Permanent Mission of Antigua and Barbuda to the United Nations.

MELISSA KERR. Eurasian, Russian, and East European Studies, Georgetown University.

IGOR KRUPNIK. Research Anthropologist, Department of Anthropology, Smithsonian Institution.

LEELO LASS. Secretary, Embassy of Estonia.

ROBERT LAUNAY. Professor, Department of Anthropology, Northwestern University.

BENJAMIN LAZARUS. Eurasian, Russian, and East European Studies, Georgetown University.

CHARLES LEBLANC. Professor and Director, Center for East Asia Studies, University of Montreal.

RONALD LEE. Author, Goddam Gypsy, An Autobiographical Novel.

PHILIP E. LEIS. Professor and Chair, Department of Anthropology, Brown University.

MARIA JUKIC LESKUR. Croatian Consulate, Cleveland, Ohio.

RICHARD A. LOBBAN, JR. Professor of Anthropology and African Studies, Department of Anthropology, Rhode Island College.

DERYCK O. LODRICK. Visiting Scholar, Center for South Asian Studies, University of California, Berkeley.

NEIL LURSSEN. Intro Communications Inc.

GREGORIO C. MARTIN. Modern Language Department, Duquesne University.

HOWARD J. MARTIN. Independent scholar.

HEITOR MARTINS. Professor, Department of Spanish and Portuguese, Indiana University.

ADELINE MASQUELIER. Assistant Professor, Department of Anthropology, Tulane University.

DOLINA MILLAR.

EDITH MIRANTE. Project Maje.

ROBERT W. MONTGOMERY, Ph.D. Indiana University.

THOMAS D. MORIN. Associate Professor of Hispanic Studies, Department of Modern and Classical Literatures and Languages, University of Rhode Island.

CHARLES MORRILL. Doctoral candidate, Indiana University.

CAROL A. MORTLAND. Crate's Point.

FRANCIS A. MOYER. Director, North Carolina Japan Center, North Carolina State University.

MARIE C. MOYER.

NYAGA MWANIKI. Assistant Professor, Department of Anthropology and Sociology, Western Carolina University.

KENNETH NILSON. Celtic Studies Department, Harvard University.

MARTIN NJOROGE. PhD. SRF/UPenn Postdoctoral Fellow, Graduate School of Education, University of Pennsylvania.

JANE E. ORMROD. Graduate Student, History, University of Chicago.

JUANITA PAHDOPONY. Carl Perkins Program Director, Comanche Tribe of Oklahoma.

TINO PALOTTA. Syracuse University.

ROHAYATI PASENG.

PATRICIA PITCHON. Researcher/Writer, London, England.

STEPHANIE PLATZ. Program Officer, Program on Peace and International Cooperation, The John D. and Catherine T. MacArthur Foundation.

MIHAELA POIATA. Graduate Student, School of Journalism and Mass Communication, University of North Carolina at Chapel Hill.

MANSAH PRAH. Dean, Faculty of Social Sciences, University of Cape Coast, Ghana.

LEOPOLDINA PRUT-PREGELJ. Author, Historical Dictionary of Slovenia.

J. RACKAUSKAS. Director, Lithuanian Research and Studies Center, Chicago.

J. RAKOVICH. Byelorussian-American Cultural Center, Strongsville, Ohio.

HANTA V. RALAY. Promotions, Inc., Montgomery Village, Maryland.

SUSAN J. RASMUSSEN. Associate Professor, Department of Anthropology, University of Houston.

RONALD REMINICK. Associate Professor of Anthropology, Cleveland State University.

BRUCE D. ROBERTS. Associate Professor of Anthropology, Department of Anthropology & Earth Science, Minnesota State University, Moorhead.

LAUREL L. ROSE. Philosophy Department, Carnegie-Mellon University.

ROBERT ROTENBERG. Professor of Anthropology, International Studies Program, DePaul University.

CAROLINE SAHLEY, Ph.D. Researcher/Writer, Cleveland, Ohio.

VERONICA SALLES-REESE. Associate Professor, Department of Spanish and Portuguese, Georgetown University.

MAIRA SARYBAEVA. Kazakh-American Studies Center, University of Kentucky.

DEBRA L. SCHINDLER. Institute of Arctic Studies, Dartmouth College.

KYOKO SELDEN, Ph.D. Department of Asian Studies, Cornell University.

ELIZABETH SERLEMITSOS. Chief Advisor, National AIDS Council, Zambia.

ENAYATULLAH SHAHRANI. Central Asian Studies Department, Indiana University.

ROBERT SHANAFELT. Department of Sociology & Anthropology, Georgia Southern University.

TUULIKKI SINKS. Teaching Specialist for Finnish, Department of German, Scandinavian, and Dutch, University of Minnesota.

JAN SJÅVIK. Professor, Scandinavian Studies, University of Washington.

MAGDA SOBALVARRO. Press and Cultural Affairs Director, Embassy of Nicaragua.

PAMELA SODHY. History Department, Georgetown University

MICHAEL STAINTON. Researcher, Joint Center for Asia Pacific Studies, York University.

RIANA STEYN. Department of Anthropology, University of South Africa.

PAUL STOLLER. Professor, Department of Anthropology, West Chester University.

CRAIG STRASHOFER. Researcher/Writer, Cleveland, Ohio.

SANDRA B. STRAUBHAAR. Assistant Professor, Nordic Studies, Department of Germanic and Slavic Languages, Brigham Young University.

DAVID STRAUB. Masters Program in Central Eurasian Studies, Indiana University.

VUM SON SUANTAK. Author, Zo History.

MURAT TAISHIBAEV. Kazakh-American Studies Center, University of Kentucky.

CHRISTOPHER C. TAYLOR. Associate Professor, Anthropology Department, University of Alabama, Birmingham.

FATIMA TLISOVA. Kennedy School at Harvard.

EDDIE TSO. Office of Language and Culture, Navajo Division of Education.

DAVID TYSON. Foreign Broadcast Information Service, Washington, D.C.

NICOLAAS G. W. UNLANDT. Assistant Professor of French, Department of French and Italian, Brigham Young University.

GORDON URQUHART. Professor, Department of Economics and Business, Cornell College.

CHRISTOPHER J. VAN VUUREN. Associate Professor, Department of Anthropology, University of South Africa.

DALIA VENTURA-ALCALAY. Journalist, London, England.

CATHERINE VEREECKE. Assistant Director, Center for African Studies, University of Florida.

CAMILA VERGARA. Journalist, New York.

KORA BATTIG VON WITTLESBACH. Department of Romance Studies at Cornell.

GREGORY T. WALKER. Associate Director, Office of International Affairs, Duquesne University.

GERHARD WEISS. Department of German, Scandinavian, and Dutch, University of Minnesota.

PATSY WEST. Director, The Seminole/Miccosukee Photographic Archive.

WALTER WHIPPLE. Associate Professor of Polish, Germanic and Slavic Languages, Brigham Young University.

ROSALIE WIEDER. Researcher/Writer, Cleveland, Ohio.

JEFFREY WILLIAMS. Professor and Chair, Department of Sociology, Anthropology, & Social Work, Texas Tech University.

KOSTAS YIAVIS. Lecturer in Modern Greek, Cornell University.

GUANG-HONG YU. Associate Research Fellow, Institute of Ethnology, Academia Sinica.

RUSSELL ZANCA. Associate Professor of Anthropology, Northeastern Illinois University.

COUNTRY INDEX

PREFACE

The Worldmark Encyclopedia of Cultures and Daily Life, Second Edition, contains over 500 articles exploring the ways of life of peoples of the world. Arranged in five volumes by geographic regions—*Africa, Americas, Asia & Oceania* (two volumes), and *Europe*—the volumes of this encyclopedia parallel the organization of its sister set, the *Worldmark Encyclopedia of the Nations.* Whereas the primary purpose of *Nations* is to provide information on the world's nation states, this encyclopedia focuses on the traditions, living conditions, and personalities of many of the world's culture groups. Entries emphasize how people live today, rather than how they lived in the past.

Defining groups for inclusion was not an easy task. Cultural identity can be shaped by such factors as geography, nationality, ethnicity, race, language, and religion. Many people, in fact, legitimately belong in two or more classifications, each as valid as the other. For example, the citizens of the United States all share traits that make them distinctly American. However, few would deny the need for separate articles on Native Americans or African Americans. Even the category Native American denies the individuality of separate tribes like the Navajo and Paiute. Consequently, this encyclopedia contains an article on the Americans as well as separate articles on the Native Americans and the Navajo. Closely related articles such as these are cross-referenced to each other to help provide a more complete picture of the group being profiled. Included in this encyclopedia are articles on groups as large as the Han of China, with over one billion members, and as small as the Jews of Cochin, with only a few dozen members. Unfortunately, although the vast majority of the world's peoples are represented in this encyclopedia, time and space constraints prevented many important groups from being included in the first edition. Twenty-three new groups have been added to this second edition, and the editors look forward to including many more culture groups in future editions of this work.

New entries include in Americas: Sudanese Americans ("Lost Boys"); in Africa: Afar, Berbers, Ewe, Guineas of Guinea Bissau, Jola, Maldivians, San (Bushmen), Sao Tomeans, and Twa; in Asia and Oceania: Brunei, Coptic Christians, Kashmiris, Moro, Rajasthanis, and Timorese; and in Europe: Alsatians, Kosovars, Maltese, Montenegrins, Serbs, Tyrolese, and Vlachs.

Over 175 contributors and reviewers participated in the creation of this encyclopedia. Drawn from universities, consulates, and the press, their in-depth knowledge and first-hand experience of the profiled groups added significantly to the content of the articles. A complete listing of the contributors and reviewers together with their affiliations appears in the front of each volume.

ORGANIZATION

Each volume begins with an introduction that traces the cultural developments of the region from prehistoric times to the present. Following the introduction are articles devoted to the peoples of the region. Within each volume the articles are ar-

ranged alphabetically. A comprehensive table cross referencing the articles by country follows the table of contents to each volume.

The individual articles are of two types. The vast majority follow a standard 20-heading outline explained in more detail below. This structure allows for easy comparison of the articles and enhances the accessibility of the information. A smaller number do not follow the 20-heading format, but rather present simply an overview of the group. This structure is used when the primary purpose of an article is to supplement a fully rubriced article appearing elsewhere in the set.

Whenever appropriate, articles begin with the **pronunciation** of the group's name, a listing of **alternate names** by which the group is known, the group's **location** in the world, its **population,** the **languages** spoken, the **religions** practiced, and a listing of **related articles** in the five volumes of this encyclopedia. Most articles are illustrated with a map showing the primary location of the group and photographs of the people being profiled. The twenty standard headings by which most articles are organized are presented below.

INTRODUCTION: A description of the group's historical origins provides a useful background for understanding its contemporary affairs. Information relating to migration helps explain how the group arrived at its present location. Political conditions and governmental structure(s) that typically affect members of the profiled ethnic group are also discussed.

LOCATION AND HOMELAND: The population size of the group is listed. This information may include official census data from various countries and/or estimates. Information on the size of a group's population located outside the traditional homeland may also be included, especially for certain groups with large diaspora populations. A description of the homeland includes information on location, topography, and climate.

LANGUAGE: Each article lists the name(s) of the primary language(s) spoken by members. Descriptions of linguistic origins, grammar, and similarities to other languages may also be included. Examples of common words, phrases, and proverbs are listed for many of the profiled groups, and some include examples of common personal names and forms of address.

FOLKLORE: Common themes, settings, and characters in the profiled group's traditional oral and/or literary mythology are highlighted. Many entries include a short excerpt or synopsis of one of the group's most noteworthy myths, fables, or legends. Some entries describe the accomplishments of famous heroes and heroines or other prominent historical figures.

RELIGION: The origins of traditional religious beliefs are profiled. Contemporary religious beliefs, customs, and practices are also discussed. Some groups may be closely associated with one particular faith (especially if religious and ethnic identification are interlinked), while others may have members of diverse faiths.

MAJOR HOLIDAYS: Celebrations and commemorations typically recognized by the group's members are described. These holidays commonly fall into two categories: secular and religious. Secular holidays often include an independence day and/or other days of observance recognizing important dates in history that affected the group as a whole. Religious holidays are typically the same as those honored by other peoples of the same faith. Some secular and religious holidays are linked to the lunar cycle or to the change of seasons. Some articles describe unique customs practiced by members of the group on certain holidays.

RITES OF PASSAGE: Formal and informal episodic events that mark an individual's procession through the stages of life are profiled. These events typically involve rituals, ceremonies, observances, and procedures associated with birth, childhood, the coming of age, adulthood, and death. The impact of twenty-first century communications and global media on customs are addressed here.

INTERPERSONAL RELATIONS: Information on greetings, body language, gestures, visiting customs, and dating practices is included. The extent of formality to which members of a certain ethnic group treat others is also addressed, as some groups may adhere to customs governing interpersonal relationships more/less strictly than others.

LIVING CONDITIONS: General health conditions typical of the group's members are cited. Such information includes life expectancy, the prevalence of various diseases, and access to medical care. Information on urbanization, housing, and access to utilities is also included. Transportation methods typically utilized by the group's members are also discussed.

FAMILY LIFE: The size and composition of the family unit is profiled. Gender roles common to the group are also discussed, including the division of rights and responsibilities relegated to male and female group members. The roles that children, adults, and the elderly have within the group as a whole may also be addressed.

CLOTHING: Many entries include descriptive information (size, shape, color, fabric, etc.) regarding traditional clothing (or a national costume), and indicate the frequency of its use in contemporary life. A description of clothing typically worn in the present is also provided, especially if traditional clothing is no longer the usual form of dress. Distinctions between formal, informal, and work clothes are made in many articles, along with clothing differences between men, women, and children.

FOOD: Descriptions of items commonly consumed by members of the group are listed. The frequency and occasion for meals is also described, as are any unique customs regarding eating and drinking, special utensils and furniture, and the role of food and beverages in ritual ceremonies. Many entries include a sample recipe for a favorite dish.

EDUCATION: The structure of formal education in the country or countries of residence is discussed, including information on primary, secondary, and higher education. For some groups, the role of informal education is also highlighted. Some articles may include information regarding the relevance and importance of education among the group as a whole, along with parental expectations for children. In addition, literacy levels are described where appropriate.

CULTURAL HERITAGE: Since many groups express their sense of identity through art, music, literature, and dance, a description of prominent styles is included. Some articles also cite the contributions of famous individual artists, writers, and musicians.

WORK: The type of labor that typically engages members of the profiled group is discussed. For some groups, the formal wage economy is the primary source of earnings, but for other groups, informal agriculture or trade may be the usual way to earn a living. Working conditions are also highlighted.

SPORTS: Popular sports that children and adults play are listed, as are typical spectator sports. Some articles include a description and/or rules to a unique type of sport or game.

ENTERTAINMENT AND RECREATION: Listed activities that people enjoy in their spare time may include carrying out either structured pastimes (such as public musical and dance performances) or informal get-togethers (such as meeting for conversation). The role of popular culture, movies, theater, and television in everyday life is also discussed.

FOLK ARTS, CRAFTS, AND HOBBIES: Entries describe arts and crafts commonly fabricated according to traditional methods, materials, and style. Such objects may often have a functional utility for everyday tasks.

SOCIAL PROBLEMS: Internal and external issues that confront members of the profiled group are described. Such concerns often deal with fundamental problems like war, famine, disease, and poverty. A lack of human rights, civil rights, and political freedom may also adversely affect a group as a whole. Other problems may include crime, unemployment, substance abuse, and domestic violence.

GENDER ISSUES: New to this edition is a section focusing on women's issues including cultural attitudes, discrimination, status, health, sexual issues, education, and work and employment. Some discussion on the group's attitudes toward homosexuality may be included in this section, where relevant.

BIBLIOGRAPHY: References cited include works used to compile the article, as well as benchmark publications often recognized as authoritative by scholars. Citations for materials published in foreign languages are frequently listed when there are few existing sources available in English.

A glossary of terms and a comprehensive index appears at the end of each volume.

ACKNOWLEDGMENTS

The editors express appreciation to the members of the Cengage Gale staff who were involved in a number of ways at various stages of development of the *Worldmark Encyclopedia of Cultures and Daily Life, Second Edition:* Christine Nasso, Barbara Beach, and Leah Knight, who helped the initial concept of the work take form; and Larry Baker and Allison McNeill, who supported the editorial development of the profiles for the first edition. Carol Nagel and Ellen McGeagh were instrumental in the planning and scheduling of the second edition of this work. Anne Marie Hacht selected the photo illustrations and provided valuable review of the entries. Marybeth Trimper,

Evi Seoud, and Shanna Heilveil oversaw the printing and binding process.

In addition, the editors acknowledge with warm gratitude the contributions of the staff of Eastword Publications—Debby Baron, Dan Lucas, Brian Rajewski, Kira Silverbird, Maggie Lyall, Karen Seyboldt, Tajana G. Roehl, Janet Fenn, Cheryl Montagna, Jeneen Hobby, Dan Mehling, Karen Ellicott, Alexander Barnes, and Elizabeth Gall—who managed interactions with contributors; edited, organized, reviewed, and indexed the articles; and turned the manuscripts into the illustrated typeset pages of these five volumes.

SUGGESTIONS ARE WELCOME: Maintenance of a work the size and scope of *Worldmark Encyclopedia of Cultures and Daily Life, Second Edition, is a daunting undertaking; we appreciate any suggestions that* will enhance future editions. Please send comments to:

Editor
*Worldmark Encyclopedia
of Cultures and Daily Life*
Cengage Gale
27500 Drake Rd.
Farmington Hills, MI 48331-3535

INTRODUCTION

by
James L. Newman

Counts vary, but a conservative one for Africa would enumerate at least 1500 distinct ethnolinguistic groups, by which is meant peoples who speak recognizably different languages and identify themselves as having their own special cultural historical traditions. Since current evidence suggests humanity took its first steps in Africa, an account of how this diversity came to be could begin over four million years ago. Space, however, prohibits such a long temporal journey, and thus our starting point will be between 10,000 and 5000 years ago when the first glimmers of today's languages can be detected. Despite their large numbers, all the indigenous languages can be placed within four classifications that are termed Khoisan, Nilosaharan, Afroasiatic, and Niger Congo. Each arose within a particular regional setting, and over time went through branchings and re-branchings, often in association with migrations, that altered population distributions in substantial ways. Fueling these migrations were changes in food economies, the development of new technologies, especially iron-making, opportunities for trade, and sometimes religious affiliation.

Joining diversity and fluidity as hallmarks of Africa's peoples is complexity. Most have arisen from multiple influences, the forces and intensities of which have varied with time and place. And while some identities have hundreds of years of history to them, others have come about more recently. European colonialism in the nineteenth and twentieth centuries was especially important to identity formation, and the colonial era was when many of these identities crystallized. Administrators of colonies needed boundaries and they drew them, usually according to what they called tribes, which were thought to be entities rooted in some unchanging past. About this the colonialists were clearly mistaken. Nevertheless the boundaries that were drawn and the names that were employed became realities that continue to define the peoples of Africa to this day. We, therefore, cannot avoid using them in our portrayal. In a few instances, errors often involving names with derogatory connotations that were given to a group by others, have been corrected. In those instances where the changes made are generally agreed upon, the old name is noted in parentheses.

KHOISAN

The Khoisan languages are best known for their clicks, which are implosively as opposed to explosively formed consonant sounds. The prototype of this language appears to have originated somewhere south of the Zambezi River, and then branched into others that spread throughout the region as well as into the savanna lands of eastern Africa, perhaps to as far north as the Tana River in Kenya. The peoples speaking Khoisan languages gathered, hunted, and fished for their sustenance, and fashioned tools out of stone, wood, and bone. They lived in bands that moved seasonally in response to changes in food availability and were comprised of 30–50 individuals.

Around 2000 years ago, groups residing near the Zambezi River in the vicinity of today's border between Zambia and Zimbabwe acquired sheep and goats and with them they migrated southward. Some eventually settled the rich grazing lands between the Vaal and Orange Rivers in South Africa, while others chose the equally productive lands in and around the Cape of Good Hope peninsula. Still others occupied the less fertile Karoo bush lands. Organized into loosely knit kinship alliances, these herders would become known as Khoikhoi (formerly Hottentot), while those who continued as hunters and gatherers are now referred to as San (Bushmen).

Both Khoikhoi and San were soon challenged by others with superior technologies. In the first centuries AD, Iron Age Bantu-speaking farmers began arriving from the north, claiming most of the better agricultural lands of the Transvaal and Natal. Then in the 1650s, Europeans took up residence at the Cape, from where they expanded inland, staking out huge land claims to support the pastoral economy they had developed. Displacement, conquest, and disease all took their tolls on the Khoisan peoples, and today only a few groups in southern Africa, such as the well known !kung San of Botswana, survive as distinct cultures. In eastern Africa, the Sandawe and Hadza of Tanzania attest to the once widespread Khoisan presence there.

NILOSAHARAN

Ten thousand years ago, the climate of northern Africa was much wetter than it is today and the area we now call the Sahara Desert contained numerous large lakes and river valleys. The rich and varied aquatic resources these provided supported growing populations, that included the ancestors of Nilosaharan speakers. During the course of the next several thousand years, their economies were enriched by the addition of livestock, especially cattle, and then shortly thereafter the cultivation of sorghums and millets. This allowed them to expand southward into the savannas bordering the equatorial rainforest, the region of Central Sudanic language family formation. Nilosaharans also occupied the grasslands and marshlands surrounding the White Nile River valley of the southern Sudan, where the Nilotic peoples, including the Nuer and Dinka, came into being. Cattle had high economic and cultural value, and competition between groups for grazing grounds and water led some groups to move southward and into the savannas of eastern Africa. The migrations began as early as 500 BC and continued into the nineteenth century, giving rise to, among others, the Samburu, Masaai, Karamajong, and Luo, and adding to the composite that would become the Tutsi.

Other Nilosaharan migrations produced today's Nubians of the Nile Valley between Aswan and Khartoum. These migrations took place in several stages during the first centuries AD, with earlier residents being either absorbed or displaced.

Another series of Nilosaharan migrations led to the formation of the Kanuri peoples of the Lake Chad region, who founded the state of Kanem-Bornu about AD 1000. Using profits derived from trans-Saharan trade, the state remained a regional power for more than 800 years

Within and around the Sahara, however, the Nilosaharans lost ground. From the east came Afroasiatic-speaking peoples, while those of Niger Congo affiliation encroached from the west. Notable survivors include the Songhai along the bend of the Niger River, who formed the core of the extensive 16th century state of the same name, and the Tibbu of the Tibesti Mountains in Chad.

AFROASIATIC

The Afroasiatic languages most likely originated in northeastern Africa somewhere between the Red Sea and Nile River. From there they have spread across a roughly crescent-shaped area extending from Kenya northward, and then westward to Morocco. One of the languages was Ancient Egyptian as seen in the hieroglyphics left behind by Pharonic Egypt. Already a highly populated area during Stone Age times, densities along the banks of the Nile River north of Aswan rose rapidly after the adoption of agricultural methods of food production some 7000 years ago. These were introduced from sources in the adjacent Levant, and included wheat and barley, as well as cattle, sheep, goats, and pigs. About 2000 years later, the many agricultural villages that dotted the landscape were politically united under the First Dynasty, beginning a span of Pharonic rule, culture, and technological achievements that would last nearly 3000 years.

South of Egypt was Nubia, an enigmatic land about which far less is known. It clearly absorbed many influences from the north and was raided regularly by Egyptians for its gold and other precious commodities. This sometimes produced considerable dislocation, including the nearly complete abandonment of sections of land from time to time. A high point was reached early in the second millennium BC with the founding of the Kingdom of Kush centered on the Dongola region of the Nile between the third and fourth cataracts. Who the founders were is unclear. The surviving inscriptions are in Egyptian, but it is unlikely that this was the everyday language of the people. Given the location, though, some branch of Afroasiatic seems most probable.

Farther south still, Ethiopia became home to the Cushitic languages. A central branch emerged in the highlands among grain cultivators who domesticated teff (a cereal grass) and finger millet (eleusine). Between 4000 and 3500 years ago, Semitic speaking immigrants from south Arabia started settling among them. One result was the introduction of Judaism, which came to distinguish people who today call themselves Beta Israel (Falasha). A broader cultural synthesis also took place and produced the peoples who founded the kingdom of Aksum. These were the ancestors of the Tigrinya, who, during the first half of the first millennium AD, built one of the world's great powers. They did so by controlling the eastern end of a lucrative Indian Ocean trade in precious commodities that included gold, ivory, and, so it seems, the biblically famous frankincense and myrrh. At its height, Aksum's territorial control extended from the confluence of the White and Blue Niles across the Red Sea to south Arabia. In the fourth century AD, the Monophysite version of Christianity became Aksum's official religion, thus making Ethiopia one of the world's oldest and longest enduring Christian strongholds. The kingdom began to decline in the sixth century, but it left a tradition that had spread throughout the highlands and would be revived by succeeding dynasties, the last being that formed in the nineteenth century under Amhara rule.

Other branches of Cushitic developed in the lowlands among herding peoples such as the Beja, Somali, and Oromo. Beginning in the eighth century, they took Islam as their predominant religion, setting in motion a regional contest between the two universal faiths that has persisted to this day.

The area west from the Egyptian Nile to the Atlantic coast became home to a multitude of Berber-speaking groups. They were initially grain farmers and herders of sheep and goats who found the fertile valleys and slopes of the Atlas Mountains a conducive environment. Others, however, developed economies more dependent on cattle and camels, the latter of which allowed them to extend into desert oases, often at the expense of pre-existing Nilosaharan communities. The most expansionary were the Tuareg, who established themselves in the Ahaggar Mountains and Aïr Highlands. From these bases, they controlled many trans-Saharan trade routes and also regularly raided settled communities south of the desert for slaves and other goods.

The impetus of Afroasiatic expansion carried some groups beyond the desert and into northern Nigeria. These would form into the Chadic peoples, with the Hausa attaining predominance. They lived in nucleated villages, with the most successful growing into fortified towns that exercised control over the surrounding countryside in a feudal-like arrangement of lords and their dependents. The largest towns were Gobir, Katsina, Zaria, and Kano, which by the thirteenth century had become major centers of both intra- and interregional trade. Each had its own area of influence and remained independent of the others. Hausa specialties were trade and skilled craft work, especially in leather, metals, and textiles. Many Hausa migrated beyond their homeland, seeking opportunities to practice their skills.

Arabic belongs to the Semitic family of Afroasiatic, and its speakers first entered Africa in large numbers with the Islamic armies that conquered the northern coastal region of the continent in the seventh century. Attacks were focused on the major cities, such as Alexandria, Cyrene, and Carthage, that had become largely Christian during Roman and Byzantine times. By this time, both empires were crumbling and the Islamic armies met little organized resistance. The soldiers were followed by holy men who went inland making converts among the Berbers. Later, other Muslim Arabs entered as nomads (Bedouin), with the major migrations occurring between the ninth and eleventh centuries. These appear to have been prompted by worsening drought conditions that had hit the Arabian peninsula. Considered by civil officials as a destabilizing factor to local economies, the nomads were forced to keep moving westward. As they did so, the Berbers lost ground, except in the mountains, where they remained dominant. In the lowlands of Morocco, an Arab/Berbers synthesis took place, creating the Maures. From here they moved southward to as far as the Senegal River valley. Also losing ground were followers of Christianity, who all but disappeared from northern Africa. The Monophysite Copts of Egypt were the exception. Though

Arabic-speaking, they resisted Islam and have continued as an important minority even to this day.

The creation of northern Africa as a region of Arab peoples dates from these events. In point of fact, however, the numbers of immigrant Arabs were never that great relative to Egyptians, Berbers, and others. Instead, many people consciously changed their identities. Arabic had become the language of political and economic opportunity and not to speak it would put one at a disadvantage. Similarly, adopting Islam was beneficial. It often was synonymous with being Arab and also linked a person to a wider and usually ascendant world of culture and commerce. The advantages continue attracting new adherents to Islam to this very day.

NIGER CONGO

The Niger Congo languages currently are more numerous and cover a larger area than all others combined. They have achieved this status as a result of migrations and subsequent divergences from a nuclear area north of the savanna/rain forest boundary in what is now Nigeria and Cameroon. A westward expansion took these peoples to the upper reaches of the Niger and Senegal rivers, where they developed agricultural systems based on fonio (a grass) and African rice. Here they seem to have encountered Nilosaharan communities, who they eventually displaced, except for the Songhai. They were proto-Mande speakers who in the late centuries BC created a series of small trading-based states based upon occupational specialties in farming, fishing, and livestock herding. The best known site is that of Jenne-jeno located within the agriculturally rich inland delta of the Niger River. It was part of a larger regional trading network that included manufactured items in stone, iron, and copper.

Jenne-jeno and others centers like it were the direct forerunners of a series of kingdoms and empires that would flourish within the region. The first that we know of was Ghana. Founded by speakers of the Soninke branch of Mande, it was already well established when described by a Muslim visitor near the end of the eighth century. Ghana grew to prominence by controlling trade in salt and gold. The salt came from mines in the western Sahara and was in demand throughout the salt-poor savanna and forest regions of western Africa. Gold, on the other hand, came from an area along the upper Senegal River known as Bambuk. It was traded across the Sahara following routes that had existed since Carthaginian and Roman times and was used by the Ghanaian royalty as symbols of their status. Accompanying gold across the Sahara were slaves, the demand for which rose following the Arab conquest of northern Africa. Used primarily as domestics and soldiers, they were valued both here and throughout southwestern Asia.

Ghana's successor was Mali. Founded by another Mande people, the Malinke, Mali reached its apogee during the middle of the fourteenth century. Prior to this Mali's leaders had become Muslims, and they made centers such as Timbuktu and Djenne famous throughout the Islamic world for their mosques, holy men, and scholars. From these and other towns, merchants traveled throughout western Africa. Many settled permanently beyond Mali's borders, creating in the process groups that would be known as Wangara, Dyula, Marka, and Yarre.

An expansionary state, at its height Mali stretched from the headwaters of the Senegal and Niger rivers, eastward to beyond the bend of the Niger, and northward into the Sahara. As a result of this great size, it incorporated many non-Malinke, which toward the end of the fourteenth century resulted in the eruption of serious factionalism. Unable to control these forces, Mali lost provinces one by one, until it finally disappeared in the sixteenth century. Taking its place as the preeminent regional power was Songhai, mentioned earlier. Its wealth and Islamic fame were even greater than Mali's, but it too was soon plagued by internal factionalism. Then in the 1590s, Songhai was invaded by forces of the Sultan of Morocco, who was seeking to control the sources of gold supplying the trans-Saharan trade. The Songhai armies were routed, despite their superior numbers. Songhai arrows and spears were no match for the Moroccan's harquebuses (early type of firearm) and muskets. With the army gone as protection, the Songhai state collapsed.

There was no immediate successor to Songhai. Instead, this portion of Africa would now be characterized by smaller, more ethnically homogeneous polities. One was Takrur, which developed along the lower and middle reaches of the Senegal River valley. It was founded by Tukolor-speakers of the Atlantic branch of Niger Congo sometime during the latter half of the first millennium AD, when it also became the first polity south of the Sahara to embrace Islam as the state religion. This served as a powerful force to preserving its unity, as did ethnic homogeneity resulting from a lack of imperial ambitions.

From Tukolor origins sprang the Fulbe or Fulani. They had adopted a cattle-oriented way of life, probably as a result of contacts with Berber-speaking nomads who had reached the area of the Senegal River valley sometime prior to AD 1000. Initially a part of Takrur, the Fulbe began moving out in search of grazing lands to support their growing herds. One route took them into the Fouta Djallon highlands, where they settled among resident Dyalonke farmers, providing livestock products in exchange for grazing rights and agricultural produce. Another route taken was along the Niger River, which brought them into the orbits of Mali and Songhai. Here they also established exchange relationships with farmers, a pattern that would be repeated many times over as they continued moving eastward, eventually reaching Hausaland. While on their moves, some Fulbe took up residence in towns and adopted Islam. They then converted the herders and the Hausa as well, it seems. The two would form a powerful alliance and help spread Islam throughout the savanna zone of western Africa during the eighteenth and nineteenth centuries.

Other important local polities that had formed early on and became locally important after the fall of Songhai were those of the Mossi, Mampruli, Dagomba, Woloff, and Serer. Each has served as a source of continuing ethnic identity.

Another area of Niger Congo consolidation and expansion took place in the savanna/rain forests borderlands near the confluence of the Niger and Benue rivers. Between 5000 and 4000 years ago, the people living here began to grow yams and oil palm to supplement gathering, hunting, and fishing. Population growth followed, leading to the formation of the Kwa and Benue Congo languages. Members of the Kwa family moved westward, eventually reaching the Bandama River, where a boundary with Mande speakers was formed. Once again under the impetus of trade, certain areas emerged as population centers. Several were close to the original Kwa hearth in Nigeria. One is represented by the archeological site of Igbo-Ukwu, located near the present city of Onitsha. It shows a relatively large population having existed by the ninth century AD, plus artifacts that came from as far away as the Mediterranean. From all accounts, this was the homeland of the Igbo (Ibo) peoples, who, over the course of the next centuries, would colonize much of the area of what is now southeastern Nigeria.

The present-day Yoruba trace their ancestry to Ife, a townlike settlement also dated to the late first millennium AD. It apparently developed at a highly strategic location that allowed Yoruba population numbers to grow and support the founding of other towns both to its north and south. That the Yoruba were highly prosperous during these times is evidenced by the large number of towns that served as centers for local kingdoms and by the quality products that were manufactured from ivory, bronze, copper, iron, and leather.

Roughly contemporaneous with Igbo-Ukwu and Ife was Benin, founded by Edo-speaking peoples. Unlike, the others, however, it grew to dominate surrounding settlements, creating a wider Benin state by early in the fifteenth century. With trade routes that reached the Hausa city states and even Songhai, Benin achieved a regional military and economic dominance that continued for several centuries to come.

Farther west, a fourth Kwa cluster developed in north central Ghana. By the eleventh century there is evidence of the existence of a substantial farming population that is thought to be associated with the origins of the Akan family of Kwa. They were connected by trade in gold and kola nuts to Ghana and Mali and this led them to expand southward into the rain forest seeking sources. By the sixteenth and seventeenth centuries a number of small, localized states had formed, but they were soon superseded in importance by Asante. Centered on Kumasi, the Asante developed a powerful kingdom whose expansion triggered the relocation of smaller groups throughout the region.

From the sixteenth through early nineteenth centuries, population developments throughout western Africa were influenced in many ways by the transatlantic slave trade. It began modestly enough with the Portuguese bartering for slaves along the Senegambia coast with the resident Woloff, Serer, and Malinke. A favorite holding point was Gorée Island. The Portuguese also traded with Akan merchants, using the fort they had built at Elmina for the storage of gold as a base of operation. The Portuguese attempted to interest Benin in supplying slaves, but its rulers showed little interest, preferring instead to keep captives for their own labor supply needs.

Demand began to accelerate toward the end of the sixteenth century, when the Dutch, French, British and others entered to supply the new plantation-based economies of the Caribbean and Brazil. It continued to grow during the seventeenth century and then reached its peak in the eighteenth century when on average 40,000 slaves were removed per year. A decline in the value of slaves due to a shift away from plantations in the Caribbean and rising abolitionist sentiments, particularly in Great Britain, caused the numbers to begin falling in the first decades of the nineteenth century and by mid-century the trade in slaves from western Africa was all but over.

Disagreements about the total number of Africans taken across the Atlantic as slaves continue to exist. It was certainly more than ten and maybe closer to fifteen million, with more than half having been obtained from sources in western Africa. The area that experienced the biggest loss by far ran from what is now the coast of Benin to Calbar, east of the Niger River delta. A secondary area was the Gold Coast. Somewhat less debatable are impacts of the slave trade. Overall, during its existence, population growth seems to have stagnated, but this hides a pattern of winners and losers. The winners, at least in population numbers and regional influence, were the better organized and militarily more powerful polities. Among these were the Igbo, Yoruba, and Asante. Rising to prominence largely as a result of slave-trading activities was the Fon state of Dahomey, which by the end of the eighteenth century contended with the Yoruba state of Oyo for regional dominance

The losers were smaller communities, some of which completely disappeared as distinct entities. A particularly hard-hit area was the so-called "middle belt" that lay between the coastal powers and those in the interior such as the Hausa and Mossi. Even today, the area is characterized by comparatively low population densities.

Politics and economics were other spheres to feel the slave trade's impacts. More authoritarian regimes emerged, backed by the guns and armies they now possessed, and agriculture and manufacturing both declined. They did so because of dislocations that those being raided experienced and because the profits from selling slaves proved far greater than those that could be earned in any other way.

Developments within Benue Congo would have even more far ranging repercussions. These were mostly due to Bantu migrations, which carried its speakers east and south to reside in virtually half of the continent. Their migrations began about 5000 years ago from the vicinity of the Cross River valley. Skilled as fisher folk and hunters, they had begun cultivating yams and other crops, and this combination of activities seems to have stimulated population growth and a need for new lands. Some groups moved east through the moist woodlands that bordered the northern margins of the equatorial rain forest. By 3000 years ago, vanguards had reached the rich agricultural lands between lakes Albert and Edward and Victoria. Here a new Bantu population nucleus formed that would serve as a source for numerous and highly complex migrations. Some led elsewhere in eastern Africa, while others took Bantu speakers to South Africa in the first centuries AD.

Apparently, what kept the Bantu moving east was a concurrent expansion of another Niger Congo linguistic group, the Ubangians. They started off with a food economy similar to the one practiced by Bantu, but enriched it with grains and livestock gained from contacts with Central Sudanic groups living to their north. The early Ubangians consolidated their position north of the equator and later branched into such modern groups as the Zande, Mangbetu, and Nzakara.

Meanwhile, other Bantu migrants had taken more southerly routes that led into the equatorial rainforest. Following river valleys, they established villages wherever the right combination of fertile soils for their crops, rich fishing grounds, and hunting opportunities could be found. This brought them into contacts with pygmoid gatherer/hunters who had entered the forests thousands of years earlier. The contacts, for the most part, do not seem to have been hostile ones. Instead, cooperative relationships were established in which the pygmoids supplied the villagers with products from the forest in exchange for agricultural commodities and manufactured goods. So close did these contacts become that whatever languages the pygmoids spoke were replaced by those spoken by the villagers with whom they associated. In time, the growth of Bantu numbers resulted in a decline in forest lands available to the pygmoids and today only a few groups such as the Mbuti and Twi remain as distinctive populations.

An important key to Bantu success was their use of iron tools. With them in hand, they could clear and cultivate more land and fashion superior arrow points and spearheads. Two sources for their adoption of iron making technologies can be identified. One is Taruga near the margins of the Jos Plateau in Nigeria. Furnaces and slag deposits have been dated to between 700–400 BC and the technologies of iron making seem to have spread from here in all directions, including to the Bantu. The second is in Buhaya in the interlacustrine region, with dates that are only a couple of hundred years later. No direct links to Taruga have been established, so developments are thought to have been independent.

Once through the rainforest, the routes followed by Bantu migrants headed in many directions and interconnected with those coming from eastern Africa. Eventually particular areas emerged as centers of population concentration. One was in the interlacustrine region, where agricultural productivity was greatly enhanced by the adoption of plantains and bananas. These had been domesticated in southeast Asia and reached the Bantu here from still unknown sources some 2000 years ago. Populations grew and by 600 to 700 years ago kingdoms had begun to form, the most prominent becoming those of Bunyoro, Buganda, Nkore, Rwanda, and Burundi. In the latter two, a cattle-based aristocracy developed from a synthesis of migrant Nilotic herders and Bantu. They would become known as Tutsi, while the vast majority of the people took on the identity of Hutu.

Other Bantu clusters in eastern Africa emerged in the highlands, especially around Mt. Kenya, producing the closely related Kikuyu-Meru-Embu peoples. Mt. Kilimanjaro became home to the Chaga, the Usambara Mountains to the Shambaa, while the uplands north of Lake Malawi were settled by the Nyakyusa. Later migrations into less fertile lowlands would produce such peoples as the Hehe, Gogo, Turu, and Nyamwezi. From the rift valley of Kenya to central Tanzania, contacts between Bantu and Nilotes were common. These contacts sometimes erupted into conflict, but for the most part, relations were peaceful and based on exchanges of livestock products for grains and other produce of Bantu fields.

Beyond eastern Africa, Bantu migrations also led them first to the most productive agricultural lands. This explains their early presence on the Transvaal, where numerous Sotho-Tswana groups developed, and along the coast and hills of Natal, which is where the Nguni settled. The polities among both remained small and basically self sufficient until the end of the eighteenth century when the Nguni Zulu began to expand. Their *impi,* or army, developed new means of warfare that allowed them to expand at the expense of neighboring groups during the first half of the next century. Destruction and dislocations often followed Zulu victories, producing what became known as the *mfecane* (scattering). Some groups completely disappeared from history, while in other instances, new ones, such as the Mfengu and Basotho, formed from the survivors.

Good quality agricultural land also accounts for the initial prosperity of the Shona of Zimbabwe. Their rise to regional prominence, however, had more to do with trade, particularly in gold. The ability to monopolize it led to the formation of the city state of Great Zimbabwe, which prospered from the twelfth to the fifteenth centuries. Thick stone walls were built to house a nobility that shipped the gold to Arab and Swahili merchants at the ports of Sofala and Kilwa in exchange for luxury items such as silks, carpets, and porcelain wares. When Great Zimbabwe lost its trade centrality to other Shona states, notably Mutapa and Batua, it went into decline and was eventually abandoned.

Another people who took advantage of the combination of productive agriculture and trade were the Kongo who resided along the banks of the lower Congo River. The kingdom they formed was already a regional power when visited by the Portuguese near the end of the fifteenth century. Commercial relations were established and the two nations even exchanged diplomatic personnel. Ivory and beeswax were traded at the outset, but early in the next century the Kongo had turned to selling slaves. Initially, this enhanced their position, but soon led to internal and external competition that resulted in the kingdom's demise in the seventeenth century.

The slave trade would continue to impact central Africa until after the middle of the nineteenth century. It fueled both the transatlantic trade, which from here supplied mainly Brazil, and a growing domestic demand for slaves by those powerful enough to secure them, such as the Ovimbundu, Lunda, Chokwe, and Lozi. By the nineteenth century it was closely tied to the ivory trade, which not only reached the Atlantic coast, but the Indian Ocean one as well. The disruptions caused by the slave trade were far greater than those experienced in West Africa and produced considerable population loss among those preyed upon. Among the hardest hit were Ubangians whose isolation kept them secluded until the middle of the nineteenth century when they were the targets of slavers coming from Khartoum.

OTHERS

There are other African peoples who derive either completely or partially from non-indigenous sources. Among those who became regionally prominent are Afrikaners, Coloureds, Swahili, Creoles, and Americo-Liberians.

Afrikaner (language Afrikaans) origins are traceable to the employees sent out by the Dutch East India Company in 1652 to establish a supply station at Cape Town for ships on their ways to and from southeast Asia. Small numbers of Dutch and other Europeans, mostly French Huguenots, continued to arrive for the next several decades, but by the turn of the century, immigration had pretty much come to an end. Those who took up farming were called Boers, and as land became increasingly scarce around Cape Town, they began moving inland, at the expense, as noted, of Khoikhoi and San. Continuing expansion led them finally to contacts with Xhosa early in the eighteenth century, initiating a series of border wars that would continue for more than 100 years.

Meanwhile, the British had superseded the Dutch at the Cape. Seeking to escape what they perceived as alien and hostile rule, thousands of Afrikaners began leaving in the early 1830s in what became known as The Great Trek. Joined by others who had wearied of constant strife with the Xhosa, they headed north across the Orange River and into the Transvaal. Here they found ideal grazing lands for their herds, much of which had been depopulated as a result of the mfecane.

The so-called Coloured people of South Africa also have their origins in policies initiated by the Dutch East India Company. To augment the labor force at Cape Town, it imported some slaves from elsewhere in Africa and then turned to sources on the Indian sub-continent and the islands of Indonesia. Sexual liaisons among them produced mixed children, as did those between Europeans and slaves, Europeans and Khoikhoi, and slaves and Khoikhoi. Some formed new groupings, such as the Rehoboth and Griqua, and most became self-consciously Afrikaner in culture, speaking Afrikaans, following the Dutch Reformed religion, and taking Afrikaner names. Eventually, all of these peoples of mixed backgrounds would be grouped together as Coloureds.

Swahili is a Bantu language, the origin of which can be traced to people who lived in small villages centered on the lower Tana River of Kenya during the first centuries AD. Some of these villages began to trade with merchants from the Arabian peninsula, who had for centuries beforehand taken advantage of the seasonal monsoons to sail between there and the Persian Gulf. The most successful grew into towns that between the ninth and twelfth centuries had produced a class of mercantile rulers who fashioned an urban culture to distinguish them from others. Included were Islam and a new language that would soon become known as Swahili. The name comes from Arabic, which had begun adding vocabulary to the language, and translates as "people of the coast."

Towns such as Pate, Lamu, Malindi, Mombasa, and Rhapta flourished from the twelfth through fifteenth centuries, but then went into decline as a result of Portuguese interventions and unstable conditions in their hinterlands that disrupted trading activities. They were revived when the Sultan of Oman decided to relocate his capital to Zanzibar in 1832 in order to better control the sources of ivory and slaves that had become so important to Oman's prosperity. The now substantial Arab presence led to considerable cultural borrowing by the Swahili that included claims of direct descent from the Prophet Muhammed, the incorporation of many more Arabic words, the use of Arabic script, and styles of dress and building. From their coastal locations, Swahili now traveled inland for the first time, establishing small communities at key commercial locations and with them went their language as a commercial lingua franca.

The Creoles of Sierra Leone are the result of population relocations that took place at the site of Freetown. The first wave landed in 1787. They were black loyalists who had fled to England at the time of the American War of Independence. Following were other refugees, such as Maroons (escaped slaves) from Jamaica, but the largest contribution came from slaves who had been freed from ships captured by the British. (The British had made slavery illegal throughout the empire in 1833 and established an anti-slavery squadron to patrol the coast of West Africa.) This new population from many diverse backgrounds created its own language called Krio and took on a strong British-based culture. They specialized in trade and from Freetown moved along the coast to wherever they could find profitable opportunities to exploit.

A second people who owe their existence to anti-slavery sentiments and activities are the Americo-Liberians. With support from an organization known as the American Colonization Society, a small number of freed American slaves was landed at Cape Mesurado in 1822, and they called their new settlement Monrovia. It grew slowly but surely and in 1839, Monrovia along with several other settlements that had formed, united to create the Commonwealth of Liberia, which secured its political independence in 1848. The Americo-Liberians modeled their constitution after that of the United States and developed a very strongly Americanized culture under the influence of Baptist missionaries.

AFAR

ALTERNATE NAMES: Danakil or Adal (older sources)
LOCATION: The Afar Triangle or Horn of Africa (Ethiopia, Eritrea, Djibouti, Somalia)
POPULATION: Between 3 to 5 million (accurate census figures do not exist)
LANGUAGE: Afar (Qafar Af)
RELIGION: Sunni Muslims, Traditional Animism, few Christians333
RELATED ARTICLES: Vol. 1: Djiboutians; Eritreans; Ethiopians; Oromos; Somalis

¹ INTRODUCTION

The Afar are an ethnic group who reside principally in the the Horn of Africa in the countries of Ethiopia, Eritrea, and Djibouti. The name Afar means "The Best" or "First" in the Afar language. Northern Afars are sometimes referred to by the Arabs as the Danakil, which refers to Danakil Desert near the Red Sea in Ethiopia and Eritrea, Southern Afars are sometimes called the Adel or Adal, a reference to the historic Adal Sultanate, which existed until the mid-1500s in the region occupied today by southern Ethiopia and Djibouti. Afars regard the name Danakil as negative and preferred it not be used to describe them.

Little is known for certain about the origins of the Afar. According to traditional accounts, there are two divisions of the Afar: *Asayahamara* (The Red Ones) and *Adoyahmara* (The White Ones). It may be that the Asayahamara are descended from a group that originally invaded from the Ethiopian highlands and who imposed their rule on the Adoyahmara.

The Afar make up about a third of the population of Djibouti and are a recognized ethnic group in Ethiopia. The Afar language (Cushitic) is spoken in the Afar region of Ethiopia, eastern Eritrea, and Djibouti. Since the Afar were traditionally nomadic herders, Afar-speakers may be further south.

The language and culture of the Afar are related to those of the Somalis and Oromos, although the Afar are a distinct ethnic group. The Afar continue to preserve and practice their traditional culture and beliefs. They have retained many ancient animistic practices.

The Afars' skin tone is generally dark brown and their facial features are similar to those of the Somalis and Oromos, although generally members of both of those groups have darker skin. The Afar are probably related to the ancient Egyptian race.

Little has been confirmed about the history of the Afar people. J. S. Trimingham, author of *Islam in Ethiopia*, offered this explanation: "Little is known about the the Afar because of their aversion to strangers. They didn't let outsiders in, so outsiders didn't learn much about them."

The ancestors of the Afar seem to have settled in farmland in the Ethiopian highlands some time before AD 1000 and primarily raised livestock. Shortly after they began a gradual transition to a more nomadic lifestyle and moved to the area they currently occupy. Since then they have been involved in many conflicts with bordering tribes and peoples.

Arab writer Ibn Sa'id writing in the 13th century, mentioned the Afar. This is the earliest known reference to the group. The Afar are also mentioned occasionally in Ethiopian history. Records include mention of Afar assisting 14th-century Ethiopian emperor Amda Seyon in a campaign. Afar are also described as assisting Emperor Baeda Maryam more than 100 years later in the 15th century.

The Afar themselves claim to be descended from Arabs, through a mythic Yemeni ancestor. This myth of origin seems unlikely, since the two groups do not share a common race, language, or culture.

The Afar language, however, and their traditional religious practice of animism points to a common history with neighboring peoples in the Horn of Africa. No written Afar records exist from previous eras.

Historically, the territory occupied by the Afar was organized into sultanates, semi-independent regions ruled by sultans. In each sultanate, the group's unique culture and customs thrived. Traditionally each sultanate was made up of several villages.

The Afar maintained a loose confederation of four sultanates. The sultans did not gain their position through heredity, but were appointed by the people.

Each Afar sultan was the religious and political leader of his clan. The Afar generally do not become involved in central political governments. They are not interested in pursuing opportunities presented to them by outsiders, although in recent years they have been cautiously open to offers of aid in such areas as medical care and to programs to improve the safety of drinking water. Throughout history, the Afar have strongly resisted domination by others, and this tradition continues into the 21st century.

The Afar have been active in Muslim-led military campaigns against the Christians who inhabited the highland regions of Ethiopia. In the 16th century, Afars fought in support of Ahmad Gran, the emir of Harar, who was attempting to establish a Muslim empire in Abyssinia (modern-day Ethiopia).

In the 19th century, the Afar also fought with the Muslim forces of the Adal kingdom, which stretched across what is now northeastern Ethipia, Djibouti, and Somalia. The Muslims were battling with the Amhara.

The Afar were also active in the Arab slave trade, serving as guides to Arab slave traders. A major slave route to Arabia crossed Afar territory. Afars continued to participate in the lucrative slave trade until 1928 (or later according to some accounts).

Since the mid-1800s and especially in the 20th and 21st centuries, interaction with external political and economic systems has caused the breakdown of the sultanates and the traditional values they represented.

The leadership of the Afar National Regional State in Ethiopia has faced many challenges as the traditional customs and culture of the Afar come under the influence of Western groups and other African cultures. During the early years of European colonization in Africa, the Afar coastal regions (part of present-day Eritrea) witnessed several battles. The Afars demonstrated tenacity and bravery in resisting the advancements of foreign forces.

The presence of foreign forces in the coastal regions of their territory threatened the sovereignty of the entire Afar nation. However, the Afars were no match for the Europeans equipped with high technology weapons. Despite persistent resistance from Afar fighters, Europeans succeeded in occupying the

AFAR

| 0 | 200 | 400 | 600 | 800 Miles |
| 0 | 200 | 400 | 600 | 800 Kilometers |

SAUDI ARABIA

Khartoum

Asmara
ERITREA

YEMEN

DJIBOUTI *Gulf of Aden*

Djibouti

White Nile
Blue Nile

SUDAN

Erigavo

Addis Ababa

ETHIOPIA

Juba

Lake Turkana

SOMALIA

Lake Albert UGANDA

KENYA

Mogadishu

coastal territory. As a result of the European presence, the Afar people were divided. The modern-day nations of Djibouti and Ethiopia (and later Eritrea) resulted.

In 1967, the territory colonized by the French changed its name from "French Somaliland" to the "French Territory of the Afars and Issas." In 1977, it became the independent nation of Djibouti.

In 1975 after an Afar sultan led an unsuccessful attempt to restore sovereignty, the Afar Liberation Front (ALF) was born in Ethiopia. In Djibouti, a similar movement simmered throughout the 1980s, eventually culminating in an Afar insurgency in 1991.

Groups of modern-day Afar may be seen camped just outside Djibouti, the capital and largest city in Djibouti. The Afar may travel to Djibouti to engage in trade or to seek medical care.

In Djibouti, where they account for almost half the population, the Afar remain under Somali domination and suffer in the ongoing struggle between Somalia and Ethiopia over the coastal territories.

2 LOCATION AND HOMELAND

The Afar live in a region often referred to as the "Afar Triangle." A large part of this triangular area is made up of the Danakil Desert, one of the earth's hottest, driest, and most inhospitable spots. The terrain is characterized by desert flatlands. There is little vegetation and limited wildlife. The Araf are among the only people who have survived life in this difficult terrain.

The Danakil Desert is a deep depression, reaching a depth of nearly 400 feet (120 meters) below sea level. One of the lowest elevations on earth, daytime temperatures may reach 50°c (145°F) in the sun. Much of the desert territory is made up of salt flats, cut by deep cracks from the sun's heat.

There are isolated mountain groups, interrupted by valleys where the thorny acacia, also known as the thorntree, grow.

The desert region is occasionally dotted with green oases of doum palm trees. The large oval yellow fruit of the doum palm tastes similar to gingerbread, giving the tree its common name, gingerbread tree. The fruit may reach two to three feet in length.

There are between 3 and 5 million Afar spread across the three countries: Ethiopia, Djibouti, and Eritrea.

3 LANGUAGE

The Afar language belongs to an Eastern Cushite group. Linguists generally identify four distinct dialects of Afar: Northern, Central, Aussa, and Baadu. Arabic is widely used with neighbors and trading partners.

The Afar language (Qafar Af), like Somali and Oromo, uses the Roman alphabet. The Afar language follows the subject-verb structure. While there is little written history, the Afar language is rich in oral traditions. There are many Afar proverbs, narratives, songs, and riddles. In addition, the Afar have a very comprehensive plant and animal nomenclature system.

4 FOLKLORE

Afar culture is oral in tradition. Afar oral literature reveals a high esteem for military prowess, with a whole repertoire of war chants. Today, Afar songs tend to extol the virtues of the camel. The Afar have a myth of origin that describes Arab ancestors traced to ancient Yemen.

Afars also think their color designations (*Asayahamara* or Red Ones and *Adoyahmara* or White Ones) came from the reddish soil of inland deserts and the white saline coastal areas.

Many Afar proverbs relate to their hot, arid environment. for example, a proverb for the salt flats worker is "As rain falls from morning clouds, so should a man cut salt early in the day."

5 RELIGION

The Afar began to convert to Islam in the 10th century after contact with Arabs. Afars adhere to the Sunni branch of Islam, but also follow many traditional animistic practices and concepts. The unique style of Islam they practice incorporates pre-Islamic beliefs, such as belief in the sky-father god, Wak. They also believe that the spirits of the dead possess power to influence the living. In addition, some Afars believe that certain trees have sacred powers.

Rituals that persist from ancient Afar animism include anointing one's body with butter or ghee (clarified butter) and the annual celebration of *Rabena*, a holiday to honor the dead.

In general, religious and community activities are governed by Shariah (Islamic law) as put forth in the Muslim holy book, the Quran. The Afars observe special days for sacrificing animals and for rainmaking ceremonies.

A small percentage of the Afar practice Orthodoxy. Christian mission sources report that Afar Christians are now engaged in producing radio broadcasts in the Afar language. The radio broadcasts use a storytelling format to recount the tales of the Old Testament.

In recent years, Christian agencies have been active in various economic, medical, educational, or cultural assistance work among the Afar.

⁶ MAJOR HOLIDAYS

The Afar observe the Muslim holy days.

⁷ RITES OF PASSAGE

Marriage is an important rite to the Afar. A first cousin is preferred as a spouse. In terms of geneology and marriage, the lines are patrilocal, that is, they follow the father's clan rather than matrilocal, that is, following the mother's clan. Divorce rates are high.

Rituals involving the genitals are practiced for both boys and controversially girls. The Afar practice infibrilation, the sewing together of the female vulva, in an effort to ensure virginity. Boys are circumcised upon coming of age and are judged for their ability to endure the pain of this procedure. Following circumcision, a boy may select the bride of his choice, although he is strongly encouraged to select a first cousin.

⁸ INTERPERSONAL RELATIONS

The Afar have traditionally kept to themselves, maintaining an isolated but mobile society.

Among the Afar, when a host offers a guest a drink of milk and the guest accepts, a bond is formed. The tradition of the bond requires that the host protect the guest if trouble arises and for avenging his death if he is killed.

The Afar people are known for their fierceness and fearlessness. They are hostile toward anyone who crossed their lands without permission. Because of the nomadic lifestyle of the Afar, any who visits Afar territory will find himself trespassing on tribal or family territory. Roads and pathways are not regarded as public walkways, since the Afar regard the territory as their own property.

Travelers may carry an official warrant from the government designed to allow travel through Afar territory. The warrant is not always honored by the Afar, however. Tradition dictates that the Afar are responsible for anything that happens on their land. Thus, they are unenthusiastic about unknown visitors. Travelers must seek permission for the Afar leaders before traveling through their territory. If permission is granted, Afar hospitality will be extended to the traveler.

The Afar maintain self-segregation from neighboring peoples. They are suspicious and antagonistic to their neighbors, especially the Somalis and other people of Ethiopia.

While the Afar are suspicious of humans who invade their land, they feel protective of all wildlife. The Afar respect and preserve their physical environment and try not to harm the meager plant and animal life sharing their hostile territory. The Afar may be largely responsible for the protection of the edangered African wild ass (*Equus africanus*), which has become extinct elsewhere in Africa.

⁹ LIVING CONDITIONS

The Afar lead a nomadic lifestyle, moving from highland to lowlands depending on the flood seasons. They carry their tent-style houses with them, packed on the backs of camels. The dome-shaped tents are made from palm ribs covered with palm mats. The tents provide shelter at night and a respite from the blistering sun during the day. The tents are erected, usually by the women, usually near water spots.

The Afar people in this area are usually found to be malnourished. Since there are few natural sources of water for the Afar people, water must be tanked in. Water is an expensive necessity for the Afar and scarcity of water often leads to conflicts. It is not uncommon for the Afar to be anemic or afflicted with malaria. Each community has a small group of men assigned to guard their herds and water. The guards are not reluctant to use violence to protect these precious resources.

¹⁰ FAMILY LIFE

The Afar people generally live in groups isolated from mainstream society. The clan, a group of extended families, is the most important political and social unit of Afar culture.

Descent is patrilineal. The Afar believe that men inherit strength of character from their fathers, but their physical characteristics from their mothers. Spirituality is also inherited from the mother. Afar men typically marry just one wife. Traditionally girls were eligible for marriage at age 10.

¹¹ CLOTHING

The Afar culture includes unique items of clothing. Men and women generally wear the same article of clothing, the *sanafil*, which is a length of fabric wrapped around and tied at the waist. The woman's sanafil was traditionally dyed brown, but modern Afar women have adopted multicolored sanafils. The man's sanafil was traditionally undyed, and that preference persists to the modern day.

Married women traditionally wear a black headscarf called a *shash*. Afar men are also known for wearing the *jile*, a long, double-edged curved dagger, at their waists.

¹² FOOD

The diet of the Afar consists of fish, meat, and sour milk. They also enjoy a porridge made from wheat flour and heavy round pancakes made of wheat topped with red pepper and ghee (clarified butter). Milk is so important to the Afar that it is also used as a social offering, given to visitors to establish a proper guest-host relationship.

Reflecting Muslim practice, food must be handled with the right hand. The left hand is used for impure purposes. Using the left hand for food, to accept a present, or for shaking hands is considered a serious affront.

The Afar enjoy a a type of palm wine made from the doum palm.

¹³ EDUCATION

Literacy levels are low among the Afar people. Education in the Afar language is still inaccessible to the majority of the rural population in the Horn of Africa. There are some schools in the more densely settled areas and in communities along the main roads. However, courses are taught in Amharic, an official language in Ethiopia. Afar families are more likely to send boys away to study than girls.

What schools do exist are overcrowded, poorly equipped, and understaffed. For children of Afar, the school year and the location of the schools does not match well with the migratory cycles of the nomadic families. Since boys and young men are likely to be among those who must travel to ten the family herds of goats and sheep, it is nearly impossible for Afar children to participate in traditional schooling.

Literacy campaigns have been undertaken by international organizations. In addition, the Afar cultural and political lead-

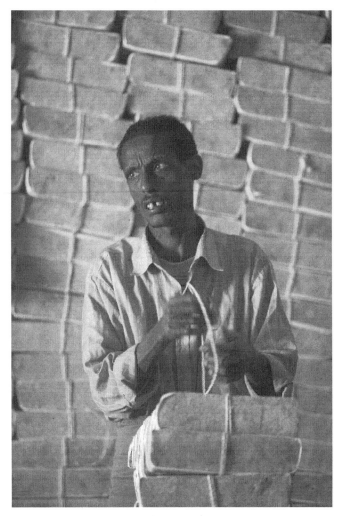

A man packing salt in Mekele in the remote Ethiopian region of Afar. (Jose Condon/AFP/Getty Images)

ers in Ethiopia have focused their efforts on improving educational opportunities, access to healthcare, and transportation. Reflecting their fiercely independent tradition, the Afar believe that they will be able to solve their own problems if these tools are in place.

14 CULTURAL HERITAGE

The Afar have a traditional type of dance, called *jenile*, which is associated with their ancient religion.

15 WORK

The Afar nomads have a unique culture. They tend their livestock, primarily sheep and goats. Sheep are raised for Islamic holiday meals and celebrations. The Afar herd their animals to find water and land for grazing. Camels are used as pack animals, but the Afar do not ride them To maintain this nomadic lifestyle, labor is divided along gender lines.

Women are responsible for setting up the burra (or camp). The burra includes two or more tents. Women manage the day-to-day running of the family's life, and when it is time to move, women repack the household goods on camel's backs for transportation. Women also milk the goats and make butter or ghee

(clarified butter). Music-making also falls to the women of the tribe.

Many Afar work at Lake Assal in the Danakil Desert mining salt. They trade the valuable salt with the Yemenis across the Red Sea, or with Ethiopians for grain. At one time, salt was cut into blocks and wrapped in palm leaves for transport. Modern miners shovel salt into large plastic bags. The Afar sell the salt that they dig from the desert, along with milk and animal hides, at markets in Senbete, Ethiopia, among other marketplaces.

The Afar living near the Red Sea are more settled. They engage in fishing and trading for a living. Governments in Ethiopia and Djibouti have urged the Afar to establish permanent settlements, but the Afar persist in sustaining their nomadic lifestyle. The Afar have not responded positively to the efforts of the Ethiopian government to encourage them to resettle in areas where irrigation systems support the enterprise of cotton farming. Only a small minority of Afars has migrated to urban areas.

In the early 20th century, the development of railroads made it possible for the Afar to transport their goods—meat, butter, milk, and hides—to new markets. This brought more Afar into contact with other ethnic groups and the urban economies of the region.

16 SPORTS

A traditional game among the Afar is *kwosso*. Kwosso is played by two teams. Each team tries to keep a ball made of rolled goatskin away from their opponents.

Few Afars engage in Western-style games or sports activities. The majority of them are nomadic pastoralists and so have little leisure time.

Among the few who enjoy sports, however, soccer is the most popular.

17 ENTERTAINMENT AND RECREATION

Entertainment media, such as television and radio broadcasts, are accessible to the small number of educated Ahar living in urban areas. The majority of Afar do not participate in recreational activities in the Western sense.

18 FOLK ART, CRAFTS, AND HOBBIES

The Afar traditionally engage in various kinds of skills such as wood and metal working, weaving, pottery, and tanning.

They weave fabric to be made into traditional clothing, including the man's *sanafil*, a white cloth wrapped at the waist and tied at the right hip. The woman's sanafil is wrapped the same way, but the fabric is dyed brown. Fabric is also woven for the optional *shash*, a black cloth that married women may choose to wear on their heads.

The Afar do some metalworking to produce tools and instruments, such as the *jile*, a curved, double-edged dagger.

19 SOCIAL PROBLEMS

The Afar are a pastoral people with a fearless reputation. Coping with the modern development of the installation of irrigation systems in the lowlands is one of the many challenges facing the Afar. The national governments, especially in Ethiopia, are attempting to displace the nomadic communities by encouraging them to establish permanent settlements and cultivate cotton, made possible by the supply of water for irrigation.

The basic necessities of life which include water, health services, education, and means of communication are largely inaccessible to the Afar people. Their nomadic lifestyle that requires them to travel long distances in search for water and pasture puts the lives of the Afar and their herds at the risk of perishing in the Danakil.

In addition, persistent border conflicts between Ethiopia and Eritrea, coupled with drought conditions, compound the problems faced by the Afar. The ongoing conflict has displaced some Afars and have made cross-border animal trading less reliable. Many Afar are malnourished and do not receive adequate medical care.

The Afar region of Ethiopia is one of the areas where the people are to a very large extent illiterate. This exacerbates the Afar's difficulty in dealing with natural catastrophes, malnutrition, war, and the HIV/AIDS epidemic.

[20] GENDER ISSUES

The Afar are a predominantly patrilineal community. There are deep-rooted traditions that have a negative impact on women's lives. The Afar customs pertaining to marriage, paternity, and dress are skewed in favor of men.

Afar believe men inherit traits such as strength of character from their fathers, but physical characteristics like height from the mother.

The division of labor is largely unequal, with women assigned more manual work than their male counterparts.

Afar families are more likely to send boys to school than girls. The fact that educational materials are lacking in the Afar language makes it even more difficult for the average person to gain access to vital information in his/her own language. According to the United Nations (UN), illiteracy severely affects Afar women more than men.

The Afar practice infibrilation, a type of female circumcision, to control the virginity and sexuality of women.

Other challenges faced by Afar women include poverty, homelessness, and lack of fresh water, disease (HIV/AIDS and others), food shortages, refugee camps requiring resettlement, political instability, and neglect.

[21] BIBLIOGRAPHY

Ahrens, J. D. *Situation of Displaced People in Afar Region.* Addis Ababa: UN-EUE Publications, 1999.

APDA. *Programme and Region Update on APDA Project Activities and General Overview of the Regional Situation.* Addis Ababa: Assaita, 2000.

Browning, V. & J. M. Little. *My Life among the Afar Nomads of Africa.* Sidney: Pan Macmillan, 2008.

Bryden, M. *Outline of a Proposed Strategy for UNICEF Engagement in Ethiopia's Afar Region.* Addis Ababa: UNDP-EUE Publications, 1996.

———. *Report on Mission to Zone 2 Afar National Regional State.* Addis Ababa: UNDP-EUE Publications, 1996.

Ethiopian Mapping Authority. *National Atlas of Ethiopia.* Addis Ababa: Government Publications, 1988.

Farah, A. Y. *A General Introduction to Obscure Society: The Pastoral Economy of the Ethiopian Afar Herdsmen in Disarray.* Addis Ababa: Save the Children Fund Publications, 1992.

Getachew, K. N. *Among the Pastoral Afar in Ethiopia: Tradition, Continuity and Socio-Economic Change.* Addis Ababa: OSSREA, 2001.

Guinand, Y. F. *Afar Region—Awash River Floods.* Addis Ababa: UN-EUE Publications, 1999.

———. *UN Inter-Agency Fact-Finding Mission to Afar and South Welo on Ethiopian Nationals Returning from Eritrea.* Addis Ababa: UN-EUE Publications, 1998.

Hayward, R. J. and E. M. Parker. *An Afar-English-French Dictionary.* London: School of Oriental and African Studies, 1985.

Insoll, Timothy. *The Archaelology of Islam in Africa.* New York: Cambridge University Press, 2003.

Kiflemariam, A., et al. *Awash River Floods: Afar Regional Survey.* Addis Ababa: UNDP-EUE Publications, 1996.

Lewis, I. M. *Peoples of the Earth (Vol.2).* London: Danbury Press Grolier Enterprises, 1973.

Olson, J. S. *The Peoples of Africa: An Ethno-Historical Dictionary.* Westport, CT: Greenwood Press, 1996.

Phillips, D. J. *Peoples on the Move.* Pasadena: William Carey Library, 2001.

Trimingham, J. S. *Islam in Ethiopia.* New York: Oxford University Press, 1952.

United Nations. *Preliminary List of Major Contributions for the Displaced in Tigray and Afar Regions.* Addis Ababa: UN Publications, 1998.

United Nations Development Program Emergencies Unit for Ethiopia. *Humanitarian Needs of War Displaced People in Northern and North-Eastern Ethiopia.* Addis Ababa: UNDP Publications, 1998.

Weekes, R. V. *Muslim Peoples.* Westport, CT: Greenwood Press, 1984.

Werner, Louis. "Djibouti: A Future in Arabic." *Saudi Aramco World,* March–April 2001, pp. 13–23.

—by M. Njoroge

AFRIKANERS

PRONUNCIATION: ahf-rih-KAHN-ers
ALTERNATE NAMES: Boers
LOCATION: Republic of South Africa
POPULATION: About 3,500,000
LANGUAGE: Afrikaans
RELIGION: Protestantism
RELATED ARTICLES: Vol. 5: Netherlanders

¹ INTRODUCTION

During the 17th century, Dutch colonists (to become known as Boers) settled at the southern point of the African continent. Over the next 200 years, British, French, and German settlers joined indigenous Africans and imported Malays to produce a unique genetic blend. In time settlers moved inland, developing their own language, Afrikaans (first as a spoken dialect and later in written form), cultural identity, and worldview. Thus, emerged the Afrikaners.

Over the next 300 years, the Afrikaners battled indigenous African peoples, established independent republics in the interior, and fought the British in two wars known as the Anglo-Boer Wars (the second is now known as the South African War). All territories were finally united on 31 May 1910 in the Union of South Africa. At this time there was a clear division between the Afrikaners (who belonged to Afrikaner political parties, spoke Afrikaans, supported Afrikaner cultural and linguistic endeavors, and belonged to one of the Dutch Reformed Churches) and British-oriented, English-speaking South Africans. In 1948 the Afrikaner-based National Party came to power and, under a strong Calvinistic religious philosophy and racist social policy, started to implement the system of *apartheid,* which separated the peoples of South Africa along color lines. To their credit, there were many Afrikaner academics, church spokespersons, and business leaders among those who finally pressured the politicians to do away with apartheid and to introduce a new South Africa. As a result, political prisoners (including Nelson Mandela) were released and majority rule was established.

The Afrikaners are a numerical, ethnic, and political minority living in South Africa. Increasingly "Afrikaner" is being defined along linguistic-cultural lines, resulting in the inclusion of persons other than whites only. This discussion aims at representing traditional Afrikaner culture and thus assumes a historical setting prior to the transition to a new democracy represented by majority rule.

² LOCATION AND HOMELAND

The Afrikaners are concentrated in the Republic of South Africa, located at the southern tip of the African continent. Geographically this includes the region between 22° to 35°s, and 15° to 33°e. This means that a large part of the country experiences summer rains. The southern tip, however, falls in the winter rainfall zone. The country is divided into a narrow coastal zone below 450 m (1,500 ft) in altitude, while the largest part is on a plateau with an altitude of more than 900 m (3,000 ft). The country actually consists of four plateaus: the coastal zone, averaging 150 m (500 ft) above sea level; the Little Karoo, averaging 450 m (1,500 ft); the Great Karoo, averaging

760 m (2,500 ft); and the High Veld, which averages 1,200 m (4,000 ft) and rises to 1,800 m (6,000 ft) in the northeast. Temperatures are remarkably uniform due to the increased altitude as one moves north. Johannesburg, the largest city, has an annual mean temperature of 15.6°c (60°F), and this varies only slightly by altitude and latitude (e.g., coastal Durban is about 6°c or 10°F warmer but is also marked by coastal winds). Rainfall (which is so critical for farming and ranching) decreases as one moves from east to west, and while South Africa enjoys a sparse average rainfall of 44.5 cm (17.5 in), this represents a relatively well-watered eastern coastal zone and a western veld tapering into the Kalahari desert (75% of the country receives less than 63.5 cm or 25 in of rain per year). The highest rainfall is in the mountain region of the southern winter rainfall zone, which receives up to 508 cm (200 in) per year.

For more than four decades the white Afrikaners (as a numerical minority) governed the country. Originally concentrated in rural areas, they have since been involved in a major process of urbanization and have become distributed over most of the country. Population figures show Afrikaans as the home language of approximately 3.5 million whites, 400,000 Coloreds, and 15,000 persons of Asian extraction. The country's total population is 47.4 million (2006 estimates).

³ LANGUAGE

Afrikaans, the language spoken by Afrikaners, evolved as a dialect spoken by pioneers on the frontier during the 18th and 19th centuries. The root stock was 17th-century Dutch, but as various linguistic groups settled in the new colonies of those days, they contributed to the emerging language. These included French, German, and English speakers. The Dutch colonial authorities brought slaves from their holdings in southeast Asia, especially Malays, and in time these people contributed to the linguistic (also the cultural, religious, and genetic) mix that was emerging. Early contact had also occurred between settlers and the indigenous Khoekhoen (herders) and San or Bushmen (hunter-gatherers), from whom vocabulary (and cultural) elements were incorporated. On the frontiers more intimate contact developed with the Bantu-speaking peoples, and once again linguistic and cultural transfers took place. The new spoken language, Afrikaans, first appeared in print during the early 19th century and since then has produced material in a wealth of literary and scientific forms. Among the unique features of the language is the double negative: *Hy wil nie speel nie* (literally, "He does not want to play not").

Personal names derive, in most cases, from a European tradition, usually given a Germanic (Afrikaans) form. It is the custom for married couples to name their first son after the husband's father and their first daughter after the wife's mother.

⁴ FOLKLORE

Early Afrikaner beliefs and traditions come from two major sources: those derived from their European ancestry, and those acquired locally due to intimate contact with indigenous peoples (Khoekhoen, San, and Bantu-speaking) and eastern immigrants (Malay and Indian). This includes childhood beliefs in mythical figures like *tikoloshe,* a diminutive urchin. As is true among many peoples, heroes and myths became intertwined as oral traditions were recounted or selected aspects recorded. As is also quite common, heroes frequently are from the political or religious realm.

Much of Afrikaner tradition recounts the exploits of pioneer leaders who with faith and fortitude "tamed" the interior of South Africa, wrestling the land from wild animals and warring native tribes. Thus, school children grew up with the names of Charl Celliers, Andries Potgieter, Piet Retief, and Gert Maritz. Much of the national folklore revolved around *Oom* (Uncle) Paul Kruger (the erstwhile president of the Afrikaner republic), for instance, recounting his experiences when he visited Queen Victoria. In the immediate past, sports heroes have emerged, particularly in the field of rugby where great physical prowess, fleetness of foot, and an accurate kicking boot have created modern heroes—often of mythical proportions.

5 RELIGION

The religion of the Afrikaner derives from Protestantism as practiced by the 17th-century Reformed Church of Holland. However, in 1685 when the French government repealed the Edict of Nantes (which guaranteed religious freedom in a heavily Roman Catholic-dominated France), Protestants fled, some going to Switzerland and others to Holland. These French Huguenots then emigrated from Holland to the Cape in 1688 to assure their religious freedom, and they added a special anti-Papist strain of Protestantism to the Afrikaner religion. They also brought a rich tradition of viniculture. After the British took over administration of the Cape in 1806, they brought English-speaking (especially Scottish Presbyterian) ministers to South Africa. Under the influence of the Swiss reformer John Calvin (and others) regarding church and state, the status of women, purity of the race, and related doctrines, a rather unique blend of Protestantism emerged in South Africa expressed by the three varieties of the Dutch Reformed Church.

6 MAJOR HOLIDAYS

Days and dates of special significance to Afrikaners are those that are associated with their religion and their national history. Many of these are no longer recognized in the new constitutional dispensation, while new holidays have been added to recognize the cultures of other ethnic groups.

Historically, religious holidays in South Africa have been tied to the Christian calendar. Christmas and Good Friday are still recognized as public holidays. Ascension Day (40 days after Easter) was once recognized as a public holiday, but was removed from the list by the Public Holidays Act of 1994. In the same act, the secular holiday of Family Day was created to replace Easter Monday and the Day of Goodwill, on December 26, replaced Boxing Day. December 16 was once celebrated as the Day of the Covenant, commemorating the day when Afrikaner pioneers beat back an attack of Zulu warriors in 1838. Since 1994, December 16 has been celebrated as the Day of Reconciliation. Other public holidays in contemporary South Africa include New Year's Day (January 1), Human Rights Day (March 21), Freedom Day (April 27), Worker's Day (1 May), Youth Day (June 16), National Women's Day (August 9), and Heritage Day (September 24).

Partly due to the Calvinistic overtones in Afrikaner society, Sundays were days of rest. Stores were closed, movie theaters were locked, organized sports were not permitted, and very

little activity took place. People were expected to attend church services. None of this applies any longer.

7 RITES OF PASSAGE

Birthdays are almost universally celebrated, usually with a party accompanied by the giving of gifts. It is expected that all infants should be baptized. Afrikaner children grow up attending Sunday school, where Biblical texts have to be memorized and simple religious instruction occurs. When young people are about 16 years old, they study catechism, learning the tenets of the Reformation and the Biblical basis of Calvinistic Protestantism. This allows for confirmation as a church member and First Communion. In many families this age also permits individual dating. To this day, the twenty-first birthday is a major celebration in which a son or daughter might ceremonially receive a key.

Adults celebrate birthdays, frequently with a *braai*—the equivalent of the American barbecue, where meat is roasted on hot coals and other dishes are prepared. Death is marked at the family level by mourning and the wearing of black dresses by women, and black ties or a black arm band by men. However, these latter practices are becoming less common. The Dutch Reformed Churches celebrate the passing of the old year and the coming of the New Year with a midnight service on 31 December. The front pew is draped in black or purple to remember those who have passed away during that year, and their names are read aloud.

Days and dates of special significance to Afrikaners are those that are associated with their religion and their national history. Many of these are no longer recognized in the new constitutional dispensation, while new holidays have been added to recognize the cultures of other ethnic groups in South Africa. The Afrikaners shown here at Voortrekker Monument are celebrating the Day of the Covenant, which commemorates the day when Afrikaner pioneers beat back an attack of Zulu warriors on December 16, 1838. (Jason Laure)

8 INTERPERSONAL RELATIONS

When meeting people it is customary to greet each person, including children, with a handshake. Friends and relatives of both genders greet each other with a kiss on the lips (this practice does not generally apply to males greeting males), accompanied by a standard question, "How are you?" Taking leave involves the same actions and the standard *"Totsiens"* ("Till we see [each other] again"). Afrikaners used to practice informal gender separation in that men would visit with men, would move aside after a meal to smoke and talk together, or would discuss national affairs with each other. Women were supposed to stay with women and talk about "womanly" affairs, such as homemaking, the servants, and the children. More recently, as women have become better educated and moved into the professions, and as men have lost some of the macho image, a more equitable relationship has developed.

9 LIVING CONDITIONS

South Africa, under Afrikaner administration, was an anomaly as had been true in many colonial and neocolonial situations. Whites lived in First World luxury, represented by housing, swimming pools, schools, hospitals, and clinics, while the same was only incidentally true for individual members of politically unrepresented groups. Afrikaners there-

fore were almost universally in a favored situation with civil service and other jobs, dependable salaries, automobiles, and electricity in their homes. Thus, they joined the consumer race to acquire the accoutrements of comfort and luxury, including televisions, videos, and computers. Because of a well-developed infrastructure, airplanes, trains and buses could deliver passengers to their destinations, while telephones served as a link for friends and people in business. There are a significant number of indigent Afrikaners.

10 FAMILY LIFE

The traditional Afrikaner family involved a young man courting his girlfriend and then formally requesting permission from her parents (especially her father) to become engaged. For three Sundays prior to the wedding, the couples' names were read in church and, if there were no objections (e.g., that one was already married or for some other legal or moral reason), the marriage was performed in church, followed by a reception. Historically, on the frontier and among farming families, Afrikaner families were large because children represented wealth and support. There also was a literal interpretation of the Biblical injunction to "go forth and be fruitful." Some Afrikaner politicians advocated a policy of large families to counter the number of non-whites and to assure the position of whites in South Africa. Today, Afrikaner families average two or three children per family. Essentially the Afrikaner family is an example of the Germanic patriarchal extended family, but under conditions of urbanization and modernization they have moved toward the individual nuclear family unit occupying a single family home or apartment. Dogs and cats are favored as pets, while the former are also bred to protect home and property. The status of women has improved over the years and today is approaching equity as regards opportunity and salary.

11 CLOTHING

The everyday clothing of Afrikaners is no different from that of any modern Western urbanite. Reaching back to frontier days when women wore long dresses and bonnets, this dress has been retained for formal folk dancing called *volkspele*. It is a pleasing sight, though becoming less common, to see the women in their multicolored long dresses and colored bonnets swirling around, accompanied by their male partners, who are also uniformly dressed in shirts, vests, and pants.

12 FOOD

The everyday meal of the Afrikaner is characterized by an emphasis on meat, starch, and cooked vegetables, and the near absence of green or fresh salads. This is particularly true of the Sunday midday meal, where it is customary to have more than one kind of meat, rice, and potatoes, at least two cooked vegetables, and dessert. The breakfast staple is some kind of porridge. In the interior, Afrikaners learned from the native peoples to make a gruel called *stywe pap* or *putu pap* ("stiff porridge" or "putu porridge"). It is common to have this porridge for breakfast with milk and sugar and also to eat it with meat or *boerewors* ("boer sausage," made of beef and pork) at a barbecue. *Braaivleis* ("roasted meat") is traditional and very common, like the barbecue. Some years ago one would only find mutton, usually ribs and chops, at a *braai*, but today all kinds of meat are cooked, and a prawn *braai* is particularly enjoyed.

Traditional foods frequently have Eastern origins, emphasizing the mixed cultural traditions. One of these is *sosaties* (marinated meat much like shish kebab), frequently included in a *braai*. Another is *bobotie*, which contains ground meat with a curry spice flavor. Deriving from the same southeast Asian origins is a twisted doughnut that is fried in hot oil and then submerged in cold sweet syrup. This *koeksister* ("cruller") is a popular delicacy. Venison has always formed part of Afrikaner dishes, as grazing animals could be hunted or culled from national parks. Fish has become very popular for those living close to the ocean, and dishes containing *snoek* (a type of fish native to the South African Cape region) are famous. Two food items that trace back to pioneer days are very common among Afrikaners: *beskuit* and *biltong*. The first is translated as "rusks" in English and comes in different varieties but essentially is a biscuit that has been oven-dried. It is usually dunked and enjoyed with coffee. *Biltong* consists of strips of dried meat, from beef or venison (and also from ostrich), which are treated with salt, pepper, and spices prior to drying. Dried fruits, either in individual pieces or in the form of a ground paste, are delicacies.

13 EDUCATION

Children go to school at age 6 and are obliged to stay in school through age 16. Most of the Afrikaans medium schools require a school uniform: girls wear the same color dress or skirt and blouse, while boys wear the same color shirt and pants. During most of the year boys wear shorts with long stockings. Each school has its own colors, and girls and boys wear blazers that display the crest of the school. Among whites (thus including Afrikaners), school attendance and literacy are nearly universal. It is common for Afrikaans students who have completed high school by successfully passing the national matriculation examination to go to one of the four primarily Afrikaans medium universities, or to a "technicon," which is more technically oriented. Since the Constitution of the Union of South Africa (1910) recognized Afrikaans and English as official languages, students have been bilingual, and many have attended one of the four English medium universities. In contemporary democratic South Africa there are now 11 official languages, recognizing each of the major ethnic groups. English, however, has established itself as the common language of commerce and of politics.

14 CULTURAL HERITAGE

A great deal of the Afrikaners' heritage is derived from and reinforced by European cultural traditions. Thus, the great number and diversity of the performing arts, musical compositions, literary creations, and expressions in ballet and dance all follow the Western European model. Obviously, South African themes have been included in many of these, as is true of the visual arts.

15 WORK

Most Afrikaners are formally employed. Coming from a rural tradition, they moved haltingly into urban forms of employment, first into civil service and education, and then into mining, industry, and business. Today they are firmly established in the urban industrial world. Among whites in the rural areas, Afrikaners predominate. Afrikaners are characterized by a Calvinistic work ethic that requires hard, industrious work. Children are raised with statements like, "Idleness is Satan's pillow," implying that idleness is the parent of vice.

16 SPORTS

Afrikaners are active sports participants. TV was not permitted in South Africa until the 1960s, then for a number of years it was only shown at night. The emphasis was on *playing* sports. Afrikaner children play a variety of games in an informal manner. Organized sports start early as boys go out for rugby, cricket, or "athletics" (which means track-and-field). Girls play netball (similar to basketball), field hockey, and participate in athletics. Sports like golf, swimming, soccer and tennis also feature. It is common to see a group of boys on an open field with a tennis or rubber ball playing single wicket cricket, or tossing a ball in a variation of touch football. Girls are more likely to be at home and to participate only in school or club sports. Intramural and league competitions are well developed in many sports, allowing students to battle for the honor of their class or their school. A dwindling number of people, particularly the older generation, engage in a competition called *jukskei*, which traces back to pioneer days. In the game, carved pieces of wood, resembling the yoke pin used on draft animals, are tossed in an attempt to knock over a stake. The game is similar to the American game of horseshoes.

Spectators flock to venues where high school, college, club, provincial, or national teams compete in all of these sports.

Traditionally Afrikaners excelled more in rugby and athletics but increasingly they have made their mark in other sports, producing world and Olympic champions.

17 ENTERTAINMENT AND RECREATION

Popular culture used to be alien and was frowned on by the elders. Thus, young people entertained themselves in folk dances, church-sponsored youth activities, and the bioscope (movies). It is now common for a group of young people to rent videos, gather at a bar or a dance, or go to a disco. Increasingly too, it has become acceptable to mix socially, and even intimately, with English-speaking persons and even members of other communities. There is a variety of theaters, lectures, and other expressions of the performing arts that are widely attended.

18 FOLK ART, CRAFTS, AND HOBBIES

In the days of frontier living, and later on farms and ranches, there existed a clear sexual division of labor. Certain things were in the man's realm, while the woman dominated domestic activities. These divisions are still sometimes carried over to the present. Women are known for quilting, crocheting, and knitting; and a beautiful doily with a circle of shells or beads covers every jug of milk. In rural areas it is common for women to make soap, bottled jellies, jams, and preserves, and do all the baking of breads, *beskuit,* and cakes. Men used to be adept at woodworking, delicate leatherworking, and the making of chairs with seats of interwoven strips of leather.

19 SOCIAL PROBLEMS

Modern Afrikaners bear a heavy, and in some cases unfair, cultural burden. That burden was created by their ancestors who accepted and reinterpreted a Calvinist Protestantism, developed a racist-based philosophy that led to the policy of apartheid, and in the process became the pariahs of the world. Not all Afrikaners agreed with the policy of their government, not all Afrikaners were racists, and not all Afrikaners accepted the social or political conditions. Yet, being Afrikaners, they are uniformly labeled. Afrikaners had been in a very favorable situation, and for some this created concern and guilt. In contemporary South Africa, also referred to as the "Rainbow Nation," a great number of legal and other actions are being implemented to correct earlier wrongs in the fields of civil rights, economic conditions, housing, etc. Today, Afrikaners are effectively facing the challenge to create a niche for themselves and to become a vital part of South African society.

South Africa's transition to democracy in 1994 brought equal rights and new opportunities to the disadvantaged sectors of the population. Unfortunately, it also sparked a dramatic increase in the rate of crime and violence—an inevitable by-product of poverty and high unemployment in the context of a new political system where social expectations are unrealistically high. Burglaries, muggings, car-jackings, rapes, and murders have all increased since the late 1990s. Afrikaners are as much the victims of this crime rate as any other sector of the population. High levels of crime have led to demands for tough action by the government as well as a return to capital punishment, which is banned in South Africa. One result has been a growing rate of emigration. Another has been the growth of private security-related services and the development of gated communities.

HIV/AIDS is a major problem in South Africa, with the adult prevalence rate at 21.5% (2003 est). The number of people living with HIV/AIDS stood at about 5.3 million in 2003, with 370 000 related deaths that year. The Afrikaners however, comprise one of the communities least affected by the pandemic.

20 GENDER ISSUES

The Constitution of the Republic of South Africa (Act 108 of 1996) guarantees many individual rights. Chapter 2[9(3)] specifically indicates that "The State may not unfairly discriminate directly or indirectly against anyone on one or more grounds, including race, gender … etc." In 2003, the Department of Education launched the Girls Education Movement (GEM) as one of the government's key gender focus programs, implemented in partnership with the United Nations Children's Fund. This program aims to ensure that girls will have access education and that their retention and achievement rates will increase. It is founded on three pillars, namely career mentorship, skills development, and advocacy.

As opposed to many communities in South Africa, particularly in the rural, patriarchal communities, Afrikaners in the country are much further along the road of gender parity. Much like other industrialized nations, Afrikaner women in South Africa are increasingly career-oriented and fill prominent positions in virtually every sector of society.

21 BIBLIOGRAPHY

De Klerk, W. A. *The Puritans in Africa: A Story of Afrikaner-dom.* London: R. Collins, 1975.

Drury, Allen. *A Very Strange Society: A Journey to the Heart of South Africa.* New York: Trident, 1967.

Giliomee, H. *The Afrikaner: Biography of a People.* Cape Town, Tafelberg, 2003.

Giliomee, H. & Mbenga, B. *New History of South Africa.* Cape Town, Tafelberg, 2007.

Harrison, D. *The White Tribe of Africa: South Africa in Perspective.* Johannesburg, Macmillan, 1981.

Wilkins, I. & Strydom, H. *The Super-Afrikaners. Inside the Afrikaner Broederbond.* Johannesburg, Jonathan Ball, 1978.

—by M. de Jongh

AKA

PRONUNCIATION: AH-kah
ALTERNATE NAMES: Pygmies; tropical forest foragers; Biaka; Bayaka; Bambenzele
LOCATION: Tropical forests of southern Central African Republic and northern Congo
POPULATION: 30,000
LANGUAGE: Diaka
RELIGION: Indigenous beliefs
RELATED ARTICLES: Vol 1: Central Africans; Congolese; Efe and Mbuti

¹ INTRODUCTION

In the U.S., the Aka are better known as "pygmies." The term *pygmy* refers to a person of short stature (usually under 1.5 meters [4 ft 9 in]) who hunts and gathers and has a strong identity with the tropical forest. It is generally a derogatory term that emphasizes their physical characteristics. Among Central African farmers, the term carries a connotation of beings closer to animals than to "civilization" (i.e., people who farm), so anthropologists currently use the term *tropical forest forager* instead. By comparison, in the United States there are the Hopi, Navajo, Lakota, Cheyenne and many other indigenous peoples, but when referring to them as a group, they prefer to be called "Native Americans" rather than "redskins." In Central Africa, the Aka, Baka, Efe, Mbuti, and other indigenous forest hunter-gatherers have generally been referred to by outsiders as "pygmies." Researchers suggest replacing the term with "tropical forest foragers" until such time that these forest people become politically organized and decide for themselves what they would like to be called as a group.

Why are the Aka short? Medical exams of children and adults indicate that their health is generally better than that of most peoples in the developing world, so their small stature is not due to lack of food. Aka children's growth is slightly slower than U.S. children's growth (as is the growth of most children in the developing world), but the biggest difference occurs when Aka children reach 14 years of age. Aka do not experience the dramatic growth spurt during the teenage years that is common in most human populations. This diminished adolescent growth is due to a lack of receptors for a particular growth hormone (IGF-I). It is also true that most mammals living in tropical forests are shorter than their savanna relatives (e.g., forest elephants are smaller than savanna elephants), which suggests that smaller size may be adaptive to the humid tropical forest.

The Aka are just one of at least 10 ethnically and linguistically distinct groups of tropical forest foragers ("pygmies") who occupy the tropical forests throughout Central Africa. Tropical forest foragers have been living in the tropical forests for hundreds, if not thousands, of years. Consequently, the Aka are referred to as the "first citizens" of the Central African Republic and Congo (much like Native Americans in the United States).

The farming peoples of Central Africa moved into the tropical forest area about 2,000 years ago and slowly established regular trading relationships with tropical forest foragers. Farmers needed game meat, honey and other forest products, and forest foragers liked the cultivated foods of farmers. Today, Aka-farmer relations are very complex, and they attend each other's funerals, births, and marriages as well as having regular economic exchanges. The farmers see themselves as superior to Aka and talk about "their" Aka. Even though Aka-farmer trading relationships may have lasted for trading generations, Aka can (and do) leave any time they feel a "patron" is not treating them well.

The Aka generally live in areas that do not have roads, but this does not mean they do not know what is going on in the world or that they have not been influenced by colonialism. At the turn of the century, the French colonizers of the Central African Republic and Congo wanted ivory, rubber, and antelope skins, and it was often the Aka who provided these items through their village trading partners. The European desire for antelope skins increased the frequency of net hunting, and the desire for ivory increased the status position of *tuma,* great elephant hunters who could communicate with the supernatural forest spirits. Because ivory trade is now banned in Central Africa, the position of *tuma* is not as important as it was 40 years ago.

There are few Aka status positions. There is no chief in the sense of a person commanding ultimate authority, yet there is the *kombeti,* who is generally more influential in subsistence and camp movement discussions. The *nganga* is the traditional healer and provides a wide range of services to the community—such as divination on hunts, curing of witchcraft, and herbal healing. The *tuma* is the great hunter who has often killed several elephants on his own. He leads spear hunts and important hunting and seasonal rituals, and organizes the training of young boys in the men's secret society. The status positions are usually held by males.

The Aka are fiercely egalitarian and independent. No individual has the right to coerce or order another individual to perform an activity against his/her will. Aka have a number of informal non-institutional methods for maintaining their egalitarianism. For instance, they practice prestige avoidance; one does not draw attention to his or her activities. There are certainly exceptional hunters, dancers, and drummers, but individuals do not brag to others about their abilities.

² LOCATION AND HOMELAND

About 30,000 Aka live in the tropical forests of southern Central African Republic and northern Congo, generally between 1° and 4°n latitude. Their east and western limits are the Oubangui River in the east and the Sangha River, respectively.

Most Aka live in remote areas of the tropical forest where the population density is less than one person per square mile. Aka women average six live births during their lifetime. About 20% of Aka children do not live to their first birthday, and many die before they reach age 15. Infectious and parasitic diseases are the most common causes of death. Approximately half of the population is under age 15, and there are approximately equal numbers of males and females.

³ LANGUAGE

There are approximately 15 ethnic groups that speak 15 languages and live in association with the approximately 30,000 Aka in the Equatorial region. The Aka language is a distinct Bantu language and classified in the C-10 Bantu language group. It belongs to the Benue-Congo group of the Niger Con-

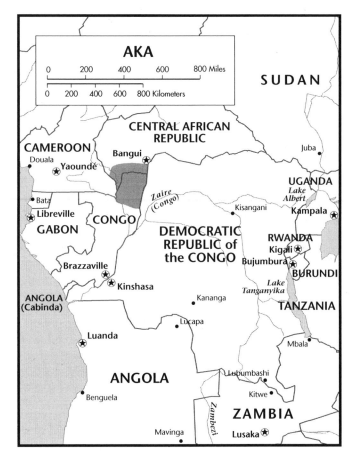

AKA

0   200   400   600   800 Miles

0   200   400   600   800 Kilometers

SUDAN

CENTRAL AFRICAN
REPUBLIC

CAMEROON
Douala
⊛ Yaoundé   Bangui   Juba

Bata   Zaire
                    (Congo)   UGANDA
⊛ Libreville   Kisangani   Lake
        CONGO   Albert
GABON   ⊛ Kampala

        DEMOCRATIC
        REPUBLIC of   RWANDA
        the CONGO   Kigali ⊛
    Brazzaville   Bujumbura ⊛
                                        BURUNDI
    ⊛ Kinshasa   Lake
                        Tanganyika
            Kananga
ANGOLA   TANZANIA
(Cabinda)
            Lucapa

    Luanda
⊛   Mbala

        ANGOLA

    Benguela
                        Lubumbashi
                            Kitwe
                Zambezi ZAMBIA
        Mavinga   Lusaka ⊛

go. In addition to their own language the Aka speak the languages of their neighbors.

The Aka speak a Bantu language called *diaka,* which is characterized by three tones. The language often sounds musical, and different tones can dramatically change the meaning of a word (e.g., *mbongo* can mean "cup," "a type of bee", or "panther"). Most Aka speak at least two other languages—the Bantu or Oubanguian language of their village trading partners and some Sango, the national language in the Central African Republic.

Aka are given personal names a week or so after birth. Personal names have meanings attached to them—for example, *Bimba* ("flea"), *Madjembe* ("intestinal worms"), *Ngunda Oti* ("without hospitality"). In the last case, a boy's mother gave him the name because, at the time of his birth, the boy's father's family did not provide her with much food. Sometimes Aka simply like the sounds of new words and use them as names. For example, Aka now use the following as personal names: *Boutros Boutros Ghali, Konvocation* (convocation from missionaries), and *Bonannee* (from "happy new year" in French). Personal names often change as one gets older, or a person may be known by several different names. Names are informal, similar to nicknames in the United States. If someone has a particular physical characteristic, or personality trait (e.g., a person with big ears, a quiet person, someone who is always sick, or a good rat trapper), people start to call the person by that name. There are no last names, but both men and women inherit a clan name from their fathers. Clan names refer to particular plants or animals that have supernatural abilities, and people who belong to a particular clan cannot eat that

plant or animal. Trails in the forest are associated with particular clans, and after marriage a couple eventually lives with members of the husband's clan.

In addition to personal and clan names, a person can also be called by a kinship term. In the United States, we are familiar with the kinship terms *mother, father, brother, sister,* and so on. Aka kinship terms are quite different in that almost everyone in the same generation has the same kinship term. For example, if you were Aka, you would call your natural father, your father's older brother, and the husband of your mother's sister by the same term—*tao.* You would refer to your brothers and sisters and all of your first cousins by the same term—*kadi.* You could refer to your grandparents and all your great aunts and great uncles by the same term—*koko.* If you had children and your brothers and sisters had children, you would use the same kinship term for all of them—*mona.* So when an Aka parent is asked, "Who are your children?" he or she recites the long list of people who in the United States would be considered nieces and nephews. Aka would feel right at home with the African-American who uses the term *bro* to refer to any man in the same generation.

⁴ FOLKLORE

Aka say that long ago they lived in villages and farmed, but one day a woman heard bees in the sky and a group of people decided to go into the forest to see where they were going. They found the bees' hive, loved the honey and, finding plenty of food in the forest, decided to stay. This is how Aka describe the origin of their life in the forest. In 2003 the oral traditions of the Aka were proclaimed one of the "Masterpieces of the Oral and Intangible Heritage of Humanity" by the United Nations Educational, Scientific, and Cultural Organization (UNESCO).

⁵ RELIGION

Aka religious beliefs are best characterized by their regional and individual variation rather than by a standardized pattern. The Aka occupy a large territory, and religious beliefs vary by area. Some Aka believe in *bembe,* a creator of all living things, but those who believe in bembe indicate that he/she retired soon after creation. *Djengi* is the most consistently mentioned, powerful, and generally benevolent forest spirit. *Djengi* has supernatural abilities, but in many ways he/she is not much different from Aka. Djengi, a spirit, can be thought of as another member of the camp whom one sees and shares with on a regular basis. Djengi shares resources with people, people visit and socialize with djengi, and there is a general trust in (if not love for) Djengi. Djengi comes into the camp in the form of a raffia mask and encourages people to have a party and celebrate in the forest spirit. Djengi asks for cigarettes, water, and other items while in camp and likes it when people dance and sing well. Djengi is a spectacular dancer, especially when the Aka are singing well. Communication with djengi takes place through a traditional healer or *tuma* who has the ability to translate the supernatural language.

Most Aka camps have a traditional healer *(nganga).* Ngangas cure all forms of illness (e.g., malaria, worms, bad luck, attack by witchcraft); see into the future to help one make decisions about travel, marriage, or friendships; and can see game animals deep in the forest while on the net hunt. The majority of *ngangas* are part-time and hunt and gather most of the day.

Ngangas acquire their knowledge through training and initiation. During initiation, the insides of their eyelids are cut, and medicine is placed in the cuts to help the *ngangas* see those things most others cannot.

Aka also believe that family members do not entirely leave this earth after they die. An ancestor's spirit *(edjo)* stays around, visits with the family, and often wants things. (One woman said that the edjo of her father knocked her down while she was walking through the forest.) Many Aka believe in witchcraft *(gundu)*, especially to explain unexpected adult deaths. Witches send poison darts *(ndoki)* into the body of a victim, and the person eventually dies from the poison unless the *nganga* can extract the dart, usually by sucking it out. If someone is accused of witchcraft, he/she may have to take a drink made from special roots. The root is believed to have supernatural power so that if a person is guilty, he/she will go into convulsions and possibly die (the root contains strychnine).

Many Aka rituals are linked to hunting and gathering, and Aka engage in a number of individual and group hunting rituals to ensure a successful hunt. To assist hunting efficiency, the net can be ritually washed of bad spirits *(kose)* or a variety of medicines *(bouanga)* can be placed on them to increase good luck. The number and types of rituals increase as hunting success decreases.

Many Aka have been contacted by missionaries, but it is difficult for missionaries to convert Aka to Christianity because the Aka move around often, and it is not possible to drive a car to most of their camps. Missionaries generally tell the Aka to stop dancing to djengi, and they are generally the only group that is trying to provide formal education and Western health care to Aka.

⁶ MAJOR HOLIDAYS

Aka do not use a numerical calendar, so they do not have specific dates that are celebrated each year, but there are holidays in the sense that there are days off to relax and party. Such holidays occur after good hunts or when large game animals, such as elephant or wild pig, have been captured. Holidays also occur during the honey, caterpillar, and termite seasons.

⁷ RITES OF PASSAGE

Aka do not have much in the way of group ritual activities. At birth, parents place protective cords made from forest vines around a baby's neck, wrists, and ankles to provide protection from bad spirits and help connect the newborn to the forest. At five or six years of age, boys are circumcised in a very informal manner. A man who is good at this comes into camp early in the morning, and the boy often runs into the forest. Everyone laughs, eventually the boy comes back, his father holds him, and the whole thing is over in five minutes. Aka are not teased if they cry and there is plenty of social and emotional support.

During the teenage years, boys and girls get their top four incisors pointed. This is done when the teenager feels ready and is conducted in a very informal atmosphere. Aka believe that pointed teeth make one look handsome or more beautiful. Some Aka, primarily teenage girls, get the bottom four incisors pointed as well. Teenagers bring in new fads from other areas. Current fads include coloring teeth with a purple dye from a forest vine, piercing the nasal septum with a small twig (girls only), and shaving stripes into one's eyebrows.

The only large, group-level ritual occurs at death. Relatives travel long distances and sing and dance for days. Camp sizes more than triple during funeral ceremonies. Teenagers go to as many funerals as possible because they are fun, and it is an opportunity to develop relationships with teenagers from other areas.

⁸ INTERPERSONAL RELATIONS

There are no formal greetings among the Aka, and people do not say good-bye, in part, because they are likely to see each other again. Aka are very warm and hospitable.

Relationships between men and women are egalitarian: men and women both contribute to the household diet, a husband or wife can initiate divorce, and violence against women is very rare. Women have their own dances and songs in which they ridicule men. Spouses can and do ridicule each other with rather crude joking, including uncomplimentary remarks about the size and shape of a partner's genitals, but for the most part the partner does not pay much attention to such ridicule.

Relations between young and old are also egalitarian in that there is minimal deference towards the elderly. Aka elders are expected to hunt and gather as long as they can, and grandparent-grandchild relations are playful and relaxed.

The Aka are fiercely egalitarian and independent. No individual has the right to coerce or order another individual to perform an activity against his/her will. Even when parents give instructions to their children to collect water or firewood, there are no sanctions if they do not do so. Aka have a number of informal methods for maintaining their egalitarianism. First, they practice prestige avoidance; one does not draw attention to his or her abilities. There are exceptional hunters, dancers, and drummers, but individuals do not brag to others about their abilities. If a man kills an elephant, he says someone else did all the work and talks about the small size of the elephant. Second, Aka practice rough joking with those who start to accumulate, do not share, or who act egotistically. For instance, if a teenager eats most of the honey before returning to camp, others will joke about the size and shape of his genitals. And third, Aka practice "demand sharing." This means that whatever one has will be given up if requested. If I like the shirt you are wearing, I ask for it and you say you really did not need it. This way most material items circulate around the camp. This is one reason Aka have been slow to take up farming. An Aka who spends three to four months farming must give everything away at harvest time when all the relatives come to visit and request food.

Sharing, cooperation, and autonomy are but a few others of the Aka core values. The community cooperates daily in the net hunt (described in the section on Work), food hunted is shared with members of the camp, and decision-making is the reserved prerogative of the individual; if one is not content with living conditions, one moves to another camp, which is easy and acceptable.

⁹ LIVING CONDITIONS

The Aka are extremely poor in terms of Western socioeconomic status and material wealth. They seldom have money and do not attend formal schools because they would be teased by the villagers and do not have money to buy books. They do not obtain Western medical care because they do not have money to purchase medicines, and clinic doctors usually discriminate against them.

Aka camps consist of 25–35 people living in five to seven dome-shaped houses. Houses are close to each other and all of them occupy an area the size of a large living room. Houses are three feet high so one cannot stand up in a house. Each family has their own house and everyone in that house sleeps together in the same bed. The house is big enough for one bed and a campfire for warmth during the night. The two or three adolescent boys in the camp share one house (the bachelor pad) while teenage girls each make their own small house. Houses are made by women, with the exception of the bachelor pads (which are often poorly constructed and leak water all the time), and are constructed from saplings and large leaves. The beds are made from logs, animal skins or leaves.

Aka move their camps about eight times a year and there are daily changes in camp composition as visitors (e.g., relatives, friends, traders) come and go, and members leave to join other camps.

Water sources are generally not contaminated because the Aka do not live in one place very long. Aka do not brush their teeth or use streams for washing. It rains frequently, so Aka simply wash off as they walk through the forest.

[10] FAMILY LIFE

The family (husband, wife, and children) is extremely important as this is the unit of production and reproduction: The family works as an economic unit on the net hunt and in a variety of other subsistence activities (e.g., collecting caterpillars and mushrooms). Additionally, the conjugal family is where most cultural skills are transmitted and acquired. The camp (*lango*) consists of 1 to 15 nuclear families, but averages around 25 to 35 individuals. Aka children grow up in an environment of trust, love, and indulgence. Infants are held throughout the day (even while sleeping), nursed on demand (four times an hour), and caregivers attend immediately to any fuss or cry. Although Aka are very indulgent and intimate with their infants, they are not a child-focused society. Parents seldom stop activities to pay undivided attention to their children.

Although the mother is the primary caregiver, Aka fathers provide more care to young children than fathers in any other society. Numerous others also help out with infant care. While in camp, infants are held by their mothers less than 40% of the time. Rather, they are transferred to other caregivers an average of seven times per hour, and they have seven different caregivers holding them during a single day.

Aka childhood lacks negative forces and violence. Seldom does one hear a parent tell a child not to touch or do something. If a child hits another child, the parent will simply move the child to another area. Corporal punishment for a child who misbehaves seldom occurs. In fact, if a parent hits a child, it is reason enough for the other parent to ask for divorce.

Generally, it is difficult for parents to get their older children to do much. When older children (7–11 years old) are asked to collect water or firewood, they often simply ignore their parents' requests. Parents may sometimes shout at their children but, more often than not, they simply go and get what they need themselves. During the teenage years, same-sex friends seem to be inseparable—they go everywhere together. Girls collect water, nuts, or fruit together, and boys take trips to the village or go on small game hunts together (hunting mice with small nets is a favorite pastime for boys.) Teenagers often travel to visit relatives and explore territories other than their own, so they may be absent from the camp for long periods.

The teenage years are a time of social and sexual exploration and teenagers are key members of the camp. They provide new and fresh energy to the camp. For example, they bring in new dances from other camps and are often the first to start dancing at night (the adults join in later). They are many times the ones to initiate changes in Aka culture (e.g., nose-piercing, breaking of relationships with villagers). In many ways, Aka parents seem similar to U.S. parents: they complain that teenagers are smoking more and having sex earlier than in the past.

First marriages occur between 17 and 21 years of age. Once a man moves his traps and spear into the house of a woman the two are considered married; there is no formal marriage ceremony. The husband must stay at the camp of his wife for two years or so, or until the first child is born and walking well. After this, "bride service," the family moves to the camp of the father's brothers. About 25% of marriages end in divorce, the majority of these being first marriages. Divorce takes place by one partner simply moving out of the house. If divorce occurs, children go with the parent they prefer.

[11] CLOTHING

The temperature never drops below 21°C (70°F) during the day. Men and women wear loincloths made of commercial fabric obtained in trade with villagers. When Aka visit the village, they put on any Western or "villager" clothes they might have. Men wear T-shirts and shorts, and women wear a cloth that they wrap around their waist.

[12] FOOD

The Aka know more about the tropical forest than do most botanists and zoologists. The Aka know hundreds of forest plants and animals, but they subsist primarily on some 60 plant species, 20 insect species, honey from 8 species of bees, and around 30 species of game. The Aka collect roots and leaves, nuts, and fruits. They collect mushrooms, termites, crickets, grubs, and caterpillars. The Aka hunt large game (primarily hog and elephant) with spears, antelope with nets, monkeys with crossbows, and rat, mongoose, and porcupine with a variety of small snare and net traps.

Although there is enormous diversity in the Aka diet, their favorite game animal by far is porcupine. Forest porcupines have fat throughout their bodies, and so are very tasty. Honey is another favorite food (the "candy" of the forest) and people spend large parts of the day looking for just a handful of honey. Aka do not hesitate to cut down an entire mahogany tree in order to get a pound of honey from its top.

Aka obtain metal pots, pans, and cooking utensils by trading game meat and other forest products with farmers. Aka do not use plates and utensils to eat. Everyone in a family eats out of two or three shared bowls of food, and they use their hands to eat. A typical meal consists of a bowl with boiled game meat in nut sauce and a bowl of some carbohydrate, usually manioc obtained through trade with farmers. The piece of manioc is picked up with one's fingers and dipped into the meat sauce.

Because the Aka live near the equator, the sun comes up at 6 am and sets at 6 pm throughout the year. Most people get up at sunrise and prepare a hot meal of leftovers from the previous evening meal. Aka then snack throughout the day as they hunt and gather. If they find fruits or nuts, they eat some immediately and save some for back at camp. The largest meal occurs after families have returned from hunting, gathering, and trading—usually at about 7 pm.

¹³ EDUCATION

Aka do not usually attend formal schools, but they begin learning about hunting and gathering when they are infants. Parents teach their 8-to-12-month-old infants how to use small, pointed digging sticks, throw small spears, use miniature axes with sharp metal blades, and carry small baskets. One- and two-year-olds use knives, axes, and digging sticks. They build play houses and imitate the dances and songs of adult life. By three or four years of age, children can cook themselves a meal on a fire; by age 10, Aka children can live alone in the forest if necessary. By age 10, they can identify hundreds of plants and animals and know all the important subsistence skills, with the exception of elephant hunting. Aka do not read or write, but they are very interested in acquiring these skills.

Catholic missionaries have started schools for Aka in a few locations, so some Aka speak French.

¹⁴ CULTURAL HERITAGE

The Aka have a reputation as being the best dancers in the Central African Republic and Congo. They are frequently invited to the capital city by the president to dance at national festivals. Aka music is unique; it has yodeling, hocketing, and polyphonic harmonies and is often heard on the national radio station.

¹⁵ WORK

The Aka are one of the last groups of people on earth to spend most of their days hunting and gathering. The tropical forest is not known for its abundance of wild edible foods, but if one has extensive knowledge of the forest it can be a land of plenty. Aka actually work fewer hours per week than do middle-class Americans, although Aka do not clearly distinguish work versus playtime: they regularly play and joke during net hunts and other subsistence activities.

Net hunting is the most important hunting technique, and it is unique among hunting techniques in that it involves the whole family—men, women, and children—and focuses on making noise rather than stalking and being quiet. Each family has a net that measures about 45 meters (150 feet) long and 2.2 meters (4 feet) high. The hunt takes place at night and begins by connecting all the families' nets together so they make a semi-circle or circle around an area about half the size of a football field. Men go to the center of the nets, women stay next to the net, and children go wherever they want. Once a sound is given to start the hunt, the men yell, scream, and pound logs on the ground to make as much noise as possible in order to wake up and scare the antelopes (most of which are nocturnal). If an animal is scared into the net, the nearest woman tackles it, grabs it behind its hind legs, and smashes its head against a nearby tree. If it is a large antelope, other women will assist in tackling and killing it. Game animals are shared with everyone in camp.

Over the course of a year, the Aka spend about 50% of their time hunting, 30% in gathering, and 20% in village work for farmers. The relative importance of hunting and gathering ac-

tivities fluctuates from season to season. For example, the Aka spend up to 90% of their time net hunting during the dry season (January to May), but during part of the rainy season (August to September) 60% of their time is spent collecting food, especially caterpillars. August is caterpillar season, and caterpillars are eaten at every meal. They can be roasted, boiled, or fried and taste like french fries. Much of the vegetable food in the Aka diet is obtained by trading game meat to farmers for manioc, corn, or other village foods.

¹⁶ SPORTS

Forest people do not play sports in the Western sense. They do, however, learn basic skills through mock hunts and other games. Children play games similar to sports that teach them about group dynamics and personal achievement. Elders teach children the strategies and techniques of hunting by pretending to be animals and showing children how to drive them into a piece of old net. The adults also play a game (more ritual than sport) resembling our tug-of-war. The purpose is to remind the community that cooperation can solve conflicts between the sexes. The tug-of-war begins with all the men on one side and the women on the other. If the women begin to prevail, one of them leaves to help out the men and assumes a deep male voice to ridicule manhood. As the men begin to win, one of them joins the women and mocks them in high-pitched tones. The battle continues in this way until the participants have switched sides and have had an opportunity to both help and ridicule the opposition. Then both sides collapse, laughing over the point that neither side gains in beating the other.

¹⁷ ENTERTAINMENT AND RECREATION

Aka do not have televisions, radios, or books. They do not have electricity, so after it gets dark they sit around fires to socialize, gossip, tell stories (often about gorillas or chimps having affairs with humans) and dance and sing. Dances usually occur about twice a week, but they are held every night during caterpillar season or when hunting is especially good.

¹⁸ FOLK ART, CRAFTS, AND HOBBIES

Aka do not have paper and pencils so their art often takes the form of body modifications—painting, scarification, haircuts, and so on. The dark juice from a fruit is used to draw designs on the face and the body that represent the sounds and sights of the forest. Scarification often takes place before a dance. Teenagers get together and cut various designs into their bodies, often around the navel. Aka use razor blades traded from villagers to cut their hair and shave their heads into some very original designs—triangles, lightning bolts, caterpillars, and so on.

¹⁹ SOCIAL PROBLEMS

Today the Aka continue to be affected by the world economy in several ways. In Bokoka, for instance, the Aka move into the village for part of the dry season, at the expense of missing the best net hunting of the year, to help the farmers with their coffee plantations. The coffee, destined for the European market, is the primary means by which villagers acquire money. Some Aka help villagers hunt elephant for ivory, while other Aka work for lumber companies in the region.

European logging companies are building roads and mills to extract mahogany and other hardwood trees (most caterpillars come from these trees). Europeans and Africans are going deeper into the forest to dig for gold and diamonds. And Western conservation groups are trying to establish national parks and reserves to save tropical forests, but this means that Aka often lose their lands.

The farmers who are the Aka's trading partners are trying to grow more and more cash crops (e.g., coffee) to buy commercial goods (e.g., radios, VCRs), and so they try to get "their" Aka to work in the fields with little or no remuneration. Consequently, traditional trading relations are breaking down and Aka now say that villagers turn into chimpanzees when they die. There is little question that both African farmers and European investors exploit Aka. Aka are quiet and self-assured, and they often respond to outside pressures by fleeing deeper into the forest. Aka are not politically organized, nor do they have the literacy skills to try and mitigate these threats to their existence.

Alcoholism and drugs are not major problems for the Aka, except in logging towns where some Aka are paid for locating hardwoods. Aka, used to immediate consumption of collected or captured foods, do not store for the future. When they are paid for their labor, they spend all their money within a day or two, often on alcohol or cannabis.

Aka do not currently have AIDS, but they know about it from all the deaths among villagers. In the past, Aka seldom had sexual relations with villagers; now they say that if they sleep with a villager, they will die from AIDS. Their hunter-gatherer lifestyle exposes them to blood of jungle fauna, thus they have among the highest rates of seropositivity for Ebola virus in the world.

[20] GENDER ISSUES

Aka male-female relations are extremely egalitarian by cross-cultural standards. Both males and females are regular contributors to the diet. Aka husbands and wives are together often and cooperate in a wide variety of subsistence tasks such as to net hunt, collect caterpillars, termites, honey, fruit, and sometimes fish. But wives are less likely to participate in cross-bow hunting for monkeys and trap-line hunting for medium size game, and never participate in spear hunts for wild pig and elephants. It is also clear that Aka men and women like to be with members of the same sex at least as much as being with their spouses. Men enjoy hunting game together, and women enjoy collecting nuts and fruit away from the men.

The political power and social prestige of Aka women is pronounced, but is not as structurally salient as that of Aka men. Aka men hold all the named positions of status—*kombeti*, *tuma*, and *nganga*—but as mentioned already, these men hold no absolute power. They influence people through their hospitality, persuasiveness, humor, and knowledge, not by their position. Aka women challenge men's authority on a regular basis and are influential actors in all kinds of decision-making. Women participate in decisions about camp movement, extramarital affairs, bad luck on the hunt, and sorcery accusations.

Autonomy within the context of group interdependence is a vital feature of Aka gender relations. Husbands and wives cooperate in a wide range of activities, but there is respect for each other's feelings and peculiarities. Husbands cannot force their wives to come on the hunt, and the wives cannot force their husbands to look for honey. Spouses can and do ridicule each other with rather crude joking (e.g., uncomplimentary re-

marks about the size and shape of their partner's genitals), but for the most part the partner does not pay much attention to the ridicule. If the couple does not get along, divorce is a matter of one partner simply moving out of the house. While men and women have clearly defined subsistence and social roles, one is not ridiculed for trying a role usually assigned to the other gender. Women carry the nets, spears, and crossbows of the men and men carry the baskets and digging sticks of the women. This sex role flexibility is seen in the different types of net hunt. On most net hunts, men go to the center of the nets and chase the game into the nets while women stand nearby to jump on and kill the captured game. But for social or environmental reasons (getting tired of doing one type of net hunt or trying to capture especially large game) the roles are sometimes reversed, and women go to the center of the nets while men stay next to the net.

Physical violence in general is infrequent and violence against women is especially rare. The lack of violence enhances female autonomy and encourages husband-wife cooperation and trust. Husband-wife conflicts do of course occur but they are usually resolved through talking, rough joking, leaving camp for awhile, or mediated assistance from other camp members.

It is essential to understand Aka gender relations, particularly husband-wife relations, if one is to understand the Aka father-infant relationship. A 2005 UNESCO report named Aka men as the "Best Dads in the World." Aka fathers have their infant within arms' reach 47% of the time. Husband and wife are together often, know each other exceptionally well, and cooperate on a regular basis in a diversity of tasks. Men and women have distinct tasks, but there are few underlying beliefs that one sex is naturally inclined to perform certain tasks. The capabilities of men and women are very similar, and therefore tasks can be reversed easily. Male and female experiences and socialization are different, but men and women know the tasks of the opposite sex. Women are also valued and respected members of the group. Aka men, however, though are similar to men cross-culturally in that men predominate in the named status positions, only men hunt large game, and polygyny is relatively common. In summary, Aka male-female relations have commonalties with male-female relations cross-culturally, but the Aka are probably as egalitarian as human societies get.

[21] BIBLIOGRAPHY

Cavalli-Sforza, Luigi Luca, ed. *African Pygmies*. Orlando, Fla.: Academic Press, 1986.

Hewlett, Barry S. *Intimate Fathers: The Nature and Context of Paternal-Infant Care Among Aka Pygmies*. Ann Arbor: University of Michigan Press, 1991.

———. "Cultural diversity among African pygmies." In: *Cultural Diversity Among Twentieth-Century Foragers*. Susan Kent, ed. Cambridge, England: Cambridge University Press, 1996.

Hewlett, S. Barry and Bonnie L. Hewlett. *Ebola, Culture and Politics: The Anthropology of an Emerging Disease (Case Studies on Contemporary Social Issues.)*. Stamford, CT: Wadsworth Publishing, 2007.

Mark, Joan T. *The King of the World in the Land of the Pygmies*. Lincoln: University of Nebraska Press, 1995.

—revised by M. Njoroge

ALGERIANS

PRONUNCIATION: al-JIR-ee-uhns
LOCATION: Western North Africa (the Maghrib)
POPULATION: 33,333,216
LANGUAGE: Arabic; Berber; French
RELIGION: Islam (Sunni Muslim)
RELATED ARTICLES: Vol. 1: Tuaregs

¹ INTRODUCTION

Algeria is one of several countries forming the Maghrib, a region in the western part of North Africa that borders the Mediterranean Sea. (Maghrib is the Arabic word referring to the direction of the sunset.) Algeria's history has been turbulent, involving repeated conquests and a particularly bitter resistance to modern European colonialism. This history has left its mark on contemporary Algeria, which from 1992 to 1998 experienced a violent civil war between the military junta running the country and a coalition of Islamist opposition parties known as the Islamic Salvation Front (FIS). Ferocious fighting killed between 100,000 and 300,000 people—the exact figures are in dispute and likely will never be known. The conflict erupted following a December 1991 election in which the FIS won by a landslide; the government quickly annulled the results, spurring outrage.

Algeria's known history can be traced as far back as 30,000 BC. Cave paintings found at Tassili-n-Ajjer and elsewhere in Algeria, dated to between 8000 BC and 4000 BC, show how ancient hunters shared a savannah region with giant buffalo, elephants, rhinoceroses, and hippopotamuses. Neolithic civilization, which is characterized by animal domestication and agriculture, developed in the area between 6000 BC and 2000 BC. Today, this area is primarily desert.

The various peoples who eventually settled in the area came to be called Berbers. Roman, Greek, Byzantine, and Arab conquerors all attempted to defeat or assimilate the Berbers into their cultures, with varying degrees of success. Phoenician traders arrived in the area around 900 BC and established the city of Carthage in approximately 800 BC in what is today neighboring Tunisia. From there, the Phoenicians established towns along the coast and in the area that would become Algeria. The Berbers were either enslaved by the Phoenicians or forced to pay tribute. By the 4th century BC, the Berbers formed the largest part of the Phoenician slave army and began to revolt as the power of Carthage weakened. In time, several Berber kingdoms were created that vied for power until the arrival of the Romans in AD 24.

The Roman conquest was disastrous for the Berbers. Tribes were forced to become settled or leave the area. For this reason, the Berbers resisted Roman rule. The Romans began their occupation by controlling the coastal lands and cultivating the area. It is estimated that North Africa produced 1 million tons of cereal each year for the Roman Empire, in addition to fruits, figs, grapes, beans, and olive oil.

Along with the Roman presence, Judaism and Christianity began to influence the Berbers. Many Jews who had been expelled from Palestine by the Romans settled in the area, and some Berber tribes converted to Judaism. Christianity arrived in the 2nd century AD and was especially attractive to slaves.

By the end of the 4th century AD, much of the settled areas had become Christian along with some Berber tribes.

In AD 429, the German king Gaiseric, backed by 80,000 Vandals (a German tribe), invaded North Africa from Spain, eventually weakening Roman control. With the decline of Roman power, Berber tribes began to return to their old lands. Meanwhile, the Byzantine emperor Justinian sent his army to North Africa in AD 533 and within a year conquered the German forces, although the Byzantines never established as firm a hold on the area as the Romans had.

The most influential conquest in the area was the invasion of Arab Muslims between AD 642 and AD 669. Nomadic Berbers quickly converted to Islam en masse and joined the Arab forces. Christian Berber tribes in Algeria converted to Islam, and in AD 711, the Muslims established firmer control in the region.

The ruling Arab view of Islam at the time was that Islam was primarily a religion for Arabs, and therefore non-Arab converts were treated as second-class citizens. Political sentiment developed among Muslims on the Arabian Peninsula, however, that rejected the Arabism of the ruling Umayyad dynasty in favor of strict equality for all Muslims. Followers of this movement, called Kharijites, spread to North Africa, and many Berbers became attracted to their message of Islamic equality and strict piety. They eventually rebelled against the Arab caliphate's control of the area and established a number of independent kingdoms.

In AD 750, the Abbasids, successors to the Umayyad dynasty, spread their rule to the area and appointed Ibrahim ibn al-Aghlab as governor in al-Qayrawan, in Tunisia. By the end of the 9th century AD, Ismaili Muslims (Shi'a Muslims who followed a more esoteric and mystical interpretation of Islam) converted the Kutama Berber tribes from Algeria and led them against the established rulers. In AD 909, the Ismaili forces established the Fatimid dynasty in North Africa.

The Fatimids were more interested in the lands to the east and left Algeria and neighboring Tunisia to Berber rule. However, considering the diverse loyalties of the different tribes, conflict became inevitable. In the 11th century, the Fatimids sent Arab bedouins to North Africa to assist their forces against other Berbers. Eventually, the influx of Arabs promoted the arabization of the entire area.

Nevertheless, independent kingdoms did manage to establish themselves in the area. The greatest of these were the Almoravids, the Almohads, the Hafsids, and the Zayanids. These kingdoms were all led by Muslim leaders who greatly encouraged learning and the arts.

Meanwhile, the Catholics of Spain were set on reclaiming southern Spain from the Muslims. Spain had become a cosmopolitan and pluralistic center of learning under Muslim rule. The Spanish conquest in 1492, however, fundamentally changed the character of the area. The new rulers forced all Muslims and Jews to convert to Christianity. Many fled to North Africa, and a sizable community of Jews settled in Algeria, Tunisia, and Morocco.

Between 1560 and 1620, Algeria became a base for privateers, or pirates. Because Muslim vessels were not allowed to enter European ports, Muslim pirates began raiding European ships. The most famous of these pirates was Khayr ad-Din, known to Europeans as Barbarossa, or Red Beard. Thanks in part to Khayr ad-Din, the Muslim Ottoman Empire (based in

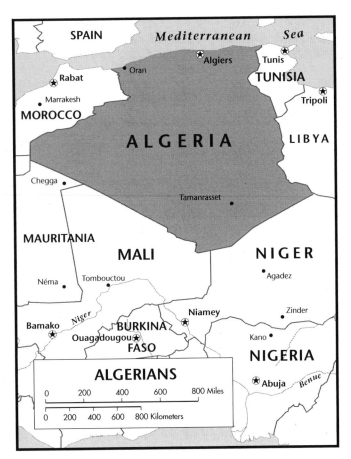

ALGERIANS

| 0 | 200 | 400 | 600 | 800 Miles |

| 0 | 200 | 400 | 600 | 800 Kilometers |

tige. All occupied areas were seized from their inhabitants and sold at extremely low prices to poor immigrants from France and other European countries. The colonists were called *colons* or *pied noirs* (black feet). Many were prisoners from France who had been exiled to Algeria.

France still had many battles to fight, however. `Abd al-Qadir, a 25-year-old Muslim, united the tribes throughout Algeria to resist the French occupation. By 1839, he controlled more than two-thirds of Algeria, creating a government, collecting taxes, supporting education, and promoting the economy. The French sent 108,000 soldiers—one-third of the French army—to defeat `Abd al-Qadir's forces. They starved the Muslim population by destroying their crops, orchards, and herds. `Abd al-Qadir was finally forced to surrender in 1847.

In 1871, another insurrection against the French broke out as a result of French economic policies, which had led Muslim areas to famine. Between 1868 and 1871, 20% of the Muslim population of the city of Constantine alone died of starvation. As a result of the revolt, France confiscated even more land.

By the time of World War I (1914–1918), a new class of European nationalists had emerged among the Algerian Muslims. Almost 200,000 Algerians fought for France during the war, and many now wanted full rights as French citizens. Some, however, wanted national independence for Algeria. The French denied both. Muslims were forbidden to become citizens in most cases unless they renounced Islam, and France considered Algeria an integral part of its nation.

During World War II (1939–1945), the Muslim opposition to France nevertheless joined the Free French forces in opposing the German Nazi invasion. Following the defeat of France by Adolf Hitler's forces, the local French government in Algeria joined the Nazi troops. At one point, they ordered that all Jews in Algeria be shipped to concentration camps in Europe. The Jews in Algiers hid in Muslim homes.

Upon the defeat of the French and German Nazi forces, the Algerians—along with Tunisians and Moroccans—asked France and the United States for independence as a reward for their support throughout the war. Their request was refused, and many of the same French leaders who had supported Hitler were reinstated in Algeria.

These events led to the Algerian War of Independence in 1954, in which Algerian Muslim nationalist parties launched a series of bombings on French military positions around the country. In August 1955, the Algerians attacked French civilians for the first time, killing 123 people in an attack in the city of Phillippeville. The French army responded by massacring as many as 12,000 Muslims. Between 1957 and 1960, the French—in what today would be called "ethnic cleansing"—forcibly removed more than 2 million Algerians from their villages to concentration camps in the plains, where tens of thousands died.

Nearly a million people—one-tenth of the Algerian population at the time—were killed between 1956 and 1962. It was one of the worst genocides in modern history. France eventually decided that the price of occupation was too high, and French president Charles De Gaulle negotiated a French withdrawal from Algeria. On 1 July 1962, Algerians voted nearly unanimously for independence, and Algeria was declared an independent country on 5 July 1962—exactly 132 years after the French invasion.

what is today Turkey) managed to spread its rule over North Africa and form a buffer against European expansion.

Many European states paid tribute to the rulers in Algeria in order to ensure the safety of their ships. Once the United States became independent of England, its ships were no longer protected by British payments and were subsequently attacked. In 1797, the United States signed a treaty with rulers in Algiers, Algeria's capital, paying tribute in exchange for safe passage.

By 1815, however, the European states were in a temporary state of peace and decided to combine forces against the North African states. Spain, the Netherlands, Prussia, Denmark, Russia, and Naples declared war against Morocco, Algiers, Tunis, and Tripoli. The United States also joined the battle, which eventually ended the practice of privateering.

In 1827, politics in France prompted the French to establish a blockade against Algiers that would persist for three years. The French monarch, Charles X, was politically weak and thought that strong action against Algiers would strengthen his popularity at home. In 1830, he decided to invade Algeria on a self-proclaimed "civilizing mission." In June of that year, 34,000 French soldiers invaded Algiers and, after a three-week battle, took the city. French troops raped women, looted the treasury, desecrated mosques, and destroyed cemeteries. Their actions set the tone for the next century of French rule.

By 1834, a new liberal government had been established in Paris. Although the government was initially opposed to the occupation of Algeria, it annexed the country and its 3 million Muslim inhabitants as a colony for the sake of national pres-

After independence, Algeria became a one-party socialist state ruled by the National Liberation Front, which had led the War of Independence. Many European companies were nationalized. French law was maintained on many civil issues, although Islamic traditions were also given representation in the law of the land. Algeria announced a strict policy of nonalignment, allying with neither the Soviet Union nor the United States.

The stagnation of oil prices on the world market negatively affected all Middle Eastern and North African states, including Algeria, which relies on oil for the majority of its revenues. Riots erupted in 1988 to protest the price of food, very high unemployment, and corruption among government officials. The riots were put down with bloody force, and hundreds were killed.

In response, the government rewrote the constitution to allow new parties to form and to liberalize the economy. The most popular of the new parties was the Islamic Salvation Front (FIS), which preached a return to traditional Islamic values and strict morality in public service. Its message had great appeal for the millions of unemployed Algerian young people. In the 1990 local elections, the FIS made substantial gains in all the major cities. In the first round of national elections in December 1991, the FIS also won large-scale victories despite the fact that the government had arrested its leaders. Fearing an FIS victory, the army took over, canceled elections, and sent 10,000 FIS activists to concentration camps in the desert; many were simply killed.

In response, civil war erupted. The exact number of dead in perhaps the most vicious civil war in North Africa will likely be never known. Estimates range from 100,000 to 300,000. Many of these deaths resulted from unprovoked raids by marauding militias attacking villages, often hacking their victims to death with hatchets.

2 LOCATION AND HOMELAND

Algeria has a population of almost 34 million, 60%–70% of whom are under the age of 30. Some 100,000 Algerians live in France, mainly for economic reasons but also because of deep historical ties. Many of these Algerians lead marginalized lives outside the mainstream of French culture, although they are third- or fourth-generation French residents. In 2006, French president Nicolas Sarkozy, for example, wondered aloud why there are no "French" players on the French national football team. The team's most famous player, Zinedine Zidane, was born in the French town of Marseille but is of Algerian descent.

Algeria is located in North Africa on the Mediterranean Sea. It is situated to the west of Libya and Tunisia and east of Morocco. The north is relatively fertile and mountainous. The south includes part of the Sahara desert. In all, more than four-fifths of the country is desert.

3 LANGUAGE

Arabic is the national language of Algeria. Before the Arab conquests, Berber was the chief spoken language. Today, Berber is still spoken in very rural areas.

Arabic, a highly evolved Semitic language that is related to Hebrew and Aramaic, is spoken by the majority of people in Algeria. Written Arabic has two forms: the first is classical Arabic, which is derived from the Quran. Modern Standard Arabic is the language of the written media throughout the Arab-speaking world. Algerians also speak many dialects of Arabic. The Algerian dialect includes many slang terms from French. The dialect also includes many Berber words, including the names for plants and areas.

The literacy rate among Algerians over 15 years of age is 70%—79% for men and 60% for women. French is widely spoken, English less so. As in all Arabic countries, the Algerians take great pride in the Arabic language, as they believe it is the language in which Allah narrated the Quran to the Prophet Muhammad.

Some of the more common Arabic words used in Algeria (as in most Arabic) are religious in nature. When pledging to do something, an Algerian Muslim says, *Insha' Allah* (If God wills it). Prior to any action, a Muslim should say, *Bismillah* (in the name of God).

Common Algerian female names are *Nafisa,* `*Aysha,* and *Farida.* Common male names are `*Abd al-Haq, Hamid,* and `*Abd al-Latif.*

4 FOLKLORE

Algeria has many legends based on the exploits of Muslim leaders who resisted the Crusaders or the French colonizers. These leaders often come from highly religious backgrounds and are considered well learned. They are called *marabouts,* or holy men, and they are believed to have *baraka,* a blessing or divine grace that allows them to perform miracles. Their burial sites are often destinations of pilgrimage, and some have become saints in the popular mind. Many people visit their graves to ask for intercession.

Most folklore in Muslim countries tells stories of important figures in religious history. One such story, which is commemorated annually throughout the Islamic world, tells of *al-Isra' wa al-Mi`raj.* According to legend, on the 26th day of the Islamic month of Rajab, the Prophet Muhammad traveled at night from Mecca, Saudi Arabia (then Hijaz) to Jerusalem. From Jerusalem, he rode his wondrous horse, al-Burak, on a nocturnal visit to heaven.

5 RELIGION

The overwhelming majority of Algerians are Muslims. The practice of Islam, however, varies from individual to individual. For example, the secular revolutionaries who fought against France in the War of Independence called themselves *mujahideen,* or "those who struggle in the cause of God." Once victorious, however, the Algerian revolutionaries created a secular state. Most Algerians belong to the Sunni sect of Islam, which was introduced by the conquering Arabs. There are still remnants, however, of the Kharijite influence, which espouses a stricter egalitarianism.

Islam teaches that God regularly sent guidance to humans in the form of prophets and accepts the earlier Semitic prophets, including Abraham, Moses, and Jesus. Muslims believe that Muhammad was the last in a line of prophets who were sent with the message that there is only one God. Muslims also believe in heaven and hell, the Day of Judgment, and angels. The Quran is the holy book of Muslims, and it teaches that in order to get to heaven, men and women must believe in God, do good works, and follow the dictates of Allah, as spelled out in the five pillars of Islam: (1) Muslims must pray five times a day; (2) Muslims must give alms, or zakat, to the poor; (3)

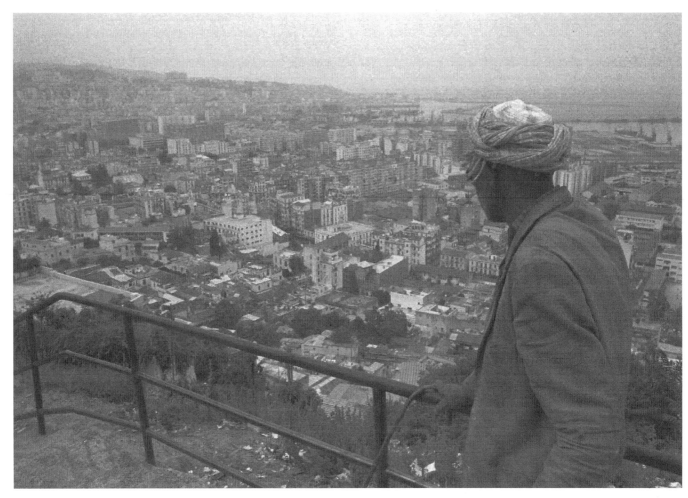

A man overlooks the captial city of Algiers. (AP Images)

Muslims must fast during the month of Ramadan; (4) Muslims must make the pilgrimage, or hajj, to Mecca; and (5) each Muslim must recite the shahada—ashhadu an la illah ila Allah wa ashhadu in Muhammadu rasul Allah—which means, "I witness that there is no god but Allah and that Muhammad is the prophet of Allah."

There are about 25,000 Roman Catholics in Algeria who remained after the French evacuation. Although there were about 140,000 Algerian Jews before the revolution, most moved to France. Today, there are only 1,000 Jews in Algeria.

⁶ MAJOR HOLIDAYS

Algeria commemorates both secular and Muslim religious holidays. One major Muslim holiday is *Eid al-Fitr,* which comes at the end of the month of fasting called Ramadan. During the month, Muslims refrain from eating, drinking, or having sex during the daytime in order to reflect on God and on the plight of the unfortunate who do not have enough food. At the end of the month, Muslims celebrate for three days. The other major Muslim holiday is *Eid al-Adha,* which commemorates the willingness of Abraham, as well as his son, to obey God's command in all things, even as Abraham was ready to sacrifice his son. This holiday falls on the last day of the *hajj* (pilgrimage to

Mecca), and pilgrims are expected to sacrifice a goat or sheep and to offer the meat to the poor.

Religious holidays are celebrated by going to the mosque for group prayers and then coming home to large meals with the family and visiting relatives. Muslims exchange gifts on religious holidays. Part of the feast is normally given to relatives and to the poor.

Secular holidays include New Year's Day (1 January); the socialist Labor Day (1 May), which commemorates worker solidarity around the world; and Independence Day (5 July). Most businesses, banks, and government offices close on these holidays.

⁷ RITES OF PASSAGE

Children between the ages of 5 and 15 are required by law to attend school. After that, they choose their preference for secondary education from a general, technical, or vocational track. Exams taken at the end of their studies decide whether students qualify for continuing education in a university, a technical institute, or a vocational training center.

Major personal events that cause Algerian families to celebrate together include births, baby-naming ceremonies, male circumcisions, and weddings. Weddings are very joyous affairs and feature customs particular to the different regions of the country. In general, marriage celebrations last for several days; the groom is responsible for the cost of the festivities. After days of singing and eating, the bride is carried off to her groom, and the union is followed by another week of celebrations.

8 INTERPERSONAL RELATIONS

Algerians shake hands when greeting one another, and kissing on the cheek between two good friends of the same sex is common. Religious men and women do not shake hands with persons of the opposite sex.

Most socialization revolves around the family. Guests are treated with great hospitality and are served pastries and sweets. Visitors to Algeria frequently find themselves invited to join strangers in tea shops and even in private homes.

Algerian men and women do very little private socializing together. The sexes are separated at most gatherings. Dating is not allowed, and marriages are therefore arranged by well-meaning families or matchmakers.

9 LIVING CONDITIONS

Upon the evacuation of the French forces, Algeria's health care system suffered. Many hospitals were destroyed by the departing French. Because of poor education, there were only 300 doctors in all of Algeria at the end of the war.

Since independence, Algeria has made great improvements in health care. After 1975, the government provided free national health care for everyone. In 1984, the government began shifting the focus of medical care to preventing disease. Instead of building large hospitals, clinics and health centers were built in many areas, and these provided free immunizations and health care. In 2007, Algeria spent 3.6% of its gross domestic product (GDP) on health care. The government spent $104 per capita on health care in 2004. In 2002, Algeria had 2002 physicians, equivalent to 1.13 per 1,000 persons; there were 62,000 nurses, or 1.99 per 1000 persons.

Housing, on the other hand, has become a greater problem than it was at the time of independence. Initially, as hundreds of thousands of French left Algeria for France, many poor Algerians were able to move into vacant properties. Other poor Algerians began building shantytowns near the cities. Unfortunately, the government did not pay much attention to the need for housing. As Algeria's population grew, the number of homes remained relatively stagnant. Today, Algeria has an acute housing shortage, and many families live together in the same home.

Algerian houses and gardens are surrounded by high walls for privacy. Inside, most homes have a central open area or patio, which is surrounded by the rooms of the house. Homes have a receiving room, bedrooms, kitchen, bathroom, and, if the family is wealthy, a second patio. The outside of the house is usually whitewashed brick or stone.

In the 1980s, Algeria began been investing heavily in transportation, though these investments were seriously derailed by the years of vicious violence. In 2004, there were 108,302 km of roadways, of which 70% were paved. There are approximately 4,000 km of railways. A rail line connects major cities and links Algeria with Morocco and Tunisia. Algeria has eight international airports, and its national airline, Air Algerie, links major Algerian cities and serves foreign destinations. There is frequent discussion of privatizing air travel in Algeria, but as of 2008, there were no private domestic carriers.

The Internet and mobile telephony are widely available in Algeria. In 2006, there were 21 mobile phone subscribers, 2.8 million land lines, 25 AM radio stations, 1 FM radio station, and 46 broadcast television stations. Algeria's Internet domain is .dz. In 2007, the country had 2,077 Internet hosts and 2.5 million regular Internet users.

10 FAMILY LIFE

Before the French occupation, Algerian family life was very traditional. Algerians lived with their extended families in tightly knit communities. A mother and father would live with their children in one home. The grandparents of the father would usually live with them. As male children married, they would bring their wives into the family as well. If a daughter became divorced or widowed, she, too, would live with the family. Children were raised by the entire extended family, and people in a town would pay close attention to the children of others in case they needed anything. Marriages were conducted by negotiation between the families of a bride and groom.

With the destruction of so many towns and villages by the French forces, extended family units broke down. Instead, Algerians developed loyalties to people who shared their particular predicament. A group of families living in a concentration camp, for example, developed loyalties to each other, similar to the blood ties of earlier times. In cities, the nuclear family started to predominate as more well-off Algerians began to imitate the French colons. The creation of modern, capitalist industry also turned most Algerians into hourly wage earners. Men and women alike worked in order to provide a minimum standard of living for their families.

In traditional Algerian society, women had generally been segregated in public life. Their primary responsibilities were raising children and taking care of home and husband. During the War of Independence, all this changed. Women were often involved in military battles, and some became commanders. Housewives became involved in planning resistance activities and hiding revolutionaries. The active participation of women led to a greater feeling of self-worth and greater self-empowerment among women. Men, too, began to change their perspectives as they learned to appreciate the contributions that women were making in all fields.

After independence, women were removed from the spotlight but continued to hold on to many of the gains they had earned during the war. As Algerian society has become more conservative in the face of economic deterioration, women's battle to maintain rights already won has taken on a greater urgency. In the last 10 years, women have become particularly politicized, engaging in demonstrations and more vocally expressing their interests.

11 CLOTHING

Two trends in clothing are currently visible in Algeria. Many Algerians, especially in the cities, dress in Western-style clothing. Many others, however, dress in traditional attire. Village men wear a *burnous* (a long hooded robe) and baggy pants, and women wear a *haik* (a long piece of cloth draped over the entire body and head). The *hijab* (a long, loose dress and hair covering) is an Islamic garment worn by many women.

During the civil war, traditional Algerian dress became politicized. The French banned women from wearing the hijab, but the prohibition had little practical effect. Women continued to dress traditionally, both as a sign of resistance to colonialism and because many Muslim women believe that their religion requires the modesty afforded by the hijab. Once independence was achieved, many women continued to wear hijab in public in order to gain greater public access. The hijab, it was felt, allowed them to interact with society as humans, not specifically as women. Recently, armed groups from the government and the opposition have begun assassinating women for dressing either in Western dress or in hijab, as they are viewed as expressing loyalty to either the military junta or to the Islamist opposition parties.

¹² FOOD

Couscous is Algeria's national dish. It is steamed semolina wheat formed into tiny granular particles that are combined with other ingredients to make a main course. Couscous can be accompanied by meat, such as lamb or chicken, and/or mixed with a variety of vegetables. Algerians enjoy combining meat and fruit, and this combination is often served with couscous. The following is a Berber dish that combines all three North African favorites.

Chicken Stuffed with Dried Fruit

3-1/2 pound chicken
5 tablespoons olive oil
1 onion, chopped
1/4 cup pine nuts or chopped almonds
1 cup mixed dried fruit (apricots, apples, pears, prunes, and raisins), soaked, drained, and chopped
salt and pepper

Preheat oven to 325°F. Heat 2 tablespoons oil in a pan, and cook the onion until pale gold. Stir in the nuts and cook for 2 to 3 minutes. Add the dried fruits and seasoning. Let cool. Stuff the chicken with the dried fruit mixture and truss. In a large, heavy, flame-proof casserole, brown the chicken in the remaining oil. Sprinkle with salt and pepper, and lay the chicken on one side. Cover the dish and cook in the oven for 1-1/2 hours, turning the chicken every 30 minutes. Leave chicken breast-side up for the last 30 minutes. Serve the chicken and stuffing with couscous.

(from *North African Cooking: Exotic Delights from Morocco, Tunisia, Algeria and Egypt,* by Hilaire Walden)

Spices are used in abundance in Algerian cooking, especially cumin, coriander, and cinnamon. Couscous can be mixed with honey, cinnamon, and almonds to make a pudding-like dessert.

Pork and alcoholic beverages are forbidden by the Islamic faith. Algeria does, however, produce wine, which it exports to Europe.

¹³ EDUCATION

Algeria has made great advances in education. At the time of independence, fewer than 1 million children were enrolled in school. The government sent many teachers to be trained abroad and hired many teachers from other countries to help make up the shortfall. Schools were built and enlarged. By 1975, 1.5 million children were in school, and by 2004, 12.5 million were enrolled. The seriousness with which the government viewed education is evidenced by the country's expenditures in the area. In 2003, Algeria spent 40% of its budget on

schooling. The results can be seen in improved literacy rates. At the time of independence, only 10% of Algerians were literate. By 2007, fully 70% of the population had achieved literacy.

¹⁴ CULTURAL HERITAGE

Algerian literature stresses themes of nationalism, land, and tradition—elements that are considered vital to the decolonization process that Algeria has undergone. Perhaps the most famous French-language Algerian writer is Albert Camus, an essayist, playwright, and novelist. In 1957, Camus won the Nobel Prize in Literature. Another great Algerian French writer was Frantz Fanon, author of The Wretched of the Earth (1961), which is considered one of the great works of postcolonial literature. Algerian-produced films have gained acclaim worldwide. The 1982 Cannes Film Festival award was won by an Algerian, Mohammed Lakhdar-Hamina, for his film *Desert Wind,* about the lives of Algerian women within traditional society. By far the most famous Algerian film is the 1966 black-and-white classic The Battle of Algiers, directed by the world-renowned Algerian director Gillo Pontecorvo. It tells the story of the Algerian War of Independence against the French and features some of the actual guerrilla fighters in the film. It won the Grand Prize at the Venice Film Festival and was nominated for three Academy Awards in the United States: best screenplay, best director, and best foreign-language film.

¹⁵ WORK

Since independence, Algeria has worked hard to industrialize its economy. The costs of industrialization and social welfare have been met by oil and natural gas production. In 2007, oil and gas made up approximately 60% of Algeria's budget revenues, 30% of GDP, and 96% of export earnings. The country has the eighth largest natural gas reserves in the world and is the fourth largest gas exporter. Algerians have recently begun mining and exporting nonfuel minerals such as mercury, phosphate, and iron ore. Algeria's GDP growth rate in 2006 was 4.6%, outpacing most of Europe and the United States. In addition to these sources of employment, Algerian laborers manufacture electronics, building materials, plastics, fertilizer, paper, clothing, leather goods, and food products. About one-third of workers are employed in the industrial sector. Although in the 1980s and 1990s, many Algerians worked in the farm sector, in 2004, only 8.1% did. In all, 61% worked in industry. Algerians who do not find work at home are often successful at finding employment across the Mediterranean in Europe. Algerian workers are commonplace in Europe, especially in France.

¹⁶ SPORTS

Algeria's national sport is football, known as soccer in the United States. Football is popular both as a spectator sport and as a participation sport played by boys and men. In the city, boys play outside housing developments. Algeria has a national team that participates in matches organized by the African Football Confederation. In 2008, FIFA (International Federation of Association Football) ranked Algeria's national team 17th among the teams in Africa and 78th in the world.
Algerians also enjoy horseback riding and swimming. Clubs that specialize in water activities are found along the Mediterranean coast.

¹⁷ ENTERTAINMENT AND RECREATION

Algeria's newspapers are published in both Arabic and French, and television shows are also produced in both languages. There are three radio networks, and each broadcasts in a different Algerian language—Arabic, French, and Berber.

Although Algeria has movie theaters, there are not enough for Algeria's population. Swimming pools in most cities and villages are very limited in number, and Western-style dance halls are almost nonexistent. Algerians are beachgoers. Summer resorts along the Mediterranean coast are popular with the middle class and are centers for swimming, water skiing, and tennis.

¹⁸ FOLK ART, CRAFTS, AND HOBBIES

Algerian handicrafts include rugs, pottery, embroidery, jewelry, and brass. Handwoven baskets are sold at *suqs* (markets) and used by customers to carry the goods they purchase.

¹⁹ SOCIAL PROBLEMS

The greatest problems facing Algeria today stem from the bitterness engendered by the long, vicious civil war. In addition to the hundreds of thousands of civilians massacred by both sides, the infrastructure of the country suffered great deterioration. The capital, Algiers, became an armed camp, with certain districts controlled by the military and the remainder run by the resistance. Both sides targeted civilians in order to spread fear and hatred.

Life has slowly returned to normal, but in 2007, several European tourists were kidnapped, some of whom died in captivity. Violence has returned to parts of Algeria since a lull in the late 1990s; though crime rates are significantly reduced, the trend is troubling for the country.

In 2007, the unemployment rate was 14%, and the percentage of the population living below the poverty rate was 25%.

The government is also faced with the question of what to do with the refugees from the disputed Western Sahara. According to 2006 estimates, 90,000 were living in squalid conditions in the southwestern part of the country. Additionally, there are approximately half a million internally displaced persons as a result of continued internal violence.

²⁰ GENDER ISSUES

Human trafficking is a significant problem, particularly among sub-Saharan women, who are often promised transit trough Algeria to the European Union but find themselves instead sold into brothels in Algeria or other destinations. Slavery is also a concern, particularly among orphaned children. During the bloody civil war, many urban, educated women sided with the moderates against the Islamists, fearing the imposition of strict Islamic laws. Still, as in many Islamic countries, many Algerian women gladly wear the abaya and the hijab, believing it to be a marker of modesty, a highly valued attribute in both Arab and Muslim culture, as well as a symbol of adherence to the teachings in the Quran.

²¹ BIBLIOGRAPHY

"Algeria: Core Health Indicators." World Health Organization, 2007.

Bourdieu, Pierre. *The Algerians.* Boston: Beacon Press, 1958.

Chrisafis, Angelique. "France Heads to Right as Political Showman Delivers Final Performance of Campaign." *The Guardian,* May 5, 2007.

Hijabm, Nadia, Mervat Hatem, Shahla Haeri, Valentine M. Moghadam, Susan Schaefer Davis, Leila Hessini, Anita M. Weiss, and Sharon Siddique. "Women and Social Reform." *Oxford Islamic Studies Online. The Oxford Encyclopedia of the Islamic World.* http://www.oxfordislamicstudies.com (accessed March 18, 2008).

Hodgson, Marshall. *The Venture of Islam: The Classical Age of Islam.* Chicago: University of Chicago Press, 1974.

Horne, Alistair. *A Savage War of Peace: Algeria, 1954–1962.* New York: Viking, 1977.

Hourani, Albert. *A History of the Arab Peoples.* New York: Warner Books, 1992.

Joffé, George. "Algeria: Year in Review 2005." *Encyclopedia Britannica Online* (accessed March 18, 2008).

Lawrence, Bruce. *Defenders of God: The Fundamentalist Revolt Against the Modern Age.* San Francisco: Harper & Row, 1989.

Memmi, Albert. *The Colonizer and the Colonized.* Boston: Beacon Press, 1965.

Mernissi, Fatima. *Beyond the Veil: Male-Female Dynamics in Modern Muslim Society.* Bloomington: Indiana University Press, 1975.

Metz, Helen Chapin, ed. *Algeria: A Country Study.* Washington, DC: Federal Research Division, Library of Congress, 1993.

"Sex and Sexuality." *Encyclopedia of the Q'uran.* http://www.brillonline.nl (accessed March 18, 2008).

Voll, John Obert. *Islam: Continuity and Change in the Modern World.* Boulder, CO: Westview Press, 1982.

Walden, Hilaire. *North African Cooking: Exotic Delights from Morocco, Tunisia, Algeria and Egypt.* Edison, NJ: Chartwell Books, 1995.

—revised by J. Henry

AMHARA

PRONUNCIATION: ahm-HAH-rah
LOCATION: Ethiopia
POPULATION: About 14 million
LANGUAGE: Amharic
RELIGION: Coptic Monophysite Christianity
RELATED ARTICLES: Vol. 1: Ethiopians; Tigray

¹ INTRODUCTION

Among the many ethnic groups in Ethiopia, the Amhara are the most populous, representing about one-fourth of the population. Their language, Amharic, is the official language of Ethiopia. From the time when modern Ethiopia was the realm of Abyssinia, the Amhara and the Tigray filled the ranks of the political elite of the country, except when the Italians controlled Ethiopia as a colony from 1936–1942. Until 1974, all Ethiopian emperors were either Amhara or Tigray. In the 2000s, Tigray dominate the Ethiopian government. Amhara remain a dominant social force, however.

² LOCATION AND HOMELAND

The traditional homeland of the Amhara people is the central highland plateau of Ethiopia. For over 2,000 years they have inhabited this region. Walled by high mountains and cleaved by great gorges, the ancient realm of Abyssinia has been relatively isolated from the influences of the rest of the world. Situated at altitudes ranging from roughly 2,100–4,300 m (7,000–14,000 ft) and at latitudes roughly between 9o to 14o north of the equator, the rich volcanic soil together with a generous rainfall and cool, brisk climate offers its population a stable agricultural and pastoral existence. However, because the Amhara were an expansionist, militaristic people who ruled their country through a line of emperors, the Amhara people can now be found all over Ethiopia.

³ LANGUAGE

The language of the Amhara people is Amharic. It is a Semitic language somewhat related to Arabic and Hebrew. Its origins derive from a Sabean language spoken by merchants and traders who migrated into Ethiopia from the Yemen region of South Arabia about 3,000 years ago. This South Arabian population settled in the highlands of Ethiopia as farmers and traders mixed with those inhabitants already present. These earlier residents are known as the Agau people. Borrowing occurred from the Agau language and Amharic emerged as it is spoken today.

⁴ FOLKLORE

Amhara culture has a wealth of folklore in the form of proverbs, legends, myths, and religious parables and anecdotes. This folklore often teaches moral lessons to children and reminds adults of proper conduct. It also provides explanations for phenomena that are otherwise unexplainable to the average Amhara peasant farmer, since scientific explanations are most often outside the realm of Amhara knowledge. A good example which shows how a story weaves explanation into a cultural institution and reinforces that institution is the phenomenon

of menstruation. How does one account for this regular emission of blood when modern knowledge of reproductive biology is outside the realm of one's culture?

The Amhara culture is patriarchal and authoritarian, emphasizing the superiority of the male over the female. The Amhara people historically had an imperialistic, militant, and expansionist government led by highly capable emperors directing armies with superior military strategies. There is much in Amhara folklore idealizing the image of the Amhara warrior who vanquishes the enemy through the shedding of the enemies' blood. In the same way that a warrior sheds the blood of his enemy, according to Amhara folklore, so God has "cursed" woman, shedding her blood each month to remind her that she is the vanquished, the servant of her father and her husband. In return for her loyalty, she will be rewarded with healthy children, a large family, and a strong man to keep her family safe. There are also stories that teach that the enemy is not to be hated but is rather to be appreciated, because without an enemy, how is a warrior to prove his worth and establish his identity and status in his community and society?

⁵ RELIGION

The Amhara people are Coptic Monophysite Christians. The population was converted to Christianity in the 4th century AD and their form of the religion has changed very little, if at all, since its beginnings in Ethiopia. Ancient Amhara culture had a writing system, and there exists a wealth of texts that have preserved the ancient teachings of Christianity in a language that is not spoken by living communities today but remains the language of the Church, something like Latin does within the Catholic religion. This is the language of Geez.

Amhara Christianity is very unlike what Westerners recognize as Christianity. Ethiopian Christianity is loaded with Old Testament religion and folklore, as well as material often considered a part of so-called "pagan" religion. Hence, we can say that Amhara religion consists of four separate but interwoven realms of religious belief. First, there is the dominant Monophysite Christian religion, including the Almighty God, the Devil, and the saints and angels in Heaven. Second, there are the *zar* and *adbar* protector spirits who exact tribute in return for physical and emotional security and who may punish, in the case of the former, or neglect, in the case of the latter, for failure to recognize them through the practice of the appropriate rituals. Third is the belief in *buda*, a class of people who possess the evil eye and exert a deadly power over the descendants of God's "chosen children." The fourth category of beliefs includes the ghouls and devils that prowl the countryside, creating danger for unsuspecting persons who cross their path. Although the Christian beliefs have been practiced since nearly the beginning of Christianity, the "pagan" elements probably go back much further.

⁶ MAJOR HOLIDAYS

Each and every Amhara person has a patron saint who is recognized on that saint's day. The celebration involves the host throwing a party for relatives and friends at his or her homestead, serving coffee and small treats, and having hours of conversation. There are major saints' days that everyone will celebrate. Sts. Mary (Mariam), Michael (Mikaeyl), Gabriel (Gahbrieyl), and George (Giyorgis). On these days chickens, sheep, or goats may be slaughtered for feasting. But there are also over 200 days of the year in the Coptic Christian calendar which prescribe fasting, such as Easter. There are also secular holidays such as Battle of Adwa Day, celebrating the victory over the Italians in 1896, and Freedom Day, celebrating the driving out of the previous communist dictatorship in 1991.

7 RITES OF PASSAGE

Marriage and death mark two major rites of passage in Amhara society. In a society where the virginity of the girl is highly valued, she is very often married very young, normally shortly after her first menstruation, but sometimes even earlier. Marriage is an elaborate celebration involving gift-giving negotiations and reciprocities, feasting, date-planning, new house-building for the couple, and so on. The day of the actual wedding is an all-day, all-night party involving feasting, drinking, and intense conversation. The bride's virginity must be proven after consummation of the marriage by a show of blood on a cloth. In the Amhara warrior tradition, the men in the wedding party wave the cloth like a flag of victory, put it on their heads, and dance and sing and drink to celebrate the victory and the consummation of the marriage. If the bride does not shed blood, implying that she is not a virgin, she risks the punishment of being hung upside down in a tree and semiasphyxiated over a smoky *qoso* fire. The groom may take a piece of glass or a razor blade to bed with him to assure that blood is on that cloth in order to preserve his honor (marrying a woman who is not a virgin is considered dishonorable).

The ritual of death is a very quiet affair. Upon the passing of an aged person the body is washed, wrapped in new funerary clothing, and, within 24 hours after death, is carried in a woven straw mat to the church, where it is buried, accompanied by the prayers of the priest. The death of a person who is younger, by accident or disease, is a time of great shock and sadness and often involves much more community activity. For a period of time after the burial, relatives and friends will come to the house of the deceased and sit for a time in quietude. The host will serve coffee, bread, and small snacks to the visitors, who offer their prayers and condolences and depart.

8 INTERPERSONAL RELATIONS

The Amhara espouse an ancient feudal culture with a considerable elaboration of outward formalities. There are prescribed behaviors of deference to persons of higher status, and a rich inventory of proverbs and parables that teach proper conduct in numerous types of situations: public behavior of children with parents and older relatives; women with their husbands; or men with older or more powerful men. But among status equals—children among themselves; men together in informal situations, such as in beer houses; women enjoying coffee together; men and the women they are with privately—here there is informality and the free expression of feeling.

9 LIVING CONDITIONS

The traditional peasant Amhara lead a life that has not changed much in the past few thousand years, because they practice an ancient form of agriculture which involves ox-drawn plow, simple irrigation techniques or complete dependency on rainfall, and simple tools for harvesting their crops of wheat, barley, hops, beans, and an Ethiopian grain called *teff*. In times past, the cool, temperate highland plateau was blessed with a fertile volcanic soil and ample rainfall to make possible three

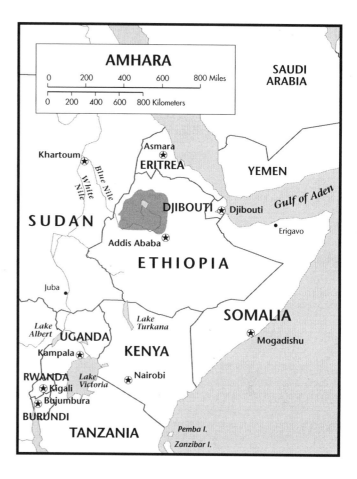

harvests per year. In recent times, the drought and famine of the 1980s, which continues in parts of the highlands to this day, has affected other regions of Amharaland. Because the new government, which took over in 1991, is unsympathetic to the Amhara people, they continue to suffer hardships from the climatic disaster, as well as from political discrimination.

In the city, the Amhara live among peoples from many other cultural groups in tightly clustered contiguous villages. Their houses are built of mud, with corrugated iron roofs. Some travelers have called Addis Ababa "the city of iron roofs." Families most often have either latrine-type toilets or no human waste disposal system at all. In most cases water is acquired from a public pipe located amid these settlements of crowded communities.

10 FAMILY LIFE

Both peasant farmers and city residents value large families. Married couples seek to have many children. Parents who have seven living children are considered to be blessed by God. Children represent a source of economic support when they are grown, a form of social security for the parents in their old age. Many children in a family promise many grandchildren who are a joy to be with, and a promise of carrying on family traditions. A family lives and works together. The day begins at dawn. The woman boils the water, roasts the coffee beans, and pounds them into the grounds that are brewed for the morning coffee. She prepares the breakfast, which is often the leftovers from dinner the night before. The children eat first

An Amhara woman with her child in Ethiopia.
(Robert Caputo/Aurora/Getty Images)

and are sent on their errands that contribute to the tasks of the household. Then the husband eats his breakfast. In the city the husband will go off to work, if he has work, while the wife remains in the village caring for hers and other children of relatives and friends. Often women have their own jobs to go to; many women own coffee or beer houses or work in hair salons. One commonly sees an unrelated child working in the house, taking care of a baby and doing simple household chores. This child may be an orphan or one who was abandoned in the streets of Addis Ababa because of extreme poverty.

¹¹ CLOTHING

The Amhara live at cold, high altitudes. Even the capital city of Addis Ababa lies at about 2,300 m (7,500 ft). Therefore, Amhara clothing is designed to conserve body heat. The Amhara of the city today commonly wear familiar Western-type clothing made in China, Singapore, and the Philippines. But many still prefer the native dress which consists of jodhpur trousers and long shirt, covered by a soft, sheet-sized cotton wrap called a *gabi*. This is worn by both men and women, but the style of these clothes varies according to the gender of the person. In the countryside, the Amhara do not wear shoes, but in

the towns and the city shoes are generally worn to protect the feet against the sharp debris of the streets.

¹² FOOD

The range of altitude in Ethiopia allows for a great variety of food crops to be grown. In the highlands the Amhara grow barley, wheat, hops, and a variety of beans. In the mid-range altitudes the farmer can grow millet and *teff,* another variety of wheat. The major export cash crop, coffee, is grown in this mid-range ecology. Coffee is an integral part of the Ethiopian cuisine as well as a major national cash crop for both internal consumption and export. In the lowlands, the Amhara grow the staple spice that is central to the cuisine of Ethiopia—cayenne pepper, which, together with a dozen other spices ground together, makes up the *berbere* sauce that is key to Ethiopian cuisine. Sugar cane is a major lowland crop the people cannot do without. Although Amhara cuisine is known to be very spicy, much of the vegetable fare need not be hot and spicy and may be favored by people with sensitive stomachs. The rate of coffee consumption is one of the highest in the world, although tea is also a very popular beverage. The eating of pork is forbidden by the Christian Amhara.

¹³ EDUCATION

The Amhara have traditionally seen formal education as under the authority of the Ethiopian Coptic Christian Church. In modern times, encouraged by the last emperor, Haile Sellassie I, secular education has become a dominant institution in the urban areas, and to a lesser extent in the countryside as well. Although in the towns and countryside secular education would appear slow compared to the Western view, in the city and in some towns Western-sponsored educational institutions provide a decent enough education to allow their students to enter the Addis Ababa University. This university provides good training in political science, economics, history, and anthropology. Many students today may attend institutions for graduate education in Europe and America, studying medicine as well as the above subjects.

¹⁴ CULTURAL HERITAGE

Some 3,000 years ago, Semitic-speaking people (very likely including Jews) from South Arabia crossed the straits of Babel-Mendab into the highlands of Ethiopia. Discovery of the fertile soils there then brought farmers as well as traders and merchants. They brought with them agricultural skills which included terracing, irrigation, canals, hydraulic devices, the plow, and the camel. They were also skilled in weaving and making incense. They brought a writing system consisting of a 256-character syllabary, and they practiced sophisticated techniques of construction which included stone-masonry. They also were familiar with and established a large-scale political system which enabled them eventually to evolve a centralized empire. The earliest and most notable example of this was the city-state of Axum where, in the mid-4th century, the emperor Ezana converted his people to Christianity.

¹⁵ WORK

In the countryside, work roles and specific tasks are segregated according to age and sex. Children collect cow dung from the fields, throw it into a hole, mix it with water, and make cow pie batter which is then shaped into round, flat pies and dried to use as fuel for the hearthfires. Women carry water back to their homesteads in large, round, narrow-necked clay jugs that can weigh over 45 kg (100 lbs). They also grind the grain, make bread from the flour, prepare the meals, and make the beer and liquor. Men plow the fields, cut the grain, litigate in court, and serve in the local militia. Both men and women look forward to the weekly market day when goods are bartered, bought, and sold, and a good deal of social activity is enjoyed. In the towns and city, numerous small businesses flourish, selling everything imaginable, and other forms of wage-labor can be found, if one is fortunate. Beggars are a very common sight in the city, and include ex-soldiers from the losing side of the recent civil war; mothers with their infant children in their arms; old men and women with no means of support; and children whose families have been lost in the war, from disease, or who have simply abandoned them because of extreme poverty.

[16] SPORTS

Soccer, known as "football," is a passion among most Ethiopians. Running is also a very popular sport, as well as a mode of physical conditioning. Amhara and other Ethiopian individuals are prime marathon runners because the high altitude prepares them well for competition in other countries. There is also the traditional sport of *ganna,* which is somewhat like hockey. The whipping contest carried out on the holiday of *Buhe* is a test of Amhara endurance and toughness. In this contest, two teams come together on a "battlefield" and whip each other until one team flees or is so badly beaten that the elders proclaim the other team the victors. This is a true test of Amhara masculinity and warrior abilities, traits which are emphasized in Amhara culture.

[17] ENTERTAINMENT AND RECREATION

In the countryside, children make their own toys such as dolls, animals, weapons, cars, etc., out of mud, sticks, rocks, rags, tin cans, and the like. Male youth engage in competitive sports. Adults drink in the drinking houses, sing, dance, gossip, and patronize the minstrels who travel from village to village singing of the news and gossip in other villages and in the city and towns. The city offers much more in the form of movie houses, electronic game parlors, drinking houses and night clubs, television videos (a booming business in Addis Ababa), and organized sports.

[18] FOLK ART, CRAFTS, AND HOBBIES

Amhara painting is a dominant art form in Ethiopia. It is usually oil on canvas or hide, and it normally involves religious themes. Paintings from the Middle Ages are known by art historians from Europe and America as distinct treasures of human civilization. The Amhara are also weavers of beautiful patterns embellished with embroidery. They are also fine gold- and silversmiths and produce delicate works of filigree jewelry and religious emblems.

[19] SOCIAL PROBLEMS

Haile Sellassie I, Emperor of Ethiopia, was the last in the line of Amhara kings who ruled Ethiopia for almost 2,000 years, with the exception in the Middle Ages of a few incursions from the Falasha Black Jews of the Simien mountains, led by the zeal-

ous Queen Gudit, and Islamic invaders, led by Ahmed Gragn. There were also Italian incursions at the end of the 19th century and again just prior to World War II. The bloody so-called "communist" revolution of 1973 ended the Amhara reign and, with drought and famine raging in the north, threw much of Amhara society into chaos. The overthrow in 1991 put an end to both the brutal dictatorship and the 30-year civil war, but it also left large segments of the Amhara people dispossessed of their land, split from their families, and more impoverished than ever before. Many thousands of Amhara, individually or with families, migrated to towns and the city of Addis Ababa to find a source of food to stay alive, and to try to establish a life until their land could be regained, if at all possible. Because people from many other cultural groups were also migrating to the city, Addis Ababa became overpopulated. Once a lovely city supporting a population of about 600,000 in the mid-1960s, by the 2000s it had swelled to nearly 4 million people.

Amhara men, farmers without city-adapted skills, could only look for day labor or go begging in the streets. Women could cook or sell beer and soft drinks in little mud huts or kiosks. If they were young and attractive, they could work in bars and prostitute themselves making much more money than domestic work could bring. Poverty has driven a preponderance of Amhara women to engage in prostitution either part- or full-time, their ages ranging from around 9 or 10 to 25 or 30 years old. The diseases of poverty accentuate the problems: HIV, tuberculosis, a variety of intestinal bacterial infections, internal and external parasites, leprosy, elephantiasis, schistosomiasis, roundworms, and tapeworms are all widespread. Current efforts to solve these problems have been too few and too weak to make any significant impact on the poverty in one of the poorest nations in the world.

[20] GENDER ISSUES

Sexuality and gender have always been issues to be worked out in traditional societies the world over. The underlying motivations include: a) explaining bodily functions, mainly of women, b) creating symbolic distinctions between the sexes through ritual and genital excision, c) maintaining male domination over reproductive females, and very importantly, d) to create a level of efficiency in work roles—who can do what work best.

Amhara organization of gender roles and the issues that arise from this, especially in modern times, are no exception to these general categories. Amhara women, as in all living species, conceive, gestate, and birth their young. The mother nurses her infant with the milk in her breasts. If she bears twins or if she hasn't enough milk for her child she may seek a lactating woman, a "wet nurse" who has either lost her child or is still lactating shortly after weaning her own child. The most fundamental bond of humans, that of mother and child, prepares the mother to nurture the child through infancy. During infancy the Amhara child is not given its Christian name until it is five years old and strong enough to survive. Until then it is called a pet name which may have no gender reference, such as "pretty little one" or "my lovely."

At forty days the male infant is circumcised. This is performed by a specialist who is expert in this operation and it is relatively simple with very little incidence of complications. After eighty days the female infant has an excision ceremony. This has some variation depending on what part of Amharaland one is in. In the central highlands of Manz the labia minor are excised with a scissors or razor blade. In the region of Gojjam, to the northeast of Manz, the clitoral hood is excised, leaving the clitoral organ exposed. These genital operations are relatively mild compared to those performed in other regions of Ethiopia and Africa. In modern times we see these customs disappearing in the capital city of Addis Ababa and the larger towns, but in the remote rural regions ancient customs prevail.

Amhara women are therefore much more closely tied to their children and the nurturance-based work roles of the homestead. Mothers teach and discipline their young children relative to their age. The work of girls and women include carrying water in large clay vessels on their back, fetching firewood and dung for fuel. When children are available they will retrieve dung and make dried cakes preparing it for fuel. Women clean, separate, and grind grain for either flour or fermentation in making beer or for distillation in making liquor. Women's work begins often before dawn and ends near midnight.

The work of men includes preparing the soil with ox-drawn plow, seeding their apportioned land with the start of the light rains. Then he has little to do until his crops are ready for harvesting. He normally enjoys life at the bars, traveling to see relatives, litigating in the court. But plowing is very hard work. Cutting the barley or wheat or bean crops is tedious. It is his work to slaughter the chickens, sheep, goats, and cattle when the occasion arises. The man is also the hunter when opportunity allows. Certain game on the highland plateau of Ethiopia are endangered species such as the Walia Ibex, Gelada Baboon, Lamergeier Vulture—a majestic bird with a ten foot wingspan, and Semien Wolf. There is protection for these animals yet, the meat of the Ibex, a species of mountain goat, is highly valued and the luxurious main of the Gelada Baboon is worn as a headdress on certain ceremonial occasions.

These gender-defined roles have been fixed by three thousand years of tradition. They have served to adapt and survive these highland populations. But in times of culture change in the more urbanized areas, who are now more in touch with world media and modern technology, culture change is evident. An amendment to the constitution of the present government has a section devoted to the rights of women. Where traditionally girls were frustrated from or directly prevented from going to school, today a girl has the right to an education. A girl's work in the home was important and much needed, but parents are realizing that a girl's education may create opportunities for her to contribute to the family in other ways. Health facilities are becoming more available to women who have had complications in birth or gynecological problems stemming from excision or infection. The Fistula Hospital was the first in the world to treat and surgically repair women torn from birthing through excision adhesions. Oprah Winfrey publicized this hospital in her drive to abolish female genital excision. Women now have greater access to legal services to address problems with husbands or to argue for higher wages or to litigate her fair share of inheritance. And today it is easier for women to enter into the political arena and serve in office. Women's Affairs Offices, called setoch guday in Amharic, are evident in many towns in the Amhara region and serve the women who seek them out. The Women's Affairs Agency is aggressively promoting the education of sex-workers in how to prevent HIV/AIDS or seek help after infection.

[21] BIBLIOGRAPHY

Buxton, David. *The Abyssinians.* New York: Praeger, 1970.

Gish, Steven. *Ethiopia.* New York: Marshall Cavendish Benchmark, 2007.

Levine, Donald. *Wax and Gold.* Chicago: University of Chicago Press, 1965.

Marcus, Harold. *A History of Ethiopia.* Berkeley and Los Angeles: University of California Press, 1994.

Molvaer, Reidulf Knut. *Socialization and Social Control in Ethiopia.* Wiesbaden: Harrassowitz, 1995.

Pankhurst, Richard. *A Social History of Ethiopia.* Trenton: Red Sea Press, 1992.

Reminick, Ronald A. *The Second Oldest Profession: Prostitution in Ethiopia.* Unpublished paper researched under Fulbright Grant to Ethiopia, 1993–1995.

———. *Structure and Functions of Religious Belief Among the Amhara of Ethiopia.* Proceedings of the First

Salih, M.A. Mohamed, and John Markakis. *Ethnicity and the State in Eastern Africa.* Uppsala: Nordiska Afrikainstitutet, 1998.

Smith, Lahra. *Political Violence and Democratic Uncertainty in Ethiopia.* Washington, D.C.: U.S. Institute of Peace, 2007.

United States Conference on Ethiopian Studies. East Lansing, Mich.: African Studies Center, Michigan State University, 1973.

Ullendorf, Edward. *The Ethiopians.* London: Oxford University Press, 1960.

—by R. Reminick

ANGOLANS

PRONUNCIATION: ang-GOH-luhns
LOCATION: Angola
POPULATION: 15 million
LANGUAGE: Portuguese, Ovimbundu, Mbundu, Kongo, Chokwe, and other Bantu languages
RELIGION: Christianity (Catholic and Protestant); indigenous religious beliefs
RELATED ARTICLES: Vol. 1: Bakongo

¹ INTRODUCTION

The territory within the boundaries of the Republic of Angola has had over 500 years of contact with the Portuguese, much of it conflictual. In 1482 the Portuguese established forts and missions along the coast and converted King Alphonso of the Kongo to Christianity. His kingdom maintained perhaps the most harmonious and equal relations with Portugal, engaging in cultural and economic exchanges.

This relationship changed dramatically with the demand for slaves. Beginning in 1483 slave trading began along the coast, penetrated to the interior in the 1700s, and subsequently passed through a series of bans. The first of the bans was in 1836, and although the Portuguese formally abolished slavery in 1875, it was not until 1911 that the slave trade ended.

Portuguese settlement in Angola began earnestly in 1575 with the founding of Luanda, originally a settlement of convicts. However, Angola's great economic potential beckoned Portuguese colonists who in the 1840s arrived in considerable numbers and began cultivating cotton, sugar, sisal and coffee. They also engaged in fishing. With the consent of the European powers, Portugal determined Angola's borders in 1891. In the early 1900s newly developed cacao and palm oil plantations were soon followed by diamond mining. Economic prosperity led to the designation of Angola as a Portuguese overseas territory in 1951. A year later, Portuguese immigrants began to flood the first *colonatos,* planned settlement projects. The Portuguese had a policy of "whitening" the population, and it became state policy for Portuguese men to go out and impregnate Angolan women. Further efforts were directed at culturally assimilating these and other Angolans under the *assimilado* policy. By 1960, only 80,000 of a population of 4.5 million people enjoyed the privileges of Portuguese citizenship, and the policy was abandoned.

Angolan resistance movements pushed back against Portuguese colonization. The People's Movement for the Liberation of Angola (MPLA) led by Agostinho Neto, the National Front for the Liberation of Angola (FNLA) led by Bakongo leader Holden Roberto, and the Union for the Total Independence of Angola (UNITA) led by Ovimbundu leader Jonas Savimbi engaged in armed resistance. The 1974 coup in Portugal, which brought down the government, ended Portugal's colonial wars in Angola as well as in Mozambique and Guinea Bissau. After a protracted struggle and two separate declarations of independence by the MPLA and UNITA, Angola gained its independence from Portugal on 11 November, 1975.

Shortly after independence, the coalition government of the MPLA, FNLA, and UNITA collapsed. Civil war followed, lasting nearly 15 years. With the Cold War in full swing, the Soviet Union backed the ruling MPLA with the assistance of Cuban troops. The United States, Zaire (now the Democratic Republic of the Congo), and China supported the UNITA-FNLA coalition, and South Africa made periodic incursions in support of UNITA. José Eduardo dos Santos succeeded Neto upon his death in 1979. In 1989, dos Santos and Savimbi agreed to elections and foreign withdrawal, completed in 1991. In the first round of the 1992 elections, UNITA perceived that electoral fraud was underway and launched simultaneous attacks around the country. In 1994, the two sides signed a peace treaty guaranteeing UNITA a share in the government and providing for the deployment of a UN peacekeeping force. Nonetheless, heavy fighting resumed intermittently up to Jonas Savimbi's death in a gun battle with government troops in 2002, which also ended UNITA's bid to overthrow the MPLA.

In the post-Savimbi era, the MPLA with international assistance disarmed, demobilized and reintegrated some 80,000 UNITA ex-combatants and thousands more of their family members into civilian life. However, head of state President José Eduardo dos Santos repeatedly postponed elections and manipulated political processes to forestall the promised transition to representative democracy.

² LOCATION AND HOMELAND

Angola is bordered by the Democratic Republic of the Congo to the north, Zambia to the east, and Namibia to the south. Cabinda, to the north, is physically separated from the rest of Angola by the Congo River and a narrow corridor of land belonging to the Democratic Republic of the Congo. To the west lies the Atlantic Ocean. The total area is 481,354 sq mi (1,246,700 sq km). The capital is Luanda. Two types of terrain characterize the country: a narrow coastal plain borders the Atlantic Ocean to the west, and an interior plateau covers the rest of the country. The climate is semiarid in the south and along the coast; in the north it varies from cool and dry to hot and rainy.

Several major rivers find their sources in the centrally located Bié Plateau, including the Cunene River flowing to the south and west, the Kuanza River flowing northwest to the Atlantic, the Kwango River, flowing northward, which joins the Congo River to the north, and the Zambeze to the east, far below Victoria Falls. The Cunene River has four hydroelectric dams.

The tallest mountains are found in the region of the Bié Plateau. To the southwest, in the Serra Xilengue, Mt. Moco rises to a majestic height of 8,594 ft. While some areas are prone to flooding, others are threatened by desertification. Oil is the main natural resource, but Angola is also rich in diamonds, gold, copper, iron ore, zinc, and manganese. Only 2.65% of the land is arable; much of it is forest and woodland (43%), and 23% is meadow and pasture. Other uses account for 32%.

A network of roads connects most of the country, although it is least developed in the southeast. Three rail lines terminating at ocean ports run approximately east to west from the interior. The longest and most important of these originates in the Katanga copperbelt of the Democratic Republic of the Congo. Since 1928 the Benguela Railroad carried the bulk of Zaire's minerals to Lobito port until rebels sabotaged the line in the 1980s. In 2008 work to reopen the line was nearing completion.

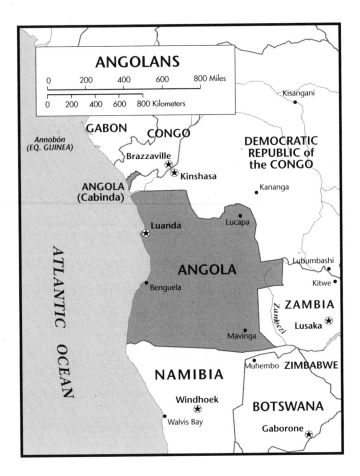

ANGOLANS

In 2000 the population was estimated to be around 15 million and was projected to reach over 20 million by 2015. The largest city was Luanda with a population of 500,000. The majority ethnic group was the Ovimbundu, comprising 37.2% of the population. The Mbundu were second at 21.6%, followed by the Kongo at 13.2%, and the Luimbe-Nganguela and the Nyaneka-Humbe at 5.4% each. Smaller groups account for the remaining 17.2% of the population. Scattered in the arid lower third of Angola are seminomadic peoples, who until the 20th century hunted and gathered. They since have adopted more sedentary lifestyles such as herding and planting.

³ LANGUAGE

Portuguese is the official language, although 95% of Angolans speak Ovimbundu, Mbundu, Kongo, Chokwe, and other Bantu languages. Portuguese remains important because it is the language of government, national media, and international relations. However, since independence, African languages have been introduced into the primary school classroom. Literacy in African languages is being encouraged and regional radio broadcasts occur in local languages.

⁴ FOLKLORE

The Kongo ethnic group to the north claims descent from the ancient Christian kingdom founded by Alfonso I in the early 16th century. Alfonso I has assumed a great importance both to Kongo identity and to Portuguese international relations history.

The first president of Angola is also its greatest hero. Agostinho Neto was both a physician and an accomplished poet. He made many contributions to *Mensagem*, a literary review with anti-colonial goals. He belonged to a group of young intellectuals responsible for shaping the country politically and culturally. Their battle cry in the early 1950s was, "Let us discover Angola." They also coined the term, *angolidade* (Angolinity), Angola's equivalent of *negritude* or "Africanization." In 1955 he published nationalist poetry. He was the founding father of the resistance movement, MPLA.

⁵ RELIGION

Angolans are extremely Christianized with as many as half of the population identifying themselves as Catholic and at least 15% as Protestant. Estimates of traditional religious practices vary, but it is likely that close to half of the population also believes or subscribes to some form of indigenous religion. The Catholic Church has at times been identified with colonialism, and therefore has gone through periods of conflict with the government. In 1949 Simon Mtoko, a Protestant, founded a Christian sect patterned after the Kimbanguists of Lower Congo (DRC). Kimbanguism, an African offshoot of Protestant Christianity, is practiced by an undetermined number of Bakongo in the northwest region of the country (see **Bakongo**).

⁶ MAJOR HOLIDAYS

Independence Day, November 11, is the national holiday. On this day the president usually makes a national address, and celebratory events such as wheelchair races are held. Other public holidays include the Day of the Martyrs in January to commemorate a huge massacre of Angolans committed by the Portuguese; *Inicio de Luta Armada* (Commencement of Armed Struggle Day) on February 4 (1961); National Hero's Day (anniversary of the birth of President Neto) on September 17; and Foundation of the MPLA Workers' Party Day on December 10 (1956). Victory Day is on March 27, Youth Day on April 14, Armed Forces Day on August 1, and Pioneers' Day on December 1. The most recent holiday is Reconciliation Day on April 4 to mark the anniversary of the end of the war approximately two months after the death of Jonas Savimbi.

Christian holy days and New Year's Day are widely celebrated. On Christmas and New Year's Day friends assume godmother (*madrinha*) and godfather (*padrinho*) relationships. They take turns giving gifts to each other; one offers the other a gift on Christmas and the other returns the gesture on New Year's. In the capital, young people are likely to spend New Year's Eve with their families until midnight, just long enough to taste some champagne, and then head for the night clubs with friends until early morning. Angolans celebrate *carnival*, (Mardi Gras) the Tuesday immediately preceding Ash Wednesday.

⁷ RITES OF PASSAGE

Indigenous traditions revolving around birth, puberty, and death still persist despite acculturation to Christianity and Western customs. For example, the Mbwela people hold masked festivals during the *mukanda* circumcision rite. In the ceremony, the *ndzingi* (masked anthropomorphic giants) dance for the young boys. Christianity has influenced the rites of passage for a majority of the population. Birth, baptism, marriage, and funeral ceremonies are marked by church rites.

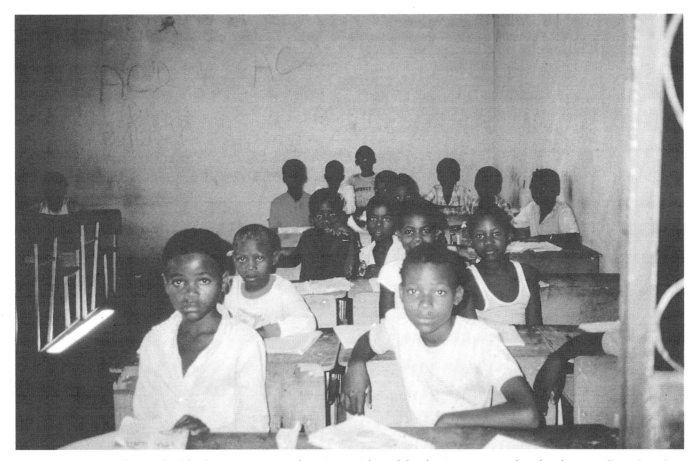

Classroom in Luanda, Angola. Schools continue to struggle against social instability, low investment, and teacher shortages. (Jason Laure)

People drink champagne and give gifts to celebrate the birth of a child. Some funeral celebrations last for days and are accompanied by feasts and drink. They can move quickly from sadness to festivity where it is fitting to celebrate a life fully lived (as opposed to mourning the loss of a child or young person).

8 INTERPERSONAL RELATIONS

High value is placed on personal relationships and greetings are essential to making and maintaining good relations. The most common greeting is the Portuguese *Ola* (Hello) followed by *Como esta*? or *Como vai*? (How are you?). Depending on the time of the day, one might hear *Bom dia* (Good morning), *Boa tarde* (Good afternoon), or *Boa noite* (Good night). Handshaking is common. A kiss on each cheek is becoming an accepted greeting among friends in urban life, although older people prefer to shake hands. Pointing is considered rude.

Young people usually choose their own spouses, but it is viewed as risky to wed someone who may not be able to bear children, and it has become customary for a serious boyfriend to wait until his girlfriend becomes pregnant before proposing marriage. In fact, the end of budding love relationships is seldom formally declared so that at some future point the boy can return and resume a sexual relationship with a former girlfriend. Once engaged, the boy brings his family and a small delegation of friends to visit the family of his girlfriend. It is common practice for the boy to bring enough cloth for his girlfriend's mother to make a dress, a western suit and tie for the father (or ranking father figure), drinks for the family and friends, and perhaps an envelope with money and a written note explaining intentions to be read before all gathered.

As sexual intercourse is considered a normal part of life, straight men and women may have occasional interludes with members of the same sex, and such encounters do not lead to anxious self-questioning about sexual orientation.

9 LIVING CONDITIONS

Living conditions deteriorated dramatically, especially for the Ovibundu over the course of the civil war, and have not returned to pre-war levels. The majority of Angolans still do not have access to clean water, health care and medical facilities, and a dependable food supply. Some 10 million people live on less than $1 a day, over 40% of children under the age of five are underweight for age, and life expectancy for the average adult is 45 years. On the Human Development Index, which measures general well-being (life expectancy, education, and standard of living), Angola ranks 162nd out of 177 countries.

Houses are typically made out of local materials, with mud or cinderblock walls and thatched or galvanized iron roofs. In Luanda, where space is limited, apartment living is becoming more common. However, since 2002 more than 50,000 people have been evicted from their houses to make room for luxury housing in Luanda.

¹⁰ FAMILY LIFE

Families tend to be close-knit nuclear units with strong extended kin relationships. Until the war, there was little need for orphanages or hospices as working family members took in those needing special care. However, the large number of casualties and land mine victims in the prime of life has meant that children, elderly people and kin have had to assume greater responsibility for their families, which has raised tension and stress in family life.

Most ethnic groups are both matrilineal and patriarchal, meaning that males inherit from their mother's brother. In the Mbundu ethnic group, a daughter would join her husband in his village, and a son would join his mother's brother's village. The Ovimbundu ethnic group has a double inheritance system, both matrilineal and patrilineal.

¹¹ CLOTHING

In the towns and cities, Western-style clothing is common and urban Angolans go to great lengths to be in sync with the latest fashions in clothing, accessories, cell phones, and sunglasses—much of which is imported from Brazil. Angolan youth prefer casual jeans and T-shirts, except for special occasions. The villages remain more traditional, where women wear *panos*, African wrap-around batik garments. Body tattoos on young people are catching on, but are rare in rural areas. Some groups such as the Mukubao in the southern province of Kuando Kubango are very traditional and do not wear clothing.

¹² FOOD

Those who can, eat three meals a day. A good breakfast consists of bread, eggs, tea, or coffee. On occasion, mothers may prepare a special breakfast treat of sweet rice *(arroz doce)*, which is a mixture of rice, milk, eggs, sugar, and a twist of orange or lemon rind for flavoring. If the noon-day meal is heavy, something light like soup will be served for supper.

The staple foods include cassava, corn, millet, sorghum, beans, sweet potatoes, rice, wheat, and bananas. Typical noon-day meals in the north consist of a ball of manioc dough called "funge bombó" (cassava flour mixed with boiling water) with fish, chicken, or meat. People everywhere enjoy pounded cassava leaves *(kizaka)*. In the south a maize meal dough ball is preferred called "funge" or "pirao" in Portuguese.

Specialty dishes include *mwamba de galinha*, a palm-nut paste sauce in which chicken, spices, and peanut butter are cooked, creating a delightful aroma. The abundance of fresh and saltwater fish provides the opportunity for an unusual combination of fresh and dried fish in a unique dish, *kalulu, the key ingredients of which are African eggplant, gumbo, and red palm oil.* Beans cooked in palm oil also are popular. However, *cabidela*, chicken cooked in chicken's blood sauce and eaten with rice and cassava dough, stands out as one of Angola's mouthwatering delights.

Angolans also drink a lightly fermented corn beverage called "kissangua." A version of this drink is made from sprouted whole sorghum grains. It is lacto-fermented, slightly alcoholic, fizzy, and highly nutritious.

¹³ EDUCATION

Education is compulsory between the ages of 7 and 15 years, and is provided free. However, at the primary level education tends to be of low quality, and high schools are rather elite. For both girls and boys, primary enrollment is 37% while secondary enrollment is 18%. Overall, 56% of males are literate compared with 28% of females. Schools continue to struggle against social instability, low investment, and teacher shortages. Private schooling exists, but is costly.

Angola has two well-established universities: The Catholic University of Angola (CUA) and Agostinho Neto University, the public university in Luanda. However, the three campuses of Agostinho Neto have been devastated by poor economic conditions resulting from the war. Other universities include the Universidade das Lusíadas with a campus in Benguela and one in Lobito. Parents who can manage it, send their children to study abroad in Cuba, Russia, and more popularly, the United States.

¹⁴ CULTURAL HERITAGE

As in most of sub-Saharan Africa, orality has characterized literature in Angola since time immemorial. It is generally agreed that written literature began in 1850 with a book of verse by José da Silva Maia Ferreira. Since 1945 and the liberation struggle, strong links developed between literature and political activism. Many MPLA leaders and members, including Agostinho Neto, took part in this movement. From 1975 until the early 1990s, Angolan writers had to be affiliated with a quasi-governmental organization in order to be published.

Music is closely linked to African oral history. Angolan musicians made their own instruments such as *clochas* (double-bell) and marimbas. Percussion, wind, and string instruments are found throughout the regions. The bow lute *(chilhumba)* is played in the south during long journeys; the lamellophone *(likembe)* is popular in the east. Musical performances often include dancing. Members of the Ngangela ethnic group in the east dance masked. The choreography is distinguished by a young woman catching a man on her shoulders.

Traditional music has strongly influenced popular music. While older people may enjoy Angolan music from the 1970s, young people prefer upbeat rhythmic Angolan *kizomba* music, danced closely together by couples. Cape Verdian music is also considered *kizomba* and is popular. Angolans love their own "semba" music, which has complex secondary and tertiary rhythms that accompany the main beat. Couples dance *semba* much like *kizomba*, but the steps are authentically Angolan. Much of the internationally known Angolan music goes by the name "bonga," but really is *semba* music. Because many Angolan professionals were educated in Cuba, the older crowd also appreciates Cuban and "bachata" music from the Dominican Republic. In the late 1990s, techno music, "kuduru" (literally "hard ass"), became the rage among young Angolans. Kuduru is strongly syncopated, uses rap lyrics, and provides a break from close dancing.

Angola's cultural heritage is tied to the Portuguese language and to a colonial past shared by four other African countries. Along with Mozambique, Guinea Bissau, Sao Tomé and Principe, and Cape Verde, Angola is a member of "The Five," meaning the African Lusaphone countries. They meet regularly to promote culture, trade, and political relations among themselves. Many new buildings in Angola reflect influences of 15th-century Portuguese architecture, some of which still stands. For example, ancient forts, churches, and homes built by Portuguese colonists are found around Luanda.

[15] WORK

Labor and productivity in Angola suffered immensely from the abrupt departure of 90% of the white settlers in 1975. Before leaving, however, the colonials destroyed factories, plantations, and transportation infrastructure. Owing to the subsequent insurgency, the labor force never fully recovered. Today some 71% of Angolans are engaged in agriculture, but mostly in subsistence, which produces only 10% of the gross domestic product (GDP). By contrast, only 10% of the population is engaged in industry, which accounts for 62.6% of the GDP. Angola's cash cow is petroleum, and provides 89.9% of Angola's exports while diamonds provide 5.5%. However, with the exception of artisanal diamond mining, neither is a major provider of jobs. Recently, many young people have found jobs in teaching and in health services. Many Angolans living on the coast supplement their income by fixing up and renting out their homes.

[16] SPORTS

Soccer is the most popular participant and spectator sport, played by both girls and boys. In 2006 Angola was one of only four sub-Saharan countries to qualify for the World Cup. The "Citadel" in Luanda is one of Africa's largest stadiums. A new spin on soccer is "fustal," which is played indoors or outdoors on smaller courts in urban areas. Competitions often are organized between members of the television and radio stations for special entertainment. Basketball is also popular. Since winning its first-ever basketball medal at the Nairobi University Games, the Angola national team won three consecutive All-African championships. Backboards and baskets have sprung up on street corners everywhere. Handball, volleyball, and track and field round out the most popular sports. Angola also has nearly a dozen international chess masters. Children enjoy a traditional game, *ware*, which is played by moving stones around a board either carved from wood, or dug out of the clay soil.

[17] ENTERTAINMENT AND RECREATION

The advent of the satellite dish has made television an increasingly popular form of entertainment in Luanda and other urban centers. The dishes are status symbols and allow Angolans to supplement the government-run station with an array of channels from all over the world. Angolans connect with world popular culture by watching Brazilian shows (in Portuguese), MTV, and American movies with Portuguese subtitles. Residents in apartment buildings lower their costs by sharing the same satellite dish. While cinemas remain a more popular form of entertainment up-country, video rental stores are mushrooming in Luanda, and home video is part of an urban trend toward home entertainment.

[18] FOLK ART, CRAFTS, AND HOBBIES

Luanda's three museums, including the Museum of Anthropology, contain a fine collection of African art and handicrafts. Non-commercial masks and sculptures vary according to ethnic group, and symbolize rites of passage or changes in seasons, and play important roles in cultural rituals. Artisans work with wood, bronze, ivory, malachite, and ceramics. The Lunda-Chokwe in the northeast provinces are uniquely known for their superior plastic arts.

Ten years ago, the Ministry of Culture stifled art by monopolizing control over art production and marketing. Recent deregulation has made handicraft production a blossoming cottage industry. Stylized masks, statuettes, and trinkets (airport art) now flood the popular Futungo tourist market on the outskirts of Luanda. This art may not reflect the deep cultural beliefs of the people, but it provides work and a source of income for people with artistic skills. Shoppers at Futungo market are treated to musicians playing traditional instruments such as *marimbas, kissanges, xingufos* (big antelope horns), and drums, giving the feeling of a village festival.

[19] SOCIAL PROBLEMS

Angola's social ills are myriad. The country still has between 2 to 10 million land mines buried in roads, trails and fields. At least 80,000 people have suffered injuries from those mines and are in need of psycho-social counseling and healing. Ex-combatants are especially susceptible to lawlessness and vice, and they risk returning to the bush as a way of life. The Kimberley Process, launched in 2003, has helped to curb trade in "blood diamonds," but thousands of artisanal miners dig and pan for diamonds in alluvial pits. Many internally displaced persons (IDPs) are still without homes, land, and a dependable source of food. Poor governance and corruption are also rife. It is estimated that $4.2 billion in oil revenues disappeared from government coffers between 1997 and 2002. If these revenues had been invested in Angola's social sector, poor health access, lack of shelter, unemployment, and low productivity could be things of the past.

[20] GENDER ISSUES

As in many parts of Africa women work as hard as or harder than men, but enjoy fewer rights and privileges. Women cultivate the fields, gather wood and water, and do domestic chores. In the village, women typically raise between 6 and 12 children. Because abortion is legal only to save a woman's life, many abortions are performed in secret and under unsafe conditions.

The gap between women's rights in towns as compared to rural villages is quite pronounced. In urban areas, women have fewer children and compete for male-dominated jobs. They drive cars, study at university, vote, occupy non-combative positions in the army, and serve as traffic policewomen. In recent history, five women ministers have led government ministries including oil, fisheries, and culture. Five women are Public Ministry magistrates, and there are three women judges. After the 1992 elections, women won 9.5% of the seats in the legislature, although 5% fewer than in the First Republic. One woman heads a political party and was a candidate in the 1992 elections.

Women's rights groups such as the Organization of Angolan Women are helping to establish literacy programs and health units for women, and ensure that polygynous families have sufficient wealth to support more than one wife.

[21] BIBLIOGRAPHY

"Angola." In *Africa South of the Sahara 2007*. London: Europa Publishers, 2008.
Angola. Paris: Editions Delroisse, n.d.

Collelo, Thomas, ed. *Angola, A Country Study*. 3rd ed. Washington, D.C.: Federal Research Division, Library of Congress; for sale by the Supt. of Docs., US GPO, 1991.

James, W. Martin. *Historical Dictionary of Angola*. Metuchen, NJ and London: The Scarecrow Press, Inc., 2004.

Sommerville, Keith. *Angola: Politics, Economics, and Society*. Marxist Regimes Series. Boulder, Colo.: Lynne Rienner, 1986.

—by R. Groelsema

AZANDE

PRONUNCIATION: uh-ZAHN-day
LOCATION: From upper Nile basin in the southern Sudan to the borders of semitropical rain forests in the Democratic Republic of the Congo
POPULATION: 3.8 million in all countries
LANGUAGE: Azande (Niger-Congo group)
RELIGION: Beliefs revolving around ideas associated with *mangu* (witchcraft); Christianity
RELATED ARTICLES: Vol. 1: Sudanese; Central Africans; Congolese; Zairians

¹ INTRODUCTION

The ethnic term *Azande* refers to a culturally diverse group of peoples who, over the past 200 years, have been brought together under the governance of a number of distinct kingdoms. They call themselves Azande but others call them simply *Zande*. Other alternate names are Azande, Zandi, Pazande, Sande, and Badjande. Little is known of their history prior to this period and reliable first-hand accounts of the Azande only began to appear toward the middle of the 19th century. By the 1950s, however, the Azande had become well-known to anthropologists through the ethnographic monographs written about them by British anthropologist Sir Edward Evan Evans-Pritchard. Indeed, one of the lasting classics of modern anthropology, his *Witchcraft, Oracles and Magic among the Azande,* is still cited in contemporary textbooks. It is widely accepted that the ancestors of Azande society migrated from the west, from what is now the Central African Republic, into the Democratic Republic of the Congo and the southern region of the Sudan, beginning perhaps 300 years ago. Because of their relative physical isolation from colonial centers of governance, the Azande practiced many traditional beliefs and customs well into the 20th century. Azande now live across the borders of three modern nation-states, and in recent decades they have been more exposed to the effects of market economies, missionary education, and related phenomena, so generalizations about the Azande as a whole are difficult to make.

² LOCATION AND HOMELAND

Reliable estimates of population figures for the Azande are not available. As of 2008 it was estimated that some 3.8 million people considered themselves ethnically Azande. Azande territory covers a vast expanse of land—some 500 miles from east to west—from the fringes of the upper Nile basin in the southern Sudan to the borders of semitropical rain forests in the Democratic Republic of the Congo. Azande are found in the Maridi, Yambio, and Tambura districts in the tropical rain forest belt of Western Equatoria (a state in southwestern Sudan) and in Bahr el Ghazal (a region in southwestern Sudan). The Azande are also found in the Democratic Republic of the Congo and Central African Republic; areas, which originally constituted part of the great Azande Kingdom destroyed by the Belgian, French, Mahdists of Sudan, and finally the British in the context of the European scramble for Africa.

The open savannah forest laced with streams that comprise the Nile/Congo divide marks most of Azande country. Changes in micro-environmental zones have a direct impact on modes of production, principle subsistence crops and modes of settlement of the Azande. Throughout this region of Africa, there is a season of intermittent rain (roughly from April to October), followed by a dry season (from November to March) when rain seldom falls. In pre-colonial times, Azande homesteads were typically dispersed. A common pattern was for men who shared patrilineal ancestry to live in the same general area. A circular hut was the primary living space, and this was surrounded by gardens of one to two acres where a man and one or more of his wives cultivated staple crops, from sorghum to cassava. Footpaths through the savannah forest interconnected homesteads of closely related relatives. An expanse of uninhabited terrain separated one such cluster of homesteads from the next. Homestead clusters were typically located near one of the many streams transecting the countryside, as streams provided fishing and other resources. During the colonial period, many Azande were forced to move from this type of settlement in an alleged effort to eradicate sleeping sickness. The result was that many Azande found themselves living in European-style villages of parallel straight streets, often living next to people who were strangers rather than kinsmen. This change had a significant impact on Azande culture in general, and particularly on Azande notions of witchcraft (see **Religion** and **Interpersonal Relations**).

3 LANGUAGE

The Azande were an expanding secondary series of kingdoms at the time of European domination in Africa. The Azande speak Zande language. The linguist Greenberg (1963) classified the Azande language as one of the Niger-Congo group. The Azande are a Bantu group and their language is similar to the other Bantu languages. Approximately five dialects of Azande are spoken throughout the area they occupy. Dialects include Sango in Central African Republic and Dio and Makaraka (Odio) in Sudan. The speech of the Azande in Sudan is fairly uniform, with a few exceptions (Mbomu, Sueh-Meridi, Bile, Bandiya, Bamboy, Bomokandi, and Anunga. In the contemporary world, most Azande also speak rural dialects of Arabic, French, or English. The Azande language is a tonal tongue, so that significant semiotic usages result from different pitches used in pronouncing identical lexical units.

4 FOLKLORE

Traditional Azande culture was rich and highly developed as is common in non-literate societies. The anthropologist E. E. Evans-Pritchard collected hundreds of Azande folktales and legends and published as many as he could in the Azande language with English translations. Probably the most important and comprehensive collections of this genre are found in Evans-Pritchard's book, *The Zande Trickster*.

The most famous Zande tales all center on the imagined activities of the trickster Ture. The character of a trickster is common to folklore throughout the world. Typically, the trickster is an animal or human protagonist who inverts the standards of expected behavior, who flaunts and ridicules the accepted order of things by doing the inverse. In Evans-Pritchard's understanding, Ture could be regarded as a collective manifestation of Azande personality. The animals act and talk like persons because people are animals behind the masks social convention makes them wear. What Ture does is the opposite of all that is moral and all us can see ourselves in Ture. The

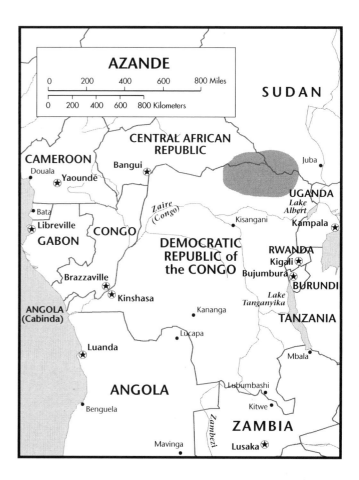

Azande character of Ture is also closely related to an important element of traditional Azande folklore known as *sanza,* or "double-speak." Evans-Pritchard wrote that *sanza* "includes any remark or action which is intended to be oblique, opaque, ambiguous, any words or gestures which are intended to suggest a meaning other than they have in themselves, which have, that is, a double meaning, a manifest meaning and a hidden one." Azande use *sanza* in conversations between princes and commoners, husbands and wives, at beer parties, and in the language of love.

There is no one single myth that describes the origin of the Azande people. The general Azande belief is that people return to life after death, reincarnated as an animal (often a lion). The most important royal chiefs may be reincarnated as leopards, pythons, snakes, warthogs, or rats. Some believe that lightning is the reincarnated spirit of a royal clan chief. When an animal dies, it signifies the end of that specific life force. Thus, Azande man will only kill an animal in self-defense.

5 RELIGION

Historically, the Azande practiced animism. Modern Azande are more likely to practice Christianity. Their traditional beliefs revolve around magic, oracles, and witchcraft. The Azande term *mboli* might be translated as "divinity" or "god." In explaining misfortune, death, and the complications of life, Azande more typically assigned the responsibility to *mangu* or "witchcraft" rather than to *mboli*. Witchcraft is believed to be an inherited substance in the belly that lives a fairly autonomous life, performing bad magic on the person's enemies. Indeed, Evans-Pritchard, the best-known ethnographer of Azande custom and belief, suggested that a Western notion of divinity was largely a consequence of foreign ideas in Azande discourse, the result of Islamic and Christian influences. During the period of British colonial rule in this part of Africa, policy dictated that formal education was to be provided by practitioners of various Christian faiths. Thus, becoming Christian was often a consequence of becoming literate. At the present time some Azande profess faith in Islamic principles and others profess Christianity, but beliefs about causation, death, and misfortune still revolve around *mangu*.

6 MAJOR HOLIDAYS

The Azande clans, which consist of several families with a common ancestor or ancestors, gather for important occasions, including weddings and funerals.

7 RITES OF PASSAGE

When an Azande woman becomes pregnant, tradition and superstition dictates that she avoid certain foods, including water buck meat and mene, a type of sweet potato. These foods are believed to cause miscarriage.

When the child is born, there is no special ceremony. When the infant is four days old, a fire of green leaves is made at the threshold of the house. The green leaves create a smoky fire and the mother, with the infant in her arms, sits in the smoke for a short period. The smoke is believed to give the newborn infant strength. After the fire dies out, the ashes and any remaining leaves are strewn on a path leading to the village. This action is believed to protect the infant from illness and disease.

Before colonization, boys were often initiated into manhood by serving the Azande nobility. Later, a ritual circumcision, held in the forest, became common, although this practice has also been discontinued. Modern Azande perform circumcision on their boys when they reach the age of nineteen. This circumcision ritual is unrelated to Islamic practices.

The Azande do not circumcise girls. Rather, girls are initiated into their gender role by observing and assisting their mothers. Traditionally, in order to marry, an Azande male had to present the bride's family with a ritualized payment (called "bride-wealth"), often consisting of a number of iron spears. As of the 21st century, the bride-wealth is more commonly paid in cash or in the form of material goods, such as cloth, cassava, or goats.

The Azande have no special ceremonies connected with marriage.

8 INTERPERSONAL RELATIONS

Social identity was largely established by membership in a specific kinship group, by the division of labor, by an over-arching patriarchal social order, and by the hierarchical order of Azande political life. Thus, one was either born a commoner or a member of the royalty, or was incorporated into one or the other through warfare or slavery.

One of the central facets of life among the Azande is their belief in witchcraft, which is used to explain and cope with all kinds of adversity, both great and small. Rather than singling out particular individuals as witches, the Azande believe that anyone is capable of causing the misfortunes of another person by ill will toward that person—even if he is unaware of do-

ing so. (Women are excluded from the tradition surrounding witchcraft.) When something bad happens to an Azande, he must first find out who caused it. For minor problems, an Azande consults an oracle that he reaches by rubbing two pieces of wood together as he tries out the names of different suspects. The perpetrator is identified when the pieces stick together instead of rubbing smoothly against each other. For major misfortunes, the "chicken oracle" is consulted. In one version of this procedure, poison is placed on the beak of a chicken. If the chicken dies when a certain individual is named, then that is the guilty party. Once the perpetrator of misfortune has been pinpointed, the aggrieved party confronts him and asks him to stop his witchcraft. On hearing of his misdeeds, the "witch" has no trouble believing that he is indeed the cause of his tribesman's misfortunes and makes amends by expressing his goodwill toward the victim and spitting on the wing of the dead chicken.

Azande witchcraft encompasses every conceivable adverse occurrence, from tripping over a tree root to adultery and murder (for which the oracles were traditionally submitted to a type of court). Witchcraft practices are also associated with social standing within the tribe because they give an added measure of status and control to wealthy householders, who often use their chickens to consult the oracle for a less fortunate kinsman or neighbor who doesn't have enough chickens of his own.

9 LIVING CONDITIONS

In pre-colonial times, Azande lived in dispersed settlements where patrilineal relatives tended to live in close proximity. In colonial times, efforts were made to relocate Azande into European-designed towns. Traditionally huts were made of wood and mud, and each individual homestead was surrounded by gardens tended largely by women. In polygynous marriages (marriages in which one man had more than one wife), each wife had her own hut where she lived with her minor children. In the past, hamlets such as these were interconnected by footpaths through forest and open savannah. The introduction of bicycles and automobiles during the colonial period had a dramatic impact on inter-hamlet relations, especially in terms of the introduction of cash crops and a market economy.

In the past, when Azande lived in dispersed settlements, communal diseases were rare. Personal health was largely affected by bacterial diseases typical to subtropical environments. Malaria, sleeping sickness, and schistosomiasis (a waterborne disease) were common causes of death in pre-colonial Azande country. Many Azande have gained Western knowledge of medicine in recent decades.

10 FAMILY LIFE

Azande society is divided into the royal clans and commoners. The royal clans, known as the Avungara are descended from Gbudwe, a strong leader, and his two sons, Yambio and Tambura. Most commoners were incorporated into the Azande through wars, conquest, and other means of assimilation. Azande settlements consist of single households made up of a man and his wife (or wives).

Azande follow certain social norms. Children are reared but by their birth mother and all the patrilineal kin living in nearby homesteads. Children are taught how to cultivate domesticated plants at an early age. Young boys are taught about hunting and fishing.

11 CLOTHING

Azande women wear cloth skirts. Infants and children wear necklaces made from chains of metal rings. Some Azande also have their heads wrapped in cord, which is thought to protect their brains from malevolent spirits. In the past, Azande musicians wore costumes consisting of a cloth skirt, an elaborate headdress, and beads and bangles on the arms and around the ankles.

12 FOOD

The traditional dietary staple of the Azande is a type of millet called *eleusine*. In the western portion of the group's territory, this has been replaced by cassava. Other crops include rice, maize, sorghum, squash, legumes, okra, peanuts, greens, and bananas. To supplement their diet, the men hunt game and the women catch fish. Chicken and eggs are considered delicacies, as are termites during the dry season. Beverages include palm wine and spirits made from cassava.

13 EDUCATION

Some Azande live in towns with modern educational facilities. Access to Western-style education has had both social and political effects. In some areas, power traditionally held by the royal elite has passed to educated commoners.

14 CULTURAL HERITAGE

Both vocal and instrumental music, as well as dance, play a significant role in Azande culture. The most common traditional musical instrument of the Azande is a small, bow-shaped, harplike instrument, often decorated with a small carved human head at one end. The Azande also make a variety of other instruments, many with designs that incorporate human or animal forms. One is a mandolin-like stringed instrument modeled on the human figure, with a peg approximating a head perched atop an arched neck and legs and feet at the base. Another is the *sanza*, made of wood or hollowed gourds, which is similar to a xylophone but in the shape of a dancing woman, with arms and legs jutting out from the body of the instrument. Other typical instruments include a bell in the shape of a stylized human figure with the arms used as handles and various drums shaped like cattle.

In addition to a variety of functional items, Azande artwork includes carved wooden sculptures thought to have been given as gifts by tribal chiefs.

15 WORK

The Azande have developed an agrarian lifestyle in response to their physical environment. They engage in subsistence farming because their homesteads are typically established a long distance from the markets. Food crops produced include maize, cassava, telebun (millet), yams, fruits: mangoes, citrus, pineapples, palm trees (from which they extract ombiro—palm oil), and coffee. They also have exotic and economically important hardwood trees such as mahogany and teak. The Azande hunt, using traps, nets, and heavy spears, and fish in the streams that flow through the countryside.

In 1948 the Equatoria Project Board (EPB) was established to develop the economic potential of the Zandeland. The Azande were encouraged to grow cotton as a cash crop. Enterprises were established to gin cotton and weave cloth and to produce edible oils, soap, and other products from cotton. This project helped link the Azande economy to other markets in south Sudan.

16 SPORTS

Typical sports among the Azande include sparring (one-on-one fighting), which serves as a way for males to practice their combat skills.

17 ENTERTAINMENT AND RECREATION

Singing and dancing are major forms of entertainment among the Azande, especially at feasts and other celebrations. Storytelling is another popular form of recreation.

18 FOLK ART, CRAFTS, AND HOBBIES

Functional artwork includes wood, bark, and pottery storage boxes. The distinctive Azande throwing knife, the multibladed *shongo*, is used in combat. It is made of copper or steel and adorned with elaborate patterns. Some of these knives are also used as bride-wealth (payment a man makes to acquire his wife). Other folk art includes pots, wooden utensils, and woven mats and baskets.

19 SOCIAL PROBLEMS

Although relative calm was restored to Sudan by the 2005 pact between the SPLA and the Khartoum government to end the civil war, at the time of this writing in 2008, the Azande, along with hundreds of thousands of the people living in the southern Sudan, had fled the Sudan to live in neighboring countries, including the Democratic Republic of the Congo, Uganda, and the Central African Republic. As a result, much of traditional Azande culture and custom is endangered or has ceased to exist.

Still, security is an issue among the Azande. There have long been tensions between the Azande and the Dinka. From across the Congo border there were accounts of abuses of Azande refugees by armed groups and returning refugees returning to Sudan have been accompanied by Congolese refugees.

Infectious and parasitic diseases like malaria, diarrhea, HIV-AIDS, and sleeping sickness pose a grave danger to the Azande population.

21 GENDER ISSUES

Traditional Azande society was highly patriarchal. Women's roles were limited to the domestic sphere. Women were responsible for raising the children, farming, preparing food, and completing the household chores. Men held all positions of public authority, with women being subservient (in a lesser, obedient position) to their husbands. A marriage was arranged by contract between two families and involved the exchange of goods, known as bride-wealth. Commoner men typically had just one wife, but nobles, and in particular kings, had many wives.

[20] BIBLIOGRAPHY

Allen, Tim. "Witchcraft, Sexuality and HIV/AIDS among the Azande of Sudan." *Journal of Eastern African Studies*, vol. 1, no. 3 (November 2007): 359–396

Baxter, P. T. W., and A. Butt. *The Azande and Related Peoples of the Anglo-Egyptian Sudan and the Belgian Congo.* London: International African Institute, 1953.

Buckner, M., D.M. Anderson, and D.H. Johnson. (eds.) "Modern Zande Prophetesses." In *Revealing Prophets: Prophecy in Eastern African History.* London: James Currey, 1995.

De Cock, K. M., D. Mbori-Ngacha, and E. Marum. "Shadow on the Continent: Public Health and HIV/AIDS in Africa in the 21st Century." In *The Lancet,* vol. 360, no. 9326 (July 2002): 67–72.

De Schlippe, P. *Shifting Cultivation in Africa: the Zande System of Agriculture.* London: Routledge and Kegan Paul, 1956.

De Waal, A. *AIDS and Power.* London: Zed Books, 2006

Engel, David M. "Law. Culture and Ritual: Disputing Systems in Cross-Cultural Context." *Law and Society Review.* December 1, 2007, 924.

Evans-Pritchard, E. E. *The Azande: History and Political Institutions.* Oxford: Clarendon Press, 1971.

———. *Witchcraft, Oracles and Magic among the Azande.* Oxford: Clarendon Press, 1937.

———. *The Zande Trickster.* Oxford: Clarendon Press, 1967.

Evans-Pritchard, E. E. (ed.) *Man and Woman among the Azande.* London: Faber and Faber, 1974.

Gero, E. *Death among the Azande of the Sudan (Beliefs, Rites, Cults).* Bologna: Nigrizia Press 1968.

Gillies, Eva. "Zande." In *Encyclopedia of World Cultures,* edited by J. Middleton. New Haven: Yale University Press, 1996.

Horton, R. "African Traditional Thought and Western Science. 1 and 2." In *Africa,* vol. 37 (1967) 50–71 and 155–87.

Mair, L. *Witchcraft.* London: Weidenfield and Nicholson, 1969.

Pagey, G. "Resurgence of Sleeping Sickness in Southern Sudan." In *Journal of Rural and Remote Environmental Health,* 2003.

Reining, C. C. *The Zande Scheme.* Evanston, IL: Northwestern University Press, 1966.

Schildkrout, Enid. *African Reflections: Art from Northeastern Zaire.* Seattle: University of Washington Press, 1990.

—Reviewed by M. Njoroge

BAGANDA

PRONUNCIATION: bah-GAHN-dah
ALTERNATE NAMES: The King's Men
LOCATION: Uganda
POPULATION: About 3 million
LANGUAGE: Luganda
RELIGION: Christianity (Protestantism and Roman Catholicism); Islam
RELATED ARTICLES: Vol. 1: Ugandans

[1] INTRODUCTION

The Baganda of Uganda are sometimes referred to as "The King's Men" because of the significance of the role of the *Kabaka* (King) in their political, social, and cultural institutions. Until 1967, the Baganda were organized into a tightly centralized, bureaucratized kingdom. From 1967 until 1993, there were no kingdoms in Uganda due to their abolishment by the national government. In 1993, the national government reinstated the Kabakaship by permitting the coronation of Ronald Muwenda Mutebi II as the 36th king of the Baganda in a line of succession extending back to AD 1400 to the first king known as Kintu. In the middle of the 19th century, the Kabaka ruled an area extending about 150 miles around the northwestern shores of Lake Victoria in what is now the nation of Uganda. He ruled over a hierarchy of chiefs including village, parish, subcounty, and county levels of stratification. Chiefs collected taxes in the form of food and livestock, and distributed portions on up the hierarchy, which eventually reached the Kabaka's palace in the form of tribute. Chiefs were also responsible for settling disputes and maintaining roads in their respective jurisdictions. The Kabaka made direct political appointment of all chiefs so as to maintain control over their loyalty to him. Kabakas were chosen from the Lion clan, whereas commoners from the other 40 clans were eligible to become chiefs or even rise to the position of *Katikkiro* (prime minister).

Another category of powerful men known as *Batongole* were commoners who were given land throughout the kingdom so they could serve as spies and informers for the Kabaka in case a Katikkiro sought to foster a rebellion, which they sometimes did. Commoner families hoped to enhance their fortunes by providing wives to powerful men, especially the Kabaka, who in some cases had hundreds of wives. These wives were then in a position to obtain "favors" for their families. Young boys were sent regularly to live with chiefs, or to the King's palace where they served as pages in the hope of being eventually rewarded by political appointments. The Baganda have many stories and songs that sing the praises of their Kabaka, as well as honoring commoners who have risen to the rank of Katikkiro.

The King's Palace was generally located on a hill, which on the occasion of his death served as his burial ground, with his successor choosing another hill for his palace. The King's Palace contained hundreds of household compounds that were occupied by his many wives, pages, and chiefs, all of whom were expected to reside in the Kabaka's palace for significant periods of time in order to demonstrate their loyalty to him. Chiefs served as military commanders of the army and navy, which provided a powerful defensive force as well as a mechanism for invasion of neighboring kingdoms to steal slaves, ivory, and women.

Many rituals surrounded the person of the king. For example, commoners had to lie face down on the ground in his presence. The Kabaka's only direct social interaction was with the Katikkiro, and he generally ate alone. His hairstyle sometimes resembled that of a rooster to symbolize his virility, and he has been described as walking like a lion to further symbolize his power. The mother of the Kabaka had the title of *Namasole* (Queen Mother). One sister was selected to be his *Nalinnya* (Queen Sister). Each of these women had her own palace and chiefs while remaining distinctly inferior to the Kabaka. Nevertheless, the Namasole could often exercise much influence over her son.

Today, the Kabaka has only ritual functions and no political power. He was removed of his power so that tribal differences would not interfere with the formation of a nation state. Baganda are presently divided on their beliefs about the role of the Kabaka in the nation state. All Baganda participate in the Ugandan governmental system, which has 39 districts and a national president. These districts contain separate units that were formerly part of the Kingdom of Buganda. Formal education in schools and a national university have replaced the old system of informal education embodied in the page system as a means of upward mobility. Nevertheless, the kingdom and associated institutions remain a strong force in the cultural practices and values of the Baganda.

2 LOCATION AND HOMELAND

The Baganda, who number about 3 million people, are located along the northern and western shores of Lake Victoria in the East African nation of Uganda. The former Kingdom of *Buganda* is bounded on the north by the former Kingdom of Bunyoro, on the east by the Nile River, and on the west by the former kingdoms of Ankole and Toro. To the south of Buganda is the present country of Tanzania. The Baganda are the largest tribe in Uganda, and the Kingdom of Buganda is the largest of the former kingdoms. Kingdoms were abolished as political institutions in the 1960s by the national government of Uganda. The Baganda are located 2° north of the equator to 1° south of the equator, but the temperature is moderate because the altitude varies throughout the region from 900 to 1,500 m (3,000–5,000 ft) above sea level. The former Kingdom of Buganda, with a total area of about 65,000 sq km (25,096 sq mi) comprises slightly more than one-fourth of Uganda's total land mass. Kampala, the largest city in Buganda and Uganda, has a mean temperature of 21°C (69°F), ranging from a high monthly mean of 28°C (83°F) to a low monthly mean of 17°C (62°F). Rainfall averages 114 to 127 cm (45–50 in) per year, and it comes reliably each year in a heavier rainy season lasting from March–May and a lighter season that lasts from August–December. Most Baganda are peasant cultivators who live in rural villages, where the homes are strung out along hills that are themselves usually about 150 m (500 ft) above valley floors consisting of papyrus swamps or forests. Rich red clay on the hills, a moderate temperature, and plentiful rainfall combine to afford the Baganda a generous environment for the year-round availability of plantain, the staple crop, as well as the seasonal production of coffee, cotton, and tea as cash crops. Some Baganda reside in towns and in Kampala, working in a variety of white-collar and nonprofessional occupations; nevertheless,

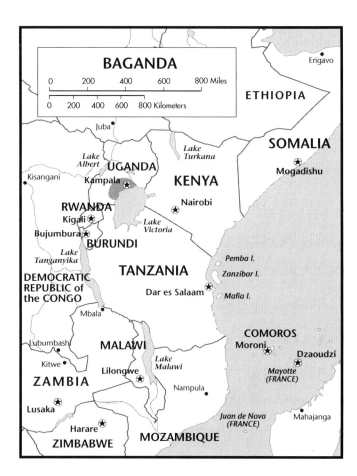

these Baganda maintain close ties with their agrarian roots in villages, while also frequently practicing "urban agriculture" in town homesteads by growing crops in small available areas and by keeping goats, chickens, and, occasionally, cows.

3 LANGUAGE

The Baganda speak a Bantu language called Luganda, which is a member of the Niger-Congo family of languages. In these languages, nouns are made up of modifiers known as prefixes, infixes, and suffixes. These modifiers vary depending on noun classes, such that word stems alone have no grammatical meanings. The stem *ganda,* for example, has no meaning in Luganda, but the term *Buganda* means the location or kingdom where the *Baganda* people live. Objects belonging to Baganda people, or to an individual *Muganda* person, are referred to as *kiganda* things. Like many other African languages, Luganda is tonal so that some words are differentiated by their pitch. For example, the word for excrement and the word for water *(amazzi),* while spelled the same, carry different meanings according to their pitch. Luganda is very rich in metaphor and in verbal genres, such as proverbs and folktales.

Children learn speech skills early in childhood that prepare them for adult life in a verbally rich culture. The clever child is one who can masterfully engage his or her peers in a game of *ludikya,* or "talking backwards." For example, *omusajja* ("man") becomes *jja-sa-mu-o.* Words in sentences appear in their same order. Another version of this game involves inserting the letter *z* after each syllable containing a vowel, followed by the vowel in that syllable. In this version, *omusajja* would become *o-zo-mu-zu-sa-za-jja-za*. Both boys and girls play *ludikya,* which they claim is frequently done to conceal secrets from adults. Many homes participate in the evenings in collective riddling games *(okukokkya)* involving men and women of all ages. A person who successfully solves riddles is awarded villages to rule and becomes a chief. Some examples of common riddles are:

> I have a wife who looks where she is coming from and where she is going at the same time (a bundle of firewood, since the two ends are similar).

> I have a razor blade which I use to shave hills (fire which is used to burn the grass for planting).

> When my friend went to get food for his children, he never came back (water in a river).

> My man is always surrounded by spears (the tongue which is surrounded by teeth)

4 FOLKLORE

The content of riddles, myths, legends, and proverbs all combine to provide for the Baganda an account of their ethnic origin and history, as well as explanations for the workings of the everyday world of people and objects that make up their culture and environment. Speech-making is especially valued and adaptive in a highly stratified society like Buganda where upward mobility was traditionally achieved by an aggressive, verbal manipulation of others through such means as cleverly turned compliments, exaggerated humility, or what the Baganda refer to as *kufukibwa,* the art of being ruled.

The most significant legend involves Kintu, the first Kabaka, who is believed to have married a woman called Nambi. First Nambi had to return to heaven where Gulu, her father, objected to her marriage because Kintu did not know how to farm but only how to obtain food from cattle. Nambi's relatives, therefore, tested Kintu in order to determine his suitability as a spouse. In one test Kintu was asked to identify his own cow from a herd, a difficult task given that there were many cows like his own. By chance, a bee told Kintu to choose the cow on whose horns he would alight. After several large herds were brought to him, Kintu reported that his cow was not among them, while continuing to watch the bee that remained on the tree. Eventually, Kintu, with the help of the bee, identified his cow, along with several calves that had been born to his cow. The amazed father eagerly gave his daughter's hand in marriage, prodding them to hurry to leave for Kintu's home before *Walumbe* (Death) would come and want to go with them. Gulu warned that they should not come back even if they forgot something for fear that Death would follow them. They left carrying with them cows, a goat, fowl, sheep, and a plantain tree. Unfortunately, over the protests of Kintu, Nambi went back to obtain grain that had been forgotten. Although she tried to run away without Death, she was unsuccessful. After many years of happiness on earth, Walumbe began to bring illness and death to children and then adults. Up to the present day, Death has lived upon the earth with no one knowing when or whom he will strike.

We see in this legend an account of the origin of the Baganda people, as well as answers to fundamental questions about the origins of such things as crops and livestock. Death is implicated in this account as an unfortunate happenstance resulting from disobedience to king or parents. Obedience is a prime value of Kiganda morality. Kintu's partnership with the bee is one example of a common motif in Kiganda folklore where animals are the subject of numerous folktales that illustrate moral themes. Animal pairs, such as "the Leopard and the Hare," "the Lion and the Crocodile," and the "Cat and the Fowl," are familiar subjects to all Baganda. Proverbs, which are abundant, are prime sources of moral instruction for young people. Some examples of Kiganda proverbs are:

> He who has not suffered does not know how to pity.

> The stick which is at your neighbor's house will not drive away the leopard.

> An only child is like a drop of rain in the dry season. He who likes his mother's cooking has not traveled.

> He who passes you in the morning, you will pass him in the evening.

> You have many friends as long as you are prosperous. That which is bent at the outset of its growth is almost impossible to straighten at a later age.

5 RELIGION

The majority of present-day Baganda are Christian, about evenly divided between Catholic and Protestant. Approximately 15% are Muslim. Each of these major denominations is headquartered on a major hill in the Kampala area, reflecting the past practice of each major institution being constructed on a specific hill, a practice originated by the Kabakas. In the latter half of the 19th century, most Baganda were practicing an indigenous religion known as the *Balubaale* cult. This cult consisted of national gods who had temples identified with them. Each temple had priests who served as oracles on behalf of their respective god. Similar to the Greek pantheon, these gods were each concerned with specific problems. For example, there was a god of fertility, a god of warfare, and a god of the lake. The Supreme God known as *Katonda* had created everything, and the Baganda paid homage to him upon awakening each morning. Katonda's power was seen in proverbs. The following are some examples:

> What God put in store for someone never goes rotten.

> Katonda gives his gifts to whomsoever he favors.

> God's favors should not be refused.

Katonda was also known by other names, such as *Mukama* (the Master), *Lugaba* (the Giver), and *Liisoddene* (the Great Eye). The Baganda also believed in spiritual forces, particularly the action of witches, which were thought to cause illness and other misfortune. People often wore amulets to ward off their evil powers. The most significant spirits were the *Muzimu* or ancestors who visited the living in dreams and sometimes warned of impending dangers. These spirits resided in the vicinity of the homestead and could be reincarnated if their names were bestowed on an infant, for which there was a special ceremony.

Christianity and Islam, both monotheistic religions, were not incompatible with the Kiganda belief in a High God. Nevertheless, throughout the second half of the 19th century, bitter rivalries and bloodshed prevailed as Kabakas, chiefs, and

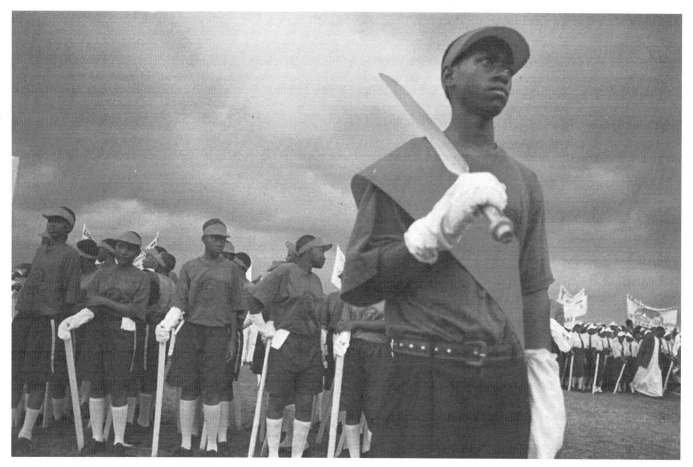

Ugandan high school students, all members of the Baganda tribe, wait for their turn to parade before their monarch during a day of tribal celebration. Three of Uganda's four traditional monarchies, Baganda, Batoro, and Banyoro, were restored in 1993.
(AP Images/Brennan Linsley)

Katikkeros became variously aligned with Anglicans, Roman Catholics, and Balubaale believers. During this period, a number of Baganda pages were put to death for allegiance to their Christian faith and are recognized today as martyrs and saints by the Roman Catholic tradition. Contemporary Baganda are considered to be extremely religious, whatever their faith, although the Balubaale cult no longer exists. Beliefs in ancestors and the power of witches are still, however, quite common.

⁶ MAJOR HOLIDAYS

Religious holidays are very significant in Buganda, especially Christmas for Christians and Ramadan for Muslims. Attendance at funerals is a major ceremonial and social event. People travel from all parts of the nation to attend funerals, which last many days.

⁷ RITES OF PASSAGE

In the indigenous life cycle, the Muganda person passes through stages, such as *omwana* (child), *omuvubuka* (youth), and *omusajja* or *omukazi* (man, woman), until at death one becomes an *omuzima* (spirit) and, therefore, a candidate for reincarnation. Although there is no Luganda word for fetus, the being inside the mother is nevertheless considered to be living and separate from the mother. Thus, if a pregnant woman dies, her fetus is extracted and buried separately. During preg-

nancy, the woman remains physically active, often working on her farm or *shamba* (garden) until the time of delivery. The pregnant woman is typically seen carrying food or water on her head, while often carrying her previous baby on her back. Birth is attended by midwives and female relatives. The umbilical cord is retained for later use in a ceremony called *Kwalula Abaana,* in which the child is seated on a mat along with other members of the father's clan (being a patrilineal society) who are to receive their clan names. The new infant is a source of considerable joy and is passed around to visitors for their pleasure. Should twins be born, special rituals are performed and the parents receive names indicating that they are the mother and father of twins. Each twin is given a special name in accordance with his or her gender and birth order.

The childhood years, beginning at about the age of seven, are characterized by the expectation that both boys and girls will conform in their behavior to what the Baganda refer to as *mpisa* (manners). This includes such things as being obedient to adults, greeting visitors properly, and sitting correctly (for girls). Tasks are assigned to boys and girls, although girls have more consistent work expectations than do boys. Girls are charged with the care of their younger siblings, whom they carry on their backs and to whom they sing lullabies, especially when their mothers are working in their *shambas* (gardens) or marketing. Boys are frequently asked to run errands for family members or to babysit.

Nowadays, children as well as teenagers pursue educational opportunities to enhance their career objectives in the modern nation state. Traditionally, teenage boys and girls were occupied with their political careers or marital prospects, respectively. Sex education for females was and is more systematic than it is for males. The father's sister (*Ssenga*) is for girls the most significant moral authority, as she represents the patrilineal extended family of which the girl is a member. Grandmothers instruct girls soon after their menstruation, during a period of seclusion, about sexual matters and future domestic responsibilities. The Baganda are quite prudish about public displays of sexuality, and affection between the sexes is reserved for private occasions. Kissing is a recent innovation. Traditionally, tickling of the hand, breast, or stomach area by either sex was considered sensuous. A common complaint of young school girls today is that their elders did not teach them anything about sex so they must now seek advice and sexual instruction from popular pamphlets and the mass media.

Among the Baganda, marriage and the birth of children are generally still prerequisites for adult status. Today, most Baganda men and women no longer live out their lives only in the context of the Buganda Kingdom. Baganda can be found in all of the modern occupations and live throughout the world from where they regularly return or seek to return to their homeland, especially for burial. The old person (*mukadde*) is happy if he or she has achieved success in the world and if they have grandchildren, who are a particular source of joy for them and their clan.

8 INTERPERSONAL RELATIONS

The Baganda place paramount emphasis on being sociable, often in a clever and assertive way so as to achieve upward mobility. Verbal skills and manipulative styles are seen in the daily life of work, school, courtship, and marriage. Individualism and being alone are not valued. In fact, a person who spends too much time alone may be thought to be a spy or a witch. Elaborate greeting rituals best symbolize the importance attached to being sociable. One of the first things that a child learns is how to greet others properly in the high-pitched voice that is considered to be respectful. Propriety requires that neighbors exchange lengthy greetings when meeting along the road. Greetings vary according to the time of day, age of participants, and length of time since previous encounters. When city folk return to their villages, formal greetings may take upwards of 15 minutes.

In Kampala, greetings are far less frequent and shorter in duration than in rural areas. Also, women in Kampala are much less likely to kneel while greeting men or other social superiors, a custom still prevalent in rural areas. Sociability is at a premium during social events, especially at burials and funerals when villages can seem deserted because their members are away, staying in temporary shelters constructed to accommodate guests who have amassed for several days of feasting, drumming, and dancing.

Dating and courtship are significant in the lives of most Baganda in their younger years. Both men and women value men who are able to flatter through verbal expertise and their power of persuasion. Common phrases of endearment include: "Your eyes are big and shiny like a light"; "Your teeth are as white as elephant tusks"; "You are as slender as a bee"; "You are my twin"; and a recent addition to a man's repertoire, "You are worth a million dollars." Women, too, are verbally adroit. Although she should not flatter a man, a woman is expected to deceive him (*okulimba*) into thinking that he is her only suitor. In physical features, there are numerous preferences that include moderation in height, weight, and skin color. Eyes should not be too large, "like a fish," nor too small, "like a hole in the cow's skin." In girls, a small space between upper front teeth (*muzigo*) and horizontal lines in the neck (*ebiseera*) are especially desirable. Baganda of all ages are very well dressed and admire those who dress well.

9 LIVING CONDITIONS

Rural homes located among banana groves or *shambas* (gardens) are usually made of wattle and daub and have thatched or corrugated iron roofs. More affluent farmers live in homes constructed of cement, with tile roofs. Some homes have electricity and running water, but for many water must be fetched from a well or collected when it rains. There commonly is a separate cooking house where cooking is done on an open wood fire. A latrine is located behind the house in the shamba. Household furniture usually consists of a wooden platform bed with a mattress, a table, and wooden chairs. Woven straw mats are used for sitting by women and children, although some homes have sofas and arm chairs. Urban homes, by contrast, are typically of concrete with corrugated iron or tile roofs and glass windows. Indoor plumbing, indoor kitchens, electricity, and toilet facilities are common in the city. Radios are frequent in both rural and urban homes. Photographs and other pictures are typically on display on the walls to commemorate family members, political figures, or religious personages.

On the whole, Baganda enjoy a fairly high standard of living in Uganda through income obtained from land rentals, agricultural produce sold for cash, and wage labor as clerks, teachers, and craftspeople, often combined with agriculture. Some Baganda in rural areas are fishermen, carpenters, mechanics, or conveyors of produce to market via bicycles, a more common vehicle than the automobile. All Baganda have daily access to a plentiful food supply, given their year-round growing season. On the other hand, Baganda suffer from malaria, given the presence of swampy areas harboring the malarial-infected mosquitoes. A particular form of childhood protein-calorie malnutrition known as kwashiorkor is frequently seen as a result of early weaning and a protein-deficient diet of matooke (plantain staple).

10 FAMILY LIFE

Traditionally, the term for marriage, *jangu enfumbire* ("come cook for me"), symbolized the authority patterns that prevailed in the typical household. The husband/father was supreme, and in the domestic sphere emulated the authority of the Kabaka in the wider political system. Children and women knelt to the husband in deference to his authority, and he was served his food first. Baganda children frequently describe feelings of fear and respect for their fathers and warm attachment for their mothers. One should never marry a person from one's own clan lest clan sanction and sickness result. Marriage is, therefore, exogamous in terms of clans, although Baganda tend to marry within their own tribe.

After marriage a new household is established, usually in the village of the husband. Most marriages are monogamous, although polygamy was not uncommon in the past. Co-wives lived in separate, but adjacent, houses while the husband had his own house in front of the women's quarters. Affinal relatives (*Bako* or in-laws) are afforded great respect, and Baganda avoid physical contact with one's mother- or father-in-law. Brothers- or sisters-in-law are often close and affectionate. Children's surnames are taken from the father and easily identify the clan from which they come. In addition to not marrying within one's own clan, it is taboo to eat the clan totem. Some common totems are: leopard, civet cat, anteater, otter, dog, cow, buffalo, bush buck, sheep, crow, and elephant, as well as yam, bean, and mushroom.

11 CLOTHING

The rural Muganda woman typically wears a *Busuuti,* a floor-length, brightly colored cloth dress with a square neckline and short, puffed sleeves. The garment is fastened with a sash placed just below the waist over the hips, and by two buttons on the left side of the neckline. It can be worn throughout pregnancy by simply loosening the sash, since the skirt portion consists of several yards of material. Traditionally, the busuuti was strapless and made from bark-cloth. The busuuti is worn on all festive and ceremonial occasions, even in Kampala where Western-style clothing predominates on a daily basis. The indigenous dress of the Baganda man is a *kanzu,* a long, white cotton robe. On special occasions, it is worn over trousers with a Western-style suit jacket over it. Younger people wear Western-style clothing. T-shirts with international celebrities on them are particularly popular. Slacks, jeans, skirts, suits, and ties also prevail.

12 FOOD

The staple food of the Baganda is *matooke,* a plantain that is steamed or boiled and commonly served with groundnut sauce or meat soups. Sources of protein include eggs, fish, beans, groundnuts, beef, chicken, and goats, as well as termites and grasshoppers in season. Common vegetables are cabbage, beans, mushrooms, carrots, cassava, sweet potatoes, onions, and various types of greens. Fruits include sweet bananas, pineapples, passion fruit, and papaya. Before eating, a bowl of boiled water and soap are passed around for each person to wash his or her hands. Steaming matooke is mashed and placed upon banana leaves in a basket, then covered by more leaves in order to keep the food hot. Portions of matooke are mixed in with the soup or sauce and eaten together. Although Baganda have cutlery, most prefer to eat with their hands, especially when at home. Drinks include indigenous fermented beverages made from bananas *(mwenge),* pineapples *(munanansi),* and maize *(musoli).* Bottled beers fermented in national breweries are especially popular in the cities and towns, as are soft drinks. Coffee and tea are common hot drinks, and many homes recognize "tea time" in the afternoon as a special heritage from the British colonial days. Traditionally, women did not eat eggs or chicken, but this custom is very rare at present. Women also traditionally ate separately from men on mats on the floor. Nowadays, the urban family tends to eat at the table together. Baganda women take great pride in their cooking, and for most it is considered inappropriate for a man to enter the cooking area. Knowledge of the over 40 varieties of plantain used in cooking is a special domain in which women excel. They also have a working knowledge of agriculture. Two or three meals of plantains per day are customary. Metal cooking pots and pans, cutlery, dishes, and glassware are now ubiquitous, although in rural areas bottled gourds and ceramic containers are not uncommon.

13 EDUCATION

Missionaries introduced literacy and formal education into Uganda in the 19th century, going on to establish in subsequent years a large number of schools and hospitals throughout Uganda. Baganda were among the first converts and, therefore, among the first literate population in Uganda. The Baganda value modern educational opportunity and will often sacrifice a great deal to obtain schooling for further advancement. Members of a family will combine resources to support a particularly promising student, who upon the completion of that education is expected to help his or her relatives. Rural areas contain primary schools often made of wattle and daub. Secondary schools vary in quality, and there is tremendous competition to get into the better ones. Kings College Budu, for example, a secondary school where Baganda royalty have studied, also accepts commoners. Accordingly, schooling serves as a leveling mechanism in modern society, much as the old page system did previously. Fostering of children was traditionally an acceptable practice in order to place children in advantageous homes such as those of a chief. Today, the modern boarding school is a favorite mechanism of upward mobility. Currently, both boys and girls attend school in large numbers, making formal education an important means of mobility for women also. The Baganda value literacy highly and have long maintained a vernacular press with a rich tradition of publishing books, pamphlets, songs, stories, and poems in Luganda and English, the national language. Makerere University in Kampala attracted many Baganda in the 20th century who went on to outstanding careers in law, medicine, and other professions.

14 CULTURAL HERITAGE

Today, Baganda are among the best songwriters, playwrights, poets, novelists, artists, and musicians in Uganda. Performing arts have a long history of development in music and dance. The Kabaka's Palace was a special place where royal dancers and drummers regularly performed. Each clan had its own particular drum beat. Most Baganda households contained at least a small drum for regular use in family singing and dancing. Drums were used to announce special events such as the birth of a child or the death of a person. The most significant drums, however, were the royal drums, called the *mujaguzo,* which numbered 93. Drums varied in size and each had its own name and specific drum beat. Drums were made from hollowed-out tree trunks and cowhide or zebra skin. Other musical instruments included stringed instruments, such as fiddles and harps, and woodwind instruments, such as flutes and fifes.

Dancing is frequently practiced by all Baganda, beginning in early childhood, and the best dancers and musicians are renowned for their skills. Baganda dancers are remarkable for their ability to move their hips swiftly to the beat of alternating drums playing simultaneously. Today, Uganda dancers and musicians are frequently seen performing abroad. In Kampala, they can be seen entertaining regularly in night clubs, bars, and other public locations.

Basketry is still a widespread art, especially mat-making by women. These mats are colorful and intricately designed. In addition to creating useful household containers, woven basketry and coiled basketry are also widespread arts that serve as the foundation for stockades, enclosure fences, and houses.

15 WORK

Most Baganda are peasant farmers, but others live in towns and in the city of Kampala and work at various white-collar and nonprofessional jobs.

16 SPORTS

Football (soccer), rugby, and track and field are common, popular sports in Uganda. Baganda boys participate in all these sports, while girls participate in track and field. Traditionally, the Baganda were renowned for their skills in wrestling, which was considered to be their national game. Males of all ages participated in this sport. Wrestling events were accompanied by beer-drinking, singing, and drumming. It was, however, considered inappropriate to defeat the Kabaka. Other traditional outdoor games by boys include the competitive throwing of sticks and a kicking game in which boys stand side by side and attempt to knock over the other boy.

17 ENTERTAINMENT AND RECREATION

Children play games involving a chief for boys or a mother role for girls. *Okwesa*, played by both boys and girls, is a game of strategy involving a wooden board and stones or beans that are placed in pockets in the board. Verbal games are played frequently, especially at night and in the company of grandparents.

18 FOLK ART, CRAFTS, AND HOBBIES

In addition to basketry and musical instruments, the manufacture of products from bark-cloth was and continues to be significant. The bark from a species of fig tree called *mutuba* is soaked in water, then beaten with a wooden mallet. This yields a soft material that is decorated with paint and then cut into strips of various sizes. Larger strips traditionally were used for partitions in homes, while smaller pieces were decorated with black dye and worn as clothing by women of royalty. Later, bark-cloth dress, particularly reddish tan-colored bark-cloth, became the national dress. Today, one rarely sees bark-cloth dresses, which have been replaced by the cotton cloth Busuuti. Bark-cloth is found today as decorative placemats, coasters, and designs on cards of various sorts. It is also rare to find traditional pipes, pots, and other ceramics, which in the past were elaborately decorated functional objects, in use today.

19 SOCIAL PROBLEMS

The Baganda have had some problems integrating their political culture into the nation state of Uganda. The first president of independent Uganda (1962) was Sir Edward Mutesa, who was also King of Buganda. The first prime minister, with whom he shared power, was Milton Obote, who was from a district outside of Buganda. Within four years, Obote had abolished the kingdoms, and Mutesa fled Uganda and eventually died in exile. In 1971, Obote was overthrown by Dictator Idi Amin,

under whose presidency all Ugandans, including the Baganda, suffered greatly from political and social oppression, death, and the loss of personal property. Currently, the Baganda participate in what is widely considered to be a national recovery from the havoc and dissension of the Obote and Amin years.

Since the mid-1980s, AIDS has resulted in many deaths among friends and family members and is a source of great grief for Baganda. Caring for the children of parents who have died of AIDS is an especially serious problem. Nevertheless, this disease has been the subject of a spirited public education effort through mass media and theatrical productions, as part of a broad public educational effort toward prevention. These efforts led to the first substantial declines in HIV prevalence in Uganda. Nevertheless, the epidemic remains serious in, with infection levels highest among women (7.5% compared to 5.0% among men) and urban residents (10% compared to 5.7% among rural residents).

20 GENDER ISSUES

In terms of gender relations, patriarchy is central to Baganda culture. In pre-colonial times there was a strict division of labor among the Baganda, where women did most of the agricultural work, while men often engaged in commerce, politics, and warfare. In recent times, the Museveni government has taken steps to elevate the plight of women as a major development issue. The Museveni administration has encouraged women to participate in politics and other aspects of public life. In 2008, each of Uganda's districts had a female member of parliament. One-third of all local council seats are reserved for women. As a result, women make up about 24% of the legislature. There are active women's rights groups, including the Uganda Women Lawyers Association (FIDA-U), Action for Development, and the National Association of Women Judges. However, in spite of these advancements, women are often targets of violence and sexual abuse. Women who reveal their HIV-positive status to their spouses are often beaten and sometimes murdered by their husbands.

In terms of human rights, Uganda's past has been checkered with torture and abuse, and according to some human rights organizations, these abuses continue in present-day Uganda. The army has been accused of committing atrocities against the populations in northern Uganda, and security forces are alleged to routinely torture suspects and members of the opposition. Homosexuality is illegal under Victorian-era legislation still in force in Uganda and many other English-speaking countries in Africa. The laws reflect a deep aversion among many Africans to homosexuality. But, the truth remains that gays and lesbians exist in Uganda, although they pay a high price for their sexual orientation, often facing discrimination, and even torture and imprisonment.

21 BIBLIOGRAPHY

Fallers, L. A., ed. *The King's Men: Leadership and Status in Buganda on the Eve of Independence*. New York: Oxford University Press, 1964.

Howard, P. L., & Nabanoga, G. "Are there Customary Rights to Plants? An Inquiry among the Baganda (Uganda), with Special Attention to Gender." *World Development 35*, no 9 (2007): 1542-1563.

IRIN. "Uganda: Humanitarian Country Profile." http://www.irinnews.org/country.aspx?CountryCode=UG&RegionCode=EAF.

Kavulu, David. *The Uganda Martyrs*. Kampala: Longmans of Uganda, Ltd., 1969.

Kiyimba, A. "Gendering Social Destiny in the Proverbs of the Baganda: Reflections on Boys and Girls Becoming Men and Women." *Journal of African Cultural Studies* 17, no 2 (2005): 253-270.

Kilbride, Philip, and Janet Kilbride. *Changing Family Life in East Africa: Women and Children at Risk*. University Park, PA: Pennsylvania University Press, 1990.

Lugira, A. M. *Ganda Art*. Kampala: OSASA Publications, 1970.

Roscoe, Rev. John. *The Baganda: An Account of Their Native Customs and Beliefs*. London: Macmillan and Co., 1911.

Southwold, Martin. "The Ganda of Uganda." In *Peoples of Africa*, edited by James L. Gibbs, Jr. New York: Holt, Rinehart and Winston, 1965.

— revised by E. Kalipeni

BAKONGO

PRONUNCIATION: buh-KAHN-go
ALTERNATE NAMES: Kongo
LOCATION: Congo River region (Angola, Democratic Republic of Congo, Republic of Congo)
POPULATION: 5.45 million
LANGUAGE: Kikongo
RELIGION: Christianity, Kimbanguism, and indigenous beliefs
RELATED ARTICLES: Vol. 1: Angolans; Congolese

[1] INTRODUCTION

The solidarity of the Bakongo people has a long history based on the splendor of the ancient Kongo kingdom and the cultural unity of the Kikongo language. Founded in the 15th century AD, the kingdom was discovered by the Portuguese explorer Diego Cao when he landed at the mouth of the Congo River in 1484. As trade developed with the Portuguese, Mbanza Bata, located south of the Congo, became the capital, later known as San Salvador. Portuguese missionaries baptized King Nzinga, who adopted the Christian name Alfonso I. Within a few years, the kingdom was exchanging ambassadors with Portugal and the Vatican.

By the end of the 16th century, the Kongo kingdom had virtually ceased to exist. Incursions by neighboring groups from the east severely weakened it, and it became subservient to Portugal. In the 17th century, British, Dutch, and French slave ships reportedly carried 13 million persons from the Kongo kingdom to the New World. Ironically, the monarch and his vassals profited financially from the trade as their kingdom crumbled beneath them. In 1884–85 at the Conference of Berlin, the European powers divided the kingdom among the French, Belgian, and Portuguese. By the end of the 19th century, little remained of the once great Kongo civilization.

The 20th century witnessed a resurgence of Kongo nationalism and culture. Inspired by the prophetic teachings of Simon Kimbangu, thousands of Bakongo and other Congolese joined his initial followers. Belgian persecution of Kimbangu encouraged anticolonial sentiment and eventually Kimbanguism became a springboard for Congolese independence. In addition, the zeal for the past of European historians and missionaries such as Georges Ballandier and Father Van Wing, spurred Bakongo intellectuals to demand immediate independence in 1956. They founded a political party, whose candidates won the vast majority of municipal seats in 1959, leading to the election of President Joseph Kasavubu, a Mukongo, as the Congo's first president.

While Kongo secessionist movements have come and gone, the early 21st century marks an upsurge in revivalist fervor, which at times has been violent. A movement to establish a Kongo federal state composed of five provinces would bring together Bakongo living in the southern Republic of Congo (Congo-Brazzaville), the Angolan enclave of Cabinda, the lower province of the Democratic Republic of the Congo (DRC, Congo-Kinshasa), and northern Angola. Its name would be *Kongo Dia Ntotela* (the United States of the Kongo). In January and February 2007 Bunda Dia Kongo (BDK—Kingdom of Kongo) protested alleged corruption during the 2006 gubernatorial elections within Bas-Congo province of DRC. The pro-

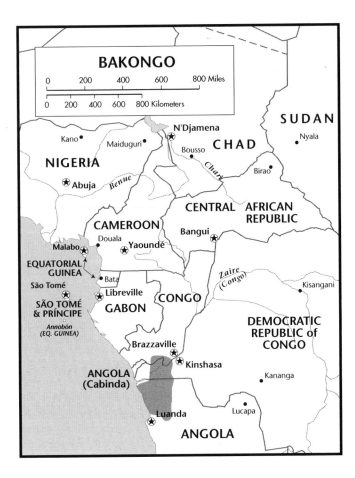

BAKONGO

tests resulted in government forces shooting and killing more than 100 persons—mostly civilians. In February and March 2008 government soldiers shot and killed scores more and burned their houses in an effort to restore state authority. The BDK has called for the establishment of an "ethnically pure" kingdom for the Bakongo.

² LOCATION AND HOMELAND

The Bakongo are a composite of peoples who assimilated the Kongo culture and language over time. The kingdom consisted of some 30 groups at its inception. Its original inhabitants occupied a narrow corridor south of the Congo River from present-day Kinshasa to the port city of Matadi in the lower Congo. Through conflict, conquest, and treaties, they came to dominate neighboring tribes, including the Bambata, the Mayumbe, the Basolongo, the Kakongo, the Basundi, and the Babuende. These peoples gradually acculturated and through intermarriage became indistinguishable from the Bakongo.

At its apex, the nuclear kingdom covered about 300 sq km (116 sq mi). Its boundaries extended as far as the Nkisi River to the east, the Dande River to the south, the Congo (Zaire) River to the north, and the Atlantic Ocean to the west. The greater kingdom of the 16th century extended another 100 km (62 mi) east to the Kwango River and 200 km (124 mi) further north to the Kwilu River. Today, the Bakongo peoples still live in their ancestral homeland. It is quite mountainous and subject to a dry season lasting from May to August/September. Of the three ecological zones to the south of the Congo River, the hilly

middle zone receives the most annual rainfall (1,400 mm/55 in) and has relatively fertile soils and moderately warm temperatures. Consequently, it is more densely populated than the dry, sandy coastal region and the infertile arid plateau to the east.

There are about 5.45 million Bakongo. They are the largest ethnic grouping of the Republic of the Congo accounting for nearly half of the population (1.9 million). In Angola, they are the third largest group, making up 13% of the population (1.9 million) and in DRC they number about 1.65 million.

³ LANGUAGE

The Bakongo speak various dialects of Kikongo, similar to the Kikongo spoken in the ancient kingdom. These dialects differ widely across the region; some are almost mutually unintelligible. To further its nation-building efforts after independence, the government of the former Zaire created a standardized version of the language, which incorporated elements of the many variants. Standard Kikongo is used in elementary schools throughout the Lower Province and Bandundu, and is called Mono Kotuba or Kikongo ya Leta (State Kikongo).

⁴ FOLKLORE

Legends trace Bakongo ancestry to Ne Kongo Nimi, who is said to have had three children, whose descendants, grouped into three clans, form the Kongo nation. The children of Ne Kongo Nimi were called Bana ba Ne Kongo, literally the children of Ne Kongo. The abbreviation became Bakongo. Proverbs, fables, legends, and tales occupy an important place in daily life. Some popular legends are only recognizable by their core content, since storytellers add their own spice and take great liberties in embellishing the traditional legends. One popular character, Monimambu, is known to the Bakongo and other peoples through oral and written literature. He is not a hero—rather he is a fictional figure with human foibles and feelings who has some successes but makes mistakes, too. His adventures are entertaining, but the stories not only amuse, they instruct as well. A favorite animal figure in Bakongo tales is the leopard.

The Bakongo recognize Dona Beatrice as a Kongolese heroine. Born Kimpa Vita, she became a Christian martyr, and later a symbol of Congolese nationhood. She lived in a time of great crisis. Rivalries had torn apart the kingdom, and the capital of San Salvador had lain in ruins since 1678. In 1703, at the age of 22, Beatrice sought to restore the grandeur of the Kongo. She warned of divine chastisement if the capital were not reoccupied. Within two years she established a new dogma and teaching and renewed the church. But her opposition to foreign missionaries led to her demise. Beholden to the Portuguese, King Pedro IV arrested her. She was tried by a church tribunal for heresy, condemned, and burned at the stake. Her idealism and sacrifice inspired a tradition of mysticism among the Bakongo, and she is considered a precursor to the 20th-century prophet Simon Kimbangu (see **Religion**).

⁵ RELIGION

The Bakongo were among the first sub-Saharan African peoples to adopt Christianity, and, as a kingdom, had diplomatic ties with the Vatican. In the colonial period, Belgian missionaries established Catholic seminaries in the villages of Lemfu and Mayidi and built mission churches and schools throughout Lower Congo.

Many Bakongo overlay their Christianity with traditional beliefs. According to the traditional religion of the Bakongo, the creator of the universe, called Nzambe, resides above a world of ancestor spirits. Many people believe that when a family member dies a normal death, he or she joins this spirit world, or village, of the ancestors, who look after the living and protect the descendants to whom they have bequeathed their lands. Spirits of those dying violent and untimely deaths are thought to be without rest until their deaths have been avenged. Sorcerers are employed to divine the agent responsible for the death through the use of fetishes or charms called *nkisi*. In addition, healing practices and traditional religion go hand in hand. Traditional healers called *nganga* may be consulted for herbal treatments or to root out *kindoki* (witches practicing black magic, who are thought to cause illness through malice, and to eat the souls of their victims by night).

In the 1920s, Simon Kimbangu, a member of the English Baptist Mission Church, claimed to have received a vision from God, calling him to preach the Word, and to heal the sick. He taught the law of Moses and repudiated sorcery, fetishes, charms, and polygamy. When his ministry acquired anti-clerical anti-colonial overtones, the Belgians arrested him and sentenced him to death. Later his sentence was commuted to life in prison, where he died in 1951. Kimbanguism gained legal recognition from Belgian authorities in 1959, and through cooptation of its leaders, the Kimbanguist church became a staunch supporter of President Mobutu after independence. Officially known as "The Church of Christ on Earth by His Special Envoy Simon Kimbangu," believers number somewhere between 1 and 3 million.

6 MAJOR HOLIDAYS

Bakongo celebrate the national political holidays of their respective countries as well as Christmas and Easter. Those who are Kimbanguists make an annual pilgrimage to the Kamba River to honor their prophet. At the river they offer sacrifices, pray, ask for blessings, and take some of the water, which is considered holy. Kimbanguists believe in Jesus as the son of God and therefore commemorate Christmas and Easter. In addition, they celebrate April 6, which marks the beginning of Kimbangu's healing ministry; October 12, which marks his death; and May 25, which marks the birthday of Papa Dialungana, their spiritual leader.

In the DRC, the Bakongo celebrate Parents Day, August 1, along with their fellow citizens. On this holiday people go to the cemeteries in the morning to spruce up the family graves. The grave sites may be overgrown with tall dry elephant grass, which is burned away, creating an Armageddon-like atmosphere. In the evenings, families get together to share a festive meal with the extended family.

7 RITES OF PASSAGE

The Bakongo believe in a close relationship between the unborn, the living, and the dead. If they are Christian, they baptize their children. At birth, there is a ritual called a *kobota elingi* (which literally means "what a pleasure it is to give birth"), a party to which friends and relatives come to share in the parents' joy and to celebrate the continuity of the family.

Until recently, initiation *(Longo)* held a critical place among the rites of passage. *Longo* teaches children the secrets of Bakongo traditions essential to assuming the responsibilities of adulthood. During *Longo*, children learn adult behavior, including control of their physical and emotional reactions to evil, suffering, and death. The ceremonies differ in form, duration, and name among the different Bakongo subgroups. In the past they lasted up to two months. Gradual westernization and rigid school calendars mean that fewer children undergo the rite.

Death is a passage to the next dimension, the spirit village of the ancestors (see **Religion**). In the past, Kongo tombs were remarkably large, built of wood or stone, and resembled small homes into which the family of the deceased placed furniture and personal objects. The corpse was dressed in fine apparel and placed in a position recalling his trade. Graves these days are often marked with no more than concrete crosses. But some are works of art that still reflect Portuguese influence and display statues of friends and family mounted on and around the tomb.

8 INTERPERSONAL RELATIONS

Bakongo are friendly people who typically greet each other both verbally and by shaking hands. The familiar greeting in Kikongo is *Mbote, Tata/Mama. Kolele?* ("Hello, Sir/Madam. What news?"). Respect for authority figures and the elderly is shown by holding the left hand to the right wrist when shaking hands. Men commonly hold hands in public as a sign of friendship. Children are always supposed to receive objects with two hands.

Although young people may initiate courtship, marriage is often the product of family intervention, with older siblings or extended family members suggesting prospective mates.

9 LIVING CONDITIONS

Living conditions are austere for most Bakongo. Rural families typically live in one- or two-room mud brick huts with thatch or tin roofs, and without electricity. Cooking is done mostly outside. Windows are unscreened, allowing access to flies and mosquitoes. Water sources are mostly unprotected and subject to contamination. Infectious and parasitic diseases in the DRC cause more than 50% of all deaths. Children under five, who make up 20% of the DRC population, account for 80% of deaths. Their daily diets are generally deficient in vitamins, minerals, and protein. Despite poor road networks, much of the produce of the Lower Congo region feeds urban populations in Brazzaville, Kinshasa, and Luanda.

10 FAMILY LIFE

The Bakongo family lives as a nuclear unit and is rarely polygamous. Although women typically give birth to as many as 10 children, diseases and other illnesses claim the lives of many while they are still infants or toddlers. Nevertheless, children are a sign of wealth, and parents consider themselves blessed to have many children.

The Bakongo are matriarchal. Children belong to their mother's lineage, and the maternal uncle exercises jurisdiction over them even while their father is alive, wielding great power but also carrying great responsibility. The maternal uncle decides where his sister's children will study and what vocation they will pursue. If a man succeeds in life but refuses

A wooden figure with nails, belonging to the Bakongo, dates to around the 16th–20th century. (Getty Images)

ple drink coffee and eat French bread, which is baked locally throughout the region.

The midday meal is the largest of the day. Bakongo enjoy one of several sauces, eaten with *fufu* or with rice. Cassava leaves *(saka saka)*, pounded and cooked, are always a favorite. Dried salted fish *(makayabu)* or pilchards are added to make a rich *saka saka*. Another local favorite is pounded sesame seeds *(wangila)*, to which small dried shrimp are added. Pounded squash seeds *(mbika)* seasoned with lots of hot pepper and wrapped in banana leaves are sold at roadside stands, and are a popular snack for travelers. The most common dish is white beans cooked in a palm oil sauce of tomatoes, onions, garlic, and hot pepper. The beans are eaten with rice, *fufu*, or *chikwange* (a cassava loaf prepared in banana leaves).

Supper generally consists of leftovers, but *chikwange* with a piece of *makayabu* covered in hot pepper sauce may be found at local markets in the evening, and is very satisfying with beer. "Kin sept jours" (meaning Kinshasa seven-day loaf) is a giant *chikwange* so large that it purportedly takes a whole family a week to eat it.

The Bakongo are fond of palm wine. Palm juice is tapped from the top of the coconut palm trunk. It ferments within hours and must be drunk the next day. On Saturday and Sunday afternoons, people sit under mango trees, enjoying the milky, tangy substance. They also make sugar cane wine *(nguila)*, fruit wines, and homemade gin (cinq cents). It is customary to pour a small amount on the ground for the ancestors before imbibing.

13 EDUCATION

By virtue of their close and sustained contact with European missionaries, the Bakongo have enjoyed relatively high levels of literacy and education. Currently, most parents want to send their children to high school and beyond, but many children from average families are obliged to drop out, at least temporarily, for financial reasons. Thus it is not uncommon to find 20-year-olds in some high schools.

14 CULTURAL HERITAGE

Kongo court art ranks with that of the Bakuba of Kasai and the Baluba of Katanga, tribes of the southeastern DRC (Democratic Republic of the Congo). One type of statue—the *mintadi,* or "chief"—was a large piece of sculpture designed to "replace" the chief at court while he was at war or visiting the king in San Salvador. These statues, of which few remain, were sculpted of stone or wood and showed the chief's rank. Another type—"maternity"—depicted a mother and child. In their resemblance to portrayals of the virgin Mary, these show a Catholic influence and are notable for both their non-stylized realism and their serenity.

Besides its reservoir of oral literature, Kikongo has a centuries-old written tradition. Kikongo verse is rich in proverbs, fables, riddles, and folktales. Parts of the Bible were translated into Kikongo in the latter part of the 19th century.

15 WORK

Except for the urban migrant, most Bakongo are subsistence farmers with small patches of cassava, beans, and vegetables. Fruit tree plantations are abundant in some areas. Generally, crop cultivation is only moderately productive because of the dry climate and infertile soils along the coast and into the

to help the family, he may be censured by his uncle. On the other hand, in the case of certain misfortunes, the uncle himself may be blamed—uncles have been stoned when they were suspected of wrongdoing. The European patriarchal tradition has weakened this once monolithic system.

11 CLOTHING

In ancient times, the Bakongo wore clothing made from bark softened by pounding. However, through their long association with the West, the Bakongo adopted Western apparel at an early date. Photographs from the late 1880s show them wearing suits over their sarongs. They generally are considered very proper dressers by other Congolese. Women adopt the latest local fashions and hair styles, which change every few months. The mainstay is the African sarong *(pagne)*. Many families are forced to buy used clothing at the markets; children typically sport T-shirts, shorts, and cotton smocks for everyday wear.

12 FOOD

The Bakongo typically eat three meals a day. For breakfast, a village family eats a pasty dough-like ball made from cassava flour *(fufu)* with yesterday's sauce. More urbanized peoplateau regions. Along the coast, however, fishing provides a livelihood for many people. Despite the building of the large Inga dams, the promise of industry touted in the 1970s never fully materialized. Recent protests in Bas-Congo DRC have carried overtones of refusing employment to outsiders, and to restricting work and business opportunities to residents of the province.

16 SPORTS

In all three countries home to the Bakongo, soccer is the national participant and spectator sport. Boys and young men play it wherever and whenever possible. As a rule, though, people find much less time to play sports than in the West. Even on Sundays, they may cultivate their fields or tend fruit trees in order to ensure a good harvest.

17 ENTERTAINMENT AND RECREATION

Besides playing and watching soccer, people love to tell stories. In rural areas people grow up listening to and learning to narrate tales. In addition, nearly everyone enjoys music and dancing. Kinshasa and Brazzaville are centers for African music, which is enjoyed throughout the continent. The larger cities are famous for their live music and nightclubs. Young people, especially, are continually learning the latest dances. In recent years the advent of satellite TV has made it possible for the more affluent to be entertained in their homes. But affordable video houses have become a popular means for the general public to enjoy movies and music videos.

18 FOLK ART, CRAFTS, AND HOBBIES

Traditionally, Bakongo artisans have excelled in wood carving, sculpting, painting, and stone work. An example of their intricate carving is found in their wooden bowl covers that have protruding human busts for handles. They also specialize in scepters, ankle bells, cow-tail fly swatters, and bottles for medicinal and magical powders, often displaying images of people and animals. Masks, on the other hand, have been less important to the Bakongo than to other people, such as the Luba.

One unique type of folk art is the fetish, which is an animal carved from wood and driven full of nails. The Mayumbe near the coast paint calabashes (gourds), embellishing them with hunting scenes and colorful geometric designs.

19 SOCIAL PROBLEMS

The Bakongo face many of the same problems as their fellow citizens in their countries. They must cope with uncontrolled urbanization, collapsing state health infrastructure, lack of well-paid jobs, economic instability, and discontent among youth for lack of opportunities. In DRC, Bakongo have longstanding grievances with the national government that their farm produce, natural resources and other sources of revenues to the national treasury far exceed the benefits they receive in state services.

Social problems are not entirely separable from political issues. As noted, Kongo nationalists have never accepted the division of their ancient kingdom at the conference of Berlin in 1884–85. They argue that the partition was a unilateral European decision in which no Congolese participated. Consequently, since the 1950s in Angola, Holden Roberto and the National Front for the Liberation of Angola (FNLA) opposed first the Portuguese and then the Popular Movement for the Liberation of Angola (MPLA) regime; their goal was the reunification of the Bakongo spread across three countries. Tragically, their protests and uprisings resulted in repression and massacres, including "Bloody Friday" on January 1993 when between 4,000 and 6,000 Bakongo were killed. In Angola, Bakongo still are viewed with suspicion by the regime because of their support during the civil war for the National Union for the Total Independence of Angola (UNITA). It would be difficult to estimate the cost of these allegiances in terms of lost social and economic development, but Bakongo clearly have paid and continue to pay dearly for their separatist ideas.

20 GENDER ISSUES

Women have not benefitted equally from development, and traditionally they have had to take a subservient role to men in political, social, and economic affairs. Women and girls still perform the majority of household chores including fetching water, collecting firewood, cooking and caring for children. They also plant, weed and harvest crops, and tend household gardens. Most girls, because they are expected to help their mothers with this workload, do not complete primary and secondary school. While women produce around 60% of the food, they receive only a fraction of agriculture extension services and generally do not own land. Some are subject to sexual violence though not nearly on the scale as experienced by women in eastern Congo. Nevertheless, initiatives like schooling for girls and women's savings and credit cooperatives have gone a long way to empowering women.

21 BIBLIOGRAPHY

Africa South of the Sahara 2007. London: Europa Publications Ltd., 2008.

Balandier, Georges. *Daily Life in the Kingdom of the Kongo: From the Sixteenth to the Eighteenth Century.* London: George Allen and Unwin Ltd., 1965.

Hilton, Anne. *The Kingdom of Kongo.* Oxford: Clarendon Press, 1985.

MacGaffey, Wyatt. *Religion and Society in Central Africa: The BaKongo of Lower Zaire.* Chicago: University of Chicago Press, 1986.

Martin, Marie-Louise. *Kimbangu: An African Prophet and his Church.* Grand Rapids, MI: Eerdmans, 1975.

—by R. Groelsema

BAMANA

PRONUNCIATION: bah-MAH-nah
ALTERNATE NAMES: Bambara
LOCATION: Republic of Mali
POPULATION: 4–5 million
LANGUAGE: Bamanankan
RELIGION: Islam; indigenous religion
RELATED ARTICLES: Vol. 1: Malians

1 INTRODUCTION

The Bamana live in the Republic of Mali. The development of a Bamana ethnic identity dates back to the pre-colonial states of Segu and Kaarta. According to oral tradition, Biton (Mamari) Kulubali founded the Segu kingdom (named after its capital) in about 1712 when he was banned from his own village after a dispute. His age mates followed him, and together they organized raids on surrounding communities. Their ranks were swelled by men whose freedom they purchased (e.g., men who had committed crimes or fallen into debt bondage) and by others who joined voluntarily. Extending his raids over an ever-larger territory, Biton gradually came to control the entire Middle Niger region. Some members of the Kulubali clan resisted his authority and migrated westward into the area of Kaarta where they founded a second Bamana state.

Biton Kulubali died in 1755. His sons quarreled over his succession and ultimately lost the throne to the military commander Ngolo Jara. Ngolo brought back stability and expanded the boundaries of the kingdom. The state was at its largest and strongest during the reigns of Ngolo's son Monzon and his grandson Da Monzon. The Scottish explorer Mungo Park, the first European to travel in this part of West Africa, visited Segu during the reign of Monzon in 1796 and again in 1805. Internal strife began again after the death of Da Monzon in 1827, and central rule became weaker. Al Hajj Umar Tal, a Muslim cleric from the Futa Toro (now Senegal), took control of Kaarta in 1855 and conquered Segu in 1860 in the course of a *jihad* (military struggle). He was succeeded by his son Amadu, who retained power in Segu until the French conquest in 1890. Bamana villages in Kaarta and in the former Segu kingdom resisted the imposition of colonial rule but finally succumbed to superior military power. The French established an administrative center in Segu and reinstalled a descendent of the Jara dynasty as a local figurehead but soon accused him of fomenting a revolt and executed him. A French administrator then governed the territory until Mali gained its independence from France in 1960. Segu has been the capital of Mali's fourth region since then.

2 LOCATION AND HOMELAND

The Bamana compose the largest of Mali's ethnic groups, numbering more than 4 million. They predominate on both sides of the Niger River between Bamako and Kè-Macina, northwest of Bamako, and between the Niger and Bani rivers southeast of Segu. Bamana families and groups of families also live among other ethnic groups elsewhere in the country. Large numbers of rural men and women move to Mali's cities, especially to the capital Bamako, to earn money during the long dry season or to establish themselves permanently. Others seek work outside the country. Côte d'Ivoire was a favorite destination until the eruption of the civil war in 2002.

3 LANGUAGE

The Bamana language (*Bamanankan*) belongs to the Mande group of languages, which are a branch of the Niger-Congo family of African languages. A national orthography for Bamana was developed after independence but the spelling of most personal and place names still reflect French writing conventions; for example "Ségou" rather than "Segu." The language is tonal so that the meaning of words changes depending on the tone of a particular syllable. (*So* with a low tone, for example, means "horse," whereas *so* with a high tone means "house.") Definite and indefinite articles are also marked by raising or lowering the tone. The language is semantically rich. Bamana convey this when they say *"Bamankan kònò ka dun"* ("The Bamana language is profound").

Since Segu is considered the Bamana heartland, the dialect of Bamana spoken in and around Segu is said to be the most authentic form of the language.

4 FOLKLORE

The foremost Bamana heroes are the king Da Monzon Jara, the king's bard Tinyetigiba Dante, and his warrior chief Bakari Jan Koné, whose deeds are celebrated in the epic of Da Monzon. This epic telescopes certain historical figures and events before and after Da Monzon's reign. In recent memory, Da Monzon's popularity even overshadows that of the kingdom's founder Biton Kulubali, although the popular Segu band Super Biton, which has represented the region at the biennial National Arts Festival, is named after the latter.

5 RELIGION

Al Hajj Umar Tal (see **Introduction**) and his successors tried to eliminate Bamana religious practices but they did not convert people by force. Bamana men and women embraced Islam of their own volition over the course of the 20th century. The vast majority are Muslims today.

Indigenous Bamana religion was anchored in respect for the ancestors, village protective spirits, and several secret societies. The abode (*dasiri*) of the village protective spirits is in a grove near the village where the villagers would collectively make annual sacrifices. Individuals and households could obtain blessings through sacrifices to ancestors at household shrines as well as to village protective spirits at the *dasiri*. Six major secret societies (*ndòmò, kòmò, kònò, koré, ciwara,* and *nya*) were instrumental in social and religious life. Only men could become members. Historical evidence suggests that there were also some female societies in the past. Not all of the six societies were represented in each village or area occupied by Bamana. All young boys were once initiated into the ndòmò society, where they participated in annual rituals and learned self-discipline. Once circumcised, a boy could join one or more of the other societies in his area. Members were required to participate in meetings and rituals and refrain from discussing the knowledge they acquired with non-members. Non-members were unable to approach the area where rituals were held; sometimes they even had to remain in their houses when rituals were taking place in the village. In such instances, a bell signaled the beginning and end of the curfew. Although the societies differed in the scope and content of their esoteric knowledge, rituals, symbols, and practices, they all upheld community values and sought to protect the community against misfortune and harm by individuals (e.g., through sorcery). Divination through procedures such as geomancy, throwing cowries, or animal sacrifice was used widely when important decisions had to be taken.

6 MAJOR HOLIDAYS

Traditionally, Bamana observed either Monday or Thursday as a day of rest. During the agricultural season, they suspended work in the fields on that day and relaxed around pots of home-brewed beer. Very few observe these days any longer due to labor migration and widespread conversion to Islam. The Bamana New Year, the first day of the lunar month *jominé*, is still recognized by some, but everyone now celebrates the national holidays (see **Malians**).

7 RITES OF PASSAGE

Ethnic differences in the celebration of rites of passage in Mali have diminished as a result of conversion to Islam and increased urbanization. Many Bamana women in rural areas still give birth at home with the assistance of a midwife. New mothers stay home and rest with the baby for seven days until a naming ceremony is held. The household elder chooses the name in consultation with the infant's father. If the family is Muslim and has no preference, the local *imam* (religious leader) will select a name and say prayers. In the rural areas outside Segu, village men assemble for the name-giving ceremony and make a small monetary contribution, but women do not bring gifts of cloth for the mother as in the city.

Village boys of roughly the same age are circumcised together and remain secluded until their wounds are healed. The same holds for girls who are excised (i.e., have part of their clitoris removed). Whether or not excision should continue is increasingly being debated. Excision is a pre-Islamic practice which many Bamana retained when they became Muslims. It was considered parallel to circumcision, and each was seen as playing a vital role in the unfolding of female and male sexuality respectively. Celebrations at the end of seclusion have also diminished considerably. In the past, when boys and girls were teenagers by the time of circumcision/excision, these rituals signaled the end of childhood and the "coming out" of the new adults was a joyous affair with much feasting, visiting, and dancing. Young women were considered marriageable thereafter and young men ready to court women. The future in-laws of girls who were already betrothed would come bearing gifts.

Weddings follow the transfer of gifts from the groom's to the bride's family (bride wealth) and are held in the home of the groom. In rural areas, entire villages or neighborhoods participate in the festivities and help the groom's family feed the guests by bringing cooked food. Friends and acquaintances of the groom come from near and far, offering their best wishes and monetary contributions. The bride is accompanied by a throng of female relatives, and her trousseau is opened and displayed for the village women. Some of the cloth she brings with her is distributed among her husband's female relatives. After the wedding, the bride spends only a few days with her husband and returns home for several weeks before joining him permanently. In the past weddings were held during the dry season, but they are now often celebrated during the rainy season when young people return from labor migration. Wed-

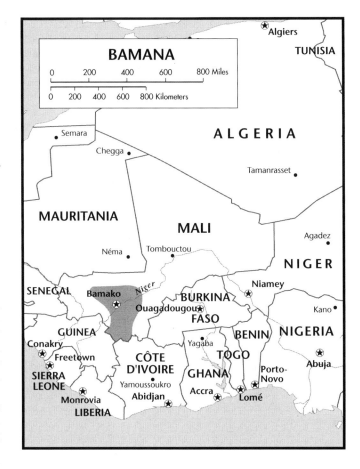

dings are equally important social occasions in the cities. Since space is more limited than in the rural areas, some of the festivities take place in the street in front of the groom's home. Families block off part of the street and erect tents to accommodate guests and musicians.

Muslim Bamana funerals are simple and differ little from others in Mali. Among non-Muslims, the death of an old woman or man gives rise to festivities celebrating the person's life, especially if (s)he has numerous children and grandchildren.

8 INTERPERSONAL RELATIONS

Learning the etiquette of greeting and hospitality is part of the socialization process of any Bamana child. The greeting ritual involves a rhythmic exchange of inquiries and responses concerning the interlocutors' well-being and establishes their membership in social groups. If the two people know each other, they inquire about family members and friends. If they are strangers, the host seeks to locate the guest socially through questions posed in greeting. During the greeting, the interlocutors lower their eyes. A younger person always shows respect by not looking an elder in the eye while greeting. Following the greeting, a visitor is offered a drink of water and a place to sit. Depending on the nature and length of the visit, a guest may also be offered food and a parting gift (e.g., a chicken or other local product). A visitor (relative, friend, neighbor, or stranger) who arrives at mealtime is always invited to join in the meal. One way to honor a guest is to offer him or her a kola nut. Most visiting takes place on the veranda or in the courtyard, but if a visitor is invited to enter someone's house, he or she traditionally removes his or her shoes.

Even among people who see each other daily, greetings are very important. There are greetings for virtually all occasions and activities. Someone returning from the market, for example, is hailed, *"I ni dògò"* (literally: "You and the market").

9 LIVING CONDITIONS

As is the case with rural Malians of other ethnic groups, rural Bamana have few material comforts. Their houses are generally made of mud bricks and have no electricity or running water. Women and young girls carry all water for drinking, cooking, and bathing home from the nearest well. They cook over an open fire in the courtyard or, during the rainy season, in a kitchen house. Each married woman is entitled to her own house with an attached bathing area and toilet. If a man has more than one wife, he must provide this for each one. A man with multiple wives frequently also has a small house of his own where he keeps his personal belongings and entertains guests. The most prevalent consumer goods include clothing, emaille bowls, garden chairs, kerosene lamps, flashlights, transistor radios, bicycles, and motor bikes. Those who do not own or have access to a bicycle or motor bike generally travel by foot or donkey-cart between rural villages.

Health problems and treatment options are generally the same as for other Malians. Because the majority of rural Bamana engage in agriculture, they are prone to work-related injuries and infected wounds.

10 FAMILY LIFE

The households of Bamana cultivators are usually multi-generational, including a man and his wife or wives, and their sons with their respective wives and children. Social relations are governed by an age and gender hierarchy. Men are ranked according to their biological age and women on the basis of their marriage into the household. Those who are older have more authority than their juniors and men have more authority than women. This principle is mitigated by various factors including earning capacity and personal dynamism. Moreover, elder women are an important force within the household by virtue of having worked and born children for their husband's family. Decisions concerning the household are made by the eldest male in consultation with his brothers or grown sons. Women are now often consulted in decisions regarding the marriage of daughters and sons, and they are able to influence decisions even when they have no direct input.

Family members cooperate in the cultivation of household fields and the crops, and/or the proceeds from their sale, provide food for the household meals and resources for agricultural improvements, marriage expenses, and other household needs. The wives of the men in the family are responsible for meal preparation. They cooperate in pounding grain unless they are able to pay for having it ground by machine, and they take turns cooking. Elder women are freed of these duties once daughters-in-law can assume them. Family members eat together, usually in same-gender groups. Since meals are taken in the courtyard for most of the year women can often overhear conversation among men and vice versa. There may also be conversation and banter back and forth. Married women host friends, visiting relatives, or their husband and his guests at their own house.

In order to generate income that is under their personal control, both men and women can grow specialty crops, produce handicrafts, or engage in small trade during the off-season or during leisure hours. Individual women and men also have the right to own chickens, goats, sheep, or cattle in addition to any animals which all members of the household may own jointly. If conflict arises and cannot be managed, jointly owned land and animals are divided, and the household breaks up into smaller units.

11 CLOTHING

Contemporary Bamana women and men dress like other Malians. Traditionally, women spun cotton and men wove it into strips that were sewn together into clothing for young and old of both genders. In the early part of the 20th century, adult male attire consisted of a tunic and ample knee-length pants that closed with a drawstring, both often dyed a rust brown by a man's wife or mother. Women traditionally wore a hand woven wrap skirt in multi-colored patterns or designs done in a mud-dye technique. They wore a piece of similar cloth around the upper part of their bodies. Basic jewelry included gold ear and nose rings for women and a single gold earring for men.

12 FOOD

The basis of the diet in rural areas continues to be millet and, to a lesser extent, sorghum and fonio. Rice is increasingly popular but not eaten every day. Millet (or sorghum and fonio) is pounded by hand or machine-ground and then prepared as a gruel (for breakfast or as a light meal) or as a stiff porridge or couscous. Both porridge and couscous are eaten with various sauces made of hot pepper and ground baobab leaf or peanut paste. Dried fish is often used for flavoring the sauce because most people cannot afford meat or chicken every day. Smoked or fresh fish is more commonly eaten than either chicken or meat. Apart from okra and sorrel, vegetables are only gradually entering the rural Bamana diet. *Ngòmi* is a millet pancake fried in shea butter oil (from the shea tree) and eaten with sauce or sugar water. Finally, a traditional Bamana liquid food, often eaten between meals, is *dègè,* which is made of finely ground millet flour and cream that are allowed to sour. At the time of consumption, it is diluted with water and sweetened with sugar. Young women who have been on labor migration occasionally prepare foods they have learned to cook in the city (e.g. pasta) as special treats.

13 EDUCATION

Educational statistics are not broken down by ethnic group. Bamana children and youths are represented in the secular schools as well as in the *madrasas* and Quranic schools prevalent in Mali. Many rural villages still do not have any school and children have to walk to the nearest village or town to attend. Secondary schools are located mainly in cities and in administrative centers such as county seats. This means that students from outlying areas must board if they want to continue their educations beyond elementary school.

14 CULTURAL HERITAGE

The tomb of Biton Kulubali, founder of the Segu kingdom, is located on the banks of the Niger in Sikoro, a few kilometers from Segu. Nearby is the reconstructed room from where Biton is said to have conducted the affairs of state. The symbol of Segu is the *balanzan* tree (*acacia albida*), which loses its fine leaves during the rainy season. In 2005 Segu hotel owners joined with local nongovernmental organizations (NGOs) and city representatives to organize the first Festival on the Niger in order to showcase regional cultural traditions and promote cultural tourism. The festival has been held every February since then and also brings national musical talent to the city.

Music is an integral part of all Bamana rituals and celebrations, with drums providing the major musical accompaniment. Young men who have the talent and interest learn drumming by working with accomplished drummers. Bands usually consist of three drummers who play in a neighborhood or village. Bands that gain a reputation have the opportunity to perform for a fee on special occasions. Women and men dance in same-sex groups. Hunters' associations have bards who make music with a lute (*donso ngoni*) that is accompanied by a scraper (a baton-like metal instrument). Another type of lute was used during secret society rituals. Women have their own musical instrument, the *gita*, used as an accompaniment to singing. The *gita* of married women consists of a calabash (gourd) turned upside down on a piece of heavy cloth and is struck with two wooden batons (similar to chopsticks). The *gita* used by unmarried girls is a calabash decorated with an incised pattern and cowry shells; it is tossed shoulder-high with both hands and turned at the same time to make a percussive sound.

Although Bamana figure among Mali's writers, oral literature has the widest audience and includes a variety of genres. Apart from the epic, there are tales, proverbs, and riddles. Children in particular exercise their intellect by telling riddles.

Puppet theater and mud cloth, discussed below, are part of the Bamana cultural heritage.

¹⁵ WORK

Agriculture continues to employ most Bamana but it is rarely the only source of income. Those who remain in the rural areas combine it with other income-generating activities, ranging from market gardening to craft production, small trade, and construction. Bamana women work in the fields alongside men, but households with enough male labor may free them from planting and weeding to pursue other activities. In the past, Bamana prided themselves on being accomplished cultivators. Young men could show prowess by excelling during collective work parties in the fields. When the village youth group worked in someone's field, it was accompanied by drummers and adolescent girls who sang to urge the men on in their work.

Seasonal or longer-term labor migration is a widespread means of supplementing rural incomes. The majority of male migrants pursue a variety of occupations in the urban informal sector while young women work as domestic servants in urban households. Like other Malians, Bamana also seek work outside the country. Women and men who complete their schooling enter a variety of occupations appropriate to their educational achievement.

¹⁶ SPORTS

Soccer is a popular sport introduced by Europeans. There are no traditional sports, although male dancing involves acrobatics such as somersaults.

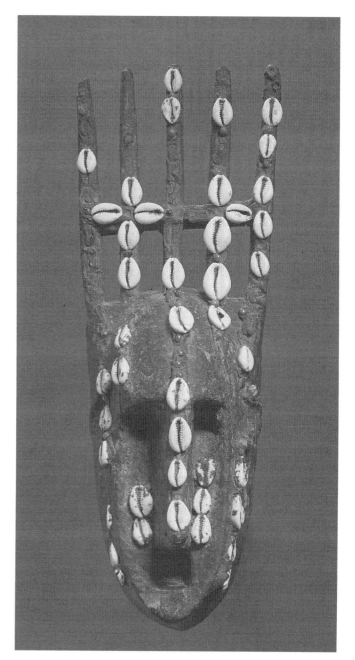

A N'domo mask with wood, shells, and seeds, from the Bamana culture, Mali. (Bridgeman Art Library/Getty Images)

¹⁷ ENTERTAINMENT AND RECREATION

Theater has long been popular among the Bamana, in small villages as well as in urban neighborhoods. In the rural areas, it is generally organized by the local youth association. One type of theater, known as *kotèba*, satirizes local practices and individuals. A favorite entertainment related to kotèba is comedy whereby a man or woman dressed outrageously acts the part of a buffoon known as *koréduga*. A second type of theater, *sògòbò*, may involve either puppetry or costumes made of reeds, cloth, and masks worn by men. The puppets represent animals, spirits, and human characters, including white colonial officials. They are commissioned from a blacksmith-carver. Performances involving reed costumes are generally held only at night at the beginning of the harvest season. Villages vie with each other for the best performances and some reach national acclaim. Both kotèba and sògòbò are done with live drumming and a male chorus.

The departure of young men and women during the long dry season has greatly diminished rural entertainment during this time of year. Weddings animate villages at the beginning of the rainy season with visitors and musical entertainment. Village youth groups invest in microphones and amplifiers since they are now considered a requirement for successful musical performances. In the absence of live performances, people of all ages listen to the radio or to music on cassettes. Socializing with friends, neighbors, and relatives remains a primary form of recreation.

18 FOLK ART, CRAFTS, AND HOBBIES

Weaving was once a widespread dry season occupation for Bamana men but it has declined considerably since the 1990s. Some men still weave blankets of home- or machine-spun cotton in red and white or black and white checks and stripes. Mud cloth (bògòlan fini), a cotton textile for ritual purposes and everyday wear, was traditionally painted by and for women in black- or brown-white geometric patterns using vegetable dyes and fermented clay. Over a decade ago it was adapted for fashionable wear, bags, and wall hangings and marketed nationally and internationally. Malians embraced it as an emblem of national identity and African Americans began wearing it as a symbol of pride. Malian artists played an important role in this transformation. Since its production for the national and international market place, men have also become involved in painting mud cloth.

Blacksmiths have historically not only made iron objects but also carved masks used in rituals, including the famous antelope headdresses seen in many museums. Wives and mothers of blacksmiths are skilled potters.

19 SOCIAL PROBLEMS

There are no social problems that are unique to the Bamana as an ethnic group. The consumption of fermented drinks, especially millet beer, on ritual occasions was common in the past but is now limited to those who continue to practice their indigenous religion. As Malian citizens, the Bamana are covered by the human and civil rights observed at the national level.

20 GENDER ISSUES

The discussion of family life above provides a glimpse into Bamana gender relations and shows that they are cross-cut by age and other forms of social status. Gender ideology places men above women but daily life allows for considerable ambiguity and flexibility. Since family land is inherited through the male line, women have to integrate their husband's home upon marriage. Rural married men who work in Bamako for extended periods of time increasingly take their wives with them during the early years of marriage. Once they have children however, women generally have to stay in the village unless the husband decides to relocate permanently to the city. A man with two wives may have one accompany him to the city while leaving one behind in the village. In sum, couples are often separated for months at a time because families cannot earn an adequate income in the rural areas. The revision of the Malian family law code, once passed, will improve women's juridical status.

21 BIBLIOGRAPHY

Arnoldi, Mary Jo. *Playing with Time.* Bloomington: Indiana University Press, 1995.

Ba, Adam Konaré. *L'épopée de Segu. Da Monzon: Un Pouvoir guerrier.* Lausanne, Switzerland: Pierre-Marcel Favre, 1987.

Festival Segou, Mali. www.festivalsegou.org/ (June 2008).

Hoffman, Barbara E., ed. "Gender in the Mande World." *Mande Studies 4,* 2002.

McNaughton, Patrick. *Secret Sculpture of Kòmò: Art and Power in Bamana (Bambara) Initiation Associations.* Philadelphia: ISHI, 1979.

Rovine, Victoria L. *Bogolan: Shaping Culture through Cloth in Contemporary Mali.* Washington and London: Smithsonian Institution Press, 2001.

Zahan, Dominique. *The Bambara.* Leiden: E. J. Brill, 1974.

—by M. Grosz-Ngaté

BANYANKOLE

PRONUNCIATION: bahn-yahn-KOH-lay
LOCATION: Ankole in southwestern Uganda
Population: 400,000
LANGUAGE: Runyankole; English, KiSwahili (two national languages)
RELIGION: Christianity (Roman Catholicism, Church of Uganda—Anglican, Fundamental Christianity); indigenous Kinyankole religion
RELATED ARTICLES: Vol. 1: Ugandans

¹ INTRODUCTION

The Banyankole, who numbered about 400,000 people at the turn of the century in 2000, are located in southwestern Uganda. This former kingdom is well known for its long-horned cattle, which were objects of economic significance as well as prestige. The *Mugabe* (King) was an absolute ruler. He claimed all the cattle throughout the country as his own. Chiefs were ranked not by the land that they owned but by the number of cattle that they possessed. Chiefs ruled over pasture lands. Although both chiefs and herdsmen possessed cattle, the ultimate ownership of all cattle was in the hands of the Mugabe. Cows were exchanged by chiefs or herdsmen for wives but could not be killed, except for a small number of bulls for sacrifice or food. The Banyankole conform to a pattern of social stratification famous in Uganda and its neighboring countries of Rwanda and Burundi, which is, namely, the division of society into a high-ranked pastoral caste and a lower-ranked agricultural caste. The Bahima are cattle herders who despise farming and do not marry the Bairu farmers who reside on a chief's estates and provide the chief with vegetable foods. The Bairu also care for goats and sheep for themselves and for the Bahima.

The Mugabe regularly held court where he resolved disputes involving more than 50 cows, or cases of wives deserting their husbands. The Nganzi was the favorite chief who decided which disputes would be heard by the Mugabe. The Nganzi alone had the right to enter the Mugabe's rooms at any time. The kingdom was divided into 16 districts headed by a chief appointed directly by the Mugabe. At his appointment, a district chief was given several hundred cows as a gift from the Mugabe. Ordinary cattle herders were free to settle wherever they chose in search of good pastures and wise leadership. Chiefs regularly held courts to resolve minor conflicts. Every year agents from the Mugabe traveled throughout the kingdom in search of taxation in the form of 1 cow per 50 cows in a homestead. Chiefs had no right to levy taxes on those in their districts.

In 1967, the government of Milton Obote, prime minister of Uganda, abolished kingdoms in Uganda, including the Kingdom of Ankole. This policy was intended to promote individualism and socialism in opposition to traditional forms of social stratification. A cash economy and private ownership of land promoted in the colonial era, set in motion by the British in the early 20th century, had earlier served to diminish the authority of chiefs in favor of wealthy farmers or herders. By World War II, the Bairu owned as many cattle as the Bahima. Nevertheless, cattle are still highly valued among the Banyankole, and the Bahima are still held in high regard.

² LOCATION AND HOMELAND

Ankole lies to the southwest of Lake Victoria in southwestern Uganda. Its area equals about 15,540 sq km (6,000 sq mi). It appears that sometime during the 17th century or before, cattle-keeping people migrated from the north into central and western Uganda and mingled with indigenous farming peoples. These migrants adopted the language of the farmers but maintained their separate identity and authority, most notably in the Kingdom of Ankole. The Kingdom of Buganda bordered Ankole on the east, and the Kingdom of Bunyoro constituted its northern border. Lake Edward was a natural border to the west.

The country was well suited for pastoralism, given its large areas of rolling plains covered with abundant grass. The land lies about 1,370 m (4,500 ft) above sea level, with some hills rising to as high as 2,740 m (9,000 ft). Valleys sometimes have papyrus grass or are wooded. Today, nomadic herders prefer to move to those areas of Ankole where fresh grazing land and water supplies are available, although these lands are diminishing because of a high rate of population growth.

³ LANGUAGE

The Banyankole speak a Bantu language called Runyankole, which is a member of the Niger-Kordofanian group of language families. In many of these languages, nouns are composed of modifiers known as prefixes, infixes, and suffixes. Word stems alone have no grammatical meaning. For example, the prefix *ba-* signifies plurality; thus, the ethnic group carries the name *Ba*nyankole. An individual person is a *Mu*nyankole, with the prefix *mu-* carrying the idea of singularity. Things pertaining to or belonging to the Banyankole are referred to as *Ki*nyankole, taking the prefix *ki-*. The pastoral Banyankole are known as *Ba*hima; an individual of this group is referred to as a *Mu*hima. The agricultural Banyankole are known as *Ba*iru; the individual is a *Mu*iru.

⁴ FOLKLORE

Morality is primarily a communal concern, for which folklore provides a repertoire of legends and tales constructed to impress upon the young standards for proper behavior through contradictions and dilemmas contained in the stories. Storytelling is a common means of entertainment, with both men and women excelling in this verbal art form. Riddles and proverbs are also emphasized among the Banyankole. Of special significance are legends surrounding the institution of the kingship, details of which provide a historical framework for the Banyankole. The perhaps legendary Bachwezi, thought to be forebears to 20th-century kingdoms in central and western Uganda, are credited by the Banyankole for pastoralism, religious cults, and social distinctions found among them. They also established the Banyankole, in Kinyankole terms, as the successors of this large, regional empire. Neighboring societies, such as the Banyoro, have traditions that contest this view in favor of legends more favorable to their own claim to succession.

Folk tales concerning morality contain many examples drawn from royalty, cattle, hunting, and other central concerns of the Banyankole. After work in the evening, parents and grandparents socialize children into the community through stories *(ebyevugo)*, proverbs *(efumu)*, and riddles *(ebiito)*. Animals figure prominently in Kinyankole tales. For example,

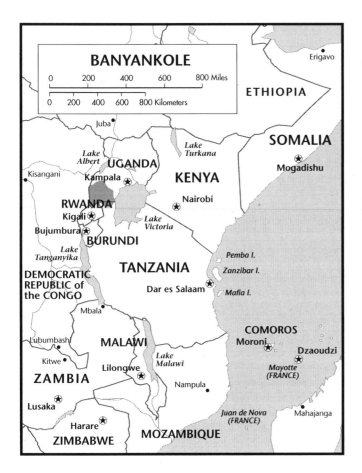

BANYANKOLE

one well-known tale concerns the Hare and the Leopard. The Hare and the Leopard were once great friends. When the Hare went to his garden for farming, he rubbed his legs with soil and then went home without doing any work, even though he told Leopard that he was always tired from digging. Hare also stole beans from Leopard's plot and said that they were his own. Eventually, Leopard realized that his crops were being stolen, and he set a trap in which Hare was caught in the act of stealing. While stuck in the trap, Hare called to Fox, who came and set him free. Conniving Hare told Fox to put his own leg into the trap to see how it functioned. Hare then called Leopard, who came and killed Fox, the assumed thief, without asking any questions. The Banyankole recite this story to illustrate that you should not trust easily, as Leopard trusted Hare, nor should you act quickly before contemplation, as Leopard did in killing the innocent Fox.

Folk tales are recounted to teenage Banyankole during the time of courtship in order to provide a moral context for gender relations. The story of the King and the Hyena, for example, illustrates what might be told to young girls who are wasting their time chasing boys instead of learning to resist temptations for future rewards, especially the attainment of a successful marriage. In this story, the King sent a chief to find people or animals who were starving so that he could give from his own abundance. The Hyena accepted the invitation to the King's palace in order to get meat, butter, and milk, although he was warned that he must overcome four temptations on the way there. After resisting other tempting foods along the way, Hyena could not resist big bones and fat meat. When told that

he could not visit the king, Hyena did not worry since he expected to return to eat the foods that he had resisted previously. Unfortunately, the river of milk, the valley full of soup and fat meat, and another valley full of roast beef had all dried up. Hyena, therefore, sadly returned to his cave, where he starved to death.

Another tale for those young people contemplating marriage, called "The Woman Who Stole Locusts," involves a man who went to a far-off country to find a wife. He chose a very beautiful girl, even though he was warned by his friends that she had a reputation for bad manners. Sure enough, while back home, food began to disappear mysteriously, especially the delicacy, cooked locusts. After it was discovered that his new bride was the cause, she was returned home, and he reclaimed the bride-wealth he had given for her.

⁵ RELIGION

The majority of Banyankole today are Christians who belong to major world denominations, including the Roman Catholic Church, or the Church of Uganda that is Anglican. Fundamental Christianity, such as Evangelicalism, is also common. For example, the Balokole are self-identified as "saved" through a rejection of personal sin and an acceptance of Jesus Christ as Lord and Savior. Public confessions of such sins as adultery and drunkenness are common, as well as rejection of many traditional secular and religious practices. The Balokole, for instance, no longer practice extensive milking or bloodletting from cows. They believe that this "sin of greed" deprives the calf of its mother's strength and milk. The Bahima Balokole have, therefore, taken up agriculture to supplement their diet. Bride-wealth and the old customs of blood-brotherhood have been rejected in favor of Christian marriage and unity in the blood of Christ. All indigenous forms of religion are rejected outright.

The element of indigenous Kinyankole religion that survives most directly today is the belief in ancestor spirits. It is still believed that many illnesses result from bad behavior to a dead relative, especially paternal relatives. Through divination it is determined which ancestor has been neglected so that presents of meat or milk and/or changes in behavior can appease the ancestor's spirit in order to address the misfortune spiritually. Banyankole respect ancestors, name children after them, and believe that ancestors communicate with the living in dreams.

Prior to the Christian missionary movement in the 19th century, Banyankole believed that God, known as Ruhanga, lived in the sky. Ruhanga created humanity in the form of a man called Rugabe and his wife Nyamate. Rugabe and Nyamate gave birth to a long line of kings who became deified. These gods had special temples and priests often in the royal compound, and tended to be concerned with helping people to solve special problems. There were, for instance, a god of fertility, a god of thunder, a god concerned with earthquakes, and deities for specific clans and their affairs. The present dynasty of kings is believed to be descendants of previous kings who have become gods. There was a strong belief in the spiritual power of the royal drum, which symbolized the benevolent tendencies of the Mugabe ("The Bountiful"). Requests made to the drum for food were never refused, making hunger quite rare in the old economy.

6 MAJOR HOLIDAYS

As the majority of Banyankole are now Christian, they celebrate Christian holidays, such as Christmas and Easter.

7 RITES OF PASSAGE

After the birth of a child, the placenta and umbilical cord were traditionally treated with elaborate ritual by the midwife who had assisted in the birth. This was thought necessary to protect the mother and her child from harm. The midwife was also skilled in herbal medicines that were used to lessen the pains of birth and to ease difficult deliveries. The birth of twins was considered catastrophic. Members of the family were confined to the homestead and could not leave until rituals, including the slaughter of a sheep, had been performed. Naming also involved a ritual in which relatives gathered together to "call one of them." Names depended on the alleged wishes of one of the ancestors, the day or season of the child's birth, or other special circumstances.

At about the age of four months, among the Bahima, a boy was placed by his father on the backs of two cows that were dedicated to the boy. After this, a hole was scraped in the floor of the hut into which the child was made to sit while he was given the name of one of his ancestors. Among the Bairu, the naming ritual for boys was similar but did not involve cows. Many East African societies train infants to sit in association with naming ceremonies and may even have special sitting ceremonies once the child has achieved this milestone. The training results in children learning to sit unassisted about one month earlier than Western children do.

In early childhood, children began to learn the colors of cows and how to differentiate their families' cows from those of other homesteads. During this time, boys and girls played together. Young boys built small models of huts; girls made head coverings out of grass. Boys were taught how to make water buckets and knives. Girls were taught how to make milk-pot covers and small clay pots. By later childhood, around seven or eight years of age, boys were expected to be useful and were taught how to water cattle and calves. Girls helped by carrying and feeding babies; they were also expected to learn to wash milk-pots and to churn butter.

Among the Bahima, girls began to prepare for marriage as early as eight years of age. They were kept at home and given large quantities of milk in order to grow fat. They were also encouraged not to exercise and to spend most of their time sitting, talking, and making bead ornaments. Today, heaviness is still valued. Teenage eating disorders, such as anorexia nervosa and bulimia, are not evident. Among the Banyankole, the father's sister (paternal aunt) was (and still is) responsible for the sexual morality of the adolescent girl. Girls were expected to be virgins before marriage, and this aunt attended the rituals and was required to verify the virginity of the bride. Today, schools, peer groups, popular magazines, and other mass media are rapidly replacing family members as sources of moral and family education for teenagers.

Traditionally, adulthood was initially recognized through the establishment of a family by marriage, the acquisition of large herds of cows for Bahima, and of abundant crops for Bairu. Happiness, and also full adult status, was achieved by both men and women through the rearing of a large family. Special occupations, crafts, storytelling, and musical expression in song and dance were some of the pastimes enjoyed.

Presently, death and burial are experienced largely through the ideology of Christian religions. Nevertheless, public weeping and wailing are still practiced, and members of the extended family are expected to attend the burial. People are expected to shave their heads as a symbol of mourning. Among the Bahima, cows are slaughtered for the funeral meal. In the past, all the full-grown bulls of the dead man's herd were slaughtered for consumption at the funeral. Occasionally, widows of a dead man committed suicide by hanging or by poison to express their grief. The Mugabe, too, ended his life by poison if he thought that his powers were waning. At his death, fires in the royal compound were extinguished, and the royal drum was covered. All work stopped throughout the kingdom, and all people had their heads shaved. The Mugabe's dead body was put on a cowskin and later transported to a forest where the royal tombs are located.

8 INTERPERSONAL RELATIONS

Social relations among the Banyankole cannot be understood apart from rank. In the wider society, the Mugabe and chiefs had authority over less wealthy herders (Bahima). The Bahima had authority over the Bairu. Within the family, husbands had authority over wives, and older children had authority over younger ones. Brothers were held in higher regard than were their sisters, although siblings of the opposite sex were frequently very close.

The death of the Mugabe symbolically illustrates his power over the kingdom. All work ceased, and any couples engaged to be married had to marry on the day of the Mugabe's death or else the man had to look for another wife. All princes and princesses wore bark-cloth clothing instead of their regular cowhide robes. Accession involved a son (usually the eldest) who had been selected by the Mugabe before his death. This prince was given a royal stool upon which he sat for his installation ceremonies. Not infrequently, however, some of his brothers chose to fight him, and civil war resulted. When the new Mugabe was determined through battle, fires would be lit once again throughout the kingdom. New chiefs were then named to oversee his cattle. The new Mugabe's mother was elevated to the rank of queen mother. She appointed her own chiefs and had her own royal homesteads throughout the kingdom. The Mugabe chose his favorite sister to be the "Munyanya Mukama," and she, too, ruled over royal estates. She frequently married royalty from neighboring kingdoms in order to create political ties with them.

In the ordinary households of both Bahima and Bairu, social relations mirrored the royal social organization. Inheritance typically involved the eldest son of a man's first wife, who succeeded to his office and property. A man might, however, choose a favorite son to be his successor. Thus, relations between fathers and sons and between brothers were formal and not infrequently strained. Mothers and their children, and brothers and their sisters, were often close. Because women could not officially own property, mothers generally expected their sons to care for them in old age. Husbands might have multiple wives, given that polygyny was not uncommon. Daughters were valued because they attracted bride-wealth upon their marriages, and sons were important for carrying on the family name. Brothers respected their sisters who brought wealth into the family when they married and left home. The most marginal person in this system of social relations was the childless woman because she could not inherit property because of her gender, nor did she have any sons to support her in old age.

Social relations in the community centered around exchanges of wealth, such as cows and agricultural produce, through the system of ranked authority and kinship. Marriage and bride-wealth were, and continue to be, significant also. The ideal person was one who was intensely involved in matters of family and community welfare. A person who was a loner and, therefore, did not involve himself or herself in the ongoing social life of the community was held in ill repute. The most significant way that community solidarity was and still is expressed is through the elaborate exchange of formalized greetings. Not to engage in these rituals is a sign of non-membership in the community. Greetings vary by the age of the participants, the time of day, the relative rank of the participants, and many other factors. Anyone, even the Mugabe, meeting an elder has to wait until the elder acknowledges that person first.

9 LIVING CONDITIONS

The Mugabe's homestead was usually constructed on a hill and measured about 0.40 km (0.25 mi) at its broadest part. It was surrounded by a large fence made from basketry. A large space inside the compound was set aside for cattle. There were special places for the houses of the king's wives, and for his numerous palace officials. There was a main gate through which visitors could enter, with several smaller gates for the entrance of family members. Waiting rooms were housed near the main gate, and visitors were announced by a gatekeeper. Covered passages connected houses inside the compound. Special names were given to the homes of the king's pages and to those of his favorite wives. There was also a special home used by the Mugabe before he went to war. Occasionally, the king's compound had over 100 homes reserved for the royal wives and their attendants. A fence set off space for his wives from areas used by servants, pages, and other residents. The royal palace was set among other dwellings occupied by prominent chiefs, brewers of the royal beer, and specialists such as woodcutters and drummers. The Mugabe moved his palace every other year in order to provide for the cows a clean environment that was free of insects. Bahima maintained homes much smaller than the king's, but modeled after it in appearance.

The Bairu traditionally built homes about 4.25 to 5.5 m (14–18 ft) in diameter, 2.75 or 3 m (9 or 10 ft) tall, and in the shape of a beehive. Poles of timber had woven over them a framework of basketry made of millet stems and chords of papyrus fiber. A thick layer of grass frequently covered the entire structure. The ground that served as a floor had on it a fireplace made from large stones. Household possessions included cowskin bedding, water pots, iron hoes, and iron knives. Sometimes goats and sheep were tied inside near the walls of the hut.

Today, housing makes use of indigenous materials such as papyrus, grass, and wood, but homes are now primarily rectangular. Such homes usually are made from wattle and daub with thatched roofs. Cement, brick, and corrugated iron are now common in the construction of homes, particularly by those Banyankole who can afford these relatively expensive materials. Currently, household possessions typically include Western-style chairs, tables, couches, and beds. Radios are commonly present, and a growing number of the affluent possess televisions. Photographs are especially valued and can be seen displayed prominently inside the house, along with calendars, magazine cutouts, and posters. Teenagers enjoy keeping personal albums containing photographs of themselves and their friends taken on special occasions and trips. The family photo album is kept by the parents. These albums are often shared with visitors as a means of socializing on an initial visit.

In the past, Banyankole traveled primarily by foot. With the exception of married Bahima women, most Banyankole could and did walk distances of many miles on a regular basis. Today, the bicycle is a popular means of transportation used for visiting and for transporting goods to market. In the past, paths through the countryside were maintained by chiefs for ease of portage of materials to the Mugabe's palace and for military security. Today, in addition to dirt roads, tarmac roads are available for public vehicles and private automobiles. Speed taxis are popular as a means for travel between towns such as Mbarara and the major city of Uganda, Kampala.

The Banyankole have enjoyed a relatively high standard of living with a rich food base. Nevertheless, diseases such as sleeping sickness and malaria have been problematic historically. Currently, HIV has inflicted many families in Ankole, but government-sponsored HIV prevention programs are in place. Teenage girls do not suffer from eating disorders that are common in the West, most likely because the culture values plumpness rather than thinness.

10 FAMILY LIFE

Among the Bahima, a young girl was prepared for marriage beginning at about the age of 10, though sometimes as early as 8, when she was prevented from having any interaction with men. She was expected to consume much milk and beef so that she could attain a desired plumpness. She was encouraged to give up all forms of exercise, resulting in her having difficulty walking. In contrast to Bahima men, girls were considered attractive by becoming as fat as possible. Marriages often occurred before a girl was sexually mature, or soon after her initial menstruation. For this reason, teenage pregnancies before marriage were uncommon. Polygyny was associated with rank and wealth. Bahima pastoralists who were chiefs typically had more than one wife, and the Mugabe sometimes had over 100. Marriages were alliances between clans and large extended families. On occasion, poor herdsmen, often brothers, pooled their resources so as to share a wife. This practice known as polyandry, or fraternal polyandry when brothers are involved, enabled a poor man not only to pay cows as a marriage fee for his wife, but with his co-husband's help he was in a position to maintain her after marriage as well. The eldest brother went through the marriage ceremony, and all the children were considered to be his for purposes of inheritance. Levirate marriage occurred when a woman became the wife of her deceased husband's brother. This custom served to keep women who had married into the family, and their children, as integral parts of the extended family.

The Bahima and the Bairu did not, as a rule, intermarry. Among both groups, premarital virginity was valued. A marriage fee was required among the Bairu, but this was not as elaborate as among the Bahima. Commonly, 14 goats were given by the prospective groom to his future father-in-law. The goats were then distributed by the father-in-law to his brothers and to a favorite sister, all members of his extended patrilineal family, as well as to his wife's brother from the extended family from which he had obtained his own wife. The 14 goats were in actuality an exchange for rights to the children who would belong to the prospective husband's family and not to their mother or to her family. Among the Bahima, marriage exchanges were much more elaborate, but the same principals operated. When the bride came to take up residence with her husband, she was received by her future father- and mother-in-law by sitting on their laps. Later, while sitting on a mat, the couple sprinkled each other with grain, then stirred millet flour in boiling water to symbolically illustrate that a new domestic unit had been established. Exchanges of food and gifts occurred thereafter for several days between the two families, to the accompaniment of music, dancing, eating, and beer-drinking.

Today, Christian marriages are common. What has persisted is the value attached to extended families and the importance of having children as a measure of a successful marriage. Polyandry and polygyny have been replaced largely by monogamy, the prescribed form of marriage of Christian religions. Marriages have been delayed, given the attendance at school of both girls and boys. One consequence of this delay has been a rise in teenage pregnancies out of wedlock. Girls who become pregnant are severely punished by being dismissed from school or disciplined by parents; for this reason, infanticide, now more common than in the past, is sometimes practiced by schoolgirls, given that abortion is not legal in Uganda.

11 CLOTHING

Dress differentiates Banyankole by rank and gender. Chiefs traditionally wore long robes of cowskins, compared to ordinary citizens who commonly were attired in a small portion of cowskin over their shoulders. Women of all classes wore cowskins wrapped around their bodies and covered their faces in public also. On a journey or when traveling to visit friends, Bahima women were carried in a cowskin-covered litter for fear that walking would tire them. In more modern times, cotton cloth has come to replace cowskins as a means of draping the body. For special occasions, a man might wear a long white cotton robe with a Western-style sports coat over it. A hat resembling a fez may also be worn. Women cover their bodies, heads, and partially their faces with dark-colored cotton cloth. Today, Banyankole wear Western-style clothing. Dress suitable for agriculture, such as overalls, shirts, and boots, is popular. Teenagers are attracted to international fashions popular in the capital city of Kampala. International business, travel, and education enable the introduction of the latest fashions from abroad, as well as the dissemination of Ugandan clothing, jewelry, handbags, and other crafts to other countries.

12 FOOD

Bahima herders consume milk and butter and drink fresh blood from their cattle. Cereals domesticated in Africa—millet, sorghum, and eleusine—dominate the agricultural Bairu sector. Milking is done by men, while butter-making among the Bahima and the majority of the farming among the Bairu are the responsibility of women. The staple food of a herder is milk. Beef is also very important. When milk or meat are scarce, millet porridge is made from grains obtained from the Bairu. Buttermilk is drunk by women and children only.

When used as a sauce, butter is mixed with salt, and meat or millet porridge is dipped into it. Children can eat rabbit, but men can eat only the meat of the cow or the buffalo. Women consume mainly milk, preferring it to all other foods. The agricultural Bairu keep sheep and goats, which are used primarily by the pastoralists for trade and sacrifice. Unlike the farmers, herders never eat chickens or eggs.

The Mugabe had established times for consuming milk, which was obtained from royal herds and given to him by his pages. He drank milk four times in the morning and four times in the evening. For example, the Mugabe drank milk before going to bed and also was awakened throughout the night to drink milk. He was regularly smeared with fresh butter, especially in the morning, by one of his wives. A bull or fatted cow was killed daily to serve to visitors at the royal compound. Some of these visitors were chiefs who ate at the same time as the Mugabe after sitting with him in court. On these and other occasions, the Mugabe ate alone. Beer made from millet was regularly consumed by the Mugabe, and he commonly had a meal of beef and beer before his nightcap of milk. Beer was also popular throughout the population as an indispensable part of ceremonies such as weddings and funerals.

Today, land and cattle are privately owned in those areas known formerly as the Kingdom of Ankole. This has resulted in migration and resettlement locally and to areas elsewhere in Uganda. Herders have moved to areas where population density is still low and where grazing lands are available. Population growth has also contributed to migration and changes in traditional patterns of subsistence. A cash economy now complicates further the old system of barter and exchange between farmers and herders.

13 EDUCATION

Formal education was introduced into Uganda in the latter part of the 19th century. Today, Ankole has many primary and secondary schools maintained by missionaries or the government. In Uganda, among those aged 15 years and over, about 50% are illiterate. Illiteracy is noticeably higher among girls than among boys. There is a problem of teenage pregnancy among girls that forces them to leave formal education. Schools in Ankole are a significant source of the transmission of national and international values and skills needed for life in modern-day Uganda. At the same time, schools seek to maintain indigenous Ankole cultural values. Runyankole is taught in primary schools.

In the past, girls and boys learned cultural values, household duties, agricultural and pastoral skills, and craft specialization through the process of observation and participation. Instruction was given where necessary by parents, fathers instructing sons, and mothers instructing daughters. Elders, by means of recitation of stories, tales, and legends, were significant teachers also. A girl was instructed by her father's sister on matters of household responsibility and sexual morality.

14 CULTURAL HERITAGE

All schools have regular performances and competitions involving dances, music, and plays that make use of traditional Ankole materials. Where appropriate, instruction also makes use of Ankole folklore and artistic expression through a long-standing process of Africanization of the curriculum.

15 WORK

Traditionally, among the Bahima, the major occupation was looking after cattle. Every day, the herder traveled great distances in search of pasture. Young boys were responsible for watering the herd. Teenage boys were expected to milk the cows before they were taken to pasture. Women cooked food, predominantly meat, to be taken daily to their husbands. Girls helped by gathering firewood, caring for babies, and doing household work. Men were responsible for building homes for their families and pens for their cattle.

Among the Bairu, both men and women were involved in agricultural labor, although men cleared the land. Since land was very plentiful, a piece of land could be farmed for several years, then abandoned for a time so it could be replenished. Millet was the main food crop. Secondary crops were plantains, sweet potatoes, beans, and groundnuts. Maize was considered a treat by the children. Children participated in agriculture by chasing birds away from the fields. Frequently, they made scarecrows that resembled people from grass and sticks. On some occasions, they shouted or banged flat boards together. At times, husband and wife slept in a small hut in their fields in order to protect their crops from wild animals. Reaping was done by men and women, and winnowing was done by women. The harvest season was a time in which there was little work and a great deal of free time for parties and marriage ceremonies. Surpluses of food were given to the pastoral chief as a form of taxation.

A notable difference in labor distinguished Bahima women from Bairu women. The former did very little physical labor apart from everyday household routines. They took care of the milk-pots and churned butter. They also spent a great deal of time caring for their personal appearance and were expected to be plump as a sign of beauty. Bairu women worked hard and, in many homes, performed the bulk of agricultural labor. They also spent much labor grinding grain into flour using stone implements.

16 SPORTS

Sports, such as track and field and soccer, are very popular in primary and secondary schools. Children play an assortment of games including hide-and-seek, house, farming, wrestling, and ball games such as soccer. Ugandan national sporting events are followed with great interest in Ankole, as are international sporting events.

17 ENTERTAINMENT AND RECREATION

Radio and television are important means of entertainment in Ankole. Most homes contain radios that have broadcasts in English, KiSwahili (the two national languages), and Runyankole. Programming includes educational themes involving topics such as nutrition, livestock management, health, and language instruction. Stories, plays, and news are popular. Teens, especially, enjoy musical shows that offer a variety of sounds from Uganda, elsewhere in Africa, and overseas. Books, newspapers, and magazines also are enjoyed by the people. Birthday parties for children are a regular form of entertainment involving birthday cakes, cards, and gifts.

Social events, such as weddings, funerals, and birthday parties, typically involve music and dance. This form of entertainment includes not only modern music, but also traditional forms of songs, dances, and instruments. Drums used to ac-

company dances are water-pots filled with different levels of water. Drumsticks are made of reeds and fiber. Men commonly beat on the drums, and women use rattles about 30 cm (1 ft) long, made from hollow reeds filled with seeds. In one popular dance form, the dancers hold their arms high above their heads in imitation of cattle horns, while hissing and stomping their feet in a rhythmic fashion. Both men and women, particularly among the Bairu, enjoy dancing. It is not uncommon for older Banyankole to congregate together at ceremonies to engage in traditional dance and song. Younger people often gravitate towards the radio or "boom box" to listen to popular, often international, music.

The drinking of alcoholic and nonalcoholic bottled beverages is common at festivities. In the past, the brewing of beer was a major home industry in Ankole, which provided beer for drinking in ceremonies, especially at harvest time. Traditional beer was made from millet, and wine was made from plantains. A large wooden trough was used for fermenting.

18 FOLK ART, CRAFTS, AND HOBBIES

The Mugabe assembled at his palace, or arranged for their residence elsewhere, the best artisans in his kingdom. Carpenters, ironworkers, potters, musicians, and others were permanent features of the royal homestead or were in constant contact with it. Carpenters came from the Bairu who had inherited knowledge of their crafts from their fathers. Wooden artifacts commonly used were: stools, milk-pots, meat-dishes, water-pots, and troughs for fermenting beer. Among the commoners, it took as many as six carpenters and dozens of friends to fell a tree and to prepare it for making beer. Ironsmiths also belonged to the Bairu. Smiths obtained their materials locally for the manufacture of spears, knives, and hammers.

Potters obtained clay from swamps that were abundantly distributed throughout the region. The clay was coiled into shape, then fired to become permanent. Every family had a member who specialized in making pots. Some pots were considered very beautiful, particularly those with long, slender necks. Pipes for smoking, however, displayed the finest artistic creativity. All Banyankole of both sexes enjoyed smoking tobacco, and young women particularly enjoyed chewing it. Most homes grew tobacco somewhere near the house. The tobacco leaves were dried in the sun, then rubbed into small pieces for smoking. Small colored beads were used to decorate clay pipes, which came in various shapes and sizes, and walking sticks. There were special guardians at the Mugabe's palace who watched over his tobacco pipes, along with other royal possessions such as spears, stools, and drums. Only the king had wooden drums made from cowhide; others used clay water-pots as a percussion instrument. Graphic art was not common, although rectangular designs did appear on the interior walls of some homes, especially those of royalty.

Traditional industries are not nearly as significant as in the past. Household possessions and artifacts show the many social changes that have occurred in Ankole; nevertheless, one can still observe the use of traditional pipes, water-pots for music, decorated walking sticks exchanged at marriage, and the use of gourds and pottery.

19 SOCIAL PROBLEMS

The political culture of Uganda continues to balance tribal, regional, and national interests. The prime minister of Uganda in 1962 at independence from England was Milton Obote from Northern Uganda. He was hostile to kingdoms in Uganda, considering them to be outdated and incompatible with socialism. In 1966, all kingdoms, including Ankole and the Mugabe, were outlawed. Obote was overthrown by dictator Idi Amin in 1971. During Amin's reign in the 1970s, all Ugandans suffered from political oppression and the loss of life and property. Obote took over once again in 1980 after the overthrow of Amin and ruled oppressively. Currently, Yoweri Museveni, who was elected president in 1986, is credited with leading Uganda in an economic recovery and toward democratic reform. Banyankole take special pride in Museveni's birthplace, which is in Ankole. Nevertheless, resistance to Amin and Obote has resulted in the destruction of towns and villages in Ankole and neighboring villages.

Since the mid-1980s, AIDS has been a source of great sorrow for numerous families who have lost relatives, friends, and other loved ones to this dreaded disease. In Uganda, there has been a strong national effort to educate the public through mass media about AIDS prevention. Orphaned children continue, however, to be a serious problem for those families stricken by AIDS, as well as for the greater society.

Population pressure, in spite of AIDS, remains a threat to adequate pasturage and a pastoral way of life. Warfare in neighboring countries such as Rwanda has contributed to population growth, as refugees have regularly come into the region. Many Rwandans are now fully integrated into the Ankole society and are full citizens of the nation of Uganda.

20 GENDER ISSUES

As in all patriarchal societies, gender roles were strictly defined among the Banyankole. These roles were defined to reinforce and perpetuate the relationship of male dominance and female subordination. While women were supposed to do all the agricultural and domestic household chores, they were not allowed to sell the produce of their labor, reserving that right for men. Women were also not allowed to own cattle or land. Even today, through socialization within the family, in educational institutions, and in other social spheres, boys and girls are conditioned to behave in certain ways and to play different roles in society.

In male-headed households, men determine the amount of land to access for farming and type of crops to be grown. Women are not supposed to speak in public. They are supposed to take care of domestic issues, such as raising children and preparing and cooking food, while men dominate the public sphere. Men control the major sources of household income, such as livestock, land, and the sale of crops produced by women. Men control the household budget, dictating what can be bought and how money is to be spent. Rules of inheritance are guided by the cultural context in which land, livestock, and important assets are passed down to men from one generation to the next. However, the fact that the Banyankole continue to recognize sisters and mothers as important people within the family, is an indication that originally they had a matrilineal succession, in which women wielded considerable political and economic power. Also, the importance of princesses among the Banyankole attests to the fact that their societies might have initially been matrilineal.

In recent times, the Museveni government has encouraged women to participate in politics and other aspects of public life. Today, each of Uganda's districts has a female member of parliament, and one-third of all local council seats are reserved for women. As a result, women make up about 24% of the legislature. There are active women's rights groups, including the Uganda Women Lawyers Association (FIDA-U), Action for Development, and the National Association of Women Judges. However, in spite of these advancements, women are often targets of violence and sexual abuse. Women who reveal their HIV positive status to their spouses are often beaten and sometimes murdered by their husbands.

In terms of human rights, Uganda's past has been checkered with torture and human rights abuses, and, according to some human rights organizations, these abuses continue in present day Uganda. The army has been accused of committing atrocities against the populations in northern Uganda, and security forces allegedly torture suspects and members of the opposition on a routine basis. Homosexuality is illegal under Victorian-era legislation still in force in Uganda and many other English-speaking countries in Africa. The laws reflect a deep aversion among many Africans to homosexuality. But, the truth remains that gays and lesbians exist in Uganda, although they pay a high price for their sexual orientation often facing discrimination, and even torture and imprisonment.

21 BIBLIOGRAPHY

Bahemuka, Judith Mbula. *Our Religious Heritage*. Nairobi, Kenya: Thomas Nelson and Sons, Ltd., 1984.

Hansen, Holger Bernt, and Michael Twaddle, ed. *Uganda Now: Between Decay and Development*. London: James Currey, Ltd., 1988.

Kiwanuka, M. S. M. *The Empire of Bunyoro Kitara: Myth or Reality*. Kampala: Longmans of Uganda, Ltd., 1968.

Mushanga, Musa T. *Folk Tales from Ankole*. Kampala: Uganda Press Trust, Ltd., n. d.

Njongu, K. & Orchadson-Mazrui, E. "Gender Inequality and Women's Rights in the Great Lakes: Can Culture Contribute to Women's Empowerment." http://portal.unesco.org/shs/en/files/9186/11387168911Presentation_-_Liz_Orchardson.pdf/Presentation%2B-%2BLiz%2BOrchardson.pdf. (October 2008).Roscoe, Rev. John. *The Banyankole: The Second Part of the Report of the Mackie Ethnological Expedition to Central Africa*. London: Cambridge University Press, 1923.

———. *Twenty-Five Years in East Africa*. London: Cambridge University Press, 1921.

— revised by E. Kalipeni

BEMBA

PRONUNCIATION: BEM-bah
LOCATION: Northeastern Zambia
POPULATION: 3,600,000 Bemba or Bemba-speaking
LANGUAGE: Bemba; English
RELIGION: Protestantism; traditional beliefs; Roman Catholicism; African Christianity; Islam
RELATED ARTICLES: Vol. 1: Chewa; Tonga; Zambians

1 INTRODUCTION

The Bemba are a matrilineal group that occupy the northeastern part of Zambia, an area of about 51,800 sq km (20,000 sq mi). The language and culture of the Bemba are very similar to those of other ethnic groups that live around them, for example, the Bisa, the Aushi, the Tabwa, and various subgroups in Luapula Province. The Bemba and the related peoples belong to the wider group usually referred to as the Central Bantu. The Bemba came to their present location from west of the Luapula River in the Congo as offshoots of the great Luba peoples during the great Bantu migrations of the 16th and 17th centuries. Once they were well established in their present habitat, the Bemba organized themselves into an expansive but loosely united state under a paramount chief, known as Chitimukulu (the Great Tree), and subchiefs belonging to the royal Crocodile clan. They were characterized as a warlike and fearsome people by early European travelers and explorers, such as David Livingstone. Zambia was colonized by the British in the early 1890s when the British South African Company, under the direction of the British-born South African business tycoon and politician Cecil Rhodes, began to expand into the area. The former name of Zambia was Northern Rhodesia, named after Cecil Rhodes and his company that won concessions by signing treaties with local chiefs to mine the rich copperbelt area.

Zambia obtained independence in 1964 under the leadership of President Kenneth Kaunda, who ruled Zambia for 27 years under a one-party state. After unrest in 1990, multiparty politics were instituted. President Kenneth Kaunda lost the presidential elections held in 1991 to Frederick Chiluba, a former trade unionist and leader of the Movement for Multiparty Democracy (MMD). By the end of Chiluba's first term as president (1996), the MMD's commitment to political reform had faded in the face of re-election demands. In the presidential and parliamentary elections held in November 1996, Chiluba was re-elected. Kaunda had been barred from running in these elections and his United National Independence Party (UNIP) boycotted them; the elections were also deemed neither fair nor free by non-governmental organizations and international observers. In the elections held in 2001, Chiluba was constitutionally barred for running again although he attempted to change the constitution to allow him to run again for a third term but this failed under pressure from the electorate. The 2001 elections saw the MMD presidential candidate Levy Mwanawasa declared the victor by a narrow margin. During his rule Levy Mwanawasa has been credited with attempting to root out corruption unlike the Chiluba's government, which was largely seen as corrupt. Under Mwanawasa's leadership, Chiluba was arrested and charged with several counts of embezzlement and corruption, crimes he was said to have committed during his tenure in office as president of Zambia.

2 LOCATION AND HOMELAND

The Bemba and related groups live in the northeastern high plateau of Zambia, an area with elevations ranging from 1,200 to 1,500 m (4,000–5,000 ft) above sea level. Although the area is well watered, the soils are generally poor and are covered by bush, scrub, and low trees typical of an African savannah environment. Lakes Mweru and Bangweulu are prominent geographical features on the plateau. Tall grass grows around the lakes, mixed with remarkable patches of dense evergreen thickets, which are eventually replaced by savannah woodlands as one moves away from the lake basins. Because of the presence of dense tree cover and unbroken savannah forest, the Bemba have been described as a forest people. The climate on the central plateau is quite pleasant with temperatures ranging from 13°C to 29°C (55°–84°F), and the area gets an adequate rainfall of about 114 cm (45 in) per year. Although the Bemba proper are a small group, their influence is visible in the numbers that speak the Bemba language and thus make the Bemba appear to be a dominant ethnic group in Zambia. Chibemba is used as a lingua franca in Zambian cities. It is estimated that of the 11.3 million people in Zambia, 32% (or 3,600,000 people) are Bemba or Bemba-speaking, 18% (2,034,000) are Maravi, 15% (1,695,000) are Tonga, 8% (904,000) are Barotze, and the remainder are ethnic groups such as the Mambwe, Tumbuka, and Northwestern peoples.

3 LANGUAGE

In Zambia, as in many southern and central African countries, there is a multiplicity of languages belonging mostly to the Bantu family of languages. For example, the name for elephant in Bemba is *nsofu*, in Tonga it is *ndopu*, while in Luyana it is *muzovu*. "To die" in all three languages is *kufwa*, and a child in all three languages is *mwana*. In short, these languages share a similar vocabulary. But in spite of their common origin, many of these languages are distinct from each other, characterized by a loss of mutual comprehensibility. It is therefore quite common for a modern-day Zambian to be multilingual, speaking a maternal or first language as well as several other languages such as Bemba and English. As noted in the preceding section, the Bemba group is the most dominant ethnic group in Zambia, and Bemba as a language is the most commonly spoken maternal language, with 32% of the population (or 3,600,000 people) speaking this language. One of the Bemba dialects has become the lingua franca of the cosmopolitan urban population of major Zambian cities such as Kitwe and Ndola. The prominence of Bemba can be traced back to the days of the powerful paramount chief Chitimukulu and his kingdom that presided over an expansive area. However, in today's Zambia, English plays an important role as the national language, the language of prestige and power spoken by an influential bureaucratic elite. Education from secondary school to university is also taught in English. While English is good as a unifying language since no ethnic group can identify with it, it has its disadvantages in that the majority of the population who are not fluent in English are excluded from the modern economy and development.

⁴ FOLKLORE

There is one interesting myth in Bemba oral tradition that deals with the origins of the Bemba group. There are many partial and varying oral renditions to this myth. The myth begins by noting that long ago in the land of Kola, there lived White and Black people, but after a quarrel the White people sailed away to get rich in Europe, while the Black people remained under their chief Mukulumpe Mubemba. The name Bemba comes directly from this chief's last name. The chief then had sons with Mumbi Mukasa Liulu, a heavenly queen who had fallen from the sky and who belonged to the "Crocodile clan" *Ng'andu*. Due to internal quarrels within the royal family, the sons fled, taking with them a group of loyal followers. After much traveling and many conquests, the surviving sons and followers settled in present-day Bemba territory and established a centralized form of government with a paramount chief, named Chitimukulu, "The Great Tree," in reference to their original ruler, from whose heavenly mother they all trace descent. By war, they expanded the Bemba control over conquered territories, and internally the Crocodile clan consolidated control and political authority over other rival clans. The full narration and interpretation of the myth, also called the Bemba Charter Myth, reveals a story that is rich in its oral, political, religious, and ritual dimensions. In general, the Bemba rely heavily on folklore, myths, and the oral tradition to pass on vital information about beliefs, customs, and culture from one generation to the next.

⁵ RELIGION

Similar to other peoples of the Bantu family, the Bemba have their own form of traditional religion in which they believe in the existence of a single high god, Leza, who is far removed from everyday life and lives in the sky. He is omnipotent and controls things such as thunder and both women's and men's fertility, and he is the source of magic power. Christian missionaries of various denominations came to Zambia during the era of colonization in the late 19th century and converted many of the peoples of Zambia, including the Bemba, to Christianity. However, few Zambians as of today have totally abandoned all aspects of traditional belief systems, so much so that the religion of most people in Zambia and among the Bemba can be considered to be a transition from traditional systems to Christianity. Those who strictly adhere to traditional religion have been greatly influenced by Christian teachings and its trappings as well. Due to the similarities in the overall structure of Christianity and indigenous religions, most people do not see any contradictions between the two and are likely to practice both religions simultaneously. In general it is estimated that 34% of Zambia's population are Protestant, 27% hold to traditional beliefs, 26% are Roman Catholic, 8% are African Christian, and the rest follow other Christian sects, Islam, and other faiths.

⁶ MAJOR HOLIDAYS

The major national holiday in Zambia is Independence Day on 24 October. Zambia obtained its independence from Great Britain in 1964 on 24 October. During this day every year there are celebrations arranged in major urban areas and throughout the country. There is much drinking, dancing, and singing. In the afternoon, people congregate in stadiums to watch a game of soccer between major leagues, or to see the national

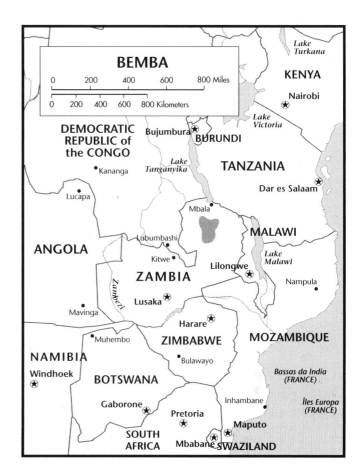

team play a friendly match with a national team from a nearby country such as Malawi.

⁷ RITES OF PASSAGE

Among the Bemba, there is no initiation ceremony for boys. Girls go through an initiation ceremony called *Chisungu,* a puberty rite that initiates girls through the symbols of life and death in order to give social form and meaning to their sexuality. A girl whose breasts have started to develop is secluded for anywhere from six weeks to three months to undergo the Chisungu ceremony. A series of rites representing the duties of the girl as cook, gardener, hostess, and mother are carried out in an initiation hut, as well as in the surrounding bush. During the ceremony there is much drumming, dancing, singing, and drama symbolic of the acoustic uproar which the Bemba associate with the whole of cosmic and human forces. One of the worst things that could happen to a girl is to bear a child before she has been initiated. Her child would then be considered a creature of ill-omen and both the father and the mother could be banished. Although still practiced in rural and urban areas, the Chisungu ceremony is slowly disappearing because most girls grow up in Christian families and go to modern schools, which have become a new rite of passage. School teachings and subjects such as biology are at variance with the teachings of Chisungu, which perpetuates male dominance and the acceptance of rigid inferior sex roles for women. Nevertheless, many people in Zambia in general, and among the Bemba in particular, believe that initiation ceremonies are part of their cultural and moral heritage and that such initiation ceremonies should continue, or even be incorporated into the school curriculum.

8 INTERPERSONAL RELATIONS

Seniority is important among the Bemba and largely determines interpersonal relations. Shaking hands is the normal way of greeting, particularly among members of the same age set. There also exists a joking relationship between members of different clans. Among the Bemba a clan is defined as a descent group whose members trace their descent from a common ancestress, i.e., a grouping of several matrilineal lineages. The Bemba people have about 40 clans, and most clans have a partner clan with which they joke and can intermarry. Marriage of individuals from the same clan is not usually permissible. Most clans are named after living things such as plants and animals. Two clans in partnership usually have names that are associated and show the type of joking relationship. For example, the Crocodile clan is the partner of the Fish clan, because crocodiles eat fish. A member of the Crocodile clan can tease or ridicule a member of the Fish clan by saying, "You are my meal today." A member of the Fish clan can answer back that if it had not been for the fish, the crocodile wouldn't have seen the light of day, and it would have starved to death.

At beer parties it is common for men and women to drink from the same container, usually an earthenware pot with a wide mouth. The beer is poured into the pot and everybody takes a few sips from the pot as it is passed around. It is bad manners to refuse a sip.

9 LIVING CONDITIONS

The Bemba live in rural villages built up around a number of matrilineal extended families. Their main occupation is subsistence agriculture in the form of shifting cultivation. Each family grows its own food and is largely self-sufficient. *Chitemene* shifting cultivation is the main agricultural system, a system where crops are grown in the ash from burning the collected, stacked branches that have been lopped and chopped. Early in the dry season, a family selects an area to be cut. The cutting of the trees is solely a man's job; the women and children collect the chopped branches and pile them into heaps which are then burnt. The women are also responsible for selecting the seeds and sowing them on the ash beds, as well as digging and sowing garden mounds around the villages on which vegetables are grown. Finger millet and cassava are the main crops, but sorghum, maize, beans, and peas are also grown. Due to the poor condition of the soils, the field is abandoned after a few years and new gardens are opened. As the population has increased, the system is beginning to break down and vegetation is chopped down before it has fully regenerated. Bemba territory is not urbanized so that many people still live a rural way of life. Disease is very much a part of Bemba society. Tropical diseases such as malaria and bilharzia, as well as malnutrition, are quite common and tend to be very debilitating and sometimes lethal. On average, life expectancy at birth is about 40.3 years for males and 40.6 years for females. Life expectancy has declined during the past decade due to HIV and AIDS which has resulted in increased adult mortality. It is estimated that 16.5% of Zambia's population is HIV positive.

Most people in the Bemba heartland still live in villages of 30–50 huts made of wattle and daub with a grass thatched roof. The village also serves as the basic political unit and is administered by a headman to whom the majority of the villagers are related. Once the fertility of the soil around the village has been exhausted, the village may be relocated to some other suitable location. This is a direct consequence of the *chitemene* system of shifting cultivation and necessitates the building of impermanent structures. Material possessions also tend to be minimal. A household might own a bicycle, a radio, and a few other trinkets of modern life. Before the arrival of the Europeans, the Bemba had no form of storable wealth. Today most households are characterized by a limited cash flow to cover basic needs. Consumer goods are rarely bought, and cash income is earned only when there is need for it. There are some households that are progressive and earn a substantial amount of cash through poaching, fishing, and casual labor to enable them to buy goods exceeding basic needs. Transportation is largely by foot, although long-distance travel is by buses that occasionally visit the remotest parts of the rural areas.

10 FAMILY LIFE

"Family" among the Bemba refers to the extended family that includes several generations, much like a clan. The extended family serves as the corporate property-holding unit and a cooperative work group that in most instances shares food, gifts, money, and other amenities of life. It is a form of social security for those having less access to wealth. Within the extended family system of classificatory kinship ties, an individual generally has several "mothers," several "fathers," and a host of "sons" and "daughters." Polygamy was permissible and quite common among the Bemba, but statistics to show its current levels are not available. Chiefs once needed additional wives because of their obligations of hospitality which entailed the preparation of large amounts of food, brewing beer, and the cultivation of large fields. But the coming of Christianity and modernization has weakened the practice of polygamy.

Since the Bemba are a matrilineal society, large payments in money or goods are not required at the time of marriage, as is commonly done in patrilineal societies. In order to become engaged to a girl, a young man is expected to offer a small betrothal present to the parents of the girl, in the form of a piece of cloth, a rooster, or something of small value. Once married, the young son-in-law moves to the wife's village and performs tasks for his parents-in-law. In the past, girls were often engaged before puberty and performed chores for their future husband such as sweeping the hut and drawing water. Before puberty, boys and girls are encouraged to play together and can indulge in "puppy love" without any sanctions. However, as soon as girls reach puberty, sexual contacts with men are prohibited until marriage. These days, boys and girls find their own mates either at school or in surrounding villages and then inform their parents about their love. Marriages can be carried out either under modern statutory law patterned along the British system, or under Bemba customary law.

11 CLOTHING

Before the arrival of the Europeans, the most common type of cloth was that made from bark, which was worn around the waist by women as a loincloth. Today most Zambians, including the Bemba, wear modern dress. Although the clothing for men is Western (shorts, pants, and shirts), the designs and fashion for women's dresses are typically of Zambian or African origin.

¹² FOOD

The staple food for the Bemba is finger millet which is ground into flour. A thick porridge is made from the flour and is eaten with a relish, a side dish of vegetables or meat. Two other important staple crops are cassava and maize. Cassava is poor in nutrients but is easy to grow and can stay underground for a number of years before it is harvested. The importance of maize has increased over time, and it is likely to take the place of finger millet as the main staple. Other important crops that comprise the Bemba diet include peanuts, beans, edible gourds or squash, pumpkins, cucumbers, sweet potatoes, bananas, and cowpeas. Due to the presence of the tsetse fly, large livestock such as cattle and goats are not kept. However, the Bemba supplement their diet in numerous ways by hunting small game, fishing, and gathering wild fruits. These activities provide much needed food during certain months and years of famine when food becomes scarce. Honey, insects such as caterpillars and grasshoppers, fruits, and wild plants are collected throughout the year. Fishing also adds much needed protein to the diet. Fishing using fish traps and fish poison is conducted during the months of February, March, and April when the rivers are full of water. Dogs are usually kept not as pets but for hunting purposes, particularly for small game such as bush pig and duiker (a small antelope). All kinds of implements are used for hunting purposes, ranging from old-fashioned guns to spears, nets, pits, traps, and axes.

Food prohibitions and taboos are not common among the Bemba, except in certain circumstances, such as soon after marriage when a son-in-law might be prohibited from eating the food cooked by his mother-in-law, or when a girl undergoing the *chisungu* initiation ceremony might be restricted from eating certain foods.

¹³ EDUCATION

At the time of independence in 1964, the educational infrastructure was underdeveloped in many parts of Zambia due to colonial neglect. Very few people were literate prior to 1964. Since independence, the government of Zambia has devoted substantial amounts of funds to educational development. The educational system in Zambia is similar to the British system in which students spend eight years in primary school, four years in secondary school, and another four years in college. The University of Zambia has a limited capacity of about 4,000 students, and entry into the university is very competitive. Because fees are not charged at any level of the educational system, the only obstacle to education is the availability of schools, particularly in rural areas where full primary schools are rare. The national literacy rate in Zambia has increased dramatically from a low of about 10% in 1964 to a high of 70% today. However, since the Bemba live far from the main centers of development, their literacy rates could be much lower than this.

¹⁴ CULTURAL HERITAGE

Like many peoples of Africa, the Bemba have a rich cultural heritage that is centered around an oral tradition of conveying information from one generation to the next. Very little of the Bemba's folklore has been written down. Traditional music is part of daily life from initiation rites and marriage ceremonies to hunting parties.

¹⁵ WORK

In traditional Bemba society, although males are heavily involved in clearing new fields, they are primarily occupied with political affairs and trade. Agriculture is largely the domain of women, who are responsible for most of the food. With the introduction of the modern economy during the era of colonization, men began to migrate for wage opportunities in the copper mines of the copperbelt of Zambia, and further afield to South Africa. As a result of large-scale migration of young men to the mines, the rural areas contain a large proportion of women; agriculture is therefore stagnant because of the lack of male labor to clear trees. Census statistics indicate that Bemba areas are second only to the Eastern Province of Zambia in their shortage of men. The absence of men in rural areas has had a major negative impact on agricultural productivity, the economic standing of women and children, marriage, and family life. In most cases, women have become poorer than in the past when men were present.

¹⁶ SPORTS

Throughout Zambia, the most popular sport played by children and young men is soccer. The national team of Zambia has had some prominent Bemba soccer players.

¹⁷ ENTERTAINMENT AND RECREATION

In trading centers throughout the Bemba region, beer pubs are a common part of the landscape, where people gather to drink both traditional and bottled beer. Television is available in Zambia, but few people in rural areas can afford to buy a television set. Like among the Chewa of Malawi, children in Bemba territory keep themselves busy through the many traditional games they have developed. Among the popular games and activities are mice hunting expeditions, hide and seek at night, tug-of-war and the nguli game (which is essentially a spinning top a carved cylindrical piece of wood, about three inches long, with a sharp pin on the bottom). Men often play nsolo, a more demanding game, much like chess, often played under a shady tree at the edge of a village, or at the mphala or insaka (men's meetinghouse). Village children make their own toys such as cars made from dry cornstalks, scrap materials, and discarded wires as well as other innovative playthings. As such children become responsible, self-reliant, and creative given the fact that parents and children rarely have money to spend on expensive (or even cheap) toys. Many of these activities help to improve children's learning and social skills.

¹⁸ FOLK ART, CRAFTS, AND HOBBIES

The Bemba people are not generally known for having developed a complex folk art culture, although iron-smelting was practiced until the 1940s. A Bemba man has four basic implements: an axe used for clearing the bush and cutting wood; a hoe for farming; a spear for hunting; and, in the past, a bow. Woodcarving is less developed compared to other peoples in the region, and weaving is unknown among the Bemba. Perhaps the best crafts among the Bemba are pottery and baskets, although these also tend to be simple and fragile.

¹⁹ SOCIAL PROBLEMS

Zambia has been relatively stable during the post-independence era, and inter-ethnic fighting has not been a major problem. However, due to economic difficulties during the 1970s and 1980s, the government has faced internal unrest from time to time. Shortages and unemployment in the cities, and widespread misery in rural areas, triggered discontent among the top-ranking leaders in government, the political party, the business community, and university students, which culminated in multiparty democracy in the early 1990s and the peaceful removal from power of President Kenneth Kaunda in 1991. Apart from the economic malaise of the rural areas, the Bemba were far removed from the centers of these conflicts, with the exception of those living in the major urban areas.

[20] GENDER ISSUES

There are pervasive inequalities between women and men in Zambia today, more so among the Bemba where women are supposed to traditionally be subservient to men. These inequalities can be traced to pre-colonial indigenous traditions, the colonial and post-independence eras. During the colonial era the introduction of the labor migration economy where men were allowed to migrate to mining and large scale plantation agricultural areas left women and old people in rural villages in charge of subsistence agriculture. Among the Bemba and other groups in Zambia women are prized for marriage and their access to secondary and tertiary education is much lower than for men and boys. Thus, wage employment in urban centers is regarded as suitable for men. Women tend to be confined to jobs related to their roles as care givers and nurturers—nurses, teachers and secretaries—low wage jobs.

In rural areas women are the backbone of subsistence agriculture producing most of the food while men are away in urban areas. Women take care of child-rearing and house-running. In Bemba subsistence society women do the weeding, sowing, and harvesting. Male activities in rural areas are fewer than female, more spaced out and less repetitive.

Recent statistics from the Human Development Report indicate that women in Zambia are more likely to be poor than men: 65% of women are poor, compared to 52% of men, and child poverty has also increased. In particular, women heads of household were more likely to be poor: 70% of female-headed households are extremely poor compared to 57% of male-headed households. Thus gender inequality in rural and urban areas is well entrenched in Zambia.

Human rights are enshrined in the Zambian constitution. However, with reference to homosexuality, Zambians are divided in how to approach it. Currently Chapter 87 of Zambia's Penal Code Act describes homosexuality as an "offense against morality." The issue of homosexuality in Zambia came to the forefront in 1998 when for the first time in the country's history, the Zambian homosexual community decided to come out in the open, and form an organization called Lesbians, Gays, Bisexual, and Transgender Association (LEGATRA) to champion their cause. This led to an uproar by the Zambian community, both in support and against it with the majority vowing to reject it at all costs. The political and Christian establishments in Zambia have condemned homosexuality as unbiblical and against human nature and pointed out that this abnormality has no right to exist in society or ask for support from the government.

[21] BIBLIOGRAPHY

Aldridge, Sally. *The Peoples of Zambia.* London: Heinemann Educational Books, 1978.

Brelsford, W. V. *The Succession of Bemba Chiefs: A Guide for District Officers.* Lusaka: Government Printer, 1948.

Kaplan, Irving. *Zambia: A Country Study.* Washington, D.C.: The American University, 1984.

Maxwell, Kevin B. *Bemba: Myth and Ritual: The Impact of Literacy on an Oral Culture.* New York: Peter Lang, 1983.

Richards, Audrey I. *Chisungu: A Girl's Initiation Ceremony Among the Bemba of Northern Rhodesia.* London: Faber and Faber Limited, 1956.

Stromgaard, Peter. "A Subsistence Society Under Pressure: The Bemba of Northern Zambia." In *Africa* vol. 55, no. 1, 1985: 39–59.

Tembo, Mwizenge S. "Games and Toys in Traditional Zambia." In *World and I,* vol. 14, no. 6 (1999): 232.

—by E. Kalipeni

BENINESE

PRONUNCIATION: ben-uh-NEEZ
ALTERNATE NAMES: (former) Dahomey
LOCATION: Benin
POPULATION: 8.3 million
LANGUAGE: French (official language); Fon and Yoruba in the south; Bariba and Fulani in the north; over 40 other languages
RELIGION: Animism; Christianity (Catholicism); Islam
RELATED ARTICLES: Vol. 1: Songhay; Yoruba

¹ INTRODUCTION

The name Benin comes from an ancient West African kingdom located in present-day southern Nigeria. Until 1972, Benin was called Dahomey, named for the pre-colonial Kingdom of Dan Homey. Benin's history is most easily thought of as pre-colonial, colonial, and independent. Until the French and Portuguese developed ports at Ouidah in 1752 and at Porto Novo in 1894, a succession of kings contested and ruled Benin. European contact consisted mostly of intense slave trading, in which Dahomey's kings engaged for 300 years until it was abolished in 1885.

French domination of the area began in 1863 when France made Porto Novo a protectorate. International pressure had been mounting to end slave traffic from this port, and the French also wanted to counter British influence in neighboring Nigeria. Thus, in the 1880s the French fought a series of battles with the Dahomians, and within 15 years overthrew the last of Dahomey's kings. French missions and schools were less successful in converting Beninese to Christianity, than in graduating thousands of highly qualified students, including several well-known writers and scholars.

Benin gained its independence on 1 August 1960. Ethnic conflict and army insurrections followed leading to six military coups, a socialist revolution, a state-run economy, and near economic disaster. In 1990 however, pro-democracy demonstrations and a national conference ended General Kérékou's 18-year rule. In 1991, Nicéphore Soglo became president through competitive elections, marking Africa's first democratic transfer of power from a dictator. In 1996 and 2001 Kérékou was returned to power at the ballot box, although there were irregularities in the latter election. Student demonstrations and strikes also signaled growing impatience with delayed prosperity. Thomas Boni Yayi succeeded Kérékou in 2006 and earned international attention for his high-profile fight against corruption and his staunch support of free markets.

² LOCATION AND HOMELAND

Benin is a small West African country about the size of Pennsylvania. It is flanked to the north by Niger and Burkina Faso, by Nigeria to the east, and by Togo to the west. It has an Atlantic coastline of 125 km, where the principal cities of Cotonou and the capital of Porto Novo are situated. Benin is about 700 km in length, and 325 km in breadth at its widest point. The flat and sandy coastal plain is interspersed by lagoons. Its warm temperatures (70–85°F) and two rainy seasons contrast with the northern, thinly wooded savannah where there is only one short rainy season and temperatures reach over 110°F.

An important hilly region in the northwest has elevations of up to 2,500 ft, providing Benin with a water reservoir.

In 2008 estimates placed Benin's population at 8.3 million, growing at about 2.6% a year. The population is young, with nearly half of all Beninese under 15 years old, and only 2.4% over 65. If not for the large number of exiles who left the country in the 1970s, the population would be much higher. The semi-desert north is sparsely populated with 12 persons per sq km, while the coastal south supports as many as 240 persons per sq km in urbanized areas. In just 32 years the rate of urbanization increased from 7% in 1960 to 38% in 1992. Nevertheless, three out of four Beninese live in villages. Of the more than 42 ethnic groups, the Fon make up 40%, and four other groups—the Adja, Bariba, Yoruba, and Aizo/HouJda—account for another 40%. The remaining 20% is spread across the Fulani, Kotokoli, Dendi, and other groups.

³ LANGUAGE

The peoples of Benin speak 51 languages, making it one of the most linguistically diverse countries in the world for its size. French is the official language, and has served to unify Benin. The two major vernaculars in the south are Fon and Yoruba, while in the north Bariba and Fulani dominate. As many as 18 languages are used in education, adult literacy, the media, and broadcasting. High schools teach English as one of the two foreign languages.

⁴ FOLKLORE

Benin's nickname, "Land of Songs," testifies to the role of singing in daily life. Through singing, people express their feelings and narrate their history. Songs are melodious, controversial, satirical, or dramatic to convey the proper emotion. Each ethnic group has its own songs and dances.

Behanzin, king of Dahomey in the late 19th century, towers above the landscape as a national hero. He became king during a period of challenge and intrigue, and went to war with France over a tributary state, Porto Novo, which France had made a protectorate. His kingdom was no match for the superior firepower of the French, and after many battles—some of them victories—he escaped to the bush. Eventually he surrendered and was exiled, and he died in Algeria of pneumonia in 1906. In 1928 his remains were brought back to Benin, where he was reburied with full military honors.

⁵ RELIGION

The majority of Beninese practice animist religion. Some 42% are considered Christian, with about 27% of these Catholic. Pope John Paul II's first trip to Africa included a visit to Benin in 1980. About 24% of the population subscribes to Islam, introduced by Arab, Hausa, and Songhai-Dendi traders from the north.

Beninese animists recognize some 5,000–6,000 deities among the Fon, Yoruba, Mina and other coastal groups. Cult leaders are fetishers, diviners, and venerators of spirits. One of the most famous cults, the Python Cult, or the Cult of the Great Serpent, reveres a deity native to the pre-colonial kingdom of Ouidah in the south. The main temple is an unprepossessing structure across from the cathedral, but it houses huge defanged pythons. Churchgoers typically worship at both places on Sundays. In earlier times, Catholic priests attempted to eradicate the cult, but the local population resisted, burning down missions and chasing out the priests. Kérékou also tried to disgrace, imprison, and brand the fetishers as national traitors. The government has since adopted a collaborative approach, and enlisted fetish priests in national development.

⁶ MAJOR HOLIDAYS

Beninese celebrate 12 national holidays, which are an eclectic mix of animist, Muslim, Christian, and secular holidays. The Muslim Tabaski feast and the month long fast of Ramadan, as well as the Christian holidays of Christmas and Easter, have become ecumenical holidays. Formerly, Independence Day, August 1, was celebrated with parades, folkloric dances, and gala evening balls, but 18 years of Kérékou's revolutionary rule gave a certain ambiguity to patriotic celebrations. Difficult financial times also have made it harder to celebrate, and most Beninese spend national holidays quietly with their families, enjoying a good meal.

⁷ RITES OF PASSAGE

Beninese family life, social stability, and tradition depend on rites of passage. The rites are festive occasions and opportunities to restore balance when death occurs. Baptisms are community celebrations. Seven days after birth, a baby's head is shaved completely, the baby receives a name, and family and friends offer prayers for the parents and the child. Friends bring gifts, usually small sums of money, a sheep is butchered, and eating and dancing follow until early in the morning.

Relatives often help choose mates for their nieces and nephews, cousins, and younger sisters and brothers. After a period of engagement, a young man offers gifts of jewelry, clothing, shoes, suitcases, and if his wealth permits, a refrigerator, to his fiancée. This secures the bride-price. Then, a small delegation of the groom's uncles and aunts visits the representatives of the future bride to propose marriage. The groom's side brings money and 40 cola nuts, symbolic of respect and harmony. If their proposal is accepted, the cola nuts are divided among the bride's family and friends, and the date is set.

Weddings are festive and cause for much feasting and celebration. Traditional weddings can last for weeks. The bride is secluded with a few friends and taken care of by elderly women. They apply *enJe*, a stain, to the palm of the hands and soles of the feet, which eventually turns black. The night before the wedding, the bride sits upon a wooden mortar and is washed by the women. In the morning prayers are offered, and the groom brings additional gifts of shoes and African cloth. Traditional strips of cloth woven together serve to make the wedding gown. The bride wears special sandals, and sometimes the groom's clothing will match that of the bride.

⁸ INTERPERSONAL RELATIONS

As in much of Africa, people typically greet each other even if they are strangers passing on the street. Upon waking in the morning, children wash their faces, brush their teeth, and then directly greet their parents good morning. In Fon, one greets another person with "Good morning" (AH-FON Ghan-Jee-Ah), "How are you?" (Ah-Doh Ghan-Jee-Ah), "Thank you" (Ah-Wah-Nou), and "Good bye" (OH-Dah-Boh). The Muslim form of greeting involves asking about another's family's well-being, and shaking hands is interrupted each time by touching the right hand to the breast. Visitors always are offered a glass of water and, if it is meal time, are expected to join in sharing some food. In the north, people traditionally do not shake hands, though this is changing. When visiting an older family member or a distinguished member of the community, one kneels before the elder in respect.

⁹ LIVING CONDITIONS

Living standards remain low. Benin ranks 163rd out of 177 countries in human development. In rural areas, one of two households does not have a safe water supply, and only one in three has access to proper toilet facilities. Malaria, acute respiratory infections, diarrhea, measles, and malnutrition are common. Life expectancy is 55.4 years, and 76 of 1,000 children born will not live to reach their first birthday. Many Beninese are food insecure, especially in the north where insufficient rains and locust infestations devastate crops. About one in four children under five are moderately malnourished and approximately 40% of pregnant women are anemic. Nearly half of all Beninese women still give birth at home without professional assistance.

Despite these serious problems, Benin is improving the health and living environment of its youthful population. The constitution of 1990 made special provisions for the survival, protection, and development of children, which included guarantees for their education. Benin ratified the Convention on the Rights of the Child in August 1990, one of the first 22 countries to do so. Benin participates in a comprehensive health plan known as the Bamako Health Initiative, which is bringing medicines to the vast majority of the approximately 400 rural health clinics. Of all children under one, 73% are fully immunized against diphtheria, polio and tetanus (1992).

The main roads in Benin are paved, and travel from the coast to the north by bush taxi or minivan is easy. Secondary roads can be rugged and cause considerable wear and tear on vehicles. Together, Benin has 600 miles of paved roads and another 5,000 miles of unpaved roads.

¹⁰ FAMILY LIFE

Beninese place a high value on family and are close-knit. Nuclear families composed of the parents and children may often include a niece or nephew, cousin, grandchild or grandparent. The sense of extended family builds out from this core to include cousins and more distant kin within the clan or lineage. Even these relatives may be referred to as brother and sister.

On average, Beninese women will be expected to have seven pregnancies in their lifetime, but families of 4–6 children are becoming the norm. Typically, the village family—including children if they are not in school—leaves the hut early in the morning only to return late in the day after working the fields, which may be at quite a distance. After the evening meal there may be storytelling around a fire. The institution of family remains resistant to social pressures and most often, if a child is born out of wedlock, the parents will marry so that the child receives a proper upbringing. In polygamous relationships, wives have their own huts in the village, or if in town, apartments in the same house, and share common kitchen and living facilities. Nonetheless, polygamous relationships can lead to quarreling and often add tensions to family life.

¹¹ CLOTHING

On the coast, women typically wear African *pagnes* of striking colors and patterns, often with a matching head scarf. Muslim women wear a three-piece cloth outfit, with one piece wrapped around the waist and falling to the ankle, a second wrapped around the chest and reaching around the knee, and a third covering the head. Once married, Muslim women always cover their heads in public. Men traditionally wear *boubou*-style cotton shirts over pants, which may or may not be of matching patterns. Increasing in popularity is the West African embroidered boubou for men and women, which requires many hours of skill to sew and embroider. Boubous of this quality are very expensive, costing into the hundreds of dollars, and are reserved for special occasions. A cheaper substitute for many people is used clothing (*fripperie*) shipped in large bales on container ships from Europe and the United States.

¹² FOOD

Despite pockets of food scarcity and insecurity, a great variety of foods exist in Benin and diets vary considerably from south to north. Taboos, handed down in the family, may prohibit the consumption of fish, goat, and beef, depending on the taboo. The staple food is *la pate*, made by adding boiling water to corn, millet, cassava, or sorghum flour. The accompanying sauces are cooked for a long time and seasoned with onions, tomatoes, garlic, and peppers. Sauces may be based on vegetables or pounded leaves, and may include fish or meat. As elsewhere in Africa, la pate is dipped into the sauce, and is eaten with the right hand. Traditional households eat porridge for breakfast, made from millet, corn, yams, or manioc.

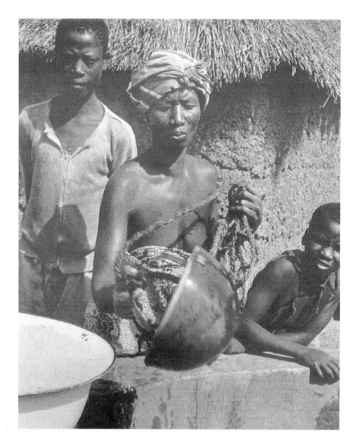

A mother and her two sons at a well. (AP Images)

Other specialties in Benin include *gari*, which is grated manioc, soaked and pressed to remove the natural traces of cyanide, and then cooked in a pot until dried, making a very fine semolina. Gari is enjoyed with peanut-cake snacks. To make peanut cakes, the oil is pressed from the peanuts, and then sugar or salt is added depending on the desired taste. Then the paste is fried. If in need of a quick snack, merchants on street corners in southern towns offer deep-fried dumplings made from pounded bananas or beans. Many Beninese enjoy soft drinks and beer, but these require spare cash. Local drinks include natural lemonade and limeade, palm wine (*sodabi*), and beer and gin made from millet (*chapalo*).

¹³ EDUCATION

Benin's former reputation as Africa's "Latin Quarter" was earned for the high number of Beninese college graduates. Today, its education system faces major challenges. High unemployment has led to a reevaluation of the sacrifices required for Western schooling and young women are pressured to marry rather than finish school. Combined primary, secondary, and tertiary school enrollment was only 50% in 2004, but Beninese were making gains in adult literacy. In 2005 the government estimated that about 35% of all adults could read and write, compared with 23% in 1989.

¹⁴ CULTURAL HERITAGE

Beninese animism, dance, and music have a long and rich history. Perhaps the best known of the traditional dances belong

The great challenge currently facing Beninese is finding work. Because of the scarcity of decent jobs, as many as 75% of city dwellers work in the informal sector as peddlers, pushcart operators, and the like. In the villages, most Beninese work in agriculture, forestry, and fishing. The current scarcity of work means that men may spend more time away from the home. (Cory Langley)

to the Fon people of the southern region. These dances may be performed specifically for a ritual, such as the *rada* rite, which is one of the three principal cults of Vaudou from the ancient Allada kingdom. Fon dance is becoming modernized, and musical accompaniment is played on a mix of traditional drums and modern instruments such as electric guitars and synthesizers. Beninese musicians depend on skilled craftspeople to produce traditional instruments of high quality, and villages like Adjarra produce over 50 kinds of tam-tams.

Many cultural traditions have roots that can be traced to former kingdoms. In the northeast, Nikki is the capital of a former kingdom whose origins go back to the 15th century. The Baribas, who are wonderful riders, inhabit the area and organize diabolical displays of horsemanship announced by long trumpets that produce unusual noises.

15 WORK

A great challenge facing Beninese is finding gainful employment at a living wage. Because of the scarcity of decent jobs, as many as 75% of city dwellers work in the informal sector as peddlers, hawkers, and pushcart operators. In the villages, most Beninese (62%) work in agriculture, forestry, and fishing. About 60% of women work in agriculture alone. The principal subsistence crops are manioc, maize and yams, and cash crops include oil, coconut palms, and cotton. Fishing, textiles, a soap

factory, and breweries employ less than 7% of the labor force. Nearly a quarter of all children between the ages of 5 and 14 in Benin work. In total, these children number about half a million workers.

Beninese are counting on a recently completed hydroelectric dam on the Mono River to provide power for future industrial projects that will lead to quality jobs. There is some hope that unexplored mineral deposits and offshore oil field development, now underway, will provide additional well-paying jobs.

16 SPORTS

The Beninese national sport of soccer is played and watched by Beninese everywhere the competitive urge strikes. It is played mainly by boys and young men. The national team is nicknamed "The Squirrels," and has qualified once for the Africa Nations Cup (2008), but never the World Cup. There also are national teams for tennis and rugby. While not a sport in the western sense, traditional dancing is also extremely popular. Teamwork is an essential ingredient, and Beninese compare and rate dancers and musicians for their agility, creativity, technical skill, and stamina.

¹⁷ ENTERTAINMENT AND RECREATION

Entertainment preferences and possibilities vary greatly from urban to rural areas. In the towns and cities where electricity is available, Beninese have the option of watching state-run television. However, many people with the means or savvy are buying and hooking up to satellite dishes. A small proportion of the population has video cassette recorders. Cinemas are always popular. By contrast, electricity has yet to arrive in most villages. There, people make their own fun. Ceremonies, holidays, and traditional feasts constitute the bulk of community recreation. Baptisms, in particular, occur frequently and provide one of the most common forms of entertainment. A village of between 300–400 people may have up to 30 baptisms a year.

¹⁸ FOLK ART, CRAFTS, AND HOBBIES

The royal history of ancient Dahomey is visible in the work of Beninese artists. The palace museum, which contains royal sepulchres and bas-relief sculpture of great intricacy, offers models of this ancient tradition. Beninese artists produce highly refined weaving and sculptures reminiscent of their ancestors' tradition. Tapestries are woven that use symbols and totems of the royal family. Sculptors fashion masks, tables, boxes, scepters, and armchairs. Much Beninese art is inspired by Benin's royal past, and carries on ancient traditions.

Crafts reflect artistic and practical needs. For example, craftswomen make pots of all sizes for carrying and storing water. Blacksmiths not only produce works of art, but are in great demand as bicycle, motorcycle, and automobile repairmen.

In the north, one finds a wide range of handmade instruments, from twin drums to calabashes that produce various tones and pitches to small Beninese guitars. One unique Beninese creation that mirrors life is the Sombas Dwellings. These are miniature round-tiered huts with turrets, resembling fortified castles. Artists have built these realistic models upon escarpments with deep valleys, waterfalls, lawns, and trees.

¹⁹ SOCIAL PROBLEMS

Benin's major social problems revolve around lack of economic opportunity, poor law enforcement, and the need for public services. High unemployment, low wages, and overdependence on the informal sector are driving educated people to take manual jobs such as driving motorcycle-taxis. Worse however, is the large number of street children, some of whom become prostitutes to support themselves, and others who are subject to trafficking. While the law prohibits human smuggling, Benin is a source, transit point, and destination for trafficked persons, mostly children who are forced into labor or sexually exploited. Some trafficking occurs as "vidomegon," a form of servitude in which children are forced to work under an arrangement between two families. Benin's central location in West Africa has made it a transshipment point for illicit drugs from Nigeria to Western Europe and the United States.

²⁰ GENDER ISSUES

Serious gender issues include discrimination against women, domestic violence, and female genital mutilation (FGM). About 17% of women have undergone FGM. Rape and underage marriage (under 14 years of age) are prohibited, but weakly enforced. In rural areas, a tradition of abduction and rape by a groom of his prospective bride persists despite efforts by government and nongovernmental organizations (NGOs) to eradicate it. Though not as prevalent as in Ghana, trokosi ("wives of the deity") is practiced. Trokosi involves sending a young virgin to work at a shrine in hopes that her servitude will atone for a past sin or crime of a family member. These young women are often exploited as sex slaves by traditional priests.

For some time Beninese women have played leading roles in the home and they continue to make many decisions regarding home economics and child care. The husband's job has been to act as the main supporter of the family. Nowadays, the scarcity of work means that men may spend more time away from the home. The consequent demands on Beninese women have forced them to find work outside the home tending small gardens or engaging in small businesses all the while caring for the family. Although women outlive men by 5%, only half as many women can read and write as men, and only about three quarters as many women as men are enrolled in primary, secondary, and university-level schools.

²¹ BIBLIOGRAPHY

Africa South of the Sahara 2007. London: Europa Publishers, 2008.

Boko, Sylvain, et al, eds. *Women in African Development: The Challenges of Globalization and Liberalization in the 21st Century.* Trenton, NJ: Africa World Press, 2005.

Cornevin, Robert. *La Republique Populaire du Benin: Des Origines Dahomeennes a nos Jours.* Paris: Editions Maisonneuve et Larose, 1981.

Decalo, Samuel. *Historical Dictionary of Benin.* 3rd ed. Lanham, MD, and London: The Scarecrow Press, Inc., 1995.

Herskovits, Melville J. *Dahomey: An Ancient West African Kingdom.* Vols. 1 and 2. Evanston, Illinois: Northwestern University Press, 1967.

Miller, Susan Katz. "Sermon on the Farm." *International Wildlife.* March/April 1992: 49-51, 1992.

Monserrat Palau Marti. *Société et Religion au Benin.* Paris: Maisonneuve et Larose, 1993.

Roese, Peter M. *A Popular History of Benin: The Rise and Fall of a Mighty Forest Kingdom.* New York: P. Lang, 2003.

—by R. Groelsema and M. C. Groelsema

BERBERS

PRONUNCIATION: BUR–bur
ALTERNATE NAMES: Imazighen (plural; singular, Amazigh)
LOCATION: North Africa (Morocco, Algeria, Tunisia, Libya, and Mauritania)
POPULATION: 25–36 million (exact statistics are unavailable)
LANGUAGE: Berber (also called Tamazight)
RELIGION: Sunni Muslim, Ibadite

1 INTRODUCTION

The name Berber may have originated with the Romans. The details of the origins of the Berber people are not known for certain, but the Berbers are generally considered the original population of North Africa. It is likely that the Berbers descended, perhaps thousands of years ago, from people who expanded west from an eastern origin along the southern rim of the Mediterranean Sea.

The Berbers, who inhabit regions across North Africa, have witnessed numerous invasions and occupations. Invaders have included Phoenicians, Romans, Vandals, Byzantines, Arabs, Spanish, Turks, and the French. Despite many attempts by colonizing people to eradicate or absorb the Berbers, their culture survived.

The Berber population is distributed across the countries of North Africa. Generally speaking, it is likely that most northwest African Arabs are of Berber origin. While precise statistics are not available, experts estimate that 35–80% of the all Berbers live in Morocco, with the remainder distributed throughout Algeria, Libya, and Tunisia. In Tunisia, Berbers comprise about 15–33% of the population.

Berber groups inhabiting coastal North Africa identify themselves by the terms Kabyles and Rifs. Others living further inland identify themselves as Chaouis, Siwis, Chleuhs, Mozabites, and Tuaregs.

The Berbers of northern Algeria number approximately 4 million. They have kept their original language and culture. The Berbers of northern Morocco are sometimes called the Rifs or Riffis. In southern Morocco, the Berbers, with a population of about 8 million, are sometimes known as the Chleuhs. Other groups include the Tuareg of the Sahara and the Chaouis of Algeria. There are also about 4 million Berbers living in Europe. Some inhabitants of the Canary Islands are also considered Berber.

Between 642 and 669, the Arabs sent their first military expeditions into the Maghrib region of North Africa, which resulted in the spread of Islam. In 711, Tariq ibn Ziyad, the Berber governor of Tangier, Morocco, crossed into Spain. Later Islamic Spain (Al Andalus) was under the leadership of the caliph of Damascus, Syria. Nevertheless, the largest group of Moors (a general term used to describe Muslim people in Spain and Portugal) was made up of North African Berbers.

The countries of North Africa gained their independence in the 20th century. Tunisia and Morocco became independent in 1956 and Algeria in 1962. The countries then established Arabic as their official language, replacing French and/or Spanish. As a result, most Berbers had to study and know Arabic, with no opportunity to use their own language at schools.

North African states identified themselves as Arab nations, ignoring the existence and the culture of the Berbers. Political tensions arose between Berber groups and governments in North Africa over linguistic and cultural issues in the decades following independence. Berber culture was discriminated against in some cases. For example, giving children Berber names was once prohibited in Morocco.

In response to the demands of the Berbers, Morocco and Algeria modified their policies. Algeria defined itself in the constitution as an Arab, Berber, and Muslim nation. As of 2008, Berber is a national language in Algeria and is taught as a noncompulsory language in the Berber-speaking areas. In Morocco, Berber is now taught as a compulsory language regardless the ethnicity.

The Berbers are ethnically—but far from politically—the dominant part of the populations of Morocco, Algeria, Tunisia, and Mauritania. Isolated Berber-speaking groups are found all over North Africa, from along the Atlantic in the west to Egypt in the east. A colorful nomadic Berber tribe, the Tuaregs, whose male warriors wear blue dresses and indigo-colored veils, still roam the Sahara desert.

Berber authors, from ancient times until today, have gained world recognition. An Oregon State University web site dedicated to Berber studies lists Berber authors Saint Augustine, Tertullian, Apuleius, Arnobius, Franto, Saint Cyprian, Lactantius, Ibn Khaldun, Ibn Battuta, Jean Amrouche, Kateb Yacine, and Mouloud Mammeri. The site notes that, through history, these authors have been identified as Roman, Arab, or French. Many of the authors wrote in a language other than Berber. The Berber language is only recently winning recognition as an official language.

2 LOCATION AND HOMELAND

Berber culture is centered in North Africa and the Mediterranean region, although Berber influence is felt as far east as Egypt and even stretches to the Canary Islands in the Atlantic Ocean. The sphere of Berber influence includes the countries of Algeria, Libya, Mali, and Niger, with large pockets in Morocco and smaller ones in Tunisia along the Mediterranean shores of North Africa. Berbers tend to live in desert regions like the Sahara and in the Atlas Mountains. Berbers comprise a clear majority of the population of North Africa in terms of race, but many Berbers deny their identity, choosing to describe themselves as Arab.

The Berbers, whose total population is estimated at 36 million, are principally concentrated in Morocco and Algeria, with significant communities also living in Tunisia, Libya, Mauritania, Mali, and Niger. In addition there are about 4 million Berbers living in Europe, primarily in France. An estimated half of the ethnic Berbers living in Europe describe themselves as Berbers. In terms of race, Berbers represent the majority of the population in Morocco and Algeria and more than half the population in Tunisia and Libya. As Arabization has swept away the indigenous language and the Berber identity from many regions, many people with Berber ancestry are now claiming to be Arabs. In terms of identity, Berbers represent 40% of all Moroccans, 30% of all Algerians, 15–33% of all Tunisians, 10% of all Libyans, and 0.5% of all Egyptians, making up more than 20 million people. Genetic evidence appears to indicate that most North Africans (whether they consider themselves Berber or Arab) are predominantly of Berber origin and that populations ancestral to the Berbers have been in the area since the Upper Paleolithic era.

Although stereotyped in the West as nomads, most Berbers were traditional farmers, living in the mountains relatively close to the Mediterranean coast or dwelling in the oases found in the desert. The Tuareg of the southern Sahara, however, were nomadic. Some groups, such as the Chaouis, were herders who moved with their herds seasonally. Their various dwelling places included deserts, areas near rivers, plains, and mountain ranges.

Most rivers are not navigable, but they have been a major source of water for irrigation. The plains are cultivated with a variety of crops, such as oranges, figs, olives, almonds, barley, and wheat. The homelands of the Berbers experience a wide variety of weather conditions. The desert is hot and dry, while the coastal plains have mild temperatures. In the summer the mountains are hot and dry, but in the winter they are cold, rainy, and often snowy.

³ LANGUAGE

Berber is primarily a spoken language. The Berber languages are mainly spoken in Morocco, Algeria, Mauritania, Tunisia, and Libya. The primary Berber language is known as Berber to Europeans and as Shilha to Arabs. The Berbers themselves call the primary language Amazigh or Tamazight. The language forms a branch of the Afro-Asiatic linguistic family. The wide dispersion geographically of the Berber people has led to the development of as many as 300 different dialects. A number of tribes, including the largest ones (the Rif, Kabyle, and Tuareg) have their own dialects.

Modern Berbers are engaged in ongoing efforts to develop and gain acceptance of a written form of their language. A Berber alphabet has existed several thousand years, but has not enjoyed widespread use.

Berber languages and dialects include Central Atlas Amazigh (Tamazight) and Riffi (in northern Morocco), Kabyle (Algeria), and Tachelhit (or Tashelhiyt, central Morocco). There is a strong movement among speakers of the closely related northern Berber languages to unite them into a single standard language.

Although an alphabet for the Berber language has existed for a few thousand years, the written language has been disrupted through history by invaders and conquests in North Africa. The language was first written in an alphabet still used by the Tuareg; the oldest dated inscription is from about 200 BC. Later, between about AD 1000 and 1500, Berbers, especially those living in Morocco, wrote their language using the Arabic alphabet. Since the 20th century, Berbers, especially the Kabyle, have begun using the Latin alphabet.

In Morocco, approximately 3–4 million speak Tachelhit, a form of Berber; another 3 million speak another Berber dialect known as Central Atlas Amazigh (Tamazight).

After independence, all the North African Maghrib countries pursued a policy of Arabization and tried to eliminate French as the language of education, literacy, and power. A side-effect of these policies was to suppress the use of Berber languages.

In the early 2000s, Berbers were becoming more vocal in their protests over the loss of their language and culture. In Morocco and Algeria—especially Kabyle—the issues was being addressed by the government. Both Morocco and Algeria

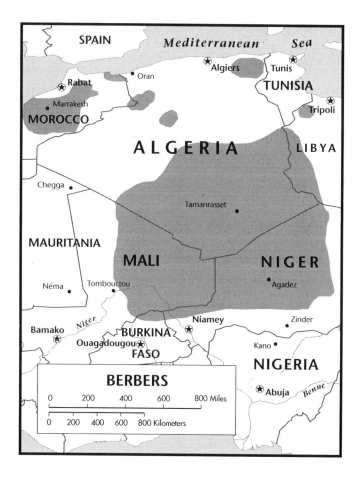

are introducing Berber language instruction in some schools. In its 2007 report on Algeria, the US State Department noted that "Access to print and broadcast media for Tamazight and Amazigh culture continued to grow. Tamazight programming also increased on the non-Berber language channels, as did advertisements in Tamazight on all television and radio channels. Beginning in the 2006–2007 scholastic year, the Tamazight language was officially taught in primary schools, starting in the fourth grade in 17 predominantly Berber provinces."

⁴ FOLKLORE

The folklore traditions of northern Africa have been deeply influenced by Islamic cultural traditions. Most folklore in Muslim countries concerns important figures in religious history, such as the prophet Muhammad. According to the tale, *al-Isra wa al-Mi'raj,* on the 26th day of the Islamic month of Rajab, the Muhammad traveled at night from Mecca (a city in what is now Saudi Arabia, then known as Hijaz) to Jerusalem. From Jerusalem, he rode his wondrous horse, al-Burak, on a nighttime visit to heaven. This legend is celebrated every year throughout the Islamic world.

Berbers have many legends based on the exploits of Muslim leaders known as marabouts. The marabouts resisted the religious Crusaders and the French colonizers of North Africa. They are believed to have had *baraka,* a blessing or divine grace, that allowed them to perform miracles. The burial sites of marabouts are destinations of pilgrimages, and many Berbers regard marabouts as saints.

Other Berbers believe in spiritual beings called *jinn.* Jinn are said to take on the forms of animals. To ward off these spirits, Berber Muslims wear a charm, known as an amulet, with verses from the Quran printed on it, as protection. They also wear the "hand of Fatima," a charm in the shape of the right hand, to protect against the evil eye.

Often, women in the countryside believe in (and might practice) *sihr,* a type of witchcraft primarily involving the use of potions. A potion might make someone fall in love or it might invoke a curse as revenge.

5 RELIGION

Prior to conversion to Islam in the 8th century the Berbers had polytheistic and animistic religious practices. The beliefs of the indigenous Berber people of North Africa were influenced primarily by the beliefs of their Egyptian neighbors, as well as by other people who lived in the area, such as the Phoenicians, Jews, Greeks, and Romans.

Berbers who adhere to a specific religion are outnumbered by those who profess no religion. However, many Berbers are Muslim (mostly of the Sunni sect), but there is also a Christian community (mainly Roman Catholic) and an even smaller Jewish community. Muslim Berbers' beliefs are exactly the same as those of Sunni Muslims elsewhere. However, Islam practiced in rural North Africa places a strong emphasis on *baraka* ("blessing") and on a belief that descendants of Muhammad can perform miracles. Shrines to these important figures are scattered throughout the countryside. Living representatives are turned to for mediation of conflicts.

There is no Islamic intermediary between man and God. However, every rural community has a teacher, called a *fqih* who trains boys and young men to recite the Quran. The community hires the fqih to lead the prayers in the mosque and to deliver a sermon each Friday.

The fqih also prepares the charms that carry verses from the Quran, which many Berbers wear in the belief that the charm will cure disease and prevent bad luck. Elements of witchcraft and sorcery that require Arabic writing are the responsibility of men; any such activities that do not involve writing are believed to be the responsibility of women.

6 MAJOR HOLIDAYS

Berbers observe both secular holidays and the Muslim religious festivals of the lunar year. The two major Muslim holidays are Eid al-Fitr and Eid al-Adha. Eid al-Fitr is a three-day celebration that takes place after the month of fasting called Ramadan. Eid al-Adha commemorates the willingness of Abraham to obey God's command and sacrifice his son, Isaac. This Eid al-Adha feast, where every householder must sacrifice a sheep, occurs in the last month of the Islamic year and coincides with the hajj, the pilgrimage to Mecca. People making a pilgrimage are expected to sacrifice a goat or sheep and offer the meat to the poor. Every Muslim must make this pilgrimage at least once during his or her lifetime.

Muslims celebrate their religious holidays by going to the mosque for group prayers. Afterward, they return home to large meals with family and visiting relatives. They also exchange gifts on religious holidays.

The secular holidays include New Year's Day (January 1) and Labor Day (May 1). Labor Day commemorates worker solidarity around the world. Berbers might also observe the holidays of their native countries.

7 RITES OF PASSAGE

Major Berber ceremonies are related to birth, marriage, and death. In addition, the first haircut and circumcision are rites of passage for boys. Circumcision is practiced by all Muslims. Most Berbers circumcise boys at around two years of age, but a sect that lives in south-central Morocco waits until boys are five or six to perform circumcision. There is no female circumcision.

Marriage ceremonies are the most important and elaborate Berber rituals. Marriage between first cousins is permitted. (This it typically a son marrying his father's brother's daughter.) Most marriages are between members of families within the same tribe section. Polygynous marriages are permitted with each co-wife having her separate dwelling or household.

Widows are often considered an inheritance by a male family member. It is not uncommon for two brothers to marry two sisters. Normally only a husband can initiate divorce (except in cases of impotence). A frequent cause for divorce is childlessness.

When death occurs, Berbers may attribute the cause as either natural or supernatural. If the deceased person is a man, his body is washed and enshrouded by a ranking Muslim man. If the deceased person is a woman, the body is attended to by another woman. Every community has a cemetery.

Burial takes place soon after death. A person who dies early in the day is buried later that day; a person who dies during the night is buried the next morning.

For burial, the body is laid with its face turned toward Mecca. An Islamic leader recites from the Quran as the body is placed in the grave. Attendance at funerals is restricted to men. The relatives of the deceased host a feast seven days after the death. Among the Rif group of Berbers, a widow hosts a feast forty days after her husband's death. Forty days theoretically marks the end of the mourning period for all Berbers, but most widows observe a three-month mourning period. This extended mourning period between widowhood and remarriage helps remove any question of paternity in case of pregnancy.

8 INTERPERSONAL RELATIONS

All close relatives, whether patrilineal or matrilineal, are typically addressed by the appropriate kin term. Alternative, they may be addressed by name. If the relative is especially close, he or she may be addressed by the kin term plus the name. The same form of address is also used for elders.

Berbers shake hands during greetings and farewells. It is common for close friends of the same sex to hug and exchange kisses on the cheeks. People of the opposite sex, if they are not religious, may shake hands; religious men and women avoid shaking hands with persons of the opposite sex. The most common greeting is the phrase *Al-salamu alaykum,* which means "May peace be upon you." The response is *Wa alaykum al-salam,* or "May peace be upon you also."

Most socializing revolves around the family. Guests are treated with warm hospitality and are served pastries and sweets. At most social gatherings, men socialize with each other and the women socialize with each other; the two groups remain separate. Boys and girls are kept apart through most of childhood. Dating is never permitted, and it is considered inappropriate and shameful for unmarried males and females to socialize; premarital sex is strictly forbidden. Premarital sex carries especially strong stigma for girls. A girl who loses her virginity outside of marriage brings great shame to her family's reputation. Marriages are arranged, either by the families or with the help of a matchmaker.

⁹ LIVING CONDITIONS

For centuries, Berbers have struggled for power with other Arab groups in North Africa. The Barbary Coast of North Africa was known as a place where Arab and Berber pirates would prey on ships on the Mediterranean Sea.

Many traditional Berbers raise sheep and cattle. However, some Berbers subsist by working at menial jobs, such as grinding flour at a mill, doing woodcarving, quarrying millstones, and making pottery or jewelry. Berber women generally carried out housework and handicrafts, such as weaving and making pottery.

Berbers live a rural lifestyle. Housing is typically a dwelling made of clay or a tent made of goatskin. In some larger Berber settlements, houses may be constructed of stone. Many modern Berbers perform migrant work in Spain or France.

For nomadic peoples, a number of factors, including colonialism, population pressure, and environmental change, has led them to develop permanent settlements. Very few Berber groups still move freely around the desert. Most have created permanent homes, with only some members moving with the herds for seasonal grazing. Permanent settlements have more access to health care and education.

¹⁰ FAMILY LIFE

Everywhere in North Africa, except among some of the Tuareg groups of the Central Sahara, descent is patrilineal and residence is patrilocal. Over a century of French rule and the long wars for independence led to a breakdown of the traditional extended family unit. A mother and father would live in one home with their children, including grown sons and their wives. The grandparents would usually live with them. All members of the family would take their meals together.

If a daughter became divorced or widowed, she would return home to live with her family. In modern times, many Berber men have traveled to Europe to find work, so their wives are now filling the role of head of the household in rural areas.

In Berber households, it is common for older children to help care for their younger siblings while their mothers do household work. In most families, the grandparents also take an active role in childrearing. Thus grandparents and grandchildren develop a close bond. Segregation of boys and girls begins when children reach six or seven years of age and the boys begin to help manage the family's herd of goats. By the time they reach puberty, which traditionally is not long before the age to marry, the practice of socializing exclusively with others of the same gender is fully ingrained. Land is passed on from father to son.

¹¹ CLOTHING

The traditional attire is a one-piece, floor-length, hooded dress, known as a jellaba. It is worn by both men and women. Western attire is often worn under the jellaba. In cold weather, many men cover their jellabas with a hooded cloak called a burnus. Religious and/or conservative women cover their hair in public.

Berber women wear long, colorful dresses, often covering their heads with straw hats. Berber women historically had tattoos on their foreheads, cheeks, or necks. However, this custom is slowly fading away. Rural men often wear turbans, which they replace with a knitted skullcap when going to a mosque.

¹² FOOD

Berber cuisine differs from one area to another within North Africa. However, most Berber diets include corn, barley, sheep's milk, goat cheese, butter, honey, meat, and wild game.

The best known and most common food among all Berbers is couscous. In fact, some historians credit the Berbers with inventing couscous, which is made from semolina flour. Couscous has been known as a North African dish since the 11th or 12th century. Berbers have different names for couscous, including *shekshu* and *sishtu*.

In Algeria, couscous is called *kisksu* or *ta'am*, meaning "food" or "nourishment." This gives an indication of the importance of couscous as a daily staple. In Tunisia, couscous may be called *kiskisi* or *kuksi*. Couscous grains may be large (and are then called *muhammas* or *burkukis)* or very fine. The fine-grained couscous is generally reserved for use in making sweet dishes, often involving almonds, raisins, or apricots.

Couscous and tagine (a type of stew) is the principal dish for special feasts and celebrations. Tagine is prepared in a single pot and requires few utensils for its preparation. The traditional tagine pot is ceramic, with a pointed dome-shaped lid. The tagine is typically simmered for hours, and is based on inexpensive cuts of meat, seasoned with spices. Thus, it is well-suited for preparation by both nomadic and rural cooks.

Preparing and serving couscous symbolizes happiness and abundance. Besides tagine, couscous may be served with meat, fish, vegetables, and spices. For a simple meal, couscous was cooked with sour milk and melted butter. This traditional food of the nomadic Berbers has found many variations among modern, more settled Berbers.

¹³ EDUCATION

After the countries of North Africa gained independence in 1950s and 1960s, most were clear in their language policy: Arabic became the exclusive official language of the country and the role of the languages of previous colonization, namely French and Spanish, was minimized. There was no mention of Berber as a national language or minority language and no prospect for making any room for this language in the national official landscape.

Berber had no place in the educational system in Morocco, especially at the primary and secondary school levels. This forced a whole generation of children to enter school in a language they had never spoken before, contributing to a higher dropout rate among Berber children.

Challenges faced by those who spoke only Tamazight extended from the education system to other official spheres, such as the healthcare system and the legal system. Arabic and French dominated in hospitals and official government agencies.

Berber activists blame Arabization for the high illiteracy rate in Morocco—an estimated 48% of its citizens cannot read—because Berber children often drop out when confront-

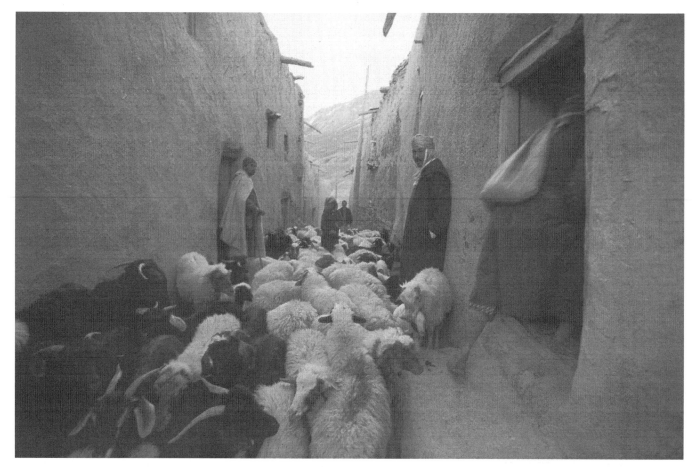

Sheep pack a street in a Berber village in Morocco. The mountain Berbers, isolated in Morocco's High Atlas Range, are proud of their traditional culture, now largely lost to their urban kin. (AP Images/Alexandra Boulat/VII)

ed with teachers who speak only Arabic. In state schools, the first language taught is standard Arabic, followed by French. At the secondary school level, English, Spanish, or German is introduced. At the university level, a growing number of students are choosing to study the Berber language and culture.

By 1994, the Berber movement had grown strong enough to persuade King Hassan II of Morocco to encourage integration of the Berber language into the public education system. His son, Mohammed IV, succeeded him in July 1999, and continued to support the use and preservation of the Berber language.

Mohammed IV established the Royal Institute of the Amazigh Culture (IRCAM) in 2001. (IRCAM is commonly called the Royal Institute of Berber Culture when referred to in English.) In September 2003 teaching Berber in public schools became a reality. However, this was not a simple undertaking. Teaching Berber involved learning the Tifinagh script, in addition to the Roman and the Arabic scripts already being taught.

In the past Berber children had been educated in the mosque, where they focused on religion and some rudimentary math. This was seen as important work and the fqih (religious instructor) is a highly respected member of the community.

However, religious education along was not adequately preparing Berber children for life in contemporary society. Berber ativists succeeded in convincing the government of Morocco

to support the preservation of the Berber language and culture through the primary schools.

With improved health care and widespread availability of immunizations, more Berber children survive to adulthood. It is important that they receive an education that prepares them to function as citizens in North African society. It is clear that more a formalized, urban, and modern style of education is needed.

Berber oarents acknowledge that their children will not be able to support themselves by herding and farming. It is inevitable that Berber children will give up the rural or nomadic life to find employment in urban areas. Life in the city requires a sort of training beyond what is available through the mosque. Many Berber and especially Tashelhit students move through the traditional (mosque-based) educational system to become religious teachers. Berber students are enrolling in increasing numbers in the religious universities in Morocco, and some eventually join the faculty.

14 CULTURAL HERITAGE

The Berber culture has its typical art and symbols, as well as its unique music that provides continuity through history. The ancient Berber culture is extraordinarily rich and diverse, with a variety of musical styles. These range from bagpipes and oboe (Celtic style) to pentatonic music (reminiscent of Chinese music)—all combined with African rhythms and a very important stock of authentic oral literature. These traditions have been kept alive by small bands of musicians who travel from village to village, as they have for centuries, to entertain at weddings and other social occasions with their songs, tales, and poetry.

Berber mothers have been largely responsible for the survival of the Berber language and cultural identity. Mothers share traditional stories and beliefs with their children. Women also preserve cultural traditions through the handicrafts such as tapestry, jewelry, tattoos, and pottery. In October 2001, the Royal Institute of the Amazigh Culture (IRCAM) was established in Morocco to preserve Amazigh culture and language.

¹⁵ WORK

Important traditional Berber crafts were blacksmithing, basketry, and utilitarian woodwork, such as the making of plow handles and yokes. However, blacksmithing was typically considered a low-status occupation for men.

Berber women produced handmade pottery. In some areas, men also produced pottery, but it was considered low-status work. There is strikingly little economic specialization by Berber men. Silversmithing and saddle-making, occupations formerly practiced by rural Jews, were skills learned by some Berbers. Most Jews migrated to Israel when that country became an independent state in 1948, leaving silversmithing and leatherwork to Berbers and Arabs who remained in North Africa.

In pre-colonial times, Berber men were occupied with feuding and warfare. Modern Berber men are occupied with agriculture, herding animals, and, occasionally hunting. Berber women manage the household and perform all housework. However, preparing tea for guests is a special task reserved for the men of the household.

The management of the household engages the entire family. Women do the housework and are called on to help the men with the grain harvest. In addition, women are responsible for carrying the harvested grain in baskets to be threshed.

Men build the houses but women whitewash the walls. Women also smooth and clean the floors. Women are also frequently the ones to haul animal manure to the collective manure pile. Women milk the animals and fetch water for the animals and the household. Gathering firewood also falls to the women.

If a Berber household includes poultry and rabbits, the women care for them. Marketing the family's goods was traditionally the responsibility of the men, but sometimes elderly women, especially in poor families, would work the family's stall at the market. In modern markets, women are as numerous as men, due in part to the absence of some adult men who have migrated to Europe for work.

By around age six, boys (and some girls) herded goats on the slopes. Older girls helped care for the family's younger children. As emphasis on schooling has increased, many boys (and to a lesser degree, girls) enroll in school and are no longer available for household chores.

¹⁶ SPORTS

Before the French colonized North Africa, some traditional sports were played in the village communities or in the nomadic settlements. After the introduction of modern sports in accordance with French colonial policy, the traditional sports were threatened.

Modern sports, particularly football (soccer), spread rapidly throughout North Africa. North Africans in general, and Berbers in particular, relished the opportunity to contest against European teams. As a result of the introduction of modern sports, national sports organizations were established. These helped contribute to a sense of national identity among the countries of North Africa.

After independence from France, North African nations introduced policies of modernization and centralization. Through the modern educational system and the process of establishing an independent government, the playing of traditional sports was discouraged. These sports were viewed as primitive and backward and threatening to the development of the modern nation. Along with traditional religious practices, traditional games were criticized for being filled with superstition.

Modern sports, however, cwere encouraged as the newly-independent nations worked to form a national identity and to find ways to compete internationally.

¹⁷ ENTERTAINMENT AND RECREATION

Ritual ceremonies serve partly as recreation and entertainment and often include music and dance. Storytelling is another favorite traditional pastime. Small bands of musicians travel from village to village, as they have for centuries, to entertain at weddings and other social occasions with their songs, tales, and poetry.

A traditional equestrian performance is practiced during cultural festivals. A performance on horseback oftens ends a traditional Berber wedding celebration. This performance is considered a form of martial art, symbolizing the strong bond between men and horses. Groups made up of hundreds or thousands of riders perform during festivals. Sports, television, and radio provide recreation for increasing numbers, especially in the cities.

Nomadic people traditionally enjoyed games involving sticks, stones, and drawing on the sandy desert ground around their settlements. These games are similar to tic-tac-toe, hopscotch, or mancala.

¹⁸ FOLK ART, CRAFTS, AND HOBBIES

Much Berber art is in the form of jewelry, leather, and finely woven carpets. The forms of Berber artistic expression, at least in the modern period, are primarily linked to utilitarian objects—pottery, weaving, and architecture—and to jewelry. All are characterized by predominantly geometrical, nonrepresentational patterns. Neither the forms and patterns nor the techniques appear to have changed significantly since ancient times, and they can be related directly to forms found in the Mediterranean basin from as early as the Iron Age. These art forms are not original or exclusive to Berbers. Still, the Berber culture has consistently produced artistic works for centuries.

Examples of Berber artistic expression include the massive earth and adobe structures, known as *ksars,* in southern Morocco. These architectural fortifications were constructed from packed earth, with towers and facades decorated with inscribed pattersn.

Berbers are also known for Kabyle and Chawia pottery, which are unique in their variety. Designed with elegant forms and elaborate applied patterns, this style of pottery is easily recognizable.

Berbers are also well known for their silver jewelry, which is embossed with intricate patterns and inlaid with stones. Some examples feature enameled cloisonné as well.

Berbers are also known for textiles produced throughout North Africa, but particularly in southern Tunisia and in central and southern Morocco.

[19] SOCIAL PROBLEMS

Politicians in North Africa who take strong political stands in support of the Berber cause rarely reach high positions in their governments. Arabization is blamed for the continued poverty of most Berbers. Fifty percent of Moroccans live on less than $50 a month, and most of the poor are Berbers.

Government jobs are off-limits to those who speak only Berber, and Berber is prohibited in the courts; all legal documents must be translated into Arabic. One government-affiliated channel, 2M, broadcasts a mix of Arabic and French. The other, RTM, broadcasts predominantly in Arabic, with only 5 to 10 minutes a day of news in Berber.

Political tensions have risen between Berber groups and governments in North Africa during the 1980s, 1990s, and into the 2000s. Berber activists argue that the Arabic education system, the lack of programs in Berber on state radio and television, and the absence of an entity in charge of preserving the Berber cultural heritage is threatening what is left of it.

In response to the demands of the Berbers, Morocco and Algeria have modified their policies. Algeria included language in its constitution declaring that the country is an Arab, Berber, and Muslim nation. Currently in Algeria, Berber is a national language and is taught as a non-compulsory language in the Berber speaking areas.

In Morocco, Berber is now taught. Nevertheless, Berber organizations have denounced the Moroccan education charter dealing with language and culture as insufficient. They point out that only two of its 100 articles deal with the question of Berber in school. The first said Berber could be used in primary school only to "facilitate the learning of the official language"— Arabic. The second said that certain universities would have the means to study the Berber language and culture.

[20] GENDER ISSUES

Islam at its foundation was a liberator of women. For the first time in recorded Arab (and Western) history, women gained part of their father's inheritance and were given rights in both marriage and divorce—it took centuries for European Christian societies to grant women rights to property, especially in marriage where a woman was considered to be owned by her husband.

Berber women's lives are changing and dynamic. In urban areas, women are quite similar to Western women in their political rights and economic behaviors. They have more access to education and so tend to have fewer children than rural women and also to work in more formal economic sectors. In rural areas, labor is often divided with women responsible for childcare, food production, and domestic tasks, while men are involved in herding and agricultural production for sale. However, as men migrate to urban areas to look for jobs, more women have to take responsibility for traditionally men's tasks, as well as their own. This has many implications as women gain access and ex-

perience in public affairs and daughters become more crucial to fulfilling domestic responsibilities. Whether urban or rural, women and girls are usually responsible for bringing water to the house for bathing, cooking, and cleaning.

Berber women, like other Muslim women, are said to live in a male-dominated society with rigid sexual stratification. The seclusion and control of the sexual practices of a woman increase a man's status and power. This view has become more prevalent with the process of Islamization in Morocco, as elsewhere.

[21] BIBLIOGRAPHY

Abou-Nassr, J.M. *History of the Maghrib in the Islamic Period.* Cambridge: Cambridge University Press, 1987.

African Studies Center at Michigan State University. africa.msu.edu (December 2008).

Agnaou, Fatima *Gender, Litearcy and Empowerment in Morocco.* New York: Routeldge, 2004.

Gellner, Ernest, and Charles Micaud, eds. *Arabs and Berbers: From Tribe to Nation in North Africa.* London: Duckworth, 1973.

Hargraves, Orin. *Culture Shock! Morocco: A Guide to Customs and Etiquette.* Portland, Ore.: Graphic Arts Center Publishing Co., 1995.

Herndon, David. "Morocco: Freewheeling With the Berbers in the Atlas and Sahara." *National Geographic Adventure* (July/August 2000): 78-83.

Julien, Ch. André. *History of North Africa: Tunisia, Algeria, Morocco, From the Arab Conquest to 1830.* Trans. from the French by John Petrie. Ed. R. Le Tourneau. London: Routledge & K. Paul, 1970.

Keohane, Alan. *The Berbers of Morocco.* London:Hamish Hamilton, 1991.

Kossmann, Maarten G., and Joseph Stroomer Hendrikus. "Berber Phonology," In *Phonologies of Asia and Africa (Including the Caucasus),* edited by Alan S. Kaye. 2 vols. Vol. 1. Winona Lake: Eisenbrauns. 461–475, 1997.

McDougall, James. *Nation, Society and Culture in North Africa.* Portland: Frank Cass, 2003.

McGuinnes, Justin. *Marrakech and the High Atlas Handbook.* Bath: Footprint Handbooks, 2001. Montagne, Robert. *The Berbers: Their Social and Political Organisation.* Translated by David Seddon. London: Frank Cass, 1973.

Oregon State University. "Berber North Africa: The Hidden Mediterranean Culture." oregonstate.edu/nehberber/rationale.html (December 2008).

Shatzmiller, Maya. *The Berbers and the Islamic State.* Princeton: Markus Wiener Publishers, 2000.

—by M. Njoroge

BURKINABE

PRONUNCIATION: bur-kin-ah-BAY
ALTERNATE NAMES: (former) Upper Voltans
LOCATION: Burkina Faso
POPULATION: 15,264,735
LANGUAGE: French, Gur Group (Niger-Congo family of languages), Bobo-Dioulasso
RELIGION: Islam, traditional religions, Christianity
RELATED ARTICLES: Vol. 1: Dyula; Mossi; Tuaregs

¹ INTRODUCTION

Burkina Faso is one of the economically poorest countries in Africa, and one of the least known to Americans. Known as Upper Volta until 1984, the former French colony has struggled against drought, isolation with respect to transportation for exports, and a general lack of money for development. The new name, Burkina Faso, was adopted as part of the Revolution of 1983 to signify a fresh start for the country, and is a name created from words of three languages in the country to mean "country of upright or incorruptible men." The shorter form Burkina is commonly used; Burkinabe is the adjectival form of the name and is the singular and plural term for the country's citizens.

Burkina Faso was one of the last parts of Africa to be conquered by Europeans. The French conquered it in 1896–97, just ahead of expeditions of the British from what is now Ghana and Germans from Togo. The French, much more than the British, intended to assimilate the peoples they ruled to French values and institutions. However, the lack of money to support the colonial regime in Burkina Faso meant that the French had to rely upon the traditional rulers, especially the kings and chiefs of the Mossi, the largest ethnic group, to administer the colony.

The colony went bankrupt during the Great Depression, and from 1933 until 1947 Upper Volta was divided between Soudan (now Mali), Niger, and Côte d'Ivoire. The restoration of the colony was due in part to the postwar alliance of pro-independence African political leaders like Félix Houphouët-Boigny in the latter colony with the French communist party, the only French party willing to even consider such a step. Upper Volta was recreated in order to reduce Houphouët-Boigny's territory and to reward the leading Mossi king, the Mogho Naba, for his support in turning out unpaid labor to extend the Abidjan railroad, the country's link to the outside world, from the Western city of Bobo-Dioulasso to the capital, Ouagadougou.

Burkina Faso became independent in 1960, but it remains closely linked to France. In the 1960s and 1970s, three civilian governments were overthrown by the military in bloodless coups-d'état, but series of coups in the 1980s turned Upper Volta from a major recipient of Western foreign aid to a revolutionary government and back again to a country cooperating with the World Bank's "Structural Adjustment" program to increase free-market economies.

By the early 1900s the French had imposed taxation on the new colony, taxes required to be paid in French francs. This required Burkinabe peoples, who previously had used cowry shells from the Indian Ocean as money, to grow, mine, make, or do something that French were willing to pay for, which was the intent of the tax program. Because little could be grown for sale in Burkina, many people worked as migrant laborers in the coffee and cocoa farms and mines of the British Gold Coast Colony and the Côte d'Ivoire. For the first two-thirds of the century this migration was largely seasonal, as the agriculturally dead dry season at home in Burkina coincided with the peak demand for farm labor in the coastal countries' farms.

Since the 1960s, the original, seasonal migration has given way to longer-term settlement in these countries. Burkinabe were 11% of the population of Côte d'Ivoire in the 1988 census. There the Mossi are said to be the second-largest ethnic group. Burkinabe who once worked as laborers on Ivoirien farms now have cocoa or coffee farms of their own, or work in urban trades and professions.

Many Burkinabe, especially Mossi, served the French colonial army. The famous troops known as the "Senegalese Sharpshooters" (*Tirailleurs Sénégalais*) were in fact recruited all over French West Africa, and Burkinabe were especially heavily represented. Mossi and others from Burkina Faso fought for France in both world wars, in Indo-China, and in Algeria. For many years the pensions of these veterans were such an important source of foreign currency to the Burkinabe government that the president would personally hold the cabinet post for veterans' affairs.

The country gained independence from France in 1960, and Maurice Yameogo became the first president. Yameogo was overthrown in a military coup in 1966 because of rampant corruption in his administration. For two decades, the country continued to experience political instability. In 1983 Thomas Sankara took control of the government and conducted a nationalist and socialist policy that placed priority on the rural population. He came to be seen as a champion of the people. However, he remained unpopular with tribal chiefs and the government elite. In 1987, he was ousted and assassinated by his second in command, Blaise Compaore, who has remained in power since then, in spite of adopting a constitution in 1991 that allows multi-party elections.

² LOCATION AND HOMELAND

Burkina Faso is located in West Africa, in the interior savanna north of Côte d'Ivoire, Ghana, Togo, and Benin. It is bounded to the west and north by Mali and by Niger to the east and north. It is slightly larger than Colorado. Most of the country is gently rolling savanna, with grasslands dotted with trees and areas of scrub brush. The country is infrequently broken by rock outcroppings or small mesas.

The population of Burkina Faso was estimated to be 15.3 million people in 2008. A French sample survey of 10% of the national population in the early 1960s estimated that 48% of the population was Mossi and 10.4% Fulani (Peulh). Other ethnic groups made up 4–7% each; these included the Bisa, who were the original inhabitants of the southern part of the country where the Mossi states formed; Gourmantche, who are related to the Mossi and have traditional states east of them; and Gourounsi, Lobi, and Dagari, peoples on the southern and western edges of the Mossi kingdoms who share a similar way of life and speak related languages, but who do not have political organizations larger than clans defined by kinship relations. The Bobo and Senoufo in western and southwestern Burkina are culturally and linguistically related to the Mande-speaking peoples of Mali.

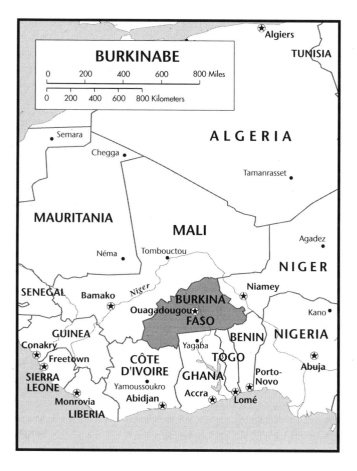

BURKINABE

0   200   400   600   800 Miles

0   200   400   600   800 Kilometers

Arabic, the bulk of Burkinabe history, law, and tradition was passed down orally.

5 RELIGION

The resistance of the Mossi and Gourmantche to the widespread introduction of Islam to the West African savanna during the 10th–11th centuries was a consequence of the close connection between political power and its validation by traditional religion. For a man to rule others, he must have received the religious right to do so, the *nam*, conferred only on one chosen and installed as a chief or king according to religious tradition. Occasional Mossi kings did convert as individuals but without lasting consequences. Mossi and other Burkinabe cultures, however, have many elements of Islamic origin.

The traditional religion of the peoples of Burkina is similar to that of many African peoples. There is a three-part view of the supernatural. An all-powerful god created the world and remains a force, but is too distant and important to have much interest in the activities of human beings. Less powerful, but more important, are spirits of earth and air that govern rainfall and soil fertility; these are tied to local places and affect local conditions. Offerings and prayers to them are made at natural features like rock outcrops or sacred trees.

Third, and most important in the success of daily life, is the influence of one's ancestors. Burkinabe peoples, again like many African societies, see the family as extending across time, from founding ancestors through those members alive now, to unborn future generations. Living members have a responsibility to their ancestors to maintain family land and to marry and have children to carry the family into the future. The ancestors watch over their living descendents and can reward or punish their behavior.

There has always been Muslim Mossi, especially long-distance traders for whom Islam was a common bond with traders elsewhere in the savanna. There are Mossi farmers who are descended from traders, however, who remained Muslim. The peoples closer to the great Muslim societies north, east, and west of Burkina have experienced proportionately greater Muslim influence. Moreover, when the French conquest suggested that the traditional supernatural powers were insufficient to protect people, there was greater conversion to Islam and Christianity.

Current figures estimate the Muslim population at 50%, with 40% following traditional religions and 10% Christian; the latter are mainly Roman Catholic due to the French colonial history. The first African cardinal, Paul Zoungrana, was the archbishop of Ouagadougou and a Mossi. The Protestant population is around 1% and represents the work of American missionaries.

6 MAJOR HOLIDAYS

Originally, the national holidays were December 11, the anniversary of the proclamation of the Republic of Upper Volta in 1958, and August 5, anniversary of the date of full independence in 1960. After the 1983 revolution led by Thomas Sankara, the national holiday became its anniversary, August 4. The government and schools also observe all the major Christian and Muslim holidays, including Easter, Christmas, *'id al-Fitr*, the end of the month's fast of Ramadan, and the festival of Tabaski (*'id al-Kabir)*, when Muslim households sacrifice a

The 48% figure for the Mossi has been suspected of being a deliberate undercount in order to deny a demographic majority to the people who already dominated the new nation's government. Because ethnicity remained a sensitive subject, the national censuses of 1975 and 1985 did not publish ethnic totals for the whole population. Current estimates are based on those 35 year-old figures. On that basis, roughly 5 million Burkinabe are Mossi. A 1996 United States government figure estimates only 24% for the Mossi, while a 1995 linguistic reference book estimates Mossi at 53% of the population.

3 LANGUAGE

French is the official language of the country, of schools, and official publications. Except for the Mande-related languages of Bobo-Dioulasso and the west of the country, most Burkinabe speak languages of the Gur group within the large Niger-Congo family of languages. Gur-speaking peoples in Burkina and adjacent parts of Benin, Togo, and Ghana share a generally similar way of life as millet farmers, with some (like the Mossi and the Dagomba and Mamprussi in Ghana) having kingdoms and chieftaincies, while others are organized only along kinship principles.

4 FOLKLORE

The Mossi and Gourmantche peoples of Burkina are notable in the history of the West African savanna in that their ruling elites did not convert to Islam when others did. While there always have been Muslims in Burkina who were literate in ram to honor God's testing of Abraham's faith by asking him to sacrifice his son Isaac.

7 RITES OF PASSAGE

There are no rites of passage at the national level, except for universal events like school graduations. The ethnic groups in Burkina Faso do mark the various transitions in a person's life with public rituals. These include the formal naming of a baby and its announcement to the community at a set time after its birth, the circumcision and instruction of pre-adolescent boys and (separately) girls, marriage as the assumption of full adult status, and funerals, which mark the moving of the deceased from living elder to watching ancestor. Burials, necessarily soon after death in a tropical country, are distinct from funerals, although both are public ceremonies. Funerals may come years after a death, when the next of kin (usually the eldest son) is able to be present and to afford the cost of the ceremony and associated feast.

8 INTERPERSONAL RELATIONS

While cities and towns always have existed in Burkina, the vast majority of the population has lived in rural farming communities. The 1985 national census showed 12.7% of the population living in towns of 10,000 or greater, up from 4.7% just after independence in 1960. The two biggest cities, Ouagadougou and Bobo-Dioulasso, had estimated populations in 1991 of 634,479 and 268,926; the next largest town in the 1985 census had a population of 38,902. Recent estimates indicate that the two biggest cities, Ouagadougou and Bobo-Dioulasso, had populations of 1,181,702 and 435,543 respectively. The bulk of the population, then, lives in villages surrounded by neighbors who usually are also relatives, since land is allocated by kinship ties. That in turn reinforces a society in which people are conscious of the ongoing family to which they belong, for whose well-being they are responsible, and whose land they farm and live on, but do not individually own and cannot sell. Respect for those older than oneself is a cornerstone of Burkinabe (and most African) societies.

A poor country with limited resources, Burkina offers little in the way of social security payments. This means that even urban wage-earners maintain links to their rural families, where they have an absolute right to land and support in their old age.

9 LIVING CONDITIONS

For those who live in rural villages, life has changed little over the centuries, although some modern conveniences have been introduced. Most people live in adobe houses with thatched roofs. Electricity is available only in towns and cities; therefore, radios are battery-powered and lanterns are kerosene or battery-powered. As the population has increased, firewood for cooking is increasingly difficult to find and women must walk greater distances for it. In rural areas water for drinking, cooking, animals, and washing comes from wells; the building of deeper, cement-lined wells has increased the number that do not go dry during the dry season, and made hauling water easier. Water is carried from the well to the house in large pottery containers carried on the heads of women.

Health issues remain significant. Malaria is chronic and widespread; anyone falling ill with another disease most likely already has malarial parasites and is weakened. The cost of im-

ported malaria-suppressing medicines puts them out of reach for most Burkinabe. Measles remains a significant cause of death for children, even though it could be prevented if the resources were available.

During the 1970s, the world's largest public health project was launched by the World Bank and other aid agencies in Burkina to reclaim fertile river-edge land from "river blindness," or onchocerciasis. This disease, caused by a parasite transmitted by black-fly bites, can lead to blindness after heavy exposure and has caused people to abandon villages and fields along the few year-round rivers. The "oncho" project has succeeded in reclaiming the land, but helicopter spraying must continue in order to suppress the black flies.

Major roads increasingly are being paved, which makes van and truck transport faster and less wearing on the imported vehicles. The single railroad, which runs from the sea at Abidjan in Côte d'Ivoire through Bobo-Dioulasso to Ouagadougou, has been extended north to Kaya and eventually will reach another 200 km to valuable manganese deposits. Most individuals cannot afford a private car, but there is a widespread network of vans linking rural communities with cities and towns. There are international airports at Ouagadougou and Bobo-Dioulasso, with flights to other cities in West Africa and to Europe, particularly to France.

Bicycles and motorbikes are the most widely owned transport. Donkeys traditionally were used as pack animals and now are also used to draw carts to haul goods and firewood.

10 FAMILY LIFE

Most Burkinabe societies are patrilineally based; communities of men linked through their fathers live with the wives and children on land that in principle their ancestors cleared from uninhabited brush. In the past, married sons and younger brothers were likely to live with their father or older brother; there is a tendency to smaller households as more men have a wider range of economic options beyond the joint sharing of family farming. In the southwestern part of the country where Burkina, Ghana, and Côte d'Ivoire come together, ethnic groups transfer some rights and goods through the male line of kinship, and others through the female. That is, a man's tools, for example, might be inherited by his sons, but his cattle would go to his sister's sons.

Marriage in Burkina, as in much of Africa, is a matter of paramount concern to families because it is the means by which the entire family is perpetuated. The incest taboo means that women to bear children must come from outside the patrilineal family, so bringing in "strangers" is a necessity for the family. Marriages are arranged, therefore, and involve group meetings between both families. While there always have been ways for couples who wanted to marry to do so, by and large most marriages are not the result of individual emotions and desires, but are part of the overall family's way of making the connections needed to bear a next generation.

11 CLOTHING

Pre-colonial Burkina grew cotton, which was spun into thread by women and woven into strips of cloth by men; the cloth was exported by donkey caravan in large rolls to other parts of West Africa and was sewn into broader panels to make clothing in Burkina and elsewhere.

Donkeys traditionally were used as pack animals and now are also used to draw carts to haul goods and firewood. (Corel Corporation)

Modern Burkina grow increasing amounts of cotton, which is still an important export. It is made into printed cloth panels 1 by 2 m (about 3¼ by 6½ ft) in size in a Burkinabe factory. The factory-made and imported cloth is what most Burkinabe wear. Shoes also are manufactured in Burkina.

Traditionally, women wore a long cotton skirt wrapped around their waists; recently, tops have been added in rural as well as urban areas. Men wore cotton shirts and trousers, or Muslim-influenced embroidered robes. Sewing machines now are used for the intricate embroidery formerly done by hand. Urban residents tend to wear variations on an increasingly worldwide style of dress. Used American cut-off jeans have become the everyday working dress of farmers.

12 FOOD

Throughout Burkina, millet and sorghum are the staple foods. Porridge made from millet flour, called *tô* in West African French, is the main food. A cider-like beer brewed from sorghum is the main drink for all except Muslims and Protestant Christians, who do not drink alcohol.

Millet porridge is boiled to a loaf-like firmness, and pieces are broken off with the right hand, dipped in sauce, and eaten. The stew-like sauce is made from vegetables, leaves, and spices, and also may contain meat, which provides most of the flavor and vitamins to the meal. Meat, especially mutton and beef, is

a luxury item not frequently eaten and even less often eaten by itself as a meal. Chickens and guinea fowl are the main sources of meat. Dried fish is traded down from the Niger River in Mali and Niger; as the lack of lakes and rivers in Burkina limits local fishing.

Corn (maize) is increasingly grown to be roasted and eaten, but it remains a secondary crop because it exhausts soil nutrients more quickly and requires more water than millet. Peanuts are grown and are eaten fresh, boiled, roasted, and ground into sauces. Rice was domesticated long ago in West Africa as well as in Asia and is grown in western Burkina. Rice tends to be a luxury food, served for special events like weddings. Even in rural areas, French-style bread is increasingly available and is, like leftover porridge, a breakfast food. High-quality wheat bread (for which flour must be imported) is eaten daily by everyone in the larger cities and towns.

13 EDUCATION

Except for Muslim Koranic schools and the three-month initiation schools that accompanied the circumcision of pre-adolescent boys, traditional Burkina education came from living with, watching, and assisting one's older family members and neighbors.

The French colonial government, anxious to save money, left education in the hands of Roman Catholic missionaries, who did not have many schools. Around 1970, only 7% of Burkinabe children of elementary school age attended school. That figure has increased, but access to education is far from universal. A 1995 estimate for the population over age 15 reported an overall literacy rate of 19.2%, 29.5% of men, and 9.2% of women.

Access to post-elementary education is competitive and limited by the smaller number of schools; there is one university, in Ouagadougou. There are a few job opportunities for those who do get a Western education.

14 CULTURAL HERITAGE

Besides the renowned tradition of wood carving, Burkinabe society has a rich heritage of folk tales and oral tradition. Their music consists of drums, flutes, and stringed instruments. In the western part of the country there are many players of the balophon, a xylophone-like instrument with dried gourds serving as resonators for the vibrating pieces. FESTPACO, the Ouagadougou film festival, is the leading film festival in all of Africa, and one of the major cultural events of any kind for the entire continent.

15 WORK

Burkina Faso only recently has begun to integrate more modern occupations into its farming tradition. While no one is without exposure to modern conveniences and new technologies, most people still live the sort of lives, doing the same sort of work, as their ancestors have done for centuries.

16 SPORTS

Soccer and bicycle racing are the major sports; no urban holiday is complete without a bicycle race. Beyond that, there is little in the way of sports. There is a national basketball team, but few are involved in the sport. Hunting is work more than sport, involving either food-seeking or control of agricultural pests.

17 ENTERTAINMENT AND RECREATION

Radio is the important means of linking people in Burkina to the outside world. Personal, as well as local, national, and world, news is broadcast. Television is minimally present; there is one station each in Ouagadougou and Bobo-Dioulasso, broadcasting only two hours per weekday and five hours on weekends to 12 sets for every 1,000 people in 2000.

Movies are important, although theaters are limited to the larger towns and cities. More importantly, relatively few movies are made in Africa, or in African languages, so that the movies people see usually are from foreign cultures and in foreign languages without dubbing into local languages. Films from India are widely screened in Africa. This is changing, however, and Burkinabe filmmakers are playing a major role. The main film festival in Africa is FESTPACO, the Festival Panafricain du Cinéma d'Ouagadougou. Burkinabe filmmakers like Gaston Kaboré and Idrissa Ouédraogo are making feature-length films that increasingly are seen in Europe and North America, but also, because they are in Moré, are fully accessible to at least half the Burkinabe population.

18 FOLK ART, CRAFTS, AND HOBBIES

Societies in Burkina, especially in the western part of the country, produce some of the most famous African art, which is carved wooden masks worn by ritual dancers who personify animal or other spirits. Patterned cloth is both woven and tie-dyed, and leather bags, cushions, and hats are widely known.

19 SOCIAL PROBLEMS

Burkina shares with other countries the problems that come with increasing urbanization and a greater output of students than there are jobs for them to fill. In relative terms, however, neither problem is as advanced as in many other African countries. The overall lack of economic infrastructure also means that Burkina is heavily influenced by economic decisions elsewhere. The country's money is the CFA (African Financial Community) Franc, the currency of most of formerly French West Africa. In 1994 the value of the CFA franc was cut in half relative to the French franc and other currencies. This had a major effect on those earning wages or salaries paid in CFA, but it affected as well the price everyone pays for increasingly necessary imported products like tires or radios or wheat flour for bread.

Burkina Faso was long noted in modern Africa as having more political freedom than most countries, even when (paradoxically) there was a military government. African governments face the task of meeting many demands with few resources, which can lead to an inability to accomplish much, in turn leading to a military seizure of power in the name of honesty and efficiency. Burkina had the distinction of two bloodless military coups, eventually returning power to civilian rule. When younger officers led by Thomas Sankara seized power in 1983, however, there were casualties from fighting and from executions of political rivals. Sankara himself made a strong effort to break the country from its dependence on foreign aid, but in 1987 was killed by his associates, who continue to rule the country. Burkina has multiparty elections, but they have been extensively boycotted by parties that argue that the government is manipulating the political system.

Alcohol and drugs are not major problems. While there is a brewery in the country, the cost of commercially produced alcohol is too expensive for most people to consume in quantity. The traditional millet beer is alcoholic, but it is an established part of both traditional society and household organization and is therefore a culturally controlled substance. Kola nuts, rich in caffeine and the basic ingredient in cola drinks, are widely chewed and are a routine gift to a host. Imported from Ghana to the south, they are the preferred stimulant for Muslims, who do not drink alcohol.

20 GENDER ISSUES

As in most African countries, traditional practices have kept women in a subordinate position. In the traditional setting, a woman is considered to be property that can be inherited upon the death of her husband. As such, traditional law does not recognize inheritance rights for women. Women suffer from frequent domestic sexual abuse and violence, and no specific laws have been put in place to protect women. Abusive husbands go free, since there are no legal channels to investigate or prosecute their actions. Another problem for girls is that they are married early in life. It is estimated that about 52% of women are married before the age of 18.

However, female excision (commonly known as female genital mutilation) was abolished in 1996. A committee known as The National Committee for the Fight Against Excision was also established in 1996 to work toward the complete eradication of this practice in Burkina Faso. Estimates indicate that up to 70% of girls and women had undergone the procedure before it was abolished in 1996. Since then, incidences of excision have declined by about 40% and more than 400 people have been sentenced for performing the practice.

Women are responsible for subsistence agriculture, and few are involved in the more lucrative private sector. In terms of their representation in parliament, women held only 11.7% of the seats and formed about 25% of the government workforce in 2008. Many of the women in government earn low wages, as they generally hold low paying jobs. In terms of human rights, excessive poverty has many Burkinabe living deplorable lives with no access to basic human rights. Child labor, child trafficking, violence, and discrimination against women and children are quite rampant in the country. People have also been arrested without charge or trial. Excessive force is often used against civilians with official impunity.

[21] BIBLIOGRAPHY

Cordell, Dennis D., Joel W. Gregory, and Victor Piché. *Hoe & Wage: A Social History of a Circular Migration System in West Africa*. Boulder, Col.: Westview Press, 1996.

Decalo, Samuel. *Burkina Faso*. Oxford, England; Santa Barbara, Calif.: Clio Press, 1994.

Evenson, R. E. and M Siegel. "Gender and Agricultural Extension in Burkina Faso." *Africa Today* 46, no 1 (1999): 75–92.

Haddad, L. and T. Reardon. "Gender Bias in the Allocation of Resources Within Households in Burkina Faso: A Disaggregated Outlay Equivalent Analysis." *The Journal of Development Studies* 29 no 2 (1993): 260–276.

McFarland, Daniel Miles. *Historical Dictionary of Upper Volta (Haute Volta)*. Metuchen, N.J.: Scarecrow Press, 1978.

McMillan, Della E. *Sahel Visions: Planned Settlement and River Blindness Control in Burkina Faso*. Tucson: University of Arizona Press, 1995.

Skinner, Elliott P. *African Urban Life: The Transformation of Ouagadougou*. Princeton, N.J.: Princeton University Press, 1974.

———. *The Mossi of Burkina Faso: Chiefs, Politicians, and Soldiers*. Prospect Heights, Ill.: Waveland Press, 1989.

— revised by E. Kalipeni

BURUNDIANS

PRONUNCIATION: buh-ROON-dee-uhns
LOCATION: Burundi
POPULATION: 8.7 million
LANGUAGE: Kirundi, French, Swahili
RELIGION: Christianity, indigenous beliefs
RELATED ARTICLES: Vol. 1: Hutu; Tutsi

[1] INTRODUCTION

Rwanda and Burundi are two African countries whose borders were not arbitrary creations of 19th-century European powers. Both had centuries-old kingdoms before European rule. However, colonial rule did bring separate and competing kingdoms under a central government. Formerly the Tutsi *mwami* (king) occupied the apex of rulership, followed by the princely class. A lower stratum consisted of Tutsi and Hutu masses where much intermarriage occurred. Hutu serfs, obligated to work for the Tutsi elite, were the lowest social class. As of the early 2000s, the Hutu comprised 85% of the population, the Tutsi 14%, and the Twa, a pygmoid group, 1%.

German rule began in 1899, but the victors of World War I gave the colony to the Belgians under a League of Nations mandate in 1916. The Belgians reinforced growing Tutsi political and economic domination by ruling indirectly through them. Since independence in 1962, Hutus have rebelled against exploitation. The Tutsi elite have strongly resisted change in the balance of power. The resulting cleavage has created recurring ethnic violence on a horrendous scale.

Since 1962, some 300,000 Burundians, mostly Hutus, have been killed and nearly a million more displaced. Massacres of thousands of people occurred in April 1972, August 1988, January 1992, and in late 1993. Presidents and prime ministers have come and gone, as if by a revolving door. Though Ndadaye, a Hutu, was elected democratically in June 1993, he was overthrown in an army coup and killed along with several prominent Hutu officials and politicians in October 1993. In 1994 the death of his successor (along with Rwanda's president) in a mysterious airplane crash over Rwanda unleashed renewed fighting that lasted for 12 years.

In late 2000, the Arusha Peace and Reconciliation Agreement, brokered by Nelson Mandela, ushered in a transitional period of power-sharing between Tutsis and Hutus that culminated in free and fair elections in 2005. A new constitution was also adopted that year, and in 2006 the majority Hutu government (under President Pierre Nkurunziza) concluded a ceasefire with a Hutu liberation force, which ended major fighting. In the meantime some 25,000 combatants and child soldiers were demobilized, disarmed, and reintegrated into Burundian society.

Burundi still faces many challenges, not the least of which is to make its unique ethnically-balanced bicameral Parliament consisting of a National Assembly and a Senate work for peace. In the 100+ seat Parliament, 60% of the seats are reserved for Hutus and 40% for Tutsis (with at least 30% being women overall). A National Independent Electoral Commission appoints additional seats to ensure ethnic representation. In the 54-seat Senate, 34 members are elected by indirect vote with the remaining seats assigned to ethnic groups and former chiefs of state, all of whom serve five-year terms.

2 LOCATION AND HOMELAND

Burundi is somewhat larger than Maryland, but has 8.7 million people (estimate 2008), making it one of Africa's most densely populated countries. Rwanda borders Burundi to the north, the Democratic Republic of the Congo (former Zaire) to the west, and Tanzania to the south and east. Lake Tanganyika and the Ruzizi river on the floor of the Western Rift valley form a stunningly beautiful natural border with the Congo. A breathtaking escarpment towers over the Ruzizi to the west.

Most of Burundi is high plateau of 1,400–1,800 m (4,600–5,900 ft). A range to the east rises to above 1,800 m. In the uplands, temperatures are mild with an occasional frost. The average temperature in the valley is near 27°c (80°f). Most of the population is concentrated on the fertile soils at 1,500–1,800 m (4,900–5,900 ft), which increases competition for scarce lands. The Twa are thought to be the first to inhabit the area. Hutus arrived between the 7th and 14th centuries, while the Tutsi migrated to the region beginning in the 15th century. A few thousand Europeans, Indians, and Pakistanis live in the capital of Bujumbura. The kingdoms of Urundi and Ruanda historically had been adversarial, and their successor republics remain rivals.

3 LANGUAGE

Two official languages are spoken in Burundi—Kirundi and French. Many Burundians along the western shore and in Bujumbura also speak the East African trade language of Swahili. A traditional greeting in Kirundi is *Amashyo* (May you have herds [of cattle]). The reply is *Amashongore*, meaning, "I wish you herds of females." The language is full of references to the virtues of cattle and wishing one herds is metaphoric for health and good fortune.

4 FOLKLORE

Folklore is expressed through music, dance, and storytelling. Literature, for example, is passed down to younger generations in spoken forms of poetry, fables, legends, riddles, and proverbs. Many epic poems concern peasants, kings, ancestors, and cattle. In telling these tales, a skilled narrator transforms ordinary Kirundi into very poetic forms. "Whispered singing" transcends simple spoken and musical renditions. Men sing quietly along with the traditional instruments, *inanga*, a zither-like instrument, and *idono*, which resembles a stringed hunting bow (see **Cultural heritage** *and* **Folk art, crafts, and hobbies**).

5 RELIGION

Most Burundians profess Christianity, with 62% subscribing to the Roman Catholic faith, and 5% to Protestant faiths. Less than 10% of the population is Muslim. Those holding indigenous beliefs account for 28% of the population, though aspects of African traditional religion overlay the non-indigenous faiths. Former Pope John Paul II visited Burundi in September 1990 to support the constitutional transition.

6 MAJOR HOLIDAYS

The national holiday of Burundi is Independence Day, July 1 (1962). Hard times have dampened enthusiasm for lavish celebrations. Moreover, Burundi's endemic coups have rendered political holidays meaningless.

Being a predominantly Roman Catholic country, Burundians celebrate the Christian holidays including the Assumption, the Ascension, All Saints' Day, and Christmas. Beginning in 2005, the government also recognized the Islamic holy days of Eid al-Fitr (end of Ramadan), and Eid al-Adha (end of Hadj). On the traditional holiday calendar, *umuco* (or *akaranga)* used to be an occasion for traditional gamesmanship. Men would compete in archery and spear-throwing competitions. Soccer and other imported sports replaced these after the arrival of the Europeans. However, Burundians still enjoy dancing, drinking, and feasting on traditional foods on this day.

Of all the holidays, the most celebrated is Christmas. Christmas is an occasion for buying new clothes and wearing them to church. Women and children especially look forward to showing off their latest acquisitions. After church, people return home to spend the day with family and friends, enjoying a good meal and beer.

7 RITES OF PASSAGE

As in much of Africa, rites of passage are important markers in the life cycle. Six days after birth, babies are presented to the family in the *ujusohor* ceremony. The mother receives flowers for her hair and gifts of money and beer are customary. Christian parents and their families generally baptize their children one month after birth. After the child begins to toddle, it receives a name in the *kuvamukiriri* ceremony. The paternal grandfather gives the child a proper name, a clan name, nicknames, and if not already baptized, the child receives baptism if the parents so choose. From an early age to adolescence, children learn family and community values and are expected to assume responsibility in their teenage years. As a result, Burundian children show a maturity rare in American children of the same age.

Initiation rites were once extremely important in Burundian society. Today few Burundian children are initiated, although most of their grandparents were. European missionaries taught that the practice was heathen and pagan and all but eradicated it. The Roman Catholic Church has replaced the initiation rite with the Christian rite of First Communion where groups of children follow a lengthy period of religious instruction that culminates in their induction into the church as adults.

8 INTERPERSONAL RELATIONS

Burundians generally are gregarious people and visit each other without announcing it ahead of time. Typically, they greet each other by shaking hands with the right hand. Among friends of the opposite sex, it is acceptable to greet by touching cheeks three times. Friends of the same sex also may greet this way and may offer each other a firm hug, grasping each other's shoulders. In former times, it was common for someone of lesser status to shake hands with a person of higher status by holding his or her right arm with the left hand while shaking hands. This was to show respect for social status. This custom is dying out with the disappearance of servitude.

People have a set of gestures for pointing and calling people that is particular to Central Africa. They point to someone by

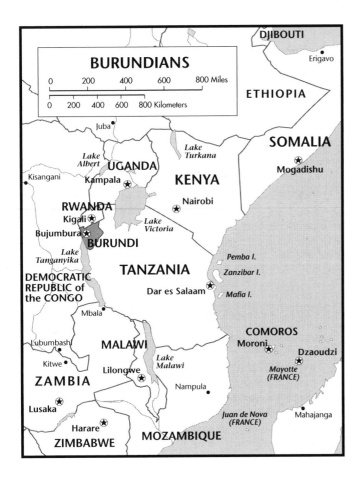

BURUNDIANS

0   200   400   600   800 Miles

0   200   400   600   800 Kilometers

towns, its infrastructure deteriorated during the war, leaving many without water, electric, and sanitation systems. Many rural houses are mud brick with thatch or tin roofs. Traditional huts formerly were made from reeds and canes. Some are cylindrical in shape, and mud walls may be whitewashed. In towns, concrete hollow block houses with galvanized iron or clay tire roofs are common. Burundi has many good masons and carpenters, but they tend to be under-paid and under-employed.

About 93% of Burundi's roads are unpaved. Some villages are reached only after hours of bouncing over dirt roads, which are prone to flooding and washing out. Bicycles and motor scooters provide human transportation and carry heavy loads of produce, such as bananas. The Catholic Church often supplies outlying areas with consumable goods through member cooperatives.

10 FAMILY LIFE

In Burundian society, the man of the household holds the authority. Women do the housework, raise the children, fetch water, collect firewood, cook the meals, and wash the clothes. They also tend gardens of cassava and sweet potatoes and raise produce for sale at the weekly market. A Kirundi expression says that women are revered for their childbearing and, as such, also make good planters. The girls help with domestic chores and with tending their younger siblings.

Some men have more than one wife, but polygamy is disappearing in modern Burundian life. Christianity and economics have changed attitudes about matrimony. The church strongly discourages polygamous behavior through sanctions and peer pressure. Weddings, bride prices, and wife maintenance are costly. Moreover, land pressures and the costs of educating children have led to smaller families. About 9% of women take modern contraceptives, and most practice traditional methods of family planning.

Correcting children in Burundi is not only the responsibility of parents, but also that of the extended family, friends, and acquaintances. If they do not correct bad behavior, they may be accused of shirking their communal duty.

Burundians rarely keep pets, but their cattle are prized possessions and occupy much of their time. Boys, for example, are often given the responsibility for tending the family's cows and goats. Because cattle give status, wealth, and security, buying a cow puts money in the bank. Some wealthy elites have accumulated as many as 2,000 head.

11 CLOTHING

Burundian traditional apparel consists of cloth wraparounds (*pagnes*), which women, girls, and elderly men still wear in the rural areas. The male pastoralists wear two pieces of cloth tied on opposite shoulders with a cord tied around the waist. The shoulders are bare and the cloth reaches the knees. Women wear shirts or blouses, *pagnes*, and scarves over their heads. In cool weather, they wear sweaters over their blouses. When women go out in public they wear a dress with a *pagne* over the top tied around the shoulder and one tied around the waist. Many people go barefoot in the village. Older women might wear a large colorful piece of cloth tied in front, which reaches the feet.

People place great importance on looking their best. Even on low budgets, they keep their clothing washed and pressed. If they wear shoes, they must be shined. Bujumbura at night

holding the arm out with the palm open and upward. Pointing at someone with one's index finger is very rude. Similarly, calling someone to come near is done by extending the arm with the palm turned down and bringing the fingers toward oneself. People, especially women, may give directions by pointing with lips pursed and the face extending toward the direction indicated.

Burundians have proper ways of giving and receiving things. Children learn to offer both hands when receiving an object, especially from an adult. This is a sign of respect and good upbringing.

9 LIVING CONDITIONS

After 12 years of civil war (1994–2006), living conditions are showing improvement. Nevertheless by African and world standards, life is extremely difficult for the average person. On the Human Development Index (HDI), which measures chances for good health and longevity, educational opportunities, and decent standard of living, Burundi ranked 167 out of 177 countries worldwide in 2007/08. Twenty-one percent of the population does not have access to clean water; 45% of children aged 0–5 were underweight (2002); 68% of the population lived below the poverty line (2002); and there is a 38% chance of not living past the age of 40. A high population growth rate (3.4% est. 2008) placed additional stress on job creation and basic services.

Bujumbura, the capital, formerly was a jewel-like town on the northeastern tip of Lake Tanganyika. However, like other or on Sundays has a cosmopolitan feel. Men and women who take great pride in their appearance, known as *sapeurs,* wear the latest fashions with great flair. The men dress up in suits and ties and the women in Western dresses and pumps. Young people are fond of stonewashed jeans and T-shirts.

12 FOOD

The staple foods in Burundi are tubers, plantains *(matoke),* and beans. Burundians are most fond of sweet potatoes and cassava served with different types of beans, greens, and cabbage. They also enjoy cassava pounded into flour, boiled in water, and stirred until it produces a thick paste *(ugali). Ugali* is sometimes made from maize. Burundians enjoy fresh, dried, and smoked fish from Lake Tanganyika and from rivers such as the Ruzizi.

People occasionally eat meat, though given their reverence for cattle, it should not be their own animal and not a cow. It is taboo to heat or boil milk because that might interfere with their cows' milk production. People also are not supposed to drink milk on the same day that peas or peanuts are eaten. Cattle and people live so close together that the health and fertility of the animals are thought to reflect on that of their owners.

Villagers typically rise early and forego breakfast. They return for a large noonday meal. At night they may eat leftovers or have tea, but tea requires extra cash. Children eat porridge and drink milk in the morning. In the cities, French bread is very popular, and European beverages such as coffee and tea have become common fare.

Burundians produce their own traditional drinks, including banana beer *(urwarwa)* and sorghum beer. Although they are fond of these in the villages, in Bujumbura Primus German-style beer is favored. Anytime someone has extra money, they invite their friends to go out to a streetside or neighborhood bar *(buvette)* for a round. Thus, if you are invited, you do not pay for even one round of drinks, but when you invite, you pay all the rounds until your pockets are empty.

13 EDUCATION

Burundians place a high importance on formal schooling, although informal home schooling begins when a child first understands right from wrong. Until 1954, church missions ran all the primary schools, and some of the best schools still are faith-based. The University of Burundi in Bujumbura founded in the 1960s is the only institution of higher learning.

A typical school day begins as early as 7:00 a.m. and finishes at 1:00 p.m. In some cases overcrowding has forced schools to hold two sessions a day, even in the evenings, so that more pupils can be accommodated. Because of the war, however, enrollment rates declined over at least a ten-year period. In 2004, the combined primary, secondary, and tertiary school enrollment was 38% those eligible, with only 83% as many girls as boys enrolled. Most children dropped out of school after reaching grade five. The literacy rate in 2004 was 41% and only 78% as many girls as boys (older than 15) could read and write. In 2005 President Nkurunziza made primary schooling free, and efforts were underway to equalize educational opportunities between Tutsi and Hutu and between the traditionally neglected north and the south, where two-thirds of the schools are located.

14 CULTURAL HERITAGE

Burundi maintains its rich cultural heritage based in part upon its past royal families. An example of how people perpetuate tradition in new forms is seen in the "tambourinaires," a folkloric drumming and dance troupe of Gishora, in Gitega province east of Bujumbura. In the past, the king initiated a group of boys from select families whose privilege it was to beat sacred drums. The drums could only be played under specific conditions, mainly for ceremonial purposes.

Today, the drums have become a popular attraction as an incarnation of this sacred heritage. As many as 25 men of all ages play huge drums carved from tree trunks, about three feet tall. They beat the drums with two sticks about 18 inches long. Even boys play. They wear red and white cloths tied in the traditional way, one over each shoulder with a cord around the waist. Dancing is very athletic. It consists of leaping high into the air and spinning around. They tell legends and folktales during the performance. Some dancers use wooden shields and spears and wear headbands and armbands of beads.

Burundians make several traditional instruments that they play during family get togethers (see **Folk Art, Crafts, and Hobbies**).

15 WORK

The vast majority of people (93%) work in subsistence agriculture and cattle herding. Subsisting means they produce staple crops such as sweet potatoes, bananas, corn, sorghum and manioc on small plots for their own consumption. A small percentage of the population grows coffee, cotton, and tea or works on larger plantations. The government employs 4% of the population in the civil service. Industry and commerce account for 1.5%, and services account for 1.5%. Those who fall between occupational cracks earn their living in whatever way possible. Some, for example, repair anything from watches to shoes. They set up their repair stands on sidewalks and take them down at the end of the day. Unfortunately, these jobs pay as little as $1.50 per day, which is not enough for a living wage. Because of underemployment, about 85% of the rural population and 55% of town folk live below the absolute poverty level.

16 SPORTS

Burundians are soccer fanatics. Soccer is played wherever space permits and where people have the leisure time to do it. Any kind of ball suffices, and makeshift goals mark parking lots, fields, streets, and any relatively horizontal surface. Schools have introduced other sports, such as basketball, volleyball, and European handball. In villages, the churchyard and adjacent school usually serve as a meeting place for school and community sports. Burundians love their national team, The Swallows, but the team continues to disappoint as it has never reached the World Cup or African Nations' Cup finals.

17 ENTERTAINMENT AND RECREATION

Entertainment and recreation are far more modest pursuits in Burundi than in Western countries. Socializing at home or sharing a beer and a meal with friends often passes for entertainment. Most people own portable radios and tune into their favorite FM stations for news, music, and radio dramas. Where electricity is available, people enjoy watching television. How-

In Burundian society, women are revered for their childbearing and girls help with domestic chores and with tending their younger siblings. (Cynthia Bassett)

ever, only a small percentage have satellite dishes (which are expensive) and the rest tune into the government station, Burundi's only TV outlet. On weekends, programming generally includes soccer matches. Television is increasingly available in rural areas thanks to solar power. But if one has a large herd to care for, watching the cows may be entertainment enough.

Bujumburans really enjoy nightlife and are fond of a variety of popular music. They dance to all kinds of music—Congolese, Malinke, Zuluka, American, rap, reggae, funk, and other styles. The Internet is gaining popularity. In 2006 it was estimated that some 60,000 people got information, news, and entertainment from this source.

18 FOLK ART, CRAFTS, AND HOBBIES

Burundians produce many crafts of excellent quality. Among the best of these are mats and baskets serving many different purposes. Papyrus roots, banana leaves, and bast (a strong woody fiber) are the raw materials for the baskets. Historically, a well-made basket was a symbol of status, not for sale, although baskets were traded occasionally for cows. Nowadays, skilled women are paid to teach young women the trade. The Twa people are skilled in making pots for their own use and for the tourist market. Wood carving has a long tradition and carvers produce highly intricate bas-relief drums and mortars for the tourist market. While drums formerly were part of religious ceremonies and provided music for social occasions, they now are produced as works of art for sale.

Burundian craftsmen make fine instruments such as the thumb piano (*ikembe*). The *ikembe* has 11 metal bands and the sounding box may have designs burned into the top for decoration. The *indingiti* is a traditional banjo or violin with a single string played with a bow. The *inanga* is an eight-stringed instrument with a large sounding board, played on its side. The musician plays it by crouching behind the instrument and plucking the strings like a harp. The *umuduri* is a musical bow with one string with three calabashes attached to the bow for amplification. Musicians use two sticks with a small calabash on the end to stroke the string.

19 SOCIAL PROBLEMS

Burundi faces several serious environmental and health threats, among them HIV/AIDS, which nationally runs at about 6% of the population. Infection rates are highest in urban areas. Other issues include poverty, school drop-out rates, weak rule of law, public corruption, large refugee populations (31,000 in 2007), and human trafficking. The minority Batwa people are deprived of land, although the government has instituted programs to provide them with free school books, health care, and two acres of land.

The most urgent matter is to find and develop lasting peace between the Hutu and Tutsi. The recent civil war resulted in more than 200,000 deaths, forced more than 48,000 refugees into neighboring Tanzania, and displaced 140,000 people internally. Some 3,000 children were pressed into combat by the various armed groups. Burundians must continue to redress political imbalance, skewed land ownership, and the disparity in economic wealth between these two ethnic groups. Land pressure, population growth, and a deteriorating environment make conflict resolution even more urgent.

[20] GENDER ISSUES

Gender presents a mixed picture in Burundi. On the one hand, women face legal and societal discrimination in inheritance laws, property rights, access to credit, jobs, and equal pay for equal work. Traditional practice encourages wife-beating, and it is culturally taboo to discuss it in public. A survey conducted in 2007 indicated that as many as one-third of women in Bujumbura were beaten at home. As a form of terror during the war, rape was widespread. Although it is illegal, prostitution is widely practiced. Many fewer girls attend and complete school than boys. Thus, to be growing up female in Burundi carries with it many serious challenges.

On the other hand, a strong women's voice is emerging for the first time in Burundi. This is exemplified by Marguerite Barankitse, who has given refuge to more than 10,000 orphan children. She affectionately refers to these children—who come from all three ethnicities—as Hutsitwa (a combination of Hutu, Tutsi, and Batwa). Burundian women gained world attention in 2000 when they utilized the Arusha Peace process as a popular public forum to advocate for their interests and rights. Although they fell short in achieving all their goals (for example, the UN refused to declare sex crimes as "crimes against humanity"), they nonetheless won more than 30% of the seats in Parliament in 2005. Women also occupy 17 of 54 Senate seats; the vice president of the republic and president of the Parliament are women. Some 400–500 women's self-help groups now participate in rotating credit schemes, lobby the Parliament to change laws, and help solve women's problems.

[21] BIBLIOGRAPHY

Africa South of the Sahara 2007. "Burundi." London: Europa Publishers, 2008.

Castermans, Philippe et Jean. *Au Burundi: Entre Nil et Tanganyika—le pays des Tambours Sacrés.* Bruxelles: Didier Hatier, 1990.

Cazenave-Piarrot, Francoise et Alain Cazenave-Piarrot et Albert, Kimenyi, Alexandre. *Kinyarwanda and Kirundi Names: A Semiolinguistic Analysis of Bantu Onomastics.* Queenston, Ontario: Edwin Mellen Press, 1989.

Daley, Patricia O. *Gender and Genocide in Burundi.* Bloomington: Indiana University Press, 2008.

Krueger, Robert and Kathleen Tobin Krueger, and Desmond Tutu. *From Bloodshed to Hope in Burundi.* Austin: University of Texas Press, 2007.

Lemarchand, Rene. *Burundi.* Cambridge: Cambridge University Press, 1996.

Ntibazonkiza, Raphael. *Burundi: Au Royaume des Seigneurs de la Lance: Une Approche historique de la Question Ethnique au Burundi.* Bruxelles: L'ASBL "Bruxelles—Droits de l'Homme," 1992.

—by R. Groelsema

CAMEROONIANS

PRONUNCIATION: kam-uh-ROON-ee-uhns
LOCATION: Cameroon
POPULATION: 18.5 million
LANGUAGE: English, French, 24 African languages
RELIGION: Islam, Christianity, indigenous beliefs
RELATED ARTICLES: Vol. 1: Fulani

[1] INTRODUCTION

Cameroon's present borders tell the history of European great powers' competition and the results on the battlefields of World War I. What began as a German colony in 1885 was surrendered to the British and French in 1916. These colonizers partitioned the country in 1919 and obtained protectorship of their respective portions from the League of Nations in 1922. Protectorate status changed to official trusteeships in 1946 by the vote of the United Nations. The British administered West Cameroon as part of Nigeria, while the French made East Cameroon part of French Equatorial Africa (along with Chad, Gabon, and Congo).

In 1955 Cameroonian insurgency movements led to internal self-governance, which became full independence in 1960. The UN-sponsored plebiscite in 1961 resulted in northern British Cameroon voting to become part of Nigeria, while southern British Cameroon joined with East Cameroon in a bilingual federal republic. Cameroon's first president, Ahmadou Ahidjo, declared a one-party state in 1966. In 1972 a unitary constitution and a strong presidential government replaced the Federal Republic, and the country's name became United Republic of Cameroon. In 1982, Ahidjo handed power over to his prime minister, Paul Biya. Biya dropped "United" from the country's name in 1983. He remains in power despite allegations that his party rigged the multiparty elections of 1992, and that in the presidential elections of 2004 his party erected substantial barriers to registering voters and allowed fraudulent balloting.

[2] LOCATION AND HOMELAND

Larger than California, Cameroon is one of Africa's most diverse countries, physically and culturally. Its crossroads location at the lobe of West Africa earned it the nickname, "the hinge of Africa." When Portuguese explorers first went up the Wouri River in 1472, they found the estuary teeming with shrimp. The *Rio dos Camaroes* (River of Shrimp) as they named it, became "Cameroon." From Lake Chad at 13°n latitude, Cameroon extends southward to 2°N of the equator. Cameroon borders Nigeria to the west and north, Chad and the Central African Republic to the east, and Equatorial Guinea, Gabon, and Congo to the south.

The climate varies markedly with the latitude and the terrain, from humidly tropical along the coastal plain, to cool in the mountainous west, to semi-arid and hot on the flat and sometimes rolling northern savannah. The vegetation also changes from tropical rain forest in the southwest to semi-desert in the northern reaches. Buttes, inselbergs, and ancient volcanic cores offer picturesque landscapes in the north. To the west lies a long line of rounded mountains of volcanic origin. Mt. Cameroon, an extinct volcano, is the highest point in West Africa at 13,500 ft.

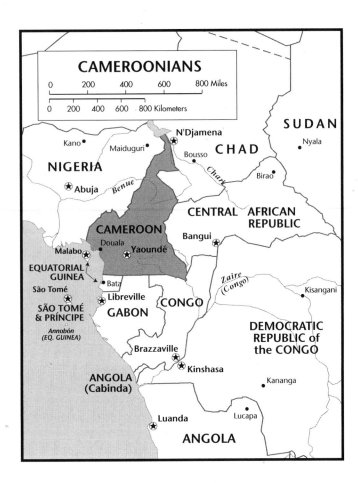

CAMEROONIANS

Cameroon's 18.5 million people come from seven major ethnic groups, primarily Fang, Bamiléké, Bamum, Duala, Luanda, Basa, Fulani. However, by some counts, as many as 200 ethnic groups exist within Cameroon's borders. One way of thinking about an ethnic group is to see it as the most extended level of the family. People of the same group usually have origins, history, homeland, language, customs, and name in common. Africans most anywhere identify with their "home" villages, though they may never have lived there.

Since independence, Cameroon has experienced a great rural exodus to the cities. Currently more than 30% of the population is urban. The population is densely concentrated in the south, near the port city of Douala, and in the northwest province around Bamenda. The north, which is primarily land for grazing and cotton production, is sparsely populated. Like most African countries, Cameroon is a country of youth, where 41% of the population is younger than 15 years old.

³ LANGUAGE

Cameroonians speak some 24 African languages. In the north, people speak Saharan and Chadic languages, and Bantu languages are spoken in the south. Cameroon is unique in that it has adopted both English and French as its official languages. Though French is dominant and a movement to make French the only official language is alive, northwest and southwest provinces hold tenaciously to English and are unlikely to give in without a major fight.

⁴ FOLKLORE

Cameroonian folklore consists of many intriguing myths and legends from the diverse cultural groups. However, one example from Bamoun recalls how traditional society once treated twins. In former times when a woman gave birth to twins, she presented them directly to the Sultan. A chicken was sacrificed to safeguard them and to ensure their good behavior. The mother then returned home with them and fed them meat. It is said that Bamoun twins have an extraordinary capacity for chewing meat even before teething. At age five, they returned to the palace to stay. The Sultan raised them as his own children, giving them a good education. As they grew older, the Sultan consulted them as his advisors on important decisions. Today, twins still are called *Nji* (chief), but the Sultan no longer raises them and their former power has diminished greatly.

One of Cameroon's foremost heroes of near mythical status is Douala Manga Bell. The people living near Douala chose him to protect their property from German colonizers. The Germans were attempting to expropriate the city of Douala and its surrounding lands, an explicit violation of an 1884 treaty. The Germans responded to organized resistance with armed force and arbitrary arrests. Finally, they captured Douala Manga Bell and tried him for high treason. They condemned him and a companion to death by hanging in 1914. Douala Manga Bell thus became a martyr-king. Cameroonians remember his heroics and the bravery of his companions in songs and theatrical performances, passed down from generation to generation.

⁵ RELIGION

Cameroon is evenly divided between Christians and Muslims each accounting for about 40% of the population. Whereas Christians predominate in the south, Muslims comprise the majority of the population in the north (roughly north of Garoua). As elsewhere in Africa, many people combine aspects of traditional African religion and animist beliefs with their Christian and Muslim faiths. One example of this overlay involves healing. A *marabout* (teacher and diviner) may advise a sick person to write texts from the holy Quran on a prayer board. The patient then prays by reciting the texts. Next, he dilutes the ink from the board and drinks it, in effect, ingesting the holy words.

If Cameroonians are divided by regional differences and language, there is much harmony and little religious strife amongst people of different faiths. Indeed, communal celebration of Muslim and Christian holidays has resulted in much crossing over from one faith to the other (see **Major Holidays**).

⁶ MAJOR HOLIDAYS

Holidays elicit various forms and degrees of celebration, mainly depending on one's region and religious faith. For example, May 20 (National Day), which commemorates the change from a federal to a unitary government in 1972, inspires much greater celebration from Francophones than from Anglophones. The residents of the western provinces increasingly see this holiday as a reminder of the power they gave away to the French-speaking majority when their regional assembly was abolished. The inverse is true of Youth Day, which Anglophones (especially before unification) celebrated for three days. The championship finals for soccer and track and field events highlighted this holiday, formerly called "Empire Day."

Typical housing in Cameroon. In the villages, most homes are made of mud and thatch, but these gradually are being replaced by concrete hollow block and galvanized iron roofing. Migration and squatting are common near the cities, resulting in shantytowns where people live without basic conveniences. (AP Images)

Similarly, traditions vary for Christmas and New Year's. The Francophones hold great celebrations for New Year's Day, while Christmas for the Anglophones means pageantry, feasting, and best behavior. On Christmas Eve and Christmas Day, for example, people wear new clothes and go to church. Children put on costumed reenactments of Christ's birth and give poetry recitals. They are judged and the winners perform later at the chief's palace. Near Wum, people form large groups and go from village to village eating, drinking, dancing, and socializing. The feasting is so joyous that Muslims join in the celebrations and go to church. Likewise, for the Ramadan feast, Muslims invite their Christian friends to help them celebrate their main religious holiday.

7 RITES OF PASSAGE

Traditional rites of passage are losing the significance they once had in Cameroonian society, especially where communities westernize or Western schooling is becoming dominant. Formerly, circumcision was one of the most important rites. It represented the shedding of youth and embracing of man- or womanhood. The transition occurred swiftly within the time frame of the initiation, which lasted from a few weeks to a few months. Upon completion of the rite, a "new" man would build a home, marry, and start a family. A "new" woman would no longer play as a girl, but she would assume the responsibilities of wife and mother.

Nowadays, Christian beliefs, especially from the Protestant faith, are replacing traditional ways. The strict application of Protestant catechism may not distinguish between the cultural and religious forms of initiation. Dancing with masks, for example, may be mistaken for idolatry. Schooling also interrupts the initiation schedules. Consequently, baptisms, First Communions, and weddings may outshine initiation, even though church ceremonies do not entirely replace traditional ways of celebrating passage.

8 INTERPERSONAL RELATIONS

The language of greeting depends on the region, but in French one typically says, *Bonjour, comment ça va*? (Hello, how are you?), and in Pidgin English one says "How na?" People shake hands and some kiss on the cheek according to the French custom, especially younger people in urban areas. People call someone by extending their arms, palm facing down, and bringing the fingers in and out. Pointing is rude, as is crossing legs at the knees or in the presence of someone with higher authority. The right hand is used to pass or accept objects.

Dating between couples is more commonly seen in the capital and big cities, and marriages are still arranged by family and relatives throughout the country. Visitors appear frequently and unannounced, and relatives commonly stay and are fed for lengthy periods.

Two teenage boys standing beside their homemade bikes in Cameroon. (David Johnson)

⁹ LIVING CONDITIONS

Despite favorable agricultural conditions and offshore oil, Cameroon ranks 144th out of 177 countries in terms of human development. Cameroonians face many of the same challenges as other Africans. Almost 7 children out of 100 do not live until their first birthday. Life expectancy at birth is 53.3 years. Unsanitary practices make waterborne diseases such as diarrhea, dysentery, and parasites very common. Rural health is improving as fewer village women and young people haul water from streams and springs. Instead, thanks to newly developed sealed wells, they can pump water by a foot pedal. In the villages, most homes are still made of mud and thatch, but these gradually are being replaced by concrete hollow block and galvanized iron roofing. In the capital and other cities, electrical power reaches many neighborhoods. Still, migration and squatting are common, resulting in shantytowns where people go without basic conveniences. Bathing and washing clothes in local streams are common.

Most of the main national roads are paved, two-lane highways. An incomplete stretch from east of Yaoundé to Ngaoundéré in the northeast is easily traversed by train. Good train service is also available from Yaoundé to the port of Douala. However, once off the main roads, the terrain can be rugged and some roads are blocked in the rainy season. Most people still travel by taxi bus and bush taxis, which are usually crowded high on top with plastic water containers, sacks
al, and chickens.

¹⁰ FAMILY LIFE

Cameroonians typically have large families with at least six children. Families are larger if the head of household has more than one wife. Grandparents and great grandparents generally live in the same compound as their offspring. The elderly command great respect and influence decisions, but the male family head usually leads in important matters. Women shoulder much of the work, tending fields, gathering firewood, and hauling water besides taking care of the children and doing the housework. One practical reason why families are large is that children help at a very early age. As soon as they are old enough, they tend fields with their mothers and siblings. It is common to see a four-year-old girl carrying a baby brother or sister on her back or doing chores around the house.

¹¹ CLOTHING

Traditional dress is found mostly in villages. In the north, Muslim men wear boubous, which are cotton pants over which a waist-, knee- or ankle-length robe is worn. Boubous typically are white, but also are made of other colors. Women wear multicolored flowing robes and cover their heads in public. Although women wear *pagnes* (sarongs) in the north, they are more popular in the south. The *pagne* is multipurpose. Not only does it serve as a wraparound skirt, but a second piece can be used to hold a baby to one's back, provide shade for the head, or give warmth on chilly mornings. A turban, usually from the same fabric, covers the head. Cameroon's high-quality cotton makes excellent cloth of traditional African patterns and designs.

In the towns, people wear these clothes too, but are also likely to wear Western pants and shirts. The younger generation wears jeans and T-shirts. Women typically wear blouses over their sarongs. As in many African countries, market traders also sell used clothing from Europe and the United States, which has been shipped by the bale. Children are likely to wear these as everyday clothes.

12 FOOD

The staples are corn, millet, cassava, groundnuts, plantains, and yams. These are made into *fufu*, a stiff paste, which is rolled into small balls and dipped into stews. A favorite is *Jamma Jamma*, spicy greens, served at the large noon meal. Women and the younger children typically eat together near the cooking fire. People eat out of communal bowls with their right hands, taking care to wash their hands before eating. In the cities or among the more "modernized" Cameroonians, people eat with kitchen utensils much like in the United States. Breakfast for the urbanite might include locally grown coffee, cocoa, or tea with milk and lots of sugar, and some freshly baked hot French bread.

Fruit abounds in Cameroon. Because of seasonal climate variation, one finds oranges, grapefruit, limes, bananas, pineapples, and coconuts in abundance. Common beverages include coffee, tea, palm wine, soft drinks, and beer, all of which are produced locally. Cameroonians love beer as evidenced by the number of breweries, the many brands, and the important role that beer plays in social encounters, parties, ceremonies and feasts.

13 EDUCATION

In Cameroon, education is bilingual, provided by government, missionary, and private schools. At state schools, education is free of charge. The government subsidizes other schools. Primary school begins at six years of age. Children begin high school at the age of 12 or 13, and continue until 19 or 20. High school has two cycles, which vary from the Anglophone to the Francophone region. In 2005 the combined primary, secondary, and tertiary enrollments were 62%, a fairly high ratio for Africa. Similarly, more than two-thirds of adults were literate. The government has established five regional campuses of the University of Yaoundé, each with a different area of specialization. Approximately one of three adults cannot read or write.

14 CULTURAL HERITAGE

The current popularity of Cameroonian modern written literature, film, and *makossa* and bikutsi music owes its success to an extremely rich and diverse cultural past. In 1974 the Cameroon government decided to protect this heritage by organizing a national culture festival. For Cameroonians, traditional culture expresses beliefs and tells stories about the physical and supernatural worlds. Therefore, it is impossible completely to separate culture, religion, and art from each other.

In traditional society, people still perform ancient rites with music, dance, masks, and statuettes. Among the Mouktélé in the north, music and dance are closely linked to farming and growing cycles. Young women play flutes (*madij*) when the millet sprouts from the earth. As harvest approaches in October, they are joined by young people playing bark flutes (*talok-*

waï). Others stamp rhythmic beats on the earth with their feet. The neighboring Toupouri dance to tam tams, cover their bodies with butter, and apply a red mineral powder to their chests.

The Bamoun of Foumban play dirge music at night to accuse a person of a serious crime. Fortunately, this gruesome procedure occurs rarely. With lifeless voices, singers march deliberately, hitting iron bells, and tapping on buffalo-skin bags. Fang musicians and storytellers dance and play the *mvet*, a harp-sitar that uses calabashes as acoustical amplifiers. They tell fables and legends, and narrate heroic events. The Pygmies all sing, improvising many parts and hitting sticks together to celebrate after a successful hunt (see **Folk art, crafts, and hobbies**).

15 WORK

Most Cameroonians (70%) work in agriculture as subsistence farmers, herders, and plantation workers. The remaining 30% are divided fairly equally between services (17%) and industry (13%). Like much of Africa, formal jobs with regular salaries and benefits in Cameroon are scarce, and tend to be in the public sector. With an unemployment rate of about 30%, most Cameroonians in the service sector make their livings doing informal jobs such as peddling goods on the street, tending market stalls, or providing the odd service. For example, one 70-year-old Cameroonian woman, Noubissi, is a traditional healer. Her profession is semi-formal in that it is protected by a Cameroonian labor union. She casts out evil spirits while burning herbs that she uses to treat her patients. She specializes in gynecology, pediatrics, female sterility, birthing, and infant health. She only prescribes natural medicines made from herbs that she herself gathers in the forest. Her unfading clientele suggests her efficacy. When asked how she cures people she answers, "Only God knows. He guides my hands."

16 SPORTS

Cameroonians are soccer fanatics, and rightly so. Cameroon's national team, "The Lions," qualified for the 1982, 1990, 1994, 1998 and 2002 World Cups, and went to the 1990 World Cup quarterfinals. In the 2008 Africa's Cup of Nations, Cameroon was defeated by Egypt in the championship match. Young men and boys play soccer with any kind of ball on nearly any kind of field, giving Cameroonians a constant source of entertainment. In 2008 Cameroon and China signed agreements to construct multi-million dollar soccer stadiums, Olympic-sized swimming pools and other world-class sports infrastructure in Doula, Yaoundé, Bafoussam, and Limbe. Other popular sports include basketball, tennis, and handball. Some men are fond of chess and checkers.

17 ENTERTAINMENT AND RECREATION

Socializing at baptisms, weddings, and parties or going out to night spots where music is played and people dance often passes as entertainment; and at these venues Cameroonian *makossa* music defines much of the popular culture. People play it everywhere: on their transistor radios, at truck stops and taxi stands, in pubs and restaurants, and in nightclubs. Musicians such as Manu Dibango and Sam Fan Thomas became international celebrities. A blind Bamiléké singer, André-Marie Tala, nicknamed Ray Charles, topped the charts in the 1970s. The music is hard-hitting with a tight, fast-paced rhythm that has spawned a number of rivals among them the extremely popular *bikutsi*. *Bikutsi* comes from the Beti people around Yaoundé and means "to beat the earth." It is danced at parties, weddings and funerals and has generated controversy for the sexual content of its lyrics and suggestive dancing styles. Current top artists are Patou Bass and Ovasho Bens.

Cameroonian television consists of the government station, which has limited broadcast hours. However, with the coming of satellite dishes, Cameroonian audiences increasingly tune into world culture beamed from outer space.

[18] FOLK ART, CRAFTS, AND HOBBIES

Cameroonian art is rich and meaningful. Through art, people tell their history, or express their beliefs about nature, procreation, leadership, divinity, and the afterlife. Artists use their natural materials to sculpt, carve, shape, and fashion objects to help them express their understanding of the world to younger generations. Art objects include "elephant" masks; wooden, bronze, and bead-covered statuettes; carved pillars and bed posts; woven baskets; and pottery. The *Tso* dancers of the Kuosi (one Bamiléké community) wear fabulous, intricately beaded elephant masks when a chief or an important dignitary dies. Statuettes with fat cheeks symbolize good eating, while protruding bellies represent fecundity.

Many other crafts have cultural, practical, or monetary value. Craftspeople fashion tam tams and various kinds of flutes. Contemporary artists copy ancient forms and sell their art to tourists who come to visit Cameroon for its cultural heritage, natural beauty, and national parks.

[19] SOCIAL PROBLEMS

Cameroon's social problems—unemployment, crime, government corruption, human trafficking, forced child labor and money laundering—are in part due to a stalled political transition from authoritarian one-party rule to multiparty democracy. Newspapers regularly carry stories alleging civil rights abuses, beatings, and even fatalities related to government crackdowns on public protests, demonstrations and strikes. Some of the violence stems from the rivalry between the Anglophone west and the Francophone east. In the 1990s the government sent troops into the western provinces to quell demonstrations.

Cameroonians also face serious economic and social challenges. The population growth rate is nearly 3%, which means by the year 2015 Cameroon will have a population of almost 23 million, most of it younger than 20 years old. The demand for education, health, and jobs will be very great. Moreover, intensive and unsustainable land uses are contributing to deforestation, overgrazing, desertification, poaching, and over fishing. Some reports indicate that Cameroon has become a transshipment point for drugs that formerly transited through Nigeria.

[20] GENDER ISSUES

Cameroon is a male-dominated society where women face unequal treatment under customary and statutory law, and discrimination in private sector employment, the civil service, political appointments, and in the country's social hierarchy. Women are expected to raise children, cook and do household chores, work in the fields, fetch water and firewood, and generally do not go out on their own to socialize in public unless it is at the market or running errands. About 20% fewer girls than boys enroll in primary, secondary, and tertiary institutions, and about 30% fewer women than men are literate. Considered property of their husbands, women generally do not own land or inherit property when their husbands die. Girls are subject to trafficking, early forced marriage, and rape.

Female *Bikutsi* musicians and performing artists like K-Tino, who sees herself as a Cameroonian suffragette, use their music to liberate and emancipate Cameroonian women.

[21] BIBLIOGRAPHY

Africa South of the Sahara 2007. London: Europa Publishers, 2008.

Debel, Anne. *Le Cameroun Aujourd'hui*. Paris: Les Editions Jeune Afrique, 1985.

Gaillard, P. *Le Cameroun*. Paris: Editions L'Harmattan, 1989.

Lobe, Iye Kala. *Doula Manga Bell: Heros de la Resistance Doula. Grandes Figures Africaines*. Paris: ABC, 1977.

Mbaku, John Mukum. *Culture and Customs of Cameroon*. Westport, CT: Greenwood Press, 2005.

—by R. Groelsema

CAPE VERDEANS

PRONUNCIATION: kayp VUHRD-ee-uhns
LOCATION: Cape Verde; United States
POPULATION: 300,000
LANGUAGE: Portuguese (official language), Crioulo
RELIGION: Catholicism with *Crioulo* aspects

¹ INTRODUCTION

It is not improbable that Phoenician sailors sailing from Carthage in the 5th century BC were the first to see the volcano of Fogo as they navigated along the African continent. There is some reason to believe that Arab sailors were aware of the islands by the 10th or 11th centuries. Certainly for seven centuries before Columbus, Arabs and Jews had occupied large regions of Iberia and had made seminal contributions to the related sciences of navigation, astronomy, cartography, and naval design. This was critical input for the Portuguese navigators.

It was sea captains sailing for Prince Henry "The Navigator" during Portugal's Golden Era of Maritime Exploration who began to sail along the upper West African coast in the early 15th century. Looking for new trade routes, African gold, and a way around the Arab world, they reached modern Senegal in the 1440s, and it was between 1455 and 1462 that the Cape Verdean islands were reached. The Cape Verdean archipelago had no known precolonial inhabitants; its entire history, from 1455 until its independence in 1975, was as a colony of Portugal.

While sailing for the Portuguese, before his New World voyages, Christopher Columbus sailed down the West African coast to Al Mina in coastal Ghana. Because Cape Verde was a normal Portuguese port of call, we may safely assume that he stopped in the islands in the late 1480s. It is certain that he was in Cape Verde on his third trans-Atlantic voyage. Queen Isabella of Spain also wanted him to investigate reports of African ships from the empire of Mali deep in that region of the Atlantic; nothing was found.

Vasco da Gama, hurrying back from his raids in East Africa and India, was also in Cape Verde, but his preoccupation was with his dying brother and avoiding Muslim sailors whom he feared would seize his ships, which he deliberately sank in Cape Verdean waters. Sir Francis Drake, famed for circumnavigating the globe and defeating the Spanish armada, was no friend to Cape Verde after looting and burning its main towns.

Charles Darwin and his ship, the *Beagle,* stopped in Cape Verde on the epic and scientifically pioneering voyage that led to the proof of evolution. Darwin's voluminous notes and drawings done in Cape Verde record an amazing diversity of animal and plant life and the unique aspects of Cape Verdean volcanic geology. Even the Lindberghs made a brief Cape Verdean stop during their famed air flight around the Atlantic rim.

² LOCATION AND HOMELAND

Although there are tens of thousands of Cape Verdeans residing in New England, many Americans have heard little of Cape Verde and its deep roots in the lands of West Africa. The Republic of Cape Verde is an archipelago nation of nine main islands, found about 300 mi off the west coast of Senegal. The horseshoe-shaped archipelago has two island groups: The Barlavento (northern, windward) islands include Santo Antão, São Vicente, Santa Luzia (uninhabited), São Nicolau, Sal and Boa Vista. The Sotavento (southern, leeward) islands are composed of Maio, São Tiago, Fogo, and Brava. Some islands are flat and sandy (Boa Vista and Sal), others provide a moonscape terrain (São Nicolau and Santo Antão) and mountains (Fogo) that tower over 9,000 ft above the sea. The capital of Praia is located on the largest island of São Tiago, while Mindelo is the main town of the north on São Vicente.

Located at the same latitude as the Sahara desert, Cape Verde suffers from severe ecological conditions. The hot and dry climate and periodic droughts have made agriculture always marginal. Cape Verdeans long have had to turn to the sea for support from fishing, whaling, and sea salt production. Perhaps above all, Cape Verdeans have a very long pattern of labor emigration to Europe, Brazil, and North America to escape the difficult conditions in the islands and send economic support back home. The Cape Verdean diaspora continues to be critical to the islands' remittance-based economy, but there has been a great growth in tourism and foreign investment that has brought in considerable funds and important economic development on which the nation now relies.

³ LANGUAGE

Although Portuguese is the official language and many other languages are also known, it is *Crioulo* that is most widely spoken in Cape Verdean homes and clubs. Like other Creole languages, the Cape Verdean tongue is unique and follows its own grammar, lexicon, and style. Telephones, televisions, literature, films, press, poetry, and radios all enrich and strengthen Crioulo communication. Women often are considered the bedrock of Cape Verdean society, especially when it comes to preserving Crioulo linguistic skills.

⁴ FOLKLORE

Cape Verdean folklore is very rich in its intermingling of Portuguese and African sources as well as its own traditions. One popular set of tales relates to *Nho Lobo*, the clever wolf whose folksy wisdom can play an important role in teaching life's lessons and basic values.

⁵ RELIGION

Most Cape Verdeans are devout Catholics, and very active church life provides for core values and stability in the community. Important saint days are widely recognized; in fact, many of the islands are named for the saint days on which they were discovered. There also are unique *Crioulo* aspects of religion. For example, the *mastro* ceremony involves a post or mast that is colorfully decorated with fruits to honor a saint. Religious carnivals and parades in the islands or in the United States also are common. Aside from floats and marchers, one also may see a Cape Verdean man "wearing" a man-sized boat model in the line of march as his feet provide the locomotion and he appears to be the captain and crew. In recent years, revivalist Protestant sects have made inroads in Cape Verde.

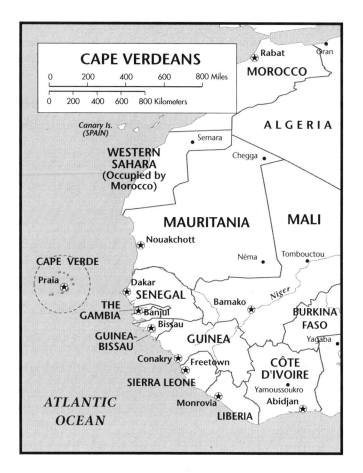

CAPE VERDEANS

0   200   400   600   800 Miles

0   200 400 600 800 Kilometers

MOROCCO
Rabat
Oran

Canary Is.
(SPAIN)

WESTERN
SAHARA
(Occupied by
Morocco)

Semara

ALGERIA

Chegga

MAURITANIA   MALI

Nouakchott
Néma   Tombouctou

CAPE VERDE

Praia

Dakar
SENEGAL   Bamako

THE
GAMBIA   Banjul
Bissau

GUINEA-
BISSAU   GUINEA
Yagaba

Conakry   Freetown

SIERRA LEONE

ATLANTIC
OCEAN   Monrovia

LIBERIA

BURKINA
FASO

CÔTE
D'IVOIRE
Yamoussoukro   Abidjan

6 MAJOR HOLIDAYS

Important holidays include 20 January (the assassination of President Amilcar Cabral) and 5 July (Independence Day). Other religious holidays surround Christmas, Easter, Carnival, and various saints' festivals. The *tabanka* festival incorporates African types of shrines with a Portuguese religious parade, particularly during the celebration of Saint John.

7 RITES OF PASSAGE

The main transitions in life are noted after birth with the First Communion, at marriage, and by cemetery burial at death. Farewell parties for migrants and for returning visitors have become so established that they approximate a rite of passage.

8 INTERPERSONAL RELATIONS

Within the family and within the wider Cape Verdean community, social networks are reinforced continually. These ties are critical when job-hunting, obtaining loans, seeking marriage partners, and conducting general social life. Cape Verdeans are highly involved in social clubs, voluntary and service associations, and community affairs. The warmth, caring, and sharing within Cape Verdean families and among friends is widely recognized. National and ethnic pride provide a strong social cement for these relations.

9 LIVING CONDITIONS

Generally, Cape Verde is strongly influenced by Portuguese culture and architectural styles and is similar to coastal Brazil in general atmosphere. Piped water and electricity are common in the main towns, but in rural areas may be lacking. Houses showing an African influence feature the round *funco* style from West Africa. They are built with Cape Verdean stone, but still may have an African-style conical thatch roof.

Modern technology now includes water desalinization and even wind-powered generation of electricity, as well as widespread use of televisions and telephones. Most main roads are paved with cobblestones and, although quite narrow, they do allow for a reasonable flow of motor traffic. The main towns have intra-urban bus transport and are connected to other towns by vans and taxis. Inter-island communication is maintained by ferryboats and frequent airplane connections. Relative to Europe or America, the living conditions in Cape Verde have numerous deficiencies. Compared with neighboring West Africa, however, living conditions are far advanced.

A substantial process of urbanization is unfolding in Cape Verde, especially to the cities of Praia and Mindelo. Traffic and parking are sometimes problems along with the high cost of imported fuel for public and private transportation.

10 FAMILY LIFE

The warmth and generosity of Cape Verdean family life is deeply rooted in culture and history. Sharing a pot of *cachupa* (stew) with family, neighbors, and drop-ins is normal. A great deal of sacrifice is made to educate children, and academic achievement and employment success are sources of great family pride.

11 CLOTHING

Western-style clothing is standard, especially for men and children. Women sometimes incorporate their unique *panos* (a cloth woven on the West African narrow loom). These *panos* are used as sashes for dancing and also can be used as a wrap for carrying babies. At times in early Cape Verdean history, the *panos* were used as currency in a barter economy. Women also have unique styles of tying headcloths. Used clothing from Europe and New England sometimes arrives in metal barrels *(bidon)* to be sorted and resold to meet domestic needs.

12 FOOD

Cape Verdean foods include *cachupa* (stew), *conj* (soup), *djagacida* (chicken with rice), *gufong* (cornbread), and other *Crioulo* favorites. Recipes often involve corn, rice, and couscous as a starch base and, if meats are included, the most common are pork, chicken, and fish (especially tuna). A wide variety of tropical fruits is readily available, including mangoes and bananas. Several islands produce Cape Verdean rum *(grog)* from distilled sugar cane. Cape Verde is not self-sufficient in food production and must rely on imported corn and wheat. Historically, droughts have caused famines that have starved 15%–20% of the population and caused others to flee.

13 EDUCATION

Cape Verdeans long have prided themselves on a relatively high standard of formal education, especially relative to other West African nations. This is due, in part, to the tradition of seminary education at the seminary in São Nicolau and because of the high degree of out-migration, which gave Cape Verdeans additional access to education. There are higher secondary

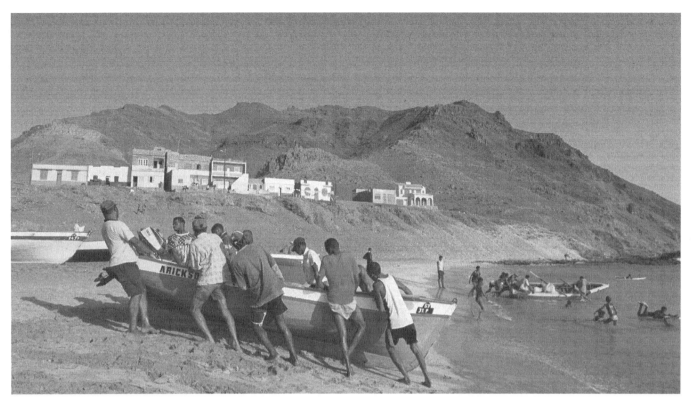

Fishermen drag a small boat up onto the shore on the island of Sao Vicente. The islands of Cape Verde offer visitors mountains for hiking, pristine beaches, and lots of water sports, like wind surfing and scuba diving. (AP Images/Armando Franca)

schools in the major towns, and elementary schools throughout the islands. Teacher-training and technical schools are also present. Post-secondary and university level education is now advancing in Cape Verde with the foundation of the University of Cape Verde as well as the Jean Piaget University, both in Praia. In Mindelo private colleges are also underway to meet the great demand for modern training and research.

14 CULTURAL HERITAGE

The roots of Cape Verde's population are found among mainland Portuguese, Azoreans, Sephardic Jews, Moors, political exiles like the *degredados*, and African peoples such as Fula, Balante, Wolof, Mandingo, Manjaco, Papeis, and Bissagos. The diversity of these origins has resulted in a *Crioulo* amalgam of Luso-African traditions. In this sense, one may say that Cape Verde is not only the westernmost extension of Africa, but also the easternmost extension of the Caribbean, and a southern extension of Europe.

Slavery helped to build Cape Verde. It was largely from the islands that the Portuguese crown monopolies based their slave trading economy from the 17th–19th centuries. Coastal middlemen called *lançados* traded with the victorious kingdoms in the slave wars required by the trade. Slaves were not only part of an important economy, but were used on Cape Verdean plantations of sugar cane and tropical products, as well as for general labor and household services.

It was quite ordinary for slave owners to have children with their servants. In fact, that is the original source of the evolution of the *Crioulo* population. Other slaves such as the *badius* fled to remote and interior portions of the larger islands

and developed their communities there. Still other slaves were "seasoned" in Cape Verde and exported to the New World, especially to regions in northern Brazil. While slavery is an undeniable part of Cape Verdean history, the sustained patterns of brutality and racism clearly are more muted than elsewhere, in large measure because of the synthesis of the Luso-African population.

Today, more Cape Verdeans live in faraway diaspora communities than in the homeland. Cape Verdeans are found throughout Africa, Brazil, and Portugal, as well as in Senegal, Italy and Holland, and in southeastern New England. In these places, Cape Verdeans long have been involved in maritime trades, such as fishing, sealing, whaling, and docking, and more recently, as agricultural and industrial workers. Financial assistance from Cape Verdeans living overseas are a critical factor in the present island economy.

The crews of the famed American whaling and sealing ships were heavily represented by Cape Verdeans. As a consequence, American consular interests are among the oldest in Africa. American naval presence in Cape Verde was significant.

15 WORK

Agriculture and fishing in Cape Verde are conducted at subsistence level or for small scale exports. The most significant export is its workforce, often as contract laborers. Remittances from Cape Verdeans around the world continue to be a very important source of financial stability.

Historically, thousands of Cape Verdeans have found work on ships devoted to whaling, sealing, slaving, and fishing, but it was in the 19th century that more regular numbers began to arrive in America with the intention of permanent immigration. During these times, a chief source of employment was as longshoremen, or in agricultural work, especially the cranberry industries of Cape Cod. The seasonal nature of this work made factory jobs more attractive and through the 20th century, when not limited by immigration quotas, they arrived seeking jobs in textiles and other manufacturing. Today, Cape Verdeans are found in every walk of life, including education, major sports, medicine, the arts, banking, commerce, and construction.

Youthful unemployment and marginal work is a serious problem in Cape Verde. This is particularly difficult among those Cape Verdeans who have been deported from the US and Europe and arrived with more liabilities than assets to themselves and Cape Verdean society.

16 SPORTS

Many sports are popular in Cape Verde, especially soccer. Basketball has shown increasing popularity. Swimming, surfboarding, scuba diving, track and field, and long-distance running also are growing. There is even a golf course and horseback riding stable on São Vicente. A very popular game in Cape Verde is *ouri*, a "pit and capture" game board that can be dated directly back to ancient Egypt.

17 ENTERTAINMENT AND RECREATION

Cape Verdean entertainment is centered around the home, where dances, parties, and receptions are very popular. Inside and outside the home there are rich varieties of popular music, both imported from the diaspora communities and synthesized in the Crioulo traditions. These forms range from the European-origin *mazurkas* and *valzas*, to the polyrhythmic *batuko*, and modern popular music of *funana* and *finaçon*. Perhaps most famed of all are the *coladeiras* and *mornas*, which capture the painful burdens of the Cape Verdean soul or *saudade*.

Lively post-colonial literature includes poetry, short stories, and novels. Cape Verde even boasts of its own neoclassical *Claridade* literary movement, much of it written in Portuguese and *Crioulo* and increasingly translated to English and French.

18 FOLK ART, CRAFTS, AND HOBBIES

A wide array of folk arts are found in Cape Verde, including sewing and crocheting for women and a revived interest in the production of *panos*. Men enjoy building ship models, carving of wood and cow horn, making shell horns, and carving pipes. Modern arts can be found in exhibitions and galleries that show textiles, pottery, wood carving, sculpture, painting, drawing, and photography.

19 SOCIAL PROBLEMS

Cape Verde increasingly is suffering from a rising use of illegal drugs and alcohol and an increased incidence of HIV/AIDS. Struggles with self-identity also are common. Apparently the personal use of drugs and alcohol is also linked to a rise in the overseas illicit drug trade and other smuggling activities. With the rise in tourism there are also more reports of the sex trade that could cause increased incidence of HIV/AIDS.

20 GENDER ISSUES

The national liberation parties of Cape Verde (the PAIGC and PAICV) had long put forth the full liberation of women as one of their central goals. A number of women were incorporated into leadership positions within the PAIGC's fighting forces during the nationalist armed struggle. The Party insisted that at least two of the members of *tabanka* (village) committees be women. The Uniao Democratica das Mulheres (UDEMU) was formed by the PAIGC in the mid-1960s. During the armed struggle period (1963–1974) fought in the mainland but led by Cape Verdeans, UDEMU assisted in the mobilization of women for the war effort. UDEMU was replaced by the Commissão Feminina (Women's Commission) toward the close of the war, and while it has been replaced it belongs in the historical evolution of female empowerment in Cape Verde.

After the 1981 coup in Bissau, the PAIGC changed its name to the PAICV. Similarly, the UDEMU which had represented women in both nations was changed to the Organizão de Mulheres de Cabo Verde (OMCV). The OMCV is organized by sectors which contain all "base groups" in a district as well as an administrative body. The OMCV continued much of the work of the former organization, and it functioned as a women's auxiliary of the single party. The position of women in Cape Verde remains hard with relatively high levels of illiteracy, hard physical work, a high level of machismo, and a relatively low level of participation.

While educational opportunities for women have been expanded since independence, the male-dominated nature of the social and familial structure is in need of further changes in various ways. Certainly the position of women has improved markedly given the traditions based in colonial patriarchy and male supremacy. Now the rights of women are legally protected. For example, children born out of wedlock must legally be supported by their fathers and the status of "illegitimacy" has been abolished.

The numbers of women in industry and tourism are increasing even though the overall numbers of industrial jobs are few. There are now women members in the Assembleia Nacional Popular. Women are commonly found in the health and educational services where such possibilities were limited during colonial rule.

Of particular importance is the male "brain drain" away from Cape Verde leaving the population composed disproportionately of women. Ironically, while their income is thereby reduced or reliant on remittances from absentee husbands, it has made the remaining women more self-reliant and codependent. It is impossible to overlook the hardships that women face, however, the spirit of liberation, social mobility and empowerment is now very significant in Cape Verde. Women are rapidly expanding into new roles and occupations and probably greater numbers of women more than men are seeking higher education that is now available in Cape Verde.

Similarly, new issues such as family planning, birth control, domestic violence, poverty and prostitution, abortion, and AIDS have also entered the picture. OMCV sectors sometimes help to organize *jardins* and pre-school teachers to provide day care and pre-school training for children. There are a number of Cape Verdean women writers, perhaps best known are Orlanda Amarilis and Yolanda Morazzo. The literary works of A. A. Goncalves reveal many of the complexities of the lives of

Cape Verdean women. Since independence, March 8, International Women's Day, has been observed in Cape Verde.

21 BIBLIOGRAPHY

Carreira, António. *The People of the Cape Verde Islands: Exploitation and Emigration.* Archon Books, 1982.

Halter, Marilyn. *Between Race and Ethnicity: Cape Verdean American Immigrants 1860-1965.* Urbana: University of Illinois Press, 1993.

Lobban, Richard A., Jr. *Cape Verde: Crioulo Colony to Independent Nation.* Boulder, CO: Westview Press, 1995.

Lobban, Richard A., Jr. and Paul Khalil Saucier. *Historical Dictionary of the Republic of Cape Verde.* 4th ed. Lanham, MD: Scarecrow Press, 2007.

—by R. A. Lobban, Jr

CENTRAL AFRICANS

ALTERNATE NAMES: CAR

LOCATION: Central African Republic

POPULATION: 4.5 million

LANGUAGE: French and Sango (official languages), Ubangian group (Niger-Congo family of languages)

RELIGION: Islam, Roman Catholic, Protestant, indigenous religious beliefs

RELATED ARTICLES: Vol. 1: Aka

1 INTRODUCTION

The Central African Republic (CAR) is a landlocked country the size of Texas in central Africa. The CAR was a French colony (Ubangi-Shari) from 1899 until independence in 1960. Prior to the arrival of the French in the nineteenth century, the peoples of the CAR were divided among numerous small kingdoms and sultanates. Trade in ivory, slaves, iron, and agricultural products along the Upper Ubangi River and across the Sahara to North Africa and the Mediterranean.

While the arrival of colonial forces put an end to the slave trade, the economic system they imposed brought further hardship and misery to the Central African people. Most of what is now the CAR was divided up into "concessions," large parcels of land turned over to private companies for exploitation. All of the natural wealth of the land—including the rights to the labor of the people—was considered the property of the various concession owners. Rubber, coffee, cotton, diamonds, and labor were among the primary products these companies sought to exploit. Forced labor and relocation along newly built roads caused many people to flee the European colonists just as they had fled Arab slave raiders engaged in the trans-Saharan trade in previous centuries. Famine and disease were the most immediate outcomes of this migration. It was only as the result of a highly publicized visit to the Ubangi-Shari by the famous French novelist André Gide in 1921 that the practice of forced labor and the concession system finally was abolished.

Under the leadership of Barthélemy Boganda, a former priest, schoolteacher, and member of the French National Assembly, Central Africans were finally able to throw off the bonds of French colonial rule in 1960. Unfortunately, Boganda never would see the fruits of his labor, for he died under mysterious circumstances in a plane crash shortly before independence from France was granted. His nephew, David Dacko, became the first president of the CAR but lost power to Jean-Bidel Bokassa after a coup d'état in 1964. Bokassa brought initial prosperity to the CAR, but he quickly became obsessed with power and grew increasingly autocratic. In 1976 he crowned himself emperor of the Central African Empire in a ceremony that cost one-third of the entire annual budget for that year. Embarrassed by the lavish lifestyle and increasingly despotic habits of Bokassa, the French intervened in 1979 and returned Dacko to power. As of 2008 the CAR had a democratically elected president, Ange Félix Patassé. However, the stability of the CAR is threatened by increasing involvement in conflicts in neighboring Chad and Sudan.

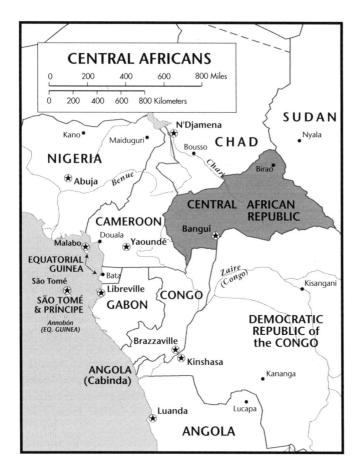

CENTRAL AFRICANS

| 0 | 200 | 400 | 600 | 800 Miles |
| 0 | 200 | 400 | 600 | 800 Kilometers |

SUDAN

Kano   Maiduguri   N'Djamena   Nyala

NIGERIA   Bousso   CHAD

Abuja   Benue   Birao

CENTRAL   AFRICAN
REPUBLIC

CAMEROON   Bangui

Douala   Yaoundé

Malabo

EQUATORIAL
GUINEA   Bata

São Tomé   Libreville   CONGO   Kisangani

SÃO TOMÉ   GABON
& PRÍNCIPE

Annobón
(EQ. GUINEA)   Zaire
(Congo)

DEMOCRATIC
REPUBLIC of
the CONGO

Brazzaville

ANGOLA   Kinshasa
(Cabinda)   Kananga

Luanda   Lucapa

ANGOLA

2 LOCATION AND HOMELAND

The CAR is home to approximately 40 different ethnic groups, most of which speak languages belonging to the Ubangian branch of the Niger-Congo language family. The primary ethnic groups of the CAR are Banda, Gbaya, Ngbaka, Ngbandi, and Zande. A number of smaller Bantu-speaking groups are found along the southern border of the CAR, and a handful of Sahelian groups are found along the northern border. With a population of just 4.5 million in an area of 240,535 sq mi, the CAR is one of the most sparsely populated countries in the world. From east to west, the CAR measures 900 miles; from north to south it varies from 260 to 475 miles. The CAR shares its 2,700-mile border with five countries: the Democratic Republic of the Congo and the Republic of Congo to the south, the Sudan to the northeast, Chad to the north, and Cameroon to the west. The CAR was called Ubangi-Shari in the colonial period since its landmass falls primarily in the watershed of these two rivers.

In terms of geography, the CAR spans all three of Africa's major types of landscape. To the extreme south is the dense equatorial tropical rain forest, which is home to the CAR's earliest inhabitants, the pygmies. The middle portion of the country, where the bulk of the population lives, is woodland savanna. In the northern part of the country the savanna gives way to the Sahel, a semidesert band that separates the Sahara desert from the grasslands. The terrain of the CAR consists primarily of gentle rolling hills with a few small mountains in the northwest and the northeast. In the middle portion of the

country, the savanna is occasionally broken up by rocky outcroppings called *kagas*. As in the rest of the region, there are two seasons: dry and rainy. In the rain forest band, the rainy season lasts nine months, from March until December, tapering off to just three to four months of rain in the northern Sahel region.

3 LANGUAGE

The 40 ethnic groups of the CAR are unified by the national lingua franca, Sango. This language is a variety of Ngbandi, which was used along the Ubangi river and into the interior for trading purposes before French colonization. Sango was then spread throughout the colony by the soldiers and workers employed by the colonial government. These hired forces were recruited from the coastal regions of Africa and themselves spoke a variety of African languages. Upon arrival in Ubangi-Shari they adopted Sango, both for communicating with the local population and for speaking among themselves. By the time Protestant missionaries arrived in the colony in the 1920s, Sango was already so widely spoken that Protestant and later Christian missionaries began using it in their work. The association between Christianity and the use of Sango has strongly contributed to its ongoing spread. Today 98% of the population of the CAR speaks Sango at least as a second language. In Bangui, the capital, and other major cities, young people who are not ethnically Sango increasingly learn Sango as their first language.

Another important language spoken in the CAR is French, which is the official language along with Sango. While Sango is the language that most Central Africans speak on a daily basis, French is the language of government and education. Many Central Africans are trilingual: They speak their ethnic language with other members of their ethnic group, especially within the family; they speak Sango in church, the marketplace, and whenever they meet someone from a different ethnic group; and they speak French at school, when dealing with the government, or when speaking to foreigners.

4 FOLKLORE

Since each ethnic group has its own language, each also has its own oral tradition, including mythical heroes and storytelling formulas. With the emergence of national identity and culture associated with the common national language, Sango, there has emerged a body of folklore known to Central Africans from all ethnicities. The central figure in this national folklore is *Tere*, a clever and witty man of supernatural powers who outsmarts his opponents with tricks and guile. Though originally a figure from Banda mythology, *Tere* has become such a central figure in Central African oral tradition that in Sango his name is now synonymous with the act of storytelling itself.

Oral tradition plays a very important role in the education of children in the CAR, for it is through these stories that they learn important lessons about the origins of the natural world, morality, traditional healing, and hunting. In days gone by, such stories would be told by the older generation to the younger while sitting around a fire in the evening. Today this tradition continues, with these stories being told over the radio and on television. The storyteller frequently incorporates a song into his story, which the entire audience will sing along with him. The refrain of these songs is frequently the moral of the story. The catchy tune and clever lyrics help the listener remember the main point of the lesson.

5 RELIGION

Most Central Africans are Christian, with 35% of the population being Protestant and 18% being Catholic. The remainder are Muslim or practice indigenous religions. In addition, many Central Africans incorporate indigenous practices of ancestor worship, or animism alongside Christianity or Islam. In local religious systems, each person is assigned a *totem,* which is an animal spirit that is passed on from generation to generation. Some *totems* are sacred to an entire ethnic group, while others are specific to individuals. In both cases, one may never eat the animal associated with one's *totem.* If possible, when a person is dying, he or she will pass on his or her *totem* to a young child, usually a son or grandson. In this way some Central Africans may end up with several *totems* that they believe give them special insights, characteristics, and protection.

Traditional priests, or witch doctors, are called *nganga.* The priest is in communication with the spirits of the ancestors who indicate to him their pleasure and displeasure. If a Central African has a problem, for example a series of bad harvests or poor luck in hunting, he or she may go to the *nganga* if it is suspected that displeased spirits are at the root of the problem. The *nganga* serves as a medium to the spirits and frequently will order a ritual sacrifice (usually a chicken) to placate them. He will bless the fishing nets and hunting spears and may order additional offerings, such as eggs and white chickens, to be left in the sacred spot of the ancestors. These sacred spots usually include an altar on which a figurine of the spirit has been placed.

6 MAJOR HOLIDAYS

Independence Day, celebrated December 1 and known locally as *Premier Décembre,* is the major important holiday in the CAR. It honors the day that Barthelemy Boganda declared the independence of the country and is celebrated with parades and much official pomp and circumstance. In many respects this is a day of remembrance of Boganda himself, who is rightfully considered to be the father of the CAR nation. On this day Central Africans show their patriotism and respect by dressing in their finest attire and participating in the activities. Schoolchildren and social organizations of every type assemble to march before local and national dignitaries. Afterwards they feast on roast goat, gazelle, or pork, which few Central Africans can afford to eat on a daily basis. The adults may drink beer or wine, while the children are given the rare treat of soda.

7 RITES OF PASSAGE

The most important rite of passage among Central Africans is circumcision, which serves as a symbol of initiation to both adulthood and the various ethnic groups. Many ethnic groups, particularly those in the northern part of the CAR, practice circumcision on both boys and girls just as they are entering puberty, around the age of 13. Historically in rural areas, circumcision takes place over a three-month period when groups of up to 30 boys or girls are taken from the village to live in a secret camp in the forest or savanna. Here they are given intensive training and education in the spiritual beliefs and practices of their ethnic group. They also are taught about sexual reproduction and the responsibilities they will bear as full-

fledged members of society. Young women are instructed to be faithful and obedient to their husbands and young men are instructed to provide for their wives and children. When the initiation period is over, they are marched back into the village where they are greeted with much celebration, dance, and fanfare. The newest members of society are given presents of money and clothing, and special feasts are held in their honor. Once they have completed this rite of passage, they have the right to take a spouse.

With urbanization, male circumcision increasingly takes place in a hospital and the practice of female circumcision is discouraged by the government. Even if circumcision does not actually take place, the removal from society for educational purposes and initiation still takes place, though the period increasingly is only a matter of a few weeks rather than months. Many young people, particularly in the larger urban areas, no longer speak the language of their ethnicity and it is only during circumcision, when they are sent to their ancestral village, that they learn something of their ethnic language and customs.

Honoring the deceased also plays a very important role in Central African society, for it symbolizes the transition from the living to the spiritual world, when a living person passes on to become a venerated ancestor. Depending on the social status of the deceased, periods of mourning may last anywhere from a few days to years. In the first few hours after the death of a close relative, male family members are expected to display their grief by shaving their hair off, and women are expected to abstain from any type of personal grooming and adornment. An all night vigil around the corpse will be held the first night, with much singing and dancing to help coax the spirit into the other world. The body is promptly buried at sunrise the next day, with the head pointing north for men and south for women. Depending on the wealth and status of the deceased, the vigil may continue for up to two weeks. During the mourning period the immediate family maintains proper decorum by refusing to wear brightly colored clothing and to participate in any pleasureful activities. At the end of the mourning period, there is a celebration with dancing, good food, and much gaiety. The day after this celebration the family will symbolize the return to normal life by putting on a new set of clothing.

8 INTERPERSONAL RELATIONS

Greeting and leave-taking are very important in Central African society because they are considered not just acts of politeness but also indicators of respect. Central Africans begin each day by greeting the members of their family with a handshake and an inquiry into how they slept. Whenever a new person enters a group of people, the newcomer is expected to first greet the most important person (e.g., oldest person, honored guest, or chief, etc.) with a handshake and then greet each and every person assembled in the same way. Failure to do so would be construed as a great insult. When leaving a group, a second handshake is required of each person. Among close friends, particularly men, a sign of intimacy and friendship is the following of the handshake with a snap of the fingers, produced jointly by both parties. Women and men both shake hands, but increasingly women are adopting the French practice of kissing on both cheeks.

Central Africans have many hand gestures that mean very specific things. For example, the gesture for calling someone over is very similar to a wave good-bye in the West and is done by outstretching the hand palm toward the person and clasping the hand. Also, when indicating the height of a person, the hand is held vertically at the level of the face, for animals the palm is held horizontally to indicate the top of the head. To refer to a person using the gesture of an animal would be construed as a great insult.

Visiting friends and family play a prominent role in Central African society, with Sunday afternoons and holidays being given over to this practice. On these days many Central Africans will put on their finest clothing and set out to go calling on friends either at home or in public places. Most visits to homes are spontaneous and unannounced, but when a visitor arrives—even a stranger— at the very least a chair in the shade and a drink of cool water is offered. Frequently, a small meal will be offered, which the host and guest will eat together. Sharing food, even if it is just a few boiled peanuts, is an important aspect of Central African culture because it symbolizes the strong emphasis placed on togetherness and community. Even if one is not hungry, in Central African society it is looked down upon to refuse a meal when offered. Instead, one should eat at least a few bites out of politeness.

⁹ LIVING CONDITIONS

The CAR is one of the poorest countries in sub-Saharan Africa and, as a result, it is plagued with a low standard of living and high death rate from disease and malnutrition. Life is particularly difficult for children who are the most vulnerable to disease and parasites. Most Central Africans live in mud-brick huts with grass roofs and without running water and electricity. While such homes are in general clean and comfortable, they offer little protection from malaria-carrying mosquitoes. In addition, most children go barefoot and are thus susceptible to other parasites that are spread through the waste of animals, particularly pigs. In large villages, each home or group of homes has a latrine and children are instructed to use it, which helps ensure that the drinking supply will not be contaminated. All too often, however, these latrines are built too close to the well or stream that supplies the drinking water.

Transportation is a major problem in the CAR. There are few paved roads, most of which are in poor condition. Few Central Africans own cars and most must depend on *trafiques*, or bush taxis, to get from one place to another. These bush taxis are almost always filled well beyond the designed capacity of the vehicle. The roof of the bus or van is piled high with passengers' luggage and goods. On buses heading toward the cities are sacks of food and live goats and chickens; on buses heading out of the city and toward the countryside are new pots and pans and other consumer goods such as soap and cloth. During the rainy season, when many roads turn to mud, it can take weeks to get from one end of the country to the other. All passengers must be prepared to sleep on the ground wherever the bus stops for the night or breaks down.

¹⁰ FAMILY LIFE

Though there are not normally formal marriage ceremonies, certain social customs are strictly followed to recognize new unions. Before a man and a woman can live together as husband and wife, the family of the man must pay a bride-price to the family of the bride. This payment is viewed as a form of marriage license or as a token of sincerity. The exact sum and terms of payment are worked out between the families of the two parties and may range anywhere from a few goats and chickens to large sums of money. If the marriage fails due to infertility or infidelity of the woman, the family of the man can demand a return of the money. No marriage is official until a child has been born.

Once a couple starts to produce children, frequently a younger sister or cousin of the wife will come and live with them to help relieve the mother's burden. The young assistant is in many respects an apprentice, learning how to keep house and to care for babies and children. The size of the household also may be further augmented by the temporary adoption of a sibling's children, either so that these children may attend better schools or so that their parents can spend more time working to make a living. It is rare to find a child being raised alone or with just one sibling. The more typical scenario is for five or six children of varying degrees of blood relatedness being raised as brothers and sisters.

¹¹ CLOTHING

Traditional Central African cloth is made out of the bark of a certain tree that grows in the rain forest and that becomes soft and pliable when beaten. In the precolonial period, most clothing consisted of a loincloth made out of this barkcloth or of a skirt made from braided raffia, which comes from a type of palm tree. Colonization and trade with Europe brought about the introduction of cotton cloth, which is frequently dyed in bright and colorful patterns. Most women today wear such cloth in a form of dress known as *pagne*, which is tied about the waste like a skirt and worn together with a matching blouse made of the same material. Clothing is a potent symbol of wealth, and genuine European prints from the United Kingdom and the Netherlands are the most sought after.

For casual wear, men may also wear matching shirt and pants made from colorful printed cloth, but for important occasions they wear European-style clothing. Central African men never would wear shorts in public, because they are the attire of children and reminiscent of the clothing of the European colonists. Increasingly, men and women alike are adopting the West African custom of wearing outfits known as *shada* made of colorful batik cloth that has a design in the weave. Outfits made out of this cloth are embellished with elaborate embroidery and may cost hundreds of dollars apiece. Less fortunate Central Africans wear secondhand European and American clothing bought for a few cents apiece at local markets.

¹² FOOD

The staple food of the Central African diet is cassava, which is a starchy root that originated in Brazil and was introduced in Africa by the Portuguese. Unlike millet, the traditional Central African staple, cassava is a hardy plant that can be grown easily in a variety of climates and even in very poor soil. To prepare the cassava for consumption, it first must be soaked in water for three days to leach out the traces of cyanide that occurs naturally in the plant. After soaking, the roots are peeled and broken into pieces to be dried in the sun. Just before eating, the dried cassava is ground into a fine flour that is used to make the mainstay of Central African cuisine called *gozo*. This is a firm paste made by adding the cassava flour to boiling water.

Most Central African meals consist of *gozo* served with a sauce made with meat, fish, and/or vegetables. One favorite everyday dish, called *ngunja,* is made with the dark green leaves of the cassava plant. Most sauces, including *ngunja,* are thickened with peanut butter, which gives them added protein and flavor. Onions, garlic, tomatoes, and mushrooms are also basic elements of Central African cuisine and are found in many national dishes. On special occasions, goat and chicken are the dishes of choice. In rural areas many people continue to enjoy wild game such as snake, monkey, and elephant.

The communal aspect of eating is reinforced by the fact that everyone eats with their fingers from a central common dish. Men and women, however, do not eat together unless they are related and in private. Women do all the cooking and they serve the food. A Central African meal consists of one bowl of sauce accompanied by one ball of *gozo,* both of which are served covered with intricately decorated gourd shells to keep them warm. Before eating, everyone washes their hands in a basin that is passed from person to person and waits for the oldest person or honored guest to begin. Also, no one may take a piece of meat until this person has done so.

Depending on the size of the household and their financial resources, usually only one meal is cooked per day and served at the noon hour. In the evening and for breakfast the next day, leftovers are eaten. The diet is supplemented with fresh fruit such as oranges, bananas, pineapples, guava, mangoes, and avocados, which grow in abundance in the CAR. French-style bread is available in the larger towns and cities where it is eaten for breakfast or in place of *gozo* with a meal. The CAR produces coffee, which Central Africans of all ages drink sweetened with ample quantities of sugar and softened with condensed or powdered milk.

¹³ EDUCATION

Most Central Africans born since independence in 1960 have attended at least some primary school, but very few have received further education. Only one eighth of all children go on to high school and of these only 1 in 10 will actually finish. To earn a high school diploma, students must take an exam called a *baccalaureate* which very few people are able to pass. All those who pass, and who have the money, are then able to go on to the one university in the country, the Université de Bangui. At all levels, parents are expected to pay a fee for the education of their children. Failure to pay is one of the major reasons why many children leave school at a young age.

In government-sponsored schools, the official language is French and, as a result, most young people today have learned at least a small amount of French. Typically, children begin their education in Sango and gradually make the transition to French so that by the time they reach high school, classes are conducted entirely in French. The ability to read and write in French is directly linked to one's educational level. Because the orthographic system of Sango is closely related to that of French, young people who learn to read and write in French, by virtue of being native speakers of Sango, know how to read and write in this language as well. Older people who never have attended school are often able to at least read Sango, thanks to the many years of literacy projects conducted by the various Christian missionary societies. Recently, the CAR government has begun a secular literacy program aimed at farmers in rural areas.

¹⁴ CULTURAL HERITAGE

The CAR has a rich tradition in music and dance, which is expressed as part of the celebration of every major holiday and event. In traditional society, music and dance were believed to facilitate communication with the spiritual world and played an important role in the belief system of the people. The primary musical instrument is the conga drum, which is made by stretching a piece of wet leather over a hollowed-out length of log. While these drums come in all shapes and sizes, some stand up to a yard tall and can be heard several miles away. In the early and pre-colonial period, a special type of drum called a *linga* was used for communicating between villages in a specially devised code. Xylophones made with wood and gourds are another common musical instrument. In traditional society, specific songs and dances were associated with different events and would only be performed at this time. For example, certain songs are performed only at funerals and others only during circumcision.

Though music and dance have changed considerably with modernization and exposure to Western culture, they retain great significance in modern Central African society. Music and dance have been incorporated into Christian worship, where services are often punctuated with lively singing and elaborately choreographed dance. Conga drums and xylophones are still popular in rural areas, but today electric guitars, keyboards, and snare drums are increasingly common in urban areas. Popular recorded music sung in Sango is heard all over the country and is very pervasive. In buses, taxis, restaurants, and bars, either the radio or a cassette player is almost always providing background music. Increasingly, African American music such as rap, reggae, and hip hop are also becoming popular.

¹⁵ WORK

There is, for all intents and purposes, no manufacturing in the CAR. At one time in the 1970s, Central Africans produced their own cloth, shoes, beer, and soap, and even assembled cars. Today only the soap factory and one of the two breweries remain in operation. Timber and diamonds are the most important industries in the CAR, generating between them 75% of the CAR's export earnings. Unfortunately, these industries employ few people. Most Central Africans are subsistence farmers, growing most of the food they consume and just a bit more that they sell to get money to buy the things they cannot grow, such as soap and cloth. A limited number grow cash crops such as coffee or cotton, but demand for these exports on the world market has been falling for the past several years as competition from other parts of the world has increased.

¹⁶ SPORTS

Central Africans are avid sports enthusiasts, with soccer and basketball among their greatest passions. Athletic clubs in virtually every city and town sponsor soccer teams that compete for regional and national championships. On Saturdays throughout the CAR, makeshift soccer stadiums become a major focus of social life as fans of all ages come together to watch back-to-back matches. Here young men come to court young women, old men come to gather and chat, and children come to frolic on the sidelines. The mayor of the town or chief of the village is usually in attendance, as are all the other local dignitaries. The presence of vendors selling grilled meat, peanuts, and bananas add a festive air to the occasion. Particularly good soccer players enjoy considerable status and prestige in their hometowns, especially if they go on to play in the national soccer league. Basketball was introduced in the 1970s by American Peace Corps workers, who built courts at high schools throughout the country. There is a national basketball training center in Bangui, and in 1988 the CAR national team astounded the continent by winning the African championship.

17 ENTERTAINMENT AND RECREATION

In Bangui, the capital, there is locally produced television in Sango and French. These shows are very popular and in the evening those rare individuals who have both electricity and a television will place the set outside so that all the neighbors can watch. It is not unusual to find 40 or 50 people gathered around a television in the evening watching storytellers, the local news, or an old French movie. In rural areas, where there generally is neither electricity nor television, some people will improvise with generators and video recorders. Usually, such events are by paid admission only and feature American action films or Chinese karate films. There is only one national radio station in the CAR, Radio Centrafrique, which broadcasts news, information, stories, and music. Radio is a major source of entertainment for those fortunate enough to have shortwave radios and batteries to operate them.

One of the most popular activities for Central Africans of all ages is dancing. In even the smallest towns there is usually at least one gathering place with a cemented dance floor and a cassette player. In the evening such places are popular with young adults who come to listen to the latest music from Bangui and the Democratic Republic of the Congo and to dance. In villages and cities of all sizes, there are frequent occasions when drumming and dancing take place. Most notably, funerals and circumcision celebrations typically involve several days of singing and dancing.

18 FOLK ART, CRAFTS, AND HOBBIES

Traditional art in the CAR takes a variety of forms including ebony carvings, pottery, weaving, and hair braiding. In the southern part of the country, near the rain forest, skilled artisans produce a host of ebony products that are popular with Central Africans and tourists alike. Statuettes, figurines, and animal carvings are the most common, though they also produce a number of household items such as combs, plates, and pestles. In the past, each ethnic group produced distinctive pottery that could be identified by the patterns and designs found on the outside. Today, however, only a few ethnic groups continue this tradition because most people have switched to aluminum and steel pots which are more durable and last longer. Traditionally, however, all cooking was done in clay earthenware pots that also were used for storing water, grain, or oil.

In the savanna region of the CAR, where the grass can grow 12 feet high and a variety of reeds may be found, the weaving of mats and baskets is a common activity. By dyeing the grasses and reeds different colors, elaborate patterns may be woven into the mats and baskets, giving them greater aesthetic appeal and increasing their value.

Hair braiding and tying is one of the principal social activities of women as well as a major outlet for their artistic talents. Some hair designs are so complex and intricate that they may take up to eight hours to complete. Central Africans are best known for the "sputnik" design, which involves winding strands of hair very tightly with string so that they stand straight out in all directions.

19 SOCIAL PROBLEMS

The post-colonial history of the CAR, like so many African countries, has been characterized by autocratic rule and restriction of basic civil liberties. The first president, David Dacko, was overthrown by his cousin, Jean-Bidel Bokassa, in a coup d'état. Bokassa became infamous for crowning himself emperor and rumors that he killed children. He fashioned himself to be a modern-day Napoleon who had absolute power—including life and death—over his subjects. He was driven from power in 1979, and Dacko was brought back only to be deposed once again in another coup, this time by André Kolingba. Kolingba ruled the CAR with a tight grip until 1993, when the first democratic elections brought Ange Félix Patassé to power. Patassé was Bokassa's prime minister and has proven himself to share many of his former boss's autocratic tendencies. Successive Central African governments have paid lip service to human and civil rights, at the behest of Western donors, but have done very little to ensure that these rights are guaranteed.

Corruption and AIDS are the biggest social problems facing the CAR today. In a country where governmental favors are routinely bought and sold and only the ethnic group associated with the president can succeed in society, it is no wonder that development of the country has been so slow in coming. AIDS is having the effect of wiping out a significant portion of the generation aged 20–40, which is putting a strain on older people who are being forced to care for children orphaned by this tragedy. Further exacerbating this problem is ongoing urbanization and rapid population growth, both of which contribute to declining living standards.

20 GENDER ISSUES

Intense poverty has made life difficult for many Central African women. Maternal mortality rates are among the highest in the world and the average life expectancy for women is only 44 years. Nonetheless, women are highly valued in Central African society, particularly for their work as mothers. Mother's Day has grown into a celebration of women in general and it serves to recognize the labor and sacrifice that all women make in CAR society. On this day men do all the cooking and cleaning, while the women sit in the shade and are served by men. Some men add humor and a festive touch to the occasion by wearing women's clothing as they go to the market and carry out other duties normally assumed by women. Often, a few days before the celebration, a son will buy his mother a chicken and some beer, which will assure her that she is loved and appreciated. On Mother's Day, the son will prepare the chicken himself and serve it to his mother.

21 REFERENCES

Bennafla, Karine. *Le commerce frontalier en Afrique centrale: acteurs, espaces, pratiques.* Paris: Karthala, 2003.

Carpenter, Allan, and Janice Baker. *Enchantment of Africa: Central African Republic.* Chicago: Children's Press, 1977.

Donnet, Nadine, Jean-François Le Borgne, and Jean-Luc Piermay. *Géographie: La République Centrafricaine, Collection André Journaux.* Paris: Hatier, 1967.

Giles-Vernick, Tamara. *Cutting the Vines of the Past: Environmental Histories of the Central African Rainforests.* Charlottesville: University of Virginia Press, 2002.

Grellet, Gérard, Monique Mainguet, and Pierre Soumille. *La République Centrafricaine, Que Sais-Je?* Paris: Presses Universitaires de France, 1982.

O'Toole, Thomas. *The Central African Republic: The Continent's Hidden Heart.* Edited by L. Bowman, *Profiles: Nations of Contemporary Africa.* Boulder, CO: Westview Press, 1986.

Sammy, Pierre. *Empire Centrafricaine: Géographie.* Paris: Hatier, 1977.

Strong, Polly. *African Tales: Folklore of the Central African Republic.* Mogadore, OH: Telcraft, 1992.

Vennetier, Pierre et al. *Atlas de la République Centrafricaine, Les Atlas Jeune Afrique.* Paris: Éditions Jeune Afrique, 1984.

Woodfork, Jacqueline. *Culture and Customs of the Central African Republic.* New York: Greenwood Press, 2005.

—revised by C. Breedlove

CHADIANS

PRONUNCIATION: CHAD-ee-uhns
LOCATION: Chad
POPULATION: 10.1 million
LANGUAGE: French, Arabic (official languages); more than 100 local languages
RELIGION: traditional African religion, Islam, Christianity
RELATED ARTICLES: Vol. 1: Fulani

¹ INTRODUCTION

The peoples of Chad possess a rich, ancient past dating to prehistoric times. If the mysterious Anasazis of the southwestern United States immortalized themselves in their 14th century rock art at Canyon de Chelly, so too have the unknown peoples of the northern Chadian desert (Ennedi Region), whose rock paintings date to 7,000 BC. This region's claim to be humanity's cradle recently was supported by linguistic research indicating that three of the four sub-Saharan language groups originated between Lake Chad and the Nile Valley. Many more discoveries undoubtedly will be made, because Chadian archeological sites of great potential remain unmapped and unexplored.

An era of empires marked the central Sahelian zone of Chad from around AD 900–1900. Their economic basis was the control of the trans-Saharan trade routes passing through the region. The survival of kingdoms depended on their ability to fight, which they did with cavalry. Two of the strongest and most durable of these were the Kanem-Borno and the Baguirmi and Wadai. The Kanem-Borno was situated to the northeast of Lake Chad and was formed from a confederation of nomadic peoples, who regarded their leaders as divine kings. The influence of Islam in the 10th century caused dissension and factionalism among those who saw the advantages of conversion and those who resisted in favor of their traditional beliefs. Strategically-spaced wells and oases favored the south-to-north trade of natron (sodium carbonate), cotton, kola nuts, ivory, ostrich feathers, perfume, wax, and hides, and foremost, slaves. From the north came salt, horses, silks, glass, muskets, and copper. The kingdom succumbed to invasions from eastern Sudan in the late 19th century.

The demise of Kanem-Borno coincided with the arrival of French dominance in the region, which was secured after considerable effort at the Battle of Kousseri in 1900. Chad was the lowest colonial priority for the French, and they made only halfhearted attempts to unify, administer, or develop it. In fact, the French ruled through sultanates in much of eastern Chad. In the south, where the French established missions and schools, the Sara peoples resisted forced labor, resettlements, and French-imposed prices for cotton. Under lieutenant-governor Félix Eboué, Chad supported the Free French under Charles de Gaulle in World War II. This act gave Chad greater, though still very limited, recognition and resources from France.

Since independence in 1960, ethnic, political, and religious factionalism, mainly between forces of the Muslim north against the Christian and animist south, has created much political and economic turmoil. Under authoritarian President Tombalbaye (1960–75), Chad experienced a general economic downturn and repressive government. Labor policies favored

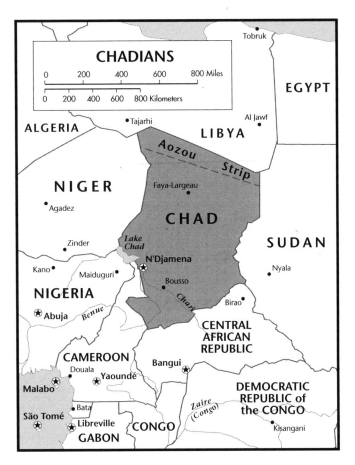

the more Westernized southerners, leading to ethnic conflict and rebellions in eastern and northern Chad. Mutineers killed Tombalbaye in 1975, which ushered in a period of civil war lasting until 1982. Two of the rebel leaders, Goukouni and Habré, came from competing Toubou clans in the north, and were bitter rivals. In 1980, under the transitional government of national unity (GUNT), units of five separate Chadian armies patrolled the capital of N'Djamena. Habré gained power in 1982, but his government was subjected to Libyan attacks in support of Goukouni. In 1990 a former military commander in chief, Idriss Déby, invaded from Sudan and took tenuous control, fending off several coup attempts and military insurrections. Lawlessness, strikes, and civil disorder have characterized the constitutional transition begun in 1992 and dragging on throughout 1994. In July 1996, Déby was elected president under the new constitution, and formed a government that included several opposition members.

In June 2005, a controversial national referendum removed constitutional term limits and paved the way for a third five-year term for Déby. Subsequently, Déby abolished the "future generations" provision in the oil law, which had been imposed by donors to set aside a percentage of oil revenues for future Chadians. Since 1998, Déby and his ethnic minority have continuously had to stave off rebellions, the most recent of which laid siege to the capital in early 2008.

2 LOCATION AND HOMELAND

Nation-building in this country of about 10.1 million has been complicated by factors of geography, religion, ethnicity, and linguistic differences in Chad's diverse population. Some 200 ethnic groups speak more than 100 distinct languages, which has enriched Chad culturally, but made the creation of a national identity and unity virtually impossible. The mainly Muslim populations of the north are nomadic or semisedentary herders and livestock breeders. The sedentary Sara groups in the south traditionally practice animism, but some have adopted Christianity. Population density is extremely low, from 0.15 per sq km in the Saharan zone, to 13 in the southern zone, where 45% of the total population lives. Only 22% of the population lives in towns and cities. N'Djamena, the capital, is by the far the largest city with a population estimated at 721,000 in 2005.

The colonial borders created a landlocked country, far from oceans and seas. Chad borders Libya to the north, Sudan to the east, the Central African Republic to the south, and Cameroon, Nigeria, and Niger to the west. With an area roughly equal to Idaho, Wyoming, Utah, Nevada, and Arizona combined, Chad stretches over 1,100 miles from north to south, and covers three climate and vegetation zones. Rainfall diminishes from 1,200 millimeters in the south to negligible amounts in the northern Sahara. In the middle lies a semidesert band called the Sahel, which has a long dry season and is subject to creeping desertification. Temperatures here regularly exceed 100°F in April and May, the hot season. From Lake Chad, an inland delta and the fourth-largest lake in Africa, the land gradually rises. Magnificent sand dunes cover the land in the north, and great, isolated piles of rocks interrupt the landscape in the eastern and southern regions. Oases with their date palms dot the northern desert. Mountain ranges cover stretches of the southwest, east, and far northwest. Emi Koussi, a dormant volcano, crowns the Sahara, reaching over 10,000 feet in elevation.

3 LANGUAGE

French and Arabic are Chad's official languages, but more than 100 local languages are spoken. These fall into 10 major groups belonging to three of Africa's four major language families. Chadian Arabic includes more than 30 dialects, which people throughout the country use to communicate with each other. For example, in a radius of 10 miles around Lake Fianga in the Mayo-Kebbi Region, people speak Toupouri, Moundang, and Fulfulde, which requires them to find a common language of communication.

4 FOLKLORE

Given the plethora of ethnic identities in Chad, it is difficult to name a specific national hero or myth without neglecting another. However, many Chadians revere Félix Eboué, in whose memory a magnificent monument in N'Djamena was erected. Many Chadians are familiar with the Sao, the earliest people known to have inhabited the region surrounding N'Djamena. Legends held that the Sao were giants possessing great strength. They could run long distances in just hours, and pull up trees like blades of grass. Sao women could lift huge ceramic granaries holding an entire year's harvest with a single hand. At independence, French history was parodied, when a famous speaker, André Malraux, supposedly declared, "Mister the President, the Saos are your Gauls."

⁵ RELIGION

In Chad, the religious and social spheres are closely intertwined. Nominally, Chadians profess one of three religious traditions: traditional African religion (35%), Islam (55%), or Christianity (10%). In fact, percentages can be misleading because religion seldom exists in pure form. Muslims and Christians tend to incorporate a number of traditional beliefs into their faiths.

Traditional religion, referred to as animism because all things are thought to have life force, focuses on ancestors and place, but is specific to ethnic group. In general, animism holds that a supreme being created the world, then retired from active intervention in it. In order to maintain harmony in the world, recently departed ancestors intervene between the living and their earliest forebears. When misfortune strikes, ritual acts that include prayers, sacrifices, and libations are performed in order to restore balance. Two examples illustrate this concept in Chad. Among the more centralized societies, such as the Moundang, rulers are associated with divine power and therefore intercede with supernatural forces to maintain equilibrium in society. The Mbaye, a Sara cultural group, believes that spirits inhabit places and natural phenomena such as water, lightning, and the sun. Because the sun spirit can render good or cause harm, it must be pacified. Diviners and sorcerers are thought to possess the ability to communicate with spirits, for good and evil purposes respectively.

Islam came to Chad well before the 1300s, and spread throughout the two northern tiers. Islam mixed with traditional African religion, but in some beliefs, Chadian Muslims are very strict. For example, during the holy month of Ramadan, Muslims fast and do not swallow their saliva from sunrise to sunset.

Catholic missionaries arrived in the 1920s and 1930s, and because of French and Italian political differences, the Vatican delayed establishment of a vicarate within Chad. Catholics are mostly concentrated around the Pala diocese in Mayo-Kebbi, whereas Protestants are spread more generally throughout the south.

⁶ MAJOR HOLIDAYS

Secular holidays such as Independence Day hold less interest in general for Chadians than Muslim and Christian holidays. Traditional holidays having to do with seasons and harvesting are festive occasions, too. For example, in the Mayo-Kebbi region, the millet harvest in September–November and the New Year in December are marked by the coming out of the Toupouri chief who, prior to that, is confined to his lodge for an entire month. In his royal dress, the chief marches slowly and regally, accompanied by dignitaries. Musicians playing long calabash horns salute him, as do dancers and a line of bare-breasted maidens. Afterwards, the local hosts serve a sumptuous meal of grilled goat meat, rice and stew, and *boule* to visitors who come from great distances (with cassette recorders and video cameras) to witness this annual event.

⁷ RITES OF PASSAGE

Knowledge of the world and its processes is passed to successive generations by males in Chad's predominantly patrimonial societies. The greatest transformation occurs from childhood to adulthood, and requires that children be prepared to assume social responsibilities. In the south, the Sara *yondo,* a male initiation ceremony, illustrates the significance of passage rites in Chadian society. Elders gather with boys in designated sites every six or seven years for several weeks during school vacations. Prior to Western schooling, the ritual lasted several months. During the initiation, the elders transfer authority. Having thus assumed manhood, the sons and brothers no longer associate with their mothers and sisters as before, and must eat and live separately. Similar ceremonies for girls teach them household responsibilities and respect for male authority.

⁸ INTERPERSONAL RELATIONS

As in other regions of Africa, greeting and leave-taking are important parts of human relations. Muslims exchange a series of greetings, asking about the other person's well-being, and that of his wife and family, too. After each exchange, one touches a hand to the breast to signal gratitude that it is so. It is an honor to receive visitors and customary to offer a glass of water if not something to eat as a sign of hospitality. In the dusty Sahel, hosts usually offer their visitors water to wash their faces, hands, and feet. In the south, visitors may find themselves welcomed by a large calabash of millet beer, which they must finish before leaving.

⁹ LIVING CONDITIONS

Chad ranks near the bottom (170th out of 177 countries) on the human development index (HDI), which measures living standards, education, and life expectancy. In 2008, life expectancy was estimated to be 47 years. Living conditions are very harsh and rudimentary in most rural areas of the country. Travel is difficult and precarious. In the desert-like regions, sand and dirt tracks crisscross in the thorn trees and scrub brush. Overloaded trucks, sometimes with flatbed trailers, move along these tracks at about 20 miles an hour, carrying passengers and goods to remote areas of the country. Trucks often bog down in mud holes during the rainy season. In 2008, Chad had only about 160 miles of paved roads in the entire country.

Medical care is spotty, especially in the northern zones, and patients must travel great distances for treatment. For lack of transportation or familiarity with modern medical care, many simply do not seek treatment in clinics or hospitals. Many Chadians depend on rain-fed agriculture, but civil war, successive droughts, and infestations of locusts render a large portion of the population food insecure. As a result of these factors, about 37% of children between 0–5 years old are underweight for their age. For every 10 children born, one dies in infancy.

In Sahelian towns, Chadian homes typically are built inside walled compounds and abut to the compound walls. Mud bricks held together with straw and camel dung are used to make the walls and the roofs. Houses consist of one or two rooms and are dark, with one or two small windows. Their primary use is for sleeping in the cooler and rainy seasons, and for storage of household belongings. Kitchen rooms are often separate, although meals often are cooked outside in the compound. In the hot dry season, Chadians sleep outdoors. People enjoy sitting under hangars made of reed mats hung upon tree limb frames. Dry pit latrines are typically located in the remotest corners of the compounds. Huts in small villages are round, and less permanent and consist of stick walls and thatched roofs. In the desert, nomads' homes may be no more than temporary frames covered with tarps.

The sun, heat, and blowing sand in the north require clothing that covers the entire body except for the face. Men often wear light cotton pants under white cotton robes, and a white or red-and-white scarf, which they wrap around their heads in the form of a turban.
(United Nations)

Throughout the Sahel, water must be drawn by ropes and rubber buckets from communal wells over 125 feet deep. In larger villages, water service may be available through local entrepreneurs. Donkeys carry several water buckets per trip in leather saddle bags, one on each side of the donkey's back. The bags open from the bottom to release the water into receptacles in the compound. Unfortunately, about 58% of the population lives without access to an improved water source. Untreated drinking water is a major source of disease and parasites afflicting children and adults.

10 FAMILY LIFE

In Chad, nomadic, semisedentary, and sedentary ways of life affect family life and structure. For example, the main social unit of the nomadic Toubou and Daza of the Sahara is the clan. However, individuals often live with people from other clans in groups of around 100 people. In Toubou families, one often finds a male head of household with one or two wives, the children, and a couple of relatives. Women participate in making decisions. In their husbands' absence they manage household operations, including changing pastures, moving tents, and cattle trading. Camps of families form and disband seasonally. Clan relatives are scattered over the region; therefore, individuals usually find kinsmen in most settlements. Families and clans influence, but do not overrule, individual preference for marriage partners. Marriages between blood relatives fewer than four generations apart are forbidden. By contrast, the semisedentary Arabs of the Sahel identify with the *kashimbet*, a unit composed of an elder male or group of males, their wives,

and descendants. Unlike the nomads, Arabs usually remain with their group of kin.

11 CLOTHING

Clothing styles vary according to climate zone and ethnic group. The sun, heat, and blowing sand in the north require clothing that covers the entire body except for the face. Men often wear light cotton pants under white cotton robes, and a white or red-and-white scarf, which they wrap around their heads in the form of a turban. Women wear robes that cover the entire body except face, hands, and feet. Boys wear simply cut cloth shirts and pants, while girls may wear cotton shirts with wraparound cloth skirts. Everyday clothing becomes extremely worn from hard use and washing. Many nomads and Arabs wear sandals or go barefoot. In the south, people dress like Central Africans in colorful cotton print shirts and pants for men, and wraparound skirts and tailored shirts for women. Chadian cotton is renowned for its long strands of high quality and can be bought from the local factory.

Chadian women adorn themselves with interesting jewelry. Toubou women wear silver nose rings, while Arab women wear copper and bronze wrist and ankle bracelets, and heavy earrings that cause large openings in the lobes. Many ethnic groups distinguish themselves with decorative facial and body tattoos. Women commonly wear leather amulets to ward off evil spirits. Others wear necklaces containing colonial coins. Among the older Toupouri and Massa women in the south, one finds lip adornments. These are metal or wood plugs that pierce the upper and lower lips to indicate marital status.

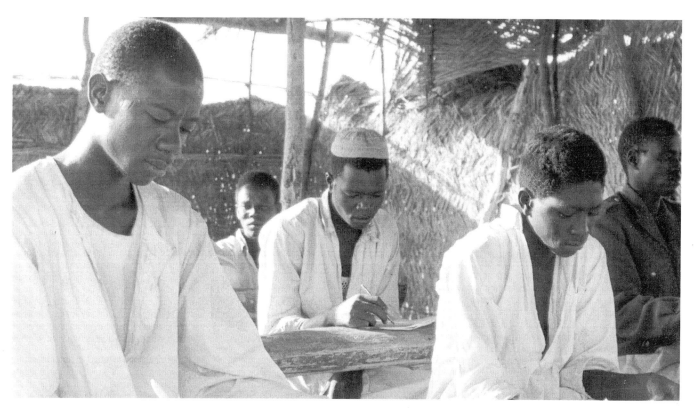

Students studying to be instructors at Koukou Angarana in Bahr Azoum, Chad. To get a diploma, students must pass a state exam that has a 36% pass rate. Future elementary-school teachers take four years of general subjects, followed by two years of teacher training. (International Labour Office)

12 FOOD

Despite the harsh climate, Chadians grow a large variety of food. The staples are sorghum and millet. They are harvested and stored in huge ceramic or round thatched granaries, with conical thatched roofs, raised a few feet above the ground. The grains are put to versatile culinary uses, including the noon-day meal. The millet is pounded to flour by using a mortar and pestle. Often two girls will share the task, taking alternating strokes. From the flour they make a round, ball-like dough (*boule*) by adding boiling water. It is similar to *gozo* in the Central African Republic and *fufu* in the Democratic Republic of the Congo and is eaten with the right hand. In the Sahel, Chadians are fond of okra and meat sauce. Sauces are flavored with onions, tomatoes, garlic, salt, and hot pepper. Men and women typically eat separately, and men are served first. Millet also makes a delicious porridge, which is sweetened and eaten to break the fast during Ramadan. A fermented version of millet (*bili-bili*) is the most popular item on market days in the south. It is served from large calabash gourds and poured into calabash bowls. The sudsy brew has a sour, smokey flavor. Calabashes must be emptied completely before the drinkers retire. As proof that no beer remains, the calabash is tipped over on its side.

Chadians supplement their diets with many other foods such as squash, beans, peanuts, sesame seeds, and cucumbers. In the north, fruits include limes and dates, whereas one finds guavas, bananas, and mangoes in the south. Travelers find grilled goat meat with dried hot pepper, and freshly squeezed lime at "truck stop" eateries in Sahelian roadside villages. It is especially delicious when fresh-baked French bread is available. Chadians also enjoy many kinds of fish. Huge river perch, known as *capitain*, are taken from the Chari and Logone Rivers. They are so named because French officers always demanded the largest of the catch, so naturally they went to the captain.

13 EDUCATION

Formal Western schooling only recently came to Chad. Protestant missions began establishing primary schools in the 1920s, followed by Roman Catholic and state schools. Until 1942 Chadian children had to go to Brazzaville (Congo) to attend high school. Nowadays, primary school is compulsory, although only one in four children actually attends. There are far more elementary and high schools in the south than in the north. Students who make it to high school attend either a four-year program (*collége*) or a seven-year program (*lycée*). To get a diploma, students must pass a state exam, the bac, which has a 36% pass rate. Future elementary-school teachers take four years of general subjects, followed by two years of teacher training.

Ten years after independence, Chad opened its first university for the 1971–72 academic year. In 1983–84, the university had an enrollment of 1,643 students with 141 teachers. Unfortunately, civil war disrupted education at all levels, and university archives were looted during battles in N'Djamena in 1979 and 1980. Besides the effects of the war, limited financing, overcrowding, and the classical French curriculum have made it difficult for Chadian children to excel in school. Model schools now are switching to teaching French as a foreign language. A surprising statistic is that despite a combined primary, secondary, and tertiary enrollment of only 37.5%, almost half of the population can read and write in French or Arabic. This result may be attributed to high attendance at Quranic schools where children learn basic Arabic and recite the Quran.

14 CULTURAL HERITAGE

Many Chadians express their cultural heritage through ceremonial dress, music, and dance, which link the material and supernatural worlds. The Chadian national folkloric ballet is particularly famous. Chadian craftsmen produce instruments of extremely high quality using materials such as wood, animal gut and horns, and calabashes. Among the principle instruments are tam-tams, pottery drums, goat-horn whistles and flutes, and gourd-calabash horns. The latter often are stained, burned with intricate designs, and decorated with animal hair. Chadians also excel at making five-stringed harps and *balafons*, which are similar to xylophones, and consist of a several resonant wood bars, each sized and sculpted to give the desired pitch, and lashed to a frame. Beneath the wood keys are gourds, which amplify the sound. Village headmen still maintain specially designed drums in their compounds, used to send urgent messages, such as announcing the death of an important person, to the people of the local and neighboring communities.

15 WORK

By world standards, Chad is one of the most undeveloped countries. More than 80% of Chadians are engaged in subsistence farming, herding, and fishing. Prior to exporting oil, cotton, the biggest cash crop, provided more than 50% of the country's foreign earnings. Most industrial jobs are found in light industries including textiles, meatpacking, beer brewing, and the manufacture of natron, soap, cigarettes, and construction materials. In late 2003, ExxonMobil's consortium began pumping oil in the southern region of Eastern Logone via a 650-mile pipeline through Cameroon to the port of Kribi on the Gulf of Guinea. But owing to corruption and diversion of proceeds to arms instead of infrastructure, Chadians have yet to benefit from the jobs and economic growth that the oil boom was expected to generate. In the foreseeable future, Chadians likely will continue to make their livelihoods mainly in the subsistence sector.

16 SPORTS

Coping with natural hazards and political upheaval has not given Chadians much time for recreational sports. While hunting and fishing may provide leisure sport activity for foreigners, Chadians hunt and fish out of necessity. Children and young people do play organized soccer, European handball, and basketball. In the cities, soccer club teams compete with one another, and the game is played wherever space permits. Apart from these, horse racing is practiced in makeshift hippodromes in the Sahel, northeast of N'Djamena. Arabs and certain other groups are excellent riders, have fine race horses, and organize races each Sunday throughout the dry season.

17 ENTERTAINMENT AND RECREATION

In contrast to American teenagers, most Chadian young people never have gone to the movies or watched a movie on a video cassette recorder or DVD player. Many have never seen television. In 2008 there were only six radio stations and one (government) television station in the country. The total number of Internet users was well under 100,000. It is safe to say that with the exception of a small urban elite, Chad remains one of the few places in the world insulated from American and Western pop culture. To the extent that Chadian entertainment exists, it consists of social and cultural events and ceremonies, which include dancing, drumming, and musical performance (see **Cultural heritage**).

18 FOLK ART, CRAFTS, AND HOBBIES

Traditional folk art in Chad serves aesthetic as well as functional purposes and has a long history dating to the iron age. Artists and craftsmen belong to castes, which are select groups of people who once married only among themselves. They have learned, mastered, and passed on the traditions and techniques of their manual craft to sons and daughters. In ancient times, a mystical, religious quality characterized blacksmithing. Kings wanted to monopolize the magical process of producing weapons such as arrow tips, spears, and daggers. They also recognized the usefulness of iron household, farming, and hunting tools such as knives and hoes. Having descended from this heritage, Chadian artists still produce a wide range of articles of genuine artistic merit and practical utility. These include musical instruments, masks, jewelry, ceramic pots, and bronze statuettes and figurines. Craftspeople spin cotton fabrics and weave strips of cloth that are sewn together to make durable garments. They also fashion leather goods from sandals to amulets. Of particular note are the practical and attractive gourds and pyroengraved calabashes, whose designs can be traced to ancient Babylonia. The gourds serve as kitchen utensils, measures, and food and drink receptacles.

19 SOCIAL PROBLEMS

Chadians have endured political anarchy, lawlessness, rebellions, and civil war since independence. They now live with the oil resource curse. In 2005, Transparency International ranked Chad along with Bangladesh as the world's most corrupt country. The southern oil fields produce more than 160,000 barrels of oil a day, yet four out of five Chadians live below the poverty line (less than $2/day).

In addition to coping with poverty, Chadians along the eastern border with Sudan have been subjected to cross-border raids. Refugee children are recruited to fight in rebel groups from both Chad and Sudan, and some 200,000 internally displaced people have been forcibly moved several times owing to inter-ethnic attacks. The violence and disruption have increased the number of orphans and caused additional stress on caregivers. The hosting of some 230,000 refugees from Darfur and more than 40,000 refugees from Central African Republic also has increased pressure on land and local communities, speeding the pace of environmental degradation. Competition with local people for wood, water, grazing land, and goods and services has led to anti-refugee sentiment. Prostitution has become particularly rampant in the southern Dabo oil fields area.

[20] GENDER ISSUES

While the law prohibits discrimination based on gender, and prohibits rape, prostitution, and domestic violence against women, Chadian customary law and society inherently favors men. Wives traditionally have been considered property of their husbands, and have limited recourse to justice under the law. Husbands may also at any time enter into a polygynous relationship without their wives' consent. Although the first wife has the right to request that her marriage be dissolved, she must pay back the brideprice and other marriage costs. While French code provides for the right of women to own and inherit property, in practice most inheritance cases are adjudicated in favor of men. In rural areas women do most of the agricultural labor, household chores, raise the children, and enjoy little free time. Gender bias will continue to be an issue in the future as only 31% as many females as males are literate, and only 60% as many females as males attend primary, secondary, and tertiary schools.

[21] BIBLIOGRAPHY

Africa South of the Sahara 2007. "Chad." London: Europa Publishers, 2008.

Chad: The True Picture. Boulogne: Editions Delroisse, n.d.

Chapelle, Jean. *Le Peuple Tchadien: Ses Racines, sa vie quotidienne et ses Combats.* Paris: L'Harmattan, 1980.

Decalo, Samuel. *Historical Dictionary of Chad.* 3rd edition. Lanham, MD: The Scarecrow Press, Inc., 1997.

Tubiana, Joseph, Claude Arditi, and Claude Pairault, ed. *L'Identité Tchadienne: L'heritage des Peuples et les Apports extérieurs.* Paris: Editions L'Harmattan, 1994.

U.S. Department of the Army. Federal Research Division, Library of Congress. *Chad: A Country Study.* 2nd ed., Edited by Thomas Collelo. Area Handbook Series. Washington, DC: 1990.

—by R. Groelsema and M. C. Groelsema

CHAGGA

PRONUNCIATION: CHAH-guh
ALTERNATE NAMES: Chaga, Waschagga, Jagga, or Dschagga
LOCATION: Kilimanjaro region in northern Tanzania
POPULATION: 1,500,000
LANGUAGE: Kichagga, Swahili
RELIGION: Christianity, Islam
RELATED ARTICLES: Vol. 1: Tanzanians

[1] INTRODUCTION

On the southern slopes of Mt. Kilimanjaro, Africa's highest mountain, live the Chagga people, also called Chaga, Waschagga, Jagga, or Dschagga. Administratively, the area lies in the Kilimanjaro region in northern Tanzania, south of the border with Kenya. The region is further divided into three districts—Hai to the west, Rombo to the east, and Vunjo in the center.

Traditionally the Chagga people belonged to different clan groups ruled by *mangis* (chiefs). Examples of clan group names include *Moshi, Swai, Marealle, Lvimo,* and *Mrema.* The area was thus divided into independent chiefdoms. The chiefs were known to wage wars against each other and at times to form alliances between themselves in their struggle for power. Thus, the number of chiefdoms declined over the years. By 1968, there existed 17 chiefdoms, namely Machame, Kibosho, Mamba, Mwika, Kibongoto, Uru, Usseri, Kirua Vunjo, Mkuu, Marangu, Mashati, Arusha Chini, Masama, Kahe, Old Moshi, Kilema, and Keni-Mriti-Mwengwe. The chiefdoms were further divided into subunits called *mitaa.*

After independence, through Nyerere's socialism and integration policies, the rule of Chiefs was diminished and later the system of chiefdoms was abolished in Tanzania. Tanzania obtained independence in December 1961 and Julius Kambarage Nyerere (1922–1999), a socialist leader who led Tanganyika from colonial rule, was elected president in 1962. One of Africa's most respected figures, Julius Nyerere was a politician of principle and intelligence. Known as Mwalimu (teacher), he had a vision of education that was rich with possibility. Nyerere voluntarily relinquished power in 1985, but the legacy of his nation building efforts can be found throughout the country. Beginning in the mid-1980s, under the administration of President Ali Hassan Mwinyi, Tanzania undertook a number of political and economic reforms. In January and February 1992, the government decided to adopt multiparty democracy from single party rule. Legal and constitutional changes led to the registration of 11 political parties. Two parliamentary by-elections (won by the ruling Chama Cha Mapinduzi [CCM] party) in early 1994 were the first-ever multiparty elections in Tanzanian history. In October 2000 Tanzania held its second multi-party general elections. The ruling CCM party's candidate, Benjamin W. Mkapa, defeated his three main rivals, winning the presidential election with 71% of the vote. In 2005 Benjamin Mkapa retired after 10 years in power. During the elections of December 2005 ruling party candidate Jakaya Kikwete was elected president by a decisive margin.

[2] LOCATION AND HOMELAND

Mount Kilimanjaro has two peaks. Kibo is the main snow-capped peak. Mawenzi is the jagged second peak connected to

Kibo by a saddle. Vegetation on the mountain is varied. The lowest plains form the bushland, and maize, thatch grass, and fodder are grown there. Next lies the coffee and banana belt, where the Chagga have their homesteads. The Chagga people do not live in villages in the rural areas. Instead, each family has its own homestead in the middle of a banana grove. This is known as a *kihamba* (plural *vihamba*). Household plots are next to those of the same clan. With increased population density and division of land holdings, there are hardly any unoccupied areas between the various lineage territories.

The Chagga population has risen steadily from 128,000 in 1921 to 832,420 in 1988 to 1.5 million people in 2003. Overpopulation has forced some Chagga people to move to the lowlands and migrate to urban areas such as Dar es Salaam and Arusha.

³ LANGUAGE

The main language spoken by the Chagga people is Kichagga, which differs in dialect between the different Chagga regions. Despite these differences in dialect, the Chagga people can understand one another. The dialectic differences help an individual detect which region another person is from.

Almost all Chagga people also speak Swahili, the national language in Tanzania. Swahili is the medium of instruction in primary schools and is used in the workplace. English is the medium of instruction in secondary schools and institutions of higher learning. Those persons fortunate enough to obtain advanced education have some understanding of English.

⁴ FOLKLORE

Chagga legends center on *Ruwa* and his power and assistance. Ruwa is the Chagga name for their god, as well as the Chagga word for "sun." Ruwa is not looked upon as the creator of humankind, but rather as a liberator and provider of sustenance. He is known for his mercy and tolerance when sought by his people. He has provided bananas, sweet potatoes, and yams. Some Chagga myths concerning Ruwa resemble biblical stories of the Old Testament.

The various chiefdoms have chiefs who have risen to power through war and trading. Some famous past chiefs include Orombo from Kishigonyi, Sina of Kibosho, and Marealle of Marangu.

⁵ RELIGION

Christianity was introduced to the Chagga people about the middle of the 19th century. By the end of the 19th century, both Protestants and Catholics had established missions in the region. Today those regions where the Catholics had established themselves, such as Kilema and Kibosho, are predominantly Catholic, and those regions where Protestants were established, such as Machame, are mainly Protestant. The Christian influence spread both through preaching and through the provision of education. With the adoption of Western religions, traditional Chagga beliefs and practices have been reduced and synchronized to the new Christian beliefs. Prayer books and hymnals have been translated into Kichagga.

Islam was introduced to the Chagga people by early Swahili caravan traders. Islam brought a sense of fellowship not only with the Chagga of different regions, but also with Muslims of other ethnic groups.

⁶ MAJOR HOLIDAYS

Major holidays celebrated by the Chagga people are both secular and religious. The main government holidays presently celebrated are New Year's Day (January 1), Union Day (April 26), Workers Day (May 1), Peasants Day (August 8), and Independence Day (December 9). On government holidays, the public rests and offices and shops are closed. Government rallies are held around the country, with military parades and speeches made by government officials.

The major religious holidays of both Christianity and Islam are celebrated. The major Christian holidays are Easter weekend and Christmas. The major Muslim holidays are *Id-el-Fitre*, *Id-el-Hajji*, and *Maulid*. Religious holidays are a time when family members make an effort to gather. People in urban areas try during these times to visit the rural areas for family gatherings. After the religious ceremonies are over, families gather for celebration and merrymaking. They feast on goat, chickens, and cattle, and drink both local and traditional brews.

⁷ RITES OF PASSAGE

For the Chagga, dying without children means the end of the lineage. A Chagga proverb—"He who leaves a child lives eternally"—illustrates the Chagga belief that people live through their descendents. It is used as a blessing or in congratulation on the birth of a child. After the birth of a child, a Chagga mother remains inactive and indoors for three months, during which time she is taken care of by her husband and in-laws. It is the duty of a woman's husband and family to supply her with milk, fat, blood, and other nourishing food. After three months, a mother may appear in public and resume normal life.

A child may be considered unlucky for several reasons. If a child cut its upper teeth first, it is considered unlucky. A child conceived too soon after the death of another child is also considered unlucky, as are twins. In the past, an unlucky male child was killed; an unlucky female child and her mother were returned to the woman's parents.

Children are taught to do small chores around the homestead as soon as they can walk. Girls' duties include grinding corn and cleaning out cattle stalls. The boys' main duty is to herd cattle. A rite called *Kisusa* is carried out when a child is about 12 years old. This rite is performed to curb unruliness in a child. The youth's relatives attend the ceremony, which is conducted by a female elder and a young man who has already undergone the rite. A goat is slaughtered and divided into portions for consumption and sacrifice. The elder woman and initiated youth sing songs of good morals and talk to the initiate about good behavior. For a month, the youth's behavior is closely watched, and he is often corrected. When the elder woman is satisfied with the initiate's behavior, friends and relatives are invited for a purification ceremony of singing and offering prayers to the ancestors. The same ceremony is repeated a month later.

In the past, both young men and young women were circumcised. *Maseka* is the term used for uncircumcised boys. There was a general circumcision that would take place corresponding with the circumcision of the chief's son. There was no particular age for circumcision, but youth were generally circumcised during the cooler months from June to August. The circumcised youth are called *Mangati*, and they now form a *rika* (generation group) and are given a name referring to the specific circumcision age group. Examples of *rikas* include *Kimakamaka* (youth), *Mbarinoti* (elders), and *Merisho* (old men). The age classes ended with the German occupation of Tanzania. The circumcision of boys now usually takes place in a hospital, where the conditions are more sterile. Female circumcision is now discouraged.

Traditionally, before young males were allowed to marry, the *Ngasi*, or initiation ceremony, took place. The youth would reside in the forest to keep the initiation process a secret from young women and children. There the youth received instruction on manhood, went hunting and endured various ordeals, especially the cold weather. The female equivalent of the initiation ceremony was called *Shija* and was performed after the young women were circumcised. All initiated young women underwent two months of instruction together in a banana grove, returning to their homes at dusk each day. They were instructed in Chagga rituals, sexuality, procreation, and menstruation. Initiation ceremonies no longer take place, as they were abolished by the Germans.

At death, the old Chagga custom was to bury only those corpses of married persons in huts. Husbands were buried inside their senior wives' huts, under the milk store. After viewing in the cattle stall, the corpse is buried seated or lying facing Kibo (Mount Kilimanjaro). Relatives were chosen to keep watch over the grave until the ceremony of shaving took place. Family members usually shaved their heads on the third day after burial. This was followed by the distribution of the deceased's property. About two years after the burial, amid ceremony, the bones were removed from the hut and moved to a sacred spot in the banana grove. It was against Chagga law to bury childless persons, unmarried persons, and children. Childless adults were deposited in the bush with their belongings. Youth and children were placed in the banana grove. The banana grove is viewed by the Chagga people as the family graveyard. Currently all corpses are buried according to either Christian or Muslim rituals. Wealthier Chagga living in the urban areas may decide to transport a corpse back to the homestead for burial. Most families wear black or drab clothing as a sign of mourning.

8 INTERPERSONAL RELATIONS

Greetings are important in Chagga culture. There are different greetings depending upon the time of day. The Machame may greet each other in the morning with *nesindisa,* while the Kibosho use *shimboni.* Greetings are exchanged before any other exchange of words or actions. When joining a group of people, it is customary to greet each person in the group. Elders are usually greeted first by the younger generation; younger people are required to show respect to the older generations. It is believed that the more senior a person is, the closer his or her contact with ancestors. Even when passing a person on the road, greetings are exchanged inquiring after one's journey, with the visitors usually initiating the greetings.

Specific behavioral norms are maintained between various persons in Chagga society. These are based on a show of respect, non-hostility, or distance. A newlywed woman would cover her head and squat in the presence of her father-in-law, thereby showing respect to and distance from him. The father-in-law is similarly required to avoid the daughter-in-law. A friendship ritual is held after the birth of a first child to remove some conditionalities of behavior between the in-laws. A wife

is required to always face her husband on approach lest she be accused of cursing him.

Relationships between men and women were based on social segregation. Publicly, male and female couples do not hold hands. Public show of affection through bodily contact is considered highly inappropriate between the sexes. It is considered acceptable, however, for male companions and female companions to hold hands out of affectionate camaraderie. Traditionally, men and women were socially segregated. Couples did not eat together at home; mothers usually ate with their children, while the father ate by himself. At social gatherings, men and women kept to themselves in separate clusters. Currently, men and women still sit separately at social functions and even in churches.

During celebrations, guests generally drink and dance in separate groups, according to generation. The older, married people make one group, while the younger people make up the other. This is because the older group may get quite rowdy. They prefer to be able to speak freely among themselves without having to worry whether the conversation is appropriate for the younger generation. Married couples, especially of the younger generation, may eat and socialize together at smaller gatherings.

When visiting, one is expected to arrive with a gift for the host family. A visitor staying for some time is expected to help with the family work. Visiting family and friends usually takes place during the late afternoon hours when most of the farm work is done. If a visitor arrives at mealtimes, he or she is invited to partake of the meal. It is considered an insult to refuse; one must at least pretend to eat a little. When departing, a visitor is escorted part of the way by the host and family. Even in urban areas, a visitor may drop in anytime and is always warmly welcomed.

9 LIVING CONDITIONS

The traditional Chagga house was conical and grass-thatched. Alternatively, a flatter, curved, banana-leaf-roofed house could be built. Because these houses tended to be large, up to 7.5 meters (25 feet) round and over 6 meters (20 feet) high, they were built with the assistance of other villagers. The doorway formed the only opening in the house's walls.

By the end of the 19th century, Swahili houses were introduced, initially constructed by chiefs. These houses were rectangular, with walls made of wattle (interwoven sticks) and mud, and thatched roofs. Today, these houses are more commonly built with cement walls and corrugated metal roofs. Wealthier Chagga families have built elaborate houses on their property.

The infrastructure in the region is more developed than in most other regions in Tanzania. The major roads are either tarmacked or all-season dirt roads. Buses transport villagers daily to and from Moshi town and other regional locations. Wealthier individuals may even own small trucks and pickups. These provide rides to villagers who may agree to ride in the back in exchange for a small fare. Most villagers, though, prefer to walk when visiting neighboring areas and villages. Piped water is provided through village taps and water pumps. Electricity is provided throughout the Kilimanjaro region at low cost from the 'Nyumba ya Mungu' dam. Phone lines may be seen crisscrossing the area, providing this service to those able to afford it. Many villagers have access to such facilities. Today, the landlines are being replaced by the ever proliferating cell phone.

The Chagga people are adapting to modern life within a rural setting. Their child mortality rate has fallen due to access to mother and child health services, health education, and immunization services. Small health facilities are available in rural areas, with larger hospital facilities in urban areas.

¹⁰ FAMILY LIFE

Traditionally, the Chagga marriage ceremony was a long process, starting with the initiation of betrothal proceedings and continuing long after the couple was married. In the past, parents initiated their children's betrothal, subject to the children's agreement. The groom assured himself that the bride consented to the marriage by inviting her and her friends to visit him. A married male relative of the groom was chosen to be the *mkara,* the person who oversaw the marriage transactions and the marriage itself. This man and his wife, also called a *mkara,* were like the best man and matron of honor to the couple. In times of marital conflict, they became mediators and advisors to the couple. Bridal payments were made over the wife's lifetime.

Today, Christian couples are married in churches. In Christian weddings, the young woman is brought to the church by her family and friends, and there she meets the groom. Following the ceremony is a reception given by the groom's family. Later, the couple may leave for a short honeymoon if they reside in an urban area. In rural areas, the couple leaves for the father-in-law's homestead, where a second celebration will take place a few days later. Throughout the marriage negotiations and celebrations, there is much drinking and feasting.

The groom is required to build his own house in which the couple lives together after marriage. After the birth of the first child, the husband moves into a *tenge* (hut), and the mother lives with her children.

Due to the Christian influence, marriages are now often monogamous. Chagga couples have an average of six children. Great importance is placed on having a son to continue the linage. The first male child and female child are considered to be of the father's side and are named accordingly. The second male child and female child are considered to be of the mother's side and are also named accordingly, and so on with the other children.

Chagga families sometimes keep dogs and cats, but they are not inclined to keep other kinds of animals.

¹¹ CLOTHING

Traditionally, Chagga clothing was made of cowhide. With contact with the outside world, the Chagga started to wear imported bead ornaments and imported cloth wraparound garments. These colorful pieces of cloth are used as wrappers around the body and are called *kangas* and *kitenges*. The cloths may be worn over a dress, or may be used to carry babies on the back or hip. Women may purchase cloth from the marketplace or shops and sew their dresses and skirts. Men may also purchase cloth and take it to a tailor to make trousers or a shirt. Elder women still prefer to wrap long cloths over their clothes.

Women and girls do not wear short clothes in public except during sports. Men generally do not wear shorts in public either. Shorts are considered for sports and schoolboys. Sec-

ondhand clothing from overseas *(mitumba)* is sold at the marketplace and is in great demand by the low-income people.

¹² FOOD

The staple food of the Chagga people is bananas. It is also their main source of drink; they produce beer with the addition of eleusive, a grain. The Chagga plant a variety of food crops, including a variety of bananas, millet, maize (corn), beans, and cassava. They also keep cattle for meat and milk, as well as goats and sheep. Due to limited land holdings and grazing areas, most Chagga people today are forced to purchase meat from butcher shops.

Pregnant women are fed on milk, sweet potatoes, fat, yams, and butter; these are considered female foods. Bananas and beer are considered male and not to be eaten by pregnant women. During the three months after delivery, a lactating mother is fed with a special dish made up of blood and butter, called *mlaso. Kitawa,* a special dish of bananas and beans is also prepared for her. *Mtori,* a soup dish prepared from bananas and meat, has spread in popularity in other parts of Tanzania.

¹³ EDUCATION

The initial classroom education available to the Chagga was in the Christian missions. Many Chagga wished for their children to receive this education and paid for it through the sale of their coffee crop. Chagga who could obtain some training rose in status in their local areas. Boys often outnumbered girls in the education facilities, because education was not considered as important for girls as for boys. Many parents also believed that it was a waste of money to educate daughters who would move to other households at marriage.

After Tanzania's independence, all Chagga people were encouraged to attend at least primary level education. By 1971 primary education was provided free by the government, and all children seven years of age and older were required to attend primary level education for at least seven years. This was followed by four years of secondary education for those who passed the national examination at the end of the first seven years. Today many private secondary schools are available in the Kilimanjaro region, providing an alternative for those not lucky enough to continue in government schools. There are also alternative trade and business schools for those students wishing to acquire skills.

Older people are involved in adult literacy programs. Many Chagga can read and write Swahili or Chagga.

¹⁴ CULTURAL HERITAGE

Wooden flutes, bells, and drums make up traditional Chagga instruments. Dancing and singing are part of almost every celebration. The Chagga have different types of dances depending on the occasion. *Rosi,* the war dance, is performed by males only. The *irirui* dance was danced by everyone at various occasions. With exposure to other ethnic groups and Western culture, the Chagga have shown a liking for various types of music. Swahili songs produced by various Tanzanian bands may be heard frequently over the airwaves in public places such as shops and buses. West and Central African music and dance forms are also gaining in popularity, and it is not uncommon to hear such songs at celebrations such as wedding feasts. Western music and dance such as reggae, pop, and rap are also popular with the youth.

The Chagga have rich oral traditions and have managed to record most of their history. They have many legends and songs, and proverbs are used to guide youth and convey wisdom. "A snail cannot destroy the grove," for example, refers to the fact that a person should aid others in distress without fear of being harmed.

15 WORK

Traditionally, Chagga work has been centered on the farm and is divided into men's work and women's work. Men's work includes feeding goats, building and maintaining canals, preparing fields, slaughtering animals, and building houses. Women's work includes firewood and water collection, fodder cutting, cooking, and cleaning of the homestead and stalls. Women are also in charge of trading in the marketplace.

In Kilimanjaro, coffee is still the principal cash crop. With ever diminishing land holdings, Chagga men are forced to seek employment in the urban areas. The wife is usually left to tend the homestead and children, and her husband visits only periodically. Eventually, his wife and family may join him in the urban area.

The more educated a person is, the better his or her chances of finding employment. Many Chagga young people work as clerks, teachers, and administrators, and many engage in small-scale business activities. Quite a few shop owners and street corner vendors all over the country are Chagga. The Chagga are known for their sense of enterprise and strong work ethic.

Women in rural areas are also forming income-generating groups involved in activities such as crafts and tailoring. These groups—promoted by churches, government agencies, non-governmental organizations, donor agencies, and political parties—help to increase their members' respectability and prestige in their communities. The groups offer an additional source of income for women outside their farming activities.

16 SPORTS

Chagga children first encounter sporting events at school. Primary school children are encouraged to participate in inter-school competitions that often lead to inter-regional and national championships. Favorite sports at school are soccer, netball, and athletics. At secondary schools, Chagga youth may be exposed to more sports such as basketball, table tennis, and volleyball.

Following the national soccer league is a national pastime greatly enjoyed by the Chagga. On the weekends, proper and makeshift soccer fields are crowded with both spectators and players alike.

17 ENTERTAINMENT AND RECREATION

For many years there were no television stations in Tanzania, so radio broadcasts were a major source of entertainment. Many households have transistor radios, and a favorite pastime is listening to radio plays and sports programs. On occasions of major broadcasts and matches, the Chagga often gather around a radio in a public meeting place, usually with a local brew on hand.

In the past, only the wealthy Chagga could afford television sets. They would tune in programs broadcast by neighboring Kenyan stations. Now many Chagga people own televisions and VCRs. This has led to the opening of many video lending libraries in the town of Moshi. Action movies are the most popular. On weekends, some public meeting places offer video shows for a small fee.

18 FOLK ART, CRAFTS, AND HOBBIES

Traditionally, the Chagga made their own utensils, mainly from wood. These items included small bowls, huge beer tubs, spoons, and ladles. Iron items included bells, ornaments, hoes, and spears. The Chagga made their own weapons and animal traps. Chagga musical instruments include wooden flutes, bells, and drums. Basket weaving was also common, although this art is now dying out as more items are bought at local stores.

19 SOCIAL PROBLEMS

Like other Tanzanians, the Chagga face the problem of declining standards of living. Tanzania has faced a period of economic hardship that has severely affected the government's ability to provide adequate social services. Schools and health facilities are run down, which affects the quality of service provided. It is not uncommon to find children sitting on a school floor, and hospitalized patients without medicine. The government has been forced to charge nominal fees for some services that were once free; it has also encouraged the establishment of private facilities to provide similar services. In response, many private schools and health facilities have opened in the Kilimanjaro region. The region now has the highest number of private secondary schools in Tanzania, attracting students from around the country.

Lack of adequate farm land is forcing Chagga youth to seek work away from the *kihamba*. Many are now involved in business and trading, which takes them out of the region to places such as Dar es Salaam, Mwanza, and even into Kenya. Sellers come to local markets such as Ndishi with goods such as cooking oil, soap, and sandals. Other traders transport goods such as bananas to outside markets. All this upheaval has led to a breakdown in social values and an increase in sexual promiscuity. This in turn has brought about an increase in the number of children born out of wedlock and an increase in sexually transmitted diseases, especially AIDS. The increase in AIDS cases is believed to be related to this migration to urban areas. AIDS awareness programs have been initiated to help deal with the problem.

Loss of Chagga culture is another consequence of outside contact. Some youth are dropping their Chagga names, and are using Christian or Muslim names that hide their cultural identity. Intermarriage with other tribal groups is causing the Chagga to bury their cultural identity and adopt a more generalized Tanzanian one that is easily influenced by Western cultures.

The political scene has changed in Tanzania from a single party in 1965 to multi-party politics in 1992. This has encouraged more Chagga to be politically active by forming and joining new political parties. There is an increasing cohesion of the Chagga people along party lines and a renewed sense of cultural identity. However, multi-party politics are still in their infancy, and it is hoped that the country can steer clear of the political confrontation that has plagued neighboring countries.

[20] GENDER ISSUES

In Tanzania, as in many other African countries, women seeking more rights and gender equity face problems created by traditions and customary laws which often discriminate, oppress, and exploit women. Most often women are deprived of their rights to education, information, technology, the means of production such as land, as well as owning property even where the constitution and some laws provide room for gender equality. In Tanzania for example, inheritance laws marginalize women and girls where women are often seen as less equal in status and stature than men. Most institutions and organizations are structured hierarchically and dominated by males. Women's specific needs and interests are often taken less seriously with little regard for gender equality in spite of the constitution guaranteeing such rights for everyone irrespective of gender. It is in this context that we need to understand and place the rights of women in Chagga society.

In the present-day modernizing cultural context, Chagga women have slowly begun to change their roles in society. The increasing participation of Chagga females in modern secondary school and higher education has resulted in dramatic changes with regard to Chagga women's participation in cultural, social, and economic activities. A common saying among educated Chagga women is "education is my husband." An educated Chagga woman empowered with her western style education might go on to have children without marrying. She can have a modern job as a secretary or a bank clerk to sustain her household without a man being present. Even in traditional Chagga society, married women maintain close ties with their natal families and have a reputation for being strong-willed and stubborn and having "excessive power." There is no question that the growing power Chagga women enjoy in the modern world is a direct result of their schooling, which is used as cultural capital. Today more than half of the graduates of local secondary schools in Chaggaland are girls and a disproportionate number of Chagga women are found in national universities. Thus modern education has become a form of female inheritance, bestowing upon them independence from the male dominated culture. In short, Chagga women have shown that in modernizing society, it is possible for women to wield some power through education, a factor which opens the door to female empowerment.

With reference to homosexuality, sexual acts between males are illegal in Tanzania. Sections 154 to 157 of the Tanzanian penal code criminalize sexual relationships between men. The penalty for a person who is convicted with this offence is a maximum sentence of 14 years in prison. Sexual acts between women are not mentioned in the penal code. This does not mean that female homosexuality was unknown when the laws were enacted. Rather, that it was not considered a threat to society and was thus largely accepted and tolerated. The penal code is applicable on the Tanzanian mainland but not on the semi-autonomous island of Zanzibar. In 2004 Zanzibar enacted a law criminalizing female homosexual acts. In Zanzibar, sexual acts between women are punishable by a maximum prison term of five years; the same prison term also applies to gay men. Gays or lesbians who celebrate their union in a manner that approximates a marriage ceremony or who live together as spouses in Zanzibar can be subjected to seven years imprisonment if convicted. However, with more activism it is hoped that in the near future restrictions on homosexuality will be eased.

[21] BIBLIOGRAPHY

Bulow, Dorothy. *Power Prestige and Respectability*. Denmark: Center for Development Research, 1995.

Dundas, Charles. *Kilimanjaro and Its People*. London: Frank Cass & Co., 1968.

Emanatian, Michele. "Everyday Metaphors of Lust and Sex in Chagga." *Ethos* 24, no. 2, (1996): 195–237.

Howard, Mary. "Socio-economic Causes and Cultural Explanations of Childhood Malnutrition among the Chagga of Tanzania." In *Social Science and Medicine*, vol. 38, no. 2, (January 1994): 239–251.

Moore, Sally F., and Paul Puritt. *The Chagga and Meru of Tanzania*. London: International African Institute, 1977.

Pelt, P. *Bantu Customs in Mainland Tanzania*. Tabora, Tanzania: TMP Book Department, 1971.

Reader, John. *Kilimanjaro*. New York: Universal Books, 1982.

Setel, Philip. "Getting AIDS is Like Breaking Your Shaft in the Shamba." In: *Energy, Disease, and Changing Concepts of Manhood in Kilimanjaro*. No. 168. Boston: Boston University African Studies Center, 1993.

Soini, Eija. "Changing Livelihoods on the Slopes of Mt. Kilimanjaro, Tanzania: Challenges and Opportunities in the Chagga Homegarden System." *Agroforestry Systems* 64, no. 2 (2005): 157-167.

Stahl, Kathleen M. *History of the Chagga People of Kilimanjaro*. London: Mouton and Co., 1964.

Stambach, A. "'Education is My Husband': Marriage, Gender, and Reproduction in Northern Tanzania." In *Women and Education in Sub-Saharan Africa: Power, Opportunities, and Constraints*. Edited by Marianne Bloch, Josephine A. Beoku-Betts, B. Robert Tabachnick. Boulder, CO: Lynne Rienner Publishers, 1998.

—revised by E. Kalipeni

CHEWA

PRONUNCIATION: CHAY-wah
LOCATION: Malawi; Zambia; Mozambique
POPULATION: 9,300,000 in Maravi group
LANGUAGE: Chichewa; English
RELIGION: Protestant; Roman Catholic; traditional beliefs; Islam
RELATED ARTICLES: Vol. 1: Mozambicans; Zambians

¹ INTRODUCTION

The Chewa, one of the Bantu peoples, live in central Malawi and spill over into parts of Zambia and Mozambique. Related groups such as the Nyanja and Mang'anja are found in southern Malawi. Together, the Chewa and related peoples are known as the Maravi group. Pushed by wars, disease, and other maladies from their original homeland around the Congo area, the Maravi were the first group of Bantu peoples to move into present-day Malawi during the early part of the 16th century. As a matter of fact, the name Malawi is derived directly from the term Maravi. The Maravi found fertile lands for settlement in the plains and valleys of central Malawi. Other Bantu groups such as the Tumbuka, Tonga, Yao, Lomwe, and Ngoni moved into Malawi long after the Maravi group had successfully established itself.

From their initial settlement at the southern tip of Lake Malawi, the Maravi began to disperse to different parts of the country. The group that migrated westwards into central Malawi and eastern parts of Zambia came to be known as the Chewa. Another splinter group moved into the Lower Shire valley of southern Malawi and became known as the Mang'anja. The era of the European and Arab slave trade during the 18th and 19th centuries ravaged the Mang'anja and the Chewa. Some areas in southern Malawi were completely depopulated. In the latter half of the 19th century, Malawi was colonized by the British and became known as Nyasaland. Malawi gained its independence from the British in 1964 under the leadership of Dr. Kamuzu Banda, a Chewa from central Malawi. Dr. Banda ruled Malawi as a dictator from 1964 to 1994, when democracy was finally restored in a dramatic but peaceful transition. Dr. Banda and his Malawi Congress Party lost the elections to the United Democratic Front (UDF) led by Bakili Muluzi, a former protégé of Dr. Banda.

President Bakili Muluzi ruled Malawi from 1994 until 2004 after two consecutive terms in office when he was replaced by his handpicked successor, Dr. Bingu wa Mutharika, in the general elections that were held in 2004. In 2002 he proposed an unpopular amendment to Malawi's constitution that would have allowed him to run for a third term, but this was abandoned due to demonstrations against him. During Muluzi's tenure as president, his administration was marred by scandal and corruption, particularly due to the sale of Malawi's reserves of maize to other countries shortly before the onset of a drought, which resulted in famine throughout the country. The millions of dollars realized from the sale of Malawi's food reserves have never been turned over, and it is widely suspected that it wound up in foreign accounts belonging to Muluzi and his supporters. Even after relinquishing power as president, Muluzi remains the head of the UDF. Soon after the take-

over of government by Bingu wa Mutharika in 2004 a dispute between Muluzi and Mutharika arose. This resulted in Mutharika leaving the UDF and forming his own party, the Democratic Progressive Party, in February 2005. In contravention of the two term limit as stipulated in the constitution, Muluzi announced in March 2007 that he would seek the party's nomination as its presidential candidate in 2009. The constitution refers to a limit of two consecutive terms of five years per term. Muluzi and his supporters believe that this enables him to run again after being out of office for a term while the majority of the population believe he is barred from running as president for the rest of his life after serving the two consecutive terms. Sentiments are rife in Malawi to amend the constitution so the word "consecutive" is removed.

² LOCATION AND HOMELAND

About the size of North Carolina, Malawi, an elongated landlocked country, is located in east-central Africa. It stretches for about 900 km (560 mi) from north to south and varies in width from 15 km to 160 km (9–100 mi) from east to west. The prominent geographical features include the spectacular Rift Valley occupied by Lake Malawi, Lake Malombe, and the Shire River; high mountains and plateaus; and high plains such as the Lilongwe Plains—the heartland of the Chewa people. Lake Malawi takes up nearly 20% of Malawi's land area.

The presence of mountains, plains, valleys, and plateaus in close proximity results in dramatic variations in climate, soils, rainfall, flora, and fauna. Because of the varied topography, the country experiences moderate and relatively comfortable temperatures throughout the year, ranging from a low of –9°C (15°F) during the cold season in June, to a high of 29°C (85°F) during the dry, hot season in October. The highest temperatures are found along Lake Malawi and in the Lower Shire Valley, which is only 70 m (230 ft) above sea level. In these areas temperatures can get as high as 38°C (100°F). Climate in the plateaus and high plains such as the Lilongwe Plains is mostly temperate.

Lilongwe, the post-independence capital city of Malawi, is located in Chewa-dominated central Malawi. Established in the early 1970s, Lilongwe has grown rapidly and boasts a population of about 744,400 people. In terms of ethnic composition, Malawi is a conglomeration of 15 different ethnic groups, with the Maravi complex (Chewa and Mang'anja) as the most dominant group. The Maravi account for 58% (or 7,540,000 people) of the total population of Malawi, currently estimated at 13 million people. Other significant ethnic groups include the Lomwe (18% or 2,340,000), the Yao (13% or 1,690,000), and Ngoni (7% or 910,000). However, Chichewa is also spoken in Zambia, Zimbabwe, Mozambique and Tanzania (where it is known as Nyanja or Chinyanja). It is estimated that the total population that speaks this language in these four countries numbers upwards of 9,500,000 with the majority (7.5 million) resident in Malawi. The presence of this language in Zambia, Zimbabwe, Tanzania and Mozambique is testament to the migration of the peoples of Malawi both during the pre-colonial, colonial, and post-independence era. During the pre-colonial era as Malawi began to fill up with people there was a Chewa diaspora into surrounding areas of Zambia and Mozambique. Once colonial rule was established, young Malawian men were encouraged by the British to migrate to Zambia and Zimbabwe to work in the mines and plantations there. The presence of

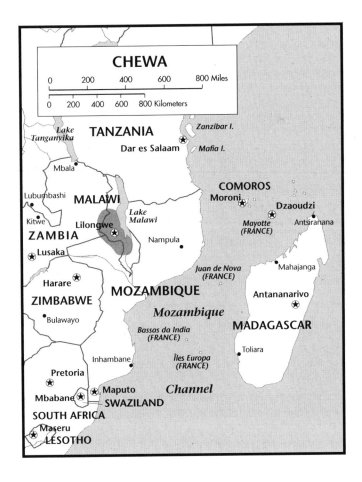

a sizable population of Chewa or Nyanja speakers in the surrounding countries can be explained by these migrations.

³ LANGUAGE

During the colonial era, Nyanja was the unified and standardized language for government and educational purposes in Malawi (then called Nyasaland). It was and remains the main language of all the peoples who have been grouped together as the Maravi for historical and cultural reasons. Two main dialects of Nyanja are clearly identifiable: Chichewa, spoken in the central region of Malawi and extending into Zambia; and Mang'anja, spoken in southern Malawi. Chichewa has risen to become the alternate name for Nyanja; it is understood widely throughout the country and hence qualifies as the lingua franca. English and Chichewa were decreed the national languages of Malawi during Dr. Banda's dictatorial rule. Although few Malawians speak English, it is the main business language and is used for official purposes in government offices and the private sector. English is also taught in schools as a second language. The persistence of English as one of the official languages of Malawi is largely due to the legacy of British colonial rule. In the post-Banda era, other ethnic groups are calling for the promotion of their languages, particularly Tumbuka, Yao, and Lomwe. These languages were suppressed and could not be aired on the only national radio during Dr. Banda's dictatorial rule in favor of Chichewa.

The pre-colonial dispersal of the Chewa peoples in various habitats and environments resulted in several dialects of the language. The Chewa people who settled along the shores of Lake Malawi and the banks of its outlet, the Shire River, referred to themselves as aNyanja, the "lake people", and their particular variety of Chichewa came to be called Chi-Nyanja, or simply Nyanja, the language of the lake people. The Chichewa word for a large expanse of water is Nyanja. Those who moved into the interior, the area of tall grass, called themselves aChipeta, the dwellers of the savanna land. The word for tall grass (savanna) in Chichewa is chipeta.

⁴ FOLKLORE

The Chewa have a rich set of beliefs, customs, and practices, all of which are central to group cohesion and survival. Much of the folklore among the Chewa dates back to the era before the arrival of European settlers, missionaries, and Christianity, and the stories have survived the pressure from Westernization and Christianity. Central to the customs and beliefs is the rich oral narrative expressed in the form of storytelling and songs about daily conditions of life such as birth, death, growing up, gender roles, polygamy, and marriage. Given the fact that the Chewa are mostly rural and engage in subsistence agriculture for their livelihood, it is no surprise that their folklore also dwells on issues of drought, fire, famine, and rainmaking.

Perhaps one of the central figures in Chewa myths is Mbona, a rainmaker among the Mang'anja of Southern Malawi. The story of this mythical hero runs much like that of Jesus Christ. He was the only son of his mother, conceived without a man, and was persecuted and eventually killed by his own people after performing miracles in the form of successful rainmaking dances in times of persistent drought. The story of Mbona has developed into the Mbona cult, a sacred oral text.

⁵ RELIGION

The main religion among the Chewa is Christianity, which was introduced by both Catholic and Protestant missionaries in the latter half of the 19th century. It is estimated that 34% of Malawi's population is Protestant, while 27% are Catholic, 19% hold to traditional beliefs, and 16% are Muslim. Although many of the Chewa people were converted to Christianity, most concurrently adhere to both traditional beliefs and Christianity. Indigenous religion among the Chewa revolves around a single supreme being, called by various names such as Chiuta, Mphambe, Leza, Mulungu, etc., and the veneration of departed spirits of ancestors, generally termed Mizimu. It was therefore easy for the Chewa and Mang'anja to adopt Christianity, which seemed to have a similar structure to their traditional beliefs.

Traditionally, in times of calamity, the chief would offer sacrifices of beer, goats, fowl, and flour to the spirits of his ancestors at a special shrine, with all his subjects in attendance. It is not uncommon today for a Chewa to consult a traditional diviner, who might order the offering of a sacrifice in the form of a pot of beer or a chicken to avert personal calamity. One key aspect of traditional religion that has survived colonial and Christian prohibition is the all-male Nyau secret society, which performs traditional rites of passage.

⁶ MAJOR HOLIDAYS

One of the major holidays in Malawi is Independence Day on 6 July. Malawi obtained its independence from Great Britain in 1964 after almost 70 years of British rule. On 6 July each year, roads in urban areas are decorated with the Malawian flag.

During the day, political rallies are held with speeches made by prominent politicians. Women are encouraged to wear either the colorful Malawi Congress Party uniform or the current ruling party's colors (blue for the Democratic Progressive Party or yellow of the United Democratic Front), and to perform traditional dances in stadiums for political dignitaries and all to see. It is indeed a joyous occasion followed by a night of feasting and dancing. One other significant secular holiday is 3 March, in remembrance of those who died during the struggle for independence. On this day prayers are offered in churches throughout Malawi and somber music is broadcast on the radio.

7 RITES OF PASSAGE

Devout Roman Catholics and/or Protestant Christians follow the Christian code of conduct in terms of baptism, marriage, and death. However, in much of Chewa society, traditional rites of passage are still an integral part of growing up. Generally, Chewa and Mang'anja boys between the ages of 12 and 16 are initiated into a semisecret society called Nyau, "The Great Dance." It is literally an association of masked dancers whose masks come in all types, from wooden masks to basketry-manufactured animal likenesses, and who parade in the villages. The masked dancers portray the spirits of the dead who have returned from the grave to conduct initiation and funeral rituals. If a Chewa man has not been initiated into the all-male Nyau society, he does not command full adult male status. During initiation, boys are secluded in the bush for instruction and discipline for about three days. Each village has its own association, but membership gained at one village is acceptable at other villages.

Girls from age 9 to 16 undergo a series of puberty and initiation rites known as *chinamwali*, which are administered by elderly women instructors called *anankungwi*. In present-day Chewaland, one finds two types of girls' initiation, one that is church-sponsored and the other that is purely traditional. The church-sponsored initiation ceremony instructs girls in a Christian way. The traditional initiation ceremony, which can last as long as two to three weeks, teaches young girls traditional customs as they relate to issues of sexuality and reproduction. Usually the women of the village accompany the young girls into the bush and put them through a course of teasing and instruction, returning each evening to the village for dancing and feasting. Drums are used to create a rhythm for dancing and singing songs, some of which illustratively teach the girls the body movements performed during sexual intercourse. In the bush, the young girls are given advice about cleanliness and politeness. They are admonished not to enter their parents' bedrooms and to avoid their male friends because sexual relationships out of wedlock result in pregnancy and might lead to diseases such as gonorrhea and AIDS. It is only after the initiation that a girl becomes a woman. In traditional Chewa society, women are in charge of issues of reproduction and make a secret of it; men are never allowed to witness births and are never told how a child is born. On the other hand, men make a secret of death through their all-male Nyau secret cult.

8 INTERPERSONAL RELATIONS

To greet each other, men and women of the same age group will shake hands vigorously. Hugging is not common in Malawi. When a man greets his mother-in-law, he has to stay at a distance from her and greet her verbally; no handshaking between the two is allowed since they are in an avoidance relationship. A daughter-in-law, however, has a close relationship with her mother-in-law. When one receives a guest it is customary to prepare food, preferably a chicken, and it is considered rude manners for the guest to decline any food that might be served, even if he or she has already eaten. When an older person is talking to a younger person, it is considered rude for the younger person to look directly into the face of the older person. A younger person is supposed to bow or look to the side, or even squat on the ground, when being addressed by an elder. Kissing in public is frowned upon. It is considered an offense for boys and girls that have gone through initiation ceremonies to enter their parents' bedrooms or huts. When growing up, boys are discouraged from performing tasks that are considered women's business such as entering the kitchen, washing pots and dishes, drawing water from the well, or fetching firewood. Before initiation, girls and boys are encouraged to play together, but after initiation they should stay apart until married. However, in urban areas modern forms of dating are quite common.

9 LIVING CONDITIONS

Only 17% of Malawi's population is urban and very few of the urban population are Chewa. The majority of the Chewa live in rural areas in nucleated villages where subsistence farming is the primary economic activity. In rural areas there is little access to modern amenities of life such as health care facilities, schools, and electricity. Among the major debilitating diseases are malaria during the rainy season, bilharzia, intestinal worm infections, tuberculosis, measles, and, recently, the proliferation of the HIV/AIDS pandemic. It is estimated that over 16% of the adult population in Malawi is HIV positive. The general health of the population is poor, and the time spent being sick, attending curative services, looking after the sick, or attending funerals is very great for most of the people. Malnutrition of all forms and anaemia are also quite common. The primary cause of malnutrition is not a lack of food as such, but rather the prevalence of certain traditional customs and beliefs about foods, patterns of eating, food distribution within the family, sources of food for the household, methods of processing, and the general customs and value systems. The result of the poor state of health is manifested in the high rates of early childhood mortality. The mortality rate for children under the age of five currently stands at 178 deaths per 1,000 live births, and the infant mortality rate is estimated at 113 deaths per 1,000 live births. Life expectancy is low, only 46 years for men and 46.7 years for women.

There does not seem to be a particular pattern in the arrangement of huts in any given village. The arrangement of huts and the type of domestic architecture is determined largely by location and the availability of building materials. Generally, the Chewa and Mang'anja live in compact villages, which in the past were essential for defense against attack from other ethnic groups, such as the Ngoni and Yao, and occasionally from lions. The huts are either circular or oblong with wattle walls, plastered outside and inside with mud and roofed with thatch. It is not unusual to find a modern type of house in rural areas, built in a rectangular fashion using bricks, cement, and corrugated iron sheets for the roof, with sawn timber doors and glass windows. In urban areas such as Lilongwe, housing is in short supply and the majority of people are forced to live in shanty towns and other low-income areas. In the city of Lilongwe, journey to work for the low-income groups is mostly on foot, by minibus, or by bicycle. It is quite common for people to walk 10 miles round-trip to and from work every day.

¹⁰ FAMILY LIFE

The Chewa and Mang'anja are matrilineal in their kinship system. Descent and inheritance are passed through the female line. The marriage process is simple and involves the appointment of marriage sureties, called *ankhoswe,* with the maternal uncle as the principal sponsor. Although boys and girls choose their own partners, a marriage cannot be recognized as valid without the approval of maternal uncles. Residence is matrilocal and the husband establishes the household in the wife's village. A father has no control over children born in a marriage, since such children are considered to be members of the mother's matrilineage and are therefore under the guidance of the maternal uncle.

Divorce is also relatively simple and quite common. A man can be divorced on a number of grounds such as failing to perform marital tasks, e.g., hoeing for his mother-in-law. Although rarely practiced these days, a successful son-in-law can be given a second wife if his first dies, or even while the first wife is still alive, as a gesture of gratitude for his satisfactory services. Polygamy, the practice of having more than one wife, used to be common, but its extent is hard to determine in contemporary Chewa society. National-level census estimates indicate that about 33% of Malawi males over the age of 40 have more than one wife.

Girls enter into marriage at a median age of about 17 years. Fertility rates are very high and a woman can expect to bear seven children by the time she goes through the 15–44 year reproductive age range. Having many children is considered to be very desirable since a man or woman with many children is considered rich, as are his relatives both by birth and marriage. More children serve as a means of social security in old age, and they provide much needed labor in herding livestock and farming.

In urban areas and even in rural areas, weddings are increasingly being conducted in churches and receptions usually follow soon thereafter, similar to marriage ceremonies in industrialized countries. For those who can afford it, the bridegroom wears a Western-style suit while the bride wears the typical Western white wedding dress with a veil.

¹¹ CLOTHING

In urban areas, women usually wear a skirt and a blouse or a modern colorful dress. The most common form of dress for women in rural areas is a loincloth tied around the waist, and a blouse. Men wear pants, shirts, shorts, and occasionally a suit. Middle-income professionals are always nicely dressed in Western-style suits. During Dr. Banda's dictatorial rule, there was a strict dress code where women could not wear slacks, shorts, or miniskirts, while men could not wear long hair. This dress code was repealed in 1994 under the democratically elected government of Bakili Muluzi. In spite of the repeal of the dress code, Malawi's clothing continues to be conservative. For women, this means skirts that do not show knees and do not fit too tightly. Malawians consider women's thighs to be suggestive, therefore they must be covered at all times.

¹² FOOD

The Chewa diet consists mainly of *nsima* (thick porridge) made from maize flour that is rich in carbohydrates and poor in protein. To compensate for the lack of protein in maize flour, nsima is eaten with a side dish called *ndiwo* made from a variety of leafy vegetables, beans, poultry, eggs, game, meat from livestock, fish, insects, etc. There are a number of beliefs, customs, and taboos that restrict certain categories of people, such as pregnant women and children, from eating certain side dishes. Because of these beliefs, diets may be unbalanced for certain segments of society, resulting in malnutrition. For example, pregnant women are forbidden to eat eggs for fear of bearing bald-headed babies. Like women, children are forbidden to eat eggs and rabbits lest they develop bald heads and twitching noses like rabbits. In most cases, children are fed on gravy and salt water with nsima, while the father and other males are given top priority—the best side dishes such as eggs and poultry. Whatever remains goes to the women. The wife is expected to look after her husband first, the children next, and herself last.

Nsima with ndiwo is sometimes eaten twice a day, at lunch time and at dinner time, but most of the time this main dish is offered only at dinner time since the mother is busy with other chores during the day such as farming, drawing water from the well, fetching firewood, and so on. In the interim, children have to make do with snacks such as roasted cassava, roasted maize, sweet potatoes, sugarcane, wild fruits, or wild insects such as roasted grasshoppers, flying termites, etc. Men, too, sometimes experience food restrictions such as not eating *thelele*, a slimy liquid-like vegetable, since it is believed that they can lose their virility. In urban centers such as Lilongwe, the high-income groups tend to have a diversified diet, while the low-income groups tend to be restricted in what they can afford.

¹³ EDUCATION

In Malawi there are two major systems of education, namely, the formal and the informal. The informal or traditional system of education (see **Rites of passage**), which is still very much a part of rural society, is encouraged by the government on the basis that it instills respect for tradition and culture. The formal education system is patterned along the British system, which consists of three tiers: primary, secondary, and tertiary. The students who do extremely well in the Malawi Certificate Examination at the end of the four-year secondary school program (and these are few in number) are then selected to attend the five constituent colleges of the University of Malawi. In recent years, adult literacy rates have seen dramatic improvements rising to 54% for females and 75% for males aged 15 years and over who are able to read and write Chichewa, English, or both languages. There is no national service for students in Malawi. Census data in Malawi indicate large gender differentials as well as regional disparities in educational attainment. For example, in 1987, for every 100 females in school there were 152 males. School attendance rates for all age groups are higher for males than for females.

¹⁴ CULTURAL HERITAGE

There is a rich musical and dance heritage among the Chewa and the Mang'anja of central and southern Malawi. In traditional settings, songs are sung at initiation rites, rituals, marriage ceremonies, or during post-harvest celebrations. There are puberty songs, praise songs, funeral songs, work songs, beer-drinking songs, coronation songs for chiefs, etc. It is not uncommon to see women sing as they go about their daily chores. Women employ sung poetry as a strategy in defining and interpreting gender roles, especially as they concern a negotiation of their standing in society. Several traditional dances are also popular among the Chewa, especially during weddings and other festivals. For example, *mganda* is an all-male dance from central Malawi in which about 15 men form a troupe. Each of the dancers uses some kind of a local saxophone made from a gourd, and they sing and dance in unison following a complex series of steps. The female counterpart of *mganda* is *chimtali,* usually performed at weddings. A group of women dance in a circle with a drum in the center and seductively gyrate their hips, bosoms, and the like. There is also the all-male Nyau masquerade dance at initiation and funerary rituals. The masked dancers are accompanied by several drummers and a women's chorus.

In addition to the traditional dances, there is also the modern popular culture imported from abroad or from regional music centers such as the Democratic Republic of the Congo and South Africa. This type of music includes reggae music, disco, breakdance, rap, etc., currently popular in bars and beer- and dance-halls.

During the post-independence era, Malawi in general has also seen the rise of a few internationally recognized literary scholars such as the famous poet, Jack Mapanje, the veteran historian and fiction writer, Paul Zeleza, and others who include Steve Chimombo, Legson Kayira, Chipasula, Rubadiri, and Felix Munthali.

¹⁵ WORK

Approximately 90% of the people in Malawi live in rural areas where subsistence farming is the primary economic activity, growing a variety of crops such as maize (the staple food crop), beans, sorghum, peanuts, rice, pumpkins, cassava, and tobacco (the main cash crop). The formal and informal sectors in the major urban centers of Malawi employ only a quarter of the labor force population. Evidently, as population continues to grow rapidly, land resources are becoming scarce and it is unlikely that the subsistence sector will continue to meet the needs of each household.

¹⁶ SPORTS

During the colonial era, the British introduced soccer to Malawi, and it is still the main sport throughout the country, especially in the urban areas of Lilongwe, Mzuzu, Zomba, and Blantyre. The Malawi national team is quite a force in southern Africa's soccer competitions and has on occasion won a number of regional championships. Soccer clubs compete for a number of prized trophies throughout the year. Every Saturday and Sunday, thousands of people converge on Civo Stadium in Lilongwe, and Chichiri Stadium in Blantyre, to watch various clubs play skillful soccer. Even in rural areas, soccer is the most common sport among school children. Basketball is also a growing major sport.

¹⁷ ENTERTAINMENT AND RECREATION

In terms of entertainment and other recreation activities, young professionals in urban areas flock to Western-style clubs and bars. In rural areas, girls and boys may perform traditional and modern dances in the moonlight to entertain themselves and other spectators. There is no television in Malawi, but upper- and middle-income families may own a TV and VCR. Individual families may thus be able to treat themselves to a rental movie.

For young boys and girls in rural areas there is a rich repertoire of games which keeps them busy all day and in the evenings. Among the most popular games for rural children are hunting small game such as mice and rabbits, hide-and-seek at night, tug of war, and many others. As one of the most cherished activities, hunting mice is usually a daylong group expedition for boys. This activity provides important skills for the future in terms of instilling hunting skills, building team cooperation, and providing a little food for each boy's household in addition to being fun and exciting. In rural villages hide-and-seek is played at night under bright moonlight. Rules prohibit hiding inside a house, and this adds extra excitement. Outdoors in the dim light offered by the moon, boys and girls in teams scurry and scamper around the village darting from place to place seeking better hiding spots, adding mystery, challenge, and enjoyment to the game for both hiders and seekers.

¹⁸ FOLK ART, CRAFTS, AND HOBBIES

In spite of the fact that the Chewa of central Malawi are not known for their art and are rarely mentioned in art history literature, they do exhibit a rich tradition of basketry and carved masks, which includes two large and intricate basketry masks known as *Kasiyamaliro* and *Chimkoko.* These masks are used in initiation rituals for the men's Nyau secret society. In urban areas, one also tends to find a rich variety of wood carvings, oil paintings, and other beautiful works of art depicting various indigenous village scenes and daily ways of living, for sale to tourists.

¹⁹ SOCIAL PROBLEMS

Malawi has 15 different ethnic groups which live in relative peace and harmony with each other. Inter-ethnic warfare is rare and uncommon. During Dr. Banda's dictatorial rule, human rights violations were quite common. Persons suspected of being critical to Dr. Banda's rule were detained without charge or trial, tortured, and sometimes assassinated. Under the previous government of Bakili Muluzi and the current government of Bingu wa Mutharika, human rights conditions have improved somewhat and people seem to be freer in expressing themselves and in openly criticizing government policies. However, the economic conditions, particularly inflation, have gotten worse because of drought that hit the country hard between 1999 and 2003, economic mismanagement and corruption in government circles under Muluzi's government, and worsening terms of trade. During 2006–2008 the country experienced a bumper crop of maize due to good rains and government subsidized fertilizer distributed to needy smallholder farmers in rural areas.

[20] GENDER ISSUES

In traditional matrilineal Chewa society women play a central role in cultural and economic activities. The land and the village belong to women. When a man gets married, he traditionally has to leave his village to reside in his wife's village, farm his wife's fields and beget children for his wife's lineage rather than his own. Should the marriage end in divorce or should the woman be widowed the property and children automatically go to the wife and her people and the man leaves his wife's village empty handed. However, since the advent of colonial rule many Chewa traditions with regard to gender issues have undergone transformation resulting in the lowering of women's status. It can be argued that the deterioration in the status of women among the Chewa is not a reflection of "traditional Chewa society" but rather something that came to Malawi via the contact with Europeans in the 16th century and subsequent colonization. The status and power of women during the pre-colonial period was far much healthier than it is today. There is a saying in Malawi that men among the matrilineal societies are forever grateful to the British for liberating them from the tyranny of the matrilineal code of conduct that was often in favor of women than men. In pre-colonial times, women played significant roles in economic, political and spiritual spheres of their communities. Women were often the most powerful spiritual figures, some became very powerful rulers of their territories as queens and paramount chiefs, and even today, they continue to play significant roles in producing food and propelling the Malawian economy.

Modernization and the ensuing social and economic transformation has brought about the erosion of the high status women used to enjoy in traditional settings. In the modernized society of today, they have been relegated to the position of "second class citizens." In an era of HIV/AIDS women have experienced the brunt of the epidemic due in large measure to their deteriorating and unequal status to men. Today, women are often married off early without regard to their potential or actual educational achievement, and are generally not allowed to partake in economically gainful activities that might lend them a semblance of empowerment. Their economic and social vulnerability is often made worse by the lack of formal educational investment in them, which leaves them without access to information vital to their reproductive health and to knowledge and prevention of diseases such as AIDS. The sad truth is that women in Malawi tend to have smaller entitlement bundles than do men because they have lower wages and are not as likely to be highly educated, or to receive government assistance, or benefit from international aid programs. Women are frequently denied education beyond primary levels because they are primed for marriage rather than careers. They are subsequently constrained in their choices of occupation, and the areas of employment offering livable wages are especially scarce.

With reference to sexual activities, the Chewa had a detailed code of conduct that regulated sexual relations between men and women and sex between those of the same gender. Homosexuality, adultery, and bestiality (i.e. sex with animals) were forbidden and sometimes punishable by death. In present day Malawi, homosexuality is illegal under the penal code and considered an "act against the order of nature." Foreigners caught in homosexual acts have been deported. Malawi nationals engaging in homosexual activities can and have been imprisoned or detained without charge or trial.

[21] BIBLIOGRAPHY

Chilivumbo, Alifeyo. "The Cultural Consequences of Population Change in Malawi." In *The Consequences of Population Change.* Washington, DC: The Center for the Study of Man, Smithsonian Institution, 1974.

Faulkner, Laurel Birch. "Basketry Masks of the Chewa." In *African Arts,* 21 (May 1988): 28–31.

Helitzer-Allen, Deborah. *An Investigation of Community Based Communication Networks of Adolescent Girls in Rural Malawi for HIV/STD Prevention Messages.* Washington, D.C.: International Center for Research on Women, 1994.

Johnstone, Patrick J. St. G., and Jason Mandryk. *Operation World.* Minneapolis, MN: Bethany House, 2001.

Newitt, M. D. D. "Early History of the Maravi." *Journal of African History* 23, no. 2 (1982): 145–162.

Ntara, Samuel Josia. *The History of the Chewa (Mbiri Ya Chewa).* Wiesbaden: Franz Steiner Verlag GMBH, 1973.

Schoffeleers, Matthew J. *River of Blood: The Genesis of a Martyr Cult in Southern Malawi, c.A.D. 1600.* Madison, WI: University of Wisconsin Press, 1992.

———. "The Zimba and Lundu State in the Late Sixteenth and Early Seventeenth Centuries." In *Journal of African History,* vol. 28, no. 3 (1987): 337–355.

Schoffeleers, Matthew J., and Adrian Roscoe. *Land of Fire: Oral Literature from Malawi.* Limbe: Popular Publications, 1985.

Tembo, Mwizenge S. "Games and Toys in Traditional Zambia." *World and I* 14, no 6 (1999): 232.

Timpunza Mvula, Enoch Selstine. *Women's Oral Poetry as a Social Strategy in Malawi.* Bloomington, IN: Department of Folklore, Indiana University, Ph.D. Dissertation, 1987.

Yoshida, Kenji. "Masks and Secrecy Among the Chewa." In *African Arts,* vol. 26, no. 2 (April 1993): 34–45.

—by E. Kalipeni

COLORED PEOPLE OF SOUTH AFRICA

ALTERNATE NAMES: Coloureds, Coloreds, Brown People
LOCATION: South Africa (especially Western Cape and Northern Cape Provinces, urban areas)
POPULATION: 4.2 million
LANGUAGE: Afrikaans, English
RELIGION: Christianity, Islam

¹ INTRODUCTION

The word *colored* in a racial context is considered by many to be pejorative or disparaging, but it is widely used to this day in serious discussions of South Africa's social and economic issues because it describes an important population entity and because nobody has been able to come up with a better or more accurate term for this purpose. It is fairly common for the term *colored* to be preceded by the phrase "so-called" as a demonstration of the speaker's ambiguous feelings. They were categorized as such by means of the Population Registration Act, No 30 of 1950. They number approximately 4.2 million and are the descendants of European settlers from the Netherlands, Germany, France, indigenous people of South Africa, especially the San and Khoekhoen, and slaves from the Dutch East Indies who were brought to the country during the 18th and 19th centuries.

The "Colored" population suffered many indignities under apartheid in terms of education, health care, and basic exclusion of other privileges, like marrying a person of another race. When apartheid laws were introduced after 1948, many communities were forcibly removed from their original residential areas. District Six in Cape Town is an example of such an area where forced eviction of "Colored" families took place because it was earmarked for urban restoration. Many of these families were moved to the Cape Flats areas with its associated problems of gangsterism, vigilante groups, etc. Since democracy in 1994, however, all the people of South Africa have the right to live wherever their economic position and preference permit.

Most coloreds tended to work as domestic servants, farm laborers, and fisher folk, but large numbers were also involved in the skilled trades like masons, tailors, and seamstresses with which craftsmanship they are associated to this day.

Culturally and economically, coloreds were always more closely associated with the dominant white population than were Africans. They spoke the same languages (English and Afrikaans), worshiped in the same churches (mostly Christian Protestant, but also some Catholic), enjoyed the same foods, wore the same kind of clothes and—especially in later years—enjoyed the same sports and pastimes. In spite of this common heritage, they were never fully integrated into white society. Today there is still a fairly widespread sense among coloreds that they continue to be victims of discrimination in South Africa, but this time at the hands of the black majority government. In a recent news report, a colored South African was quoted as protesting: "We weren't white enough in the old regime and now we're not black enough." This perception is based on allegations that, in narrowing the economic gap between whites and blacks, the government is willing to remove many of the gains achieved by coloreds through their own hard work and sacrifice. It is but one delicate problem among the many difficulties facing the young democracy.

Subgroups were and, often still today, are recognized among the coloreds. The dominant subgroup is the so-called Cape Coloreds who are, as was indicated, descended from various indigenous people and European settlers and are mainly to be found in the Western Cape region and in the Northern Cape. The 1950 Population Registration Act in fact made allowance for six sub-categories of coloreds, and some of these still self-identify as distinct communities. Examples of such communities are the Griquas, Malays, Rehoboth Basters (of Namibia), and the Nama.

The Griqua and Nama, together with people like the Korana, more properly can be identified as Khoekhoen (previously Khoikhoin), who were conventionally grouped with the San (Bushmen) under the term Khoesan (Khoisan) due to the similarity in their click languages. Contemporary identity for communities such as these is a complex matter. The Griqua for example, are still regarded as "Colored"—even the identity documents of many still carry this designation. However, they have a strong sense of identity and number approximately 300,000. As descendants of mostly Khoekhoen and Afrikaner communities, they formed a distinct group as early as the 17th century.

For some Griqua people it has been possible to register as Griqua while others who legitimately trace Griqua descent prefer not to be identified as such. It is also possible to "become" Griqua by, for example, marrying into the Griqua community or by joining the Griqua movement through membership in the Griqua Independent Church. As a group however, they have obtained international recognition and in 1998 already, the United Nations awarded them, one of South Africa's oldest peoples, First Nation status.

The Cape Malay is also a large subgroup, primarily centered in particular neighborhoods of the Western Cape Province and number about 180,000. They are descended from the indigenous Khoekhoen, slaves brought to South Africa by the Dutch East India Company and European settlers. They have retained many cultural elements from their diverse origin but they are recognized as a distinct and close-knit community, mostly because of their Islam religion and location.

The same Act in fact also made allowance for a category "Other Colored" for those who did not obviously qualify for the sub-categories mentioned above. An example of such a group is the Buys community at Buysdorp near Louis Trichardt (Makhado) in Limpopo Province. The settlement has approximately 400 permanent residents, all of whom are related to one another, but many more live and work elsewhere in South Africa. They are the descendants of the well-known Coenraad de Buys (grandson of French Hugenot Jean du Bois) who had married several indigenous women and settled in the area even before the Voortrekkers (Boer pioneers) had established the first settlement of white people in the Limpopo Province at the town of Schoemansdal. They, too, have a fierce sense of identity and prefer not to be categorized as belonging to the general "Brown"/"Colored" grouping.

Those first few of the Karretjie People (see elsewhere in this volume) who eventually obtained identity documents were also classified "Colored," but as itinerant people of the Great Karoo region of South Africa, they also regarded themselves as distinct, as descendants of a First People of South Africa, the Xam Bushmen.

2 LOCATION AND HOMELAND

Most of South Africa's colored people live in both the urban and rural areas of the Western Cape (main city: Cape Town) and Northern Cape Provinces, where they have numerical superiority and constitute influential political and cultural groups. However, they have also migrated to other major centers and significant concentrations can be found around the cities of Johannesburg, Pretoria, Port Elizabeth, East London, and Durban. There are also important groups in the neighboring nations of Namibia (see elsewhere in this volume) and Zimbabwe.

In the Western Cape Province—regarded as their traditional homeland—colored people play a vital role in the economically important agriculture industry (fruit, wine, wheat and dairy products), not only as farm laborers but also as managers, skilled artisans, and increasingly as property-owning entrepreneurs. They are also a dominant group in the fishing industry that has grown up in the rich cold waters of the country's west coast, where the Benguella Current has helped to create excellent trawling and line-fishing conditions. In the cities, many members of the colored community are engaged in trades such as carpentry, plumbing, auto repair, and construction, but they are also prominent in professions such as health care, accounting, law, and education.

3 LANGUAGE

Colored South Africans speak two languages, mainly Afrikaans, but also English. Afrikaans is a language found only in South Africa that evolved from the Dutch spoken by the early white settlers with influences from other groups who settled in the country. In an informal setting, such as day-to-day life at home, it is not unusual for coloreds—and to a lesser extent other groups—to combine the two languages in a distinctive local dialect that is very colorful and expressive. This local dialect has little formal written literature, but it is widely popular and accepted as a phenomenon that has given Cape Town its special character. It is particularly effective when used in a humorous context and in the light-hearted songs known as "moppies." In formal settings, however, colored speakers use either formal English or Afrikaans.

Among the Griqua for example, who were also formally classified colored and are still generally regarded as such, there is a concerted effort to revive their original Khoekhoen/click language. Khoekhoen is a surviving dialect and is taught in a school in the Richtersveld area. Researchers in the Great Karoo region have also found individual Karretjie People who could still speak a "southern" Griqua/Korana dialect.

4 FOLKLORE

Because of their historical association with whites, coloreds share the general folklore heritage common to the Western world. However, there are also some (dwindling) legacies that apparently came from the early mingling with slaves from the Dutch East Indies–notably the telling of *goël* (literally, to practice magic) or ghost stories, which are frequently as amusing as they are alarming. One of the features of Cape Town in summer is the strong southeast wind known as the "Cape Doctor." Sometimes it blows so hard that people can hardly walk in the city and the harbor closes to shipping. Southeaster time, when windows are rattling and doors are creaking, is ideal for the telling of *goël* stories.

5 RELIGION

The colored people of Cape Town observe two main religions—Christianity (mostly Protestant, but also some Catholicism) and Islam, which plays an influential role in a large sector of the population. In urban areas where colored people live in large numbers, it is common to hear the faithful being summoned to prayer from mosques. Local leaders of both major religions were prominent during the struggle against apartheid. Some, such as the Reverend Allan Boesak, became familiar figures on the international stage as pressure built up against apartheid. Boesak is still active as a public commentator. Because of the powerful influence of Islam, many colored people take an intense interest in events in the Middle East and other parts of the world where the interests of their fellow Muslims are at stake. Both Christianity and Islam are seen as factors in the emergence of a strong conservative element in the colored community.

Amongst the Griqua, their "Independent Church" has been an important mechanism for mobilization and cultural revival.

6 MAJOR HOLIDAYS

For more than 100 years, Cape Town's colored community was associated with an annual New Year's Day "minstrel" parade through the streets of the city and along the main roads leading into town. Neighborhoods formed troops that dressed in colorful satin costumes and marched or danced behind guitar and banjo bands. Each troop had its own combination of colors. When they all arrived at central sports fields, they competed for trophies to the delight of large crowds of spectators. According to historians, the tradition began in the 19th century, when a local baker dressed up a group of people to advertise his breads and cakes. But, it was largely abandoned during the latter days of apartheid because many members of the community felt the name "Coon Carnival," by which it became known, was derogatory. Since democracy the tradition was revived and the citizens of Cape Town are again enjoying the minstrel bands and their humorous songs.

A traditional song is "January, February." Its words consist only of the 12 months of the year, sung to a catchy tune and rhythm. Everyone knows this song, and spectators often join in when the band marches by. There are many other songs—some funny, some sad—but all are unique to the spirit of the Cape and its people. Another well-known traditional song describes the arrival off the Cape of the Confederate raider Alabama during the American Civil War. Thousands of people climbed to the top of Signal Hill overlooking Cape Town to see the warship and witness any battles that might take place with Yankee enemies. The event is remembered in a universally known song called *Daar Kom Die Alabama* ("There Comes The Alabama").

More serious is the annual competition between Malay choirs—choirs made up of the descendants of workers who were brought to the Cape during the days of the Dutch East India Company, which established a replenishment station and vegetable garden at the Cape of Good Hope in 1652. Their songs range from localized versions of modern tunes to traditional ballads and joke songs called "moppies." An especially delightful moppie tells the story of a baboon trying to learn how to swim. He learns very quickly when he sees a crocodile in front of him and a shark behind.

The official public holidays of South Africa of course apply to the coloreds as well and these are: New Year's Day, January 1; Human Rights Day, March 21; Good Friday and Family Day, which vary; Freedom Day, April 27; Worker's Day, May 1; Youth Day, June 16; National Women's Day, August 9; Heritage Day, September 24; Day of Reconciliation, December 16; Christmas Day, December 25; Day of Goodwill, December 26.

7 RITES OF PASSAGE

Birthdays are celebrated by parties where the guests bring gifts. Baptism of infants, confirmation, and first communion are celebrated among Christian colored people. On their 21st birthday, many young adults in South Africa receive a symbolic key to adulthood.

However, as part of the revival of Khoekhoen/Griqua culture and a renewed awareness of an own identity, a number of "Kaptyns" or Chiefs are again recognized. The *nâu* inauguration ceremony for such chiefs has been resurrected in some quarters. It involves slaughtering a sheep, the use of its blood for purification, the slow circular movement of the participants whose feet are bathed in the blood, the tasting of bitter *boegoe*

and sweet honey—symbolic of both bad and good times—and finally, an oath of loyalty is taken.

A few other traditions and rituals that still persist include (in Griquastad, an important Griqua town): the *hokmeisie* or girls' initiation ceremony; the *mokwele* or betrothal ceremony; and the marriage ceremony involving a special dance, *stapdans*.

8 INTERPERSONAL RELATIONS

Even though there was legal separation of races in South Africa for most of the 20th century, there was always contact between whites and coloreds. Culturally, the two groups shared similar interests and background. They listened to the same music and saw the same movies (even though theaters were segregated), used the same school textbooks and lived in close proximity (although residential areas were largely separate). They met in the workplace, stores, and the street. As a result, close friendships were formed and feelings of mutual respect developed, even though the previous regime did everything possible to keep racial and ethnic groups separate. Until 1986 it was illegal for members of different race groups to have sexual relations, for example, and people were actually prosecuted for breaking this law. Thus, the removal of all race laws has been easy for whites and colored to adjust to in terms of their relations with each other. Relations between coloreds and members of the black majority are tenuous in the new system. There have been some tensions based on the perception by coloreds that the majority regime may not always have colored interests in mind.

9 LIVING CONDITIONS

Under apartheid, whites enjoyed most of the advantages and privileges in terms of education, health care, land allocation, and so forth. Next in the pecking order were coloreds, followed by blacks. For example, when the transition to non-racial democracy took place in 1994, the student-to-teacher ratio in white schools was 18 to 1; in colored schools, it was 22 to 1 and in black schools it was 50 to 1. Coloreds lived in close proximity to their white neighbors even though there was a large income gap between the two groups. When most of the apartheid laws were introduced after 1948, many colored people were forcibly moved from their traditional residential areas to segregated suburbs and townships. This development was bitterly resented and resisted, and it resulted in the destruction not only of well-established communities but of families themselves. Forced removals remain one of the worst memories of the old South Africa. It created problems that are still beyond solution in many cases. One of the most resented examples occurred in the center of Cape Town, where an area known as District Six was earmarked for urban renewal. District Six was the traditional home of many colored families, and it certainly needed renewal. But, it was renewed for whites and the original inhabitants were moved to bleak townships on the sandy Cape Flats, where crime, alcoholism, and other social ills soon became rampant. These townships and suburbs still exist (as do many of the problems they created) but colored people can now live wherever their economic status allows and they have increasingly moved into formerly exclusive white suburbs. Some communities of coloreds like the Buyses and the Dunns have preferred to stay in and hang on to their own exclusive pockets of the land—in the far northern Soutpansberg of the Limpopo Province and the Province of KwaZulu-Natal, respectively.

10 FAMILY LIFE

Colored families tend to be extended, conservative, and mutually supportive. In fact, it was largely these qualities that enabled the community to survive the difficult earlier years. The sense of interdependence is inclined to translate to neighborhood and community as well.

11 CLOTHING

Colored South Africans wear clothing, both formal and casual, similar to that worn by people in major industrial nations anywhere in the world. Young people wear jeans, sneakers, and T-shirts just like their counterparts in the United States and Canada, and baseball caps have become popular too. Jackets and ties are becoming less common in more formal venues, such as the workplace, largely following the trends elsewhere in the world.

12 FOOD

Colored people are renowned for their culinary skills and have contributed more to South Africa's heritage in this area than any other group. They are especially famous for wonderful stews—known as *bredies*—which are traditionally made with mutton and lamb and prepared with a base of tomatoes, cabbage, or local plants known as *waterblommetjies*. Also popular are small, triangular pies known as *samoesas*, which contain a curried mince mixture. *Samoesas* are ideal for snacks or lunch and are often served as appetizers or at cocktail parties. The influence of the Dutch East Indies is strong, especially in the lasting popularity of curries that can be served warm or cold, strong or mild. A special favorite is curried fish, which is prepared with local *hake* (known as stock fish) or a local deep-sea fish called *kingklip*, or *snoek*, which looks rather like the familiar barracuda. Among working men, it is common for the midday meal to consist of a loaf of bread with the inside hollowed out and the hole filled up with a *bredie*. This substantial meal gives a worker plenty of energy for the rest of the day's labor.

13 EDUCATION

Education has long been seized upon as the road to self-improvement among the members of South Africa's colored community. As a result, families will save and sacrifice to send their children to the best available schools and colleges. In the past, colored people were allowed to attend only those institutions designated for their use. While these schools were better equipped than those allocated to black Africans, they were nevertheless inferior to the schools for whites. In the present open society with free access to facilities and institutions, colored students increasingly feature prominently in the best schools and foremost universities.

14 CULTURAL HERITAGE

In spite of disadvantages in educational opportunities, the so-called "colored schools" and the University of the Western Cape (originally exclusively for coloreds) have produced notable figures in the fields of medicine, law, government, diplomacy, the arts, engineering, commerce and industry and education itself. Some of South Africa's finest writers and poets, such as the internationally acclaimed Adam Small, come from the colored community. The cultural revival amongst particularly the Griqua people has been instrumental in both a renewed empha-sis on a nearly forgotten heritage and a revitalized awareness of identity. An important focus of this cultural revival and identity is personified by two women. Krotoa ("mother" of the Khoekhoen) had special musical and linguistic skills but was adopted by Jan and Maria van Riebeeck (who established the first Dutch settlement at the Cape). They changed Krotoa's name to Eva and "polluted" her lifestyle. The other is Saartjie Baardman, who was taken to Europe in 1810 and paraded in front of the British and French public. Her remains were repatriated to South Africa in 2002 and ceremonially buried in the Eastern Cape where she grew up.

In keeping with the above, the Griqua recognize their own *Volksimbole* (National symbols). In addition to their Independent Church, they have a *Volksvlag* (National Flag) with the colors, bottle green (fruitful life), red (Blood of Christ), white (peace), blue (the color of heaven, pure love) and sea green (derived from the Karoo *kanniedood vetplant*—succulent), a *sinnebeeld* (symbol), which is the *kanniedood* (ad finem) because it is so hardy and durable; and finally a *Volkslied* (National Anthem) *God Eewig, Groot en Goed* (God Eternal, Great and Good), which is sung in Dutch.

15 WORK

During apartheid coloreds were kept by law out of the best jobs and the best schools and forced to travel long distances each day to low-paying jobs. The result has been a high incidence of crime, alcoholism, and other social ills. Remarkable leaders, however, have emerged from the community to address these problems and turn them around. A focus on education has produced doctors, scientists, lawyers, industrialists, and artists in record numbers for such a small community. Many members of the colored community are now anxious about current government trends, which they fear will lead to their becoming victims of affirmative action for Africans. They do not want to lose what they have gained over the years at such great cost. The community's leaders do recognize, however, the unfairness of the old system, a system in which, as recently as 1990, a colored child was 24 times more likely to be helped by a welfare grant than a black child.

16 SPORTS

The most popular sports are soccer, cricket, rugby, and track and field. Now that the community has the opportunity to develop socially and economically, there is increasing interest in the sports of tennis, swimming, golf, yachting, wind- and wave-surfing, and individuals are excelling and gaining national colors in these sports. South Africa has an ideal climate for all outdoor sports and the colored community is as active as any other in the country. Hiking and mountaineering are also extremely popular, especially in the Western Cape, where there are interesting climbs that are easily accessible and the weather is mild for much of the year. On weekends, it is common for families and friends to get together for picnics and barbecues at the beach, alongside a river, or in a backyard.

17 ENTERTAINMENT AND RECREATION

For the most part, the colored community's entertainment is the same as that of people in any other industrialized society—pop and classical music, the movies, dances and nightclubs, and radio and television. Some members of the community have gone on to become entertainers with international reputations as singers and musicians.

[18] FOLK ART, CRAFTS AND HOBBIES

Colored people enjoy varied hobby activities typical of citizens of an industrialized society.

[19] SOCIAL PROBLEMS

Many of the community's problems can be directly attributed to the treatment it received when South Africa was governed by a system that separated people according to race. The result was a relatively poor education because schools were not given the same facilities afforded to "white" schools and because many people had to abandon schooling at an early age to help support the family. Compounding this situation were the breakups of communities and even families as people were moved into townships and suburbs defined by the race of their inhabitants. In addition, many coloreds were kept in low-paying jobs because of job-discrimination laws.

It was inevitable that social ills, such as alcoholism, poor health care and a rising crime rate, would result. Not all of these negative factors have been eradicated yet, but under the new democratic system all South Africans—regardless of race—have an equal opportunity to live a better life. The colored community has shown the resilience and character through the years to take full advantage of their new hard-won rights. Some of the community's leaders are anxious to ensure that its people will not be abandoned by the black majority in the effort to provide a completely level playing field; this concern is a hotly debated political issue in South Africa today.

South Africa no longer conventionally issues birth rate, health, mortality rate, and other statistics by community or race, but the HIV/AIDS figures for the country as a whole are much worse for certain sections of the nation, including for example, the colored townships. For South Africa, the HIV/AIDS adult prevalence rate was 21.5% in 2003. That year there were 5.3 million people living with HIV/AIDS. In 2003, HIV/AIDS deaths totaled more than 370,000.

[20] GENDER ISSUES

The Constitution of the Republic of South Africa (Act 108 of 1996) entrenches individual rights and protection. Chapter 2 [9(3)] specifically indicates that "The State may not unfairly discriminate directly or indirectly against anyone on one or more grounds, including race, gender [and other categories]." But the reality is, particularly in the erstwhile exclusively colored townships and mainly due to social and domestic problems still experienced there, women still bear the brunt of discrimination, particularly alcohol-induced verbal and physical abuse.

For those coloreds who have "graduated" out of such depressed and repressing circumstances gender roles are increasingly changing, as is the case for other South African communities. The leader of one of the prominent opposition political parties, Patricia De Lille, is a case in point. Similar trends are apparent in the academic, arts, and economic spheres of life.

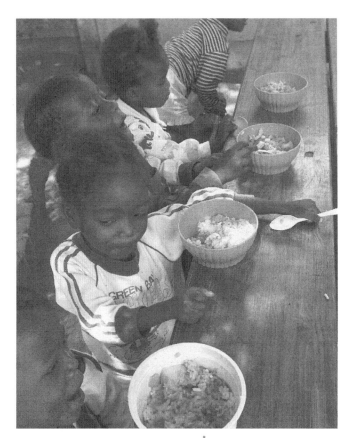

A group of children enjoy their lunch at the Sparrows Nest, a home run by Sparrow Ministeries, in Roodepoort, South Africa. Sparrow Ministeries cares for adults and children with HIV/AIDS. Researchers have released reports estimating that AIDS could kill as many as 7 million South Africans by 2010. (AP Images/Denis Farrell)

[21] BIBLIOGRAPHY

De Jongh, M. "Exclusivity, Hybridity and Community: Negotiating Place, Ethnicity and South African Realities." *Anthropology Southern Africa* 29 (3&4), 2006.

Green, Lawrence G. *Tavern of the Seas.* Cape Town: Timmins, 1953.

South Africa Yearbook 2007/8. Pretoria: GCIS, 2007/8.

Venter, Al J. *Coloured. A Profile of Two Million South Africans.* Cape Town: Human & Rousseau, 1974.

Waldman, L. *The Griqua Conundrum: Political and Sociocultural Identity in the Northern Cape, South Africa.* Ph.D. Johannesburg: University of the Witwatersrand, 2001.

Wilson, Monica and Leonard Thompson, ed. *The Oxford History of South Africa II (1870–1966).* Oxford: Clarendon, 1971.

—revised by M. de Jongh

COMORIANS

PRONUNCIATION: kuh-MAWR-ee-uhns
LOCATION: Comoros Islands
ALTERNATE NAMES: Mauri or the Mahorais
POPULATION: 798,000
LANGUAGE: Arabic, French, Comorian (Shikomori)
RELIGION: Islam (Sunni), Catholicism

¹ INTRODUCTION

The Comoros Archipelago—comprising Grande Comore (Njazídja), Anjouan (Nzwani), Mayotte (Mahore), and Mohéli (Mwali)—was originally named by Arab sailors who visited the islands in the late 6th century. They called them *Juzu el Kumar* ("islands of the moon" in Arabic) because of their brightness during the full moon. Before the arrival of the Arabs, Africans of the Wamakuwa and Bantu tribes had been living on the islands, organized in clans, and had originated the Comorian language, which is still spoken today. The Comoros was also visited by sailors from East Asia, Persia, and Israel. More Arabs arrived on the islands between the 12th and 17th centuries, transforming their social structures and introducing sultanates. The Comorians are a blend of settlers from the past: Iranian traders, mainland Africans, Arabs, and Malagasy.

In the early 15th century, Portuguese visited the region. (In 1527, the Comoros islands appeared on a world map designed by Portuguese cartographer Diego Roberso.) Sailors from the Netherlands, France, and other European countries, all attracted by the islands' geographically strategic position eventually followed them. In the early 17th century, pirates used the Comoros as a base from which to attack and rob merchant vessels. In 1841, King Andreanantsuli of Madagascar, having previously declared himself sultan of Mayotte, sold the island to the French. Later in the 19th century, Ramanetaka, another Malagasy king, formed a relationship with the local authorities on Mohéli, modifying its system of local rule and establishing another sultanate. The Comoros became a French protectorate in 1886. They were placed under the authority of the French governor general of Madagascar in 1908 and given their own internal administration in 1912.

In 1958, the political status of the islands was modified by a referendum, which gave them the status of a self-governing French overseas territory. Said Mohammed Cheik became the president of the Council of Government. In a December 1974 referendum, a majority of the Comorians of the four islands voted for independence from France. Dissatisfied with the prospect of losing all four islands, the French scheduled another election in July 1975 that permitted each island to choose its own political status.

Opposing this French move to divide the islands, Ahmed Abdallah, president of the Council of Government, unilaterally declared independence for all the islands on 6 July 1975 and was installed as the nation's first president. Less than a month after the Comoros' independence, France established a military presence on Mayotte, and while the former colonial power was affirming its control of Mayotte, European mercenaries, led by the notorious French soldier of fortune Bob Denard, destabilized the other three independent islands by overthrowing the governments and killing the presidents. Since its independ-

dence, Comorians have requested the reintegration of the island of Mayotte through a United Nations resolution.

A state-owned newspaper, Al Watwany, began operations in July 1985, first as a monthly and soon afterward as a weekly. An independent weekly, L'Archipel, began publishing in 1988. A news agency, Agence Comores Presse, is now based in Moroni, and France has provided funds for establishing a national television service. In 1989 Comoros had an estimated 61,000 radios and 200 television sets.

In addition to national broadcasts on FM in Comoran Swahili and French, Radio Comoros in 1993 broadcast internationally on the shortwave band in Swahili, Arabic, and French. An independent commercial FM radio station, Radio Tropique FM, began broadcasting in 1991, although it and its director, political activist Ali Bakar Cassim, were both the object of government ire over the station's readiness to criticize the Djohar regime.

On 3 August 1975 Ali Soilihi, assisted by French mercenaries, overthrew Abdallah's government, implementing a socialist-inspired self-sufficiency policy that boosted the Comorian economy. On 12 November 1975 the Comoros was admitted to the United Nations as a nation composed of four islands—Grande Comore, Anjouan, Mohéli, and Mayotte. In May 1978 European mercenaries once again led by Denard, who had placed Soilihi in power, overthrew the government and assassinated him. Denard took control of the Comoros and restored Ahmed Abdallah to power. For more than a decade Abdallah ruled the country, backed by Denard and his mercenaries. He changed the name of the country to the Federal Islamic Republic of the Comoros.

In November 1989, when President Abdallah anticipated negotiating with France on the question of the Comorian island of Mayotte and planned to expel the mercenaries, they assassinated him and seized control of the country for several weeks. France and South Africa arranged their surrender and subsequent departure. Five months later, Said Mohammed Djohar the former head of the supreme court, was elected president. A few months before the end of President Djohar's five-year term, history repeated itself when Bob Denard, supposedly on parole in France, seized President Djohar and forced him into exile to Réunion, a French Overseas Department island. Once again Denard took control of the country for several weeks. Pressured by the Comorian government and the international community, France sent its marines to withdraw Denard and his mercenaries.

In March 1996 Mohammed Taki Abdoulkarim was elected president. A year later, because of the incomplete independence of the Comoros and chronic political instabilities conceived by some Europeans, on 3 August 1997 the residents of Anjouan and Mohéli declared an unrecognized independence and requested to return under French administration, which France denied.

In 1997, the islands of Anjouan and Mohéli declared their independence from the Union of Comoros. However, the islands were reunified as the Comoros again in 2002, a new constitution mandated the election of a president of Anjouan along with presidents for the other two islands and a federal president. Mohamed Bacar, who had led the separatist government since 2001, was elected for a five-year term as President of Anjouan. His term expired on 14 April 2007, and the President of the Assembly, Houmadi Caambi, became acting president from April 2007 to 10 May 2007.

Comorian federal troops tried unsuccessfully to take control of buildings in Anjouan and install a replacement president as mandated by a court in May 2007. The Union government delayed the holding of an election on Anjouan due to alleged irregularities and intimidation, but Bacar nevertheless printed ballots and held a sham election in June, claiming a landslide victory of 90%.

In October 2007, the African Union (AU) imposed travel sanctions on Anjouan's President Mohamed Bacar and other government officials and froze their foreign assets while calling for fresh elections. In February 2008 the Comoros rejected the AU's extended sanctions against Anjouan and instead opted for a military solution.

In March 2008 hundreds of Union government troops began assembling on Moheli, which is closer to Anjouan than the larger island, Grande Comore. Foreign troops from Sudan, Senegal, Libya, Tanzania, and France arrived to offer support for the operation to invade and secure the Comoros. Anjouan promised to hold new elections in May 2008, which the South African president supported as a way to resolve the crisis. The proposal and the invasion went ahead.

² LOCATION AND HOMELAND

The Comoros Islands, located between Madagascar and the east coast of Africa, cover 2,170 sq km (838 sq mi). The national capital, Moroni, located on Grande Comore, has over 30,000 inhabitants. The climate of the Comoros is tropical, with a warm rainy season from November to April and a mild dry season from April to October. The total population is approximately 530,000 people, of whom more than 30% live in urban areas. The population increases about 3.5% per year, with an annual birthrate of 50 births per 1,000 population and an annual death rate of more than 10 per 1,000 population. The age structure of the population of Comoros is similar to that of many developing countries, in that the republic has a very large proportion of young people.

Grande Comore (Njazídja) covers a total area of 1,145 sq km (442 sq mi). Geologically speaking, it is the youngest island in the archipelago and is dominated by an active volcano, Mt. Khartala (7,900 ft/2,408 m), with the world's largest crater. Its last eruption was in 1977. The island of Anjouan (Nzwani) is triangular, roughly 97 km (60 mi) on each side, and a total area of 424 sq km (164 sq mi). It is the most densely populated island in the archipelago, with 210,000 people. Mayotte (Mahore) is the westernmost island in the archipelago, with an area of 374 sq km (144 sq mi). As the first island to be settled by Europeans, Mayotte was the most resistant to the establishment of a strong Islamic culture by Arab inhabitants. Mohéli (Mwali) is the smallest of the four islands, with an area of 290 sq km (112 sq mi).

³ LANGUAGE

Arabic, French, and Comorian are the official languages of Comoros. The Comorian language, *Shikomori*, is derived from the Bantu culture and related to Swahili and Arabic. A different dialect of *Shikomori* is spoken on each of the four islands of the Comoros: *Shinjazídja* on Grande Comore, *Shindzuani* on Anjouan, *Shimwali* on Mwali, and *Shimaore* on Mayotte. De-

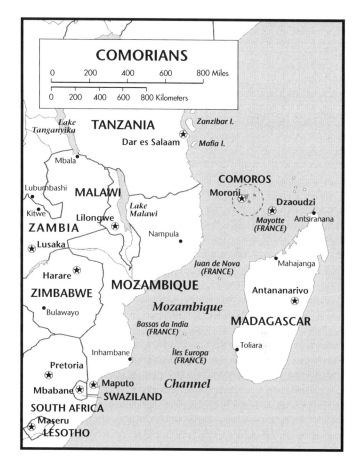

spite some phonetic and semantic differences among the dialects, its speakers understand each other.

Comorians do not have surnames in the Western sense. Instead their proper names are followed by those of their fathers, as in Sofia Muhammad-Sofia, the daughter of Muhammad. Most Comorian proper names have specific meanings. For example, the name *Mdahoma* means "long life," *Karihila* means "fearless," and *Shujai* means "hero." Departing from the traditional Comorian names, some Comorians today use Arabic or Christian names. The Comoran people are a blend of African, Arab, and MalayoIndonesian elements. A few small communities, primarily in Mahoré, speak Kibushi, a Malagasy dialect. The principal Comoran Swahili dialect, written in Arabic script, is related to the Swahili spoken in East Africa but is not easily intelligible to East African Swahili speakers. Classical Arabic is significant for religious reasons, and French remains the principal language with which the Republic of the Comoros communicates with the rest of the world.

Comorian, or *Shikomor* is a descendant of Swahili with Arabic influences. About 57% of the population is literate in the Latin alphabet, more with the Arabic alphabet; total literacy is estimated at 62.5%. Comorian has no native script, but both Arabic and Latin scripts have been used.

⁴ FOLKLORE

Comorian folklore is dominated by both African and Islamic traditions. Like some other Muslims, there is a widespread belief among Comorians that events occur according to Allah's will, and that human beings cannot control their destinies. Certain local myths are related to Islam. In the north of Grande Comore, for example, it is believed that at the present site of Lac Salé ("salted lake"), a village was flooded because its inhabitants refused to give water to a sharif (supposedly a direct descendant of the prophet Muhammad).

Some widespread beliefs are related to African divinities, such as the belief that a diviner (*mwalim*) or *jinn* (spirits) should be consulted before any social activity or ceremony. Such consultations may require special rites, financial outlays, and animal sacrifices.

Mt. Khartala on Grande Comore is said to have been created by the shock that occurred when King Solomon's ring fell on the island while he was being chased by *jinns* from Saba (present-day Ethiopia). It is said that when the ring sank in the Indian Ocean, it was eaten by a fish.

5 RELIGION

Islam is the state religion; some 98% of Comorians are Sunni Muslims. About 2% are Catholic, and evangelical believers represent only 0.1% of the population. There is at least one Catholic church in the capital of each island. Surprisingly, however, mosque attendance is very low. Mixed with their Islamic practices, there is a strong involvement in occultism and spirit possession.

6 MAJOR HOLIDAYS

The Comoros have two types of holidays: religious and national holidays, the latter include New Year's Day (January 1); a holiday commemorating the death of President Said Mohammed Cheik, the first president of the self-governing Council government (March 16); Labor Day (May 1); and Independence Day (July 6). Religious holidays include the celebration of the prophet Mohammed's birth; *Miraj*, the day when the latter went to visit paradise; *Idd el Fitri*, which marks the end of Ramadan; and *Idd el Adha*, primarily a day to remember one's ancestors. Religious holidays conform to a lunar calendar.

7 RITES OF PASSAGE

In the Comoros, each stage of human life is celebrated by a specific ceremony. Newborn babies and their mothers are kept secluded to avoid the "evil eye" of possible enemies for the first seven days after birth. During this period several religious rituals take place, and only very close relatives are permitted to visit them. After the seven days, friends can see them. Some bring gifts, which may range from a ring to a cow to a tree.

At the age of six, children are sent to a Quranic school, where they learn the Islamic code of conduct, and later to a Western-style primary school. Four to five years later, when they are able to read the entire Quran, a special ceremony called the *Hitimiya* is organized. This ritual is simultaneously a ceremony of a personal recognition and a rite of passage to adolescence. At this time, boys are circumcised.

Traditionally, the eldest daughter in a family does not leave her house after the *Hitimiya* unless she is escorted by a member of her family and covered with a *shiromani* or *lesso* (colorful local shawls). At present, this tradition is only practiced in some rural areas.

At the age of 15, boys traditionally leave their families and build huts where they sleep and socialize with their friends. Yet they still participate in family activities and play a role in public events in their villages. When this phase is over, they are ready to marry, once they have the approval of their families. They can celebrate with either a simple marriage or the *anda* (grand marriage).

For Grand Comorians, the anda is not only a wedding festivity; it is also a social, economic, and cultural rite. Several stages and ceremonies should be accomplished before a man becomes a "respectful man." The grand marriage is cost prohibitive and associates the whole community. On the other islands, the structure is similar but less expensive.

Anda promotes a man to a personal social achievement and hierarchy and/or validates his political status. It also provides prestigious status to a woman and her family. In order to access the highest social hierarchy grade and personal prestige, one should celebrate one's own anda and also have one for a daughter or niece. Thus, it is not uncommon for someone to marry at the age of 20 and celebrate a grand marriage 30 years later.

Depending upon the family (either rich or socially well-integrated), the grand marriage can begin at the day of someone's birth, reach its peak during the marriage celebration, and continue even after the person's death. However, a simple marriage is reserved for marginal families and those who choose not to celebrate a grand marriage.

Birthday parties are celebrated only in urban areas, yet those born during the month of Maulid (the month corresponding to the Prophet Mohammad's birth) celebrate with a religious ceremony.

8 INTERPERSONAL RELATIONS

Comorians are known for their politeness, humor, hospitality, and harmony. Sharing and helping others are considered mandatory in all circumstances, to the point where the very notion of thanking someone is considered odd, because help is always expected and even taken for granted.

The Comorian greeting is very lengthy and may even include inquiries about one's neighbors, pets, or cattle. In public, men shake hands, and some young people slap each others' hands. Older women greet each other verbally or grasp each others' hands. *Kwezi*, either preceding or succeeding a sentence, is a common term of respect used when addressing a person older than oneself. It is considered impolite to address people by their family names. When addressing an older person with whom one is not familiar, proper forms of address are *mjomba* (uncle), *mbaba* (father), or *mdzade* (mother). If one knows the person's child, niece, or nephew, these appellations are followed by the name of the younger relative (e.g. *mbaba* Ali if the son's name is Ali, or *mjomba* Nema if the nephew's name is Nema).

It is considered rude to lose contact with close family or friends, and regular visits are the norm. When someone intends to travel abroad, everyone in the community is informed, and gifts are given by friends and close family members before a trip. The traveler is also expected to bring gifts for those at home upon returning.

Officially, dating is forbidden, as Islam forbids relationships between unmarried couples.

9 LIVING CONDITIONS

Comoros is among the world's least developed countries, with high birth and death rates, and a population growth rate that is roughly twice the world average. In the 1980s, a large proportion of all housing still consisted of the traditional straw huts with roofs made from cocoa leaves, although there were also dwellings made from brick, stone, or concrete.

About 60% of the Comorians live in cities; but whether in rural or urban areas, housing on the island is generally poor. The average life expectancy was 56 years in 1992, when it was estimated that nearly one-third of all children died before the age of five. Leading health problems include malaria, tuberculosis, and leprosy. By 2005, life expectancy was 62.2 years.

There is a ring road on each island. Many of the smaller roads are usable only for part of the year. Grande Comore has an international airport at Hahaia, and there are airfields on the other islands.

10 FAMILY LIFE

Despite the intrusion of foreign customs, Comorian culture retains a strong traditional concept of the family, whose members are linked by blood, marriage, or adoption. Friends may also be considered family. The coherence provided by this tradition has played a tremendous role in social and daily life, fostering solidarity and preventing delinquency and crime. Polygamy is an acceptable practice among the Comorians. Among men who can afford it, the preferred form of marriage appears to be polygyny with matrilocal residence. The first marriage is formally initiated with the grand marriage when possible, subsequent unions involve much simpler ceremonies. The result is that a man will establish two or even more households and will alternate residence between them, a reflection, most likely, of the trading origins of the Shirazi elite who maintained wives at different trading posts. Said Mohamed Djohar, elected president in 1990, had two wives, one in Njazidja and the other in Nzwani, an arrangement said to have broadened his appeal to voters. For men, divorce is easy, although by custom a divorced wife retains the family home. Children are expected to help with family duties such as farming, fishing, and caring for the animals. Each family is affiliated with a political party, a bond based on personal relationships rather than on the party's policies or actions.

11 CLOTHING

French colonization modified the Comorian mode of dress. Although young people wear Western style clothing, traditional clothing is still common among the adults. Traditional clothing, still worn by older women, is very colorful. They either wear a long dress and cover themselves with a *lesso* or *shiromani* (traditional shawls), or they wear a *chador,* a combination head covering, veil, and shawl worn by women in many Muslim countries. Younger women wear Western clothes but still cover themselves with a lesso. Only women in cities wear pants. While in town, a Comorian man will typically wear a white cotton garment and a knee-length shirt, sometimes with a white jacket and white skull cap. Out of town, a long cloth sarong (colorful skirt) is worn. Most women wear long, colorful cotton dresses with bright shawls as face coverings. Others prefer wearing black robes that cover their heads. Older men wear a traditional cloth called an *ikoi* covering their lower body, a long white robe called a *kandu,* and a *kofia,* an embroidered hat.

12 FOOD

Comorian food reflects a combination of influences, mostly African but also Arab and Indian. The main fare in the Comorian diet consists of products cultivated on the islands, except rice, which is imported from Asia. Most Comorian cuisine is spicy. The basic diet of the Comorians consists of rice, potatoes, corn, fish, coconuts, and bananas. Other crops that are grown are sweet potatoes, citrus fruits, and pineapples.

Breakfast varies from one island to the next. On Grande Comore, people drink hot tea with bread, grilled breadfruit, or leftovers. On Anjouan and Mayotte they drink a hot soup made from leftover rice. The residents of Mohéli drink hot tea and eat grilled cassava or breadfruit with fish. Lunch is similar on all four islands and may include cassava, tarot, green bananas, potatoes, breadfruit (grilled, fried, or boiled) or rice with *madaba* (cassava leaves), fish, and imported meat. Rice is the main dish for dinner. The most common beverages are fresh water and fruit juice. Alcohol and pork are forbidden by the Muslim religion. On Anjouan and Mayotte, a local beer, *trembo,* made from coconut juice is tolerated. The Comoros islands have an abundance of fruit, including mangoes, papayas, oranges, coconuts, and pineapples, varying with the specific season and region.

Before exposure to Western influences, Comorians ate on a mat placed on the floor using their right hands, a practice still followed in rural areas. In urban areas, people eat at tables with Western utensils.

13 EDUCATION

The Comorian educational system is based on both Islamic teachings and the French model. All education is free. Each village has several Quranic schools and at least one French primary school. However, due to economic problems, the majority of students find it hard to finish primary school.

There is a *collège* (junior primary) and three to five *lycées* (secondary schools) on each island, as well as a couple of technical training schools and a teacher training college. For higher education, since the 1990s many private primary and secondary schools have emerged.

14 CULTURAL HERITAGE

Comorian music and dance are based on African, Arabic, Malagasy, European, and southern Indian traditions. Comoran society and culture reflect the influences of Islam and the traditions of East Africa. The former provides the basis for religion and law; the East African influence is evident in the language, a Swahili dialect, and in a number of pre-Islamic customs. Western, primarily French, influences are also prevalent, particularly in the modern educational sector, the civil service, and cultural affairs. Lavish wedding ceremonies are common and highly regarded. This wedding ceremony, which can cost as much as the equivalent of $20,000 to $30,000, involves an exchange of expensive gifts between the couple's families and feasts for an entire village. The gift giving and dancing that accompany the grand marriage have helped perpetuate indigenous arts in silversmithing, goldsmithing, folk song, and folk dance.

15 WORK

Subsistence agriculture and fishing are the Comorians' chief sources of income, employing roughly 80% of the labor force, with a smaller number engaged in trade. In families engaged in farming or fishing, children generally work alongside their parents, although the legal minimum age for employment is 15. In the 1990s, teachers and other government employees, as well as dock workers, began to unionize. Most of the islanders work as farmers or fishermen, while a few breed cattle, sheep, goats, and donkeys. A small number work in industry or in jobs relating to tourism. The island of Mayotte is very poor and undeveloped. Due to the shortage of good farmland, much of the food must be imported.

16 SPORTS

Soccer (known as football) is a popular male sport in the Comoros. Each village has at least two football teams. Women only participate as spectators. Volleyball and basketball are also common in urban areas, where some women are involved in sports. Comoros participated in its first Olympic games in Atlanta in 1996.

17 ENTERTAINMENT AND RECREATION

Public conversation is a very common form of male entertainment in the Comoros. Each village has several public places called *bangwe* where men of the same generation or social and cultural background meet every day, particularly from 4 to 6 pm and from 8 pm until midnight. All social games and activities take place at the bangwe. *Mrenge*, a mixture of boxing and wrestling, was once a popular game on the islands and is still occasionally played on Anjouan and Mayotte. The influence of Western culture has dominated Comorian society, and some Comorian games are unfortunately now disappearing or are considered uncivilized, such as *mbio za ngalawa* (boat racing) and *ngome za ngombe* (cattle wrestling). For recreation they enjoy dancing, singing, and playing instruments, especially horns and drums.

Older men enjoy playing dominoes, cards, and *mraha*, a seed-and-board game well known in Africa and the Pacific Islands. Movie theaters have declined since the introduction of the VCR. On weekends, young people organize picnics or barbecues on the beach. In each major city there are a couple of nightclubs. Young people also commonly surf the Internet.

18 FOLK ART, CRAFTS, AND HOBBIES

The Comoros, especially Anjouan, are known for their wood-carvings and dolls. Other traditional crafts include the brightly colored red and orange cloth worn by Comorian women, as well as jewelry and embroidered Muslim hats.

19 SOCIAL PROBLEMS

Comorians have no real ethnic or racial divisions. Nevertheless, there are traditional hostilities between urban and rural dwellers and between fishermen and peasants. Yet since the illegal occupation of Mayotte by France in 1975, divisions have emerged between residents of Mayotte and other Comorians of the independent three islands. Political instability is a major problem facing the Comorians. More than a dozen coups d'état conducted by Western mercenaries in the years since 1975 have led to political instability on the islands.

The physical needs of the Comorians are numerous. Major problems in Mayotte include poverty, disease, and hunger. Educational levels are low and only 68% of the population is literate. The economy is struggling and unemployment levels are very high. There is a shortage of hospitals and doctors, and many suffer from illnesses and chronic malnutrition. Hygiene is poor due to the fact that the Comorians have a poor water supply. Such problems contribute to a high death rate, especially among young children.

20 GENDER ISSUES

Among the men who can afford it, the preferred form of marriage appears to be polygyny with matrilocal residence. The result is that a man will establish two or even more households and will alternate residence between them, a reflection, most likely, of the trading origins of the Shirazi elite who maintained wives at different trading posts. Women have to contend with an alternating husband. For men, divorce is easy, although by custom a divorced wife retains the family home.

Although women play a limited role in Comorian culture, in which polygamy is legal, their matriarchal tradition gives Comorian women the last word on important issues pertaining to household affairs. Also, atypically for an Islamic society, they may leave their husbands without any official notice or legal decision.

Despite their lower economic status, women married to farmers or laborers often move about more freely than their counterparts among the social elite, managing market stands or working in the fields. On Mwali, where traditional Islamic values are less dominant, women generally are not as strictly secluded.

Islamic law recognizes only male ownership and inheritance of land. In Comoros, however, certain landholdings called *magnahouli* are controlled by women and inherited through the female line, apparently in observance of a surviving matriarchal African tradition.

Girls are somewhat less likely than boys to attend school in Comoros.

Although the 1992 constitution recognizes their right to suffrage, as did the 1978 constitution, women otherwise play a limited role in politics in Comoros. By contrast, in Mahoré female merchants sparked the movement for continued association with France, and later, for continued separation from the Republic of the Comoros.

Due to restricted religious and political beliefs, women cannot plan their own families. The use of contraceptives is irreligious in the largely Islamic community.

21 BIBLIOGRAPHY

Damir, Ben Ali, Paul Ottino, and Georges Boulinier. *Tradition d'une lingée royale des Comores*. Paris: Editions l'Harmattan, 1986.

Gemma Pitcher and Patricia C. Wright *Lonely Planet World Guide: Madagascar and Comoros*. Portland, OR: Lonely Planet Publications, 2004.

Hornburger, Jane M., and Alex Whitney. *African Countries and Cultures*. New York: David McKay, 1981.

Johnstone, Patrick and Jason Mandryk. *Operation World*. London: Milton Keynes, 2005.

Malyn Newitt *The Comoros Islands: Struggle Against Dependency in the Indian Ocean.* Boulder, Colorado: Westview Press, 1984.

Martin, Jean. *Comores. Quatres Îles Entre Pirates et Planteurs.* Paris: Editions l'Harmattan, 1983.

Martin, Jean and Harriet Ottenheimer. *Historical Dictionary of the Comoro Islands.* Rowman & Littlefield Publishers, 1994.

Ottenheimer, Martin. *Marriage in Domoni, Husbands and Wives in an Indian Ocean Community.* Prospect Heights, IL: Waveland Press, 1985.

Said, Islam, Moinaescha Mroudjae, and Sophia Blanchy. *The Status and Situation of Women in the Comoros.* New York: United Nations Development Programme, 1989.

Verin, Pierre and Réne Battistini. *Les Comores.* Paris: ACCT-Nathan, 1987

—revised by M. Njoroge.

CONGOLESE (BRAZZAVILLANS)

PRONUNCIATION: kahn-go-LEEZ
ALTERNATE NAMES: Congo-Brazzavillans
LOCATION: Republic of the Congo
Population: 3,903,318
LANGUAGE: French, Lingala, Kikongo, Sangha, Bateke, 60 others
RELIGION: Christianity (Catholic), animism
RELATED ARTICLES: Vol. 1: Bakongo

[1] INTRODUCTION

In October 1997, the Republic of the Congo swore in a new president after waging a four-month civil war that killed thousands and left Brazzaville, once one of the most peaceful and smoothly run capitals in Central Africa, in ruins. Five years after the first democratic elections, private militias installed an unelected government. The civil war was partially fueled by the prize of the country's offshore oil wealth, which motivated many of the warlords. The army split along ethnic lines, with most northern officers joining President Denis Sassou-Nguesso's side and most southerners backing the rebels. By the end of 1999, the government, which was backed by Angolan forces, had taken most of the key positions, and the rebels agreed to a ceasefire. However, remnants of the civil war militias, known as Ninjas, have remained active in the southern Pool region.

The Republic of Congo is one of sub-Saharan Africa's main oil producers, though 70% of the total population of about 3.9 million lives in poverty. In 2004 the country was expelled from the Kimberley Process, which is supposed to prevent conflict diamonds from entering the world supply market. This followed investigations that found that the Republic of Congo could not account for the origin of large quantities of rough diamonds that it was officially exporting. However, reports of battle and corruption do not do justice to the Republic of the Congo. It has long been the education and banking center of the Central African region. During World War II, it was the capital of the Free French movement led by Charles de Gaulle against the Nazis and France's Vichy government. Its leaders were unabashedly Communist during the latter half of the Cold War, trading vigorously with China and the Soviet Union.

Mention "The Congo," and many people think of the jungles made famous by the writings of Joseph Conrad in *The Heart of Darkness*. The Republic of the Congo is located directly across the Congo (or Zaire) River from the Democratic Republic of the Congo (known as Zaire until mid-1997), the setting for Conrad's novel. The river that divides the two Congos is the second longest in Africa, after the Nile, and carries the largest potential supply of hydroelectric power in the world.

Brazzaville is Congo's capital, sitting directly across the great river from Zaire's pulsating capital, Kinshasa. But, Kinshasa seems a world away from the sleepier city on the opposite bank. Brazzaville is calm and orderly, boasting relatively reliable transportation links and utilities, and a crime rate significantly lower than that of Kinshasa and indeed many other African cities. Pointe-Noire, the Congo's industrial and

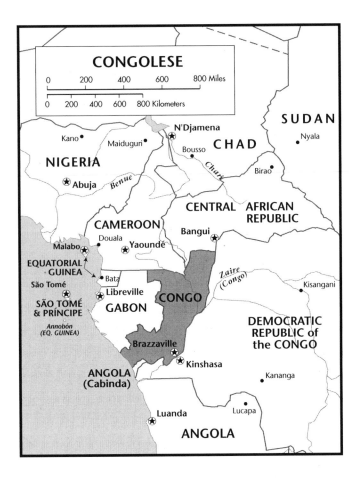

petroleum center, is located on the Atlantic coast and boasts a dredged harbor that can accommodate oil tankers from around the world.

The Portuguese discovered the mouth of the Congo River in 1482 and began trading with the Kongo kingdom, which had been consolidated in the 14th century. Slaves and ivory attracted the interest of other European countries, and in 1883, explorer Savorgnan de Brazza signed treaties with the Bateke, a tribe located to the north, ceding the entire region to France.

Today, the Congo continues its close relationship with France, despite achieving independence in 1960. Its currency is tied directly to the French franc, and France remains its chief trading partner.

2 LOCATION AND HOMELAND

The Congo straddles the equator, most of the land covered by dense tropical forest. It is hot, very humid, and rains an average of 178 cm (70 in) per year. Wooded savanna, river valleys, and a small coastal plain make up less than half of the total land area, which is 342,000 sq km (132,000 sq mi), about the size of Montana. The Congo's entire eastern and southern borders are washed by the Congo River. The magnitude of this river in the lives of Congolese, past and present, cannot be underestimated. Over 1,600 km (1,000 mi) of unbroken navigable water serves as a veritable highway for huge barges and dugout canoes, carting people and produce through Central Africa. People eat from it, live on it in houses built high on stilts, take

electric power from it, and hand pieces of it down through the generations, in the form of inheritable fishing rights.

Inland, there are many lakes and marshes, one of which is the legendary home of a water-dwelling dinosaur known locally as Mokele-Mbembe, considered somewhat of a national treasure, and hunted, but never seen, by groups of eccentric Western scientists. Better documented are elephant, hippo, lowland gorilla, lion, chimpanzee, pangolin, bushpig, dozens of ungulates, crocodile, and tropical birds. The two major environments that comprise the Congo, forest and savanna, are pure contrasts. In most of the forest, one cannot see more than a few yards. On the savanna-covered plateaus, one can see for miles. In the dry season, miles of fire, set by lightning or the game-hunter, ring the horizons.

3 LANGUAGE

French is the administrative language of the Congo, with Lingala, Kikongo, Sangha, and Bateke the most widely spoken native languages. There are 60 other languages in the Congo, crisscrossing national boundaries. There is another kind of Congolese language though, and that is the language of the talking drum. For generations, messages have been sent from village to village by the regulated beat of special drums, usually situated near the compound of the village chief. In the past, everyone within earshot understood the meaning of the various rhythms. There were rhythms for death, birth, marriage, or the impending arrival of a dignitary. Talking drums still are used, but they are losing their original relevancy in lieu of radio, shortwave, and television.

4 FOLKLORE

The Congo is rich in folkloric tradition, and generalizations are difficult in a country with dozens of ethnic groups. Typically, however, heroes and personalities tend to take the form of animals. Each family, or sometimes an entire village or clan, will have its own totem, an animal whose spirit and characteristics represent the group's unity. These animals are imbued with mystical powers, are responsible for the creation of the ancestral lineage, and revered through storytelling and surrounding ritual and taboo.

5 RELIGION

The vast majority of the population identifies itself as Christian, primarily Catholic. Many continue to hold animist beliefs and do not consider them contrary to monotheism. Local animists long believed in one supreme god before the arrival of European missionaries. Its name is Nzambi and can best be described as the omnipotent spirit of nature. One of the Congo's creation myths tells of Nzambi's great illness, back when the Earth was still completely covered with water. In his fits of coughing, he spat up the sun, moon, stars, animals, and people. So, the world was born by opportune accident.

6 MAJOR HOLIDAYS

The Congo's national holiday is celebrated on August 15 and commemorates the country's independence from France begun on that day in 1960. Independence Day is celebrated in streets, courtyards, houses, and bars. Beer and palm wine are consumed in large quantities, and the preferred dish on this special occasion is chicken and rice. Chicken, or any form of animal protein, for that matter, often marks a special occasion. Less than 1% of the land in the Congo is used for animal husbandry, and most meat is either hunted or imported at great expense.

Other holidays include Christmas and New Year's, Easter, All Saints Day, and June 10 (National Reconciliation Day).

7 RITES OF PASSAGE

Because many Africans believe in the spirit life of their ancestors after death, funeral and mourning rituals are accorded great importance. But, the ritual life of the Congo is changing quickly with urban migration fueled by wage labor. For traditionalists, the period of mourning can be very involved and intensely onerous. Widows typically shave their heads, dress in rags, and bathe infrequently. They sometimes are required to live by themselves in a house far removed from the center of the village, forbidden to talk with anyone or look a person in the eye. Their only food might be leftovers from their in-laws' table, never to include meat or fish. This state of affairs can last anywhere from one month to the rest of a widow's life, depending on the ethnic group, village, and piety of the family. Widowers, understood to have important work to do outside the home, including fathering more children, might be expected to wait a year before remarrying, as a sign of respect to the dead wife.

A ritual surrounding marriage, practiced less now than in the past, attests to the traditional importance of premarital virginity for girls. It is interesting to note that this ritual appears in different forms throughout the world, particularly the Near East.

Once a couple has decided to marry, both the man and the woman undergo a course in "domestic education," taught by the elders of their own gender within the family. It is assumed that the woman is a virgin, and she must receive some sexual instruction in order to contribute to a successful union. On the morning after the wedding night, the women from both sides of the family arrive early, while the couple is still in bed, to inquire pointedly about the previous night's events. Was consummation successful? Were all parties satisfied? Was there blood evident to prove the virginity of the bride? If the answer to any of these questions is no, then the husband has the right to ask for his bride-price back and annul the marriage.

8 INTERPERSONAL RELATIONS

Different cultures express greetings in different ways and so it is in the Congo, with its many cultural heritages. Common for some groups is to greet close relatives not seen for a long time with a bear hug. Among friends and acquaintances, there is the two-handed shake. While in neighboring Gabon, kissing alternate cheeks three to four times is prevalent even in the villages, it is a Western custom seen in the Congo almost exclusively in the modern cities.

There is a marked formality in communication among Congolese, a style that is shared throughout Central Africa. Even a business meeting should begin with a polite inquiry into the other person's well-being, that of their family, and an indication of the honor that their presence bestows. Public recognition of social hierarchy is very important, and agreement with an elder, boss, or anyone of higher status is valued above directness.

9 LIVING CONDITIONS

The Congo is a poor country by Western standards. It is far from the poorest country in Africa, however. It currently ranks 16 out of 52 on the United Nations Human Development Index for Africa, which ranks countries according to quality of life based on income levels, literacy, and other criteria. This relative wealth is primarily due to the existence of petroleum.

Outside of the cities, houses commonly are built out of mud brick and are in constant need of repair. Many can afford corrugated zinc roofs on their homes, and those who cannot use thatch. Buildings in urban areas are usually made out of concrete blocks, and there are several steel and glass office towers in Brazzaville, though they have been severely damaged by the war.

Whether poor or wealthy, Congolese take immense pride in their homes. Mud-brick houses are ringed with handmade, well-maintained fencing. Decorative flowers and bushes are planted in a front yard that is scrupulously cleared of weeds and grasses in an effort to keep away snakes, rats, and insects. Cooking often takes place in the front of the house over an open fire, where the women prepare the food, and everyone else gathers. Small villages are arranged with straight, perpendicular streets of dirt and a wide boulevard through the center.

Larger towns and cities are relatively clean and well-planned. Utilities, such as electricity and water, are available, if not affordable to everyone. This is not the case throughout the interior. Villages not on the power grid often use gas powered generators for communal purposes during restricted hours. Watching a wrestling match on a television placed in front of the local bar is but one example.

Although nearly two-thirds of the Congo's citizens live in or between the two major cities of Brazzaville and Pointe-Noire, making it one of the most urbanized populations in Africa, there is ample room for small farms and gardens, and most Congolese are engaged in some type of subsistence farming. They know how to farm and produce just enough food to feed their families and perhaps fill a stall at the vegetable market.

10 FAMILY LIFE

The average Congolese woman bears six children during her lifetime. Still, the Congo has one of the lowest population densities on the continent. In the past, most marriages were arranged by family members. Today, this is much less common. Often, a man proposes to a woman with a gift of money. Then, once both families are in agreement, a "dot," or bride-price, is paid by the groom to the bride's parents. While this custom has no legal status, it is ancient and taken quite seriously. If a couple divorces, in many instances, the husband can demand his money back.

A visitor to the Congo might remark that women do most of the work it takes to run a family and a household. They are responsible for planting, harvesting, food preparation, water fetching, child care, and housework (which can include putting on a new roof or erecting a fence). Men traditionally are responsible for hunting, clearing the forest for gardens, or, in the city, engaging in wage-labor.

The word "family" has a somewhat different meaning in the Congo than in the West. The nuclear family is not necessarily the standard unit. Family means an extensive network of relatives, including aunts, uncles, cousins, grandparents,

While the government, by its own admission, has ignored the rural economy for decades, there is, in spite of this, a relatively high density of rural primary schools.
(International Labour Office)

nieces, and nephews. Matrilineal cultures, such as many in the Congo, identify the older brother of one's mother as the prime male role model and caretaker. Cousins on one's mother's side are considered brothers and sisters. If each woman has six children, there are many siblings.

The extended family plays the role in society that the state has taken over in many Western countries. Indigent, sick, or disabled people are rarely sent to institutions, such as nursing homes, left to live on the street, or live on welfare. Their care is the family's responsibility, and the burdens of this responsibility can be spread among the dozens of people that constitute a family.

¹¹ CLOTHING

Central Africans take care in their dress in general, and Congolese are no exception. Whether a person has means or not, people in the street, the market, and in offices can be seen in pressed, colorful, hand-tailored garb. *Bous-Bous*, the colorful strips of cotton cloth essential to any Central or West African wardrobe, can be dressed up or down. They also are used as head wraps and turbans by Congolese women. Office workers and bureaucrats dress much the same as they do in the West.

¹² FOOD

While a visitor to the Congo will marvel at the abundance of greenery, this does not mean that agriculture is flourishing.

Rain forest soil is very nutrient-poor and, despite additional areas of savanna and river valley, only 2.5% of the Congo's soil is under cultivation. Foodstuffs commonly grown on this percentage include bananas, manioc, peanuts, coffee, cocoa, taro, and pineapples. Some livestock is raised, but over 90% of the country's meat is imported.

Congolese cultures abound with food taboos, many related to village, family, or even individual totemistic beliefs. It is strictly taboo for anyone to eat the meat from an animal that is his or her totem.

¹³ EDUCATION

For a long time, Brazzaville was considered the educational capital of Central Africa. Many educated people over the age of 50 in neighboring Gabon, for instance, who did not study in Europe, went to school in the Congo. While the government, by its own admission, has ignored the rural economy for decades, there is, in spite of this, a relatively high density of rural primary schools. Brazzaville has one university and a regionally famous painting school called L'École de Poto-Poto. Murals by Poto-Poto students can be found throughout the streets of Brazzaville. The literacy rate is estimated at 75% for adults.

¹⁴ CULTURAL HERITAGE

"Every Congolese learns to sing," so it is said. Singing has long been used to alleviate the tedium of work. There are songs about fishing, planting, and how to use a hoe, paddle a canoe, or pound manioc with a giant mortar and pestle. Musical instruments include myriad drums, guitar, and the *sanzi*, a small wooden box with metal teeth that are plucked by the thumbs, like a hand-held piano.

Congolese are also prolific storytellers. Passing tradition to other generations orally kept ethnic histories and the arts alive before the advent of literacy. Since the introduction of French and written language, however, the Congolese penchant for storytelling has found a new outlet, and its novelists, playwrights, and poets have gained celebrity throughout Francophone Africa. Jean Malonga, Henri Lopes, Soni Laboue Tansi, Marie Leontine Tsibinda, and Guy Menga are some of the best known.

There is a pre-modern pharmacological wisdom of rain forest-dwellers that now is beginning to be tapped by modern scientists. A deep knowledge of the forest is a rich, yet vanishing part of the Congo's cultural heritage, and while the average life expectancy of a Congolese has never been over 54 years, people in this region long have found local solutions to their health problems.

¹⁵ WORK

During the Communist regime, all land was officially state-owned, meaning by extension that all work on it was work for the state. This may have had something to do with the resulting underdevelopment of the agricultural sector over the decades. Conversely, the urban bureaucratic class exploded during this time. Between independence and 1970, after seven years of Communist rule, the civil service grew by 636%. Salaries for state workers ate up almost 75% of the national budget. These expenditures were paid for by oil revenues and foreign subsidies. With the change of governments, and the pressing need to reduce foreign debt, the Congo has significantly reduced the size of its bureaucracy.

[16] SPORTS

As all over Africa, soccer is the most passionately followed sport. Also popular are karate, handball, basketball, and volleyball, as both participant and spectator sports. Television devotes a lot of time to sports coverage. Now, with satellite capability, one can follow the French Open tennis tournament in a thatched bar deep in the bush.

[17] ENTERTAINMENT AND RECREATION

Sports, singing, dancing, music, storytelling, and visiting relatives are pastimes everywhere in the Congo. In the city, there are movies, some theater, and discotheques. Fishing is also considered recreational, as well as work. There is always sitting down to a cold Primus beer or glass of palm wine to pass the afternoon in gossip.

[18] FOLK ART, CRAFTS, AND HOBBIES

Traditionally, Congolese art was created to serve religious or ceremonial functions, rather than for pure aesthetic reasons. Masks, weaving, pottery, and ironwork were often abstract, depicting the human head or animals. Much of the local expertise in crafts has been lost, although a government agency and an ethnicity museum in Brazzaville are trying to preserve what knowledge and artifacts are left. With an active painting and literary community in the Congo, new forms continue to emerge.

[19] SOCIAL PROBLEMS

The Congo suffered four months of war in a battle to overthrow the president of its very tenuous democracy. Violent death, dislocation, and general social breakdown are among the immediate problems the Congolese face. HIV and AIDS are also a major worry for the people of the Congo. Although infection rates are not as bad as elsewhere in eastern and southern Africa, it is estimated that at least 5.3% of the population between the ages of 15 and 49 years is HIV-positive. The prevalence rates range from 1.3% in the north to 10.3% in the south, where civil unrest still lingers.

There are tens of thousands of indigenous Pygmies in the Congo, considered to be the first inhabitants in the area. While equal rights are officially protected in the Congolese constitution, Pygmies are heavily discriminated against. They have been turned away from public hospitals when seeking medical care and are not represented in government. Those working in the formal sector, such as the logging industry, do not receive equal pay for equal work. Pygmy slavery used to be institutionalized in what is now the Congo, and while it is technically illegal, a form of indentured servitude is said to still exist. Discrimination against Pygmies is not exclusive to the Congo, but it exists all over Central Africa.

[20] GENDER ISSUES

Women in the Republic of the Congo are underrepresented in positions of influence. For example, they control only 11.1% of the seats in parliament, attaining this figure in 2005 when President Sassou-Nguesso increased the number of women in the cabinet to 5 from an original 2 out of 35. The insecurity and displacement that occurred because of the fighting in the southern parts of the country have increased the vulnerability of women and adolescent girls to HIV/AIDS. Women under the age of 35 are twice as affected as men, with 61,000 women over the age of 15 living with HIV, out of about 100,000 adults aged 15 and above who are living with HIV. Human rights violations are quite common. Opponents to the government are routinely arrested and remain in custody without charge or trial.

There is no law against homosexual behavior in the penal code. However, there is no legal protection against discrimination based on sexual orientation, nor is there legal recognition of same-sex couples. The government stand on homosexuality is that it does not exist in the Congo.

[21] BIBLIOGRAPHY

BBC. "Country Profile: Republic of Congo." http://news.bbc. co.uk/2/hi/africa/country_profiles/1076794.stm (September 2008).

Biebuyck, Daniel P. *Congo: Tribes & Parties.* London: Royal Anthropological Institute, 1961.

Coppo, Salvatore. *A Truly African Church.* Eldoret, Kenya: Gaba Publications, AMECA, 1987.

IRIN. Republic of the Congo: "Humanitarian Country Profile." http://www.irinnews.org/country.aspx?CountryCode =CG&RegionCode=GL (September 2008).

Kempers, Anne Grimshaw. *Heart of Lightness.* Portsmouth, NH: P.E. Randall Publisher, 1993.

Vansina, Jan. *Paths in the Rain Forest.* Madison: University of Wisconsin Press, 1990.

Warkentin, Raija. *Our Strength is in Our Fields: African Families in Change.* Dubuque: Kendall/Hunt, 1994.

—revised by E. Kalipeni

CONGOLESE (ZAIRIANS)

PRONUNCIATION: kahn-go-LEEZ
ALTERNATE NAMES: Congo-Kinshasans
LOCATION: Democratic Republic of the Congo (DRC—the former Zaire)
POPULATION: 66 million
LANGUAGE: Lingala; Swahili; Ciluba; Kikongo; French (language of government)
RELIGION: Christianity (Catholicism, Protestantism, African Christianity)
RELATED ARTICLES: Vol. 1: Azande; Bakongo; Efe and Mbuti

¹ INTRODUCTION

The Democratic Republic of the Congo (DRC—the former Zaire) is Africa's third-largest country roughly equal in size to the United States east of the Mississippi River. Its boundaries were drawn arbitrarily at the Conference of Berlin in 1884–85. More than 300 ethnic groups, who speak between 300–600 dialects and languages live within those boundaries.

Archeological evidence from the Shaba, Kasai, and the Lower Congo regions indicates that this part of the world is one of the oldest cradles of human habitation. Prior to European colonization, the peoples of the DRC were part of empires, kingdoms, and small forest village communities. Perhaps the most renowned kingdom was the Kongo, established as early as the 15th century. This Christian kingdom had diplomatic relations with Portugal, Spain, and the Vatican. To the east, the emperor of the Lunda Empire maintained relations with the Portuguese and traded with Arabs on the coast of the Indian Ocean. The legendary prosperity of the Kongo Kingdom and the Luba Empire was cut short by slave trafficking, which eventually caused them to collapse.

The DRC has gone through several name changes, from "The Independent State of the Congo," to "The Belgian Congo," to "The Democratic Republic of the Congo" in 1960, to "Zaire" in 1971, and back to "The Democratic Republic of the Congo" in 1997. At the Berlin Conference, the European powers gave King Leopold II of Belgium sole proprietorship of the territory. Leopold ruled it as his personal fief through ruthless agents, who coerced local populations to meet quotas for red rubber and ivory. Those failing to meet quotas had their hands chopped off. Forced labor killed some 10 million Congolese between 1880 and 1910. When these atrocities became public, the Belgian state took over the colony to avoid further embarrassment. However, oppression and exploitation continued.

In the 1960s and 1970s, rebellions and secessions threatened the sovereignty of the country, but were beaten back with the assistance of the United Nations and foreign troops. Imminent revolt forced the Belgians to grant independence to the territory in 1960. Prime Minister Lumumba, who had socialist tendencies, was killed in February 1961. CIA and Belgian involvement brought Mobutu to power in 1965. Mobutu Sese Seko, whose name means "the one who will last forever," plundered the country's resources and impoverished his fellow citizens. His fortune, once estimated at over $8 billion, made him one of the richest men in the world. Mobutu had been Africa's longest-ruling leader when he was forced into exile in May 1997. He died in Morocco in September 1997.

In April 1997, with the backing of Rwanda and Uganda, rebel forces under Laurent Kabila marched on and captured Kinshasa, the capital. Laurent Kabila was assassinated in January 2001 and succeeded by his son, Joseph, who headed a transitional government in 2003, and was elected president in 2006. An elected national assembly was installed in September 2006, and provincial assemblies in early 2007, which in turn elected senators as well as provincial governors.

² LOCATION AND HOMELAND

The DRC extends from the Atlantic Ocean in the west to the snow-capped Ruwenzori Mountains (the "Mountains of the Moon") in the east. Straddling the equator, the DROC shares borders with nine states: the Republic of Congo, Central African Republic, Sudan, Uganda, Rwanda, Burundi, Tanzania, Zambia, and Angola. The mostly highland plateau is broken up by hilly and mountainous terrain, and a vast central basin drains into the Congo River. A chain of deep-water lakes formed by the Great Rift Valley fault line lie on the eastern border. Moving away from the equator, a rainy and a dry season begin to alternate. In the drier highlands, temperatures can drop to 5°C (40°F) at night.

The DRC claims the second-largest remaining rain forest in the world, and some of the world's largest deposits of minerals and precious metals. It is rich in copper, tin, manganese, coltan, and cobalt. Industrial diamonds abound in the Kasai Regions. Gold deposits have been identified in Orientale Province. The Inga Dam on the lower Congo River harnesses energy from the world's second-largest flowing volume of water. However, commercial logging threatens fragile ecosystems in the central basin and along the fertile eastern corridor.

The DRC's population is growing at about 3.2% yearly. By the year 2020, it is expected to reach 90 million people. Population density varies greatly from extremely dense urban centers to the sparsely populated central basin. The rural eastern corridor, bordering on Uganda, Rwanda, and Burundi contains about 29 persons per sq km (76 persons per sq mi). Six ethnic groups account for more than 69% of the population, but no single group dominates the others numerically or politically. The Luba make up 18%; the Kongo, 16%; the Mongo, 13.5%; Rwandese, 10%; Azande, 6%; and Bangi and Ngale, 6%.

³ LANGUAGE

In spite of the many dialects spoken throughout the DRC, four national languages predominate. Foremost among these is Lingala, which is spoken in the equatorial region, in the capital, and along the Congo River. Lingala is the main lingua franca (common language) thanks in part to former President Mobutu, who made speeches in Lingala and popularized it in the civil service. It also became the language of preference in the army and in Congolese music.

Swahili is the second lingua franca, spoken throughout the northeast, eastern, and southeast parts of the country. Tshiluba is spoken in the two Kasai regions, and Kikongo is spoken in Bas-Congo. French is officially used in government, and in education at university and high school levels. In public elementary schools, French is often taught as a second language. It is common to find people speaking a national language at the market, French in school, and their mother tongue at home.

⁴ FOLKLORE

Folklore is communicated in many ways, including literature, art, music, and dance. It is a means of carrying on tradition from generation to generation. Each ethnic group has its own legends and folk tales, though similarities exist. Animals figure importantly in these. For example, the rabbit is identified with intelligence and cunning, while the crocodile is associated with something bad, such as an unforgiving traffic cop, or an overzealous ticket-taker on the bus.

A deep appreciation for Congo's rich past is seen through a former popular television figure, *Grandpère* (grandfather), who told folk tales in a village setting, recalling former times when this tradition took place around an evening fire. Since the purpose of the tales was to teach while entertaining, Grandpère frequently expounded on the morals of these stories and of their application to daily life. Children, as well as adults, now watch a similar program in four of the national languages. In Swahili the program is called, "Hadisi Njo," and in Lingala "Lisapo Nge." These titles are actually the way storytelling begins with the storyteller saying "Lisapo Nge!" and the audience replying "Onge!" Children considered it a great honor to appear on the Grandpère show.

⁵ RELIGION

Nearly half of all Congolese practice Catholicism, and another third are Protestant, yet Christian and traditional beliefs are blended together. For example, at holy Mass, protection of the ancestors is often implored. People also dance in the liturgy and offer in-kind gifts, including goat, cassava, fish, fruits, and vegetables. In 1921, Simon Kimbangu, claiming to be a prophet of Jesus Christ, led a religious revival against colonialism. Some 17% of the population now profess a form of African Christianity. In recent years Protestant sects led by charismatic preachers have gained large followings in towns and cities. The popularity of these churches is based in part on the hope they hold out to their parishioners, for whom survival has become a daily challenge. It also reflects the failure of institutionalized churches to respond to people's everyday needs.

Traditional belief holds that all things have life and deserve respect, even inanimate objects like rocks. Life never ends, and no separation exists between the living and the dead. Offering the ancestors a drink by pouring some beer on the ground is symbolic of this belief. Nzambe, assisted by the spirits of ancestors, is the supreme being from whom all things derive. The *Nganga-Nzambe,* the "doctor of God," is called upon in times of need to intercede with sacrifices and prayers. When evil befalls someone, it is assumed that a person or a bad spirit is responsible. It is up to the Nganga to find the cause and appease the person or spirit who is displeased.

⁶ MAJOR HOLIDAYS

The increasingly difficult political and economic climate in the DRC has dampened popular celebrations of secular holidays. June 30, Independence Day, is celebrated in the capital with speeches, parades and folk dancing, but political holidays such as May 20, the day that Mobutu's Popular Revolutionary Movement Party (MPR) was founded, have been taken off the calendar. Christmas, New Year's Day, and Easter are festive occasions for family visiting, and if means permit, are celebrated with roast goat or cow.

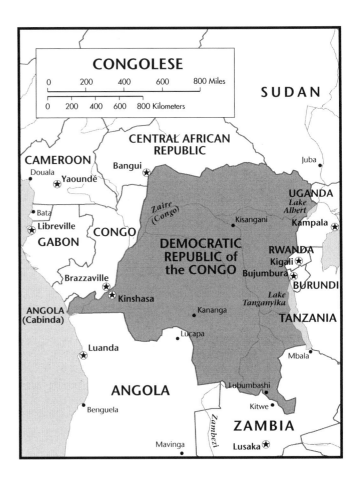

Parent's Day, August 1, is a unique holiday. In the morning Congolese celebrate the dead, and in the afternoon, the living. Residents of Kinshasa, for example, go to the cemeteries early to clear and spruce up family graves. Fires are set to burn away the tall weeds and elephant grass, which at the end of the rainy season are very dry but so thick as to be impenetrable. As the grasses burn, tomb stones, grave markers, and crosses appear through the smoke and flames. Visitors dodge these uncontrolled fires to sweep off their ancestors' graves and perhaps enjoy a meal at the site with them. Adults then return home to eat again together with the children.

⁷ RITES OF PASSAGE

In the DRC, children are a symbol of wealth, and all births are celebrated with joy. However, in the dominant patriarchal system, boys are more desired because they perpetuate the family name. *Kobota elingi,* the joy of giving birth, is celebrated with friends, who bring gifts, food, and drinks to the parents. They also help out with household chores and caring for the baby. The more respected the parents are, the more help they are likely to receive.

Prior to colonization, boys and girls passed to adulthood through initiation rites. Boys were circumcised and taught the elders' wisdom and the values of their culture. Girls were never circumcised, but they were brought to a secret place and taught how to succeed in marriage and to raise a family. Nowadays, male circumcision occurs soon after birth. Because of social changes in the cities, young men and women are usually

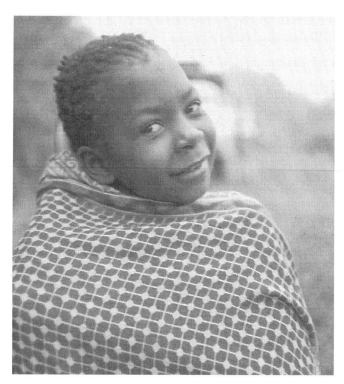

Zairian families traditionally tended to be large, with 10 or more children. The number of children per family is shrinking, especially in urban centers. (Jason Laure)

taught about life and their culture by a family member such as an uncle or aunt.

Congolese believe in life after death, but death still remains a mystery, especially in the case of a child, young person, or young adult. Blame or responsibility must be assigned so that their spirits may rest. When an elderly person dies, however, it is believed that their spirits watch over family members. Funeral ceremonies, *matanga*, vary according to ethnic group. In the villages, the corpse is washed and kept in the house until burial. In the cities, it is taken out and laid in a bed underneath a canopy of palm branches. Mourners comfort the family by bringing gifts, and by sitting on the ground with the family and praying.

⁸ INTERPERSONAL RELATIONS

Congolese are extremely gregarious and commonly stop to greet friends, and even strangers, on the street. When socializing, they typically walk around in small groups of two or three. It is customary to shake hands when meeting people, and when taking leave of them. When greeting an older person, one waits for the elder person to offer his or her hand. If the hand is not offered, one gives a slight bow with the head. If the hand is offered, the younger person reaches out with the right hand and rests the left hand on the right arm near the wrist. Children should receive objects from adults, even from each other, with both hands.

During the Mobutu era, strangers greeted each other with the title, "Citoyen" (Citizen). They now use the French "Monsieur," "Madame," or "Mademoiselle." However, a less formal and popular address is simply "Papa" or "Mama." There are several ways to greet people depending on time of day and the nature of the relationship. In the morning a Lingala-speaker greets by asking, "Hello, is that you? *(Mbote, Yo wana?)*, Are you awake? *(Olamuki?)*, How did you sleep?" *(Olalaki malamu?)*. Asking someone how they are consists of literally asking, "What news?" *(Sango nini?)*. The typical reply would be, "No news!" *(Sango te)* meaning, "Fine." It is not considered impolite to drop in on someone without giving prior notice. In fact, announcing a visit signals something important, like a marriage request, in which case the visitor brings along a sack of rice, a goat, and several cases of beer.

Congolese place great importance on family and social relations. A grandparent affectionately refers to his or her grandchild as "little husband or wife," and the grandchild refers to the grandparent in the same way. A woman light-heartedly addresses a neighbor as "father-in-law" *(bokilo)* because she likes his young son, whom she calls her "little husband." Many people call friends and even strangers "brother-in law" or "sister-in-law," which is a way of building friendships and avoiding conflict.

⁹ LIVING CONDITIONS

The majority of Congolese find it challenging to send their children to school, pay for health care, and even to eat one or two meals a day. Many middle-class urbanites who once had dependable salaries and were people of means now eat once a day or less. Half-finished houses take years to complete. Many goods are priced in US dollars to hedge against inflation. The Human Development Index (HDI), which measures general well-being according to life expectancy, education, and standard of living rates the DRC 168 out of 177 countries.

Health care is generally available in cities and town centers, but unless patients can afford to pay for bandages, medications, and other basic supplies, they will not receive treatment. Before the outbreak of AIDS, clinics and hospitals routinely reused needles. Some 54% of the population does not have access to improved water sources, 31% of children aged 0–5 are underweight for their age, and the probability of not surviving past age 40 is about 41%.

Homes in the village are often made from mud brick, and thatch or galvanized-iron roofing. They are clean, but not mosquito-proof. People use kerosene lamps, and women and children haul water from nearby springs, rivers, or common wells. It is difficult in these conditions to avoid bacteria and children often suffer from a variety of air- and water-borne diseases such as diarrhea and dysentery. In the towns, some houses have electricity, running water, and flush toilets. However, large sections of Kinshasa that once enjoyed 24-hour electricity now receive on average six hours of power a day.

The most common form of transportation in the DRC is on foot. People walk everywhere, and women and girls balance huge loads on their heads—anything from wash basins full of fruit to buckets of water. The extremely poor condition of DRC's once vast road network makes it impossible to travel easily from one region to another. Air travel, which is risky and expensive, is practically the only way to travel from Kinshasa to Lumbumbashi or to Goma and Bukavu in the east. River travel is the other most dependable means of reaching the hinterlands. River boats and dug-out canoes are perhaps the best way to bring goods to market and to travel especially in the central Congo basin.

10 FAMILY LIFE

Children are a blessing, a sign of wealth and a social safety net for parents in their old age. Families of 10 or more children are not unusual though family size shrinks with education and affluence. The financial difficulties associated with paying bride prices, housing, and other costs delays marriage. Many couples now either co-habit or marry in their thirties. Polygyny is practiced, but since second wives are not recognized by church or state, men tend to keep a second wife or girlfriend (deuxième bureau—second office) at another location.

In the extended family, marriages may be seen as alliances among families, clans, and ethnic groups with similar interests, and therefore parents and older siblings will search for a suitable spouse for their children and younger brothers and sisters from among members of the same ethnic group. A couple often participates in separate traditional, civil, and religious ceremonies. The traditional ceremony consists of exchanging gifts between the two families. The bride-price, which includes money, clothing, a Coleman lantern, or cattle, has been paid long before the wedding. The bride-price creates an alliance between the two families and the couple, and it represents the wealth that women bring to African society as mothers and workers. The civil ceremony consists of exchanging wedding vows before a government representative. The official reminds the couple of their family and civic responsibilities, and also confirms that the bride-price has been accepted. The bride and groom are expected to furnish cases of beer and soft drinks for the official. Finally, at the church, the bride might wear a Western-style wedding dress. In rural areas, wedding celebrations can last weeks, punctuated with singing, dancing, and feasting.

11 CLOTHING

In the DRC, people dress up in public. If they cannot afford fancy clothes, they wear washed and neatly pressed second-hand clothing. Sloppiness is not considered a virtue. In the 1970s, under Mobutu's "authenticity program," the government banned westernized business suits for men, and replaced them with collarless suits, or *abacost,* meaning "down with suits." Neckties and bow ties were also replaced by scarves and matching handkerchiefs in the front pockets.

Similarly, women were not permitted to wear wigs, Western pants, jeans, or miniskirts. Even today as those rules no longer apply, women prefer African wraparounds (*pagnes),* tailored in creative styles with bright, colorful African patterns. Highly trained and skilled tailors and dressmakers have made an art form of styling the pagne and blouse, and many fabrics are given names. In addition, made-to-order bracelets, rings, earrings, and necklaces of ivory, malachite, gold, silver, copper, and diamonds are prized. In inflationary times, quality fashionable clothing and jewelry are investments that hold value. Congolese styles have caught on elsewhere in Africa, and have given the DRC a leading reputation for African dress.

12 FOOD

Congolese love to eat, but have increasingly had to tighten their belts because of the economy. Breakfast may be no more than sweet *cafe au lait* (coffee with milk) with a baguette of French bread that can be dunked in the coffee. The noon meal is the most important and requires considerable time to prepare, including a trip to the market to buy ingredients. The staples are cassava, rice, potatoes, plantains, and sweet potatoes or yams, accompanied by a sauce of greens, fish, or meat depending on the region. Typically, a family eats from the same bowl of sauce, and from a large dough-like ball of cassava flour or corn flour (*fufu)* or a mixture of the two. Before eating, hands are washed (a basin of warm water, a bar of soap, and a towel may be passed around). Supper consists of leftovers or tea and bread. In rural areas men and women tend to eat separately, particularly at parties and ceremonies. People eat with one hand, usually the right. Congolese would normally cook more than they can eat because one never knows when visitors might drop in. Under normal circumstances it would be extremely rude not to offer, or not to accept, food and drink.

A favorite sauce is made from cassava leaves (*saka saka),* which are pounded and cooked. Fish is often added to saka saka. Other traditional foods include pounded sesame seeds (*wangila),* squash seeds (*mbika),* steamed chicken or fish (*maboke),* shiskabobs (*kamundele),* and plantain dough (*lituma).* In some regions, people consider caterpillars, grubs, roasted crickets, and termites to be delicacies. In the Equatorial region, wild game such as elephant, monkey, hippopotamus, and crocodile are enjoyed. The DRC is perhaps best known for *mwamba,* a sauce made of palm-nut paste, in which chicken, meat, and fish are cooked. Mwamba is cooked over a low fire, and is eaten with rice, fufu, or *chikwange* (cassava prepared in banana leaves).

As for drink, fondness for beer is legendary, but in the village, palm-wine is the favorite. This drink is fermented after being tapped from the top of the coconut palm, drawn into a gourd overnight, and collected early the next morning. On Saturday and Sunday afternoons, people sit in the shade of a mango tree, consuming the milky, tangy substance. Banana-beer, sugarcane-wine, fruit wines, homemade gin, and passion fruit juice are some of the other drinks produced throughout the country. Pouring a small amount of drink on the ground for the thirsty ancestors is customary before drinking.

13 EDUCATION

Education is not required by law, and many children drop out of school to work when parents are unable to pay fees, book rentals, and buy school uniforms, copybooks, pencils, and other supplies. In 2005 the combined primary, secondary, and tertiary gross enrolment ratio was 33.7%. The adult literacy rate for people aged 15 years and older was 67%.

Secondary school begins with a two-year middle school program (*cycle d'orientation).* The main goal is to evaluate student strengths and weaknesses, and orient students for future study and career choices. The four-year high school program includes the following general options, depending on the school: Literature, Science, Business, Nursing, and Education. A high school diploma must be earned by passing a rigorous state exam, and for many it becomes the final degree. Public university, plagued by strikes and overcrowding, closes frequently. Consequently, many private universities have opened over the past few years. Parents with means or connections send their children to private boarding schools for high school, and to university in South Africa or Europe.

Because pay is low and erratic, teaching is no longer a prestigious vocation. Teachers supplement their income by working on the side. Inability to make a living wage has also led to bribes for grades. Many public school classrooms lack basic supplies such as blackboards and chalk. In some schools, children must take their own stools. A unique Congolese institution that puts responsibility on the pupils to keep up their schools is *salongo*. *Salongo* brings the students together to spruce up school buildings, clean school yards, and remove overgrowth from school grounds and sports fields.

14 CULTURAL HERITAGE

Congolese dance music, referred to as "Sukus" in the United States, has been popular throughout sub-Saharan Africa since the 1950s and continues to gain international popularity. It is a combination of jazz, traditional music, and Latin-influenced rhythms. The instrumentation consists of electric guitars, keyboards, trumpets, saxophones, conga drums, and Western-style drum sets. Lyrics in Lingala comment on society, give advice, make political statements, criticize behavior, or simply relate love stories. Songs typically are divided in half. They begin with a slow section, and end with a fast-paced beat. One song can last for as long as 20 minutes.

Congolese are imaginative dancers, constantly inventing new dances which come and go almost monthly. Colorful names depict the dance movements and gestures, such as *dindon* (the turkey), *caneton* (the duckling), *volant* (the steering wheel), and Apollo (astronauts' space-walking on the moon). Music is heard just about anywhere even on domestic flights. Drumming and dancing are part of any festive occasion, be it greeting the president at the airport, frolicking in the village under a full moon, or performing at a cultural event. The national folkloric ballet has gained an international reputation.

From ancient times, Congolese peoples have used their oral literature to carry on traditions, customs, and social values. Modern written literature has been built on this oral foundation. It varies widely from classical to popular forms and is written in French as well as in national languages. Drama is one of the most popular forms of literature today.

15 WORK

One of the greatest challenges facing the Congo is to create work opportunities for its citizens. Industry employs only 10% of the work force, mainly in mining, timber extraction, oil palm processing, textiles, chemicals, and food processing. Services employ about 12% of the labor force. The rest of the work force is either without work or employed in the informal sector in subsistence agriculture and petty trades. Informal work provides no regular salary, health insurance, pensions, or other benefits. Since the closure of Gecamines, the national mining company, some 20,000 skilled jobs with benefit packages have been lost. The impact of these closures on mining cities like Kolwezi has been devastating to infrastructure and the local economy. While industrial mining is beginning to return, some 2 million miners labor under harsh conditions panning for diamonds, copper, gold, and coltan, which is used in making cell phones, DVD players, and computers.

16 SPORTS

Soccer is the national pastime, played or watched virtually throughout the country. Competition with African national teams is so intense that when the national team defeated the Moroccans for the Africa Cup in the 1970s, the returning players were welcomed like royalty and given houses, cars, and large sums of money. Congolese (then Zairians) were treated to a national holiday.

People love playing cards, chess, checkers, and board games. A traditional board game called *Mangula* is played mainly in rural areas by men. One version consists of a carved wooden board with two rows of shallow pockets separated by a divider. The game begins with some small stones in each pocket. Player One moves and continues according to the number of stones he picks up. Each time he lands, he picks up his opponent's stones in the pocket opposite him across the divider, and uses these stones to continue his play. When he fails to pick up any stones, his opponent takes his turn. The first person to displace all his opponent's stones to his side of the board wins.

17 ENTERTAINMENT AND RECREATION

Most people do not have disposable income to go to cinemas, to eat out, to go to night clubs, or to pay for entertainment. Their entertainment is restricted to socializing with family and friends, watching TV (in towns and cities), and telling stories or dancing in the village square on special occasions. Video houses hooked to satellite TV have gained in popularity for watching soccer tournaments and movies. In the cities young people and adults enjoy going out on Saturday night to socialize, listen to music at outdoor pubs, dance at night clubs, and watch theatrical events.

18 FOLK ART, CRAFTS, AND HOBBIES

The DRC is famous for its traditional folk arts and crafts. Artists and craftspeople produce ceramic pots, reed mats, woven baskets, woodcarvings, chess games, sand paintings, handmade clothing, and jewelry. Children are very inventive, recycling tomato cans and metal hangers to design cars that are steerable, and airplanes with hatches that open.

In general, African art is functional, but increasingly tourist art generates income. Formerly, masks were assigned power to intercede with the divine. Some are still only brought out on very specific occasions for initiations and for solving community problems. The Bakuba people from the Kasai regions still produce wood sculptures, masks, and statuettes that may be used to enhance fertility, and to chase away evil spirits. In recent times, a distinct genre of oil paintings, found in many Zairian homes, wryly reflects the magnitude of contemporary social challenges. In these paintings, snakes or lions within striking distance of unsuspecting human prey depict impending doom.

19 SOCIAL PROBLEMS

Congolese must conquer hunger, political repression, and political and economic instability, and meet their basic daily needs. People work hard for very little. Many people resort to "*Article 15*" or "*debrouillez-vous*," which means, "make do in whatever way possible." Kids leave school early, girls prostitute themselves, civil servants steal, police officers extort, and military personnel loot and pillage. Enormous human losses caused by HIV/AIDS and the Ebola virus challenge Congolese to care for the sick and orphaned. A hidden tragedy is that generations of Congolese children may be growing up undernourished on a basic diet of cassava, which is extremely poor in nutrition.

Nonetheless, Congolese are learning to cope with these scourges. Compared to the United States, drug use is uncommon, and serious crimes as Americans know them are rare.

For all their problems, Congolese are resilient people, who are making do with *"Article 15."*

20 GENDER ISSUES

The value of women and girls to Congolese society is recognized through the bride price (la dotte), which is payable by the groom's family to the bride's family in order for marriage to proceed, and it can be quite considerable involving both in-kind and cash payments. However, women and girls are subservient to men and boys in social, economic and political spheres of life, and under the law women do not possess the same rights as men. For example, a woman must obtain her husband's permission before opening a bank account, conducting a real estate transaction, and applying for a passport.

A woman found guilty of adultery could be sentenced up to one year in prison while a man would unlikely be subject to a penalty. Women are not permitted by law to work at night or to accept employment without their husband's consent. They typically do most of the household work, fetch water and firewood in the village, and in the public and private workplace they receive less pay for doing the same job. They rarely occupy political posts or positions of high authority and responsibility. As noted (see **Social Problems**) women and girls are subjected to trafficking, forced labor, prostitution, and rape, but the government is either unable or unwilling to protect them and to provide justice for them under the law.

21 BIBLIOGRAPHY

Diallo, Siradiou. *Le Zaire Aujourd'hui.* Paris: Les Editions Jeune Afrique, 1984.

Hochschild, Adam. *King Leopold's Ghost: A Story of Greed, Terror, and Heroism in Colonial Africa.* London: Pan MacMillan, 1998.

Huybrechts, A., et al. *Du Congo au Zaire: 1960–1980.* Bruxelles: CRISP, 1980.

Kelly, Sean. *America's Tyrant: The CIA and Mobutu of Zaire.* Washington, DC: The American University Press, 1993.

Nzongola-Ntalaja, Georges. *From Zaire to the Democratic Republic of the Congo.* Second Revised Edition. United Nations: Nordiska Afrikainstutet, 2004.

Stengers, Jean. *Congo: Mythes et Realites: 100 Ans d'Histoire.* Paris: Editions Duculot, 1989.

Wrong, Michela. *In the Footsteps of Mr. Kurtz: Living on the Brink of Disaster in the Congo.* New York: HarperCollins, 2001.

—revised by R. Groelsema and M. C. Groelsema

COPTIC CHRISTIANS

ALTERNATE NAMES: Copts
LOCATION: Egypt
POPULATION: 6.8 million-8.3 million (2007 estimate/includes 1.2 million Coptic Christians who reside outside Egypt)
LANGUAGE: Arabic, Coptic
RELIGION: Coptic Orthodox Christianity

1 INTRODUCTION

The Coptic Christians are a distinct religious community in Egypt and the Coptic Orthodox Church is the largest Christian institution in the Middle East. The origin of the community dates to the childhood of Jesus, who was said to have traveled to Egypt with his father, Joseph, and mother, Mary. The apostle Mark, a follower of Jesus, brought Christianity to Egypt during the rule of the Roman emperor Nero in the 1st century AD, and Copts regard Mark as the first patriarch of their church. Mark's proselytizing helped spread Christianity from the city of Alexandria throughout Egypt. Writings from the New Testament that date to AD 200 have been found in Bahnasa. A fragment of a document found in upper Egypt contains a portion of the Gospel of St. John in the Coptic language.

Copt scholars and writers played an important role in the formation of early Christian theology. The Catechetical School of Alexandria was founded in AD 190 and soon became the most important site for religious instruction among Christians. The school also taught science, mathematics, and the humanities. Monasticism, or the practice of renouncing worldly pursuits in order to pursue a spiritual path, began in Egypt in AD 300 and influenced Coptic beliefs in submission and humbleness. A Copt known as St. Anthony was the world's first Christian monk. By the end of the 4th century AD, hundreds of monasteries had formed in the hills of Egypt.

Coptic Christians were part of the Byzantine family of Christians until the universal Christian church split following the Council of Chalcedon (the Fourth Ecumenical Council) in AD 451. The council, based in Rome, ruled that Jesus was both fully human and fully divine, or of two complete natures. This ruling diverged from beliefs of the Coptic Christians and other followers of what has come to be known as the Eastern Orthodox Churches. Eastern Orthodox followers believe that the humanity and divinity of Jesus are united and that the son of God has one, not two, natures. As the universal church split, Copts suffered a great deal of persecution from other Christians, and their strength as a religious community weakened. Arabs invaded Egypt in AD 649 and were able to use the weakness in the community to convince hundreds of thousands of former Christians to convert to Islam. By the end of the 12th century, Egypt had become a predominantly Muslim country. Muhammad the Prophet, the founder of Islam, however, had an Egyptian wife and emphasized the need for new converts to practice kindness toward Copts. Coptic Christians were allowed to practice their faith freely and suffered little discrimination as long as they paid a special tax to the Arab regime. The Copts suffered periodically from Muslim hostility and were at times prohibited from building new churches, testifying in court, or practicing their religion in public.

The position of Copts improved in the early 19th century under the rule of Muhammad Ali. The Egyptian state lifted tax rules imposed on the community and no longer separated Copts from Muslims administratively. By 1855 Copts were serving the Egyptian army and joined with Muslims in asserting a sense of a national Egyptian identity during the 1919 revolution in Egypt. The Coptic church has enjoyed a remarkable revival since the middle of the 20th century. The church is strongest in Egypt, with approximately 9 million followers. However, missionary efforts and the emigration of Copts from Egypt have led to the establishment of Coptic Christian communities throughout the world.

² LOCATION AND HOMELAND

Copts live throughout Egypt, and traces of their cultural, historical, and spiritual influence can be found in every province. Egypt is located in northern Africa. It is bordered by the Mediterranean Sea, between Libya and the Gaza Strip, and the Red Sea north of Sudan. Egypt's land also includes the Sinai Peninsula.

With an area of 1,001,447 sq km (686,622 sq mi), Egypt is slightly bigger than the states of New Mexico and Texas combined. That land area is largely desert, with small oases scattered throughout the land. All but about 5% of the country's land is uninhabitable. More than 97% of the population lives in the Nile Valley, which runs the length of the country. The Nile faced seasonal flooding until the Aswan Dam was built in southeastern Egypt. The dam has allowed for a small agricultural area to thrive. Most residents, however, live in cities along the Nile, particularly around Cairo. Overcrowding has prompted the government to reclaim desert areas through the pumping of water from Lake Nasser. Southern Egypt is largely rural and Copts who inhabit these areas are generally poorer and less well educated than those who reside in the more prosperous north.

Part of the Sahara Desert lies in Egypt. Coptic monasticism historically has brought men to Egypt's deserts to practice asceticism for periods of time. As a result, a rich array of Coptic culture can be found near the Khargo oasis. Living conditions in the deserts are extremely harsh. The climate throughout Egypt is generally hot and dry in the summer with temperatures reaching 21 to 36°c (69 to 97°F) in July and more moderate in the winters. Temperatures in December average from 8 to 18°c (46 to 64°F). Egypt receives only 5 mm (0.20 in) of rainfall per year on average although as much as 203 mm (8 in) might fall in the Nile Delta. A hot, dusty wind known as *khamasiin* blows in Egypt through the spring.

³ LANGUAGE

The word Copt is derived from Gibt, which was an Arabic form of the Greek term of Aigyptos. The Greek term was derived from Hikaptah, which was the ancient Egyptian name for the first capital city of Memphis. The Coptic language shares a philological affinity with the ancient tongue of Egypt's pharaohs and continues to be used in liturgical rituals. However, most Copts speaks Egypt's official language of Arabic. Some also use English and French for business or social affairs. Coptic language and literature courses are offered at a few European universities, a Coptic Studies program at American University–Cairo, and some Coptic Orthodox Churches.

Coptic Christians often define their affiliation to their religion through the naming of babies. It is customary to choose a Coptic name over a more common Egyptian name that might be associated with Islam.

⁴ FOLKLORE

Copt stories from the medieval period remind humans of the importance of prayer, fasting, and doing good works in the name of God. Many of the stories contain both Coptic Christian and Egyptian Muslim influences. Some were first written in Arabic, but used in Christian homilies throughout Egypt.

One such story relates to a figure named Luqman the Wise, a Christian preacher. In one story, Luqman the Wise chastises those who neglect such practices by telling them that they risk allowing a rooster to become better than them.

> Luqman the Wise says:
>
> "O my son, don't let the rooster be better than you!
>
> For it, when the night is half spent, beats
>
> its wings and cries out to God in praise.
> So if a lowly bird that has no value praises God, how can it be that a
>
> noble human being, whom God has set above all the creatures, does not
>
> praise God and ascribe him holiness at all times?"

In another story, Luqman the Wise's words emphasize the freedom and strength of the Copts in preserving their religious practice amid the threat of persecution from Muslims:

> Also, Luqman the Wise says:
>
> "God has humbled the people of the world
>
> with two traits: death and poverty.
>
> Were it not for death, no stubborn tyrant would submit.
>
> Were it not for poverty, no free people would serve slaves."

⁵ RELIGION

The Book of Isaiah in the Old Testament contains a prophecy of the formation of a Christian community in Egypt. In chapter 19, verse 19, Isaiah writes, "In that day there will be an altar to the lord in the midst of the land of Egypt, and a pillar to the lord at its border." In line with that prophecy, many Biblical figures saw Egypt as a refuge from famine and persecution. Mary and Joseph, the parents of Jesus, also are believed to have spent time in Egypt when Jesus was a small child. Many churches have been built at sites where the Holy Family was believed to have sought shelter, and other landscape features, such as caves and trees, are known as resting points for the family.

Coptic Christianity leans toward the mystic and spiritual. Religious instruction continues at the Catechetical School of Alexandria, where scholars use allegorical and spiritual methods to interpret and teach scripture. Numerous saints and ascetics are associated with the Coptic Orthodox Church. Many of these individuals attained martyrdom during the centuries of persecution that Copts suffered under Byzantine rule.

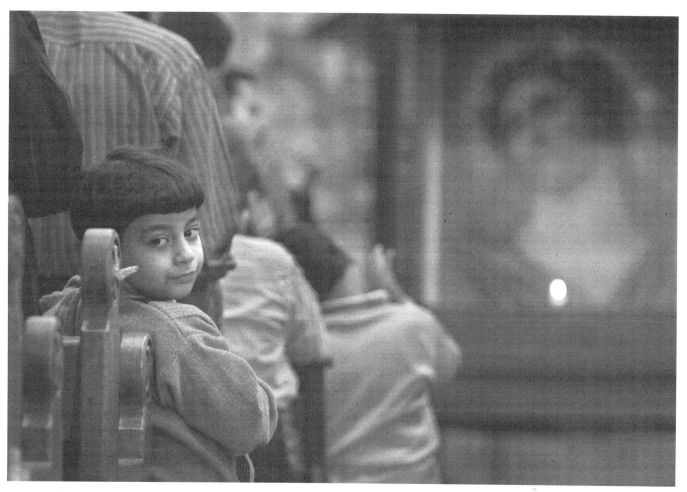

A young Coptic Christian boy at church services in the St. Maximus Church, Alexandria, Egypt. (AP Images/Ben Curtis)

One of the most prominent symbols of the Coptic Church is the Coptic cross. The most common Coptic cross consists of two bars of equal length that are crossed perpendicularly at the center. There are three points at the end of each bar, symbolizing the Trinity. The total of 12 points on the cross further symbolizes the 12 Apostles. In some forms, the cross will contain a circle, either at the center or at the top. Copts adapted the cross soon after the apostle Mark brought Christianity to Egypt. The Copt use of this cross continues a belief among pre-Christian Egyptians that the symbol represented eternal life.

Many Coptic Christians regard asceticism as a way of life. The level to which asceticism is practiced among Coptic Christians varies considerably. Nevertheless, most believe that the path to enjoyment of the divine spirit lies in a minimizing or full renouncing of worldly pursuits. This belief leads some to practice celibacy. Women traditionally would live together in a single house in the cities to assist each other spiritually, while men who chose to be celibate would live in simple huts in villages. Others would go to Egypt's deserts. Nearly a dozen monasteries still exist in Egypt's deserts, and at least six convents for Copts are still operating in Egyptian cities.

The Coptic Christian worship service is lengthy and rich with ritual. Worship includes the singing of hymns, the reciting of liturgies, fasting, and numerous feasts throughout the year. The full congregation, including children, participate in the service.

6 MAJOR HOLIDAYS

Egypt established Coptic Christmas as a national holiday in 2003. The celebration of Christmas generally falls around January 6 or 7 and ends with a 45-day fast that some Copts observe. Shops and government services for both Muslims and Christians are closed in Egypt on that day. Other major holidays include Epiphany, Palm Sunday, Easter, Pentecost, Ascension, and Annunciation. These holidays, along with Christmas, are known in the Coptic Christian world as the Seven Major Feasts. A series of fasts precede the major feasts. The church also celebrates what are known as the Seven Minor Feasts: the Circumcision of the Lord, Entrance into the Temple, Entrance into Egypt, Transfiguration, Holy Thursday, Thomas Sunday, and Great Lent.

7 RITES OF PASSAGE

Copt babies are traditionally washed during a special service eight days after their birth and baptized in the church. A special liturgy is recited in the new child's honor. The death of a congregation member results in two services—a funeral that takes place at the church and a special prayer three days after the death at the home of the deceased.

[8] INTERPERSONAL RELATIONS

Most Egyptians take a relaxed, patient approach to life. The term *ma'alesh* translates to mean "don't worry" or "never mind." The phrase is used when conflicts arise, as a way of pointing out that the concerns are not serious and will soon pass. A sense of community and the importance of generosity are emphasized among all Egyptians and personal needs at times are dismissed as secondary to community needs. Social relationships between Coptic Christians and Muslims are generally cordial, and Copts in Egypt follow the prevailing Egyptian attitude toward life.

Copt families historically lived separately from Muslims in Egypt. Cities contained certain quarters where Copts would congregate, and some villages were inhabited entirely by Copts. That practice of separation has declined considerably since the modern Egyptian nationalistic movement of the early twentieth century, and most Copts are fully integrated into modern Egypt's Islamic-based society. The Coptic Orthodox Church, however, bans marriage between Coptic Christians and Muslims and will excommunicate those who marry outside the church. The church also prohibits intermarriage between Copts and Jehovah's Witnesses, although Copts are allowed to marry people of other Christian denominations.

[9] LIVING CONDITIONS

Living conditions have been improving in Egypt since the mid 1960s. The death rate has fallen from 19 deaths for every 1,000 births in 1965 to approximately 5 deaths for every 1,000 births as of mid-2007. Life expectancy in mid-2007 was estimated at 74.2 years for women and 69 years for men.

Medical facilities still are limited in rural areas. As a result, diseases such as typhoid and bilharzia continue to be problems. Doctors and volunteers visit villages with medical caravans, and the government has established a daily four-hour satellite television program on health topics. Although every city has a hospital, it is only the private, most expensive hospitals that are equipped with state-of-the-art technology.

A large gap between the wealthy and poor continues to exist in Egypt. This is reflected in housing found in the country. Housing conditions range from the spacious, elegant villas for the wealthy to dirty, slum-like dwellings for the poor. Many people live in apartment buildings in Egypt's crowded cities. While the buildings are often unattractive and dirty on the outside, the interiors are well maintained and clean. As more people crowd into cities, shanty towns have sprung up. Conditions in these areas are unclean and unsafe. Huge cemeteries surround Cairo, and some of the poorest residents have begun to inhabit old tombs illegally.

Rural homes tend to be small and built as closely to each other as possible so that Egypt's sparse agricultural land can be used for farming.

[10] FAMILY LIFE

Egyptians value both the nuclear and extended family. Brothers are required to protect their sisters and often accompany them in public. While extended families traditionally lived in one household, the increased urbanization in Egypt's cities is making the nuclear household more common. Marriages often are arranged between cousins, and many young adults will care for their parents in old age. Coptic Christians share similar family values.

Coptic life also centers around the church. An entire family customarily will choose a priest as a family counselor and will make regular personal confessions to that priest. Worship is family oriented, with both male and female adults as well as children participating actively in the service.

[11] CLOTHING

Copt weavers developed many fabrics that contained ornately designed patterns in pre-Islamic Egypt. The patterns often contained images of landscape scenery, animals, and religious iconography. Long, loose-fitting tunics displayed the intricate, colorful work.

Today, most Coptic Christians dress as Muslims and others in Egypt do. The traditional dress of men in Egypt is the *gallabeyya,* which is a long robe. Males continue to wear the traditional dress in cities but also will wear Western business suits and more casual Western attire. Copt women usually follow the tradition in Islamic countries of covering the body in public, although they will wear Western styles of clothing occasionally in cities. Copt women in rural areas particularly will wear black headscarves and long, loose-fitting dresses that drape the entire body. In churches, it is common for worshippers to remove their shoes before entering.

[12] FOOD

Foods among Coptic Christians are flavored with spices such as cumin, garlic, onion, and allspice, and many vegetarian dishes have emerged in the Coptic Christian cuisine because of the fasting rules that the church observes. In the Coptic tradition, a partial fast and abstinence from meat are recommended on nearly 200 days out of each year. Meals during these fasting periods often include fava beans, lentils, grape leaves, tomatoes, and potatoes.

During non-fasting periods, Copts, like other Egyptians, eat rice, bread, fish, lamb, chicken, and turkey.

It also is customary to pray before and after a meal. Even when the meal does not contain meat, menus are quite elaborate. It is customary throughout Egypt not to eat everything placed on a plate as a way of complimenting the host for providing such an abundance of food. Foods are generally eaten with the fingers of the right hand, although Western utensils are used for eating occasionally in cities.

[13] EDUCATION

Copt children attend schools in Egypt, which are free through the university level. The UN Development Program estimated that 91% of all Egyptian children were enrolled in primary schools in 2003 and that 88% were enrolled in secondary schools. In addition, Egypt has twelve public universities and 8,674 privately funded schools and universities. The country also has 125 technical and vocational schools. As of 2005, about 1.76 million students were enrolled in higher educational institutions. Class sizes in Egypt are quite large with as many as forty-three to sixty-two students being taught by a single instructor. The government plans to build 2,000 additional schools by 2012 and has initiated a program for teacher training.

Instruction in Egyptian schools is primarily in Arabic, although English and French also are taught. The role of the Coptic Christian community in Egypt is largely ignored in primary and secondary schools. As a result, Copt children learn about their language and culture primarily at home or through the church. Some steps are being taken to change that situation. The American University-Cairo recently established a Coptic Studies program in which the language, literature, and culture of the Copt community is taught.

The Copt's ancient school, the Catechetical School of Alexandria, was destroyed in the early Islamic era. It was reestablished, however, in 1893 and currently has campuses in Alexandria and Cairo in Egypt and in New Jersey and California in the United States.

14 CULTURAL HERITAGE

There is a rich heritage of Coptic Christian chants, music, iconography, and tapestry associated with the Coptic Orthodox Church. Much of this heritage has been ignored by Egypt's Muslim-majority community until recently. Now, efforts are underway to revive and restore Coptic arts. Many churches are receiving money from the government and international aid groups to restore the distinctive architecture of their sites. Paintings on the walls of the churches and in monasteries in Egypt's deserts also are being restored. A Coptic museum in Cairo also is being renovated, and religious sites have been added to a governmental list for restorations.

Much of the cultural revival of Coptic arts, language, and literature has resulted from the growth of Copt communities overseas.

15 WORK

Egypt's educational system emphasizes rote learning over critical thinking. That style of education, coupled with a lack of trained teachers, has not prepared young Egyptian adults well for the labor market of the early 21st century. The adult literacy rate was 55.6% in 2003, which is extremely high relative to other countries.

Most Egyptians work in the government, and many, including many Coptic Christian men, are conscripted to complete a term of service in Egypt's military. Approximately one-third of Egyptians works in agriculture and grows corn, wheat, cotton, rice, barley, and fruits. Others work in tourism or at ports along the Suez Canal, an important source of income for Egypt. Much of the population lives below the poverty line. Women account for only one-fourth of Egypt's income.

16 SPORTS

Soccer is Egypt's national sport. Besides playing soccer, Egyptians enjoy playing tennis, swimming and horseback riding. Although a tradition of playing sports does not exist in Copt communities, Coptic Christians also take part in similar activities.

17 ENTERTAINMENT AND RECREATION

Egyptian cities have a number of cinemas where Egyptian and foreign films are shown. Egypt's film-making and television programming have received acclaim throughout the Middle East. Television plays a big part in daily leisure lives, even in the rural areas. Men often gather at coffee shops to play backgammon and dominoes and to converse with friends. Women tend to socialize primarily in the home or at places such as markets.

For Copts, the church is a center of social life. Churches organize summer camps for youth, pilgrimages to holy sites within Egypt as well as the rest of the Middle East, and offer many opportunities for socializing before or after services. The rise of Islamic fundamentalism in Egypt and resulting attacks on Copts has prompted many Copts to turn inward and isolate themselves from the Muslim mainstream. Many have turned to their churches for protection and solace.

18 FOLK ART, CRAFTS, AND HOBBIES

The Coptic tradition of pattern weaving in the early Christian era led to the creation of many elaborately designed bed sheets and covers, towels, napkins, tablecloths, curtains, and wall hangings. Much of this textile work continues today, and is marketed in tourist centers. An "s-twist" of thread characterizes the Coptic textiles. Flax fibers used to make thread are washed and then spun into thread in a counter-clockwise direction. Many Coptic crafts developed in monasteries, and practices of weaving, leather binding, painting, and woodwork continue into the present day.

19 SOCIAL PROBLEMS

Egypt revised its constitution in 1981 so that legislative principles would draw their source from the Islamic Sharia. About 90% of Egyptians are Sunni Muslim and look to Islam to govern decisions on marriage, divorce and inheritance. However, tensions are growing between secularists and fundamentalist Muslims in Egypt. While secularists support a state that allows for religious difference, a free press, and cultural diversity to flourish, some religious fundamentalists within Islam would like the government to enforce a great adherence to Islamic principles in schools, public policies, and the arts. Egypt's growing population, limited natural resources, and reliance on the Nile River for water are straining the country's resources. Nearly one out of five Egyptians lives below the poverty line, and even though less than 3% of the country's land is usable for agriculture, nearly one-third of the people draw their income from agriculture. Islamic fundamentalists believe that more compliance with Islamic law could help alleviate Egypt's problems.

The fight over secularism has generated some hostilities against Coptic Christians since the 11 September 2001 terrorist attacks on the United States and the wars in Afghanistan and Iraq. U.S. president George W. Bush has referred to the war against terror as a "crusade." The term "crusade" evoked memories of the centuries of bitter warfare between Muslims and Christians for some fundamentalists who have responded by looting Copt businesses, attacking churches, and harassing Copt individuals. Coptic Church leaders have tried to quell the hostility by appealing to the Quran and its calls for compassion. Pope Shenouda III is the present head of the Coptic Orthodox Church. He frequently infuses his prayers with references to Arab poetry and Muslim religious messages. His goal is to press for national unity in which Copts will remain free to practice their faith under a benevolent Islamic state.

20 GENDER ISSUES

Egypt enacted a family reform law in 2000 that allowed for women to initiate divorce from a spouse. Although the law made it possible for a woman to leave an abusive spouse, it does not allow for the woman to collect alimony and requires that she return any money that was given to her or her family at the time of her marriage.

Rules against divorce are even more prohibitive in the Coptic Christian community. The Coptic Orthodox Church prohibits divorce and strictly forbids women to have abortions. In recent years, some women have converted to Islam in order to divorce their husbands. These conversions have presented difficulties in the Coptic community because Egypt's Islamic code often forces children of a parent who converts to Islam to abandon the church and become Muslim. The Coptic Orthodox Church also has condemned marriage between gays and lesbians.

[21] BIBLIOGRAPHY

Arab Republic of Egypt. Culture Grams: World Edition. Ann Arbor, Mich.: ProQuest LLC, 2008

Coptic Orthodox Church Network. http://www.copticchurch. net (October 2008).

Economist Intelligence Unit: Country Profile: Egypt. Economist Intelligence Unit Inc., 2007

Golia, Maria. "Remembrance of Things Forgotten: Egypt's Valuable Coptic Architecture Has Until Recently Been Overlooked but Interest Is Reviving." *The Middle East* (May 2007): 60–62.

Knickmeyer, Ellen. "Egypt's Coptic Christians Are Choosing Isolation: Violent Clashes With Majority Muslims and an Increase in Separate Institutions Help Sever Centuries-Old Ties, *Washington Post Foreign Service,* July 7, 2008.

Malaty, Fr. Tadros Y. *Introduction to the Coptic Orthodox Church, its History, Beliefs, and Practices* (Alexandria, Egypt), www.copticchurch.net/topics/thecopticchurch/index.html (August 2008).

"Pope Shenouda Warns Copts That Marriage With Jehovah's Witnesses is Ground for Excommunication, Divorce," 2002. *WorldWide Religious News,* April 19, www.wwrn.org (August 2008).

Saad, Michael. "A Christian Appeal to Islam," *Christian Century,* February 23, 2000.

Swanson, Mark N. "Common Wisdom: Luqman the Wise in a Collection of Coptic Orthodox Homilies." Currents in Theology and Mission, 33.3 (June 2006): 246(7)

"The Christian Coptic Orthodox Church of Egypt," 2006. Encyclopedia Coptic , http://www.coptic.netEncyclopedia-Coptica/ (8 August 2008).

—by H. Gupta-Carlson

CREOLES OF SIERRA LEONE

PRONUNCIATION: CREE-uhls of see-AIR-a lee-OWN
LOCATION: Sierra Leone
POPULATION: 150,000–190,000
LANGUAGE: Krio
RELIGION: Christianity with remnants of traditional African religion

[1] INTRODUCTION

The Creoles are a culturally distinct people of Sierra Leone. Their ancestors were liberated slaves from London, Nova Scotia, Jamaica, and parts of West Africa. They were brought as immigrants to the coast of Sierra Leone, where Britain established a haven for liberated slaves in 1787 and a colony in 1807. After passage of the Anti-Slavery Act in 1807, the British navy patrolled the West African coast, intercepted slave ships bound for the Americas, and released their captives in Freetown. From 1808 to 1863 thousands of liberated Africans came to Freetown, and by 1830 the crown colony had become home to more than 10,000 people, who by virtue of adoption and intermarriage became the Creoles.

By the late 1800s, the Creoles had become prosperous through trade and aspired to emulate the culture and manners of Victorian England. Trade grew between the Creoles and the peoples of the interior. In 1895, the British and French signed a treaty, establishing the current boundaries of present-day Sierra Leone, and the following year the British proclaimed the interior a protectorate.

In the 20th century, the racial stratification of the British Empire hurt the Creoles. Many were restricted to low-level civil service posts. Political reform in 1951 created new opportunities for the Creoles. In 1967, Dr. Siaka Stevens, a Creole and former Freetown mayor, was elected prime minister, a post he held until 1985, when violent strikes and demonstrations forced him to step down in favor of General Joseph Saidu Momoh, a Limbe. Overall, Creole political dominance diminished in the post-independence period as elections based on one-man one vote took root and new parties favored the numerically superior Temne and Mende peoples.

Momoh's rule ushered in twenty years of great political and social upheaval. The period was marked by four coups, brutal executions, and 11 years of rebellion and civil war fueled mainly by illegal diamond trading (1991-2002). Foreign troops and UN peacekeepers eventually restored peace and order, but not before thousands were killed and maimed, and more than two million people left homeless.

In 1999 the assault on Freetown by the Revolutionary United Front (RUF), and its campaign "operation no living thing" targeted the Creoles. Importantly, it made clear for all to see the dangers of long-term privilege and the horrific power of envy and discontent. By the end of 2005, most of the peacekeepers had left the country, and free and fair presidential elections occurred in 2007. As of the mid-2000s, a fresh urgency for balanced and equitable development throughout the country seemed to be prevailing.

² LOCATION AND HOMELAND

The Creole homeland is a mountainous, narrow peninsula on the coast of West Africa, about 32 km (20 mi) long and 16 km (10 mi) wide. At its northern tip lies Freetown, the Sierra Leonean capital. The mountains towering above Freetown and its harbor inspired the Portuguese explorer Pedro de Cinta to name them " *Sierra Lyoa*" ("Lion Mountains"), which later became Sierra Leone. The local African name was "Roma-ron"—"place of the mountain." Town and location names such as Aberdeen Bay, Murray Town, Hill Station, Gloucester, Wellington, Hastings, York, and Kent testify to subsequent British influence.

The whole of Sierra Leone covers some 72,500 sq km (28,000 sq mi), roughly the size of South Carolina. The nation is bounded by Guinea to the north and east, and Liberia to the south. At 10° to 13° north latitude, Sierra Leone lies roughly at the same latitude as Panama.

The peninsula's mountain range is covered by tropical rain forests split by deep valleys and adorned with impressive waterfalls. White sand beaches line the Atlantic coast. During the rainy months, from May to November, monsoons dump as much as 15 cm (6 in) of rain in one hour. The mountains receive more than 500 cm (200 in) of rain annually.

All together, Sierra Leone is home to at least a dozen major ethnic groups, including the Koranko, the Mende, the Temne, the Fula (Peul), and the non-Muslim Vai. Groups that arrived before the end of the 18th century are known as "early settlers"; all others, including the Creoles, are the "later settlers."

³ LANGUAGE

Krio, a language distinct from West African pidgin, is the mother tongue of the Creoles, less than 15% of whom are literate in English. It is widely spoken throughout the country at markets and in the workplace where it is understood by as much as 95% of the population. However, it is only the first language of about 10% of the population. The fear that Krio is becoming polluted by English (which is popular among youth) has prompted a movement to teach it more systematically in the schools.

In addition to adapting many English words into its vocabulary, Krio incorporates syntactic, semantic, and phonologic elements of West African languages and bears similarities to Gullah and Jamaican Creole. But Krio also has been influenced by other European languages. For example, "sabi" is of Portuguese origin, and "boku" is of French origin. In its pure form, Krio is practically unintelligible to the outsider.

⁴ FOLKLORE

Creoles have inherited a diverse array of tales from their ancestors. Especially popular with children, they amuse and provide instruction in Creole morals, values, and traditions. Among the best loved are stories about the spider. Children delight in his cleverness and grow nervous when his tricks get him into trouble. The following is a typical spider tale:

Once the spider was fat. He loved eating, but detested work and had not planted or fished all season. One day the villagers were preparing a feast. From his forest web, he could smell the mouth-watering cooking. He knew that if he visited friends, they would feed him as was the custom. So he called his two sons and told both of them

to tie a rope around his waist and set off in opposite directions for the two closest villages, each holding one end of the rope. They were to pull on the rope when the food was ready. But both villages began eating at the same time, and when the sons began pulling the rope, it grew tighter and tighter, squeezing the greedy spider. When the feasting was over and the sons came to look for him, they found a big head, a big body, and a very thin waist!

⁵ RELIGION

While most Sierra Leoneans (60%) subscribe to Islam, Creoles are deeply proud of their Christianity, which blends with remnants of traditional African religion (see **Rites of Passage**). The early immigrants either brought their Christian faith with them or were schooled by missionaries. In 1827, the English Church Missionary Society established the first college in West Africa, Fourah Bay College (now the University College of Sierra Leone), to train missionaries. Samuel Ajai Crowther, a liberated African and the first pupil to attend the college, became the first African bishop of the Church of England in 1864. Presently, there are some 15 different faiths and more than 70 churches in Freetown.

⁶ MAJOR HOLIDAYS

Coups, dictatorial rule, war, and financially hard times have dampened enthusiasm for Independence Day and other secular holidays. However, Creoles celebrate Christmas and Easter with much feasting. Children receive new clothes and gifts of money from their parents and relatives on these occasions. One popular holiday in Freetown is the end of the Muslim Ramadan fast. On this night, young boys carry thin paper lanterns attached to wooden frames. The parade begins at 11:00 pm, and parties with singing and dancing are held throughout the night.

⁷ RITES OF PASSAGE

Despite their outwardly Western ways, Creoles practice certain African rituals in connection with rites of passage. One such ceremony is the *awujoh* feast. Of Yoruba origin, awujoh is held to win the protection of ancestral spirits for newborns and newlyweds and gain wisdom regarding death. Awujoh is believed to appease angry ancestors and attain their guidance when someone dies.

At death, the pillows and blankets of the deceased are stripped off the bed because they are associated with the death struggle. Pictures are turned toward the wall. At the wake, relatives and friends sing spirituals and church hymns. (Aku Creoles sing songs in Yoruba: "This world, this world, is not ours.") People clap loudly to make sure the corpse is not merely in a trance. The next day the body is washed, placed in expensive shrouds, and laid on a bed for a final viewing. Then, it is placed in a coffin and taken to the church for the service and then to the cemetery for burial.

The mourning period lasts one year. On the third, seventh, and fortieth day, *awujoh* feasts are held. The feast on the fortieth day marks the spirit's last day on earth. The family and guests eat a big meal. At a certain point, everyone is called to witness as portions of the meal, including beverages and kola nuts, are placed into a hole for the dead. The family and friends may talk into the hole to discuss their problems with the dead. They throw kola nuts on the ground to determine whether they have been heard and to see whether foul play was involved in the death. At the end of the year, the family holds another awujoh followed by the *pull mohning* day—the end of mourning. The mourners wear white, visit the cemetery, and then return home for refreshments.

8 INTERPERSONAL RELATIONS

The Creoles are a sociable people, given to joking and teasing. Their gregarious nature is often expressed in gestures, such as hand slapping and handshaking. A common greeting in the morning is "Ow de body?" Historically Creoles have been united by their privileged social status, enjoying membership in many elite social clubs. In Sierra Leone, the Masons have traditionally been dominated by Creole men.

Traditional attitudes are still noticeable in Creole dating and marriage customs. For example, marriage is still viewed as a contract between two families. Therefore, parents or other family members seek out prospective mates for their kin from hardworking, well-to-do families. Dating ends when a mate has been chosen and the groom's parents set a "put stop" day, after which the girl can no longer entertain other beaus. "Put stop" has a scripted ceremony in which each family plays a part. Out of several possibilities, the groom's family indicates the young lady of its choice, who is always the last to enter the room. On the evening before the wedding, the groom's friends treat him to "bachelor's eve," a rowdy last fling before marriage.

9 LIVING CONDITIONS

Creole families typically live in two-story wooden houses reminiscent of those found in the West Indies or Louisiana. Despite their dilapidated appearance, they have a distinctive air, with dormers, box windows, shutters, glass panes, and balconies. Several of them were burned or destroyed during the war, yet it is surprising how many of them have survived for over 200 years. The elite live in attractive neighborhoods like Hill Station, above Freetown. A large dam in the mountains once supplied reliable water and electricity, but in the aftermath of the war tanker trucks and pickups with makeshift tanks deliver water to the neighborhoods. People light their houses with kerosene lamps and cook on gas- or wood-fired stoves.

At rush hour, downtown Freetown is congested with Landcruisers, Volkswagens, and Japanese cars. Broken-down cars are abandoned and left to rust in the "car cemeteries" of Freetown's back streets. Most people travel by taxi. Fares are negotiated before the ride, with the passenger usually offering half of what the driver demands. Pickup trucks (lorries) with wooden benches in the back provide rural transportation. These are efficient but overcrowded and carry rice bags, cassava, bushels of fruit, and chickens, as well as people, and sport a variety of colorful graffiti. Buses ply the main roads between provincial cities but are more expensive.

Freetown once had a reputation for being the "white man's grave" because of its endemic malaria. Large, deep drainage canals now carry off much of the monsoon rain, reducing the number of flies and mosquitoes. But social and physical infrastructure destroyed during the war will take many years to restore. Health care is still not available to many Sierra Leoneans, the HIV/AIDS rate hovers around 7%, and life expectancy is 41 years. In 2007 Sierra Leone received the lowest Human Development Index (HDI) rating in the world, placing 177th out of 177 countries (measuring standard of living, health, and education).

10 FAMILY LIFE

Creoles live in exogamous nuclear families, but the extended family is important to them. Family members who do well are expected to help those who are less fortunate, assisting poorer relatives with school fees and business or job opportunities. Women typically shoulder the greatest domestic burdens, unless the family has hired helpers. In families with limited means, the women care for the children, clean house, do the marketing, cook meals, wash dishes and clothes, and carry wood and water.

11 CLOTHING

In the 19th century, Creoles wore European dress to imitate upper-class English manners and find acceptance in the higher ranks of society. Early settlers arrived dressed in European clothes, and the liberated slaves who came later were given English clothing. Woolen suits, bowler hats, stiff upright collars, white gloves, and cigars were the most obvious outward signs of a gentleman's acculturation. For her part, the civilized lady spent lavishly on the fashions of the day, usually imitating styles seen in magazines. Manual laborers acquired suits, which they wore on Sundays and holidays, and for weddings and funerals. In the fields, men wore pantaloons and vests, while at home women wore the traditional African wraparounds (*lappa*). Children often ran naked in the streets.

Today, pop fashions—jeans, T-shirts, and sneakers—are very much de rigueur for young people. However, the older set still dresses conservatively in European suits and dresses. On Sunday mornings, the Anglican and Catholic elites of Freetown turn out in their Sunday finery at the Regent Church service high above the capital. For every day, women wear simpler Western dresses, skirts and blouses, or the lappa with an African blouse.

12 FOOD

Creoles typically eat three meals a day, the largest enjoyed in the morning or near midday. The staple noonday meal is *foofoo,* a dough-like paste made of cassava tubers pounded into flour. Foo-foo is always eaten with a "palaver sauce" or "plassas," which is a spicy dish consisting of leafy greens embellished with tripe, fish, beef, salt pork, and chicken. Red palm oil heated to a near boil forms the base of the sauce. Foo-foo and sauce must be eaten with the fingers of the right hand. A West African specialty, jollof rice, is also popular. This is a one-pot meal, most likely of Wolof origin. Other favorites include rice with various sauces, rice bread, and salad. Unless they are teetotalers, Creoles enjoy alcoholic drinks such as beer, gin, and palm wine. Fruit juices are made from pineapples, mangoes, and oranges.

13 EDUCATION

In the 19th century, the European notion of "bringing civilization to the heathen" provided a rationale to educate Creoles and hold them up as models for their pagan brethren. Indeed, the British made more public funds available per capita in Sierra Leone than in Britain itself in the early part of the century. Since a proper education assured upward mobility, Creoles sent their children to Fourah Bay College or to a British university. Now the University of Sierra Leone, Fourah Bay College, founded by missionaries in 1827, was once the "Athens of West Africa." Based on this educational privilege, Creoles supplied the colony with lawyers, doctors, clergy, upper-level civil servants, and businessmen.

In the 20th century, schooling in Sierra Leone became universal. In 1987, tuition fees were abolished for government-funded primary and secondary schools making schooling more accessible than before. However, the war forced many schools outside Freetown to close. Though Creole children—by virtue of living in Freetown—fared better than most during the war, they also suffered school closures, teacher shortages, and substandard facilities. Sierra Leone lags behind much of the world with a literacy rate of 35% and a combined school enrollment of 45%.

¹⁴ CULTURAL HERITAGE

In the late 1800s, the Creole upper class was far more concerned with literary societies, public lectures, piano recitals, and dignity balls than with African drumming and dancing. They thought that Gumbay and Shakee-shakee dances were unseemly and unfit for civilized people. Creole attitudes toward indigenous dance have changed, and Creoles participate in Sierra Leone's internationally famous National Dance Troupe, which has members from all ethnic groups. In 1992, the troupe included sixty singers, dancers, and musicians.

The Creoles are still known for their intellectual and literary contributions. Creole educators, theologians, authors, dramatists, and poets have pioneered a burgeoning literature in the Krio language. The following stanza from a poem by Thomas Decker offers a glimpse into this body of work:

"Slip Gud"

Slip gud, o, bedi-gial!	Sleep well, my "baby-girl!"
opin yai lilibit	Open your eyes a little bit
en luk mi wan minit	Look, just for one minute
bifo you slip.	Ere you fall asleep.

¹⁵ WORK

Creoles are found in all occupations and vocations. They farm, fish, trade, teach, and sell artwork and handicrafts. Many have left manual jobs for office work and other status jobs, only to find that these do not pay enough to support large families. Both men and women operate small businesses, such as food stands and restaurants. A growing number of Creoles have found employment in start-up non-governmental organizations (NGOs) many of which provide social and civil rights services in post-conflict Sierra Leone.

¹⁶ SPORTS

The favorite Sierra Leonean sport is soccer, called football in West Africa. Schools of all sizes have teams, and in even the smallest villages, games are played every evening. Although children may play without soccer shoes, they usually have uniforms. Though inspiring, the Leone Stars—the national team—have never qualified for World Cup finals.

¹⁷ ENTERTAINMENT AND RECREATION

Creoles enjoy going to movies, watching television, listening to the radio, and following soccer. Radio Sierra Leone was established in 1934 and is the oldest broadcasting service in English-speaking West Africa. Now transistor radios with shortwave and FM capabilities are found in even the smallest villages. With the growth of satellite television, the number of channels and the service area have expanded dramatically from Freetown to the hinterlands. Programs from the United States and England are very popular.

Recreational opportunities abound in and around Freetown. On weekends, especially Sundays, the beaches at Aberdeen are filled with soccer players, swimmers, joggers and casual strollers who come to see the fisherman bring in their catches, or who simply enjoy people-watching. Kabobs and cold drinks can be found in the many beach cabanas, seaside restaurants, and informal refreshment stands.

A favorite pastime for girls is hair braiding, which can take an entire weekend. Boys enjoy checkers and other games, while adults like to exchange visits with their friends. One of the regular forms of entertainment both in Freetown and in rural areas is the central market. In the villages of Kent, Sussex, and York, there is a designated market day every week. People come from miles around not only to buy and sell, but to dress up and exchange the latest news and gossip, with the added stimulation of fresh palm wine or beer.

¹⁸ FOLK ART, CRAFTS, AND HOBBIES

In the 19th century, the Creole elites favored "high-brow" hobbies, such as reading, playing instruments, and writing poetry, over crafts and folk art. Nowadays, small-scale arts and crafts centers flourish in Freetown, catering mainly to foreign tourists. Miranda Burney Nicol (Olayinka) and Phoebe Ageh Jones are two artists whose works have been distributed internationally. Cloth dyeing (batik) is a traditional craft that has recently been revived.

¹⁹ SOCIAL PROBLEMS

The Creoles' problems are inseparable from those of other Sierra Leoneans. There are few jobs for school graduates and dropouts alike, which has increased the number of beggars and hawkers. The weak economy has encouraged other social problems like prostitution. Families that have taken in relatives must deal with the added stress that comes from belt-tightening and overcrowding. In Freetown, relentless migration from the provinces has increased congestion, pollution, and crime. Basic services barely function, and the government, businesses, and civil society need to do a much better job of controlling corruption. There is a genuine concern about the effects of almost a generation that has largely missed formal education.

While these problems seem daunting, the country is now in an intensive rebuilding phase, as is its neighbor to the south and east, Liberia. If handled properly, the next decade could present Creoles and their neighbors new opportunities to put the past behind and to find a common way forward. Young Creoles and their friends face a difficult future, but they also represent a generation with new ideas and potential solutions to old problems.

²⁰ GENDER ISSUES

Creole women are the backbone of their families and of society. They manage the household and rear the children; many work outside the home. Virtually all Creole girls receive at least primary formal schooling, and the vast majority complete secondary school and beyond. The first Creole girl graduated from Fourah Bay College in 1938. The Church Mission Society founded the Annie Walsh Memorial School for girls in 1849, and many of its graduates in turn founded schools of their own. Hannah Benka-Coker has had a statue erected in her honor at the Freetown Secondary School for girls.

As a result of educational opportunity, many Creole women became influential in the women's movement in the early 1900s that culminated in the right to vote (for women of status) in 1930. Constance Horton, later Mrs. Cummings-Jones, became the first woman elected to a municipal council in Africa in 1938. Having been active in church associations, Creole women used their organizing skills to advocate for women's rights in the 1950s. Subsequently, many of them attained high positions in their respective professions. For example, Mrs. Constance Cummings-John was mayor of Freetown in 1966. In 2008 the executive directors of the Sierra Leone NGO association and of the Center for Good Governance were Creole women.

Nonetheless, Creoles and Sierra Leonean women face gender discrimination in the workplace. They also face inheritance laws and property rights laws that favor men over women. Rape and domestic violence are not uncommon, but are surrounded by a culture of silence. Although it is difficult to know how many of the victims are Creole, it is safe to assume that Creoles are affected. The Ministry of Social Welfare, Gender and Children's Affairs is poorly funded, relies mainly on donor assistance, and has few programs to support efforts to further the rights and progress of women in Sierra Leone.

[21] BIBLIOGRAPHY

Adebajo, Adekeye. *Building Peace in West Africa: Liberia, Sierra Leone, and Guinea-Bissau.* Boulder, Colorado: Lynne Rienner, 2002.

Africa South of the Sahara 2007. Sierra Leone. London: Europa Publishers, 2008.

Fyle, C. Magbaily. *Historical Dictionary of Sierra Leone.* Lanham, Md.: Scarecrow, 2006.

Greene, Graham. *The Heart of the Matter.* New York: Viking, 1948.

Harris, Joseph E., ed. *Global Dimensions of the African Diaspora.* 2nd Edition. Washington, DC: Howard University Press, 1993.

Paracka, Daniel J., Jr. *The Athens of West Africa: A History of International Education at Fourah Bay College, Freetown, Sierra Leone.* New York and London: Routledge, 2003.

Spitzer, Leo. *The Creoles of Sierra Leone: Responses to Colonialism, 1870-1945.* Madison: University of Wisconsin Press, 1974.

Wyse, Akintola. *The Krio of Sierra Leone: An Interpretive History.* London: C. Hurst and Company, 1989.

—by R. Groelsema

DINKA

PRONUNCIATION: DEEN-kuh
LOCATION: Sudan
POPULATION: 500,000 to 1 million
LANGUAGE: Dinka
RELIGION: Monotheistic-worship of Nhialic
RELATED ARTICLES: Vol. 1: Nuer; Shilluk; Sudanese

[1] INTRODUCTION

Numbering between 500,000 and 1 million people, the Dinka are one of the largest ethnic groups in the republic of Sudan. Their presence in this region of Africa was noted thousands of years ago by Egyptian and later Greek travelers and geographers. The Dinka belong to a larger group of historically related cultures that anthropologists have referred to as the Nilotic peoples of Africa—Dinka, Nuer, Atuot, Shilluk, and Anuak—all of whom live in the upper Nile region of southern Sudan. General observations about the Dinka and related Nilotic peoples figure in the narratives written by Arab slave traders who entered their country in the 16th, 17th, and 18th centuries. Perhaps their reputation as fierce warriors was earned during this period, as the Dinka successfully resisted Arab presence. In the middle of the last century (c. 1840–1880), the Dinka also resisted efforts on the part of a Turkish administration in the northern Sudan to administer, tax, and otherwise harass them. In 1898, a condominium (joint) form of government was created between Egypt and Great Britain, and from this time until the Sudan gained independence from Great Britain in 1956, the Dinka were only marginally affected by British colonial presence. In 1983, a civil war erupted in the Sudan, pitting the largely Arab and Muslim northern Sudan against the black African peoples of the south. Lasting into the 1990s, the war has had dire consequences for the Dinka and other Nilotic peoples. Tens of thousands of Dinka have died, and countless others have become refugees in either the northern Sudan or the many countries bordering the Sudan. Rebel groups and international human rights organizations have accused the Sudanese government of attempting genocide against the Dinka.

[2] LOCATION AND HOMELAND

A careful census of the Dinka has not been attempted since the mid 1950s, at which time it was estimated that the Dinka numbered more than 1 million; in 2008 estimates place the Dinka population at somewhere between 500,000 and 1 million. Dinka country extends from 6° to 10°N latitude and from 26° to 32°E longitude. This vast region forms a seasonal swampland as the Nile floods from its high ground in Uganda into the flat, saucer-like geography of the southern Sudan. The extreme differences between the wet and dry seasons have a dramatic effect on many aspects of Dinka life. During the season of rains, human population densities increase as people are forced to settle in areas that are higher than the Nile floodwaters.

Because of civil war, large numbers of Dinka have migrated from southern Sudan to the northern Sudanese capital of Khartoum, as well as to Kenya, Uganda, Europe, and the United States. There are no precise data on the actual number of Dinka now living elsewhere. As of the mid-2000s, thousands of internally displaced Dinka were beginning to return to their home villages in southern Sudan.

3 LANGUAGE

Linguists classify Dinka as a major language family in the Nilotic category of African languages. Historically, it is most closely related to Nuer and Atuot, languages spoken by peoples living in close proximity to the Dinka. The Nuer and Atuot languages, however, are more closely related to each other than they are to Dinka.

ENGLISH TERM	ATUOT /NUER	DINKA
cow	*yang*	*weng*
beer	*kung*	*mou*
incest	*rual*	*akeeth*
husband	*cou*	*nwc*
wife	*cek*	*tieng*
child	*gat*	*mieth*
war spear	*mut*	*tong*

The Dinka have a diverse lexicon with which to describe their world. It is estimated that the Dinka language has more than 400 words to refer to cattle alone—their movements, their diseases, and their variety in color and form. The Dinka's very perception of color, light, and shade in the world around them is in these ways inextricably connected with their recognition of the color configurations in their cattle. Without their cattle color vocabulary, they would have scarcely any way of describing visual experience in terms of color, light, and darkness.

4 FOLKLORE

The Dinka tradition of oral literature is extensive and a considerable amount has been recorded. In this tradition, two figures stand out prominently, a legendary figure known as Col Muong, and another known as Awiel Longar. Col Muong figures in many stories as a man who has an enormous appetite for all things in life. When he is hungry, he is said to eat an entire herd of cattle or an entire field of grain. Stories about him seem to indicate that people should do the best they can with what they have rather than focus on their own individual needs. Awiel Longar figures as the common ancestor of all Dinka peoples. Awiel is thought of as a culture hero who showed people how to live and, indeed, brought them life. Dinka folklore is also rich in "just so" stories about the origins of customs, the behavior of animals, and everyday life.

5 RELIGION

Dinka religious beliefs have been described and analyzed in detail by the late British anthropologist R. G. Lienhardt in his book, *Divinity and Experience: The Religion of the Dinka*. The Dinka term *Nhialic*, Lienhardt suggests, is best translated as "creator" and in this regard Dinka religion may be regarded as monotheistic. Ultimately, *Nhialic* is thought to be the source of all life and death. Mediating this distant, though approachable, image are a series of lesser manifestations of the creator's power. These are known to the Dinka by a series of "refractions" or manifestations of divinity to which Dinka dedicate ritual sacrifices and libations. Rituals are performed at births, deaths, to cure disease, and in times of crises.

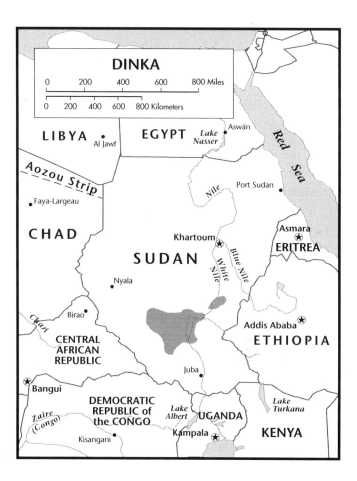

6 MAJOR HOLIDAYS

Celebrations take place in the autumn, when the whole tribe is together. Religious sacrifices may be made on special occasions. To honor their traditional spiritual and political leaders—called "masters of the fishing spear"—the Dinka enacted day-long ceremonies marked by large public gatherings and the sacrifice of many cattle. By ritually "killing" these men, Dinka collectively asserted their power to control the spiritual powers governing human life.

7 RITES OF PASSAGE

Like other cattle-keeping people of southern Sudan and eastern Africa, the Dinka mark significant life-passage events with informal but significant ritual occasions. Thus, birth, marriage, and death are all marked by standardized customs involving public ceremonies, and are typically accompanied by animal sacrifice. In the passage to adult status, young men, rather more than young women, are publicly recognized. Adult males decorate initiates' heads with a series of deep gashes that form scars that last a lifetime, publicly proclaiming their newly attained adult status.

8 LNTERPERSONAL RELATIONS

When men become adults, they no longer refer to themselves by their birth names, but instead adopt "ox-names"—derived from characteristics of their favorite cattle, typically with complex metaphorical reference. Thus, a man may be known as Thiecdeng ("club of divinity") or Acinbaai ("a man who never

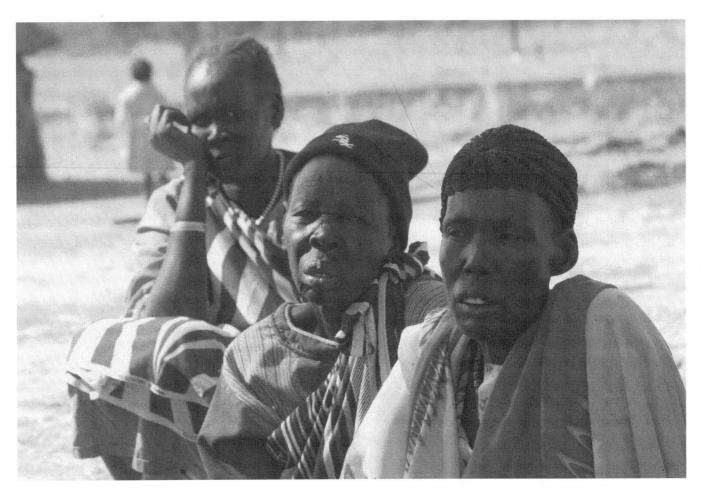

Sudanese refugees from the Ngok Dinka tribe wait in the village of Dokra in central Sudan. (AP Images/Alfred de Montesquiou)

leaves his herd of cattle"). Children's names are often chosen to reflect circumstances of their birth. Thus, one may be called Kueric ("born in the middle of a path in the forest"), Amoum ("the one who survives his dead brothers"), or Ayumpuo ("the one who cools the heart").

Meals are generally eaten in an informal manner. The only explicit strictures involving eating are that unmarried people of similar age who have no close kinship cannot eat in each other's company.

⁹ LIVING CONDITIONS

Round huts, approximately 4.5 m (15 ft) in diameter, were formed with clay, with 1.5- to 2-m (5- to 6-ft) walls, covered with conical thatched roofs. Homesteads such as these were typically surrounded by a garden and separated one from another by an open expanse of savannah forest. Garden soil would typically maintain its fertility for 10 to 12 years. Following this, the area would be set afire and a new homestead erected nearby, in a manner anthropologists call "slash and burn" horticulture.

Because the Dinka population is fairly dispersed (though less so in the season of rains), communicable diseases have traditionally been uncommon. On the other hand, given its subtropical location, Dinkaland is subject to a fair number of

endemic diseases, including malaria, dysentery, and other waterborne diseases.

¹⁰ FAMILY LIFE

Polygamy (the practice of marrying more than one person) is common among the Dinka, although many marriages are monogamous. Men of high social standing may have as many as 50 to 100 wives. In polygamous marriages, wives cooperate in performing household duties, although each is responsible for rearing her own children. Upon marriage, a man pays his wife's family a certain number of cattle, usually between 30 and 40. The Dinka consider it extremely important to have children, which they regard as assuring their immortality.

Traditionally, following marriage a man established a homestead near his father. Around her homestead, a woman would cultivate a garden in a plot ranging from one to two acres, raising sufficient food to feed her family throughout the year. Cash was not a factor in traditional food production, so kinship relations provided a means to assure that if some relatives' gardens failed in a particular year, food could be shared by all.

Even though much of Dinka public life is dominated by men (e.g., ritual and political leaders are male; sacrifices are always led by men), women play a very significant and even powerful role in local life. Many important myths and rituals have powerful feminine symbolism.

11 CLOTHING

The Dinka wear very little clothing and no shoes. The men go naked, and the women may wear goatskin skirts. Both men and women wear strings of beads around their necks. Women also wear bangles on their arms and legs, and they may also wear elaborate jewelry in their ears.

12 FOOD

In the rainy season, milk from cows is plentiful, and this supplements the horticultural diet based primarily on millet. During the dry season, Dinka subsist mainly on fish and other freshwater resources, supplemented by reserves of millet.

Dinka have traditionally produced all the material resources needed to sustain their livelihood via a mode of production that combined horticulture with pastoralism, fishing and occasional hunting. The staple horticultural crop was millet. Ground nuts were introduced in the 1930s and added an additional source of protein to the Dinka diet. Women usually provide a morning meal of millet, sometimes mixed with milk or beef broth. A second meal is prepared as evening approaches. Depending on the season, the millet staple will be supplemented with fish, meat, or other domesticated crops such as beans, tomatoes or rice (now purchased from small rural markets). Cooking oil is produced by crushing the nuts of shea trees and pounding the pulp into oil. A number of species of chili peppers provide condiments. Women cook all meals with the help of their daughters. Women grow a variety of gourds to make containers for cooking and preparing food, and they also use earthenware pots for storing and boiling water.

On ritual occasions, cattle were sacrificed and slaughtered, although cattle (cows) were kept mostly for their milk rather than meat. In the dry season, cattle were occasionally bled by tying a cord around the animal's neck, pulling it tight, then piercing a vein in the animal's neck. The blood was collected in a gourd, mixed with milk, and then boiled, producing a high-protein "pudding." When milk was plentiful, particularly in the rainy season, it was also preserved in a cheese form by mixing a quantity of fresh milk with a smaller portion of hot cow urine. Milk prepared in this form could be stored for as long as three months.

13 EDUCATION

The Dinka lacked any formal system of education until literacy was introduced via mission schools beginning in the late 1930s. Even today, most Dinka lack literacy skills. Indeed, to some, writing is suspected to be a form of political control, and thus many people have never sought to become literate. During the Colonial period in the southern Sudan, English was the only acknowledged language of mission education and administration. During the course of the first civil war in Sudan, in 1964 the government expelled missionaries from the southern Sudan and declared Arabic to be the national language. Regional dialects of Arabic have since emerged in Dinka country. At the time of this writing, very few Dinka have received a formal education because the educational system, along with the majority of social services, has disappeared due to war.

14 CULTURAL HERITAGE

Like many other semi-nomadic peoples throughout the world, the Dinka do not have a substantial heritage of plastic arts; song and dance, however, play an important role in their culture. A set of drums for dancing is found in every Dinka settlement. Like many other aspects of Dinka life, artistic expression is associated with cattle, which they often imitate in their songs and dances. Because the Dinka identify so closely with their herds, when a tribesman sings a song praising his cattle, he is, in effect, praising himself. Songs serve many other functions as well. There are battle songs, songs of initiation, and songs celebrating the tribe's ancestors. In symbolic "song battles," singing can also defuse tensions and avert bloodshed among this highly volatile people.

Following is a typical Dinka song:

O Creator who created me in my mother's womb
Do not confront me with a bad thing
Show me the place of cattle,
So that I may grow my crops
And keep my herd.

15 WORK

Tending herds of cattle and growing millet form the basis of the livelihood and economy of the Dinka. As the main channel and hundreds of tributaries of the Nile begin to flood during the season of rains (roughly April to September), people move with their herds of cattle to higher ground. Here, during the season of rains, the millet and other crops are planted. With the coming of the dry season and abating flood waters, people drive their herds back toward rivers and tributaries where the cattle are pastured. Labor among the Dinka is clearly divided along gender lines, with men in their 20s and 30s devoting their time to cattle-herding. Women are responsible for growing crops (although men perform the heavy work of clearing new fields for planting). Women also cook and draw water from wells and rivers. Each homestead normally plants two millet crops every year, as well as okra, sesame, pumpkins, and cassava. One of the ways that Dinka boys are prepared for adulthood is by being given a small flock of sheep and goats to tend.

Although many Dinka want to preserve their traditional way of life, they find that, because of the consequences of civil war and the need to participate in "modern" as well as "traditional" society, the past they once knew may be gone forever.

16 SPORTS

Dinka men engage in mock sparring, using spears or sticks and shields, in order to develop their fighting skills.

17 ENTERTAINMENT AND RECREATION

Because much of the Dinka population disperses to follow the herds during the dry season, important social events such as marriages are more common during the rainy season. People live in more compact settlements at that time, and milk and millet are plentiful. Seasons during which there are droughts or unusually heavy rains likewise have a dramatic impact on local social life. Dinka social life is also closely tied to religion.

[18] FOLK ART, CRAFTS, AND HOBBIES

Dinka men make spears and fishing hooks. The women make cooking pots using coils of clay, which are formed into the desired shape and then smoothed over. Sharp tools are used to etch patterns in the clay, and color is applied with a stone, after which the pot is fired in a hole in the ground that is covered with burning straw and dung. Besides making pots, which are also essential for carrying water, Dinka women weave baskets and sleeping mats.

[19] SOCIAL PROBLEMS

Since the civil war that began in the 1980s pitting the northern and southern regions of Sudan against each other, numerous Dinka villages have been destroyed by burning or bombing. Thousands of Dinka women have been raped and their husbands castrated in their presence. Young girls have been found brutally murdered. Many Dinka have been abducted and sold as slaves in the northern Sudan. Violence against the Dinka is now on a level that has no precedent in their remembered past.

[20] GENDER ISSUES

As the late Godfrey Lienhardt noted in an article he wrote on the relations between the sexes among the Dinka, vis-à-vis many other African cultures, Dinka women and men have equivalent status. Indeed, early on in their socialization, young boys recognize their utter dependence on their sisters and mothers, who provide for their basic subsistence. As adults, men likewise recognize that their aspirations to become founders of lineages are entirely dependent on the birth careers of their wives. In the contemporary world and in the aftermath of two civil wars and immigration to a wide variety of countries, much has changed in all of Dinka culture, including gender relations.

[21] BIBLIOGRAPHY

Beswick, Stephanie. *Sudan's Blood Memory: the Legacy of War, Ethnicity, and Slavery in early South Sudan*. Rochester, NY: University of Rochester Press, 2004.

Burton, John W. "Dinka." *Encyclopedia of World Cultures*. Boston: G. K. Hall, 1992.

Deng, Francis Mading. *Dinka Cosmology*. London: Ithaca Press, 1980.

———. *Dinka Folktales: African Stories from Sudan*. New York: Africana Publishing, 1974.

———. *The Dinka and Their Songs*. London: Oxford University Press, 1973.

Lienhardt, R. G. *Divinity and Experience: The Religion of the Dinks*. Oxford: Clarendon Press, 1961.

Ryle, John. *Warriors of the White Nile*. Amsterdam: Time-Life Books, 1982.

—by J. W. Burton

DJIBOUTIANS

PRONUNCIATION: juh-BOOT-ee-uhns
ALTERNATE NAMES: Jibouti
LOCATION: Djibouti (Horn of Africa)
POPULATION: approximately 833,000
LANGUAGE: Afar, Somali
RELIGION: Islam
RELATED ARTICLES: Vol. 1: Eritreans; Somalis

[1] INTRODUCTION

Djibouti (also Jibouti) is the name of both a small country and its seaport capital. This land's former name was the French Territory of the Afars and Issas and, before that, French Somaliland. Occupying an area roughly the size of New Jersey, tiny Djibouti, sandwiched between Ethiopia, Somalia, and Eritrea on the east coast of Africa, was the last French colony in Africa.

The area that today is Djibouti was populated for centuries by two groups of once entirely nomadic herders, the Afar and a branch of the Somali people known as the Issa. The French opening of the Suez Canal in 1869 and later British control of this strategic artery of global commerce resulted in intervention across the Horn of Africa by European powers, changing this area from a global backwater to a strategic point in world commercial and naval movements. The canal became the pivot for European domination of most of Asia, the eastern half of Africa, and the Indo-Pacific seas. As European powers competed for strategic advantage, coaling stations for merchant and war fleets became essential. In 1892 France abandoned its commercial center in the city of Obock and transferred it southward, across the Gulf of Tadjoura, to the city of Djibouti, which possessed a better harbor. By 1899 the newly prosperous port city had 10,000 inhabitants, as it drained trade from nearby older ports. Planning began for a French railroad to Addis Abeba, capital of Ethiopia, recently unified and expanded under the Amhara. Meanwhile, in 1894, France had merged its protectorates in the area into French Somaliland (present-day Djibouti). Djibouti's strategic global location remains its chief commercial and military importance.

Commerce grew in the city during the early part of the 20th century, while in the colony's hinterland, the Afars and Issas, the two main ethnic groups, engaged in continued fighting. By 1935 France had ended most open fighting between the two peoples and, occasionally, against French troops. France proclaimed its neutrality during the Italian conquest of Ethiopia in 1935–1936, but tilted toward the Ethiopians, eventually using its base in Djibouti to aid the Ethiopian resistance against their fascist occupiers. On 23 December 1942 Vichy forces in French Somaliland surrendered to British and Free French forces.

French Somaliland became an Overseas Territory of France in 1946. In part because of pressures from pan-Somali nationalists, President Charles de Gaulle of France in 1966 announced a referendum, held in 1967, to determine the future of the colony. This referendum reaffirmed the desire of the majority of the population to remain part of the French community. The colony was renamed the French Territory of the Afars and Issas. Movements for independence continued, nevertheless, and the territory became independent, as Djibouti, on 27 June 1977. The Issa control the government.

President Hassan Gouled Aptidon became and remains head of state. In 1981 Djibouti formally became a one-party state headed by a directly elected president. Aptidon was re-elected in 1981 and 1987. The Afar minority felt excluded in this political process. In 1991 an Afar-based armed rebellion began with the Afar gaining control of much of the country-side. Accordingly, in 1992, President Aptidon presented a multiparty constitution that was ratified by the citizenry. However, Aptidon's dominant political party, the People's Rally for Progress, has no effective opposition. In 1993 Aptidon achieved a fourth term, in Djibouti's first "multiparty" presidential election. The Afar opposition largely boycotted the election, and unrest continues. Some fighting continued through 2000. Ismael Omar Guelleh won his first term as president in 1999 and his second term in 2005, with 100% of the vote. The legal code is based on French civil law, with local Islamic additions.

During the first Gulf War, the French military used Djibouti as its staging base of operations and continues a presence in that country, with ships, aircraft, and armored vehicles. In 2001 Djibouti leased a former French Foreign Legion base to the U.S. It is now shared with France and is part of the U.S. Central Command. Since 2002 a U.S. task force combining all of the armed services and the State Department provides, from the base, humanitarian and development aid to Djibouti. Besides the French military presence, which contributes to the Djibouti economy, the U.S. bases several hundred troops as part of its campaign against regional "terrorism." Djibouti is America's sole base in Africa. From there the U.S. launched its attacks during 2007–2008 against fundamentalist Islamic forces in Somalia. The Djibouti economy centers mainly on the country's strategic location for transshipment of freight and refueling of ships. Ethiopian exports and imports comprise about 85% of port enterprise.

2 LOCATION AND HOMELAND

With a territory of some 23,200 sq km (8,950 sq mi), Djibouti has a population, in 2007, estimated by the UN at 833,000 but the real number could be nearer half as many. About two-thirds of Djiboutians live in Djibouti city, the capital. The country of Djibouti extends inland about 88 km (55 mi), from the north and south shores of the Gulf of Tadjoura, a narrow inlet of the Gulf of Aden. It lies on the western shore of the Bab el-Mandeb (Arabic for "gate of tears"), a strategic strait 27-km (17-mi) wide joining the Gulf of Aden to the Red Sea, and thus, via Suez, Atlantic to Indo-Pacific commerce. Besides the sea, Somalia, Ethiopia, and Eritrea border Djibouti. The country's Red Sea coast stretches some 800 km (500 mi).

The land of Djibouti comprises arid, rugged highlands often 900 m (3,000 ft) or more in elevation, with peaks at 1,620 m (5,400 ft) and 1,980 m (6,600 ft), and basaltic steppe and desert plains having salt lakes and normally dry streams. Lake Assal is the lowest point in Africa, at 155 m (508 ft) below sea level. Once called by Europeans "the valley of hell," Djibouti is a land of permanent intense heat and drought. The Somalis call the terrain *guban* (burnt land). In its northeastern third, the land is tropical desert; the remainder is tropical steppe with a coastal desert fringe. Grass and herbaceous plants, such as thornbush, grow singly and in patches, awaiting seasonal rainfall, about 50 cm (20 in) in the mountain heights and 13 cm (5

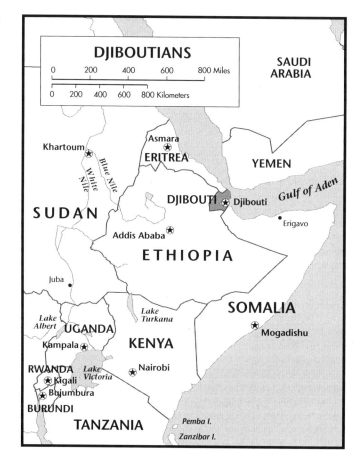

in) in the deserts. Only a few mountain peaks sport continuous vegetative cover. When the briefly seasonal flow in watercourses ends, herds of livestock depend on permanent wells. No surface streams from the Ethiopian highlands penetrate as far as Djibouti.

Djibouti contains two indigenous ethno-linguistic groups, the Afar (sometimes also called the Danakil) and the Somali. (Djibouti Somalis primarily belong to the Issa clan of the Dir clan-family, which covers two-thirds of Djibouti and extends into adjacent Somalia and Ethiopia.) Each group's links of language, culture, patrilineal kinship, and Islam provides internal unity. Such multiple bonds do not prevent intra-ethnic strife, especially among the Somalis. Besides the Afar, who make up perhaps 35% of the population, and Somalis, who account for as much as 65%, there are also small Arab, French, Ethiopian, and Italian minorities. Periodically, large numbers of refugees displaced by warfare have crossed the border into Djibouti from Ethiopia and Somalia.

3 LANGUAGE

The official languages of Djibouti are French and Arabic, but the everyday languages of most of the people are the Eastern Cushitic languages, Afar and Somali, of the two main ethnic groups. Educated Afars and Somalis speak French. The Somali tongue of Djibouti belongs to the "common dialect" group, found in much of Somalia and used in broadcasts.

A young Djiboutian woman and her father. City dwellers wear Western-style clothing, while those in rural areas wear the loose clothing typical of desert dwellers. (Jason Laure)

⁴ FOLKLORE

The Somali Issa have a myth of origin that portrays their common ancestor—named 'Aqiil Abuu Taalib—as a holy man from Arabia. They have hymns (*qasiidas*) in his honor, and his shrine (*maqaam*) is in Djibouti, where he is said to have appeared miraculously. The Somali's oral tradition also includes storytelling and poetry. Poetry traditionally recited in the villages by special readers called *gabaye* was a way of recording the community's history and customs, as well as current events. The Somali tradition of oral poetry may be in danger as nomadic Somalis have begun learning to read and write.

The Afar maintain some lore that dates back to their original, pre-Islam religion, including a belief in the powers retained by the spirits of the dead, and a belief in the existence of groves and trees with sacred powers. One traditional practice part of this belief system is anointing one's body with butter or *ghee* (a clarified butter commonly used for food and other purposes). Another is the annual celebration of a feast of the dead called *Rabena*.

⁵ RELIGION

Whether among the Afars, Somalis, or Arabs, the religion of Djibouti is Islam. Somalis generally follow the Sunni sect, while Afars are Sufi Muslims, with the former people more devout than the latter. As elsewhere in the world, Islam accommodates local practices. For the orthodox, religious and community activities are governed by the *shari'a*, the canon law of Islam. The greater the orthodoxy, the more the control of women by men. Pilgrimage and scheduled prayer and fasting, such as during Ramadan, are expected. Islam does not transcend ethnicity and thus does not impose a unity on different Muslim peoples, such as the Afars and Somalis. Among the Afars, survivals from the pre-Islamic cosmology of their sky-father deity, Wak, are evident, including days for animal sacrifice and rainmaking ceremonies. (For more about religion in the Horn of Africa, see Eritreans section 5.)

⁶ MAJOR HOLIDAYS

Local Muslim saints' days associated with the Afar and the Issa are popular among their respective groups. Among the Somalis, various devout dervish orders have their own particular and universal observances, such as the Prophet Muhammad's birthday. Many Afars and Somalis are uninformed about the symbolic, mystical content of their own holidays. In Djibouti most urbanites and town residents attend Friday prayer at their mosque.

⁷ RITES OF PASSAGE

As among most of the peoples of the Horn, adult status for the Afars and Somalis requires a genital operation, with or without ceremony, usually in childhood. For Afars and Somalis, boys are circumcised and girls undergo clitoridectomy, a practice intended to ensure their chastity. See section 20.

8 INTERPERSONAL RELATIONS

Djiboutians show great respect to their elders and, in general, for the dignity of others. With their nomadic tradition, Djiboutians historically have not had the chance to forge strong relationships with neighbors, and clan membership plays a prominent role in an individual's social relationships and social standing, which is also determined (for men) by courage in combat. Clan solidarity is reflected in the following Somali saying: "I against my brother; I and my brother against my cousin; I, my brother, and my cousin against the world." (In recent decades, the Somali clans of Djibouti and neighboring Somaliland have been dormant from time to time. However, Somali clan solidarity is important in warfare, both against other clans and against the U.S.)

Among the pastoral Afar, accepting a drink of milk signifies the formation of a bond between a guest and host that includes a responsibility to protect the guest should trouble arise and to avenge his death if he is killed.

Djiboutis, Eritreans, and most Ethiopians share a strong taboo, common among Islamic peoples, involving the left side. The left hand is regarded as unclean and is supposed to be used only for personal hygiene purposes and never for such activities as eating, accepting a present, or shaking another person's hand (which would be considered an unforgivable insult).

9 LIVING CONDITIONS

Living conditions vary greatly, from affluent upper-class Arab businessmen and the educated Afars and Somalis of the country's elite, to undernourished herders with scant possessions and scrawny livestock. Government and Catholic organizations provide some humanitarian aid to the impoverished. Life for women is arduous, as it is generally among nomadic peoples across Africa. Major health threats include severe malnutrition, malaria, and tuberculosis. In 2003 the estimated number of people having an HIV infection was 9,100. Estimated in 2007 as having one of the world's lowest average life expectancies, of 55 years, and an infant mortality rate of 100 per 1,000 live births, Djibouti has a health crisis.

A paved road links Djibouti to the heavy-duty Aseb-Addis Abeba highway, but the road into Northern Somalia is barely usable. A meter-gauge railroad operates to Addis Abeba. Djibouti city has international airline and ship services to the outside world. The city has contained a free port, since 1949. The harbor is enclosed by land, dredged to depths of 12–20 m (40–65 ft). Modern fueling facilities and a floating dry dock round out the facilities of this strategic port.

10 FAMILY LIFE

The Djiboutian family averages six or seven children. A marriage is considered as much a union of two families as of two individuals. Divorce is an accepted and common part of the culture. Practicing polygyny, Muslim men traditionally can marry as many as four women. Each wife raises her own children, and her household is in charge of a specific task, such as agricultural work or tending to livestock. Although polygyny is common among the Somali people, Afar men usually have only one wife. Among the Afar, girls were traditionally eligible for marriage when they turned ten; boys when they had killed

their first man (a feat often attested to by the castration of the victim).

11 CLOTHING

Unlike women in many other Muslim countries, women in Djibouti do not wear veils, although married Afar women wear a black head scarf. City dwellers wear Western-style clothing, while those in rural areas wear the loose clothing typical of desert dwellers. The traditional outfit of the Afar is a garment called a *sanafil*, consisting of a cloth tied around the waist and reaching to the calves (with a knot at the right hip for men and at the left for women). The wealthier Afar wear another piece of cloth, the *harayto*, slung over their shoulders. Afar men are known for the long, sharp, double-edged dagger, called a *jile*, which they wear at their waists. Among the nomadic Somali in rural areas, the men wear a garment similar to the sanafil of the Afar, while the women wear a long, brightly colored cloth called a *guntina*, wound around their torsos and knotted at the right shoulder.

12 FOOD

Among the nomadic herders of Djibouti, their livestock (goats, sheep, camels, and cattle) provides the main dietary staples— milk and meat. They also may obtain grain or vegetables through barter. Sheep and goats provide common fare, while beef is reserved for special occasions. Grain is typically roasted and eaten one grain at a time. A favorite delicacy is a thick flatbread made from wheat and eaten with a sauce made from *ghee* (clarified butter) and red pepper. A papyrus root called *burri*, which grows in some areas, is combined with milk to make porridge.

Most Djiboutians observe Islamic dietary laws, which include a ban on eating pork and consuming alcohol. Smoking hashish and chewing chat leaves, both narcotics, are as moral as alcohol is immoral.

13 EDUCATION

Until after World War II, Catholic missions provided the infrequent formal education, outside of Koranic schools. A French-style curriculum is used in the growing number of government schools. Practical training of a limited kind is given to many pastoralists, who frequently must round out earning a livelihood with seasonal work in the city or on the railroad. The estimated literacy rate in 2003 for those 15 and older was 68%.

14 CULTURAL HERITAGE

The Afar have a traditional type of dance, called *jenile*, which is associated with their ancient pre-Islamic religion.

The Somali have a venerable tradition of oral poetry and song. Their poetry makes heavy use of alliteration.

The visual fine arts of the Somalis have been strongly influenced by Islam, which, for example, does not allow humans or animals to be represented in artwork. Popular motifs are flowers and imaginary creatures.

15 WORK

Labor other than the traditional herding of the nomads in rural areas is concentrated in the city of Djibouti. Major employers include the food and beverage industry, shipping, construction, and shipbuilding, as well as the national railway. High rates of unemployment and underemployment exist.

[16] SPORTS

Few Djiboutians engage in games or sports activities in the Western sense. Some enjoy playing and watching soccer games.

[17] ENTERTAINMENT AND RECREATION

In rural areas, Djiboutian women enjoy spending their free time visiting with each other. Often, they engage in crafts such as weaving or needlework during these social sessions. Men enjoy congregating and drinking coffee. In villages, towns, and cities, the market serves as an important place for people to socialize. City dwellers enjoy movies and other urban pursuits. Television and radio broadcasts are in French, Afar, Somali, and Arabic. The government owns the television station and the principal newspaper. Voice of America and BBC transmitters supplement the state controlled radio.

[18] FOLK ART, CRAFTS, AND HOBBIES

Somali women use natural fibers to weave rugs, mats, and other objects. Ornamental jewelry, popular with both men and women, is made from silver, and glass, stone, or wooden beads. Pottery is made without a wheel by hollowing out a ball of clay and molding it into the desired shape. Other popular craft items include decorative wooden cups and spoons.

[19] SOCIAL PROBLEMS

Three of the five points of the single star of nationalism on the flag of Somalia symbolize the Somali-inhabited territories in Kenya, Ethiopia, and Djibouti. This star signifies that all Somalis should be unified under one flag. Such reunification may never be realized in the Horn of Africa, but the view continues to cause strife. Pan-Somaliism has been especially curtailed following the protracted civil wars in Somalia, and the breaking away of (formerly British) Somaliland in the north from the warring south. At the base of broad social problems are almost no cultivable land and scant freshwater resources.

The Afars were almost continuously in arms against the government of President Aptidon, and have sought greater autonomy. This so-called Afar problem crosses state boundaries into Eritrea. If the Afars of Djibouti succeed in their quest for greater autonomy, some observers speculate that the next step would be a drive for unification with the Afars of Eritrea. So long as the French military remains in Djibouti, the partitioning of the country along ethnic lines remains unlikely.

[20] GENDER ISSUES

Throughout the Horn of Africa and across a wider span of the continent, male and female "circumcision" is part of gender socialization and reinforced in the core aspects of a cosmology. The "circumcision" operation on females does a permanent anatomical and physiological damage and a psychological limiting of natural human development. Regarding the female circumcision only, from their own socialization, Westerners report mutilation and barbarous treatment. However, a relativistic native view also exists. (For more about cosmologies of the Horn, see Eritreans, sections 5 and 20.)

In the Horn—as among the Somalis, Afar, Tigrayans, Amhara, Kunama, Nara, Beja, and variably among the Oromo, etc.—values and norms regarding women include that their sensuality must be controlled and diminished, permanently. To this end, the clitoris of a female infant or child is unsanitarily excised (amputated), thus insuring, it is said, that she will not be overly active sexually. Among the Afar, this rite is marked with song. No men are present during or may in any way observe the operation, performed by an old, experienced woman. By the operation, which a few do not survive, the female will make a good and true wife for one of god's chosen, a male. No male would marry a female not having undergone this clitoridectomy. For that matter, no woman desires to marry a man "uncircumcised like a dog." Female "circumcision" is not a communal rite of intensification but an individual rite of passage in society. For a male, circumcision can be either, depending on the particular culture.

Among the Somali, Afar, and other peoples of northeastern Africa, especially Muslims, the surgery for clitoridectomy is extended to include excision of part or all of the labia majora and labia minora of the vulva and, then, infibulation. Infibulation has the paired wounds from the surgery fastened for healing together as one unbroken line of flesh. A slender reed or stick is placed in the wound to allow a small opening for urination and menses. Upon the happy day of marriage, the young bride is "unfibulated" by an experienced woman but the inexperienced groom could do so. Some reports of "reinfibulation" of a wife given particular circumstances exist. The practice of infibulation goes back at least to Pharaonic Egypt.

Infibulation controls that a female is a virgin before marriage to her husband, preventing consensual and forced coitus. In the Horn, both female clitoridectomy (and any infibulation) and ordinary male circumcision are marks of gender membership, and usually eligibility for marriage, in a particular society.

[21] BIBLIOGRAPHY

Ahmed, Ali Jimale. *Daybreak Is Near: Literature, Clans, and the Nation-State in Somalia.* Lawrenceville, NJ: Red Sea Press, 1996.

Cassenelli, Lee V. *The Shap Eritrea: A Country Handbook.* Asmara: Ministry of Information, 2002.

Country Profile. Djibouti. London: Economist Intelligence Unit, 2004.

Dubois, Collette and Frederick C. Gamst. "Djibouti, City." *Encyclopaedia Aethiopica* 2 (D-Ha):183-185. Ed. by Siegbert Uhlig. Wiesbaden: Harrssowitz Verlag, 2005.

Gamst, Frederick C. "Conflict in the Horn of Africa." In *Peace and War: Cross-Cultural Perspectives.* Ed. By Mary L. Foster and Robert A. Rubenstein. New Brunswick, NJ: Transaction Books, 1986.

Houstin, Nicole, ed. *Atlas de Djibouti.* Paris: Editions Jeune Afrique, 2007.

Lewis, Joan M. *Blood and Bone: The Call of Kinship in Somali Society.* Lawrenceville, NJ: Red Sea Press, 1994.

Morrow, James. *Djibouti.* Philadelphia: Mason Crest Publishers, 2004.

Saint Veran, Robert. *Djibouti: Pawn of Africa.* Metuchen, NJ: Scarecrow Press, 1981.

Schraeder, Peter J. *Djibouti.* Santa Barbara, CA: Clio Press, 1991.

The Shaping of Somali Society: Reconstructing the History of a Pastoral People, 1600-1900. Philadelphia: University of Pennsylvania Press, 1982.

Thompson, Virginia, and Richard Adloff. Djibouti and the Horn of Africa. Stanford, CA: Stanford University Press, 1968.

Uhlig, Siegbert, ed. Encyclopaedia Aethiopica, 4 vols. Wiesbaden: Harrssowitz Verlag, 2003–2008.

U.S. Department of the Army. Federal Research Division, Library of Congress. Ethiopia: A Country Study. 4th ed. Edited by Harold D. Ofcansky and LaVerle Berry. Area Handbook Series. Washington, DC: Government Printing Office, 1993.

—by F. C. Gamst

DYULA

PRONUNCIATION: Joo-lah
LOCATION: Mali, Burkina Faso, and Côte d'Ivoire (Ivory Coast)
POPULATION: 300,000
LANGUAGE: Mande; Arabic; French
RELIGION: Islam
RELATED ARTICLES: Vol. 1: Burkinabe; Ivoirians; Malians

¹ INTRODUCTION

In many dialects of the Mande language, the word *dyula* means "trader." Most Dyula people trace their origins back to the land of Manden, the heartland of the great medieval empire of Mali, along what is now the border of the modern nations of Guinea and Mali. Gold from Mali was transported across the Sahara Desert in exchange for rock salt mined in the Sahara. It was the search for new sources of gold that first led traders from Mali to what is now northern Ghana. Along with gold, they also began exporting kola nuts, which only grow in the rain forest region along the Atlantic Coast, but which became a prized item of luxury consumption in the interior of West Africa. Even after the decline of the Mali empire, these trade links between the desert, the grasslands, and the forest were maintained. Traders continued to move southwards towards the forest, settling in communities along the trade routes.

Some of these trading communities established themselves as minority groups among peoples such as the Senufo, the Kulango, and the Abron, with very different languages and cultures from their own. These minority groups came to call themselves, very simply, *Dyula*—"traders." Here, they continued to participate in the long-distance trade between the forest and the desert. Indeed, their words for "north" and "south" are *kogodugu,* literally, "the land of salt," and *worodugu,* "the land of kola nuts." However, they also specialized in producing and selling various luxury items, especially woven cloths, to their neighbors. Even nowadays, a Dyula village or neighborhood is easily identified by the number of its looms.

For the most part, the Dyula lived peacefully under the rule of kings or chiefs from other groups. However, around AD 1700, a Dyula named Sekou Wattara seized power in the large trading town of Kong, in northern Ivory Coast. Under Sekou's rule, Kong became a major military power, sending out raiding parties as far north as the Niger River, and staving off the armies of the mighty empire of Asante to the southeast. Kong's military might was short-lived, but it continued to be a major trading center until its destruction at the end of the 19th century.

At the end of the 19th and the beginning of the 20th centuries, most Dyula communities were incorporated into various parts of French West Africa. Many Dyula were active in the movement for independence, rallying to the Rassemblement Démocratique Africaine (RDA) party.

² LOCATION AND HOMELAND

The Dyula homelands are now divided between several African nations: Mali, Burkina Faso, and Ivory Coast, between roughly 8° and 12° north latitudes and 2° and 7° west longitudes. This is an area of savanna, with one annual rainy season. Since

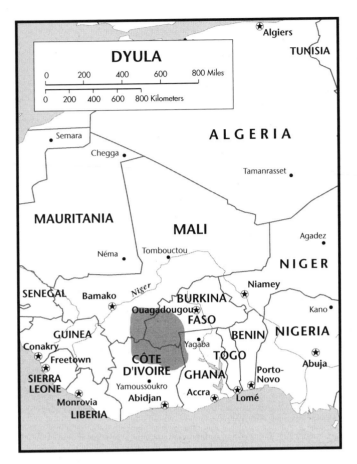

lary, augmented by numerous loan words, both from French (e.g., *mobili* for "automobile"; *montoro* for "watch"; and *seta-dir*, "that's to say") and from Arabic (e.g., *hakili*, "intelligence"; *wakati*, "time"; and the days of the week).

Because the Dyula are Muslim, many given names *(togo)* are also of Arabic origin: Mammadou, Saidou, Khadija, Fatouma-ta. Dyula often give their first-born children the name of their own father or mother. Often a man will not, for example, call a son he has named after his own father by the child's proper name, just as many Americans hesitate to call their own parents by their first names; rather, he will call him *ba*, "father," *gbema*, "grandfather," *cekoroba*, "old man," or some equivalent term.

Many Dyula clan or family names *(jamu)*—Coulibaly, Kone, Wattara, Cisse, Saganogo, Toure—are widespread throughout much of West Africa, linking Dyula families with distant "cousins" far away.

⁴ FOLKLORE

Women and children sometimes recite folk tales in the evening. Speakers will vie with one another to see who can recite stories the most dramatically and rapidly, without hesitating. Typically, such stories are about clever heroes who use their wits to escape danger, or about jealousy within the polygynous family between co-wives and between children of different mothers.

Dyula men will more likely tell religious stories; since they are Muslim, these are typically about prophets—not only Muhammad, but also Jesus as well as Old Testament prophets. They also have a deep concern for their own history and relate accounts of events in their communities or about the deeds of their family ancestors.

⁵ RELIGION

The Dyula are all Muslim and have been ever since their arrival in their present location. Indeed, Islam and trade were (and still are) closely associated throughout much of West Africa, especially in the savanna. However, in the past, Dyula communities included two different hereditary categories of Muslims: "Scholars" *(mori)* and "Warriors" *(tun tigi,* or *sonongi* in Kong). Members of "Scholar" clans were expected to conform fairly rigorously to Muslim codes of religious behavior: praying five times a day; fasting in the daytime during the month of Ramadan; and abstaining from alcoholic beverages. "Warriors," on the other hand, might drink beer, and pray and fast irregularly. Adolescent "Warrior" boys were initiated into secret societies called *lo*. The initiation process took seven years, during which the boys underwent various ordeals and were taught the *lo* secrets, for example, about powerful spirits embodied in the *lo* masks, some of which were considered so dangerous that only initiates were allowed to see them. Certain "Scholar" families, on the other hand, were known far and wide for their Islamic learning. Kong, for example, was widely known as a center for scholarship as well as trade. About 50 years ago, the initiation societies were abolished, as many Dyula came to feel that such practices were not proper for Muslims.

⁶ MAJOR HOLIDAYS

Dyula holidays are all associated with the Muslim ritual calendar. Because the Muslim year is lunar and not solar, these holidays take place at a different time each year according to

this is in the southern stretches of the grasslands, towards the tropical rain forests to the south, rainfall is relatively plentiful compared to drier regions of the Sahel, to the north. In any case, from their arrival in their present homeland, migration has been a fundamental feature of the existence of this people of traders. Consequently, during the colonial period, Dyula readily migrated to the large towns and cities that sprang up in southern Ivory Coast, in search of better prospects. Nowadays, there are at least as many Dyula living in southern Ivory Coast as there are in their home communities. It is very difficult to estimate their total population, not least because many migrants from other regions to the cities of Ivory Coast are also now called "Dyula." The total Dyula population probably numbers about 300,000 people.

³ LANGUAGE

The Dyula speak a dialect of the Mande language, which is very widely spoken over much of West Africa, in Mali, Senegal, Guinea, Gambia, Sierra Leone, Liberia, Ivory Coast, and Burkina Faso. The Dyula can easily understand many other dialects (Bamana, Malinke) of the language. Mande is a tone language, though there are only two tones. As traders, the Dyula are quite skillful at understanding others—Africans as well as Europeans—who mispronounce their language. Perhaps because this is a trade language, which many Africans speak as a second language, the grammar is relatively simple. There are no genders or noun classes, plurals are formed regularly, verbs are not conjugated, and verb tenses are easy to learn. However, the Dyula dialect has a rich and idiomatic vocabu-

Western reckoning and cannot be associated with any particular season. *Tabaski* celebrates the annual time of the Hajj, the pilgrimage to Mecca. Everyone dresses in their best finery, and all men pray together at the mosque. When they come home, each family that can afford it sacrifices a ram and distributes part of its meat to friends and relatives. *Sunkalo* (the Dyula name for Ramadan) is a month of fasting, but only during the daytime. Throughout the month, at sundown, people prepare elaborate meals. While older men observe the month with additional prayer, young girls perform special dances *(kurubi don)* where they beat the rhythm on special long, thin gourds painted for the occasion. *Donba* (literally "big dance") is the celebration of the Prophet Muhammad's birthday, and, as its name suggests, is a particularly joyous occasion.

⁷ RITES OF PASSAGE

Seven days after the birth of a child, there is a relatively informal naming ceremony, where the infant is given its Muslim name. In the past, there were elaborate rituals to mark the passage into adolescence: initiation into *lo* societies for "Warrior" boys, excision (female circumcision) for girls. Both of these rituals have been abolished on the grounds that they are improper for Muslims.

Weddings are very elaborate affairs, involving several types of ceremonies. Older men formalize the marriage arrangements in the *furu* ceremony, in which a bundle of kola nuts previously wrapped in string is ceremonially untied, marriage gifts are officially presented, and all present witness the transaction and bless the marriage. During this time, in the *konyo mina* ceremony, the bride dances around the village, proud to be the center of attention but also sad to renounce the freedom of adolescence. The festivities often last a week, while the bride and groom remain secluded in a hut. Usually, in any year, all weddings in a single village take place on the same day, so that this is a festival for the entire community and not just the families of the bride and groom.

Funerals are more or less elaborate depending on the age and status of the deceased. The corpse is washed and buried as quickly as possible in an unmarked grave, after it has been prayed over, in accordance with strict Islamic rules. However, commemorative ceremonies may be held on the third, seventh, and fortieth days after burial, as well as one year afterwards. Such ceremonies may involve the reading of prayers, sermons delivered by local scholars, and the distribution of ritual gifts *(saraka)* to a wide variety of individuals and groups. Funerals of very old and important people may indeed be festive occasions, marked with singing and dancing, to commemorate the rich and full life of the deceased.

⁸ INTERPERSONAL RELATIONS

As traders, the Dyula were always accustomed to traveling far and wide. When visiting any community, an individual always needed an established host *(diatigi),* who was responsible for taking proper care of the "stranger" *(lunan)* for as long as he or she chose to stay. Indeed, a "stranger" might decide, or even be asked, to stay for life, settling down in the new community.

The Dyula, as also befits traders, are very sociable, and elaborate greetings are an important part of everyday life. People will routinely inquire about each others' health and about their family. Greetings also include Muslim blessings *(duaw),* which

are usually fairly routine but, in some circumstances, can be quite elaborate.

In the past, young unmarried men and women were allowed to take official boy- or girlfriends *(teri)* with the knowledge and consent of their parents. Sex play, but not full sexual intercourse, was permitted for such lovers. Marriages, however, were arranged by parents, and it was very rare that boy- and girlfriends would marry one another. This practice of taking an official, publicly recognized lover before marriage has been discontinued.

⁹ LIVING CONDITIONS

Because of their involvement in trade, the Dyula have always enjoyed a relatively high standard of living compared to many of their neighbors. They enjoy dressing well, eating well, and, when they can afford them, owning luxuries such as radios, cassette recorders, televisions, and automobiles. Old-fashioned mud huts with thatched roofs have been almost everywhere replaced by concrete houses with corrugated iron roofing. These modern houses are less likely to burn down and are easier to maintain, though in fact they are less comfortable than thatched huts. In larger towns, modern houses often also have running water; electricity is available, not only in town, but in many villages nowadays.

¹⁰ FAMILY LIFE

All the families in any village who belong to one clan and who descend from a common ancestor live together in a neighborhood called a *kabila*. A large village can contain as many as 20 such neighborhoods. The group has a chief and resolves disputes in a meeting where all adult men in the clan can air their grievances. Traditionally, Dyula preferred to marry cousins within their own clan neighborhood. The proportion of such marriages is declining, but they are still common, especially in rural areas.

As Muslims, Dyula men are allowed up to four wives. Indeed, about half of all married men have more than one wife— a very high proportion, even for West Africa. However, some of these wives are widows who have remarried men their own age late in life. Islam dictates that husbands should treat all wives equally. Indeed, Dyula women enjoy considerable freedom. The stereotypical notion that Islam inevitably leads to the oppression of women certainly does not hold true with the Dyula. Women often actively earn money of their own outside the home, for example, by trading in the market.

¹¹ CLOTHING

As weavers and traders, the Dyula enjoy fine clothing. Cloths are traditionally woven in narrow strips, which are then sewn together to make a rectangular blanket. Elaborate patterns require great skill. For example, weavers have to be very careful when weaving a checkerboard pattern that the squares on each strip of cloth will match with those on the next strip. Women would tie one such blanket around their waist, and another over their shoulders, with a third used to carry a baby. Men would dress in elaborate robes, often delicately embroidered.

Nowadays, men usually wear Western-style clothing on ordinary occasions, reserving fine robes for special occasions. Women generally buy machine-produced cloths, which are much cheaper than the handwoven variety, and so the Dyula tradition of weaving is in decline.

12 FOOD

Dyula usually eat three meals a day, supplemented by snacks, which can be obtained from street vendors. Breakfast consists of porridge made from corn, rice, or millet. The midday meal is usually the most elaborate. Rice or pounded yams are supplemented with a sauce or a stew, such as meat cooked in peanut sauce. These sauces are generally quite spicy. The evening meal often consists of a spongy pudding called *to,* made from corn or millet flour, typically accompanied by an okra sauce.

Eating is invariably a social activity. Any friend or relative, even a casual acquaintance, who happens to drop by when a person is eating will be asked to partake of the meal. It is extremely rude not to invite someone to share one's meal, although the invitation can be politely declined by saying, "I'm full."

13 EDUCATION

As Muslims, the Dyula have a long tradition of literacy in Arabic. Boys from "Scholar" families would begin from the age of seven to learn to read and write Arabic script. Initially, such education stressed the ability to be able to recite any written passage, without necessarily understanding its meaning. A special ceremony called *Kurana jigi,* "putting down the Quran," was held when a boy was able to recite the entire Quran. Some boys, and indeed adult men, would decide to pursue their studies further, and most communities contained individuals with considerable skill at reading and writing Arabic. Large Dyula towns like Kong were great centers of learning, attracting students from far and wide.

Dyula parents were initially reluctant to allow their children to pursue a Western-style education, which they feared would undermine their religious values. Nowadays, however, most boys and girls are sent to school, where they learn to read and write French. Recently, modern Muslim schools have been established in larger towns, where Dyula children can follow a combined curriculum in Arabic and in French; however, such schools are not always officially recognized by the government.

14 CULTURAL HERITAGE

Unlike some other Mande peoples, the Dyula have no professional "bards" or *griots* as they are sometimes called (*jeli* in Dyula). Singing and music-making are not in any way professional occupations. On holidays, at weddings, or on other special occasions, groups of young men and women, as well as older women, will sing (sometimes improvising as they go along) and dance through the community. Such activities, however, are generally considered improper for older men.

15 WORK

As traders, the Dyula have always valued occupations linked in one way or another to the marketplace. Even as farmers, they tend to treat agriculture as a business, growing cash crops like tobacco (in the past) or (nowadays) cotton, or planting coffee and cocoa in southern Ivory Coast, rather than simply growing food to feed their own family. Weaving was formerly the most widespread occupation. When sewing machines were introduced, many Dyula eagerly adopted the profession of tailor.

In the past, work was intimately tied to the family. Sons would work under the authority of their father, and young-

er brothers would work for their older brothers, at least until they were married and had families of their own. In this way, a group of weavers in the same family would be able to pool their work and sell it more profitably. Nowadays, work is more individualized. Parents, uncles, or older brothers no longer control the salaries of their younger relatives. Tailors, for example, rely on the labor of apprentices, rather than on family members.

16 SPORTS

Until about 40 years ago, wrestling was the most popular sport among Dyula boys. Individuals and teams from each clan neighborhood would regularly compete with one another. However, the sport has lapsed. Now, soccer is undoubtedly the favorite sport, as is true in much of Africa.

17 ENTERTAINMENT AND RECREATION

Radios are very common among the Dyula. Radio Mali regularly broadcasts in the Bamana language, which Dyula can understand effortlessly, although young people often listen to other stations that broadcast in French. Cassette recorders are also very popular. Young people listen to tapes of pop stars, sometimes from America but also from Africa: Alpha Blondy, a leading reggae musician from Ivory Coast, sings in English and French as well as Dyula. Homemade cassettes of traditional African music are also available in the marketplace, alongside cassettes of Muslim sermons, to which pious Muslims will listen for entertainment as well as for their religious content. In larger towns, televisions are commonplace, even in comparatively modest homes. In the evening, television is particularly popular with women and adolescents, who will cluster around the set of a relative, friend, or neighbor if they have none of their own.

18 FOLK ART, CRAFTS, AND HOBBIES

Although the demand for elaborate, handwoven cloths has fallen off a great deal, there are still many Dyula weavers. A few Dyula villages have developed successful cooperatives, where they produce tablecloths and napkins and other items explicitly aimed at the tourist market.

19 SOCIAL PROBLEMS

Handwoven cloth, once the mainstay of the Dyula economy, can no longer compete with machine-produced textiles. It remains a luxury item, but its value and the size of the market have plummeted. Finding employment or a source of dependable income is a problem for the Dyula, as it is with all other peoples in the region. The recent devaluation of the CFA, the unit of currency in much of French-speaking West Africa, has made prospects for young people even bleaker, at least in the short run.

These economic strains have put increasing pressure on family units. Extended families no longer pool their resources, and fathers no longer can rely on the labor of their sons, or older brothers on their younger brothers. This increased independence expresses itself in other ways, too; young men and women now generally marry partners of their own choice, and women are not married off in early adolescence. However, such freedom has also led to rapidly rising rates of childbirth outside of wedlock.

During the colonial period and throughout the 1970s and 1980s, many Dyula settled in the southern part of Côte d'Ivoire, one of the most prosperous regions in West Africa due to coffee and cocoa plantations. Beginning in the 1980s, the economic bubble began to burst, and immigrant Dyula became the targets of increasing xenophobic sentiments. The situation deteriorated after the death in 1993 of President Félix Houphouët-Boigny, who had ruled the country for over thirty years. The political turmoil led to riots in which Dyula and other Muslims were often targeted. After a failed military coup, a rebel government established itself in the north of the country, in the heart of the Dyula homeland. By 2008, the two sides had come to an agreement, although the situation remains tense in much of the country.

[20] GENDER ISSUES

In principle, Dyula women were supposed to remain under the authority of men—fathers, brothers, or husbands. However, they were never secluded, and in fact, enjoyed a considerable degree of autonomy. In particular, women were often allowed (if not encouraged) to engage in independent economic activities, such as trading produce in the market. While wives had a claim on their husbands' income and could sue for divorce for lack of support, men had no right to any of their wives' earnings.

As Muslims, Dyula men could marry up to four wives, although it was unusual for men to have more than two wives. In the past, Dyula women were married in early adolescence while men married much later. Adolescent girls had little or no say in their choice of husbands. However, once they were widowed or divorced, they were relatively free to marry whom they pleased. As of the 21st century, young women are usually allowed to choose their husbands and are not pressured to marry so young. According to Islamic law, men do not have to specify their reasons for divorce, whereas women have to sue for divorce on specified grounds. In fact, women are far more likely than men to seek divorce.

[21] BIBLIOGRAPHY

Launay, Robert. *Beyond the Stream: Islam and Society in a West African Town.* Berkeley, CA: University of California Press, 1992.

———. "The Power of Names: Illegitimacy in a Muslim Community in Côte d'Ivoire." In *Situating Fertility: Anthropology and Demographic Inquiry,* edited by Susan Greenhalgh. Cambridge: Cambridge University Press, 1995.

———. "Spirit Media: The Electronic Media and Islam among the Dyula of Northern Côte d'Ivoire," *Africa,* 67, 3 (1997): 441–53.

———. *Traders Without Trade: Responses to Change in Two Dyula Communities.* Cambridge: Cambridge University Press, 1982.

Launay, Robert, and Marie Miran. "Beyond Mande Mory: Islam and Ethnicity in Côte d'Ivoire," *Paideuma,* 46 (2000): 63–84.

Warms, Richard L. "Commerce and Community: Paths to Success for Malian Merchants." *African Studies Review* 37 (1994): 97–120.

Wilks, Ivor. "The Transmission of Islamic Learning in the Western Sudan." In *Literacy in Traditional Societies,* edited by J. R. Goody. Cambridge: Cambridge University Press, 1968.

—by R. Launay

EFE AND MBUTI

PRONUNCIATION: AY-fay and mm-BOO-tee
ALTERNATE NAMES: Bambuti
LOCATION: Ituri forest in northeast Democratic Republic of the Congo (former Zaire)
POPULATION: Approximately 35,000
LANGUAGE: Bambuti languages
RELIGION: Traditional tribal beliefs
RELATED ARTICLES: Vol. 1: ?

[1] INTRODUCTION

Researchers believe that hunters and gatherers have lived in the rainforests of central Africa for more than 6,000 years. Because of their relative isolation, misconceptions about them abound. Their small stature has led to the use of the term "pygmy," and in some instances they are mistakenly referred to as dwarfs. Indeed, some of their African neighbors thought of them (and still do) as less than human.

The name *pygmy* itself inadequately describes these peoples, as it emphasizes physical size to the detriment of other characteristics. Pygmies are indeed short of stature: men are about four and half feet tall and women are about an inch shorter. More importantly, however, pygmies are forest dwellers who share cultural traits with similar peoples living in the forests of equatorial Africa. They have a unique culture, set of values, and lifestyle that are all undergoing great change. Their adaptation to change may teach other cultures how to cope with radical disruptions to their societies.

In many respects, pygmies represent the antithesis of modernity. Just 30 years ago they possessed only the bare essentials for their livelihoods. They did not seek to create surpluses in goods, and they had no use for money. Government was simple: decisions for a particular band were made by common consent, and dissenters were free to leave and join another community if they wished. The forest, their "mother," had the capacity to supply their every need.

Traditional values of interdependence and sociality are being replaced by independence and individuality. Today, under environmental challenges and pressures to acculturate, pygmy society is changing rapidly. Political rebellions in the Ituri area following Congolese independence in 1960 hastened some of these changes. But efforts by former President Mobutu's government to remove pygmies from their forest habitat and to assimilate them into Congolese society wreaked the greatest physical and social havoc on them. The experiment with "emancipation" nearly drove them to extinction and had to be called off.

Since 1997, pygmy survival has been threatened further by wars, which have drawn as many as eight countries into conflict in Eastern Congo. Of the more than five million people that have died of war-related and humanitarian causes in the east, thousands have been pygmies. They have been the primary victims of the scramble for 'conflict' and 'blood' diamonds, gold, and other resources. By 2008, peace in the forested region was not yet guaranteed, as major armed groups had yet to disarm.

In spite of the political and natural threats to their survival, pygmies have proven resilient to adversity. They currently en-

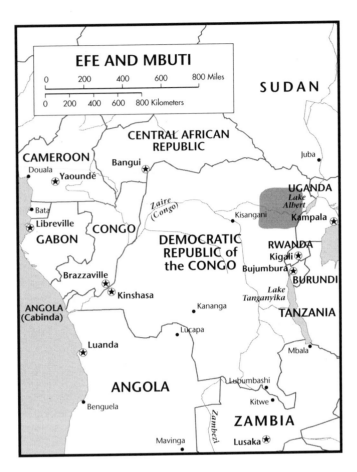

EFE AND MBUTI

SUDAN

CENTRAL AFRICAN REPUBLIC

CAMEROON
Douala • Bangui • Juba
• Yaoundé
UGANDA
Lake
Albert
• Bata Zaire (Congo)
Kisangani • Kampala ⊛
• Libreville
CONGO
GABON DEMOCRATIC RWANDA
REPUBLIC of Kigali ⊛
the CONGO Bujumbura ⊛
• Brazzaville BURUNDI
Lake
• Kinshasa Tanganyika
ANGOLA • Kananga TANZANIA
(Cabinda)
• Lucapa
Mbala •
• Luanda
ANGOLA Lubumbashi •
Kitwe •
Benguela • ZAMBIA
Zambezi
Mavinga • Lusaka ⊛

gage in more sustained and deeper contacts than before with African village communities on the fringes of the forest. A long-time student of the Mbuti pygmies, Colin Turnbull, believes that should the equatorial forest be destroyed, the pygmy devotion to "forestness" will help them adapt "and find a new source of sanctity in the here and now." Turnbull feels that by studying the pygmies, Western populations can learn to re-think what is "backward" and what is "advanced." Seeing how the pygmies adapt to change may help us reassess our own social contexts.

2 LOCATION AND HOMELAND

Pygmy peoples live in scattered groups throughout the equatorial band of Africa, primarily in an area within five degrees on either side of the equator. However, pygmy units range as far north and west as Benin and as far east as the Great Lakes of the Rift Valley. This discussion focuses on the groups of the Ituri forest in northeast Democratic Republic of the Congo (formerly Zaire), including the Efe and their close relations to the south. Although they differ by language and hunting strategies, they share a core culture. Collectively, the Efe and three other groups of the Ituri are called the *Bambuti*. While there are as many as 35,000 Bambuti, researchers estimate that no more than 20,000 pure-blooded Bambuti remain in the world.

The Bambuti live within a 130,000-sq-km (50,000-sq-mi) tract of the huge 648,000-sq-km (250,000-sq-mi) Ituri forest. The Ituri lies on the equator in the northeastern part of the Congo River basin, between 0° to 3°N, and 27° to 30°E. Elevations in this area range from 700 to 1,000 m (2,300 to 3,300 ft). The terrain is rolling, covered by primary rainforest.

Trees reach heights of 30–60 m (100–200 ft) before their canopies spread out, allowing only filtered sunlight to reach the understory below. In areas where the forest has been cleared and allowed to grow back, thick tangled underbrush impedes movement. Rain falls nearly every afternoon except during the dry season of January and February. Many small streams only a few miles apart run continuously, and several large, fast rivers intersect the forest. Temperatures are fairly constant, ranging from 20°C (70°F) at night to highs of 27°C (80°F) during the day, unless the sky is overcast.

The pygmy populations of the Ituri occupy specific territories within the forest, and they generally do not hunt or gather on another's territory. Each unit also trades with various African ethnic groups (referred to as "Negroes" or "villagers") living on the fringes of the forest. Although not the most numerous, the Efe occupy the largest territory across the northern and eastern parts of the Ituri. Their trading partners are the Sudanic-speaking Mamvu and Walese Africans. Pygmies trade forest products such as honey, meat, rattan, and thatch leaves in exchange for the Walese's plantains (see **Interpersonal Relations**).

3 LANGUAGE

Sustained contact with African groups over long periods has all but led to the extinction of Bambuti languages. Nevertheless, researchers distinguish three linguistic groups that speak dialects of three major African languages. Some tonal patterns remain as well. Efe pygmies have retained their language to a recognizable extent.

4 FOLKLORE

Pygmies anthropomorphize animals, meaning that they give forest animals attributes of people. Certain animals represent clans, sexes, and individuals and they become very real people. Both pygmies and their village hosts have invented stories about these animals, and they assign special attributes to Mr. Turtle, Mr. Gray Antelope, or Mr. Chimpanzee. For example, Mr. Turtle is a wise and tricky individual, whereas the smallest antelope is king of the beasts. Animal stories thus serve to teach about human behavior and relationships.

5 RELIGION

Religion in pygmy life increasingly reflects borrowings from neighboring African groups. The Bambuti attribute the wealth and goodness of the forest to Muungu, a high deity, the greatest of forest gods, who supplies all of their needs. The forest is like a mother and father to them, providing food, clothing, shelter, warmth, and affection. Pygmies believe in totemic spirits (*sitana*), who live in rock piles, hollow trees, and holes in the ground, and they stay clear of these places if possible. They also believe in a water animal called *nyama ya mai* in Swahili, who is responsible for any serious water mishaps. If someone drowns or a canoe tips over, they will say the water animal did it. If sickness strikes that cannot be cured by pygmy remedies, pygmies will seek treatment from a village witch doctor to suck out "disease objects" with herbs or by cupping with animal horns.

Pygmies also practice certain magical rituals called *anjo* to help control the weather and enhance hunting. Their main concern is to delay rain and storms until the hunt is over. For example, the Efe may burn leaves of the wild pepper plant to

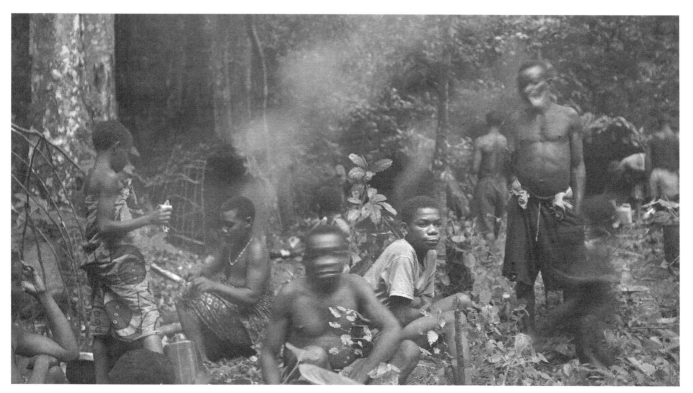

Mbuti pygmies at a forest hunting camp in the Democratic Republic of the Congo. (National Geographic/Getty Images)

stop storms. Other weather superstitions have to do with picking certain flowers or dropping stones into streams, which they see as causes of rain. Before hunting, Bambuti groups light fires in the morning during hunting season to "warm the forest" for good luck. Efe women sometimes light smoky fires at mid-day to keep the weather clear for hunting. Mbuti children light smoky fires to purify the hunters who will cause bloodshed in the sacred forest. Pygmies tie the leaves of the species that their prey enjoys on their bows, and they sometimes burn these leaves and rub the ashes on their bodies. When dividing the catch, the elder cuts a small piece off of the heart of an animal and tosses it into the forest for good luck.

The most important ritual ceremony is the *molimo,* which is held whenever hunting becomes unproductive or a special problem demands resolution within the band. Traditionally, this ritual was very secret and kept hidden from women and children, although more recently the molimo has been performed in villages. The ceremony begins with a long, mournful cry from the forest, goes to a birdcall, then to a growl, and back to a birdcall again. The men at the campfire answer the call, which is made with a wooden trumpet, but represents the voice of the forest. After the main ceremony is over, the women and children join the men, circling the campfire in one direction, while the men circle in the other. The ceremony may last several days, until it is felt that the molimo has answered their request.

6 MAJOR HOLIDAYS

Holidays hold little meaning for the Bambuti other than as opportunities for parties. The end of *Nkumbi,* the honey feast dance, and other ceremonial activities may be thought of as traditional pygmy holidays (see **Rites of Passage** *and* **Cultural Heritage**).

7 RITES OF PASSAGE

The Bambuti have gradually been assimilating village rituals, but birth in pygmy society is treated without any ritual. In former times, girls went through initiation, the *elima,* but this practice has fallen away. Boys increasingly attend a village circumcision school *(nkumbi),* which is held every three or four years depending on the number of boys between the ages of 9 and 14 who are ready for circumcision. The boys leave their parents for several months and live in close association with the village boys, who are their hosts. They learn the secrets and are circumcised together. At the end of the ceremonies, their parents come to dance and get drunk with the village boys' parents. Thus, each group of boys belongs to an age-grade, much as American high school students identify with their graduating class or college students identify with a fraternity. When strangers meet, they ask, "What class do you belong to?" Because each class acquires a name from a significant event during its initiation, they reply, "I'm a hurricane," or "I'm a great army worm," or something similar. These ceremonies bond boys of the same age together and also cement relationships between villagers and pygmies.

Marriage takes place soon after puberty, leaving little time for courtship. Nevertheless, at puberty, youthful chivalry at the hunt gets publicized, and much flirtation back in the camps occurs. Inter-band visits offer occasions for youth to get acquainted and to engage in marital prospecting.

When a Mbuti dies, members of the deceased's family mourn by covering themselves with white clay. The women organize weeping and wailing sessions, which last for several days. Funerals also offer occasions for wine drinking. Once a wake is over, the band usually moves camp.

8 INTERPERSONAL RELATIONS

Pygmies place great importance on respect for each other, and children learn this early. In principle, children of the same age group remain on equal footing throughout their lives and call each other *apua'i*. Their games teach them to be social, interdependent, and synergistic in problem-solving. Evening campfires offer adults daily opportunities to discuss and resolve disputes. Anyone who speaks from the center of the camp must be listened to. Members of a band gang up on wayward members to enforce rules and maintain harmony in the group. Individuals and families visit other pygmy camps for months at a time to socialize with family members and to prospect for marriage. These visits break up the monotony of daily life.

Relations between the Bambuti and villagers are also very important. Researchers have disagreed on whether this relationship is essentially dependent, independent, or interdependent. The first view sees pygmies as vassals of the villager overlords. The second sees them as fully independent if they so choose because the forest supplies them with everything they need. Contact with villagers offers an agreeable change of pace, but is voluntary and temporary. The third view finds a mutual interdependence between pygmies and villagers with neither side holding an advantage. Each has something the other wants and needs.

Villager-Pygmy relationships are based on the claim of villages to about 100 square miles of forest. Villagers thus act as hosts to pygmy families living within their territory. Each supplies the other with necessities the other is unable to get on his own. For the pygmy in pre-colonial days, this included scouting in the forest for enemies of a village. A visitor to a village will often see bunches of plantains lying on the ground waiting to be picked up by pygmies at their convenience. The relationship is interfamilial and is inherited on both sides from father to son. If a pygmy leaves a villager to ally with someone else, it is regarded as "divorce." In former times, inter-village warfare sometimes erupted when villagers attempted to woo pygmies away from each other.

9 LIVING CONDITIONS

Living conditions have deteriorated dramatically since 1998 due to the fighting. Traditionally, material comfort, wealth, and security were the least of the pygmies' concerns. They trusted the forest to provide their needs, which, by most standards, were extremely minimal. The Bambuti needed spears, bows and arrows, and nets for hunting; pots to cook in; huts to sleep under; and loin cloths to wear. They traded forest products to villagers for items difficult to obtain such as salt, knives, and metal tips for their weapons. However, at the dawn of the 21st century, the forest people were very much engaged in a struggle for survival.

Pygmy settlements are rustic, temporary camps situated within 50 yards of a stream suitable for drinking. Their igloo-shaped huts have open doors. Huts are made of bent saplings that form a frame onto which large *mongongo* leaves are tied. Mats or leaves generally serve as beds and cooking is done on open fires near the huts. People simply relieve themselves in the forest near the camp.

After one to three months in one place, animals, fruit, and honey become scarce, and the stench of refuse and human waste becomes unbearable. The community packs up and moves to another site, but never to an abandoned camp site. The women pack their pots, axes, and whatever they own into baskets, which they strap to their backs; babies travel on top of the packs. The men carry their weapons, elephant spears, and bows and arrows.

From April to June, if the rainy season is particularly severe, preventing hunting, widespread hunger may sometimes occur, as it did in 1980. People's resistance to infectious diseases lowers, and conflicts over food are more frequent. When pygmies fall ill, they treat themselves with medicinal herbs and bark. They give each other enemas for diarrhea and intestinal disorders, which are frequent. Dysentery is common; pneumonia is less common, but deadly. Pygmies are quite resistant to disease overall, and the most frequent cause of premature death is falling from trees or being hit by a falling tree limb during a storm. Pygmies go everywhere on foot and cover great distances in little time. Their size allows them to pass under low limbs and tangles. Villagers and other outsiders seem very clumsy in the forest by comparison. The Bambuti use their hands to grasp branches and remove fallen clutter and tangles from trails as they go, tossing dead wood into the nearby understory. The noise created by this tactic also serves to mislead and distract game during a hunt.

National Park set-asides like that of Kahuzi-Biega in South Kivu pose new threats to way of life. Bambuti increasingly live near or alongside a forest area they can no longer access because it has been designated as a protected area or a national park. In one case, Pygmies confined to living on an island in miserable circumstances have complained that they are dying of hunger while they are not allowed to fish, which is one of their traditional sources of food.

10 FAMILY LIFE

Family life among the Bambuti is much different from that in the West. The Bambuti learn the value of interdependence and sociality as children. Children call all women in the camp *Ema* (mother) because they are all mothers to pygmy children. Nursing goes on long after a child can walk and talk, and mothers often swap and adopt children of their sisters and close friends.

Efe pygmies live in small camps of fewer than 50 residents. Mbuti pygmy camps usually have two to three times as many people because net-hunting requires communal participation. Individual households are nuclear families (*endu*) consisting of a husband, a wife, and their children. Families are patrilineal, meaning that they trace their lineage through the male line to a common male ancestor. Pygmies are exogamous and may not marry anyone to whom they know they are related.

Marriages are exchanges between families. Mutual affection and chivalry can play a part, but generally a man offers a sister, niece, or cousin to his wife's brother or male relative. Divorce is common, and if a marriage does not last, this often also causes the divorce of the couple who arranged the marriage. A woman often initiates divorce simply by packing her things (including small children) and moving back to her family's camp. If she has boys, they return to their father when they are old enough to hunt. The typical marriage is monogamous because pygmy women are scarce.

¹¹ CLOTHING

Villagers like to joke that when they first encountered pygmies, the pygmies wore no clothes at all. Pygmies deny this and insist that they have always worn loin cloths. Traditional cloth is made from the inner bark of vines. Men generally process it, which involves pounding, wetting, and working it until it is soft and pliable. Acculturation has increased the use of cotton fabrics in pygmy dress. Used clothing has also become more common. The Bambuti enhance their appearance by scarification (scarring) on the face. Some women also wear bead necklaces. Both men and women improve their appearance by filing their teeth to a point.

¹² FOOD

The Efe diet is seasonal depending on the rains. From late June to mid-September, honey, fruits, and nuts are most abundant in the forest. At this time, pygmies move their camps into the forest, but they return to the villages often to trade for peanuts, plantains, and other foods. By late September, rivers have overflowed, and forest conditions are extremely wet for hunting. The Efe move back to the edge of the forest, where the women help with village gardens while the men hunt. During the dry months up to February, men spend time helping villagers clear garden areas, while women assist with rice harvesting. In February and March, the forest has dried sufficiently to permit good hunting conditions. The Efe move back into the forest and then emerge again in April or May to forage in abandoned gardens for cassava and sweet potato tubers. Pygmies feel obliged to hand over all honey and elephant meat to their hosts, but they will eat all they can first. They do not store or preserve game.

Pygmies typically eat two to three meals a day, one in the morning before the hunt, possibly one at noon, and one in the late afternoon after the hunt. They enjoy many forest delicacies, ranging from *pangolins* (an armadillo-like animal) to reptiles and insects. They have a favorite recipe for fried caterpillars. They wrap a caterpillar in a piece of leaf and place it next to the fire. Toasting it as one would a marshmallow, it is then dropped into a pot of boiling palm oil and cooked. When finished, the caterpillars look something like fried shrimp.

Food taboos are associated with clan, sex, or individuals. Pygmy clans identify with animals that performed a kind deed or may have helped an ancestor through a crisis. They make these animals their totems and are not allowed to hunt, eat, or even be around them. If they encounter one in the forest, they will run the other way. For men, the taboo will usually be a species of a hunted animal such as an antelope or monkey; for women, the totem is usually a slow-moving animal such as a porcupine or snake. Women and children may eat frogs and toads, but men abstain from these. Chimpanzees and leopards are rarely hunted and eaten, and they may be totems for some clans. The totems are not their ancestors, but they do represent very real people. To violate the taboo would bring sickness, misfortune, and even death. To respect it binds the clan members sharing the totem, even though they may be separated by great distances.

¹³ EDUCATION

The Bambuti have evaded formal education. In camp, children learn basic skills, such as tree-climbing, before they walk. Boys practice shooting bows and arrows at the age of three. As they grow older, boys accompany men on the hunt, while girls learn to gather food, cook, and make huts. This basic education is complete by the age of six or seven.

¹⁴ CULTURAL HERITAGE

The Bambuti have not developed a written literature and do not create graphic arts. Perhaps their most important cultural legacy is their sense of family, their community reliance, and their belief in the forest. Some pygmies are accomplished storytellers and tell folktales about forest spirits and legends about ancestors. Pygmies enjoy singing and dancing, especially on moonlit nights. They stamp on the ground or on hollow logs and, if they can, they borrow drums from their villager hosts.

One of the gayest and happiest dances occurs during the honey feast. Pygmies celebrate the honey dance after days of feasting on honey. Women form an inner ring and circle around a bonfire, while men form an outer ring and circle in the opposite direction. The men pretend to seek honey and come near the women. The women play the role of bees, humming and droning. They pick up burning branches from the fire, with which they menace the men to remind them of the dangers of bee stings.

¹⁵ WORK

Formerly, pygmies worked just enough to supply their basic needs. Principally the men hunted and the women gathered. When they had surpluses, they traded them for articles and food from African villagers. The forest products they traded were generally meat, honey, fruits, and building materials. In exchange, they received plantains, yams, corn, cloth, and iron tools. Women also tended villager gardens and men occasionally helped villagers clear land. While the Bambuti continue to trade, today they are more concerned with having cash, so they seek surpluses in their hunting and have become more competitive with each other. The unfortunate reality, however, is that exposure to villagers has increased their visibility and therefore their vulnerability to exploitation by combatants, who rape the women and utilize the men as free labor.

Hunting and gathering still form the core of the Bambuti's livelihood in the forest. Mbuti hunting is a group affair done with nets. Each net is owned by one to four men, and a minimum of seven nets are required for a successful hunt. Women and children scream, shout, and beat bushes to frighten animals toward the nets, which are strung over bushes about four feet high. The animals become entangled in the nets behind which the men are hiding. Once netted, large game such as hogs, bushbucks, and an occasional okapi must be killed with spears. The Efe men often hunt alone either for monkeys with poison-tipped arrows or for duikers, small African antelope, by perching in fruiting trees. They obtain the poison from the juice of the kilabo plant. A mere scratch with this poison can cause death.

¹⁶ SPORTS

Forest people do not play sports in the Western sense. They do, however, learn basic skills through mock hunts and other games. For example, every camp has a designated play area for children next to streams (*bopi*) that is off limits to adults. Here children play games similar to sports that teach them about group dynamics and personal achievement. Of similar importance, the elders teach children the strategies and techniques of hunting by pretending to be animals and by showing children how to drive them into a piece of old net.

The adults also play a game (more ritual than sport) resembling our tug-of-war. The purpose is to remind the community that cooperation can solve conflicts between the sexes. The tug-of-war begins with all the men on one side and the women on the other. If the women begin to prevail, one of them leaves to help out the men and assumes a deep male voice to ridicule manhood. As the men begin to win, one of them joins the women and mocks them in high-pitched tones. The battle continues in this way until the participants have switched sides and have had an opportunity to both help and ridicule the opposition. Then both sides collapse, laughing over the point that neither side gains in beating the other.

[17] ENTERTAINMENT AND RECREATION

The Ituri forest is one of the world's last refuges from cinemas, televisions, videos, IPODs and internet. The Bambuti relax after a day's hunt by sitting on home-made four-legged stools in front of their huts, talking and smoking. Conversation may be directed at everybody or may be between two people, but it is audible to all. People talk about what they did that day or what they are going to do the next. They may joke about someone's clumsiness, and they often get up in the night to urinate or smoke and continue their conversations. Pygmies also celebrate a good hunt, especially an elephant kill, with feasting and dancing. An elephant kill is an act of courage, and they know the meat and ivory will trade well.

When they move to village outskirts, pygmies socialize with villagers while bartering their game. On moonlit nights, they stay late to drink wine and dance. The pygmies put on outlandish performances to entertain villagers in exchange for beverages. A few elderly men stay behind in the camp to smoke hashish and stand guard against thieves.

[18] FOLK ART, CRAFTS, AND HOBBIES

Pygmies have little time and interest for crafts and hobbies. If they need a tool such as a mortar and pestle to prepare food or medicine, they often wheedle it from their villager hosts. Pygmies fashion their own nets from *lianas* (vines) and make belt pouches, baskets, and mats from grasses. They craft stools and chairs from sticks and branches.

[19] SOCIAL PROBLEMS

Prior to independence, pygmies remained outside the mainstream of society and politics. An internal system of camp debate and consensus allowed every adult to express his or her opinion. No chief or formal council imposed rules. Instead, an informal oligarchy of leaders led decision-making and maintenance of law and order.

However, post-independence wars, nation-building, and national park set-asides have disrupted customary ways. Logging, illegal mining, road-building, and commerce have further eroded the isolation of the forest peoples. Indeed, the plunder and smuggling of coltan into Rwanda has wreaked havoc on the environment and has been the cause of many pygmy deaths in Ituri. Ironically, coltan is a natural resource for chips used in cell phones, computers and other electronics. Pygmy values, beliefs, and way of life are increasingly jeopardized by uncontrolled illegal exploitation of resources for which they have no use.

Even more devastating to the pygmies is the presence of various armed groups all of which have exploited the forest people as cheap (or free) labor, raped pygmy women, and retaliated against pygmy communities for allegedly cooperating with enemy groups. The armies and militias have used them as hunters and guides for their special knowledge of forest trails. In addition to rape, one human rights group found evidence of mass killings and cannibalism by armed combatants against the forest people. Sexual exploitation has resulted in a high rate of gonorrhea among Bambuti, which researchers believe accounts for a low birth rate among pygmy women.

[20] GENDER ISSUES

Pygmy society is relatively egalitarian for its lack of the typical gender issues stemming from societal discrimination, marginalization of girls, unfair inheritance laws, disputed abortion rights, and workplace inequality. The critical role women play in survival no doubt accounts for this consideration. However, one of the forest people's key gender problems is inter-clan disputes over women and children. Pygmies lose about 14% of their women to marriage with villagers. Reciprocal marriage exchanges are therefore difficult to fulfill because families often have uneven numbers of females. Patricians and younger males harass, capture, and come into armed conflict with each other over "sister exchange." Thus, many males must live well past puberty while waiting for a wife. These bachelors can cause serious problems when they tryst with married women or with girls in their endogamous clan.

[21] BIBLIOGRAPHY

Bailey, Robert C. and Robert Aunger, Jr. "Significance of the Social Relationships of Efe Pygmy Men in the Ituri Forest, Zaire." In Mary H. Pulford, ed., *Peoples of the Ituri.* Orlando, FL: Harcourt Brace College Publishers, 1993.

Bailey, Robert C. and Irven Devore. "Research on the Efe and Lese Populations of the Ituri Forest, Zaire." In Mary H. Pulford, ed., *Peoples of the Ituri.* Orlando, FL: Harcourt Brace College Publishers, 1993.

Bailey, Robert C. and N. R. Peacock. "Efe Pygmies of Northeast Zaire: Subsistence Strategies in the Ituri Forest." In Mary H. Pulford, ed., *Peoples of the Ituri.* Orlando, FL: Harcourt Brace College Publishers, 1993..

Clayton, Jonathon. "Pygmies Struggle to Survive in a War Zone Where Abuse is Routine: A Threatened People are Taken Advantage of by Everyone." *TimesOnline.* December 16, 2004.

Farnham, Kay. N.d. *The Pygmies of the Ituri Forest: An Adventure in Anthropology.* Gage Educational Publishing, Ltd.

Pulford, Mary H., ed.. *Peoples of the Ituri.* Orlando, FL: Harcourt Brace College Publishers, 1993

Putnam, Patrick and Carleton S. Coon. "The Pygmies of the Ituri Forest." In Mary H. Pulford, ed., *Peoples of the Ituri.* Orlando, FL: Harcourt Brace College Publishers, 1993.

Turnbull, Colin M. *The Forest People.* New York: Simon and Schuster, 1962.

———. *The Mbuti Pygmies: Change and Adaptation.* New York: Holt, Rinehart and Winston, 1983.

—by R. Groelsema

EGYPTIANS

PRONUNCIATION: ih-JIP-shuhns
LOCATION: Egypt (northeastern Africa)
POPULATION: 80 million
LANGUAGE: Arabic
RELIGION: Islam (Primarily Sunni; minorities of Shia and Sufi); Coptic Christian; other Christian denominations. [Fewer than 1,000 Jews.]

¹ INTRODUCTION

The Arab Republic of Egypt is more commonly known as Egypt. Throughout Egypt's 6,000-year history, it was the focus of ambitions of many foreign powers, who wished to dominate this country that occupies a strategic position linking the continents of Africa and Asia. Conquerors of Egypt have included the Ptolemies, Romans, Greeks, Arabs, Fatimids, Mamluks, Ottomans, French, and British. Britain was the last colonial power to conquer Egypt. British forces withdrew in 1954, leaving Egypt independent under the leadership of President Jamal 'Abd al-Nasir.

A key event in the ancient history of Egypt was the unification of Upper (southern) and Lower (northern) Egypt, by the legendary King Menes, in the third millennium BC. This began the famous Pharaonic Age, in which a god-king, or pharaoh, held power over all of Egypt. The legacy of the pharaohs is preserved in the pyramids and in the stories etched in stone in hieroglyphic symbols across the face of Egypt.

A second key event, one of the most influential in the development of modern Egypt, was the Arab Muslim conquest in AD 641 by 'Amr Ibn al-'As. This conquest led to the spread of the Arabic language and Islamic religion across Egypt. This was not affected by the absorption of Egypt into the Ottoman Empire in 1517, since the Ottomans were themselves also Muslim, and Islamic institutions were maintained. An attempt to free Egypt from Ottoman rule, led by Muhammad 'Ali in the first half of the 19th century, failed. The British occupied Egypt in 1882 in order to control the Suez Canal and safeguard the British route to India. Egypt never became a British colony, but it did become part of the British Empire, with Egyptian King Faruk as ruler.

In 1952, a group of Egyptians called the Free Officers, led by Lieutenant Colonel Jamal 'Abd al-Nasir, overthrew King Faruk. 'Abd al-Nasir became President of Egypt in 1954 and immediately began a series of nationalizations, including the nationalization of the Suez Canal in 1956, a move that infuriated the countries that depended on safe passage through the canal. This led to the 1956 Tripartite Invasion of Egypt by Britain, France, and Israel. Following threats that the Soviet Union would attack Britain and France if they did not withdraw from Egypt and pressure by the United States on Britain and France, by the end of the year, the three forces had all withdrawn. As Israel withdrew from the Sinai, it destroyed roads, railroads, and military installations. During Nasir's presidency, Egypt was also embroiled in the June 1967 Arab–Israeli War, in which Israel occupied Egypt's Sinai peninsula.

Upon Nasir's death in 1970, Anwar Sadat became president of Egypt. During his term, Egypt launched the 1973 Arab–Israeli War across the Suez Canal, hoping to recapture the Sinai from Israel and liberate Palestinian territories that had also been occupied by Israel in 1967. Although the goals of the war were not achieved, Sadat nevertheless felt victorious because his forces had inflicted heavy damage on the Israeli forces.

In 1977, in a move that took the world by surprise, Sadat visited Israel in preparation for peace negotiations. By 1979, President Anwar Sadat of Egypt and Prime Minister Menachem Begin of Israel had signed the Camp David Peace Accords, ending the progression of Egyptian-Israeli wars and returning the Sinai to Egyptian sovereignty in 1982. There have been no Egyptian-Israeli wars since Camp David and, following a period in which Egypt was shunned by the Arab world for forging a separate peace with Israel, Egypt now plays the role of mediator between Israel and other Arab nations, working to promote a comprehensive peace in the region.

President Sadat was criticized in some domestic circles for his peace overtures toward Israel. He was also increasingly criticized for the economic program he introduced in 1974, known as *Infitah*, or "the opening." Infitah focused on cutting back the size of the huge public sector by reducing government spending and restricting the hiring of new employees by the government. Previously, every university graduate was guaranteed a job in the public sector. Under Sadat, this promise of employment was curtailed, leaving thousands of university graduates without jobs. Infitah also had an adverse effect on the cost of living, by removing many subsidies on food and thus leading to rampant inflation. Sadat grew increasingly frustrated as he tried to deal with increasing opposition to his political and economic reforms, and he enacted new laws meant to give himself more power and curtail public criticism. As the opposition became more intense, Sadat reacted by arresting at least 1,500 opponents in September 1981. One month later, on 6 October 1981, Sadat was assassinated by a member of an Islamic opposition group, known as the *Jihad* (holy struggle) organization.

Husni Mubarak succeeded Sadat and has been president of Egypt since October 1981. Mubarak has followed Sadat's lead by continuing to pursue Infitah and by upholding the peace with Israel. He has allowed political parties to operate but maintains a ban on Islamic parties and the state of emergency imposed after the death of Sadat remains in force more than one-quarter century later. When the Islamic opposition gets out of line, as it has increasingly done in the 1980s and 1990s, Mubarak authorizes hundreds and thousands of arrests. There are at least three Islamic trends in Egypt. Many in the general population tend to be religiously observant—fasting, praying, and dressing conservatively, but seeing no need to make Islam into a political force. Second, a mainstream, politically active Islamic opposition group, known as the Muslim Brotherhood, seeks to change the Egyptian legal system by basing it on Islamic *shari'a*, or law. The Brotherhood, or *Ikhwan* as they are known in Egypt, have renounced the use of violence against the government and seek to impose Islamic law by working from within the political system. The third Islamic trend is militant and is represented by the Jihad organization. This group seeks to impose Islamic law on the country by overthrowing the current government. Battles between Jihad members and Egyptian security forces have become frequent, causing President Mubarak to crack down on Islamic political opposition, even against members of the Ikhwan.

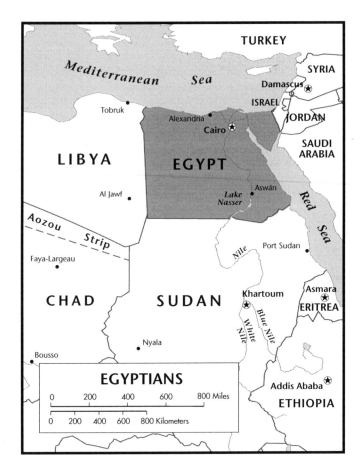

² LOCATION AND HOMELAND

Egypt has a population of about 80 million, with 99% of its people living along the banks of the Nile River. Population density in the Nile Valley is one of the highest in the world, exceeding 1,500 persons per sq km. The population grows by 1.7% per year. Sixty percent of Egypt's population is under the age of 25.

The country occupies approximately 1 million sq km in north-eastern Africa. Of this, only 35,000 sq km (the Nile Valley and Delta) are cultivated. The rest of the land consists of the Western (Libyan) Desert, the Eastern (Arabian) Desert, and the Sinai Peninsula. Egypt is bordered on the west by Libya, on the south by the Sudan, on the east by the Red Sea, on the northeast by southern Israel, and on the north by the Mediterranean Sea. The Nile River runs through Egypt from Sudan, flowing from south to north and ending at the Mediterranean Sea. Three central African rivers flow into the Nile. These are the White Nile, originating in Uganda; the Blue Nile, originating in Ethiopia; and the Atbarah, also originating in Ethiopia. Along the banks of the Nile lies the Nile Valley and Delta, an extensive oasis on which 99% of Egypt's population lives.

³ LANGUAGE

All Egyptians speak Arabic, the national language. Arabic is a highly evolved Semitic language related to Hebrew and Aramaic. Written Arabic is in the form of classical Arabic or a simpler version called "modern standard," which is the form taught in schools throughout the Arab world and originally based on the Quran. This Arabic is used in the media, government, and literature throughout the Arab world, tying the Arab world together culturally. Egyptians speak two major dialects of Arabic. In Cairo and most other urban centers, to mention just one of the many differences between colloquial Egyptian Arabic and the Arabic spoken in most of the rest of the Arab world, the sound *j* is pronounced as *g* (as in the word "girl"). Thus, a boy whose name is pronounced "Jalal" in most of the Arab world is known is "Galal" in Cairo. In most of the countryside, however, the *j* sound is maintained. In Cairo, the word for carrot is *gazar*. In the countryside, and in most of the Arab world, it is *jazar*. A mountain in Cairo is *gabal*, and in the countryside and most of the Arab world it is *jabal*.

Common boys' names are *Ramadan* and *Sha`ban*, which are also the names of Islamic months. Other common names are *Gamal, Mohammad*, and *Ahmad*. Common girls' names are *Mona, Su`ad, Magda, Fatima*, and *Lobna*. Egyptians often use nicknames for friends and relatives. Very common nicknames are *Mimi* for Mohammad, and *Fifi* for Fatima.

⁴ FOLKLORE

Some of Egypt's most popular legends are stories of liberation from foreign rule and domination. Ahmad Arabi is famous for his opposition to British and French interference in Egypt's finances in the late 19th century, and Sa`ad Zaghlul is famous for his opposition to British domination during the early 20th century.

Most folklore in Muslim countries tells stories of important figures in religious history. One such story that is also cause for annual commemoration throughout the Islamic world is that of *al-Isra' wa al-Mi`raj*. According to legend, on the 26th day of the Islamic month of Rajab, the Prophet Muhammad traveled at night from Mecca, Saudi Arabia (then Hijaz) to Jerusalem. From Jerusalem, he rode his wondrous horse, al-Burak, on a nocturnal visit to heaven.

Another item of folklore commonly believed in some Islamic communities, including Egypt, is that evil spirits, called *jinns*, live in haunted places. Jinns are demons that are believed to take on the form of an animal or human. Some Egyptians also believe in the "evil eye" and take measures to prevent being inflicted by it.

⁵ RELIGION

About 90% of Egyptians are Sunni Muslims, 8.5% are Coptic Christians, and 1.5% are other Christian denominations—Greek Orthodox, Eastern and Latin Rite Catholics, and Protestants. There are fewer than 1,000 Jews in Egypt. Christianity came to Egypt during Roman rule in the 1st century AD. The Copts have been a significant minority in Egypt since medieval times. They are led by a patriarch based in Alexandria, Egypt—Pope Shenudah III—and he is known as the pope of the Coptic Church worldwide.

Islam, Egypt's national religion, teaches that Allah (the Arabic word for God) regularly sent guidance to humans in the form of prophets. Islam accepts the earlier Semitic prophets, including Abraham, Moses, and Jesus. Muslims also believe that Muhammad was the last in the line of prophets sent with the message and that there is only one God. Muslims believe in heaven and hell, the day of Judgment, and angels. The Quran is the holy book of Muslims, and it teaches that, in order to get to heaven, men and women must believe in God and do good works by struggling in God's way. Belief and good deeds are tightly bound together in Muslim literature.

The Islamic religion has five pillars: (1) Muslims must pray five times a day; (2) Muslims must give alms, or *zakat*, to the poor; (3) Muslims must fast during the month of Ramadan; (4) Muslims must make the pilgrimage, or *hajj*, to Mecca; and (5) each Muslim must recite the *shahada—ashhadu an la illah ila Allah wa ashhadu an Muhammadu rasul Allah*—which means "I witness that there is no god but Allah and that Muhammad is the prophet of Allah."

6 MAJOR HOLIDAYS

Egypt commemorates Muslim religious, secular, Coptic, and Roman Catholic holidays. One major Muslim holiday is *Eid al-Fitr,* which comes at the end of the month of fasting, *Ramadan.* During Ramadan, Muslims refrain from eating, drinking, or having sex during daylight hours, in order to reflect on God and on the plight of the unfortunate who do not have enough food. At the end of the month, Muslims celebrate *Eid al-Fitr* for three days. The other major Muslim holiday is *Eid al-Adha,* which commemorates the willingness of the Prophet Abraham, as well as his son, to obey God's command in all things, even when Abraham was told to sacrifice his son.

It is traditional to buy new clothing for these two holidays, and the shops of Cairo and other urban centers stay open later than usual before the holidays. Swarms of people fill the streets, shopping for clothing for these exciting events. The religious holidays are celebrated by going to the mosque for group morning prayers and then coming home to large meals with family and visiting relatives. Part of the feast is normally given to relatives and to the poor. Egyptian children are given small amounts of money by visiting relatives. Other Islamic holidays that are celebrated to a lesser degree are the Islamic New Year, the Prophet Muhammad's birthday, and the Tenth of *Muharram.* The latter is the tenth day of the Muslim month of Muharram, commemorated because Moses led the Israelites out of Egyptian slavery on this day. The Prophet Muhammad instructed all Muslims to fast on this day.

Orthodox Christians celebrate Christmas on 7 January and Easter on a different date each year. All Egyptians celebrate *Sham al-Nisim,* a Coptic holiday with Pharaonic origins, on the first Monday after Easter.

Secular holidays include New Year's Day (1 January); Sinai Liberation Day (25 April); Labor Day (1 May); Mother's Day (31 March); Evacuation Day, commemorating the withdrawal of the British (18 June); Revolution Day (23 July); National Day (6 October); and Victory Day (23 December).

7 RITES OF PASSAGE

Egyptian boys are circumcised, usually at birth, but often later in the child's youth. The birth of a baby is an important event, and the baby's first week of life is commemorated on the seventh day with a celebration called the *subu`.* Graduation from high school is also important, although many of Egypt's children do not finish 12 years of school because they drop out to help their families earn a living. A 2005 study by UNICEF reports that primary school attendance is above 90% for both boys and girls.

Marriage is an important rite of passage, but increasingly Egyptian men and women are getting married in their late 20s and 30s. This is based more on financial ability to support a family than on a preference for delayed marriage. In order to get married, a man must typically provide a furnished apartment at the very least and also have an expensive wedding ceremony. Millions of Egyptian men simply cannot afford this considerable expense. Some charitable organizations are attempting to help by providing weddings free of charge, but this serious social issue is a cause of great concern to the government.

All adults hope to conduct the Islamic *hajj,* or pilgrimage to Mecca, sometime before their death. Those who do so are thereafter given the title *Hajj* preceding their name, such as *Hajj* Mustafa (man) or *Hajjah* Fatima (woman). Upon a loved one's death, the burial is carried out as soon as possible, preferably on the same day. The condolence period lasts for three days, during which mourners recite passages from the Quran. If the deceased was a public-sector employee, his or her family receives a death benefit from the government to help it deal with the loss.

8 INTERPERSONAL RELATIONS

Egyptians are very friendly people, and even the poorest among them will show hospitality to a stranger. The Egyptian greeting is typically "*as-salamu `alaykum,*" or "peace be with you," and the response is "*wa `alaykum as-salam,*" or "and peace be with you as well." Egyptians shake hands upon greeting, although two men or two women who have not seen each other for a while might kiss on the cheek. An unmarried man and woman, however, would not kiss due to Muslim and social mores, and a very pious man and woman might not even shake hands. In formal situations, a man is referred to as *sayyid* (Mr.), a married woman as *sayyida* (Mrs.), and a single woman as *anisa* (Miss). Anyone with a doctorate or a Ph.D. or a medical degree is referred to respectfully as "Doctor," even in informal settings. Children must show respect for their elders and can never refer to an adult by his or her first name without attaching "aunt" or "uncle" to the name. Thus, a child would address a female adult acquaintance as "`*Amti* (Aunt) Fatima," and a male adult acquaintance as "`*Amo* (Uncle) Muhammad." The same words are used to address a child's actual aunt and uncle.

Dating in the Western sense between the sexes is a social taboo because Islamic values prohibit an unmarried man and woman to be alone together. Public ritualized socializing is widespread, however, and the parklands built along the Nile are crowded with young couples sitting on benches, sharing meals or tea, and even exchanging flowers. Marriage tends to be arranged by matchmakers, although a man and woman who are interested in each other may declare their intentions to their families, formally (publicly) announce their intention, and then see each other in the presence of a third party, usually a family member. Such careful measures are the society's way of preserving the dignity and honor of their children and making sure that girls remain virgins until they are married. Premarital and extramarital sex are strictly forbidden.

9 LIVING CONDITIONS

The government increased spending on health care after the 1952 Revolution, and the result has been a decrease in the infant mortality rate and an increase in life expectancy. Diarrhea and the dehydration that sometimes accompanies it account for many deaths among infants and children. One reason for this is the lack of safe water for drinking and cooking among

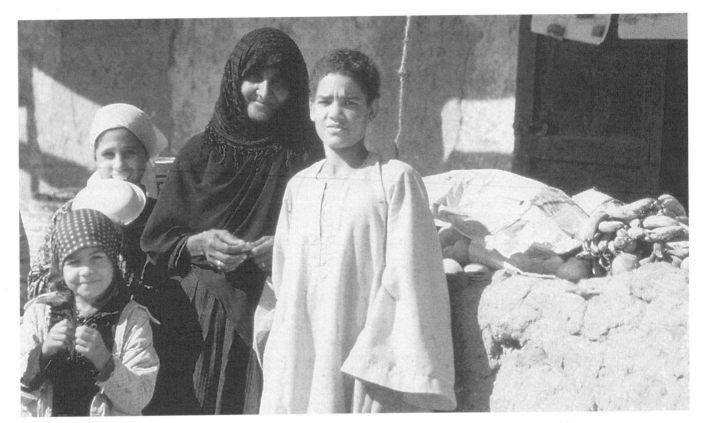

Egyptian children are taught to show respect for their parents and other adults, and children are given responsibilities at a young age.
(Cory Langley)

25% of the population. Among adults, the main causes of death are respiratory and digestive ailments. In 2003, there was about one physician per 835 inhabitants, and almost as many certified nurses. The country has public, government-run hospitals and clinics as well as more expensive, private hospitals and clinics. There are also numerous low-cost clinics located in neighborhood mosques and run by Islamic charitable organizations. These are frequented by both Christian and Muslim patients and are often considered to be better providers of health care than government clinics.

The rapidly growing population of Egypt is a challenge to authorities responsible for meeting the housing needs of the country. Population size, coupled with a shortage of skilled laborers and construction materials, has resulted in a shortage of affordable housing. Nowhere is this more evident than in the mausoleums of Cairo's cemeteries, where more than 500,000 poor people have set up their homes. The cemeteries are so populated that they are now called "The City of the Dead." One fifth of all Egyptians live in the 400 slums that surround Cairo. The majority of Egyptians live in crowded apartment buildings in very densely populated communities. Some people have built semi-legal housing of wood, cardboard, and metal on the flat rooftops of apartment buildings. There is little space for single-family houses, although these can be found in a few areas. The government has been trying to deal with the urban crowding by building new cities on the outskirts of Cairo. These include *Madinat Nasr* and *The Tenth of Ramadan* towns. While some families have been eager to move to these new towns, Cairo is

still more attractive to most people because of the lack of employment in the new areas.

One of the most prosperous established sections of Cairo is Zamalek, a small island in the Nile River, where the per-capita income is $15,000 per year, in contrast to the $150 per-capita income in some of the slums.

¹⁰ FAMILY LIFE

The family is the center of social organization. Every Egyptian is expected to get married and produce children in order to continue the family lineage. When a child is born, the parents' new roles are acknowledged with new titles: The father becomes *Abu* ("father of") the new child, and the mother becomes *Ummu* ("mother of") the new child. Thus, the parents of a child named *Ahmad* are known as *Abu Ahmad* and *Ummu Ahmad*. The father is the head of the household, and he is responsible for providing for the family. The mother manages the household and is the primary caregiver and child rearer. Many wives now work to help support the family, but they are still responsible for maintenance of the home. Today's families tend to be primarily nuclear (parents and their unmarried children), whereas not long ago most Egyptians lived in extended families. Urbanization and migration in search of employment have split up extended families. Upon marriage, a son tries to arrange for housing near his parents, and it is common to find a family trying to add apartment units to its dwelling in order to prepare housing for its sons. Sons who cannot afford to live independently might bring their brides to their parents' home and live with the family until independent living arrangements can be made. A daughter who gets married moves into her new husband's home, and the best "catch" is a man who already has his own apartment and doesn't have to rely on his parents. Single sons and daughters, for the most part, stay at home until they are married.

Children are taught to show respect for their parents and other adults, and children are given responsibilities at a young age. Girls help their mothers with housework and take care of their younger siblings. Boys in poorer families are expected to learn a trade early on, often interrupting their chances to attend school. It is not uncommon to find poor children selling merchandise on street corners in order to contribute to the family income. Children of wealthier families have the luxury of focusing most of their attention on school. Enrollment of girls in rural areas lags behind that of boys, and girls drop out of primary school more frequently than boys.

11 CLOTHING

Walking through Egypt's cities, one finds a myriad of clothing types, ranging from the traditional *galabiyya* worn by men and *milaya* worn by women to the Islamic *shari`a* worn by women to Western-style business suits and dresses. The galabiyya, Egypt's national attire for men, is a long, robe-like garment with long sleeves and trim around the neckline. The galabiyya tends to be light in color, with gray, beige, and white being the most common colors. The galabiyya is worn over a shirt and slacks, and is worn mainly by traditional older Egyptian men. The milaya, worn by Egypt's traditional older women, is usually black, and is also a long robe-like garment with long sleeves. It is worn over a light dress. Women wearing the milaya also wrap their heads in a black scarf or shawl.

The Islamic *shari`a* attire is worn by religious women, usually women who are younger than those who wear the milaya. Shari`a dresses are common in university settings and in the work place. This dress is also long, with long sleeves and buttons down the front, resembling a long jacket. Some religious women also wear long skirts and dresses that differ from Western wear only by virtue of their length and full-body coverage. Any woman wearing the shari`a dress or the long dress-like religious attire will also don a long scarf that she wraps around her head. Some of these scarves are quite beautiful, with hand-stitched sequins and/or beads. Fashion-conscious religious women might also wear fancy little hats over their scarves. Scarves, hats, and religious attire are color-coordinated, with the long dresses and skirts being much more brightly colored than the shari`a attire, which usually has a solid neutral tone.

Many Egyptians wear typical Western attire, and Western clothing shops abound in the city. Women wear dresses and skirts—usually below the knee in length. Women also wear slacks and suits. These women generally do not cover their heads. Men wear Western business suits, slacks, jeans, and so on. In the cities, the Western look is the most common, although Islamic attire is becoming increasingly popular for women, particularly in universities.

12 FOOD

Most of the population consumes bread, rice, beans, fruits, and vegetables on a daily basis. Those who can afford to also eat red meat, poultry, and fish.

The typical Egyptian breakfast consists of *ful mudammas* (fava bean dip) with pita bread, hard-boiled or scrambled eggs, and a cup of hot tea with boiled milk. There are two major variations of ful mudammas, and recipes for them follow.

Ful mudammas with tomato

1 15-ounce-can cooked fava beans
¼ cup olive oil
1 small onion, chopped
4 ounces tomato sauce
½ teaspoon salt
¼ teaspoon black pepper
¼ teaspoon paprika
A few sprigs of fresh parsley
pita bread

In a skillet, sauté the chopped onion in the olive oil until the onion is transparent. Add salt, pepper, and tomato sauce. Drain and rinse the fava beans, and add to the tomato mixture. Cook over medium heat 5 to 7 minutes, stirring occasionally. Pour into serving dish, and garnish with paprika, parsley, and olive oil. Eat with pita bread.

Ful mudammas with lemon and garlic

1 15-ounce-can cooked fava beans
½ cup water
2 tablespoons fresh lemon juice
¼ teaspoon garlic powder
¼ teaspoon salt
¼ teaspoon black pepper
¼ cup olive oil
¼ teaspoon paprika
a few sprigs of fresh parsley
pita bread

Drain and rinse fava beans. Place beans in a skillet, and add 1/2 cup water. Heat over medium heat, allowing water to evaporate. Add lemon juice, garlic, salt, and pepper and cook 3 to 5 minutes, stirring occasionally. Pour into serving dish, and garnish with paprika, parsley, and olive oil. Eat with pita bread.

Ful mudammas is available in carryout restaurants in almost every neighborhood in Egypt and is an inexpensive yet nutritious meal. The same restaurants that serve ful also serve *ta`miyya*, known as *falafil* in most of the Arab world and in the West. Ta`miyya is a deep-fried patty made of a dough-like paste that consists of fava beans, onions, garlic, cumin, coriander and parsley. The patties are served in sandwiches with pickles, and are often a quick meal at lunch time.

Egypt's national dinner is a spinach-like vegetable known as *mulukhiyya*. This leafy vegetable is a member of the hibiscus family and is grown in abundance in Egypt. When in season, Egyptians pick the leaves off the stems and cook them fresh. Out of season, mulukhiyya is available dried. Middle Eastern and Greek stores in the United States sell dried and/or frozen mulukhiyya. A recipe for mulukhiyya follows.

Mulukhiyya

1/3 pound dried mulukhiyya
1 whole chicken, cut into pieces
1 quart water
1 teaspoon salt
¼ teaspoon black pepper

Egyptian social worker Sahar Rabie gives a demonstration about bird flu at the Community Development Association in the village of Tawfiqiya at the outskirts of Fayyoum, Egypt. In an area where chickens used to roam freely, as the local population has become aware of, and frightened by, the disease, chickens have been slaughtered or locked away. (AP Images/Nasser Nasser)

6 to 7 cloves of garlic, mashed or finely chopped

2 tablespoons olive oil

1 tablespoon dried coriander

Boil the chicken pieces in water, skimming off and discarding the froth that appears during the boiling process. Add salt and pepper, and cook chicken until tender (about 30 minutes). Add mulukhiyya and simmer for 20 minutes, stirring occasionally. Meanwhile, sauté garlic in olive oil. Add coriander to garlic and stir well. When mulukhiyya soup is finished cooking, pour garlic mixture into soup and simmer another 2 minutes. Serve mulukhiyya over a bed of rice or eat with pita bread.

Ful, ta`miyya, and mulukhiyya are Egypt's most popular foods. Other common foods include stuffed cabbage leaves, stuffed grape leaves, *musaqqa`a* (eggplant and tomato casserole), macaroni baked with béchamel sauce, shish kebab, and *shawirma* (gyro) sandwiches.

Common desserts include *kunafa,* a baked pastry made of layers of shredded wheat dough and nuts and covered with syrup; *baqlawa* (baklava), a baked pastry made of layers of filo dough and nuts and covered with syrup; and *basbusa,* a baked caked made of semolina flour and soaked in syrup.

Common drinks include hot tea with mint, Turkish coffee, a licorice root drink known as `*irk sus,* and fresh fruit juice—including carrot juice and sugar cane juice squeezed fresh by street-side vendors.

Because they are predominantly Muslim, Egyptians do not consume pork and are prohibited from drinking alcoholic beverages. The latter, however, are served in expensive restaurants, hotels, and a few pubs and drinking establishments, even in relatively poorer areas of Cairo.

13 EDUCATION

Before the 19th century, most education in Egypt was religious and for boys only. Theological seminaries, mosques, and churches taught males to read and write Arabic and to memorize religious texts. Secular education was established in the early 19th century by Egypt's ruler, Muhammad `Ali. In 1873, the first school for girls was built. When Egypt was under British administration, between 1882 and 1922, public education was not expanded, but many private schools were established. And, although education for all children was proclaimed a national goal after the British withdrawal from Egypt, by 1952 some 75% of the population over 10 years of age was still illiterate, with 90% of females over 10 years of age were illiterate.

After the Free Officers Revolution in 1952, educational opportunity was expanded, and government spending on education increased. Enrollment in schools doubled in the first decade after the revolution and doubled again in the following decade. Enrollment rates continued to increase after 1975, although not at such dramatic rates. In 1981, the government decreed that all children must complete the first 9 years of school—6 years of compulsory primary school and 3 years of compulsory preparatory school. By 2005, 88% of children between the ages of 7 and 12 were enrolled in primary school. Attendance rates in secondary schools dropped off dramatically in rural areas, where in 2005 only 6% were in regular attendance. Despite these disparities in educational opportunities 2005 reports from the US government say 71% of the population above 15 is literate.

Education at all levels is free, from primary school through university education. The school system, however, is greatly overpopulated with students and has a chronic shortage of teachers. In 2005 the ratio of students to teachers was 86 to 1 and 99 to 1 for female teachers. In recent years, some schools have operated two shifts per day to cut down on class size. Many teachers find it more lucrative to work abroad in other Arab countries, where class sizes are much smaller and the salaries are much higher. Many teachers offer private tutoring in order to bring home extra income. This means that many children spend time outside school trying to improve their education. The cost of tutoring is often too high for the poor, who frequently complain that their children are being forced, by an inadequate educational system, into private lessons which they cannot afford.

Students are required to pass a series of end-of-the-year exams in order to make it from one level in the school system to the next. This is particularly important at the end of middle school, when grades determine the type of high school a student will attend. Those who do well in middle school attend an academic, college-prep secondary school. Others might attend a technical or vocational school or, if their grades are very discouraging, they might simply drop out.

At the end of high school, students take another set of exams. Secondary school students whose grades merit have the option of enrolling in a university. Egypt's leading universities are Cairo University, Alexandria University, 'Ein Shams University, Asyut University, and the American University at Cairo. The first four of these are public universities, and the last is private. In addition, there are a number of smaller universities throughout the country. There are a variety of technical institutes of higher learning available for those who do not make it into college. These schools offer training in such fields as hotel management and secretarial services.

14 CULTURAL HERITAGE

Ancient Egyptians left behind a rich artistic heritage in the form of pyramids, pharaonic painting and sculpture, hieroglyphics, and architecture. The Egyptian pharaohs believed in life after death and built 75 pyramids that would serve as their dwellings after death. The best known of these, The Great Pyramid, was built about 2690 bc at Giza. (Earlier pyramids were constructed in Saqara) It contains more than 2 million blocks of limestone, some weighing up to 15 tons. Pyramids and wall sculptures are found in Giza, in Upper Egypt (the south), in the Valley of the Kings, in Luxor and Karnak, and on Philae Island. The Cairo Museum houses a large collection of antiquities. The museum displays about 100,000 exhibits, including some of the coffins excavated from the pyramids and treasures from the tomb of Pharaoh Tutankhamun (King Tut).

Literature is greatly enjoyed in Egypt, and Cairo's publishing companies generate an abundant supply and variety of literary works. The Cairo Book Fair is a major annual event in which recent international publications are featured with great fanfare. A variety of literary forms are enjoyed in Egypt, with short stories, poetry, and novels being quite popular.

One of Egypt's most famous authors was a blind essayist named Taha Husayn (d.1973), whose literary output was immense. Some of his writing has been translated into English, including *Tales from Egyptian Life* and *An Egyptian Childhood* (an autobiography). The modern Egyptian novelist best known in the Western world is probably Naguib Mahfouz, (d. 2006) winner of the 1988 Nobel Prize for Literature. Virtually of his Mahfouz's work has now been translated, the better known of which include such classics as *Midaq Alley* and *The Cairo Trilogy*. Mahfouz had a penchant for writing about the lives of ordinary Egyptians, particularly the poor and middle classes. His stories feature observations of the socio-economic and political conditions of Egyptian society, with direct and indirect commentary on issues such as women's emancipation, polygamy, the British occupation of Egypt, and the Egyptian response to that occupation.

15 WORK

Agriculture is the largest source of employment in Egypt—32 percent of Egyptians work in this sector. Farmers plant *berseem* (clover) for livestock feed, as well as corn, wheat, vegetables, rice, cotton, and fruit. Since 1974, when the government announced economic reforms that would include industrialization, rural residents have flocked to greater Cairo in search of employment. Cairo's population grew from 7 million in 1976 to 20 million in 2006. Those who find work with the manufacturing sector work in industries such as iron and steel, aluminum, and cement. Some work in oil production, and others produce consumer goods.

Despite the industrialization that has taken place, Egypt's cities do not offer enough employment opportunities to the migrant masses. Urban residents thus end up depending on the government for jobs, and the waiting period can be as long as 10 years. When attempts to find work fail, the unemployed migrate to neighboring countries in search of employment. From the late 1970s to the early 1980s, 90% of new jobs were either provided by the public sector or were in neighboring oil states. In 2005 the government introduced some free market reforms, taking tentative steps away from the state dominated economic model championed by Egypt's still revered President Nasir. As a result of these reforms there was a large rise in the stock market, GDP grew at approximately 6–7% a year for 2005–2007. Little of this increased wealth saw its way to the poor of the Cairo or the rural areas.

The unemployment rate in 2007 was 10.1%. After agriculture, Egypt's major employment sectors are industry (17%) and services (51%). Twenty percent of Egyptians live below the poverty line. The per capita GDP is 5,400 US dollars per year.

Many who do work hold more than one job to make ends meet. This is particularly true for public sector employees. It is common to find a man (seldom a woman) working at a government-run factory during the day and moonlighting in a second job at night.

16 SPORTS

Egyptians take soccer, which they, like the rest of the non-American the world, call football, very seriously. Competitions are held among the many teams nationwide and are broadcast on radio and television with great enthusiasm. National soccer teams also compete in regional soccer competitions with other Arab and African states. The national team has won the African Cup of Nations a record six times and won its second consecutive title in 2008 in an upset victory over favored Cameroon. FIFA currently ranks the team as the 29th best in the world. Swimming and scuba diving are enjoyed along the beaches of the Mediterranean Sea and the Red Sea. The Red Sea in particular is considered one of the great diving locations in the world. Indoor swimming pools and tennis courts are located in sports clubs, but generally only the middle class and wealthy can afford these.

17 ENTERTAINMENT AND RECREATION

There are more than 100 cinemas in Cairo, some run by the government and others privately owned. There are also many cinemas in Port Sa'id and Alexandria. Egyptian-made movies range from comedy to drama and often attempt to convey a political message relevant to contemporary political and economic conditions. One famous actor, 'Adil Imam, is renowned for his comedic movies, but has recently ventured onto political turf in his movies, *Terrorism and Kebab* and *The Terrorist*. In both films, Imam plays the lead role of a young Egyptian inadvertently caught in a web of poverty and anti-state terrorism.

Cairo has about 17 theaters, and Alexandria has about 6. Egyptian theaters host a variety of shows, including opera, orchestra, folk art, and choral troupe performances.

Egypt has been the home of many musical performers known throughout the Arabic-speaking world. Solo singers Um Kalthum, Farid al-Atrash, and 'Abd al-Halim Hafiz (all now deceased) were classical performers whose songs were known to last up to two hours each. While the classical style is still popular, there is now a new style of Egyptian music that blends the classical with more Western-sounding music. Muhammad Munir and "Four M" are samples of this new sound, which is very popular with the younger generation. Music cassettes are sold by street vendors. These are very popular and cost about $1 to $2 each.

Television entered the lives of Egyptians in the mid-1960s, and by the 1980s had become quite common. Televisions are even common among the residents of the cemeteries. Egyptian TV has a wide variety of programming, including comedy, music and dance shows, cartoons, and soap operas. Families are glued to their TV sets in the evening when the nightly soap operas come on. With the proliferation of satellite television, Egyptians can now watch American and European television entertainment and news channels as well.

Egyptian children generally play in the many open fields in their neighborhoods, but new parks have also been built. There are a limited number of amusement parks, the main one called "Sinbad" and located in Cairo. Toys are not very common and did not arrive in Egypt in significant number until the mid-1980s, when fathers returned from jobs in the oil countries, gifts in hand. Although many stores now have ample supplies of toys for children, most people do not spend their money on such luxuries. Children who are fortunate enough to get toys often go out of their way to take care of them, even if this means placing the toy out of reach to keep it from being damaged.

18 FOLK ART, CRAFTS, AND HOBBIES

The stores of Khan al-Khalili in Cairo cater predominantly to tourists and feature the hand-made crafts of local artisans. Media such as wood, brass, copper, glass, mother-of-pearl, leather, silver, and gold are cut, shaped, and engraved to form a multitude of items. Some of the most creative handicrafts for which the Egyptians are noted include wooden jewelry boxes covered with mother-of-pearl, engraved silver and hand-painted serving trays, and leather ottomans with intricate designs. Jewelry stores sell handcrafted bracelets, necklaces, rings, and earrings made of silver and gold. In the small village of Kirdasa, in addition to these handicrafts, the stores specialize in hand-made women's dresses that feature embroidery, sequins, and beads.

One of the most unique forms of folk art in Egypt is *hajj* painting. As a Muslim completes his or her pilgrimage to Mecca, a local artist paints the new pilgrim's front door with a mural symbolizing the hajj. Most hajj paintings are found in the villages.

19 SOCIAL PROBLEMS

One of Egypt's biggest problems is socio-economic frustration. Unemployment and underemployment have resulted in a high level of poverty and despair. Among the many effects of this situation is a growing attraction to religion: in 1986, according to government accounting, there was one mosque for every 6,000 Egyptians; by 2005 there was one mosque for every 745 people. A lack of affordable housing has forced hundreds of thousands of Egyptians to live in the mausoleums of Cairo's cemeteries. There are now 400 slums around the capital city. Shanty towns and slums continue to appear all over the metropolitan Cairo area. Housing is poorly constructed, services are few, and basic needs such as drinkable water and sewage are non-existent. The growth of slums has correlated with an increase in crime, violence, and religious militancy. Thefts such as pickpocketing and purse-snatching are common in metropolitan Cairo. Although violence rarely accompanies thefts, there are acts of violence within families and between religious militants and state security forces. White-collar crime is commonplace and includes embezzlement, diversion of subsidized goods, tax evasion, and bribes to officials. Another major problem is the illegal use of drugs. Although hashish has been smoked in Egypt for centuries, recently there has been an increase in the use of "hard" drugs such as heroin and cocaine.

Egyptian prisons are overcrowded. This is due in part to the arrest of criminals, but also to an ongoing political conflict between the government and the opposition. Clashes between government forces and religious opponents to the government periodically take place, sometimes resulting in hundreds of political opponents being arrested. The casualty list during clashes is sometimes quite high. One study found that total casualties (killed and wounded) during state–militants confrontations in the periods of heaviest demonstration in the late 1980s and 1990s went from 322 in 1992 to 1,106 in 1993. (The 1994 figure was 659, and the 1995 figure was 620.) International human rights organizations, such as Human Rights Watch and Amnesty International, have been critical of the Egyptian government's handling of militant opponents to the regime. The major criticism is that not only violent opponents, but also nonviolent political opponents, are being denied their political and civil rights in the state's attempt to maintain control over opposition forces. Political protests of even the most benign sort are regularly put down with brutality and overwhelming force. Human Rights Watch also reports regular, arbitrary arrest of street children in Cairo and Alexandria. The authorities subject them to beatings, sexual abuse, and deny them access to basic human amenities.

²⁰ GENDER ISSUES

Egyptian society is marked with sexual inequality in myriad forms. The streets of Cairo are world renowned among female travelers as being rife with sexual harassing behavior. Men routinely follow, whistle at, and in other ways humiliate women, both Egyptians and tourists. Human Rights Watch reports that both family and criminal law continue to discriminate against women. Criminal law is lax in legislating against violence against women and where laws do exist, they are routinely ignored. A well documented incident occurred in October 2006 in a busy downtown area in which gangs of men, celebrating the end of holy month of Ramadan, attacked scores of women on the streets as police looked on doing nothing. Several women were set upon by dozens of crazed men who stripped them naked. Much of this violence was captured on mobile phone videos and distributed around the world via the Internet.

Small steps in improving the rights of women have been taken in very recent times. In 2007, the Egyptian judiciary received its first female judges and in June 2007, the government banned female genital mutilation.

²¹ BIBLIOGRAPHY

Abed-Kotob, Sana. *Egypt's Political Instability: The Analysis of Influential Factors.* Ph.D. Dissertation. College Park, MD: University of Maryland, 1992.

Abdelhadi, Magdi. "Cairo Streets Target Women." BBC News Online. 1 November 2006 http://news.bbc.co.uk/2/hi/middle_east/6106500.stm (September 2008).

Handoussa, Heba. *The Burden of Public Service Employment and Remuneration: A Case Study of Egypt.* Monograph commissioned by the International Labor Office, Geneva, May 1988.

Human Rights Watch. *Country Summary: Egypt.* 2008, www.hrw.org (September 2008).

Ibrahim, Saad Eddin. "Reform and Frustration in Egypt." In *Journal of Democracy* 7, no. 4, (1996): 125–35.

Metz, Helen Chapin, ed. *Egypt: A Country Study.* Washington, DC: Federal Research Division, Library of Congress, 1991.

Oweiss, Ibrahim M., ed. *The Political Economy of Contemporary Egypt.* Washington, D.C.: Georgetown University, Center for Contemporary Arab Studies, 1990.

Slackman, Michael. "Generation Faithful Stifled, Egypt's Young Turn to Islamic Fervor." New York Times. 17 Feb 2008.

Sullivan, Denis. *Private Voluntary Organizations in Egypt: Islamic Development, Private Initiative, and State Control.* Gainesville, FL: University Press of Florida, 1994.

Wikan, Unni. *Tomorrow, God Willing: Self-Made Destinies in Cairo.* Chicago: University of Chicago Press, 1996.

—revised by J. Henry

EMBU

PRONUNCIATION: EM-bo
LOCATION: Embu in the Eastern Province of Kenya
POPULATION: About 450,000
LANGUAGE: Kiembu
RELIGION: Christianity; indigenous Embu religion
RELATED ARTICLES: Vol. 1: Kenyans

¹ INTRODUCTION

The Embu are a Bantu-speaking people who are closely related to the Gikuyu of Ndia and Gicugu to the west, the Mbeere and the Kamba to the southeast, and the Chuka and the Meru to the north. As the Embu proverb goes, *Mwana ti wa muciari umwe*—a child does not belong to one parent. These communities share common ancestry and origins. Despite speaking a Bantu language (Bantu came from central Africa), the agricultural Embu and Mbeere are one of the few Kenyan peoples whose oral traditions seem to locate their origins within Kenya, in fact very close to their present location to the southeast of Kirinyaga (Mount Kenya). Tradition also speaks of a time when they were hunter-gatherers and used to live in "caves," meaning rock shelters or hollow trees in forests, much as the indigenous Kenyan groups of hunter-gathers such as the Okiek ("Ndorobo") did until the 20th century. Tradition further states that the Ndorobo interacted with the Embu a long time ago before the Ndorobo were either displaced or left when the forests began to be converted to farmland.

The origin of the Embu is still unclear, but there are two explanations. From historical accounts, the Embu are believed to have migrated from the Congo Basin together with their close relatives, the Kikuyu and Meru People. This migration was perhaps due to conflicts like slavery. It is believed that they migrated as far as the Kenyan Coast, since the Meru elders refer to Mpwa (Pwani or Coast) as their origin. The conflicts there, perhaps slave trade by Arabs, forced them to retreat northeast to the interior of Kenya, and they settled by the slopes of Mt. Kenya. They refer to this location as the place of the Lord, the owner of the snow ("Nyaga") or ("Njeru" meaning white)—hence the name "Mwenenyaga" or "Mwenenjeru."

Oral history on the other hand traces the Embu to the Northeastern Bantu who came from a dispersed area in the Taita hills near Mount Kilimanjaro. From here, this Bantu group migrated to the coast, then turned northward to a mythical place called Shungwaya between the Tana and Juba rivers in Somalia. Shungwaya became the second dispersal area from which various Bantu groups started moving out about AD 1200-1300. One such group, known as the Nyika, migrated northeast and then southward to the region of Mount Kenya. During the migration, the Nyika broke up into other smaller groups that are now known as the Kamba, Gikuyu, Meru, Chuka, Embu, and Mbeere. It is likely that the Embu arrived in their present home by AD 1425. They fought and expelled a people known as the Gumba, who were the original inhabitants of the territory.

On the contrary, the Embu ancestral origin myth goes on to indicate that the Embu have been on their land since the beginning of time. Embu mythology claims that the Embu people originated from Mbue Njeru in the interior of Embu, close

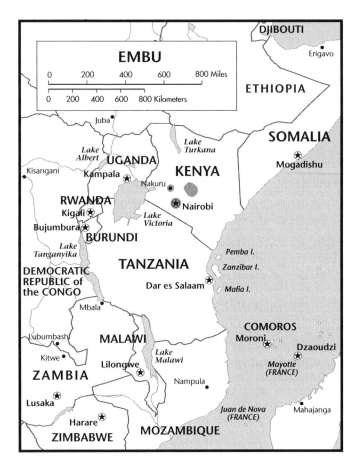

own territory. The Embu also fought with the Maasai, who came from the south to raid for cattle, and the British, who colonized Kenya in 1920.

The battles against the British were ideologically different from the previous ones. In 1900, the British built the first administrative post at Fort Hall to control the rebellious Gikuyu. By 1904, the Gikuyu of Ndia and Gicugu, Embu's neighbors, had been conquered by the British. From here, the British organized military expeditions against the Embu who had refused to accept British rule peacefully. With the help of the Mbeere and the Gikuyu of Ndia, the British conquered the Embu around 1906. However, Embu resistance against foreign rule continued, more in the form of passive rather than armed resistance. To maintain order, Embu Station was established, first as a military station, and then as an administrative center. The last time the Embu fought against British rule was in the 1950s during the Mau Mau rebellion, which lasted for almost 10 years. This time the Embu and the Meru joined the Gikuyu to fight for Kenya's independence, which came on 12 December 1963.

The Embu were traditionally organized into a patrilineal system through which descent was traced and inheritance handed down. Embu society was first divided into moieties (two major social groups), which consisted of numerous clans. In turn, each clan was made up of various lineages, with a lineage consisting of a number of minor lineages or extended families. Within this system of social organization, Embu males were also divided into age-groups which represented different levels of authority, status, and responsibility. Along with the age-group system existed an administrative ruling structure with the father as the senior authority within a household, above which came the ridge council serving as a minor lineage in a particular area. Above the ridge council were the clan council and the warrior leaders' council. The warrior council executed the decisions or rules made by the clan council. The warrior leaders' council also made and executed decisions regarding war, the protection of people and property, and the execution of justice. Above all was a council known as Kiama Kia Ngome, a type of supreme court which dealt with civil and criminal justice for the entire Embu country. It heard and made decisions on the most serious cases such as murder and sorcery. All of these (mostly judicial) councils were made up of elders who were highly regarded for their wisdom, fairness, and religious/medical knowledge. These elders, regardless of the council level, were known as *athamaki* (rulers), and they ruled the Embu. There were no chiefs in Embu until the British "invented" them.

Today, the Embu participate in the democratic political process. Initially, the Embu people never aligned themselves with a single political outfit. They spread out across the ruling party (for instance KANU) and even the opposition (for instance the Democratic Party and FORD-Asili) in the 1990s. Embu politics would not be complete without the mention of the Nyaga family that has dominated local politics since pre-colonial Kenya. However, in the 2000s the Embu have largely aligned with and overwhelmingly voted alongside their Agikuyu cousins in what is commonly known as the Mt. Kenya caucus or otherwise the Gikuyu, Embu, Meru Association (GEMA or MEGA). Most of the Embu as of 2008 belonged to the Party of National Unity (PNU) which was one of the partners in Kenya's Grand Coalition government.

to Runyenjes town. The mythology claims that God (Ngai) created Mwenendega and gave him a beautiful wife by the famous Mbui Njeru waterfall—hence her name "Ciurunji." The couple was blessed with wealth, and their descendants populated the rest of Embu. The Embu believe that they descended from Mwenendega who lived in a small grove, which now bears his name, near the present location of the town of Runyenjes. This grove is still protected as a sacred place. One day Mwenendega saw a very beautiful woman bathing in a stream nearby. Her name was Nveta, and it is said that she was not an earthly woman. After much persuasion and praises of her beauty, she agreed to live with him and not return to her people. They had many children. Their first two children were a boy called Kembu and a girl called Werimba. When Kembu impregnated Werimba, the two were expelled from home. They founded their new home elsewhere and bore children who also married each other and bore more children. All these children came to be known popularly as "children of Kembu," and later, Embu, in short.

Since Mount Kenya lies within the lands of this cluster, these groups collectively are known as the Mount Kenya Bantu. Although over the years they have traded with each other, there are also many accounts of the wars that they have fought with each other either to capture livestock (cattle, sheep, and goats) or gain territory belonging to the other. Two of the more famous battles occurred around 1870 and 1890 when the celebrated war hero, Njeru Karuku, led the Embu successfully against the Chuka. In 1900 the Embu defeated the attacking Kamba and drove them back across the Tana River into their

2 LOCATION AND HOMELAND

Embu is located on the southeastern slopes of Mount Kenya, where the altitude ranges from 1,100 m to 2,100 m (3,500-7,000 ft) above sea level. It is situated between longitudes 37°E and 38°E and latitudes 0°S. The most important geographical feature is Mount Kenya, which stands at 5,199 m (17,058 ft) above sea level. On a clear day, the permanent ice on the mountain shines very brightly, projecting unimaginable beauty and power, while the twin peaks, Lenana and Batian, stand out majestically. The total area is about 714 sq km (276 sq mi). Embu is part of the Eastern Province of Kenya. The capital town is also called Embu and serves as the district and provincial administrative center. To the south of Embu are to be found their cousins, the Mbeere people, in Mbeere District. Previously, the Embu and Mbeere were in one district, Embu District, and just referred to as the Embu people. To the west, Embu neighbors are the Kikuyu in Kirinyaga and Nyeri districts. The Meru people in Meru South District border Embu to the Southeast.

The numerically smaller Mbeere (around 100,000, as compared with an Embu population of around 450,000) live to the south of the Embu in the lower Kiangombe Hills. Despite their proximity to the British during the colonial period (Embu town was a major colonial center), the Mbeere have always kept themselves apart (and have been kept apart) from the Kenyan mainstream. The Kiangombe Hills are only barely fertile and poorly watered, dominated by thorn scrub and dust, which meant that the British had little interest in the area or the tribe, who were consequently left to themselves. As a result, some aspects of traditional culture lingered longer in Mbeere than they did in Embu, although nowadays they are both pretty much part of modern Kenya.

In 1918, the population of the Embu was estimated at 53,000 people. This population reached 85,177 people by 1962; 101,770 by 1969; and 180,400 by 1979. The Embu constitute roughly 2% of the Kenyan population. Some 17% of the Embu live in major urban centers like Nairobi, Mombasa, and Nakuru. By 1989, the population of Embu was projected to reach 228,144 people, increasing to 265,769 by 1993. In 2008 the Embu population was about 450,000. The population estimate may include Chuka and Mwimbi-Muthambi. Between 1969 and 1993, the Embu population growth rate ranged from 4.1% to 3.1% per year. This, coupled with a lack of employment opportunities in the rural areas, is causing many people, especially males, to migrate to the urban centers. However, most Embu, like many Africans, are culturally and economically tied to the land, and most of those who move to the cities maintain strong links to the rural homeland to which they eventually return, die, and are buried. The urban residents are also the ones who introduce elements of modernization to the rural areas.

3 LANGUAGE

Kiembu (the language of the Embu) belongs to a large cluster of languages known as Bantu. It is a language that is rich with proverbs and idioms. Although not emphasized today, mastery of proverbs and idioms once demonstrated intelligence and brought a person honor and respect. By using proverbs, people could talk about a particular subject or person without being specific or openly ridiculing a person, thereby avoiding social antagonism. But the greatest mastery in the use of proverbs and idioms was the choice of context in which the intended message was conveyed without ambiguity. For instance, the proverb, "Hungry stomachs have no ears," can mean many things, but if it is invoked in the context of a case hearing, it means the council needs a fee from both parties, usually in the form of a goat, to be eaten by the elders as they continue to listen to the case. In the context of widespread civil disobedience, the meaning is that hungry people are poor listeners to the advice or rule of their rulers.

One can also learn a great deal about the Embu traditions, social norms, and individual behavior from the names given to people. Traditionally the Embu derived most of their names from animals, such as Njiru or Mbogo (buffalo), Nthia (antelope), Njoka (snake), Ndwiga (giraffe), Njuki (bee), Njogu (elephant), Nyaga or Kivuti (ostrich), Ngoroi (columbus monkey), or Munyi (rhinoceros). The reason for this is unclear, but one explanation is that Embu parents, who lost many children in infancy, wanted to ensure that their children would grow to maturity, just as the young of wild animals did, without much care. Other Embu names came from natural phenomena such as Mbura (rain), Riua (sun), Nduma (darkness), etc. Some other names were, and still are, derived from behaviors associated with certain well-known individuals. For instance, a mother might name her son Kinyua (one who drinks much) after a grandfather who drank too much porridge or beer. A daughter may be named Marigu after a female relative who had the habit of carrying food wherever she went, or Maitha if she were a cruel or harsh woman.

Kiembu or Kimbeere are dialects of the same language, with 85% lexical similarity between them. Also closely related are the languages of their geographical neighbors, the Kikuyu and Chuka (73% similarity), Kamba (66%), and Meru (63–65%). Up to 70% also speak Swahili.

4 FOLKLORE

To the Embu, the myth about their origins from Mwenendega and Nveta remains the most important of all their myths and folk tales. However, the most fascinating part of the myth, and one that draws fear and reverence, concerns Nveta's real identity and clan membership. One day, as Nveta and Mwenendega were drinking beer, the latter asked her why no beer or any other gift had ever been sent to them from her people. Mwenendega also wanted to know who her people really were and where they resided. All of a sudden, Nveta became very angry and ordered the children into the house. She looked up to heaven as if she were praying and within a short moment there was lightning and thunder that had not been heard before in the land of the Embu. Very heavy rain fell that completely flooded their home, covering their house and their livestock. After that, Mwenendega and Nveta disappeared and could only be seen by good fortune.

Other heroes of the Embu include famous prophets, medicine men, and warriors. Ireri wa Irugi (*wa* stands for "son of") was perhaps the most famous of all the prophets. It is said that he was able to communicate with Mwene Njeru (God), and that is why he was able to prophecy future events. One such event, and the most famous, was the coming of the white people. He warned people that he had seen strangers coming from the east towards Kirinyaga (Mt. Kenya). They had with them an iron-mouthed animal that would be used to collect all nations (ethnic groups) to one place where they would be helpless. The coming of the British soldiers from the eastern side of

Embu land, and the subsequent conquest of the Embu, is seen as the fulfillment of the prophecy.

Gacogo wa Karaini was regarded as the highest religious leader of the Embu. He was also a skilled medicine man and circumciser. Being a religious leader, people from all over Embu and beyond sought his blessings and advice. His medicine and charms had the reputation of being very effective in curing various ailments and in protecting one from any harm, such as sorcery. He was so revered that people addressed him as Mutia, or "the respected one."

Mwoca wa Minano is remembered as one of the greatest Embu warriors ever to live. His courage and skill in planning war tactics and raids won him much respect among all the people. He is credited for maintaining a very strong defense on the eastern border with the Gikuyu. He is most remembered for leading Embu warriors in a fierce battle against the British in about 1903. During this battle he killed a white soldier and took away his gun. When it was realized that the dead white soldier was uncircumcised, Mwoca was very disappointed because he thought all along he had fought with a "man," and not a "child."

5 RELIGION

The origins of the Embu religion are not known, but by the time the white people came, the Embu had a very well-established religion.

The Embu worshipped one God whom they called Mwene Njeru, meaning "the owner of the sun." Despite the spread of Christianity, some people, particularly very old men and women, still believe in Mwene Njeru, who is omnipresent. When Mwene Njeru visits Embu, he has favorite places, of which the most important is Kirinyaga. From the mountaintop he can see the whole of Embu and what the people are doing. Other places include all the sacred groves, *matiiri* (sacred places of age-groups), and very big trees. Mwene Njeru is believed to be the source of all goodness, but he also punishes the people when they disobey him or do wrong to one another. People, led by the most sacred elders, sacrifice a goat that is all one color to Mwene Njeru to ask or thank him for his blessings, to end a catastrophe (e.g., drought, epidemics), and for his protection. The concern for long life is at the heart of the Embu religion. To live into very old age, and therefore to enjoy the respect and privileges accorded to the elders, is a clear demonstration of how much one is blessed by Mwene Njeru.

The Embu also believe in the spirits or *ngoma*. However, they distinguish between two kinds of spirits: the "evil spirits," and the "ancestral spirits." Evil spirits are malevolent—they bring misery to the people without provocation. Even when seen, they are not easily recognizable, and sometimes they may be heard singings but are not visible. They are not offered sacrifices but rather are bribed with some meat or animal blood. Ancestral spirits, on the other hand, are good spirits who protect people from evil spirits and other misfortune. But they also discipline people when they are disobedient. People appease them with sacrifices but do not worship them as they worship Mwene Njeru. When seen, they are easily recognizable as deceased relatives. It is believed that they form families, raise children, cultivate, and keep animals, just as they used to when they were alive.

The Embu have a saying that "no one dies a natural death." Death is always attributed to some evil magic or sorcery.

Events that are beyond human explanation are often attributed to the power of magic and sorcery. For instance, why should a tree fall and kill only one of the two people standing by it? To the Embu, this is not a question of chance but rather of somebody using magic to kill another person. There is also the belief that some people have the skill to use magic and sorcery to turn others into "fools," cats, dogs, snakes, etc. Faced by such powerful forces, people turn to diviners and medicine men for protection.

No accurate figures are available on Embu subscription to the Christian and other foreign religions: a recent estimate was two-thirds traditional religion, one-third Christian, though it seems much more likely that the reverse is true, and that Christians are in the majority.

6 MAJOR HOLIDAYS

The only holidays that the Embu celebrate are the national holidays such as Independence Day, Labor Day, Christmas Day, and New Year's Day. These holidays are marked by celebrations, which involve eating and beer-drinking, and of course, those formally employed do not have to show up for work. The most important national holiday is Independence Day, which is celebrated on December 12 every year. This is the day on which Kenya gained its independence from Britain in 1963, ending nearly 100 years of colonial rule. There are marches in major urban centers by school children, administrative police, and various other organized groups. In the capital city of Nairobi, celebrations include parades by various units of armed forces, an air show by the Kenyan Air Force, traditional dances by various ethnic groups, performances by school choirs, and lastly, a speech by the president of Kenya. Various dignitaries from overseas and from other African countries are also invited to attend.

7 RITES OF PASSAGE

In the old days among the Embu, the birth of a child was celebrated as a special event because a child was viewed as the "wealth" of a lineage or clan and also brought recognition and respect to both parents. Failure to bear a child was, and still is, viewed as a misfortune on both parents or as the result of a curse or sorcery. This could result in a man either marrying a second wife or the dissolution of the marriage. The birth of a boy was announced with five ululations (*ngemi*) and the birth of a girl with four. After ululations, the baby was given a name. Four days (for a girl) or five days (for a boy) after birth, a ritual known as *kuumagarua*, or "to be taken out" (to be introduced to the outside world), was performed. An older girl presented the baby girl with a tiny bundle of firewood, similar to that carried by adult women, and an older boy presented the baby boy with a small bow and arrow. This symbolized the lifetime chores, and the different worlds, of the two sexes. Today this ritual is not performed. Most children are born in hospitals and, instead of going through the ritual of being "taken out," they are baptized in church in accordance with the teachings of the parents' denomination. Immediately after birth, the mother gives the baby an Embu name and during baptism the baby receives a Christian name.

After birth, circumcision for boys and clitoridectomy for girls were the most crucial rituals in a person's life-cycle. A boy's first instruction in tribal knowledge came from his father around the homestead's fireplace, but a man's life as a full member of the tribe began in earnest at his circumcision shortly after puberty. His readiness to be circumcised was indicated by the payment of a goat called *mburi ya nduo*, the "goat of circumcision." Another goat was paid when the time for circumcision came, which entitled him to get married. This goat was called *mburi ya nthumbi* (the "goat of the cap"), and was named after a cap made for him by recently circumcised men to indicate his newly acquired status. Traditionally, boys were circumcised between the ages of 18 and 22, while the girls underwent clitoridectomy between the ages of 14 and 18. The ritual initiated both girls and boys into adulthood. The girls had to be initiated before their first menstruation; otherwise, they could only marry a married man.

During the ceremony both boys and girls were expected to prove their courage, and thereby their readiness to accept adult responsibilities, by withstanding much pain without crying or moving. In Kenya, clitoridectomy is now illegal and the practice has almost disappeared. However, the circumcision of boys is still viewed as very important among the Embu. Currently, the circumcision ritual has been transformed from that of a public ceremony to a very private affair carried out in the hospital with the initiate under general anesthesia. But regardless, it is still associated with courage and responsibility. Today, one does not immediately assume the responsibilities of marriage but may go on with schooling, get a job, and then prepare to marry. Marriage, whether in the old days or at present, is considered very important and everybody is expected to marry and have children. It is by bearing children that the Embu think of a person as "complete."

On matters of death, the Embu did not bury their dead before the 1920s. They believed that the burying of the dead body was like burying "fertility." Rather, they left the dead bodies in the forest under a tree. Those who handled the dead body underwent a cleansing ritual to rid them of "pollution." But most significantly, the Embu believed in life after death, that the body's spirit did not die but lived on and, depending on the behavior of the living relatives, could be benevolent or malevolent. Today, the Embu inter their dead through a religious burial. There are no public cemeteries. A person is buried on the land owned by the family. Usually only the members of a family know where the grave is because it is marked with just a few stones or some planted flowers. The relatives of the deceased are exempted from work on the day of death, and this custom is still observed today. Death, as the last stage in the life cycle, is one event that the Embu do not celebrate.

8 INTERPERSONAL RELATIONS

Greetings, as a sign of politeness, well-wishing, and good behavior, constitute one of the most important aspects of Embu culture. Failing to greet somebody is always taken as an insult, immediately creates tension between the parties involved, and almost always results in a harsh criticism or rebuke by the person not greeted. The common and formal greeting begins by asking a person about his or her health. After the appropriate response, the two parties shake hands. One should not, under any circumstance, refuse to shake another person's hand. People of generally the same age or status let their eyes meet as they greet each other and shake hands. Young people greeting elderly people usually avoid eye contact, as a sign of respect, by looking either down or sideways. Among the Embu there is no such thing as times for visiting or not visiting. A household not

visited regularly is said to lack hospitality. A visitor is always offered food or something to drink, like tea. If it is during a mealtime, a visitor joins in sharing whatever food is available. There is an Embu saying that "a mother cooks more than her family can finish" so that there is always some for a visitor. Refusing an offer of food, without an appropriate explanation, is considered an insult to the person offering the food. More seriously, the refusal may be taken to imply that the food is poisoned or bewitched.

Dating practice has changed from a very strict code of behavior to a more relaxed and less culturally structured practice. When a boy meets a girl that he likes, he may straight away express his love for her, or send another boy or girl to convey his love message. He may also write to the girl asking her to be his girlfriend. If the girl's response is favorable, then the two start seeing each other regularly and in public. The boy may also start visiting her in her home more openly. However, dating is not expected to lead to marriage until the boy's father goes to visit (at the son's request) the girl's father to seek permission for marriage and to initiate marriage plans.

For a long time men from neighboring communities like the Gikuyu, Meru, and Kamba have come to get brides from the Embu, while the Embu men enjoy high regard from marriageable girls in the same tribes. With the advent of Kenya nationalism, this high regard has permeated to the entire nation, and now the Embu form one respected unit of the Kenyan social fabric.

Value is also attached to the extended family and Embu nomenclature enhances this relationship. Embu parents name each of their children after one of their relatives on either side, but never after themselves. Those relatives, to use Western terms, may be the child's grandparents, aunts, uncles, and even distant relatives. The main significance of this naming practice is that: (1) it gives honor or recognition to the person after whom the child is named; (2) it creates a special relationship between the child and the person she or he is named after; and (3) creates a particular bond between the parents and the child and the person after whom the child is named. All this influences and dictates the behavior between all the individuals involved.

On intercommunity relations, the Mbeere are closely allied to the Embu, to whom they are related. In times of famine—which strikes the Mbeere more frequently than the Embu—the Embu would supply staple food like maize and beans in return for goats, skins, sorghum, and pigeon peas. Historically, the Embu also fought for the Mbeere, on a famous occasion in which the Kamba tried to oust the Mbeere from their land. The Embu and Mbeere jointly own sacred groves (*matiiri*) in Mwea, which is one of their traditional places of origin.

The Embu were fierce warriors who, although rarely raiding other tribes, always stood firm in defense of their territory and people. Many occasions are on record where the Embu had to fiercely repulse Kamba and even the dreaded Maasai invasions. They also rose against the British in the Mau Mau fight for Kenya's independence. The fact that the tribe was and continues to be considerably small explains the relatively small impact on the history of Kenya.

9 LIVING CONDITIONS

The standard of living is very low because of very low income and lack of economic opportunities. Like many other people in the rural areas of Kenya, the Embu live under very difficult health conditions. Most families use pit latrines, obtain water from the rivers, and very rarely get good medical care. The Ruvingazi and Kapingazi Rivers border Embu town to the west and the east respectively and are a key source of domestic water to many Embu families. Health services, mostly provided by the government, are inadequate and very poor. In order to treat less serious ailments, people buy medicine from retail shops or rely on herbalists.

Until the "Emergency" of the 1950s, when the Mau Mau began their fight for freedom, five or six family homesteads constituted a typical settlement. The "Emergency" however led to the creation of larger villages, both for protection, and under pressure from the British who wanted tighter control over the area. People built their own houses using locally available materials. Houses were traditionally the classic thatched cone roofs on a circular base, but are nowadays mostly rectangular buildings covered with corrugated or flat metal sheets, although the traditional round houses are more common among the Mbeere. The walls are generally still constructed in the traditional way, with narrow spaces between upright poles stuffed with leaves and mud. Apart from the family house, the other homestead structures were a kitchen (sometimes part of the family house), the man's house, a grain store, and millet store. However, some wealthier people are beginning to build stone houses with ceramic tile roofs. In most houses there is no electricity or telephone. Fire and kerosene lamps are the primary source of light.

Most families make their living through small-scale agriculture. Coffee and tea are the main cash crops. Traveling is mainly by *matatu* (privately operated small van/truck-like vehicles), bicycles, and walking. People walk as much as 32 km (20 mi) in a single day.

¹⁰ FAMILY LIFE

The Embu are a patrilineal society in which women are subordinate to men. Women are assigned all the domestic chores of child care, food preparation and storage, family care, firewood collection, fetching water, and growing food. Women are also involved in the marketing and buying of small amounts of food crops. This labor burden increases if the husband is away on wage employment. Women who have attained higher education and have formal employment are able to escape this labor burden.

Families generally live on small farms in compounds. Family size among the Embu varies widely depending on the family type. Families are predominantly nuclear. On average there are about seven people per household. There is also the extended family consisting of parents, married sons and their families, and unmarried daughters. In this type of family, there may be as many as over 25 people living together. Polygyny is common. A man can take several wives if he can afford it, although nowadays this is becoming rare.

The Embu people practice exogamous marriage. Marrying within one's clan is taboo as incest because all clan members are relatives. However, with the breakdown of the clan system, clan affiliation is becoming less significant and the rule of exogamy is almost forgotten. Consequently, marriages are taking place between clan relatives. Marriage involves the payment of bride-wealth to the bride's family. In the old days, bride-wealth used to be in the form of livestock, i.e., cattle and goats, but at present, it is paid in the form of money. Contrary to popular misconception, people do not think of the bride-wealth practice as "buying" a wife. It is thought of as a way to thank the parents for bearing and bringing up a daughter to maturity and thereby making it possible for a man to have a wife. Bride-wealth payment is also a measure of a man's commitment to his wife and responsibility for his family. However, like many other traditional practices, bride-wealth is also disappearing, especially among the highly educated. A mother and her children lived in the main family house where the household goods were stored. Marriageable girls lived with their mothers, and suitors were entertained there. The father would sometimes share his house with his uncircumcised sons, but once circumcised but not yet married they would build their own dwelling or live in the grain store.

Family size was an indicator of a man's social and economic success. A man's riches were formerly judged by how many wives and children he had; that is, family size was an indicator of the social and economic status of a person. For example, Senior Chief Muruatetu, probably one of the most famous Embians, not only had 16 wives and many children, but he was also a respected administration officer for the colonial government and independent Kenya. An entire village bears his name, and a school is named after him.

¹¹ CLOTHING

The Embu used to wear clothes made of animal (sheep, goat, cattle) skins. These clothes gave way to cotton clothes and Western-style clothing introduced in the early 1900s. Today, clothing is just as modern as in any other modern society. Women's clothing is more colorful than men's, which is usually one solid color. Women do not wear pants, as men do. Very little jewelry is worn (e.g., earrings), and only young women wear it. Before the changes brought by modernization, both men and women wore jewelry (necklaces, bracelets, earrings, ankle and knee bracelets), though women wore more than men. Both men and women also decorated their bodies in the same fashion, e.g., scarification, filed teeth, V-shaped fillings between the upper two incisors, and pierced and extended ear lobes. The youth of both sexes wore long hair, while the elderly had clean-shaven heads. Because of all these changes, there is really no traditional dress. The dress code now tends towards the Western mode.

¹² FOOD

A wide variety of food crops are cultivated in Embu. These include maize, beans, bananas, potatoes, yams, arrowroots, cassava, and sugar cane. In addition, a few animals, e.g., cattle, sheep, goats, and chickens, are raised. It is primarily from these food sources that the Embu make their dishes. There are three main foods that are made: *nyenyi, kithere*, and *ngima. Nyenyi* is the most traditional of the Embu dishes. It is a mixture of maize, beans, bananas, and green vegetables. It is cooked in a big clay pot. Once cooked, the ingredients are mashed together until well mixed. *Kithere* is basically a mixture of maize and beans. Today, people add to this mixture some vegetables, potatoes, and meat, but the ingredients are not mashed together. *Ngima*, popularly known as *ugali* in Kiswahili (also described as thick porridge), has become very popular, especially in urban centers. It is simply a mixture of white corn flour (*mutu wa mbembe*) and water. Water is boiled in a pot, then corn flour is added until the thickness required is reached. The mixture is cooked for 10–15 minutes while turning it with a wooden spatula (*mwiko*). It is then eaten with meat stew, bean stew, or even roasted meat.

Today the most special foods are *mucere* (rice) and *chapati* (unleavened flat bread). These are expensive foods that have to be purchased from shops and are therefore only served on special occasions, such as when entertaining important guests, or on holidays such as Christmas. The traditional special food that is still popular is roasted goat meat. The slaughter of a goat and the roasting of the meat is a practice done on very special occasions. To slaughter a goat for a person is a demonstration of high respect for that person or the importance of the friendship that exists between the two people. Tea has replaced millet and sorghum porridge as the common daily beverage. It is taken any time of the day, unlike other foods that are eaten as midday and evening meals.

Household utensils are rare in most homes. The most important are modern cooking pots, plates, cups, and silverware. Although clay pots are still in use, they are not regularly used. The wooden *mwiko* has remained unchanged and has actually grown in popularity. Most of the utensils in many households are imports and have for the most part replaced the traditional ones.

Also gone are most of the food taboos that were once observed by the people. For instance, it was taboo for: (1) men and women who had drunk cattle blood to eat the meat of wild game; (2) circumcised men and women to eat chicken, for it was considered children's food; (3) women to eat eggs; (4) men to drink milk after eating the meat of wild game; and (5) women to eat the meat of a cow that had died in labor. The only taboos that are still observed are those that prohibit the eating of monkeys, clawed animals, and snakes.

Food is very central to Embu customs, particularly those that govern people's behaviors and attitudes towards others. Food is something to be shared, and to be accused of being a selfish person (*mundu muthunu*) is not only a terrible insult but also labels a person as unworthy to receive other people's assistance, including food. When there is no food to be offered to a visitor or a person passing by, an explanation is usually offered. The Embu have many stories and proverbs that teach the morality of food-sharing. Also related to the moral significance of sharing is the belief that it is very bad manners to try to eat more than others, particularly if the people are eating from the same bowl.

13 EDUCATION

With the free primary and secondary education programs undertaken by the Kenyan government since 2003, the literacy rate in Kenya in 2008 stood at about 49%. Among the Embu, literacy is very high because of an overwhelming enthusiasm by parents to send their children to school. Good education is viewed as the path to a better life both for the children and the parents. Children are the social security of their parents in old age, and as such, parents invest as much as they can in the education of their children.

Under the current educational system, children start school at the age of six. They spend eight years in primary education, four in secondary (high school) education, and four in university education. Most children now finish primary and secondary levels, but few get into the university. It is the dream of

every parent to have a child go to the university because of the increased opportunities for a better-paying job upon graduation. The cost of education and the rate of unemployment are both increasing, and these factors could lower the level of literacy in Kenya.

14 CULTURAL HERITAGE

Among the Embu, as in many African cultures, music and dancing are inseparable. Once the musical instruments set the rhythm, people begin to sing and dance. Today, most of the dancing and singing is performed in churches and in elementary and secondary schools. School children practice various traditional dances for competition with other schools. There are also dance troupes that entertain visiting leaders and dignitaries with traditional songs and dances. Through traditional dances and songs, as well as stories, riddles, and proverbs, the Embu traditions, folklore, social norms, and history are passed from one generation to the next. The publication of the book *Ndai, Nthimo, Na Ng'ano Iri Ukua Wa Aembu* in Kiembu has become an invaluable record of Embu riddles, proverbs, and stories for future generations.

The rich local cultural and natural heritage also feeds the tourism industry. Much abounds to entertain tourists and visitors, not least the Embu people themselves who carry about their daily life with a deep sense of filial attachment to each other. They are a hospitable people, almost always welcoming visitors and eager to help. This has endeared them to their neighbors and to strangers from afar. The district plays host to the renowned Mt. Kenya to the north. Mountaineering therefore preoccupies most locals and visitors. Mt. Kenya remains a unique tourist attraction with hordes of foreigners and local people flocking to its slopes to savor the allure of its beauty and majesty. Numerous expeditions set out each year to scale the slopes to the mountain top. It is an enthralling experience, especially watching the sun rise in the horizons in the early morning from the highest Batian mountain peak. This climb is a real achievement; it calls for great stamina and resilience.

Other attractions in the region are the huge Karue hill towering high along the Embu-Meru highway. It is a magnificent view, made of a huge crested rock, at the top of which has grown two unique eucalyptus trees. From such a bird's eye view, one can see the entire of Embu. Nearby this hill are two magnificent waterfalls in close proximity which color the sky in white as their waters fall down, then converge to form one big Ena river that then meanders downstream to encircle the Karue hill. Completing the scenery is the Kirimiri hill nearby. Though not open for tourism, it is home to a diverse array of wildlife.

Generally, it seems likely that the last hallmarks of Embu culture may disappear over the next few decades as Western culture and Christianity continue to erode traditional values. Already, much if not all of the traditional music has vanished, and the relevance of traditional forms of government, such as the Nthuke Age-Sets, are becoming increasingly obscure.

15 WORK

The Embu are an industrious lot regarding the wide variety of economic activities they are engaged in. They value hard work and scorn laziness. Hard work, as the Embu say, builds character and prosperity. Hard work also makes a person highly eligible for marriage. Every healthy person is expected to work to benefit oneself and others. There is a very clear division of labor by gender. The Embu have successfully taken up modern lifestyles, as shown by excellence both in academia and the overall national growth. Numerous schools and colleges train hundreds of youth each year to become well equipped not just for agricultural work but also for formal employment and entrepreneurship.

The Embu traditionally rely on agriculture, though a large number have become traders. The Embu are farmers who also rear cows, goats, and sheep. With the advent of colonialism, many cash crops were introduced. For long these have offered a lucrative alternative source of livelihood for the people. The most widespread cash crops to date are coffee, tea, and macadamia nuts. These are mainly grown for sale with little being processed for domestic consumption.

In the formal sector there are areas of employment that tend to be dominated by males (e.g., administration and management) and by females (e.g., nursing, secretarial work, and primary-level teaching). The same work ethic is expected of students by their parents. A man's riches were formerly judged by how many wives and children he had.

16 SPORTS

For almost everybody, both children and adults, soccer is the most important sport. To boys, anything that is round, regardless of size, is a soccer ball. One of the most popular radio programs is the broadcast of national and international soccer tournaments. Although soccer is mostly a school-organized sport, the spectators are local people. For girls, netball (somewhat similar to basketball) is very popular and is also a school-organized sport. Track and field sports, or "athletics," are also very popular in schools at every level and are highly encouraged by the government. In addition to all these popular sports, there are many other games that children play, such as jumping rope, to entertain themselves.

17 ENTERTAINMENT AND RECREATION

In the whole of Embu there is only one movie theater, in Embu town. This provides entertainment mostly to urban residents and people with higher incomes. Once in a while there is a mobile cinema vehicle which moves through the rural areas showing films, most of which are educational documentaries. Wealthy families with access to electricity have television sets. Others who can afford television sets but have no electricity run them using solar-energy panels or car batteries. Until recently, people could only see one channel, which was government-controlled. Now there are over eight channels, one of which is CNN. Television shows include those produced locally and those imported from various countries. Old and young men would normally congregate in pubs and homes where DSTV is connected, to watch European soccer and other games.

As mentioned earlier, church choirs and dancing, in some religious sects, also provide some entertainment. Spectator sports such as soccer and athletics provide much needed entertainment. Pop music by Kenyan, African (especially Zairian), and Western artists is very popular with young people.

18 FOLK ART, CRAFTS, AND HOBBIES

The Embu are known for bee-keeping. Beehives are made from a tree trunk and are then hung on a tree for the bees to build honeycombs inside. Women are skilled weavers, particularly using fiber strings to make baskets (ciondo). Fiber strings are stained with vegetable dyes to produce multicolored bands on the baskets. Today, commercially produced strings of different colors are also being used to make very beautifully decorated baskets. Following the reform of the education system, other Embu arts and crafts, such as leatherwork and woodcarving, are being reintroduced to Embu children.

19 SOCIAL PROBLEMS

Over the years, Embu society has experienced rapid population growth. This has resulted in widespread land fragmentation whereby a man has to subdivide his land among his sons. Taken to the third generation, this has resulted in land ownership being fragmented to small strips of land not conducive to economic activity. In lieu of this, landlessness and the subdivision of family land into small plots for the purpose of inheritance are already major social and economic problems. This is creating much tension among family members as well as within the whole society. It has also resulted in food shortages and the inability to raise livestock because of the lack of grazing lands.

Alcoholism, a national problem, is not yet a serious problem in Embu, but conditions are developing that could turn it into a very serious socioeconomic and health problem soon. Following the liberalization of the economy, new and cheap alcoholic drinks commonly known as Keg, high in alcohol content, have been introduced to Embu. They are very popular compared to the high-priced, low-alcohol, bottled beers. The fact that there is very little social stigma attached to alcoholism, and that alcoholism is not viewed as a health problem or disease but rather as an indication of personal weakness and lack of control, may help to increase the problem. There is also a complete absence of any education regarding the consequences of alcoholism. The drinking of alcohol in the rural areas of Embu is primarily a male activity. Women who drink alcohol in public places are looked down upon. But in general, alcoholism among women is also increasing.

20 GENDER ISSUES

Although it appears that Embu society was originally matriarchal, a woman's role today is largely restricted to her functions as wife, mother, and farm worker. There was one woman at the time of the colonial conquest who managed to become chief, but was subsequently betrayed by jealous men. Her name is Cierume. Among the Embu, a woman's life is literally marked by her circumcision at adolescence, which allows her to become married and bear children. It is during this initiation that she begins to acquire knowledge about the realities and responsibilities of life, and the cultural values that surround her. The practice of clitoridectomy is becoming rarer today.

Nonetheless, uncircumcised girls still face stigmatization, and women in that position will usually have to leave their homeland (through choice or by force), for an uncertain future in the slum towns of Nairobi and elsewhere. Change, however, may be in the offing if a recent nongovernmental organization (NGO) report on gender roles among the Embu is correct: as a response to rapid population growth and overcrowding, many respondents declared that roles were no longer gender-based since changing circumstances had led to the disintegration of the indigenous social matrix.

21 BIBLIOGRAPHY

Browne, O. *The Vanishing Tribes of Kenya*. Westport, CT: Negro University Press, 1970.

Embu Historical Texts. Nairobi: East African Literature Bureau, 1974.

Fedders, A. and C. Salvadori. *Peoples and Cultures of Kenya*. Nairobi: Transafrica, 1979.

Haugerud, Angelique. *The Culture of Politics in Modern Kenya*. Cambridge: Cambridge University Press, 1995.

Huntingford, G. W. B. "The Peopling of the Interior of East Africa by its Modern Inhabitants." In *History of East Africa*. Vol. 1, edited by R. Oliver and G. Matthew. London: Oxford University Press, 1967.

Muriuki, G. *A History of the Kikuyu, 1500-1900*. Nairobi: Oxford University Press, 1974.

Mwaniki, K. H. S. *The Living History of the Embu and Mbeere*. Nairobi: Kenya Literature Bureau, 1973.

———. *Ndai, Nthimo na Ng'ano iri Ukua wa Aembu*. Nairobi: East African Literature Bureau, 1971.

Mwaniki, N. "The Consequences of Land Subdivision in Northern Embu." *The Journal of African Policy Studies* 2, no. 1 (1996): 53–87.

Swinimer, Ciarunji Chesina. *Oral Literature of the Embu and Mbeere*. Nairobi: East African Educational Publishers, 1997.

Were, G. S., and D. A. Wilson. *East Africa Through a Thousand Years: A History of the Years AD 1000 to the Present Day*. New York: African Publishing Corporation, 1968.

—revised by M. Njoroge

THE ENGLISH IN SOUTH AFRICA

LOCATION: South Africa
POPULATION: About 3.6 million
LANGUAGE: English
RELIGION: Christianity; Judaism
RELATED ARTICLES: Vol. 5: English

1 INTRODUCTION

Though whites of English-speaking descent make up only about 8% of South Africa's population of 44 million, their culture and their language are powerful influences in a country where more than three-quarters of the people are blacks. English is one of 11 official languages in South Africa (the others are Afrikaans, Ndebele, Pedi, Sotho, Swazi, Tsonga, Tswana, Venda, Xhosa and Zulu) but it is one of the most widely spoken. A foreign visitor to South Africa who speaks only English will have no difficulties at all getting about and being understood. English is the principal language of business and tourism, English-language newspapers are published daily and can be obtained everywhere. Public signs and notices are always posted in English.

With South Africa's economy expanding rapidly into the global market place and with computerized personal communications becoming a feature of the workplace as well as schools and colleges, a good working knowledge of English is regarded as an essential requirement for young South Africans of all communities who want successful careers in business and the professions. English is taught in all the schools, is the medium of instruction (sometimes in addition to Afrikaans) in all universities, and is continuing to be a dominant force in South Africa's young democracy even though the constitution requires recognition of all the official languages.

The international status of English as the language of many of the world's leading countries is one of the reasons for its continued dominance in South Africa. Books, magazines, movies, TV shows and musical recordings flood into the country from the English-speaking world—mostly from the United States and Britain but also to a lesser extent from Canada, Australia, and New Zealand—and are popular and influential. The pop stars and cultural icons of America and England are popular in South Africa too and going to the movies is a regular pastime. South Africa has vibrant media and entertainment industries of its own and, while a local African flavor often adds spice and a special character to these activities and Afrikaans music is undergoing a popular resurgence, the impact of the international English-speaking world is seen clearly in tastes and trends.

Throughout most of the 20th century, South Africa's political life was dominated largely by white Afrikaners, descendants of settlers who began to arrive in the 17th century, mostly from the Netherlands but also from France and Germany. After April 1994, when South Africa became a non-racial democracy and Nelson Mandela was elected the first black president, control of the country passed into the hands of the black majority and apartheid was finally abandoned. Although they were never in political control in the 20th century, Eng-

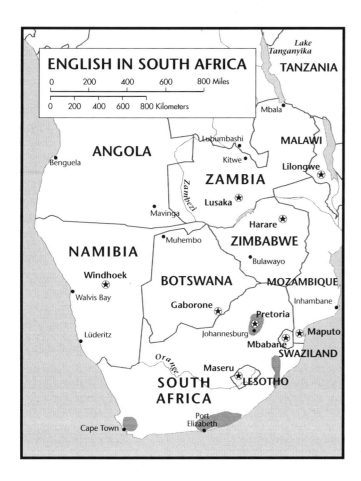

ENGLISH IN SOUTH AFRICA

lish-speaking South Africans were prominent in commerce and industry and the professions throughout much of this period—and remain influential as one of the best-educated and most affluent sectors of the population.

2 LOCATION AND HOMELAND

White English-speaking South Africans have historic and language ties to Britain but they do not regard themselves as British expatriates. They see themselves as South Africans, an important sector of a racially and culturally diverse nation. They live throughout the country but are concentrated mostly in and around the cities and urban areas—the coastal cities of Cape Town, Port Elizabeth, East London and Durban, and the inland cities and towns of Johannesburg, Pretoria, Bloemfontein, Grahamstown, and Kimberley.

South Africa has an estimated 44 million people and about 9.6%, or 4.2 million, are whites. English South Africans make up less than half of that group. Their presence in the country goes back to the end of the 18th century when Britain seized control of the Cape of Good Hope, the first white settlement area in Cape Town, during the Napoleonic Wars. The British government encouraged its citizens to emigrate to the Cape—mostly to establish a buffer between African tribesmen and farming colonists on the eastern frontier—and the first sizable group of 4,000 began to arrive in 1820. These 1820 settlers faced enormous day-to-day difficulties in making their new lives in the wilderness, but they prevailed and brought much needed skills to the colony. Their legacy is still strong, espe-

cially in the eastern Cape around Port Elizabeth, East London, and the university town of Grahamstown.

Their presence also contributed to a major event in South African history—the Great Trek during which Afrikaner farmers migrated inland to escape British rule. The Great Trek, roughly equivalent to America's western migration of the 19th century, brought the Afrikaners (known as the Boers) into conflict with African tribes, notably the Zulus in what is today the province of KwaZulu-Natal. Eventually, the British government went to war with the Zulus, defeating them after a number of bloody battles and establishing the British colony of Natal. At the turn of the century, British forces defeated two republics founded by the migrating Boers in the Anglo-Boer War (now known as the South African War) and the whole of the country was incorporated into the British Empire. In 1910 South Africa became a self-governing dominion within the British Empire. Throughout this turbulent history, English-speaking South Africans settled widely.

3 LANGUAGE

English was established as a mother tongue in South Africa in the 19th century. It is little different from the English spoken elsewhere in the world but has a distinct flavor, accent, and character and has absorbed, informally, a number of words and sentence structures from other ethnic and racial groups. Some of these words have crept into usage abroad—such as "trek" for a journey and "veld" for the prairie. In an analysis of South African English pronunciation, the *Collins English Dictionary* cites the words "yes," "kettle," and "axle," which are commonly pronounced "yis," "kittle," and "eksel." South African English slang has borrowed some structures from Afrikaans, such as: "She threw him with a stone" and "I am going to the shop, will you come with?" It has also taken some words from African languages, such as "indaba," which means a gathering. Some phrases are unique to South African English, such as "just now," which means "soon but not right at this time."

4 FOLKLORE

Since they share their language with English-speaking peoples around the world, English South Africans also share in the special anniversaries, legends, and myths that are part of the international culture of the language. They celebrate Christmas in the traditional way with gifts, family gatherings, and dinner and get together for parties and celebrations on New Year's Eve when the midnight hour is greeted with hugs and kisses and the singing of *Auld Lang Syne*—a familiar scene around the world. In coastal ports like Cape Town it is common for ships to sound their sirens to greet the New Year.

The community has nothing like Halloween but, until fairly recently, they marked Guy Fawkes Day (November 5) with fireworks and bonfires. Guy Fawkes Day recalls an unsuccessful attempt to blow up the British Houses of Parliament. Today, however, private use of fireworks is banned in many areas because of the danger to lives and property and the event is rapidly passing out of memory. Apart from that, there is little folklore uniquely associated with English South Africans.

5 RELIGION

Religious beliefs are an important part of the daily life of many South Africans. The major faiths are Christianity, Hinduism, Islam, and Judaism. Religion has played a key role in the history of the country, especially in its opposition to racial discrimination known as apartheid. Religious leaders, such as Archbishop Desmond Tutu of the Anglican Church in South Africa, became politically prominent in their campaigns for equality and democracy. Nearly all of the denominations were involved in the anti-apartheid struggle—Catholics, Methodists, Lutherans, Baptists, Presbyterians and others. Most English South Africans belong to protestant Christian denominations with a lesser number but significant number adhering to the Catholic Church.

A small number—about 200,000—are Jews who tend to live mainly in the affluent areas of Johannesburg and Cape Town. Jewish influence in South Africa is much larger than the community's numbers would indicate. English-speaking Jewish South Africans have leadership positions in medicine and law, commerce and industry, and education and politics, and many have excelled in sport and the arts. The first South African to be posted to Washington as the country's ambassador during the transition away from apartheid was Jewish.

6 MAJOR HOLIDAYS

The English of South Africa observe the country's national and religious holidays. These include Human Rights Day (March 21), Good Friday (changes yearly), Family Day (changes yearly), Freedom Day (April 27), Worker's Day (May 1), Day of Reconciliation (December 16) and Christmas Day (December 25).

7 RITES OF PASSAGE

The rites of passage for English South Africans would be familiar to their counterparts in other parts of the world. One of the earliest events is kindergarten at age five or younger, followed by primary school at age six. Junior school starts at age eight and high school at age 13. After graduation from high school—known as matriculation in South Africa—it is common to go on to a technical college or to a university. Colleges and universities are seldom referred to as "schools" in South Africa, except in some instances as "school of medicine" or "school of law."

Reaching the age of 18 when it becomes legal to drive, to vote, and to drink alcohol is an important rite of passage. The 21st birthday is the most important rite of passage when it is usual to present the celebrant with a silver key to adulthood.

After university graduation—and sometimes before—it is common for young English South Africans to travel abroad. Typically, they travel to Britain and the European continent (11 or 12 hours away by air) but increasing numbers are traveling to the United States, Asia, Australia and New Zealand. Because of the expense involved, many try to get work during their travels, and it is not uncommon to find them working as farm laborers, maids, nannies and in other casual jobs before moving on to the next stage of their journey. There are currently for example, thousands of young South Africans working in London and this has become a kind of rite of passage in itself.

8 INTERPERSONAL RELATIONS

In the past, English South Africans—like other communities in the country—tended to keep to themselves with most social contacts confined to members of their own group. Several social and political trends have changed that situation. The most dramatic change was the transition to democratic government,

which began by stages in the 1980s and was consummated in 1994. This has brought whites and blacks together in schools, colleges, the workplace, and on sports fields with an intimacy that did not exist before. As a result, different communities are being exposed to customs and personal practices that may be different from their own. For instance, in some rural African areas it is still considered polite to sit down and not to speak first when a prominent person or someone elderly enters a room. English South Africans have been taught traditionally that younger people should stand up as a mark of respect and greet a more senior person first. They are learning that their own way is not necessarily the only or correct way for everyone. All communities serve in a volunteer defense force and this development has further demolished past barriers. Previously, this was by conscription for white and "coloured" 18 year old males only.

Another major influence was the introduction of television in South Africa in 1975. Before that time, there was only radio with separate language channels. TV programs sometimes alternate the languages or have subtitles, which means that, for the first time, English-speaking South Africans were being exposed to other tongues and cultures, also from abroad, under the powerful influence of entertainment.

All these trends have tended to break down the barriers between social groups in South Africa. One of the most memorable examples of this was the nationwide celebration when South Africa won the Rugby World Cup in 1995 and again in 2007. Rugby is still played mainly by whites and particularly by Afrikaans-speakers. However, the whole nation reacted joyously when the national team won these tournaments. All the games had been broadcast live. In 2010 South Africa is hosting the FIFA World Cup (soccer/football), which is also providing South Africans with a common focus.

9 LIVING CONDITIONS

Transition to democracy has opened up equal opportunities for everyone, and there are no longer legal barriers to communities living in each other's previously restricted areas. However, political change has come much faster than economic change and many blacks still live in poverty while many English South Africans continue to live the relatively privileged life-style that was once considered their right. The typical successful white South African lives in a style similar to his or her counterpart in the United States—in single-family houses on wide suburban streets or in apartments or semidetached row houses with neighborhood playgrounds, shopping centers, and cinemas. As the economy grows and blacks take advantage of new employment and educational opportunities, they are increasingly achieving a similar comfortable standard of living. There is some concern, however, that this applies mostly to a new black elite.

10 FAMILY LIFE

The social stability provided by the family unit is recognized by the government, which has a policy of supporting family cohesion. In English South African families it is not unusual for both parents to work during the day and for younger schoolchildren to be cared for by live-in domestic workers when they come home in the afternoon. Marriage nowadays usually occurs in the late twenties to early thirties. With high interest rates and sharply rising property prices, it has become more common for older children to continue to live at home for longer than they would have in the past and even—if the property is large enough—for families to build separate structures that allow either the children or the elderly parents to live nearby but separately for privacy. It is a case, perhaps, of a tight economy contributing to family cohesion. English South African families celebrate the traditional events such as birthdays, anniversaries, special achievements in school or in sports, and often take vacations together, renting cottages or apartments at the seaside. These days it is common for family members who live apart to communicate daily with each other by computer e-mail or cellular/mobile telephone. Family pets are popular with one or two dogs and cats being the norm.

11 CLOTHING

Day-to-day clothing is similar to that worn by middle-class people throughout the world. Increasingly, however, it is common to find men shedding jackets and ties in the work environment, following a trend set by the previous president Nelson Mandela who made colorful open-neck shirts fashionable, even at formal meetings. Schoolchildren are required at most schools to wear school uniforms. Sometimes, these uniforms are still the traditional blazer and tie for both boys and girls, which can be hot and uncomfortable during the summer, but many schools have opted for open-neck clothes. Jeans, shorts, and T-shirts are popular on weekends. Young English South Africans spend much of their money on leisure clothes. They strive to conform to current fashion trends.

12 FOOD

The meal associated traditionally with English South Africans is the English-style roast beef or lamb with roast potatoes and Yorkshire pudding prepared on Sunday morning and eaten at a family lunch—followed by a nap. That may be turning into a myth, or at least a memory, as life-styles permit less time in the kitchen and a desire to eat lighter and less costly food. Similarly, the traditional breakfast of bacon and eggs often gives way today to coffee or tea and toast or one of the many breakfast cereals familiar to Americans. Fruit is also a popular first meal of the day. There are usually three meals each day—breakfast, a sandwich at lunch, and dinner in the evenings. Dinner could consist of grilled steak with fried or baked potatoes, or fried or baked fish, which is especially popular in coastal cities, washed down with beer or wine or plain water. In winter, stews are popular. Known as *bredies,* they can be made with mutton or beef and any kind of vegetable. English South Africans like to garnish their food with a pickled relish called chutney, and many enjoy a bread spread called Marmite, a dark-colored yeast extract with a salty taste. Fast foods are gaining in popularity, and hamburgers are frequently eaten—to the concern of some diet specialists.

13 EDUCATION

South Africa has a literacy rate of some 86.4 percent for those over 15 in the nation at large, but for the English-speaking community the rate is almost universal. Education is compulsory to the age of 16 and it generally takes 12 years to obtain a high school diploma or senior certificate, which is required to continue studies at a technical college or university. University undergraduate degrees generally take three years to complete with longer academic years than are usual in the United States.

An additional year of study after a bachelor's degree can lead to an honors degree, followed by further work for master's degrees or doctorates. These days, it is becoming more difficult to get a good job without at least a bachelor's degree or a technical college diploma. Many families devote a great deal of time, energy and resources to education and will sacrifice to ensure that their children are well prepared for a future in which advanced technology will play a key role in everyday life. In a tight economy many find it hard to keep their children in the classroom for extended periods.

14 CULTURAL HERITAGE

English South Africans have inherited a rich local cultural heritage, mostly in the area of literature in which writers have achieved international renown for their depiction of dramatic events against a South African background. Probably the best-known such writer is Alan Paton whose novel *Cry the Beloved Country* explores the impact of racism on whites as well as blacks. It has been made twice into American movies. An extremely popular author is Herman Charles Bosman who, writing in English with an Afrikaans flavor, takes a humorous look at daily life in a rural community. Other writers who have achieved international fame include Nadine Gordimer and J. M. Coetzee while other South African writers, such as André Brink (Afrikaans) and Njabulo Ndebele, have made major contributions to English literature in South Africa. Playwright Athol Fugard has also achieved international fame with his dramatic portrayals of life through South Africa's race-tinged prism. Western classical and pop music is popular but many English South Africans have developed a taste for African music, such as the close harmonies found in the singing of groups like Ladysmith Black Mambazo. American musician and entertainer, Paul Simon, has done much to bring the charms of this kind of music to an international audience.

15 WORK

A typical work week ranges from 40–46 hours, and a legally mandated minimum wage is adjusted from time to time. Until 1979, special classes of labor were reserved for workers by race. However, in the late 1990s, this situation started changing. Some English-speaking South Africans expressed concern over black economic empowerment (BEE) programs, in which special consideration is given to employing and promoting blacks. Some claim now that this has led to a new kind of apartheid in which whites are unable to get jobs and promotions because of their skin color. Few disagree with the need for affirmative action, but many argue with the way in which it has been implemented, given that South Africa is some 14 years into democracy with a post-apartheid generation now at school. Policymakers hope that the problem will ease and disappear eventually as a growing economy opens up job opportunities for all.

16 SPORTS

Because of the country's generally benign climate throughout the year, outdoor sports are very popular. The most popular sports are rugby, soccer, and field hockey played in winter, and cricket in summer. Tennis, golf, track and field athletics, competitive cycling, and swimming are also extremely popular. Lawn bowls, played mostly by older folk but also by a growing number of young people, has a large following. American-style baseball has a few adherents but is not nearly as popular as cricket, which—in the view of some—has joined rugby as a national obsession. Wind-surfing, surfboard riding, and both fresh- and salt-water yachting are enjoyed all year long while hiking and mountaineering have many adherents. Sports events that attract the largest crowds in the country's many fine stadiums are rugby, soccer, and cricket. Events that attract thousands of spectators as well as participants include annual road marathon races in Cape Town and Natal. Professional horse racing also has a large following and two races in particular—the Cape Metropolitan handicap and the Durban July—are major media events where the fashions worn by the race goers get as much attention as the horses. South Africa has produced world and Olympic champion individuals and teams in many of its sports.

17 ENTERTAINMENT AND RECREATION

Popular recreation attractions in South Africa include Kruger National Park and several game reserves. Entertainment facilities include symphony halls, theaters, movies, nightclubs, and discos. The annual National Arts Festival held in Grahamstown is a major event featuring mainly English plays, music, and arts, and also crafts stalls.

18 FOLK ART, CRAFTS, AND HOBBIES

The English in South Africa enjoy the varied hobbies of citizens of an industrialized nation.

19 SOCIAL PROBLEMS

South Africa's transition to democracy in 1994 brought equal rights and new opportunities to the disadvantaged sectors of the population. Unfortunately, it also sparked a dramatic increase in the rate of crime and violence—an inevitable by-product of poverty and high unemployment in the context of a new political system where social expectations are unrealistically high. Burglaries, muggings, car-jackings, rapes, and murders all increased since the late 1990s. English-speaking South Africans are as much the victims of this crime rate as any other sector of the population and it has led to demands for tough action by the government as well as a return to capital punishment, which is banned in South Africa. One result has been a growing rate of emigration. Another has been the growth of private security-related services and the development of gated communities.

South Africa's transition also made it a target for foreign narcotics traffickers who saw the opportunities in newly opened borders for a major international transshipment point. Illicit drugs are now being shipped through South Africa to North America and Europe in a network that has made it hard to trace their origins. Nations with more experience in dealing with this cruel trade are helping South Africa address the problem, but drug trafficking has boosted crime within the country and is a major societal concern.

HIV/AIDS is also a major problem, with the adult prevalence rate at 21.5% (2003 est.). The number of people living with HIV/AIDS was estimated at 5.3 million (2003) and the number of deaths caused by the disease was estimated at 370,000 deaths in 2003.

20 GENDER ISSUES

The Constitution of the Republic of South Africa (Act 108 of 1996) specifies individual rights and their protection. Chapter 2[9(3)] specifically indicates that "the State may not unfairly discriminate directly or indirectly against anyone on one or more grounds, including race, gender,…etc.". This is observed in practice by all government agencies. For example, the Department of Education runs a program, the Girls Education Movement (GEM), launched in 2003. It is a key program supporting and fostering education for girls and was implemented in partnership with the United Nations' (UN) Children's Fund.

This program aims to ensure that girls not only have access to education, but that they stay in school and succeed. GEM was founded on three pillars: career mentorship, skills development, and advocacy.

Through GEM, girls are placed in partner companies during their Easter, winter, and spring school breaks, to discover first-hand how skills acquired in school and the skills-development program relate to the workplace.

They are exposed to a structured job-shadowing program and to new and exciting career paths in the fields of mathematics, science, and commerce. The GEM Skills Development Program aims to address gender disparities through education and advocacy.

Compared to many other communities in South Africa, the English in the country, even in rural areas, are much farther along the road of gender parity. Much like their counterparts in other industrialized nations, English women in South Africa are career-oriented and fill prominent positions in virtually every sector of society.

21 BIBLIOGRAPHY

Butler, G. *The 1820 Settlers*. Cape Town, Human & Rousseau, 1974.

Mallaby, Sebastian. *After Apartheid*. New York: Random House, 1992.

Paton, Alan. *Towards the Mountain, An Autobiography*. Cape Town: David Philip, 1980.

Reader's Digest Illustrated History of South Africa. Cape Town: Reader's Digest Association, 1994.

South Africa Yearbook 2007/08. Pretoria: Government Communication and Information System, 2008.

Suzman, Helen. *In No Uncertain Terms, A South African Memoir*. New York: Knopf, 1993.

—by M de Jongh

EQUATORIAL GUINEANS

PRONUNCIATION: ee-kwuh-TOR-ee-uhl GHIN-ee-uhns
ALTERNATE NAMES: Equatoguineans
LOCATION: Equatorial Guinea (island of Bioko, mainland of Rio Muni, several small islands)
POPULATION: 616,000
LANGUAGE: Spanish (official); Fang; languages of the coastal peoples; Bubi, pidgin English and Ibo (from Nigeria); Portuguese Creole.
RELIGION: Christianity, African-based sects and cults

¹ INTRODUCTION

Equatorial Guinea has recently gained prominence around the world as one of the smallest African states now awash in oil. Prior to this discovery, it was one of the least-known African countries comprising the rectangular-shaped island of Bioko (formerly Fernando Po) and the mainland, Rio Muni. Portuguese explorers landed on Fernando Po in 1471–72 and made it part of the commercial sphere of Sao Tomé. The islanders strongly resisted the slave trade and attempts to occupy their homeland. The Portuguese gave the island and parts of the mainland to Spain in a treaty in 1787. However, Spanish administration of Fernando Po only began in 1858. Nevertheless, Equatorial Guinea is the only sub-Saharan country that uses Spanish as its official language.

In the latter 19th century, European missionaries and descendants of Liberians, Sierra Leonians, Nigerians, and liberated slaves (Fernandinos) developed large cacao, coffee, and tobacco plantations on Fernando Po. Cameroonians, Fang (from Rio Muni), more Nigerians, and Liberians immigrated to the island to work the plantations. However, in 1976, the island was greatly depopulated when the government expelled 25,000 Nigerians. After the coup in 1979, Obiang Nguema renamed the island, Bioko, but the residents have resisted this name. Since 1979, Nguema has resided as head of state on the island, protected by his praetorian guard of 600 Moroccan soldiers.

Since independence in 1968, the country has been ruled by the despotic Nguema family. Equatorial Guinea's first head of state, Francisco Macias Nguema, Obiang's uncle, was Africa's worst despot. A Fang from the Esangui clan on the mainland, he dissolved the country's multiparty system in 1970 and replaced it with a single party, the *Partido Unico Nacional de los Trabajadores* (PUNT). Macias murdered politicians and government administrators, executed members of the opposition, and exiled most of Equatorial Guinea's educated and skilled workforce. One-quarter to one-third of the population was murdered or exiled during his tenure.

In 1979 defense minister Obiang Nguema Mbasogo, Macias' nephew, overthrew his uncle in a coup and eventually executed him. Obiang has ruled since with members of the Esangui clan dominating the government. He has won a series of fraudulent elections, the last in 2002. Legislative elections in 1999 and 2004 also were dismissed as highly flawed, and in May 2008 legislative and local elections of a similar ilk confirmed Obiang's firm grip on power.

Since 1981 at least seven real or imagined coups have been attempted. The most recent occurred in 2004, implicating Mark Thatcher, son of the former British Prime Minister, for having bankrolled the coup attempt. Rumors in 2008 reported Obiang as suffering from cancer and perhaps willing to step down in favor of his son Teodorín, who served as Forestry Minister. Despite a thriving economy fueled by oil, Equatorial Guinean exiles have been hesitant to return to the country because of persistent human rights abuses, corruption, and crime.

² LOCATION AND HOMELAND

Besides Bioko island and the mainland, Equatorial Guinea comprises several small islands. A cluster of small islands—Elobeyes and de Corisco—lies just south of the mainland. Rio Muni is situated between Gabon to the south and east and Cameroon to the north. Bioko is part of a geologic fault line extending from the island of Annobon (Equatorial Guinea), some 700 miles to the southwest, all the way to Tibesti in northern Chad. A range of volcanic relief is apparent along this line including Mt. Cameroon (13,000 feet), only 32 kilometers from Bioko and visible from there on a clear day.

Both the mainland and the islands receive abundant rainfall—more than eight ft annually. Three extinct volcanoes form the backbone of Bioko, giving the island fertile soils and lush vegetation. The Pico de Basile rises to more than 10,000 feet above sea level. The mainland coast is a long beach with no natural harbor. A narrow coastal plain rises sharply to a forested plateau, and small ranges of low mountains reach nearly 4,000 feet in elevation.

Equatorial Guinea's population is about 616,000 (est. 2008), one-fourth of which lives on Bioko. For its physical size, the ethnic composition of Equatorial Guinea is unusually complex. The Ntumu Fang occupy the mainland north of the Mbini river and the Okak Fang live to the south of it. Together, the Fang peoples form the majority (80–90%) of Mbini, and the Kombe, Balengue, and Bujeba tribes occupy the coastal areas. Bioko's population is a mixture of the Bubi, its original inhabitants, the Fernandino, long-settled immigrants from nearby West Africa, and Fang migrants, who now dominate the military and civil service. Malabo (formerly Sta. Isabel) on the island of Bioko is the administrative capital for the entire country. Bata is an important regional capital on the mainland and was periodically the site of the national government for three or four months each year in the 1980s.

³ LANGUAGE

Spanish is the official language. Well-educated Equatorial Guineans speak Spanish Castilian with a proper lisp. Inhabitants of Rio Muni speak Fang and languages of the coastal peoples. On Bioko, the islanders speak mainly Bubi, although many island people use pidgin English and Ibo (from Nigeria). The 1,500 residents of the island of Annobon speak Portuguese Creole.

⁴ FOLKLORE

The Fang tell many stories and folktales through the personage of animals. These tales serve to illustrate lessons of life. One animal in these fables is as clever as the fox, wise as the owl, and diplomatic as the rabbit. The islanders call him *ku* or *kulu*, the turtle. One tale concerns a divorce and child custody case between a tiger and a tigress. Each animal of the forest opines on who should get possession of the child. In the tradition of male dominance, they believe the tiger deserves parentage, but before rendering a verdict, they want to consult the *ku*. The *ku* hears each side of the case and asks them to return the following day at lunchtime. When they are assembled the next day, he appears in no hurry to give his opinion and instead bathes in a large mud puddle. Then he cries as if overcome with grief. The animals are mystified and ask him to explain. He replies, "My father-in-law died while giving birth." The tiger finally interrupts with disgust, "Why listen to such rubbish? We all know a man cannot give birth. Only a woman has that ability. A man's relationship to a child is different." The *ku* replies, "Aha! You yourself have determined her relationship with the child to be special. Custody should be with the tigress." The tiger was unsatisfied, but the other animals agreed that the *ku* ruled correctly.

5 RELIGION

Most Equatorial Guineans profess some form of Christianity, but many African-based sects and cults persist. For example, the Bubis practice a syncretic religion where indigenous beliefs and Christianity have been joined in a monotheistic religion.

Though not a religion per se, Macias invented his own personality cult, which he attempted to inculcate through the Catholic church. In 1974 he ordered priests to read the following message during the mass: "Never without Macias, always with Macias. Down with colonialism and with ambition." He decreed that churches hang his portrait in their sanctuaries. Inscribed was the message: "Only and unceasing miracle of Equatorial Guinea. God created Equatorial Guinea thanks to Macias. Without Macias, Equatorial Guinea would not exist." He recruited youth spies to report on "subversive" clergy and expelled, imprisoned, and executed bishops, priests, and pastors suspected of resisting. In 1975, he closed all mission schools. Obiang has permitted freedom of worship, but surveillance and repression of the clergy continues.

Equatorial Guinean religions are similar to African religions elsewhere in that they revolve around a supreme being and lower-level deities in the spirit world that may assist or bring misfortune to people. To guard against misfortune, the Fang invoke guidance and protection from ancestors who held leadership positions when they were living. The Fang carry their skulls and bones with them as relics for communicating with the ancestors' spirits.

Equatorial Guinean sects are infamous for their alleged human sacrifices and necrophagy. A report in 1926 claims that the Fang tore out the hearts and genitals of their victims, sometimes eating them. In 1946 one observer claimed that Fang sorcerers practiced cannibalism during ceremonies. Reports on one sect claimed that members had to take turns bringing in cadavers, or if one was not available, to kill a victim or otherwise be killed. The rationale for necrophagy is that one acquires the attributes and the power of the person ingested.

The earliest European accounts of necrophagy date from the mid-19th century. It is not clear however, the extent to which the slaving middle men, the Ndowe, invented stories to scare the Fang and the Europeans, both of whom came to depend on the Ndowe for slaves. Moreover, European explorers may have misunderstood the significance of human skulls and body parts found stored in and near Fang homes. It is possible that what Europeans saw was earlier evidence of a modern Fang cult. The Fang still conserve skulls and body parts as relics to which prayers are addressed and transmitted by the ancestor

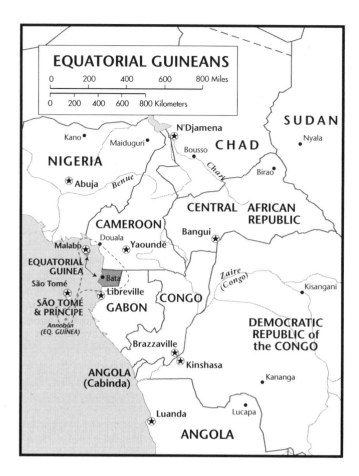

to God. The remains also scare away evil spirits, but they are now hidden in secret places out of public view.

6 MAJOR HOLIDAYS

Equatorial Guineans recognize 12 public holidays. Independence Day is October 12, but a special celebration is reserved for Armed Forces Day, August 3, which also is known as the *golpe de libertad* (the freedom coup that overthrew President Macias). On that day, in the main square of Malabo, the president's motorcade passes flanked by motorcycles and elite Moroccan guards on foot. They run to keep pace carrying walkie-talkies as they go. After the government ministers have passed, delegations of singers, dancers, and musicians from the barrios of Malabo and the villages take their turn. Guitarists, drummers, and women in grass skirts are among them. Perhaps the most outrageous characters in the parade are the "lucifers," dancers in tennis shoes wearing looping horns, colored streamers, pompons, leopard-skin cloth, a pillow stuffed in the pants, and seven rear-view mirrors taped to the nape of the neck. Cuban laborers of African descent from the 19th century imported the costume and the tradition.

7 RITES OF PASSAGE

Equatorial Guineans of various ethnic groups mark life's passages—birth, puberty, marriage, and death with rites and rituals because these bridge present generations to the ancestors, who may be invoked for assistance, guidance in decision-making, and protection. The Fang communicate with ancestors via rites performed in secret societies. Elders initiate new members into secret societies to which outsiders may never belong, nor even observe. The Bubis of Bioko offer sacrifices of buffalos, sheep, goats, chickens, and ducks and sometimes saltwater fish on rites of passage occasions.

The elaborate funeral rites of Bubis show their belief in the hereafter and in reincarnation. Villagers announce a death by drumming on a hollow log. The drums at dawn and at dusk sound while the community observes a moment of silence. Someone reads the most important acts of the defunct. Only the most basic tasks such as digging yams for the daily meal may be performed until the funeral is over. A designated elder of the village chooses women who will wash the corpse and embalm it with a red creme, *Ntola*. All community members except pregnant women and children participate in ceremonies of singing and dancing and accompany the corpse to the grave site. Before taking the corpse from the house to the cemetery, the mourners sacrifice a male goat and pour its blood over the corpse. This is repeated several times on the way to the cemetery. The corpse is then placed in the fetal position in the grave so that it may be born again. Family members leave personal objects with the defunct, which will serve in the hereafter for daily labor. Grave robbery is punished by amputation of hands. After burial, mourners plant a branch of the sacred tree, *Iko*, on the tomb.

8 INTERPERSONAL RELATIONS

Equatorial Guineans love to tell stories and to joke around, but they also show respect for people of a certain status. For example, they reserve the title of "Don" or "Dona" for people of high education, wealth, and class. This might be a government minister, a plantation owner, or an important businessman. Equatorial Guineans are very ebullient people. They readily shake hands and greet each other. The typical morning greeting is the Spanish, *buenos dias*.

9 LIVING CONDITIONS

Living conditions in Equatorial Guinea have fluctuated greatly over the years. Prior to independence in 1968, the country was a showcase for exports of cocoa, coffee, timber foodstuffs, palm oil, and fish. Then President Macias' corrupt regime systematically impoverished the country through political repression and neglect. By 1990 the country had to import staple foods such as palm oil and fish. About four-fifths of the population reverted to making its living in subsistence agriculture in the jungles and highland forests. Average income by the late 1990s was less than $300 per year, and life expectancy was only 45 years. Many children died of preventable diseases like measles.

All this began to change in the mid-1990s with the discovery of off-shore oil. In 2008 with a current daily production of some 400,000 barrels a day, Equatorial Guinea boasted the fourth-highest per capita income in the world. Its gross domestic product (GDP) per capita was $44,000, putting it ahead of Switzerland, Canada, and Britain. Life expectancy rose to over 60 years. However, because a few senior government officials own most of the businesses and control most of the country's wealth, oil dividends do not reach the vast majority of Equatorial Guineans.

About 50% of the population lives in poverty without access to potable water and sanitation. On the main island, small rectangular wood plank or palm thatch houses lack electricity and indoor plumbing. Simple beds are made out of polished bamboo slats lashed together and mounted on larger bamboo posts. On the mainland, huts are made of cane and mud walls with tin or thatch roofs. In some villages, the cane walls are only chest high so that the men can watch the goings-on of the village. Women and girls wash clothes at streams or wells and usually hang them up or lay them out on a clean section of the yard to dry. Children are expected to help carry water, collect firewood, and run errands for their mothers.

10 FAMILY LIFE

The family and the clan are critical institutions in Equatorial Guinean life. It is important that people know their ancestry and family life is geared toward perpetuating the lineage. Marriage in Fang society is exogamous and descendance is patrilinear. Families are polygynous and men may have several wives, mainly for prestige and for economic reasons. Bubi society is primarily endogamous, meaning that people marry within the same lineage. Bubi society also is matriarchal—people trace their lineage by their mother's line. In ancient times, Bubis were allowed to marry a sibling as long as he or she did not have the same mother. Bubis therefore place great importance on having girls because they perpetuate the family. A family without girls would risk extinction. Thus, Bubis consider girls to be the eyes of the home, *que nobo e chobo*, the paper that perpetuates the family. The boys are thought of as the pillars of the house because they sustain the household.

No reliable statistics exist on the percentage of households headed by women or how many women work in different sectors of the workforce. Nonetheless, women typically do the housework and bear five to six children. Men customarily assume authority in the household because, as one Bubi proverb says, "a chicken never will crow at dawn."

11 CLOTHING

Equatorial Guineans do their best to look sharp in public. For those who can afford them, Western-style suits and dresses are de rigueur for any professional or business activities. Businessmen wear three-piece pinstriped suits with vests and neckties, even in the extremely hot, muggy weather of the island. Women and girls go out neatly dressed, wearing pleated skirts, starched blouses, and polished shoes.

Children in the villages wear shorts, jeans, and T-shirts, though tailored cloth dresses are popular for girls. The women wear bright, colorful loose-fitting sarongs with African patterns. They usually wear head scarves too. Older women may wear a large, simply cut piece of cotton cloth over a blouse and sarong. People with little money often make do with secondhand American T-shirts and other clothing. The wearer is usually oblivious to what a T-shirts says, including sometimes very bawdy messages. Many people go barefoot, or wear flip-flops and plastic sandals.

12 FOOD

The staple food of Equatorial Guinea is coco yams (*malanga*), plantains, and rice. The island coco yams are among the tastiest in Africa and grow well in Bioko's rich soils where rainfall is plentiful. People eat little meat other than porcupine and forest antelope, a large rodent-like animal with small antlers. Equatorial Guineans typically supplement their diets with vegetables from their home gardens and with eggs or an occasional chicken or duck on special occasions. Fish are abundant in the coastal waters and provide an important protein source in an otherwise starchy diet. Many people cook on open wood fires, either on the floor of their houses or in the open yard.

¹³ EDUCATION

Formal education at all levels has suffered much under the Nguemas. In the 1970s, many teachers and administrators were liquidated. Many Spanish teachers, most of them priests, left the country in 1978 to return later. Cuban and UNESCO-funded teachers also left the country because of assassinations and ministerial paralysis. In the 1980s, only two public high schools existed, one in Malabo and the other in Bata. In 1987, a UNESCO mission found that of 17 schools visited on Bioko, not one had blackboards, pencils, or textbooks. Children learned by rote hearing and repetition. In 1990 the World Bank estimated that 50% of the population was illiterate. But in 1993, no one could provide statistics on basic indicators such as primary-school enrollment and number of schoolteachers. Fortunately, there has been some windfall from oil revenues, and modest investments in education have improved school infrastructure, teacher capacity, and quality of curricula.

¹⁴ CULTURAL HERITAGE

The cultural heritage of Bioko dates to Paleolithic and Neolithic periods. Archaeologists have discovered stone tools such as axes and hoes. At this time, stone mortars and pestles also were in use. People made jewelry from snake vertebrae woven with raffia to make armbands and bracelets. The precolonial period was unproductive in cultural growth because of the severe depopulation of Rio Muni and the islands during the slave trade.

Fang art and magical beliefs are closely linked. The main traditional instrument of the Fang, the Mvett, typifies this relationship. The name "Mvett" also applies to the Fang sagas. The religious-mystic order of the Bebom-Mvett is the caretaker of the "Cycle of Legends of Engong." The "Cycle" is for the Fang nation what the Old Testament is for Christians and Jews. The Mvett instrument is a harp-zither made of three gourds, the stem of a leaf of the raffia plant, and cord of vegetable fibers. Mvett players are highly respected by Equatorial Guineans of Fang background.

¹⁵ WORK

Bubi society is divided by function: farmers, hunters, fishermen, palm-wine collectors, and, in former times, the royal police of the supreme chief. A supreme priest blessed the yam plantations and protected the sacred fire. Bubis traditionally refused contact with Europeans and refused forced plantation labor in coffee and cocoa.

In rural areas, most Equatorial Guineans still practice subsistence farming. They grow tubers, bush peppers, cola nuts, and fruits. Women do four-fifths of the work. Men clear the land, and women do the rest, including carrying 187-pound baskets of yams on their backs to market. Along with the oil industry has come a variety of new jobs at the ports and in services such as bars, restaurants, and domestic work. However, because oil production is off-shore, the number and types of good-paying jobs are limited, and most of job creation has been in low-paying unskilled work.

Equatorial Guinean children in the villages wear shorts, jeans, and T-shirts, though tailored cloth dresses are popular for girls. (United Nations)

¹⁶ SPORTS

Equatorial Guineans are avid soccer players. They also maintain a keen interest in table tennis which they got from Chinese aid workers. The assassination of the minister of youth and sports in 1976 greatly paralyzed organized sports in Equatorial Guinea. At independence, there were some 40 soccer fields in the country, which were rebuilt in the late 1970s and early 1980s by the Spanish. The Spanish also sent professionals to retrain players at a level required for international competition. Equatorial Guinea participated for the first time in the Olympics in 1984 at the Los Angeles games.

¹⁷ ENTERTAINMENT AND RECREATION

Like Africans on the continent, Equatorial Guineans enjoy socializing with family and friends and do not need invitations to visit each other. It is common to see them playing cards, checkers, and chess with friends. Almost any occasion will spark dancing and singing. No formal party is needed. Men especially go to pubs to socialize and drink. Various African musical styles from Makossa of Cameroon to Congolese music are popular with youth.

Part of the reason for this vibrant socializing had to do with restrictions on electronic media. Until 1981 the country had only two radio stations, one on the mainland and the other on Bioko that broadcasted propaganda and personality cultism for the Nguemas. Since then, the Chinese built new installations that include broadcasting in Spanish and local languages. The stations also play music from Cameroon and Nigeria. Today, the BBC and Radio France International are available on FM broadcasts from Malabo and are popular.

Television has remained under strict government control for fear that it could become a democracy tool. In 1982 most of the 200 color televisions in the country were owned by Spanish technical assistants. By 1984 the number of televisions had risen to 1,500. In the late 1980s, Malabo had two non-functioning movie theaters used for government events. In 1990, the entire island of Bioko had no functioning cinemas, bookstores, or newsstands. Today, to get information and entertainment that otherwise would be available on TV, Equatoguineans spend hours in dozens of Internet cafés in Bata and Malabo listening to music, reading news and opinions on websites of exiles (which are critical of the government), and generally accessing a window on the outside world.

18 FOLK ART, CRAFTS, AND HOBBIES

Folk art is rich and varies according to ethnic group. On Bioko, the Bubi people are known for their colorful wooden bells. The makers of the bells embellish them with intricate designs, engravings, and shapes. Musicians ring these bells by turn or in combinations during the folkloric dances of the *Kacha*.

In Ebolova, women weave baskets more than two feet high and two feet across to which they attach straps. They use these to haul produce from their fields and garden tools. Equatorial Guineans make many hats and other objects, especially baskets of all kinds, from raffia and palm leaves. Some baskets are so finely woven that they hold liquids such as palm oil.

19 SOCIAL PROBLEMS

The oil boom has created new jobs, but along with the influx of wealth has come a number of social problems. Equatorial Guinea is ranked as the tenth-most corrupt country in the world and is a staging point for drug trafficking between South America and Europe and a destination for trafficked children. Trafficked persons come from neighboring Benin, Nigeria, Gabon, and Cameroon, and work as farmhands and household servants. Girls are particularly vulnerable to sexual exploitation either as domestic servants or in the commercial sex trade. By 2008 the government had taken steps to get children off the streets and to control trafficking, but the lack of hard data made it impossible to determine the extent of the problem.

20 GENDER ISSUES

The status of women is improving gradually. However, in rural areas women still perform most of the household and agricultural work, and excessive drinking by men, wife beating, and female sexual abuse are reported frequently with little will on the part of the police and courts to prosecute the perpetrators. These problems have reached the attention of the president's wife, who led a campaign in 2007 to raise public awareness on spouse abuse. The government also launched a major crackdown against prostitution to curb trafficking.

Progress in education for girls is being made. By 2008 women and girls had a literacy rate of 78% (compared to 93% of males), and girls' enrollment rates were climbing with 81% as many girls as boys enrolled in primary, secondary, and tertiary education. Also in 2008 there were 20 women in the 100-member parliament and six women in the cabinet including the Ministers of Labor and Women's Issues.

21 BIBLIOGRAPHY

Africa South of the Sahara 2007. "Equatorial Guinea." London: Europa Publishers, 2008.

Asangono, Alejandro Evuna Owono. *El Proceso democratico de Guinea Ecuatorial.* Madrid: CEIBA, 1993.

Boriko, Emiliano Buale. *Guinea Ecuatorial: Las Aspiraciones Bubis al Autogobierno.* Madrid: Iepala Editorial, 1988.

Fegley, Randall. *Equatorial Guinea: An African Tragedy.* New York: Peter Lang, 1989.

Klitgaard, Robert. *Tropical Gangsters: One Man's Experience with Development and Decadence in Deepest Africa.* New York: Basic Books, 1990.

Lewis, Marvin. *An Introduction to the Literature of Equatorial Guinea.* University of Missouri Press, 2007.

Liniger-Goumaz, Max. *Connaître la Guinée Equatoriale.* Conde-sur-Noireau: Editions des Peuples Noirs, 1986.

———. *Historical Dictionary of Equatorial Guinea.* 2nd ed. African Historical Dictionaries, No. 21. Metuchen, N. J. and London: Scarecrow Press, 1988.

———. *Comment On S'empare d'un Pays: La Guinée Equatoriale.* Genève: Les Editions du Temps, 1990.

———. *Who's Who de la dictature de Guinée Equatoriale: Les Nguemistes 1979-1993.* Genève: Les Editions du Temps, 1993.

—by R. Groelsema

ERITREANS

PRONUNCIATION: eh-rih-TRAY-uhns
ALTERNATE NAMES: Ertra
LOCATION: Eritrea (Horn of Africa)
POPULATION: 4.9 million
LANGUAGE: Ethio-Semitic Tigrinya, Tigre, and Amharic (Amharinya); Eastern Cushitic Afar and Saho; Central Cushitic Bilin Agaw; Nilo-Saharan, Kunama, Nara; Beja (Bedawi); Indo-European English and Italian, spoken by some; Arabic, spoken in the coastal cities and by the Rashaida.
RELIGION: Sunni Islam, Orthodox Christianity
RELATED ARTICLES: Vol. 1: Tigray; Djiboutians

¹ INTRODUCTION

Modern Eritrea was born in the crucible of a large-scale, devastating, 30-year civil war during which more ammunition was exploded than in all of the North African campaigns of World War II. A number of separate Eritrean guerrilla movements, nearly destroyed from feuding with each other, gradually united. By 1991, they had won a war against combined Ethiopian, Cuban, and Soviet forces. These forces at times numbered 150,000–200,000 troops backed by at least $5 billion in direct Soviet and inadvertent U. S. military aid.

Eritrea's history intertwines with that of Ethiopia of which it had long been a northern frontier. Italians established a commercial foothold in Mitsiwa (Massawa) and Aseb in 1869, and took control of the ports from the Egyptians during the period 1882–85. Thus, Italy gained its first bases in the strategic Horn of Africa. In 1887 at Dogali, Ethiopian Emperor Yohannes, a Tigrayan, turned back Italian thrusts into the interior of Eritrea from Mitsiwa but the Italian army eventually took control of Eritrea. To facilitate Italy's expansion in the Horn, construction of the Eritrean Railway began at Mitsiwa in 1888 as a military line for the planned enlargement of what became the colony of Eritrea on 1 January 1890.

A little known continental catastrophe of the Italian invasion of Eritrea began in 1889 when the Italian army imported Indian cattle into the colony. The cattle carried the virus for rinderpest (from the German cattle-plague), then unknown in Africa. By 1897 the plague had spread to South Africa, killing about 90% of all African cattle, while decimating populations of buffalo, giraffe, wildebeest, and other wild herbivore game. Mass starvation began for humans across Africa. Without plow oxen, about a third of the Eritreans died.

In March 1896, the Ethiopian's decisively defeated at Adwa the Italian army, pushing it back into Eritrea and forcing Italy to turn its resources to developing this colony. From Eritrea, Italy successfully invaded Ethiopia in 1935–36. In 1941, British forces from Sudan quickly defeated the long-entrenched Italians in Eritrea. Through 1952, a British military administration controlled Eritrea, while the government in London considered whether to annex the western part of Eritrea to the Anglo-Egyptian Sudan. In 1952 the United Nations voted to make Eritrea a semi-autonomous federated unit of Ethiopia. In 1953, a former Italian communications base just west of Asmara, Eritrea became one of the largest U.S.-intelligence-gathering facilities, monitoring communications from the Eastern

Bloc and Middle East. During the 1950s, then strategic Ethiopia was the largest recipient in Africa of U.S. economic and military aid.

In 1962, Emperor Haile Selassie I, an Amhara, forcibly annexed Eritrea as a province in his Ethiopian empire, thereby kindling rebellion. During this period, U.S.-supplied planes buzzed low over Asmara and the countryside to monitor the terrain and to stifle Eritrean insurgency. By the 1970s, U.S. intelligence turned to satellites to gather global electronic transmissions and no longer required land facilities. Ethiopia thus gradually became less strategic, and U.S. aid to the country declined. Suppression of the Eritrean insurgency became increasingly less acceptable to the Americans. The U.S. began to rebuff Haile Selassie's requests for more arms to counter Communist influences in the Horn and Red Sea regions.

In 1974, Haile Selassie was overthrown by a faction known as the *Derg* (Amharic for committee). A provisional government was formed under Lt. General Aman Andom, an Eritrean who was later executed by the Derg. Next, Brigadier General Teferi Benti headed a new government, and the Derg proclaimed a socialist state of Ethiopia. In 1975, the rival Eritrean Liberation Front and Eritrean People's Liberation Front ended most of their differences and overran all of Eritrea, except for Asmara, Mitsiwa, and Berentu. In 1976, socialist Ethiopia broke ties with the U.S. and signed a military compact with the USSR. The next year, the Derg executed General Teferi and his colleagues and installed Lt. Colonel Mengistu Haile Mariam as head of state. With Soviet support, in 1977, Cuban and Ethiopian forces repelled a Somali invasion of the Ogaden in southeastern Ethiopia. During 1978–1981, the civil war against the Derg raged in Eritrea province and a parallel insurgency grew in Tegre province on the southern border of Eritrea. In both provinces, the insurgent fronts espoused Marxist ideas and were dominated by the Tigrayan ethnic group. It is not often remembered that Marxist ideology fired the Eritrean rebel groups. In 1978, additional Ethiopian forces, now freed from combat in the Ogaden, entered Eritrea and retook most of the countryside.

To secure Eritrea politically and economically, the Communist government of Ethiopia in 1982 mounted large-scale military campaigns against both the Eritrean People's Liberation Front (EPLF) and the Tigrayan People's Liberation Front (TPLF). Trained by the Eritreans, the Tigrayans eventually formed the core of the Ethiopian People's Revolutionary Democratic Front, which eventually defeated Ethiopia's Communist government.

From 1983–84, the all-important rains failed and a drought ensued. With climatic aridity across northeastern Africa, the military policies and Stalinist central planning of Ethiopia's Derg created catastrophic famine in 1984–85. Western nations sent massive food aid to the beleaguered Communist government in Ethiopia, thereby aiding some seven million under the threat of starvation. At the same time, with this food, the West helped the Derg implement its plan of forced resettlement of peasants out of the north and away from the influence of the liberation fronts.

During 1985, the Derg's offensives against the Eritreans and Tigrayans continued. Owing to poor economic planning, the famine persisted in Eritrea and northern Ethiopia. The insurgent fronts gradually captured large amounts of Soviet tanks, artillery, other ordnance, and even Soviet advisors.

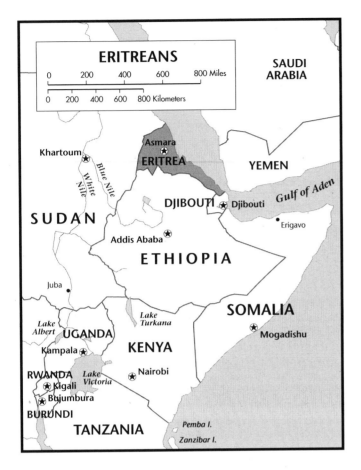

ERITREANS

By 1989, the Ethiopian government's largely conscripted military forces lost battles across Eritrea and Tegre provinces, died by the thousands, and surrendered in droves. Ethiopia, accordingly, began peace negotiations with the Eritreans. During 1991, the peace talks continued in Washington, while the insurgents' hold on Eritrea broadened. With U.S. prodding, on 21 May 1991 President Mengistu Haile Mariam resigned and fled Ethiopia, while the victorious Tigrayans, under Meles Zenawi, encircled the country's capital, Addis Abeba. The Stalinist Marxist government of Ethiopia surrendered on 27 May 1991. The Eritreans now completely controlled Eritrea, under Issaias Afwerki, who received military training in China during 1966. Outside of Asmara, near Kagnew, a Soviet "elephants' graveyard" grew: many hundreds of T–54 tanks, armored personnel carriers, and army trucks. De facto independence now existed for Eritrea.

Sovereignty became a reality for Eritrea on 27 April 1993, when virtually everyone in this land voted in a UN-certified referendum calling for independence from Ethiopia. On 24 May 1993 the Tigrayans controlling Ethiopia granted independence to the Tigrayans controlling Eritrea. Eritrea became the 52nd independent state in Africa and joined the United Nations and the Organization of African Unity (OAU) within the same week. Consequently landlocked Ethiopia, then a country of about 54 million, had its two seaports, Aseb and Mitsiwa, inside the sovereign country of Eritrea. At first, Eritrea was a friendly ally but then became a warring enemy and now is a hostile neighbor of Ethiopia. The same can be said of Ethiopia's relations with Eritrea.

During 1998–2000, Eritrea and Ethiopia fought another war with each other having heavy casualties and great loss of treasure for the two impoverished countries. After a truce, the United Nations has peace-keeping forces along the border of the two hostile countries, in a seemingly permanent Temporary Security Zone. In December 2006, Ethiopia invaded Somalia as a U.S. surrogate to suppress the Islamic Courts Union then controlling and stabilizing Somalia and befriended by Eritrea. In 2007 Ethiopia accused Eritrea of aiding militarily the fundamentalist Somalis opposing Ethiopia and the U.S. The Bush administration contemplated labeling Eritrea a rogue state, along with North Korea and Iran. In September 2007 the Eritrean government denied accusations that it aids terrorists in the Horn of Africa. The Eritrean Mufti (Jurist of Islamic Law), Sheik Al Amin Osman, announced in March 2008 that the peaceful relations among Eritrean Christians and Muslims were commendable.

The Eritrean People's Liberation Front reorganized into the People's Front for Democracy and Justice (PFDJ). Habte Selassie Bereket headed a Constitutional Commission providing a constitution in 1997, in time for national elections for a permanent government, but it is a charter still not fully implemented. Eritrea thereby became a presidential republic with a unicameral parliament. Issaias Afwerki became Eritrea's president and head of state. Eritrea is a one-party state governed by the PFDJ. Nongovernmental publishing ceased in September 2001. The government controls TV and radio stations. A private press is forbidden for matters of national security. In 2007 the activist organization Reporters without Borders placed Eritrea last on their world list regarding freedom of the press. Eritrea's legal system is based on the imperial Ethiopian legal code of 1957, with amendments and additions.

Fundamentalist Islamic groups in Sudan, a former ally of the Eritreans, aiding the fundamentalist Eritrean Islamic Jihad, strove to overthrow the secular government of Eritrea, which guarantees the freedom of all religions. Consequently, in 1995, Eritrea announced that it would support opposition groups bent on overthrowing the government of President Omar Hassan al Bashir in Sudan. Eritrea's undemarcated border with Sudan has been a concern of tension between the two countries but the tension now subsides.

² LOCATION AND HOMELAND

Eritrea (official name, Ertra) is named for the Red Sea (Latin, *Mare Erythraeum*). About the size of Pennsylvania, some 117,600 sq km (45,400 sq mi), Eritrea had a population, in 2007, of about 4.9 million people. Nine ethnic groups make up Eritrea. Almost a million Eritreans are scattered across the globe, because they fled the ravishes of civil war. The highland capital of Asmara (pop. about 400,000) is a pleasant, Italianate city, with broad, palm-lined boulevards as well as narrower, packed streets, and sunny, mild weather year-round. Using the Ethiopian calendar, the city boasts thirteen months of springtime.

Just north of the strait of Bab el-Mandeb, Eritrea's Red Sea coast stretches 1,014 km (630 mi), from Ras Kasar to Ras Dumeira. Besides the sea, Sudan, Djibouti, and Ethiopia bound Eritrea. The country comprises savanna, rugged highlands, and semidesert and desert plains. Scattered acacias and junipers dot the savanna, and almost all original forest cover long has been cleared, after some 3,000 years of plow agriculture. From east to west, topographically, Eritrea consists of a low coastal desert plain, some 16 to 89 km (10 to 55 mi) wide and including the Kobar Depression, descending to 116 m (380 ft) below sea level. A steep ascent of the northeastern escarpment of the Abyssinian Plateau reaches a level of almost 2,440 m (8,000 ft); descends gradually through Asmara, at 2,345 m (7,694 ft); slopes to Keren, at 1,390 m (4,560 ft); declines to Akordat, at 621 m (2,038 ft); and ends, as a steppe plain, on the Sudan border, at about 430 m (1,400 ft). Aridity increases the further west one travels from Asmara, which has 53 cm (21 in) of rain per year and an annual average temperature of 16.7°C (62°F).

3 LANGUAGE

Eritrea contains at least nine indigenous ethnic-linguistic groups. Native Eritrean languages include Ethio-Semitic—of the South Semitic branch of the Semitic family—Tigrinya and Tigre; Beja (Bedawi); Eastern Cushitic Afar and Saho; Central Cushitic Bilin Agaw; and Chari-Nile—of the Nilo-Saharan superfamily—Kunama and Nara. The related Eritrean languages, Tigrinya, and Tigre, the last of which is the language of no single ethnic group, are often confused. Perhaps 200,000 people largely in semi-pastoral groups, in the lower plains and on islands off the coast north of the Tigrayans, speak Tigre. Tigre-speakers include the eastern Beni Amirs; the western Beni Amirs speak Beja. Ethio-Semitic Amharic (Amharinya); Central Semitic modern Arabic; and Indo-European English and Italian are also spoken by some Eritreans. Arabic, a local language, is spoken in the coastal cities, along the Sudan border, and by the Rashaida pastoralists; English is the language of instruction in the secondary schools and higher education; and Italian is known by some in Asmara and other cities. The Semitic, Cushitic, and Omotic language families found in the Horn of Africa all belong to the Afro-Asiatic superfamily, including also Chadic, Berber, and ancient Egyptian families.

4 FOLKLORE

There is no folklore common to all nine ethnic groups of Eritrea. Religious folklore—Orthodox Christian, Muslim, Roman Catholic, and various pagan faiths—is shared among the respective adherents of each faith and is part of the cosmology of each of the nine cultures. (For cosmology, see sections 5 and 20 and section 20 of Djiboutians.)

5 RELIGION

Eritreans are, roughly, half Christians and half Sunni Muslims. Some Protestantism is found and Roman Catholicism exists, centering on Our Lady of the Rosary Cathedral in downtown Asmara. Enda Mariam is the principal Orthodox house of worship in Asmara, and the impressive Jamie el-Khulafa'e el-Rashidin Mosque is near the city hall. Roman Catholicism was introduced with Italian colonialism. Tigrayans who are Muslim have the designation Jebarti, thus setting them apart from Christians.

The native Ethiopian Orthodox Christianity is often mistakenly labeled as Coptic; however, it has the Alexandrian rite under the aegis of the Patriarch of Alexandria. Adherents of this Ethiopian Christianity consider themselves the legitimate heirs of the Israelites of the Old Testament. According to the traditional *Kebra Nagast,* written in the ancient Ethio-Semitic liturgical language, Ge'ez, the God of Israel transferred His abode on earth from Jerusalem to Aksum, Ethiopia. Indeed,

the religion of the Ethiopian Christianity is *be-orit* (by the Old Testament), and the central room of every church, the holy of holies, contains not an altar with the host, but a replica of the Ark of the Covenant *(tabot).* According to local beliefs, the original ark and the remnants of the true cross are hidden under separate mountains in Eritrea-Ethiopia, considered the holiest of lands. Another belief has the Ark secluded in a church of Aksum, Ethiopia.

Orthodox Christian priests both sing and dance in their ceremonies. Services are in Ge'ez, ancestral to Tigrinya, Tigre, and Amharic. The monarchs, of which Haile Selassie (whose name means "Power of the Holy Trinity" in Amharic) was the last, purportedly descend from King Solomon and the Queen of Sheba. Ethiopian Orthodox believers are monophysite Christians, that is, they do not subscribe to the creed that Christ has two natures, human and divine. Rather, they believe that Christ has only a unified nature.

Religion is more than a body of rituals and creeds. For most of the world's peoples it is the core of their particular cosmology. Religious cosmology is a worldview providing the unifying, overarching ethos of a society and its culture, for example, of Tigrayans, Kunama, Afar, Beja, Bilin, etc. Such cosmology is grounded in supernaturalism and human social relations with a spirit realm. It has values and practices fostered by supernaturalistic interpretations of the world, as it is concomitantly conceived. The ever-changing religious cosmology of each Eritrean society is a body of socially learned belief collectively carried by the members of that people. It is handed down from generation to generation. The cosmology of a society provides satisfying answers to the underlying "how's," "why's," "where's" questions of life. It is a people's conceptualization about how their universe functions; why it functions in particular ways; and where their conceived universe is situated in space and time. A religious cosmology, then, answers humankind's age-old questions of existence. (See **Gender Issues** below and **Djibouti Gender Issues** for further discussion of cosmology in the Horn of Africa.)

6 MAJOR HOLIDAYS

The religious holidays of Eritrea are those of Islam and the Ethiopian Orthodox Church. The Ethiopian Orthodox holidays, *Fasika* and *Timkat,* and the Muslim holidays are geared to a lunar rather than solar calendar; thus, their dates vary. Major Muslim holidays include Eid el-Fitr in the spring, Eid el-Fahta in the summer, and Eid el-Nabi (the Prophet's birthday) in the summer.

Religious days of the Orthodox Church accord with the Ethiopian Calendar, which differs from the Gregorian one commonly used in Western countries (and now Eritrea's standard calendar as well). Thus, for example, Christmas falls on 7 January. Easter *(Fasika),* Epiphany *(Timkat),* and *Meskel* (Finding of the True Cross on 27 September), are the major Christian holidays. Christian congregations also have their own localized holidays, for a particular saint or angel.

Secular Eritrean holidays exist as well. These include New Year's Day on January 1, Women's Day on March 8, Labor Day on May 1, Independence Day on May 24, Martyrs' Day on June 20, Beginning of Armed Resistance Day on September 1, and (Western) Christmas on December 25.

Officially, nowadays, a 24-hour clock exists; Eritrean Time is GMT plus 3 hours. Traditional folk in the country and many townspersons, however, keep the ancient mode of time reckoning, with a cosmology reflecting nature. They determine approximate time from the position of the sun during daytime. Here the first hour of the day begins at dawn and the twelfth hour ends at dusk. A second 12-hour demi-cycle follows, until dawn.

⁷ RITES OF PASSAGE

Eritreans mark major life events within the religious traditions of either Christianity or Islam. Major Christian rituals include baptism, weddings, funerals, and second funerals forty days after death. As among most of the peoples of the Horn, adult status for the various Eritrean ethnic groups requires a genital operation, with or without ceremony, usually in childhood. Boys are circumcised and girls undergo clitoridectomy, a practice controlling their sexuality. The vast majority of women of Eritrea have undergone this ritual. (For more on clitoridectomy, see Djiboutians section 20.)

⁸ INTERPERSONAL RELATIONS

There are no common greetings shared by all nine Eritrean ethnic groups. However, it is not uncommon for people to hold hands while talking, and to kiss twice on each cheek when greeting. Respect for one's elders is paramount in all behavior.

⁹ LIVING CONDITIONS

Eritrea is one of the world's poorest countries. During 1993 per capita per year income was estimated at between $70 and $150, compared to $330 for most of sub-Saharan Africa. For 2007 this income was questionably estimated at about $1,000. During the devastating civil war perhaps 200,000 Eritreans were killed; facilities for wage employment—factories, mines, and plantations—were destroyed; and roads, railroads, and port structures were torn apart. At the end of the war, 80% of Eritreans were dependent on foreign food aid. Thus jobs for the multitudes of displaced persons are necessary, but the required development capital is almost nonexistent. Until 1995 the former guerrilla fighters working for the new government collected only a basic living allowance rather than a salary. Additionally, with tens of thousands of returning refugees and the war's desolation, an acute housing shortage exists.

The average life expectancy of Eritreans at birth is 60 years. In 2007 the infant mortality rate was estimated at 45 deaths for every 1,000 live births. In 2003, the incidence of adult HIV infection was an estimated 2.7%

A highway network connects all the cities of Eritrea with Ethiopia and Sudan. The 95-cm-gauge Eritrean Railway, destroyed during the civil war, is reconstructed from Mitsiwa (Massawa) to Asmara, but not yet from Asmara to Akordat. Asmara and Aseb provide air service to the outside world. Both Mitsiwa and Aseb have recently improved deep-water ports with cargo-hoisting capabilities and covered storage but which Ethiopia no longer uses. A rebuilt highway from Mitsiwa to Asmara and a new coastal one from Mitsiwa to Aseb enhance foreign trade.

¹⁰ FAMILY LIFE

Arranged marriages are the rule in Eritrea. Among the Tigray, the contracts governing arranged marriages included provisions for divorce, and it is not unusual for both men and women to marry more than once. Women in Eritrea have formed the National Union of Eritrean Women, which has some 200,000 members.

¹¹ CLOTHING

Eritreans in urban areas wear Western-style clothing. A common traditional costume of men and women in both Eritrea and Ethiopia is the *shämma*, which consists of a large piece of cotton cloth wrapped around the body to form a dress-like garment, with a smaller piece of the same fabric used for headgear, either a scarf or hood. The cloth has a brightly colored, decorated border, sometimes including silk in the weave, which is arranged at the hemline. Plastic sandals are the most common footwear among Eritreans. In some areas of Eritrea, men and women wrap a piece of cloth around their waists and knot it to form a skirt-like garment; this may be worn with or without a shirt or other top. In the torrid Danakil region of the Afar, women are nude from the waist up. A typical hairstyle among Eritrean women is the *shiurba*, in which the hair is worn braided across the top and sides of the head and loose at the back. Many Christian Eritreans have crosses tattooed on their foreheads. In rural areas, some married women wear gold bands in their noses.

¹² FOOD

Among the main dietary staples in Eritrea is a flatbread made from a native cereal grain (called *teff* in Amharic and Tigrinya) and eaten with a spicy pepper-laden stew. Other grain staples include barley and wheat. There are many varieties of barley and wheat cultivated, with different ethnic groups growing different types. Tigrayan varieties of wheat include *desaleny* and *ayiquertem,* and of barley, *saida* and *saisa*. Sorghum and coffee are both common ancient crops; safflower, a native oil seed, and an ancient form of flax are both cultivated for oil and food. Chick peas (known as *shimbra* to Tigrayans) are an important food staple. Goats, sheep, cattle, and even camel meats are relished, depending on the ethnic group. Coffee is drunk, with a pinch of salt, often in elaborate ceremonies of coffee preparation for honored guests. During the course of a fragrant half-hour, red coffee berries could be plucked from the tree and roasted on a griddle. The blackened beans are then ground in a mortar, and the grounds are boiled in a pot. Finally, the black liquid is poured into cups and enjoyed as a social occasion.

¹³ EDUCATION

The estimated literacy rate in 2003 for Eritreans was about 59%. Islamic Koranic and church schools traditionally have instructed a few males in literacy. Those becoming Islamic or Christian clergymen received advanced education in religious schools. Some of the monastery sites of higher education date to the beginnings of Christianity. Since 1941, secular government schools were developed somewhat and then curtailed by the civil war. By 1964, as the civil war began its intensity, about 200 elementary and 9 secondary schools had some 44,000 pupils. In 1973 Eritrea possessed 17 secondary schools. As of 1994, about 42% of children were enrolled in elementary school. There were 37 pupils for every teacher and 68 for every textbook. In the early 21st century, over 800 schools provide instruction, with a university and a technical institute proving post-secondary education.

A common traditional costume of men and women in both Eritrea and Ethiopia is the shamma, which consists of a large piece of cotton cloth wrapped around the body to form a dress-like garment, with a smaller piece of the same fabric used for head-gear, either a scarf or hood. (Cory Langley)

14 CULTURAL HERITAGE

Tigrayans have a 3,000-year-old literary tradition, and have practiced iron metallurgy for over 2,500 years. Traditional musical instruments of the Eritreans include pipes, harmonicas, and the *kirir*, which resembles a guitar. The Tigre people have a sacred artistic tradition within Christianity that includes music (directed by monastically trained men) as well as Biblical illumination, scroll making, and icon painting.

15 WORK

About 85% of all work resides in the traditional agricultural sector, comprising cultivation of crops and husbandry of livestock. The average Eritrean remains a ruralist, unaccustomed to the demands of working in the modern cash economy. A few large-scale commercial farming enterprises exist, producing cattle, cotton, sisal, tomatoes for canning, and garden vegetables. Modern industries providing wage employment include textiles, tanning, leather and plastic shoes, fishing, and salt production. In addition, small enterprises abound, such as oil-seed pressing, flour milling, soap making, plastic container fabricating, and tire retreading. Eritrea smelts steel from the many Soviet military vehicles littering the countryside, thus beating swords into plowshares.

The rebuilding of the Eritrean Railway is developing groups of skilled craftspeople—machinists, boilermakers, black-smiths, pipe fitters, sheet-metal workers, welders, electricians, timber sawyers, stone masons, and carpenters. These skilled workers comprise a body of instructors for training the unskilled, unemployed segment of the workforce. Additionally, the schedule and safety demands of railroading help workers develop discipline and work habits they need to be successful in industrial settings.

16 SPORTS

The majority of Eritreans are traditional rural cultivators and pastoralists with little opportunity for sports. Among those who enjoy sports, soccer is the most popular. During the war for independence, rebel fighters would gather to watch matches. A traditional game among the Afar is *kwosso*, in which the goal is to keep a ball made of rolled goatskins (resembling a soccer ball) away from the opposing team. Eritrean athletes compete in international track and field events and become national heroes. Bicycle racing is a popular spectator sport centering on the killing Tour of Eritrea, from the coastal desert up the steep escarpment almost 2,440 m (8,000 ft) to the summit and, then, downgrade to Asmara.

17 ENTERTAINMENT AND RECREATION

Urban dwellers, especially teens, enjoy dancing at clubs. Today the main boulevard of the capital city, Asmara, is lined with

The Tigrayan people weave coarse grasses into baskets. (Cory Langley)

open-air cafes, bars, and patisseries. Television is available in Eritrea, with broadcasting in Tigrinya and Arabic. There are also radio broadcasts, as well as government controlled newspapers. These print media are mainly enjoyed by the educated elite, however. The majority of Eritreans do not participate in recreational activities in the Western sense.

18 FOLK ART, CRAFTS, AND HOBBIES

Among the typical Tigrayans, little exists in the way of arts and crafts, except for weaving coarse grass mats. Church art and written music among priests and monks are exceptions. The concept of a hobby is unknown and not applicable to these people.

The Tigrayans practice *Qene*, an intellectually challenging spoken duel using especially composed poetry verses. At wedding and other occasions, Tigrayan men perform a dance that includes jumping rhythmically up and down while singing. Songs may be traditional, or newer, such as "Addis Abeba" ("New Flower"), after the capital of Ethiopia founded in the 1880s.

19 SOCIAL PROBLEMS

To minimize ethnic divisiveness, the Organization of African Unity resisted all separatist movements on the continent until the 1990s. The separation of Eritrea from Ethiopia marks the first redrawing of borders in Africa, a continent with over 1,300 ethnic groups, some of which at times are fratricidal. The leadership of Eritrea faces the challenge of marshalling the

country's diverse peoples to build an economically viable and politically secure state, with almost no financial and material resources.

In the wake of its devastating civil war and the war of 1998–2000, Eritrea faces the challenges of continuing to repair its damaged infrastructure, finding employment for the former rebel fighters, and providing services for the many thousands of people disabled in the fighting. Other social problems include a low per capita income, lack of medical facilities, a housing shortage, and a large part of the population in the armed forces.

20 GENDER ISSUES

Cosmology is a view of the ordering of the world, a blueprint of the way things are. With their religious cosmologies, humans reduce the seeming chaos in the experiential world to a purported, often logically circular, meaningfulness. Cosmology allows an apparent certainty for action and thought and an apparent guide for rational behavior, including gender relations. Throughout the Horn of Africa, socialization into the male and female genders is reinforced in the core aspects of a cosmology such as its values, norms, statuses and roles, and etiquette. Gender is the socially learned cultural overlay a society places on biological sex, either of the two categories in which humans are divided regarding reproductive functions. In other words, gender means what it is to be male or female and just how "male" or "female" one should be.

For Eritreans of various ethnic groups, the creator god of each people is a male. For the Christian Tigrayans and Muslims, he is the God of Abraham (named, respectively, Egziabeher [Lord of the Sky] and Allah [the God]); for the Afar, he is Wak; and for the Kunama, he is Anna.) In each religious cosmology, he intends males to dominate women, deemed to be the lesser of the two sexes. Women were created by god for the purposes of obeying and serving their husbands, including by rendering domestic services and bearing and nurturing children for them. Males have a monopoly on controlling religious knowledge. Men alone become religious practitioners who interpret the cosmology providing the matrix of a culture.

In Islamic societies the low status of women stems largely from pre-Islamic patriarchal (control by males) traditions rather than directly from the more recent Quran. However, in Islam and Eritrea's pre-Islamic religions, blood from menses is believed ritually polluted. Whatever the root source, in Islam women's rights are constricted. Accordingly, in these cosmologies, women are viewed as potential ritual polluters of humans and nature. Such views help rationalize the holding of religious and political power exclusively by men.

Religious cosmology contains myth, or an explanatory "history" of supernatural and human beings who were or are important actors in a particular cosmic concept of the universe. Myths are sacred tales, passed from generation to generation, with dogmatic rather than verifiable content. Myth not only explains cosmological states and processes, it justifies the orders of things in the world. For example, Eve is the originator of sin; therefore, women are punished in childbirth by labor pains. In some accounts Eve (woman) is a mere derivative of Adam (man). Especially in its mythic aspect, cosmology supports and either realistically or symbolically exemplifies the core values and norms in a culture. In turn, cosmology and its related values are reflected in and reinforced by ritual, for example, a father giving a bride to the groom.

As they relate to values and norms, most cosmologies contain moralisms, or ideals of conformities with generally accepted standards of goodness in character and behavior. Myths often reinforce charters or explanatory rationales for the reason why things are the way they are. In this way the institutions and social order of a society are vindicated. Given the existence of a particular background cosmology for a society, a monocultural person rarely looks beyond the "proofs" engendered by the elements of this worldview, including for gender. Socialized to a particular cosmology, a person consciously and unconsciously selects, rejects, and fits information to fashion a satisfying consistency regarding his or her world vision. Accordingly, males and females in patriarchal and other societies, such as those in Eritrea, do not believe but, instead, know the social and ritual superiority of men over women. (For some thought-provoking gender issues, see Djibouti, section 20.)

21 BIBLIOGRAPHY

Africa Watch. "Eritrea: Freedom of Expression and Ethnic Discrimination in the Educational System: Past and Future." *Human Rights Watch/Africa* 5 no. 1 (January 12, 1993).

Bauer, Dan F. *Household and Society in Ethiopia: An Economic and Social Analysis of Tigray Social Principles and Household Organization*, 2nd ed. East Lansing: African Studies Center, Michigan State University, 1985.

Berg, Lois A. *An Eritrean Family*. Minneapolis: Lerner Publications, 1997.

Brooks, Miguel F., ed. *Kebra Nagast (The Glory of Kings)*. Lawrenceville, NJ: Red Sea Press, 1995.

Cliffe, Lionel, and Basil Davidson. *The Long Struggle for Eritrea*. Trenton, NJ: Red Sea Press, 1988.

Connell, Dan. *Getting Home Is Only Half the Challenge: Refugee Integration in War-Ravaged Eritrea*. Washington, DC: U.S. Committee for Refugees, 2001.

Country Profile. Eritrea. London: Economist Intelligence Unit, 2004.

Davidson, Basil, et al., ed. *Behind the War in Eritrea*. Nottingham: Spokesman, 1980.

Duffield, Mark, and John Prendergast. *Without Troops and Tanks: Humanitarian Intervention Ethiopia and Eritrea*. Lawrenceville, NJ: Red Sea Press, 1994.

Eritrea: A Country Handbook. Asmara: Ministry of Information, 2002.

Erlich, Haggai. *The Struggle over Eritrea, 1962-1978: War and Revolution in the Horn of Africa*. Stanford, CA: Hoover Institution Press, 1983.

Gamst, Frederick C. "Beja." In *Muslim Peoples: A World Ethnographic Survey*, 2nd ed. edited by Richard V. Weeks, vol. 1, pp. 130–137. Westport, CT: Greenwood Press, 1984.

———. "Bilin." In *Muslim Peoples: A World Ethnographic Survey*, 2nd ed. edited by Richard V. Weeks, vol. 1, pp. 162–167. Westport, CT: Greenwood Press, 1984.

———. "Conflict in the Horn of Africa." In *Peace and War: Cross-Cultural Perspectives*, edited by Mary L. Foster and Robert A. Rubenstein, New Brunswick, NJ: Transaction Books, 1986.

Gayim, Eyassu. *The Eritrean Question: The Conflict between the Right of Self-Determination and the Interests of States*. Uppsala: Lustus Forlag, 1993.

Gebre-Medhin, Jordan. *Peasants and Nationalism in Eritrea*. Trenton, NJ: Red Sea Press, 1989.

Henze, Paul B. *Layers of Time: A History of Ethiopia*. New York: St. Martin's Press, 2000.

Keneally, Thomas. *To Asmara: A Novel of Africa*. New York: Warner Books, 1989.

Machida, Robert. *Eritrea: The Struggle for Independence*. Trenton, NJ: Red Sea Press, 1987.

Mesghenna, Yemane. *Italian Colonialism: A Case of Study of Eritrea 1869-1934*. Lund: Lund University. 1988.

Normile, Dennis. "Driven to Extinction. Rinderpest." *Science*, vol. 319 (2008):1606–1609.

Papstein, Robert. *Eritrea: Tourist Guide*. Lawrenceville, NJ: Red Sea Press, 1995.

Pateman, Roy. *Eritrea: Even the Stones Are Burning*. Lawrenceville, NJ: Red Sea Press, 1997.

Research and Information Center on Eritrea. Bibliography on *Eritrea*. New York, 1982.

Sherman, Richard. *Eritrea: The Unfinished Revolution*. New York: Praeger, 1980.

Tekle, Amare. *Eritrea and Ethiopia; From Conflict to Cooperation*. Lawrenceville, NJ: Red Sea Press, 1994.

Tesfagiorgis, Gebre Hiwet. *Emergent Eritrea: Challenges of Economic Development*. Trenton, NJ: Red Sea Press, 1993.

Uhlig, Siegbert. *Encyclopaedia Aethiopica*, 4 vols. Wiesbaden: Harrssowitz Verlag, 2003–2008.

U.S. Department of the Army. Federal Research Division, Library of Congress. *Ethiopia: A Country Study*. 4th ed. Edited by Harold D. Ofcansky and LaVerle Berry. Area Handbook Series. Washington, D.C.: Government Printing Office, 1993.

Yohannes, Okbazghi. *Eritrea: A Pawn in World Politics*. Gainesville, FL: University of Florida Press, 1991.

—by F. C. Gamst

ETHIOPIANS

PRONUNCIATION: ee-thee-OH-pee-uhns
ALTERNATE NAMES: Abyssinians
LOCATION: Ethiopia
POPULATION: 52 million
LANGUAGE: Amharic; English; French; Italian; Arabic; various tribal dialects
RELIGION: Coptic Monophysite Christianity; Islam; indigenous religions
RELATED ARTICLES: Vol. 1: Afar; Amhara; Fulani; Oromos; Tigray

¹ INTRODUCTION

Evidence of Ethiopia's past reaches back to the dawn of human existence. The 1974 discoveries of paleoanthropologist Dr. Donald Johanson and his team first revealed an ancient female ancestor of humanity that he named Lucy. She was found in the northeast quadrant of Ethiopia in the Awash river valley at a site called Hadar. She was dated at about 3.5 million years old and was a member of a prehuman species called Australopithecus. The casts of her bones now reside in the Cleveland Museum of Natural History. Her actual bones are locked in a large vault in the National Museum in Addis Ababa, the capital city of Ethiopia. Subsequently, many other bones were found of the same age and were called Lucy's family. In 1992–94, paleoanthropologist Dr. Tim White and his team found even older bones, discovered 45 miles southwest of Hadar, which now has brought our ancestry back to possibly 4.5 million years ago. More recently, paleoanthropologist Dr. Yohannis Haile Sellassie and his team, also working in the Afar region discovered remains that reach back more than 5 million years to the chimpanzee-hominid species boundary. These exciting discoveries teach us much about not only how old our prehuman ancestors are, but also that we all emerged from a common ancestral family. Ethiopia is the homeland of us all.

For millennia primitive peoples hunted and gathered their subsistence in the resourceful valleys and highlands of what we now know as Ethiopia. The word "Etyopya" is from the ancient Greek meaning "The land of people with burnt faces." It was an area of continuous population movement. Peoples from the Saudi Arabian mainland crossed the narrow straits of the Bab el Mandeb at the southeastern extremity of the Red Sea bringing their culture and technology with them and settled into the northern reaches of Ethiopia. Peoples of the Sudan to the west and the peoples of the desert to the east were also in a state of migration and many found Ethiopia to be hospitable and they settled among and mixed with populations who originally came from other lands. A major factor encouraging these movements and settlement was trade. Food items and spices, salt bars used as currency, gold and precious stones, domestic animals and wild animal skins, and slaves; material goods found in one area and not in other areas became sought after and stimulated the migrations of traders and their families and the growth of market towns. This activity has persisted for 2,000 years and continues into the present.

Peoples of the vast rolling highland plateau, commonly known as Abyssinia, found rich volcanic soils to grow their crops in an abundance that permitted large aggregates of peo-

ple to live together. With such large groups of people complex political organizations formed. Centralized kingships became a dominant type of institution, which to the observer, looked something like the feudal systems of the European middle ages. Until the 19th century these autonomous fiefdoms were dominant in the highlands. Then in the mid-19th century, Emperor Menelik consolidated these fiefdoms and many other tribal groups into one empire. This consolidated empire was a continuation of a long line of Abyssinian emperorships that lasted until 1974, when Emperor Haile Sellassie I was overthrown in a bloody revolution that persisted until 1991, when two major northern peoples swept down and took power and formed what the new government calls a "democratic" revolution.

² LOCATION AND HOMELAND

Ethiopia is situated on the eastern "horn" of the African continent. It is bound by the Red Sea to the northeast, Sudan to the west, Kenya to the south, and Somalia to the east. A great cleavage in the African continental plate runs south from the Red Sea all the way into the Indian Ocean. This major geological formation is known as the Great Rift Valley. In Ethiopia, the Great Rift Escarpment forms what is considered to be one of the more spectacular regions on earth—at 14,000 ft one can look straight down into an abyss of fog and clouds and hear the eagles, hawks, antelope, ibex, monkeys, and hyenas calling in the distance below. Looking out onto the valley's lowlands, when the afternoon winds have blown the fog and clouds away and before the rains come in the late afternoon, one can see the desert lowlands with vast, steep-walled mountains rising from the valley floor some 3,000–6,000 ft. These are called *amba* and are the remains of extinct volcanoes that accumulated gradually over a period of thousands of years.

To the south in the Great Rift Valley, one finds steaming thermal lakes where underground water broke free with quaking earth and came to the surface, creating a series of lakes extending down through sub-Saharan east Africa. The lush forests of southern Ethiopia, its rich alluvial river and lake soils, and the plentitude of fish and land animals and birds, provided ample food resources for numerous tribal peoples who still inhabit this region and sustain cultural traditions that reach back 10,000 years. Today, within the national boundaries of Ethiopia some 52 million people reside, comprising more than 80 separate cultures and languages.

³ LANGUAGE

Since it was the Amhara people who dominated vast regions of Ethiopia for some 2,000 years and maintained a line of kings governing Abyssinia, their language, Amharic, has become the dominant language of the country. It is a Semitic language, having similarities to both Arabic and Hebrew. Because of the significant influence of Great Britain from the 19th century onward, and because of the presence and influence of America in the 20th century, English has become the second dominant language of this country. Generally, both Amharic and English are the languages of business, medicine, and the academic disciplines. But language and culture in Ethiopia are very complex because of the many other linguistic and cultural influences. One finds a family of northern languages in Eritrea. The Cushitic family of languages are spoken by a majority population of Oromo peoples in the central regions of Ethiopia. The desert-dwelling peoples of the southeast speak dialects of

Somali. In the south and southwest we find the Omotic family of languages spoken by numerous smaller tribal groups. Many of these languages, especially those spoken by the minority tribal groups, have no written traditions, and the cultures of these peoples are carried on by oral traditions. They are called nonliterate cultures, but there is no devaluing of these peoples because they exist without writing. One language of Ethiopia is not spoken by any cultural population at all. It is called Geez, an ancient Ethiopic language used in Coptic Christian religious contexts by the clergy. Scriptures are written in Geez, and prayers, chants, and songs are uttered in Geez within the Ethiopian Christian Church. Geez functions something like Latin in the Catholic religion.

Languages from the West are also well recognized: French because of French enterprises in the early part of the 20th century, building a railroad and establishing schools, and Italian because of the Italian occupation during World War II. Today most automobile and refrigerator parts have Italian names. Arabic is a dominant language of business among people dealing in commerce with Arabia and the Middle East.

⁴ FOLKLORE

Every culture has its own body of folklore, myths, legends, song, poetry, stories, and parables, all revealing the identity of the culture and the common sense of morality and tradition among the people of that culture. It would take an encyclopedia of folklore to illustrate the examples from the many cultures of Ethiopia. Here, one myth, the Abyssinian story of Solomon and Sheba, may serve as an example of the usefulness and significance of myth and folklore in one particular culture.

Meqedes, Queen of the land of Sheba (in Amharic she is also known as Saba), knew of King Solomon's great wisdom and wished to visit him in the land of Israel. So she summoned a businessman, a trader who traveled far and wide and knew the paths to Israel. She gave him delicate perfumes and scents from a variety of barks and flowers and sent him to offer these to King Solomon, who accepted them with curiosity and anticipation, wondering about this new queen from the land of Ethiopia. The trader returned with the good news that King Solomon would be interested in meeting her. She gathered her retinue of handmaidens, cooks, body guards, and slaves and set off to the land of Israel by boat up the Nile and by camel across the great deserts.

King Solomon personally greeted Saba at his gate and they introduced themselves. Solomon invited Saba and her retinue to a great feast. Then the King invited Saba to sleep with him. The Queen refused politely but with resolution. That night, King Solomon took Saba's maidservant to bed with him and they sleep together. The next evening King Solomon and Saba dined together. The King had instructed his cooks to make the food very spicy and salty. Then that night, the King invited Saba to sleep with him, promising not to touch her so long as she does not take anything belonging to the King—if she did, he could have her. Saba agreed to this and went to bed with King Solomon. That night Saba awoke with a great thirst and drank some of Solomon's water. He caught her and reminded her of their agreement. They slept together and he impregnated her with new life.

The Queen of Sheba returns to her land and in time bears a child, whom she names Menelik. As Menelik grows through

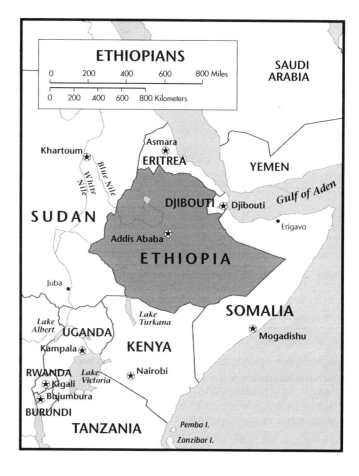

childhood, Saba, also known as Meqdes, teaches him about his father, King Solomon, and he draws a picture of his father to keep near as a remembrance. As a young man, Menelik travels back to the land of Israel to meet and know his father. Menelik, who will succeed his mother to the throne of Sheba in the land of Abyssinia, remembers the great ark and the tablets that were handed down by God to Moses on Sinai. He arranges with his retinue to have the Ark of the Covenant taken from its place and brought back to the land of Sheba without the knowledge or consent of the Israelites. Back in his native land, Menelik installs the Great Ark in the Church of St. Mary at Axum, thereby sanctifying the land of Sheba and legitimating the origin and royal line of the Solomonic dynasty.

This myth exists to this day. It is a very important myth because it gives the Abyssinian peoples a sense of historical identity. It also legitimated or justified the emperor's right to rule by linking the Abyssinian people with God, Moses, and the Holy Ark of the Covenant—the critical link being Menelik, sired by King Solomon, who was of the royal line of kings sanctioned and blessed by God. And, if you read closely, you can get a bit of the flavor of Abyssinian culture: the sending of sentient gifts to beg an invitation, Solomon's craftiness at having conjugal relations with Meqdes, the Queen of Sheba, and Menelik's absconding with the Ark from Israel and installing it at Axum, thereby transferring that great power to his own land. And, as with any culture one studies, folklore is an expression of a people about themselves and how they see and feel about the world in which they live.

5 RELIGION

Religious belief and ritual vary with each culture existing within the boundaries of Ethiopia. With over 80 languages spoken, one can find over 80 cultures and over 80 religions. Yet one finds commonalities and overlaps in religious belief and ritual. In general, there are three major religions practiced by Ethiopian populations: Coptic Monophysite Christianity, Islam, and indigenous (or what some people used to call pagan) religion. Ethiopian Coptic Christianity was adopted by the Abyssinian peoples (north central highland populations) in the 4th century. This religion has not changed very much in the almost 2,000 years it has been practiced by Ethiopians of the highlands. This form of Christianity still contains many of the Hebraic and pagan elements that one would expect to find during the time when Christ's disciples were preaching to the villagers of Galilee. If you traveled into the highland countryside today and mingled with the peasantry and came to know their way of life, you would feel as though you were walking into the times of the Old Testament. Ethiopian Christianity is a museum of early Christian life, and for that reason is a very important area of study.

Whereas Ethiopian Christianity is practiced by a minority of the total Ethiopian population, Islam is practiced by the great majority of the Ethiopian population. It must be stressed that each culture practices their religion in their own way and makes many distinctive interpretations that other cultures do not share. So one finds many different cultures of Ethiopia practicing Islam, each interpreting the Koran a bit differently, and each with a slightly different nuance of practice from the other. One notable ritual practice is the chewing of *qat*, or *tchat*. This is a plant that grows in proliferation and is a multi-million dollar industry in Ethiopia with exports to several Middle Eastern countries. The leaves are most often bitter to the taste and provide a mild stimulant that can keep one awake through the night. Often these people will work very hard at their jobs of trading or farming through the morning, and then at noon they will cease their work and chew for the rest of the day, socializing, praying, and attending to nonessential business.

The third major category of Ethiopian religion is indigenous religion. This is a generic term for the ancient religions practiced often by tribal peoples who live by 10,000 year old traditions. Sometimes one finds the overlay of a Protestant religion taught by missionaries living amongst a particular people, or a thin appearance of Islam which came as an outside influence. But, these ancient religions have served the people well, adapting them to the world and allowing them to survive with vitality and spirit to this day.

One cannot leave issues of religion without mention of the Falasha, or Bete Yisroel, the Hebraic people of Ethiopia who practice an ancient, pre-Talmudic form of Judaism. From the 11th through the 13th centuries these people formed a powerful political entity in the very high reaches of the Semien Mountains and for a period of time controlled the Abyssinian population. Because they were vanquished by the Abyssinians at the end of the 13th century, they became landless and made their living working in metal, clay, cloth, and tanning hides. They existed as a despised caste group that other peoples were, nevertheless, dependent upon because of their fine crafting skills. Because of the upheavals of famine and civil war—at one point they were caught in the crossfire of that war—and

because of high-level political manipulations, two massive Israeli airlifts brought the majority of these people to Israel, their promised land.

6 MAJOR HOLIDAYS

Although the majority of holidays are of a religious nature—and they are numerous—there are some secular holidays recognized by all Ethiopians alike. The Ethiopian New Year is celebrated in September because they use the Julian calendar, which contains 12 months of 30 days, plus a 6-day "month" which ends their year. New Year's Day is a time of celebration, during which the people slaughter chickens, goats, and sheep, and sometimes a steer. They welcome the New Year with singing and dancing. The other major holiday today can be translated as "Freedom Day" or "Independence Day," and celebrates the northern fighters sweeping down into Addis Ababa and ousting the former dictatorship after a 30-year civil war. During both holidays there are parades, feasts, and dancing to the traditional Ethiopian music.

7 RITES OF PASSAGE

Birth is not a very significant time for rites of passage in Ethiopia, because the family is anxious about the survival of the newborn and does not know whether their god will take the infant or let it gain strength through childhood. Infant mortality may vary between 20% and 40% depending on the particular people and where they live. For the Christian and Islamic groups, genital cutting marks a rite of passage into the religious world and provides cultural identity for the boys and girls involved. For the boys it is a simple circumcision ceremony. For the girls, depending on the cultural group, her operation may vary from an excision of the labia minor or clitoral hood, to a more radical clitoridectomy. For many groups in Ethiopia, marriage is a significant event in which the couple assumes the full responsibilities which include work roles and the rearing of children who will carry on the family name and maintain the family estate.

Among the highland Ethiopians, the virginity of a bride is considered extremely important, and her virginal blood must be in evidence upon the marital bed sheets before this first marriage is legitimated. The funeral ritual is the other major rite of passage in which the community grieves and celebrates the passing of the spiritual body into the realm of God.

8 INTERPERSONAL RELATIONS

Throughout Ethiopia one finds both formal and informal ways of relating to others. The formal method of communication and relation lubricates the busy comings and goings and business of everyday living, prevents potential conflicts from coming to the surface, and provides a threshold through which people may enter into more informal conversation if they wish. Among the Amharic speakers in Ethiopia (most people speak Amharic even if it isn't their mother tongue, because it is the national language), when greeting an acquaintance, one will say *tenayistilign* ("may God give you health for me"), and the other will answer in kind. Then the first speaker will say *dehna neh?* ("you are fine?") if he or she is speaking to someone familiar. The other will answer, *awon, dehna negn* ("Yes I am fine"). They will question each other about their wives, children, and other close relatives. This can be repeated over and over again several times before they lapse into conversation.

Then, if they are close and wish more of each others' company, there will be an invitation to one's home. It is an honor to be invited because it means you will feast with them and drink beer and liquor, spending hours in warm conversation telling all the news one can remember. Normally, if one is invited to another's home, one should bring a gift. The traditional visiting gifts in Ethiopia include coffee or sugar, a bottle of liquor or honey wine, or fruit or eggs. The giving of food and drink is practically a sacred act.

9 LIVING CONDITIONS

Many Americans and Europeans have learned of the drought and famine in Ethiopia which has left parts of that country devastated. However, this is just one part of Ethiopia—the north central region—that has been affected, aggravated by a civil war that persisted until 1991. There are really four major ecological zones that determine particular living conditions for Ethiopians. To the east are the desert nomads, whom *National Geographic* considers to be one of the toughest and most ferocious peoples on earth. They live with their camel and cattle herds in one of the most hostile places on earth, the Afar Desert and Danakil Depression, where temperatures can climb to 140°F. Salt bars are still mined here and sold as currency. In contrast, the great highland plateau rises from 9,000 to 14,000 ft, with fertile soils allowing rich harvests for large populations of Abyssinians living in a fairly complex political system.

Work roles are distinctive among men and women. Women start the day at dawn, get the water, make the coffee, prepare the grains for the day's meals, and care for the children. Men get up a bit later and, depending on the season, will till the soil with plowshare and oxen, allow the animals to fertilize it with dung, harvest the grain crops, and defend the homestead in times of strife. Men usually have much more leisure time than the women. But through the day there is always time for coffee parties and much gossip and lively conversation. Adults and children tell stories by the hearth fires at night and retire between 10:00 pm and midnight. To the south, one finds tribal peoples living in a horticultural ecology, cultivating food-giving plants around the homestead, and whose daily rounds are not too different from the peasant farmers in the highland. The fourth way of life is the urban life, mostly in small towns. Even Addis Ababa, the capital city, is more a conglomeration of villages or neighborhoods with straight-sided, mud-walled houses topped by corrugated iron roofs. The city is teaming with automobiles and large Italian trucks. The presence of pre-formed concrete buildings marks the establishment of government and big business and a few palaces mark the royalty of an earlier era.

Health is the major problem in the cities, where many diseases flourish in a dense population with very little access to modern medicine because of the poverty and shortage of cash to purchase antibiotics. By World Bank standards, Ethiopia is one of the poorest countries in the world, yet one finds traces of a growing middle class. What is striking to the observer is the contrast between the majority of very poor, many living on the street under plastic, and a noticeable chosen few living sumptuous lives in palatial homes with satellite dishes on their roof tops.

10 FAMILY LIFE

Among the Christian population monogamy is the rule, allowing one spouse. Among the Muslim population a man may have up to four wives if he can afford them, but normally one finds men with one wife. Ethiopians love to have large families because children are considered wealth: they are a source of labor; they are social and emotional support; and they are an old couple's social security. Peasant farmer families often live in large extended families in homesteads where each house serves as a room with a special function, such as the kitchen house, the bedroom house, the party house, the toilet house (although most rural people go in the trees), and the guest house; all are surrounded by walls of stone and thornbush to keep out the wild animals, such as leopard, hyena, and wild dog. One will normally find three generations of family living together, sharing the work and the pleasures of family life. Most families have one or more dogs that they keep tied on a short rope (to make them vicious) in order to intimidate intruders who might consider stealing a goat or a chicken or two.

Grandparents are highly valued because they are the teachers of the young. They tell their grandchildren stories of their history, their religion, and the best way to gain power and influence in the community. Women are considered inferior to men, as both men and women will attest. Women are reminded of their inferiority by the physical superiority of their husbands and by God, who has cursed them by shedding their blood every month—shedding their blood the way a warrior vanquishes his enemy.

11 CLOTHING

A great variety of clothing can be found in Ethiopia, from the elaborate and colorfully embroidered white dresses of women and the tailored white shirts and jodhpur trousers of men, to the naked tribal peoples of the southwest whose only clothing in the past was iron bracelets, beads, gypsum and ocher paints, and elaborate designs of scars. Today more and more of these peoples have donned clothing, but only as a decoration.

12 FOOD

The traditional Abyssinian cuisine is a complex of a variety of foods. The *berebere* is a hot sauce primarily of cayenne pepper but which also includes 12 other spices. It is heavy and rich, cooked with a good deal of butter. The meat that goes with this sauce includes chicken, sheep meat, goat meat, and beef. Pigs are not eaten anywhere in Ethiopia except by the Europeans and Americans. Pork is considered disgusting and is taboo, according to the ancient Hebraic custom. No meal is complete without a variety of fresh vegetables, both cooked and raw. Cheese, like a dry cottage cheese, is eaten, but not to a great extent. Fish is also eaten, though it is not a popular dish among the native Ethiopians. People sit around a tall circular basket (mesob) with a flat top, where the large round sourdough bread is laid and the various foods put down upon it. Food is eaten with the fingers—no finger-licking please! At the beginning and at the end of the meal, the hostess will come around with hot steaming towelettes to clean one's fingers. The meal is finished with coffee brewed from locally grown beans. Some of the richest coffee beans found anywhere in the world are produced in Ethiopia and, while some are exported, much are grown for one's own personal consumption and enjoyment.

In traditional Abyssinian cuisine, people sit around a tall cir-cular basket (mesob) with a flat top, where a large disk of flat sourdough bread is laid and the various foods put down upon it. Food is eaten with the fingers by pinching it and picking it up with a piece of the bread. (Camille Killens)

13 EDUCATION

Traditionally, in the rural regions, which is most of Ethiopia, education was primarily for boys and young men and was accomplished within the domain of the church. Today, government schools dot the countryside and teachers from the capital city and the larger towns go out and take up their professional roles in these schools. In the city and larger towns, schools have always played an important role in the secular education of the children. Today in the city, girls and young women are fighting to be educated. More and more opportunities are opening up for women with the help of international enterprises which are boosting the faltering economy.

14 CULTURAL HERITAGE

Traditional Ethiopia boasts distinctive genres of music, dance, and among the Abyssinians, a literature predominantly religious in nature. Its millennia of relative isolation has allowed a unique tradition of music, similar to Indian or Arabic styles, as well as painting which is largely religious and akin to the Byzantine, where we find highly stylized features of people with very large eyes. But today, a growing number of artists are creating powerful images of their times with oil and watercolor and in sculptural forms.

15 WORK

In the rural countryside the traditional work of boys and girls and men and women has continued relatively unchanged for 1,000 years. It is the work of farming in the highlands. In the deserts it is nomadic herding of camels, goats, and cattle, traveling from water place to water place in an annual circuit. In the Rift Valley and the surrounding regions of the south and southwest, it is the gardening of horticulturalists, cultivating the *ensete* plant that looks like a banana tree, but whose trunk pulp is prepared and eaten. It is only in the towns and the city that industry and business have proliferated. Most work involves independent shops selling fabric goods, hardware, food, drinks, and numerous coffee and pastry shops, mostly run by women.

16 SPORTS

Many Ethiopians are crazy about soccer, normally called "football" as the American version of football is unknown. Ethiopians of the towns and cities are also very conscious of the great talents of Ethiopian athletes in the Olympic sports. The marathon is the forte of Ethiopians. Long-distance running is a very popular sport even at the local level, and Ethiopians, both men and women, are very health- and sport-conscious. But, of course, there are numerous traditional sports that persist: the wrestlers and stick fighters in the tribal south, the whipping battles of the northern would-be warriors, and a variety of children's ball and stick games found among most peoples of Ethiopia. But, the women are the dancers. They rarely compete in sports. Sport is the arena of young men. Women cheer the men and encourage them to be fierce so they can be proud of them and consider them worthy partners in marriage.

17 ENTERTAINMENT AND RECREATION

In the rural countryside children play spontaneously, making animals, dolls, balls, toy weapons, automobiles, and such out of the available resources at their disposal—mud, clay, rags, sticks, tin can scraps, and the like. Male youth engage in competitive sports. Adults drink and talk and dance, especially during holiday celebrations which occur almost weekly in Abyssinian culture.

There are also traveling minstrels—men and women who travel from village to village, town to town, singing bawdy songs and the gossip of the day or week. With their music they invite spectators to sing with them and dance and joke. And in return they "beg" for money, which they receive unbegrudgingly, especially from their slightly inebriated audience. In the city of Addis Ababa and a few northern towns one can find movie houses showing B-grade films from America, Italy, and India. Bars and night clubs proliferate, complete with music and dance. Although there is only one television station, video tape rental and VCRs are a booming business.

18 FOLK ART, CRAFTS, AND HOBBIES

Throughout Ethiopia, artisans ply their trades, serving both the aesthetic and practical interests of their customers. Workers in clay make biblical figurines, coffee and cooking pots, water jugs, and plates to set food on (but not to eat off). Blacksmiths forge plowshares, iron rings for bracelets, neck ornaments, and items to attach leather thongs to—bullets, cartridge casings, spear heads and knives. Woodcarvers craft chairs, tables,

Crowded marketplace in Harrar, Ethiopia. Most urban work involves independent shops selling fabric goods, hardware, food, drinks, and numerous coffee and pastry shops. (United Nations)

goblets, and statuary. Painters paint oil on canvas, traditionally religious images for which Ethiopians are widely known. Modern painters incorporate the traditional art of their culture with their own interpretations of their world today, sometimes with spectacular results. Weavers hand-spin their own cotton thread and weave it into intricately designed cloth and embellish it with highly detailed and colorful embroidery. This is then used in clothing, including scarves, shirts, dresses, and capes.

19 SOCIAL PROBLEMS

Of social problems there are many, so numerous it can be daunting and discouraging for those European national agencies who wish to help. Many Westerners know of the thirty years of civil war in the north, unrelenting drought, widespread famine, and massive loss of life. Add to this the inaccessibility of modern medicine, except for the urban upper class, rampaging diseases like tuberculosis, intestinal bacterial infections, and HIV in an overcrowded capital city, unrelieving and ubiquitous urban poverty, widespread prostitution, and homelessness. Crack cocaine has found its way into the capital city. Corruption is present in the commercial bank and other major national institutions. There are uncontrolled violations of human rights in the countryside and in the capital city including politically motivated arbitrary imprisonment without trial, detention and torture, and summary executions.

The Derg regime, which overthrew Emperor Haile Sellassie I in 1974, was itself overthrown in 1991 after a 17 year reign ending a 30 year war waged by the northern provinces of Eritrea and Tigray. In 1993 the new ruling government of Ethiopia recognized the sovereignty of Eritrea, sanctioned by the United Nations. Henceforth, a series of military confrontations occurred setting off the Ethiopian-Eritrean War whose precipitating circumstances were disputes over the Ethiopian-Eritrean boundaries in an area of barren, noncultivable land around a few remote towns. Skirmishes continued into 2008 and this continuous warfare is compounded by the Ethiopian Army's incursions into Somalia attempting to bolster the existing government against Islamic rebel fighters. The fighting over national boundaries in the eastern desert Ogaden has strained the Ethiopian Army's forces on all fronts.

As military campaigns continue other agencies are beginning to address these massive social problems. A small group of American Peace Corps volunteers have been installed, small private clinics, funded by Ethiopians, staffed often by doctors from Europe and America, are springing up like mushrooms in the capital city and in larger towns. Faint incursions of foreign businesses are being established and developed in the capital city, which could help pump the Ethiopian economy to some degree. Several reservoirs are planned, some are now being built, and many small dam projects are under construction, especially in the drought-ravaged north. There are several tree-planting projects under way to begin addressing the problem of a thousand years of wanton tree cutting. There are only faint glimmerings of hope in a country which has been all but forgotten by the wealthiest nations in the world. But the Ethiopian spirit is strong and the children of Ethiopia are vibrant and enthusiastic, nurtured by loving relatives who do what they can to engender promise for the next generation.

20 GENDER ISSUES

Since the establishment and stabilization of the new government in 1994 and the subsequent writing of a new constitution, women's rights has been a target issue of government and nongovernmental agencies at all levels. At present there are no less than 15 government agencies dedicated to addressing women's rights issues. There are eight United Nations agencies focused on gender issues and women's affairs. There are 37 international nongovernmental organizations (NGOs) whose projects include the rights of women and the securing of economic stability in women's affairs. Furthermore, there are 47 local NGOs around the country addressing a variety of gender issues involved with economic development, political participation, and health problems which include female genital excision customs.

A group of locally organized agencies under the umbrella title HUNDEE is dedicated to a variety of local concerns including female empowerment, women's rights, food shortage vulnerability, and the integration of a number of agencies for a greater efficiency of operation. A notable influence in Ethiopian affairs is the Women's Affairs Association, or Setoch Guday in Amharic. These women are dedicated to actualizing the newly established Articles of the Constitution declaring equality and empowerment of women in modern Ethiopian society. Their general objectives are to raise the consciousness of women regarding their rights, to inform a variety of agencies as to women's rights, conduct research into the status of women, conduct training groups teaching strategies for asserting the rights of women, build economic cooperatives to provide economic independence in the hopes of diminishing the incidence of prostitution, and to extend the reach of women's associations in order to implement women's constitutional rights.

21 BIBLIOGRAPHY

Amnesty International. *Ethiopia. Accountability Past and Present: Human Rights in Transition*. London: International Secretariat, 1995.

Ben-Ezer, Gadi. The Migration Journey: The Ethiopian Jewish Exodus. New Brunswick, NJ: Transaction Publishers, 2006.

Buxton, David. *The Abyssinians*. New York: Praeger, 1970.

Campbell, Andrew. *Ethiopia*. North Mankato, MN: Smart Apple Media, 2007.

Finneran, Niall. *The Archaeology of Ethiopia: Shaping an Identity*. NY: Routledge, 2007.

Johanson, Donald, and David Brill. "Ethiopia Yields First 'Family' of Early Man." *National Geographic,* December 1976, 790–811.

Levine, Donald. *Wax and Gold*. Chicago: University of Chicago Press, 1965.

Marcus, Harold. *A History of Ethiopia*. Los Angeles: University of California Press, 1994.

Milkias, Paulos. *Haile Selassie, Western Education, and Political Revolution in Ethiopia*. Youngstown, NY: Cambria Press, 2006.

Pankhurst, Richard. *A Social History of Ethiopia*. Trenton: Red Sea Press, 1992.

Reminick, Ronald A. *Structure and Functions of Religious Belief Among the Amhara of Ethiopia*. Proceedings of the First United States Conference on Ethiopian Studies, East Lansing, Michigan State University, 1973.

———. "The Second Oldest Profession: Prostitution in Ethiopia." Unpublished paper researched under a Fulbright Grant to Ethiopia, 1993–1995.

Ullendorf, Edward. *The Ethiopians*. London: Oxford University Press, 1960.

White, Tim, et al. *Australopithecus Ramidus, a New Species of Early Hominid from Aramis, Ethiopia. Nature* 375, (4 May 1995).

—by R. A. Reminick

EWE

ALTERNATE NAMES: Eibe, Ebwe, Ehwe, Efe, Eve, Eue, Gbe, Vhe, Krepe, Krepi, Popo
LOCATION: Ghana, Togo, Benin
POPULATION: 3.1 million people
LANGUAGE: Ewe
DIALECTS: Anglo (Anlo, Awlan), Awuna, Hudu, Kotafoa, Adan, Agu, Aveno, Be, Gbin, Ho, Kpelen, Togo, Vlin, Vo.
RELIGION: Christian and traditional religion

¹ INTRODUCTION

The Ewe are a people found primarily in three countries of West Africa, namely Ghana, Togo, and Benin. They are concentrated in southeastern Ghana east of the Volta River, in southern Togo and the southwestern portion of Benin. They are a collection of a group of people who speak Ewe as the main language, but with different dialects. Each group is also known by a different name, such as Anglo (Anlo, Awlan), Awuna, Hudu, Kotafoa, Adan, Agu, Aveno, Be, Gbin, Ho, Kpelen, Togo, Vlin, Vo, and so on. Other slightly different cultures that are closely related to the Ewe include the Adja, Oatchi, Peda, and Fon. Even though these other groups speak languages that are incomprehensible to Ewe, they are considered to be part of the Ewe cultural group.

Although the Ewe people are said to have originated from present-day southern Togo in the Tado region, it is thought that the original group of Ewe migrated south from Nigeria to their present area at some time in the 13th century. The Adja Kingdom of Tado in southern Togo, situated along the Mono River, is an area that has been constantly populated since prehistory and is well known for its metalworking and other crafts. Most Adja people today still live in and around Tado. The Ewe and Fon are considered to be the descendants of the Adja people who migrated from Tado and intermarried with other groups as they moved in different directions towards southeastern Ghana and Benin.

In the 18th century, as Europeans began to explore West Africa, the Ewe came into contact with this new group, who instituted a new type of trade: slavery. The Ewe homeland was strategically located for the Atlantic slave trade. The Dutch, English, and the Danes all traded in slaves from this region, making it a center for the Atlantic slave trade. Some Ewe groups were middlemen in capturing other unfortunate ethnic groups, including some of their own, to be sold into slavery to the Europeans, who transported them to the New World in North America. Once slavery came to an end, the Ewe people fell under British colonial rule in Ghana and German rule in Togoland, on the Togolese side. When the Germans lost World War I, Togoland was given over to the French as a protectorate. Thus, the Ewe people, as is the case in most African countries, find themselves split into two: the Ewe of Ghana and the Ewe of Togo. The Ewe people of Ghana are aligned with the British while those of Togo are aligned with the French.

² LOCATION AND HOMELAND

As noted above, the Ewe people are located in three different countries, with the majority found in Ghana and Togo and a few in Benin. They are located between the Volta River in Ghana and the Mono River (to the east) in Togo. The Atlantic Ocean forms the southern boundary. The northern boundary is just past Ho in Ghana and Danyi on the western Togolese border all the way to Tado on the eastern Togolese border. The Fon and other related ethnic groups are concentrated in the southeastern part of Benin. As such, extended families may find themselves in two different countries.

In terms of climate and geography, the Ewe homeland has several distinct features as one moves from the coast into the interior of these three countries. The coastal zone is generally flat with many palm trees, from which palm oil and palm wine are obtained. Immediately inland there is swampland, lagoons, and small lakes, which provide much needed aquatic resources, such as fish. Immediately after this zone of lagoons there is a rolling plain, characterized by red lateritic and sandy soils, followed by the forest zone at an elevation of about 700 meters above sea level. Temperatures are quite high along the coastal zone as well as inland, ranging from 20–35° C (68–95° F) throughout the year. There are mainly two seasons: the dry and rainy season. The dry season runs through November to March while April through May and September through October are characterized by heavy rains.

³ LANGUAGE

The language of the Ewe people is also known by the name Ewe. It is a Niger-Congo language spoken in Ghana, Togo, and Benin by approximately five million people. It is a national language in Togo and Ghana. Ewe is an umbrella term of a collection of dialects and/or related languages referred to as Gbe languages, which are spoken from the eastern portion of Ghana all the way to the western part of Nigeria. In addition to Ewe, Fon and Aja are two other principal languages of the Gbe cluster. There is no question that the Ewe, Adja, Guin, and Fon languages are very closely related, all originating centuries ago with the people of the royal city of Tado. Numerous dialects exist inside the family of Ewe proper, such as Anlo, Kpelle, Danyi, and Be. Adja dialects include Tado, Hweno, and Dogbo. Fon, the language of the Kingdom of Dahomey, includes the Abomey, Xweda, and Wemenu dialects.

In linguistic terms, Ewe is a tone language much like other Gbe languages. When the first missionaries came to Ewe homeland during the 18th century, they transformed Ewe into a written language, using the Latin alphabet with some extra letters derived from the International Phonetic Alphabet to represent certain sounds. In terms of tone and nasalization, an n is placed after vowels. Tone is generally unmarked, except in some common cases, which require disambiguation, e.g. the first person plural pronoun *mí*, "we," is marked high to distinguish it from the second person plural *mi*, "you," and the second person singular pronoun *wò*, "you" is marked low to distinguish it from the third person plural pronoun *wo*, "they/them."

⁴ FOLKLORE

Ewe culture and tradition is rich in folklore, poetry, myths, and songs. The Ewe groups in present day Ghana note of their escape from their original homeland in Togo to establish themselves in their present location. The escape, which happened in the 15th century, is commemorated in an annual festival known as the Hogbetsotso Za. Today, many of the stories told in folklore recite the impact of the Atlantic slave trade on their

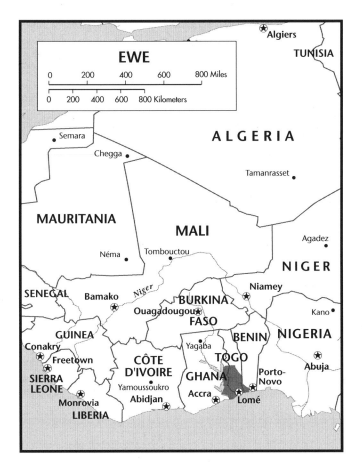

society. The frequent raids for slaves by European slave traders, who would navigate their ships easily to the shores of the ocean for their human cargos, left an indelible mark on the memory of the Ewe people. Thus, oral tradition, such as folklore, myths, and songs, recant the loss of entire settlement populations.

Folklore and poems teach society about the virtues of valor, hard work, and a common purpose and destiny. For example, a poet or storyteller might refer to the leopard, an animal used throughout Africa to symbolize skill, cunning, and physical strength. It may also be used to indicate royal, political, and spiritual power. Another story talks of the headless crab, a narrative that establishes the crab's origin and its moral significance for the present. Narrated to children, it is a cautionary story that suggests to the children the need to know how to manage relationships with friends. The story of the jealous twins shows the perils of competition within the family and, more specifically, betrayal among brothers. It explores the contradiction inherent to peer-relationships in the family. Siblings from the same mother/parentage (here epitomized by twins) are expected to feel the strongest bond and to take care of each other and their family, but at the same time, each brother has to assert himself individually.

Other stories use the omnipresent *kente* textile, a specialty weaving skill of the Ewe people. Furthermore, names of settlements in Ewe folklore might refer to the rich natural resource base and beauty of the landscape in the Ewe homeland. For example, Keta, one of the early settlements of the Ewe in Ghana, means "the head of the sand," referring to the fertile, sandy soils around the settlement. Denu, which means "the beginning of palm trees," is an important plant that provides palm oil and palm wine.

5 RELIGION

In their traditional religion, the Ewe believe in the existence of a supreme being called Mawu, who created everything in the world. Associated with the sky, Mawu is remote from the daily affairs of man, leaving that to lesser deities. For example, one of the lesser gods is Torgbi-nyigbla, the head of the nature gods (*tro*) associated with war and thunder. They also practice Afa divination and the Legba cult, which include deities such as *dulegba* (settlement protector) and *alegba* (individual protective deity). There are other deities who come from outside Eweland, such as *vodu* and *dzo* (amulets). More importantly, the Ewe people denote Se as the word for law, order, and harmony, and see the deity Se as the maker and keeper of human souls. Se is also considered to embody destiny.

As noted earlier, Eweland was at the heart of the trans-Atlantic slave trade, in which thousands of Ewe and Fon people were taken to the New World. The slaves took many aspects of their religion with them, so much so that they have transformed Catholicism to reflect this heritage. For example, aspects of Fon and Ewe religion are imbedded in Christian cults in Haiti, Brazil, Cuba, and Jamaica, where voodoo (vodoun) and the cult of Shango are practiced, just to mention a couple of examples. In Eweland itself, the arrival of Christian missionaries introduced a new religion: Christianity. Today, the majority of Ewe people declare themselves to be Christian, although most Ewe are concurrently involved in both Christian and traditional religious practices.

6 MAJOR HOLIDAYS

In addition to national and/or Christian holidays, the Ewe people have had their own traditional holidays, some of which are still observed today. Examples of these holidays include the Yam Festival, their own New Year celebration that falls in September, and other remembrance days for the dead. The annual festival of Hogbetsotso Za commemorates the day the Ewe fled from their homeland in Togo because of the harsh rule they endured at the hand of one of the kings. Government sanctioned national holidays in Ghana include January 1 (New Year's Day), March 6 (Independence Day), May 1 (Workers' Day), July 1 (Republic Day), December 25 (Christmas Day), and December 26 (Boxing Day). There are other Christian and Muslim holidays that are also observed by the adherents of each religion.

7 RITES OF PASSAGE

Many African cultures have initiation ceremonies that mark the rite of passage into adulthood. The Ewe people are no exception in this regard. Among the Ewe, initiation ceremonies for men and women or boys and girls are in line with their beliefs in a supreme being and lesser deities. Boys are circumcised and named on the seventh day after birth, while infant girls are named and welcomed into society by having their ears pierced on the seventh day after birth. Men and women are initiated into the many traditional cults (the most famous of which is voodoo or vodoun) as members or as priests and priestesses of the many deities in Ewe religion. Some individuals are initiated into the various guilds, for example, the weaver's guild.

The pantheon of lesser deities in Ewe religion includes Yewe, Afa, Eda, Nana, and Mamiwota, with the first two as the most popular. Individuals are also initiated into a specific cult under a specific deity, to whom they will then direct their worship. If one is initiated under Yewe (the god of thunder and lightning), that individual is given a new Yewe name, and the old name is discarded and can never be used again. However, those who pledge their allegiance to Afa (the god of divination) keep their original names after being initiated into the Afa cult. Music and dance are at the heart of all the initiation ceremonies, with much jubilation and festivities at the end of the initiation. Some of the initiation rituals of Ewe cults are elaborate and extremely painful. For example, an initiate into the voodoo cult can be isolated for a minimum of two months and a maximum of nine months. The initiate is sequestered in an initiation hut, where he or she remains physically, socially, and psychologically isolated from the community at large. During the period of seclusion, they learn the culture of their cult, including its songs and dances while speaking only the language of the cult. Scarification is another aspect of the initiation process, where detailed cuts are made on the initiate's back, as well as on the forehead and cheeks.

There are several ways in which an individual can be selected for initiation into some of these cults. In many instances, young females are given to the cult by their families. Should an individual be unwilling to be initiated, she can forcibly be abducted into the cult as directed by the deities and/or spirits of the dead. The view is that the young female initiate is an incarnation of a deceased member of the cult. Women have also been abducted into the cult as a result of transgressions committed against the cult, such as breaking into a cult house or insulting a cult member. Often these cases are resolved through the payment of a fine, but if the person is unable to pay the fine, the cult will sometimes forcibly take the person into the cult. Sometimes individuals are initiated into the cult when they fall ill and are diagnosed as "wanted by the cult." In order to cure the sickness, the person must submit himself or herself to the cult.

8 INTERPERSONAL RELATIONS

Interpersonal relations are an important aspect of Ewe society. These are geared toward maintaining a level of communal solidarity and general stability in the village. Conflicts, although sometimes violent, can be resolved peacefully between two feuding groups without the intervention of a third party. Dance and drumming are seen as the fabric that ties the community together in the pursuit of a collective destiny and in the essence of their shared experience. Every member of society is expected to participate in the dance and drumming. Those who refuse to participate in the festivities of music and dance are viewed as excommunicating themselves from society. Punishment of such noncompliance behavior may come in the form of denial for a proper burial.

9 LIVING CONDITIONS

Ewe people live mostly in villages and towns and survive on subsistence agriculture and trading activities. Many of the houses are built of mud bricks in a rectangular fashion with grass-thatched walls and roofs. Some houses are built of concrete brick with corrugated iron sheets for roofing material. Along the coastal zone there are numerous huts built of palm-

fronds, with grass or palm-thatch for the roofs. Members of an extended family often live in one compound with a cluster of huts surrounded by a mud wall or palm-frond fence. In both Ghana and Togo, some Ewe people live in large towns and cities, such as Tema and Aflao in Ghana and Lome, Kpalime, and Tsévié in Togo. In rural areas, a large village may have a central market, where on certain designated days people from surrounding settlements may come to trade agricultural produce and other goods.

10 FAMILY LIFE

The Ewe people follow the patrilineal system of tracing descent. Members of a clan can trace their descent to a male ancestor. Furthermore, clans can be divided into lineages that are branches in which individuals can trace their descent back to a common male ancestor. Each lineage is led by a male head, who is usually the oldest surviving member of the group. He is in charge of the lineage and its affairs, often having a final say in all decisions and settling any disputes that might arise among the members of the lineage. He is also responsible for the maintenance of ancestral shrines, often acting as the chief priest for the lineage with duties of leading ceremonies, acting as the link between the living and the dead, pouring libations and lifting prayers to the ancestors, and managing common property for the benefit of all members.

The nuclear family, composed of husband, wife, and children, is an integral part of the Ewe lineage even though it is the smallest part. Marriage is considered to be an extended family affair rather than simply between man and woman. Polygamy, the act of a man marrying several wives, is also allowed, although many men prefer to have only one wife. Elders are given a lot of respect and power in Ewe culture, so much so that sons, even when married and occupying the position of head of their respective households, are expected to abide by the decrees of their fathers.

11 CLOTHING

The Ewe people are master weavers of the cloths known worldwide as *kente*. The Ewe have a long history of weaving Kente cloth and legend has it that in the Asante wars against the Kpetoe area, weavers were captured who as prisoners of war taught the Asante how to weave. On the other hand the Asante people have their own legend that holds that they learned weaving from a spider.

Kente is the main form of clothing for the Ewe. It can be made into dresses for women or shirts and pants for men. The chiefs often wrap themselves in a large and beautifully embroidered kente cloth. In modern times, Ewe weavers make kente cloth primarily for sale through markets drawing buyers from all over Ghana and surrounding countries. Some of their cloth finds its way to markets in North America and Europe.

Ewe weavers utilize the narrow-strip loom, similar to that used by the Asante, which serves as evidence of mutual influence between the weavers of the two groups. One distinctive type of Ewe cloth features a rich variety of weft float inlaid pictures (in a zig-zag pattern across the width of the fabric) on a cotton background. Often a rich variety of objects, ranging from animals such as cows, sheep, and horses to human figures, ceremonial stools, hats, trees, and flowers, and household objects such as dining forks, are depicted on these cloths.

Ewe women perform a traditional dance during a funeral in Woe, Ghana. (AP Images/Madison J. Gray)

¹² FOOD

Among the Ewe, forest crops, such as plantain, cassava, co-coyam, and tropical yams, form the basis of the staple food. The starchy foods are pounded into flour to make the staple *akple*, a thick porridge that is taken with okra soup or stew made of common vegetables and some animal protein, such as fish, chicken, and goat meat with palm oil and hot peppers. Palm nut and peanut soups are considered a delicacy. Corn is increasingly becoming an important food crop among the Ewe. In urban areas, rice and bread have become the foods of choice for those who can afford them. Palm wine made from the fermented sap of the oil palm is the preferred drink among the Ewe while those who reside in urban areas feast on bottled European-style beer.

¹³ EDUCATION

In traditional Ewe society, children are socialized according to the customs and culture of the Ewe as they grow up. The cultural emphasis is on community and individual destiny as dictated by the gods and the spirits. Moral values through stories, myths, and legends are inculcated in the children by storytellers. The arrival of the German missionaries in the 1840s, and later the British and French, added a new layer of modern education among the Ewe. Over the years, Western education has been well entrenched in Ewe society with over 60% of eligible school aged children attending schools from primary through secondary school education to college or university level.

Today, Ewe people are among the highest educated groups in both Ghana and Togo. They consider themselves to be the human resource basket of these countries providing intellectual material at the University level as well as white collar jobs in the civil and private sectors of the economy. In addition to obtaining a modern education, many are naturally gifted in handicrafts, such as tinsmithing, iron smelting, building and construction, carpentry and joinery, weaving kente textiles, and so on. They also pride themselves on their music and for adhering to certain core values, such as honesty and hard work. These skills are a testament to their high levels of attainment of a modern and western oriented education with literacy rates of as high as 60% of the population with the ability to read and write a language.

¹⁴ CULTURAL HERITAGE

Music and dance is one of the most enduring aspects of Ewe cultural heritage. The Ewe express their emotions through songs, drumming, and dancing. Songs are an integral part of funerals, festivals, weddings, storytelling, and other happy or sad occasions. When women are pounding yams or cassava into flour to make *fufu* (a hard porridge), they will often sing songs. Fishermen pull their nets with music and farmers will sing while tending to their gardens. Weaving of kente cloth is also an important aspect of Ewe culture that dates back to their origins in this region.

15 WORK

Ewe who still reside in rural areas or on the coast and the many lagoons immediately after the Atlantic Ocean still practice a subsistence form of livelihood. Many are still peasant farmers who cultivate crops such as corn, cassava, and yams with some livestock, such as goats and chickens. Those on the coast and in the inland lagoons and lakes engage in artisanal fishing. There is also a great deal of trading that goes on in rural areas largely carried out by women. The highly educated Ewe residing in the big towns and cities, such as Accra and Lome, are employed in the modern as well as the informal economy.

16 SPORTS

One of the most enduring sports in traditional Ewe society was wrestling between men. In the modern era, soccer has become the premier sports for the peoples of Ghana, in addition to other European introduced sports, such as tennis, cricket, and basketball.

17 ENTERTAINMENT AND RECREATION

To pass time, the Ewe people devised all kinds of activities, which included an assortment of games, dances, and music. The games were and still are enacted with songs, which make them interesting and enjoyable. Many of these games are done during a full moon at night.

18 FOLK ART, CRAFTS, AND HOBBIES

Ewe people have a long-standing tradition of arts and crafts. The most important is the weaving of kente cloth, mostly done by men. Pottery is another craft that is done by women. The beautiful pots are used for storing water and cooking purposes. They also have the tradition of iron smelting and smithing to produce various implements.

19 SOCIAL PROBLEMS

Social problems among the Ewe are similar to the ones prevalent throughout Ghana. Although the government established the Ministry of Women and Children's Affairs to promote the welfare and rights of children and protect them from defilement, incest, underage marriage, and sexual abuse against minors, violations of these rights continue to take place throughout the Ewe region in Ghana and Togo. The most widespread problem is the use of child labor. Children are used in market centers, for fishing, stone quarrying, and food vending. Female child laborers are particularly vulnerable, as they are sometimes forced into prostitution or are sexually exploited. Underage and forced marriage for girls continues to be a main human rights abuse in some parts of Ghana. HIV/AIDS is another intractable problem for the country of Ghana as a whole in spite of the fact that HIV/AIDS rates have stabilized at 2.7%.

20 GENDER ISSUES

Among the Ewe, traditional patriarchal views continue to hinder the advancement of women's rights. Traditional religion, culture, and marriage customs continue to reinforce the low status of women in Ewe society. Women are often denied the right to inherit property or land and many become destitute once the husband dies or once they are divorced. Early and forced marriages for girls are often justified by parents claiming that the girl had been promised to the man when she was young and that the man had spent money looking after her while she was growing up. Women also frequently experience domestic violence. The custom of *trokosi* among the Ewe puts young girls in a constant vulnerable position. Among the Ewe cult system young girls, usually virgins, are offered to shrines to atone for a crime committed by a family member. While in bondage, the girls become not only free labor, but also sex objects for the fetish priest. If the *trokosi* bears a child while enslaved, the child becomes the property of the shrine.

21 BIBLIOGRAPHY

Avorgbedor, Daniel K. "Freedom to Sing, License to Insult: The Influence of Haló Performance on Social Violence Among the Anlo Ewe." *Oral Tradition* 9/1 (1994): 83-112.

Awoonor, Kofi. *Guardians of the Sacred Word: Ewe Poetry.* New York: Nok Publishers, 1974.

Beckwith, Carol, and Angela Fisher. *African Ceremonies.* New York: Harry N. Abrams, 1999.

Cottrell, Anna. *Once Upon a Time in Ghana: Traditional Ewe Stories Retold in English.* Leicester: Troubador, 2007.

Dennis, Ahiagble Bob. *The Pride of Ewe Kente.* Accra: Sub-Saharan Publishers, 2004.

Dzobo, N. K. *African proverbs: guide to conduct : the moral value of Ewe proverbs.* Cape Coast, Ghana: University of Cape Coast, Dept. of Education, 1973.

Greene, Sandra E. *Gender, Ethnicity, and Social Change on the Upper Slave Coast: A History of the Anlo-Ewe.* Portsmouth, NH: Heinemann, 1996.

Kwaku, Ken. "Tradition, Colonialism and Politics in Rural Ghana: Local Politics in Have, Volta Region." *Canadian Journal of African Studies / Revue Canadienne des Études Africaines.* 10, no. 1 (1976): 71-86.

Meyer, Birgit. *Translating the Devil: Religion and Modernity among the Ewe in Ghana.* Trenton, NJ: Africa World Press, 1999.

Rosenthal, Judy. *Possession, Ecstasy, and Law in Ewe Voodoo.* Charlottesville: University Press of Virginia, 1998.

Steckle, J. *The Effects of Industrialization on Food Consumption Patterns; A Study of Two Ewe Villages.* Legon: Institute of Statistical, Social and Economic Research, University of Ghana, 1972.

Verdon, Michel. *The Abutia Ewe of West Africa: A Chiefdom That Never Was.* Berlin: Mouton Publishers, 1983.

—revised by E. Kalipeni

FULANI

PRONUNCIATION: foo-LAH-nee
ALTERNATE NAMES: Fulbe; Peuls, Fula, Fulah, Foulah and
    Fellata (Sudan) and Futa Toro, Futa Jallon or Fulas Pretos
    (in Guinea and Senegambia), or Bororo in some parts of
    Nigeria.
LOCATION: From the western part of West Africa (Senegambia)
    to Chad in the east (some groups reaching as far as the
    Nile river in the countries of Sudan and Ethiopia); largest
    concentrations in Nigeria, Senegal, and Guinea
POPULATION: 12 million
LANGUAGE: Fulfulde, Arabic, French, or English
RELIGION: Islam
RELATED ARTICLES: Vol. 1: Beninese; Chadians; Ethiopians;
    Guineans; Nigerians; Senegalese; Sudanese

¹ INTRODUCTION

The Fulani peoples (also known as *Fulbe* or *Peuls*) of West Africa are among the most widely dispersed and culturally diverse peoples in all of Africa. They have a population of more than six million. Many Fulani trace their beginnings to the Senegambia area where, as early as 1000 years ago, they adopted a pastoral livelihood and began moving about with their herds of cattle. By the eighteenth century some had migrated as far east as the Niger and Benue Rivers (now in Nigeria). In the eighteenth and nineteenth centuries, some Fulani populations, which had become devoted to Islam, initiated *jihads* (Islamic holy wars) in several West Africa locales, seeking to spread or purify the Islamic religion. These events figure prominently in the histories of most Fulani groups, especially among those who emerged as religious and political leaders in the new kingdoms that resulted from the wars.

Fulani, a name that originated in northern Nigeria, is the most popular name currently used for these people. The terminology and sayings included in this section are from the Adamawa dialect, spoken in northeastern Nigeria and northern Cameroon.

Today, one finds both nomadic, pastoral Fulani *(mbororo'en)* and settled Fulani *(Fulbe wuro)*. The pastoral Fulani (full-time cattle keepers) move about with their cattle for much of the year, while the settled Fulani live permanently in villages and cities. Although these two "types" of Fulani share a common language, origin, and some cultural features, they regard themselves as only distantly related. The settled Fulani are mostly concerned with the Islamic religion, whereas the pastoralists' concerns are more with their cattle.

The present population of Fulani might be about 12 million, with another wider regional population of various bilingual speakers of Fulani and other local languages. The Kano Chronicle provides a significant historical record to the Fulani and Hausa people they came to dominate in the 18th and 19th centuries during the Fulani jihads. This is most particularly the case of the Fulani jihad of Uthman dan Fodio as well as regional jihads in the Guinea highlands.

² LOCATION AND HOMELAND

Questions of Fulani origins are disputed by scholars, but a solution is that a primordial intrusion took place from the east and then a westward spread, but during the time of the greatest Fulani jihads, return migrations from Senegal also took place. This was especially true with their horse cavalry for conquest periods and with extensive trade networks in periods of consolidation.

The Fulani populations are now found all over the savanna and semi-arid zones of West Africa to the south of the Sahara desert. This area, which has only a short rainy season, is particularly suitable for pastoralism or a combination of pastoralism and agriculture. The general distribution of these people ranges from the western part of West Africa (Senegambia) to Chad in the east, with some groups reaching as far as the Nile River in the countries of Sudan and Ethiopia. The dispersal across the continent occurred while herdsmen and their families sought to find better pasture land, to escape conflicts with settled peoples in several West African kingdoms, or to visit the Islamic holy land in the Arabian Peninsula. The largest concentrations of Fulani are in the countries of Nigeria, Senegal, and Guinea, where Fulani were involved in the holy wars and settled down, became the ruling class, and intermarried with the local populations.

³ LANGUAGE

Fulani belongs to the sub-branch of Atlantic language family, but there are many loan words from Berber and Arabic. Despite their wide geographical distribution, the Fulani peoples believe they generally belong to the same ethnic group, but with sub-groups and different dialects. The language is known as Fulfulde (or Fula or Pulaar). There are similarities in the grammar and vocabulary of the different groups, but communication among Fulani from different regions is difficult (although not impossible). There are at least five major dialects of this language (Futa Toro, Futa Jallon, and Masina in the west and Central Nigeria; and Sokoto and Adamawa in the east). Thus, for example, a Fulani from Adamawa in Nigeria would only understand a few words when speaking with a Fulani from Senegal. As Muslims, many Fulani can read and write Arabic. Nowadays, many can also speak either French or English, depending on which European country colonized their region.

⁴ FOLKLORE

Because most Fulani are Muslims, much of their history and worldview derives from Islam. Local groups recognize important historical figures who helped spread Islam in their land and acquired additional spiritual and magical powers due to their religious devotion. Moreover, as many communities have lengthy genealogies, recollections (sometimes exaggerated) of important religious and historical figures abound in terms of their wealth, success in battle, devotion to Islam, and superhuman deeds. Despite the significance of Islam, some modern-day Fulani recount traditions of the pre-Islamic origin of the Fulani. These traditions state that cattle, as well as the first Fulani family, emerged from a river, began the migrations across Africa, and gave birth to children who founded the various Fulani groups.

Fictional stories or folktales *(taali)* are popular among all Fulani. Adults or storytellers gather children before bedtime

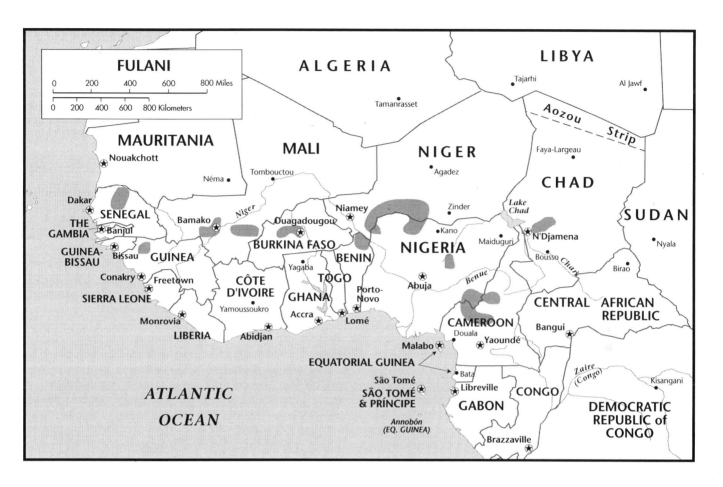

to recite the stories, which usually have a moral. Among the pastoralists are many stories pertaining to their cattle and migrations. Among all Fulani, stories discuss the adventures of animals such as squirrels, snakes, hyenas, and rabbits, some of which are extremely clever. Some discuss men and women, Islamic teachers, and children. All Fulani groups have riddles, proverbs, and sayings which, together with the stories, are used to help educate children about the culture and practices of the society as well as to entertain them.

An example of a saying in Fulfulde is: *Tid'd'o yod'ad'd'o* ("Work hard and succeed"). An example of a Fulani proverb is: *Hab'b'ere buri ginawol* ("Actions should be judged according to intention" or literally, "Deliberate acts could be worse than insanity").

5 RELIGION

As the Fulani adopted Islam, they acquired a set of beliefs about the world and their new faith. They also have obligations as Muslims, such as praying five times a day, learning to recite the holy scriptures *(Quran)* by heart, fasting in the daytime for one lunar month each year, making the pilgrimage *(hajj)* to the Islamic holy land in Mecca, and giving alms to the needy. The most important duty is to declare one's true faith in Islam and that Mohammed was a prophet sent by Allah.

One should note that the Fulani are Sunni Muslims, but are also influenced by the Muslim brotherhoods that are widespread across the Sahel as well as other syncretic beliefs and practices. The intensity of religious belief among the Fulani varies by membership in those who are more actively engaged in pastoralism and less inclined to be devout and are more syncretic versus those settled Fulani who are more devout and more inclined to be engaged in religious activism and jihads.

6 MAJOR HOLIDAYS

All Fulani participate in Islamic holidays *(Id),* namely the feast after the fasting period and the feast of the birth of the Prophet Mohammed. On these days, people pray in thanksgiving to Allah, visit their relatives, prepare special meals, and exchange gifts such as gowns or cloth. Fulani also observe the national holidays of various African nations in which they reside.

7 RITES OF PASSAGE

Islam has influenced many Fulani holidays and ceremonies. Shortly after a child is born, a naming ceremony is held in which the child is given a name following Islamic law and practice. Around the age of seven, boys are circumcised, followed by a small ceremony or gathering in their household. Shortly after this time, they begin performing herding or farming activities, sometimes on their own. At this age, girls help their mothers. Also around this time, most children begin attending school. When they are close to puberty, the children socialize in the markets or other communities. Girls are usually betrothed in marriage during their early to mid-teens, while boys remain as *sukaa'be* (handsome young men) until around the age of 20. At that time, they start a herd or obtain a farm and marry with the intent to start a family. Following ceremonies in which the bride and groom are prepared for marriage, the families of the betrothed contract the marriage under Islam. By middle age, a man may be known as a *ndottijo* (elder, old man) who has acquired wisdom over the years.

8 INTERPERSONAL RELATIONS

All Fulani have an elaborate code for interacting among themselves and with other people. The code, known as *pulaaku*, prescribes certain morals and etiquette which the Fulani believe distinguish them from other people; some regard it as sacred. *Pulaaku* prescribes *semteende* (modesty and reserve), together with *munyal* (patience) and *hakkiilo* (common sense, care), which must be shown in public, among one's in-laws, and with one's spouse, all as a sign of respect for the others and for one's own dignity. Fulani thus tend to avoid showing off with people outside their group, although they are supposed to demonstrate kindness (*end'am*) among their kin. The pastoral Fulani may have developed *pulaaku* to help them preserve their economic independence and their identity and to avoid being assimilated into other groups. Nowadays, all Fulani throughout West Africa strongly adhere to this code of behavior. Islam, which also prescribes modesty and reserve, has tended to reinforce this code.

9 LIVING CONDITIONS

Among the pastoral Fulani, life can be extremely harsh. They often live in small, temporary camps, which they quickly dismantle as they often move in search of pasture and water. Some move mainly between wet and dry season camps or small villages. Transportation is often on foot, although some families have donkeys, horses, and camels. Because of the settlements' distance from towns, modern health care is not readily available. Traditional healers, whose medicines and practices have been perfected over the centuries, are more commonly consulted.

Fulani who have settled in towns are more inclined to visit modern health-care facilities such as clinics and hospitals than are the pastoral Fulani. In the cities they also have access to modern transportation, including cars and buses, and they usually reside in large family houses or compounds.

The Sahel in general is relatively underdeveloped so that Fulani are facing various difficulties of finding adequate employment in the modern sectors of the economy that require new educational and technical skills.

10 FAMILY LIFE

Among the Fulani, life centers around the family. This includes one's immediate kin, such as parents and siblings, but it also includes the extended family (cousins, aunts and uncles, and distant relatives), whose members are all treated as close kin. In the rural areas, these groups tend to live close together and join in work efforts; in the towns and cities, they tend to be more dispersed. Each kin group (*lenyol*) normally recognizes a common male ancestor who lived several generations ago and founded the family.

In the towns, women manage the very large Fulani households and families. Many women are in seclusion due to the Islamic prescription for the extreme modesty of women. Among the pastoralists, the women help support their families through the trade or sale of milk, and they often walk miles each day to the markets or towns to do so.

Marriage is a very important institution among the Fulani. Male family members usually choose a spouse for a child, usually among relatives (particularly cousins) and social equals. This practice helps to keep wealth (cattle and land) in the family and to maintain the moral and physical purity of each group. Polygyny (multiple wives) is not uncommon in Fulani society, as a man's wives all help with domestic work and can bear him many children. They also bring him prestige, particularly if they are modest in behavior and dress.

All Fulani communities have leaders of sorts, known as *ardo'en,* who influence or guide their peoples in an informal manner. Beginning with the holy wars and the settlement of Fulani populations, some individuals have acquired formal power and authority over their peoples and have become chiefs (*laamb'e*). Some of the larger Fulani communities have had emirs (*laamiib'e*) who reigned over their court and subjects in royal fashion.

Fulani traditionally prefer endogamous marriage with parallel cousins, especially patrilateral and they follow patrilineal descent with patrilocal post-marital residence.

11 CLOTHING

There are a great variety of dress codes and styles among the different Fulani groups, but all are proud of their beauty and physical features, which in some respects resemble those of North Africans. Typical Fulani features include tall stature, long limbs, light skin, and relatively long and soft hair. In a broad sense, the married men and women follow the Islamic dress code in which modesty is prescribed. The men wear large gowns and trousers and caps, and women wear wrappers and blouses. As a sign of modesty, married Muslim women wear veils when they leave their household.

Pastoral men also wear Islamic dress, but it is not as elaborate as among the settled Fulani men. Women wear blouses and wrappers but not veils. Among the pastoralists, younger men and women adorn themselves with jewelry and headdresses, and they plait their hair. During certain festivals, young pastoral men wear makeup to accentuate their features, including their eyes, their pointed noses, and their lips, which they line with white paint. They dance for the women and sometimes choose a marital partner.

12 FOOD

Most Fulani value cattle and their diet usually includes milk products such as yogurt, milk, and butter. They prefer not to slaughter their cattle for food, but purchase basic foodstuffs, including meat, in the market. Each morning they drink milk or gruel (*gari*) made with sorghum. Their main meals consist of a staple food or heavy porridge (*nyiiri*), made of flour from such grains as millet, sorghum, or corn, which they eat with soup (*takai, haako*) made from tomatoes, onions, spices, and peppers, and other vegetables such as okra, spinach, or baobab leaves.

13 EDUCATION

From birth, Fulani children receive a rigid education to socialize them into the customs and identity of their society and prepare them for the harsh environment in which they live. All adults and senior children help educate the younger children through scolding, reciting sayings and proverbs, and telling them stories. Children also learn through imitation. In many

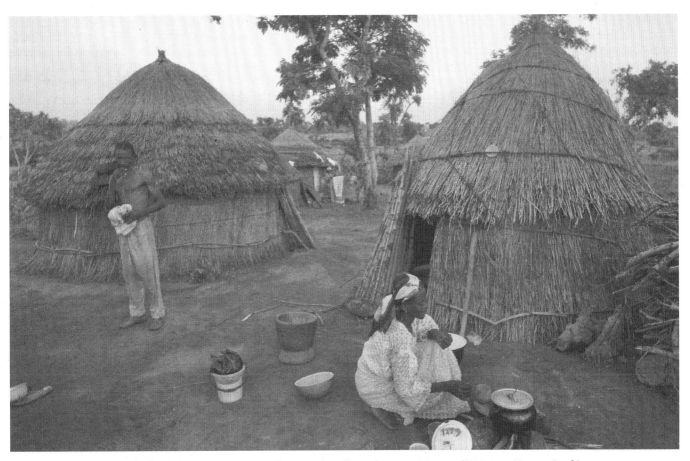

A Fulani woman cooks outside her house in the village of Daruga, Nigeria. (AP Images/George Osodi)

communities, children from about the age of six attend Islamic *(Qu'ranic)* school, where they study and recite the scriptures and learn about the practices, teachings, and morals of Islam. Nowadays, settled Fulani children attend primary and secondary school, and some eventually enroll in universities. It is more difficult for the children of pastoral families to attend school, as they are often on the move. In some countries, however, special efforts are being made to place these children in school or to build mobile schools that follow them during their migrations.

14 CULTURE

Among the Fulani, music and art are part of daily life. Work music—with song, drums, or flutes—is found among those in rural areas working in the pasture, the fields, or the market. Court music (drumming, horns, flutes) and praise-singing are found among those in towns, especially in the palace or during festivals. The praise singers discuss community histories, leaders, and prominent individuals, whereas religious singers may cite Islamic scriptures. Most commonly, art occurs in the form of personal adornments such as jewelry, hats, and clothing, and of architecture.

For many Fulani, however, their most important cultural feature is their character or *pulaaku* (as discussed in the section on interpersonal relations). Fulani should be reserved and demonstrate a strong sense of shame *(semteende)* in all their dealings outside their household, with strangers, and with cer-

tain kinds of kin. For example, it is considered shameful if a Fulani eats outside his household. A proverb thus states, *Pullo nastan luumo wade, nastatta luumo semteende* ("It is better to die than be shamed in public"). These behavioral norms, in the Fulani view, distinguish them from members of other tribes or ethnic groups. Among the pastoral Fulani, herdsmanship *(ngainaaka)* is also a very important aspect of their culture. The settled Fulani still value cattle, and many of them own herds, but they lack the extreme enthusiasm for cattle as found among the true pastoralists.

With such an extensive multinational African distribution of the Fulani, they are found in all walks of life, in sports, military, commerce, arts, and politics. Among the most prominent personages of Fulani origin are three heads of state of Nigeria, including the President Umaru Yar'Adua. In Guinea-Conakry those with family names such as Balde and Diallo, or Alfa Yaya, or Alfa Molo were prominent leaders of Fulani origin, and the first president of Cameroon, Ahmadu Ahidjo, also shares this ethnicity.

15 WORK

All Fulani communities have a relatively rigid division of labor according to age and sex. Men's and women's domains are highly segregated, and children assist their parents, but they also have their own chores around the house, on the farm, or in the pasture.

Men tend the cattle, work in the fields, or have formal employment in the city. They also play an important part in decision-making about farming, herding, migrating, and other family matters. Many men are either full or part-time Islamic scholars or teachers. In the settled communities, Fulani men pursue a variety of occupations such as work in the government, as Islamic teachers and scholars, in education, in business, or, to a lesser extent, as traders.

Women's primary role is managing the household (cooking, cleaning) and caring for the children. Among the pastoralists, the women also set up and dismantle camps, tend the small animals (sheep and goats), and trade or exchange milk products in nearby towns and markets to obtain the foodstuffs they themselves do not produce. Most married women in the towns are housewives, but a few work as teachers, nurses, or secretaries. A few supplement their own or their husband's income with trading items such as jewelry, clothing, spices, cigarettes, or beverages— often from within their own household.

16 SPORTS

Young pastoral men participate in a kind of sport known as *sharro*. This is a test of endurance and bravery in which young men lash each other to the point of intolerance. They do so as they enter manhood, but some continue to participate in the practice until they become elders. Among the settled Fulani, there are a great variety of traditional local sports and games, including wrestling and boxing. Western sports such as soccer and track and field are now found in communities and schools. Wealthy Fulani also participate in horseracing and polo.

17 ENTERTAINMENT AND RECREATION

Among the pastoral Fulani, children participate in different kinds of dances—among their immediate friends and kin, when they meet in the market, or when kin groups gather during the rainy season. Among the settled people, musicians and praise-singers perform at festivities such as weddings, naming ceremonies, and parties and Islamic holidays. Today, most Fulani appreciate Western music and own radios. Among the settled Fulani, one commonly finds stereos, televisions, and VCRs.

18 FOLK ART, CRAFTS, AND HOBBIES

Fulani women make handicrafts in their spare time, including engraved calabashes or gourds, weavings, knitting, and baskets. Some of these items are used or displayed in the household, and many are given as gifts to other women or kept as part of a woman's or her daughter's dowry for marriage. In contrast with some of their neighboring peoples, Fulani men are less involved in the production of crafts such as pottery, iron-working, and dyeing. They believe that these activities, which are undertaken in the public, may bring shame upon them, and they prefer to purchase such wares from the craftsmen among other peoples.

19 SOCIAL PROBLEMS

The pastoral Fulani are currently facing many problems. Drought often reduces their water supply and pasture, and disease may also strike the herds. As the population of West Africa has grown, there is less land available for herding, and conflicts with settled people have increased. The modern governments are also curtailing the Fulanis' movements or trying to force them to settle down. The result is that Fulani herds have declined dramatically, seriously threatening the pastoral Fulani livelihood, although many still find a way to survive. Some settled Fulani are also faced with relative poverty, as most of the countries they live in simply do not have enough resources and funds. Nevertheless, all Fulani find comfort in the fact that their kin are always willing to help those facing hardship. In addition to regional drought, desertification and unemployment are severe issues faced by modern Fulani.

20 GENDER ISSUES

Common with African Islamic societies in general the social position of women is structured with the culture-religious organization of society in which patriarchy, patrilineality, possible but limited polygyny, and patrilocal residence provides for specific domestic roles for women. Within the domestic framework there are some options open to women in the informal economy, particularly in gendered spaces that focus on food and clothing production. At the same time, this is being contested by new social movements and forces that empower women in terms of legal, economic, and human rights, as well as the necessity to bring more women into economic production along with more males moving out of the traditional compounds in search of work and opportunity. Thus, gender roles in modern Fulani society are both steadfast and traditional, while being contested by the powerful forces of change. This gender contestation is particularly acute in Nigeria whereby the federal state seeks centralization on one hand, while empowering the various states to solve their own problems. For Fulani regions which are seeking a post-colonial strengthening of Islamic law the torque between these counterforces has been problematic.

21 BIBLIOGRAPHY

Bivins, Mary Wren. *Telling Stories, Making Histories: Women, Words, and Islam in Nineteenth-Century Hausaland and the Sokoto Caliphate.* Portsmouth, NH: Heinemann, 2007.

Bocquene Henri. *Memoirs of a Mbororo: the Life of Ndudi Umaru, Fulani Nomad of Cameroon.* New York: Berghahn Books, 2002.

David, Nicolas. "The Fulani Compound and the Archaeologist." *World Archaeology*, 3(2), 1971, 11–131.

Hopen, C. E. *Pastoral Fulbe Family in Gwandu.* London: Oxford University Press, 1958.

Johnston, H. A. S. *The Fulani Empire of Sokoto.* London: Oxford University Press, 1967.

Ndukwe, P.I. *Fulani.* New York: Rosen Publishing, 1996.

Reisman, Paul. *Freedom in Fulani Social Life.* Chicago: University of Chicago Press, 1977.

Stenning, Derrick. *Savanna Nomads.* London: Oxford University Press, 1959.

—revised by R. Lobban

GABONESE

PRONUNCIATION: gab-uh-NEEZ
LOCATION: Gabon (western Central Africa)
POPULATION: About 1,485,832
LANGUAGE: French; 45 local Niger-Congo languages
RELIGION: Roman Catholicism; Protestantism; Islam; animism

¹ INTRODUCTION

Gabon's stability keeps it in the shadows. An African country that has not been afflicted by wars, drought, or chronic uprisings, it tends to stay out of the press and has long held an unchallenged position in the "French sphere of influence."

The peopling of what is now Gabon was a slow and steady process. Pygmies and other forest dwellers have been living there for millennia. Around 1500 bc, Bantu people from the northwest began to migrate into the area, slowly spreading out over the next 2,500 years, differentiating into the more than 40 ethno-linguistic groups that exist today. Later migrations during the period of the slave trade, and again in the 19th century, have further enriched the mix. The southern kingdom of Loango grew in the years before European contact, but most people led simple lives of autonomy, living in villages among extended family. For many centuries, people kept small plots where they grew yams, greens, and later, bananas. Horticulture was supplemented, and often overshadowed, by hunting meat and gathering wild plants from the forests or savannas. Archaeological evidence suggests the existence of iron smelting in Gabon since the 4th century bc.

Europeans arrived in the 15th century. First came the Portuguese, then the Dutch, British, and French. Rarely did they venture beyond the coast. Their interests were slaves and ivory, and trade increased dramatically in the 18th century. Loango became a center for a vigorous trade in slaves, who were captured farther inland and sold to Europeans at the coast by members of more powerful tribes. It is estimated that by 1840, 2.5 million slaves had been taken from West Central Africa.

In the late 19th century, France became the colonial power in Gabon and continued to be heavily involved in political and economic affairs after Gabon's independence in 1960. There are more French expatriates living in Gabon now than during the colonial period.

² LOCATION AND HOMELAND

Gabon covers 103,347 square kilometers. It is slightly smaller than the state of Colorado. Gabon is on the West Coast of Africa, centered on the Equator. It borders Equatorial Guinea and Cameroon to the North, and the Republic of Congo to the East and South. The capital, Libreville, is on the West Coast in the North. Libreville ("Free town") was the landing place for a ship of freed slaves in the 1800s and later became the capital.

Over 80% of Gabon is tropical rain forest, with a plateau region in the South. There are nine provinces named after the rivers that separate them. There are roughly 1,485,832 Gabonese (2008). There are equal numbers of men and women. The original inhabitants were the Pygmies, but only a few thousand remain. Of the total population, 60% live in the cities while 40% inhabit the villages. There is also a large population of Africans from other countries who have come to Gabon to find work. Gabon retains its colonial frontiers as drawn by the Europeans in 1885.

Tropical forest covers 80% of the country, the rest consisting of grassy savannah and high plateau. There are two dry seasons and two rainy seasons, but the equatorial climate is very hot and humid year-round. The major geographical feature is the Ogooue River, which flows east to west, splitting the country into two. It is the largest river between the great Niger and Congo rivers, and its watershed drains the whole of Gabon.

Gabon is becoming a country of urbanites. The major cities besides Libreville are Port Gentil, with its oil reserves; Oyem, with its vital trade with Cameroon to the north; Franceville, gateway to the Bateke Plateau; and Lambarene, made famous by Albert Schweitzer and his hospital. This riverine port, 125 miles from the capital, accessible by paved road only in 1996, still has one of the best hospitals in Central Africa.

³ LANGUAGE

The national language is French, mandatory in school. It is spoken by the majority of the population under the age of 50. The use of a common language is extremely helpful in the cities, where Gabonese from all of the different ethnic groups come together to live. Most Gabonese speak at least two languages, as each ethnic group has its own language as well. The educated Gabonese speak Parisian French, while the rest of the country speaks a version of French that has absorbed the rhythm and accent of their local language.

There are 45 local languages in Gabon, many of them shared with neighboring countries. Some of the larger ethno-linguistic groups are Fang, Punu, Nzebi, Myene, and Obambe/Teke. These languages are mutually unintelligible—but as with other languages in the Niger-Congo family, deploy consonant groupings, like in *Ndjole* (*n-jolay*), as well as open, rounded vowel pairs, as in *antsia ama* (*anchiama*). Because of this linguistic diversity, French has become the true lingua franca (common language) and is the official national language. The business of government, education, marketing, publishing, and socializing is conducted in French. Unfortunately, as a result, many young Gabonese cannot speak the language of their grandparents.

⁴ FOLKLORE

Because Gabonese languages were not written down until the 19th century, storytelling has long been the way to teach children and to transmit tradition to people of all ages. Each ethnic group has its own stories, but common are morality tales involving animals like the wasp that loses the affections of a mate due to excessive pride in his slim waist and lovely striped coat.

With nationalization have come national folk heroes. One is Charles Tchorere, a soldier who fought as a captain in the French army against the Germans in World War II. He is remembered for bravery in distant battles and for the honor he bestowed upon his nation.

⁵ RELIGION

There are several different belief systems in Gabon. About 75% of Gabonese identify themselves as Roman Catholic, 20% as Protestants, less than 1% as Muslim, and the rest as animist. In reality, however, many Gabonese hold animist beliefs while at the same time practicing Christianity or Islam. Animism, a body of beliefs held by tribal and pre-industrial people the

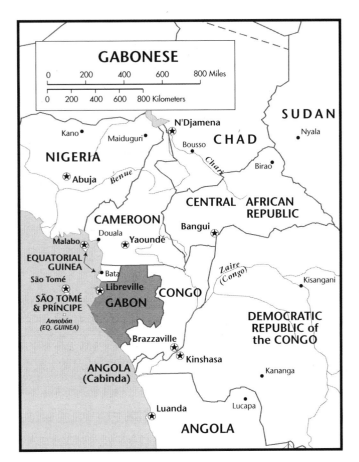

⁶ MAJOR HOLIDAYS

Because of the ethnic diversity of such a small population, national holidays take on universal significance. The most important is August 17, commemorating Gabonese independence from France. Towns, large and small, have a central square called "Place de l'Independence" where the Gabonese flag is flown, and speeches and traditional dancing take place. In the capital there is a military parade. While most Gabonese are Christian, New Year's Day sees more celebration than Christmas or Easter.

⁷ RITES OF PASSAGE

The passage from life to death is considered the most important rite of passage in Africa due to the importance of spirit ancestors. In Gabon, funerals are elaborate affairs at which mourners close to the deceased stay awake for days, attending to the body. What used to be quite common in the past, though much less so now, is the remarriage of a widow to a close relative of her departed husband, usually a younger brother. This custom is logical when one considers the traditional practice of paying *dot* (bride-price), wherein a husband or his family pay a woman's family for the privilege of marrying her. After dot is paid, the marriage and resulting children are considered legitimate, and the woman's labor then belongs directly to her husband's family. If the husband dies, it is his family who still has rights to her labor and future fertility, and hence the responsibility for her welfare and that of her children.

There are few universal rituals in multi-ethnic Gabon, but those surrounding *Bwiti* are remarkable for their adoption from the Fang by other groups. The *Bwiti* cult grew out of a demographic crisis at the turn of the last century, when sexually transmitted disease caused infertility among women and a declining birth rate throughout the country. Bwiti began as a set of rituals performed by women to ensure fertility. It is now described by Gabonese as a secret society of both men and women who perform these rites in an attempt to purify the body and spirit for many reasons. While the Bwiti rituals combine dancing, singing, and drinking, as in many Gabonese celebrations, the central element is the ingestion of *iboga,* a wild plant found only in Gabon. *Iboga* is a hallucinogen, and if enough is taken, subjects will go into a trance, perhaps entering a spirit world were the ancestors reign. Once in this world, questions are asked of the dead about how to arrange matters here in the world of human habitation. After death, bodies are rubbed and embalmed to remove rigor mortis. Because of the tropical climate, the bodies are interred within two days. They are buried in a wooden coffin. The deceased then joins the ancestors who are to be worshipped in Bwiti ceremonies. They can be asked for advice, about remedies to diseases, etc. There is a *retraite de deul* ceremony one year after death to end the mourning period.

⁸ INTERPERSONAL RELATIONS

Gabonese greetings among strangers are reserved, and a quick handshake is standard for both social and business occasions. A foreigner visiting a private home for the first time will be offered beer, but conversation may not begin immediately. It is often said by Gabonese that chattering too much with a new guest assumes a familiarity that may be disrespectful. It does not take long, however, to get to know people, and those introduced through family are soon greeted with flourish. Friends

world over for thousands of years, generally does not identify a human-like god that is concerned with activities on Earth. Animist gods are abstract and amorphous, and inanimate objects can hold spiritual power. It is the spirits of ancestors who aid or obstruct human endeavor. These beliefs are simultaneously held with Bwiti, an ancestral worship. There are also several thousand Muslims, most of whom have immigrated from other African countries.

Several rituals and holy places exist. The Bwiti ceremonies, performed to worship the ancestors, are led by *ngangas* (medicine men). There are special wooden temples for these ceremonies, and participants dress in bright costumes, paint their faces white, remove their shoes, and cover their heads.

Witchcraft is also an element of animism which exists in Gabon; belief in evil spirits and sorcerers who can conjure them is quite common. Among traditionalists, death itself is not a natural phenomenon, but can only be explained as the work of a malevolent spirit or the malfeasance of a neighbor skilled in casting spells.

Wines are made from palm trees and sugarcane. The palm wine, in conjunction with a hallucinogenic root called *iboga*, is used during ceremonies for death, healing, and initiation. In small doses, iboga acts as a stimulant, making it useful for all-night ceremonies. In larger quantities, it is hallucinogenic, allowing participants to "see their ancestors." Food and wine are offered to the ancestors during the ceremonies, and both men and women partake in these rituals, which are full of drumming, singing and dancing meet each other with a series of four kisses, two on each cheek, as in parts of France. Sometimes just a touching of cheeks will do. Men often walk holding hands, a sign of filial affection. Among older Gabonese, separation of the sexes is the norm at social gatherings.

The expression of young love has changed over the years. Young couples in the city go to movies, dance, and visit as in the West. But traditionally, marriages were often arranged, usually between a young girl and older man, so the opportunity for dating within one's age group was limited.

9 LIVING CONDITIONS

Living conditions in Gabon are generally better than in the rest of Africa. Two reasons for this are the abundance of oil and exportable timber and the low population.

While there are no Gabonese starving from drought or living in squalid refugee camps across borders, there are many who live in impermanent huts, lack electricity and plumbing, don't have access to schools or medical facilities, and have little hope of entering the formal economy.

Health facilities are inadequate. Hospitals are ill-equipped, and patients buy their own medications from pharmacies before treatment can begin. Malaria, tuberculosis, syphilis, AIDS, and other infectious diseases are widespread and virtually untreated. Many villagers also turn to the *ngangas* for remedies, as modern health care is expensive and far from their residences.

As in the rest of Africa, there is a drastic difference between rural and urban living conditions. Downtown Libreville and Port Gentil boast luxury apartments with satellite dishes, Mercedes, and supermarkets. Cities are then ringed by shanties, filled with immigrant workers from other African countries. Rural areas are decidedly poorer. There are few jobs and little farming beyond what can feed a family. One reason for this is the lack of investment by the Gabonese government, like many African governments, in agriculture-related infrastructure. Although most Gabonese know how to farm, almost all of the nation's food is imported.

As a building material, cement is seen as a sign of wealth. All of the government buildings are constructed in cement. In the capital, it is easy to differentiate between buildings that were styled by Gabonese and those done by outside architects. In the villages, the architecture is different. The structures are impermanent. The most economical houses are made from mud and covered in palm fronds. There are houses built from wood, bark, and brick. The brick houses are often plastered with a thin layer of cement with roofs made from corrugated tin. A wealthy family might build with cinder blocks. In addition to the houses, both men and women have distinctive gathering places. The women each have a *cuisine*, a kitchen hut filled with pots and pans, wood for fire, and bamboo beds set against the walls for sitting and resting. The men have open structures called *corps de guards*, or gatherings of men. The walls are waist high and open to the roof. They are lined in benches with a central fire.

10 FAMILY LIFE

Families in Gabon tend to be large, and women have an average of five children. Some ethnic groups are matrilineal; immediate family includes not only parents and siblings, but also the mother's parents and siblings. The government is actively encouraging births due to a belief that the population is simply too small. As a result of this policy, as well as a generally lax cultural attitude toward sex, many young Gabonese women become pregnant with no husband. Families stay together. When a couple is wed, they move to the husband's village which holds his extended family including brothers, sisters, parents, aunts, uncles, grandparents, children, nieces, and nephews. It is common for families to share a home with their parents and extended relatives. Everyone is welcome and there is always room for one more.

Polygyny—the taking of more than one wife—is legal in Gabon, although it is required for couples entering state-sanctioned marriage contracts to register as either "polygamous" or "monogamous."

Women's property rights are difficult to protect without a legal marriage certificate, but there are many couples that don't have this. Interestingly, the French word for "woman" is also used to signify "wife." *Ma femme* is how many women in couples are identified. This may or may not imply legal marriage, but her betrothal to a man is understood—she will often already have his children and will consider his family her in-laws.

11 CLOTHING

Today, most Gabonese wear Western-style clothing. Men wear suits and ties to the office, and blue jeans and T-shirts during the weekend. Women wear dresses and skirts of a Western cut, with material of a colorful African print and the detailed embroidery work done by tailors all over West and Central Africa. A more traditional item is the *boubou*, a flowing top that varies in length from knee to floor. Ceremonial occasions call for elaborate boubous with loose-fitting matching pants underneath for men and double-wrapped *pagnes* for women. A *pagne* is a colorful strip of African cloth used for everything from casual wraparounds to slings for tying a baby to its mother's back. Earlier, raffia was the most commonly used cloth. It is made out of a kind of grass, woven tightly to form a stiff but malleable material.

12 FOOD

The cat is eaten on special occasions among the Fang. It is traditionally eaten by men and is reputed to bestow longevity, as the cat is notoriously hard to kill. The staple of most Gabonese, however, is manioc root. It is ground, soaked, and fermented in a labor-intensive process that can take weeks and appears in the markets resembling a block of cheese wrapped in a banana leaf. Manioc leaves are also eaten and look like spinach when cooked. Another common source of carbohydrates is the banana. These are not small, sweet bananas, which also exist, but larger, harder bananas known in the Americas as plantains.

The staples vary little among the groups in Gabon. The groups share a landscape and climate and thus are able to produce the same kinds of things. Bananas, papayas, pineapples, guavas, mangoes, bushbutter, avocado, and coconuts are the fruits. Eggplants, bitter eggplants, feed corn, sugarcane, peanuts, plantains, and tomatoes are also found. Cassava is the main starch. It is a tuber with little nutritional value, but fills the stomach. Its young leaves are picked and used as a vegetable. Protein comes from the sea and rivers, as well as from bush meat hunted by the men.

Dancers from a traditional Gabonese dance group perform during the Fete des Cultures in Franceville, Gabon.
(Desirey Minkoh/AFP/Getty Images)

Favorite meats include wild monkey, bushpig, pangolin (a small armored mammal resembling an armadillo), and gazelle. Shrimp, crab, and a variety of fish are harvested from the ocean, carp from the Ogouee River, and tilapia from rural fish farms. Most rural households keep chickens, and while there are a few pig and cattle enterprises in Gabon, most domesticated meat is imported from countries with less humid environments more conducive to stockraising. With a year-round growing season, trees produce a vast array of fruit and nuts. The palm nut is used to make palm oil, a necessity in every kitchen. Coconuts, pineapples, mangos, and lemons are sold on practically every street corner.

The Gabonese habit is to eat the largest meal in the middle of the day. Schools, offices, and businesses shut down between noon and 3:00 pm, and people can go home for lunch. Leftovers are usually served in the evening, unless there is a special occasion, when the main meal is eaten later, accompanied by lots of beer, palm wine, and Coca-Cola.

13 EDUCATION

In theory, Gabon offers free universal education. In reality, many villages don't have schools, and some children have to travel long distances or relocate to attend. The adult literacy rate is 63%. Schools use the French system, which allows for 13 years of formal education, and a final state exam called the *Baccalaureate*. Public schools tend to be crowded, with 30–100 students to a classroom. In rural areas, schools often lack essential materials like books and chalkboards. The children begin school at age five or six. When there is no money for books and supplies the children will not attend school. Sometimes a wealthy relative will be called upon to provide these essentials. Both boys and girls attend school until they are 16 by law. Girls may drop out of school due to pregnancy and the boys continue with school or begin to work.

The Omar Bongo University in Libreville offers two to three year programs in many subjects, as well as advanced studies in select fields. The University of Science and Technology in the south is relatively new and diversifies the options. These schools are dominated by upper-class men. Women have a difficult time excelling in academics, as the subjects and standards are structured for men. Some Gabonese study abroad in other African countries or in France, at both undergraduate and graduate levels.

14 CULTURAL HERITAGE

With over 40 distinct cultures in Gabon, national heritage becomes important. While Gabon has changed more rapidly than perhaps any other African country, there is an acute sense of an ancestral "Africanness" that spans ethnicities. The first stanza from the Gabonese national anthem is suggestive:

United in concord and brotherhood
Wake up, Gabon, dawn is upon us.
Stir up the spirit that thrills and inspires us!
At last we rise up to attain happiness.

The International Center for Bantu Civilizations was created in Libreville in 1983, and there is a Gabonese Museum featuring Gabon's history and artistic relics. There is also a French Cultural Center in the capital that displays artistic creations and features dance groups and chorales. There is an annual cultural celebration as well, with performances by musicians and dancers from many different groups in celebration of Gabon's diversity.

Much of Gabon's literature is strongly influenced by France, as many authors received their schooling there. Writers use French, newspapers are in French, and television is broadcast in French. Radio programs use both French and local languages, however, and there is mounting interest in the history of Gabon's peoples.

The Fang make masks, baskets, carvings, and sculptures. Organized clarity and distinct lines and shapes characterize Fang art. *Bieri*, boxes to hold the remains of ancestors, are carved with protective figures. Masks are worn in ceremonies and during hunting sessions. The faces are painted with white and black features. Myene art centers around Myene rituals for death. The female ancestors are represented by white painted masks, which are worn by their male relatives. The Bexota on the other hand use brass and copper to cover their carvings. They use baskets to hold ancestral remains.

15 WORK

A relatively large percentage of the Gabonese population works directly for the state, living in a provincial capital or a large town. One salaried worker will support several to dozens of other people on his or her salary. Many more work in the informal sector selling produce, driving unregistered taxis, or tailoring. Income is supplemented by family plantations, often kept by members living in rural areas, but also kept in small plots around the cities.

Work in Gabon stops between the hours of noon and 3:00 pm because of the heat. Most buildings outside of downtown Libreville are not air conditioned.

16 SPORTS

As in most of Africa, soccer is the national sport. Basketball, for both men and women, and martial arts are very popular. The most common game played by all ages is checkers—every bar and café has a board and pieces fashioned out of soda pop or beer bottle tops.

17 ENTERTAINMENT AND RECREATION

Gabon borrows heavily from Western popular culture. Traditional pastimes fight an uphill battle with American and French television, music, and the antics of sports heroes. Central African music is also very popular.

The most common form of entertainment, for old and young alike, is visiting. Neighbors, friends, and relatives from the same village stroll in the evening, make unannounced social calls, and gossip. While television and radio have made inroads into even the most remote villages, oral culture and face-to-face interaction is an integral part of Gabonese life to a much greater extent than in the West.

18 FOLK ART, CRAFTS, AND HOBBIES

Gabon is known for some of the world's most outstanding masks and statuary, particularly those produced by the Fang in the north, where a high level of artistic abstraction of the human face and figure influenced artists such as Pablo Picasso. Particular to southern Gabon are soapstone carvings of female heads called *Pierre de M'bigou*. These heads are now considered somewhat of a national symbol and can be seen on stamps and business logos. However, with the drastic changes brought by modernity, most of Gabon's craft traditions have been lost.

19 SOCIAL PROBLEMS

In 1990 Gabon made the transition from a one-party state to multi-party democracy. People on the street, in bars, and in the classroom feel freer now to criticize their government and the president. Gabonese like politics, and spirited debates often ensue. Labor, student, and women's groups request permits to hold rallies and protest marches, and usually receive them.

Women's rights are of particular interest in Africa, where traditional gender roles are quite strong. In Gabon women can own property, sue for divorce, and hold public office, but family law recognizes only female—not male—infidelity as grounds for divorce. Domestic violence and absentee fatherhood is prevalent, and, as in America, they are problems that often remain behind closed doors.

A problem that doesn't remain behind closed doors is alcoholism. With a bar on nearly every corner, no regulation of consumption, and a traditional taste for homemade beer and wine, Gabonese are copious drinkers. While many Gabonese believe that drugs are a serious problem in their country, it is nothing compared to the alcoholism.

Despite these problems most Gabonese are proud of their country, with its abundant natural resources, relative wealth, and incredible natural beauty. The PNLS (National Program to Fight Against AIDS) has an office in every major city. It sells condoms and educates women on family planning and pregnancy. There is also a Forests and Waters office in every city, working to protect the environment and wildlife from exploitation, though its effectiveness is questioned. The World Wildlife Fund has ecological and sociological research and wildlife preservation projects in the north and on the coast, and the United Nations supports agricultural advancements in the north by sponsoring extensionists and providing training and mopeds. The United Nations Children's Fund (UNICEF) is also present, working against child prostitution and infant mortality. A German organization, GTZ, funds the organization of the Gabonese National Forestry School. The Peace Corps is active in Gabon as well, with programs in construction, health, agriculture, fisheries, women in development, and environmental education.

20 GENDER ISSUES

In general Gabonese men assume a dominant role over Gabonese women. Men make the financial decisions and control the activities of the family; however, Gabonese women are known to be outspoken and frequently influence family decisions. In the government, the military, and the schools, men hold the vast majority of positions of responsibility and power. Alternatively, women do the majority of the manual labor for the family. Gabonese women typically assume a role of homemaker; few work or engage in activities outside the home.

Gabonese families are generally large. Women are responsible for raising their many children, farming, preparing food, and carrying out various household chores.

Men assume responsibility for housing. Most men build a house for the family and construct a separate area for each wife to use for food preparation. Men also handle the business transactions related to any cash crops the family may produce. In addition, men may fish, work in construction, or take menial office jobs in the cities. Women may also work in the cities, typically in the service sector. A few exceptional women have risen to positions of responsibility, but most positions of power in the workplace are held by men. Children may help with such chores as laundry, kitchen clean-up, and housecleaning.

[21] BIBLIOGRAPHY

Aicardi de Saint-Paul, Marc. *Gabon: The Development of a Nation.* London: Routledge, 1989.

Alexander, Caroline. *One Dry Season.* London: Alfred A. Knopf, 1989.

Balandier, Georges, and Jacques Maquet. *The Dictionary of Black African Civilization.* New York: L. Amiel, 1974.

Barnes, James Franklin. *Gabon: Beyond the Colonial Legacy.* Boulder, CO: Westview Press, 1992.

Decalo, Samuel. *The Stable Minority: Civilian Rule in Africa, 1960–1990.* Gainesville, FL: FAP Books, 1998.

Gardinier, David E. *Gabon.* Santa Barbara, CA: Clio Press, 1992.

——. *Historical Dictionary of Gabon.* Boulder, CO: NetLibrary, Inc., 2000.

Gray, Christopher J. *Colonial Rule and Crisis in Equatorial Africa: Southern Gabon, c. 1850–1940.* Rochester, N.Y.: University of Rochester Press, 2002.

Griffiths, Ieuan L. L., ed. *The Atlas of African Affairs.* 2nd ed. New York: Routledge, 1994.

McElrath, Karen (ed.). *HIV and AIDS: A Global View.* Westport, CT: Greenwood Press, 2002.

Murray, Jocelyn, ed. *Cultural Atlas of Africa.* Rev. ed. New York: Checkmark Books, 1998.

Vansina, Jan. *Paths in the Rainforest.* Madison: University of Wisconsin Press, 1990.

—revised by M. Njoroge

GAMBIANS

PRONUNCIATION: GAM-bee-uhns
LOCATION: The Gambia
POPULATION: 1.7 million
LANGUAGE: English, Wolof, Mandinka, Jola, Fula
RELIGION: Christianity, Islam, traditional African beliefs
RELATED ARTICLES: Vol. 1: Malinke

[1] INTRODUCTION

The Gambia (the name is written with a capital T) is a country of about 4,000 sq mi (10,000 sq km) occupying both banks of the River Gambia for a distance of about 200 mi (320 km). It is surrounded, except for the coastal region, by Senegal.

Around AD 750, a people who made stone circles and who were associated with iron working came from the north and occupied the middle zone of the north bank.

In later centuries, the most important migrants were the Mandinka from Mali in the east, coming as hunters, warriors, and farmers. From the north came the Wolof with their powerful cavalry forces, who conquered the Serer on the north bank. South of the Bintang Creek and in the Kombo region were the Jola and the Bainunka, the latter now largely absorbed into other groups. Later groups of cattle-keeping Fulbe (known in Nigeria as Fulani) arrived. They came from the north on the Senegal River, from Masina in the east, and Firdu in the south. Sometimes they lived beside Mandinka communities, at other times they remained separate, moving frequently in search of water and pasture. The most recent migration is that of the Serahuli (known as Soninke in Senegal), though some families had undoubtedly come centuries earlier. Their major migration took place at the end of the 19th and beginning of the 20th century. They are agriculturalists who also specialize in long distance trade.

The river was visited by early Portuguese explorers, such as Cadamosto in 1455, whose traders gradually settled at various points on the river, seeking gold, ivory, and hides. The English began exploration in the early 17th century, searching for sources of gold, especially in the upper river. An early attempt at colonization in the lower river was made by the small Baltic state of Kurland in 1651. But they were dispossessed by the English who captured a fort they had built on what is now James Island. The French, moving along the coast, claimed the right to trade at Albreda on the north bank.

The accounts of early writers show that the present-day peoples had already settled in the areas they occupy today prior to colonization. After the establishment of colonies in the West Indies and in America, slaves began to be exported from the region. Some were criminals being sold as a form of punishment, but most were war captives brought from the interior. Occasionally individuals were kidnapped by the slave traders trying to fill up their cargo. With the English law against international slave trading in 1807, the town of Bathurst was built on the island of Banjul (later renamed St. Mary's) to control the mouth of the river. Wolof from Gorée in Senegal, who were traders and artisans, formed a major part of the new town. People freed from slave ships captured at sea and refugees from local wars were also settled in the area. Bathurst was renamed Banjul after independence. Another island, MacCarthy Island, was acquired upriver in 1823 as a base from which to protect traders and as a refuge for escaped slaves.

In the middle of the 19th century it was realized that groundnuts (peanuts), which grew well, provided an oil much in demand in Europe. These became the major export of the country. The land, however, was torn apart by religious wars set off by a militant Muslim element known as the Marabouts, who sought to convert nonbelievers (locally known as Soninkes). From time to time, the English tried to bring about peace, as constant warfare destroyed both trade and agriculture. Sometimes they reached an accommodation with the Muslims, while at other times they supported the non-Muslims.

While British possessions were limited to land near the mouth of the river and a few upriver sites used for trading, the French began moving south in Senegal. The Treaty of Versailles of 1783 had granted the British exclusive rights to the river but said nothing about land. Eventually, in 1888 an agreement was reached with France, granting the British 10 kilometers on each bank. The boundary did not take into account natural features or existing political divisions. Surveying to determine the boundaries took place from 1891 to 1896.

Once the boundary was established, the English created a protectorate system of government, signing agreements and governing through local rulers supervised by British "Traveling Commissioners." Many of the traditional ruling families had, however, been wiped out during the Soninke/Marabout wars, and Muslim rulers had taken their place. Tension between the groups was still strong, and many small districts had to be created to relieve the tensions. But local warfare ceased, slave trading was abolished, and a system of local government developed.

The Gambia became independent in 1965 under D. K. Jawara. A republic was declared in 1970, Jawara becoming the nation's first president. He continued to be reelected, surviving an attempted coup in 1981 led by a left-wing extremist. Senegalese forces helped restore him to power. As a result, a Senegambian Confederation was created to bring the countries closer together, but the agreement had collapsed by 1989. The main cause of friction was the fact that Gambians imported vast quantities of goods for sale across the border, often managing to avoid paying customs duties.

Gambia currently has a multiparty political system. The Constitution of the Second Republic of Gambia provides for elections by universal suffrage for adults 18 and older. The ballot is a secret one, and elections must be held every five years. The country's National Assembly includes 45 elected members and four nominated members. The president, popularly elected for a five-year term, is both the chief of state and head of government.

The country's administration is divided into the capital territory (the seat of government), the adjoining Kombo Saint Mary area, and the provinces. Each province has five divisions, each one headed by a commissioner. These divisions are further subdivided into districts locally administered by head chiefs.

The judicial system resembles that of other common law jurisdictions. There is a single system of courts, forming a hierarchy. The subordinate courts consist of Khadis courts, district tribunals, and magistrate courts. At the higher level are the Supreme Court, the Court of Appeal, and the Privy Council. The latter is the highest court of appeal for The Gambia.

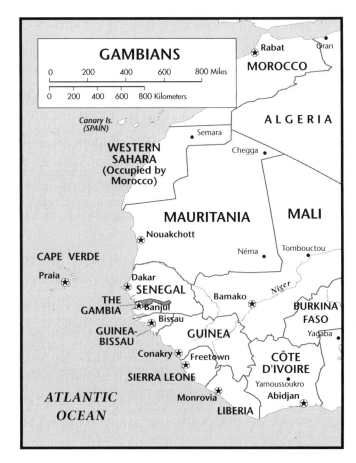

In 1994 a military coup was led by four army lieutenants headed by Lt. Yayha A. J. J. Jammeh. President Jawara fled the country. The coup was said to be prompted by the widespread corruption of politicians. The constitution was suspended, political activity forbidden, and the press restricted. A period of rule by decree followed. In 1996 a new constitution, largely determined by the military, was written. Lt. Jammeh, then at the rank of colonel, resigned to stand in presidential elections, all former politicians being prohibited from taking part. Consequently, he was elected in September 1996. Jammeh was reelected in 2006, and the next elections were scheduled for 2011.

With the exception of the Fulani, ethnic groups are highly stratified. This stratification is a remnant of the great empires that once ruled the country. In each group, status was essentially inherited from the father. The rulers also inherited their status and administered a feudal domain.

2 LOCATION AND HOMELAND

The Gambia is a multiethnic country; major ethnic groups include the Fula, Jola, Mandinka, Serahule, and Wolof. There is no part of The Gambia that is inhabited by one single ethnic group. This close dwelling has led to a sharing of many cultural traits among the groups, which has led to a movement toward a Gambian national culture. There has been a concentrated effort to represent the various minority ethnic groups in government. In addition to indigenous ethnic groups, there has also been an annual migration from Senegal, Guinea, and Mali.

Many people from those countries come to trade in groundnuts (peanuts) and stay to settle.

The Wolof and the Mandinka are the major ethnic groups. The Wolof live mainly in the capital, Banjul. The Mandinka are the largest single ethnic group in the country. These groups represent the former Empire of the Wolof in the Senegambian region and the Mandingo Empires of Mali and Songhai. Creoles form a large element within the local elite. Additionally, there are Mauritanians, Moroccans, and Lebanese in the country. These groups are mainly traders and shopkeepers. English is commonly spoken by members of all ethnic groups since it is the official language of the country. Each ethnic group speaks its own language as well. Harmony among ethnic groups is the general rule, so much so that The Gambia is considered to be a melting pot of West African ethnic groups.

With a population growth rate of 2.72% per year and fertility rate of 5.13 children per woman, the population in 2008 was estimated at more than 1.7 million, making it the most densely populated country in West Africa. The majority of the country's population belongs to eight indigenous tribes. These are: the Mandinka (about 41% of the population); the Wolof (15%); the Fula (19%); the Jola (10%); the Serahuli (8%); the Serer (2.5%); the Aku (0.8%); and the Manjago (1.7%). The ethnic groups were all affected by the Atlantic slave trade and domestic slavery.

The River Gambia is affected by tides on its eastern boundary. Owing to low rainfall in recent years, the intrusion of salt water has now extended far upriver, hindering rice cultivation in areas previously used for agriculture. In its lower section the river is broad and bordered by extensive mangroves. Inland is a low sandy plateau where the villages are built and farm land cultivated. In the middle section the mangroves fade out, and the banks are bordered by grasslands and palms. Ocean-going vessels, which once went as far as Kuntaur (150 mi upstream), now stop at Kau-ur (120 mi upstream) due to increasing silting. In the past, silting created many islands in the middle section, but only one is inhabited—MacCarthy Island. In the upper river the banks become higher and are backed by low-lying land, which floods during the rainy season. The largest town is Basse, a major trade center and administrative headquarters for the Upper River Division.

Beyond the boundary, in Senegal, the Barrakunda Falls are found—really a rocky ledge, which hinders navigation. The river continues in a southeasterly direction, with much twisting and turning, another 400 miles to its source in Guinea. Owing to rocks, sandbanks, and narrow channels, the river cannot be used except for an occasional canoe.

³ LANGUAGE

Mandinka is spoken throughout the country. Wolof is the language of the capital, Banjul, and the middle river area, though the dialects differ. Wolof is also the language of commerce. Because the Fulbe people migrated from different regions, a number of dialects can be heard.

The most common variety of Jola spoken is that of Fonyi (Foñi). The language of government and education is English, though local languages may be used in the lower grades of provincial schools.

All the languages have rich vocabularies. There are numerous proverbs and a wide range of traditional idioms. Children have word games, such as riddles, tongue twisters, and sometimes secret languages of their own.

There are grammars and dictionaries for Wolof, Mandinka, and Fula. Religious and instructional materials have been translated into these languages. Traditional tales and legends have been recorded and translated into written form.

⁴ FOLKLORE

All groups have rich heritages. Legends, mostly relating to events in Mali, Guinea, and Senegal, are related by professional entertainers, who are known locally as *griots*. The Wolof call them *gewel*, and the Mandinka, *jalolu*. The narration is accompanied by a musical instrument and the listeners are expected to respond to the narrator with appropriate interjections.

Folktales are abundant. One group tells of the adventures of Hare and Hyena, the precursor to the Brer Rabbit and Brer Fox tales in English. Hare is seen by the Wolof as a gewel, who is able to talk his way out of any trouble. Non-gewel regard Hare as a trickster. Usually tales are told after dark by mothers to small children. A common folktale is one in which an unjust situation occurs. The situation is remedied by a son or daughter, often with the help of a spirit or an old woman who has been courteously treated. Those who caused the trouble are punished, and the sufferers end up rich and happy again. A whole series of family values is reinforced in the tales. Trouble comes to those who break taboos—for example, a daughter should be obedient and polite, a son should be brave, the old should be treated courteously, strangers should be received hospitably, etc.

Proverbs are used in everyday speech; for example, "However long a stick is in the river, it cannot become a crocodile," means that a stranger can never become a true native, and "The best medicine for a person is another person," stresses the importance of human relations.

⁵ RELIGION

The majority of people are Muslim (90%). Christians (9%) are found mainly in the urban areas. Only a few hold on to traditional beliefs. In the Jola area there are still a few shrines where offerings are made to spirits believed to influence human destiny.

From an early age, children are taught to recite and copy verses from the Quran. Discipline in Quranic schools is strict. Most stop after learning the essentials, but a few go on to more advanced Arabic studies. The main tenets of Islam are the observation of the month of fasting (Ramadan), when food and drink are prohibited during daylight hours; saying the five daily prayers; if possible, going on the pilgrimage to Mecca; giving alms to the needy; and belief in Allah as the only God. The major religious festivals are occasions of celebrations—the Muslim New Year, Muhammad's birthday, the feast at the end of Ramadan, and *Tabaski (Id el kabir),* commemorating Abraham's sacrifice of a sheep in place of his son.

Christian missions—the Roman Catholic Mission, the Methodist Mission, and the Anglican Church—established churches, built schools, and played a major part in education. Mission work outside the capital is limited and is primarily associated with education and social development.

There are a number of traditional religious practitioners as well as Muslim imams, Catholic priests, and Protestant ministers. Each traditional group has its own practitioners.

There are no places that are sacred to all peoples; each ethnic group has its own particular local shrines. Muslims go to Mecca on pilgrimage, and Catholics increasingly travel to Rome and other Catholic holy places.

Each group has its own particular beliefs concerning the afterlife and death. Catholics and Muslims tend to combine the particular traditional beliefs of their ethnic group with more universal Catholic or Muslim beliefs.

6 MAJOR HOLIDAYS

Official holidays are New Year's Day (January 1), Independence Day (February 18), and Liberation Day (July 22), commemorating the military coup. Christmas is also observed by all. It is marked by special watchnight services at the Christian church and children singing carols. From Christmas week to the New Year, large lanterns (fanal) in the form of ships and houses, lit by candles or batteries, are paraded around the streets, accompanied by drumming. During this period many traditional masked figures—the kankurang, with a dress of leaves and red bark (Mandinka), and kumpo (Jola), like a revolving haystack—join in the festivities.

Christians in Sanjul celebrate the feast of St. Mary (August 15), the patron saint of the island. Easter is also observed. The Muslim festivals, listed in the section on religion, depend on the lunar calendar, so dates vary from year to year when judged by the Western calendar.

7 RITES OF PASSAGE

The major stages of life are marked by special rites. After birth a child remains indoors for seven days, and various protective devices are made. Then, the baby is brought out for naming. Its head is shaved, which marks a change in status. The name is bestowed, prayers said, and an animal, usually a fowl but sometimes a sheep, is sacrificed. The meat is eaten later in the day. The child is then regarded as a Muslim.

In childhood there are initiation ceremonies for boys, which involve circumcision and a period of training "in the bush." They learn to endure hardship, obey orders, respect their elders, and understand traditional wisdom. Some boys are circumcised early in life at hospitals or clinics, but still have to undergo the training later. Girls, except for the Wolof, have a similar period of training. Wolof girls often have a ceremony of lip tattooing, which is regarded as a test of courage.

Marriage for women also represents a rite of passage—separation from their family of birth and incorporation into their husband's community. Marriage is a long process. An engagement may take place while the girl is still young. The husband performs services for his in-laws and has visiting rights. At a later date the marriage is formally arranged at a mosque ceremony attended by representatives of the families concerned. Marriage money to be paid is discussed. Later ceremonies involve the formal transfer of the bride to her husband.

Death also represents a transition. A service is held at the mosque before the body is taken to the burial ground. A "charity" (alms) is made on the third and the 40th day, the last marking the final separation when the deceased is considered to have joined the ancestors. Traditional Jola ceremonies involve the slaughter of many cattle and the firing of guns.

Food is important at ceremonial occasions, such as naming ceremonies, betrothals, marriages, and deaths. At these occasions, meat is served along with Jollof rice and fruit. The more food, the more successful the occasion.

8 INTERPERSONAL RELATIONS

In general, Gambian ethnic groups prize tranquility of life, and their manners tend to ease the attainment of that goal. Gambians tend to be soft-spoken and gentle in demeanor, seeking to avoid noisy conflicts and striving toward quiet settlement of disputes. People ask about one another's families.

The exchange of greetings is an important social skill. Greetings differ according to the time of day, the place, whether within the family or in a formal social occasion or a passing situation, and on the age and relative social status of the participants.

The initial greeting is the Arabic salaam aleekum ("Peace unto you"), to which the reply is maleekum salaam. The general greetings follow, such as "Have you spent the day in peace?," or "Have you spent the night in peace?" depending on the time. The reply is always "Peace only." Surnames are exchanged. If one does not know a person's surname it is appropriate to ask. This is to honor the clan of the person spoken to. One can ask where the person has come from, so that one can ask about the people there too, either in general terms ("How is your father?," or "How is your wife?") or by name. Upon leaving one says "I am going," and one is asked to convey information about their destination.

When visiting, the person who arrives initiates the greetings. If one reaches a door where knocking would not make a sound one says "kong, kong" instead. A person should greet one of higher rank, or superior position, such as a village head, chief, or religious teacher. People of equal rank often address each other at the same time. The code of greetings must be followed before any other business is raised.

9 LIVING CONDITIONS

The Gambia is beset by a host of diseases, of which malaria is the most prevalent. Because of the vast areas of swamp it is impossible to control the mosquitoes that carry the disease. On the other hand, smallpox has been eradicated, sleeping sickness has become rare, and polio and leprosy are under control. But infant mortality is high. Diseases, such as measles, whooping cough, and pneumonia, are often fatal to small children. A program of immunization is helping matters. Poor waste disposal and contaminated water lead to intestinal infections. HIV/AIDS has also increased in recent years.

Modern health care is found in urban centers and sporadically in villages. Medicines are in short supply and are expensive. Hospitals and clinics are unable to meet the needs of the people. To receive attention requires a wait of many hours. In 2008 the ratio of doctors to the population was 1:15,000. The infant mortality rate was 65.24 deaths/1,000 live births. The death rate was 11.81 deaths/1,000 population. Life expectancy at birth was about 55.64 years. The HIV/AIDS adult prevalence rate was 1.2% and the number of people living with HIV/AIDS was 6,800.

Supermarkets and stores have a wide range of products, but most are too expensive for the ordinary person to afford. Among young people there is a great demand for cassette players and transistor radios. Businessmen, politicians, senior civil servants, professionals, such as lawyers and doctors, and those employed by international bodies maintain a high standard of living with cars and Western-style furnishings.

In rural areas most houses are built with mud walls. The outside and floors may be cemented. The roof is thatched when circular houses are made, but corrugated sheeting is used with square and rectangular houses. In some villages bamboo matting and reeds are used to form walls. In the hot climate these are quite comfortable.

An inadequate water supply now presents problems. With a shortage of rain in recent years, and with the intensive clearing of vegetation for cultivation, streams have dried up and the general water table has fallen. Deeper wells have had to be dug. Where pumps have been installed, their maintenance has often proven difficult.

At one time there were river steamers, which went up and down the river. Now there are only a few small vessels used by tourists for short trips. People generally travel by road, using converted trucks, which carry goods and passengers, small buses, "bush taxis" (ramshackle old vehicles), and a few large government buses, which are always extremely overcrowded. Crossing the river is a slow business. Most vehicle owners prefer not to cross, but let their passengers off at the ferries to find alternative transport on the other side.

In Banjul, a large influx of motor vehicle traffic conveys people from suburban areas to work and school. In the evening there is a rush hour out of town. With heavy road traffic and overloaded vehicles roads rapidly deteriorate and are difficult to maintain. Where earth roads still exist they become corrugated and develop potholes from the rains.

10 FAMILY LIFE

In rural communities people live in compounds consisting of a series of houses around an open courtyard. These are inhabited by a group tracing descent in the male line. There are distinct men's and women's sections. Small children stay in their mother's house. Adolescent boys have a house of their own. At night a woman goes to join her husband.

The oldest man of the lineage settles disputes and allocates land. Each man farms on his own land and contributes to a common millet farm. Women have their own rice fields and cultivate gardens in the dry season. An enormous amount of labor, cooking, drawing water, washing clothes, caring for small children, gathering wild products, farming, and gardening falls on their shoulders, though daughters are expected to help as much as they can. A man can marry up to four wives. Most marriages tend to be arrangements between families, but a young man may state a preference that he would like his family to follow. If a girl has her mother's support, she may refuse a marriage she dislikes. In urban situations there is greater freedom of choice. A husband can divorce his wife by pronouncement in front of witnesses; a woman must go to the chief's court. A divorced woman can marry again by her own choice. A widow may also remarry after a period of mourning, though if she has children, she normally marries someone in her husband's lineage so that the children continue to be brought up in the same compound. In the villages, age groups unite people. The young men perform communal labor and organize entertainment. There are corresponding groups for youths and girls.

All societies except for the Jola and some Fulbe have a strongly stratified social system that includes an old-ruling family from which the chief was chosen, high-ranking powerful families, and ordinary peasant farmers. Smiths, musicians, and leatherworkers formed special castes, each marrying within their own category. In the old days there were also slaves, those born as slaves, and more recent captives. Consciousness of social status is still important when it comes to marriage, but the drift of people to urban centers and education have tended to obscure many of the old distinctions.

Each ethnic group has its own marriage, residence, and kinship patterns. Additionally, Islam and Christianity have their own regulations. Any particular marriage pattern, kinship system, or residence pattern depends upon a confluence of variables.

Marriage in The Gambia is regulated by either customary, Shariah (Muslim), or general law. Customary law is reserved for all non-Muslims and covers inheritance, land tenure, tribal, and clan leadership, as well as other relationships. Shariah law is primarily for Muslims and covers marriage and divorce. General law is based on British law. Rape is illegal in the case of both married and unmarried women and, along with assault, is a crime. The law does not differentiate between married and unmarried women in this regard. Any person who has carnal knowledge of a girl under the age of 16 is guilty of a felony (except in the case of marriage); incest is also illegal. These laws are generally enforced.

Infant care generally follows West African patterns. Women have general responsibility for child care. Young girls carry their siblings around with them.

There are variations in the domestic units of the various ethnic groups of The Gambia. The social structure of the pastoral Fulani is egalitarian, in marked contrast to that of other Muslim groups, such as the Hausa, and to most sedentary Fulani. The influence of Islam on kinship patterns is evident in the general preference for cousin and other intralineage marriages. Most men are polygynous, the typical household unit comprising the family head, his wives, and unmarried children. Other Islamic groups, such as the Soninke, follow the same general pattern. The Wolof are noted for their double descent kinship system. A household unit usually has a nuclear family or a polygynous unit. There may also be other close kin living together. The vast majority of The Gambia's ethnic groups are patrilineal and patrilocal. This tendency toward male groups is strengthened through Islamic affiliation, as 90% of the population is Muslim. Even the Soninke, who practice double descent, have developed a bias toward the patriline.

11 CLOTHING

Clothing of locally made cloth is worn by rural people when working on their farms. Herdsmen also wear the traditional type of dress. Children who go to school wear uniforms made of imported cloth, each school having its own colors. Boys wear shorts and shirts, and girls wear skirts and tops.

Women wear a long skirt, generally of local cloth, with a loose upper garment of imported cloth. Another cloth is used to carry a child on the back. Women always wear "a head tie," a large square of material that can be tied in a variety of fashions. Hairstyles are elaborate and show both age differences and changing trends in fashion. On festive occasions women, particularly the Wolof, wear many layers of clothing.

Males wear elaborate robes for religious ceremonies and special festivals. In offices Western-style clothing is generally worn. There is a large trade in second-hand clothes from the United States. Young men like to copy American fashions with jeans, T-shirts, and baseball caps.

12 FOOD

Two hundred years of British colonialism added Western food to the diet available in The Gambia. In addition, each ethnic group has its own cuisine.

The Jola prepare a dish, *caldu*, that is made from fish (typically rock bass) and served with rice. Because the Jola live in a forested zone, they make use of many leaves and fruits in their diet. They are skilled at collecting, processing, and preserving plant materials for cooking.

Some people in Banjul are fond of dishes prepared with palm oil, such as *fufu*, which is made from mashed cassava. The Mandika have a dish called *domoda*, which is rice served with a rich sauce of vegetables (sometimes supplemented with meat or chicken) stewed in groundnut (peanut) paste. Sauce ingredients may include tomato puree, peppers, onions, limes, and okra.

The Wolof use *chere* (steamed millet flour), which requires skillful preparation. Dried baobab leaf powder is added to the millet flour, and the mixture is formed into balls that are served with sauce. A favorite dish is *benachin* (literally "one pot"), which requires much attention to prepare. Ingredients must be added in the proper order and cooked for the right length of time, before adding them all to rice for the final stage. *Yassa* is grilled chicken that has been marinated in lemon juice, vinegar, onions, pepper, and oil. The marinade then becomes the sauce for serving with rice. In urban areas a popular dish is fish with rice (*cheb u jen*), flavored with garlic, lemon, bay leaf, pepper, and tomatoes.

The Mandinka eat rice as their main food, though some millet is used. The Jola are also rice cultivators. The upriver Wolof depend on millet and sorghum, but urban Wolof use rice. The Fulbe and Serahuli use millet and sorghum. Roots crops, like cassava and yams, are used sparingly.

In general, a small snack is taken in the morning, such as pap, fruit, or leftovers from the previous day. A light meal is taken in the middle of the day, and the main meal eaten in the evening. Men eat from a common calabash, or bowl. If several families are present in a compound, each household may contribute a dish. Women and children eat separately. When a boy matures and develops good manners he joins the adult men. Eating is done with the right hand, the hands being washed before a meal. The left hand is used only for unclean tasks.

The staple food, boiled or steamed, is served with a sauce of leaves, flavored with dried fish or shellfish, and vegetables. In the rainy season many varieties of leaf are available. In the dry season garden products, such as tomatoes, eggplant, okra, bitter tomato, shallots, onions, are grown. Children eat wild fruits. Mango trees are abundant in most villages, as are papaya (pawpaw). In the western zone, oranges, limes, and bananas are cultivated.

Meat is rarely eaten except for major festivals, though boys sometimes hunt small animals. Chickens are kept for such occasions as naming or marriage celebrations, or to honor an important visitor. Near the coast there is always fresh fish, but most fish consumed is sun-dried or smoked. Where cattle are kept, curdled milk is used with millet.

Gambian women wear a long skirt, generally of local cloth, with a loose upper garment of imported cloth. Another cloth is used to carry a child on the back. (AP Images)

13 EDUCATION

In 1990 the literacy rate for adults (aged 15 and over) was estimated at 27%. But there was a marked difference between men and women, the rate for men being 39%, for women 16%. School enrollment has been increasing. In 1991–92 the rate of enrollment in primary schools (the first 6 years) was 59% for boys and 48% for girls. For secondary schools the rate was 16% in 1987. Literacy in Gambia is defined as those 15 and older who can read and write. In the total population, the literacy rate was 40.1% in 2003; 47.8% for males and 32.8% for females.

Socialization is generally through imitation and proverbs. Older children, especially girls, care for their younger siblings. Generally, male children accompany their fathers, while girls follow their mothers. Segregation by sex is common, and children tend to follow their parents' example and occupations. Males tend to be dominant over females. Religion plays its role in supporting the established order. European missionaries have helped bring in Western ideas and modern employment options to the country.

Any community member can correct any child. Folktales and proverbs illustrate moral ideas.

Education, in theory, is free and universal for primary school. In practice, that is not always the case. Urban areas tend to have better schools and more reliable attendance.

In urban areas a higher proportion of children attend school. In rural areas children are expected to help their parents in daily work, so they are reluctant to send their children

About 75% of Gambians are engaged in agricultural crop production and raising livestock. (United Nations)

off to school. In some communities there is a conflict between Islamic schools and Western schools. Islamic instruction is generally held in the very early morning, or by firelight after dark, and does not conflict with daytime work.

Relatively few of The Gambia's people advance to higher education. In fact, there are no universities in The Gambia, but in the late 1990s, university extension programs were offered for the first time. There is a teachers' training college where instruction is provided in the fields of education, agriculture, health, and domestic science, but there is no university. For advanced level instruction Gambians go overseas to universities in Europe or America. Once they have obtained a degree they may be reluctant to return to low-paying jobs in The Gambia. Many have found work with international organizations, such as the United Nations Development Program (UNDP) and the World Health Organization (WHO), and have gone to work elsewhere in Africa.

14 CULTURAL HERITAGE

Music and song are important in Gambian culture and can be divided into two types: personal music and group music. First, there is personal (individual) music. A man sings as he weeds or paddles a canoe. A Fula plays a one-stringed fiddle when

herding cattle and sings to sooth restless animals at night. A woman or girl sings a lullaby to a small child. A young man plays a flute when guarding a millet field. A watchman plays a musical bow at night. Blacksmith's apprentices play rhythms as they pump their bellows.

Second, there is group music. In many cases dancing is also involved. The group repeats a chorus or claps hands while a lead singer or drummer sets the pace. Children play singing games. There is singing when groups work in the fields, so that they hoe in unison. Traditional warriors' songs are sung to give boys courage as they go for circumcision. Wedding ceremonies have a variety of songs sung at different stages.

Finally there is music performed by professionals to an audience, either to patron families or at a formal concert. The Mandinka *kora*, a 21-stringed instrument, the xylophone, and the Wolof *xalam* (an ancestor of the guitar), are played by professionals who undergo a long apprenticeship and belong to a special caste.

Songs are also sung for special ceremonies, to bring rain, or to effect a cure. Historical songs about former kings and wars and many praise songs are sung mainly in the context of honoring rulers. Praise songs may be sung when a griot feels he can demand a reward and at naming or wedding ceremonies. There are special hunters' songs (now rare) played on a stringed instrument known as the *simbongo,* designed to attract and charm dangerous animals and commemorate major hunting achievements. Challenge songs are sung at wrestling matches.

Broadcasting has provided a new outlet for musicians, and traditional music of all types can be found on records, cassettes, and compact discs.

Dancing takes place at most ceremonies and also serves as general recreation in the evening. In the latter instance it is young people who participate. Girls and young women dance as individuals in response to a drummer. In urban situations a variety of dances derived from elsewhere in Africa, the West Indies, and America may be found.

There are a variety of works in English by Gambian authors, including plays by Gabriel Roberts; poetry by Lenrie Peters, Malick Faal, Tijan Sallah, Swaebou Conateh, and Kahadija Saho; novels by Lenrie Peters and Ebou Diba, and short stories by Tijan Sallah and Nana Humasi (Nana Grey-Johnson).

There is some government support but The Gambia is a poor country and can spare little for the arts. Increasingly, there are collections of folk tales, poetry accompanied by the Kora, a lute-like instrument, and novels. No Gambian novelist has reached the stature of other Africans, such as Chinua Achebe or Wole Soyinka, but there are promising young Gambian authors.

In Graphic arts, the masks of The Gambia are well known and appreciated. In performing arts, the Kora, a lute-like instrument, accompanies much singing and dancing. There are many collections of these performances on audio and videotape.

15 WORK

About three-quarters of the people are engaged in agricultural crop production and livestock raising. About 80% of the population is comprised of subsistence farmers. A majority of these subsistence farmers are women. Groundnuts make up the majority of export products. Millet is also grown widely in the country. There is very little manufacturing in the country. The

Fulani specialize in dairy products and trade them for grain and other products.

There is limited small-scale manufacturing, such as processing groundnuts, smoking fish, and preparing hides. The fact that there is very little manufacturing in The Gambia has resulted in liberal trade policies and the encouragement of tourism. The rapidly growing population of 1.7 million is divided between a rural majority and a growing urban minority. The private sector of the economy is led by tourism, trading, and fishing. The Gambia's high population growth rate has diluted the positive effects of economic expansion. The Gambia's per capita gross domestic product (GDP) was about $1,300 in 2007.

A number of people are employed in service occupations, such as house building and furniture making. Many are engaged in trade, both full-time in shops and markets in urban centers, and others part-time, when farming has ceased. Smuggling constitutes a substantial economic activity. A number of people are engaged in the tourist industry in hotels, as guides, selling arts and crafts, transportation, etc.

In agriculture there is a division of labor, the women being concerned with rice cultivation and dry-season gardening, the men with millet and groundnut farming. Farm work using traditional hoes for ridging and weeding was extremely arduous, but the introduction of animal traction—ox plows, weeding machines pulled by donkeys, and carts for transportation of crops—has eased the burden. At the same time, it has necessitated more thorough clearing of the land, resulting in soil depletion.

16 SPORTS

Soccer is the main field sport. International matches are played in a major stadium built by the Chinese. Basketball is becoming an increasingly popular activity among teenagers. Tennis and golf are played mainly by those who have lived abroad or by expatriates.

17 ENTERTAINMENT AND RECREATION

Radio Gambia broadcasts the early morning call to prayer, followed by readings from the Quran. News is broadcast in English and the major Gambian languages (Mandinka, Wolof, Fula, Jola, and Serahuli). There are occasional programs in other tongues. There are broadcasts for schools in the mornings and early afternoons.

A television station was opened in 1995. Video cassettes are available. Businessmen run a number of small movie theaters, many films coming from India.

The National Dance Troupe performs primarily for tourists. Wrestling competitions are popular during the weekends.

Board games include a form of checkers played with black and white counters on a board, *ludo* (Parcheesi), and *wori*, in which counters are moved around a board with six cups on each side, the aim being to outnumber and capture the opponent's counters at the end of each move. Among young men card games are popular.

18 FOLK ART, CRAFTS, AND HOBBIES

Wood carving, traditionally limited to the making of implements and utensils, such as bowls, mortars, pestles, and canoes, is now geared towards the tourist market. Carvings of animals, decorative masks, model canoes, and drums are made for sale to tourists.

Goldsmiths and silversmiths make earrings, brooches, bracelets, etc., and are especially noted for their filigree work.

Pottery is primarily utilitarian. Water jars, cooking pots, and bowls are made, the best work coming from the upper river region.

Leatherworkers make sandals and covers for charms, which are worn by nearly everybody.

Weaving is a traditional art, the cloth being woven on narrow looms. The strips are sewn together to make cloths worn by women as skirts. Locally made cloth is worn in most traditional ceremonies. Formerly *pagnes* were dyed with indigo, but now imported dyes are used.

Dyeing has reached a high standard, Serahuli women being noted for their skill. Imported textiles are often used as a base, and artistic batik works are produced for the tourist market. Tie-dye and "resist" techniques are used to make a great variety of designs.

Basket work such as winnowing and storage baskets is primarily utilitarian.

A special art is the making of lanterns in the shape of ships or houses from paper fastened to a wooden framework, which are lit by candles or batteries and paraded around town during Christmas week.

19 SOCIAL PROBLEMS

In the constitution of 1970 a major section was devoted to human rights. The Gambia became the location of the African Center for Democracy and Human Rights Studies. Various local support groups were formed. Discussions on the rights of women, the rights of children, and police procedures were free and open. This was changed by the military government in 1994. The old constitution was abolished, and it was held that human rights were now irrelevant. Political activity was forbidden, freedom of the press restricted, and criticism of the government forbidden. Arrests for political reasons became common. The death penalty, abolished in 1993, was reinstated. The official party line that was expressed was that health, education, and improved agriculture were all that mattered. Democracy could not be expected to flourish under conditions of poverty. The right to development was placed above civil and political rights.

Though the country is Muslim, alcohol has always been freely available. In urban areas there are some cases of alcoholism. Marijuana grows easily in the country, and a number of youths have become addicted. Severe drug laws are now in effect.

20 GENDER ISSUES

Most women are engaged in subsistence farming. As in much of West Africa, men clear the land for cultivation and women do the work of planting, tending, and harvesting the crops. Men control tree crops in The Gambia, while women control subsistence gardens.

Women's income from subsistence farming at one time exceeded men's incomes from other activities. Landowners, most of whom were men, felt their authority was undermined by this circumstance and began to try to curtail women's farming activity. They used the county's new interest in environmental preservation to restrict women's ability to farm (and therefore limited women's earning power).

Traditionally Gambian women are subordinate to men. Polygyny is prevalent, even in groups without traditional patrilineal descent. The growth of Islam has strengthened men's roles and their ability to control women in their family.

According to law, women have equal rights in employment. However, most Gambian women are engaged in subsistence farming where the laws are neither relevant nor observed.

All ethnic groups have traditional patterns of inheritance in which priority is given to the male survivors. Islam, however, under Shariah law, provides a portion of a men's estates for widows.

²¹ BIBLIOGRAPHY

Davison, Jean, ed. *Agriculture, Women, and Land: The African Experience*, 1988.

Gamble, David P. *The Gambia*. Oxford: Clio Press, 1988.

McPherson, Malcolm F., and Steven C. Radelet, eds. *Economic Recovery in the Gambia: Insights for Adjustment in Sub-Saharan Africa*. Cambridge, MA: Harvard Institute for International Development, 1996.

Magel, Emil A., trans. *Folktales from The Gambia: Wolof Fictional Narratives*. Pueblo, CO: Passeggiata Press, 1984.

Mark, Peter. *The Wild Bull and the Sacred Forest: Form, Meaning, and Change in Senegambian Initiation Masks*. Cambridge: Cambridge University Press, 1992.

Moss, Joyce, and George Wilson. *Africans South of the Sahara*. 1st ed. Detroit: Gale Research, 1991.

Mriphh, Edrisa Sagnia. *Classical Gambian Recipes*. Banjul: Edrisa Sagnia Mriphh, 1983.

Sallah, Tijan M. *Wolof*. New York: Rosen Publishing Group, 1996.

Schroeder, Richard A. *Shady Practices: Agroforestry and Gender Politics in The Gambia*. Berkeley: University of California Press, 1999.

Wright, Donald R. *Oral Traditions from The Gambia*. Athens, OH: Ohio University Center for International Studies Africa Program, 1979 and 1980.

Zimmermann, Robert. *The Gambia*. Chicago: Children's Press, 1994.

—revised by M. Njoroge

GHANAIANS

PRONUNCIATION: gah-NAY-uhns
LOCATION: Ghana
POPULATION: About 23 million
LANGUAGE: English, Akan, Hausa, more than 25 African languages
RELIGION: Islam, Christianity

¹ INTRODUCTION

Modern Ghana was established in 1957, when colonial subjects of the Gold Coast ended more than 75 years of British rule. Ten years prior to independence, these colonial subjects conducted a non-violent movement consisting of boycotts, demonstrations, and mass strikes against the British. One of the leaders of this anti-colonial movement, Kwame Nkrumah, became the first elected head of state. As the first independent nation south of the Sahara, the country was named for the ancient empire of Ghana, a thriving commercial center known to Arabs and Europeans in the 10th century as the "land of gold." Ethnic groups in the northern part of modern Ghana such as the Mamprussi claim a historical connection to ancient Ghana, which was located in present-day Mali.

In the 50 years since independence, Ghana has witnessed four military coups, the first in 1966 and the most recent in 1981. Presently, Ghana is a constitutional democracy with a multi-party system. The executive branch of government consists of 20 cabinet-level ministers and 10 regional ministers. The legislative branch of government, the National Parliament, consists of 230 members. Ghana is divided into 10 administrative units referred to as regions, which are subdivided into districts. Thus, members of parliament are elected representatives from these districts. National elections for the presidency and the parliament are held every four years. Women hold 10% percent of the seats in parliament.

² LOCATION AND HOMELAND

Today about 23 million Ghanaians inhabit a rectangular shaped country consisting of 239,460 sq km. Roughly the size of the state of Oregon, Ghana is bound to the south by the Atlantic Ocean and has a coastline stretching more than 350 mi. Otherwise Ghana is surrounded by French-speaking countries: Burkina Faso on its northern border, on the east by the Republic of Togo, and on the West by La Cote d'Ivoire. Major rivers of Ghana include the Ankobra, the Ofin, the Pra, the Tano, and the famous Black and White Volta.

Although it is a small tropical country located just north of the equator, the geographical terrain and climatic zones of Ghana are varied. The humid southern regions, marked by coastal plains and rain forest, receive upward of 200 cm of rainfall annually. Faced with harmattan (dust-laden) winds four months out of the year, the savannah lands of the northern regions only receive about 100 cm of rainfall annually. The country's central regions are marked by plateaus and escarpments which extend for over 200 km and where the annual rainfall is about 150 cm. As is the case with all tropical countries, Ghana has two seasons: the wet season begins in April and ends in October, and the dry season lasts from November to March.

In the mid-nineteenth century, Horatio Bridge, captain of an American ship, was so impressed with the city of Accra that he declared, "My impressions of Accra are more favorable than of any other place which I have seen in Africa...Accra is the land of plenty in Africa. Beef, mutton, turkey, and chickens abound; and its supply of European necessaries and luxuries is unequalled." Currently the nation's capital, Accra is still a bustling international city with a population just over two million. A cultural center for the Asante, Kumasi is another large historical city, with a population of 1.5 million. Four other cities in Ghana have populations ranging between 200,000 and 300,000. The larger cities tend to be the capitals of Ghana's 10 administrative regions. For instance, Tamale, a city of 300,000, is the capital of the Northern Region. However, the majority of Ghanaians, about 60%, live in small towns and villages.

While there are distinct regional differences in the architectural styles of Ghanaian houses, this is not the case in the urban centers. Most urban houses are single- or two-story family units made of cement. Apartment buildings over 10 stories are rare in most urban centers. However, towering office buildings dot the landscape in cities such as Accra and Kumasi. The pre-colonial central city is often composed of mud and cement houses with corrugated zinc roofs. Exclusive suburbs have the large two-story houses surrounded by compound walls and shaded by palm and fruit trees.

The indigenous architectural styles are found in the rural communities. In the southern and central regions of Ghana, one finds the rectangular-shaped adobe or wattle house with a thatched roof. In the northern regions, one finds the circular adobe house with a concentric thatched roof or the rectangular adobe houses with the flat roof. Among the Gurensi of northern Ghana, women paint the beautiful geometric designs found in their circular adobe homes.

³ LANGUAGE

Although English is the official language of government and business, Ghanaians speak more than 25 distinct African languages belonging to the Niger-Kongo language family. Akan is the first language of more than 50% of Ghanaians; speakers of this language include the well known Asante and Fante, as well as eight other ethnic groups. Other languages spoken by large numbers of Ghanaians include Ewe, Ga, Guan, and Gur. Most Ghanaian speak two or more African languages. Multilingualism has always been a feature of African societies, stimulated to a large degree by regional and long distance trade. About 200 years ago Muslim merchants introduced Hausa, a Nigerian language, into commercial centers such as Accra. Today, Hausa has become a lingua franca facilitating intergroup communication throughout Ghana. A weekly show is broadcast in Hausa on the national radio station.

Upon arriving at the international airport in Accra, travelers may observe colorful billboards with the word "Akwaaba," or *welcome*, written in bold letters. To welcome passengers in the Akan language seems reasonable since it is the first language of half of Ghana's population. Below are typical Akan greetings one may hear in southern Ghana:

Eti Sen	Hello!
Wo ho ti sen	How are you?
Me ho ye	I am fine.
Me ho wo ekyere	See you later!

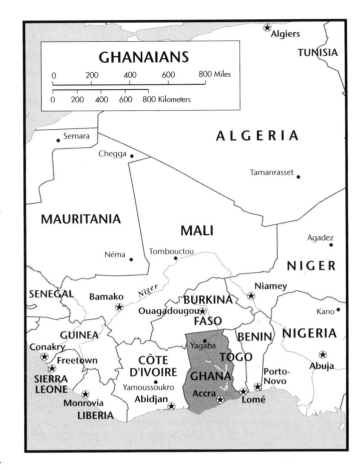

As a result of the Trans-Atlantic slave trade, Ghanaian personal names are found in various parts of the Americas. Among the Fante and most ethnic groups in the southern regions of Ghana, at least one of the names given to a newborn designates the day of birth. In the Carolinas, for example, "Essie" and "Effie" are the shortened forms of Fante "day names" given to females born on Wednesday and Friday. The Akan day name "Kudjoe" is commonly given to males among the people of Jamaica, Surinam, and the Sea Islands off the coast of South Carolina and Georgia.

⁴ FOLKLORE

In pre-colonial times, the history of most Ghanaians was preserved by oral historians. In the case of the highly centralized Akan kingdoms, trained court historians preserved the history. The oral traditions of a state society are "fixed texts" and must be recited in a precise manner, word for word. In addition to preserving group history, among the Tallensi of northern Ghana, the legend of Mosuor serves as a charter for the political and ceremonial relationships which exist between chiefs. Today, many of the great leaders of Ghana's different ethnic groups are also included in school history books. A grade-school pupil does not have to be Asante to learn of Yaa Asantewa, the queen mother who declared war on the British in 1900.

Storytelling is one of the most important recreational activities found among Ghanaians, especially in rural villages. While stories are used to teach children morals, social norms, and history, they are also used as a form of social control among the adults. Such stories may allude to the improper behavior of local adults without revealing their names. Just as storytelling is a crucial element of primary curriculum in the American school system, Friday afternoons are set aside as a time for storytelling in Ghanaian schools. Students are encouraged to share with the class stories which they have been told by their parents and grandparents.

Among the Akan- and Guan-speaking peoples, folktale characters include the tortoise, hare, vulture, and crow. However, Anansi the spider is the most popular animal character. Anansi defeats his larger foes through intelligence, humor, and cunning rather than through the use of physical force. Some of these spider tales, referred to as "Anancy tales" by Jamaicans, were introduced into the Caribbean by enslaved Akans forced to work on plantations in the 18th century.

5 RELIGION

Prior to the introduction of Islam and Christianity in Ghana, the concept of a supreme being was common in the majority of the indigenous religious systems. It was a belief in the power of intermediary mystical beings such as ancestral spirits and lesser deities that made these religions the target of 19th-century Christian missionaries. Islam was introduced into northern regions of Ghana as early as the 14th century among people such as the Mossi. The Larabanga Mosque south of Tamale was built as early as the 15th century.

Whether an individual is Christian or Muslim, he or she is reluctant to totally divorce themselves from certain aspects of the indigenous religions, especially community-wide festivals commemorating the ancestors. In Cape Coast, each August the Fante sponsor the Oguaa-Afahye Festival, an agricultural festival. It attracts Fante from all over the Central Region and family and friends from various parts of the country. Although ancestral reverence is central to this festival, the participants may represent a variety of Christian denominations including Anglicans, Baptists, Catholics, A.M.E. Zion, and members of various independent churches.

During the 1930s, some African Christians became dissatisfied with mission churches controlled by white missionaries. They left to create independent Christian sects, sensitive to both the spiritual needs and cultural values of Africans. For instance, the Harrist Church, which was founded in La Cote d'Ivoire in 1913, spread to southwestern Ghana within a few years. The first Harrist church was established in Ghana by Maame Tani, a healer, and Papa Kwesi Nackabah, a preacher. Not only does the Harrist Church give women a greater role in religious affairs, it sanctions polygyny. The Harrist Church also incorporates African dance and song into devotional services.

6 MAJOR HOLIDAYS

Ghanaians celebrate Independence Day on March 6 and Republic Day on July 1. The government often sponsors major parades in the large cities on national holidays. On such occasions, teenagers and young adults enjoy beach parties. The two religious holidays recognized by all are Christmas and Damba, which marks the birth of the Islamic prophet Mohammed.

Every month of the year, one or more festivals are held in some part of Ghana. For instance, during the month of August, while people of the Northern Region celebrate the Damba Festival, the Ga people of Accra sponsor the Homowo Festival,

a celebration of female puberty rites. While most festivals may have political or economic significance, Ghanaians use festivals to express their appreciation to the divinities for good health, prosperity, and a bountiful harvest.

7 RITES OF PASSAGE

The cycle of life from birth to death is marked by some type of celebration in Ghana. Throughout southern Ghana, ethnic groups carry out special naming ceremonies for the newborn. The Ga host a naming ceremony for the newborn infant eight days after birth. Family members and friends may sponsor numerous small ceremonies to mark the child's growth. For instance, among the Adkye-Ga, a newborn's mother or female relatives will dress the infant in waist beads, believed to protect the baby from disease and evil spirits. On a practical level, this string of beads adorning the baby's waist holds the diaper. Once a boy is toilet trained he no longer wears waist beads. A female, however, may wear her waist beads for the duration of her life, simply lengthening the string and adding beads to accommodate changes in her body.

Many ethnic groups in Ghana sponsor events which mark adolescence. Among the Ashanti and other Akan groups, nubility rites are held for a female once her menstrual cycle is regularized. The nubility rite lasts for several days and is conducted by the Queen Mother and elderly members of the girl's matrilineage. As a series of life-affirming spiritual and religious activities, this ritual does not involve any type of genital mutilation. The adolescent female is educated in the moral standard and behavior necessary for her to become a successful mother, wife, and member of her community.

The nubility rite includes activities such as a stool ceremony, a ritual bath, dancing, and pouring libation to thank God, the earth, the ancestors, and the community for having protected the girl. Other ceremonial activities include the presentation of gifts from guests, distribution of food on behalf of the girl, a hair-cutting ceremony, the ceremonial dressing of the girl, and the eating of a ritual meal.

8 INTERPERSONAL RELATIONS

Among Ghana's diverse groups, custom stipulates how greetings should be delivered and received. Among the Akan peoples, one can not initiate a conversation without first extending the proper greeting. To do otherwise, one risks being labeled as rude and uncivilized.

9 LIVING CONDITIONS

There is an average of five people living in each house in Ghana. In towns and cities, some housing has been built by the government or by organizations and companies to provide housing for their employees.

10 FAMILY LIFE

The dominant family structure in Ghana is the extended family, and the influence of descent groups is still very strong. From birth to death, Ghanaians are members of either a matrilineal or patrilineal descent group. The Fante of the Central Region, like all Akan-speaking groups, trace descent through the female line; children belong to their mother's lineage. The Tallensi of the Northern Region reckon descent through the male line and children are members of their father's lineages. These

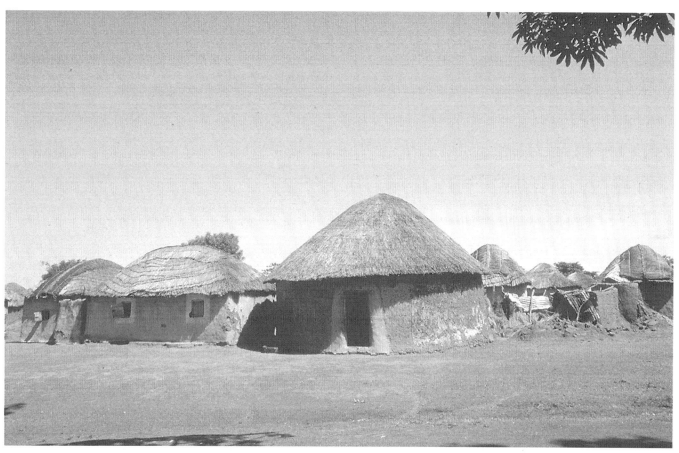

A Ghanaian rural family compound. The dominant family structure in Ghana is the extended family, and the influence of descent groups is still very strong. From birth to death, Ghanians are members of either a matrilineal or patrilineal descent group.
(Corel Corporation)

unilineal descent groups regulate marriage, hold property jointly, perform important religious activities, and provide members with the security of a mutual aid system. Members of a Tallensi patrilineage are obliged to participate in certain ceremonies which revere and pacify their ancestors. Adult members of a Fante matrilineage will be expected to offer financial assistance to children other than their offspring.

Most Ghanaians believe that marriage is a family matter rather than a contract between two individuals. In both urban and rural communities, marriage requires the approval of the family and involves some type of bridal payment (a prescribed set of gifts given by the potential groom to his fiancée's family). Today, young adults wishing to marry may choose one or a combination of wedding ceremonies: the traditional, civil, Christian, or Islamic wedding ceremony.

11 CLOTHING

On a daily basis Ghanaians may choose to dress in either African or Western-style clothes. A woman who chooses to wear the "kaba and slit," a matching blouse and long skirt made from African cloth, is considered to be as appropriately dressed as one wearing a Western business suit.

While certain types of woven cloth and clothing designs may be associated with a specific ethnic group, they are becoming a part of the national dress. For instance, although the *fugu* is a shirt worn traditionally by elderly men on ceremonial occasions, among the northern peoples such as the Dagomba and the Kasena, it is now worn by men all over the country. In fact, this striped cotton shirt was often worn by the former head of state President Rawlings.

All students attending elementary, secondary schools and college wear uniforms; however, it is not uncommon to see urban teenage boys dressed in the fashionable blue jeans worn in American cities. On special occasions, custom dictates that people wear traditional clothing. For instance, the Ashanti must wear the hand-stamped *Adrinkra* cloth at funerals. Throughout Ghana, men and women holding traditional political titles have specific clothes worn only on ceremonial events. Among the Ga, on ceremonial occasions chiefs must wear the expensive machine-made *bazin* cloth, draped in the toga style. In addition to dictating clothing to be worn by nobility, there are rules regarding hairstyles, makeup, jewelry, and footwear. The Fante Queen Mother must wear a natural hairstyle and the traditional hand-made sandals associated with nobility at all public ceremonies.

12 FOOD

Ghanaian cuisine is very savory, and the use of cayenne, allspice, curry, ginger, garlic, and onions is common in most dishes. Stews are some of the nation's most popular dishes;

the national dish is groundnut peanut stew, which may include chicken or beef. Another common dish is *palava* sauce, a spinach stew which may use fish or chicken. A spicy rice dish cooked in tomato sauce and meat, Jollof Rice, is eaten by many Ghanaians, and is the antecedent to the red rice dish eaten by African-Americans in the coastal Carolinas. Ghanaians also eat black-eyed peas; the dish "red-red" is black-eyed peas cooked in palm oil and served with rice and fish.

While urban dwellers may include bread, oatmeal, and ice cream in their diet, most rural folk rarely eat Western food. For breakfast, Fante villagers may eat fish and kenkey, a fermented corn dish. The first meal of the day for an Ewe family living in Accra may include an egg and large bowl of oatmeal sweetened with local honey. The main staples served with Ghanaian meals are rice, millet, corn, cassava, yams, and plantains. The latter four may be fried, roasted, or boiled.

Some of the fast foods sold by urban street vendors include roasted plantain or peanuts, corn on the cob with pieces of coco nuts, and beef kebabs. In all of the cities, there are hundreds of small restaurants, referred to as *chop bars*, serving indigenous cuisine at reasonable prices. Women tend to be the owners and employees of these small chop bars.

13 EDUCATION

After independence in 1957, the Ghanaian government introduced free education, assuming all educational expenses for students from the time they entered primary school until they completed university. Still today, after introducing nominal tuition fees in the 1980s, educational expenditures represent more than 25% of the national budget. Unlike Western countries, the Ghanaian government assumes the bulk of the operational cost for secondary boarding schools, both public and private. While public boarding schools are located in all 10 regions of the country, private institutions tend to be located in or near the major urban centers. Achimota School is an example of a public coeducational facility located in Accra and Sammo Secondary Technical School, located in Cape Coast, is an example of a private boarding school.

Competition to the nation's secondary schools and institutions of higher education is very intense. Two entrance examinations, one for secondary school and the other for the university, weed out all but the most exceptional students. As is the case throughout the continent, the number of female students decreases drastically at the upper levels of the educational system.

Government guaranteed loans have been introduced to help students finance their education at public universities and professional and technical colleges. Four of Ghana's public universities are located in the southern and central areas of the nation: the University of Ghana, the University of Cape Coast, the University of Science and Technology, and the University College of Education. More recently, the government established the University of Development Studies at Tamale in the Northern Region. In the past 10 years, several private universities have been established. Several of the private universities were established by religious bodies such as the Seventh Day Adventists who own the Valley View University in Accra, and Central University College which was established by the Central Gospel Church. The first tertiary institution in Ghana modeled on the American liberal arts college is Ashesi University. There are also several public institutions of higher education similar to American community colleges which offer training in fields such as nursing, teaching, fashion design, and computer programming. Such institutions include polytechnics and nursing training and teacher training colleges which are located in all the country's regions.

14 CULTURAL HERITAGE

Music and dance are intimately interwoven in most parts of African. Ghanaian choreographer A. M. Ipoku asserts, "...one can see the music and hear the dance." When attending night clubs or house parties, Ghanaians dance to high life, reggae, or rhythm and blues. When attending Christian churches, Ghanaians sing Western-style hymns or gospel music. It is not unusual to hear gospel music at the funeral of some Christians.

Traditional music and dance are performed at all coronations, festivals, and the funerals of high-ranking members of a community. Among the Ga of southern Ghana, during the Homowo Festival which introduces adolescent girls to the public, musicians play the traditional drum music, *Kpanlogo*. In the north, the final funeral ceremony of a beloved person of high status among the Dagomba may include musical performances by more than six groups, each playing a distinct musical style. The dances performed also vary, the most important dance being the *Baamaya*. These dancers have bells tied to their feet and waists, wear headdresses, and wave fans while they perform fascinating and strenuous movements.

The drum is by far the most important musical instrument among southern ethnic groups; however, the xylophone dominates the music of northern groups. Both instruments are made in a variety of sizes. Other traditional instruments include various types of rattles such as the *shekere*; clapperless bells; and wind instruments such as the bamboo flute and single-note trumpet made from animal horns, ivory, or wood. Popular music using Western instruments does not pose a threat to Ghana's rich musical heritage. For instance, the installation ceremony of a new paramount Asante chief requires a new pair of *atumpan drum*, also known as the talking drum. As is the case with many African languages, the Ashanti language is tonal. Following the high-low pitches of the Akan language, the atumpan recites proverbs and poems recounting the valor of warriors and singing the praises of chiefs. Presently, the atumpan is played at the opening session of the National Assembly in Accra and is used in radio broadcasts to announce the news.

One of West Africa's most renowned composers and ethnomusicologists is the Ghanaian J. H. Kwabena Nketia, a professor at the University of Ghana. He translates the traditional elements of Ghanaian music into contemporary idioms, and some of his best known compositions include *Bolga Sonata for Violin and Piano* and *Canzona for the Flute, Oboe, and Piano*.

Prior to independence from the British, the literary arts were very limited. For instance, the works of only two playwrights were published prior to independence. The first Ghanaian to publish a play was Kobina Sekyi in 1913; Sekyi's *The Blinkards* is a satirical comedy that questions the increasing Anglicization of indigenous culture. Also during the colonial period, Ferndinand Kwasi Fiawoo, an Ewe of eastern Ghana, wrote three plays in Ewe which were well received by readers and audiences.

The first Ghanaian to publish a novel was Joseph Ephraim Casely-Hayford, *Ethiopian Unbound* in 1911. It was over 30 years later before another Ghanaian writer would be published—*Eighteenpence* by R. E. Obeng in 1943.

After independence, the literary arts began to flourish; literary journals such as *Drum* and *Okyeame* published the short stories and poetry of such writers as Ama Ata Aidoo, Efua Sutherland, Kwesi Brew, and Kojo Kyei. Unfortunately, during the nine years that Kwame Nkrumah served as head of state, the creativity of Ghanaian writers was seriously censored. In 1960, Nkrumah shut down the *Drum*. Only poets concerned with patriotic or nationalist issues, such as Michael Dei-Anang and Yaw Warren, escaped the scrutiny of the government.

After the overthrow of Nkrumah's government in 1966, an impressive group of writers emerged. Well known playwrights include Kofi Awoonor, Efua Sutherland, and Joe Graft. Novelists include Kofi Awoonor, Ayi Kwei Armah, and Ama Ata Aidoo. Ghanaian poets who are recognized by an international audience include Atukwei Okai, Kofi Awoonor, and Vincent Odamtten. Poets as well as other creative writers do recognize the impact of their respective oral heritage on the literary arts. Ewe oral poetry, *halo*, has been a major influence on the poetry of Kofi Awoonor in terms of structure and rhythm.

15 WORK

Ghana has a diversified economy consisting of light manufacturing, mineral production, and agricultural production. Gold is one of the country's most abundant mineral resources, and in recent years it has superseded cocoa as the leading foreign exchange earner. Other minerals mined and exported include diamonds, manganese, and bauxite. In 2008 offshore oil was discovered in commercial quantities in Cape Three Points, which is located in the Western Region. It is expected that this discovery will boost the economy and provide more jobs.

In the last 25 years there has been a boom in the timber industry. Although tracks of virgin rain forest such as the Kakum National Park in the Central Region are protected by the government, community groups throughout the country are concerned about the adverse effects of deforestation. Various women's and youth groups sponsor tree-planting projects. Ghanaian farmers are keenly aware that deforestation causes erosion, gradually decreasing agricultural yields.

A large proportion of the population is engaged in subsistence farming. In most groups, men carry out the heavy work associated with preparing the fields, but women and children plant, weed, and harvest most food crops. Principal food crops produced for domestic consumption include cassava, maize, millet, plantains, peanuts, rice, yams, leafy vegetables, beans, and fruits. Many women sell their surplus food crops to urban traders in order to earn cash.

Introduced during the colonial era, cocoa is still Ghana's leading export crop and is processed by Europeans to make chocolate. In most farm communities cocoa cultivation is dominated by the men. Among the Ewe, women own only 4% of the total cocoa acreage. Women farm the food crops and must be involved in the petty retail trade, food processing, or artisan work in order to earn money.

Although farmers raise chickens, cows, goats, sheep, and pigs, fish is indeed the staple protein food among Ghanaians. Fishing is an important economic activity, connecting communities from the farthest extremes of the country. There are hundreds of fishing villages located along the Atlantic coastline. During the fishing season, small crews of men in brightly

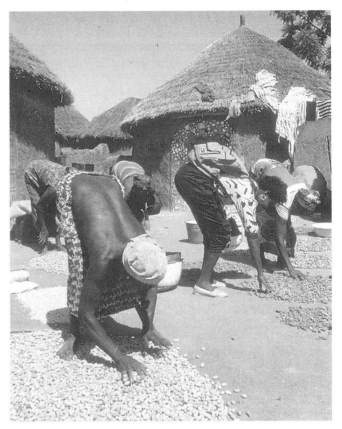

Ghanaians drying peanuts. Ghana's national dish is peanut stew, which may include chicken or beef. (Corel Corporation)

painted canoes cast their nets into the Atlantic Ocean. Most fishermen have mastered both lagoon and deep sea fishing. The fish they catch is processed and marketed by their wives or female relatives. Women are responsible for the selling of fresh, smoked, salted, and fried fish in the Makola Market and other smaller markets in Accra. Some Ga women travel hundreds of miles to sell their product in the markets of cities such as Kumasi, Ho, and Tamale. Historically, and still today, the fish trade is a major economic resource open to Ga women.

Processing foods for Western markets is a slowly developing but lucrative business venture in Ghana. Commercial fishing companies with expensive boats and high-tech equipment supply an increasingly large number of American and European supermarkets and restaurants with tuna and lobster. Some women's cooperatives have begun raising and processing snails, known as escargots in metropolitan restaurants in European cities.

Women are well represented in the labor force, but also tend to work in the informal sector of the economy, mainly as petty traders in sales and retail. Professional women cluster in occupations such as nursing and teaching. In the corporate world, women are underrepresented in managerial positions and dominate the clerical positions. Lack of capital is the main reason why few women have been able to establish independent businesses; banks and loaning institutions discriminate against them.

The manufacturing sector of the economy is growing at a slower pace and includes wood processing, food processing, textile, brewing, and distilling. Few of these products are exported outside of the African continent. However, the handicraft industry is thriving and exports are increasing. Traditionally woven clothes, leather bags, bead necklaces, and beautifully carved masks and stools are sold in many large American cities. Currently, many African-American secondary and college graduates adorn their robes with *kente* scarves produced by Asante weavers.

16 SPORTS

The most popular spectator sport in Ghana is soccer. Every major city supports one or more professional teams and a stadium—Asante Kotoko in Kumasi, the Venomous Vipers in Cape Coast, and the Hearts of Oak in Accra. The Black Stars, Ghana's national team, is made up of the best players from these various teams. Ghanaians playing abroad, such as Michael Essien, who plays for the English soccer team Chelsea, return home to play with the Black Stars during international matches such as the Africa Cup or the World Cup. On any given weekend it is not uncommon to find teenage boys or men competing in soccer matches. Soccer for females is gaining in importance, and a female soccer league was launched in April 2008.

While soccer is the sport of the masses, basketball and tennis are replacing cricket in popularity among the elite. Females attending secondary schools and institutions of higher education tend to excel in sports such as track and handball.

17 ENTERTAINMENT AND RECREATION

After World War II, the concert party, a type of comic opera performed in the Akan language, became the most popular form of entertainment in the coastal towns. This folk theater is a fusion of Akan performing arts, especially masquerade and Anansi stories, influenced by Western musical and dramatic traditions. While the theatrical form used is similar to slapstick humor, there are both moral and political overtones in the performance. Today, there are over 50 concert party troupes who perform in both urban and rural areas. The events open at nine o'clock with a dance and live band playing popular tunes. Two hours later, the troupe performs a comical play which lasts until two or three o'clock in the morning. Generally, the band ends the concert with a selection of music.

18 FOLK ARTS, CRAFTS, AND HOBBIES

Although the British manufactured goods introduced during the colonial period decreased certain cottage industries, Ghana has maintained a rich art and craft tradition. While certain crafts such as batik were introduced in the 1960s, others such as pottery have been practiced for thousands of years. In pre-colonial times, those ethnic groups that were organized in kingdoms boasted many full-time artisans. Weavers and smiths were full-time artisans in Kumasi, capital of the Ashanti kingdom. Today, Asante smiths still produce the incredible beautiful gold jewelry for the monarch, and the weavers produce the kente clothe worn by royalty.

Pottery, the country's oldest craft, dates back to 4000 bc, and women still throw pots of various sizes without the wheel. The perfectly round clay pots produced by Shai women, known throughout southern and central Ghana, are used for storage and cooking. Akan women are some of the few female sculptors in Africa; their clay figures are idealized portraits of deceased chiefs or important elders in their society. Beads commonly found in markets throughout Ghana are also produced by women. Among the Krobo people in the eastern part of Ghana, beads are used in several socio-religious ceremonies, including puberty rites for adolescent girls.

As mentioned above, many Ghanaian groups continue to use traditionally woven cloth for special occasions. Throughout Ghana, men are the weavers. Men in northern societies such as the Dagomba make leather products and weave the fugu shirt described earlier.

19 SOCIAL PROBLEMS

The minimum working age is 15, but custom and economic necessities often force children to work at a younger age. The government has established agencies to help protect children. Ethnic tensions in the northern parts of Ghana eased somewhat in the 1990s, although they have not completely disappeared.

20 GENDER ISSUES

Any visitor to Ghana will notice the high visibility and dynamism of women in commercial and social life. They are found on the streets carrying their wares on their heads, selling in shops, in the markets, or from tables set up on pavements. Women in Ghana also play important roles managing church, home, and community activities. Among the matrilineal communities, some royal women become queen-mothers, and perform political and ritual functions. However, despite their high visibility in daily life, few women occupy positions of authority in formal power structures. After elections in 2000, only 19 women were elected to a parliament of 200. In 2004, although 100 women contested the parliamentary elections, only 25 were elected.

Women in Ghana are faced by constraints such as a lack of education, training and skills, low rates of utilization of productive resources such as land, and poor literacy rates in comparison with men. According to a major social survey, the Ghana Living Standards Survey (GLSS 4) for 2000, 44.1% of women as compared to 21.1% of men had no formal education.

This has a direct effect on women's capacity to take up formal sector jobs and leadership positions. Thus the majority of women in Ghana are self-employed. Their main activities are petty trading, food processing, and marketing food crops. Although this makes them highly visible, their businesses tend to be small-scale, home-based and loosely structured with limited management expertise and weak infrastructural support.

Due to their low levels of literacy and skills, women tend not to be able to improve their opportunities, and they remain in low-skilled, low-status and low-paid jobs.

The underlying causes of the constraints are deep-seated traditional social attitudes and socio-cultural practices and beliefs which are slow to change. Also, the Judeo-Christian traditions tend to reinforce patriarchal cultural practices and beliefs, and this makes Ghanaians adopt conservative attitudes toward issues such as homosexuality and fashions and fads which are thought to be "Western."

Efforts have been made by both the state as well as civil society organizations to bridge the inequalities that persist between men and women. In 1975 the National Council for Women and Development was established as the national machinery to promote the advancement of women, following from the first United Nations Conference on Women. Since January 2001 the national machinery has been transformed and elevated to a full ministry, the Ministry for Women's and Children's Affairs (MOWAC), headed by a minister of state who has cabinet status. MOWAC has worked with academia, NGOs and members of legislative bodies to research and review aspects of Ghanaian laws which do not promote the advancement of women. Ghanaian women have a long history of organization and association and many belong to groups with a variety of interests. Such groups could have any of the following interests: religious, professional or occupational, micro-finance, self-help, politics, women's rights, or charity.

Feminist groups such as Abantu for Development and Netright have been at the forefront of activities to support the empowerment of women, and also to support them when they venture into formal power structures and take up public office. Since the 1980s, the collective efforts of the state and civil society have brought about a number of achievements for gender issues in Ghana. Notable examples are the establishment of the passing of PNDC Law 111 or the Intestate Succession Law, the establishment of the Girls' Education Unit of the Ministry of Education, the passing of The Children's Act, the amendment of the Criminal Code to suppress trafficking in women, the establishment of a Domestic Violence and Victims Support Unit within the Ghana Police Service, and the passing of a Domestic Violence Bill. Particularly since 2000 some women's rights groups have begun to form networks. One such network was very instrumental in mobilizing the public to support the passing of the Domestic Violence Bill in 2007. Another network had earlier mobilized the public to support a Women's Manifesto which was presented to President Kufour in 2005.

In spite of the activities by both the state and civil society to improve the status of women in Ghana, and the increasing levels of awareness of women's and gender issues in the country, challenges to women's empowerment and leadership still persist. Although the status of women in Ghana has improved greatly during the last 25 years, there is still room for more progress.

[21] BIBLIOGRAPHY

Aidoo, Agnes Akosua. "Asante Queen Mothers in Government and Politics in the Nineteenth Century." In *The Black Woman Cross-Culturally*, ed. Filomina Chioma Steady. Cambridge: Schenkman Books, 1981.

Atumpan: The Story and Sounds of the Talking Master Drum of the Ashanti. Produced by Mantle Hood. Institute of Ethnomusicology, UCLA. Videocassette.

Awumbila, Mariama. "Women and Gender Equality in Ghana: A Situational Analysis." In *Gender Training in Ghana: Politics, Issues, and Tools*. Dzodzi Tsikata, ed. Accra: Woeli Publishing Services, 2001.

Bridge, Horatio. *Journal of African Cruiser*. London: Dawson of Pall, 1968.

Cole, Herbert M., and Doran H. Ross. *The Arts of Ghana*. Los Angeles: Museum of Cultural History, 1977.

Convention on the Elimination of all forms of Discrimination against Women. New York: United Nations, 2005.

Duncan, Beatrice Ekua. *Women in Agriculture in Ghana*. Accra: Friederich Ebert Stiftung, 2004.

Hay, Margaret Jean, and Sharon Stichter, ed. *African Women South of the Sahara*. New York: Longman Publishing, 1995.

Nketia, J. H. Kwabena. *The Music of Africa*. New York: W. W. Norton & Co., 1974.

Priebe, Richard K., ed. *Ghanaian Literatures*. New York: Greenwood Press, 1988.

Robertson, Claire. *Sharing the Same Bowl*. Bloomington: Indiana University Press, 1984.

Wilks, Ivor. *Forest of Gold: Essays on the Akan and the Kingdom of Asante*. Athens: Ohio University Press, 1993.

—revised by M. Prah

GIKUYU

PRONUNCIATION: kee-KOO-yoo
ALTERNATE NAMES: Kikuyu; Gekoyo
LOCATION: Kenya
POPULATION: 6.8 million
LANGUAGE: Gikuyu; English and KiSwahili (national languages)
RELIGION: Christianity (Roman Catholicism, Anglicanism, fundamentalist groups, African Separatist Churches); ancestor spirits (Mungiki etc)
RELATED ARTICLES: Vol. 1: Kenyans

¹ INTRODUCTION

The Gikuyu, like the white settlers in the early 20th century, were attracted to the highlands because of cool temperatures, fertile soils, and abundant rainfall. Prior to the arrival of the Gikuyu, hunters and gatherers known as the Dorobo occupied the area. Although the exact date when the Gikuyu began to occupy the central highlands is not known, their oral history refers to a cycle of famines, which helps to tie their presence to a point in history. For example, the "Famine of Sweeping the Courtyard" occurred probably before 1637 and the "Famine of Small Bones" occurred later, sometime in the mid-18th century. It is known, therefore, that by the early 1600s (well before the arrival or Europeans), the Gikuyu were concentrated at Ithanga, 80 km (50 mi) southeast of the mountains that rise near the confluence of the Thika and Sagana rivers.

Oral traditions of all the tribes of Kenya agree that people began to migrate in different directions, eventually becoming the separate groups that exist today. The Gikuyu themselves moved west, from where the Gikuyu creation myth picks up the story.

The history of the Gikuyu becomes further complicated for historians and anthropologists with the inevitable intermarriage and interaction that occurred (and still occurs) between the various tribes and groups.

Having migrated to their current location about four centuries ago (in the 1600s), the Gikuyu make up Kenya's largest ethnic group. The Gikuyu attribute their origins to sacred intervention by their god Ngai who sometimes resides on Mt. Kenya, which, for the Gikuyu, is a sacred place.

The Gikuyu have featured very significantly in the development of contemporary Kenyan political, cultural, and social life. The Land and Freedom Movement (referred to pejoratively as the "Mau Mau" Movement) during the 1950s was primarily a Gikuyu guerrilla war in response to British imperialism, which had alienated Gikuyu from their farming lands in favor of white settlers. Many of these settlers owned farms bigger than the states of Rhode Island or Delaware. On these farms Gikuyu were required to do forced labor, especially providing labor for cash crops such as coffee and tea. A "hut tax" in 1901 was imposed on every Gikuyu household so that men were forced to migrate into the growing city of Nairobi or on to the white-owned farms to earn money so as to pay taxes. The Gikuyu nationalist Jomo Kenyatta became the first president of Kenya at its independence in 1963. He is revered amongst the Gikuyu for his leadership against colonialism and for his status as the father of his country.

Today, the Gikuyu, like other Kenyan ethnic groups, participate in a democratic political system. Political participation is primarily through election to a parliamentary seat (of which there are 210 in Kenya) or through direct election to the national presidency. Most of the Gikuyu belong to one major political party, the Party of National Unity (PNU), one of the major partners in Kenya's "Grand Coalition" government as of 2008. The other major partner in the coalition government is the Orange Democratic Movement (ODM).

The Grand Coalition government was the culmination of a peace deal brokered by former UN Secretary General Kofi Annan when violence broke out among Kenya's ethnic groups following the announcement of the disputed December 2007 presidential election results. Members of the Gikuyu community (from which the incumbent President Mwai Kibaki hailed) suffered most of the violence where over 1,000 people were killed and over 500,000 displaced from their own homes.

As of 2008 the Gikuyu were as much part of the ruling coalition government as other Kenyan citizens. Mwai Kibaki was the second Gikuyu to become the president of Kenya since 1964 when Kenya became a republic. He was elected for a renewable five-year term in 2002 after former African strongman Daniel Moi retired from office and active politics. Other outstanding Gikuyu personalities in history include Jomo Kenyatta, the first president of Kenya; Dedan Kimathi, the celebrated leader of the "Mau Mau" Movement; and Wangu wa Makeri, a legendary woman who ruled Gikuyuland.

² LOCATION AND HOMELAND

Official figures released in January 2007 estimated the population of Kenya at 36.1 million. The Gikuyu are the largest ethnic group in Kenya numbering about 6.8 million of this population. The overall population growth rate for Kenya, however, dropped from 2.82% in 2005 to 2.75% in 2006. This drop can be attributed to disease and to more effective methods of family planning.

Although the Gikuyu live throughout Kenya, they are primarily located in two of Kenya's eight provinces. These two provinces, Nairobi Province and the Central Province, are in the central area of the country. Due to their numerical superiority and early 20th century colonial association with British settlers in the highlands, the Gikuyu have been well positioned to occupy a central position in Kenyan social life.

The capital city of Nairobi lies just on the southern boundary of the area traditionally occupied by the Gikuyu people. Thus, many Gikuyu now are counted among this city's inhabitants of about 3 million people. Ancestral homes are to the north of Nairobi in the towns of Murang'a, Nyeri, and Kiambu. Gikuyuland is a dissected plateau of about 160 km (100 mi) from north to south and 48 km (30 mi) from east to west. Its elevation ranges from about 900 m (3,000 ft) to over 2,300 m (7500 ft) above sea level. The plateau features deep gorges and parallel ridges. Rainfall due to the high altitude is very plentiful. On the eastern side of the plateau, the ecology is comparatively arid dominated by a grassland zone. To the west of this area, the elevation increases giving rise to more rainfall and woodlands with good potential for agriculture. The largest ecological area is characterized by high altitude and rainfall where foliage is abundant and population is heaviest. Since the Gikuyu rely heavily on agriculture, this is the area of significant cash crops such as pyrethrum, coffee, and tea. Soils are deep and red here providing a fertile ecology for the growth of traditional crops such as sweet potatoes, bananas, millet, sorghum, arum lily, yams, cowpeas, and maize, which is the staple throughout Gikuyuland.

Gikuyu also raise cattle, sheep, and goats. They use the hides from the cattle to make bedding, sandals, and carrying straps and they raise the goats and sheep to use for religious sacrifices and purification.

³ LANGUAGE

"Kikuyu" is the Anglicized form of the proper name and pronunciation of Gikuyu. The Gikuyu refer to themselves as the Agikuyu people. The Gikuyu are generally fluent in three languages: Gikuyu, KiSwahili, and English. The official language and the medium of instruction at all education tiers in Kenya is English. All children receive instruction in this language in school beginning with primary school and continuing through university. KiSwahili is a national language that is widely used as a language of trade and commerce especially by those for whom formal education has not been possible. KiSwahili is also taught in the schools from primary through secondary school. When traveling outside the central highlands, the Gikuyu use either English or KiSwahili. Radio, television and mass media publications are richly available in these two languages throughout Kenya.

The Gikuyu language, however, can be thought of as the language of preference in home and community and is spoken by, and passed on to, children at home. Gikuyu is taught in primary schools throughout Gikuyuland. Gikuyu is classified as a member of the Benue-Congo family of languages. It is grouped among the Bantu languages within this system of classification. These languages are widespread throughout central and southern Africa, which indicates a common culture history stretching over and uniting ethnic groups over a vast geographical area. Bantu languages have a common grammatical structure and cognate words shared as a language heritage. For example, in Gikuyu, as in other Bantu languages, nouns are grouped into classes and are modified by variations in prefixes, infixes, and suffixes to signify attributes such as plurality, singularity, size, human versus non-human status, and tense to name but a few. For instance, the stem "ndo" has no meaning except when modified. For example, the word "mondo" means man and the word "ando" means men. In KiSwahili, also a Bantu language, the stem "tu" is modified in the word man as "mtu" and "watu" as men or people. The term Bantu, which is used for the language family of which Gikuyu is a member, therefore, means "the people" while "muntu" means "a person."

There are varieties within the Gikuyu language. There is the Southern Gikuyu (Kiambu, Southern Murang'a), Ndia (Southern Kirinyaga), Gichugu (Northern Kirinyaga), Mathira (Karatina), Northern Gikuyu (Northern Murang'a, Nyeri) dialects. Lexical similarity of Gikuyu is about 73% with Embu language, 70% with Chuka language, 67% with Kamba language and 63% with Meru.

If technological advancement is any guide, the Gikuyu language has a bright future. With the liberalization and growth of technology in Kenya, the Gikuyu language is claiming its place on the airwaves through such FM stations as Kameme FM, Inooro FM, and Coro FM. It is also establishing itself on the Internet where members interact in the Gikuyu language. Various writers, including Ngugi wa Thiong'o, the celebrat-

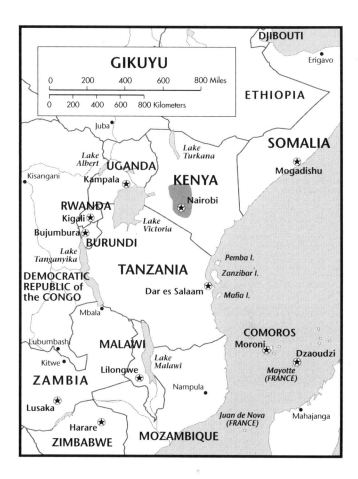

ed Kenyan novelist, have come out to promote the Gikuyu language.

⁴ FOLKLORE

The origin myth of the Gikuyu teaches that Ngai ("God") carried the first man, Gikuyu, atop Mt. Kenya, also known as *Kiri-nyaga*, which is translated as the "Shining Mountain" or "Mountain of the Light." Ngai showed him the bountiful land spread out below the mountain. He was told that his sons and daughters would inherit the land and multiply. They would enjoy all of the abundance provided by the land. Gikuyu was given a wife named Mumbi meaning "Creator" or "Molder," and together they had nine daughters. Ngai said that whenever problems arose, the people should make a sacrifice and gaze at Mt. Kenya so as to be assisted. One day, Gikuyu was unhappy at not having a male heir so he pleaded with Ngai to provide a son for him. After appropriate rituals, Gikuyu went to a sacred tree where he found nine men waiting to greet him. He arranged for these men to marry his daughters provided they agreed to live under his roof and abide by a matrilineal system of inheritance. In time, many grand and great-grandchildren were born. Still later, each daughter came to head her own clan, thus giving rise to the nine clans of the Gikuyu people. The legend continues that in time the kinship system changed from a matrilineal to a patrilineal one. It is believed this happened because the women became excessive in their domination over men. Polygyny (one man and several wives) from then on replaced polyandry (one woman and several husbands) as a marital practice. Nevertheless, the women were able to maintain their names for the main clans. There was actually a 10th daughter but the Gikuyu considered it to be bad luck to say the number 10. When counting they used to say "full nine" instead of 10. To this day, most women carry one of these names. The names are Wanjiru, Wambui, Wanjiku, Wangari, Waceera, Wairimu, Wangui, Wangechi, Wambura, and Wamuyu.

The Gikuyu origin myth validates their system of kinship and gender relations. Spiritual life centered around belief in a high god and sacred places such as Mt. Kenya. Solidarity for family and community in naming practices and family inheritance is made sacred. Above all, land which continues to be the primary value for Gikuyu and which was contested during the colonial era against the British settlers can be understood to have far more than economic utility. Land is indeed a gift from God.

There are a number of other important legends that provide "cultural heroes" who performed great feats in the past. Among these are Karuri who was a past ruler of legendary proportions. Another is Wamugumo who was a noted giant believed to have been able to eat an entire goat by himself. He could clear land that took many men a long time to accomplish, and he was able to kill lions, buffalo, and leopards with ease. A famous woman called Wangu wa Makeri ruled during the period of the matriarchy. During this time, it is believed that women were allowed to have many husbands, especially young men, and the old men did all of the work.

Folktales and riddles combined with myths to provide for young people a strong sense of values recognized by the community as making up Gikuyu culture. Grandmothers were excellent storytellers and devoted a great deal of time to the telling of stories. Some common riddles include "A man who never sleeps hungry?"=fire (which is lit throughout the night); "My son lives between spears"=the tongue; and "My child travels without rest"=the river (always flowing). Proverbs are numerous and constantly changing to reflect current times. For example, one proverb teaches that "A good mortar does not correspond to a good pestle," to show that successfully matching a husband and a wife may be difficult. Another proverb widely heard is "When the hyenas come, nobody will give shelter" which shows that in periods of panic, "it is every man for himself." Common sense is taught by most proverbs such as "When one goes on a journey, he does not leave his bananas cooking in the fire."

Children enjoy telling and listening to a wide assortment of folktales all of which serve to instill values in them. These tales involve stories about animals and people with such titles as "The Hyena at the Crossroads," "The Poor Woman and the Hog," "Two Girls and Their Gourds," and "The Woman and the Bird." Games are played involving speech acts such as competitive riddling and tongue twisters. One tongue twister refers to a child who saw a tadpole and ran away and when the tadpole saw the child, it also ran away. In Gikuyu, one says "Kaana ka Nikora kona kora kora, nako kora kona kaana ka Nikora kora."

⁵ RELIGION

The Gikuyu today are prominently represented in a variety of Christian churches which include Roman Catholicism, Anglicanism, fundamentalist groups, and African Separat-

ist Churches. The significance of belief in a high god, Ngai, is maintained or was transferred to the Christian-centered belief in monotheism. Ngai created everything. He lives in the sky and is invisible. Sometimes he lives on Mt. Kenya which in Gikuyu is called *Kiri-nyaga* meaning the "Mountain of the Light" or "Shining Mountain." He should only be approached when problems are serious such as involving life and death questions. During periods of famine or epidemic diseases, the elders on behalf of the entire community approached him.

Other spiritual realms in addition to monotheism have also persisted into contemporary life. Important among these are the ancestors. These departed relatives were concerned with all matters especially those considered to be not important enough to seek Ngai's attention. Matters of everyday health, for example, deeply involve the ancestors who intervened to cause sickness when their interests were not upheld. "Traditional doctors" were popular as resources for diagnosing which ancestor had been responsible for a particular disease and for information as to how the ancestor may be appeased.

Religious ceremonies were commonly included in public prayer. Invoking through prayer the blessings of Ngai or the ancestors generally started these ceremonies. One common prayer includes the following supplications: "Praise ye Ngai. Peace be with us. Say ye, that the elders may have wisdom and speak with one voice. Say ye, that the people may continue to increase. Say ye, that sheep and cattle may be free of illness. Say ye, peace be with us." Significantly, the elders led public prayers that served to validate their authority over affairs of the community by establishing a direct line to the high god that ran directly through them. Renowned elders stood out as prophets who were in a position to provide insights as to the wishes of Ngai. Some prophets are venerated in tribal history as most helpful during community crises concerning epidemics and drought. Currently, one can observe on occasion farmers thanking Ngai at harvest time for a plentiful bounty.

Prophets and seers cut a significant niche in Gikuyu religion. Examples included Mwathi wa Mugo and Mugo wa Kibiru. These prophets are believed to have predicted the coming of the White settlers, the struggle for freedom and the role of the Gikuyu in the political leadership of postcolonial Kenya. They gave religious and political guidance to the community.

In the past, religious values emphasized community solidarity and discouraged what may be referred to as "rugged individualism." Gikuyu learned that family and community welfare was paramount over their individual interests. Authority was vested in those individuals such as elders and prophets who were believed to know what was best for all people. Expressions of individuality and solitary life were not encouraged. Someone perceived to be outside the group might be accused of being a witch and could be killed by the elders. At the same time, considerable security and important meaning in life was provided in this Gikuyu system of social/spiritual culture. That was so because all human life was spiritual and communal. The landscape itself that made up the environment was composed of "sacred" places and objects. For example, the fig tree still has important symbolic significance harkening back to the period when Ngai sent Gikuyu forth to take up residence near Mt. Kenya. Many rituals were performed in the vicinity of a fig tree.

It is clear that the Gikuyu religious system provided a set of answers and solutions to problems of everyday life and misfortune. At the same time, successful experiences were also accounted for by emphasizing conformity to religious values. The ancestors as both kinsmen and spiritual entities are especially well positioned to give a strong sense of family values as reinforced by religious belief. They can be reincarnated in the form of names so that as long as there is a Gikuyu society, the ancestors will live on. The body itself was far less significant than the name or memory of a dead person. In fact, frequently bodies after death were simply discarded in the bush perhaps to be eaten by wild animals such as the hyena.

Today members of the outlawed, quasi-political/religious Mungiki sect are attempting to bring back traditional rituals. Their members claim they are a group of traditionalists interested in re-introducing and promoting traditional way of life among the Gikuyu ethnic group. They pray as they face Mount Kenya, which they believe to be the home of their god Ngai. The Mungiki have adopted the dreadlocks worn in the 1950s by members of the Mau Mau Movement.

⁷ RITES OF PASSAGE

The Gikuyu are well known for the emphasis that they placed on rituals, which occurred at the time of adolescence. Prior to the arrival of the Europeans, there was a custom known as Ngweko. Periodically, elders supervised, in a special location, occasions where young people would gather together and spend private time with each other for the purpose of getting to know members of the opposite sex. At this time, young people paired off according to mutual attraction and, for most couples, experimental lovemaking was practiced. Such lovemaking did not always result in sexual intercourse. Should a young girl become pregnant however, the boy responsible was held accountable and was expected, in time, to marry the girl that he had impregnated. The Gikuyu considered Ngweko to be a form of indigenous education in sexual knowledge. It is said that Ngweko (fondling), since it was associated with sexual reproduction, was considered by the society to be a sacred act of carrying out the orders of their God to reproduce. Many elder Gikuyu believe that the missionaries made a mistake when they labeled Ngweko as sinful. The schools that were established to educate the people in modern culture did not include anything about sexual education. Perhaps for this reason, since the co-educational boarding school became a common place where young people often experimented with their sexuality without any education, teenage pregnancies have become a major social problem in Kenya including the Gikuyu. It is important to note that in the Ngweko system, supervised sex was permitted but self-control for both boys and girls was emphasized.

Both boys and girls, prior to participating in Ngweko, undergo numerous rituals including operations on their genital organs. The purpose of these rituals is to enable young people to bond into groups and to develop a sense of peer group solidarity with those people with whom they have undergone painful experiences together. Clitoridectomy was, and to some extent still is, practiced by the Gikuyu and is the topic of much debate by Africans and others. A middle ground position appears to be emerging that grants the social significance of adolescent ritual while wanting to eliminate clitoridectomy even under hospital conditions where it still occurs. The boys continue to be circumcised, a practice widespread in Africa (unlike clitoridectomy) and commonly found in many other parts of the world as well. Supporters of initiation note that the Gikuyu recognize the equal significance of boys and girls by subjecting each to initiation ceremonies together.

The Gikuyu word for circumcision of either sex is *irua*. There are many dances and songs which take place during initiation ceremonies and these are called *mambura* (rituals or divine services). During initiation ceremonies, the Gikuyu history is publicly rehearsed so as to impart a sense of community solidarity. Each irua group is given its own special name according to events of the day, such as war or famine. Initiation ceremonies involve special foods, and the selection of a sponsor to impart knowledge and to supervise the young person. After several days of instruction, boys and girls are taken together to a compound for their circumcision. Numerous friends and relatives gather for singing and dancing throughout the night. A special feast is made for the parents of the children. The day before the operation, there is a ceremonial dance known as *matuuro*. The girl has her head shaved, but does not participate in a race undertaken by boys. The winner is thought to have been favored by Ngai (God). In another ceremony, boys and girls are organized into lines according to seniority. They take an oath never to reveal Gikuyu secrets to outsiders. Senior warriors then take boys and girls to a special place where they participate in more ceremonies involving being sprayed with medicines that are thought to enhance bravery and endurance. Songs sung on these occasions emphasize community solidarity and bravery.

The next day the physical operations occur. The girls are operated on by a woman considered to be an expert and the boys by a man also considered to be experienced in these matters. In the operation, the girls sit together on a cowhide rug. Female friends and relatives cluster around in a circle. Males are not permitted anywhere near this event. The girls are held by their sponsors and are doused with cold water to reduce pain. While the *moruitha* performs the clitoridectomy, each girl is expected to remain stoic so as not to be seen a coward by the onlookers. After the girl is covered with a new dress, applause and cheering burst forth from the onlookers. The girls retire to a special place for several days where their wounds heal. During this time, close relatives and friends bring special foods and treats for the girls. For several months, the girls do not do any work. Their parents now may wear brass earrings as a sign of their seniority. This symbolizes that their child has now been reborn, not as their child, but as a child of the whole community. Boys' circumcisions mirror that of girls' clitoridectomy ceremonies in most details.

The Gikuyu organized their experience of adolescence very differently from modern life in Kenya. While many elder Gikuyu people still maintain strong relationships with others with whom they were initiated, younger teens are not receiving community socialization comparable to their parental and grandparental generations. While mandatory painful initiation ceremonies may well be best thought of as a vestige of the past, many Kenyans lament what they perceive to be a rising tide of individualism and lack of peer group solidarity among the young. One of the most interesting challenges for young people in Kenya is to work out for themselves what is most appropriate for them to emphasize in choosing to combine old customs with modern ones. This issue is a prominent theme among Kenyan intellectuals and the mass media and is the subject of stories, plays, and other programs on Kenyan radio and television.

8 INTERPERSONAL RELATIONS

Social relations in contemporary Gikuyu society are played out primarily in the context of the local community, school, and church. Dating, courtship, friendship, and family life are significant concerns around which people construct their social lives. There is more evidence today for individual choice in these matters than in the past where very strong principles of age stratification and gender distinction dominated social life.

In the past, boys were organized into sets consisting of groupings of local boys initiating at one time. These sets were grouped into larger groupings, called regiments, made up of boys from elsewhere and from one's local area that had been initiated at the same time. Boys in a common set or regiment proceeded through life together and exercised authority over sets and regiments coming after them. Tribal political authority was vested in one of two older generations that were responsible for governmental decisions involving war and peace and daily conflict resolution. Every generation inherits the name of that generation to which the grandfather belongs. Thus, there is a constant alternating of two generational names, an older and younger. The principle of age determined whom a man or a woman might marry or have sexual relationships with. For instance, a man could have no sexual relations with a girl who was a member of his own set generation. They were considered to be initiation "brothers" and "sisters." The men's regimental organization served as a police force. The older regiments basically interpreted tribal law and made significant decisions while the younger regiments enforced their decisions. Warrior regiments were active in defending communities from raids from neighboring societies or for carrying out raids elsewhere. Thus, the structure of Gikuyu age stratification provided a workable framework for the functioning of society around social needs for procreation, defense, and social regulation.

Within this framework, every Gikuyu knew precisely how best to relate to other people. Social relations such as dating, visiting, and greeting others properly were all prescribed by age (and gender) according to an ubiquitous principle of stratification.

9 LIVING CONDITIONS

The Gikuyu enjoy an abundant resource base arising from their vantage position in the central highlands of Kenya. Much of the region was, therefore, free of malarial mosquitoes and the tse tse and other flies as sources for human and animal disease. Gikuyuland was in the past, and many ways still is, a granary for the Gikuyu and their neighbors. The Gikuyu have experienced success in commercial farming and many other businesses that have been a significant source of revenue for those Gikuyu now in a position to own and maintain large estates and an affluent life-style. Still, many other Gikuyu reside in slums that have grown rapidly in urban areas, especially Nairobi. In this city, many of the thousands of street children, now homeless, come from Gikuyu towns where they have suffered from family dislocation and poverty due, in part, to the uneven income distribution in Kenya. The globalization of the world's economy has been particularly hard on poorer nations such as Kenya. Additionally, many Gikuyu, like some other Kenyans, have lost their sense of community responsibility so

cherished in the past. This is a constant theme in the writing of Ngugi wa Thiong'o as well as other Kenyan writers.

In the past, all Gikuyu had sufficient access to food, housing, and other materials even though successful people had more than others. Gikuyu houses were round with wooden walls and grass thatched roofs. Neighbors generally helped in the construction of a home in exchange for beer and meat. Building materials were collected from local materials. Women were considered responsible for thatching, and a carefully thatched house was highly valued. Good thatching provided protection from the rains and the sun during the dry season. Homes were made according to plan with the man's home being much simpler than the woman's. A husband and wife typically lived in separate houses although the woman's house had spaces for her children and her sheep and goats. The better-built homes sometimes lasted for more than 10 years, but re-thatching was an annual event.

10 FAMILY LIFE

Marriage and family life revealed the Gikuyu preference for large families and big compounds. It was considered a religious obligation to have children in response to the command of God to multiply. Four children, two boys and two girls, was the ideal. Boys were desirable because they carried on the family name, which was passed on through the male line. Girls were desired to attract bride wealth in cows and goats which could be, in turn, used to obtain wives for their brothers, and later to have children for those families in which they married. When a girl married and bore children for her new family, she began a family journey that saw her become more powerful as she bore children affiliated to her husband's family. Her children stayed with her in her home separate from their father. Polygyny (one man and more than one wife at a time) was valued as a means to provide large families. Women, too, often preferred polygyny to monogamy (one man and one woman) and, not infrequently, assisted their husbands in finding younger wives. Elder wives had clear lines of authority over younger wives and supervised them in affairs of the compound. Given the importance of age stratification in Gikuyu social organization, it may be said, too, that a woman actually married into an age set as well as the extended family of her husband. When her husband entertained his age set friends, it was considered appropriate for them to sleep with his own wife. This was not considered adultery unlike clandestine affairs held in secrecy, a practice that was severely punished. Thus, in married life, one also sees the basic value of sharing and communalism so significant in all areas of Gikuyu life.

The marriage ceremonies were lengthy and involved stages of progression which first included the initial meeting of the aspiring son-in-law with his prospective parents-in-law. The girl's assent was needed at this meeting before events could proceed to later stages. These events included parental visits, exchanges of goods as bride price spread out over time, and eventual movement of the girl herself into the home of her husband. The marriage itself is finalized when, prior to her movement to her new family, the boy and his relatives come to the girl's house bearing numerous gifts all specifically earmarked for her relatives who were most responsible for her upbringing. The actual movement, not infrequently, took on a rather dramatic public capturing of the girl at some point when she was unaware. Girls arrived in their new homes quite willingly on the whole even though they might have been "captured" to get there. For a period of many weeks after establishing residence in her new compound, rituals and exchanges continued to occur to symbolize the girl's transitional stage between her old and new families. She was frequently visited by her girlfriends, and had her own special places in the compound where she could retire alone for private reflection.

Nowadays, marriage no longer involves all of the rituals and exchanges previously emphasized. Nevertheless, there is still bride wealth, significant involvement of parents in the choice of their children's spouses, and the very high value attached to having children. Marital ceremonies no longer involve Gikuyu religious beliefs which have given way to Christianity, both mainstream and independent churches, and Islam.

Gikuyu family identity is carried on through nomenclature. This is executed by naming the first boy after the father's father and the second after the mother's father. The same goes for the girls; the first is named after the father's mother and the second after the mother's mother. Following children are named after the brothers and sisters of the grandparents, starting with the oldest and working to the youngest. Along with the naming of the children was the belief that the deceased grandparent's spirit that the child was named after, would come in to the new child. This belief was lost with the increase in life-span because generally the grandparents are now still alive when the children are born.

11 CLOTHING

In the past, Gikuyu adults dressed in animal skins, especially sheep and goatskins. Skin tanning was a vital industry for which many men were renowned as specialists. Women's attire includes three pieces, an upper garment, a skirt, and an apron. Men wore a single garment covering the entire body. Young men preferred bare legs made possible by wearing short skirts, especially those made from a kid because of its smooth hairs. Elders wore more elaborate skins often made of fur and, sometimes, aprons worn in ceremonial dances. European clothing is now commonplace throughout Gikuyuland.

Although in rural areas women nowadays wear multi-colored cotton dresses and skirts and blouses, it is common to find girls wearing Western style trousers and even miniskirts. Men generally wear Western style trousers and shirts with jackets and ties for formal occasions. Casual and trendy clothes like jeans and T-shirts are common on weekends and holidays across the gender divide. Women who wish to emphasize an African look can be seen wearing long pieces of colorful cloth worn in skirt-like fashion wrapped around a shorter dress.

12 FOOD

Farm produce and meat were abundant in the past and presently provide Gikuyu with an excellent nutritional resource. Maize, made into a thick porridge called *ugali*, is the national dish of Kenya. Ugali is eaten with meat, stews, *mandondo*, *njahe* or traditional greens known as *sukuma wiki*. Ugali and *irio* are popular on a daily basis in Gikuyuland. Irio, a specifically Gikuyu dish, is a mixture of the kernels from cooked green corn boiled with beans, potatoes, and chopped greens. In the past, the Gikuyu had a regular and intense ceremonial calendar involving considerable feasting. Boiled and roasted meat were constantly being consumed along with beer on these occasions. In the past, the brewing of beer was a cooperative

activity between men and women. Beer was made from sugar cane, maize, and millet. Gourds were used to contain the strained juices for fermenting.

Today, bottled beverages have generally replaced traditional beer on daily and social occasions. Distilleries in Kenya provide an assortment of beer and soft drinks. Eating meat is a mainstay today on all ceremonial occasions. A major form of recreation, especially on Sundays, is visiting special places for *nyama choma* (roast meat). Goat meat is the most popular choice although it is more expensive than beef. Chicken, as in the past, is also a regular treat. Bottled beverages and meat are integral parts of the nyama choma recreational event. Although the traditional ceremonial calendar is largely a thing of the past, Gikuyu maintain an intensely social existence involving regular attendance at funerals and weddings. These events would be unthinkable without an abundant supply of meat and bottled beverages.

13 EDUCATION

Traditionally, Children were imparted knowledge through a socialization process that began very early in the life cycle. Infants were sung lullabies emphasizing tribal values and, as the child grew, he listened intensely to tales, riddles, and proverbs, which had moral messages. Even after the coming of formal schools in the colonial era, a special time was set aside for the telling of folktales to test students' memories and knowledge. In the past, boys, prior to initiation, played games that emphasized leadership roles and involved bows and arrows, spears, and slings to instill skills in marksmanship. Little girls cooked imaginary dishes and played at making pots and grinding grains. Dolls were also made with local clay and grass. As children matured, boys were trained by their adult male relatives, and girls by their mothers, grandmothers, and older sisters. For example, boys were taught how to differentiate large herds of cattle or goats by their color, size, and horn texture. Fathers and grandfathers also taught youngsters boundaries of their land, clearing techniques for land prior to farming, and extensive information about the family genealogy. In a society where kinship operated as a principle for the exchange of food and labor, family genealogy was as crucial to know as knowledge about plants and animals. Mothers taught girls knowledge of crops, soils, weather and other significant details of food production.

Today, the traditional informal educational system has been, by and large, replaced by formal education. In Kenya, including Gikuyuland, there has been an attempt to make formal education more sensitive to traditional values and knowledge than was the case during the pre-independence colonial era. One of the disadvantages of emphasizing only knowledge relevant for life in the modern world, such as literacy and world geography, is that, for example, elder women who were the "teachers" no longer teach knowledge about wild plants potentially edible during famine as it was in the past. Sex education is no longer taught as in the past. Reaching a reasonable balance between the old and the new in the current school curriculum is a constant challenge faced by Gikuyu educators. The idea that education is closely linked to the community still persists. Harambee ("let's pull together") primary and secondary schools are constantly being built throughout Gikuyuland and elsewhere in Kenya. Nevertheless, young people now have excellent opportunities for schooling even though it is too costly for many families. Money is raised for these schools by individual donations, but those wishing to show solidarity with the community often give it publicly at feasts. The illiteracy rate in Kenya is approaching 50%, but it is lower in Gikuyuland.

¹⁴ CULTURAL HERITAGE

Music and dance, along with storytelling, were all emphasized in the past. Dancing by men and women was mandatory at initiation ceremonies, weddings, and other public events. People of all ages enjoyed dancing. There were three basic kinds of musical instruments in the past: drums, flutes, and rattles. The last were used for private pleasure while drums and flutes were significant at dances. Song was woven into the fabric of everyday life. There were songs for babies; songs sung by girls while threshing millet and by boys while practicing archery; songs sung by families and community members during weddings and funerals; songs sung by community members and initiates during initiation ceremonies; songs concerning everyday problems of life and love that were sung around the campfire; songs for drinking; songs that concerned cultural heroes both past and present; and songs sung in praise of ancestors and the high god, Ngai. In brief, Gikuyu life was unthinkable without the joy of singing, dancing, and musical expression, participated in by all members of the community.

Much remains of the older patterns of musical and dance appreciation. Although the traditional instruments and dance steps are now rarely seen, attendance at school dances and nightclubs is a major form of recreation by old and young alike. Gikuyu songs composed to meet everyday challenges can still be heard on the radio. Storytelling is now supplemented by a very impressive written literature. This printed material includes children's literature where tribal stories and tales are made available to youngsters. One such book entitled *Nyumba ya Mumbi* graphically illustrates the Gikuyu creation myth. Novelists, journalists, poets, and other writers are numerous in Kenya including many from Gikuyuland. Perhaps the most famous of these writers is Ngugi wa Thiong'o, whose many stories, plays, and novels have catalogued the Gikuyu struggle for national identity throughout the 20th century. His work includes material about the land and freedom movement, the impact of Europeanization on traditional Kenya society, and increasingly the alienation experienced by many Kenyans as the traditional ethic of communalism gives way to modern forms of excessive capitalism and greed. Ngugi wa Thiong'o has written world famous literature in both English and Gikuyu. Some of his work is performed in theater in rural areas in Gikuyuland.

¹⁵ WORK

There was, in the past, a very strong division of labor by gender. Nevertheless, men and women worked together as well as separately in tasks that complemented each other. Gikuyu parents raise boys and girls very differently. The girls are raised to work in farming and the boys usually work with the animals. The girls also have the responsibility of taking care of a baby brother or sister and also helping the mother out with household chores.

Each woman had her own plots of land where she cultivated the crops such as sweet potatoes, millet, maize, and beans. A woman cultivated her land and had the freedom to do as she pleased with its produce beyond providing food for her chil-

dren and husband. Men were responsible for heavy labor such as clearing the land and cutting down trees. Household tasks for women involved maintaining her own granary and supervising the feeding of sheep, goats, and cows that were kept at the homestead. A polygamous husband had his own hut apart from his wives where he ate with friends or his children and was served food by his wives. On a daily basis, women, together with their children, collected firewood, water, and produce from the garden. There was also a division of labor by gender concerning industries. Some men were ironsmiths, manufacturing for the community such things as knives, arrowheads, bracelets, axes, hammers, spears, and other utilitarian tools. Only women were potters. Pottery provided for household needs and, for the better potters, was the source of marketing exchanges to obtain foods and material objects. There is a well-known proverb that characterizes the best potters who may be in a good position for valued exchanges as "the good potter cooks with broken pots." Women also excelled in making baskets, and men tended to specialize in skin tanning.

The informal educational system of the Gikuyu involved children and young people learning economic tasks from adults and specialists through direct observation and often apprenticeship. Work-related education frequently involved storytelling that highlighted environmental factors such as crops, weather, and ecology. Elder women sometimes told these stories as a form of entertainment. In one story entitled "Ngiciri and Madam," a man wants to get married to a girl who is being pursued by many other men. To help him, he enlists the assistance of birds to which he gives millet. Doves are given sorghum so as to enlist their aid in his competitive strategies to get the girl. They help him pass a test given to him by the girl's family. In this test, he must demonstrate his knowledge by separating into piles millet, sorghum, maize, and castor oil seeds that have been mixed together. His other test requires that he eat an entire bull in one night to show his power. Because he knows not only what seeds birds enjoy, but that hyenas like cattle bones, his friend, the hyena, helps him secretly to consume the bull just as the birds had helped him separate the seeds into separate piles. The hero of this story wins because he knows his environment and understands that animals and humankind have fates that are intertwined.

The Gikuyu remain intensely agricultural and devoted to their land. Cash crops are now significant, but still the traditional division of agricultural labor is very much in place. Modernization of the economy has made social and class differences more evident than in the past. Though they are traditionally agricultural people and have a reputation as industrious people, many Gikuyus are now involved in business. Most Gikuyu still live on small family plots but many of them have also seen the opportunities in business and have moved to cities and different areas to work. They have a desire for knowledge and they believe that all children should receive a full education. Gikuyu have a strong reputation for money management and it is common for them to have many enterprises at one time. The majority of those in hawking businesses in urban centers in Kenya are the Gikuyu.

Since they also practice animal husbandry, the Gikuyu use the hides from the cattle to make bedding, sandals, and carrying straps and they raise the goats and sheep to use for religious sacrifices and purification

Through formal education and accumulation of private capital, many Gikuyu are now very wealthy and enjoy affluent lifestyles. Professional occupations, as well as employment in factories and other working class jobs, now differentiate the Gikuyu into social categories based upon income. Nevertheless, among most Gikuyu, there is still a strong sense of ethnic solidarity and heritage in cultural values. In Kenya's multiparty democratic system, for example, Gikuyu of various economic classes primarily belong to one of two political parties, both of which are overwhelmingly Gikuyu in membership.

16 SPORTS

Sports are popular throughout Gikuyuland where schools sponsor competitive games for boys and girls. Spectators enjoy soccer (football) and track and field events. One can see people of all ages playing a board game known as *bao* in which players attempt to capture the seeds of their opponents. The game involves a wooden board containing holes in which seeds are placed. A player seeks to capture his opponent's seeds using a complex strategy whereby his opponent's seeds end up on his side of the board. This indigenous African game of strategy known as *bao* in KiSwahili is widespread in Africa and is now played elsewhere in the world. In the past, the Gikuyu boys enjoyed games such as wrestling, weightlifting, and club throwing. There were district mock fights pitting young boys from each area against their counterparts from elsewhere. Wrestling produced stars who were widely praised throughout the country. Girls played hide and seek and jumping games while still young, but became increasingly more involved with household responsibilities and marriage as they approached mid-teen age.

17 ENTERTAINMENT AND RECREATION

The Bomas of Kenya is a prominent, national dance troupe in which Gikuyu dances are prominently featured. Schools have regular dance and singing competitions where traditional art forms are preserved.

Gikuyu, like other Kenyans, enjoy watching television, listening to the radio, and going to movie theatres. Radio and television regularly feature content derived from Gikuyu tradition. As mentioned above, there are radio stations and internet communication that offer a wide range of entertainment in Gikuyu genre. Such entertainment includes comedies, folk music and oral narratives to name a few. The radio stations that broadcast their entertainment content exclusively in Gikuyu language include: Inooro FM, Kameme FM, and Coro FM among others. There are books and magazines published in Gikuyu language e.g *Matigari,* by Wa Thion'go. There are also comedies, music, and movies produced in Gikuyu and available in tape, video, and Internet formats.

Traditionally, Gikuyu would also attend dances as a form of entertainment. There were dances for men alone, women alone, and men and women together.

18 FOLK ARTS, CRAFTS, AND HOBBIES

Traditional industries and crafts have been largely replaced by tourist and commercial markets. The most notable persistence is in basket making, which is in the hands of women. The Gikuyu *keondo* (basket) is now popular in Europe and America where it is a widely used handbag or bookbag used by students. The keondo is a knitted basket made in various shapes, colors and sizes. These baskets are knitted from strings gathered from shrubs and sometimes have Gikuyu geometric designs. The folk arts promoted basketry and the manufacture of clay figurines. The figurines are made from local materials such as clay, discarded wire, and grass. Manufactured objects depict solitary or communal daily life such as children playing, elders in various kinds of clothing, people dancing, bicycling, singing, and so on. Adornment, hairstyles, and clothing are featured on figurines to describe various mixtures of the old and new stylistic preferences.

19 SOCIAL PROBLEMS

Perhaps the primary social problem of the Gikuyu is how best to manage their comparative success in the context of Kenyan commerce and politics. The political opposition sometimes focuses on the Gikuyu, aiming at offsetting their numerical and commercial power. The Gikuyu have expanded into regions outside of their central highlands homeland. Many Gikuyu, therefore, are now wealthy immigrants, as it were, who are often seen by local groups elsewhere in Kenya as interlopers and landgrabbers. Hence, the Gikuyu have Gikuyuphobia as a major challenge to contend within the modern Kenya. As mentioned previously, members of the Gikuyu in the diaspora bore most of the brunt of post-election violence in 2007–2008, and in politically-instigated clashes in 2002, 1997, and 1992.

Management of current social problems in Kenya, such as alcoholism and HIV, sometimes poses difficult challenges for Gikuyu families. On alcoholism, it is noteworthy that prior to the arrival of the Europeans, distilling was unknown. In the past, traditional beers and wines were made by fermentation only. Such drinks were not likely to produce alcoholism and often had nutritional value. Today, consumption of distilled beverages is common, and driving of automobiles on poorly maintained roads has contributed to what is among the highest rate of accidental death due to driving anywhere in the world.

The issue of land ownership is still a thorn in the flesh for most members of the Gikuyu. They have to reckon with displacement in the diaspora due to political violence and tribal hatred. Most of the land in the Gikuyu ancestral area is in the hands of the few, leaving many others to live as squatters.

There is also the security issue posed by the Mungiki sect (see section one, *Introduction*). The activities of the sect involving groups of suspicious looking youths, many donning dreadlocks, assaulting women, taking unusual oaths, and engaging in strange prayers and ritual beheadings among other practices have led to violent confrontations with authorities. In the wake of such a confrontation, many youth have been killed, arrested, or have been forced to flee their homes and villages.

20 GENDER ISSUES

Through the process of socialization within the family, in educational institutions and other social spheres, boys and girls are conditioned to behave in certain ways and to play different roles in society. They are encouraged to conform to established cultural norms through a reward-punishment system.

The role and status of women in Gikuyu society is changing for the better compared to many other Kenyan or African societies. There is a tendency towards a matrilineal system of family among the Gikuyu. Clearly, the Gikuyu were originally a matriarchal society. This could be traced back to the Gikuyu leadership, folk literature, and the Gikuyu nomenclature systems among others. It was rare in traditional Africa to have women as rulers in society.

Gikuyu folklore acknowledges women's leadership in their history. A notable legendary figure is Wangu wa Makeri, a woman famous for her cruelty. She would literally sit on men at public functions, which caused Gikuyu men to plot her overthrow. According to folklore, the men conspired to impregnate all Gikuyu women on one night. The resulting pregnancies would incapacitate the women, allowing the men to assume power easily.

Gikuyu clans are named to honor the legendary nine daughters of Mumbi, reflecting the importance of women's influence in Gikuyu history.

Indeed, in Gikuyu nomenclature, it is possible to find a son of a single mother bearing the maiden name of his mother as his surname. This underlines the significance that the Gikuyu society attaches to the mother.

Among the Gikuyu, in the case of divorce or separation, children typically stay with their mother, and not their father, as would be expected in most patriarchal societies.

Modern Gikuyu women in the 21st century are not restricted to the functions of wife, mother, and farm worker. Many Gikuyu families secure formal education for their girls starting from the kindergarten through post-high school. Thus, women in Gikuyuland have been able to compete successfully with men in the workforce. Modren Gikuyu women have found careers in politics, law, religion, and healthcare, spheres traditionally dominated by men.

Although in many subsistence economies women work on the farm and are intricately connected with their land, they do not have ownership over the land they work. Traditionally among the Gikuyu, if a man had more than one wife, he was responsible for clearing bushes to create a farm plot for each wife. Each wife's plot was close to her own hut, away from the other co-wives. The woman's younger son would inherit this plot after his mother's death. They usually allowed an unmarried daughter to have a plot of her own on which she could build a house. It is significant that daughters could hope to have the right to land ownership.

21 BIBLIOGRAPHY

Arnold, Gay. *Modern Kenya*. New York: Longman, 1981.

Bottignole, Silvana. *Kikuyu Traditional Culture and Christianity*. Nairobi: Heinemann Educational Books (E.A.) Ltd., 1984.

Davison, Jean. *Voices from Mutira: Lives of Rural Gikuyu Women*. Boulder, CO: Lynne Rienner Publishers, 1996.

Dinesen, Isak. *Out of Africa*. New York: Random House, 1972.

Gakuo, Kariuki. *Nyumba Ya Mumbi: The Gikuyu Creation Myth*. Nairobi: Jacaranda Designs, Ltd., 1992.

Johnston, Toni, et al. *Kenya: Gender, Facts and Figures*. New York: Alfred A. Knopf, 2003.

Kenya in Pictures. Minneapolis, Minn.: Lerner Publications Co., 1988.

Kenyatta, Jomo. *Facing Mount Kenya: The Tribal Life of the Gikuyu*. New York: Random House, 1965.

Kimani Njogu. *Culture, Entertainment and Health Promotion in Africa*. Nairobi: Twaweza Communications, 2005.

Lambert, H. E. *Kikuyu Social and Political Institutions*. London: Oxford University Press, 1956.

Leakey, Louis. *Mau Mau and the Kikuyu. London: Methuen, 1952.*

Liyong, Taban lo. *Popular Culture of East Africa: Oral Literature*. Nairobi: Longman Kenya Ltd., 1972.

Mukabi-Kabira, Wanjiku. "Storytellers and the Environment." In *Groundwork: African Women as Environmental Managers*. Nairobi: English Press Limited, 1992.

Muriuki, Godfrey. *The History of the Kikuyu 1500-1900*. Nairobi: Oxford University Press, 1974.

Presley, Cora Ann. *Kikuyu Women, the Mau Mau Rebellion, and Social Change in Kenya*. Boulder, CO: Westview Press, 1992.

Stein, R. *Kenya*. Chicago: Children's Press, 1985.

Themes in Kenyan History. Athens: Ohio University Press, 1990.

Thiong'o, Ngugi wa. *Decolonizing the Mind: The Politics of Language in African Literature*. London: Heinemann, 1986.

Webb, Lois Sinaiko. *Holidays of the World Cookbook for Students*. Phoenix, AZ: Oryx, 1995.

—revised by M. Njoroge

GUINEANS

PRONUNCIATION: GHIN-ee-uhns
LOCATION: Guinea
POPULATION: 10.2 million
LANGUAGE: French, Pulaar (Fulfulde), Susu, 30 African
    languages
RELIGION: Islam, Christianity, traditional religions
RELATED ARTICLES: Vol. 1: Fulani; Malinke

¹ INTRODUCTION

People have inhabited the territory now known as Guinea since the stone age. Ancestors of the coastal and forest peoples lived in Guinea before the birth of Christ. They hunted and gathered or grew rice in small communities. Early peoples of the savannah and central plateau were part of larger empires and kingdoms. The Malinkes of Upper Guinea trace their ancestry to the founders of the great Mali Empire (AD 1200–1350). Songhay rulers transformed Mali into a still greater empire which flourished into the 16th century. Ancestors of the Peuhl group began migrating to the central plateau in AD 600.

Portuguese explorers first visited the Guinean coast in the 15th century, but sustained European contact came from slave traders. In the early 1800s the French moved south from Senegal to establish trading posts along the coastal estuaries. These inlets and estuaries offered hiding places for slavers, allowing trade to continue until the end of the American civil war. European powers fixed Guinea's modern political boundaries during the scramble for Africa in the 1880s. From 1850–1900, the Peul and the Malinke fought a series of battles with the French. Eventually, Samory Touré, now a national hero, surrendered to the French in 1898. For the next 60 years, the French ruled Guinea through canton chiefs who collected taxes, maintained order, and raised armies for the colonizer.

Guinea set a precedent for many African countries when it rejected President DeGaulle's offer in 1958 to become part of a greater French world community. Led by Sékou Touré, the Guinean "revolution" deteriorated into totalitarian rule and dictatorship. A period of isolation and persecution reigned during which two million Guineans fled their country for personal safety and economic survival. In 1984, Sékou Touré died during heart surgery in Cleveland. A 10-year period of free market liberalization and democratic change led by General Lansana Conté followed.

In 1993 General Conté entered civilian life and won Guinea's first multi-party presidential elections. However, widespread manipulation and vote-rigging occurred, raising questions of Conté's legitimacy. Flawed presidential elections in 1998 and again in 2003 (which were boycotted) consolidated his power even if they did not legitimate it in the eyes of his opposition. A contentious national referendum in 2003 cleared the way for Conté to run for a third consecutive term, removing age restraints on the presidency, and essentially making him "president for life." But an attempt on his life in 2005 signaled his widespread unpopularity.

In 2006–7, national strikes led by trade union and civil society activists turned violent, resulting in the deaths of hundreds of civilians. However, the protests forced major political concessions, including one that reestablished the post of prime minister with extensive powers, and the right of civil society to approve the designee to that position.

² LOCATION AND HOMELAND

Guinea is somewhat smaller than the state of Oregon. It shares borders with Guinea-Bissau and Senegal to the north; with Mali and Cote d'Ivoire to the east; and with Liberia and Sierra Leone to the south. In all, Guinea spans 450 miles from east to west, and about 350 miles from north to south, curving southeast from the Atlantic. Guinea's population is young—44% is 14 years old or younger—but it is growing slower than most African countries at just under 2%. Estimates place the total population over 10 million. Another 2 million Guineans live abroad having fled persecution under Sékou Touré. Density is highest in the capital of Conakry, in parts of the Fouta Djallon plateau, and in areas of the Forest Region.

Guinea has four distinct geographical regions: Maritime Guinea, Middle Guinea, Upper Guinea, and the Forest Region. Each of these regions is home to one of four major ethnic groups. On the monsoonal coastal plain live the Susu (15%). This region receives up to 4 meters of rain yearly, two-thirds of it in July and August. During those months it rains hard nearly every night and sometimes for days on end. Brackish estuaries reaching many miles inland make rich fishing grounds. The region produces rice and many fruits, including pineapples.

To the east on the Fouta Djallon plateau live the Peul (36%). Also called Fulani, these people make their livelihoods herding cattle on the sandy highlands and farming in the fertile valleys that wind far below. This picturesque region includes buttes, escarpments, waterfalls, and rock faces 2,000–5,000 feet in elevation. Some forested portions are home to antelopes and monkeys. Further east and southeast lies the western frontier of a great savannah, which spreads eastward at 1,000 feet in elevation into the Ivory Coast and Mali. This is the home of the Malinke (23%) and the headwaters of the Niger River. The region is sparsely wooded and interrupted by rocky spurs. Farmers grow wet rice, *fonio*, peanuts, and sweet potatoes in the river valleys, and herders raise cattle on the high plains.

To the south is the humid Forest Region, which ranges from 1,500 to over 4,000 feet. Mt. Nimba, Guinea's tallest point (5,748 feet) lies in the extreme southeast. The rainfall is more balanced, and the highlands produce rice, maize, cassava, kola, oil palms, bananas, and coffee. The major ethnic groups are the Guérzé, Kissi, Toma, and Mano. They also have members living in Sierra Leone, Liberia, and Cote d'Ivoire (Ivory Coast). These groups share some cultural characteristics and together make up 15% of the national population.

³ LANGUAGE

The peoples of Guinea speak 30 languages, including the colonial language, French. French is used widely in government and is the language of instruction in high schools and universities. Aside from French, the languages in widest use are Pulaar (Fulfulde), which is spoken by the largest ethnic group, the Peul. Susu is gaining converts because it is the lingua franca (common language) of the capital.

⁴ FOLKLORE

Each ethnic group has its own myths, legends, and folktales. Of these, the Sundiata epic of the Malinke group has had a great impact on Malinke cultural, social, and political iden-

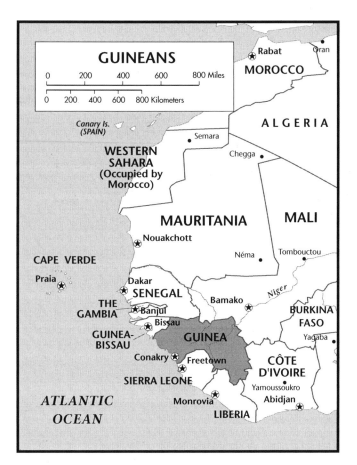

tity. It also has gained international literary fame as an epic poem. In 1960, a history professor published the poem in written form for the first time. The epic tells the story of a crippled boy, Sundiata, who rises to lead armies and saves his people from an evil warrior-king, Soumaro Kanté. Sundiata wins the Battle of Karina in AD 1206 and establishes the Mali Empire. Historically, we know that the battle occurred and that the victors drew up a charter to govern the kingdoms of the new empire. The charter has codified behavior and social relations for 800 years.

⁵ RELIGION

The vast majority of Guineans (80%) profess Islam. Christians, mainly Catholic, make up 10% of the population. Traditional indigenous African religion overlays these outside faiths and accounts for the rest. Islam came into West Africa via North African Muslim traders beginning in the 8th century AD. By AD 1000 ruling groups had adopted it as their faith too. The Peul established Islam in Guinea through a series of jihads (holy wars), notably that of El Hadj Oumar around 1850. Samory Touré, an anticolonial warrior and empire ruler, also imposed Islam by jihad around 1880 in Upper Guinea. Islam sustained itself because of its compatibility with traditional customs and family structure. It also allowed former slaves or their descendants in the Fouta Djallon to improve their social and economic standing in Peul society. The Friday work day ends at 1:00 pm so that Guineans may pray at the mosque.

Guineans rely strongly upon their traditional spirit beliefs and resort to marabouts (dervishes believed to have supernatural powers) and fetishers in times of trouble. The least Islamicized region is the Forest Region, where males continue to practice secret rites in the "sacred forest." The Coastal Region has the largest number of Christians, where the missionary presence since the 19th century was strongest.

⁶ MAJOR HOLIDAYS

Besides the month-long Ramadan fast, one of the most celebrated holidays in the country is the Muslim feast of *Tabaski*. Tabaski celebrates the sparing of Abraham's son, who was saved when God provided a lamb for sacrifice. Trucks bring thousands of sheep and goats from upcountry to the capital for sale. By Islamic custom, butchers must slaughter animals by cutting the throat and allowing the blood to flow. On the morning of the feast, people colorfully dressed in their new clothes fill the streets and carry their prayer mats to mosque. The remainder of the day is spent greeting friends and feasting with the family.

On August 17, people remember the day in 1977 when women protested the market police and the laws that forbade private trade. Sékou Touré gave in to the demands and abolished the restrictions. Nowadays, everybody celebrates the day as a national holiday. Government officials honor women in ceremonies throughout the week. On the morning of the holiday, women sweep the streets of the capital.

⁷ RITES OF PASSAGE

Whatever their commitment to Islam, most Guineans still hold to some traditional beliefs and combine the two in everyday life and ritual. One example is circumcision. In both religions circumcision is a necessary rite. In Islam it suggests purification, while in traditional beliefs it has a supernatural quality. Islam advises that circumcision take place on the seventh day, the fortieth day, or when a child reaches the age of seven. Mystery cults and secret societies that worship animal or nature spirits initiate new members at puberty. In both cases, circumcision takes place and satisfies both religions.

Rites of passage remain important to Guineans of all ethnic groups and are cause for family and community celebration or observance. At baptisms, the father whispers the baby's name into its ear so that the child alone knows its name. Names tell about the family, its caste, and ancestors. Weddings, too, are cause for celebration. After the ceremony at the mosque, couples are married civilly at a government office. When the magistrate asks if anyone objects to the marriage, a friend accuses the couple in jest of having broken their vows. The accusation lightens the ceremony with humor and amusement. Then the groom offers a symbolic sum of about 50 cents to the magistrate. In the evening, the family closes off the street where the reception of music and dancing take place. Women come up to the musicians in small groups, waving the equivalent of $5 and $10 bills high above their heads and putting these on the musicians' heads.

Muslims bury their dead on the day after death and hold eulogy ceremonies 40 days after death. At Malinke ceremonies, family and friends gather to pray and recite the Quran. Mourners help the family pay expenses by giving offerings to the prayer leaders. They throw wadded up bills into the circle where the reciters are sitting. A praise-singer and his assistant, masters of ceremony, mention by name those who contribute and the amount they give.

8 INTERPERSONAL RELATIONS

Greetings are an important part of everyday life. Guineans call this custom *salaam alekum*, meaning offering the "peace of God." People would consider it rude not to greet their friends, officemates, or co-workers first before assuming the tasks of the day. Greetings involve asking each other questions about the well-being of the family. People touch their right hand to their heart to show respect, sincerity, and thanks to God. Men and women usually do not shake hands with the opposite sex. Friends who have not seen each other recently place their hands on the other's shoulders and touch cheeks three times.

In urban settings, Western-style dating is common. In rural areas, a young man might come to visit a fiancée at her home. Friends go out together to parties in towns or meet at community gatherings in the villages. Visiting is usually spontaneous, and it is customary to offer a glass of water to the visitor.

9 LIVING CONDITIONS

Nearly half of the population lives below the official poverty line, but living standards are gradually improving. Since the 1990s, life expectancy at birth has increased from 45 to 50 years, and the infant mortality rate declined from 13.4 (1996) to 8.7 babies out of 100 (2008 est.) that did not live to reach their first birthday.

Houses typically are made of mud brick with thatched roofs in round or rectangular form. Those who can afford more durable structures build with concrete and galvanized iron roofing. Running water is uncommon, even in the cities, where several families might share a common stand pipe. Latrines are usually dry pits, but as many as one-third of households in Conakry lack toilet facilities. Inadequate garbage collection in the capital allows enormous trash piles to litter the streets. Despite the construction of two major dams on the Konkouré River, electricity remains sporadic in the capital, with neighborhoods taking turns to receive power under "load-shedding" arrangements.

To compensate for poor landline telephones, most urbanites use cell phones while in rural areas messages are still commonly sent via friends and family by word of mouth. People are used to walking great distances, whether in the country or city. In the cities, most people commute to work and travel to market in crowded minivans. The fare costs about 10 cents. Conakry also has many taxis, usually worn-out Toyotas that fit two passengers up front and squeeze four into the back.

10 FAMILY LIFE

If they have the means, men may take up to four wives by Muslim law. Among the Peul, it is not unusual to find men aged 60 and above who have wives in their teens. Their wives may be younger than their children and even their grandchildren. Such families often number well over 20 children, with ages varying 40 or more years. Wives of the same husband usually live in separate houses apart from each other, or in separate huts within the same compound. Children refer to their "step mothers" as co-mothers (*co-mères*). Women play important income-generating roles in some families by trading, selling at the market, and working small businesses.

Among some groups, endogamy is widespread, meaning that individuals marry within their own clan. In these cases, family members may be related in two or three ways, as cousins and as nieces or nephews, or aunts and uncles simultaneously.

11 CLOTHING

Guineans have made an artform of *boubous*, which they slip over their heads and wear over matching pants. Their color and quality speak about the owner's wealth. Tailors make stylish boubous from *bazin* cloth, which has intricate designs in the weave. Women's outfits may be white or a single bright color, upon which tailors sew elaborate embroidered designs. The embroidery thread comes in all colors. If a tailor is unfamiliar with a design, Guineans bring a picture or a model to copy. Both men and women's boubous are open at the side for style and to allow air circulation in hot and humid climates. Women generally wear matching turbans or head scarves, while men often wear a Muslim skull cap or stylish white or blue wool cap. Guineans usually reserve these for special occasions or Friday prayers, as the complete outfit costs a few hundred dollars. Cheaper versions feature simpler designs and less expensive cloth for use at home and work. The Peul are famous for their indigo dyes and batik patterns. Women, especially of the Forest and Coastal regions, also wear African-style wraparounds (*pagnes*) with matching blouses or European blouses. European shirts and trousers are popular too, but it is less common to see men in Western suits and ties.

12 FOOD

The menu boards of local Guinean restaurants in towns and cities typically announce three offerings: greens, peanut, and meat stews. Invariably, white rice accompanies the stew. Some coastal people enjoy palm nut stew, which is eaten like soup. Most Guineans eat these sauces for the midday meal between 10:00 and 1:00. At night families eat leftovers or may have porridge, bread, and tea.

Ethnic groups usually have their own specialties. The Peul, for example, are fond of thick sour milk poured over a fine grain, called *fonio*. Families and friends may share this mixture together, each with a soup spoon, reaching into the calabash bowl. For supper, the Susu prepare an Ivorian dish called *achecké*, which is finely graded manioc cooked briefly in oil and eaten with grilled fish or chicken. A popular dish from Senegal is *riz gras*, literally "fat rice." People order this dish with fish or meat mixed with cabbage, carrots, squash, and cassava heaped over rice cooked in oil. In the Fouta Djallon, people drink a beverage similar to coffee which comes from the forest and contains antimalarial properties. In the Forest Region, palm wine is a favorite drink. Fruits are abundant in Guinea; citrus, pineapples, bananas, and mangoes are common. Guinea's variable climate allows for oranges the year-round.

Some taboos exist. Certain coastal peoples do not eat monkeys because they believe them to be people who once did not observe Friday prayers. Most Muslims refuse to eat pork, and if strict in their practice, do not drink alcohol or smoke.

13 EDUCATION

Literacy rates are improving, but only 30% of the population over 15 years old is literate in French. Parents want their children to attend school, but high levels of unemployed graduates raise questions about the usefulness of schooling. Many obstacles prevent children from completing primary school. In the rural areas, parents often need extra help in the fields or with household chores. School fees are high for many families, and sometimes children must walk distances up to six miles to attend school. Crowding and low standards are common in public elementary and high schools; therefore, parents with the means usually send their children to private schools. Dropout rates are high, and less than 25% of children go on to high school. In the 1970s the government "Africanized" the textbooks and the curricula to make learning more relevant. The government used civics classes to teach students party propaganda and doctrine.

In the 1970s and 80s, technical schools with low standards graduated thousands of agricultural extension agents, to whom the government guaranteed employment. These guarantees no longer exist leaving most university graduates unemployed and looking for work. Through technical assistance, foreign donors help the government build schools, train teachers, develop curricula, and manage education, but enormous challenges remain especially in rural areas.

[14] CULTURAL HERITAGE

Guineans have a rich cultural heritage. Performances of music and dance mark special occasions and holidays. Traditionally, music and dance served ritual purposes at birth, initiation, and death, or seasonal cycles of planting and harvesting. People danced on their way to harvest a field. Peul musicians typically play handcrafted flutes, drums, and stringed instruments, and use calabashes to beat out rhythms. Malinke traditional music currently is blending with traditional forms. The men drum and play *balafons* (xylophones) while women wearing elaborate boubous dance with graceful arm movements, suggesting butterflies. In the Forest, one popular hunter's dance consists of masked dancers in bark, raffia, and animal skin costumes walking swiftly on stilts. Forester drummers are highly accomplished and send messages with their drum beats to neighboring communities. Drumming is a major Guinean art form, and apprentices learn from the masters over a period of years. During Sékou Touré's time, the government supported the arts, and Guineans produced some of Africa's finest theater and folkloric ballets in international competitions.

Guineans excel in literature. Malinke and Peul traditional *griots*, or praise-singers, are bards who narrate past traditions through story and song, often with musical accompaniment. They are skilled professionals trained in their art by members of their family and profession. Authors such as the Malinke Camara Laye have produced written work of international acclaim in French. His novel, *The African Child* (*L'Enfant Noir*) tells of a child growing up in the Malinke homeland. The child's father is a goldsmith, and he learns about spirits and taboos from his parents. The novel is often used in the American university classroom in French and literature courses.

[15] WORK

The lack of jobs continues to plague the country. Following structural adjustment in 1984, more than 50,000 Guineans lost their civil service jobs, and since then the ranks of university graduates and skilled workers looking for work has continued to swell. Guinea's economy is dependent on bauxite exports for 85% of its foreign earnings, but almost no processing of the ore occurs in the country. Therefore, few Guineans benefit from this major industry, and of the nearly 3.7 million people in the labor force, approximately three out of four work in subsistence or plantation agriculture, which accounts for only 24% of the gross domestic product.

[16] SPORTS

Guineans are avid soccer players and during the 1970s produced some of Africa's most competitive teams. Basketball is also popular, and schools arrange competitions. In the towns, children and young men play soccer wherever space allows. In Conakry, this means placing four large rocks as goal posts in the street. Since few people own cars, streets make convenient playing fields. Girls play versions of hopscotch. A less popular game that men play is the French game of "bocci ball."

[17] ENTERTAINMENT AND RECREATION

Entertainment and recreation revolve mostly around socializing, rites of passage, and sporting events. The few city parks found in Conakry like Ignace Deen and the 2nd of October are not well kept, are unsafe at night, and aside from joggers, are not generally frequented. Conakryites wishing to get away from it all on weekends may spend Sundays at small resorts outside of town such as the *Chien qui Fume*, named for its rock formations resembling Snoopy the Dog lying on his doghouse smoking his pipe. Marriages often are held on weekends and the wedding parties provide entertainment and recreation at hotels or in the street.

Few Guineans can afford televisions or satellite dishes, and those who do must cope with electrical outages. When the power is on, neighbors gather round on the sidewalk to watch popular regional theatrical productions broadcast on Guinea's government station. Similar to American serials, these plays in the local languages are about daily life and teach about human foibles, solving community problems, and coping with social challenges.

Guineans also go to the movies and to musical performances featuring musicians from around Africa. Miriam Makeba, who once was married to the late Kwamé Touré (Stokely Carmichael), lived in Guinea and gives performances on her return visits. The discos play a variety of Guinean, Cuban, Zairian, Senegalese, and American music. In rural areas, teenagers are no longer shut off from international popular culture. It is becoming more common to find generators, solar panels, and satellite dishes in remote villages where a night's entertainment can be had for a small admission fee.

[18] FOLK ART, CRAFTS, AND HOBBIES

Besides modern tourist art, Guineans still produce significant folk art and crafts. Some ethnic groups excel in painting pottery, masks, house walls, and tombs. The Kissi people have made stone sculpture statuettes for 500 years for rituals and to communicate with ancestors. The Baga people on the coast make wooden busts of females, the *Nimba*. These fecund images have become the national symbol of art.

Guineans are reviving their handicrafts industries. For example, the Peul make leather sandals of very high quality, and women weave decorative raffia place mats and baskets. In cooperatives, women dye fabric for making clothing, tablecloths, and napkins. Local weavers still produce cloth strips for traditional garments, and tailoring and embroidery have remarkable artistic merit.

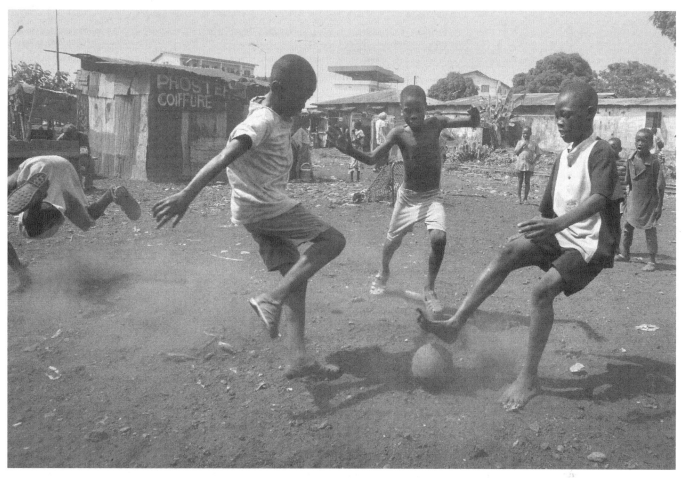

Young Guinean children play soccer on a dirt pitch by railroad tracks in the capital of Conakry. (AP Images/Ben Curtis)

19 SOCIAL PROBLEMS

Guinea has not fully recovered from the persecutions, tortures, and starvation of thousands of political prisoners in the 1960s and 70s. Reforms in the political system have improved civil and human rights, but the government remains highly intolerant of dissent. In 1985, 50 Malinke officers were shot after an alleged coup attempt, and more than 100 people died in ethnic-related conflict during the 1993 elections. In 2006–07, nationwide strikes and protests over depressed wages, the lack of jobs, and a growing discontent with pace of political reform turned violent and resulted in the deaths and injuries of hundreds of youths. In Guinea, people aged 15–40 are considered to be the youth of the country. It is this group that is becoming especially impatient with the lack of services, poor governance, and few work opportunities. Corruption is seemingly everywhere and has widened the gap between the haves and the have-nots.

20 GENDER ISSUES

Gender presents a paradox in Guinea. On the one hand women are strong and assertive, but on the other they are subject to societal discrimination, prostitution, and female genital mutilation. In 1977 it was a women's march that forced Sékou Touré to abandon his failed economic policies. Yet in 2008 women are weakly represented in politics with 20 of 114 parliamen-

tary seats, 1 governor and 2 prefects, 3 cabinet members, and 5 of 26 Supreme Court justices. Though the Ministry of Social Affairs and Women's and Children's Issues has created greater awareness of gender discrimination, in general women have fewer rights than men, are easily divorced under Muslim law, are disadvantaged by inheritance laws, and in rural areas are subject to the heavy demands of childbearing, childrearing, and subsistence farming. There is a national women's empowerment plan (2007–11), but it is slow to get off the ground.

21 BIBLIOGRAPHY

Africa South of the Sahara 2007. "Guinea." London: Europa Publishers, 2008.

Kaplan, Robert. "The Coming Anarchy." *The Atlantic Monthly,* February 1994.

Nelson, Harold D. et al, ed. *Area Handbook for Guinea.* Washington, D. C.: American University, 1975.

—by R. Groelsema

GUINEANS OF GUINEA-BISSAU

PRONUNCIATION: GHIN-ee-uhns
LOCATION: Guinea-Bissau
POPULATION: 1.6 million
LANGUAGE: Portuguese, Crioulo, Balanta, Pulaar, Malinke
RELIGION: Indigenous African religion, Islam, Christianity
RELATED ARTICLES: Vol. 1: Guineans; Fulani; Malinke

¹ INTRODUCTION

Guinea-Bissau has been inhabited since the Stone Age. Early peoples in this coastal area hunted and gathered or grew rice in small communities. These communities were swept into the kingdom of Gabu, which became part of the great Mali Empire in AD 1200–1350, and then within the orbit of the Songhay Empire that flourished into the 16th century. In 1546, as the unifying power of Songhay declined, Gabu exerted its independence and gradually became semi-autonomous. Portions of this ancient kingdom existed until 1867.

Portuguese explorers first visited the coastal islands and mainland in the 15th century. Nuno Tristao is credited with exploring and mapping the area in 1446. Portuguese colonists soon followed and gained trading rights from the Portuguese government. The most valuable commodity soon became human slaves, and Guinea-Bissau became a center for the Portuguese slave trade in Africa. In the early 1800s, the French moved south from Senegal to establish trading posts along the coastal estuaries. These estuaries and other inlets offered hiding places for slave traders, allowing the trade to continue until the end of the American civil war. In 1879, Portugal changed Guinea-Bissau's status from a possession to a separate colony, which provided greater autonomy for the European settler community. Soon after, the Conference of Berlin (1885–86) reaffirmed the colonial boundaries in West Africa, giving the Portuguese undisputed control over the Cape Verde islands, the offshore islands of Bissagos, and the Guinea-Bissau mainland between the French possessions of Senegal and Guinea.

In 1951, Portugal attempted to reassert control from the metropole by designating its African colonies, including Guinea-Bissau, as overseas provinces. Five years later, dissidents founded the African Party for the Independence of Guinea-Bissau and Cape Verde (PAIGC) and began to wage a guerrilla war against the Portuguese. Its leader, Amilcar Cabral, was assassinated in 1973, but the overthrow of the Salazar government in Portugal paved the way for independence of Portuguese Africa. An agreement in August 1974 led to independence on September 10 with Cabral's brother, Luis de Almeida Cabral, as president. Cape Verde gained its independence a year later, and for five years the two countries shared the PAIGC as a common party. However, Guinea-Bissau remained a single party state because of fears of a return to Portuguese rule.

Nearly 30 years of political upheaval followed. Joao Bernardo Veira deposed Cabral in a military coup in November 1980 and established a government of crony capitalists. Agricultural production increased overall, but Veira's government was deposed by rebels in May 1999. Malam Bacai Sanha, the former head of the parliament, became the interim president. In 2000, Kumba Yala, a former teacher and popularist leader of the independence movement, was elected president in the country's first multi-party elections. However, an army rebellion that year threatened the fledgling democracy and led to the death of General Ansumane Mane. In September 2003, Yala was deposed in a military coup, and Henrique Rosa was appointed president of a transitional government. In March 2004, parliamentary elections returned a plurality to the PAIGC and Carlos Gomes Junior became prime minister. However, in October the chief of the armed forces was killed in a mutiny over back pay. In 2005 Veira returned from exile in Portugal to stand for elections. The second national round of multi-party elections was held in June 2005 and returned Veira to the presidency. The contest was fought bitterly by Uala and Sanha resulting in a run-off between Sanha and Veira. Veira eventually was declared the winner, but Sanha and his PAIGC party alleged fraud. Sanha finally accepted the results in September. In April 2007, Prime Minister Aristides Gomes resigned after being censured by parliament. A no confidence vote for his government paved the way for Martinho N'dafa Kabi to be appointed his successor.

Internationally, Guinea-Bissau has maintained good relations with Senegal and Guinea. Both neighbors sent troops to support Veira in the late 1990s to repel insurgents. In return, Veira's government attempted to dislodge Casamance rebels who established bases in Guinea-Bissau in order to launch cross-border attacks on Senegalese government troops.

² LOCATION AND HOMELAND

Guinea-Bissau is one of Africa's smallest countries. It is approximately the size of Switzerland or slightly under three times the size of Connecticut. It is wedged between Guinea to the south and east and Senegal to the north. Its coastline spans 299 km (186 mi), and it encompasses an archipelago of islands about 48 km (30 mi) off the coast. In all, Guinea-Bissau counts 36,120 sq km (13, 946 sq mi).

Guinea's eight regions reach from a swampy coast to gradually rising savanna in the east. Mangroves and winding estuaries provide rich fishing grounds along the highly indented coastline. Sparsely wooded savanna dominates the eastern reaches. The highest point of the country is in the northeast about 305 m (1,000 ft) above sea level. This area joins the northern reaches of the Guinean Fouta Djallon plateau. From June to November, monsoonal rains pound the coast, where up to 4 m (13 ft) of water falls annually. Two-thirds of this rain falls in July and August. The reverse is true for the rest of the year when cooler dry winds blow off the deserts of north central Africa.

Guinea-Bissau's population is young. About 41% is 14 years old or younger and population growth is at about 2% per year. The population consists of four main ethnic groups and several smaller groups. The largest group is the Balanta (30%), followed by the Fula (20%), Manjaca (14%), Mandinga (13%), and the Pepel (7%). The Balanta occupy the central region and the Fula the north, while the Manjaca, Mandinga, and Pepel have settled mostly in the coastal areas. In addition, Cape Verdean expatriates, Syrian Lebanese, and some Portuguese are found in the capital of Bissau and in secondary towns. Two of the groups—the Fula and the Mandinga—form part of greater transboundary ethnic groups living in Senegal, Mali, Guinea, and beyond. The Mandinga trace their ancestry directly to the founders and rulers of the Mali Empire.

³ LANGUAGE

The peoples of Guinea-Bissau speak Portuguese, Crioulo, and several African languages. Portuguese is used widely in government and is the language of instruction in high schools and universities. Aside from Portuguese, the languages spoke regionally are Pulaar (Fulfulde), which is spoken by the Fula, and Mandinka, which is spoken by the Mandinga group. Guinea-Bissau is a member of the Lusophone states of Africa, which include Mozambique, Angola, Sao Tomé and Principe, and Cape Verde.

⁴ FOLKLORE

Guinea-Bissau, like most African countries is rich in folklore. Elders and professional storytellers recall myths, legends, and tales handed down over generations. Their stories often feature animals whose cleverness, foibles, and personalities illustrate human character and experience. The glories of past empires, such as the Mali and Songhai Empires of the 13th and the 15th centuries AD, also serve as backdrops for folkloric exposition. In the retelling of such stories, Guineans become part of the peoples of greater West Africa who share ancient cultural traditions.

Some folklore, having emerged from the decolonization period, is more recent. It recalls a colonial past of repression, servitude, and humiliation broken by revolutionary struggle. For Guinea-Bissau's youthful population, the revolutionary war of the 1950s seems like ancient history. Leaders of the liberation struggle, like Amilcar Cabral, born in 1924, are now revered national heroes and have entered the pantheon of national folklore. Through their poems, speeches, and armed struggle, they have become larger than life.

⁵ RELIGION

Nearly half (45%) of the population is Muslim. The Muslim community dominates the commercial sector and, increasingly, the government. Despite centuries of Catholic missions, dating to the Portuguese explorations along the Atlantic coast, Christians account for only 5% of the population. African indigenous religion overlays these faiths with at least 50% of the population practicing some form of African traditional religion.

In African traditional religion, ancestors exercise power over their living descendants through spirits. Spirits may be evoked through offerings at household shrines or at shrines staffed by priests, witches, and traditional doctors. In coastal villages, one finds many such shrines, to which animals are sacrificed, and local alcohol and food are offered. People mainly visit the shrines to seek advice and protection or to make special requests. Guineans abroad often return to visit the shrines. However, if they are unable to do so in person, they send remittances to relatives to make sacrifices and say prayers on their behalf.

⁶ MAJOR HOLIDAYS

Guineans celebrate nine holidays per year, including Christmas, New Year's, International Women's Day, and Labor Day. Two holidays are dedicated to Muslim feasts: Korité, which celebrates the end of Ramadan, and Tabaski, the Feast of the Sacrifice (of Abraham's son). The Anniversary of the Killing of Pidjiguoiti, National Day or Independence Day (September 24), and the Anniversary of the Movement of Readjustment (November 14) are also commemorated.

The biggest holidays are faith-related. Carnival was once identified with Catholic Crioulo culture, but is now a popular multi-ethnic festival. In a sense, the entire month of Ramadan has become a holiday, as fasting during the day and feasting at night slow the pace of work. Korité celebrations of special meals and gatherings with family and friends may last from two to ten days. Tabaski begins with prayer at the mosque, followed by feasting and gift giving among families and friends.

⁷ RITES OF PASSAGE

Rites of passage vary by ethnic group and by religion, but uniformly celebrate birth, puberty, adulthood (marriage), old age, and death. Muslims traditionally name their children at baptisms, when the father whispers the baby's name into its ear. Names are significant because they normally have meanings that tell about the family, its caste, and its ancestors.

Circumcision marks the attainment of puberty, suggesting purification in Islam, and also a mystical supernatural dimension for traditionalists. For girls and boys, this ritual is the most important because it is the gateway to adulthood and full participation in society. In some cases, a child may be circumcised at a younger age. Islam advises that circumcision take place on the seventh day, the fortieth day, or when a child reaches the age of seven, but depending on the beliefs of the family, it may be carried out in peer groups and conducted as part of a weeklong rite of initiation. Girls, however, may be circumcised as infants.

Weddings are cause for festive celebrations. For Muslims, after the religious celebration at the mosque, couples will also need to be officially married by a civil administrator at a government office. These ceremonies may be held on the same day. In some areas, the passage to death is the most celebrated event as it marks the afterlife, and still more importantly, ancestorhood (see Religion). At funerals, wealthy families may have hundreds of people in attendance and will slaughter several cattle for feasting. Non-Muslims may make gifts of food and local palm wine as ritual offerings. The deceased will be wrapped in several layers of expensive cloth. Muslims bury their dead on the day after death and hold eulogy ceremonies 40 days after death.

⁸ INTERPERSONAL RELATIONS

Guineans are extremely social people and spend considerable time greeting friends and maintaining relationships. The Muslim greeting, *salaam alekum*, meaning the "peace of God," is commonly shared not only among practicing Muslims, but also by people who may be greeting each other in a Muslim neighborhood or region. The common reply is alekum salaam, meaning "and peace with you." It is considered rude not to acknowledge someone by offering a verbal greeting, by bringing one's right hand to one's chest, or by shaking hands (only with the right hand) in most company. However, it is unusual for men and women to shake hands with each other, especially in the village. Greetings often involve asking questions about one's well-being and that of their family.

Guinea-Bissau is an affective society where relationships largely are determined by birth. The strongest link is to the nuclear family, which may include mother, father, and siblings, and in polygamous households, a co-mother and her children. Cousins usually are thought of as brothers and sisters. The strength of this bond gradually weakens as the relationship widens to the clan or lineage and ethnic group. But, the power of these relations is seen in the importance people attach to membership in various associations that include peer groups, hometown associations, secret societies, and intertribal relationships.

In rural areas, rights to land are determined locally. Rules vary according to tribe, but generally land is passed down in the family through males. Among the Manjaco and Papel, rice fields are inherited by a sister's sons, who as caretakers and custodians of the trust, determine which family members receive which portion of land. In any case, it is expected that members of a kinship group help each other till and harvest their fields. Not to do so would be to invite ostracism, a punishment of the worst kind.

Affective relationships are often hierarchical and demand proper respect. A child must show deference to his parents and older siblings, while adults and young adults must defer to their elders. Again, not to do so would be seen as disrespectful. Because of the hierarchy of these relationships, people are used to authority figures, secrecy, and limited decision-making.

Affective relationships have economic dimensions. The Mandingo are born into castes, which historically have promoted skills, trades, and vocations. Blacksmiths, storytellers, pastoralists, agriculturalists, doctors, and herbalists are determined by caste, and these societies have established long traditions and rules that govern relations between members of different castes. The Fula know who among them descended from a slave or free family. Social mores are changing, but it is a gradual process.

9 LIVING CONDITIONS

Living conditions for most people are difficult. On the Human Development Index (HDI), which measures chances to live long, be educated, and have a decent standard of living, Guinea-Bissau ranks third to the last out of 177 countries. Wealth is concentrated in the hands of a few elites distinguished by their Mercedes Benz cars, fancy suits, and the latest electronic gadgets.

In contrast, most people live in small rectangular houses with galvanized iron roofs, or cylindrical huts made of dried mud and thatched roofs. These homes typically have no windows or chimneys to vent smoke. Cooking may be done outside with firewood and large stones, on which a kettle is placed. Malaria, tuberculosis, and other life-threatening diseases are rampant. Most people cannot afford western medicines, and those that can, may find them beyond their expiration date. Affordable health care means seeking out local healers and diviners and making sacrifices at shrines. Fewer than 60% of

people have access to potable water and 40% will not live past the age of 40.

10 FAMILY LIFE

For the subsistence farmer, family life revolves around seasonal work in the fields, supplemented with weekly markets and punctuated by visiting with family and friends. Families rise early, usually at dawn, have a meal of porridge or stew, and walk long distances to their fields. If the children are not in school, they will accompany the adults to help with weeding, harvesting, or tending babies and small children. Girls help their mothers fetch water, carry firewood, and wash clothes at the river or stream. Despite the heavy work, children find time to play, and boys will be seen kicking a soccer ball in the village squares. Evenings are a time for eating the large meal of the day. Depending on the tribe, men may eat separately from the rest of the family. Evenings also are a time for relaxing and storytelling, and during full moons, dancing and drumming may take place. In town and country, baptisms, weddings, funerals, and holidays are times for getting together to celebrate, to grieve, and to share experiences. City children may have better chances for schooling, but many of them must peddle wares and do domestic chores to help generate income for the family.

11 CLOTHING

By and large, Guineans have little discretionary income for expensive clothing. Hence, everyday work clothing consists of hand-me-downs and used clothing purchased at local markets. Western clothes, t-shirts, and sports jerseys from American universities and professional sports teams have found their way to Africa in bulk shipments of used clothing. People are conscientious about how they look though, and if at all possible, they dress up to go out in public.

In coastal areas it is common to see women wearing brightly colored pieces of cloth (wraps or lappas) with matching blouses and headscarves, although these are found throughout the country. Men may wear eye-catching prints that have been made into shirts and trousers. Children wear these as well. Many men wear *boubous*, which are flowing cotton robes with open sides, worn over matching pants. Their color and quality speak to the owner's wealth. The higher the quality of cloth and the more exquisite the tailoring, the greater one's wealth. They may wear matching skullcaps. Women wear a version of these that comes in three pieces: a wrap that ties around the waist and a matching blouse and headscarf. Friday prayers and holidays are the best times to observe and appreciate fine clothing.

12 FOOD

Guineans are fond of white rice, which is a staple for coastal people and also imported to feed urbanites. In the interior, millet is the staple crop. Both are enjoyed with a variety of sauces typically cooked in a base of palm oil, onions, and tomatoes, supplemented with meat, fish, chicken, pounded seeds, greens, or peanut pastes. These stews vary somewhat by tribe and region, but they are cooked in large kettles over wood fires. For lack of refrigeration, mothers or their helpers will buy produce daily at the local market. Millet, peanuts, seeds, and other ingredients are pounded in a mortar and pestle. The coast is known for its fresh fish, while upcountry, guinea hens, and beef are popular. On ceremonial occasions, people eat large quantities of meat and, unless proscribed by religion, consume large quantities of palm wine, rum, or other local beverages.

13 EDUCATION

The government has made education universal, but in practice only one in three children actually attends school. Schools are often built in or near villages in three- to five-classroom structures. Children are not unaccustomed to walking a few miles to school. Pencils, textbooks, and chalk—materials taken for granted elsewhere—are in short supply, and families may need to pay extra for them. But, the greatest challenge at the primary and secondary levels is teachers. Teachers prefer to live and teach in towns where quality of life is higher. Low pay and erratic salaries hurt motivation.

At the university level, the few Guineans who obtain scholarships study abroad. In colonial times, only a few students—primarily of Cape Verdean ancestry—received higher education. They went to Portugal. In the 1970s, those with the right connections went to East Germany, the Soviet Union, Cuba, and China for their degrees. During the revolutionary era, the government embarked upon an ambitious literacy program led by the well-known educator-activist, Paolo Freire. The program was meant to be universal, but given the extreme challenges facing the country, it failed to have lasting effect.

14 CULTURAL HERITAGE

Like most of Africa, Guinea-Bissau's cultural heritage is embodied in sculpture, music, dance, and theater. The national media support the performing arts in telecasts and radio broadcasts, which are extremely popular. Guineans have passed down their history and literature orally through storytelling and song. Only recently have these been the subject of written accounts. One notable example is the writings of Amilcar Cabral, who led the armed struggle for independence. Cabral's influence is still felt through his masterful speeches on national liberation. Crioulo fiction has also gained popularity thanks to Guinean writers of Cape Verdean ancestry, such as Fausto Duarte and Joao Alves da Neves. Duarte, a government employee educated in the Portuguese assimiliçao (assimilation) program, distinguished himself as one of the earliest African novelists, first writing in Portuguese and later in Crioulo. He died in 1953.

15 WORK

Guineans start working early in their lives as children. Many of them are subsistence farmers and artisanal fisher folk, living off their own produce. Women and children also perform domestic tasks. Children herd goats and cattle. Market trade is usually conducted by women. Those lucky enough to find employment in the public sector have steady work, but barely make a living wage. As elsewhere in Africa, many people count on remittances from friends and relatives abroad. Trade and commerce are mostly of the petty variety and relatively unimportant for the GDP. In Bissau, men drive taxis or load and unload ships at the docks. *Pontas*, former colonial concessions now owned by members of government, are worked by landless peasants who receive farm implements from the landowners

so they can grow cash crops. However, the sharecroppers must give a portion of their harvests or profits to the landowner.

16 SPORTS

Either as spectators or players, Guineans love soccer. All other sports, such as basketball, though played by schoolchildren, pale in comparison. One bi-annual tournament in West Africa is named for Guinea-Bissau's national hero, Amilcar Cabral. The Amilcar Cabral Cup has never been won by, but has been hosted by, Guinea-Bissau three times since it began in 1979.

17 ENTERTAINMENT AND RECREATION

Most forms of entertainment and recreation are fairly simple and do not depend on electricity. In the village, swapping tales around a fire in the evening, a boys' game of soccer with an undersized plastic ball, or a game of checkers in front of a market stall may be all there is for entertainment. One popular game that is played throughout West Africa is *Ouri* (also called Wari), which is played on a wooden board with seeds and six pockets. The object of the game is to capture more seeds than one's opponent. Since the game has only 48 seeds, capturing 25 is sufficient to win. Ceremonies and feasts provide opportunities to socialize and to meet members of the opposite sex.

In the towns, small bars and coffee shops, internet cafés, TV, and DVDs provide ready forms of entertainment. Soccer fans watch matches on TV, at clubs with satellite dishes, or at the national stadium. At night, discotheques attract people of all stripes. Guineans love to dance the *passada*, a highly suggestive Portuguese-African dance with lots of pelvic motion and rhythm. The local music beat is called *gumbe*. Men tap out the rhythms to gumbe on giant gourds cut in half, which they float upside down in a basin of water. Lyrics to gumbe music are in Crioulo and are sung throughout the country. Gumbe artists from the 1980s and 1990s used their songs to protest against the dictator-president, Joao Bernardo Vieira. Gumbe has borrowed heavily from Congolese soukous, French Antillean zouk, and rap, reggae, and salsa. Cover charges at most discos are high, but in reality almost anyone can get in to forget about their problems in their music and dance.

18 FOLK ART, CRAFTS, AND HOBBIES

Art generally has a religious, mystical, and otherworldly significance. Each ethnic group has its own arts and crafts, and some, like the Baga of the southwestern coast, have achieved world recognition for their woodcarvings. The Baga, who number perhaps only 60,000 people, are divided between Guinea-Bissau and the Republic of Guinea to the south. They make wooden busts of females, the *Nimba*, which are fecund images. Owing to their distinctiveness, Nimba have become internationally renowned as superior works of art. In addition to finer forms of art, Guineans also make tourist art and crafts, such as animal carvings, rattan baskets, jewelry, and toys made from tin cans, but there is limited demand for such items.

19 SOCIAL PROBLEMS

Guinea-Bissau has many social problems stemming from cultural, social, economic, and political causes. Women face discrimination, and most children do not finish primary school. Schoolgirls often face sexual advances from teachers and older students. Extreme poverty has forced many girls and women into prostitution, and a growing number of boys living on the streets of Bissau have become part of gangs. Some children are trafficked, especially to Senegal, where boys are sold to work for religious leaders (marabouts), and forced to beg on the streets to pay for their upkeep and schooling. Buying and selling of child brides is a reality, and child labor is common.

Government corruption and neglect is part of the problem. Government posts are seen as opportunities for self-enrichment, and officials do little to enforce laws or regulate behavior. Judges and policemen are poorly trained and paid and commonly take bribes, and prisons fail to measure up to minimum standards of decency. While the personal use of illicit drugs is not the problem it is in Westernized countries, Guinea-Bissau has become a transit point for international narco-traffickers smuggling Columbian cocaine to European markets. Journalists who report on the drug trade have received death threats. In the absence of strong checks and balances, Guinea-Bissau has a powerful executive and a system that has encouraged military coups and counter coups. Political instability, coupled with crime and unemployment, has encouraged many of the best-educated Guineans, who are most needed in leadership positions, to leave the country. This brain drain has deepened poverty and social injustice for most people.

20 GENDER ISSUES

As elsewhere in sub-Saharan Africa, gender issues are prominent on the social agenda, and a number of human rights organizations have mobilized—usually with foreign donor assistance—to defend women's rights and bring balance to gender roles in Guinea-Bissau. Women and girls have less job mobility, complete fewer years of schooling, do most of the subsistence farming, and enjoy far less protection under the law than men. There is, for example, no law against wife beating, and many women are subjected to violence as a means of settling disputes in the home. While the law prohibits rape and prostitution, the government provides little enforcement, and women are harassed sexually. Certain ethnic groups do not allow women to own or inherit property.

Girls are also subject to female genital mutilation (FGM), which is practiced widely throughout the country. Known as *Fanado*, it is estimated that 45% of women aged 15–49 are excised. As many as 2,000 girls (including infants) undergo this procedure annually, often under unhygienic conditions. Fanado is steeped in religious and cultural tradition, and the cutters, who are women, often learn the practice from their mothers and grandmothers, and earn their livelihoods from it. Families pay between $10–$15, not including gifts, to have their girls circumcised. Even non-Muslim women who marry Muslim men will undergo Fanado, because during the holy month of Ramadan, Muslim men will refuse to take food from an uncircumcised woman. Uncircumcised women are also not allowed to pray in the mosque. In June 2008, government launched a program to ban the practice, but it is likely to take years before it is stopped.

21 BIBLIOGRAPHY

Africa South of the Sahara 2007. Guinea Bissau. London: Europa Publishers, 2008.

Chabal, Patrick. *Amilcar Cabral: Revolutionary Leadership and People's War*. New York and Cambridge, U.K.: Cambridge University Press, 1983.

Forrest, Joshua. *Lineages of State Fragility: Rural Civil Society in Guinea Bissau*. Athens: University of Ohio Press, 2003.

"Guinea Bissau." *CIA World Factbook*. https://www.cia.gov/library/publications/the-world-factbook/geos/pu.html (October 2008)

Lobban, Richard Andrew, Jr., and Peter Karibe Mendy. *Historical Dictionary of the Republic of Guinea-Bissau*. Third Edition. Metuchen, NJ and London: The Scarecrow Press, Inc., 1999.

—by Robert J. Groelsema

GUSII

PRONUNCIATION: goo-SEE
ALTERNATE NAMES: Kisii, Kosova, Guzii, Ekegusii Gisii,
   Abagusii, Kissii, Kisi
LOCATION: Western Kenya
POPULATION: 2.1 Million
LANGUAGE: Ekegusii
RELIGION: Christianity mixed with ancestor cult beliefs
RELATED ARTICLES: Vol. 1: Kenyans

¹ INTRODUCTION

At the end of the 1700s, Bantu-speaking populations were dispersed in small pockets at the northern, southern, and eastern margins of the Kisii highlands and in the Lake Victoria basin. Around 1800, the highlands above 1,515 meters (4,970 feet) were probably uninhabited from the northern part of the Manga escarpment south to the river Kuja. At that time, the lowland savanna was being settled by large numbers of agropastoralist peoples ancestral to present-day Luo and Kipsigis, dislodging the smaller Bantu groups from their territories on the savanna. The Gusii settled in the Kisii highlands, while other culturally and linguistically related groups remained along the Lake Victoria Basin or, as the Kuria, settled in the lower savanna region at the Kenya-Tanzania border. The establishment of British colonial administration in 1907 was initially met by armed resistance that ceased after World War I.

Contrary to other highland areas in Kenya, the Gusii were not subject to land alienation. The seven subdivisions of Gusiiland were converted into administrative units under government-appointed chiefs. The first missions established were Roman Catholic in 1911 and the Seventh Day Adventist in 1913. The mission activity was not initially very successful, and several stations were looted. After Kenyan independence in 1963, schools were built throughout the area; roads were improved; and electricity, piped water, and telephones were extended to many areas. By the 1970s, the land shortage had begun to make farming unprofitable, and education of children for off-farm employment has since become important.

The Gusii's strong clan affiliations began to break down in the mid-1800s. As of the 21st century, Gusii chiefs represent clans in the local Kenyan administration and participate actively in Kenya's multiparty politics. In the 2007 general elections Gusii voters supported both the opposition and the ruling party. As a result, Gusii representatives are divided between the two major political parties that make up Kenya's ruling "Grand Coalition" government. Many members of the Gusii community were victims of the post election violence that swept through Kenya in January 2008. Thousands were displaced and hundreds killed.

² LOCATION AND HOMELAND

Gusiiland is located in western Kenya, 50 kilometers (31 miles) east of Lake Victoria. Since pre-colonial times, abundant rainfall and very fertile soils have made Gusiiland one of the most productive agricultural areas in Kenya. Between 70% and 80% of the land is arable. The region is bounded by latitudes 0°30' and 1°00's and longitudes 34°30' and 35°00'E. Since 1989, the Gusii have occupied as a single ethnic group Kisii and Nyami-

ra Districts. The area is a rolling, hilly landscape on a deeply dissected plain at altitudes of 1,190 m (3,900 ft) in the far northwestern corner of the territory to 2,130 m (6,990 ft) in the central highlands.

The mean maximum temperatures range from 28.4°C (83°F) at the lowest altitudes to 22.8°C (73°F) at the highest elevations. The mean minimum temperatures are 16.4°C (61.5°F) and 9.8°C (50°F) respectively. Rain falls throughout the year with an annual average of 1,500 to 2,000 millimeters (60 to 80 inches). There are two peak seasons of rainfall: March to May is the major rainy season; September to November is the minor rainy season. In the 19th century, much of present-day Gusiiland was covered by moist montane forest. Today, all forest has been cleared, very little indigenous vegetation remains, and no large mammals are found.

The Gusii population is estimated at 1.65 million as of 2007, up from 1.3 million in 1989. The Gusii are among the most rapidly growing populations in the world, increasing by 3% to 4% per year. The region where the Gusii live is one of the most densely populated in Kenya. The Gusii population is also young, with around 50% of the population being under the age of 15 years. The high population growth rate is due to the cultural attitude that having many children ensures security in old age. This has led to low use of family planning methods.

The average woman bears approximately nine children; infant mortality is relatively low (about 80 per 1,000 live births), especially in comparison to other areas of sub-Saharan Africa.

Most Gusii live in rural areas, although many have left the traditional tribal lands for urban centers (in Kenya and elsewhere around the world) to seek education, employment opportunities. Outside the tribal area, the group's language, Ekegusii (and materials in Ekegusii), is little used and may be in danger of being lost.

³ LANGUAGE

Ekegusii is a Western Bantu language. Naming customs include naming a child after a recent event such as the weather at the time of the child's birth. Most common is to use the name of a dead person from the father's clan for the first name and one from the mother's clan for the second name. Some common names refer to the time of migrations. For example, the woman's name *Kwamboka* means "crossing a river." Another aspect of the language is its close relationship to Gusii culture, where talking about personal emotional states is not condoned. Hence, questions about a person's mental state are answered with statements about physical health or economic situation.

There is little literature available for teaching Ekegusii, except for some elementary works in form of folktales, short stories, songs, and proverbs. To date, the Holy Bible and Christian hymnals remain the major translations and only rich source of written Ekegusii. Ekegusii is dependent on tone differentiation. Ekegusii has not developed specialized vocabulary and everyday words for new and emerging globalized experiences, such as hip hop music, information technology, commerce, communications, and travel. This makes the language ill-equipped for modern communication. Ekegusii speakers find that their language lacks words for such everyday items in modern society as radio, television, video, and computer. To the disadvantage of would-be speakers and learners of Ekegusii, Kenya's country's education system does not place much emphasis on the learning of various tribal languages and tribal languages

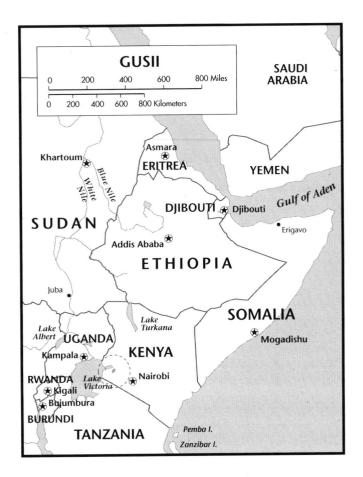

GUSII

0   200   400   600   800 Miles

0 200 400 600 800 Kilometers

are not included in national examinations. Therefore, young people have little motivation to develop proficiency in tribal languages.

4 FOLKLORE

Gusii oral traditions contain a number of prominent persons who are linked to historical events, notably the period of migrations into the current homeland and the coming of the British. These figures are usually men, but a few women are also remembered. There are two historical figures linked to the establishment of the most populous section, the Kitutu. These are Nyakanethi and her stepson Nyakundi, who fortified themselves in the highland to the north and gave shelter to families who fled from attacks by neighboring peoples. These people were given a home in Kitutu with Nyakundi as their chief.

Other "heroes" are related to the establishment of the colonial administration. The prophet Sakawa, who was born in the 1840s and died around 1902, is reputed to have foretold the arrival of the British in 1907 and the building of the district capital Kisii Town.

In 1907–08, a prophetess called Moraa tried to incite rebellion against the British. In 1908 she gave her stepson, Otenyo, magical medicines that would protect him from bullets and sent him to kill the British officer, G.A.S. Northcote. Although Otenyo wounded Northcote with his spear, the British District Officer survived and later became the governor of Hong Kong.

5 RELIGION

Before the advent of Christianity, the Gusii believed in the existence of one God who was the originator of the world but did not directly interfere in human affairs. Instead, it was the ancestor cult, together with ideas about witchcraft, sorcery, and impersonal forces that provided a complex of belief in suprahuman agency. The ancestor spirits (ebirecha) existed both as a collective and as ancestors and ancestresses of the living members of a lineage. They were not appropriated until there was tangible evidence of their displeasure such as disease, death of people and livestock, and the destruction of crops.

The community is about 82% Christian and 18% traditional religion. Most Gusii today claim to be adherents of some Christian church. There are four major denominations in Gusiiland: Roman Catholic, Seventh-Day Adventist, Swedish Lutheran, and the Pentecostal Assemblies of God. Active Seventh-Day Adventist members are oriented toward European family ideals and practice a form of protestant ethic. Although churches are very active, aspects of non-Christian beliefs continue to permeate the life of most Gusii. Afflicted by misfortune, many Gusii visit a diviner (omoragori) who may point to displeased spirits of the dead and prescribe sacrifice.

Diviners (abaragori), who are usually women, determine the cause of various misfortunes. A variety of healers also exist. Abanyamoriogi (herbalists) use a variety of mixtures of plants for medicines. Indigenous surgeons (ababari) set fractures and treat backaches and headaches through trepanation (needles). Professional sorcerers (abanyamosira) are normally hired to protect against witchcraft and to retaliate against witches. Omoriori, the witch smeller, ferrets out witchcraft articles buried in a house. Witches (omorogi) can be men or women but are usually the latter. They are believed to operate in groups who dig up recently buried corpses and use body parts as magical paraphernalia and eat the inner organs. Witches usually kill their victims through the use of poisons, parts of corpses, and people's exuvia (skin). Witchcraft among the Gusii is believed to be an acquired art handed down from parent to child.

6 MAJOR HOLIDAYS

Only the national holidays of Kenya are celebrated.

7 RITES OF PASSAGE

Mothers have the ultimate responsibility for the care and socialization of children, but they delegate a great deal of care taking and training to other children in the homestead. Mothers seldom show physical or verbal affection for children and fathers take very little part in child rearing. Gusii infants are raised to understand and behave according to the codes of shame and respect that apply to their relationships to persons in adjacent generations. Children cease sleeping in their mother's house when they are still very young. Grandparents play a supportive role and are supposed to inform grandchildren about proper behavior and sexual matters.

The most elaborate and socially important ceremonies are associated with initiation and marriage. Initiation involves clitoridectomy for girls and circumcision for boys. The ceremony is supposed to prepare children as social beings who know rules of shame (chinsoni) and respect (ogosika). Girls are initiated at the age of seven or eight, and boys a few years later. Initiations are gender-segregated, and female and male specialists perform the operations. Afterward, there is a period of seclusion for both genders.

The traditional Gusii wedding is no longer performed. It was an extremely elaborate ritual that lasted several days. The rituals emphasized the incorporation of the bride into the groom's lineage and the primacy of male fertility. Among wealthier people, it has been replaced by a wedding in a church or before an administration official.

Funerals take place at the deceased's homestead, and a large gathering is a sign of prestige. Women are buried beyond the yard on the left side of the house, and men are buried beyond the cattle pen on the right side of the house. Christian elements such as catechism-reading and hymn-singing are combined with the traditional practices of wailing, head-shaving, and animal sacrifices to the dead. The preferred person to dig the grave is the deceased's son's son. Before burial, the corpse is dissected in order to ascertain whether death was caused by witchcraft. After burial, the widow or widower is restricted to the homestead for a few weeks to two months, when ritual activities, including a sacrifice, are performed. One basic funeral theme is fear of the dead person's spirit. The deceased, enraged for having died, may blame the survivors and must therefore be placated with sacrifices.

8 INTERPERSONAL RELATIONS

Daily interactions follow strict rules of polite behavior, which can be translated as rules for avoiding sexual shame (chinsoni) and rules governing respect (ogosika). These rules are many and complicated. They regulate proper behavior between women and men, between generations, and between different kinds of kin. For example, although brothers and sisters and anyone within the same generation may joke with each other and talk about sexual matters, this is prohibited between adjacent generations. A father may not set foot in his son's house; a son-in-law has to avoid his mother-in-law; a daughter-in-law must not come too close to her father-in-law (she cannot even cook a meal for him). In everyday interaction, the expected behavior is one of respect and deference by young people toward older people as well as by women toward men. The Gusii are very decorous and careful about personal appearance and avoid showing themselves even partially naked. Similarly, bodily functions must not be mentioned or implied between adjacent generations or between women and men. Going to the lavatory is a laborious undertaking because one must avoid being seen on the way there.

A Gusii person distinguishes her or his own father and mother by specific terms: tata ("own father") and baba ("own mother"). Likewise, parents distinguish their children as momura one ("own son") and mosubati one ("own daughter"). However, all women and men of the same generation are considered "brothers" and "sisters." All women and men in one's parents' generation are called tatamoke ("small father") and makomoke (small mother). All members of the next generation are omwana one ("my child"), grandchildren's generation are omochokoro ("my grandchild"), and grandparents' generation are sokoro ("grandfather") and magokoro ("grandmother").

Hospitality and respectful treatment toward strangers is common, but the Gusii are also very reserved, polite, and in many ways suspicious about others' intentions. Although interpersonal conflicts are common, people should not show outwards signs of anger. Instead, aggression emerges as witchcraft accusations and attempts at sorcery toward enemies. The strong emphasis on outward peace and emotional control results in explosions of violent behavior under the influence of alcohol.

One always greets strangers met on the footpaths between the farms, as well as acquaintances of one's own generation, with a simple phrase similar to our "Hi, how are you?" ("Naki ogendererete"). However, if one visits a homestead or meets a relative, a more complete greeting ritual is necessary, which includes inquiring about each other's homes, children, and spouses. Unannounced visiting is not considered polite; a message should be delivered beforehand. A visitor enters a reception area, and a child comes and gives him or her a chair and takes anything he or she may be carrying. Neighbors or other visitors may come and engage in casual conversation, but the hosts usually do not appear until something to drink, usually tea, has been brought forward.

Body language is reserved and gesturing is kept to a minimum. Between persons of unequal status, such as young and old or man and woman, the person of lower status should not look directly into the other's eyes.

Interactions between unmarried youth were once strictly regulated, but young men and women today meet and socialize in many places outside the home. Premarital sex is common, and many girls end up as single mothers. Western ideas of love are common, and youth write love letters to each other and visit friends' houses where they dance and talk.

Today, intermarriage does occur between Gusii and people of other ethnic groups.

9 LIVING CONDITIONS

Before colonialism, the extended polygynous family was spatially divided into two components: the homestead (omochie), where married men and women and their unmarried daughters and uncircumcised sons lived, and the cattle camps (ebisarate) in the grazing areas where resident male warriors protected most of the cattle. The British abolished the cattle camps in 1913. In the late 19th century, most Gusii were settled in dispersed farmsteads, although in North Mugirango fortified villages were built for protection against Kipsigis raids. A homestead consisted of wives' houses, houses for circumcised boys, and possibly a small day hut for the husband. Married men did not have any separate houses for sleeping but alternated between their wives' houses. A compound had several elevated granaries for millet. The traditional Gusii house (enyomba) was a round, windowless structure made of a framework of thin branches with dried mud walls and a conical thatched roof. Today, the Gusii continue to live in dispersed homesteads in the middle of farm holdings. Modern houses are rectangular, with thatched or corrugated iron roofs, and cooking has been moved from the house to a separate kitchen structure.

The hilly nature of the district leads to serious soil erosion and makes road communication difficult, especially in the rainy season when many roads (only 10% of which are paved) become impassable.

Health facilities are inadequate, unevenly distributed and lacking in essential medicines. There are a number of hospitals—including the government-run facility in Kisii town and the Mission Hospital in Tabaka—but the bed occupancy rate is 160.3%. The major diseases in Kisii are malaria, anemia, pneumonia, meningitis, tuberculosis, measles, and gastroenteritis. The first AIDS cases in Kenya were recognized in 1984 (1987 in Kisii district), but it is now believed that 1 in every 18 adults is infected with HIV in all areas. Over 70% of AIDS cases are aged 20–49 years, the most economically active age group and also the best educated and skilled.

Infant mortality has been declining for several years and the acceptance of immunization programs is increasing, but a large proportion of children are believed stunted due to poor nutrition. Water is easily available from rivers, wells, springs, roof catchments and boreholes, although the only treated water supply is found in Kisii Municipality. In recent years Kisii highland has had new water treatment stations among others one at Birongo serving parts of Nyaribari central and Chache and also Kitutu Masaba.

Intensive farming in hilly regions has increased the rate of soil degradation and erosion, while the application of farm chemicals has polluted surface and groundwater sources. More than 90% of rural household energy needs come from wood, but the district is no longer self-reliant and other sources such as biogas are being encouraged.

[10] FAMILY LIFE

During the pre-colonial period, the exogamous, patrilineal clan (eamaate) provided the largest unit for cooperation. Clans were part of clan clusters with a bird or a mammal as totem but without any common organization. At the lineage level (riiga), patrilineal descent and marriage defined commonly recognized access to land and provided the rationale for corporate action. During the colonial period, indigenous political and social organization became conceptualized as a segmentary lineage system where units from the clan cluster, clans, and clan segments became defined according to a genealogical grid with an eponymous ancestor at the top.

Today, all land is registered in individual men's names, but the land market is still limited, and sales are uncommon. Men have ultimate rights to the management and use of land through inheritance. Women still have no birthrights to their parents' land. The vast majority of women can only obtain access to land through marriage. However, a few employed women buy land in other districts. Since the initial registration in the 1960s, land has not been surveyed, and much land is still registered in the name of dead fathers or grandfathers. A man usually transfers land to his wife and sons when the eldest son marries. Land is ideally divided equally between wives under the supervision and witness of local male elders. After division, the husband often retains a small plot (emonga) for personal use.

Marriage can be established through the payment of bride wealth, in the form of livestock and money, by the husband to the wife's family. This act establishes a socially sanctioned marriage through which a woman and a man become defined mothers and fathers. Residence is at the husband's home. Divorce is rare and entails the return of the bride wealth. At the death of a husband, a widow chooses a husband among the deceased's brothers. Until the 1960s, everyone got married as soon as possible after puberty. However, at the end of the 1960s, elopements started to increase in number, and the period between the inception of a cohabiting union and payment of bride wealth has become progressively more and more extended. In 1985 at least 75% of all new unions between women

and men were established without the payment of bride wealth. The lack of bride wealth means that a union is without social and legal sanction, and this has resulted in the formation of a socially and economically marginalized stratum of single mothers without access to land. This has been accompanied by a decline in the value of bride wealth payments for peasant women from about 13 adult Zebu cows in the first half of the 1950s to about three adult Zebu cows in 1985. Employed women, such as nurses and lawyers, fetch high bridewealth—15 to 45 Zebu cows (although their bride wealth is frequently paid in cash and European cows).

Households are based on nuclear or polygynous (multiple-wife) families. Each wife maintains her own household and there is little cooperation between co-wives. With the decline in polygyny, a domestic unit typically consists of a wife and husband and their unmarried children. It may also include the husband's mother, and for shorter periods, younger siblings of the wife. Until the birth of the first or second child, a wife and her mother-in-law may cook together and cooperate in farming. Married sons and their wives and children usually maintain their own households and resources.

[11] CLOTHING

Western-style clothing is always worn.

[12] FOOD

The staple vegetable food is corn, which is ground into flour. Corn flour is mixed into boiling water to form a thick dough-like paste (obokima) that is eaten with all meals. A meal usually consists of fried cabbage, tomatoes, and some potatoes. Depending on how well-off the family is, meat in the form of chicken or goat may be served. The meat is eaten with one's fingers, forming the obokima into a spoon, with which other food is scooped up and eaten. Other popular foods are sour milk, goat intestines, and millet porridge. Finger millet was the traditional staple before the introduction of corn and is considered an extremely nourishing food, which is necessary for pregnant women. It is a kind of "power food" that is believed to strengthen a person's physical and mental power and increase a man's sexual prowess.

[13] EDUCATION

Education is in high demand, and there are about 200 high schools, the majority of which are community-supported. There are also a number of private schools. With the introduction of free primary and free secondary education in Kenya, enrollment at these levels has shot up. Most well-to-do families, however, send their children to private schools, where the cost is prohibitive for many but quality of learning is high. Although primary and now secondary schools are free, there are other costs involved such as books, building fees, and so on. A majority of Gusii between 6 and 24 years old have attended school. By the 1980s, fewer than 50% of all Gusii children attended secondary school, but all attended primary school. Female enrollment in secondary school is at 45%, while adult literacy is 56% (high in relation to much of Kenya). However, fees for secondary school are in excess of KSH5000 per year. The government has only scrapped the tuition fees for public secondary schools, for most children primary school is the highest level of education open to them. Private schools have grown in number in the district. They often do better in the region.

¹⁴ CULTURAL HERITAGE

Older people know many traditional songs, and the favorite instrument is a lyre (obokhano). Most cultural rites and practices such as the naming of children, rites of passage, traditional marriage, dance, burial customs, and cultural institutions have been ignored with many adopting aspects of foreign cultures largely due to lack of understanding and knowledge. This unfortunate scenario has resulted in a generation that shuns Ekegusii and Abagusii culture.

¹⁵ WORK

The pre-colonial staple crop was finger millet, which was grown together with sorghum, beans, and sweet potatoes. Plant food was complemented by meat and milk from livestock and wild vegetables. At the end of the 19th century, the cultivation period was two years, with a fallow period of three to six years. By the 1920s maize had overtaken finger millet as a staple food crop and cash crop. Other important contemporary crops include cassava, pigeon peas, onions, bananas, potatoes, and tomatoes. In the 1930s, coffee was already being grown on a limited basis, and by the 1950s Gusiiland had become established as a producer of coffee and tea. Cultivation takes place with iron hoes and ox-drawn plows. Livestock was formerly more numerous, but farmers still keep cattle (both local Zebu and European stock), goats, sheep, and chickens. High population density has forced the Gusii to utilize every available space for agriculture, and families today are unable to produce enough food for subsistence needs. In addition to farming, many Gusii engage in outside employment, either locally or in the large urban centers.

In the late 19th century, women were primarily responsible for cultivation, food processing, cooking, brewing, fetching water and fuel, and housecleaning. Population density has led to pressure on land as almost all land in Kisii district is put to maximum agricultural use. Tea and coffee processing and soda bottling constitute Kisii area's manufacturing industry, but retail and wholesale businesses exist in market centers despite the lack of cooling facilities for preserving perishables. Men were concerned with warfare, house- and fence-building, clearing of new fields, and herding. Although women performed most of the cultivation, men participated to a much higher degree than is the case today. Young unmarried men and boys undertook herding in the cattle villages. Initiated, unmarried daughters assisted in cultivation. Since the early colonial period, the division of labor has gradually changed to the detriment of women. As men have withdrawn from cultivation, women are obliged to perform most of the same tasks as they did in the precolonial era in addition to most tasks involving men's cash crops.

The annual growth rate in paid employment is 3.5%, but this is barely keeping up with the current population growth rate. There are many societies such as savings and credit cooperatives (SACCOs) concentrated in Kisii Town according to members' occupations or primary cash crop as well. The informal sector is involved in repair, metal fabrication, furniture making, and the sale of secondhand clothes, while the soapstone that is found in the area of Tabaka provides a reasonable resource for the carving industry.

Income is largely unevenly distributed, with an average income per capita of KSH2000 (approximately US$30 in 2006), although most appear to earn KSH1000–1500. Many are severely impoverished.

¹⁶ SPORTS

Wrestling used to be a popular sport for men but has declined. Various Western athletic activities have been introduced. The most popular sport among boys is soccer, and most schools have a soccer field. Other sports include table tennis, netball, and cycling.

¹⁷ ENTERTAINMENT AND RECREATION

Traditional dancing and music were once popular, but there exist few outlets in the countryside today for such entertainments. Much recreation, especially among men, consists of drinking beer, either indigenous or bottled. Watching soccer on television and listening to the Gusii FM Radio station also form large part of modern Abagusii entertainment.

¹⁸ FOLK ART, CRAFTS, AND HOBBIES

In pre-colonial Gusiiland, a variety of goods were manufactured-iron tools, weapons, decorations, wooden implements, small baskets for porridge, and poisons. Pottery-making was limited, and most ware was imported from the Luo. The most notable in terms of technical complexity and product value among the Gusii industries was the smelting of locally obtained ore and the manufacture of iron implements. Blacksmiths did not form a special caste as is so often the case in African societies. Smithing was a remunerative industry reserved for men, and blacksmiths became wealthy and influential.

The Gusii soapstone carvings have received international distribution and fame. The stone is mined and carved in Tabaka, South Mugirango, where several families specialize in this art. The craft is bringing a sizable income to the area through the tourist trade. In 2007 the master carvers and classic soapstone carvers of Kisii Tabaka were awarded an exclusive license to produce hand carved stone caricatures of characters from "The Simpsons" cartoon, via 20th Century Fox and Craft Village UK.

¹⁹ SOCIAL PROBLEMS

Alcoholism and violence toward women are the most severe social problems. Traditionally, only older people were allowed to drink large amounts of indigenous beer (amarua). Today, social control over drinking has broken down, and traditional beer and home-distilled spirits are served in huts all over the district. Probably close to 50% of the young adult and middle age population are regular drinkers, with a larger proportion of men than women. This heavy drinking leads to violence, neglect of children, and poverty. The Gusii also have high murder rates compared to the rest of Kenya. Although violence toward women (such as rape and regular beating) has been part of Gusii culture since earlier in this century, alcohol-influenced behavior is probably involved in its increase.

Until the ravages of AIDS hit western Kenya, the Gusii also had one of the fastest growing populations in the world. The effect of all this, not surprisingly, has been far from pacific. Kisii town is now Kenya's second most violent place, after Nairobi; instances of mob justice in the form of lynching suspected witches, for example, surged in the 1990s, and the unemployment rate remains one of the country's highest. Witchcraft and perception of witchcraft has also been a major problem among the Gusii lately. In a recent incident about 15 people suspected to be sorcerers were lynched.

The Gusii have long fled from stronger and more aggressive enemies such as the Luo and Maasai. Yet somehow, despite centuries of having been scattered about western Kenya through force of arms, their identity and their social cohesion has remained intact. There have been many disputes with other ethnic groups over the years. Land is the main reason tensions have existed between various ethnic groups, such as the Maasai, Kalenjin and Kipsigis. Shifting boundaries between ethnic groups have created tensions.

20 GENDER ISSUES

The exploitation of women in Gusii society is a serious human-rights problem. According to customary law, which is usually followed in the countryside, women cannot inherit or own land, cattle, or other resources. This makes them completely dependent on men for survival and attainment of any future security. Until a woman has adult sons, she is under the authority of her husband and has to ask permission from him to leave the homestead.

Women do most of the work in feeding their families, and many husbands spend time drinking and visiting friends while their wives work in the fields and take care of the household. Although not all husbands beat their wives, such behavior is considered acceptable and is not uncommon.

Finally, the Gusii practice female genital mutilation, which, although prohibited by national law, still flourishes. At the age of 8 or 9, girls are brought together by their mothers in August for collective circumcision ceremonies. The practice is almost universal among the Kisii. However, according to one source there has been a shift from "traditional" to "sanitized" methods, whereby parents are now paying large sums of money to medical professionals to perform the rite on their daughters.

21 BIBLIOGRAPHY

Fedders, Andrew and Cynthia Salvadori. *Peoples and Cultures of Kenya*. Nairobi: Transafrica, 1979.

Hakansson, N. Thomas. "Bridewealth, Women and Land: Social Change among the Gusii of Kenya." *Uppsala Studies in Cultural Anthropology* 9. Stockholm: Almkvist and Wiksell International, 1988.

Hakansson, N. Thomas. "Detachable Women: Gender and Kinship in Processes of Socioeconomic Change among the Gusii of Kenya." *American Ethnologist* 21 (1994): 516–538.

LeVine, Robert A., et al. *Child Care and Culture: Lessons from Africa*. Cambridge: Cambridge University Press, 1994.

LeVine, Robert A. and Barbara B. LeVine. *Nyansongo: A Gusii Community in Kenya*. Six Cultures Series, Vol. II. New York: John Wiley and Sons, 1966.

LeVine, Sarah. *Mothers and Wives: Gusii Women of East Africa*. Chicago: University of Chicago Press, 1979.

—revised by M. Njoroge

HAUSA

PRONUNCIATION: HOW-suh
LOCATION: Hausaland in West Africa (northwestern Nigeria and in adjoining southern Niger)
POPULATION: 22 million
LANGUAGE: Hausa, Arabic, French or English
RELIGION: Islam, small native cults
RELATED ARTICLES: Vol. 1: Nigerians; Nigeriens

1 INTRODUCTION

The Hausa are the largest ethnic group of West Africa, with a population of some 22 million, with another wider regional 15 million bilingual speakers of Hausa from northern Cameroon to northern Ivory Coast. Because of their wide geographical distribution and intermarriage and interaction with different peoples, the Hausa are a heterogeneous people, with a variety of cultural and physical features as well as diverse histories.

The Hausa generally recognize a common origin. They acknowledge a common mythical ancestor (Bayajidda) who, according to tradition, migrated from Baghdad in the 9th or 10th century ad. Along the way, he stopped at the kingdom of Bornu (now in northeast Nigeria) and married the daughter of the king, but was forced to leave her behind. He then fled west and helped the king of Daura slay a snake that was depriving his people of water, and he was given the Queen of Daura in marriage as a reward. Bayajidda succeeded as the king of Daura, and his son, Bawo, who founded the city of Biram, had six sons who became the rulers of other Hausa city-states. Collectively, these are known as the *Hausa bakwai* ("Hausa seven") and include Kano, Katsina, Rano, Zazzau, Daura, Gobir, and Biram. Bayajidda is said to have borne another son with a concubine, and this son fathered seven other children. Each established city-states far away from Daura, which became known as the *banza bakwai* ("bastard seven"). They include Kebbi, Zamfara, Gwari, Jukun, Yoruba, Nupe, and Yauri. Thus, by the 15th century, a number of relatively independent city states had emerged, which competed with each other for control of trans-Saharan trade, slaves, and natural resources. From that point, the various city-states trace their history independently of each other, each with its lists of kings who have ruled since that time.

During the 19th century, Hausaland was unified during an Islamic holy war (*jihad*) led by a Fulani scholar, Usman d'an Fodio. (Islam had arrived in the area by the 14th century.) The *jihad* sought to correct the impure ways of the Hausa Muslims and convert those who were still "pagans." All of the land of the Hausa (*k'asar Hausa*) and some other territories were united under the rule of d'an Fodio, and later his sons. They directed political and religious affairs in the land from the capital at Sokoto until the British arrived and colonized the area in about 1900. Even during colonial times, the city-states and their leaders maintained some authority and autonomy, and many Hausa traditions and customs have been preserved until recently.

Among the Hausa origin myths, the snake, water, and western migration themes have been alleged to link the Hausa with ancient Meroe on the Nile. Hausa communities outside of Hausaland are commonly known as zongos. Hausa communities in the 15th and 16th centuries found themselves in a regional power vacuum with the decline of Bornu-Kanem to the east, Songhai to the west, and being restrained by the northerly Berbers and the long-standing southward migration of the Sahara. The Kano Chronicle provides a significant historical record to the Hausa and Fulani people. While there are important aspects of collaboration between these two groups, generally one can say that the 18th century Fulani jihads put the Hausa in a relatively subordinate position.

2 LOCATION AND HOMELAND

Hausa peoples are concentrated mainly in north central Nigeria and in adjoining southern Niger, an area that is predominantly semi-arid grassland or savanna. Hausaland consists of a number of large cities surrounded by rural agrarian communities that grow mainly millet, maize, and sorghum during the region's 4- to 5-month rainy season. The cities are among the greatest commercial centers of sub-Saharan Africa. Hausa peoples are found dispersed throughout West Africa, Cameroon, Togo, Chad, Benin, Burkina Fasso, and Ghana. Some are found as far away as Sudan and Congo Republic. They have settled permanently or temporarily in these locations as traders.

3 LANGUAGE

Hausa is the most widely spoken language in West Africa. It is spoken by an estimated 22 million native speakers, plus an additional 17 million second-language speakers. The Hausa language, from which these people take their name, belongs to the Chadic sub-branch of Afro-Asiatic language family of Africa, which has strong affinities to Arabic in the north. Perhaps one-fourth of the Hausa vocabulary derives from Arabic, and more recently terms from Fulfulde (see **Fulani**) and Kanuri languages, as well as English, have been incorporated. Many Hausa can read and write Arabic, and many can also speak either French or English. There are five main dialects of Hausa in northern Nigeria, in addition to variations on the language in the Hausa diaspora in such places as Ghana, Benin, and Togo.

4 FOLKLORE

The Hausa have a rich system of folklore, some of which has been influenced by the Islamic religion. The system includes stories (tatsunya)—of animals, men and women, young men and maidens, and heroes and villains—which usually have a moral. Many include proverbs and riddles to help convey a message to the audience, which is often comprised of children. The stories sometimes involve a trickster who appears as a spider and demonstrates both cunning and greed. Hausa folklore also includes exaggerated stories or traditions (labaru) of important figures or events in the Hausa past (such as battles or notable rulers). In these, folklore merges with history. The Hausa origin myth includes Bayajidda the serpent slayer who was rewarded by marriage the Queen of Daura, who, in turn, had the founding sons of the Hausa's seven original towns.

5 RELIGION

Since the penetration of Islam into Hausaland in the mid-14th century, most Hausa have become extremely devoted to the Islamic faith. Muslims believe in Allah and Mohammed as his prophet. They pray five times each day, read the holy scriptures, fast during the month of Ramadan, give alms to the poor, and

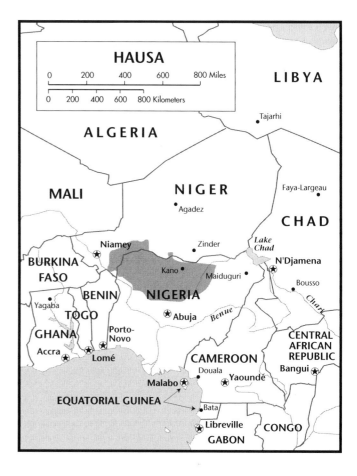

aspire to make the pilgrimage (hajj) to the Muslim holyland in Mecca. The religion affects nearly all aspects of Hausa behavior, including their dress, art, house types, rites of passage, and laws. In the rural areas, there are still a few communities of peoples who do not follow Islam. These people are referred to as *Maguzawa*, and they worship nature spirits known as *bori* or *iskoki*.

The Hausa are Sunni Muslims, but are also influenced by the Muslim brotherhoods that are widespread across the Sahel as well as other syncretic African beliefs and practices. Some Hausa, known as maguzawa, tend more toward non-Islamic African beliefs. Bori cults are built around spirit possession and exorcism and are especially attractive to women and marginalized peoples.

6 MAJOR HOLIDAYS

The Hausa annual cycle follows the Islamic calendar. Feast days (Id) take place following the month of fasting (Ramadan), following the pilgrimage to Mecca (hajj), and on the birthday of the prophet Mohammed. At this time, families usually sacrifice a ram in thanksgiving, celebrate with their relatives and friends, and give each other gifts. Hausa also observe the national holidays of Nigeria.

7 RITES OF PASSAGE

About a week after a child is born, it achieves personhood when it is given a name during an Islamic naming ceremony. Boys are usually circumcised at around the age of seven, although there is no rite of passage associated with this. At around this same age, both boys and girls study the Qu'ranic scripture, which they must learn by the age of 13.

In their mid- to late teens, young men and women may become betrothed in marriage. The marriage ceremony may take place over several days, first among the bride and her family and friends, when she is prepared for marriage. Male representatives of the bride's and the groom's families contract the marriage according to Islamic law, usually at the mosque. Shortly thereafter, the couple will be brought together, often with a small celebration.

Upon the death of an individual, Islamic principles for burial are always followed. The deceased is washed, prepared for burial, wrapped in a shroud, and buried facing eastward toward the Islamic holyland of Mecca. Prayers are recited, and family members receive condolences. Wives mourn their deceased husbands for about three months.

8 INTERPERSONAL RELATIONS

In contrast to some other Nigerian peoples, Hausa tend to be quiet and reserved. This may be due to the influence of Islam and their close association with Fulani (Fulbe) peoples, who are known for extreme reserve and shyness. Thus, when Hausa interact with other, unrelated peoples or strangers, they tend to exercise restraint and not show emotions. Likewise, when a Hausa interacts with certain kin (such as senior siblings, in-laws, or one's spouse or parents), reserve and respect must be shown. This may entail, for instance, not uttering the name of one's spouse or parents or talking quietly. In-laws or co-wives may be avoided altogether. To the Hausa, this is a demonstration of respect. By contrast, relaxed, lively, affectionate, and at times playful relations exist among certain other kin such as junior siblings, grandparents, and grandchildren, or among cousins.

There are no formal age groups among the Hausa. From an early age, however, children develop friendships with their neighbors that may last a lifetime. In some towns, youths may form associations whose members play or dance together until they marry.

9 LIVING CONDITIONS

Hausa reside in both rural and urban areas. In the rural villages, they usually live in large households (gidaje), which are inhabited by a man, his wives, his sons, and their wives and children.

In large cities, such as Kano or Katsina, most Hausa live in the old sections of town or in newer quarters built for civil servants. Many non-Hausa (particularly Yoruba, Igbo, Nupe, and Kanuri) have moved to these cities and occupy what are called "stranger quarters" (sabon gari). Hausa housing ranges from traditional extended family compounds (inhabited by a male, his wives, and his sons and their families) to relatively modern, single-family houses in new sections of cities or government residential areas.

In rural areas, most people get around on foot or bicycle, but they use public transport (buses, taxis) when traveling long distances. Hausa cities have public transportation, and many residents have cars.

Modern health care is available throughout Hausaland, except in remote villages. People can seek medical help in clinics and hospitals, although there is sometimes a shortage of medicine. Some people also consult traditional healers who administer local remedies (magani), many of which prove very effective.

Northern Nigeria is relatively underdeveloped; the Hausa are facing various difficulties of finding adequate employment in the modern sectors of the economy that require new educational and technical skills.

10 FAMILY LIFE

As throughout Africa, family life is extremely important among the Hausa. Ties of kinship are elaborate, particularly through the male line, and relatives cooperate in economic activities such as farming and trading in the rural areas or in business activities in the urban areas. Kin aspire to live near each other to socialize and provide mutual support. They also contract marriages for junior members, who ideally are related (i.e., cousins). Under Islamic law, a man may marry up to four wives. Principles of kinship and descent are most elaborate among the aristocratic Hausa of Fulani descent, who trace their ancestry back to the time of the jihad in the 19th century. These people are known as Hausa-Fulani.

Most married Hausa women observe seclusion; they stay in the home and only go out for ceremonies or to seek medical treatment. A few can go out to their place of work. When they do go out, they should be modestly dressed (i.e., with a veil) and are often escorted by children.

Hausa generally do not recognize themselves politically as one unit but rather identify with the individual Hausa "states" that have persisted from earlier times. Each state has an emir (Sarki) who is flanked by a council (majalisa). States as territories are divided into districts, which are administered by government and local officials. Lastly, village chiefs and ward heads control affairs of villages or sections of cities.

11 CLOTHING

Hausa men are recognizable throughout West Africa by their elaborate dress. Many wear large, flowing gowns (gare, babban gida) with elaborate embroidery around the neck and sometimes down the front. They also wear colorful embroidered caps (huluna). Hausa women, like women of neighboring groups, wear a wrapper made of colorful cloth with a matching blouse, head tie, and shawl. Some of these cloths are extremely expensive, and women collect them, together with gold jewelry, as a sign of status and wealth.

12 FOOD

The Hausa eat a variety of foods that derive from their predominately agricultural livelihood. Their staples consist of grains, namely sorghum and millet, together with maize, which are ground into flour for a variety of foods. Rice may also be used as a staple. Breakfast often consists of porridge and sometimes cakes made of fried beans (kosai) or wheat flour (funkaso). Lunch and dinner usually include a heavy porridge (tuwo) that is served with a soup or stew (miya), and dinner is the main meal. Most soups are made with a base of ground or chopped tomatoes, onions, and peppers. To this are added other vegetables such as spinach, pumpkin, okra, and other leafy vegetables, and spices that are found locally. Small quantities of meat are used, and beans, peanuts, and milk may also add protein to Hausa diets. Milk products are obtained from the pastoral Fulani (Fulbe) peoples. Nowadays, as many Hausa women engage

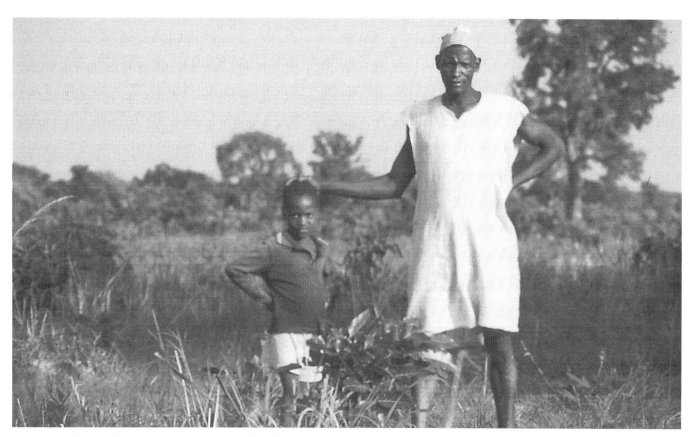

A Hausa father and son in their work clothes. Many Hausa men have more than one occupation. In rural areas, they farm and also engage in trade or craftsmanship. In the towns and cities, they may have formal jobs that they may supplement with trade. (Jason Laure)

in the trade of cooked foodstuff, many families or individuals purchase snacks or meals outside the household as needed.

¹³ EDUCATION

From birth, Hausa children are socialized in the household by their relatives, especially women, through imitation, scolding, reciting sayings and proverbs, and storytelling. From about the age of six, they attend Islamic (Qu'ranic) school and learn to recite the scriptures and learn about the practices, teachings, and morals of Islam. By the time they reach adulthood, many achieve high levels of Islamic scholarship.

Western education was established in Hausaland during the early 20th century. Children began attending schools built by the British Colonial government, first at the primary level, and then at the secondary level. One of the first and finest universities in all of Africa, Ahmadu Bello University, was founded in Zaria in the 1940s. Since Nigeria received its independence in 1960, many schools and universities have been built by the Nigerian government, and a majority of Hausa children, especially in urban areas, are now able to attend school, at least to the primary level.

¹⁴ CULTURAL HERITAGE

Culture (al-ada) is one of several features that distinguish a Hausa person from members of other ethnic groups, in addition to his origin (asali), his adherence to the Islamic religion (addini), and his mastering the Hausa tongue (yare). Hausa culture includes the Hausa mode of dressing, particularly the

big gown and cap, along with several other customs, such as dancing and marriage ceremonies. The Hausa also identify closely with their music, particularly that of the praise-singers who sing about community histories, leaders, and prominent individuals. Hausa culture also includes individual character, known as mutumci or hali. In their personal dealings, Hausa seek to strike a balance between being assertive and being thrifty, which benefits them in their business dealings, and having a strong sense of shame (kunya) and respect among strangers as well as kin.

¹⁵ WORK

Hausa society has a strong division of labor according to age and sex. The predominant activities are trade, especially in the towns, and agriculture in the rural areas. Hausa women, although they are usually secluded (except at harvest time in the rural areas), have occupational specialties, including processing, cooking, and selling foods. They also sell cloth weavings, pots, medicines, vegetable oils, and other small items. They do so with the help of their children or servants, who go to other houses or the market on their behalf.

Male children help their fathers with farming; young girls help their mothers around the house, care for the younger children, or go out and trade. Recently, some of the women's trading activities have declined as children have been enrolling in school during the hours their mothers need help.

Many Hausa men have more than one occupation. In rural areas, they farm and also engage in trade or craftsmanship.

They grow food crops and cash crops such as cotton and peanuts. In the towns and cities, they may have formal jobs, such as teaching or government work, which they may supplement with trade. Some individuals are full-time traders with shops or market stalls, while others engage in long-distance trade of cattle and skins to other parts of Nigeria or to neighboring countries. Many Hausa are full-time Islamic scholars.

16 SPORTS

Both wrestling (kokawa) and boxing (dambe) have been popular sports among the Hausa. Wrestlers and boxers form distinct groups in Hausa communities, until recently being defined by distinctive dress and hairstyles. Children at a young age become apprentices of more experienced individuals. Eventually they participate in the competitions. For entertainment or on religious holidays, people are summoned to arenas or markets for the matches. Music, particularly drumming, accompanies the competition. Magical potions or charms (magani) are used to enhance the performance. Both boxers and wrestlers wear special loincloths during the competitions, and the boxers also wear special bracelets and a cloth wrapped around one hand, which serves as a boxing glove. During a match, a wrestler will choose an opponent and the two will wrestle until one is thrown to the ground. Boxers fight until one is either brought to his knees or falls flat on the ground.

More recently, other sports have been introduced into Hausaland. In particular, horseracing and polo are found among the nobility. Soccer is popular among practically everyone, and it is now considered Nigeria's national sport.

17 ENTERTAINMENT AND RECREATION

From a young age, Hausa children participate in dances, particularly when they meet in the market. Storytelling, local dramas, and musical performances have also been common forms of entertainment until recently. Musicians perform at various festivities such as weddings, naming ceremonies, and parties, as well as during Islamic holidays. Today, Western forms of entertainment are popular. Western music, including rap and reggae, are common, as are television programs imported from the United States and England. Nowadays, one often finds stereos, televisions, and VCRs in the homes of Hausa people, airing a mix of traditional Hausa entertainment and that of the West.

18 FOLK ART, CRAFTS, AND HOBBIES

Among the Hausa, music and art form an important part of culture and everyday life. Work songs often accompany activities in the rural areas or in the markets. Court music (drumming, horns, flutes) and praise-singing are found among those in towns, especially among the nobility. Some of the Hausa praise-singers (marok'i) have achieved national prominence.

Hausa are well-known for their craftsmanship. There are tanners, leatherworkers, weavers, carvers and sculptors, ironworkers and blacksmiths, silver workers, potters, dyers, tailors, embroiderers, and so on. Their wares (such as jewelry, hats, cloth, and utensils) are sold in the markets throughout Hausaland and in much of West Africa. North African, Islamic forms and motifs have influenced much of Hausa art, design, and architecture, which includes Arabic characters and geometric designs.

19 SOCIAL PROBLEMS

Problems and hardships among the Hausa today are caused by the physical and political environment in which they live. Geographically, most of Hausaland is in the northern savanna and Sahel zones near the Sahara desert, which are prone to drought. Crops fail if rainfall is not timely or sufficient. Most people do not have the means to purchase the necessary foodstuffs and may suffer during harsh weather. Some must migrate to the cities in search of work.

Since gaining its independence, Nigeria has also witnessed a host of problems associated with managing the new country and its government. Political instability, military dictatorships, corruption, and lack of unity among Nigeria's more than 200 ethnic groups are among the many problems that have plagued the country. Even though Nigeria is one of the world's largest suppliers of oil, much of the wealth has not been properly invested in economic and social development.

Consequently, among the Hausa, as among all other peoples of Nigeria, poverty is widespread. Its manifestations include poor nutrition and diet, illness and insufficient health care, inadequate educational opportunities, and a relatively low standard of living in contrast with much of the Western world. Nevertheless, the richness of Hausa culture and society offsets many of these hardships, and there is reason for optimism that living conditions will gradually improve as the people of Nigeria gain more experience as citizens of the new nation.

In short, the central problems in Hausaland remain practical issues of employment and social services, while the main cultural and religious issues rest in the torque between conservative Islamic values in a modern federal African nation.

20 GENDER ISSUES

In all Islamic societies the position of women has certain specific cultural and religious expectations requiring modesty and domestic functions. In this context the stresses of modern life have caused both changes and threats to this long established cultural order. In northern Nigeria in particular the tension between a secular federal state and local provincial autonomy has been very contentious at times. Among the issues was the case of Amina Lawal who was charged with adultery and was sentenced to death by stoning according to a harsh interpretation of Islamic law. This was never carried out but was a difficult issue of the federal government along with parallel cultural issues regarding a Nigerian beauty contest. On the other hand the legendary Hausa Queen Aminatu is noted for her military prowess and is much celebrated, but even her role is disputed by some theologians and historians.

21 BIBLIOGRAPHY

Coles, Catherine, and Beverly Mack. *Hausa Women in the Twentieth Century*. Madison: University of Wisconsin Press, 1991.

Koslow, Philip. *Hausaland: The Fortress Kingdoms. Kingdoms of Africa*. New York: Chelsea House Publishers, 1995.

Smith, Mary. *Baba of Karo: A Woman of the Muslim Hausa*. New Haven, CT: Yale University Press, 1981.

Smith, M. G. "The Hausa of Northern Nigeria." In Paul Gibbs, ed., *Peoples of Africa*. New York: Holt, Rinehart, and Winston, 1965.

—revised by R. Lobban

HUTU

PRONUNCIATION: HOO-too
LOCATION: Rwanda, Burundi
POPULATION: Approximately 16–17 million
LANGUAGE: Kinyarwanda, Kirundi, Swahili, French, English
   Christianity with aspects of traditional belief, spirit cults
RELATED ARTICLES: Vol. 1: Burundians; Rwandans

¹ INTRODUCTION

The term *Hutu* refers to the majority of people who live in the African countries of Rwanda and Burundi. The Hutu people share cultural traditions with the other inhabitants of these countries, the Tutsi and the Twa, and all three groups speak the same Bantu language. The contemporary social situation in Rwanda and Burundi is the result of a complex history that brought these diverse peoples together.

Scholars, as well as the people of the two countries themselves, disagree over the precise meaning of the label *Hutu*. In practice, there are two senses of the name. First, *Hutu* may be used to refer to ethnic origins. In this sense, it refers to people of Bantu origins who share a common history as farmers. In its second sense, it indicates social status, referring to the fact that the Hutu traditionally belonged to a low-ranking social category, similar to a caste, and were subordinate to the higher-ranking Tutsi, who formed an aristocracy. Lowest in the status system were the Twa, a group of hunters and foragers known more commonly as "pygmies."

Like the two different meanings of the name *Hutu*, there are two prevalent interpretations of the group's history, both of which have assumed mythic proportions and are often used for political purposes.

The first myth of history has the effect of justifying Hutu hatred of the Tutsi. It overemphasizes the ethnic divisions of the past. It suggests that the Tutsi are a distinct race of conquerors who have enslaved the Hutu and Twa for hundreds of years, making use of the widely accepted belief that the Hutu and the Twa were the first settlers of the region, only later to be followed by the Tutsi in the 15th or 16th century.

The second mythical version of history has been used to deny the legitimacy of Hutu claims to political representation. It depicts the inhabitants of Rwanda and Burundi as a single ethnic group whose divisions have arisen solely as a result of economics and colonialism. This version de-emphasizes the physical differences among these groups, claiming they are too ambiguous to matter. The peaceful and cooperative quality of Hutu-Tutsi relations are overemphasized, and any contemporary ethnic problems are blamed on foreigners. This myth, at its most extreme, rules out any mention whatsoever of ethnicity.

Both these versions of history are oversimplifications, but they are made believable because they have some evidence in their support. For example, the first version's emphasis on ethnic divisions is supported by studies that have found the Tutsi to be on average four to five inches taller than the Hutu. This ethnic emphasis is also supported by the fact that many Tutsi can also drink large quantities of milk without suffering the indigestion associated with the genetic condition called lactose intolerance, a finding in accord with the view that the

Tutsi were at one time nomadic cattle herders related to other tall and lean people of East Africa such as the Maasai and the Nuer.

In spite of such support, the mythical features of these contrasting historical accounts can be countered by considering the historical record, whose details are much more complex and ambiguous than the myths allow. For example, the *mwami,* the Tutsi king who ruled over Rwanda-Burundi, enjoyed some popular support from both the Hutu and the Twa. Furthermore, even in central Rwanda, where the king was strongest and most identified with Tutsi control, royal power was only solidified in the 19th century. In fact, Hutu regions of northern Rwanda remained free of his rule until the 20th century. As for the situation in Burundi, Hutu leaders were able to rise to positions of power and influence within the king's court while some whose roots were Tutsi were quite poor.

The history of the Hutu and the Tutsi is complicated still further by the fact that social relations in Rwanda and Burundi were modified by European rule. Both countries were occupied by foreign powers in the period from 1890 to 1962. Germany clearly favored the Tutsi elites during their period of military occupation, from 1890 until the end of World War I. The Belgian administrators who followed the Germans also favored the Tutsi initially, but their position became more ambiguous over time. By the 1950s, Belgian administrators and missionaries were actively encouraging Hutu leaders in their attempts to gain political control.

Rwanda and Burundi took dramatically different paths to independence in 1962. During the local run-off elections in Rwanda in 1959, open rebellion against the Tutsi broke out. Ultimately, this led Hutu leaders to abolish the kingship and take power by force. In Burundi, there was a more peaceful transition to independence, with the *mwami* initially acting as an intermediary between Tutsi and Hutu sides. This peace, however, was fragile, and Hutu efforts to gain power by force were crushed, culminating in a ruthless campaign of repression against them in 1972.

The end result of the independence process was that opposite sides controlled the two countries. In Rwanda, the Hutu established a period of rule that was to last until 1994. In Burundi, the state came to be controlled by a branch of the Tutsi. More recently, there have been attempts to reconcile the two groups, but conflicts over political power continue.

² LOCATION AND HOMELAND

Rwanda and Burundi are mountainous countries in east-central Africa. They share a common border, with Rwanda located to the north. Rwanda's northern border is with Uganda. Both countries are bounded by the Democratic Republic of the Congo (formerly Zaire) to the west and Tanzania to the east. Rwanda and Burundi are both quite small. Their total area combined is approximately 54,100 sq km (20,900 sq mi), or roughly the combined size of Maryland and New Jersey.

Population densities in the region are among the highest in Africa and have been high for many years. Burundi had an estimated 312 people per square kilometer of land in 2008, and Rwanda an estimated 407 people per square kilometer of land. The combined total population of Rwanda and Burundi was approximately 19 million in 2008. Crises in Burundi and Rwanda have produced large numbers of refugees, including thousands of Tutsis fleeing Rwanda in the early 1960s and thousands of

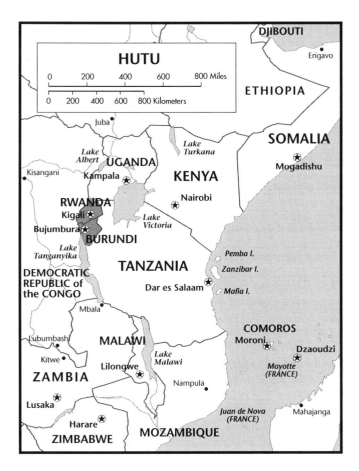

HUTU

0   200   400   600   800 Miles

0   200   400   600   800 Kilometers

Hutu fleeing Burundi in 1972, as well as the refugees generated in Rwanda in 1994. Many people of both groups have lived in refugee camps in neighboring countries, although many Tutsi have returned to Rwanda since 1994. The traditional ethnic distribution figures are usually given as 85% Hutu, 14% Tutsi, and 1% Twa. However, given the history of conflict in the region, ethnic census data should be treated with caution.

³ LANGUAGE

The Hutu, Tutsi, and Twa speak variants of a language called *Kinyarwanda* in Rwanda and *Kirundi* in Burundi These are best thought of as two dialects of a single language that falls into the Central Bantu family. They are mutually intelligible but vary in terms of pronunciation and vocabulary.

Because of the long association of Rwanda and Burundi with Belgium, and the use of French in schools, many Rwandese and Burundians speak French and have French first names. Swahili is also spoken in the region, especially along the border with Tanzania and among those who have been refugees there. English is increasingly important in Rwanda.

Personal names seem lengthy, but their meanings make them simple to native speakers. For example, the name *Mutarambirwa* means "the one who never gets tired." Individual names can also be derived from well-known events or borrowed from praise poetry.

Traditionally, the ability to express oneself well orally was highly valued. Metaphorical references to cattle and crop cultivation were commonly used in everyday speech. In re-

gions where social relations were most caste-like, with farmers expected to act deferentially toward aristocrats, status was marked in language by polite forms of address. For example, *murakoze* is the respectful form for "thank you" while *urakoze* is the informal form.

⁴ FOLKLORE

Verbal arts of the region include praise poetry, proverbs, folktales, riddles, and myths. Traditionally, these were vibrant parts of everyday life. For example, riddle-like descriptions could be worked into everyday speech: a poor person wearing a pair of ragged shoes held roughly together with a safety pin might evoke empathy by describing his shoes as a "poor broken-down old man with a spear stuck in his body." Similarly, proverbs were used in defense of an opinion or to provide a moral lesson.

Tales of the legendary figure Samadari were popular among Hutu and lower-ranking Tutsi. Samadari is a kind of trickster who was free to violate the ordinary rules of social conduct. He could openly mock the rich and the powerful and heap scorn upon wealthy cattle owners.

⁵ RELIGION

Today most Hutu are Christians, particularly Catholics, with a small percentage of Muslims. Nonetheless, African religion continues to be important for the majority as well. In the Hutus' traditional religion, the creator is envisioned as having many human characteristics. The word for creator, *Imaana*, signifies both God and God's power to create and ensure prosperity and fertility. *Imaana* was essentially benevolent but somewhat removed from the affairs of ordinary people. Perhaps because of his remoteness, elaborate tales of the creation of the universe are lacking.

Non-Christian religious expression is not uniform but one unifying factor is belief in the power of the *abazima*. These are the spirits of the dead, particularly ancestral spirits. They may bring misfortune to those who do not respect them but they may also provide spiritual aid. Offerings are made to *abazima*, and diviners may be consulted to interpret their wishes. Two of the most important spirits among the Hutu are Ryangombe and Nyabingi. In northern Rwanda, Nyabingi is associated with fertility. During ritual occasions individuals may feel they are possessed by the spirit of Ryangombe.

One mythical account of the origin of the Burundians and Rwandans—promoted by the Tutsi elites and rejected by most contemporary Hutu—legitimizes the rule of the Tutsi over the Hutu and Twa by cloaking it in the authority of religious tradition. According to this account, the first inhabitants of the region were said to be the three sons of a king: Little Twa, Little Hutu, and Little Tutsi. The story tells how the king appointed Little Tutsi ("Gatutsi") to rule over the other two as a result of their personal failings.

A variety of distinct spirit cults exist, with separate forms of worship, some including elaborate initiation procedures.

⁶ MAJOR HOLIDAYS

Holidays observed by the Hutu include the Rwandan and Burundian independence days, May Day, New Year's Day, and the major Christian holidays. Royal rituals—now no longer observed—were elaborate national affairs that included specially trained dancers and the use of giant sacred drums. Rwanda has several new holidays. These include February 1 (National Heroes Day); April 7 (Genocide Memorial Day); July 4 (National Liberation Day); and October 1 (Patriotism Day).

7 RITES OF PASSAGE

An individual's first rite of passage is the naming ceremony, which takes place seven days after a child's birth. For the first week, both the baby and the mother are secluded inside the house, but on the seventh day the child is brought out for the first time. Food and drink are prepared, and children from the area are invited to participate in the ceremony.

Marriages are legitimated by the transfer of bridewealth, a kind of compensation for the loss of the woman's labor paid by the family of the groom to the family of the bride. Bridewealth is paid in cattle, goats, and homebrewed beer. The traditional marriage ceremony itself is complex, and the details vary from region to region. Commonly, the bride's body is purified by being smeared with herbs and milk.

Upon marriage, the bride may be secluded at the father-in-law's house for several days. Her transition to full marital status is signified by the end of this seclusion. Except for marriage, there is no formal initiation process to mark the transition from adolescence to adulthood.

Death is marked by prayers, speeches, purification rituals, and restrictions on many everyday activities. Close family members are expected to refrain from sexual relations and to avoid working in the fields during the period of mourning. At the end of the mourning period, the family hosts a ritual feast.

8 INTERPERSONAL RELATIONS

Differences in social status, traditionally conveyed by posture, body language, and speaking style, figured prominently in social relations among the Hutu. Individuals of lower status were expected to show deference to those superior in rank by kneeling. However, a certain casualness of bearing and emotional expression was permissible among lower-status Hutu when they were among equals. Women were expected to defer to men, and idle conversation was frowned upon.

Customarily, relationships in Rwanda and Burundi were regulated by the movement of cattle. In a system similar to sharecropping, patrons (*bashebuja*), who were frequently Tutsi, lent cattle to clients, who were often Hutu. In exchange, the client (*bagerewa* or *bagaragu*) owed allegiance to the patron. Such relationships were called *buhake* in Rwanda and *bugabire* in Burundi.

The Hutu have separate greetings for morning, afternoon, and evening. The morning greeting—"*Warumutse ho?*"— is answered "*Waaramutse.*" The afternoon greeting—"*Wiiriwe ho?*"— is met by the return, "*Wiiriwe.*" Men take leave at the end of a visit by directly offering thanks for the hospitality provided them. Women are often expected to be less direct in ending a visit, perhaps making excuses about household obligations.

Traditionally, romantic relationships between young men and women were expected to occur within the same caste group. Socializing through such group activities as dances and church events was common, as opposed to individual dating. Today, Western-style dating is practiced in urban areas among some of the elite.

Anita Nizigama, a Tutsi, poses for a portrait with her husband, a Hutu, and their child. Nizigama's mother initially protested the marriage. In 1994, Hutus murdered about one million Tutsis. (Melanie Stetson Freeman/Christian Science Monitor/ Getty Images)

9 LIVING CONDITIONS

Despite the high population density in Rwanda and Burundi, the population remains rural. Society is organized not in villages, but as family housing units spread across the terrain. Houses were traditionally beehive-shaped huts of wood, reeds, and straw, surrounded by a high hedge that served as a fence. More recently, modern building materials and styles have been introduced.

High rates of disease and malnutrition make life difficult for the Hutu. Even before the political violence of the 1990s, the average life expectancy of a person in Rwanda and Burundi was only about 40 to 50 years. In 2008, roughly 5% of Hutu and Tutsi adults were said to be living with AIDS, with the percentage of those living with HIV much higher. Rwanda and Burundi have in the past been healthy and prosperous places, benefitting from the high elevation that offered protection from tropical maladies. Life expectancy is low not only because of extreme levels of political violence but also because of inadequate nutrition, health care, and the spread of diseases of crowding. Particularly problematic diseases include bacterial diarrhea, hepatitis A, and typhoid fever.

Although Rwanda in particular has experienced economic growth since 1994, the infrastructure in the region is not well developed. Roads are often unpaved or poorly maintained. There is no railway service.

10 FAMILY LIFE

Historically, the women of the family are responsible for the maintenance of the home and for planting, hoeing, and weeding the crops. Men and boys are responsible for pasturing the livestock and for clearing the fields; women of reproductive age are forbidden to take care of cattle.

Although love matches were not unknown, and elopements occurred, marriage in Rwanda and Burundi was often about power and relationships between families. These days, however, marriage is more often a matter of personal choice. The goal for both Hutu and Tutsi men was to have a large family with many children. Men, therefore, frequently sought to have more than one wife. Although the majority of men could not afford to be polygynous, a substantial minority did succeed in marrying more than once. Because the society was patrilineal, a woman's children belonged to the father's lineage. Hutu men were not forbidden to court Tutsi women, but marriages were rare. More common in the modern period, but still rare, are marriages between urban Tutsi and Hutu. Twa men and women were traditionally looked down upon by both Hutu and Tutsi and not generally considered acceptable mates.

11 CLOTHING

Among Hutu in rural areas of Rwanda and Burundi, modesty was traditionally not considered an issue until late childhood, so children were permitted to go about without clothing until sometime between the ages of eight and eleven years. For adults, the handmade bark-cloth skirts and hide cloaks of the past have long since given way to Western-style clothing. Handmade beaded necklaces and bracelets continue to be worn, however.

12 FOOD

The staple foods of the Hutu include beans, corn, millet, sorghum, sweet potatoes, and cassava. Milk is highly valued as a food source, as is cattle meat. Because of the social and religious value of cattle, however, people do not often butcher a cow without some ritual justification. Goat meat and goat milk are consumed as well, but they are considered proper food only for persons of low social status. Meal times are flexible, often revolving around work obligations.

Bananas and sorghum grain are fermented to make alcoholic drinks, which are consumed on social occasions and during ritual events such as ceremonies in honor of the dead.

13 EDUCATION

Literacy rates have been at times lower than 50% in Rwanda and Burundi in the vernacular (native language), and still lower in French, but seem to be improving. Rwanda currently reports a literacy rate of about 70%. In Burundi, literate Hutu were targeted for death in 1972, but education began to be encouraged again in the 1980s. There are teacher-training schools and at least one university in both Rwanda and Burundi. However, Rwanda's educational structures were disrupted by the 1994 genocide. Prior to that time, the Rwandese school system was moving toward an emphasis on education in French, but there is now a new emphasis on English, with a goal of trilingual education. The government also has the goal of providing free primary and secondary school education for all.

Quality education continues to be associated with the ability to speak a European language.

Perhaps because it is so difficult to attain, education is highly valued among the Hutu. Education, especially quality education, is considered a matter of central importance.

14 CULTURAL HERITAGE

The kings of Rwanda and Burundi maintained elaborate dance and drum ensembles, which were associated with royal power. On ritual occasions in Burundi two dozen drums were arranged in a semicircle around a large central drum. The musicians moved in a circle around the drums, each taking a turn beating the central drum. This style of drumming has survived the demise of the kingship, and the music has been recorded commercially.

Music, dancing, and drumming are still important in rural life. There are separate men's and women's dances, and both groups' styles are highly expressive. Dance movements often include rapid movements of the upper arms and body, leaping, and rhythmic foot stomping. Vocal music may be performed solo or in choral groups. Many different types of popular song are composed, including hunting songs, lullabies, and songs in praise of cattle (*ibicuba*). In some areas, in the past, a minstrel traveled from area to area singing the news and accompanying himself with a seven-stringed zither.

Rural literature takes the form of legendary tales, myths, and praise-poetry. At one time the Hutu composed poetry for the king and nobility, but praises were also sung to honor the everyday aspects of agricultural life.

15 WORK

Agricultural labor was traditionally predominant among the Hutu, with work related to cattle raising and herding more highly valued than cultivation of the soil. People of Tutsi background who cultivated the soil were often considered poor and could lose their status as nobles. In this way some Tutsi "became" Hutu. Today, a majority of Hutu are still farmers. Coffee and tea are the primary cash crops. People also seek opportunities for cash employment. In major cities industrial development has been hampered by the years of political conflict.

16 SPORTS

One of the most popular traditional forms of entertainment for both young people and adults is a variant of the game known as *mancala* in other parts of Africa and played with a wooden board that has rows of hollowed-out holes for holding beans. The beans are moved rapidly from hole to hole; the object of the game is to line up one's pieces in rows in such a way as to systematically eliminate the pieces of one's opponent. The main spectator sport in Burundi is soccer.

17 ENTERTAINMENT AND RECREATION

The capital cities of Rwanda and Burundi have movie theaters that show European and American films. The television industry itself is still under development. Television in Rwanda fosters multilingualism by broadcasting in many languages. This is in stark contrast to the genocide period during which one radio and television station used locally produced music and entertainment to broadcast hateful anti-Tutsi messages.

Music similar in style to that of the Congo and other neighboring countries is popular. Communities may also form neo-traditional drum and dance troupes for local people. Today a number of musicians from Rwanda and Burundi have achieved international recognition. Burundian musician Khadja Nin is particularly well-known for her multicultural style.

18 FOLK ART, CRAFTS, AND HOBBIES

The Hutu have traditions of basketwork, pottery, woodwork, metal work, and jewelry making. Traditionally, wood carving was not highly developed, consisting mainly of drums, quivers, shields, and stools. Metal work included such objects as copper bracelets and rings, and iron spear points. The Gisaka region of Rwanda was also known for its elaborately painted house interiors. Today, many handicrafts are being produced for the international market. In Rwanda, reconciliation between Hutu and Tutsi women has been facilitated by groups who work together to weave "peace baskets." These have been offered for sale in the United States by a major department store.

19 SOCIAL PROBLEMS

An estimated 100,000 educated Hutu in Burundi were hunted down and killed in 1972, following an invasion by rebel Tutsis. In 1993, violence at that level was once again reported. This was followed by more than a decade of intermittent conflict between the Tutsi dominated army and Hutu rebels. There was no major progress toward peace until an agreement was made in 2003. Areas of conflict and dispute continue, although a democratically elected government with a Hutu president was established in 2005.

In Rwanda, the opposite situation has occurred: the Tutsi have suffered at the hands of the Hutu. In 1962, Hutus massacred thousands of people they defined as Tutsi. Victimization of Tutsis began again in the l990s after Tutsi rebels launched an invasion from neighboring Uganda. More than 800,000 people labeled Tutsi or Tutsi supporters were killed in the 1994 genocide. Many Hutu opposition leaders were also victims.

It cannot be stressed enough that labeling political violence in Rwanda and Burundi simply as Hutu versus Tutsi is an oversimplification. In practice the killings are not so well defined. Victims have frequently been targeted because of their political beliefs regardless of their purported ethnic classification.

In 1996 thousands of Hutu civilians who had fled to the former Zaire (now the Democratic Republic of Congo) in the wake of the 1994 genocide were caught up in a civil war. This was mainly due to the fact that the civilians had fled Rwanda together with a mass of armed Hutu soldiers. The fleeing Hutu military forces from Rwanda in turn got involved in clashes with the ethnic Tutsi of Zaire (*Banyamulenge*). Subsequently, the Banyamulenge allied with the rebel leader Laurent Kabila and helped depose Zaire's infamous dictator Mobuto Sese Seko.

20 GENDER ISSUES

According to custom, women were expected to be subordinate to their husbands; those who disobeyed could be punished severely. The use of violence was considered an acceptable way for a man to discipline his wife. However, a woman might also find support from her kin to prevent the severest of abuses. While the Hutu woman might suffer indignities from an abusive husband, her status was even lower in relationship to elite Tutsi men. A Tutsi man could take a Hutu woman as a concubine, for example, and refuse her the status of a wife, depriving her and her children of legitimacy in the kinship system. The man's wives also had authority over the concubine.

More recently, moves toward gender equality have been promoted. Both Burundi and Rwanda now require that a significant percentage of its elected representatives be women. In Rwanda, the government has enacted other legislation to support women's economic and political rights as well.

Violence against women remains a problem in the area. In the lead up to the 1994 genocide in Rwanda, propaganda was particularly directed against Tutsi women, and they were frequently raped before being killed. One harmful stereotype was that Tutsi women were dangerous because they beguiled Hutu men with their beauty and seductive charms. Particularly as a consequence of the ongoing civil conflict in Burundi, women continue to be subjected to high rates of sexual violence there.

Homosexuality is rarely openly acknowledged by Tutsi or Hutu. This is also something that many people find sinful according to the doctrines of the Catholic church. In 2007 the government of Rwanda began considering a provision to the penal code that that would penalize homosexual behavior. It is already illegal in Burundi.

21 BIBLIOGRAPHY

Adekunle, Julius O. *Culture and Customs of Rwanda*. Westport, CT: Greenwood Press, 2007.

Albert, Ethel M. "Rhetoric, Logic, and Poetics in Burundi." *American Anthropologist* 66(6): (1964): 35–54.

"Anthology of World Music: Africa—Music From Rwanda." Audio CD. Rounder Select, 1999.

Carlisle, R., ed. "The Hutu." *The Illustrated Encyclopedia of Mankind*. New York: Marshall Cavendish, 1990.

Cooke, Peter. "Burundi." In *The New Grove Dictionary of Music and Musicians*. Edited by Stanley Sadie. Washington, D.C.: Macmillan, 1980.

Gansemans, J. "Rwanda." In *The New Grove Dictionary of Music and Musicians*. Edited by Stanley Sadie. Washington, DC: Macmillan, 1980.

Hatzfeld, Jean. *Machete Season: The Killers in Rwanda Speak*. New York: Picador, 2006.

Hiernaux, Jean. "Human Biological Diversity in Central Africa." *Man* 1(3) (1966): 287–306.

Keogh, P., et al. "The Social Impact of HIV Infection on Women in Kigali, Rwanda." *Social Science and Medicine* 38(8) (1994): 1047–54.

Lemarchand, Rene. *Burundi: Ethnocide as Discourse and Practice*. New York: Cambridge University Press, 1994.

Malkki, Liisa H. *Purity and Exile: Violence, Memory, and National Cosmology among Hutu Refugees in Tanzania*. Chicago: University of Chicago Press, 1995.

Taylor, C. "The Concept of Flow in Rwandan Popular Medicine." *Social Science and Medicine* 27(12) (1988): 1343–1348.

—by R. Shanafelt

IGBO

PRONUNCIATION: EE-bo
LOCATION: Igboland (Southern Nigeria)
POPULATION: 18 million
LANGUAGE: Igbo (Kwa subfamily of the Niger-Congo language family)
RELIGION: Tribal religion
RELATED ARTICLES: Vol. 1: Nigerians

¹ INTRODUCTION

The Igbo make up the second largest group of people in southern Nigeria. They are a socially and culturally diverse population, living in the southeastern part of the country. The Igbo consist of many subgroups, all speaking one language, and live in scattered groups of villages, lacking the cities and centralized kingdoms that characterize other major groups in Nigeria, such as the Yoruba and the Hausa.

When, and from what area, the Igbo came into their present territory is not known. Their origin is a subject of much speculation. The people have no common traditional story of their origins. Nor do the local traditions of the various Igbo groups provide clues. It is for this reason that some Western writers on the colonial era treated the Igbo as "a people without history." While this view is no longer considered valid, the Igbo culture historian is handicapped because there is little archaeological data from which to draw. On the basis of cultural data and fragmentary oral traditions, historians have proposed two interrelated hypotheses of Igbo origins: one, that there exists a core area that may be called the "nuclear" Igboland, and two, that waves of immigrant communities from the north and the west planted themselves on the border of this nucleus as early as the 14th and 15th centuries.

The belt formed by the Owerri, Awka, Orlu and Okigwi divisions constitutes the "nuclear" area: its people have no tradition of coming from anywhere else. It is a densely populated area, from which people migrated to the Nsukka area in the north, and into Ikwerri, Etche, Asa, and Ndokki in the south. From these areas, a secondary wave of migration took people farther to the north, south, east, and west. This was a movement that tended to homogenize Igbo culture. The main reasons for migration were population pressure in certain areas and natural disasters.

In addition to this pattern of migration from the nuclear area, there are traditions, confirmed by culture traits, of peoples that entered Igbo territory in about the 14th or 15th century. Of these, three are the Nri, the Nzam, and Anam. Some of these people claim descent from the Bini people of the Benin Kingdom to the west.

European contact with the Igbo-speaking peoples dates back to the arrival of the Portuguese in the middle of the 15th century. For nearly four centuries, the Niger Coast formed a "contact community" between European and African traders. It was a period of trade on the coast rather than one of conquest or empire building in the hinterland, or interior. The main item of commerce provided by the Igbo was slaves, many of whom came to the New World. After the abolition of the slave trade in 1807, a new trading epoch opened, with a shift to traffic in raw materials for industry: palm products, timber,

elephant tusks, and spices. With this shift, the European traders could no longer be confined to the coast. In the struggle to establish a "free trade" hinterland between 1807 and 1885, the British companies played a decisive role for Britain through their joint program, combining aggressive trading with aggressive imperialism. When, in 1900, the Protectorate of Southern Nigeria was created from the former British Niger Company's administrative area and the Niger Coast Protectorate, Igboland was already being treated as a British colony. Between 1902 and 1914, there were 21 British military expeditions into Igboland. Until 1960, Nigeria was a British colony and the Igbo were British subjects. On 1 October 1960, Nigeria became an independent nation with the political structure of a federation of states.

² LOCATION AND HOMELAND

An accurate census has been difficult to achieve in Nigeria, and the same is true for the Igbo. According to the 1963 census, the Igbo number about five and a half million. This population is very unevenly distributed, with most of it concentrated in a line, or axis, formed by Onitsha, Orlu, Okigwi, and Mbaise areas. Along this line, the density of population exceeds 1,000 persons per sq mi in many places, resulting in one of the world's most densely populated rural areas where people subsist on root crops raised through hoe cultivation. In all directions from this main population axis, the density of the population falls below the Igbo average of 350 per sq mi but remains well above Nigeria's average of 85 per sq mi.

Igboland is located in southeastern Nigeria between 5° and 6° N latitude and between 6° and 8° E longitude. The total land area is about 41,000 sq km (about 15,800 sq mi). Before it enters the Atlantic Ocean through a network of tributaries that make up its delta, the Niger River divides Igbo country into two unequal parts. The greater portion lies east of the river, the smaller one to the west. The western Igbo are territorially marked off from the Bini and Warri, their non-Igbo neighbors. On the left bank of the Niger, the eastern Igbo extend from the Niger Delta, where the Ijo and the Ogoni are their southern neighbors, to the north, where the Igala and the Tiv mark the boundary. On the eastern boundary are the Ibibio. Although separated by the Niger, the western and eastern Igbo have retained their cultural and ethnic unity. In modern times, their attitude toward political questions and their identification with their own leaders have revealed the solidarity between the Igbo on both sides of the Niger.

The Igbo country exhibits a wide variety of physical features. The Niger River contributes to this diversity. The most important rivers—Niger, Imo, Anambra, and Urasi—flow from north to south, indicating a steep northward gradient. Four distinct areas may be distinguished: the riverine, delta, central, and northeastern belts. The riverine and delta belts are low-lying, are heavily inundated during the rainy season, and are very fertile. The headwaters of the Imo and Urasi rivers serve the central belt, a relatively high plain that gradually fades into the Okigwi-Awgu plateau. The Udi highlands, which contain coal deposits, are the only coal-mining area in West Africa.

Igboland has a tropical climate. The average annual temperature is about 27°C (80°F), with an annual range of 5 to 10 degrees. The rainy and dry seasons are well marked. The former begins in April and lasts until October, when the dry season starts. Rainfall is heavier in the south than in the north. Important in the seasonal cycle are the southwest monsoon winds that bring rain and the northeast winds that are dry, dusty, and cold. These dry winds are known as the "harmattan."

3 LANGUAGE

The Igbo language is one of the speech communities in the Kwa subfamily of the Niger-Congo language family. It is marked by a complicated system of high and low tones that are used to indicate differences in meaning and grammatical relationships and a wide range of dialectal variations. Using a longitudinal dialectal profile, communities at the center and those at the poles can understand one another's dialects; but between communities at the poles, mutual understanding varies from partial to almost none. These polar dialects are the result of greater isolation.

Here are a few Igbo expressions:

English	Igbo
Hello, how are you?	Keku ka imelo?
What is your name?	Kedu ahagi?
Thank you.	Ndewo

4 FOLKLORE

The Igbo world in all its aspects is made comprehensible to the people by their cosmology, which explains how everything in the world, including material, spiritual, and social entities, came into being. Through it, the Igbo know what functions the heavenly and earthly bodies have and how to behave with reference to the gods, the spirits, and their ancestors. In their conception, not only is cosmology an explanatory device and a guide to conduct or ethics; it is also an action system that defines what they should do.

The Igbo world is a world peopled by invisible and visible forces, by the living, the dead, and those yet to be born. All these forces interact and affect and modify behavior. The survival of this world requires some form of cooperation among its members, although this cooperation may be hostile in nature. It is a world in which others can be manipulated for the sake of an individual's advancement in status, which is the goal of Igbo life. Reincarnation is seen as not only the bridge between the living and the dead, but a necessary factor in the transaction and transfer of social status from the world of the living to the world of the dead. It is a world of constant struggle that recognizes that conflicts exist and requires that people be able to adjust to changes in their lives—being "good citizens" and cooperating for the good of the group. The leader in this world is given minimal power and yet is expected to give maximum service in return, to fulfill the common goal of progress and "making the town get up."

5 RELIGION

Igbo religion is a tribal religion in the sense that its major tenets are shared by all Igbo-speaking people, but in matters of participation, it remains locally organized, with the most effective unit of religious worship being the extended family. Periodic rituals and ceremonies may activate the lineage (larger kinship unit) or the village, which is the widest political community.

While the Igbo religion is polytheistic—having many gods—the idea of a creator of all things is basic to Igbo theology. The Igbo believe in a supreme god, a high god who is all good. This god is a "withdrawn" god, who has finished all ac-

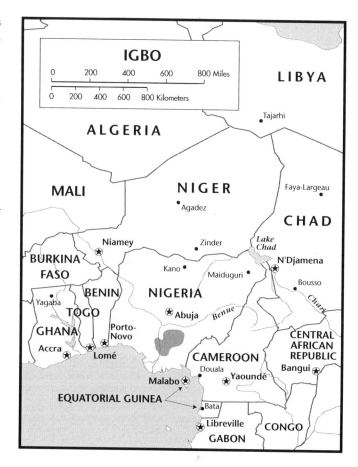

tive works of creation and keeps watch over his creatures from a distance. He is not worshiped directly: there is no shrine or priest dedicated to his service. He gets no direct sacrifice from the living but is seen as the ultimate receiver of all sacrifices made to the minor gods. He seldom interferes in the affairs of human beings, a characteristic that sets him apart from all the other deities, spirits, and ancestors. Although he may be distant and withdrawn, he is not completely separated from human affairs. He is still the great father, the source of all good. The high god is conceived of in different roles. In his creative role, he is called Chinook or Chi-Okike. To distinguish him from the minor gods he is called Chukwu—the great or the high god. As the creator of everything, he is called Chukwu Abiama.

Besides the high god, there are other minor gods called nature gods, sometimes described as kind, hospitable, and industrious; at other times they are conceived of as fraudulent, treacherous, unmerciful, and envious. They are, in general, subject to human passions and weaknesses. But, they can be controlled, manipulated, and used to further human interests. Of these minor gods, Ala, the earth goddess, is considered nearest to the people. She is a great mother, the spirit of fertility of both human beings and the land. Anyanwu is the sun god. He makes crops and trees grow. Igwe is the sky god, the source of rain.

The organization and power structure of these nature gods mirror Igbo social structure. Like the latter, the gods are seen as forming a hierarchy. But, it is usual Igbo practice to appeal to one god or to a number of gods simultaneously without any consideration of their rank or status.

In addition to the important deities, the Igbo believe in other spirits that may be either personal or impersonal, benevolent or wicked, according to the circumstances. People can keep their goodwill by treating them well. Only the wicked need fear them. Among the principal spirits are Agbara and Alosi. Forests and rivers lying on the fringes of cultivated land are said to be occupied by these spirits. Important personal spirits include Mbataku and Agwo (both of whom are spirits of wealth), Aha njoku (the yam spirit), and Ikoro (the drum spirit).

These deities and spirits have anthropomorphic characteristics (human traits). The Igbo attitude toward them is not one of fear but one of friendship, a friendship that lasts as long as the reciprocal obligations are kept.

6 MAJOR HOLIDAYS

The Igbo celebrate the major national holidays of Nigeria, including the following: New Year's Day (January 1), Easter (March or April), Nigerian Independence Day (October 1), and Christmas (December 24–26).

In addition, each town has its own local festivals. Those in the spring or summer are held to welcome the new agricultural cycle. In the fall, harvest festivals are held to mark the end of the cycle. The timing of these festivals varies from town to town.

7 RITES OF PASSAGE

Circumcision takes place about eight days after the birth of a boy and is performed by a skilled woman in the village. At this time the umbilical cord is buried. This is not marked by an elaborate ritual but its social significance is great: a child whose navel cord is not buried is denied citizenship. The child's mother selects the most fruitful oil palm tree from those that her husband shows her; the umbilical cord is buried at the foot of this tree.

Receiving a name is an important event in a child's life, for the child is socially accepted as soon as he or she is given a name. The name-giving ceremony is a formal occasion celebrated by feasting and drinking. A child may be given many names. The parents' choice of names may be dictated by the kind of birthmarks on the child's skin and by the opinion of the diviner, or seer. *Njoku* and *Mmaji,* the male and female figures of the yam deity, are conferred by divination. Other names may be given to indicate the market day on which the child was born, or a preference for male children, or a certain concern for the future of the child. The name *Nwanyimeole* ("What can a woman do?") means that a father is in need of a male child. *Onwubiko* ("May death forgive") expresses the fact that parents have lost many of their children by death and pray that this child may survive. *Chukwuemeka* ("God has done well") is a thanksgiving name for the favor received.

Before the advent of Western schooling, adolescent boys passed through a formal initiation known as *ima agwo*. Girls passed through *mgbede*, a ceremonial seclusion known as the "fat house." In southern Igbo communities this was followed by clitoridectomy, or female circumcision.

The process of betrothing and marrying an Igbo young woman is a long, ceremonious one that often takes years and is rarely accomplished in less than a year. Marriage is so important to the Igbo that nothing concerned with it is taken lightly. The process falls into four interrelated stages: asking the young woman's consent, working through a middleman, testing the bride's character, and paying the bridewealth, a kind of dowry.

Death in old age is accepted as a blessing. It is the desire of every Igbo man and woman to die in his or her own town or to be buried within its boundaries. If death occurs at a distance, the relatives bring the body home for burial. After death, the body is clothed in its finest garments, and the corpse is placed on a stool in a sitting posture, propped against the wall. In front of the corpse are placed the deceased's special treasures and the implements of his or her work. Lying or sitting in state lasts for a few hours, during which old friends and relatives come and pay their last respects to the dead. When due time has elapsed, young men wrap the corpse in grass mats, carry it out to the burial ground, and bury it. When the head of a family dies, he is buried in a deep grave beneath the floor of his house. As a general rule, burial follows within 24 hours of death.

8 INTERPERSONAL RELATIONS

The Igbo are often depicted as an egalitarian society in which almost everybody is equal. This obscures some of the regional differences in Igbo social structure. But, in spite of these differences, all Igbo share the same egalitarian ideology: the right of the individual to climb to the top and faith in the individual's ability to do so.

Within this egalitarian ideology, two criteria shape interpersonal relations: age and gender. Precedence is given to males and to seniors by birth order. This latter is the normal basis for headship of an extended family. The behavior between kinsmen and nonkinsmen is similarly regulated by this senior-junior principle. Seniors are considered the moral agents of the young. It is the duty of the children to greet their seniors first in the morning or whenever they meet. In children's play groups, leadership and authority are informally given to the older boys and girls.

The women members of an Igbo village are of two categories: the women who belong to the village by descent, who may be unmarried, married, divorced, or widowed and the women who belong to it by marriage. The Igbo woman in general enjoys a high socioeconomic and legal status. She can leave her husband at will and summon him to a tribunal where she will get a fair hearing. She marries in her own right and manages her trading capital and her profits herself. Although land rights do not normally descend through the female line, and although living in their husband's compounds makes it impossible for them to play important social and ritual roles in their own family's natal village, women can take titles and can practice medicine.

Social stratification is based on wealth. It does not matter what occupation a person engages in to provide for his old age and for his family. With this ideological approach, the Igbo distinguish between *obgenye* or *mbi*, the poor, from *dinkpa*, the moderately prosperous, and the latter from *nnukwu madu* or *ogaranya*, the rich.

9 LIVING CONDITIONS

The Igbo live in compact villages, each built around a central square, which is a clearing with a thatch-roofed mud resthouse of the village men's society and a large open space where meetings and ceremonies are held. Extending from the village, sometimes for several miles, is a wide band of farmland, divided into sections, one or two of which are cultivated each year while the others lie fallow. At the edges of the villages and along the roads and bush paths connecting them are scattered groves of oil and raffia palms.

Most villages are divided into wards, and each ward is divided into compounds. The physical structure of the compounds consists of houses crowded wall-to-wall along narrow alleyways. The entrance to a compound is usually through an ornamental gateway leading from the square. The back of the compound, at the edge of the village, is devoted to garden land where certain crops not planted on the farms are grown.

Village life has changed considerably since the discovery of oil in Nigeria. Villages became connected by roadways to urban centers, which exerted considerable influence even on the most remote areas. The government has also supported development in the rural areas. Electricity was introduced; television sets and radios are now commonplace. The houses, which were formerly made of mud walls and thatched roofs, are now constructed of cement blocks with corrugated iron roofs. Villages have running water, although it is not connected to every house.

Another important development is the network of health centers and hospitals that now dot the rural areas. Almost all villages have a health center and a nurse practitioner or a resident doctor.

10 FAMILY LIFE

There is no Igbo word for "family." The term "family" as used by English-speaking Igbo may apply to several different sorts of groups. On the simplest level is the elementary family, composed of a father and a mother and their children, that is, the nuclear family in the usual Western sense of the word. But, under the practice of polygyny, many Igbo men have more than one wife, so there is also the polygynous family, made up of a father and his wives and all their children—father, mothers, and a group of full and half-siblings. Residence is patrilocal; a woman goes to live with her husband when she marries, and sons, when they marry, do not traditionally leave home and set up separate homes their own. Thus, there is, in addition, the extended family: a father and his sons—or a group of brothers if the father is dead—their wives, sons, and unmarried daughters. The extended family usually has about 5 to 30 members.

Ideally, all of the members of the extended family live in one large compound. The ideal of Igbo family life is a big compound. Establishing a big compound depends on the abilities of the head of the compound. It is the demonstration of his personal achievement and his social status. A successful man marries as many wives as he can support, which involves providing farm plots to help the women and their dependents make a living. Polygyny is seen as imposing social and economic obligations that can be fulfilled only by a man of substantial wealth.

The compound consists of a number of economically independent households, each with a man or a woman as the head. All the heads and their dependents recognize the authority of the compound head and would not make a major political decision without first consulting with him. The compound head has numerous ritual, moral, and legal rights and obligations. In Igbo idiom, he is the "eyes of his compound members as they

are his ears." In return, he receives respect, obedience, and material tokens of goodwill.

In recent years, many changes have taken place that contradicts this ideal. Christian marriage and marriage by ordinance (law) are important innovations. Both have given women legal protection and property rights not recognized by the traditional system. This has not, however, completely eliminated polygyny. A legal limit has also been imposed on the amount of bride-price a woman's family may demand. There has been an opposite trend, however. As more women have become educated, their families have raised their expectations of bridewealth, demanding higher and higher amounts.

Among Igbo professional people, the trend is toward a nuclear family, establishment of a separate residence, and marriage based on love. Tension still exists around the issue of the amount of support that should be given to the members of the extended family, creating conflict between generations.

11 CLOTHING

The everyday clothing in urban areas is not different from that of Westerners. Traditional clothing is still worn on important occasions in the cities and every day in rural areas. There are both formal and informal attire for both men and women. For everyday use men wear a cotton wrapper, a shirt, and sandals. For formal occasions they wear a long shirt, often decorated with tucks and embroidery, over a better-quality wrapper, shoes, and a hat. Women wear wrappers for both informal and formal occasions; the major difference between these is the quality of fabric. For everyday use, the preferred material is cheap cotton that is dyed locally. For formal wear, the wrapper is either woven or batik-dyed, often imported from Holland.

The blouse for formal wear is made of lace or is embroidered . Women also wear a head tie, a rectangular piece of cloth that can be tied around the head in a number of different ways.

Both men and women have distinctive facial markings, although this is becoming less common. For women, the marking is performed as a preliminary to marriage and is called *mbubu*. The *mbubu* consists of a series of small slits made in the flesh with a pointed razor. Into these slits, pellets of tightly compressed cotton or palm leaf are inserted, and the whole is smeared with charcoal. The end result is a regular pattern of black oval blobs that stand out on the skin.

The tribal markings of the men, called *ichi*, are more elaborate and diverse. Some of the Igbo groups use them only on the face, others on the body as well. The latter is often part of the initiation ceremony. The work is done by women; the flesh is cut in a series of lines and soot from a cooking pot is rubbed into them to produce an intensely black effect.

12 FOOD

The yam is the staple food of the Igbo. To be deprived of yams creates a condition of acute distress. Whatever substitute may be offered, it cannot satisfy the Igbo palate. There are many varieties, which differ greatly in size, appearance, and flavor. Other starchy foods include rice, cassava, taro, maize and plantains.

Traditionally, the yam was the choice of food for ceremonial occasions. Nowadays, it has been replaced by rice.

A usual meal includes a starch and a soup or stew, prepared with a vegetable, such as okra or bitter leaves, to which piec-

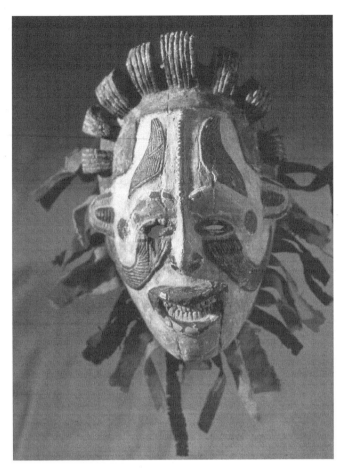

An Igbo Maiden Spirit mask, which men would wear to mimic activities of women for magical purposes. The masks would be worn during certain rituals, especially at funerals and festivities. (The Image Works)

es of fish, chicken, beef, or goat meat are added. The following recipes are very popular.

Shrimp Jollof Rice

Jollof rice of various types is popular throughout Nigeria, and among the Igbo who live near waterways it is often prepared with shrimp. Elsewhere, the protein may be chicken.

The dish is cooked until the rice grains are soft and separate, but never until they become mushy.
Ingredients:
500 g (17.5 oz) shrimp
300 g (10.5 oz) fresh tomato
20 g (0.7 oz) tomato paste
75 g (2.6 oz) onion
fresh red pepper
dry ground pepper
peanut oil
200 g (7 oz) rice
salt
300 ml (11 oz) water

Shell the shrimp. Grind the tomato, peppers, onion, and 6 to 8 shrimp together. Wash, clean, and drain the rice. Heat

the oil until it smokes slightly. Add the ground ingredients and cook for 5 minutes. Add 300 ml water and tomato paste. Bring to a boil, and add the rice, salt, and remaining shrimp. Replace cover and bring back to a boil. Heat oven to 120°c (250°F), pour rice mixture into an ovenproof dish, and place in oven. Cook until the liquid is absorbed completely. Stir to loosen the rice grains, replace the cover and allow to sit in warm oven for a few hours with the heat off and door ajar to blend the flavors.

Thin Goat Meat Pepper Soup

This dish may be served with simple shrimp stew and a salad.
480 g (17 oz) goat meat
salt
dry ground red pepper
100 g (3.5 oz) onion
20 g (0.7 oz) tea leaves
enge, crushed
20 g (0.7 oz) dried crayfish, ground
100 g (3.5 oz) dried fish (optional)

Wash the goat meat and cut into pieces. Place in a pot and add water to cover. Add salt, pepper, thinly sliced onion and crushed enge. Boil on low heat until the meat is tender. Top up water to cover and add coarsely chopped tea leaves, ground dried crayfish and dried fish. Boil for 10 minutes. Allow to stand for 30 minutes for flavors to blend well.

¹³ EDUCATION

When Nigeria gained independence from Britain in 1960, its new parliamentary government immediately set out to transform the country into a highly developed, modern nation. It set a priority on education and poured its resources into schooling its people. Universal primary education soon became the norm in southern Nigeria, where the Igbo live. Secondary education also developed rapidly. The Igbo were much involved in these efforts since education had had a long tradition among them, and they saw it as a way of moving forward. One of the first universities in the country, modeled on the American system, was established in Nsukka. This university serves the population of the entire country; however, the majority of students at Nsukka are Igbo. A sign of enthusiasm for education is the fact that in any major city of the country, the majority of civil servants are of Igbo origin.

¹⁴ CULTURAL HERITAGE

In addition to the visual arts, the Igbo cultural heritage includes music and dancing. For music making there are a number of wind and stringed instruments. These include the *ugene,* a kind of whistle made of baked clay, round in form, and about the size of a billiard ball. Chiefs are entitled to carry an ivory horn for sending out messages by powerful blasts of dot-and-dash notes. The horn is blown like a flute, and the note can be varied in length but not in pitch. Probably the most interesting of the Igbo instruments is the *ubaw-akwala,* a sort of guitar. It has a triangular body formed by three pieces of soft wood sewn together. This instrument is the favorite for accompanying songs and chants and is used by strolling singers in the evenings. Singers are much appreciated, and they must possess not only a gift for music, but poetic ability as well. They improvise their themes as the song proceeds and show great ingenuity in fitting words to tempo and tune.

Dancing is a great Igbo pastime, and it is practiced by everybody capable of movement. There are many forms—for boys, for girls, for men, for women, and for mixed groups, group dancing is associated with religious observances and festivals.

15 WORK

The traditional Igbo economy depends on root-crop farming. Yams, cassava, and many varieties of cocoyam (taro) are the chief staples and provide the majority of the population with its subsistence needs. There are other occupations besides farming, but land is considered the most important asset.

The Igbo system of land tenure is based on four principles:

1. All land is owned. There is no concept of abandonment of land or unowned land. Whether the land is cultivated or not, it belongs to somebody.

2. Land ultimately belongs to the lineage, or kinship group, and cannot be separated from it.

3. Within his lineage, the individual has security of tenure for the land he needs for his house and his farm.

4. No member of the lineage is without land.

There is a division of labor according to gender. Men clear all bushes and plant the yams with the help of the women and the children, collectively. Following the planting of yams, the main crop, plots are allocated to the women individually. Each woman plants crops, such as maize, melon, and okra, on the slopes of the hills, and plants pumpkins, beans, cassava, and taro in the spaces between the yam hills.

Trading has become an important source of livelihood for the Igbo. It is no longer possible for them to maintain the desired standard of living by depending entirely on agriculture. There are some Igbo communities where trading has surpassed farming in importance. Trading is an old occupation among the Igbo, and the marketplace has occupied an important place in their economy and life for a long time.

Many Igbo are now engaged in wage labor, with the number of people increasing constantly. The incidence of migrant labor is heaviest in the most densely populated areas. Migration is of three types: villagers seeking paid labor in more urbanized areas within Igboland, those who work in Nigeria but outside Igboland, and those who work outside Nigeria. The opportunities offered to labor, skilled and unskilled, by the economic developments of Nigeria in the past few decades have been grasped by the Igbo. The growing cities, expanding road construction, building boom, new industries, and oil explorations are creating job opportunities demanding varying kinds and degrees of skill; the Igbo are found at every level.

16 SPORTS

Wrestling is universal among boys and young men, and it is the most popular sport. Every youth who is physically capable practices it and continues to do so until he marries. There are great yearly contests in every part of Igbo country.

The other popular sport is soccer, played traditionally only by boys, but more recently introduced through the school system to girls.

17 ENTERTAINMENT AND RECREATION

In addition to rituals, dances, and traditional music, modern forms of entertainment include watching television and going to the movies and discos. Most households own radios, and there are several television sets in each village. The tradition of storytelling continues. As in the past, the Igbo also play games, including card games and checkers. Among the younger people American youth culture is popular, and most young people listen to rap and rock music.

18 FOLK ARTS, CRAFTS, AND HOBBIES

The Igbo practice a number of crafts, some engaged in by men only and some by women.

Carving is a skilled occupation and is confined to professional men. They manufacture doors and panels for houses, as well as stools, dancing masks, and boxes for kola and snuff. Tom-toms, or drums, are also the work of specialists. These are hollow blocks of wood and mostly intended not as musical instruments but for spreading information about ceremonies, festivals, and meetings. Another valued craft is that of the blacksmith. It is only practiced by people in certain towns, who are able to control production. The Awka smiths hold the leading place in the profession throughout Igbo country and beyond. They also travel to such distant parts as Bonny, Calabar, and even Lagos, plying their craft. They manufacture items of personal adornment as well as practical items such as hoes and axes. Nowadays, manufactured goods are replacing these implements.

The arts and crafts in the hands of the women include pottery making, spinning, weaving, basketry, and grass plaiting. Earthen pottery is manufactured by women skilled in the art throughout Igbo country. The pottery is limited to vessels designed for utilitarian purposes, and decoration is not developed to any great extent. Spinning of cotton is done by means of a bobbin that revolves by its own weight. Since this equipment is portable, a woman can do her spinning while trading in the market or sitting in her compound. The thread is then woven on hand looms into strips of cloth from 12 in to 15 in wide. The strips are then sewn together and can be used for a variety of purposes. Mat weaving is another of the women's crafts. The craft work of each area is distinguished by its own regional characteristics. One other art practiced by women is artistic abilities in the adornment of their persons by means of stains.

19 SOCIAL PROBLEMS

The problems that beset the state of Nigeria in postcolonial times, ranging from a civil war in which the Igbo were principal players to a series of military coups, have affected the Igbo profoundly. Among them there is a continuing distrust of the peoples of the North (primarily the Hausa) and the West (primarily the Yoruba). Although Nigeria is party to several international human rights treaties, the current government's human-rights record is poor.

The crime rate in Nigeria is high, especially in larger urban centers, but rural areas are also affected. Crimes against property generally account for more than half of the offenses. The crime wave was exacerbated by the worsening economic conditions of the 1980s.

Drug-related crime emerged as a major problem in the 1980s. Igboland has so far escaped the worst of this, but young people even here are reputedly now smoking marijuana.

[20] GENDER ISSUES

A woman in modern Igbo culture is no longer just a consumer of wealth; she is also a maker of wealth. The traditional values and expectations of the patriarchal Igbo society have changed with the breakdown of the traditional norms, the influence of other cultures, and formal education for women. Igbo women now occupy senior positions in the society just like their male counterparts.

In the past, there were a number of clear-cut expectations for both men and women exerted on the members of the community. For example in the traditional Igbo culture, a boy was expected to display masculinity and stiffness. Femininity in a boy was scorned and a boy would be scolded and beaten to discourage womanish traits. Boys were groomed by their fathers to be brave, bold, adventurous, and audacious. Girls on the other hand were brought up to be soft, subservient, and gentle. Both men and women played their gender roles in a complementary manner. These roles were so deeply indoctrinated into their everyday lives that there was little conflict between the sexes. The gender roles were so clear that a member of either gender doing the opposite of what was expected of him or her would be consider as an abomination. For example, if a girl held her father's gun, that would be an abomination. On the other hand, a girl could stay with the older women in the kitchen as they cooked and told jokes, but the same behavior would be considered unacceptable for a boy.

In traditional Igbo society, the birth of a boy was considered a more joyful occasion than the birth of a girl. For the father, the birth of a son meant the continuation of the family line and a clear path of inheritance. For a mother, the birth of a son brought acceptance in society and a sense of greater acceptance into the husband's family. The birth of a daughter, however, would be welcomed with mixed feelings, especially if she was coming after a line of other girls without a son in-between. Without a son, the father would lose hope of having someone to continue with his lineage, since the girls would grow and be married off, thus leaving the home.

In traditional Igbo society, there was clear division of labor based on one's gender. From an early age, the boy, for example, knew that his duties would include staying close to his father, washing his father's clothing, taking care of the livestock, maintaining farming implements, and gathering yam seedlings for planting. He was expected to protect the girls of the community. He would be allowed to participate in "manly" sports, such as wrestling, and he would accompany his father to social meetings and ceremonies. He was expected to establish himself as a skilled member of the society, perhaps as a farmer, blacksmith, or a shepherd. The man's movements were not restricted.

Girls, however, were taught from childhood that their world began and ended with marriage, childbirth, and caring for the needs of her husband. She was taught that the kitchen would be her primary domain and headquarters.

[21] BIBLIOGRAPHY

Achebe, Chinua. *Things Fall Apart*. London: Heinemann Educational Books, 1958.

Achufusi, G. I. "Female Individuality and Assertiveness in the Novels of Ifeoma Okoye." In *Feminism in African Literature*, edited by Helen Chukwuma. Enugu: New Generation Books, 1994.

Agbasiere, J. T. *Women in Igbo Life and Thought*. London and New York: Routledge and Francise Group, 2000.

Brydon, Lynne, and Sylvia H. Chant. *Women in the Third World: Gender Issues in Rural and Urban Areas*. Piscataway, NJ: Rutgers University Press, 1989.

Chinweizu, A. *Anatomy of Female Power*. Lagos: Pero Press, 1990.

Green, M. M. *Ibo Village Affairs*. New York: Frederik Praeger, 1964.

Ndiokwere, Nathaniel. *Search for Greener Pastures: Igbo and African Experience*. Nebraska: Morris Publishing, 1998.

Lerner, Gerda. *The Creation of Feminist Consciousness*. New York: Oxford University Press, 1993.

Obododimma, Oha. "The Semantics of Female Devaluation in Igbo Proverbs." African Study Monographs, 19 (2) (1998): 87–102.

Ottenberg, Phoebe. "The Afikpo Ibo of Eastern Nigeria." In *Peoples of Africa*, edited by James L. Gibbs. New York: Holt, Rinehart and Winston, Inc., 1965.

Ozumba, G. O. "Methodology and African Philosophy." In *Footmark on African Philosophy*, edited by A. F. Udiugwomen. Lagos: OOP, 1995.

Turner, James. "Universal Education and Nation-building in Africa." *Journal of Black Studies* 2, 1: 3-27.

Uchendu, Victor. *The Igbo of Southeast Nigeria*. New York: Holt, Rinehart and Winston, Inc., 1965.

Walaka, Jude. *The Struggle for an Inclusive Nigeria*: *Igbo's*: *To Be or Not To Be*. Enugu: SNAAP Press Ltd., 2003.

—reviewed by M. Njoroge

IJO

PRONUNCIATION: EE-jo
ALTERNATE NAMES: Ijaw, Izo
LOCATION: Niger River delta (coastal region of southern Nigeria)
POPULATION: 2 million or more
LANGUAGE: Ijo; other African languages; English for traveling, trading
RELIGION: Traditional tribal religion and Christianity

¹ INTRODUCTION

The Ijo, the fourth largest ethnic group in Nigeria, are a socially and culturally diverse people, living in the coastal region of southern Nigeria, principally in the states of Bayelsa and Rivers. Linguistic and archaeological analysis indicates that they migrated to the Niger Delta as long as 7,000 years ago. It is not known whether they were seeking refuge from mainland attackers or were attracted by the abundance of fish and the supply of salt.

The delta at first must have seemed like an isolated and easily protected area, with its maze of waterways, but later it became a major point of contact with European travelers and traders. Beginning with the Portuguese explorers in the 15th century, the region became more and more closely tied to the world economy as demands for its resources increased: first human resources—slaves—then palm oil, and most recently, petroleum. European missionaries also had a major impact as the Ijo were converted to Christianity, became missionaries themselves, and introduced schools to villages throughout the delta.

The effects of these changes varied widely, however. The Ijo were divided into 43 *ibe,* an Ijo word roughly translated as "clan(s)," and were never politically unified in the form of a kingdom or state. Those living on islands in the eastern delta formed "city-states" and monopolized the trade for slaves and palm oil; the political organization of the central delta was primarily village-based. In fact, when speaking of the Ijo it is important to keep in mind that the Ijo, like many other African peoples, never formed a neatly bounded society. For each general statement, there is usually an exception. For example, the Ijo and their language have the same name (*Ijo,* often spelled *Ijaw*), but the great range of dialects prevents Ijo speakers in the eastern and western fringes of the region from understanding one another. Only the Ijo living in the central part of the delta can understand both. But the Ijo now see themselves as a distinct people with reference to their mainland neighbors (the Igbo, Yoruba, Isoko, Beni, and others), even though the cultural differences within the Ijo-speaking population are sometimes greater than those between Ijo and non-Ijo.

The Ijo political identity took shape during the colonial period, as early as the 1940s as part of nationalist movements throughout the continent. Later, the creation of the Delta state in the 1960s responded to Ijo demands for recognition, and 30 years later the Bayelsa state was carved away from the Delta state. Political identity has been sharpened both through conflicts with the federal government and with neighboring peoples, particularly the Itsekiri and Urhobo living in the Warri area.

² LOCATION AND HOMELAND

An accurate census has been difficult to achieve in Nigeria as a whole. Estimates range from two million Ijo speakers to more than seven million of Ijo descent. The communities they occupy in the Niger Delta vary in size from several thousand to a few hundred persons, or fewer. The population size is tied closely to the topography of the delta.

There are three broad ecological zones in the delta of the Niger River. The first is fairly narrow, only a few hundred yards in places, and consists of a sandy stretch of land that marks the edge of the delta as it meets the Bight of Benin. The villages located here are small. The second zone is the area of mangrove trees and tidal floods that lies behind the beaches. Mostly seasonal fishing camps are found here, although in the eastern delta the trading organizations formed by the Ijo middlemen developed into communities with denser populations. The third zone includes the dry land that rises above the mangroves. The communities here are located along the banks of the rivers that crisscross the delta.

The waterways were the only means of transportation in the delta until a highway and bridges were built in the 1980s that crossed the northern part of the delta connecting Lagos in the east (the former capital of Nigeria) with Port Harcourt, a major city in the west. In the past the Ijo traveled extensively along the coastal waterways that extend from Cameroon to Ghana, and settled along them to work as fishermen, government employees, missionaries, and tradesmen. The Ijo are found today living throughout Nigeria and have entered numerous other occupations. During the Christmas holiday, many Ijo return to their delta communities. The high-speed motorboats that have replaced canoes reduce the trip home to a few hours' journey from the mainland, when formerly it took several days.

³ LANGUAGE

The languages spoken by the Ijo belong to the Ijoid or Benue-Congo subgroups of the Niger-Congo language family. The Igbo and Yoruba languages are also members of the latter subgroup. Because of the demands of travel and trading, it is not unusual for an Ijo to speak several African languages, as well as English or pidgin English. Beginning in primary school, English is the official language of instruction.

Ijo names usually involve a personality trait or an event. A girl might be named Oweizighe ("a male has not yet been born") because her parents had wanted a boy. The process of naming is as fluid as the names themselves. Anyone can name a newly born child, or no name will be assigned until it seems clear that the infant will survive beyond the first few months. A young person can decide to change his or her own name. For family names people use their father's first name, or his father's name, depending on factors such as the social standing of the grandfather or the place where the person lives while growing up.

⁴ FOLKLORE

The Ijo do not have a category of beliefs that can easily be called folklore. At best they have some unproven stories of how they came to move from one place to another, or how a particular custom was started. In one frequently told example, disputes among brothers over the distribution of wild game led to the splitting up of a community and the formation of a new *ibe.* In another example, some Ijo claimed that a water spirit con-

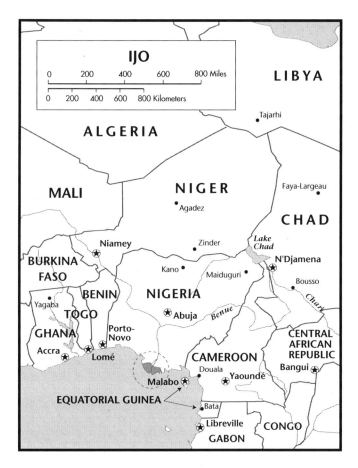

vinced them to stop female circumcision in their *ibe* after seven young women died.

Similarly, with regard to religious beliefs, those who converted to Christianity came to see traditional Ijo notions about spirits and magical powers as examples of superstitious beliefs. In contrast, they believe their own faith in a major world religion is based only on truth.

5 RELIGION

The traditional Ijo believe in a High God, called Wonyingi ("our mother"), who created and controls the destiny of everything on earth. An individual's spirit is believed to meet with Wonyingi before birth to make an agreement or contract for the person to live a particular life. This belief is tied in with a philosophy that requires each person to work hard to achieve the good fortune that may be in his or her contract. When the person's best efforts come to nothing and a person is beset by misfortune, the Ijo rationalize that it must have been part of the contract. There are several kinds of spiritual agents, however, who can help to shape a person's destiny: spirits of the dead, spirits of the bush and water, and witches.

Although the spirits of the dead are believed to go back to their own villages, it is necessary to bury the dead properly and to appease the spirits with food and drink. Before consuming a beverage, an Ijo will pour a little of it onto the ground for dead relatives to "drink." It is believed that if the spirits are unhappy, they will make a person ill, infertile, or even cause that person's death.

Spirits of the bush and water are believed to be the most common and conspicuous supernatural agents influencing the course of daily life. The Ijo appeal to the water spirits in particular by wearing elaborately carved wooden masks, decorated with chalk and feathers, on their heads. When a particularly powerful spirit is thought to be residing in a mask, people will travel long distances to ask the spirit for help with their economic, health, or other problems. Spirits may also be asked to punish a thief or protect a person from evil witches. Spirits can respond to these requests through supernatural messages (perhaps explaining why a person died) interpreted by dancers who, with shielded faces, imitate the dances the spirits were said to have performed on the sand banks. In the eastern part of the delta, elaborate masquerade dances are performed on a cyclical basis to honor village heroes.

Not all witches are thought to be bad, but they are believed to be dangerous. They may even be children, who might just as easily kill a clan member as a neighbor. At the same time, if a witch chooses to do so, he or she can protect family members from the attacks of others. The most direct way of identifying a witch comes during funerals, when the spirit of a dead person sometimes confesses to having been one. A witch discovered in this way is buried quickly, without a coffin, at the side of the river.

6 MAJOR HOLIDAYS

In recent times, the period from Christmas to New Year's Day has become a time of celebration as many Ijo working on the mainland try to return to their home villages for their annual vacations at that time. The Ijo in the western delta also have a spring festival that lasts 12 days. They welcome the new agricultural cycle with special dances for women who have been circumcised and with libations for the ancestral spirits. They also perform rituals to cast out evil spirits to symbolically cleanse the community.

7 RITES OF PASSAGE

The central Ijo have relatively few rituals to mark a person's milestones. Differing from those areas where female circumcision is practiced, the females of the central Ijo go from birth to death without any ritual to signify their first menstrual period, marriage, pregnancy, or menopause.

Similarly, rituals rarely are attached to the development of males, even at the time when they are circumcised, usually within a week after birth. In the past, when the main male occupation was collecting palm berries to produce palm oil, a boy was pelted with berries after he had climbed his first tree and cut down his first bunch of berries.

For both men and women, the most significant rite of passage is at the time of death. The status of a person is measured by the type of funeral he or she receives. The more generations of living descendants a person has, the more elaborate the funeral will be. In general, elderly persons with grandchildren would be honored with an all-night wake, a masquerade dance, drumming and dancing, and food for visitors. Those who died a "bad death"—the result of an accident, or if the person was revealed to be a witch, are buried quickly, without ceremony or coffin, on the river bank.

8 INTERPERSONAL RELATIONS

Two main criteria influence interpersonal relations among the Ijo: age and gender. Otherwise, they are remarkably egalitarian in their economic and political outlook and activities. Everyone is expected to work, even young children (from the time they are able to clean up around the compound), as well as, the most elderly members of the group. Priests of the cult houses and chiefs are also expected to help with the work, which includes farming, fishing, canoe carving, and weaving thatch for roof repairs.

The standard greeting is *noaho* ("hello"). Although the Ijo do not celebrate birthdays, they are very conscious of relative age distinctions. Younger people are expected to bow slightly at the knee when meeting someone older, and to express their respect by offering the oldest person present the opportunity to speak or to eat and drink first. Women, however, usually defer to men unless they are considerably older than the men.

At political gatherings, whether family or village meetings, men make decisions based on consensus. Although people defer to the oldest men, agreement is reached through the ability of a speaker, regardless of age, to persuade the others to accept his views.

Another form of greeting is to ask anyone passing by to "come and eat." Since Ijo villages are not subdivided by walled compounds, the open space allows people to see all those who pass by. As with the American greeting, "How are you?", the offer to join in the meal is not taken literally and is not usually accepted.

9 LIVING CONDITIONS

Village life changed considerably after oil exports became a major source of income to the Nigerian government. Closer ties to international markets created more opportunities for paid work on the mainland and in government-supported developments in the delta. Health clinics became more common, and some illnesses, such as yaws, which afflicted many children, were almost eliminated. Malaria, however, and other illnesses endemic to the tropics remain prevalent.

Since the introduction of electricity, television sets can now be found even in the most isolated of villages. The houses of thatched roofs and mud walls typical in the past have been mainly replaced by cement-block houses, some having two stories.

The change to more permanent housing is perceived by the Ijo as an improvement in their standard of living, and not simply as a status marker. Those who cannot afford to build a cement-block house are seen as being very poor. The old-style houses require constant maintenance, and thatched roofs let in both rain and snakes.

It is much more difficult to assess the benefits of the new economy to households generally. While the Ijo had been relatively independent in their ability to produce most of what they used and consumed, the post-oil era placed them in the position of having to purchase most of their household needs.

Because of the topology of the delta, villages are essentially located on islands. In the past, canoes were the main form of transportation to work on farms, to fish, and to visit neighbors on the mainland. At one time, outboard motors were used to power large canoes to ferry passengers and goods throughout the delta. More recently, high-powered motor boats have become the main means of transportation. Despite the topology,

a highway was constructed across the delta, linking Warri in the west and Port Harcourt in the east, via Yenagoa. The maintenance of this highway and bridges in this tropical environment has been a major challenge.

10 FAMILY LIFE

Women are considered to be equal to men. They provide the food for the household, by farming or fishing, and many engage in business activities to earn money to buy what they cannot produce. Although husbands are expected to contribute as well, especially in paying school expenses for their children, it is not unusual for women to pay household expenses. Women who become wage earners, working in the schools or on palm oil plantations, still maintain farms.

The Ijo family is an extended family type. Polygyny, in which one man has two or more wives, is the preferred form of marriage. Each wife has her own bedroom and kitchen, usually in a single house. Since women are expected to live near their husbands' families, and men to live near their fathers, the number of persons residing near each other in an extended family can typically be 15 or even more.

The Ijo practice two forms of marriage, both involving "bridewealth," or what the Ijo colloquially call "dowry." The small-dowry marriage requires the husband to pay a certain amount to his wife's parents and kinspeople. In the past, the payment was made in cases of gin; later it was in cash. The large-dowry marriage involves a larger payment, and only a few marriages are of this type; usually wives in these cases are not local women.

The essential difference between the two types of marriage, especially for the central Ijo, is in the lines of inheritance. The children of a small-dowry marriage trace their line of inheritance through their mother to her brother and other kinsmen. In the large-dowry marriage, the children "belong" to the father. What this means in practice is that small-dowry children have more choices of places to live when they reach adulthood: they can continue to live in their father's residence or they can move to any place where they can trace a connection through their mother's line of descent. In practice, however, other factors sometimes intervene to restrict such choices. Children are often sent to live with relatives, either because of divorce or a parent's death, or to help care for an infant when there is no older sibling in, for instance, the mother's sister's family.

Unlike many other African societies, among the Ijo, wives are not ranked within a marriage. Each is treated equally and each has equal access to her husband. This does not prevent women from becoming jealous if they see their husband favoring one of their co-wives. For some women, this is enough of a reason to make them want to be a single wife. Others claim there are advantages to having co-wives, in that they provide companionship to each other, help in feeding the husband, and aid in caring for sick children.

The inability of co-wives to live peacefully together can lead to chronic conflicts and divorce. However, the most important and acceptable reason for divorce is infertility. If a woman does not become pregnant within a reasonable time after marriage, she can divorce her husband and return the dowry. On the other hand, if the man has children with other wives and it appears that the woman is barren, the husband does not have grounds for divorcing her. If she commits adultery or refuses to fulfill a wife's role, such as cooking for him, then he can send her away and still claim a repayment of the dowry.

The Ijo do not have pets as such. Dogs have to forage for food, and rarely are petted.

11 CLOTHING

There is both formal and informal clothing for men and women. During the work day men wear shorts, often under a cloth sarong, a shirt, and sandals (some also go barefoot). For formal occasions they wear a long shirt covering a good-quality sarong, a hat, and shoes, and they often carry canes. Women also wear cloth sarongs with blouses when working during the day, and sandals (some also go barefoot). Their formal clothes consist of expensive, colorful sarongs, blouses, and head wraps. They wear shoes or sandals, and strands of beads around their waists under their sarongs and around their necks.

If clothing is seen as decorative art for the body, it should also be noted that Ijo women spend much time weaving their hair into attractive forms, and tattooing their bodies and faces by cutting designs with a razor and then rubbing charcoal into them.

12 FOOD

Fish and cassava are the "meat and potatoes" of the Ijo diet. When fish is plentiful, it is eaten at every meal. When fresh fish is expensive and scarce, so-called "ice fish"—imported frozen fish—is substituted. The Ijo plant maize (corn), plantains, and bananas, as well as many leafy vegetables and peppers. In some areas they also grow yams. Varying with the seasons, clams are found in the river, and fruits such as mangoes grow in the forest. Because of disease spread by the tsetse fly, there are few large animals in the delta. Chickens and goats are the main domesticated animals and are usually reserved for special meals when visitors arrive or a ceremony is performed. Men sometimes hunt for animals, such as deer or wild pigs. Palm wine, tapped from palm trees, offers a nutritious drink at meals and on special occasions.

Ijo generally eat three meals a day. The morning and noon meals are small; the main one is in the evening after work. Men eat together, rolling cassava into a ball— with the right hand only—and dipping it into a shared pot containing a stew of fish and vegetables. Cooked plantains or yams are added when available. Women and children eat in the same fashion from their own plate.

The Ijo wash their hands before eating, but no one eats with the left hand, which they consider "unclean." The left hand is used to wash oneself after using the toilet, and to engage in sexual activity. By holding a drink in the left hand, a person signifies that he or she has killed someone in the past.

13 EDUCATION

Two forms of education have been closely related since the advent of missionary schools in the last century: formal schooling and informal instruction in culture and livelihood. The schools themselves are accessible to Ijo throughout the delta, eventually through college level. Girls now attend school in equal numbers with boys, and the literacy rate has increased steadily. Schooling is seen as a necessary step to finding a job, and the spectacular increase in the number of schools following Nigerian independence has made teaching positions the primary kind of job available. With the advent of schooling,

however, came a rising expectation—on the part of both parents and students—that literacy would bring with it higher wages. This expectation affects the other form of education, the cultural learning that defines being an Ijo. Learning to farm and fish is still part of growing up, but these jobs are often rejected as not being suitable occupations for graduates of secondary schools. The alternative is to migrate to urban areas to look for employment, especially since teaching assignments have become more competitive because of the increasing number of graduates. Since employment opportunities are often no better in the city than in the countryside, the government has established oil palm plantations, rice farms, and other development projects to encourage Ijo people to seek jobs in their home areas.

14 CULTURAL HERITAGE

Ijo dance and music are typical of the rhythmic complexity generally found in West African music. Drums of various sorts provide music at all events. Special dances are performed to distinguish, for example, between a funeral for a person of high status and a masquerade dance honoring a water spirit. The Ijo readily add songs and dances from other ethnic groups to their own repertoire. This has continued with youths forming bands using electric guitars and other Western instruments to blast out the latest Nigerian popular songs.

Although the Ijo have no tradition of literacy, they tell stories in the evenings or when receiving guests, for instance, after a funeral. These stories often have a moral lesson and, while seemingly of a mythical nature, they are told as though they had actually happened.

15 WORK

Like the Western concept of the "Protestant Ethic," which emphasizes the inherent value of work, the Ijo similarly stress the importance of everyone's engaging in productive work. In practice, this ideological emphasis means that the Ijo do not recognize a hierarchy based on occupational status in which a political leader or religious dignitary might expect to be supported by the community. Instead, they, too, must engage in some form of productive work. With widespread education, however, as noted above, the introduction of white-collar jobs has broadened the definition of work to include more than physical labor alone.

16 SPORTS

Wrestling and soccer are two of the most popular sports for boys and young men. Soccer, also for girls, has been introduced as part of the school program, but is no longer confined to the school day.

Men's wrestling appears to have a long history. Preparations for a wrestling match in the villages against a team from another village often take on the appearance of preparations for war. In a village, a particular bush spirit that has been associated with protection in battle can be approached for similar protection in a wrestling match. In other places, wrestling matches are just a sport, and like soccer games, they draw large audiences.

Since Ijo villages are usually located near a river, most Ijo can swim. Children often compete with each other in swimming races.

17 ENTERTAINMENT AND RECREATION

With electricity came the radio and, much more recently, television. The main forms of entertainment, however, remain similar—in form, if not in content—to the way children and adults occupied their leisure time in the past. Storytelling now includes events, real or imagined, that resemble the sensationalistic "news" in Western tabloid newspapers. As in the past, the Ijo also play games, such as card games and checkers.

18 FOLK ART, CRAFTS, AND HOBBIES

Ijo masks and woodcarvings, usually depicting fish and made to be worn on top of the head, are found in museums throughout the world, and are treated as serious art by viewers and scholars. While the Ijo are not unconcerned with the beauty of their carvings, their main concern is with the utility of the object: whether a spirit is satisfied to reside there. Wood carvers, like those who carve canoes, see themselves as craftsmen, possessing a certain talent, whose aim was to satisfy public needs.

Similarly, women weave colorful and decorative sleeping mats. While their main aim is to sell the mats, like craftspeople everywhere, the Ijo recognize and appreciate the difference in quality and beauty between one mat and another.

19 SOCIAL PROBLEMS

The problems that beset the state of Nigeria in postcolonial times, ranging from a civil war to a series of military coups, affected even the most isolated villages in the Niger Delta. Nigeria's national regimes' reputation for allowing bribery to become a way of life and for abusing human rights has been well publicized. There is an irony in seeing the Ijo tradition of democratic relations at the local level being frustrated by a modernized national government that has voiced much enthusiasm for achieving democracy but appears, at times, to evolve in the opposite direction.

The pollution caused by oil extraction eliminated, for the most part, fresh fish, the most fundamental part of the Ijo diet. By the early 1990s this ecological degradation was compounded by a general loss of economic well being, lack of employment, and a growing frustration over the inequitable distribution of wealth. Ijo attacks on the oil facilities and theft of the oil itself have caused problems worldwide, particularly in the United States, which relies on Nigeria as one of its top five importing countries for most of its oil needs.

20 GENDER ISSUES

Gender has been touched upon in several sections above, and, as with the other topics, emphasis must be placed on the variations found among the Ijo. From the women in the central delta whose associations extend no further than the extended family to those living on the delta borders who belong to powerful female marketing organizations, the differences are profound. At the same time, the division of labor marked by age and gender is recognized by the Ijo themselves as being inherently balanced. Consistent with a general ethos of egalitarianism, Ijo ideology does not hold one sex to be innately superior to another. Although women never occupied political roles, this did not mean they were not political. A wife could, on occasion, rely on women in her community to forcefully punish a man who repeatedly and without reason mistreated her. Men claimed, not entirely joking, that it was prudent to marry an odd number of women to avoid them pairing up against him. In their view the odd numbered one could be counted on to cook when the others went on strike.

As in many other African societies, women play a major role in the trading economy, whether in the market place or in moving provisions and goods between markets. Their ability to accumulate wealth was not seen as unusual.

In a reflection of the role women played at critical times in the past, as when there was resistance to colonial tax impositions, Ijo women have attempted to impose their own presence by holding sit-ins at oil facilities to make the oil companies more responsive to demands for jobs and local community development.

21 BIBLIOGRAPHY

Alagoa, E. J. *A History of the Niger Delta: An Historical Interpretation of Ijo Oral Tradition.* Ibadan: Ibadan University Press, 1972.

Alagoa, E. J., and Tekena N. Tamuno, ed. *Land and People of Nigeria: Rivers State.* Port Harcourt, Nigeria: Riverside Communications, 1989.

Dike, Kenneth O. *Trade and Politics in the Niger Delta, 1830–1885: An Introduction to the Economic and Political History of Nigeria.* Oxford: Clarendon Press, 1956.

Efere, E. E., and Kay Williamson. "Languages." In *Land and People of Nigeria: Rivers State,* ed. by E. J. Alagoa and Tekena Taumo. Port Harcourt, Nigeria: Riverside Communications, 1989.

Ejobowah, John Boye. "Who Owns the Oil? The Politics of Ethnicity in the Niger Delta of Nigeria." *Africa Today,* vol. 47, no. 1 (2000):29-47.

Hollos, Marida, and Philip E. Leis. *Becoming Nigerian in Ijo Society.* New Brunswick, NJ: Rutgers University Press, 1989.

Horton, Robin. "From Fishing Village to City-State: A Social History of New Calabar." In *Man in Africa,* ed. by M. Douglas and P. M. Kaberry. London: Tavistock, 1969.

Leis, Philip E. *Enculturation and Socialization in an Ijaw Village.* New York: Holt, Rinehart and Winston, 1972.

———. "Ethnic Conflict, History, and State Formation in Africa." In *Population, Ethnicity, and Nation-Building,* ed. by Calvin Goldscheider. Boulder, CO: Westview Press, 1995.

Ukiwo, Ukoha. "From 'pirates' to 'militants': A Historical Perspective On Anti-state and Anti-oil Company Mobilization Among the Ijaw of Warri, Western Niger Delta." *African Affairs,* vol. 106, no. 425, (2007): 587–610.

Williamson, Kay. "Linguistic evidence for the prehistory of the Niger Delta." In *The Early History of the Niger Delta,* ed. by E. J. Alagoa, F. N. Anozie, and Nwanna Nzewunwa. Hamburg: Helmut Buske, 1988.

—by P. E. Leis

IVOIRIANS

PRONUNCIATION: ih-VWAHR-ee-uhns
ALTERNATE NAMES: Ivorians
LOCATION: West Africa (Côte d'Ivoire)
POPULATION: 18,373,600 (2008)
LANGUAGE: Approximately 60 ethnic languages, including Akan; Mandé; Gur (Voltaic); Kru; Dioula (the most widely spoken); Baoulé (Akan); Sénoufo (Voltaic); Yacouba (south Mandé); French (official language)
RELIGION: Islam; Christianity (both incorporate traditional indigenous beliefs)
RELATED ARTICLES: Vol 1: Aka; Dyula; Malinke

¹ INTRODUCTION

Côte d'Ivoire is a French-speaking country in West Africa. A number of important kingdoms existed in the area from early times. In the 14th century the Mali empire extended into part of Côte d'Ivoire; later empires included the Kong and the Baoulé kingdom of Sakasso. Many different ethnic groups migrated over the centuries into what became known as Côte d'Ivoire.

Early trade with Europe was based on ivory, which gave the country its name—Ivory Coast (although in 1986 the government decided that the country should be known only by its French name, Côte d'Ivoire). However, the trade in ivory led to such a decline in the elephant population that the trade virtually disappeared by the beginning of the 18th century. An elephant's head, however, still is portrayed on the country's crest. The Portuguese were the first Europeans to reach the coast of Côte d'Ivoire. The earliest recorded French voyage took place in 1483, but it was only in the mid-nineteenth century that the French firmly established themselves in the region. At first, trade was governed by treaties; later, French exploration and occupation intensified. In 1893, Côte d'Ivoire became a French colony.

The best known recent figure is the first president, Félix Houphouët-Boigny. Houphouët-Boigny came from a wealthy Baoulé chief's family. Born around 1905, he grew up to study medicine in Dakar (Senegal) and became a medical assistant, a prosperous cocoa farmer, and a local chief. He campaigned for fairer cocoa prices for African farmers and founded the country's first agricultural trade union for African planters. This trade union was quickly converted into the Parti Démocratique de Côte d'Ivoire, which is still the dominant political party. Houphouët-Boigny became a deputy to the French National Assembly (parliament) in Paris, and the first African to serve as a cabinet minister in a European government. At independence in 1960, he became the country's first president, favoring a continued close relationship with France. He promoted agriculture and led Côte d'Ivoire's economy to great success until the beginning of the 1980s, when prices for Côte d'Ivoire's two major export crops, cocoa and coffee, crashed. The drought of 1983–84 compounded the problem, as did excessive borrowing and the steep rise in oil prices. Côte d'Ivoire's economy declined dramatically as its per capita income fell from $1,290 in 1978 to $510 in 1995. Despite good harvests in 1985–86, a fall in coffee and cocoa prices, the outflow of capital, and too much government spending led to serious indebtedness. Re-

sulting austerity measures were met with protests, strikes, and riots. However, despite charges of corruption and a lavish lifestyle, Houphouët-Boigny still was revered and honored until his death in December 1993, when he was succeeded by Henri Konan Bedié.

Côte d'Ivoire was the richest of the French colonies by the late 1940s, based on the export of timber and forest products, such as palm oil and cocoa. Since independence, the strength of the economy has varied considerably, attaining average annual growth rates of 6.7% in the first two decades, then declining significantly between the beginning of the 1980s and 1994; it finally began to improve again after a 50% devaluation of the French-backed Communauté Financière Africaine (CFA) franc in January 1994.

In December 1999, a military coup—the first ever in Cote d'Ivoire's history—overthrew the government. Junta leader Robert Guei blatantly rigged elections held in late 2000 and declared himself the winner. Popular protest forced him to step aside and brought Laurent Gbagbo into power. Ivorian dissidents and disaffected members of the military launched a failed coup attempt in September 2002. Rebel forces claimed the northern half of the country, and in January 2003 were granted ministerial positions in a unity government under the auspices of the Linas-Marcoussis Peace Accord. President Gbagbo and rebel forces resumed implementation of the peace accord in December 2003 after a three-month stalemate, but issues that sparked the civil war, such as land reform and grounds for citizenship, remained unresolved. In March 2007 President Gbagbo and former New Force rebel leader Guillaume Soro signed the Ouagadougou Political Agreement. As a result of the agreement, Soro joined Gbagbo's government as prime minister and the two agreed to reunite the country by dismantling the zone of confidence separating North from South, integrate rebel forces into the national armed forces, and hold elections. Several thousand French and United Nations (UN) troops remain in Cote d'Ivoire to help the parties implement their commitments and to support the peace process.

² LOCATION AND HOMELAND

Côte d'Ivoire, a roughly square-shaped country, is located on the Gulf of Guinea. It is bordered by Liberia and Guinea to the west, by Ghana to the east, and by Mali and Burkina Faso to the north. It lies between 4° to 11°N and 3° to 8°W and covers 322,000 sq km (124,500 sq mi—slightly larger than New Mexico) and has a 530-km (330-mi) coastline along the Gulf of Guinea.

Most of the country consists of a low plateau, sloping gradually southward to the Gulf of Guinea. The plateau is broken by hills in the north and by the Man Mountains in the west, which are about 4000 ft in altitude. Much of the landscape is monotonous, although in places granite domes (inselbergs) rise out of the otherwise flat surface. The heavy surf and strong currents along the coastline have deterred traders throughout history; only in the eastern half of the country was access easier because of a narrow belt of lagoons, sandy islands, and sandbars. Côte d'Ivoire has no natural, sheltered deepwater harbors; Abidjan became the largest port in West Africa only after 1950, when the Vridi Canal was constructed to give Abidjan deepwater access from the ocean.

Climate differences have led to different types of vegetation. The southern part of the country has an equatorial climate with high temperatures and humidity. Tropical rain forest traditionally occupied this region; although much now has been cut down to provide timber for export and land for plantations of cocoa, coffee, oil palms, bananas, rubber, and other crops. In the north it is drier, with almost all the rain falling within a three-month period in the late summer. The rain forest changes into savanna woodlands characterized by increasingly shorter grasses and isolated stands of trees. Vegetation becomes increasingly sparse toward the Burkina Faso border where there is less rainfall. Four rivers, the Cavally, Sassandra, Bandama, and Comoé flow from the north into the Gulf of Guinea to the south. None of the rivers is fully navigable because of rapids and large differences in the levels of the water between the seasons.

The population of Côte d'Ivoire in 2008 was estimated at 18,373,600; it has been growing very quickly since 1975 when it was 6.7 million. The population growth rate in 2008 was 1.96%. About 40.4% are under 15 years of age; and life expectancy is a low 49 years. Abidjan's population is about 3 million and has been growing very rapidly. Grand-Bassam was the original capital of Côte d'Ivoire; it was replaced by Bingerville in 1900 and by Abidjan in 1934. Since 1983, Yamoussoukro, Houphouët-Boigny's village, has been the official administrative capital, although the government has remained in Abidjan and that city remains by far the largest and most dynamic economically.

More than 60 ethnic groups make up the population of Côte d'Ivoire, each with its own distinct language or dialect and customs. The four largest ethnic groups all have their major centers outside Côte d'Ivoire—the Akan to the east, the Mandé and Voltaic to the north, and the Kru to the west. Thus Côte d'Ivoire does not have a single dominant culture. In the past people had more in common with the people of surrounding countries than with their fellow Ivoirians. Indeed, one of the challenges of the country has been to develop a national identity, so that people consider themselves Ivoirians first and members of their particular ethnic group second. The Akan and Voltaic groups form matrilineal societies while the Mandé and Kru are patrilineal. The largest group, the Akan, includes the Abron, Agni, and Baoulé people. The Mandé are among the oldest settlers of Côte d'Ivoire and are found in the forest region; this group includes the Dan or Yacouba, the Malinké, and the Dioula. The most important peoples in the Voltaic group are the Sénoufo. The Kru or Krou group consists of a number of small ethnic groups, including the Godié, Bété, and Wè. Most live in small farming villages or as fishers along the coast.

Although these ethnic groups existed as distinct entities in the past, especially in rural areas, modernization and urbanization have led to mixing, so that ethnic lines have become far less distinct, especially in the towns and cities in the south, which are more cosmopolitan. A large percentage of the population living in the country are non-Ivoirians, having come to seek work. Most are from Burkina Faso, Mali, and Guinea, with smaller numbers from Mauritania and Senegal. In addition, there are significant Lebanese and French populations.

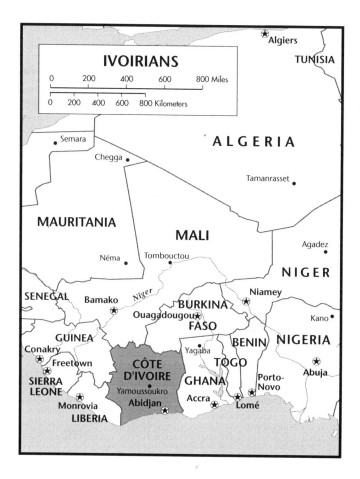

3 LANGUAGE

Although all of its approximately 60 ethnic languages belong to the Niger-Congo family, no one language is spoken by more than about a quarter of the population. Four of the eight major branches of the Niger-Congo language family are represented in Côte d'Ivoire: Akan, Mandé, Gur or Voltaic, and Kru. Dioula (pronounced Jou-lah), a north Mandé language, is the most widely spoken African language in Côte d'Ivoire, used all over the country as a market language. Other major African languages are Baoulé (Akan), Sénoufo (Voltaic), and Yacouba (south Mandé).

The official language of the country is French, which is spoken especially in the urban areas and in higher education. However, it is not spoken by the masses of the people, who prefer popular (pidgin) French or Dioula.

4 FOLKLORE

Each ethnic group has its own traditions and heroes. One of the most famous legends tells the story of how the Baoulé people arrived in Côte d'Ivoire. In their original homeland, Ghana, they wisely had stored grain in case of famine, but then were attacked by other groups when famine came. Rather than forfeit their food, their queen, Abla Pokou, led her people west into Côte d'Ivoire. Finding it impossible to cross the Comoé river, the queen sacrificed her own child to the genies of the river; they in turn, in recognition of the gift, caused the trees to bend over the river and form a bridge to a land of peace and safety. The word *baoulé* means "the little one dies."

5 RELIGION

Most people in Côte d'Ivoire follow traditional religions, revering the ancestors and believing in the spirits of nature. Even those who profess to follow one of the two major universal religions, Islam and Christianity, generally incorporate traditional practices into their religious observances and daily lives. Many follow syncretic cults loosely based on Islam or Christianity. Sorcery and witchcraft have a strong impact on people, especially in the rural areas but even in the cities. Belief in fetishes is widespread. Traditional ceremonies, dances, and funerals are all related to religious beliefs; they often involve wearing masks. Animal and other sacrifices also may play an important role.

Islam was brought to Côte d'Ivoire by Malinké immigrants from the Mali Empire of the 13th to 18th centuries and is particularly strong in the northern savannah area of the country, although the spiritual center is Abidjan, where one-third of the population is Muslim. About 40% of the population is currently considered Muslim.

Christianity was brought by the Europeans. The French established their first missionary work in the 17th century. About one-fourth of the population, mostly in southern cities, belongs to either the Roman Catholic (the majority) or Protestant churches. Some Ivoirians are followers of the Liberian prophet, William Wade Harris, who spread his version of Christianity along the coast in the early part of the 20th century; the Harrist church continues to gain adherents in urban areas.

6 MAJOR HOLIDAYS

August 7 is Independence Day. Both Christian and Muslim holidays are celebrated: Christmas, Easter, and Pentecost; and Idul Fitri (the feast at the end of the fasting month of Ramadan) and Labaski, 70 days after the end of Ramadan. The Ivorian government recognizes the following holidays: New Year's Day (January 1), Labor Day (May 1), Assumption (August 15), All Saints' Day (November 1), and Ascension Day.

7 RITES OF PASSAGE

Each ethnic group has its own traditions (see **Aka**, **Malinke**, and **Dyula**). The major transitions of life—birth, puberty, marriage, and death—all are marked with ceremonies and rituals. Among the most important are initiation rites. The Sénoufo, for example, pass their values and traditions down the generations through *poro,* an ethnic educational system that spans twenty-one years. During the initiation participants undergo endurance tests and other secret ceremonies in the sacred forest adjacent to the village. Traditionally excision festivals occurred, but these have been severely limited by the government, as have some other initiation practices.

Marriage is basically family, not individually, based. Many marriages are arranged, although in the towns and cities more young people now choose their own spouse. Marriage generally takes place early, particularly for women and especially for those in rural areas. Motherhood thus starts young. By age 14 almost one-half of the girls are married. Divorce and separation are uncommon.

Funerals are central to several ethnic groups. Among the Akan, all villagers shaving their heads mark death in a village. Among the Baoulé, burial is secret, even for someone as illustrious as the first president, Houphouët-Boigny.

8 INTERPERSONAL RELATIONS

Men clearly dominate relationships. Much respect is traditionally accorded to the elders in the village.

9 LIVING CONDITIONS

Living conditions vary enormously according to whether people live in urban or rural surroundings and according to their wealth.

More than 40% of the population lives in towns and cities. Those who are well off live in nice two- or three-story homes or in air-conditioned skyscrapers, with all the modern conveniences of electricity, running water, sanitation, paved roads, etc. They shop in well-stocked stores and at sophisticated malls. The majority who are poor, however, live mostly in overcrowded slums with none of these facilities and obtain their necessities from open-air markets and roadside stalls.

Most people still live in villages, generally with dirt roads. Although increasing numbers have electricity, many still live in simple, traditional ways, in conical, thatched roof homes, collecting their own water and firewood. Frequently children have to walk to a neighboring village to go to school or to find a clinic staffed by a nurse. Official figures indicate that there is only one doctor for about every 10,000 people in the country and they are overwhelmingly located in the cities. Most land tenure systems are based on the concept of communal ownership. Each family is granted the right to cultivate particular areas, rights that can be handed down through the generations. Almost all city office workers keep alive their ties with their agricultural villages and their links with their native ethnic group.

10 FAMILY LIFE

Households characteristically are made up of the extended family, with parents and children, grandparents, uncles, aunts, and cousins all sharing the same facilities. The family is very strong and children are much wanted. Indeed, the average Ivoirian woman has more than seven children. Women have the responsibility for taking care of the children. Babies are carried on their mothers' backs while the women work in the fields, fetch firewood or water, cook, and undertake other household chores.

This extended family system, together with ethnic and village loyalties, provides a form of social security. It also provides a mechanism for income to be redistributed. Hospitality and solidarity are a way of life; this spirit of hospitality and brotherhood is expressed clearly in these lines from the Ivoirian national anthem: "land of hospitality.... the homeland of genuine brotherhood."

Customs regarding family life vary from one ethnic group to another. For example, among the Beng (one of the south Mandé group) menstruating women may not work in the forests or the fields, touch a corpse, or cook for their husbands.

Although the law in Côte d'Ivoire allows only one wife, in practice almost one-fourth of men in the country have two or more.

11 CLOTHING

As in most of the developing world, both traditional and Western clothes are worn. Particularly in the urban areas, most people wear Western clothing—pants, or blue jeans, and shirts, although many women wear traditional brightly colored dresses *(pagnes)* with matching head scarves. In the rural areas, traditional clothing is most common. Women wear pagnes or blouses with long pieces of cloth that wrap around. Men wear shorts or wrap short pieces of cloth around their bodies. Many men have long, beautiful robes for ceremonial occasions.

12 FOOD

Yams, plantains, rice, millet, corn, and peanuts are staple foods in Côte d'Ivoire, although each region has its specialties. For example, in the northern savanna area, a common dish is rice with a peppery peanut sauce. Closer to the coast, fish with fried plantain is popular.

The national dish is *fufu*, made by pounding plantains, cassava, or yams into a sticky dough that then is served with a highly seasoned meat or vegetable sauce, called *kedjenou*. Fufu is eaten by hand with each person taking a fingerful of dough and dipping it in the sauce. The sauce, prepared from different bases, such as peanut, eggplant, okra, or tomato, can be made with chicken, beef, fish, or other meats; it is simmered like a stew in a *canari* or oven or over a wood fire. Wood is still the most common fuel except in the towns and cities.

Traditionally people grew their own food and sold the surplus. As in almost all of West Africa, markets play an important role in people's lives. In the cities and large towns, markets are periodic, held every 3, 4, 5, 8 or even 16 days. Merchants are clustered according to the product sold—kola nuts, salt, cloth, animals, leather, baskets, etc. Women are very active in the markets, selling their produce, and purchasing needed goods.

13 EDUCATION

The Ivoirian educational system is an adaptation of the French system. Very few received an education during colonial days, but after independence far more children had the opportunity to attend school. By 2008 Côte d'Ivoire had a literacy rate of about 50.9% , with 57.9% literate males and 43.6% literate females.

Primary school, which is officially compulsory, lasts for six years and secondary school for seven. Children start school generally at age seven. Secondary education is divided into two cycles, the first four years, which culminate in a certificate of the lower cycle of secondary study (the *brevet d'étude du premier cycle*—the *BEPC*), and the second cycle, whose graduates earn the *baccalauréat,* a level of learning roughly equivalent to one or two years of university study in the United States. About two-thirds of primary-school-age children attend school. About 20% continue on to secondary school. Higher education includes the university in Abidjan and a large number of technical and teacher-training institutes. School is free, although students pay an entrance fee at public schools. The public school system is supplemented by Catholic and Quranic schools. However, lack of trained teachers and inadequate equipment and supplies make it hard for most children to obtain a good education.

14 CULTURAL HERITAGE

Music, dance, and storytelling are all important in the lives of Ivoirians. Rhythm is an important part of music in Côte d'Ivoire as in almost all of West Africa. Songs are about typi-

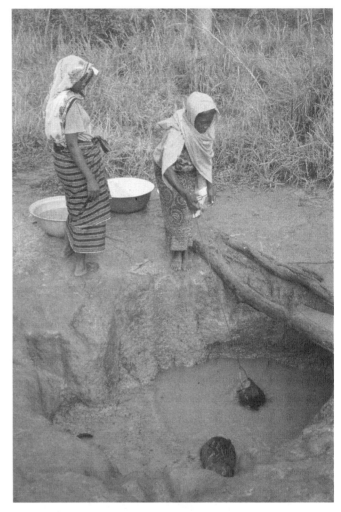

Two women in Côte d'Ivoire stand at a well to fill buckets with water. Government education efforts, supported by the World Health Organization and Global 2000, teach villagers how to protect themselves from Guinea worm and other water-borne diseases. (The Image Works)

cal topics—love, money, friendship, peace, death, and national heroes.

There is great variety in dance in the different regions of the country. It is associated with physical, spiritual, and social benefits. In Côte d'Ivoire there are three types of traditional dancing: the royal dance performed only by a king or tribal chief; the fetish dance, danced by male initiates who have undergone initiation rites in the sacred forest; and the popular dance, open to all, including women. Mask dancing, which belongs to the second category, includes performing a wide variety of twists, turns, twirls, and handstands, sometimes on tall stilts; the dancer's identity remains unknown throughout the ceremony.

15 WORK

In 2007 close to 68% of the population worked in agriculture, far less than the 84% who were farmers in 1960. In general, men clear the land and also take most of the responsibility for the cash or export crops that are grown, such as cocoa, coffee, and pineapples. Women frequently plant and tend the crops and also have the responsibility for growing food crops, such as yams, cassava, plantains, corn, and rice.

A much smaller proportion of the labor force works in industry, concerned largely with processing foods and other raw materials, and producing items such as textiles and machinery. About one-third of the population works in the service sector—more than double the proportion in 1960. Non-Africans dominate the managerial and professional ranks, and work also as mechanics, technicians, and storekeepers. Non-Ivoirian Africans mostly are employed as rural unskilled labor.

16 SPORTS

By far the most important sport in Côte d'Ivoire is football (soccer), which is played throughout the country.

17 ENTERTAINMENT AND RECREATION

Ritual ceremonies serve partly as recreation and entertainment and often include music and dance. Storytelling is another favorite traditional pastime. Griots, or bards, may sing or tell folk stories, riddles, and proverbs way into the night. Several ethnic groups have stories that revolve around a scoundrel or trickster, who is always ready to pull a fast one on his partners. Many stories relate to family relationships, such as those between son-in-law and mother-in-law.

Cinema and theater are also important. Movies are made in Côte d'Ivoire for both the cinema and television. Theater includes works by playwrights such as Bernard Dadié, Côte d'Ivoire's most famous writer, and François-Joseph Amon d'Aby. Television and radio provide recreation for increasing numbers, especially in the cities.

18 FOLK ART, CRAFTS, AND HOBBIES

The art of Côte d'Ivoire is among the most outstanding in West Africa. Weaving, woodworking, and sculpture flourish. The wooden carvings, and especially the masks, of the Dan and Baoulé people are particularly famous for their beauty and intricate designs. The masks vary considerably from region to region in their designs and purposes. Dan (Yacouba) masks, for example, generally have a somewhat abstract human face while Baoulé masks typically represent an animal or stylized human face. Some may represent antelope or buffalo with large open mouths, intended to represent evil spirits; others may be humorous as with a *kplekple,* or horned mask, representing a disobedient child. The most famous mask is often considered to be the "fire-spitter" helmet mask, said to represent the chaotic state of things in primeval times; it is a combination of hyena, warthog, and antelope.

Art works are produced not only for ceremonies, but also for enjoyment in non-ceremonial environments; carved doors and furniture, statues, and other decorative objects form an integral part of people's lives. Painted, tie-dyed, and woven textiles, pottery, worked gold and brass, and beautiful jewelry all form a vital part of Côte d'Ivoire's rich artistic heritage. Musical instruments, such as percussion instruments, drums, stringed instruments, and various transverse horns in wood, metal, or animal horn also are made. Images are made of bush spirits, pythons, chameleons, in Sénoufo art, in cast brass ornaments and in mudcloth paintings.

19 SOCIAL PROBLEMS

Côte d'Ivoire is a country of great social contrasts. Many of its current social problems arise from its difficult economic conditions. The declining standard of living and the economic austerity that occurred between 1980 and 1994 led to social upheavals, political dissension, and repression.

Poverty, exacerbated by fast population growth and rapid urbanization, underlies the lack of adequate facilities, ranging from inadequate schools and housing to inadequate access to health care, clean water, electricity, and other important elements of infrastructure. Poverty also underlies the increasing amount of crime, including violent crime, found especially in swollen urban areas like Abidjan. Urban unemployment is acute, by 2008 registering at some 40% to 50% as a result of the civil war. Yet along with the decline of real per capita income, there are those who are rich—some commercial farmers, landowners, business executives, and others whose extravagance stands in stark contrast to the misery and squalor the poor experience. Growing inequality between rich and poor exacerbates social tensions. Corruption among government officials reduces the effectiveness of government and its ability to help the country develop, and causes deep resentment among ordinary people. It is widely felt that government officials do what is good for themselves and not what is best for the country.

Côte d'Ivoire also suffers from having one of the highest incidences of AIDS and HIV infection in the continent.

Tensions also exist among ethnic groups and between political parties, tensions that become particularly apparent at election time.

20 GENDER ISSUES

In rural areas, women and men divide the labor, with men clearing the land and harvesting cash crops like cocoa and coffee, while women grow vegetables and other staples and perform most household tasks. Women also collect water and fuel, care for their families, spin and weave, and produce handicrafts and pottery to sell. In general, men hold most prominent civic and government positions, as well as the role of tribal chief in the villages. Religious roles, from shamans to Catholic priests to Muslim imams, are dominated by men.

Men dominate inheritance practices in traditional societies. Both Baoule and Senufo people belong to their mother's family group; power and land are passed down through a mother's family line to her sister's sons. In the Bete and Nyula groups, inheritance is passed down through the father's line to the sons. In most traditional societies in Côte d'Ivoire, women do not have the right to inherit land, but only to use that of their husbands or families. Legislation was enacted in 1983 to allow women greater control of their property after marriage.

Government policy encourages full participation by women in business, but generally there is a bias among employers to hiring women, whom they consider less dependable because of their potential pregnancy. Women are underrepresented in most professions and in the managerial sector as a whole. Some women also encounter difficulty in obtaining loans, as they cannot meet the lending criteria mandated by banks, including title to a house and production of profitable cash crops, specifically coffee and cocoa. However, women are paid on an equal scale with men in the formal business sector. Men continue to dominate managerial positions and enjoy the most career mobility, usually due to a higher level of education and connections with other businessmen.

21 BIBLIOGRAPHY

Center for Environment and Development in Africa (CEDA). *Côte d'Ivoire: Environmental Profile of the Coasts*, 1997.

Cohen, Michael A. *Urban Policy and Political Conflict in Africa: A Study of the Ivory Coast*, Chicago: University of Chicago Press, 1974.

Daniels, Morna. *Côte d'Ivoire*. World Bibliographical Series, Vol 131. Oxford: CLIO Press, 1996.

Eloundou-Enyegue, Parfait M. *Poverty and Rapid Population Growth in Africa: The Links between High Fertility and Poverty at the Household Level*. Rand Working Papers in Economics, 1998.

Foster, Philip, and Zolberg, Aristide R., eds. *Ghana and the Ivory Coast: Perspectives on Modernization*. Chicago: University of Chicago Press, 1971.

Grinker, Roy Richard, and Christopher B. Steiner, eds. *Perspectives in Africa: A Reader in Culture, History and Presentation*. Malden: Blackwell Publishing, 1997.

International Monetary Fund. *Enhanced Structural Adjustment Facility Policy Framework Paper, 1998–2000*. 2000.

Kashambuzi, Eric. *Critical Issues in African Development*. New York: Rivercross Publishing, 1997.

Khapoya, Vincent B. *The African Experience: An Introduction*. 2d ed. Upper Saddle River, NJ: Prentice Hall, 1998.

Meekers, Dominique. "The Process of Marriage in African Societies." *Population and Development Review* 1 (18) (March 1992): 61–78.

Moss, Joyce, and George Wilson. *Peoples of the World: Africans South of the Sahara*. Farmington Hills, MI: Thomson Gale, 1991.

Vennetier, Pierre, ed. *Atlas de la Côte d'Ivoire*. 2d ed. Paris: Jeune Afrique, 1983.

—revised by M. Njoroge

JOLA

ALTERNATIVE NAMES: Jola-Fogny, Jola-Fonyi, Diola (French)
LOCATION: Casamance Region of Southern Senegal, The Gambia, and Guinea Bissau
POPULATION: 702,000
LANGUAGE: Jola or Diola; dialects: Banjaal, Bayot, Ejamat, Fonyi, Gusilay, Karon, Kasa, Kuwatay and Mlomp
RELIGION: Islam (primary), Traditional (Indigenous) Religions and Christianity

1 INTRODUCTION

The Jola (also known as Diola in French) are a heterogenous ethnic group found in Senegal, The Gambia, and Guinea-Bissau. They comprise 10% of the population in The Gambia and 6% of the population in Senegal. In The Gambia they are concentrated in the Foni area of southwest The Gambia; hence, another name for them is Jola-Foni. In Senegal they are concentrated in the southern region of Casamance. The Casamance region is separated from the rest of Senegal by the territory of the former British colony of The Gambia. Jola people have long claimed that they are marginalized by their government that is dominated by ethnic Wolof, a majority group in Senegal. In 1982, a few years after Senegal obtained independence from France, Jola people, who form the majority in Casamance, rose up against their government demanding independence from Senegal on the basis that they were isolated geographically from Senegal proper. Since then, there have been sporadic fights between the rebel movement in the Jola homeland and the government of Senegal.

Although little is known about the origins of the Jola, it is believed that the ancestors of the present Jola people settled this region long before the 13th century, predating other groups, such as the Mande and Fula peoples. Archeology of the mouth of the Casamance River shows evidence that by AD 200 there were groups of people who were well-adapted to coastal habitats and who had spread out to the islands bordering the mouth of the Casamance River. There were advanced hunter-gatherers, as well as groups who subsisted on shellfish from the mangrove flats and fish from the ocean. Some of them practiced advanced agriculture and raised livestock, notably cattle. They also worked metal, from which they forged spears and agricultural implements.

By the time the Portuguese arrived in the middle of the 15th century, the Jola were well established and largely isolated from other groups, with very few contacts with other people in the region. When the Europeans came to the region, they instituted slavery. While the Jola fiercely resisted both enslavement and participation as middle men in the trade, other groups, such as the Manding, located along the Lower and Upper Gambia River and inland along the Middle Casamance and Geba Rivers, were involved in trade with the Europeans in slaves and gold. The Jola, located on the coastal zone, did not engage in any trade with outsiders, nor did they have any chiefs to rule, preferring rather to be acephalous societies (those without a ruling chief or head). They resisted any intrusions into the homeland by their neighbors and the new arrivals, the Europeans. As such they were considered to be a dangerous group and were bypassed by the Portuguese, who sailed past them at the

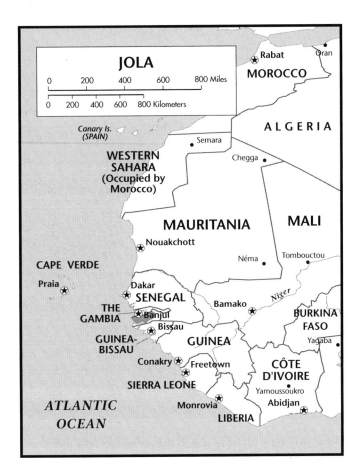

JOLA

mouth of the Casamance and Cacheu rivers in order to trade with other people further upriver.

Even when colonial rule was imposed by the British in The Gambia and the French in Senegal, the colonial rulers had great difficulty in subjugating them. Although the Jola had appeared weak and fragmented, they maintained strong stockades and an attitude of fierce independence. Over time, however, the Jola began to accept the new reality of colonialism; by 1905 they had began to pay taxes to the new European masters.

²LOCATION AND HOMELAND

The Jola are found mainly in Senegal, The Gambia, and Guinea Bissau although a small number exist in other countries in this region of West Africa. The largest numbers are located in the Casamance region of Southern Senegal. It is a strip of forested and river bottom land between The Gambia and Guinea Bissau. A substantial number of Jola live along the south bank of the Gambia River, where they farm different types of crops, particularly rice. While Senegal was colonized by the French, the British claimed the area around the Gambia River as their territory. Awkwardly, The Gambia, a small sliver of territory on both sides of the Gambia River, sticks deep into Senegal, cutting off the Casamance region from the rest of Senegal. The Jola thus feel isolated from the rest of Senegal and have, since 1982, demanded independence from Senegal. The Casamance region has seen fighting since then, between a breakaway rebel movement and government forces, making the region unstable and dangerous. A smaller number of Jola are found in the

northern part of Guinea Bissau, just to the south of the Casamance region of Senegal.

The Casamance region is regarded as the most beautiful area of Senegal. The region receives a greater amount of rainfall than the rest of Senegal. It is characterized by hot temperatures with a low-lying geography and a few hills to the southeast. It is well endowed with fertile soils that are suitable for agriculture, but it does not have high-value minerals. The regional economy is heavily dependent on the cultivation of rice and other crops. Pristine beaches along its coastline have seen an increase in the tourist industry.

Close to the coast there are thick mangroves and forests that are very compact and difficult to access. They offered protection to the Jola during times of slavery and colonization. There are a few large deer and several species of monkeys. But, what the region lacks in fauna, it makes up for in the rich variety of bird species. The turtle-doves with their characteristic songs, the francolins that fly away as soon as they see you, the calaos perched at the top of the large cheesemonger trees, the blackbirds with their shiny plumes and pretty bluish reflections, the black and white corbels, vultures, and many others are all present in the Casamance region.

³LANGUAGE

The language for the Jola is referred to as Jola or Diola. There are many dialects of this language, some of which are unintelligible to each other. Jola belongs to the Bak group of the Atlantic branch of the Niger-Congo language family. Banjaal is spoken in a small area south of the Casamance River, while Bayot is spoken around Ziguinchor, the capital city of Casamance. Other dialects are spoken in a handful of villages, such as Ejamat, Fonyi, Gusilay, Karon, Kasa, Kuwatay, and Mlomp. The multiplicity of dialects in the Jola homeland is testament to the isolation of the Jola from the rest of the peoples in this region and often from each other.

⁴FOLKLORE

Like most African societies, the Jola have a rich tradition of legends, folktales, and myths, which serve as a means of handing down traditions and customs from one generation to the next. Folktales impart moral values and prepare young people for life, as there are many lessons to be learned from the tales. There are many stories of legendary heroes who led their people into battle against other hostile ethnic groups and races. Other legends trace the origins of the Jola. For example, one folktale talks about two sisters traveling on the Senegal River. Their boat hit an object and was split in half. One sister, Aguene, drifted south to become the mother of the Jola, while the other sister, Anecho, drifted north to become the mother of the Serer people.

The use of natural surroundings and the animals that abound in these environments are omnipresent in African folktales, and the Jola are no exception to this rule. Consequently, the monkey, the hare, the lizard, the bird, the deer, the snake, the hyena, and other animals take on human characteristics of greed, jealousy, honesty, loneliness, and so on. It is through the behavior of these animals that important lessons are imparted to children. For example, one folktale tells of the adventures of Hare and Hyena. Hare is seen by the Jola as a cunning individual that is able to talk his way out of any trouble. Others see Hare as a trickster.

Many of the folktales feature an unjust situation that is remedied by a child, often with the help of a benevolent spirit or some old woman who has been treated courteously. The troublemakers end up being severely punished, while the victims end up rich and live happily thereafter. It is through folklore that family values and interpersonal relations are reinforced. If one breaks a tradition or any of the prescribed taboos, then one can expect to be punished by the supernatural world. It is expected that sons and daughters should be obedient and subservient to their elders, treating them with dignity. Strangers from afar should be treated with hospitality, and sons should be brave and help protect their homeland.

There is also a rich tradition of proverbs among the Jola and related ethnic groups. For example, "However long a stick is in the river, it cannot become a crocodile." This proverb implies that a stranger can never become a true citizen of Jola homeland. Another proverb talks about the importance of interpersonal relations and the interdependent nature of Jola people: "The best medicine for a person is another person." On nurturing independence in children: "A tree that grows in the shade of another one will die small." On learning to occupy one's position of humility and lie low when necessary: "If the dog is not at home, he barks not."

⁵RELIGION

The traditional Jola believe in the existence of a supreme being called Emit, or Ata Emit, the one who resides in the sky. They associate this entity with natural phenomena of the sky, rain, and the seasons. Similar to other indigenous religions in Africa, the Jola have shrines, charms, sacred forests, sacred lands, and secret masquerades, all of which play a central role in Jola cosmology. They worship and pray to these entities to protect their families and villages and to offer generous providence for the well-being of Jola society.

Christianity came among the Jola with the arrival of the Portuguese and other European powers, who introduced Catholicism to many converts. However, during the 20th century, there has been a shift from Christianity to Islam, because of strong influences from the northern part of the country, which is largely Muslim. Today, over 90% claim to be Muslim, with about 3% claiming to be Christians. However, the majority practice their traditional beliefs concurrently with Islam or Christianity. It is not unusual for a Jola individual to seek Western medical help for treatment and, at the same time, consult the traditional healer for herbs and amulets.

⁶MAJOR HOLIDAYS

In traditional Jola society there were indigenous celebrations for the initiation ceremonies of boys and girls. Other holidays included a celebration immediately after the rice harvest. Today, the Jola also celebrate holidays that are mandated by the modern government and those that are associated with Islam and Christianity. Official holidays in Senegal include New Year's Day (January 1), Independence Day (February 18), and Liberation Day (July 22). Christmas is also observed by all. It is marked by special watch night services at the Christian church, with children singing carols. Easter is also observed. In The Gambia, the major state holidays include New Year's Day (1 January), Independence Day (4 April), and International Workers' Day (1 May). During the holidays, people cook ceremonial food and dress up in bright traditional outfits. Other

religious holidays include Good Friday, Easter Monday, Eid-al-Fitr, Eid-al-Adha, the Islamic New Year, and Muhammad's birthday.

⁷RITES OF PASSAGE

The Jola have several initiation ceremonies for boys and girls; however, in the modern era, the introduction of Islam and Christianity has brought modifications in these traditions. Initiation ceremonies are secret affairs not to be divulged to the opposite sex. Male initiation ceremonies take place in the sacred forests. The boys undergoing initiation (which includes circumcision) are secluded for substantial periods of time, undergoing tests of endurance and training sessions in the morals and customs of Jola society. Circumcision for boys generally occurs at some time between the ages of 6 and 8. Girls also undergo an initiation ceremony at some time between the ages of 13 and 25. Girls are secluded in an initiation hut. Men are not allowed in the female initiation ceremony just as the females are not allowed in the boys' ceremony. However, in both ceremonies, boys and girls learn to endure hardship, obey orders, respect their elders, be courageous, and understand traditional wisdom.

When a baby boy is born, it is secluded for up to seven days and then brought out for naming according to the dictates of the Islamic religion. There is an animal sacrifice, usually a chicken or a goat. At this ceremony, the child becomes a Muslim. For women, marriage is an important rite of passage. Among the Jola, death is considered a rite of passage into the afterworld. Every Jola wishes for a good funeral, which is often accompanied by rituals and rites. Traditional funeral ceremonies among the Jola require a huge feast in which many cattle are slaughtered and offered as a send off sacrifice for the dead. In addition, guns are fired to honor the departed.

⁸INTERPERSONAL RELATIONS

The Jola pride themselves on their fierce loyalty to their group. They prefer an acephalous, rather than a hierarchical, political system. With a classless system in their social institutions, they are unlike their neighbors, who have *griots* (history keepers and tellers), slaves, nobles, leather workers, and so on. Because they are a classless society, all individuals are considered to be equals, although elders are to be respected by the young people. The old are respected as the repository of traditional wisdom. Extended families are loyal to one another, which results in a sense of community and interdependence.

⁹LIVING CONDITIONS

The Jola live in large villages and depend on the cultivation of crops, such as rice, peanuts, millet, some vegetables, as well as the tapping of palm wine. Peanuts (known as groundnuts) are grown as a cash crop. Usually, a village is composed of two large extended families, which intermarry as a tightly integrated community. Within the villages, the Jola live in simple homes made of mud walls and grass thatched roofs. Sometimes, bamboo matting and reeds are used to form the walls. This type of construction offers great relief in the hot climate. Those who are well off are able to construct modern rectangular homes, with corrugated iron sheets as roofing material and cement for outside and inside floors.

The village is often organized in the form of a series of compounds. A compound consists of a series of houses around an open courtyard. A grass or reed fence might enclose the houses from the outside. Members of a compound might all be related, tracing their descent to a common male ancestor. Men and women have their own huts and separate sections within the compound. At night, women may go to join their husbands in the husband's huts. Within the compound disputes are settled by the oldest man of the lineage.

The Casamance region, the homeland of the Jola, has fertile soils, which offer an excellent opportunity for subsistence farming. As a hardworking people, they produce enough food for themselves, with the excess sold to others. However, malaria is an ever-present threat because it is hard to control mosquitoes in such a swampy environment. Other diseases, such as measles, whooping cough, and pneumonia, result in high infant deaths. HIV/AIDS also poses a new threat to the Jola way of life.

10 FAMILY LIFE

For women, marriage is a second rite of passage as they often have to leave their homes to join that of their husband. Polygamy is allowed, and one can have as many as four wives. Co-wives often share household chores and responsibilities for gardening, cultivating rice, food preparation, and care of the children. Men are responsible for cash crops, such as peanuts, citrus fruits, and mangoes, which are sold to provide resources for the family. Families help each other economically and otherwise. A son might be educated by the extended family. In turn, he is expected to contribute to the extended family, should he become gainfully employed in one of the distant cities, such as Dakar. Thus, each relative is seen as a form of social safety valve in times of trouble. The entire community is also expected to gather at times of important life events, such as birth, circumcision, weddings, and funerals.

Marriage itself is a family affair, rather than an individual affair between two people. It is often a protracted process, in which girls are betrothed to a future husband while they are still young and the future husband is expected to work for his in-laws while waiting for the girl to become of age. Marriages are often blessed in a mosque, following the Islamic tradition. The marriage celebration generally involves the entire village.

11 CLOTHING

The Jola wear colorful dresses, shirts, and pants fashioned from locally made cloth. Women generally wear long skirts with a loose blouse. For religious festivals, men wear long robes of different colors, as dictated by Islam. For those who work in urban areas, suits, ties, and other Western fashioned clothes are often worn by both men and women.

12 FOOD

The main staple food for the Jola is rice. Fishing communities will usually take their rice with fish. Those in more forested areas gather and preserve various edible leaves and fruits. The Jola also like to prepare their dishes with palm oil. Cassava is another important food crop, which is pounded into flour to make a hard porridge called fufu. Fufu is usually served with stew made from beef, goat, sheep, or chicken. Yassa is a favorite dish from Casamance. It is made of chicken or fish marinated in lemon juice, pepper, and onions, and then baked. It is usually served with plain rice.

13 EDUCATION

In rural areas, modern education is not seen as important. It is often considered a nuisance that hinders children from fully participating in the daily chores of farming and raring livestock. Parents prefer to send their children to Islamic schools, where instruction takes place either very early in the morning or late in the evening leaving the children to help out with farming and raising livestock during the day. It is mostly in urban areas and towns that a modern education is valued.

14 CULTURAL HERITAGE

The Jola have a rich cultural heritage and love their many festivals throughout the year. Perhaps their most enduring legacy is their famous musical instrument, the *akonting* (or ekonting) or folk lute. It is a banjo-like instrument with a skin-headed gourd body, two long melody strings, and one short drone string. Some believe that it was a precursor to the Western banjo. Thus, music, song, and dance are an important aspect of Jola culture. Men and women sing as they go about their daily chores of gardening or while paddling canoes. During festivals, there is much drumming, singing, and dancing. At night or during the day, children may sing and dance in groups. When boys are taken into the secret forest for circumcision, they are accompanied by the singing of war songs to give them courage.

15 WORK

Most Jola are engaged in agricultural production and the raising of livestock. They are a very hardworking people. Women tend to the rice fields and vegetable cultivation while men concentrate on millet and peanut farms. They use traditional implements, such as hoes for ridging and weeding. Those who can afford ox plows use donkeys or cattle to do the cultivation. Occupations among the Jola include rice cultivation, honey collecting, palm wine tapping, fishing, oyster collecting, and other agricultural activities. Some of the women may be employed as housemaids in the households of rich Gambians. Wealth among the Jola, particularly for women, is measured in terms of how much rice she owns.

16 SPORTS

Traditionally, wrestling was an important part of Jola society. It prepared young men for the prowess of war and other conflicts. Today, the most important sporting activity is soccer. In urban areas basketball and tennis are also played.

17 ENTERTAINMENT AND RECREATION

The most common form of entertainment among the Jola is music and dancing. The Jola enjoy listening to music and dancing to the *ankonting,* as well as drumming. The many festivals and ceremonies are often accompanied by much feasting and dancing.

18 FOLK ART, CRAFTS, AND HOBBIES

The Jola have a secret society of masked dancers that often play at important events, such as funerals and initiation ceremonies. Elaborate masks are made in the form of animals, such as the large deer found in their environment. They also carve from wood many implements used in their day-to-day lives, such as drums, bowls, mortars, pestles, and canoes for fishing.

With the budding tourist industry in the Casamance region, some Jola have begun to specialize in the carving of animals, drums, and decorative masks for sale to visitors.

[19] SOCIAL PROBLEMS

Since the early 1980s, the Casamance region has witnessed political instability. Some factions among the Jola took up arms to free the region from Senegal and obtain independence or autonomous rule. Over three thousand people have been killed in the skirmishes between the rebel groups and government forces since 1982. However, in recent years tensions between the two forces appear to have eased somewhat.

[20] GENDER ISSUES

There is a clear division of labor by gender in Jola society. Women are expected to do household chores, such as cooking, cleaning, and child rearing. Furthermore, women have a lower status in comparison to men as they are considered to be dependent on male relatives. Men have the rights to what their women produce. Islamic and traditional customs, including the custom of polygamy, place women in an inferior role. Women are discriminated against when it comes to issues concerning marriage, divorce, and devolution of property upon the death of a husband.

In the modern legal systems of The Gambia and Senegal, there exist policies that attempt to promote gender equality; however, disparities by gender continue to widen. It has also been noted that female genital mutilation/cutting is practiced by about 15% of Jola. Although many programs, policies, projects, and plans have been geared towards the elimination of all forms of harmful traditional practices, especially female genital mutilation, the lack of general commitment and will on the part of government authorities has hindered their successful implementation. Domestic violence against women is also an ever-present problem, as there are no specific laws against it.

[21] BIBLIOGRAPHY

De Jong, Ferdinand. *Masquerades of Modernity: Power and Secrecy in Casamance, Senegal.* Edinburgh: Edinburgh University Press for the International African Institute, 2007.

Doyle, Mark. "Senegal's Southern Rebellion Starts to End." *BBC News*, Thursday, 16 December 2004. Available online at http://news.bbc.co.uk/2/hi/africa/4102267.stm.

Janneh, Mbalefele. *Jola History.* Banjul, The Gambia: Oral History, Cultural Archives, 1970.

Linares, Olga F. "Deferring to Trade in Slaves: The Jola of Casamance, Senegal in Historical Perspective." *History in Africa* 14 (1987): 113-139.

———. "Diminished Rains and Divided Tasks: Rice Growing in Three Jola Communities of Casamance, Senegal. In A. Endre Nyerges (Ed.), *The Ecology of Practice: Studies of Food Crop Production in Sub-Saharan West Africa.* Amsterdam, the Netherlands: Gordon and Breach Publishers, 1997.

———. "Going to the City...and Coming Back? Turnaround Migration among the Jola of Senegal." *Africa* 73, no.1 (2003): 113-133.

———. "Jola Agriculture at a Crossroads." *Canadian Journal of African Studies* 39, no. 2 (2005): 230-252.

———. *Power, Prayer, and Production: The Jola of Casamance, Senegal.* Cambridge Studies in Social and Cultural Anthropology, 82. Cambridge [England]: Cambridge University Press, 1992.

———. "State and Household Crops among the Jola (Diola) of Senegal." In John S. Henderson and Patricia Netherly (eds.), *Configurations of Power: Holistic Anthropology in Theory and Practice.* Ithaca, N.Y.: Cornell University Press, 1993.

Mark, Peter. *The Wild Bull and the Sacred Forest: Form, Meaning, and Change in Senegambian Initiation Masks.* Cambridge: Cambridge University Press, 1992.

Mark, Peter, F. de Jong, F., and C. Chupin. "Ritual and Masking Traditions in Jola Men's Initiation." *African Arts* 31, no. 1 (1998): 36-47.

—by E. Kalipeni

KALENJIN

PRONUNCIATION: KAH-len-jeen
LOCATION: Kenya
POPULATION: About 4.4 million
LANGUAGE: Kalenjin; Swahili; English
RELIGION: Christianity (Africa Inland Church [AIC], the
    Church of the Province of Kenya [CPK], Roman Catholic
    Church); Islam
RELATED ARTICLES: Vol. 1: Keiyo; Kenyans

¹ INTRODUCTION

The Kalenjin live primarily in Kenya, East Africa. A living illustration of the complex nature of ethnic identity in Sub-Saharan Africa, they are not a tribe. Rather, the Kalenjin are an ethnic grouping of eight culturally and linguistically related groups or "tribes": the Kipsigis, Nandi, Tugen, Keiyo, Marakwet, Pokot (sometimes called the Suk), Sabaot (who live in the Mount Elgon region, overlapping the Kenya/Uganda border), and the Terik.

Earlier, the Kalenjin were known collectively as the "Nandi-Speaking Peoples" or, alternatively, the "Southern Nilo-Hamites." The name "*Kalenjin*" translates roughly as "I tell you." It has played a crucial role in the construction of this relatively new ethnic identity among these formerly autonomous, but culturally and linguistically similar, tribes. The origin of the name "*Kalenjin*" and the Kalenjin ethnic identity can be traced to the 1940s. It represents a clear desire to draw political strength from the greater numbers of such an association.

Beginning in the 1940s, individuals from these groups who were going off to fight in World War II used the term *kale* or *kole* (the process of scarring the breast or arm of a warrior who had killed an enemy in battle) to refer to themselves. During wartime radio broadcasts, an announcer, John Chemallan, used the phrase *kalenjok* ("I tell you," plural). Later, individuals from these groups who were attending Alliance High School formed a "Kalenjin" club. Fourteen in number, they constituted a distinct minority in this prestigious school in a Kikuyu area. This affected their desire for some sort of outward manifestation of identity and solidarity, as the Kikuyu are not only much more numerous but also culturally and linguistically very different from the Kalenjin. These young high school students would form the future Kalenjin elite. The next step in the consolidation of Kalenjin identity was the founding of a Kalenjin Union in Eldoret in 1948, and the publication of a monthly magazine called *Kalenjin* in the 1950s.

However, throughout this process the growing sense of pan-Kalenjin identity was not forming in a vacuum; instead, it should be seen in relation to colonialism and to anti-Kikuyu feelings. The British colonial government sponsored the *Kalenjin* monthly magazine out of a desire to foster anti-Kikuyu sentiments during the Mau Mau Emergency. The latter was a mostly Kikuyu-led, anti-colonial insurgency that provoked an official state of emergency lasting from October 1952 to January 1960. Clouded in emotional arguments coming from both sides, the causes of this movement have been reanalyzed. One of the most striking elements is the tension that existed between the numerically dominant Bantu Kikuyu and the less numerous Nilotic and Nilo-Hamitic Maasai and Kalenjin.

Considering this, and the desire of the colonial government to suppress the Mau Mau movement, a policy of encouraging pan-Kalenjin identity, which was still local in character rather than a truly nationalistic movement, made sense. Benjamin Kipkorir, a prominent Kenyan scholar, stated that "the term *Kalenjin* and the concept of ethnic solidarity that later came to be associated with it . . . had its roots in the Mau Mau emergency. It may thus be said to have been a by-product of Mau Mau" (Kipkorir 1973, 74).

Kalenjin language and culture probably began forming 1,000 years ago as a result of the intermingling of Highland Nilotic migrants with ancestral Southern Cushitic speakers. The length of time the Kalenjin have been living in Kenya's Western Highlands and the Rift Valley, their homeland, is open for debate. While an earlier view claimed that these peoples have only been living in western Kenya for about 400 years, more recently a number of others have argued that the Kalenjin have occupied these parts of Kenya for 2,000 years or more.

One of the most famous aspects of Kalenjin history involves the *Sirikwa* holes. These are hollows that measure from 4.5 m to 9 m (15–30 ft) in diameter made in hillsides. Kalenjin legend has it that the Sirikwa people used these as cattle pens to guard their animals at night. Archaeological excavation at several Sirikwa holes reinforces this image: houses were built on the outside fence with the door facing inward toward the stock enclosure. There would have been only one way to enter the entire complex, and that would have been closely watched and heavily guarded.

The basic unit of indigenous political organization among the Kalenjin was the *koret* ("chor-ette") or parish. This was not a nucleated village in any sense but rather a collection of anywhere from 20 to 100 scattered homesteads. It was administered by a council of adult males known collectively as the *kokwet* ("coke-wet") and was led by a spokesman called *poiyot ap kokwet* ("poy-ought ab coke-wet"). This spokesman was not a hereditary or elected leader in the sense of a chief. He was, rather, someone who was recognized for his knowledge of tribal laws, oratorical abilities, forceful personality, wealth, and social position. At public proceedings, although the *poiyot ap kokwet* was the first to speak, all of the elders were given the opportunity to state their opinions. Rather than making decisions himself, the *poiyot ap kokwet* expressed the consensus of opinion, always phrased in terms of a group decision.

A number of *koret* formed the next level of political organization, the *pororiet* ("poor-or-e-et"). Each was led by a council, the *kiruokwet ap pororiet* ("kee-roo-oh-kwet ab poor-or-e-et"). This council consisted of the spokesmen of the individual *koret,* over whom presided two reasonably active old men called *kiruokik* ("kee-roo-oh-keek"), the "councillors." In addition, among the Nandi, there were two representatives of the *orkoiyot* ("or-coe-ee-yot"); a Nandi prophet, called *maotik* ("mah-oh-teek"); and two senior military commanders of the *pororiet's* warriors, *kiptaienik ap murenik* ("kip-ta-eneek ab mur-eh-neek").

Today, traditional Kalenjin political/territorial organization has been largely replaced with one based upon the units imposed by the British colonial structure—villages are included in sublocations, which are included in locations, which are included in divisions, districts, and provinces. Each village has a village elder, who may be seen as the equivalent of a modern *poiyot ap kokwet* and who tries to settle minor disputes and handle routine affairs. Assistant chiefs are in charge of sub-locations, while chiefs administer locations. District officers oversee divisions, and district commissioners are the highest authority in each district. Finally, provincial commissioners are the highest authorities in each of Kenya's eight provinces and are directly under the president's authority.

² LOCATION AND HOMELAND

Figures released in January 2007 estimated the population of Kenya to be 36,913,721. Of that 12% are thought to be Kalenjin, approximately 4.4 million people. Together, the Kalenjin peoples comprise Kenya's fourth-largest ethnic group. Most Kalenjin are concentrated in the Western Rift Valley and the Western Highlands.

³ LANGUAGE

The first language of the Kalenjin peoples is Kalenjin, a language of the southern section of the Nilotic branch, and part of the Chari-Nile language group of Africa. Three Kalenjin dialect clusters have been identified: one consists of the Sabaot, along with the Sebei and Kony; another is made up of Pokot, northern Marakwet, and northern Tugen; while the third dialect includes the Nandi, Kipsigis, Keiyo, Terik, and southern Tugen and Marakwet. Although these dialects are all supposedly mutually intelligible, speakers of one dialect often have difficulty understanding speakers of another. In addition to Kalenjin, most people speak Swahili and English, since both are official national languages and are taught in school, beginning with primary school education. Today it is only very old persons who do not speak at least some English.

⁴ FOLKLORE

Oral tradition was, and still is to some degree, very important among the Kalenjin. Prior to the introduction of writing, folk tales served to convey a sense of cultural history. Kalenjin oral tradition has four main genres: narratives (stories), songs, proverbs, and riddles. Stories usually contain both people and animals, and certain animals have acquired attributes that are concrete representations of character traits, e.g., hare is a trickster figure whose cleverness can be self-defeating; lion is courageous and wise; and hyena is greedy and destructive. Songs accompany both work and play, as well as ceremonial occasions such as births, initiations, and weddings. Proverbs convey important messages in very concise ways and are often used when elders settle disputes or advise younger persons. Riddles involve word play and are especially popular with children.

⁵ RELIGION

Traditional Kalenjin religion is based upon a concept of a supreme god, *Asis* ("Ah-sees") or *Cheptalel* ("Chep-ta-lell"), who is represented in the form of the sun, although this is not God himself. Beneath *Asis* is *Elat* ("Ay-lot"), who controls thunder and lightning. Spirits of the dead, *oyik* ("oh-yeek"), can also intervene in the affairs of humans, and sacrifices of meat and/or beer, *koros* ("chorus"), can be made to placate them. Diviners, *orkoik* ("or-coe-eek") have magical powers and help in appeals for rain or to end floods.

Currently, nearly everyone professes to being a member of some organized religion—either Christianity or Islam. Major Christian sects include the Africa Inland Church (AIC), the

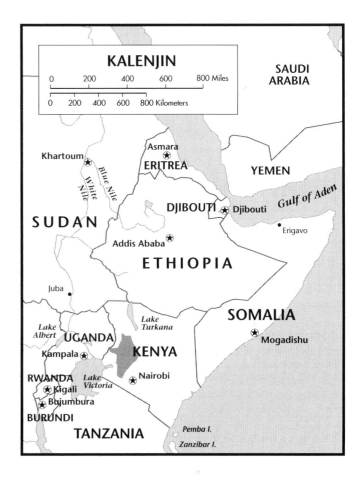

Church of the Province of Kenya (CPK), and the Roman Catholic Church. Muslims are relatively few in number among the Kalenjin. Generally speaking, only older people can recall details of traditional religious beliefs.

⁶ MAJOR HOLIDAYS

The major holidays observed by the Kalenjin are mostly those associated with Christianity (i.e., Christmas and Easter), and national holidays such as Jamhuri (Republic) Day, Madaraka (Responsibility) Day, Moi (the second president) Day, and Kenyatta (the first president) Day. At Christmas it is common for people who still live in traditional mud-walled houses with thatched roofs to give the outer walls a new coat of clay whitewash and paint them with holiday greetings (such as "Merry Christmas" and "Happy New Year").

Three one-month-long school holidays occur in April, August, and December. The first two coincide with peak periods in the agricultural cycle and allow children of various ages to assist their families during these busy times. The December holiday corresponds with both Christmas and the traditional initiation ceremonies, *tumdo* ("toom-doe").

⁷ RITES OF PASSAGE

Age is a fundamental organizing principle in all Kalenjin societies, as it across much of Africa. The status a person occupies and the roles he or she performs are still to a large degree ordained by age. For both males and females, becoming an adult in Kalenjin society is a matter of undergoing an initiation ceremony. Traditionally, these were held about every seven years. Everyone undergoing initiation, or *tumdo* ("toom-doe"), thereby becomes a member of a named age-set, or *ip-inda* ("e-pin-da"). Age-sets were traditionally "open" for about 15 years. There are eight male age-sets and they are cyclical, repeating approximately every 100 years. The *sakobei* ("sah-coe-bay") ceremony marked the closing of an age-set about every 15 years, and the elevation of a new age-set to the warrior age-grade.

These age-sets and the age-grades (e.g., warrior, junior elder, senior elder) through which individuals passed provided an important basis for traditional social structure. Among the Kalenjin, indigenous political organization was based upon the combination of cross-cutting principles of age-sets and small territorial units called *korotinwek* (singular *koret*) and larger ones called *pororisiek* (singular *pororiet*). No Kalenjin societies possessed any kind of centralized leaders such as chiefs; instead, councils of elders made all decisions.

After male youths were circumcised, they were secluded for lengthy periods of time during which they were instructed in the skills necessary for adulthood. Afterwards, they would begin a phase of warriorhood during which they acted as the military force of the tribe. Elders provided guidance and wisdom. Today age-sets have lost their politico-military function, but this principle still creates bonds between men who are members of the same set, and feelings of respect for those who are older. Female age-sets have long since lost much of their importance, and most people are hard-pressed even to remember the names of the age-sets.

In the past, only people who had borne children would be buried after death; the others would be taken out to the bush and left to be eaten by hyenas. Today at every person's death, he or she is buried, but not in a cemetery as in the United States. People are returned to their farm, or *shamba* ("sha-mbaa"), for burial. There is usually no grave marker, but invariably family members, friends, and neighbors know where people are laid to rest.

8 INTERPERSONAL RELATIONS

Chamge ("chaam-gay") or *chamuge* ("chaa-moo-gay") is the standard greeting among Kalenjin. If the encounter is face-to-face, the spoken greeting is almost always accompanied by a hearty handshake, and people often clasp their own right elbow with their left hand. The response is the same—*chamge*, sometimes repeated several times. It may be emphasized with *mis-ing* ("me-sing"), which can mean either "very much" or "close friend," depending upon the context. As a sign of respect, a younger person will greet someone of their grandparents' generation by saying, *chamge kogo* (grandmother—"chaam-gay coe-go") or *chamge kugo* (grandfather—"chaam-gay coo-go").

Americans are likely to find several aspects of Kalenjin body language to be unusual. First, holding hands after greeting is very common for people of the same sex. Even when walking, these people may hold hands or lock little fingers. But it is readily apparent that there is absolutely no sexual connotation to this behavior. Furthermore, people of opposite sexes are strongly discouraged from these and other public displays of affection. Second, in their conversations Kalenjin do not point out objects or people with their fingers. Instead, they point by turning their head in the proper direction and then puckering their lips briefly.

Taking leave of someone is accompanied by the farewell, *sait sere* ("sah-eat sarey"—meaning literally, "blessing time"), and hearty handshakes. Often people will walk with their visitor(s) a distance in order to continue the conversation and to give their friend(s) "a push." Once again, these people often hold hands, especially if they are members of the same sex.

In the past, dating and courtship were almost entirely matters of family concern. Clans were usually exogamous, i.e., one had to marry outside of one's own (and father's) clan. Today young men and women are more free to exercise their own free will, especially those who live away from home at boarding schools. They will meet and socialize at dances in town, discos, and in cafes called *hoteli* ("hotel-e") in KiSwahili. Still, when a young man decides on a wife, he and his father's family must gather together a suitable bride-price payment (often erroneously referred to as a "dowry") to be given to the bride's family. In the past this consisted almost entirely of livestock, but today it is becoming more and more common to use money in place of, or in addition to, livestock.

9 LIVING CONDITIONS

Considerable variation exists in the way that members of various Kalenjin groups make a living. For most groups, subsistence is agropastoral in orientation, based upon a combination of cultivation of grains such as sorghum and millet (and more recently maize), and livestock husbandry of cattle, goats, and sheep. Typical of East African groups, there tends to be little integration between the two activities since grazing land is usually located some distance from the fields and homesteads. Livestock are not used for traction, nor are they fed on the stubble of grain or other crop products. Often, such groups live on the face of a hillside or escarpment and cultivate nearby, as do the Keiyo and Marakwet. Among the Pokot there are two different subsistence patterns: one consists of pastoralism, involving the keeping of, and primary dependence upon, cattle, sheep, goats, donkeys, and a few camels; the other consists of agricultural production, mostly of corn today, but in the past, indigenous grains such as sorghum and millet. The pastoralists comprise approximately 75% of the Pokot.

Previously, when game populations were at higher levels and before the government ban, hunting sometimes supplemented the diet, but only among the so-called "Dorobo" or "Okiek" did it provide a major staple. The latter were forest hunter-gatherers who often resided near the Kalenjin groups.

Traditionally Kalenjin houses were round, with walls constructed of bent saplings anchored to larger posts and covered with a mixture of mud and cow dung, while roofs were thatched with local grasses. While these kinds of houses are still common, there is a growing trend towards the construction of square or rectangular houses that are built with timber walls and roofs of corrugated sheet metal, *mabati* ("ma-baatee").

Most Kalenjin are rural dwellers and do not have electricity or indoor plumbing in their houses. Radio/cassette players; kerosene lamps and stoves; charcoal stoves; aluminum cooking pots; plastic dishes, plates, and cups; and bicycles are the most common consumer items. Those people who do not have electricity but who do have televisions use car batteries for power.

10 FAMILY LIFE

Traditionally, like in most African societies, the family was central in the daily life of the Kalenjin. But by family what was meant was the extended family, not the nuclear family in the Western sense. Kalenjin residence patterns were, and still are, mostly patrilocal. That is, typically after marriage a man brings his wife to live with him in, or very near to, his father's homestead. Marriage of one man to multiple wives (polygyny) was and is permitted, although most men cannot afford the expense of such unions because of the burden of bride-price. Regardless of the type of marriage, children were traditionally seen as a blessing from God and, as a result of this, until very recently Kenya had the highest population growth rate in the world.

Slowly these patterns are changing as monogamous marriages now prevail and nuclear families are becoming more frequent. Moreover, younger people are now expressing a desire to have fewer children when they get married. This is due to the increasing expense of having large numbers of children who not only must be fed but also educated to cope in today's world. To some degree, young women are also changing their aspirations to go beyond motherhood alone and include a career as well.

11 CLOTHING

The Kalenjin were not renowned for their traditional clothing, which essentially consisted of animal skins, either domesticated or wild. Earrings were common for both sexes in the past, including heavy brass coils that tended to make the earlobe stretch downward almost to the shoulder. This is generally not practiced today, when the Western-style dress of most Kalenjin, even in rural areas, is scarcely different from that of people in nearby towns. The buying of secondhand clothes is quite common. Thus, men wear trousers and shirts, usually along with a suit jacket or sport coat, while women wear skirts and blouses, dresses, and/or *khangas* ("khan-gaaz")—locally made commercial textiles that are used as wraps (one for the top and one for the bottom). Youths of both sexes covet T-shirts with logos, especially those of American sports teams or bearing the likeness of famous entertainers.

12 FOOD

The staple Kalenjin food is *ugali* ("oo-golly"). This is a cake-like, starchy food that is made from white cornmeal mixed with boiling water and stirred vigorously while cooking. It is eaten with the hands and is often served with cooked green vegetables such as kale, called *sukuma wiki* ("sue-cooma weeky") in KiSwahili, meaning literally, "to push the week." Less frequently it is served with roasted goat meat, beef, or chicken. Before the introduction and widespread diffusion of corn in recent times, millet and sorghum—indigenous African grains—were staple cereals. All of these grains were, and still are, used to make a very thick beer that has a relatively low alcohol content. Another popular Keiyo beverage is *mursik* ("more-seek"). This consists of fermented whole milk that has been stored in a special gourd called a *sotet* (pronounced just as it appears, with the accent on the second syllable) that has been cleaned using a burning stick. The result is that the milk is infused with tiny bits of charcoal.

Lunch and dinner are the big meals of the day. Breakfast usually consists of tea (made with a lot of milk and sugar) and remains from the previous night's meal, or perhaps some store-bought bread. Mealtimes, as well as the habit of tea-drinking, were adopted from the British colonial period. Lunch is eaten

at 1:00 pm rather than at noon, and dinner is often eaten later in the evening at 8:00 or 9:00 pm. In addition to bread, people routinely buy foodstuffs such as sugar, tea leaves, cooking fat, sodas (most often Orange Fanta and Coca-Cola), and other items they do not produce themselves.

13 EDUCATION

Traditionally, education among the Kalenjin was provided during the seclusion of initiates following circumcision. This transitional phase of the rite of passage provided an opportunity to instill in young men and women all the requisite knowledge necessary to be a functioning and productive adult member of society. It was, in essence, a "crash" course in the intricacies of their culture. Nowadays, after initiation young men and women are still secluded but for shorter periods of time (one month as compared with three months in the past). The timing of the December school holiday coincides with the practice of initiation and seclusion.

In 2003 free primary school education became universal in Kenya. "Free" must be qualified however, because parents must provide their children with uniforms, books, pens and pencils, and paper, as well as contribute to frequent fund raising activities for their children's school(s). This constitutes a tremendous financial burden for families in a country where the average per capita income is about $360 per year. Post-primary school education is relatively expensive, even at the cheaper secondary schools, and entry is competitive. Tuition at the more prestigious high schools, where students must board, is very expensive. Typically, parents rely on contributions from a wide range of family, neighbors, and friends to meet the high tuition costs. Tuition at Kenya's universities is rather nominal, but the selection process is grueling and relatively few students who want to attend can do so.

14 CULTURAL HERITAGE

Traditional music and dance had many different functions. Songs would accompany many work-related activities, including, for men, herding livestock and digging the fields, and, for women, grinding corn, washing clothes, and putting babies to sleep (with lullabies). Music would also be an integral part of ceremonial occasions such as births, initiations, and weddings. Dances to punctuate these occasions would be performed while wearing ankle bells and would be accompanied by traditional instruments such as flutes, horns, and drums. Oral stories, proverbs, and riddles all convey important messages to be passed from generation to generation.

15 WORK

In Kalenjin societies, much of the work, at least traditionally speaking, is divided along gender lines. Men are expected to do the heavy work of initially clearing the fields that are to be used for planting, as well as turning over the soil. Women take over the bulk of the farming work from there on, including planting, several weedings, harvesting (although here men tend to pitch in), and processing crops. Among the Kalenjin, tradition holds that men are supposedly more concerned with herding livestock than with other pursuits. Recent evidence suggests that women, children (especially boys), and even older people are equally as likely to be engaged in animal care as men, especially in those situations where men are likely to be away from home engaged in wage work.

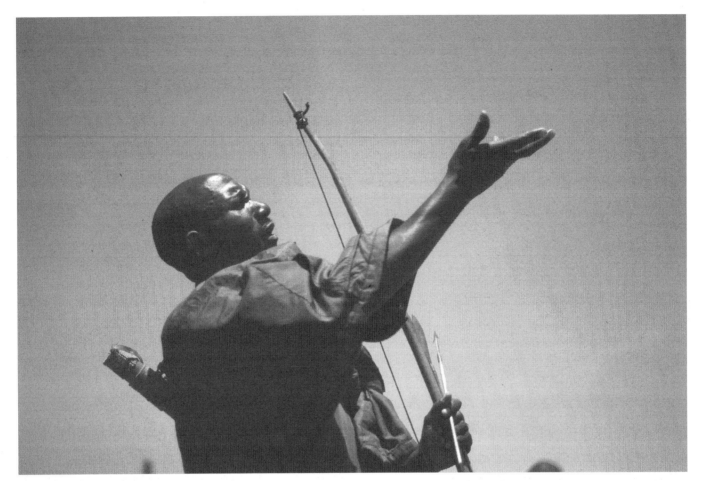

A leader of the Kalenjin tribe speaks to a group of warriors near the western Kenyan town of Chebilat. (Roberto Schmidt/AFP/ Getty Images)

In addition to all of their other tasks, women are expected to perform nearly all of the domestic work that is involved in keeping a household running. In doing so, they often enlist the help of young girls, who are expected to assist their mothers and other female relatives in chores such as fetching water from wells or streams, and collecting the firewood that most families use for cooking. Young boys will sometimes perform these same tasks but more often do things such as grazing and/ or watering livestock.

16 SPORTS

Soccer is a major sports interest of the Kalenjin, especially the youth, as it is with many other Kenyans. Nonetheless, running (especially middle and longer distances) is the sport that made the Kalenjin peoples famous in world athletic circles. St. Patrick's High School in Iten has turned out a phenomenal number of world-class runners.

17 ENTERTAINMENT AND RECREATION

In rural areas without electricity, the radio is still the main form of entertainment. KBC (Kenya Broadcasting Corporation) programs are attentively monitored, as are shortwave radio transmissions by the BBC (British Broadcasting Corporation) and the VOA (Voice of America). A small number of

people have televisions, and the only programming available is from KBC. In towns and trading centers, video parlors are becoming common, and action films are especially popular.

18 FOLK ART, CRAFTS, AND HOBBIES

In other parts of Kenya, the famous sisal bags (called *kiondo* in KiSwahili and pronounced "key-on-doe") are manufactured and marketed worldwide. Although the Kalenjin are not well known for their handicrafts, women do make and locally sell decorated calabashes (*sotet* in Kalenjin and pronounced just as it appears) from gourds. These are rubbed with oil and adorned with small colored beads and are essentially the same type of calabashes that are used for storing fermented milk.

19 SOCIAL PROBLEMS

Politically, Kalenjin fared extremely well under the presidency of Daniel arap Moi, from 1978 to 2002. Moi, a Tugen, was very generous with resource distribution in Kalenjin areas during his rule. In 2002 Moi was constitutionally obligated to step down. However he did select a successor, Uhuru Kenyatta, in hopes of continuing his influence in the ruling party, the Kenya African National Union (KANU). Unfortunately for Moi the various opposition parties united behind Mwai Kibaki, who won the presidency with approximately 65% of the vote.

Since that time KANU's influence has waned but Moi has remained an active, albeit backstage, political force. The return of the presidency to a member of the Kikuyu ethnic group resurrected a great deal of animosity among Kalenjin.

In the election of December 2007, Kalenjin overwhelmingly sided with the opposition candidate, Raila Odinga of the Orange Democratic Movement (ODM). Sadly, the disputed results of that election saw a great deal of violence, considerable loss of life and the displacement of hundreds of thousands of people. Although most of the international attention was on Nairobi, regrettably many of these actions took place in the Rift Valley Province, Kalenjin heartland, especially in and around the highlands town of Eldoret and to some extent in the Rift Valley town of Nakuru. Unsavory elements of society used the occasion to once again resurrect the idea that this part of Kenya is only for Kalenjin and that others, particularly Kikuyu, must leave. Approximately 1,500 people died in the post election violence and at least 350,000 internally displaced people are living in camps around the country

Tobacco usage and alcohol consumption continue to be common among men but not women. For decades the Kenyan government has banned the brewing and distillation of traditional homemade alcoholic beverages, including *busaa* ("boosaah"), a beer made from fried, fermented corn and millet, and *chang'aa* ("chaan-gah"), a liquor distilled from *busaa*. Nevertheless, these beverages continue to be popular with people, especially men, and provide some individuals, mostly women, with supplementary income. *Chang'aa* especially can be lethal since there is no way to control the high alcohol content (unlike that of *busaa,* which tends to have a very low alcohol content), and there are many opportunities for contamination. It is not uncommon to read stories of men dying after attending drinking parties in the Kenyan daily newspapers.

Raiding for livestock has always been part of Kalenjin culture and this continues to be true, especially among the Pokot. Now, instead of spears and bows and arrows, raiders use semiautomatic weapons like AK 47 rifles. The Marakwet in particular have continued to suffer at the hands of armed cattle rustlers, often from the Pokot. Because of their marginal status both geographically and politically Marakwet complaints to the government do very little. Poverty and a general lack of concern on the part of government continue to fuel the situation.

As is true all over Africa and Kenya, HIV/AIDS is arguably the major issue confronting Kalenjin today. Fortunately, prevalence rates in the country as a whole have dropped dramatically from 14% in 2002 to 5.1% in 2008. Moreover the HIV prevalence rate in urban areas is much higher, at 9.6 % whereas in rural areas it is 4.6%. Most Kalenjin live in rural areas. Also, a link between male circumcision and susceptibility to HIV infection has been posited, whereby circumcision significantly decreases the risk of HIV infection. One study among agricultural employees in Rift Valley Province found that Luo men, from a tribe that does not circumcise, had a significantly higher HIV prevalence (24.8%) than Kalenjin men (4.5%).

20 GENDER ISSUES

Traditionally Kalenjin culture is, like most others in Africa, heavily divided on gender lines. Along with age, gender is a fundamental organizing principle in African societies. In the past leadership was always the prerogative of adult males but recently this has begun to change. With the growth of multiparty politics Kenyan women have increasingly entered the political sphere. However, unlike other ethnic groups, such as Kikuyu or Kamba, Kalenjin women have not participated in politics to the same degree.

As part of traditional rites of passage, circumcision of both boys and girls was practiced. In the academic world the female variant has come to be known female genital mutilation (FGM) and is a very controversial subject. Although technically illegal in Kenya since 1990 it is still widely practiced by members of many ethnic groups. Among the Kalenjin its prevalence rate has recently been estimated at 47% compared with rates as high as 97% for the Somali. In several areas of Kenya, some especially progressive women have recently been promoting alternatives to traditional circumcision and instead advocating what has come to be known as "circumcision with words." An example from Keiyo District is the Tumndo Ne Leel Support Group, which started in 2003 as a community based organization. One of the unique features of this approach is that it retains the very important ceremonial and symbolic role of a rite of passage while doing away with the act of "cutting." In the process this community based organization addresses the larger issue of female empowerment in this traditionally male-dominated society.

Homosexuality is not a subject of open discussion in Kalenjin society, nor in most other Kenyan societies. Reliable data on prevalence would be nearly impossible to elicit. An institution in which two women would marry was traditionally found among the Nandi. It was usually found in circumstances where an older woman had no male heirs and thus needed a son because women cannot inherit property. The older woman became the "husband" of the younger woman and was treated for all intents and purposes as a man. The younger "wife" may have already had children with other men who had left her or died or she may already be pregnant with the child of a man who did not want to marry her. Both parties benefited from the union, which was domestic and economic rather than sexual in nature. The female husband gains descendants and promotion to male status, after spending years in the unenviable status of a barren or sonless wife. The wife is likely to be a girl for whom getting married has been difficult. If she already has children, she gains inheritance and clan status for them (Oboler 1980).

21 BIBLIOGRAPHY

Chesaina, C. *Oral Literature of the Kalenjin*. Nairobi: Heinemann Kenya, 1991.

Daniels, Robert E., Mari H. Clark, and Timothy J. McMillan. *A Bibliography of the Kalenjin Peoples of East Africa*. Madison, WI: University of Wisconsin African Studies Program, 1987.

Edgerton, Robert. *Mau Mau: An African Crucible*. New York: Free Press, 1989.

Ehret, Christopher. *Southern Nilotic History: Linguistic Approaches to the Study of the Past*. Evanston, IL: Northwestern University Press, 1971.

Evans-Pritchard, Edward Evans. *The Political Structure of Nandi-Speaking Peoples. Africa.* 13: 250–267.

Fedders, Andrew, and Cynthia Salvadori. *Peoples and Cultures of Kenya*. Nairobi: Transafrica, 1988.

Huntingford, G. W. B. *The Southern Nilo-Hamites*. Ethnographic Survey of Africa, East Central Africa, Part VII. London: International African Institute, 1953.

Kanogo, Tabitha. *Squatters and the Roots of Mau Mau*. Athens, OH: Ohio University Press, 1987.

Kiley, Sam. "Seeds of Genocide Were Sown a Decade Ago by Moi." The Observer, 6 January 2008, 37.

Kipkorir, Benjamin. *The Marakwet of Kenya: A Preliminary Study*. Nairobi: Kenya Literature Bureau, 1973.

———. *Peoples of the Rift Valley* [Kalenjin]. Nairobi: Evans Brothers Ltd., 1978.

Massam, J. A. *Cliff Dwellers of Kenya*. London: Frank Cass & Co. Ltd., 1927.

Miller, Norman, and Rodger Yeager. *Kenya: The Quest for Prosperity*. 2nd ed. Boulder, CO: Westview Press, 1994.

Moore, Henrietta. *Space, Text, and Gender: An Anthropological Study of the Marakwet of Kenya*. Cambridge: Cambridge University Press, 1986.

Oboler, Regina Smith. "Is the Female Husband a Man? Woman/Woman Marriage among the Nandi of Kenya." Ethnology, Vol. 19, No. 1 (Jan., 1980), pp. 69-88.

———. *Women, Power, and Economic Change: The Nandi of Kenya*. Stanford, CA: Stanford University Press, 1985.

Roberts, Bruce D. *The Historical and Ecological Determinants of Economic Opportunity and Inequality in Elgeyo-Marakwet District, Kenya*. Ph.D. Dissertation, University of Pittsburgh, 1993.

———. "Livestock Production, Age, and Gender Among the Keiyo of Kenya." *Human Ecology* 24, no. 2 (1996): 215–230.

———. "Always Cheaply Pleasant: Beer as a Commodity in a Rural Kenyan Society." In *Commodities and Globalization: Anthropological Perspectives*. Angelique Haugerud, M. Priscilla Stone, and Peter D.Little, eds. New York: Rowman and Littlefield Publishers, 2000.

Rosenberg, Jared. "Circumcision Reduces HIV Risk among Men in Kenya." International Family Planning Perspectives, 33.1 (March 2007): p4(1).

Sateren WB, Renzullo PO, Mason C, Wasunna M, Robb M, Langat L, Elson L. "HIV Infection among Agricultural Employees in Rift Valley Province, Kenya: Prevalence, Risk Factors, and Suitability for Vaccine Efficacy Trials. *International Conference on AIDS*. 7–12 July 2002; 14: abstract no. WePeC6185.

Sutton, J. E. G. "The Kalenjin." In *Kenya Before 1800: Eight Regional Studies*, edited by B. A. Ogot. Nairobi: East African Publishing House, 1976.

Throup, David. *Economic and Social Origins of Mau Mau, 1945–53*. Athens, OH: Ohio University Press, 1989.

"Tumndo Ne Leel: Placing Value on Kalenjin Traditions while Working to Stop FGM." *Sexuality in Africa Magazine*, 31.3 (September 2006)

—by B. Roberts

KARRETJIE PEOPLE

PRONUNCIATION: KAH-ri-ki
LOCATION: The Great Karoo in South Africa
POPULATION: Several thousand
LANGUAGE: Afrikaans
RELIGION: None

[1] INTRODUCTION

Travelers who journey between the interior of South Africa and the coast cross the vast arid scrublands of the central plateau. This is the Great Karoo (derived from a Khoekhoen or "Hottentot"— a pejorative term—word for desert), and this is where the Karretjie People (*karretjie* means "donkey cart"), can usually be seen criss-crossing the plains in their donkey carts.

Most of the Karretjie People are descendants of the earliest inhabitants of the area, the hunting-gathering Xam San (also known as "Bushmen," a term that in some quarters is regarded as pejorative but is still sometimes used by such people themselves) and the nomadic-pastoral Khoekhoen ("Hottentots"). Archaeological evidence, DNA analyses, the historical record, local folklore, and oral tradition not only confirm the early presence of the Xam San and Khoekhoen in the area, but also the changing nature of their interaction with the more recently arrived pioneer white farming community from the south. The first sporadic contacts in the 1770s were followed by extended periods of conflict, intermittent times of peace, increased competition for resources, and eventually the powerful impact of a burgeoning agricultural economy and commercialization in the rapidly developing towns. The competition for resources, at least initially, centered around two issues. First, the farmers hunted the game in the hunting grounds that the Xam San regarded as their own. When they then began slaughtering the more easily accessible domesticated stock of the farmers, they themselves became the hunted. Second, the farmers and the Khoekhoen were in competition for the same grazing lands for their stock.

Eventually though, the lifestyle of both the Xam San and the Khoekhoen were transformed. In the case of the Xam San, for example, they changed from nomadic hunters to become so-called "tame Bushmen" farm laborers. They retained, at least initially, their nomadic ways, first on foot, later with the help of pack animals, and eventually with donkey carts. A few of those who were not hunted or who had not died of some foreign disease, like the smallpox epidemic early in the 18th century, still sought refuge in remote areas or rock shelters. Finally, though, most of the Xam San squatted near towns or were drawn into the agricultural economy by becoming laborers on the white farms. Like their parents and grandparents, most of the adult Karretjie People were born on a farm and, in spite of their present truly nomadic existence, many of them have a history of having lived at least semipermanently on a farm. It was on the farms that their ancestors first learned the skill of shearing. When wool-farming as an enterprise expanded, the Karretjie People, with the help of the mobility afforded by the donkey cart, developed an itinerant lifestyle in order to exploit shearing opportunities on farms spread over a wide area.

2 LOCATION AND HOMELAND

The Great Karoo, the region frequented by the Karretjie People, is a semidesert some 260,000 sq km (100,000 sq mi) in extent and 900 m to 1,200 m (3,000–4,000 ft) above sea level. It is a summer-rainfall area with extreme temperatures in both the summer and the winter. Strong winds and dust storms characterize the months of August and September and occasionally blow for the duration of the summer. The summer rains begin with light showers in October, but temperatures remain quite low. In fact, light snowfalls are known to have occurred as late as September. Temperatures increase quite dramatically during November, and temperatures above 40°C (105°F), during the summer months until February are not unusual. Rain during the summer is sporadic and often occurs in the form of thunderstorms, when 2.5 cm (1 in) or more of rain may fall in a short time, only to be followed by a long dry period. Temperatures decrease by April, and this usually also marks the end of the rainy season.

Topographically the region consists of vast plains dotted with flat-topped hills. In the valleys and on the plains the soil layer is thin, resulting in vegetation consisting mainly of Karoo scrub and grasses, much favored by both sheep and the remaining wild game, mainly a variety of antelope and smaller animals. The Karoo has become famous for Merino sheep and, hence, wool-farming, although Angora goats for mohair, and cattle and horse-breeding, and more recently game-farming, are also to be found. None of this land is owned by the Karretjie People, but as itinerant sheep-shearers this is the area that they roam, and they certainly regard these open spaces as their domain. It is difficult to obtain accurate census figures on a moving population, but Great Karoo-wide the Karretjie People probably number several thousand although many of them have recently become sedentary and hence no longer truly itinerant Karretjie People.

3 LANGUAGE

Virtually all the Karretjie People are unilingually Afrikaans-speaking. The few exceptions include isolated elderly individuals who still speak a Khoesan dialect or a language like Griqua or Korana, the language of their forbears. The Afrikaans that most of them speak was brought to the Great Karoo by the 18th-century Afrikaner hunters and pioneer farmers. Because most of the ancestors of the Karretjie People became farm laborers and were often, at least relatively and temporarily, isolated from their own wider social network and intensively exposed to Afrikaner culture, their own language gradually lost its currency.

While mostly intelligible to Afrikaans-speakers in general, the Afrikaans that the Karretjie People speak is peculiar to them and is enriched by characteristic words and sayings, such as *skêrbestuurders,* literally, "sheep-shear managers or drivers," i.e., sheep-shearers; *klipbrille,* literally, "with stone spectacles" or "glasses," i.e., being illiterate; and *hulle regeer al weer,* literally, "they are governing again," i.e., they are arguing again.

Most personal names derive from an Afrikaner tradition, although many are peculiar to the Karretjie People. Some names follow the names of animals that are, or were, found in the area. Some common names are Mieta Arnoster (the last name is from the Afrikaans *renoster,* "rhinoceros"); Hendrik Sors, Katjie Geduld, Plaatjie Januarie (the last name literally means "January"); Meitjies Verrooi (the first name literally

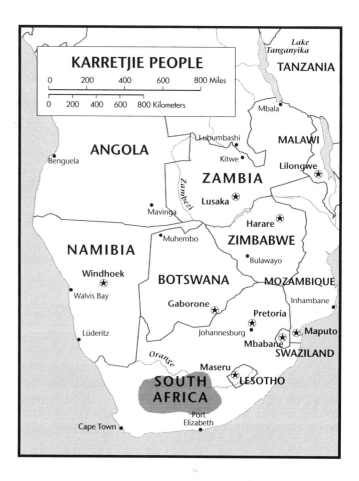

means "little maid," the "little" indicated by the diminutive "-tjie"); and Struis Maneswil (the first name is an abbreviation of the Afrikaans *volstruis,* "ostrich"). Karretjie children also have what is known as a *kleinnaampie* (literally, "small name" or nickname). For instance, the little girl Marie Jacobs is also known as Rokkies (literally, "little dress"), and her twin brother Simon Jacobs is known as Outjie (literally, "little guy").

4 FOLKLORE

The relative isolation, as individuals on farms, of the forbears of the Karretjie People resulted in them "losing" much of their early traditions and beliefs. Their relative isolation today as a community has prevented them from significantly adopting the myths and folklore of the sedentary communities in their area. Thus, there is only a vague awareness of being descendants of the earliest inhabitants of the region, and many of the few stories and folktales that the Karretjie adults do relate to their children are derived from the Afrikaners or from the teachers at the farm schools that a few of these children started attending.

A story that is told, and which serves to discipline young girls, is that of the Oranatan (probably derived from *Orang-oetang,* Afrikaans for "orangutan"). The Oranatan lives in a cave and moves around at night. He captures any young girl who ventures outside her *karretjie* shelter at night, takes her to his cave, and keeps her there for himself forever.

5 RELIGION

Although some of the Karretjie People were married in a church or by a magistrate, it is more common for such a union to be sanctioned simply by virtue of its recognition by the Karretjie community. Children from the former type of marriage take the last name of the father, while in the case of the latter type of union, they take the last name of the mother.

Very few of the Karretjie People are members of a church or a religious organization or have ever, for that matter, been exposed to religious activities. A few have been baptized by a minister of the Dutch Reformed Mission church, either in a church or by virtue of a minister visiting the farm where their parents worked. Those couples who have had a church marriage *(referred to as ge-eg, "properly" married)* are the exception, and those who live together are regarded as having an appropriately sanctioned union.

6 MAJOR HOLIDAYS

Neither religious nor secular holidays have any particular significance for the Karretjie People. The unpredictability of their employment as itinerant shearers is such that they are idle almost as many days as they are shearing. The selective observance of the national holidays of South Africa by the farmers for whom they work in large part guides the activities of the Karretjie People on such days. The Christmas–New Year period, when there is no shearing activity in any event, is a time for celebration and efforts are made to have more to eat and drink available, their meager resources permitting.

7 RITES OF PASSAGE

The passage of a Karretjie person from one social role to another is marked by very little ceremony. The transformation of a person from childhood to adulthood is probably the most significant. Boys, for example, learn to shear by helping their fathers from an early age. They "graduate" from at first shearing the less important wool from the same sheep to eventually, when they are strong and skilled enough, shearing independently. Birthdays are not marked by any ceremony, but when boys are old enough and are shearing on their own, they obtain their own *karretjie* (cart) and donkeys and are no longer regarded as children.

8 INTERPERSONAL RELATIONS

Even after a long absence, greetings between spouses, siblings, and between parents and children are often noticeably unemotional, undemonstrative, and occasionally even totally absent. When they do greet each other or others, it might be by means of a handshake. When asked, "Hoe gaan dit?" ("How are things going?"), the response may be, "Darem opgestaan" ("At least I got up [this morning]") or "Nee, die oë blink" ("No, the eyes are shining").

The small Karretjie family may share meals together and may ride together in the donkey cart to visit family or friends at a neighboring farm or another outspan (a "neutral" site or place next to the road where they erect their overnight shelters and unyoke or outspan the donkeys), but the adult males are then inclined to drink, chat, and joke with each other in a group. The women drink and socialize in their own group while the children play together. Such visiting takes place over weekends and often results in long drinking sessions, which sometimes result in arguing and even fighting.

Karretjie children play together as a group well into adolescence, although there is an increasing tendency for girls' and boys' activities to separate as they become older. A special relationship between a boy and a girl is not always clearly apparent in the sense of them sharing time and activities apart from the rest. The itinerant lifestyle, and the small and close-knit Karretjie community at a particular outspan, precludes this.

9 LIVING CONDITIONS

It is a useful rule of thumb to regard a *karretjie* (cart) as the focus for a Karretjie unit because it provides transport for each family and becomes part of the overnight shelter. A Karretjie unit does not necessarily replicate a household, however. For domestic purposes like cooking, eating, and child care the *karretjies* of parents and married children, or of married siblings, may function together as a unit. Each Karretjie family constructs its own shelter, normally in the *gang* (corridor) next to the road. Sheets of corrugated iron, plastic, and hessian are normally used to construct such a shelter, which consists of a single space with no divisions. The number of people at an outspan is relatively small, and an average of 2 to 14 Karretjie units occupy a particular outspan.

The Karretjie People suffer from the harsh extremes of temperature in this part of South Africa during winter and summer. During winter they are constantly suffering from coughs and colds. They are, however, generally in relatively good health. Adults normally seek medical treatment only in absolute emergencies, such as in the case of a difficult childbirth, chronic illness, or serious accident. In case of illness, people far from town are largely dependent on the compassion of neighboring farmers, although a mobile clinic is now reaching some of those on the outspans and farms. Although pregnant women are now advised to go to town to give birth at a hospital, most are still assisted by older women at the outspan because of the practical difficulties involved in getting to town, especially in case of an emergency.

Most of the outspans have neither clean water nor toilet facilities, and this creates extremely unhealthy conditions for the people living there. Water has to be fetched from nearby taps, windmills, or a river in one instance. The Karretjie People's health is closely related to their environmental conditions and circumstances. High infant mortality rates, low birth weight, poor diet, undernutrition, and diarrhea are significant factors that determine the quality of these people's state of health.

Although the Karretjie People tend to use plants from the natural environment for the treatment of common ailments such as colds, a mobile medical unit nowadays alleviates some of these problems. Its activities are mostly directed to preventive care, in particular family planning, and curative tasks. Mobile clinics have a regular visiting schedule and consist of medical teams with separate units. The medicines provided are fairly inexpensive, but children under six years old receive free medical treatment. In some areas, feeding schemes have been initiated by social workers, and teams try to reach people at outspans twice a week.

10 FAMILY LIFE

Karretjie families on the outspans are relatively small. Although there are a few single-parent families, most families consist of a mother, father, and from one to six children, with three children being roughly the average. Some of the families are extended by virtue of a grandchild, grandparent, or a sibling of one of the parents living with them. As soon as boys are skilled enough, they start shearing independently and, as a result, often form an independent Karretjie unit. The composition of the Karretjie unit also frequently changes by virtue of children or grandparents temporarily joining other units in order to take advantage of available resources.

Women play a significant role in the family structure but remain in a subordinate position because decision-making is done mostly by the head of the Karretjie unit, in this case the senior male and shearer. Adult women and older girls assist in packing and unpacking the donkey cart before and after traveling, they wash clothes and prepare food for the family, and they are the primary caretakers of young children.

Most Karretjie families keep pets, of which dogs and cats are the most popular. Dogs are also used for hunting purposes. When the Karretjie moves as a unit, the dogs are tied behind the cart and run along, while cats are placed on top of the load of the cart together with the old people, children, chickens, and accessories.

11 CLOTHING

The Karretjie People seldom have money to buy items such as clothes. The clothing that they own is mostly secondhand. Men wear shirts and trousers and are fond of caps, while women wear dresses and sometimes head cloths. The decorations that the Karretjie People wear are not of much value and are usually used handouts from the surrounding sedentary communities. Rings of copper and safety pins are popular.

12 FOOD

The staple ingredient of the Karretjie diet is mealie-meal (corn-meal), at least when times are "good." When shearing on a farm they buy supplies, mainly mealie-meal, sugar, coffee, and to-bacco, "on the book" (on credit) from the farmer's store. With any extra money from a shearing assignment, the Karretjie People may undertake a pilgrimage to town before returning to their "home" outspan. At other times, the "not-so-good" or "in between shearing" times, the *krummelpap* (crumbly-thick porridge) becomes *slappap* (soft porridge) and eventually *dunpap* (thin or watery porridge).

The Karretjie people do not eat at regular times. Depending on the availability of food, they normally have two meals a day, i.e., breakfast and supper. They own only the necessary utensils, such as a pot for cooking porridge, a few cans to fetch water, and sometimes only two or three spoons that a family shares during a meal.

Found on the fringe of a gravel road, the occasional carcass of a rabbit is a welcome addition to the usually depleted Karretjie menu. Snares are also set in the veld for rabbits, or antelope like steenbok and duiker. Young boys also set traps and try to entice birds into them by sprinkling a trail of porridge crumbs. The environment does not present much in terms of edible wild roots and berries, although some use is made of the Karoo vegetation for medicinal purposes. Some of the outspans offer alternative resources, such as a river for fish, including yellowfish, carp, and modderbek (literally, "muddy mouth," this fish feeds on the river bed), or prickly pears, which ensure

a juicy, vitamin-rich option during their brief bearing season in the summer.

13 EDUCATION

Until 1992 almost all the Karretjie People were illiterate, having never had the benefit of schooling or even access to a school. Since then the children have started attending farm schools in the area. The farmers or farmers' wives who run these schools fetch the children at the outspans, provide board and lodging for them by means of a government subsidy, and return them to their Karretjie homes on Friday afternoons or, depending on the particular school, only for school holidays.

Because of an adult education program, which was started in 1995, adults at some of the outspans received literacy training, as well as practical and skills training. Some of the children drop out of the farm schools for practical reasons (or because other children discriminate against them) but then participated in this adult education program.

As formal education is a recent and limited development for these communities, the process through which children are prepared for full participation in their community is still an essential function of the Karretjie unit. Informal education is part of everyday life, and the children learn by observing and imitating their parents, other adults, and siblings' activities. The experience of moving to an outspan or farm in itself is educational because they cover vast distances and frequently encounter new regions and different sets of people.

Most of the parents are anxious for their children to attend school and want them especially to learn the skills of reading and writing so that they can get a *sit* job (sitting down, e.g., clerical work) instead of a *staan* job (standing up, e.g., shearing). Some, however, admit that the schooling of their children may interfere with their mobile way of life, and that the children who do attend school are changed by the experience and often become critical of certain aspects of the nomadic way of life, and even of their own parents' behavior.

14 CULTURAL HERITAGE

With their long history of illiteracy, the Karretjie People have no recorded cultural heritage and, obviously, no literature. The Karretjie People have also lost virtually all of their oral tradition, and that which they have is quite "shallow," or relatively recent. The songs that they sing, and the music with which they identify, have all been taken over from surrounding sedentary peoples. This also applies to dancing, although here there is some measure of innovation, much of which is apparent during weekends of socializing.

15 WORK

Virtually all the males of the Karretjie People are, or will eventually become, sheep-shearers. To supplement their meager income, or to tide them over from one shearing season or assignment to another, they do odd jobs on the farms: they hoe burweed, dig irrigation furrows, erect or repair fencing, and build windbreaks for sheep *kraals* (corrals). They may also get temporary employment in a town as painters or gardeners. When the men are shearing, the women may get part-time work at the farmhouse as assistants to the domestic workers or in the garden. They may also help in the shearing shed, sorting the wool locks, extracting foreign matter like burrs from the wool, or sweeping up the wool off-cuts on the floor (young children also do this) where the shearing is in progress.

The Karretjie People are generally recognized as the best shearers in the region. Although as hand-shearers they are slower (a shearer averages approximately 30 sheep a day) than the professional teams shearing with electric machines, many farmers prefer to use them because: (1) unlike the other teams they are not unionized and hence do not drive as hard a bargain; (2) their shearing is neater; (3) the farmers claim to get along better with them because they can converse with them in Afrikaans (as opposed to many of the organized shearers, who are Xhosa-speaking); and (4) farmers do not want or have to have them permanently, or even semipermanently, on the farm.

A farmer intending to shear stops at an outspan (often one with which he has a long-standing arrangement) and informs the spokesperson of the Karretjie shearing team that he intends to start shearing on a given day. He tells them how many sheep or goats there are to shear and how many shearers he needs. A price is tentatively negotiated, and the shearers either get a prepayment there and then or receive it as soon as they arrive on the farm. This confirms the arrangement, although the contract remains verbal at all times.

The price paid per sheep shorn depends largely on the farmer, from as little as R1.00 (approximately $0.13) for the short-wooled Dorper sheep (mainly kept for the meat), to perhaps starting at R2.00 (about $0.26) for Merino sheep. Additionally, each shearing team is given one sheep for slaughter for every 1,000 sheep shorn. The shearers buy their shears, which last them for "three or four farms," from the farmer for about R40.00 ($5.10). Rations are usually bought on credit from the farmer's food store—these prices are often higher than those in town. After shearing for two to three weeks, and after deductions, the shearers may receive a net payment of as little as R40.00 ($5.10). Odd jobs pay R10.00 to R20.00 ($1.28–2.56), and women who work as temporary domestics in town have been known to be paid only R5.00 ($0.65) a day. Some farmers allow the whole Karretjie unit, i.e., not just the shearers, onto their property and occasionally even make housing available for the shearers, but most shearers claim that they do not want to stay in a proper house and prefer their own Karretjie shacks.

Outside observers often perceive the Karretjie People as trekking around haphazardly because of an eager desire or fondness for traveling. Their movements are directed, however, by an intricate interplay of seasonal, social, economic, and ideological factors that result in discernible, though flexible, regularities. Geographical mobility is a reaction to adapt to the scarcity of resources and to optimize the precarious access to available resources. The key to such survival strategies has been the ingenuity of the Karretjie People and the mobility that their donkey carts afford them.

16 SPORTS

The strenuous itinerant lifestyle of the Karretjie People, the fact that they hardly ever find themselves in the same location for any length of time, and the fact that they have been removed from the mainstream of the surrounding society for so long have together resulted in a complete lack of participation, and even an awareness of, or an interest in, organized sports activities. It is only much more recently, with the advent of limited

schooling, that some of the Karretjie children have become exposed to such activities. The small boys do however kick a ball around, if they managed to get hold of one, otherwise an empty plastic bottle serves the purpose.

17 ENTERTAINMENT AND RECREATION

The Karretjie People mostly entertain themselves. They have no access to electricity and hence have no television, but a few have decrepit portable radios, to which they listen when they have enough money for batteries. For the most part, they socialize, go visiting, go hunting (illegally) with their dogs or with snares, and, when near a river, they fish.

18 FOLK ART, CRAFTS, AND HOBBIES

Karretjie women can usually be seen mending or altering clothes and making *lappies komberse* (patchwork blankets). Men busy themselves fixing donkey harnesses and carts and repairing shoes. Little boys make *ketties* (slingshots) for hunting birds, and clay animals when their overnight shelters are near water. Little girls make their own *stokpoppe* (stick and rag dolls).

19 SOCIAL PROBLEMS

The farmers who employ the Karretjie People as shearers are not contractually bound, as the undertaking to shear and the price are both determined by verbal arrangement. These shearers are the most unprotected source of labor in one of the most protected economic sectors in South Africa. A shearer can be quite arbitrarily dismissed, often works long hours or not at all, has no insurance or guarantee of assistance in unemployment, disability, old age, or on leave, and has extremely tenuous access to medical and educational facilities.

South Africa's first democratic election on 27 April 1994 provided the Karretjie People with their first-ever opportunity to cast a vote. Although most of them were not in possession of the required identity documents or voter cards, temporary arrangements were made for many of them. But the ability to vote and the new government now in power have not changed their lives and circumstances at all. Subsequent elections have come and gone, but if anything, the Karretjie People are worse off now than they were before the first. They have, through a series of historical external interventions, progressively been denied access to the resources of the area, most significantly the main resource, land. The process that was set in motion with the arrival in the area of the first white farmers in the 1700s has produced a hierarchical and rigidly ordered social system. The process has furthermore produced in most of the residents in the area (not least of whom, the Karretjie People themselves) a collective, conditioned mind-set of tacit acceptance of the status quo—a status quo of inequity and intolerance, and a monopoly of resources that transcends the statutory transformations brought about by the election of a democratic government. The advent and expansion of game farming in the Merino-wool farming districts frequented by the Karretjie People, increased professional sheep-shearing competition and general changes in the agricultural economy of the area, have resulted in dwindling shearing opportunities. This has further forced the Karretjie People into a downward spiral of poverty. Sooner or later they have to sell their donkeys and *karretjie*, hence lose their mobility and have even less access to shearing assignments. They end up in informal settlements or squatting on the fringes of the towns in their region, scrounging to keep life and limb together.

Although in going about their daily activities the Karretjie People are cheerful, humorous, and ostensibly even optimistic, they are realistically aware of the hardships of their way of life and only too mindful of how little the future seems to hold for them. As marginal people, they not only occupy the lowest rung of the socioeconomic ladder, but in a wider community of divisions and opposition, the particular sociocultural, political, and economic niche in which they find themselves is now even more precarious and vulnerable in the extreme. The hardship and uncertainty tends to translate into feelings of helplessness and frustration, which are regularly manifested in weekend-long bouts of drinking and fighting that, on some occasions, resulted in the deaths of family members and friends.

20 GENDER ISSUES

The pattern of gender roles and relations amongst the Karretjie People have been transmitted and enculturated over generations. This is a matter both of a conditioned continuation of an inherent value system and practical considerations. The foraging Xam San, forbears of the Karretjie People, roamed the Great Karoo for centuries, the men hunting the game and fending off intruders or aggressors, the women collecting wild roots and berries and taking responsibility for the small children and domestic chores. When the Xam San themselves became the hunted with the arrival of European farmers, many of them became "tame Bushmen" on the farms. The physically stronger males became farmhands learning the requisite skills, including shearing when Merino sheep were introduced into the area. The females were employed as domestic help in the homestead. The descendants of these people retained their mobility, first on foot, then by means of pack animals and finally with the donkey cart. They adapted to the niche livelihood of becoming a floating community of shearers providing this specialist service in a burgeoning wool-farming economy. The male, as shearer was, and still is, the provider for the Karretjie domestic unit and he controls the finances. The female, as mother, generally stayed at their shelter tending to their offspring and domestic matters. Although all the Karretjie People are of small stature, the males are physically stronger and even should the possibility of females, as shearers, have been contemplated by the farmers and the Karretjie People themselves, they would have been hard put to master and sustain such strenuous activity over continuous 12-hour working days.

Although Karretjie children play together at an early age, their play and other activities separate as they become older. They learn by observing and imitating their parents' roles and responsibilities. The boys make slingshots to shoot birds, help with the donkeys and aspire to become shearers as soon as they are old, and strong, enough—in fact they join their fathers in the shearing shed at an early age and are gradually initiated into shearing. The girls make and play with dolls and help their mothers with domestic duties, fetch water and tend to those children even smaller than themselves.

So the Karretjie male as main wage-earner is also the decision-maker e.g. in terms of when to break camp, what the next destination is to be, etc. This also translates into the domestic context and husband/wife interpersonal relations. Despite the fact that women play a significant role in the family and domestic organization and situation, they remain in a sub-ordinate position in every respect—even to the extent that a husband would reprimand, castigate, and even manhandle his partner or wife if, according to him, she has been disobedient. This is of course, exacerbated when there is drinking involved over weekends.

All of this flies in the face of the fact that individual rights and particularly discrimination on the grounds of gender are protected in the Bill of Rights of the South African constitution. The circumstances of the Karretjie People are such though, that much as the benefits of citizenship are not accorded them, so too are they often essentially beyond the reach of the cornerstones of democracy.

21 BIBLIOGRAPHY

De Jongh, M. "Kinship as Resource: Strategies for Survival among the Nomads of the South African Karoo." In *African Anthropology,* 11(2) 1995.

———. "No Fixed Abode: The Poorest of the Poor and Elusive Identities in Rural South Africa". In *Journal of Southern African Studies.* 28(2) 2002.

———. "Strangers in Their Own Land—Strategies, Social Resources and Domestic Fluidity of the Peripatetic Karretjie People of the South African Karoo". In: Berland, J.C. & Rao, A. (eds.) *Customary Strangers: New Perspectives on Peripatetics Peoples in the Middle East, Africa, and Asia.* London: Praeger, 2004.

———. "Human Agency, Asymmetrical Relations and Sociocultural Systems. Itinerancy and Sedenterism in the Great Karoo of South Africa". In *International Journal of the Humanities* (3). 2006.

De Jongh, M. and R. Steyn. "Itinerancy as a Way of Life: The Nomadic Sheep-Shearers of the South African Karoo." In *Development Southern Africa,* 11(2) 1994.

Steyn, R. "Child-Rearing and Child-Care in a South African Nomadic Community." In *African Anthropology,* 11(2) 1995.

—by M. De Jongh

KEIYO

PRONUNCIATION: KAY-oh
ALTERNATE NAMES: Kalenjin
LOCATION: Kenya
POPULATION: 110,000
LANGUAGE: Dialect of Kalenjin; Swahili; English
RELIGION: Christianity (Africa Inland Church [AIC], the Church of the Province of Kenya [CPK], Roman Catholic Church); Islam
RELATED ARTICLES: Vol. 1: Kalenjin; Kenyans

¹ INTRODUCTION

The Keiyo live in the Republic of Kenya, East Africa. One of Kenya's lesser-known groups, they were known earlier as El-geyo ("El-gay-o"), a Maasai term. The Keiyo are part of a larger ethnic grouping of eight culturally and linguistically related tribes known as the Kalenjin. The length of time the Keiyo and other Kalenjin groups have been living in the Western Highlands and the Rift Valley, their homeland, is open for debate. Some scholars claim that these peoples have only been living in western Kenya for about 400 years, while others argue that such groups have occupied these parts for 2,000 years or more.

² LOCATION AND HOMELAND

Figures released in January 2007 estimated the population of Kenya to be 36,913,721. Of that 12% are thought to be Kalenjin, approximately 4.4 million people. Collectively the Kalenjin comprise Kenya's fourth-largest ethnic group, with the Keiyo numbering about 144,000 people.

The Keiyo live in the western section of Africa's Great Rift Valley in an administrative district bearing the same name—Keiyo District. Until recently, most Keiyo lived along the slopes of the Elgeyo Escarpment, a spectacular geological feature that drops in elevation from 2,590 m (8,500 ft) in the highlands to 1,070 m (3,500 ft) in the Kerio River Valley. Shortly before, and continuing after, the end of British colonial rule in 1963, many Keiyo moved up into the highlands of the fertile Uasin Gishu plateau to take up farming of cash crops.

³ LANGUAGE

As their first language, or mother tongue, the Keiyo speak a dialect of Kalenjin, a language of the southern section of the Nilotic branch, which is part of the Chari-Nile language group of Africa. There are three Kalenjin dialect clusters: one consists of the Sabaot, along with the Sebei and Kony; another is made up of Pokot, northern Marakwet, and northern Tugen; and the third includes the Nandi, Kipsigis, Keiyo, Terik, and southern Tugen and Marakwet. Although these dialects are all supposedly mutually intelligible, speakers of one dialect often have difficulty understanding speakers of another. In addition to Kalenjin, most people speak Swahili and English, since both are official national languages and are taught in school, beginning with primary school education. Today it is only very old persons who do not speak at least some English.

Most young people today have a Western or Biblical name (for example, Mary, Rose, David, or Paul) as well as a traditional Kalenjin name (for example, Kipkemoi, Kipchoge, Cheru-

tich, or Jebet). Traditionally, names for males begin with the prefix "Ki," while those for females begin with "Che" or "Je." In addition, traditional names often refer to some circumstance when the child was born. For example: Kipchoge (a boy born near the granary), Kibet (a boy born during the day), Cherutich (a girl born as the cows were coming back home), and Jepkemoi (a girl born at night).

⁴ FOLKLORE

Oral tradition was, and still is to some degree, very important among the Keiyo. Prior to the introduction of writing, folk tales served to convey a sense of cultural history. Keiyo oral tradition has four main genres: narratives (stories), songs, proverbs, and riddles. Stories usually contain both people and animals, and certain animals have acquired attributes that are concrete representations of character traits, e.g., hare is a trickster figure whose cleverness can be self-defeating; lion is courageous and wise; and hyena is greedy and destructive. Songs accompany both work and play, as well as ceremonial occasions such as births, initiations, and weddings. Proverbs convey important messages in very concise ways and are often used when elders settle disputes or advise younger persons. Riddles involve word play and are especially popular with children.

⁵ RELIGION

Traditional Keiyo religion is based upon a concept of a supreme god, *Asis* ("Ah-sees"), who is represented in the form of the sun, although this is not God himself. Beneath *Asis* is *Elat* ("Ay-lot"), who controls thunder and lightning. Spirits of the dead, *oyik* ("oh-yeek"), can also intervene in the affairs of humans, and sacrifices of meat and/or beer, *koros* ("chorus"), can be made to placate them. Diviners, *orkoik* ("or-coe-eek"), have magical powers and help in appeals for rain or to end floods.

Currently, nearly everyone professes membership in some organized religion—either Christianity or Islam. Major Christian sects include the Africa Inland Church (AIC), the Church of the Province of Kenya (CPK), and the Roman Catholic Church. Muslims are relatively few in number among the Keiyo. Generally speaking, today only older people can recall details of traditional religious beliefs.

⁶ MAJOR HOLIDAYS

The major holidays observed by the Keiyo are mostly those associated with Christianity (i.e., Christmas and Easter), and national holidays such as Jamhuri (Republic) Day, Madaraka (Responsibility) Day, Moi (the current president) Day, and Kenyatta (the first president) Day. At Christmas it is common for people who still live in traditional mud-walled houses with thatched roofs to give the outer walls a new coat of clay whitewash and paint them with holiday greetings (such as "Merry Christmas" and "Happy New Year").

There are three month-long school holidays in April, August, and December. The first two coincide with peak periods in the agricultural cycle and allow children of various ages to assist their families during these busy times. The December holiday corresponds with both Christmas and the traditional initiation ceremonies, *tumdo* ("toom-doe").

⁷ RITES OF PASSAGE

Age is a fundamental organizing principle in Keiyo society, as it is across much of Africa. Thus, the status occupied and the roles performed by a Keiyo individual are still to a large degree ordained by age. Shortly after a child is born, it is given a name. Friends and family are invited for a ceremony called *chai ya mtoto* ("cha-eye ya m toto"), meaning literally, "the child's tea." This designation derives from the slang use of the KiSwahili word for tea, *chai* ("cha-eye"), to mean payment, often in the form of bribes paid to government officials. Guests give presents and contribute money to the parents to help defer the costs of the party. In the past, the two lower incisor teeth of both boys and girls would be removed at a later age both for cosmetic reasons and to toughen the children for later initiation rites.

For both males and females, becoming an adult involves undergoing an initiation ceremony. Traditionally, these were held about every seven years. Everyone undergoing initiation, or *tumdo* ("toom-doe"), becomes a member of a named age-set, or *ipinda* ("e-pin-da"). Age-sets were traditionally "open" for about 15 years. There are eight male age-sets and they are cyclical, repeating approximately every 100 years. The *sakobei* ("sah-coe-bay") ceremony marked the closing of an age-set about every 15 years, and the elevation of a new age-set to the warrior age-grade. These age-sets and the age-grades (e.g., warrior, junior elder, senior elder) through which individuals passed provided part of the basis for traditional social structure.

After circumcision, male youths were secluded for lengthy periods of time during which they were instructed in the skills necessary for adulthood. Afterwards, they began a phase of warriorhood during which they acted as the military force of the tribe. Elders provided guidance and wisdom. Today age-sets have lost their military function, but this principle still creates bonds between men who are members of the same set, and feelings of respect for those who are older. Female age-sets have long since lost much of their importance. Among the Keiyo today, females are known by the age-set of their husband, and very few women can even recall the names of the female age-sets.

In the past, only people who had borne children would be buried after death; the others would be taken out to the bush and left to be eaten by hyenas. Today at every person's death, he or she is buried, but not in a cemetery as in the United States. People are returned to their farm, or *shamba* ("sha-mbaa"), for burial. There is usually no grave marker, but invariably family members, friends, and neighbors know where people are laid to rest.

⁸ INTERPERSONAL RELATIONS

Chamge ("chaam-gay") or *chamuge* ("chaa-moo-gay") is the standard greeting among the Keiyo. If the encounter is face-to-face, the spoken greeting is almost always accompanied by a hearty handshake, and people often clasp their own right elbow with their left hand. The response is the same—*chamge*, sometimes repeated several times. It may be emphasized with *mising* ("me-sing"), which can mean either "very much" or "close friend," depending upon the context. As a sign of respect, a younger person will greet someone of their grandparents' generation by saying, *chamge kogo* (grandmother—"chaam-gay coe-go") or *chamge kugo* (grandfather—"chaam-gay coo-go").

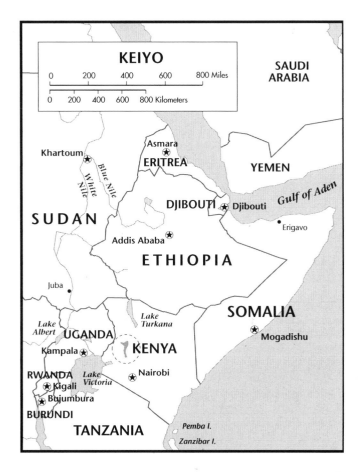

Americans are likely to find several aspects of Keiyo body language to be unusual. First, holding hands after greeting is very common for people of the same sex. Even when walking, these people may hold hands or lock little fingers. But it is readily apparent that there is absolutely no sexual connotation to this behavior. Furthermore, people of opposite sexes are strongly discouraged from these and other public displays of affection. Second, in their conversations Keiyo do not point out objects or people with their fingers. Instead, they point by turning their head in the proper direction and then puckering their lips briefly.

Taking leave of someone is accompanied by the farewell, *sait sere* ("sah-eat sarey"—meaning literally, "blessing time"), and hearty handshakes. Often people will walk with their visitor(s) a distance in order to continue the conversation and to give their friend(s) "a push." Once again, these people often hold hands, especially if they are members of the same sex.

In the past, dating and courtship were almost entirely matters of family concern. Clans were exogamous, i.e., one had to marry outside of one's own (and father's) clan. Today young men and women are more free to exercise their own free will, especially those who live away from home at boarding schools. They will meet and socialize at dances in town discos and in cafes called *hoteli* ("hotel-e") in KiSwahili. Still, when a young man decides on a wife, he and his father's family must gather together a suitable bride-price payment (often erroneously referred to as a "dowry") to be given to the bride's family. In the past this consisted almost entirely of livestock, but today it is becoming more and more common to use money in place of, or in addition to, livestock.

⁹ LIVING CONDITIONS

Most Keiyo live on relatively small family farms averaging less than 2 hectares (5 acres). They grow many different staple food crops such as corn, beans, millet, sorghum, kale, and cowpeas, as well as a variety of cash crops like coffee (small amounts), pyrethrum (related to the chrysanthemum and used in manufacture of insecticides), potatoes, and tomatoes. Most people also keep livestock in the form of cattle, sheep, and goats, and a few donkeys that are used for transport.

Before the British arrived, the Keiyo lived on the face of the Elgeyo Escarpment, while grazing their cattle in the forests at the top of the escarpment and cultivating on the escarpment shelf around their homes. Disease-resistant goats would be sent to the valley during the day, and hunting would also be carried out there. Residence on the Elgeyo Escarpment enabled productive use of multiple ecological zones and protected the Keiyo from diseases like malaria in the valley and, in the past, raids by Maasai and Nandi warriors on the Uasin Gishu plateau. Furthermore, the climate on the escarpment shelf is very moderate. The highlands can become extremely wet and cool during the rainy season, while the valley becomes devastatingly hot in the dry season. However, the escarpment provides relief from both extremes for most of the year.

Traditionally, Keiyo houses were round, with walls constructed of bent saplings anchored to larger posts and covered with a mixture of mud and cow dung, while roofs were thatched with local grasses. While these kinds of houses are still common, there is a growing trend towards the construction of square or rectangular houses that are built with timber walls and roofs of corrugated sheet metal, *mabati* ("ma-baatee").

Most Keiyo people still do not have electricity or indoor plumbing in their houses. Radios and/or cassette players; kerosene lamps and stoves; charcoal stoves; aluminum cooking pots; plastic dishes, plates, and cups; and bicycles are the most common consumer items. Those few people who do not have electricity but who do have televisions use car batteries for power.

¹⁰ FAMILY LIFE

Traditionally, like in most African societies, the family was central in the daily life of the Keiyo people. But by family what was meant was the extended family, not the nuclear family in the Western sense. Keiyo residence patterns were, and still are, largely patrilocal. That is, typically after marriage a man brings his wife to live with him in, or very near to, his father's homestead. Marriage of one man to multiple wives (polygyny) was and is permitted, although most men cannot afford the expense of such unions because of the burden of bride-price. Regardless of the type of marriage, children were traditionally seen as a blessing from God and, as a result of this, until very recently Kenya had the highest population growth rate in the world.

Slowly these patterns are changing as monogamous marriages now prevail and nuclear families are becoming more frequent. Moreover, younger people are now expressing a desire to have fewer children when they get married. This is due to the increasing expense of having large numbers of children who not only must be fed but also educated to cope in today's

world. To some degree, young women are also changing their aspirations to go beyond motherhood alone and include a career as well.

¹¹ CLOTHING

The Keiyo were not renowned for their traditional clothing, which essentially consisted of animal skins, either domesticated or wild. Earrings were common for both sexes in the past, including heavy brass coils which tended to make the earlobe stretch downward almost to the shoulder. This is generally not practiced today, when the Western-style dress of most Keiyo, even in rural areas, is scarcely different from that of people in nearby towns. The buying of secondhand clothes is quite common. Thus, men wear trousers and shirts, usually along with a suit jacket or sport coat, while women wear skirts and blouses, dresses, and/or *khangas* ("khan-gaaz")—locally made commercial textiles that are used as wraps (one for the top and one for the bottom). Youths of both sexes covet tee-shirts with logos, especially those of American sports teams or bearing the likeness of popular American entertainers.

¹² FOOD

The staple food of the Keiyo is *ugali* ("oo-golly"). This is a cake-like, starchy food that is made from white cornmeal mixed with boiling water and stirred vigorously while cooking. It is eaten with the hands and is often served with cooked green vegetables such as kale, called *sukuma wiki* ("sue-cooma weeky") in KiSwahili, and meaning literally, "to push the week." Less frequently it is served with roasted goat meat, beef, or chicken. Before the introduction and widespread diffusion of corn in recent times, millet and sorghum—indigenous African grains—were staple cereals. All of these grains were, and still are, used to make a very thick beer that has a relatively low alcohol content. Another popular Keiyo beverage is *mursik* ("more-seek"). This consists of fermented whole milk that has been stored in a special gourd called a *sotet* (pronounced just as it appears, with the accent on the second syllable) that has been cleaned using a burning stick. The result is that the milk is infused with tiny bits of charcoal.

Lunch and dinner are the big meals of the day. Breakfast usually consists of tea (made with a lot of milk and sugar) and any leftovers from the previous night's meal, or perhaps some store-bought bread. Mealtimes, as well as the habit of tea-drinking, were adopted from the British colonial period. Lunch is eaten at 1:00 pm rather than at noon, and dinner is often eaten later in the evening at 8:00 or 9:00 pm. In addition to bread, people routinely buy foodstuffs such as sugar, tea leaves, cooking fat, sodas (most often Orange Fanta and Coca-Cola), and other items they do not produce themselves.

¹³ EDUCATION

Traditionally, Keiyo education was provided during the seclusion of initiates following circumcision. This transitional phase of the rite of passage provided an opportunity to instill in these young men and women all the requisite knowledge necessary to be a functioning and productive adult member of their society. It was, in essence, a "crash" course in the intricacies of their own culture. Nowadays, after initiation young men and women are still secluded but for briefer periods of time (one month as compared with three months in the past). The timing of the December school holiday coincides with the practice of initiation and seclusion.

In 2003 free primary school education became universal in Kenya. "Free" must be qualified however, because parents must provide their children with uniforms, books, pens and pencils, and paper, as well as contribute to frequent fund raising activities for their children's school(s). This constitutes a tremendous financial burden for families in a country where the average per capita income is about $360 per year. Post-primary school education is relatively expensive, even at the cheaper secondary schools, and entry is competitive. Tuition at the more prestigious high schools, where students must board, is very expensive. Typically, parents rely on contributions from a wide range of family, neighbors, and friends to meet the high tuition costs. Tuition at Kenya's universities is rather nominal, but the selection process is grueling and relatively few students who want to attend can do so.

14 CULTURAL HERITAGE

Traditional music and dance had many different functions. Songs would accompany many work-related activities, including, for men, herding livestock and digging the fields, and, for women, grinding corn, washing clothes, and putting babies to sleep (with lullabies). Music would also be an integral part of ceremonial occasions such as births, initiations, and weddings. Dances to punctuate these occasions would be performed while wearing ankle bells and would be accompanied by traditional instruments such as flutes, horns, and drums. Oral stories, proverbs, and riddles all convey important messages to be passed from generation to generation.

15 WORK

In Keiyo society, much of the work, at least traditionally speaking, is divided along gender lines. Men are expected to do the heavy work of initially clearing the fields that are to be used for planting, as well as turning over the soil. Women take over the bulk of the farming work from there on, including planting, several weedings, harvesting (although here men tend to pitch in), and processing crops. Among the Keiyo, tradition holds that men are supposedly more concerned with herding livestock than with other pursuits. Recent evidence suggests that women, children (especially boys), and even older people are equally as likely to be engaged in animal care as men, especially in those situations where men are likely to be away from home engaged in wage work.

In addition to all of their other tasks, women are expected to perform nearly all of the domestic work that is involved in keeping a household running. In doing so, they often enlist the help of young girls, who are expected to assist their mothers and other female relatives in chores such as fetching water from wells or streams, and collecting the firewood that most families use for cooking. Young boys will sometimes perform these same tasks but more often do things such as grazing and/or watering livestock.

16 SPORTS

Soccer is a major sports interest of the Keiyo as it is with other Kenyans. Nonetheless, running (especially middle and longer distances) is the sport that has made the Keiyo and other Kalenjin peoples famous in world athletic circles. St. Patrick's High School in Iten has turned out a phenomenal number of world-class runners.

17 ENTERTAINMENT AND RECREATION

In rural areas, the radio is still the main form of entertainment. KBC (Kenya Broadcasting Corporation) programs are attentively monitored, as are shortwave radio transmissions by the BBC (British Broadcasting Corporation) and the VOA (Voice of America). A relatively small number of people have televisions, and the only programming available is from KBC. In towns and trading centers, video parlors are becoming common, and action films (e.g., those starring Chuck Norris, Sylvester Stallone, Bruce and Brandon Lee) are especially popular.

18 FOLK ART, CRAFTS, AND HOBBIES

In other parts of Kenya ,the famous sisal bags (called *kiondo* in KiSwahili and pronounced "key-on-doe") are manufactured and marketed worldwide. Although the Keiyo are not well known for their handicrafts, women do make and locally sell decorated calabashes (*sotet* in Kalenjin and pronounced just as it appears) from gourds. These are rubbed with oil and adorned with small colored beads and are essentially the same type of calabashes that are used for storing fermented milk.

19 SOCIAL PROBLEMS

Tobacco usage and alcohol consumption continue to be common among men but not women. For decades the Kenyan government has banned the brewing and distillation of traditional homemade alcoholic beverages, including *busaa* ("boosaah"), a beer made from fried, fermented corn and millet, and *chang'aa* ("chaan-gah"), a liquor distilled from *busaa*. Nevertheless, these beverages continue to be popular with people, especially men, and provide some individuals, mostly women, with supplementary income. *Chang'aa* especially can be lethal since there is no way to control the high alcohol content (unlike that of *busaa* which tends to have a very low alcohol content), and there are many opportunities for contamination. It is not uncommon to read stories of men dying after attending drinking parties in the Kenyan daily newspapers.

Considerable variation in levels of economic and social development exists in Keiyo District. The Kenyan government estimates the percentage of people living in absolute poverty is 47.82%, or about 75,000 persons. For various reasons, some of which are geographic in nature, there is much more poverty in the valley and much less on the escarpment and even less in the highlands. Considerable food insecurity exists especially in the lower areas of Keiyo, where people are being supported through famine relief. Cattle-raiding is also a major security concern in the valley area of the district. Paved (tarmac) roads are still in short supply and during the rainy season the earth roads become virtually impassable. This problem is true in all three regions of the district.

As is true all over African and Kenya, HIV/AIDS is arguably the major issue confronting Keiyo today. Fortunately, prevalence rates in the country as a whole have dropped dramatically from 14% in 2002 to 5.1% in 2008. Moreover the HIV prevalence rate in urban areas is much higher, at 9.6 % whereas in rural areas it is 4.6%. Most Keiyo live in rural areas. Also, a link between male circumcision and susceptibility to HIV infection has been posited, whereby circumcision significantly decreases the risk of HIV infection. One study among agricultural employees in Rift Valley Province found that Luo men, from a tribe that does not circumcise, had a significantly higher HIV prevalence (24.8%) than Kalenjin men (4.5%).

20 GENDER ISSUES

Traditionally Keiyo culture, like most others in Africa, is heavily divided on gender lines. Along with age gender is a fundamental organizing principle in African societies. In the past leadership was always the prerogative of adult males but recently this has begun to change. With the growth of multiparty politics Kenyan women have increasingly entered the political sphere. However, unlike other ethnic groups, such as Kikuyu or Kamba, Keiyo women have not participated in politics to the same degree. One exception is Tabitha Seii, who, since 1992, has repeatedly and bravely challenged the strongman of Keiyo politics, Nicholas Biwott. Although Mrs. Seii, a former headmistress, has never succeeded, she was appointed Kenya's High Commissioner to South Africa in 2003. In 2007 she resigned in protest and joined the opposition Orange Democratic Movement (ODM). Mrs. Seii was also a founding member of the Education Center for Women in Democracy (ECWD), a group whose mission is to increase the presence of women in leadership and decision-making positions

As part of traditional rites of passage, circumcision of both boys and girls was practiced. In the academic world the female variant has come to be known female genital mutilation (FGM) and is a very controversial subject. Although technically illegal in Kenya since 1990 it is still widely practiced by members of many ethnic groups. Among the Kalenjin its prevalence rate has recently been estimated at 47% compared with rates as high as 97% for the Somali. In several areas of Kenya, some especially progressive women have recently been promoting alternatives to traditional circumcision and instead advocating what has come to be known as "circumcision with words." An example from Keiyo District is the Tumndo Ne Leel Support Group which started in 2003 as a community based organization. One of the unique features of this approach is that it retains the very important ceremonial and symbolic role of a rite of passage while doing away with the act of "cutting." In the process this community based organization addresses the larger issue of female empowerment in this traditionally male dominated society.

21 BIBLIOGRAPHY

Chesaina, C. *Oral Literature of the Kalenjin*. Nairobi: Heinemann Kenya, 1991

Fedders, Andrew, and Cynthia Salvadori. *Peoples and Cultures of Kenya*. Nairobi: Transafrica, 1988.

Government of Kenya. *Central Bureau of Statistics, Ministry of Planning and Natural Resources,* http://www.cbs.go.ke (April 2008).

Massam, J. A. *Cliff Dwellers of Kenya*. London: Frank Cass & Co. Ltd., 1927.

Miller, Norman, and Rodger Yeager. *Kenya: The Quest for Prosperity*. 2nd ed. Boulder, CO: Westview Press, 1994.

Republic of Kenya. "Keiyo District Strategic Plan 2005-2010 for Implementation of the National Population Policy for Sustainable Development." National Coordination Agency for Population and Development, Ministry of Planning and National Development. August 2005.

Roberts, Bruce D. *The Historical and Ecological Determinants of Economic Opportunity and Inequality in Elgeyo-Marakwet District, Kenya*. Ph.D. Dissertation, University of Pittsburgh, 1993.

———. "Livestock Production, Age, and Gender Among the Keiyo of Kenya." *Human Ecology* 24, no. 2 (1996): 215–230.

———. "Always Cheaply Pleasant: Beer as a Commodity in a Rural Kenyan Society." In *Commodities and Globalization: Anthropological Perspectives*, Angelique Haugerud, M. Priscilla Stone, and Peter D.Little, eds. New York: Rowman and Littlefield Publishers, 2000. Pages 179–196.

Rosenberg, Jared. "Circumcision Reduces HIV Risk among Men in Kenya." *International Family Planning Perspectives* 33.1 (March 2007): p. 4(1).

Sateren, W. B, P. O. Renzullo, C. Mason, M. Wasunna, M. Robb, L. Langat, L. Elson. "HIV Infection among Agricultural Employees in Rift Valley Province, Kenya: Prevalence, Risk Factors, and Suitability for Vaccine Efficacy Trials." *International Conference on AIDS*, 7–12, July 2002.

Sutton, J. E. G. "The Kalenjin." In *Kenya Before 1800: Eight Regional Studies*, edited by B. A. Ogot. Nairobi: East African Publishing House, 1976.

"Tumndo Ne Leel: Placing Value on Kalenjin Traditions while Working to Stop FGM." *Sexuality in Africa Magazine*, September 2006. Volume 31. Issue 3.

—by B. Roberts

KENYANS

PRONUNCIATION: KEN-yuhns
LOCATION: Kenya
POPULATION: 36.9 million
LANGUAGE: Kiswahili; English; regional ethnic languages
RELIGION: Christianity; Muslim; traditional indigenous beliefs; independent Christian churches; small numbers of Hindus, Sikhs, Parsees, Bahais, followers of Judaism
RELATED ARTICLES: Vol. 1: Embu; Gikuyu; Gusii; Kalenjin; Keiyo; Luhya; Maasai; Oromos

¹ INTRODUCTION

Kenya is a multi-racial society of about 36.9 million people, the overwhelming majority comprising indigenous ethnic groups with the rest being Asian, Arab, and European. Arabs have, for many centuries, had historical connections with coastal Kenya, where the dominant language is Kiswahili and the major religion is Islam. Asians, mainly of Indian descent, who are significant in the professional and commercial sectors, were originally railway construction workers taken from India to Kenya by the British colonialists about 100 years ago. Europeans are primarily of British origin, having come to Kenya in search of commercial and agricultural opportunities. The "White Highlands" commonly included large, commercial farms so that indigenous Africans were displaced from their own extremely fertile land. The Land and Freedom Movement (Mau Mau) contributed, through armed resistance in the 1950s, to eventual independence from Britain. Under the leadership of President Jomo Kenyatta, Kenya became a republic in 1964, a year after winning its independence. Kenya currently is a multi-party democracy. Its government consists of a president and a legislative assembly composed of 12 members nominated by the president, 210 elected members, the attorney general, and a speaker. Kenya is divided into eight provinces under the authority of the president.

² LOCATION AND HOMELAND

The Republic of Kenya, which is 583,000 sq km, is located in East Africa on and near the Equator. The Indian Ocean is on its east coast; the neighboring countries of Ethiopia and Sudan are to the north; Somalia is to the northeast; Tanzania is to the south; and Uganda is to the west. There is considerable landform variation, ranging from the permanent snow of Mts. Kenya and Kilimanjaro, to palm-treed, tropical shores. Some areas are desert, but most land is forested or composed of rolling grassland. The major geological feature, the Rift Valley, stretches from Zimbabwe to the south to the Red Sea to the north, and is 50 mi wide and 9000 ft above sea level in some places. Numerous lakes are found along its base. Kenya's Lake Victoria is the second largest fresh water lake in the world.

Because of altitude extremes and seasonal rainfall, Kenya has regional climatic variation. Typically, there are two rainy seasons, with highest rainfall in April and lowest rainfall in January. Evenings can become quite chilly in the Central Highlands, and the coastal areas are characteristically hot and humid. Kenya's capital, Nairobi, although close to the Equator, is almost 1700 m above sea level, making it comfortably warm or cool most of the year.

Location and geological and climatic conditions combine to make Kenya a diverse and attractive place for everyday life as well as for visiting. Tourism is a major industry. Large numbers of international visitors come to witness spectacular game parks, the beautiful Rift Valley, and elaborate ocean resorts. One unforgettable sight is that of Lake Nakuru, covered with an unimaginable number of pink flamingoes. For even more excitement, one can visit the Masai Mara National Reserve with its varied wild life including thousands of wildebeest running over the land.

³ LANGUAGE

The official national languages of Kenya are Kiswahili and English. English is spoken in government, courts, universities, and secondary schools. National mass media such as newspapers and magazines, as well as radio and television, are overwhelmingly in English. Nevertheless, Kiswahili is widely spoken in everyday life as a lingua franca (common language), especially in commerce and by those who do not know English. It is the dominant language along the coast, particularly in the major port city of Mombasa. Nowadays, Kiswahili is usually taught along with English in schools throughout Kenya. Regional ethnic languages spoken at home are typically used for elementary school teaching along with English and Kiswahili. Major ethnic languages in Kenya include Kikuyu, Luo, Kiluyia, Kikamba, Samburu, and Masai, although there are numerous others. Major Asian languages are Hindi and Gujarati. A pronounced linguistic characteristic of Kenya is the multilingualism of its residents.

⁴ FOLKLORE

Prior to the modern era and before the introduction of literacy in English and Kiswahili, indigenous ethnic groups had developed a sophisticated folklore that embodied their ethnic history, as well as wisdom concerning everyday mysteries and dilemmas. In legends, the movements of people throughout East Africa, from river and lake to highland and plain, and the exploits of past leaders, were recounted in oratory. Riddles, proverbs, and sayings are still richly represented in daily speech to indicate morality and proper behavior for young and old alike. Puzzling questions such as, "Why do cats like to stay by the fireplace? Why do hyenas limp? How did circumcision come to be practiced? What is the origin of death?" are answered in folktales. Proverbs contain much wisdom, as the following examples from the Luo attest: "The eye you have treated will look at you contemptuously"; "A cowardly hyena lives for many years"; "The swimmer who races alone, praises the winner." Riddles are also commonly heard. For example: "A lake with reeds all around? The eye." Another is: "A snake that breathes out smoke? A train."

The Gikuyu people account for the origins of their customary way of life as farmers and herders in the following way. The first tribal parents, Gikuyu and Mumbi, begot their own children, who then begot children who dispersed around Mt. Kenya. These children began diverse economic activities. The story goes as follows: One grandchild's knee started swelling one day. When he opened his knee, three little boys emerged, who became his sons. In time, one of them became a hunter; one enjoyed collecting fruits and plants; and the third made fire for cooking. In time, the hunter domesticated some animals, and the collector grew some crops such as bananas, cas-

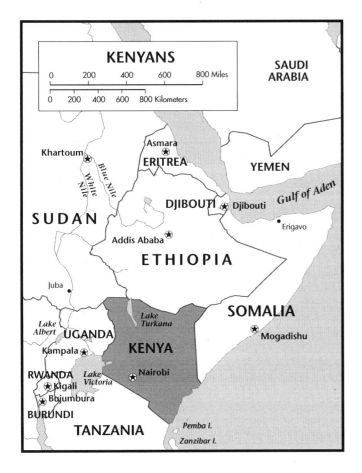

KENYANS

0   200   400   600   800 Miles

0   200   400   600   800 Kilometers

SAUDI ARABIA

Khartoum

Asmara
ERITREA

YEMEN

Blue Nile
White Nile

DJIBOUTI   Djibouti   Gulf of Aden

SUDAN

Erigavo

Addis Ababa

ETHIOPIA

Juba

SOMALIA

Lake Turkana

Lake Albert   UGANDA

KENYA

Mogadishu

Kampala

Nairobi

RWANDA   Lake Victoria

Kigali

Bujumbura

BURUNDI

TANZANIA

Pemba I.
Zanzibar I.

sava, and sweet potatoes. The third son applied fire to stones and metals and became a blacksmith. In this way, Gikuyu culture originated.

Traditionally, word games were commonly played by children who spent a great deal of time in the evenings listening to grandparents telling stories and legends. Tongue twisters such as the following might be heard among the Gikuyu: *Kaanaka Nikora kona kora kora, nako kora kona kaanaka Nikora kora* (refers to a child and a tadpole scaring each other when they come upon the other suddenly).

Coastal Kenya, particularly the city of Mombasa, had a rich Kiswahili folklore tradition, especially tales, legends, and stories of Islamic origin. The 19th century had a number of poets renowned for their popular Kiswahili poetry. Topics included advice about not being tempted by present fortune, in that misfortune could come at any time and the inability to explain strange events, such as a hyena and a goat walking arm in arm. There is also praise as well as scorn for public figures.

Although indigenous folklore is still plentiful throughout Kenya, it has been supplemented with English literary traditions in schools and universities. Modern movies, television, and radio, with their global subject matters, are popular forms of entertainment among young Kenyans. Nevertheless, radio and television regularly feature traditional folklore as part of their programming.

5 RELIGION

Kenya's religious heritage mirrors its ethnic history described previously. The majority religion is Christianity, with about 37% Protestant (including Quakers) and 25% Roman Catholic; about 4% are Muslim. The remainder practice traditional indigenous beliefs or are members of independent Christian churches that have broken away from Protestant and Catholic denominations, often over indigenous beliefs that are found incompatible with European dogma. Smaller numbers of Kenyans are Hindus, Sikhs, Parsees, Bahais, and followers of Judaism. Traditional religions generally believed in a high God, spiritual forces such as venerated ancestors, and malevolent forces such as witches. The creator God was known by different names, but was everywhere thought to be benevolent and forgiving. For example, the Abaluyia people believed that God was known as Were when he created Heaven first, then the earth. He created mankind so that the sun could have someone on whom to shine. Animals, plants, and birds were created by Were as food for mankind.

The first independent church in Kenya, and currently one of Kenya's largest, was called the Nomiya Luo Church. Its founder, Johana Owalo, was one of the early converts to Christianity around the year 1900. In 1906, he was baptized a Roman Catholic. In 1907, he had a vision and was taken to Heaven by the Angel Gabriel. Although he could enter Heaven, Europeans and Asians could not, suggesting that he was rebelling against colonialism. The Pope had also been banished because he permitted adoration of Mary and the saints. After this and other instructional visions, he left Catholicism for Anglicanism. Subsequent to this, he learned to speak Arabic and converted to the Islamic faith. In time, he began to teach that mission churches were contrary to African traditions and began to attract many followers. His beliefs are a mixture of Anglican and Catholic practices; in addition, they include a preference for traditional marital customs such as inheritance of widows by their deceased brothers, which was accepted in the Old Testament but not by Christians.

Missionary churches, while still present, are now largely in the control of a Kenyan hierarchy. For example, there is a Kenyan Roman Catholic Cardinal and a Church Province of Kenya (Anglican) Archbishop, each with numerous subordinate Kenyan bishops. Kenyan languages, music, and dance are integral aspects of religious ritual in these and other Christian communities.

6 MAJOR HOLIDAYS

Kenya celebrates as public holidays the religious holidays of Good Friday, Easter Monday, Christmas Day, and the Muslim festival *Idd-ul-fitr* (which depends on the sighting of the new moon after Ramadan). Secular holidays include New Year's Day and Labor Day (May 1). The most significant secular holidays unique to Kenya are related to their colonial struggle and subsequent independence. *Madaraka* (June 1) celebrates internal self government day, and independence day is celebrated on December 12. Jomo Kenyatta, a major leader during the struggle for independence, was detained on 20 October 1952 for a period of seven years by the colonial government; Kenyatta Day (October 20) is celebrated annually in honor of Kenya's first president and patriot. During all holidays in Kenya, schools and businesses are closed. Many residents of cities return home to rural areas for family gatherings and visiting.

Celebrations include festivities such as eating, drinking, and dancing in homes, bars, and night clubs. On such occasions, *Nyama Choma* (roasted meat) is a common treat. Goat or beef are consumed, although goat is considered the greater delicacy. On secular holidays, the Kenyan military is on parade, and politicians give speeches in public and on radio and television. Newspapers typically carry honorific testimonials to past and present political leaders.

7 RITES OF PASSAGE

Kenyans generally are raised in the context of a strong family and community ideology. Birth is typically a welcome event in all the ethnic groups of Kenya. Most births take place in hospitals or small rural clinics under the care of a midwife. Infants are commonly breast-fed and carried on the back or side in a sling of cloth. Mothers are assisted in the care of their infants and toddlers by young caretakers, who are often older siblings. For this reason, a special bond prevails between a caretaker and his "follower" in the birth order. If no girl is available, a boy can also be a caretaker. Parents desire to have both boys and girls. Boys are valued because in most societies in Kenya descent is traced through males (patrilineal), who then inherit land. The families of girls receive gifts from their future in-laws on the occasion of marriage into their family, a custom known as bride wealth. Although women may now own land, bride wealth is still common and a sign of prestige for highly educated women.

Puberty is marked in many societies by initiation rites such as male circumcision or female clitoridectomy. Circumcision serves to tie together young males into a common social group who will bond for life as they make the transition from childhood to manhood. Among the Bukusu, for example, circumcision ceremonies are held every four years. Young initiates of 12 or 13 years of age are carried on the shoulders of their male and female relatives in celebration of their new public identity. It is considered shameful to express pain while being publicly circumcised. Bukusu men from all walks of life and from all over the world return to Bukusu land to witness the circumcision of their relatives. There are, however, many societies in Kenya that do not circumcise such as the Luo, Kenya's second largest ethnic group. Most ethnic groups do not practice clitoridectomy, although it is found among the Gusii, Pokot, Kikuyu, and a few other societies. Unlike circumcision, this practice is very controversial and the subject of considerable national and international debate, even when it is undertaken with modern medical precautions. Many folk explanations for its existence, such as the control of female sexuality or the enhancement of female solidarity, are now largely discredited in contemporary Kenya.

Marriage and parenthood are still very significant events in the life cycle. Kenyans of all ethnic groups live out their lives with a strong sense of identity to their families and to their ethnic groups. Land is a strong symbol in this ideology, so that regardless of where a person lives in Kenya, there is a strong pull to return "home" whenever possible. Burial of a person of any age is a matter for not only the individual and his family and church, but not uncommonly for the person's ethnic group as well. The continued importance of being buried in one's homeland came to a dramatic conclusion in a much publicized case in Kenya known as the Otieno affair. Mr. Otieno, a Luo lawyer, had been married to a Kikuyu woman. They lived in Nairo-

bi. Mrs. Otieno, on the occasion of his death, ordered that her husband be buried in that city. Members of Mr. Otieno's clan, however, insisted that he be buried in the Western Province, the homeland of his clan. This would insure that he would be buried properly in communal clan land, according to rituals necessary to the respectful repose of his body and spirit. Public cemeteries with individual grave sites are rare in Kenya. After many months of agonizing public debate throughout Kenya by all social strata over individual rights vs. clan rights, it was determined in the High Court of Kenya that he would be buried in the clan lands.

8 INTERPERSONAL RELATIONS

Kenyans can be characterized as very gregarious and very much involved in the social lives of their families, in such a way that "rugged individualism" is not valued. Ethnic groups contain very elaborate greeting patterns that are extended ritualistically and vigorously in rural areas. The simplest and most common Kiswahili greeting is *Jambo* ("hello") to which a person replies likewise. *Jambo* or *Hujambo, Bwana* is said to a man ("You have nothing the matter, Sir?") while a woman is addressed *Jambo, mama*. If addressing more than one person, the greeting would become *Hamjambo*. The reply to this is *Sijambo,* or *Hatujambo* if with others. These greetings are usually followed by additional salutations depending on social context, time of day, weather, and so forth.

Politicians frequently seek to mobilize Kenyans for development projects by encouraging a national slogan that has interpersonal content. The late President Kenyatta initiated *Harambee* ("Let's pull together") as a national symbol, around which individuals and communities mobilized to raise money for such things as the construction of schools, hospitals, and other public works. Individuals are sponsored to attend school or to obtain medical treatment or other necessities through harambee. Today, political leaders and other prominent people attend harambee functions and give large sums of money, which are sometimes announced in newspapers or on the radio. Many Kenyans carry on their person a harambee card on which to note the amount given by a donor. Some Kenyans do not approve of this custom, although it is difficult to say no since requests may be made in public. Also, it is thought that some unscrupulous politicians may misuse the system for their own gain as a way to purchase votes.

Young people have many opportunities for social interaction, especially in the cities. Rural areas tend to have dating patterns that are supervised by family members. Attendance at funerals, where several days of rituals culminate in feasting and dancing, is a favorite venue for courtship. Secondary schools and churches in the town and country also sponsor social events where teenagers may interact. Dating in Nairobi is more elaborate and may involve nightclubs, restaurants, movie theaters, malls, and drive-in movie theaters. One club known as "The Carnivore" is very popular among secondary and university students, especially those returning from schooling in Europe and America during their holidays. The Carnivore, which is located in a Nairobi suburb, is a disco but also has an attached restaurant frequented by tourists in pursuit of zebra, antelope, and other meats.

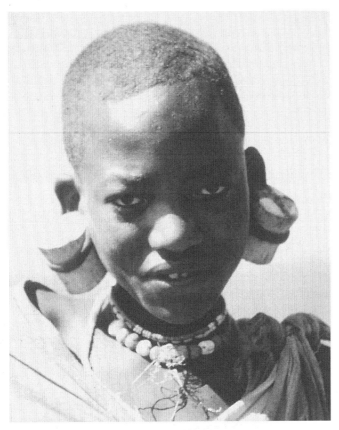

Various ethnic groups in Kenya have their own traditional dress. (Cory Langley)

⁹ LIVING CONDITIONS

The majority of Kenyans live in rural areas where electricity and running water are often not available, and roads are not paved. Homes are constructed of waddle and daub and thatch, although wealthier people do have access to more elaborately constructed homes of stone or brick and live near towns where electricity and running water are available. A growing number of Kenyans (about 25%) live in cities. Large cities in Kenya include Naivasha, Nakuru, Mombasa, and Kisumu, although Nairobi is by far the largest city. Nairobi originated at the time of the construction of the Uganda Railway in 1899. Population grew to 250,000 at the time of independence. By 1990, there were 1.5 million inhabitants residing in numerous estates and suburban areas around the city center, where businesses are clustered. In 2007 Nairobi boasted a total population of 2.8 million people in comparison to Mombasa, the second largest city with a total population of 828,500 people. A significant portion of Kenyans are middle class or richer and live in comfortable houses or even mansions in suburban areas. Nevertheless, Nairobi has many shanty towns such as Kibera or Mathare Valley, in which homes are little more than shacks built out of wood packing cases, flattened tin cans, cardboard, or other discarded items. Many who reside in these shanty towns are squatters with no ownership rights, so they can be forcibly evicted at a moment's notice. Many residents do pay rent to local landlords. Very small-scale commercial activities such as vegetable stalls, food stores, carpentry, and tailoring abound in these shanty towns. Numerous illegal activities such as ille-

gal brewing of beer, prostitution, and petty theft are common. Notwithstanding, fear of entry into the shanty towns is greatly exaggerated in more affluent parts of town where homes are fenced or walled in and typically have house guards known as *Askaris*. Their fear of robbery is not always without foundation, in that it appears to be rising in these suburban areas. The majority of residents in these shanty towns are, however, hardworking people who must face difficult obstacles to survive in situations of meager resources.

Health problems in shanty towns are generally more severe and include gastrointestinal problems and diarrhea for children, and for all people respiratory infections, occasionally cholera, typhoid, and typhus, and a growing problem of HIV infection. Most Kenyans experience periodic bouts with malaria, although this disease is generally contracted when visiting areas outside of Nairobi where malaria-carrying mosquitoes are common. Hospitals are both public and private throughout the country. No fees are charged for visits to public hospitals and for medication, although extended waiting is required and medicines are often not available.

Transportation in Nairobi includes a Kenya bus service for the city and its environs. The *matatu* (van) is an alternative form of transportation operated along bus routes and frequently in competition with them. These vans, like the buses, are severely overcrowded, especially during rush hour, so that passengers are oppressively cramped and may even get injured. The matatu driver employs a "tout," a teenager or young adult male, to yell out for passengers to board the van, to pack in as many as possible, and to collect the fare. These touts can be seen leaning from speeding matatus in a show of bravado matched only by their quick-witted tongues. Matatus are a frequent source of accidents in cities and in rural areas, where they are also common. Taxis are available for those who can afford this expensive means of transportation. The affluent frequently have their Mercedes as a show of prestige. More Kenyans now own cars than ever before, although the bicycle is a popular means of transportation in rural areas. For those traveling between cities or between town and country, Kenya rail service, Kenya airways, and a growing number of bus companies provide excellent service. International travel is available from many international carriers including Kenya Airways, from airports in Nairobi, Mombasa, and Eldoret. Those wishing to travel by sea can do so from the seaport of Mombasa.

¹⁰ FAMILY LIFE

Marriage and family are closely associated in all ethnic groups. The extended family is more important than the nuclear, monogamous family. It is not uncommon to see several generations living in the same compound or neighborhood. Nevertheless, national marriage laws recognize cultural variation. The European heritage is recognized in one legal code that privileges conjugal marriage, while prohibiting plural marriages such as polygyny and wife inheritance. These and other practices are permissible under customary law, where recognition is given to indigenous marital customs. Religiously contracted marriages are recognized for Muslim and Hindu unions under separate codes. Wife inheritance is very controversial, with traditionalists arguing that this practice ensures that widows and their children will be cared for within their husbands' extended families. The new husband assumes all of the rights and obligations of his deceased brother. National Christian churches, unlike some independent Christian churches, are generally opposed to this practice.

Bride-price, unlike widow inheritance, still continues to be a common practice and has been augmented by premarital rituals such as the engagement party, where members of the extended families of the future bride and groom formally meet each other. Families are quite large. Kenya's current total fertility rate of 4.82 children born per woman is among the highest in the world. A significant feature of family life is the obligation of extended family members to assist their kinsmen. Homes will typically have an extended family member in residence. School fees and other necessities are expected to be offered with the understanding that reciprocity will be forthcoming. Many Kenyans, even a majority in some parts of the country, experience their family life within the home of a relative. This practice occurs, in part, because it is thought unfortunate for any home not to have children, and because children are placed whenever possible in the home of a prosperous relative. Kinship terminology is also routinely extended so that one's mother's sister is called "mother," and one's father's brother is called "father." The term brother or sister is often extended to what would be called "cousin" elsewhere.

¹¹ CLOTHING

Various ethnic groups in Kenya have their own traditional dress. Maasai men, for instance, can be seen wearing red tunics and sandals as well as elaborate bracelets, necklaces, and large earrings dangling from their much-elongated earlobes. Their hair may be shaved or elaborately braided and covered with red ochre. Feathers may be worn on certain occasions. Women wear long, plain cotton dresses decorated with elaborate belts, huge necklaces, and wear long earrings. On their arms are many copper bangles. Their hair is typically shaved or quite short. A person's status in Maasai society is indicated by the size and various combinations of adornment.

European and Arabic garb are now commonplace throughout the country, even among urban Maasai. In rural areas, for example, women wear multicolored cotton dresses or skirts and blouses. Large shawl-like cloths are worn commonly as protection from rain, sun, and cold. Babies can be seen carried on the back or on the side in a sling. Scarves are worn on the head. Flat shoes or bare feet are standard. Men generally wear Western-style trousers and shirts with jackets and ties for special occasions. Dress in urban areas reflects social class differences. The most stylish and expensive clothes in the latest international styles are available for those who can afford them. Long pieces of colorful cloth are often worn as skirts, wrapped around shorter dresses or by themselves along with matching headpieces. Arabic influences are strong, especially along the coast where the fez and turban are commonplace. Asian dress is the sari for women, and white cotton shirts and pants are prevalent for men. Secondary school children usually wear uniforms to school, but dress very much like American and European youth at home and for leisure. Nevertheless, ethnic or religious variations are also apparent.

¹² FOOD

Pre-colonial food production included both agriculture and animal husbandry. Archaeological research has demonstrated that indigenous African crops included sorghum and finger millet. Later, some 2,000 years ago, crops such as bananas,

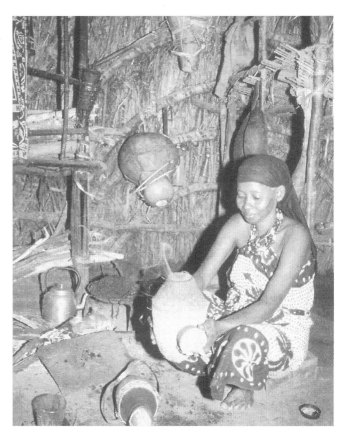

The major staple throughout much of Kenya is maize, which is made into a thick porridge and eaten with meat, stews, or indigenous greens. (David Johnson)

yams, rice, and coconuts reached East Africa from Southeast Asia. About 400 years ago, crops from the Americas such as maize and cassava spread to East Africa from West Africa. Today, the major staple throughout Kenya is maize, which is also an important cash crop as well. Pastoralism, or cattle keeping, has a long history in Kenya. By the 17th century, for example, groups like the Maasai and Turkana subsisted exclusively on cattle, which were originally domesticated and developed through breeding in the Horn of Africa and East Africa. Cattle provide meat, milk, butter, and blood. Livestock includes poultry, sheep, and goats. Many societies in Kenya combine agriculture with livestock raising.

Currently, crops and livestock raised in Kenya also include those imported from Europe during the colonial era. Examples of crops are white potatoes, cucumbers, tomatoes, and many others. Indigenous fruits such as papaya and mangoes are especially favored throughout the country. Agriculture is the major component of Kenya's economy, employing about three-fourths of the population and generating a significant amount of export earnings. Coffee and tea are the main exports. A major staple throughout much of Kenya is maize, which is made into a thick porridge called *Ugali* and is eaten with meat, stews, or indigenous greens (*sukuma wiki*). Many Kenyans eat this combination on a daily basis. It takes much practice to cook the mixture of maize meal and boiling water to the right consistency without burning it. *Sukuma wiki* is a combination of chopped spinach or kale that is fried with onions, tomatoes, perhaps a green pepper, and any leftover meat if it is available. This is seasoned with a good bit of salt and some pepper. The main staple for the Gikuyu is *Irio,* a mixture of kernels from cooked green corn and beans, potatoes, and chopped greens.

Present-day Kenyans enjoy eating in a variety of international restaurants and fast food chains. Asian restaurants are also very popular. In rural areas, children can be seen snacking on roasted maize and sugar cane. Manufactured candy and bottled drinks such as Fanta (orange soda) and colas are very popular at birthday parties and other festive occasions. Bottled beer brewed in Kenya has largely replaced traditional beers made from millet, or maize, although coconut wine is popular on the coast. Modern eating utensils are common; nevertheless, most Kenyans prefer eating their *Ugali* with their right hand.

13 EDUCATION

There are many schools throughout the country servicing young people from nursery school through university and professional training. Primary and secondary schools vary in size and quality, and education can be costly. Both secular and religious schools operate on a daily or boarding basis. Harambee schools often do not have the same resources as those with international connections through church or the state. Scholarships are available on a competitive basis for both boys and girls. Competitive sports such as football (soccer), swimming, and track and field are common. A system similar to that in the United States (8 years of elementary school, 4 years of secondary school, and 4 years of university) recently replaced a British system based on Ordinary and Advanced levels of secondary and advanced education following the primary years. The American system now includes more attention to practical subjects and local culture than did the British system, which emphasized comparatively more European historical and literary content.

Post-secondary education includes a wide variety of vocational and technical schools and a growing number of national universities and teacher training institutions. Post-graduate education includes academic subjects, law school, and medical school. There is much competition in Kenya for limited places in educational institutions, requiring many students to go abroad to the United States, Europe, and Asia for their education.

14 CULTURAL HERITAGE

A cultural mosaic characterizes Kenya's rich cultural heritage. The Muslim tradition is embodied in archaeological and written sources from the coastal region. The historical monument at Gedi, located between Malindi and Mombasa, was founded in the late 13th century. From a study of its tombs, monuments, and shards, it is clear that an urban Muslim civilization, combining indigenous African practices with those from Arabia and India, prevailed for many centuries at Gedi and elsewhere along the coast. Music, dance, and literature were associated here with a literate civilization.

The European (primarily British) heritage in Kenya is notable in Nairobi and some of its suburban areas such as Karen. The Norfolk Hotel in Nairobi opened in 1904 and was soon after nicknamed "The House of Lords" because of its predominantly European, titled visitors. President Theodore Roosevelt, among other prominent Americans, visited there also, espe-

cially to hunt big game. During the colonial era, Africans were not allowed to stay there. Today, the Norfolk retains some of its original architecture and caters to wealthy Kenyans and an international clientele. Movie viewers may remember seeing this hotel in the film *Out of Africa,* an account of the life of its author, Isak Dinesen, on a coffee farm in Kenya during the colonial period. Elspeth Huxley in her books (e.g., *Flame Trees of Thika*) gives another account of Kenya's social life and customs from the perspective of a European living at that time.

Kenya's greatest contemporary writers are world-renowned for their short stories and novels. Ngugi wa Thiong'o, the author of such books as *Petals of Blood* and *Devil on the Cross,* writes in his traditional Gikuyu language rather than English to stress the importance of communicating with all members of his society in a language that the colonialists had suppressed. His novels contain a continuing critique of social inequality in Kenya today. Grace Ogot, in books such as *The Other Woman,* has developed the short story to a high standard.

Music and dance competitions are held frequently in the schools. These cultural expressions are heavily influenced by indigenous forms. Regularly, the National Theatre hosts final competitions among students who come from all over Kenya to display their skills in indigenous dance and song. The Bomas of Kenya is a professional dance troupe that holds regular performances of traditional dance, primarily for tourists. Radio and television shows commonly have programs that feature ethnic music and songs as a popular form of entertainment. Music from the United States is popular today, especially among teenagers. Zairian music is popular among Kenyans of all ages.

15 WORK

Although Kenya has a very significant industrial base that includes processed foods, textiles, glass, and chemicals, agriculture is the mainstay of the economy. Women are engaged as subsistence farmers in those ethnic groups where agriculture is significant. Typically, men, however, clear the land and help in harvesting. In the rural economy, women also collect wood for charcoal, attend markets, and carry heavy loads. Men and women work on coffee and tea estates, these being important cash crops. Tourism is the principal source of foreign exchange and provides jobs for men and women in the hotel and game park industries. Men work as bus drivers, taxi drivers, and factory workers and play important roles in agriculture, primarily with cash crops.

Graduates of secondary schools in Kenya who do not go on to university or teacher training colleges seek technical or secretarial schooling. Training in computer technology is of growing importance, although use of e-mail and the Internet are still quite rare. All young people, however, experience difficulty in gaining employment because Kenya's infrastructure and industrial base is not large compared to its agricultural base. This is not attractive to many students, because young people do not wish to live in rural areas where social life is less varied. Government and industry have not successfully developed rural areas to guard against urban migration and a strong preference by young people to live in cities rather than in small towns or the countryside.

16 SPORTS

Clubs where sports can be practiced by members and their guests are very important in the urban areas. These clubs commonly have billiards, squash, swimming, and tennis available. Golf is available at some clubs and hotels. Cricket is also a popular sport. Automobile races are common. Over the Easter weekend, the Malboro/Epson Safari Rally attracts an international audience. At the Ngong Road Race Course, on many Sunday afternoons, horse racing is held with legalized gambling. Football (soccer) is a national pastime, with some ethnic groups comprising teams that compete against teams from industries, armed forces, and the police. Boxing is another spectator sport enjoyed periodically. Schools sponsor competitive sports for boys and girls, including soccer and track and field. In rural areas, there is a widespread game of strategy known as *Bao* in Kiswahili. This game involves a wooden board containing a varying number of holes or divisions and seeds. A player attempts to capture the seeds of an opponent through a series of complex plays whereby the opponent's seeds end up on his side of the board. National *Bao* competitions are held to determine the best players. Children play a simplified version of this game, much to the amusement of adult spectators.

17 ENTERTAINMENT AND RECREATION

Sports, theater, television, and cultural activities such as reading, dancing, and music are popular forms of entertainment and recreation. Going to movie theaters is a particularly popular amusement for younger people. International films can be seen in theaters in Nairobi and other cities. Popular films include adventure stories, martial arts, and romances. Asian moviegoers also have the choice of seeing the latest Asian films in their own languages.

Sunday is a special day, particularly for Asian families, to dine out, buy treats such as ice cream, and to walk throughout the city. Jamhuri Park, a large open area with a lake for boating and places to purchase ice cream and candy treats, is popular with other ethnic groups. On weekends and in the evenings, walking, window shopping, and shopping in malls is a frequent pastime for all Kenyans. The most popular form of entertainment, however, is visiting with friends and relatives. Much food, drink, news, and joviality are exchanged, mixing people of all ages. Visiting between rural and urban relatives is an occasion for the exchange of food from the rural area for money and material goods from the urban area.

18 FOLK ART, CRAFTS, AND HOBBIES

Carvings, batiks, basketry, jewelry, ceramics, and other indigenous crafts are made largely for tourist consumption. Masai artifacts are very popular with tourists. Development projects stimulate local cooperative groups by encouraging them to manufacture baskets, women's purses, and mats for sale. *Kiondos* are particularly popular in the United States among college students for carrying books. These are multicolored, tightly woven straw bags with leather straps. Soap stone bowls, carved animals, and other artifacts from western Kenya are also popular abroad.

Until recently, craft objects were made of various animal products, including skins and hides from zebras, giraffes, bushbuck, civet cats, and crocodiles. Such articles as shoes, purses, wallets, and musical instruments were sources of major international attraction. Jewelry, carvings, and other products made from ivory were especially valued.

19 SOCIAL PROBLEMS

Wildlife management and conservation are major concerns of the Kenya government and tourist industry. For this reason, commercial artifacts made from wild animals that are considered endangered or are living on game reserves have been banned. Tourists are now limited to photographic rather than hunting safaris. In spite of these limitations, poaching continues to be a problem. Some conservationists have expressed concerns that the elephant population (the source of valuable ivory) has grown too large in certain regions, where farmers have been killed by elephants on rampage rummaging for food in their gardens. Meeting a happy balance between animal and human environmental needs remains an elusive goal at present.

Street children can be seen in cities and large towns of Kenya. These children come from poor families in rural areas where the alcoholism of one or both parents is a contributing factor. They earn money by begging, collecting waste products for sale to wholesalers, who resell them to recyclers. Street girls often earn money through prostitution or begging. Glue-sniffing is a widespread addiction among the younger street children.

Because of the large volume of tourists and the relatively poor quality of Kenya's highways, death by motor vehicle accidents has become a major problem in the country. Alcohol use is a contributing factor, although also significant are the unavailability of spare parts and the age of most vehicles in a country where all vehicles and parts are imported. Crashes with wild and domesticated animals are not uncommon in rural areas.

From its independence until the early 1990s, Kenya had a one-party democratic system. It is now experiencing a transition to multi-party democracy, where members of the opposition parties feel that their political rights are not respected. Members of the ruling party, however, claim that political parties tend to be coterminous with ethnic groups, and that multiparty democracy promotes tribalism. Young people commonly complain that all political parties are lead by primarily very old men, leaving little visible leadership by the young or by women. Patriarchal leadership (at least in public) was a strong value in traditional political systems within Kenya. Nevertheless, there are now women judges and members of parliament in the Kenya government.

In 2007 and 2008 political turmoil in Kenya testified to the tensions and mistrust brought about by a long history of a one party system followed by a multiparty system of government that is seen as being controlled by a few greedy politicians. The country erupted in violence when the incumbent President Mwai Kibaki was controversially declared the winner of the presidential election held on 27 December 2007, which was widely believed to have been won by Raila Odinga of the Orange Democratic Movement. Hon. Raila Odinga had led in most opinion polls prior to the elections and was leading by significant margins in the earlier presidential vote returns, until the surprise announcement of Kibaki as the eventual winner. Many Kenyans were angered by allegations of electoral manipulation and went on a violent rampage in many parts of the country. Police fatally shot hundreds of civilian demonstrators, causing more violence directed toward the police and eventually degenerating into inter-ethnic conflicts. Initial targets of violence included some Kikuyu people—the community of which Kibaki is a member—living outside their traditional settlement areas, especially in the Rift Valley Province. Some of the Kikuyu also engaged in retributive violence against groups supportive of Odinga, primarily Luos and Kalenjin.

Many deaths were recorded with large numbers of homes and private properties destroyed, resulting in significant internal displacement of people. By 28 January 2008 the death toll from the violence was around 800 and by the end of March 2008 it had reached 1,600. The largest single loss of life occurred when a church providing shelter from the violence to 200 people was set alight by rioters, burning 35 people to death. The people who were sheltering there were members of President Kibaki's tribe, the Kikuyu. Another 16 people from Odinga's tribe, the Luo, were also burned to death by Kibaki supporters while sheltering in a house in Naivasha. As of April 2008, up to 600,000 people were internally displaced in Kenya due to the political turmoil.

The violence in Kenya has had serious economic ramifications not only for Kenya, but throughout East Africa, particularly for the landlocked countries of the Great Lakes region (Uganda, Rwanda, Burundi, and eastern parts of the Democratic Republic of Congo). These countries depend upon Kenyan infrastructure links (particularly the port at Mombasa) for important import and export routes. Significant shortages of gasoline were reported in Uganda as well as Zanzibar following the 2007 elections. Kenya's tourism industry came to a standstill that resulted in a loss of millions of dollars to the Kenyan economy. As of 28 February 2008 Kibaki and Odinga had signed a power-sharing and peace deal called the National Accord and Reconciliation Act, which constitutionally establishes the office of prime minister and creates a coalition government with Raila Odinga designated to be prime minister.

20 GENDER ISSUES

The recent riots and violence following the December 2007 presidential elections brought to the fore the widening gender gap in Kenya. Numerous instances of women being raped and sexual violence against women were reported in the 2008 post-election period. The gender gap can easily be illustrated in the political arena. With respect to political representation, 2.7% of elected representatives on country, urban, and municipal councils are women. In the judicial service establishment, women only account for 17.6%. Indeed, gender representation statistics from the World Economic Forum's Gender Gap Index for the year 2007 for Kenya are abysmal. Out of 128 countries Kenya is ranked 83 in terms of inequality between the sexes, and is scored at 0.651 on the gender gap index, where 0.00 equals inequality and 1.00 equals equality. On the same scale, the existence of legislation punishing acts of violence against women is scored at 0.17. In other words, violence against women largely goes unpunished. Women and girls continue to suffer from violence in the home, the community and in state custody.

During the Moi regime violations against human rights were commonplace. People were imprisoned or detained without charge or trial. Political assassinations were also a common occurrence. However, when Mwai Kibaki replaced Moi some progress was made in addressing human rights. With the recent post-election violence the little progress that had

been made in fostering human rights seems to have been shattered. Human Rights Watch (HRW) has charged that the government in 2008 was implementing a "shoot-to-kill" policy. Evidence indicates the excessive use of force, torture, and arbitrary shootings by the police. Prison conditions are also deplorable and life threatening.

With reference to homosexuality, it remains illegal in Kenya. However, lifestyles are a slowly changing in Kenya. Male homosexuality is becoming fashionable among young men and is practiced in prisons, boarding schools, colleges, and in tourist resorts along the coast. In spite of its illegality nobody gets imprisoned for homosexual acts in Kenya. Many homosexuals adopt heterosexual lifestyles in an attempt to fit into a society that finds homosexuality repugnant.

20 BIBLIOGRPAHY

Abdulaziz, Mohamed H. *Muyaka: 19th Century Swahili Popular Poetry*. Nairobi: Kenya Literature Bureau, 1979.

Bahemuka, Judith Mbula. *Our Religious Heritage*. Nairobi: Thomas Nelson and Sons Ltd., 1983.

"Kenya's Rival Politicians Reach an Agreement." *International Herald Tribune*, 28 February 2008.

Kilbride, Philip L., and Janet C. Kilbride. *Changing Family Life in East Africa: Women and Children at Risk*. University Park: Pennsylvania State University, 1990.

Liyong, Taban lo. *Popular Culture of East Africa*. Nairobi: Longman Kenya Ltd., 1983.

Ochieng', W. R., and R. M. Maxon, eds. *An Economic History of Kenya,* Nairobi: East African Educational Publishers Ltd., 1992.

Pritchard, J. M. *A Geography of East Africa*. London: Evans Brothers Ltd., 1977.

Rigby, Peter. *Cattle, Capitalism, and Class: Ilparakuyo Maasai Transformations*. Philadelphia: Temple University Press, 1992.

Shorter, Aylward. *The Church in the African City*. Maryknoll, NY: Orbis Books, 1991.

—revised by E. Kalipeni

LIBYANS

PRONUNCIATION: LIB-ee-uhns
LOCATION: Northern Africa
POPULATION: 6.1 million (includes 166,510 non-nationals)
LANGUAGE: Arabic; English
RELIGION: Islam (Sunni Muslim)
RELATED ARTICLES: Vol. 1: Tuaregs

¹ INTRODUCTION

Libya is located in a region of North Africa known as the Maghrib (the Arabic word referring to the direction of the sunset). It is bordered to the east by Egypt, to the west by Algeria and Tunisia, and to the south by Chad, Niger, and Sudan. The name *"Libya"* comes from an ancient Egyptian name for a Berber tribe that was applied by the Greeks to most of North Africa, and the term *"Libyan"* to all of its Berber inhabitants. It was not until Libya achieved independence in 1951 that its history changed from one of cities and regions to that of a modern nation-state.

Geography was the principal determinant in the separate historical development of Libya's three traditional regions: Tripolitania, Cyrenaica, and Fezzan. Until the late 1960s, each of these regions held on to its own identity, as they were separated by formidable deserts.

The history of Libya can be traced as far back as the eighth millennium bc. Archeological evidence indicates that Libya's coastal plain was home to a Neolithic culture whose peoples were skilled in the domestication of cattle and the cultivation of crops. Farther to the south, nomadic hunters and herders roamed a vast savannah rich in game. This civilization flourished until 2000 bc, when the land began to desiccate, eventually becoming what is today the Sahara desert.

The peoples who settled in the area were called Berbers. Although the origins of these nomadic tribes remain largely a mystery, evidence suggests that they migrated from the steppe regions of southwest Asia. Roman, Greek, Phoenician, and Arab conquerors all attempted to defeat or assimilate the Berbers into their cultures, with varying degrees of success. Phoenician traders arrived in the area around 900 bc and established the city of Carthage in approximately 800 bc in what is today neighboring Tunisia. The Carthaginians spread Phoenician hegemony across most of North Africa, where a distinctive "Punic" civilization came into being, and established several towns along the Libyan coast. The Berbers were either enslaved by the Phoenicians or forced to pay tribute.

While the Phoenicians were busy on the western coast of Libya, the Greeks established control in the east. By 631 bc, Greek settlers had established the city of Cyrene on a fertile highland about 32 km (20 mi) inland. Within 200 years, four more Greek cities had been established, constantly resisting encroachments by the Egyptians to the east and the Carthaginians to the west. Eventually, the Greek settlement was overrun by Persia, later to be returned to Greek control by Alexander the Great in 331 bc. However, the city-states constantly vied with each other for power, leaving them vulnerable to the expanding Roman Empire. In 74 bc, Ptolemy Apion, the last Greek ruler, bequeathed the area, collectively known as Cyrenaica, to Rome, which formally annexed the area by ad 74.

In spite of the political strife, there was much cultural and economic development in the area. The region grew rich from grain, wine, wool, and stock breeding and from the cultivation of silphium, an herb widely regarded as an aphrodisiac. A school of intellectuals known as the Cyrenaics, who expounded a doctrine that defined happiness as the sum of all human pleasures, developed in the area.

The Roman conquest of the region would prove disastrous for the Berbers. Tribes were forced to become settled or leave the area. For this reason, the Berbers resisted Roman rule. The Romans began their occupation by controlling the coastal lands and cultivating the area. It is estimated that North Africa produced 1 million tons of cereal each year for the Roman Empire, as well as fruits, figs, grapes, beans, and olive oil.

Along with the Roman presence, Judaism and Christianity began to influence the Berbers. Many Jews who had been expelled from Palestine by the Romans settled in the area, and some of the Berber tribes converted to Judaism. Christianity arrived in the area in the 2nd century ad and was especially attractive to slaves. By the end of the 4th century, many of the settled areas had become Christian, along with some of the Berber tribes.

In ad 429, the German king Gaiseric, backed by 80,000 Vandals (a German tribe), invaded North Africa from Spain, eventually weakening Roman control. With the decline of Roman power, the Berber tribes began to return to their traditional lands. Meanwhile, the Byzantine emperor Justinian sent his army to North Africa in ad 533 and within a year conquered the German forces.

The most influential conquest of the area was the invasion of Arab Muslims beginning in ad 642. By ad 644, the Muslims had established control over Cyrenaica in the east and Tripolitania in the west. The nomadic Berbers quickly converted en masse to Islam and joined the Arab forces. By ad 663, the Arabs had spread their influence to the south in Fezzan with the help of Berber troops. The Arabs used the region as a launching pad for operations against Carthage. In ad 670, the Arabs established the town of al-Qayrawan, south of modern-day Tunis, and continued to spread their influence to the west.

The ruling Arabs viewed Islam primarily as a religion for Arabs and therefore treated non-Arab converts as second-class citizens. Political sentiment developed among Muslims on the Arabian Peninsula, however, that rejected the Arabism of the ruling Umayyid dynasty in favor of strict equality for all Muslims. Followers of this movement, called Kharajites, spread to North Africa, and many Berbers became attracted to their message of Islamic equality. They eventually rebelled against the Arab caliphate's control of the area and established a number of independent kingdoms.

In ad 750, the Abbasids, successors to the Umayyid dynasty, spread their rule to the area and appointed Ibrahim ibn al-Aghlab as governor in al-Qayrawan.

In the last decade of the 9th century, missionaries from the Ismaili sect (Shia Muslims with a more esoteric and mystical interpretation of Islam) converted the Kutama Berbers to Islam and led them in opposition against the established Aghlabi kingdom. Al-Qayrawan fell in ad 909, and the next year the Kutama installed the Ismaili grandmaster from Syria, `Ubaidallah Sa`id, as *imam* (leader) of their movement and ruler of the territory they had conquered, which included Tripolitania, the northwestern section of Libya. This imam founded the Fatimid dynasty.

The Fatimids turned their attention to the east, and by ad 969 they had conquered Egypt and moved its capital to the new city of Cairo. From there, the Fatimid dynasty established a caliphate rivaling that of Baghdad. Tripolitania was left to Berber rule, and considering the diverse loyalties of the different tribes, conflict became inevitable. In the 11th century, the Fatimids sent Arab Bedouins to North Africa to assist their forces against other Berbers. Eventually, the influx of Arabs into the region promoted the arabization of the entire area.

Nevertheless, independent kingdoms managed to establish themselves. The greatest of these were the Almoravids, the Almohads, the Hafsids, and the Zayanids. The kingdoms were all led by Muslim leaders who greatly encouraged learning and arts.

Meanwhile, the Catholics of Spain sought to reclaim southern Spain from the Muslims. Spain had become a cosmopolitan and pluralistic center of learning under Muslim rule. The Spanish conquest in 1492, however, fundamentally changed the character of the area. The new rulers forced all Muslims and Jews to convert to Christianity. Many fled to North Africa, and a sizable community of Jews settled in the area from Morocco to Libya.

As Europe experienced a slow economic revival and Spanish power began to increase, the Mediterranean became a battleground for supremacy among the Hapsburg Empire, the Spanish, and the Ottoman Turks. By 1510, Spanish forces had captured Tripoli, but Spain was more concerned with lands further west and entrusted the protection of Tripoli to Malta.

By this time, piracy had become prevalent along the North African coast. Because Muslim vessels were not allowed to enter European ports, Muslim pirates began raiding European ships. The most famous of these pirates was Khayr ad-Din, known to Europeans as Barbarossa, or Red Beard. Khayr ad-Din captured several European ports, recognizing the sovereignty of the Ottoman sultan over the territory he had conquered. In 1551, the Maltese were driven out of Tripoli by the Turks. It took until the 1580s, however, for the Turks to extend their power south into Fezzan. In actuality, however, they exercised little control there.

By 1815, the European states combined forces against the North African states. Spain, the Netherlands, Prussia, Denmark, Russia, and Naples declared war on Morocco, Algiers, Tunis, and Tripoli.

Deprived of the basis of its economy, Tripoli was unable to pay for basic imports or service its foreign debt. When France and Britain pressed for payment on behalf of Tripoli's creditors, the regional ruler authorized extraordinary taxes to provide the needed revenue. The imposition of these taxes led to an outcry in the town and among the tribes that quickly developed into civil war. Eventually, the sultan sent troops from Turkey and regained control of the region.

By the early 1800s, Muhammad ibn 'Ali al-Sanusi had begun to have a profound influence on the region. Largely influenced by Sufism, a mystical branch of Islam, he incorporated teachings from both orthodox Sunni Islam and Sufism to create an austere reform movement that proved very popular among the Berbers. In Tripolitania and Fezzan, al-Sanusi gained such popularity that he was called the "Grand Sanusi." The Bedouins revered him as a saint. After his death in 1859,

his son, Muhammad, brought the Sanusi order to its peak of influence, and he was widely regarded as the *Mahdi* (a popular messianic leader in Islamic tradition).

Meanwhile, Italy turned its attention to North Africa. Becoming a unified state only in 1860, Italy had a late start in the European race for colonies, and it viewed Libya as compensation for its acquiescence to the establishment of a French colony in Tunisia. Toward this end, Italy engineered a crisis with Turkey in 1911. When Turkey refused to allow Italian military occupation, Italy declared war on Turkey. With Turkey facing troubles in the Balkans, it was forced to sue for peace with Italy, essentially turning over control of Tripolitania and Cyrenaica in October 1912.

Italian control over the area, however, was slow to consolidate because of organized resistance among the remaining Sanusi orders, especially in the south. When Italy joined the Allied powers in 1915, the first Italo-Sanusi war became a battle of World War I. At war's end, the Allied powers recognized Italy's sovereignty in Libya.

Several nationalist movements began to take shape in Libya, although there was little cooperation among them. A pan-Arabian nationalist, 'Abd ar-Rahman 'Azzam, persuaded local leaders to demand Italian recognition of the region as an independent republic. After this attempt failed, Tripolitanian nationalists met with the Sanusis in 1922 and offered to accept Idris as emir of Tripolitania. Although initially hesitant to draw the anger of the Italians, Idris accepted the emirate over all of Libya and then fled to Egypt to avoid capture, sparking the second Italo-Sanusi war.

With the ascension of Benito Mussolini's Fascist government in 1922, Italy's position on Libya quickly changed to one of brutal military pacification. The final dissolution of the Ottoman Empire by the 1923 Treaty of Lausanne opened the door for Italy's annexation of Libya.

The greatest resistance to the Italian occupation in the early 1920s was led by a religious leader, 'Umar al-Mukhtar. A veteran of many campaigns, Mukhtar was a master of desert guerrilla tactics. Leading small, mobile bands, he attacked outposts, ambushed troop columns, and cut supply and communication lines before fading back into the desert. Unable to defeat Mukhtar in a direct confrontation, the Italians resorted to a war of attrition, herding people into concentration camps, burning crops, blocking wells, and slaughtering livestock throughout Libya. Mukhtar, however, held out until his capture at al-Kufrah, the last Sanusi stronghold, in 1931. He was hanged before a crowd of 20,000 Arabs assembled to witness the event. With his death, the pacification of Libya was complete.

Libya became known as the "fourth shore" of Italy. Its annexation was seen as a way to provide resources for and to relieve overcrowding in Italy. To this end, the infrastructure of Libya was greatly improved, but only to the benefit of the Italian settlers. Most arable land was confiscated from the local tribes and given to Italian colonists, who by 1940 numbered about 110,000, or 10% of the population. Education for the Arabs during this time was completely ignored, as evidenced by a literacy rate of less than 10%. This lack of education created a dearth of skilled workers and professionals, a problem that would plague Libya for decades.

Most Libyan leaders realized that their best hope for independence lay in the defeat of Italy in a larger conflict, and

World War II (1939–45) provided them with such an opportunity. When Italy officially entered the war on the side of Germany, the Libyan leaders, including Idris, immediately threw their support, both physical and verbal, behind Great Britain. Although Britain welcomed the Sanusi support, it made no coherent statement or promise to secure Libyan independence.

In late October 1942, British troops broke through Axis lines at Alamein in a massive offensive that sent the Germans and Italians into retreat. Cyrenaica was taken in November, followed by Tripolitania in January 1943. The road to Libyan independence was long and protracted. Britain took control of Libya until the end of the war. Italy's claim to Libya was officially renounced in 1947. During this time, nationalist movements formed in Libya, and in November 1950, Idris was accepted as the leader of a unified Libya. A constitution was drafted and adopted in October 1951. On 24 December 1951, King Idris I proclaimed the independence of the United Kingdom of Libya as a sovereign state.

The vast majority of power in the Libyan government lay in the hands of the newly appointed monarch, and after the first general election in February 1952, Idris abolished all political parties. In his foreign policy, Idris maintained a strongly pro-Western stance, even agreeing to allow the United States to maintain a military base there. Although diplomatic relations were established with the Soviet Union in 1955, economic aid was refused in deference to the United States and Britain.

In spite of foreign aid, Libya remained a relatively poor and underdeveloped country until the discovery of oil in 1959, which turned Libya into an independently wealthy country in short order. The vast majority of Libyans, however, did not see much improvement in their standard of living as a result of the corruption and inefficiency of the monarchy and the unfavorable contracts of the Western oil companies. This fact, along with Libya's continued pro-Western foreign policy, led to an increasingly volatile situation among the populace and, more importantly, among an increasingly pan-Arabist army.

On 1 September 1969, in a daring coup d'état, a group of about 70 young army officers and enlisted men seized control of the government and abolished the monarchy. The army quickly rallied behind the coup and, within a few days, had control of the entire country. Popular reception of the coup, especially among young urbanites, was enthusiastic. The coup was headed by the Revolutionary Command Council (RCC), of which Captain Muammar Qadhafi was a member.

The RCC adopted a socialist philosophy but rejected communism because of its atheistic stance. The council reaffirmed Libya as an independent Arab and Muslim nation and enacted many social, economic, and political reforms. Overnight, Libya shifted from a traditionalist Arab state to an idealistic nationalist state.

As the RCC fought off initial challenges to its power, more and more authority was transferred to the RCC and, ultimately, to the hands of Qadhafi. However, Qadhafi was a highly idealistic pan-Arabist influenced by Jamal `Abd al-Nasir of Egypt. In this light, Qadhafi turned his attention to foreign affairs, leaving administrative tasks to Major Abdel Salam Jallud.

The change that Qadhafi envisioned for Libyan society began in 1973 with the so-called Cultural Revolution. The idea was to combat inefficiency and apathy in the government bureaucracy by involving large numbers of the populace in political affairs. On the economic front, the main task was the redistribution of wealth from oil revenues. A property law was passed that forbade ownership of more than one private dwelling per family. Retail and wholesale trade operations were replaced by "people's supermarkets" that were heavily subsidized by the government. While these moves were popular among poor Libyans, they created resentment among the traditional aristocracy, which led an attempt at sedition from abroad. As retaliation, a series of opposition figures were assassinated.

Libya continued to increase the amount of revenue it obtained from the sale of petroleum. Toward this end, Qadhafi suggested that the production of oil be controlled, and he strongly supported the establishment of the Organization of Petroleum Exporting Countries (OPEC). There, he expounded his policy of using oil as leverage against the Western states and Israel. As a consequence of these policies, oil production in Libya dropped by half between 1970 and 1974, even as revenues from the sale of oil quadrupled.

On the political front, Qadhafi continued to agitate for Arab unity. While many Arab leaders gave lip service to the idea of a pan-Arab state at some "time in the future," Qadhafi considered it an achievable goal in the immediate future. As such, Qadhafi eventually tried to form a federation with Egypt and Syria. Egypt, however, proved quite apathetic on this front, and the federation was struck a fatal blow in 1973 when Egypt and Syria attacked Israel without informing Qadhafi.

Relations with Western states remained troubled for some time. The major Western powers accused Libya of sponsoring terrorism in support of the Palestine Liberation Organization's aspirations to statehood. Libya was also accused of supporting the Irish Republican Army (though no credible evidence of this has ever been produced), Lebanese leftists, and left-wing movements in Europe and Japan. As a result, relations with the United States and Britain steadily deteriorated. The low point in these relations occurred in 1988, when a Pan Am airliner was blown up in mid-flight over the Scottish town of Lockerbie, killing 270 people. Libyan operatives were widely believed to be behind the attack, a fact the country officially acknowledged in 2003. After an investigation and trial lasting until 2001, a Libyan intelligence agent was sentenced to life in prison for his role in the attack. After the U.S. invasion of Iraq in 2003, Libya began a process of greater cooperation with Western powers and declared an end to what was then a secret nuclear weapons program.

² LOCATION AND HOMELAND

Libya has a population of about 6.1 million people, more than half of whom are under the age of 22. The population grows by approximately 2.3% per year, partly a result of general improvement in health conditions, which has led to a decrease in both the infant mortality rate and the death rate. More than 90% of the population identifies itself as Arab; most of the remaining minority is composed of Berbers and black Africans. Approximately 76% of the population now lives in urban areas concentrated along the coast. There are also small numbers of Greeks, Maltese, Pakistanis, Indians, and Egyptians.

Libya is located in North Africa on the Mediterranean Sea. It has an area of 1,760,000 sq km (679,536 sq mi) and a coastline of 1,800 km (1,119 mi), making it the fifteenth largest country in the world. There are some fertile highlands in the north but no true mountain ranges except in the largely empty southern desert. In all, more than 80% of Libya is covered by

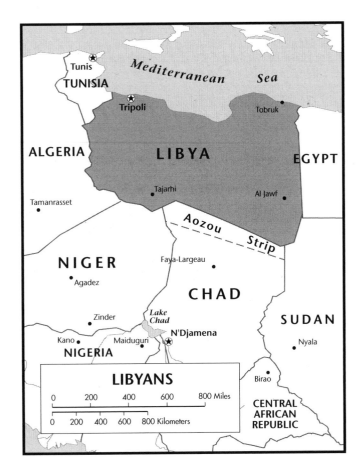

the Sahara desert. There are no rivers; a few saltwater lakes are located near the Mediterranean coast.

³ LANGUAGE

Arabic is the national language of Libya. Although the government officially discourages the use of other languages, English is the most popular second language, and it is regularly taught in school. Because the Italians failed to assimilate or educate the population during its occupation, the Italian language never caught on in Libya as French did in Tunisia, Algeria, and Morocco.

Arabic, a highly evolved Semitic language related to Hebrew and Aramaic, is spoken by nearly the entire population of Libya. Written Arabic has two forms: Modern Standard Arabic is taught in schools throughout the Arab world, while classical Arabic is an older version of the language derived from the Quran. Libyans also speak their own dialectical Arabic, which includes many slang terms, some from Berber and Italian.

In greeting, a Libyan says *as-salamu ʿalaykum*, which means "peace be with you." The response is *wa ʿalaykum as-salam*, which means "and peace be with you as well."

Common Libyan female names include *ʿAysha, Fatima, Amna, Khadija*, and *Asma*. Male names are *Muhammad, ʿAli, Yusif, Ibrahim*, and *Mukhtar*.

⁴ FOLKLORE

Libya has many legends based on the exploits of Muslim leaders who resisted the Crusaders or the Italian colonizers. These leaders, such as ʿUmar al-Mukhtar, often come from highly religious backgrounds and are considered well learned. They are called *marabouts*, or holy men, and they are believed to have *baraka*, or divine grace, which allows them to perform miracles. Though the government discourages such practice, their burial sites are often destinations for pilgrimages, and some of these leaders have become saints in the popular mind. Many people visit their graves to ask for intercession.

Most folklore in Muslim countries tells stories of important figures in religious history. One such story, which is commemorated annually throughout the Islamic world, is that of *al-Isra' wa al-Miʿraj*. According to legend, on the twenty-sixth day of the Islamic month of Rajab, the Prophet Muhammad traveled at night from Mecca, Saudi Arabia (then Hijaz), to Jerusalem. From Jerusalem, he rode his wondrous horse, al-Burak, on a nocturnal visit to heaven. This legend partly explains the importance of Jerusalem to people of the Islamic faith.

Another folk belief that is common in Islamic communities, including Libya, is that evil spirits, called *jinns*, live in haunted places. Jinns are demons that are believed to take on animal or human form.

⁵ RELIGION

The overwhelming majority of Libyans (97%) are Muslims, although a Catholic church has been built in Benghazi, Libya's second largest city. The practice of Islam varies from individual to individual. Civil law is based on religious code, or *Shariʿa*. Most Libyans belong to the Sunni sect of Islam, which was introduced by the conquering Arabs. However, there are still remnants of the Sanusi order, which was influenced by Shia doctrine through the Fatimids.

Islam teaches that God (Allah) sends guidance to humans in the form of prophets, and it accepts the earlier Semitic prophets, including Abraham, Moses, and Jesus. Muslims believe that Muhammad was the last in a line of prophets who were sent with the message that there is only one God. Muslims believe in heaven and hell, the Day of Judgment, and angels. The Quran is the holy book of Muslims; it teaches that in order to get to heaven, men and women must believe in God and do good works by struggling in God's way. Belief and action are tightly bound together in Muslim literature.

The Islamic religion has five pillars: (1) Muslims must pray five times a day; (2) Muslims must give alms, or *zakat*, to the poor; (3) Muslims must fast during the month of Ramadan; (4) Muslims must make the pilgrimage, or *hajj*, to Mecca; and (5) each Muslim must recite the *shahada—ashhadu an la illah ila Allah wa ashhadu in Muhammadu rasul Allah*—which means, "I witness that there is no god but Allah and that Muhammad is the prophet of Allah."

⁶ MAJOR HOLIDAYS

Libya commemorates both secular and Muslim religious holidays. One major Muslim holiday is *Eid al-Fitr*, which comes at the end of the month of fasting called Ramadan. During Ramadan, Muslims refrain from eating, drinking, or having sex during daylight hours in order to reflect on God and on the plight of the unfortunate who do not have enough food. At the end of the month, Muslims celebrate for three days. The other major Muslim holiday is *Eid al-Adha*, which commemorates the willingness of Abraham, as well as his son, to obey God's command in all things, even when Abraham was told to sacrifice his son.

Religious holidays are celebrated by going to the mosque for group prayers and then returning home to share large meals with family and visiting relatives. Part of the feast is normally given to relatives and part to the poor. Libyan children enjoy visiting carnivals on holidays. Other Islamic holidays, celebrated to a lesser degree, are the Islamic New Year, the Prophet Muhammad's birthday, and the Tenth of *Muharram* (the tenth day of the Muslim month of Muharram, commemorated because Moses led the Israelites out of Egyptian slavery on this day; the Prophet Muhammad instructed all Muslims to fast on this day).

Secular holidays include Independence Day (December 24) and Evacuation Day (June 11), a commemoration of the U.S. withdrawal from Wheeling Air Force base in Libya in 1970. Army Day is celebrated on August 9 and Proclamation Day on November 21.

7 RITES OF PASSAGE

Male babies are usually circumcised at birth, although some families wait until the boy reaches the age of 10 or 11. Children of both sexes are expected to help with household chores.

All children between the ages of 6 and 15 are required to attend nine years of school or vocational training. Afterward, they may attend three years of secondary school. Young boys and girls attend school together, but beginning at age 10 or 11, they attend separate schools. After school, young boys may attend schools specializing in religious training, where they learn to recite the Quran from memory.

Desert Bedouins are expected to marry and produce children in order to increase the size and power of the extended family and/or tribe. The majority of Libyan marriages are arranged by families, and even those who marry for love must have the approval of their families. Weddings take place either in a mosque or in the bride's home, with the ceremony administered by an *imam* (Muslim prayer leader). A marriage contract is signed during the wedding ceremony.

Elderly family members are cared for by their children, and none are put in retirement or old-age homes. Upon death, the deceased's body is washed, clothed in clean linen, and buried with his or her right side facing Mecca. Only men attend the funeral; women express their grief at the deceased's home by wailing.

8 INTERPERSONAL RELATIONS

Islam is central to the Libyan way of life, and this fact is reflected in Libyans' social mores and use of language. Daily life revolves around the five daily prayers that Muslims are obliged to perform. Many Libyan men attend the mosque regularly, in keeping with the five prayer times; Libyan women predominantly pray in the home. As in all Muslim countries, Friday is Libya's holy day, and the noon prayer is almost always attended at the local mosque.

The practice of Islam has also influenced the Libyan use of language. The typical Libyan greeting is an Islamic one: *as-salamu 'alaykum*, which means "peace be with you." The response is *wa 'alaykum as-salam*, "and peace be with you as well." God's name is always invoked in conversation. A Libyan will usually say *in-sha' Allah,* which means "if God wills it," when asked whether he or she plans to do something. This might appear to be indecisive, but it is actually an acknowledgment of God's role in everything one does.

A Libyan always greets guests with a cup of coffee or tea, and desert tradition requires that a guest be offered food. Hospitality is part of the Libyan code of honor. Travelers often find it difficult to navigate cities without being repeatedly asked into strangers' homes for tea and cakes.

Libya has no bars or night clubs, but there are many sidewalk cafés where men drink coffee or tea and socialize. In the evenings, most Libyans can be found at home. In keeping with Islamic teaching, alcohol is illegal in Libya, even at high-end hotels in the major cities.

It is considered disrespectful to openly criticize anyone, and courtesy must always be shown when in public. Children must respect adults. Libyans of tribal background give great importance to tribal loyalty, and strangers arouse tribal suspicion—not surprising in light of the country's history of foreign colonization. Urban dwellers, particularly in larger cities such as Tripoli and Benghazi, are more open to outside influences and ideas. Most Libyans treasure their privacy. This has been particularly true since the 1980s, when outspoken political opposition to the current regime became a punishable offense. Thus, Libyans avoid making any public comments that might be interpreted as political criticism.

9 LIVING CONDITIONS

Living conditions for most Libyans improved dramatically in the years following the 1969 coup. By the 1980s, the welfare system provided work injury and sickness compensation, as well as disability, retirement, and survivors' pensions. Workers employed by foreign firms were also guaranteed the same social security benefits as workers employed by Libyan firms. The government subsidized the underemployed and the unemployed and provided nurseries to care for the children of working mothers. As oil production in the country increased in the 1990s and 2000s, such government subsidized health care greatly improved.

A major problem for Libyans during the 1970s was the country's health care system. The Italian colonization left little infrastructure, and the lack of education provided to the Libyans meant there were few trained health care professionals, a problem that went largely unaddressed by the Idris monarchy. The RCC socialized health care in 1970, making it free for all Libyans. The first medical and dental schools were established in 1970 and 1974, respectively. Health care expenditures increased tremendously beginning in 1970. In 2001, the government spent $343 per capita on health care. From 1990 to 2004, the number of hospital beds increased from 3.5 to 5.8 per 1,000 citizens. Life expectancy at birth is 77 years, a figure similar to or higher than that of many developed nations.

Housing has proved to be a more intractable problem for the Libyan government. A 1969 survey indicated that there was a shortage of nearly 180,000 dwellings. As a consequence, the revolutionary regime invested several million dollars between 1970 and 1995, building some 277,000 houses and apartments. There is still, however, a housing shortage caused by a continued influx of population into the cities from the countryside and by a high birth rate. As a result of the growing population, shantytowns can be found on the outskirts of major metropolitan centers. These are in stark contrast to the European-style villas inhabited by the urban middle class.

The typical Libyan family lives in a state-built apartment building. Those who can afford them hang Persian carpets on the walls for decor. It is common to have at least one sofa and a few embroidered floor cushions for seating. In 2006, there were 4 million mobile phones in use. Combined land line and mobile phones provide telecommunications service to 75% of the population. There were 16 AM radio, 3 FM radio, and 3 short-wave radio stations in operation in 2005. That year, there were 12 broadcast television stations and 24 Internet hosts. Libya's internet code is .ly.

In 2002, Libya had about 83,200 km (51,670 mi) of roadways, of which more than half were paved. The main road is a 1,769-km (1,100-mi) coastal highway running from Tunisia to Egypt. An old railway, the Benghazi line, was abandoned in 1964. There are plans for a new railway system, and a railroad between Benghazi and Egypt began construction in 1993, with plans for service to begin in 2010. Tripoli and Benghazi (a city on the Mediterranean coast) both have international airports, and Libya has a national airline, Jamahiriyya Libyan Arab Airlines. A private airline, Afriqiyah Airways, connects Libya with much of Europe and Africa.

10 FAMILY LIFE

Libyan family life operated along traditional tribal, or *qabilah*, lines, until well after independence. Libyans live with their extended families in tightly knit communities. A typical household consists of a man, his wife, his sons and their wives and children, his unmarried daughters, and perhaps other relatives, such as a widowed or divorced mother or sister. At the death of the father, each son establishes his own household and repeats the cycle. Marriages are typically arranged by negotiation between the families of the bride and groom, as men and women generally are not allowed to mix socially.

The traditional roles of men and women changed noticeably after the coup in 1969. Women were granted the right to vote in the early 1960s, but they were actively encouraged to vote after 1970, in part because of the regime's hope for an expanded political base. The new regime encouraged women to pursue education and provided them with incentives to work. Working mothers were offered cash bonuses, and day care was institutionalized in the 1970s. The retirement age for women was set at 55, and laws were passed ensuring equal pay for equal work.

In spite of the government's efforts, some traditional views have been slow to change. For example, women were disproportionately represented in jobs as secretaries or clerks because of deep-seated cultural biases against the intermingling of men and women. However, by the mid-1980s, women had broken into several professional fields, most notably health care. Since 2001, the government has tried to further redefine the role of women and expand its armed forces by making military service mandatory for both sexes.

11 CLOTHING

Two styles of clothing are visible in Libya. In the cities, there is a mixture of Western and traditional garb. Girls commonly wear brightly colored dresses, and boys wear jeans and shirts. Young men and women wear predominantly modern clothing, though most women continue to cover their hair, in keeping with Islamic tradition. The traditional attire for men is a long white gown worn over a shirt and pants. Some men wear a black or white Muslim hat on their heads. Traditional women also wear long gowns and hair coverings. Most women's gowns cover both the head and body.

In rural areas, traditional dress predominates. Men of the Tuareg tribe in the Libyan desert wear black or dark blue cloaks. Tuareg men also cover their faces and hair with blue veils historically dyed with indigo, leaving only their eyes visible. The latter attire has earned them the title "People of the Blue Veil." This practice developed out of the need for protection from the desert sun and sand. Styles of dress in the cities often fall along generational lines, and it is not unusual to see people walking side by side wearing different styles of garments. Unlike in other parts of North Africa, in Libya, traditional versus modern dress has not become a charged political issue.

12 FOOD

Before every meal, a Libyan recites the Muslim expression *bismillah,* or "in the name of God." After finishing the meal, he or she then says *al-hamdu lillah,* which means "thank God."

As in other regions of North Africa, couscous is a very popular food. Couscous is semolina wheat sprinkled with oil and water and rolled into tiny grains. The grains are then steamed and ready for use in a favorite recipe. The couscous can be mixed with a number of sauces and then combined with a variety of meats and/or vegetables. Couscous is also combined with honey and milk and served for breakfast. The main meat eaten by Libyans is lamb.

Most Libyan meals are eaten with *kasrah,* a flat, round, non-yeast bread. Kasrah is often eaten with dips, such as *babaghanuj,* a dip made of mashed, roasted eggplant mixed with lemon, tahina (sesame seed) paste, and a pinch of salt.

Dates are a favorite snack, known for their abundance. Palm trees are hardy plants that grow in groups by the sea and in oases. Dates from palm trees are used in many forms by Libyans. The fruit can be eaten fresh or squeezed to make juice or date honey. Dried dates can be ground into date flour. And date pits can be roasted and ground to make date coffee.

Coffee and mint tea are popular drinks, served throughout the day. Alcoholic beverages and pork are forbidden by Islamic law.

13 EDUCATION

Before World War II (1939–45), few schools existed in Libya, resulting in a literacy rate of less than 10%. After the discovery of oil in the country in 1959, Libya invested in new schools, vocational training centers, and universities. Another education boom took place in the 1970s, following the installation of the new regime in 1969. Libya adopted a Western-style system that includes six years of primary school, three years of preparatory school, and three years of secondary school. Schooling is mandatory for both boys and girls until the age of 15. After completion of secondary school, Libyans may attend either vocational schools or universities. Libya's first university was established in 1955 in Benghazi. This was followed by universities in Tripoli, Mersa Brega, and Sabha. All schooling, including that at the university level, is free. This includes books, school supplies, uniforms, and meals. As a result of these educational programs, the literacy rate in Libya rose from an abysmal 10% during the Italian occupation to more than 92% as of early 2003.

A family walks through the Roman ruins of Leptis Magna, the largest city of the ancient region of Tripolitania. Leptis was designated a UNESCO World Heritage site in 1982 and contains some of the world's best preserved remains of Roman architecture. (Reza/Getty Images)

Problems facing the educational system stem from a lack of qualified teachers. As a result, the vast majority of teachers in Libya are expatriates. In addition, some confusion resulted when the government tried to integrate secular and religious schooling. Military training is a mandatory part of education in the school system, for both men and women, from the secondary through the university level.

14 CULTURAL HERITAGE

Traditional Libyan folk dance is a strenuous and lively form of entertainment. Music and dance troupes often perform together at festivals. Line dancing is popular, with dancers linking arms while swaying, hopping, and gliding across the stage. Singers are often accompanied by musicians who play the violin, the tambourines, the 'ud (a windpipe made of cane), the tablah (a hand-beaten drum), and the lyre.

The Libyan government maintains strict control over the production and distribution of printed matter, and all printing presses are government owned. Libraries, also government owned, have abundant collections of old religious writings but far less modern literature. Printed material that is critical of the regime or of Islam is censored.

Muammar Qadhafi spelled out the goals and ideals of his 1969 revolution in a three-volume collection, *The Green Book*,

which he produced between 1976 and 1979. The books emphasize the centrality of Islamic values to the governing of the Libyan nation, but they also stress the importance of the then-fashionable socialist ideologies of the emerging postcolonial countries, and for that they have been criticized by Muslim leaders.

Libya has produced few internationally renowned artists, though Ali Omar Ermes is a notable exception. He lives in the United Kingdom and produces paintings featuring Arabic calligraphy done with a modernist, Western sensibility. His works are in the permanent collection of the British Museum in London and the Smithsonian Institution in Washington, DC, and are collected by world-renowned private collectors such as the Prince of Wales.

15 WORK

Most workers are employed in the oil industry, the largest sector of the Libyan economy. Others work in the state-owned manufacturing firms that produce machinery, appliances, cement and construction equipment, cigarettes, clothing, leather goods, textiles, shoes, fertilizers, and industrial chemicals, as well as processed foods such as olive oil, citrus fruits, tomato paste, tuna, and beverages. Many people who were once employed in agriculture moved to the cities during the oil boom and subsequent industrial development. Agricultural workers made up about 17% of the workforce in 2004. These workers grow citrus fruits, barley, wheat, millet, olives, almonds, dates, onions, potatoes, tomatoes, and tobacco. Many farmers raise sheep, goats, cattle, camels, and poultry and produce dairy products and honey. Fishermen operating out of Tripoli bring in tuna, sardines, and mullet.

There is a shortage of unskilled laborers, attributable in large part to a high military conscription rate, but also to the increased education level of Libya's young people, which makes them look down on menial jobs. Thus, Libya has many unskilled foreign workers from neighboring countries. Libya also has hundreds of thousands of foreign technical workers, who are needed to advise on petroleum extraction and design and to construct irrigation projects.

16 SPORTS

Libyan sporting events tend to be very strenuous and spirited. Popular spectator sports are camel racing and horse racing, with competitions held on racetracks in rural areas. Football—known to Americans as soccer—is also a popular spectator sport. In 2008, Libya's national football team was ranked eighty-fifth by FIFA (International Federation of Association Football), the world football governing body. Although the Libyan team has never played in the World Cup, it came within one game of qualifying in 1986 in Mexico City. Other popular sports are basketball and track and field events.

17 ENTERTAINMENT AND RECREATION

Radio and television, with state-sponsored news, religious, and musical programming, are popular forms of entertainment in Libya. In 2004, there were 18 AM radio stations, 3 FM radio stations, and 3 shortwave stations. There are 16 officially sanctioned broadcast television stations, but satellite receivers are as ubiquitous in Libya as they are in most developing countries. In 2007, al-Libiyah, the nation's first officially sanctioned nongovernment television station, began broadcasting. There are stations in Benghazi and Tripoli that broadcast in French, English, and Italian. The movie theaters show imported foreign films. The news media is tightly controlled, and government censorship is widespread. In the Worldwide Press Freedom Index of 2007, Libya was ranked the one-hundred-fifty-fifth least free media in the world.

Libya has nine museums housing archeological, religious, and historical exhibits. Chess and dominoes are enthusiastically played, both in cafés and in homes. The country is also home to some of the best preserved archeological sites of the classical world, including the Phoenician ruins of Leptis Magna and world-famous Greek ruins at Cyrene.

18 FOLK ART, CRAFTS, AND HOBBIES

Libyan art, in keeping with Islamic beliefs, refrains from realistic depictions of people or animals. Instead, artists have a unique style known as *arabesque*, in which designs are complex, geometric, and abstract. Libyan artisans use intricate lines and geometric shapes in their carpets, embroidered goods, jewelry, leather goods, tiles, and pottery. Islamic words and passages from the Quran are often etched in elaborate calligraphy. Libyan architecture has the same restrictions, and therefore lifelike statues and adornments are not found on buildings.

Small craft shops once sold domestic artwork such as metalwork, pottery, tiles, leatherwork, and handwoven and embroidered goods, but many such shops have closed down because of the nationalization of businesses under Qadhafi, which discouraged artisans from practicing their crafts.

19 SOCIAL PROBLEMS

The greatest problems facing Libya today stem from the lack of political freedom and fluctuations in economic well-being. In the 1970s, the average income of Libyans was twice that of their Italian colonizers. Since then, however, fluctuations in oil prices have led to variations in economic well-being in Libya, causing some social distress. The steep rise in oil prices since 2003, however, has brought renewed prosperity. Seeking a share of this new wealth, workers from impoverished Asian and African countries have migrated to Libya, where they often face exploitation. Libya is also a transit country for the trafficking of humans and narcotics.

Islam in Libya has not experienced the sort of radicalization seen in neighboring Egypt and Algeria, for example. It remains, among the nations of the Maghrib (the western part of North Africa bordering the Mediterranean), a moderately religious nation, although there were relatively short-lived Islamist uprisings in the late 1990s in the nation's eastern provinces.

In 2003, Libya officially announced that its intelligence services had planned and carried out the 1988 bombing of a Pan Am airliner over Lockerbie, Scotland. Since then, many Western nations have resumed diplomatic and economic relations with the once-isolated country. United Nation sanctions against the country were lifted in 2003. The country also announced that year that it was abandoning its nuclear weapons program, which until then had only been suspected.

It is widely believed that Qadhafi's son—and, many believe, heir apparent—Sayf al-Islam Qadhafi, is the force behind Libya's recent reconciliation with the Western powers and its reintegration into the world community.

20 GENDER ISSUES

Libya is one of only a few Islamic nations that have signed and ratified the 1979 Convention on the Elimination of All Forms of Discrimination Against Women. It did so, however, subject to reservations made in deference to its interpretations of Shari'a (Quranic law).

Human Rights Watch reports that Libya maintains prisons for women and girls who have committed no crime, who have served their sentences for crimes committed, or, in some cases, who are simply seeking refuge from domestic abuse, as there are no shelters for such victims in the country. The government of Libya has rejected the report, saying these are not prisons or detention facilities but are instead "social rehabilitation facilities." Documented testimonials from women held in such facilities question this assertion.

Libya has no domestic violence laws. Rape cases of extreme violence can be and sometimes are prosecuted, but judges are given the discretion to force the woman to marry her rapist as a form of social remedy. Rape victims can also be prosecuted for adultery if they are married at the time of their rape.

21 BIBLIOGRAPHY

Copeland, Paul W. *The Land and People of Libya.* New York: J. B. Lippincott, 1967.

Gottfried, Ted. *Libya: Desert Land in Conflict.* Brookfield, CT: Millbrook Press, 1994.

Hodgson, Marshall. *The Venture of Islam: The Classical Age of Islam.* Chicago: University of Chicago Press, 1974.

Hourani, Albert. *Arabic Thought in the Liberal Age, 1789–1939.* London: Oxford University Press, 1962.

Metz, Helen C., ed. *Libya: A Country Study.* Washington, DC: Federal Research Division, Library of Congress, 1988.

Wright, John. *Libya: A Modern History.* Baltimore: Johns Hopkins University Press, 1981.

—revised by J. Henry

LUHYA

PRONUNCIATION: LOO-ee-ah
ALTERNATE NAMES: Luyia, Abaluhya
LOCATION: Western Kenya
POPULATION: 5.3 million
LANGUAGE: Several Bantu dialects
RELIGION: Christianity (Catholicism, Protestantism); Islam; some indigenous beliefs
RELATED ARTICLES: Vol. 1: Kenyans

[1] INTRODUCTION

The Luhya, Luyia, or Abaluhya, as they are interchangeably called, are the second-largest ethnic group in Kenya, after the Kikuyu. The Luhya belong to the larger linguistic stock known as the Bantu. The Luhya comprise several subgroups with different but mutually intelligible linguistic dialects. Some of these subgroups are Ababukusu, Abanyala, Abatachoni, Avalogoli, Abamarama, Abaidakho, Abaisukha, Abatiriki, Abakisa, Abamarachi, and Abasamia.

Migration into their present Western Kenya location goes back to as early as the second half of the 15th century ad. Immigrants into present-day Luhyaland came mainly from eastern and western Uganda and trace their ancestry mainly to several Bantu groups, and to other non-Bantu groups such as the Kalenjin, Luo, and Maasai. Early migration was probably due to the search for more and better land, and escape from local conflicts, tsetse flies, and mosquitoes. By about 1850, migration into Luhyaland was largely complete, and only minor internal movements took place after that due to food shortages, disease, and domestic conflicts. Despite their diverse ethnic ancestry, a history of intermarriage, local trade, and shared social and cultural practices have combined to form the present Luhya ethnic group, which still displays variations in dialects and customs reflecting this diverse ancestry.

The Luhya have been subjected to the political forces that have affected most of the other ethnic groups in Kenya. Colonization of Kenya by the British from the 1890s to 1963 forced many communities, including the Luhya, into migrant labor on settler plantations and in urban centers. Because of their numeric strength, the Luhya are considered a potent political force and have always been active in political activities in Kenya. For example, veteran politicians Michael Wamalwa Kijana and Musalia Mudavadi rose to become vice presidents of the Kenyan Government though for brief periods of time. Others have gone on to become influential members of the Kenyan society such as medical doctors, professors, educators, economists, lawyers and so on.

[2] LOCATION AND HOMELAND

The Luhya people make their home mainly in the western part of Kenya. Administratively, they occupy mostly Western Province, and the west-central part of Rift Valley Province. Luhya migration into the Rift Valley is relatively recent, only dating back to the first few years after independence in 1963, when farms formerly occupied by colonial white settlers were bought by, or given back to, indigenous Africans.

According to the latest population estimates of Kenya, the Luhya people number 5.3 million people, making up 14% of

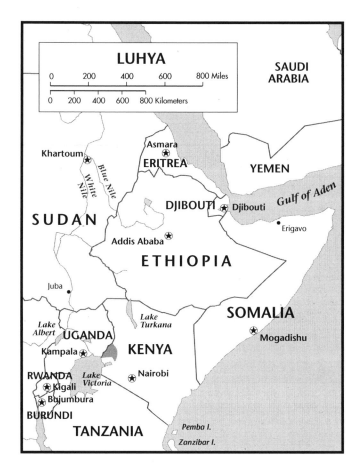

LUHYA

Kenya's total population of 36.9 million people. The Luhya are the second-largest ethnic group in Kenya, after the Kikuyu. Whereas the majority of the Luhya live in western Kenya, especially in the rural areas, there is an increasingly large number of Luhya who have migrated into major urban centers such as Nairobi in search of employment and educational opportunities. About 1,500,000 Luhya people live outside of Western Province. This is about 28.3% of the total Luhya population.

³ LANGUAGE

There is no single Luhya language as such. Rather, there are several mutually intelligible dialects which are principally Bantu. Perhaps the most identifying linguistic feature of the different Luhya dialects is the use of the prefix *aba-* or *ava-*, meaning "of" or "belonging to." Thus, for example, *A*balogoli or *A*valogoli means "people of *logoli*."

Luhya names have specific meanings or connotations. Children are named after natural climatic seasons, and also after their ancestors, normally their deceased grandparents or great-grandparents. Among the Ababukusu, the name Wafula (for a boy) and Nafula (for a girl) would mean "born during heavy rains," while Wekesa (for a boy) and Nekesa (for a girl) would mean "born in the harvest season." With European contact and the introduction of Christianity at the turn of the 20th century, Christian and Western European names began to be given as first names, followed by traditional Luhya names. Thus, for example, a boy might be named Joseph Wafula, and a girl, Grace Nekesa.

⁴ FOLKLORE

One of the most common myths among the Luhya group is the one regarding the origin of the earth and human beings. The myth holds that *Were* (God) first created heaven, then earth. The earth created by *Were* had three types of soil: top soil, which was black; intermediate soil, which was red; and bottom soil, which was white. From the black soil, *Were* created a black man; from the red soil, he created a brown man; and from the white soil, he created a white man.

⁵ RELIGION

The Luhya people traditionally believed in and worshiped one God, *Were* (also known as *Nyasaye*). *Were* was worshipped through intermediaries, usually spirits of dead relatives. The spirits had a lot of benevolent as well as malevolent power and thus had to be appeased through animal sacrifices, such as goats, chickens, and cattle.

At the turn of the 20th century, Christianity was introduced to Luhyaland as it was to the rest of the country. An extensive spread of Christianity occurred during the colonial period. The overwhelming majority of Luhya people now consider themselves Christians. Both Catholicism and Protestantism are practiced. Among the Abawanga, Islam is also practiced.

Despite conversion to Christianity, belief in spirits and witchcraft is still common, and it is not unusual to find people offering prayers in church and at the same time consulting witch doctors or medicine men for the same or different problems.

⁶ MAJOR HOLIDAYS

There are no specific holidays that are uniquely Luhya, or that celebrate Luhya achievements or culture. Rather, the Luhya people celebrate the national holidays of Kenya with the rest of the nation. Among the Abalogoli and Abanyole, an annual cultural festival has recently been initiated, but it is not yet widely adopted. The festival is held on December 31.

⁷ RITES OF PASSAGE

As is true in many African societies, having many children is considered a virtue, and childlessness is a great misfortune. Many births take place in the home, but increasingly women are urged to give birth in hospitals or other health facilities. Deliveries that take place at home are managed by older neighboring women who have experience in assisting in deliveries. Men are normally not expected at the place of delivery. The placenta *(engori)* and the umbilical cord *(olulera)* are buried behind the hut at a secret spot so they will not be found and tampered with by a witch *(omulogi)*. For births that take place in hospitals or other places outside of home, these rituals are not observed.

Until the last 10 to 20 years, initiation ceremonies to mark the transition from childhood to adulthood were elaborately performed for both boys and girls. Among other things, these rites included circumcision for boys. Uncircumcised boys *(avasinde)* would not be allowed to marry or join in many other adult activities. Nowadays circumcision still takes place, but only among the Ababukusu and the Abatiriki are the ceremonies still elaborate and largely public.

Death and funeral rites involve not only the bereaved family, but also the community and other kin. While it is known that many deaths occur through illnesses like malaria and tuberculosis, as well as road accidents, quite a few deaths are still believed to occur from witchcraft. Burial often takes place in the homestead of the deceased. Among the Luhya, funerals and burials are public and open events. Animals are slaughtered and food and drinks brought to feed the mourners. Because many people nowadays profess Christianity, many burial ceremonies, even though largely traditional in terms of observance of certain rites, do involve prayers in church and at the deceased's home. Music and dance also take place, mostly at night. Music and dance are a mixture of both traditional Luhya performances and contemporary Western-style music involving modern stereos and "boom boxes."

8 INTERPERSONAL RELATIONS

Greetings among the Luhya take various forms. The essence of any form of greeting is not just to salute the person, but to inquire of their well-being and that of their families. People take a keen interest in one another's affairs, and people are often willing to share their concerns with others. Shaking hands is a very common form of greeting, and for people who are meeting for the first time in a long while, the handshake will involve not just the clasping of hands, but also a vigorous jerking of the arm. Shaking hands between a man and his mother-in-law is not allowed among some Luhya communities. Hugging is not very common. Women may hug each other, but cross-gender hugging is rare.

Women are expected to defer to men, especially to their husbands, fathers-in-law, and the older brothers of their husband. Thus, in a conversation with any of these men, women will tend (or are expected) to lower their heads, fold their hands, and look down.

Visits are very common among the Luhya people. Most visits are casual and unannounced. Families strive to provide food for their visitors, especially tea. Dating among the Luhya is informal and is often not publicly displayed, especially among teenagers. Unless a marriage is seriously intended and planned, a man or a woman may not formally invite their date to their parents' home and introduce him or her as such.

9 LIVING CONDITIONS

The living conditions of the Luhya are not much different from those of other communities in Kenya. Major health concerns among the Luhya include the prevalence of diseases such as scabies, diarrhea, malaria, malnutrition, and, lately, AIDS. These illnesses are prevalent mainly due to poor sanitation and inadequate access to clean water and health facilities, and also because they frequently do not practice safe sex.

In the rural areas, the Luhya live in homesteads called *mugitsi* by the Avalogoli, comprising an extended family. The houses are mostly made of grass-thatched roofs and mud walls, but increasingly people construct houses with corrugated iron roofs, and in some cases, walls made of concrete blocks. The houses tend to be round or square. Because of the general poverty in rural areas, people own very few material goods, and items such as transistor radios and bicycles are considered prime possessions. Items like cars and TVs are largely lacking among the majority of these people.

People rely on public transportation, consisting of buses and vans, but travel on foot and on bicycles is also very common. Roads in the rural hinterland are not paved and tend to be impassable during heavy rains.

10 FAMILY LIFE

In the rural areas among the Luhya, people live in homesteads or compounds, with each homestead comprising several houses. In one homestead may live an old man (the patriarch), his married sons and their wives and children, his unmarried sons and daughters, and sometimes other relatives. Even though each household may independently run its own affairs, there is a lot of obligatory sharing within the homestead. Family sizes tend to be large, with the average number of children per woman reaching eight.

Women are expected to defer to men in this patriarchal society. Acts of supposed lack of deference or insubordination by women towards their husbands, father-in-laws, or other senior male relatives can result in beatings from the male relatives, especially the husband. Women do most of the domestic chores such as fetching firewood, cooking, taking care of children, and also farm work.

Marriage among the Luhya is exogamous. One cannot marry those belonging to his or her parents' clans or lineages. Polygyny (the act of a man marrying more than one wife) is not as widely practiced these days among the Luhya, but it is still fairly common among the Ababukusu subgroup. Traditionally, a request for marriage is made between the parents of the man and the woman. If the marriage is agreed upon, bride-wealth of cattle and cash, called *uvukwi* among the Avalogoli subgroup, is paid. Nowadays, however, young people increasingly get married on their own accord with little parental input. Civil and church (Christian) marriages are also becoming common. Bride-wealth is still being paid, but amounts differ widely, and payment schedules are not strictly adhered to.

Pets are kept, especially dogs and cats. Often, however, these pets are kept for utilitarian purposes. Dogs provide security, while cats catch mice. Often the dogs will have their kennels outside of the house, but cats may sleep in the house.

11 CLOTHING

Ordinarily the Luhya people wear clothes just like those of their fellow Kenyans—locally manufactured and imported dresses, pants, shirts, shoes, etc. Elementary and high school students wear uniforms to school as a national policy. Women almost never wear either short or long pants. Those who dare to do so are considered aberrant and may even be verbally assaulted by men. It is particularly inappropriate for a married woman to wear pants or a short skirt or dress in the presence of her father-in-law. Earrings, necklaces, and bangles are commonly worn by women. Men generally do not wear earrings.

Traditional clothing is worn mostly during specific occasions by certain people. In cultural dances, performers may put on feathered hats and skirts made of sisal strands. For the Luhya groups that still maintain the traditional circumcision rites (especially the Ababukusu), the initiates will often put on clothing made of skins and paint themselves with red ochre or ash.

12 FOOD

The meal regime among the Luhya involves breakfast, lunch, and dinner. Breakfast mainly consists of tea. The preferred tea is made with plenty of milk and sugar. However, milk may

Itionyi, a five-year old bull, walks through the streets of Khayega, Kenya, after defeating another bull at the Ilala ground in Kakamega. Bullfighting is a tradtional pastime of the Luhya people and features heavily in their festivities. (AP Images/Sayyid Azim)

not be available all the time, and tea may very often be taken without it. Tea without milk is called *itulungi*. For those that can afford it, wheat bread bought from the stores is consumed with tea. Tea and bread, however, are too expensive for many families to eat on a regular basis, so porridge, made of maize, millet, or finger millet flour, is consumed instead. Lunch and supper often consist of *ovukima*—maize flour added to boiling water and thoroughly mixed until cooked into a thick paste more or less like grits in the US. *Ovukima* is eaten with various vegetables like kale and collard greens, and for those who can afford it, beef or chicken. Chicken is a delicacy and is the food prepared for important guests or on important occasions.

Other foods that are consumed include traditional vegetables like *mrera* and *nderema*. Many traditional food taboos have broken down. Women, for example, were not allowed to eat chicken and eggs in the past, but this taboo has largely been abandoned. The chicken gizzard, however, is still for the most part considered men's food (particularly the male head of the household), and in many homes women will not eat it.

The main cooking utensils are pots made of steel or other metals. These are mass-manufactured in the country, as well as imported, and are bought from the stores. Clay pots are also still used by many families for preparing and storing traditional beer, and also for cooking traditional vegetables. Plates

and cups are made of either metals, plastic, or china, and are bought from the stores, as are spoons, knives, and forks.

13 EDUCATION

The literacy level among the Luhya is close to that of the country as a whole. The literacy level for the total population of Western Province where the majority of the Luhya live is 67.3%. This is slightly lower than the national average of 69.4%. Literacy among women is slightly lower than among men. Typically, most people (about 75% of the population) drop out of school after primary school education, which (since the mid-1980s) lasts eight years. The main reasons for the high drop-out rates are the stringent qualifying examinations to enter high school, and the very expensive school fees required in high school.

Parents spend a large portion of their income on their children's education in school fees, uniforms, school supplies, transportation to and from school, and pocket money. Often the family will deny itself many of life's necessities and comforts, like better housing, food, and clothing, in order to put the children through school. Expectations are consequently placed on those going to school to finish and assist with the education of their younger siblings, and to care for their parents in old age. Because very few students are able to get a university education, parents and the community are very proud of those that manage to attain this level of education.

14 CULTURAL HERITAGE

Music and dance are an integral part of the life of the Luhya people. There is a wide variety of songs and dances. Children sing songs and dance for play and (especially boys) when herding livestock. Occasions like weddings, funerals, and circumcision ceremonies all call for singing and dancing. Musical instruments include drums, jingles, flutes, and accordions. The Luhya are nationally renowned for their very energetic and vibrant *isukuti* dance, a celebratory performance involving rapid squatting and rising accompanied by thunderous, rhythmic drumbeats.

Proverbs, stories, and songs are commonly used not only for entertainment, but also for education (especially of the young), conflict resolution, and adding flavor or weight to conversations.

15 WORK

The majority of Luhya families are agriculturalists. Because of the high population density (about 900 people per sq km, or 2,450 people per sq mi) in Luhyaland, most families own only very small pieces of land of less than 0.4 hectares (1 acre) which are very intensively cultivated. Crops grown include various species of vegetables such as kale, collard greens, carrots, maize, beans, potatoes, bananas, and cassava. Beverage crops like tea, coffee, and sugarcane are grown in some parts of Luhyaland. Livestock, especially cattle and sheep, are also kept. Tending the farm is often a family affair. Because the family farm is rarely sufficient to meet all of the family's needs for food, school fees and supplies, clothing, and medical care, often some members of the family will seek employment opportunities in various urban centers in the country and remit money back to the rural homes.

16 SPORTS

There are numerous games and sports played by children among the Luhya. For girls, jumping rope is very common. The jumping is counted and sometimes accompanied by rhythmic songs. Hide-and-seek games are common among both boys and girls. Soccer is the most popular game with boys. Any open ground can serve as a playing field. Adult sports include soccer for men, and to a lesser extent, netball for women. Netball is somewhat like basketball, only the ball is not bounced on the ground. School-based sports also include track-and-field events.

The most popular spectator sport is soccer, and the Luhya are known for producing some of the best soccer players in the country. The AFC Leopards soccer team, largely comprised of Luhya players, is one of the best teams in the country. Bull-fighting is also a popular spectator sport.

17 ENTERTAINMENT AND RECREATION

Television sets are too expensive for the majority of Luhya families to afford, especially in the rural areas. This is further hampered by the lack of electricity in many of the rural areas. Radios and cassette players, however, are affordable, and these provide musical entertainment for many people. Local bars and shops also have radios, cassette players, juke boxes, and other music systems, and thus many men congregate in these places to drink, play games, and listen and dance to music. Music is mainly of local, Swahili, and Lingala (Democratic Republic of the Congo) origin, but western European and American music are also common.

18 FOLK ART, CRAFTS, AND HOBBIES

Pottery and basket-weaving are quite common among the Luhya, especially in the rural areas. Most of these are either used in the home or sold in the markets for cash. Pots are often used for brewing local beer, cooking food, and storing water. The pots are made of clay. Baskets are made from the leaves of date palms (called *kamakhendu* among the Ababukusu) that grow on river banks. Increasingly, sisal is used. The baskets are sold and are also used at home for carrying and keeping foodstuffs. Body ornaments like bangles, necklaces, and earrings are commercially mass-produced in the country or imported, and thus are not in any way uniquely Luhya in form. Among the Ababukusu subgroup, however, parents of twins wear a traditional bangle called *imwana*.

19 SOCIAL PROBLEMS

There are no human and civil rights problems that are unique to the Luhya people. Violations of human rights and civil liberties that the Kenya government has been accused of generally apply across most ethnic groups. Problems of alcoholism exist among the Luhya, but problems that are considered particularly pressing are those to do with the high population density and high population growth rate. Health problems arising from diseases endemic in Luhya areas is also of concern. The drug problem has not caught up with the Luhya to any significant degree.

20 GENDER ISSUES

Among the Luhya gender roles are assigned to men and women culturally in ways which create, reinforce, and perpetuate relationships in which males are viewed as superior and women are in a subordinate position. As already noted earlier, women are supposed to be in deference to men. When talking to her husband or male in-laws, a wife is supposed to kneel down with her head bowed and arms folded on her chest in deference to the man. Luhya boys and girls are conditioned to behave in certain ways and to play different roles in society. For example, women are supposed to do most of the domestic chores such as fetching firewood, cooking, taking care of children, and also farm work. As such the Luhya people have distinct cultural practices, especially governing the gender division of labor, marriage and women's access to resources. Due to the high rate of male out-migration, an estimated 30–60% of households are female-headed and they have to single-handedly farm their fields in the absence of men. Thus gender empowerment and equality constitute the major gender issues among the Luhya.

With reference to homosexuality, certain types of same-sex activity were tolerated in tribal tradition, but only as childish behaviors unworthy of an initiate. But in general homosexuality is not tolerated in Luhya society. In the larger Kenyan society, homosexuality continues to be illegal as a "crime against nature" under the Kenyan penal code inherited from the British colonial legal system. Homosexuality is regarded with disdain and disgust by the majority of the population, and persons arrested for homosexual activity are treated harshly by the police. In some ethnic groups of Kenya, homosexuality can be punished by death. All religious groups abhor homosexuality and condone its complete suppression. In spite of this suppression, Kenyan male prostitutes are readily available on the streets of Nairobi and Mombasa, usually catering to international tourists. They are well dressed in order to be able to enter international hotels. In most instances the prostitutes themselves are probably bisexual, many having girlfriends or wives, and consider themselves heterosexual.

[21] BIBLIOGRAPHY

Abala, Judith. "Storytelling in the Maragoli Society." Master's thesis, Ohio State University, 1989.

Abwunza, Judith. "Logoli Women of Western Kenya Speak: Needs and Means." Ph.D. dissertation, University of Toronto, 1991.

Gonza, Richard Kayaga. "The African Homestead as a School: A Case Study of the Luhya of Kenya." In *Journal of African Cultures and Religion,* edited by Michael C Kirwen. vol.2 no.1, 2007.

Government of Kenya. *Kenya Population Census 1999.* Vol 1. Nairobi: Government Printer, 1999.

Nyamongo, Isaac. "Food and Nutrition." In *Bungoma District Sociocultural Profile,* edited by Gideon Were and Osaga Odak. Nairobi: Government of Kenya, n.d.

Odak, Osaga. "Material Culture." In *Bungoma District Sociocultural Profile,* edited by Gideon Were and Osaga Odak. Nairobi: Government of Kenya, n.d.

Orawo, Charles Nyakiti. *Lwimbo: Busia-Luhya Song Dance Traditions.* Kisumu, Kenya: Lake Publishers & Enterprises, 2002.

Thomas, Samuel S. " Transforming the Gospel of Domesticity: Luhya Girls and the Friends Africa Mission, 1917-1926." *African Studies Review,* 43, no. 2, (2000): 1-29.

Wagner, Gunter. *The Bantu of North Kavirondo.* London: Oxford University Press, 1949.

Were, Gideon. *Essays on African Religion in Western Kenya.* Nairobi: East African Literature Bureau, 1977.

Were, Gideon, and Derek Wilson. *East Africa through a Thousand Years: A History of the Years AD 1000 to the Present Day.* 3rd ed. New York: Africana Publishing Company, 1987.

—revised by E. Kalipeni

LUO

PRONUNCIATION: luh-WO
LOCATION: Western Province and Nyanza Province in Kenya; Tanzania
POPULATION: Over 3 million
LANGUAGE: Dholuo; English (official); KiSwahili
RELIGION: Christianity combined with indigenous practices (Anglican church [CPK], Roman Catholicism, and independent Christian churches)
RELATED ARTICLES: Vol. 1: Kenyans; Tanzanians

[1] INTRODUCTION

Throughout the 19th century, the Luo undertook the last phase in their migrations into their present area in Kenya, moving slowly out of lower savanna grasslands into higher and cooler regions with reliable rainfall. In this migration, cattle, while still valued, were supplemented by farming and an ever increasing importance of crops in their economy. Bantu agriculturalists, with whom the Nilotic Luo began to interact, exchanged many customs with them. Some Bantu borrowed the Luo practice of knocking out the lower incisor teeth as a sign of beauty. The Luo, however, did not adopt circumcision for men, as practiced in some neighboring Bantu groups. The Luo are now found throughout Kenya, especially in Nairobi where they live in large numbers. Nevertheless, most Luo maintain strong economic, cultural, and social links to Western Kenya, which is considered by them to be their "home."

[2] LOCATION AND HOMELAND

The Luo number over 3 million people, or about 13% of the total population of Kenya (nearly 25 million people). They are, along with the Luhya, the second-largest ethnic group in the country, behind the Gikuyu. Most Luo live in western Kenya in Western Province or adjacent Nyanza Province, two of the eight provinces in Kenya. Some Luo live in Tanzania to the south of Kenya. Over the past 500 years, the Luo have migrated slowly from the Sudan to their present location around the eastern shore of Lake Victoria. This area changes from low, dry landscape around the lake to more lush, hilly areas to the east. The provincial capital of Kisumu is the third-largest city in Kenya and is a major center for Luo activities and interests.

[3] LANGUAGE

The Luo, like other Kenyans, are typically conversant in at least three languages. The two national languages of Kenya are English and KiSwahili. English, derived from the British colonial era before Kenya's independence in 1963, is the official language of government, international business, university instruction, banks, and commerce. It is taught throughout Kenya in primary and secondary schools. KiSwahili is the primary language of many coastal populations in Kenya and has spread from there throughout East Africa, including Luoland. Today, this language serves as a significant means of communication across ethnic boundaries and is most evident as a language of trade and commerce in urban markets and rural towns. Nowadays, KiSwahili is also taught in Kenyan primary and secondary schools. Both English and KiSwahili, therefore, are widely available to the Luo as a means of communication and for consumption of radio, television, and newspaper materials available in these two languages. Nevertheless, the indigenous language of the Luo, referred to as Dholuo, is for most people their language of preference in the home and daily conversation. Dholuo is taught in the primary schools throughout Luoland such that these days Luo young people are fluent in at least three languages. This is impressive when one takes into account that English, KiSwahili, and Dholuo are from three very different language families with drastically different grammatical principles and vocabulary.

Dholuo is a Nilotic language classified as a Nilo-Saharan language. This language family is spoken by Africans living in an area between the western Sudan and the middle Niger River area to the north and west of Kenya and also in Uganda where the Nilotes most closely related to the Kenya Luo reside. Dholuo is a tonal language: words differ by their pitch, resulting in an aesthetically pleasing musical quality.

Children enjoy playing language games in Dholuo. Among these is a "tongue twister" game. For example, children try to say without difficulty, "*Atud tond atonga, tond atonga chodi,*" which means, "I tie the rope of the basket, the rope of the basket breaks." "*Acham tap chotna malando chotna cham tapa malando*" means, "I eat from the red dish of my lover and my lover eats from my red dish." Most Luo, irrespective of educational attainment and occupation, prefer to speak Dholuo at home and continue to teach this language to their children. Even young Luo teenagers, who nowadays live in Nairobi and rarely visit Luoland, nevertheless have learned to speak excellent Dholuo among Luo.

Names are given corresponding to places where an individual is born, the time of day, or the day of the week. Even the kind of weather that prevailed at the time of a child's birth is noted. For example, one born during a rain storm is called Akoth (male) or Okoth (female). Cold days or those with strong winds are also significant for naming. Just about every Luo also has a "praise name," which is used among close friends.

4 FOLKLORE

The spoken word is richly elaborated among the Luo. Stories, legends, riddles, and proverbs are traditionally recited in the *siwindhe,* which is the home of a widowed grandmother. In this place, Luo boys and girls gather in the evenings to be taught the traditions of their culture. Boys, by their teens, sleep in the siwindhe lest they be teased as one who still sleeps in his mother's house. In the evening after people have returned from their gardens, they gather around the hearth to tell stories and to listen to them. In the siwindhe, however, grandmothers preside over storytelling and verbal games. Riddles, for instance, take the form of competitive exchanges where winners are rewarded by "marrying" girls in a kind of mock marriage situation. Often, friendly arguments erupt over interpretations of riddles. One riddle, for example, asks the question, "My house has no door," which is answered by "an egg." Another riddle is, "What is a lake with reeds all around?" The answer is, "an eye." Clever answers are frequently given as alternatives to these standard answers. Proverbs also enter prominently into the siwindhe discussions and are common in everyday use as well. Some examples are, "The eye you have treated will look at you contemptuously," "A hare is small but gives birth to twins," and "A cowardly hyena lives for many years."

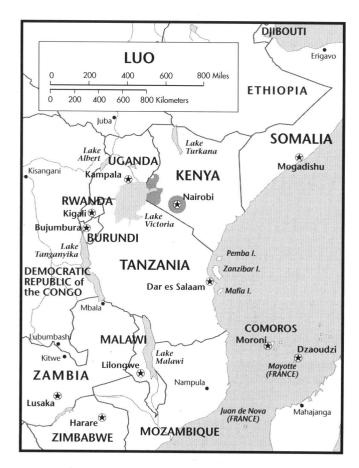

Morality tales are told both in the siwindhe and in other homes not only for entertainment but also to impress upon all listeners the proper way to cope with life's circumstances. Such questions as, "Why do people die?", "What is the value of a deformed child?", "What qualities make an appropriate spouse?", "What is friendship?", "Who is responsible for a bad child?", "Why do some people suffer?", and many others are the subject of folklore. For example, the story known as "Opondo's Children" is about a man called Opondo whose wife continuously gave birth to monitor lizards instead of human babies. These lizard babies were thrown away to die because they were hideous. Once, however, the parents decided to keep such a child, and he grew to adolescence. This child, as a teenager, loved to bathe alone in a river. Before swimming he would take off his monitor skin, and while swimming he mysteriously became a normal human being. His skin was in fact only a superficial covering. One day a passerby saw him swimming and told his parents that he was a normal human being. Secretly, his parents went to watch him swim and discovered that he was in fact normal. They destroyed his skin and thereafter, as the Luo say when measuring time, "when days more numerous than hairs on a sheep" had passed, the boy became accepted and loved by all in his community. For this reason, Opondo and his wife deeply regretted that they had thrown away all of their many monitor children. This tale constitutes a lesson teaching that compassion should be displayed towards children with physical defects.

An origin tale concerns the origin of Lake Victoria, entitled "Victoria Nyanza." For the Luo, Lake Victoria is the most significant feature of their landscape. Women are known as "daughters of the lake," and a man is known as "a lake man." In the tale there was once a time when a giant called Lowle (Lake Victoria) lived in the sky, and whenever he urinated great ponds of water were formed. This is how Lake Victoria came to be.

In another origin tale concerning death, it is told that humans and chameleons are responsible for this calamity. *Were* (God) wanted to put an end to death, which strikes "young and old, boys and girls, men and women, strangers and kinsmen, and the wise and the foolish." He requested that an offering be made to him of white fat from a goat. A chameleon was commissioned to carry the offering up to the sky where *Were* lives. Along the way, the fat became dirty and was angrily rejected by *Were*. He declared that death would continue because of this insult. The chameleon became cursed by the Luo, and ever since it must always walk on all fours and take slow steps.

Suicide and the love between brother and sister are emphasized in a tale concerning orphans. Obong'o was killed in battle with a neighboring society. This happened after his sister, Awuor, a fellow orphan, had pleaded with him not to risk his life. In her deep sorrow, after burying her brother, she committed suicide by setting her house on fire with herself and all their possessions inside. This tale reinforces the theme of love between a brother and sister, a sentiment enhanced by a system of bride-wealth. It is commonly the case that when a young man's family gives cattle and other goods to another family in exchange for his wife (and her future children who will be members of his family), it is wealth acquired from his sister's marriage that contributes to his own bride-wealth. After marriage, throughout life, brothers and sisters remain very close.

5 RELIGION

Christianity has had a major impact on Luo religious beliefs and practices. Today, there are a variety of religious communities drawing on beliefs from indigenous practices and Christianity. The Anglican Church, known as the CPK, and the Roman Catholic Church are very significant among the Luo. The offices of bishops from these two faiths are located in Kisumu. Many people, however, do not draw sharp distinctions between religious practices that have European origins and those with African origins. Mainstream churches draw on a rich Luo musical and dance tradition in their liturgies. For many Christians, the ancestors continue to play a significant role in their lives. In traditional belief, the ancestors reside in the sky or underground, from where they may be reincarnated in human or animal form. Ritual ceremonies are sometimes performed when naming a baby to determine if a particular spirit has been reincarnated. The spirits of ancestors communicate with the living in their dreams.

In the Luo religion, troublesome spirits may cause misfortunes if they are not remembered or revered. Luo refer to spirits by the term *juok*, or "shadow." Spirits in the male line are especially venerated. The Luo high god has now fused with the Judeo-Christian god. The Luo refer to God by many names that reveal his power and Christian influence. For example, *Were* means "one certain to grant requests"; *Nyasaye*, "he who is begged"; *Ruoth*, "the king"; *Jachwech*, "the molder"; *Wuon koth*, "the rain-giver"; and *Nyakalaga*, "the one who flows ev-

erywhere." Prayers and petitions are addressed to God by those in need of his assistance.

Christianity has fused most notably with traditional religious notions and customs in "independent Christian churches," which have attracted large followings. For example, the Nomiya Luo Church, which started in 1912, was the first independent church in Kenya. The founder of this church, Johanwa Owalo, is believed to be a prophet like Jesus Christ and Mohammed. Owalo was originally a student at a Roman Catholic Mission Station where he was baptized. Soon after, he began to have visions. In one of these, he was taken to heaven by the angel Gabriel. He began to question Catholic doctrine when he observed that Europeans were not permitted to enter heaven. Owalo then began to question the colonial order of his day in which the British controlled Kenya. Later, he joined with a Catholic priest and began to teach a new theology that included rejection of the pope and the doctrine of the trinity. Owalo eventually joined the Anglican church, so that presently the Nomiya Hymnal contains both Catholic and Anglican hymns. Some traditional practices rejected by some mainstream Christian churches are retained by the Nomiya church, such as levirate marriage, in which a widow marries the brother of her deceased husband. The Legio Maria is another prominent Luo independent church, with 250,000 members. This church practices the Latin Roman Catholic Mass. The Legio Maria is also tolerant of the levirate. Compared to mainstream churches, women play an important role in this church, and there is a pronounced devotion to Mary, the mother of Jesus.

6 MAJOR HOLIDAYS

The Luo recognize national holidays of Kenya and Tanzania, depending on the country where they reside. In addition, Luo celebrate the Christian religious holidays.

7 RITES OF PASSAGE

People are discouraged from noting when someone is pregnant for fear that problems might result from jealous ancestors or neighbors. Older women and midwives assist the woman throughout her pregnancy and in childbirth. The birth of twins is treated with special attention, requiring taboos on the part of the parents. Only obscene dancing and foul language by neighbors lifts the burden of giving birth to twins, which is believed to be the result of evil spirits. Babies and children are considered to be vulnerable to the "evil eye" and frequently wear amulets to protect them from evil glances.

Adolescence is a time of preparation for marriage and family life. Traditionally, girls obtained tattoos for their backs and had their ears pierced for earrings. Adornment also included armlets and bands for the waist, wrist, and ankles. Girls spent time in peer groups where considerable conversation was centered around boys and their personal attributes. Sex education was in the hands of older women, who gave advice in a communal sleeping hut used by teenage girls. Lovers sometimes made secret arrangements to meet near these huts, although premarital pregnancy was strictly forbidden. Nowadays, for education, neighborhood and boarding schools have replaced communal sleeping huts and elders, although sex education is not taught in these schools. Perhaps for this reason, teenage pregnancies are thought to be a major social problem in contemporary Luoland by most elder Luo. Now, as previously, adolescent boys enjoy more freedom from adult supervision than girls. Consequently, responsibility for teenage pregnancy falls entirely on the shoulders of girls, who generally leave school should they become pregnant.

Adults wishing to contribute to the continuation of Luo traditions maintain a rigorous involvement in the social life of their communities. For this reason, there is hearty attendance at ritual occasions, such as weddings or funerals of members of the family. Since there are no initiation ceremonies in earlier stages of the life cycle, the funeral serves as the most important symbol for family and community identity. Burials must take place in Luoland, irrespective of where a person may have lived during his or her adult years. Several years ago, a national event in Kenya centered around the death and burial of a prominent Luo man. Although he was an attorney and was married to a non-Luo woman in Nairobi, Mr. Otieno was buried in his home area against the wishes of his wife. She wanted him to be buried in Nairobi where they had lived. Mr. Otieno's clan elders, however, claimed his body for burial in Luoland because it was believed that only there could the proper rituals be performed so that his ancestor spirit could rest in peace. For example, the directional orientation of the body in the grave pertains to clan origins and migrations. The grave must be dug by a male adult related to the deceased by blood. The Otieno matter received serious discussion in the Kenya national media as it worked its way through the court system. The Kenya Supreme Court decided that the clan elders had prior rights over Mr. Otieno's body and ruled that he must be buried in Luoland. This case symbolizes the significance of sacred land, community membership, and spiritual continuity after death with clan and family.

8 INTERPERSONAL RELATIONS

Social relations among the Luo indicate a number of underlying principles from the past that continue to be very strong in present-day social life. These principles revolve around kinship, gender, and age. The Luo have what can be called a "segmentary lineage" form of social organization. This means that Luo are organized into more or less maximal and minimal kinship groups that are like the branches of a vine. Descent is traced through only the male sex (one's father) to reckon relatives from near to distant kinfolk, who align themselves with and against other such groupings for purposes of exchange, marriage, and political alliance. There is a strong emphasis in this system on the male gender, through which both men and women are placed within the kinship system. Names are received through the male line, and after marriage women go to reside in the homesteads of their husbands. Nevertheless, women are not without power and influence in this "segmentary patrilineal" system. For example, as a wife of a patrilineage, a woman builds up alliances over time for her husband's family by maintaining strong relationships after her marriage with her brothers and sisters who live at her birthplace or elsewhere. It is expected that after marriage a woman will bear children for her husband's patrilineage. It is for this reason that bride-wealth is given by her husband and his lineage mates to her family in exchange for her hand in marriage. It is this bride-wealth that has contributed to the woman's capacity to maintain warm ties throughout her life in her own birth family, which she left behind after marriage.

By having children, a woman greatly enhances her power and influence within the lineage of her husband. As the children grow older, they take special care of her interests. Perhaps as many as 30% of Luo homesteads are polygynous (in which a man has more than one wife). This contributes to solidarity between a mother and her children, and between children born of the same mother, within the context of polygynous extended families. In such families children have different mothers and a common father. Nevertheless, polygyny is commonly accepted by both men and women, provided traditional ideas and regulations are maintained. This includes, for example, a special recognition for the first wife or "great wife," whose house and granary are located prominently at the back of the homestead opposite the main gate. Subsequent wives have homes alternatively to her right and left in the order of their marriage. Sons are provided with homes adjacent to the main gate of the compound in the order of their birth. The common father for the polygynous extended family maintains a homestead for himself near the center of the compound. His own brothers, if they have not yet formed their own homesteads, reside on the edge of the compound near its center. As Luo become wealthy in Luoland or elsewhere, it is common for them to build a large house for their mother. This is especially necessary if she is a "great wife," as it is considered improper for younger wives to have larger homes than wives more senior to themselves.

The spatial ecology of the polygynous homestead symbolizes the significance of age-grading in social relations. Brothers are ranked in the homestead, and co-wives are differentiated by their age. Children are commonly reared by their older siblings who are nurses to them, carrying them about and singing lullabies to them. Male elders have a prominent place in the community. They are significant players in the politics of marriage and family alliances. This is enhanced by their control over cattle, land, and other resources. Elders are indispensable for rituals that center around important community events, such as weddings and funerals.

Visiting and being visited is the major source of pleasure for the Luo. The social principles of age, kinship, and gender obligations impose a heavy schedule of ritual obligations on Luo, irrespective of their residence. Rituals center around sickness and death, stages in the life of children, marriages, and succession to leadership in lineage and clan groupings. Attendance at funerals is a significant obligation for all Luo. There is a constant movement between Nairobi and Luoland for attendance at funerals. A powerful, prominent man or woman, for example, in Nairobi may be but a child while visiting home, where he or she behaves with great deference to Luo senior in age or to families where there is a relationship of respect based on marriage ties. At funerals, Luo consume large amounts of meat, beer, and soft drinks and socialize with friends, relatives, and members of the opposite sex. Funerals last for four days for a male and three days for a female. After the burial and expression of grief through orations and viewing of the body, there is a period of feasting and celebration. Visitors come from far and wide and are housed around the compound of the deceased where he or she will be buried. This location and the duration of the ritual is an excellent opportunity for young people to meet and observe members of the opposite sex, or for elders to discuss marriage alliances that they might wish to promote. Dating may well follow initial meetings or deliberations at the funeral.

⁹ LIVING CONDITIONS

In rural areas, houses are of several types, based on wealth and degree of permanence. A common house is made of mud and wattle walls and thatched with grass. Another style includes mud and wattle walls, but its roof is made of corrugated sheets of metal. A more elaborate and permanent type of house is built of brick walls and a roof covered with iron sheets or tiles. Bricks, iron sheets, and tiles are all items of prestige, and their ownership symbolizes success in farming, animal husbandry, or some modern occupation, such as teaching, the ministry, or shop keeping. Homes vary in shape as well as size. Some homes of the old variety made of wattle and mud are circular. Those with more permanent materials tend to be rectangular. A prosperous man who is the head of a large extended family may have several wives whose homes are situated by their rank within a large circular homestead.

Luo living in Kisumu, the regional capital, or Nairobi have homes that vary according to their relative social status. Some Luo are numbered among the very elite Kenyans whose homes are very elaborate, with facilities for automobiles, sleeping accommodations for visiting relatives, and servant's quarters. Other less fortunate Luo are numbered among those who live in Nairobi's crowded slums where homes are quite temporary, made of wattle and mud and short-lived materials such as tin, paper, and plastic.

In Kisumu, a city of about 323,000 people, the bicycle is a very important means of transportation. Bikemen serve as taxis and carry traders and passengers throughout the town and region. Some of the bicycles have hoods on them. The *matatu*, or communal taxi, and public buses are other significant conveyances seen throughout the region. For those traveling the 500 km (310 mi) between Nairobi and Kisumu, there is daily train and air service, as well as frequent buses and taxis.

Because of their marginal position in the national economy, the Luo do not have a great deal of access to medical services. Moreover, their environment is hot and humid throughout much of the year, and they live in the low-elevation malarial zone in Kenya. Malaria is a major killer in Luoland. Children's diseases, such as *kwashiorkor* (a form of protein malnutrition), are a threat in those families without access to a balanced diet or knowledge about nutrition and health standards. Medical services are a mixture of socialist and capitalist principles. Kisumu, for example, has a large public hospital where services and medicine are free. In these hospitals, there is a frequent shortage of medicine and a perception that services are not as good as those in private hospitals where patients must pay to see a doctor or to purchase drugs. There is an emphasis on preventive medicine in villages, so that most rural communities have clinics with medical health workers who place a great deal of emphasis on sanitation, prenatal care, nutrition, and other practices known to reduce the risk of disease. There is some blending of indigenous and medical ideas about the origins of illness arising from spiritual causes, such as ancestors and witchcraft, and the more recent "germ theory of disease." Many Luo participate in a dual medical belief system for any particular ailment or other misfortune.

¹⁰ FAMILY LIFE

Marriage was traditionally considered to be the most significant event in the lives of both men and women. It was thought inappropriate for anyone to remain unmarried. This was so because of the significance of the value of community and communalism over the needs and rights of individuals considered apart from family concerns. In a society without industrial technology, where subsistence depended on human labor, it can be understood why large families were adaptive for the Luo. The system of polygyny worked to ensure that all people achieved a marital status. After the death of a woman's husband, she was "inherited" by her dead husband's brother. This custom, known as the *levirate*, guaranteed that a woman remained within the extended family of her husband. Her new husband took over all of the domestic roles of his dead brother. This custom is still widely practiced in Luoland and is the subject of heated debate between those favoring autonomy and individualism over and against those more traditionally inclined. Generally, churches with international ties, such as the Anglican CPK and the Roman Catholic Church, frown on the levirate, as do women with considerable formal education. The levirate receives support from independent churches and those men and women for whom traditional values take priority in their lives. They note, for example, that in Dholuo the term for wife is "our wife," symbolizing that her marriage involves an entire family, not just herself.

The significance of bride-wealth is increasing, even among the educated. In this custom, members of the groom's family initiate a process of negotiation with the bride's family that may unfold over many years. Negotiations can be intense, and for this reason a "go-between," thought to be neutral to the interests of each family, is used. Luo believe that divorce cannot occur after bride-wealth has been exchanged and children have been born. Even if separation happens, the couple is still ideally considered to be married. Failure to have children, however, is thought to be the fault of the bride and, for this, she will be divorced or replaced by another wife. Cattle are the primary object of wealth given in bride-wealth. In determining the value of a prospective bride, her family takes into account her health, looks, and, nowadays, her level of formal education. Women with university degrees are expected to draw many cattle and they frequently, in spite of their high formal education and outward acceptance of nontraditional ideas, are offended if their suitor does not offer a big bride-wealth. Failure of men to raise a high bride-wealth presses many of them to propose elopement, a practice that is on the increase today.

A marriage custom that is now rarely practiced is referred to as *meko* ("catching"). In this practice, a woman is "dragged" by her husband's male relatives to his home, where the marriage ceremony occurs and the marriage is consummated. The timing of the meko depended on how much of the bride-price had been paid, such that it could be assumed that the marriage would, in fact, occur. Members of the girl's family, particularly her brothers, kept guard to "protect" her from being dragged. It is said that the bride was often secretly pleased with all of the attention from her brothers and her new husband and brothers-in-law. The last would thereafter refer to her as "our wife." There was, nevertheless, outward screaming and resistance on the part of the girl while being dragged.

Young people in Kenya still tend to marry within their own ethnic groups. Tribal elders frequently caution against "intertribal marriages." The more distant the ethnic group in space and customs from the Luo, the greater the cautionary warnings. For this reason, Luo intertribal marriage is most likely to occur with members from neighboring Baluya societies, which are Bantu. However, most Luo marry within their ethnic group.

¹¹ CLOTHING

Traditionally, the Luo wore minimal clothing. Animal hides were used to cover private parts, but there was no stigma associated with nudity. Today, clothing styles are largely European in origin and varies according to a person's social class and lifestyle preferences. It is not uncommon to see in remote rural areas people fashionably attired according to some of the latest tastes. In the past, for example, when platform shoes were common for women, or today when jeans are popular among teenagers, these fashions were and are popular in remote areas. Nevertheless, for those Luo living in Nairobi, for example, there is a tendency for their apparel to be very cosmopolitan by rural standards and no different from clothing styles as seen in New York or Paris.

In rural areas, most people dress according to their work routines. For example, women while farming or attending market wear loose-fitting dresses made of solid or printed cotton fabric. Wearing sandals or going barefoot is typical while working. Men wear jeans as work pants while farming. During the rainy season, the roads can become very muddy. Boots and umbrellas are especially prized by both men and women. These days, there is a strong market in second-hand clothing, making available to even the poorer families slacks, dresses, coats, undergarments, sweaters, shoes, handbags, belts, and other items. Luo enjoy dressing up for funerals and weddings and are considered to be very fashionable throughout Kenya.

¹² FOOD

Agriculture is very significant and is a primary responsibility of women. They tend to use hand hoes while men use ox plows. The primary crops are maize, millet, and sorghum. While coffee, tobacco, cotton, and sugarcane are important cash crops, cattle, sheep, goats, and chickens are also very significant, especially cattle, which are used for bride-wealth. Fish from Lake Victoria and streams are important, especially tilapia. Many foods are purchased, such as sugar, bread, and butter, which are consumed with tea on a daily basis, a custom known as "tea time" and derived from the British colonial era that ended in 1963. Tea may also be taken with cakes and occurs in mid-morning and late afternoon.

The staple food eaten several times per day is *ugali*. This is made from maize meal stirred in boiling water until it becomes a thick and smooth porridge. Ugali is always taken with an accompanying sauce, such as meats and stews. Greens *(sukumawiki)* are also frequently eaten with ugali. Maize, popular throughout Kenya, is frequently sold for money. This has led many families, when pressed economically for money for school fees or clothes, to sell their maize. For this reason, there is a periodic famine throughout Luoland that occurs every year during the long, dry season prior to harvest.

The Luo had no ideas about private ownership of land prior to the colonial period, which spans the 20th century. They followed communal principles that guaranteed that everyone was assured access to land for cultivation. Women did not inherit land but had access to the land of their husband and their own unmarried sons. Explorers who arrived in western Kenya before colonialism noted that food was very abundant throughout Luoland. With private property, however, it became increasingly impossible for the land to be made available to those without money. Land alienation and a rise in population, which in Kenya is one of the highest in the world, have caused periodic hunger for many people. Presently, there is a stigma associated with selling land; for this reason, money obtained through its sale is considered by many Luo to be "bitter"; that is, it is money that is obtained through some injustice. This money must be kept apart from transactions involving livestock and bride-wealth. Also considered taboo is money obtained through the selling of roosters. Luo homes are considered incomplete without a rooster, which symbolizes "maleness," especially fertility. After the funeral of a man, a rooster is taken from his house and eaten by his relatives. This signifies the end of his homestead. When a new homestead is founded, a man is given a rooster from his father's home.

¹³ EDUCATION

Kenya introduced a new system of education in the 1980s known as the "8-4-4 system," modeled after the American system. Luo now go eight years to primary school, four years to secondary school, and four years to college. There is the desire to make secondary school more practical than it was under the British system in which students attended primary school, followed by high school with stressful and consequential 0-level and A-level exams that determined a student's vocational placement for life. Only those with the highest scores on the A-level could proceed on to the university. The British system emphasized performance on exams that often had questions reflecting European rather than African content. The new system places more emphasis on school performance and subject matter that is more African.

Luo attend technical, secretarial, nursing, computer, teacher training, and business schools after high school as alternatives to the university. There is a new university at Maseno near Kisumu that will provide easy access for those wishing to attend university. Education is highly valued among the Luo, and they are well represented in the professions, especially university and higher-educational institutions. Nevertheless, there still remains a high level of illiteracy, especially among females. For example, in polygynous marriages there is a strong tendency for younger wives to be more educated than their older counterparts. This pattern reflects recent changes where more Luo are now recognizing the importance of sending girls to school.

The Luo success in academic pursuits may well be related to the value given to "wisdom" in their culture. Modern philosophers have applied the term "sage philosophy" to describe individuals among the Luo who, in the past and present, excel in teachings and reflections on the human condition. The Luo society is an open one. All individuals are encouraged to express themselves publicly. "Truth" *(adier)* is expressed through songs and folklore by respected elder men and women who are acknowledged as wise. Most respected, however, is the *japaro*, a term that translates into English as "thinker," who is consulted on all matters of interest to community welfare. The most famous sage until his death in the mid-1990s was Mr. Oginga Odinga, a widely respected elder and former vice-president of Kenya. He spoke out publicly during colonialism and in post-colonial politics against what he considered to be injustices. In his writings he emphasized Luo values for communal welfare and concern for preservation of traditional values. His death was deeply felt by most Luo and many other Kenyans as well.

14 CULTURAL HERITAGE

The Luo consider their entire traditional way of life to be an important community resource. There is a great deal of disagreement over what should be preserved and what should change. Customs centering around marriage and gender relations are hotly debated. It is felt that many practices should be retained from this area of life as well as from music, dance, and folklore. The Luo, however, did not develop an elaborate material culture given that they were, for much of their history, primarily a pastoral population and therefore on the move in search of pasture. They did, however, excel in the verbal arts and philosophical arts associated with successful communal life.

Songs are very popular today as in the past. Musicians nowadays praise and lament political, generational, economic, and cultural contradictions in contemporary life. Luo devote much time to listening to music and purchasing records, tapes, and CDs. Christian church music is also a form of entertainment. It is said that the short story was a well-developed art among the Luo in traditional times. Such stories were often accompanied by music. Perhaps because of the importance given to the short story in Luo culture, the most important short-story writer in Kenya today is the Luo woman, Ms. Grace Ogot. In her stories she includes many traditional themes as well as modern dilemmas, such as an educated woman living in a polygynous arrangement. Some of her best-known stories are, "The Other Woman," "The Fisherman," and "The Honorable Minister."

15 WORK

The most notable fact about the Luo agrarian economy is that women play the primary role in subsistence farming. Before the introduction of the modern money economy, the garden was the centerpiece of the women's world of work. Industrious women could amass considerable wealth by exchanging their garden produce for animals, handicrafts, pots, and baskets. Presently, there continues to be a very strong vocabulary involving farming in the Dholuo language. For example, terms distinguish the relative size of gardens, the conditions of the soil, and the quality of the landscape. There is also a rich vocabulary of farm activities. These include terms for clearing, digging, planting by scattering or placing seeds into holes, weeding, reweeding, and harvesting. Each of these terms has many constituent terms to cover fine points of variation. A complicated vocabulary also exists for farm instruments. The crops themselves are described in great detail, as are troublesome weeds. For example, concerning maize, some of the terms are: *oduma* (white maize), *nyamula* (yellow maize), *oking* (fine grain maize), and *obabari* (bigger, not-so-shapely maize grain and cobs).

A young girl is expected to assist her mother and her mother's co-wives in farming land owned by her father, brothers, and paternal uncles. Even though a girl may go to school and rise to a prominent position in society, there is often still a strong association with the land and digging. Many Luo living in Nairobi, for example, practice "urban agriculture." When returning home to the rural areas on vacation, women frequently "dig" to get vegetables to bring with them back to the city.

Men are preoccupied with livestock and have mastered an impressive vocabulary to differentiate among them. It is said that men spend a great deal of their time in "social labor" concerned with placing their cattle in good social contexts, such as bride-wealth exchanges, trading partnerships, and commercial sales. In the modern economy, cattle and goats have taken on monetary value as well as being items of social prestige in and of themselves. Men, as compared to women, have the major control over animals and those crops that are primarily cash crops. In sum, the Luo idea that work should be divided according to the principles of age and gender are still evident.

16 SPORTS

The Luo are participants in all of the major national sports currently played in Kenya. One sport, however, that receives a great deal of support is soccer. The soccer club known as Gor Mahia (Gor Mahia, like Ramogi and Lwanda Magere, was a great ancestor in Luo history) is Luo and symbolizes success for the ethnic group when they are victorious on the field. Some other ethnic groups support their own soccer teams, too. Secondary schools provide an assortment of sports for young people, giving them an opportunity to engage in competitive games such as track-and-field and soccer. Children enjoy games in the village, such as racing, wrestling, and soccer. Some boys who live near the lake are good swimmers.

17 ENTERTAINMENT AND RECREATION

Childhood play activities for girls include grinding soil on a flattened stone in imitation of adults who grind grains. Girls play "babies" with dolls made from clay or maize cobs in imitation of their mothers or child nurses who care for them. Female names are given to the dolls. Girls and boys imitate funeral ceremonies by mourning over the "death" of a playmate. Boys and girls play hide-and-seek together, and "house" by constructing small domiciles modeled after adult huts. Girls play *kora* with pieces of broken pottery or stones. In this game, stones are collected in the palm then thrown into the air. The main purpose is that more than one of the stones thrown into the air must come to rest on the back of the hand. As children reach middle childhood, between 6 and 10 years of age, separate play groups are formed by gender. Now girls spend more time at home caring for younger siblings and assisting in household duties and gardening. Boys have more freedom and combine play activities with responsibilities for herding and care of animals. One game in particular played by children and adults is *bao,* the name of a board game played widely throughout Africa. This game involves trying to place seeds on the opponent's side of the board while he or she attempts to defend against this.

Entertainment is now available through radio and television. In Luoland, programs are provided in KiSwahili, English, and Dholuo on the radio. Virtually all homes have radios, which are a significant source not only of entertainment in stories and music but also of education for health and national development. Books and printed media have now largely replaced public oratory as a means of entertainment. Nevertheless, visiting is a special joy that can be characterized as socially lively with lots of animated discussion. The verbally adroit person is still widely admired and respected.

Birthday parties are now much more important than they were in the past, when individuals did not reckon their age in years. Parents try to make their children's birthdays special with a birthday cake, cards, and gifts. Weddings and funerals, as in the past, are still major forms of entertainment for old and young alike. Church groups, clubs, women's organizations, and schools are important organizations for their members' social calendars.

¹⁸ FOLK ART, CRAFTS, AND HOBBIES

See "Entertainment and Recreation."

¹⁹ SOCIAL PROBLEMS

Luo consider their most pressing social problem to be their perceived isolation from Kenya national politics. Kenya today is characterized by a multi-party democracy. One of the consequences of the multiparty system in Kenya is that there is a tendency for members of a specific ethnic group to align themselves with a given party. This relationship between ethnicity and politics is, of course, not unique to Kenya and is found in most multi-ethnic nation-states practicing democracy. The Luo dominate within the Ford-Kenya party, one of the several opposition parties presently in Kenya. Within the Ford-Kenya party, there are Luo factions that vie for party leadership. During the colonial era and since independence, the Luo have been somewhat isolated from national leadership even though they are the second-largest ethnic group in the country. The first vice-president of Kenya, and the most significant politician in post-colonial Luo politics, was Oginga Odinga. He was instrumental in initiating the multi-party movement in Kenya in the early 1990s, after his isolation (since independence) from participation in national governments by those in power. It is felt that his isolation was intentional by those seeking to keep the Luo out of power. Another prominent Luo politician was Tom Mboya, widely admired around the world. He was killed by an assassin's bullet in 1969 while serving as the Minister of Economic Planning and Development and Secretary General of the Ruling KANU Party. His death prevented him from succeeding President Kenyatta as the president along the lines felt likely to have occurred by his numerous supporters. His death was considered by many Luo to have been politically motivated.

Specific social problems follow from what the Luo consider to be marginal political participation in Kenya. It is believed that economic development in Western Kenya is low as part of a concerted effort to isolate them from development projects. It is, in fact, true that the districts where Luo live in the west are marginal on most indicators of development. Roads are usually badly in need of repair, rates of HIV infection are comparatively high, food shortages are frequent, and infant mortality is among the highest in the country. Typical of this situation is that, although Kisumu is on the shores of Lake Victoria, nevertheless it suffers from an acute water shortage. Moreover, the municipal water supply is so badly treated that residents suffer from water-borne diseases, such as typhoid fever, amoebic dysentery, common dysentery, and diarrhea. Typically, tourism has bypassed Luoland and Lake Victoria in favor of Nairobi and the coastal area of Kenya. This is so even though Lake Victoria has many features of interest to tourists such as hippopotami, freshwater fish, and cultural attractions. All in all, there is little doubt that the facts of marginalization are difficult to deny, in spite of differences of opinion over their causes.

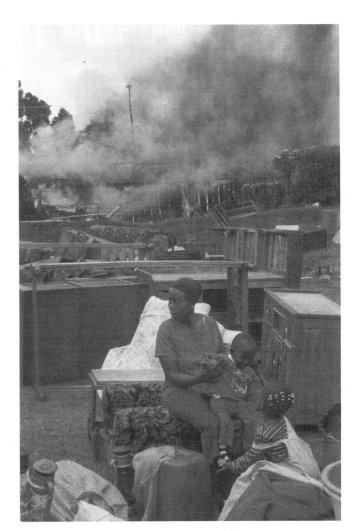

A woman from the Luo tribe sits with two children on some of the belongings they salvaged from their home. Members of the Luo tribe set fire to homes alleging they were owned by a Kikuyu. At least ten lives were lost in renewed political and ethnic clashes in western Kenya in early 2008. (Yasuyoshi Chiba/ AFP/Getty Images)

²⁰ GENDER ISSUES

Just like their neighboring Luhya, the Luo people follow a patrilineal system of kinship. Gender roles are assigned to men and women in ways that create, reinforce, and perpetuate the relationships in which males are viewed as superior and women are viewed as subordinate. Patriarchy in the Luo context has traditionally ensured that women cannot pose a challenge to male dominance. Luo boys and girls are conditioned to behave in certain ways and to play different roles in society. The Luo people have distinct cultural practices governing the gender division of labor, marriage, and women's access to resources. For example, women are supposed to do most of the domestic chores, such as fetching firewood, cooking, taking care of children, and also farm work. Because of the high rate of male out-migration, an estimated 30–60% of households are headed by females, who have to single-handedly farm their fields in the absence of men.

Kenya as a whole ranks poorly in the Gender Gap Index in terms of women's economic participation, educational attainment, health, political empowerment, maternity and childbearing, earnings, and basic rights. The AIDS epidemic has also taken a toll among both men and women in Luoland, especially in the main urban center, Kisumu. In short, gender empowerment and equality constitute the major gender issues among the Luo.

[21] BIBLIOGRAPHY

Africa News Online. "Lucrative Bicycle-Taxi Industry Losing Its Lustre." All Africa Press Service, 1996.

———. "Kisumu's Water Paradox a Boon to Illegal Dealers." All Africa Press Service, 1996.

Liyong, Taban lo. *Popular Culture of East Africa*. Nairobi: Longman Kenya, 1972.

Mwakikagile, Godfrey. *Ethnic Politics in Kenya and Nigeria. Huntington*, New York: Nova Science Publishers, Inc., 2001.

Mwakikagile, Godfrey. *Kenya: Identity of A Nation*. Pretoria, South Africa: New Africa Press, 2008.

Ocholla-Ayayo, A. B. C. *Traditional Ideology and Ethics Among the Southern Luo*. Uppsala, Sweden: Institute of African Studies, 1976.

Ogot, Bethwell. *History of the Southern Luo*. Nairobi: East African Publishing House, 1967.

Ogot, Grace. *The Other Woman*. Nairobi: Transafrica Publishers, Ltd., 1976.

Ominde, Simeon H. *The Luo Girl*. Nairobi: East African Literature Bureau, 1952.

Omondi, Lucia N. "The Role of Language in Rural Development." In *Groundwork*, edited by Shanyisa A. Khasiani. Nairobi: Acts Press, 1992.

Onyango-Ogutu, B., and A. A. Roscoe. *Keep My Words*. Nairobi: Heinemann Kenya, Ltd., 1974.

Oruka, H. Odera. *Oginga Odinga: His Philosophy and Beliefs*. Nairobi: Initiatives Publishers, 1992.

Shipton, Parker. *Bitter Money: Cultural Economy and Some African Meanings of Forbidden Commodities*. Washington, D.C.: American Anthropological Association, 1989.

The Daily Nation. *S. M. Otieno: Kenya's Unique Burial Saga*. Nairobi: A Nation Newspapers Publication, 1988.

—revised by E. Kalipeni)

MAASAI

PRONUNCIATION: MAH-sigh
LOCATION: Kenya, Tanzania
POPULATION: Approximately 880,000
LANGUAGE: Maa (Olmaa)
RELIGION: Traditional beliefs
RELATED ARTICLES: Vol. 1: Kenyans; Tanzanians

[1] INTRODUCTION

The Maasai are thought of as the quintessential cattle herders of Africa, yet they have not always been herders, nor are they all today. Because of population growth, development schemes, and land shortages, cattle raising is in decline. However, cattle still represent "the breath of life" for many Maasai. When given the chance, they choose herding above all other livelihoods. For many Westerners, the Maasai are Hollywood's noble savage—fierce, proud, handsome, graceful of bearing, and elegantly tall. Hair smeared red with ocher, they either carry spears or stand on one foot tending cattle. These depictions oversimplify the changes in Maasai life during the 20th century. Today, Maasai cattle herders may also be growing maize or wheat, rearing Guinea fowl, raising ostriches, or may be involved in tourism and ecosystem management.

In precolonial times, Africans, Arabs, and European explorers considered the Maasai formidable warriors for their conquests of neighboring peoples and their resistance to slavery. Caravan traders traveling from the coast to Uganda crossed Maasailand with trepidation. However, in 1880–81, when the British inadvertently introduced rinderpest (a cattle disease), the Maasai lost 80% of their stock. The colonizers further disrupted the life of the Maasai by moving them to a reserve in southern Kenya. While the British encouraged them to adopt European ways, they also advised them to retain their traditions. These contradictions resulted in benign neglect and allowed the Maasai to develop almost on their own. However, drought, famine, cattle diseases, and intratribal warfare in the 19th century greatly weakened the Maasai and nearly annihilated certain tribes.

Since Kenyan and Tanzanian independence in the 1960s, land tenure has changed dramatically. Modern ranching, wheat schemes, and demarcated grazing boundaries in the Maasai district are becoming common. Wage and cash economies are replacing barter. Consequently, the Maasai have begun to integrate themselves into the modern economies and mainstream societies of Kenya and Tanzania, albeit with considerable reluctance.

[2] LOCATION AND HOMELAND

The Maasai are thought to have originated in the Upper Nile Valley. Their myths speak of ascending from a broad and deep crater bounded on all sides by a steep escarpment. By the 1600s they had begun migrating with their herds into the vast arid, savannah-like region of East Africa straddling the Kenya-Tanzania border. Presently, their homeland is bounded by Lake Victoria to the west and Mt. Kilimanjaro to the east. Maasailand extends some 500 km (310 mi) from north to south and about 300 km (186 mi) at its widest point.

In 1994 estimates placed the Maasai population inside Kenya's borders at 450,000 inhabitants, and 430,000 Maasai living in Tanzania (1993 estimate). The greater Maasai nation comprises several cultural groups, which the Maasai have absorbed through conquest or assimilation. Besides their rural lifestyle, their language—Olmaa—unites them.

³ LANGUAGE

The Maasai are speakers of the Maa language, which is spoken as well by the Samburu and the Chamus living in central Kenya. Maa is a Nilotic language whose origins have been traced to the east of present-day Juba in southern Sudan. More than 20 variants of Maa exist, grouped into a northern cluster and a southern cluster. The Maasai belong to the southern group and refer to their tongue as Olmaa.

⁴ FOLKLORE

Maasai legends and folktales tell much about the origin of present-day Maasai beliefs, including their ascent from a crater, the emergence of the first Maasai prophet-magician (Laibon), the killing of an evil giant (Oltatuani) who raided Maasai herds, and the deception by Olonana of his father to obtain the blessing reserved for his older brother, Senteu (a legend similar to the Biblical story of Jacob and Esau).

One myth of origin reveals much about present-day Maasai relations between the sexes. It holds that the Maasai are descended from two equal and complementary tribes, one consisting strictly of females, and the other of males. The women's tribe, the Moroyok, raised antelopes, including the eland, which the Maasai claim to have been the first species of cattle. Instead of cattle, sheep, and goats, the women had herds of gazelles. Zebras transported their goods during migrations, and elephants were their devoted friends, tearing down branches and bringing them to the women for home and corral building. The elephants also swept the antelope corrals clean. However, while the women bickered and quarreled, their herds escaped. Even the elephants left them because they could not satisfy the women with their work.

According to the same myth, the Morwak—the men's tribe—raised cattle, sheep, and goats. The men occasionally met women in the forest for trysts. The children from these unions would live with their mothers, but the boys would join their fathers when they grew up. When the women lost their herds, they went to live with the men, and, in doing so, gave up their freedom and their equal status. From that time, they depended on men, had to work for them, and were subject to their authority.

⁵ RELIGION

In contrast to the predominantly Christian populations of Kenya and Tanzania, the Maasai traditionally place themselves at the center of their universe as God's chosen people. Like other African religions, that of the Maasai holds that one high God (Enkai) created the world, forming three groups of people. The first were the Torrobo (Okiek pygmies), a hunting and gathering people of small stature to whom God gave honey and wild animals for sustenance. The second were the neighboring Kikuyu, cultivators to whom God gave seed and grain. The third were the Maasai, to whom He gave cattle, which came to earth sliding down a long rope linking heaven and earth. While the pygmies were destined to endure bee stings, and the Kikuyu

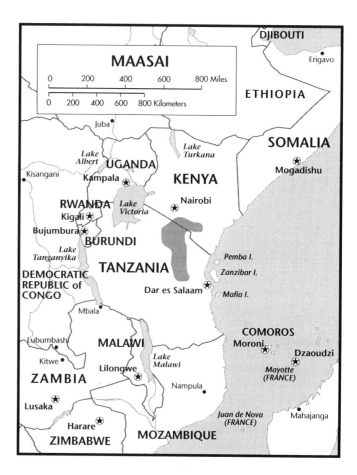

famines and floods, the Maasai received the noble gift of raising cattle. A Torrobo, jealous of the Maasai's gift of cattle, cut the "umbilical cord" between heaven and earth. For many Maasai, the center of their world remains their cattle, which furnish food, clothing, and shelter.

⁶ MAJOR HOLIDAYS

The traditional Maasai calendar has no designated holidays. It is divided into 12 months belonging to three main seasons: *Nkokua* (the long rains), *Oloirurujuruj* (the drizzling season), and *Oltumuret* (the short rains). The names of the months are very descriptive. For example, the second month of the drizzling season is *Kujorok*, meaning "The whole countryside is beautifully green, and the pasture lands are likened to a hairy caterpillar."

Maasai ceremonial feasts for circumcision, excision, and marriage offer occasions for festive community celebrations, which may be considered holidays. As the Maasai are integrated into modern Kenyan and Tanzanian life, they also participate in secular state holidays.

⁷ RITES OF PASSAGE

Life for the Maasai is a series of conquests and tests involving the endurance of pain. For men, there is a progression from childhood to warriorhood to elderhood. At the age of four, a child's lower incisors are taken out with a knife. Young boys test their will by burning themselves on their arms and legs with hot coals. As they grow older, they submit to tattooing on the stomach and the arms, enduring hundreds of small cuts into the skin.

Ear piercing for both boys and girls comes next. The cartilage of the upper ear is pierced with hot iron. When this heals, a hole is cut in the ear lobe and gradually enlarged by inserting rolls of leaves or balls made of wood or mud. Nowadays plastic film canisters may serve this purpose. The bigger the hole in the lobe, the better. Those dangling to the shoulders are considered ideal.

Circumcision (for boys) and excision (for girls) is the next stage, and the most important event in a young Maasai's life. It is a father's ultimate duty to ensure that his children undergo this rite. The family invites relatives and friends to witness the ceremonies, which may be held in special ceremonial villages called *imanyat*. The *imanyat* dedicated to circumcision of boys are called *nkang oo ntaritik* ("villages of little birds"). After completing the prerequisite requirements, the young warriors establish a village camp some miles away, called a *manyata*, where they will live with their mothers and sisters.

Circumcision itself involves much physical pain and tests a youth's courage. If they flinch during the act, boys will bring shame and dishonor to themselves and their family. At a minimum, the members of their age group will ridicule them and they will pay a fine of one head of cattle. However, if a boy shows great bravery, he receives gifts of cattle and sheep.

Girls must endure an even longer and more painful ritual, which prepares them for childbearing. (Girls who become pregnant before excision are banished from the village and stigmatized throughout their lives.) After passing this test of courage, women say they are afraid of nothing. The guests celebrate the successful completion of these rites by drinking great quantities of mead and dancing. The boys are now ready to become warriors, and the girls ready to bear a new generation of warriors. In a few months, the young woman's future husband will come to pick her up and bring her with him to live with his family.

After passing the tests of childhood and circumcision, boys become young warriors and must fulfill a civic requirement similar to military service. They live for periods of up to several months in the bush, where they learn to overcome pride, egotism, and selfishness. They share their most prized possessions, their cattle, with other members of the community. However, they must also spend time in the village, where they sacrifice their cattle for ceremonies and offer gifts of cattle to new households. This stage of development matures a warrior and teaches him *nkaniet* (respect for others), and he learns how to contribute to the welfare of his community. The stage of "young warriorhood" ends with the *eunoto* rite, with which a man ends his periodic sojourns in the bush and returns to his village, putting his acquired wisdom to use for the good of the community.

8 INTERPERSONAL RELATIONS

To control the vices of pride, jealousy, and selfishness, each child belongs to an "age set" from birth and must obey the rules governing relationships within the set, between sets, and between the sexes. Warriors, for example, must share a girlfriend with at least one of their age-group companions. All Maasai of the same sex are considered equal within their age group.

Many tensions exist between children and adults, elders and warriors, and men and women, but the Maasai control these with taboos. A daughter, for example, must not be present while her father is eating. Only non-excised girls may accompany warriors into their forest havens, where they partake of meat (*see* Food). Though the younger warriors may wish to dominate their communities, they must follow rules and respect their elders' advice.

9 LIVING CONDITIONS

Maasai living conditions may seem primitive, but the Maasai are generally proud of their unencumbered lifestyle and do not seek to replace it with urban amenities. Nevertheless, the old ways are undergoing transformation. Formerly, cattle hides were used to make walls and roofs of temporary homes during migrations. They were also used to sleep on. Permanent and semi-permanent homes resembling igloos were built of sticks and supple branches plastered with mud, and with cow dung on the roofs. They were windowless and leaked considerably. Nowadays, tin roofs and other amenities are fairly common replacements for these Spartan dwellings.

Generally, the Maasai are remarkably healthy people. Their resistance to disease stems in part from their use of medicinal herbs and bark and their dietary discipline, which includes judicious use of cattle fat. Babies receive a spoon of beef or sheep's fat daily from birth to weaning, which strengthens them and immunizes them from deadly diseases. In some Maasai groups, when a cow dies of anthrax, husbands of pregnant women give their wives a piece of the infected animal's tumor, which inoculates the fetus. The mother is likely to survive because she also was inoculated before birth. This allows the Maasai to eat the meat of sick cattle, including those that have died of anthrax, which is normally fatal to humans. Warriors regularly consume a soup made of medicinal bark to thwart common ailments.

Today a few paved trunk roads and many passable dirt roads make Maasailand accessible. The Maasai travel by bus and bush taxi much like their fellow citizens when they need to cover sizable distances.

10 FAMILY LIFE

The Maasai are a patriarchal society. Men typically speak for women and make decisions in the family. Male elders decide community matters. Until the age of seven, boys and girls are raised together. Mothers remain close to their children, especially their sons, throughout life. Once circumcised, sons usually move away from their father's village, but they still heed his advice. Girls learn to fear and respect their fathers and must never be near them when they eat.

One's age-mates are considered extended family and required to help each other. Agemates share nearly everything, even their wives. Girls are often promised in marriage long before they are of age. However, even long-term arrangements are subject to veto by male family members.

Once married, a woman leaves her family to live with her husband, automatically becoming the wife of her husband's age-mates, too. Thus, a warrior may arrive in a village, ask for a man of his age group, and oblige him to find other lodgings for the night. The wife receives the stranger with hospitality, takes care of his staff, knife, and other effects, and offers him milk and the bed across from hers. She may agree to sleep with him,

Maasai at a wedding in Kenya. (David Johnson)

but she has the right to refuse. Children from these unions belong to the woman and her husband.

11 CLOTHING

Maasai apparel varies by period, age, sex, and place. Traditionally, shepherds wore capes made from calf hides, and women wore capes of sheepskin. The Maasai decorated these with glass beads. In the 1960s, the Maasai began to replace animal-skin capes with bolts of commercial cotton cloth. Women tied these around their shoulders in different ways as capes (*shuka*) and perhaps over a dress or tied around the waist. The Maasai color of preference is red, although black, blue, striped, and red checkered cloth is also worn, as are multicolored African designs. Elderly women still prefer red, dying their own cloth with ocher. Until recently, men and women wore sandals cut from cow hides, which now are increasingly replaced by tire-strip sandals and plastic sandals and shoes.

Young women and girls, and especially young warriors, spend much time primping, and styles change with successive age groups. The Maasai excel in designing jewelry, and they decorate their bodies through such practices as tattooing, head shaving, and hair styling with ocher and sheep's fat, which they also smear on their bodies. A variety of colors are used to create body art. Women and girls wear elaborate bib-like bead necklaces, as well as headbands, and earrings, which are both colorful and strikingly intricate. When ivory was plentiful, warriors wore ivory bands on their upper arms much like the ancient Egyptians. Jewelry plays an important role in courtship.

12 FOOD

As with shelter and clothing, the Maasai depend on cattle for both food and cooking utensils. Cattle ribs make stirring sticks, spatulas, and spoons. The horns are used as butter dishes and the large horns as cups for drinking mead.

The traditional Maasai diet consists of six basic foods: meat, blood, milk, fat, honey, and tree bark. Wild game (except the eland), chicken, fish, and salt are ritually forbidden. Allowable meats include roasted and boiled beef, goat, and mutton. Both fresh and curdled milk are drunk, and blood is drunk at special times: after giving birth, after circumcision and excision, or while recovering from an accident. It may be tapped warm from the throat of a cow, or drunk in its coagulated form. It can also be mixed with fresh or soured milk or drunk with therapeutic bark soups (*motori*). It is from blood that the Maasai obtain salt, a necessary ingredient in the human diet. People of delicate health and babies eat liquid sheep's fat to gain strength.

Honey is obtained from the Torrobo tribe and is a prime ingredient in mead, a fermented beverage that only the elders may drink. In recent times, fermented maize with millet yeast or a mixture of fermented sugar and baking powder have become the primary ingredients of mead.

The Maasai generally take two meals a day, in the morning and at night, following an unusual pattern dictated by the dietary prohibition on mixing milk and meat. They drink milk for ten days—as much as they want morning and night—and eat meat and bark soup for several days in between. Some exceptions to this regime exist. Children and old people may eat corn meal or rice porridge and drink tea with sugar. For warriors, however, the sole source of true nourishment is cattle. They consume meat in their forest hideaways (olpul), usually near a shady stream far from the observation of women. Their preferred meal is a mixture of meat, blood, and fat (munono), which is thought to give great strength.

Many taboos govern Maasai eating habits. Men must not eat meat that has in any way been in contact with women or handled by an uncircumcised boy after it has been cooked. Older members do not eat meat belonging to younger ones unless they are "bribed" for the honor. A new husband does not eat his bride's food until she "bribes" him by giving him a heifer.

13 EDUCATION

There is a wide gap between Western schooling and Maasai traditional education, by which children and young adults learned to overcome fear, endure pain, and assume adult tasks. For example, despite the dangers of predators, snakes, and rogue elephants, boys would herd cattle alone with the blessing of their fathers. If they encountered a buffalo or lion, they were supposed to call for help. However, they sometimes reached the pinnacle of honor by killing lions on their own. Following such a display of courage, they became models for the other boys, and their heroics were likely to become immortalized in the songs of the women and girls.

Prior to independence, school participation gradually increased among the Maasai, but there were few practical rewards for formal education and therefore little incentive to send a child to school. Formal schooling was primarily of use to those involved in religion, agriculture, or politics. Since independence, as the traditional livelihood of the Maasai became less secure, school participation rates climbed dramatically.

More recently, there has been a concerted push by government and nongovernmental organizations (NGOs) to enroll Maasai children in schools and assimilate the Maasai into mainstream Kenyan and Tanzanian society. The elders, who have been at the forefront of resistance to change, fear that schools have become tools to strip the Maasai of traditional respect for and unity of their culture. Those who embrace modern education argue that the Maasai must adapt quickly or die.

14 CULTURAL HERITAGE

The Maasai have a rich collection of oral literature that includes myths, legends, folktales, riddles, and proverbs. These are passed down through the generations (see Folklore and Entertainment and recreation). The Maasai are also prolific composers. Women are seldom found at a loss for melodies and words when some heroic action by a warrior inspires praise. They also improvise teasing songs, work songs for milking and for plastering roofs, and songs with which to entreat their traditional god (Enkai) for rain and other needs.

15 WORK

Labor among traditional pastoral Maasai is clearly divided. The man's duty is to his cattle. He must protect them and find them the best pasturage possible and the best watering holes. Women raise children, maintain the home, cook, and do the milking. They also take care of calves and clean, sterilize and decorate calabashes (gourds). It is the women's prerogative to offer milk to the men and to visitors.

Children help parents with their tasks. A boy begins herding at the age of four by looking after lambs and young calves, and by the time he is 12, he may be able to care for cows and bulls and move sheep and cattle to new pastures. Similarly, the girls help their mothers with domestic chores such as drawing water, gathering firewood, and patching roofs. Nowadays, many Maasai perform a mixture of traditional and modern workforce labor, including ranching, conducting tourists to Maasai villages, and limited agriculture.

16 SPORTS

While Maasai may take part in soccer, volleyball, and basketball in school or in nontraditional settings, their own culture has little that resembles Western organized sports. Young children find time to join in games such as playing tag, but adults find little time for sports, or "horsing around." Warding off enemies and killing lions are sports in their own right.

17 ENTERTAINMENT AND RECREATION

Ceremonies such as the eunoto, when warriors return to their villages as mature men, offer occasions for sustained partying and much merriment. Ordinarily, however, recreation is much more subdued. After the men return to their camp from a day's herding, they typically tell stories of their exploits. Young girls sing and dance for the men. In the villages, elders enjoy inviting their age-mates to their houses or to rustic pubs (muratina manyatta) for a drink of beer.

18 FOLK ART, CRAFTS, AND HOBBIES

The Maasai make decorative bead jewelry for necklaces, earrings, head bands, and wrist and ankle bracelets. These are always fashionable, though styles change as age-groups invent new designs. It is possible for the astute observer to detect the year of a given piece by its age-group design. Maasai also excel in wood carvings, and increasingly produce tourist art as a supplementary source of income.

19 SOCIAL PROBLEMS

In the recent past, cattle theft and intertribal warfare were major social problems for the Maasai. Today, the main dilemma they face concerns adaptation to economic and social change. Key issues include land encroachment, formal schooling for children, jobs and skills development, and conserving traditional ways. Threats to their pastoral way of life have created a great deal of tension within the Maasai community, and in the foreseeable future, Maasai will struggle with the challenges of acculturation and assimilation. The Maasai may fear losing their children to Western schooling, but a modern education has increasingly become a necessity for the Maasai in order to remain competitive with their neighbors.

20 GENDER ISSUES

Male dominance in Maasai culture is enshrined in myths and folktales (see Folklore). The more benign aspects of this phenomenon are manifested in a traditional division of labor: women raise children, tend house, gather firewood, carry water, do the milking, cook (most foods) and serve guests. The taboos regarding what women can eat and do (see *Food*) are further indications of this subservience, while the woman's role in early marriage and her relationship to her husband's cohorts reveal how female submissiveness is embedded in Maasai thinking. Nonetheless, there is an abiding respect between men and women and boys and girls in Maasai culture, which has held the society together for centuries. As more Maasai children attend formal schools, and are exposed to ideas from outside the traditional sphere, gender relations will change. Whether they will reflect those of the broader Kenyan and Tanzanian societies around them, or whether they will take a different tack remains to be seen.

21 BIBLIOGRAPHY

Cronk, Lee. *From Mukogodo to Maasai: Ethnicity and Cultural Change in Kenya*. Cambridge, MA: Perseus Books, 2004.

Hughes, Lott. *Moving the Maasai: A Colonial Misadventure*. London: Palgrave Macmillan, 2006.

"Kenya." In *Africa South of the Sahara 2007*. London: Europa Publishers, 2008.

Saitoti, Tepilit Ole and Carol Beckwith. *Maasai*. New York: Abradale Press, 1990.

Sankan, S. S. Ole. "Colonial Education among the Kenyan Maasai, 1894–1962." Discussion Paper No. 4. Montreal: McGill University, 1986.

Spencer, Paul. *The Maasai of Matapato: A Study of Rituals of Rebellion*. Bloomington: Indiana University Press, 1988.

Talle, Aud. *Women at a Loss: Changes in Maasai Pastoralism and their Effects on Gender Relations*. Stockholm: University of Stockholm Press, 1988.

—by R. Groelsema

MALAGASY

PRONUNCIATION: mahl-uh-GAH-see
LOCATION: Madagascar
POPULATION: 20 million
LANGUAGE: Malagasy (Merina); French
RELIGION: Traditional beliefs; Christianity; Islam; animism

1 INTRODUCTION

The origins of the Malagasy people remain a mystery. Scholars believe the Malagasy are a kaleidoscopic mix of Indonesian, Malayo-Polynesian, and African descendants. It is not known where the original people, the *Vazimba*, came from, nor where they are today.

Supposedly, the Indonesians were the first arrivals. Then came the Arabs, the Southern Indians, and merchants from the Persian Gulf. South and East Africans followed, and eventually Europeans, starting with the Portuguese, then the Spanish, the British, and finally the French, who conquered the island in 1895.

Today, the Malagasy population of 20 million people is divided into 18 identifiable ethnic groups in addition to the Comorans, the Karane (Indo-Pakistan), and the Chinese. The white people are either *zanathan*, a French term, local-born, or *vazaha* (newcomers).

Merina live in the central highlands of the island's capital, Antananarivo or Tananarive. Their home region is called Imerina. They are thought to have come from the east of Mangoro or from the northeast, pushing back, intermarrying with, and finally conquering the original inhabitants, Vazimba.

The Merina society is hierarchical and extremely structured. Previously they were divided into three main castes: the *Andriana*, the nobles; the *Hova*, freemen who are the commoners; and the *Andevo*, slaves descended from former slaves. Today, the caste division is no longer practiced or is not obvious.

The Merina ruled Madagascar before the French assumed control in 1895. They are usually highly educated and represent the modern middle class and the intellectual elite. They can be found scattered around the island, except in the extreme north or south and a portion of the west coast, as businessmen, doctors, ministers, managers of plantations, technicians, and government officials.

Betsimisaraka, "the many inseparables" or "the many who do not want to separate," are the second-largest ethnic group, found in the east. They are cultivators. They reside in isolated villages because of differences in dialect, in ritual or local political office, in cultural practice, and in material culture. Their political organization is village-based.

Betsileo, "the numberless invincibles," are a peaceful and hardworking peasant tribe of the central highlands around Fianarantsoa or the east coast of Madagascar. They are skilled craftsmen known for their mastery at managing water for their irrigated and terraced rice and cassava fields on poor soil. They share customs, beliefs, and historical traditions similar to the Merina, but are less warlike and less well organized.

Tsimihety are "the people who do not cut their hair"—a phrase that could be a sign of mourning or a sign that they did not observe hierarchy. It may also be derived from the fact that during the 19th century, facing Marofelana bandits, Tsimihety

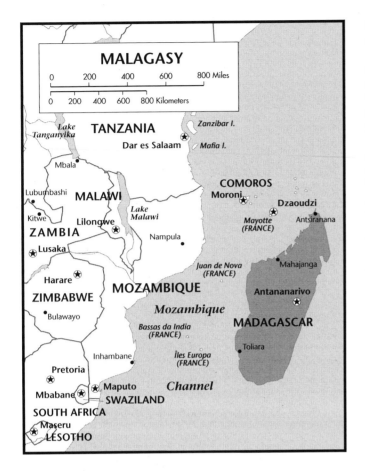

ta: nobles, commoners, and descendants of slaves. Members of each stratum marry solely within their own group.

Antandroy, "the people of the thorny brambles," are a dark-skinned, primitive, and attractive tribe who live in the arid south around Ambovombe in the east. They are a branch of the Sakalava of the west coast and worked readily for colonists all over the island. They are a large, cohesive group with a uniform set of customs.

Tanala, "the people of the forests," live in areas where forests have been cut down on the slopes inland from Manakara on the east coast. They are divided into two subgroups—the Tanala Menabe and the Tanala Ikongo—with the Menabe living in less desirable areas. The Tanala lack political organization but are skilled hunters, food gatherers, and woodsmen.

Anteimoro, "the people of the coast," live in the region of Vohipeno and Manakara on the east coast, south of the center of the island. Some have Arab blood, and traces of an Arab culture exist. They are the only group that knew how to write before the London Missionary Society arrived in Madagascar in 1818. Unique contributions from the Anteimoro include manuscripts dealing with history and religious matters, written in the Malagasy language using Arabic script. They claim to be descended from Arabs who arrived by boats from Mecca in the 13th century, married local women, and founded a kingdom.

Their society is divided into castes, with the upper level claiming to be direct descendants of Arab settlers. Their culture also is divided by age, with each group being assigned specific functions and a particular status for a given number of years. They are known for the *ombiasy* (divine healers) and *sikidy* (fortune tellers).

Bara is a name with no certain meaning. The Bara are nomads of the southern highlands around Ihosy and Betroka. They are artists, sculptors, dancers, cattle rustlers, and athletes. They are divided into four kinship groups living in different areas: Bara-Be, Bara-Iantsantsa, Bara-Vinda, and the Bara-Antevondro. They once considered agriculture degrading work; however, one can find some Baras working as sharecroppers on tobacco plantations in Miandrivazo or Malaimbandy.

Sihanaka, "those who wandered in the marshes," are found around Lake Alaotra, the largest fresh water lake on the island north of Antananarivo, west of Tamatave in Tamatave Province. They work as farmers, cattle herders, and fisherman, and are known to drain swamps to make rich agricultural land. They have features similar to the Merina and live next to them; however, they refuse to mix.

Antanosy, "the people of the island," are dark-skinned, flat-nosed, thick-lipped people. They were the first to drive the French settlers out of Fort Dauphin, in and after 1643. The Antanosy were divided by chiefdoms belonging to the noble class.

Mahafaly, "those who put taboos on things," are a dark-skinned, primitive tribe living around Ampanihy. Their kings were related to the kings of the Sakalava tribe before Madagascar was conquered. They are known for their mastery in carving the long wood staffs used to garnish their tombs.

Maka or Masombiky, "people of Mozambique," live on the west coast across from Africa, and are the only truly African descendants of the imported slaves, perhaps brought from the Mozambique Channel by Arabs from Zanzibar.

Bezanozano means "many little braids"—a name referring to their traditional hairstyle. In many ways, they resemble the

men let their hair grow long so that they might be mistaken for women and would not be attacked. They reside in the north of Madagascar. They have 40 localized kinship groups, the largest being the Antandrona, the Maromena, and the Maromainty.

The Tsimihety are often referred to as mobile semi-nomadic people because it is their custom to move around for freedom. Peter J. Wilson, in his book *Freedom by Hair's Breadth: Tsimihety in Madagascar*, observes: "Through this mobility they could express their sense of freedom and defiance of outside authority because they could always exercise what Albert O. Hirshman has called the "exit option." They are egalitarians who do not believe in the ownership or transmission of land; rather they believe that individuals are stewards with a responsibility to manage the land on behalf of their ancestors. Land belonged to those who cultivated it or to those who have ancestors buried in a particular area."

Sakalava, "dwellers in long valleys," are a tall tribe of dark brown people, formerly the most powerful of the tribes. Majunga, now called Mahajunga, is their most important city. They are associated with the Islamic groups of Madagascar's southeast. Europeans from around the coast, communities already established in the southwest, and migrant people from the eastern seaboards form the Volamena (literally, "red silver" or "gold") royal lineage.

Anteifsy, "people of the sands," lived originally on the African continent and live in the southern end of the east coast of Farafangana, in Fianarantsoa Province. They live in three stra-

Betsimisaraka, with whom they live intermingled in the sub prefecture Moramanga. They are herders and woodsmen.

Antakarana "people of the rocks," lived in the northern tip on Diego-Suarez, now Antsiranana (Cap d'Ambre to Sambirano River). They are a heterogeneous group with mixed Sakalava, Betsimisaraka, and Arab ancestry. During Merina conquests, part of the group settled on the northwest coast, where they managed to preserve considerable independence. This group became Muslim, but they still maintained traditional customs dealing with family relations and burial practices. They raise cattle and also grow maize, rice, cassava, and other crops.

Antambahoako, "the descendants of Rabevahoaka," are the smallest of the tribes. They live near Mananjary, south of the center of the east coast. They are the only ethnic group with a single common genealogy, being descended from King Raminia, who came from Mecca in the 14th century. They are no longer in contact with the Islamic world, but they retain fairly strong Muslim influences. They are divided into eight kinship groups and resemble the Betsimisaraka, whose homeland surrounds them. They are known as good fishermen and boatmen.

The Vezo are a small group of people living in the southwest part of Madagascar who, as John Mack notes in *Madagascar: Island of the Ancestors*, "do not practice circumcision, which is a central ritual elsewhere on the island, circumcision often being for men a crucial condition of access to ancestral tombs. This in itself argues for a strong African rather than Southeast Asian element in Vezo culture, and to this day they retain strong contacts with coastal peoples in Mozambique."

In the 1800s, three major movements among the Sakalava, the Betsimisaraka, and the Merina created an alliance. Nevertheless, tension was constant, particularly among the different ethnic groups who were "ultimate masters of adaptation."

On 26 June 1960 Madagascar gained independence from France.

In 1993 the government changed from a Communist dictatorship to a still-adapting free market democracy. Madagascar is being pressured by economic and environmental forces on all fronts. The economy and infrastructure continue to decay due to constant corruption and political instability. Economic reforms have been erratic. Other nations seem more interested in preserving the endangered species rather than the people.

Overall, Madagascar is ranked as one of the poorest countries in the world, suffering from chronic malnutrition, underfunded health and education facilities, a 3% annual population growth rate, and a severe loss of forest lands accompanied by erosion.

Madagascar has six governmental administrative divisions: Antananarivo or Tananarive, Antsiranana, Fianarantsoa, Mahajanga, Toamasina, and Toliary. Elections were held in February 1997. Following those elections, President Didier Ratsiraka was reinstated chief of state. (President Ratsiraka was the president of Madagascar from mid-1975 until the end of the 1980s.) However, in the 2001 presidential elections, Marc Ravalomanana shocked most outside observers when he claimed outright victory, supplanting veteran politician and longtime president of 27 years, Ratsiraka. In the elections of May 2006, Marc Ravalomanana was once again declared the winner of the presidential elections. In April of 2007 voters in a referen-

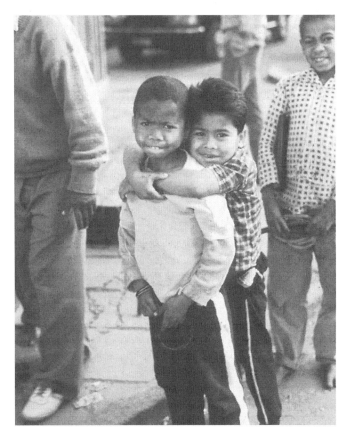

The Malagasy population is divided into 18 identifiable ethnic groups in addition to the Comorans, the Karane (Indo-Pakistan), and the Chinese. (Cory Langley)

dum endorsed constitutional reforms to increase presidential powers and make English an official language. The consolidation of power by Ravalomanana has raised questions about his authoritarian tendencies.

The legislative branch of government is a bicameral Parliament which consists of a National Assembly or Assemblée Nationale and a Senate. The National Assembly consists of 127 seats, reduced from 160 seats by an April 2007 national referendum. Members are elected by popular vote to serve four-year terms. The Senate or Senat has 100 seats; two-thirds of the seats are filled by regional assemblies and the remaining one-third of seats appointed by the president to serve four-year terms. The decentralized regional assemblies were elected in February 1997 and in the May 2006 elections.

² LOCATION AND HOMELAND

One billion years ago a piece of land broke away from Africa and moved southeast to become an island continent in the Indian Ocean—Madagascar. Many of the species of plants and animals found on the island became extinct or pursued separate evolutionary courses. As a result, 90% of all species on Madagascar are unique, found nowhere else in the world. Some of the unusual species that evolved are the lemurs, the tortoises, the *Aepyornis* (elephant birds), the tenrec, the chameleons, and other strange and exotic insects and birds.

Madagascar, located 250 miles off the east coast of Africa, is the fourth largest island in the world, after Greenland,

New Guinea, and Borneo. It is approximately 1,000 miles long and 360 miles wide, nearly the size of California, Oregon, and Washington combined.

³ LANGUAGE

Malagasy, French, and English are the country's official languages. The Malagasy language is rich in metaphor and poetic imagery and belongs to the Malayo-Polynesian family of languages. Although the Malagasy language includes many dialects, the Merina language is the official language of the state and is universally understood. The basic Malagasy vocabulary is 93% Malayo-Polynesian in origin and there is evidence of borrowings from Arabic, Bantu, Sanskrit, and Swahili.

⁴ FOLKLORE

Malagasy ancestor worship includes a celebration known as the *famadiahana* (turning over the dead). Each year, ancestors' bodies are removed from the family tomb and the corpses are rewrapped in a fresh shroud cloth. Family members make special offerings to the dead ancestors on this occasion, which is accompanied by music, singing, and dancing. Malagasy do not consider death to be the absolute end to life. In fact, Malagasy believe that after death, they will continue to be interested and involved in the affairs of their family. Malagasy believe that dead family members continue to influence family decisions and are thus honored. For this reason, Malagasy tombs are usually far more substantial in construction and luxurious than the homes of the living."

Many Malagasy believe that spirits are present in nature, in trees, caves, or rock formations, on mountains, or in rivers or streams. Some also fear the *tromba,* when the spirits of the unknown dead put people into a trance and make them dance. The one who is possessed must be treated in a ritual by an *ombiasy* (a divine healer). These ombiasis are known to have supernatural forces, particularly in the area of constellations. This is why, quite often, people consult or rely on the ombiasis to look over the ill or the dying, or to decide the proper date to have a marriage, a circumcision or a *famadiahana* (turning of the dead).

⁵ RELIGION

Traditional religion in Madagascar is identical with traditional culture; ancestral civilization determines values and behavior. All Malagasy believe that there is one supreme being called Zanahary (God) or Andriamanitra (Rakotosoa). There is no dogma or clergy. "Men who die 'leave to become God,' having powers with the rank they held in life," and "prayers are always asked for blessing with both Zanahary and the ancestors," observes Harold D. Nelson in his *Area Handbook for the Malagasy Republic.* He goes on: "about [half] of the population are Christians, divided almost evenly between Roman Catholics and Protestants; [there is a] small Muslim element; [the] rest [of the] population adheres to indigenous beliefs and practices in which [an] ancestor cult is [a] primary feature."

⁶ MAJOR HOLIDAYS

The government of Madagascar's official holidays include the following:

January 1	New Year's Day
March 29	Memorial Day
Movable	Monday Easter
May 1	Labor Day
May 8	Ascension Day
Movable	Monday Pentecost Holiday
May 25	Unity African Organization Day (UAO)
June 26	National Day
August 15	Assumption
November 1	All Saints' Day
December 25	Christmas Day

⁷ RITES OF PASSAGE

An important celebration of Malagasy culture is circumcision or *mamora raza.* Once a young boy is circumcised, the eldest male in the family is expected to eat the foreskin with a banana.

However, circumcision in the Tsimihety culture is a "hit or miss" situation which the circumciser, or *tsimijoro,* performs with or without parental consent. The term for this is *kiso lehifitra.* Tsimihety do not have a celebration or feast after the procedure, but celebrate before if the ceremony is formalized. Formalization takes place when and if the boy's father invites the *tsimijoro* and his wife's brother; both males contribute a cow to the proceedings. Then, meat is distributed to the family or close affinities. At night, before the circumcision, both families sing for the happiness of the child. The operation is performed before dawn. Special powerful water, or *rano malaza,* is poured over the penis, after which the prepuce is marked with white earth. The foreskin is then given to the wife's brother, who has to swallow it, or he might throw it over the roof of the house. The *tsimijoro* spits salted water onto the wound. After six days, the boy is thrown into a river or pond where he is bathed.

The *Vezo* do not practice circumcision, nor is female circumcision practiced in the Malagasy cultures.

⁸ INTERPERSONAL RELATIONS

On a personal level or in one-to-one relationships, the Malagasy people are hospitable, very warm, and amicable. However, in unfamiliar surroundings with unfamiliar people, they appear to be reserved, somewhat distant, or unassertive. They are not likely to be the first to initiate a conversation and are not likely to continue a conversation.

A single handshake and a "hello" is the proper greeting when people are introduced. A handshake is also used when saying goodbye. Among family and close friends, a kiss on both cheeks is exchanged at every meeting, regardless of the number of people present or how often they have met during the preceding days. The custom is for women and the young to initiate greetings when they meet elders.

A polite but simple refusal of an offering, especially food or a dance from an invited guest, is considered rude and pompous. It is better to fabricate excuses than to simply refuse politely. It is also considered embarrassing if a host does not offer a visitor a chance to sit and have something to eat and drink.

Regardless of the situation, elders and seniors are always right, and women are expected to take the modest position, particularly in public.

9 LIVING CONDITIONS

The high incidence of disease in Madagascar is a result of a nutritionally inadequate diet and insufficient medical care and sanitation practices. Malaria, schistosomiasis, and tuberculosis are common diseases, along with leprosy, bubonic plague, diphtheria, typhoid, venereal infections, tetanus, hepatitis, and gastroenteric parasites.

Madagascar is considered a third world country, and basic essential necessities such as electricity, clean water, stable housing, and transportation are hard to come by for the average citizen.

When walking the streets of Madagascar, it is evident that the people are sharply divided between an upper class and a lower class. A middle class virtually does not exist. Many upper-class homes are fenced and guarded 24 hours a day and filled with maids who work at the beck and call of their owners.

10 FAMILY LIFE

The strong and significant social value of Malagasy culture is summed up in the word *fihavanana*, which refers to both kinship and solidarity. As Nelson observes, "Family loyalties override all others, and help with expenses occasioned by marriages, funerals, and sickness continues to be a moral imperative." Help is never regarded as an exchange of economic services but, instead, as the demonstration of a moral link between kin, related or not, especially in times of death.

Most Malagasy social activities revolve around family—which usually consists of three generations—whether family members may live in one household or in a number of households. The head of the local family is usually the oldest male or father, who makes major decisions that affect the family interests, represents the family in dealings with the outside world, and reprimands those who act counter to the welfare and reputation of the family. In some instances, the oldest female plays these roles.

But the powers of the eldest male have diminished in the cities, where he can no longer protect family members as he would have in the past, or where the young can escape his control. Nevertheless, parental control remains stronger in Madagascar than in Western countries. If a father is deceased, then the eldest son assumes the role of the father and is often referred to as "father" or *dada* by the younger siblings. Daughters are required to perform household duties and to care for younger siblings, while sons go to school or are allowed to play.

In general, women are expected to care for family and domestic affairs. They are less educated than men and are hardly consulted in the decisions which affect the future of the society. They are discouraged from taking jobs away from men and are rejected from traditional male-dominated occupations. In a nutshell, women are subordinate to men, and younger Malagasy are subordinate to their elders.

An ancient ideal of having seven boys and seven girls per household is now regarded as a joke—a common thing to say to a couple who has just married. A more modern expectation nowadays is four children per household.

Most communities are represented by a *fokon'olona*, a village council in which older generations always take precedence over younger generations. They lead meetings and make final decisions. In short, the senior male is the final authority.

In many ethnic groups, there is a tendency to marry within one's kinship group and within one's social rank. Other groups, such as the Tsimihety and the southeastern groups, insist on marrying outside the kinship group to forge stronger links with other villages. Merina marriages between close kinsmen keep land inheritance by both sons and daughters continuous.

A ceremony of purification is performed in cases of marriage between close kin. Marriage between the children of two sisters is considered most incestuous of all, because it is the mother, not the father, who gives *ra* (blood) to the child according to Malagasy beliefs.

Nelson tells us, "Polygamy, which formerly was frequent, has almost disappeared except for the Muslim Comorians and some people in the south and southwest, such as the Antandroy, Antanosy, Mahafaly, and Antaisaka." However, in Tsimihety culture, marriage is either expanded or not, and trial marriages are practiced because of their belief in partnership. Adolescents are free to have sexual relations in hopes of finding someone they would like to marry. Once the adolescents have chosen, the parents are informed, and the parents inform senior kin. Then discrete inquiry by relatives on both sides begins. First, as Peter Wilson describes in *Freedom by Hair's Breadth*, they "try to find whether there already existed a kinship relationship between the two individuals, and, second, whether the households and extended family were diligent or slovenly and whether the prospective spouse was likely to have been brought up well to perform his or her role. The usual method was to contact a kinsperson who was likely to know if the person was fit or not."

Malagasy marriages are preceded by lengthy discussions, or *kabary*, by a representative from both families. As a gesture, the groom's family will give a few thousand Malagasy francs or perhaps one head of cattle, which is called a *vody ondry*, to pay for the bride. This gesture also serves as a reimbursement for the expenses and hardship incurred for raising her.

Women are expected to obey their husbands, but in practice they have a great deal of independence and influence. They manage, inherit, and bequeath property and often hold the family purse strings.

11 CLOTHING

Many of the Malagasy have come to regard anything Western as desirable and fashionable. Therefore, the markets are full of poor-quality imported clothes and imitation Western outfits. However, traditional clothing varies throughout the island.

Common clothing items include the *lamba*, which is worn somewhat like a toga, with or without additional clothing underneath. Lambas are made of bright, multicolored Malagasy patterns that usually have a proverb printed at the bottom. In some cases, lambas are used to carry a child on the women's back. Elder women wear white lamba made of fine silk, or raphia from the leaves of a tropical plant over their dress

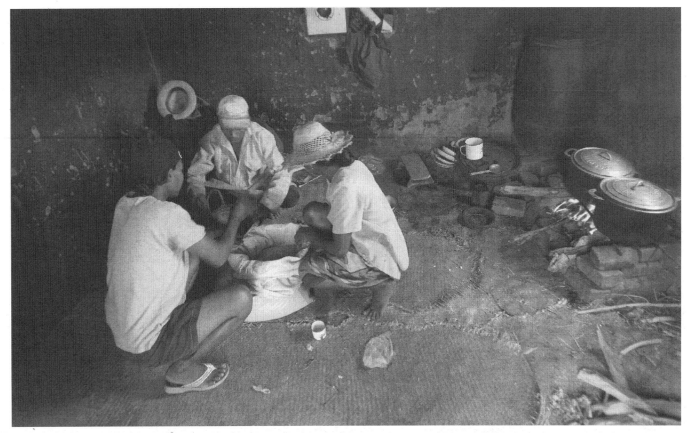

A Malagasy family prepares food in Antanetikely, Madagascar. Medical teams visit this village, south of the capital, twice a year to treat children and give them measles vaccinations, doses of Vitamin A, and de-worming tablets. The government hopes this will save thousands of children a year. (AP Images/Jerome Delay)

or blouse and skirt. It is not common for the women to wear pants.

In rural areas, men wear *malabars,* dress-like shirts made of cotton woven fiber. They are usually colored in earth tones.

12 FOOD

In Madagascar, rice is synonymous with food. If you have not eaten rice during the day, then you have not eaten, as rice is eaten two or three times a day.

Nevertheless, the Malagasy diet varies. It is common to have leftover or fresh rice for breakfast, sometimes served with condensed milk. Lunch and dinner consists of often heaping mounds of rice topped with beef, pork, or chicken with a vegetable relish. However, beef is usually served only for a celebration or an offering. The Tsimihety eat with disinterest; the cooking is bland, unimaginative, and aesthetically impoverished.

The coffee and vanilla that Madagascar supplies to the world is hardly part of the Malagasy diet. Candy, ice cream, and cake make up a small part of part of their daily or holiday diet.

It is common for a visitor or someone important to be given a basket of uncooked rice and a live chicken. Chicken is usually served to guests rather than beef. In some of the more rural areas, the Malagasy also eat fruit bats, civet cat, and lemurs. Or, like the Tsimihety, they may snack on roasted corn, roasted in-

sects, guinea fowl, and fruit. Children in particular eat roasted beetles, grasshoppers, and grubs.

A national snack called *koba* is a paté of rice, banana, and peanut.

A typical drink is *ranompango,* which is water added to a pot after all the rice but the crust has been removed and then allowed to boil, so as to take the flavor of burnt rice. Some villages produce sugar cane fermentation for rum *(betsabetsa)* or distilled rum *(laoka),* which are mostly used for bartering or for addressing ancestors, by pouring it on the ground.

Dessert usually consists of fruit, sometimes flavored with vanilla.

Some typical Malagasy dishes include:

Akoho sy voanio—Chicken and Coconut

1 chicken
1 coconut
2 tomatoes
2 onions
2 cloves of garlic
20 g of ginger
Oil, salt, pepper

Cooking Instructions:

Sprinkle chicken with salt and pepper to taste. Slice tomatoes into small cubes. Set aside.

Shred the coconut into a clean cloth. Fold the cloth around the shredded coconut. Wet the cloth using a glass of warm water. Squeeze the cloth and the shredded coconut to extract coconut milk. Discard the shredded coconut. (If obtaining a fresh coconut is not possible, you may substitute a can of unsweetened coconut milk instead.)

Add a small amount of oil to a frying pan. Sauté chicken over medium heat until cooked thoroughly.

Add onions to the pan. Continue stirring over medium heat until the onions are brown.

Add ginger, tomatoes, and garlic to pan. Sauté together briefly over medium heat.

Add coconut milk. Mix well. Reduce heat.

Simmer over low heat for 30 minutes.

Serve with rice and salad.

Serves four.

Lasary Voatabia—Tomato and Scallion Salad

In a 1-quart bowl, combine:
1 cup scallions, finely diced
2 cups tomatoes, finely diced
2 tablespoons water
1 teaspoon salt
Several drops Tabasco sauce

Stir lightly and chill.

Serve approximately 1/3 cup per portion in small dishes.

Kitoza

A popular delicacy in Madagascar in which beef is cut into strips and broiled over a charcoal fire:

Cut round steak to ¼-in thick.

Cut meat into pieces about 4 in by 2 in. Thread the strips on a fine strong cord, and hang the cord as you would a small clothesline. The meat will become quite dry in a few hours.

Put the strips over a charcoal brazier so that the meat dries to a crispness but does not burn. Remove meat immediately from the fire when it crisps.

This dish is usually eaten with a watery cornmeal mush for breakfast.

Vary Amin Anana—rice and greens

In a 4-quart saucepan:
Sauté ½ pound boneless chuck cut into ½-in cubes in 2 teaspoons oil until meat is brown on all sides.
Add 1 tomato cut into ½-in chunks.
Cook with the beef for 10 minutes.
Add 1 bunch of scallions cut into 1-in pieces
½ pound mustard greens cut into small pieces
1 bunch watercress cut into small pieces
Sauté, stirring occasionally with cover on until vegetables soften.
Add 2 cups water (or enough to cover vegetables)
1 cup rice
1 tablespoon salt
½ teaspoon pepper

Cover tightly and simmer slowly until rice is thoroughly cooked and all the liquid is absorbed.

Correct the seasoning to your taste.

Sakay, a hot red pepper, is usually served on the side with all Malagasy dishes.

¹³ EDUCATION

In 2005 over 70% of Madagascar's population ages 15 and over could read and write. The level of education achieved typically depends upon geographic area and an individual's rank and status. However, parents expect their children to reach the highest level of education possible, including a master's degree or a Ph.D. Parents commonly send their children to France or elsewhere overseas for higher education because the quality of education in Madagascar is poor.

¹⁴ CULTURAL HERITAGE

In the liner notes to the recording *Music from Madagascar*, D'Gary proclaims, "Musically speaking, Madagascar is a liberated heaven with no closed doors!" Stephane De Comarmond goes on: "Music in Madagascar can be divided in two extremes: melodic and rhythmic! The capital and High Plains of the center—most oriental-oriented—are packed with melodies and harmonies, whereas the coastal regions, which have been in regular contact with Africa, are the home of the beats." One musical form, Salegy, which in the 1960s was evident on the northern coast, has become widespread on the island with the introduction of non-traditional instruments such as the electric guitar, bass, and drums. Most Malagasy music and lyrics are about daily life.

Internationally recognized Malagasy musicians include: Earnest Randrianasolo, known as D'Gary, a Malagasy guitarist of the Bara culture. He is an original guitarist and musical visionary. He has been successful in transferring the music of many unique, traditional Malagasy instruments to a finger-picked acoustic guitar. One D'Gary song, "Betepotepo" (the name of a town) is about the desire to return to the home village. His themes include nostalgia for children, family, and village life. Other musicians include Dama Mahaleo, a Malagasy folk-pop superstar; Paul Bert Rahasimanana, known as Rossy, a group of 12 musicians; Jaojoby; Justin Vali, "the master player of the valiha"; Mama Sana, a 70 year-old valiha master; Poopy; Jean Emilien; Rakotofrah; and Kaolibera, a well-known guitarist. Another group is Tarika Sammy. Tarika means group, specifically referring to a performing ensemble. The Tarika Sammy group plays tradition-based music. The lead group is Sammy, or Samoela Andriamalalaharijaona. One song produced by Sammy is called "Mila Namana" ("I Need a Friend"); it is about feeling lonely and needing a friend. Another song is called "Eh Zalahy" ("Hi there!").

Classical music, such as music by Mozart and Dell, is played in the churches.

Some of Madagascar's unique melody instruments include: the vahila, a tubular harp; the marovany, a box zither; the kabosy, a cross between a guitar, mandolin, and dulcimer; the lokanag, a solid-bodied, Malagasy fiddle; Sodina-b, a flute made from bamboo ("B" indicates "big flute"); and Tahitahi, tiny flutes, usually of wood, gourd, or bamboo, used by Tarika

One of Madagascar's unique musical instruments is the vahila, a tubular harp. (Camille Killens)

Sammy as bird call sounds. Percussion instruments include: Ambio, a pair of resonant wood sticks that are struck together; and Kaimbarambo, a bundle of resonant grasses played many ways—sometimes called a kefafa, which literally means "broom."

15 WORK

In *The Great Red Island*, Arthur Stratton writes: "The Malagasy laborer has none of his European or American counterpart's inducements to work for fixed wages during certain hours of the day or the night, and regular days of the week, throughout the year—not even with a paid holiday in summer. The Malagasy needs are simple and his wants are easily satisfied. He is not concerned with climbing any sort of social, spiritual, or economic ladder to get within reach of any real or illusory goal on top. His concept of success does not goad him along to 'improve' himself, to keep up with the Joneses, or to buy himself some status symbols like a Cadillac or a mink coat. . . . They have no drive to occupy their minds or their hands; they like to do nothing serious at all; they have no sort of compulsion to steady occupation; they do not live from payday to payday. A Malagasy man and his family can get by very happily with highly irregular working hours amounting to no more than three or four wage-earning months of the year. The rest of the time they spend in resting up after enjoying themselves. Thus there is a chronic labor shortage in Madagascar while there is also a chronic unemployment."

Today, the French, the Creoles from Réunion, the Chinese, the Indians, and the Merina highlanders dominate in business in Madagascar.

The Chinese are known for their integrity and are appreciated in Madagascar because, when they migrated to Madagascar, they chose to live among the Malagasy on the same footing. However, they keep to themselves and operate in a different manner.

The Indians, or *karana* on the other hand, are thought to be "slippery and an unpopular lot." A marriage between a *karana* and a Malagasy virtually never happens; however, marriage between a Chinese person and a Malagasy is highly possible.

Women's role in agricultural work is often more arduous than the men's, including water carrying, wood gathering, and rice pounding, much of it to compensate for inadequate technical services in the economy. Special roles in planting and cultivation, marketing surplus crops, preparing food, and domestic crafts keep women occupied throughout the day and the year; men insist on conventional periods of repose.

16 SPORTS

Typical sports played in Madagascar are soccer, volleyball, and basketball. Other activities include martial arts, boxing, wrestling or *tolona*, swimming, and tennis.

17 ENTERTAINMENT AND RECREATION

Because most social activities center around the family, recreation and entertainment consist of family members and relatives meeting to play typical sports and to dine together.

Unique Malagasy games include games with stones, board games such as Solitarie and Fanorona, cock-fights, singing games, and hide-and-seek.

18 FOLK ART, CRAFTS, AND HOBBIES

In *Madagascar: Conflicts of Authority in the Great Island*, Philip M. Allen writes: "Malagasy artistic creativity finds itself in crisis today. In the past, Madagascar excelled in traditional architecture and sculpture—seen especially in tombs of the west and the south—as well as in oral and literary poetry, in textile design, and especially in music. Paintings remain servile to French academic styles, including determination of palette choices to render typical scenes of Malagasy life, the most popular subject for oil painters and water colorists. The imitative process results in waves of local-color celebrations for the tourist market rather than a true expression of the Malagasy creative spirit."

Madagascar is known for its basket weaving and painting on silk.

19 SOCIAL PROBLEMS

The primary social problem is poverty, and *quatre-amie*, or street children, who beg for food or search for it in the garbage. Rapid population growth over the recent past threatens biodiversity because every year nearly one-third of the island's former scrub forest and desert is set afire to keep land arable. The Human Development Report indicates that between 1990 and 2004, over 70% of the population was living below the national poverty line. Although mortality rates have declined dramatically, fertility rates are extremely high in Madagascar. Other demographic indicators such as infant mortality rates are also relatively high. Malnutrition is also rampant.

20 GENDER ISSUES

As already noted above, women are expected to care for family and domestic affairs and be subservient to men. According to the UNDP Human Development Report 2006, in 2004 the literacy rate for men was 76.5% and 65.3% for women. The primary-school enrolment ratio for male and female students had climbed to 1:1, but girls leave school more often than boys because of the burden of household chores, parents' views on the importance of girls' education, concern for girls' safety, and a lack of gender-sensitive school environments. Women are conspicuous by their absence from gainful employment and public life in Madagascar. The position of women is weakest in the political sphere: women received the right to vote and to stand in elections in 1959, yet in 2004 only 8.4% of seats in parliament were held by women. In a nutshell, women are subordinate to men, and younger Malagasy are subordinate to their elders.

In terms of human rights, Madagascar has signed or ratified five of the six principal international human rights treaties. Since 1993, human rights have been generally respected and although the death penalty remains in force, it has not been applied for more than 40 years. However, despite government commitment to human rights, judicial proceedings against people associated with the Ratsiraka government, including those suspected of human rights abuses during the 2002 crisis, were often unfair. There are reports of police brutality against prisoners and political detainees, as well as instances of arbitrary arrest and detention. Quite often prison conditions are deplorable and life threatening. Women prisoners are routinely subjected to violence and abuse including rape.

Generally, homosexuality is not condoned in rural and urban Madagascar. However, homosexuality appears to be legal in Madagascar with 21years as the age of consent. Neither homosexuality nor sodomy are mentioned in the criminal laws of Madagascar. Nevertheless the government is actively engaged in curbing sex tourism with punishment for prostitution and pornography.

21 BIBLIOGRAPHY

Allen, Philip M. *Madagascar: Conflicts of Authority in the Great Island.* Boulder, CO: Westview Press, 1995.

Hellier, Chris. "Malagasy Melting Pot: Photojournalist Chris Hellier Takes Us on a Tour around Madagascar to Meet Some of the Country's 18 Ethnic Groups." *Geographical : the Royal Geographical Society Magazine* (August 2000): 14-25.

Jolly, Alison. *A World Like Our Own.* New Haven, CT: Yale University Press, 1980.

Krabacher, T., Kalipeni, E. and Layachi, A. *Global Issues: Africa.* Dubuque, Iowa: McGraw-Hill Contemporary Learning Series, 2008, p. 74-76.

Mack, John. *Madagascar: Island of the Ancestors.* London: British Museum Publications Ltd., 1986.

Nelson, Harold D. *Area Handbook for the Malagasy Republic.* Washington, D. C.: The American University, 1973.

Sandler, Bea. *The African Cookbook.* New York: Carol Publishing Group, 1993.

Stratton, Arthur. *The Great Red Island.* New York: Charles Scribner's Sons, 1964.

Webster, Donovan. "I was caught in Madagascar. Peddled for 30 cents. Smuggled to Orlando. Sold for $10,000. I'm rare, coveted tortoise—coldblooded contraband." *The New York Times Magazine*, 16 February 1997.

Wilson, Peter J. *Freedom by Hair's Breadth: Tsimihety in Madagascar.* Ann Arbor: The University of Michigan, 1992.

World Beat. *Societe Malagache de Reproduction du Son et De L'Image.* Songs compiled by Stephane De Comarmond. Compact disc.

—revised by E. Kalipeni

MALDIVIANS

PRONUNCIATION: mal-DEEV-ee-ans
ALTERNATE NAMES: Divehi
LOCATION: Maldives, an island nation in the Indian Ocean
    southwest of Sri Lanka
POPULATION: 385,925 (2008 estimate)
LANGUAGE: Divehi or Dhivehi
RELIGION: Islam (Sunni)

¹INTRODUCTION

Maldivians are known as Divehi. They reside primarily on Maldives, an island-nation southwest of Sri Lanka. In the Divehi language, Maldives is known as Divehi Rājje, which translates as "island kingdom." Maldivians link much of their identity to islands, and the Republic of Maldives itself consists of 1,190 tiny islands that are organized into approximately 26 coral atolls. The word "dives," which is found both in the nation of the Maldivian people and in their geographic home, comes from a Sanskrit word, *dvīp,* for island. The word "dives" also is used to identify many of the other islands within the Maldives archipelago.

Maldivian society is relatively small in size. Its people draw a shared sense of identity through their history, the Divehi language they speak, and their belief in Islam. Individuals value strong community ties, loyalty to their national president, and family obligations. Modern-day Maldives earns much of its revenue through tourism, and the Maldivians are known as tolerant and respectful of those who visit their island-nation.

The Maldivian society is among the world's oldest. However, the origins of the Maldivians themselves are not entirely known. Some scholars believe the first people to arrive in the islands were sailors from Sri Lanka and southern India as early as 2000 BC. Others trace the origins to Aryans who had migrated into northern India at about the same time and continued to journey southward. Archeological evidence indicates that the earliest inhabitants practiced Hinduism and Buddhism, which also were practiced widely in southern India and Sri Lanka.

Arab and Persian sailors who began traveling trade routes through the Indian Ocean in AD 900 brought Islam to Maldives. The first recorded arrival was in AD 947, and by 1153 most Maldivians had converted to Islam. However, Maldivian culture is derived from many other sources as well. Inhabitants of some of its islands are descendents of former slaves while others claim lineage to members of Arabian nobility who arrived in Maldives while making the hajj, or pilgrimage to Mecca, that is a vital component of Islam. Intermarriage between these different peoples has made the Maldivian community rich with traditions from many cultures. The Maldivian language, Divehi, also reflects this mixing. Divehi's roots are Sinhalese and Sanskritic, which reflects the migration of people from present-day Sri Lanka and the Indian subcontinent. However, the spoken language contains many words that are of Persian, Arabian, and Portuguese influence. A fusion of several cultural traditions also is seen in traditional Maldivian medicinal practices, which include uses of Chakra, Ayurveda, and Unani.

Portuguese traders arrived in Maldives in the 16th century, invading the capital of Malé in 1558. Maldivians reacted to the Portuguese with hostility. A local uprising led by Maldivian hero Muhammed Thakurufaanu drove out the Portuguese in 1573. Thakurufaanu established Maldives as a sultanate, which remained in place until 1887 when the sultan at the time signed an agreement with British forces and made the Maldives a British protectorate.

Maldives remained under British control until 1965, first as a protectorate, then as a republic. On 26 July 1965, however, a new nation-state was formed and Maldives became independent. The modern-day country elected its first president, Ibrahim Nasir, in 1968. Nasir remained in power until 1973. Nasir was replaced by Maumoon Abdul Gayoom. Gayoom held the position until 2008 despite three armed attempts to unseat him in the 1980s and riots in 2004. Gayoom managed to stay in power largely because there was only one political party until 2005, when the government introduced more democratic reforms and legalized political parties. A new constitution was ratified in August 2008 and elections took place in October of that year. The elections resulted in a new president, Muhammad Nasheed.

In the years since independence, Maldivians have benefited from a relatively stable economy based largely on tourism, which the government introduced in 1972. Its worst economic disaster occurred in December 2004 when a devastating tsunami swept through the Indian Ocean. More than 80 people were killed in Maldives, and thousands of other residents lost their homes. The country's infrastructure also suffered heavy damage. A rebound in tourism, however, has helped the country recover. Despite growing problems of poverty and drug abuse, the close interdependent community and kinship ties that Maldivians have nurtured for centuries keep the country and its people vibrant today. Even as the country shifts to a more democratic political structure, families who are at the top of Maldives' social structure retain power. Village administrators deal with disputes at the local level by reporting them to the national government and waiting for instructions on how to proceed. More than 70,000 foreign workers also reside in Maldives. Most are from India, Sri Lanka, Bangladesh, and Nepal, and work in the tourism industry.

²LOCATION AND HOMELAND

The archipelago that makes up Maldives is in the Indian Ocean southwest of Sri Lanka. The land mass consists of 1,190 coral islands. Those islands are then grouped into 26 atolls. About 200 of the islands are inhabited by local Maldivians. An additional 80 islands maintain tourist resorts. Although the archipelago stretches in a north-south direction for 820 km (509.5 mi), the total land-mass of Maldives is fairly small, about 300 sq km (186 sq mi). That mass is roughly 1.7 times the size of Washington, D.C. Most of the islands are no more than 8 km (5 mi) in length, and the main vegetation is palm trees. About 80% of the islands' land has a very low elevations of about 1 m (3 feet). These low elevations have made Maldives quite vulnerable to rising sea levels that are being produced through global warming. Although a sea wall protects Malé, the nation's capital, many geographers predict that the archipelago may eventually become completely submerged.

Lagoons, deep blue waters, coral reefs, white sandy beaches, and palm trees characterize the appearance of the Maldivian islands. That natural beauty along with year-round balmy temperatures has helped in developing the archipelago's tourist economy. Some islands also have fresh water lakes, as well as swamplands and clusters of mangroves. The overall climate is typical of a tropical monsoon area. The weather is generally warm and quite dry from December through March, which is the northeast monsoon season. From May to October, during the southwest monsoon season, Maldives receive a great deal of rainfall. Temperatures remain relatively constant throughout the year, ranging between 25 and 30°C (77 and 86°F).

The Maldives lies along major maritime travel routes in the Indian Ocean. Winds that accompany the yearly monsoons historically made Maldives favorable to trade, and many Maldivian sailors traditionally planned trading expeditions to the Indian subcontinent and Sri Lanka around the seasonal schedule. Today, most Maldivians live in small villages and earn their living through fishing and tourism. Dolphins, manta rays, whale sharks, basking sharks, and sea turtles all inhabit the waters around the archipelago. About 13% of the land is useful for agriculture, but most agricultural activities are of a subsistence nature. Maldivian villagers plant coconut, breadfruit, taro, cassava, millet, sorghum, bananas, papaya, and drumstick (a long tough stem vegetable that tastes a little like a cross between asparagus and green beans). Maldivians also raise goats and chickens. Most homes include a small vegetable garden that provides for the needs of family members.

Maldivians obtain drinking water by sinking shallow wells into the sand. Rain percolates through the sand, which creates a series of fresh water aquifers that the islanders long have taken advantage of. These aquifers, however, are growing depleted and a loss of fresh water supplies is one major threat facing Maldivians.

The geography of the archipelago has influenced the character of the Divehi people. Generally, they consist of three ethnically distinct groups. A central group of Maldivians, who make up about three-fourths of the population, are the main group and live between an island known as Ihavandippuḷu (Haa Alif) and an island known as Haddummati (Laamu). A southern group occupies the atolls closest to the equator and makes up about 20% of the total population. The final group, the people of Minicoy, live on one long island (10 km or 6.2 mi in length) at the northern end of the archipelago. Their island is administered by India, and the Minicoy make up about 4% of the total population. The Minicoy community is both geographically and politically isolated from the rest of Maldives.

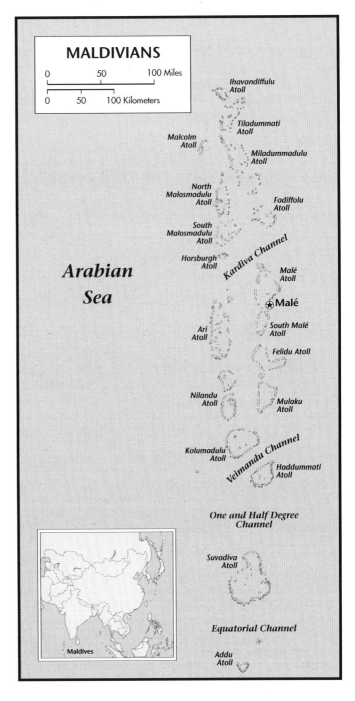

³LANGUAGE

The official language of Maldives is Divehi (Dhivehi). It is part of the Indo-Aryan language group and grew out of Sinhala (the main language spoken in Sri Lanka) and Sanskrit (the language from which many of the languages of the Indian subcontinent including Hindi were derived). Divehi is spoken only in the Maldives. On Minicoy, the area under Indian administration, the language is known as Mahl. Divehi also contains words borrowed from Arabic, Tamil, Malayalam, Hindi, French, Persian, Portuguese, and English.

Regional variants in pronunciation and vocabulary have developed across the archipelago. Malé Bas, which is the form of Divehi spoken in the nation's capitol, is considered to be the most mainstream form of the land. The language sounds distinctly different, however, in some of the southern atolls such as Huvadu, Fua Mulaku, and Addu. Variants also have developed in Haddummati and on Minicoy. Malé Bas is the main form used in writing. However, popular songs and poetry often draw on the richness of the regional variants. Divehi uses a written script, Thaana, which, like Arabic, is read from right to left.

The use of Divehi is primarily local. In business settings, English is widely used and is taught in schools. The tourist industry also has brought Maldivians into contact with numerous Europeans, and it is not unusual for those who work in the tourism industry to speak several languages in order to communicate with the Europeans who visit the islands.

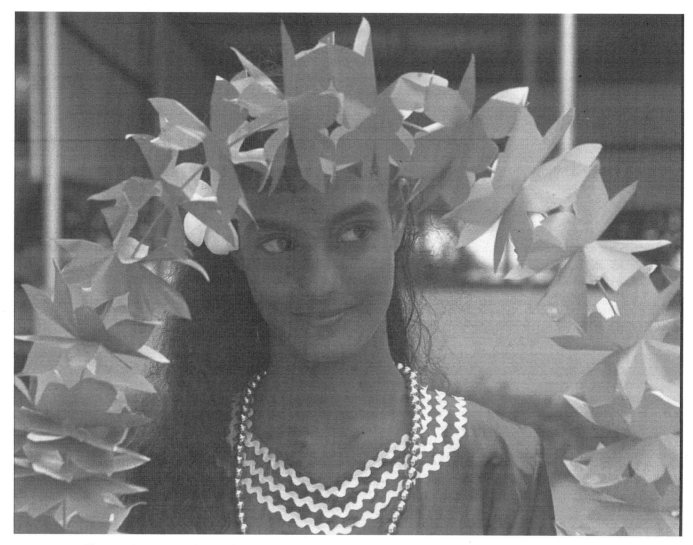

A young Maldivian girl wearing traditional finery waits outside her house to bid goodbye to leaders and dignitaries of the 9th annual South Asian Association for Regional Cooperation Summit. (AP Images/Sherwin Crasto)

⁴FOLKLORE

Much of Maldivian folklore appears to have come from Buddhist culture, and features an emphasis on the superstitious and supernatural. Many of the myths that survive today are based on the islanders' dependence on coconut trees and fish for survival. One story holds that many Maldivians died until a *fanditha* (sorcerer) created coconut trees from the skulls of the deceased settlers. In a different story, the tuna fish, a major fish eaten by Maldivians, is said to have been brought to the seas around the archipelago by Bodu Niyami Kali fanu, a mythical sea traveler who voyaged to the end of the world and found the fish at Dagas, a mythical tree.

A story about a prince from the Indian subcontinent known as Koimala is associated with the founding of the present day capital of Malé. In this story, Koimala was welcomed by Maldivians and invited to settle on a sandy bank that had been stained with fish blood. Koimala planted trees in the bank and from them, the first papaya fruit was harvested. Eventually, Maldivians accepted Koimala as their ruler. Koimala ordered a palace to be built and to name the island Maa-le Malé.

The arrival of Islam to Maldivian society also has come to be associated with a folk tale. In this story, a visiting Muslim named Abu al Barakat ul Barbari triumphed in battle with a sea demon known as Ranna Maari. That act convinced the Maldivian king to convert to Islam. The story persists, even though other versions of the story describe the visitor as a saint from Persia whose tomb occupies a central site in today's capital.

Myths of extinction preoccupy Maldivians, with some predicting that a great catastrophe will cause the islands to be submerged by the ocean. Other stories warn of evil spirits, sea monsters, and heroic sea creatures such as fishes, crabs, and seabirds. Folk tales also have arisen around local plants and trees. Some stories that came to the islands through interactions with foreigners have been adapted to fit the needs of island living.

⁵RELIGION

Maldives is an Islamic society. The Maldives government follows the Sharia (laws and practices based on the Quran), and businesses generally close for 15 minutes each time that Muslims are called to perform their five daily rounds of prayer. Nearly all Maldivian locals are Sunni Muslim, although Hinduism, Buddhism, and Christianity are practiced by expatriates and foreign workers. These practices are allowed by the government as long as they remain confined to private homes.

The government limits contact between natives and tourists, partly to protect its Muslim traditions from outside influences. As a result, most resorts have been built on previously uninhabited islands and locals generally were not allowed to spend extended amounts of time in the tourist areas. These rules are beginning to be relaxed, but contact between tourists and natives remains fairly limited.

Despite the adherence to Islamic law, Maldivians continue to use charms and spells to protect themselves from evil spirits. Most of these practices, which are related to the magical-religious system of fanditha, continue mainly in remote, rural areas. Traces of mother-goddess worship practiced by Dravidians and of Buddhism also remain a part of life within these rural settings.

⁶MAJOR HOLIDAYS

Maldivians observe all of the major Islamic holidays. Ramadan is a 30-day fasting period that occurs in the ninth month in the Muslim calendar. The observance of Ramadan greatly affects the Maldives daily way of life. Government offices close after 1:30 p.m. during that month, and businesses generally shut down at 3 p.m. The end of Ramadan is known as Kuda Eidh or Eid al Fitr and is celebrated with three days of festivities. Maldivians traditionally go back to their home islands for this festival and take part in such activities as a traditional tug-of-war game. During Bodu Eidh, the Feast of the Sacrifice, Maldivians celebrate with a week of dances, plays, sporting events, and other cultural activities. It is common during this period for Muslims who can afford to do so to travel to Mecca for the hajj pilgrimage. Maldivians also celebrate the birth of the Prophet Muhammad.

Secular holidays include Independence Day on July 26; New Year's Day on January 1, Republic Day on November 11, the day that Muhammed Thakurufaanu defeated the Portuguese in 1573.

⁷RITES OF PASSAGE

Maldivians traditionally celebrate the birth of a child with a naming ceremony seven days after the child is born. Bondibai, a sweet dish made of rice, is served. Spiced meats or chicken are given to family and friends, and the newborn receives his or her formal name. Boys undergo circumcision at age six.

Dating remains uncommon among Maldivians. Many Maldivian young men and women meet each other through group picnics to uninhabited islands that family groups arrange. It is typical to marry someone from one's own island or atoll. When a marriage is set to occur, families of the bride and groom notify their island's chief. Ceremonies are civil services with large celebrations afterwards. Most Maldivian women are in their early 20s when they marry. New couples often live in the home of the man's parents.

Upon death, family members bury the deceased within 24 hours. Memorial ceremonies honor the deceased on the third and fortieth days after the burial occurs, and on the anniversaries of the death.

⁸INTERPERSONAL RELATIONS

Maldivian culture is Islamic based. As a result, children learn at an early age to respect their elders. Greetings are relatively formal, consisting of a handshake and a smile. Women typically do not take the last names of their husbands but retain their own last names, which they inherit from their fathers.

Unarranged visits are common in Maldives. Visitors are welcomed, and both hosts and guests sit together to converse. Tea, cool drinks, and pastries typically are served. The atmosphere is casual.

⁹LIVING CONDITIONS

The traditional island home in Maldives is a one-storey compound that includes several rooms, a courtyard, and an open-air bathroom. Homes may be built of concrete or coral, and roofs are made of either coconut thatch or corrugated iron. Many homes receive electricity through generators. More and more Maldivians are abandoning the traditional way of life to seek work on resort islands. Those who work in the tourist industry often are away from their homes and families for up to eleven months out of the year. They live in cramped apartments that are located mostly in Malé. Many tourism workers save money to build dream homes on their home islands. They often spend their vacations working on these homes. Much of this construction was ravaged during the 2004 Indian Ocean tsunami, and families were relocated, often against their will.

Fishing, water-gathering, and household duties were traditional practices on rural islands. These practices continue even though work in the tourist industry is breaking up many Maldivian families. More industrial businesses also are being developed on the islands, such as fish-canning and shipbuilding.

The birth rate in Maldives is among the world's highest, with 14.84 births recorded annually for every 1,000 persons, according to 2008 statistics. Many infants do not survive; about 30.63 infant deaths are recorded for every 1,000 live deaths. The average life expectancy for Maldivians is approximately 74 years. Overpopulation is a threat, in that the islands are becoming less self-sufficient and more reliant on imported goods. Water supplies are growing brackish, and many islands face the prospect of overflowing solid waste and sewage disposal systems.

The government of Maldives has developed excellent health care facilities, with a regional hospital placed in each group of atolls and clinics on every island. However, the government does not provide much financial assistance to families in need of urgent medical care. As a result, many Maldivians prefer to first use a more traditional method of healing. Uses of herbal remedies and sand massages are common. One of the more serious health issues facing Maldivians is a blood condition known as thalassemia. The condition requires frequent transfusions, and it can be passed from one generation to the next.

10 FAMILY LIFE

The tourist economy upon which Maldivian families rely makes it difficult for families to spend much time together. It is not uncommon for spouses to be separated from each other for several months or for a parent not to see children more than once or twice a year. Nevertheless, the government emphasizes the importance of the family unit in Maldivian society and encourages the nurturing of family ties during extended holiday periods in the islands.

Men who do not work in tourism may carry out small-scale fishing enterprises. Many women also work in tourism. Those who do not work in tourism take responsibility for childrearing, cooking, cleaning, and collecting water. Women are expected to run their households even if they work outside the home. Salaries earned by resort workers typically are sent home and divided among family members. The lure of steady income that jobs in tourism offers drives some families to put education and other matters on hold so that at least one family member can take a tourism position.

¹¹CLOTHING

Temperatures in Maldives range between highs of 30°C (86°F) and lows of 25°C (77°F). As a result, most Maldivians dress casually. Men wear T-shirts with shorts, lightweight trousers, or sarongs. Women might wear a long-sleeved dress. However, many also dress quite simply in a blouse or tunic worn over a skirt or slacks. T-shirts and jeans also are common, as well as a head covering in accordance with Muslim customs.

Women generally follow Islamic dress codes and keep their thighs and shoulders covered. Women also tend to avoid wearing swim suits or bikinis, even when visiting the beach or swimming.

¹²FOOD

Traders and visitors from the Indian subcontinent, Africa, and Europe have influenced many aspects of Maldivian culture, including the Maldivian diet. Traces of Arabic, Indian, Sri Lankan, and East Asian spices, ingredients, and cooking methods can be found in Maldivian meals.

The staple diet consists primarily of rice and fish. Tuna is the most widely consumed fish. Maldivians also eat pumpkin, coconuts, papaya, pineapple, and sweet potatoes. To these basic foods are added chilis and other spices. Many Maldivians will eat betel nuts with cinnamon or cloves after meals to cleanse the digestive system and the breath. Most abstain from alcohol in accordance with Islamic codes. The most widely consumed drink is tea. During Ramadan, the Islamic month of fasting, Maldivians typically drink fruit juices and eat dates to break the fast at the end of each day.

Maldivians traditionally have eaten with their fingers, a custom also practiced in the neighboring nations of India and Sri Lanka. The right hand is generally used for eating, and it is believed that the practice of eating with the fingers completes the cooking of the food. In the past, families would eat together. Now, the practice of sharing meals is less common. Men often are gone for long periods of time on fishing trips, and many Maldivians—both male and female—are away from their families for several months working in the tourist industry. Restaurants in the tourist areas serve Indian and Sri Lankan foods as well as many European dishes. Many Maldivians working in these areas eat at such restaurants, as well.

¹³EDUCATION

Although education is not compulsory, Maldives has a highly literate population. Approximately 96% of all Maldivians over age 15 can read and write. Most attend primary schools on their home islands, although some will attend private, religious-based schools. After five years of primary school, Maldivians can attend up to seven years of secondary school.

Schools emphasize basic mathematics as well as reading and writing in Divehi and English.

At age 16, students take "O" or Ordinary Level exams. These are followed by "A" or Advanced Level exams taken at age 18. To qualify for "A" level courses, Maldivians often must leave their home islands and reside in the nation's capitol. That dislocation often prompts Maldivians to end their education after age 16 and begin working in the tourist industry to help support their families.

Maldives has one university and several colleges. Still, some Maldivians choose to attend university abroad. The government and several private organizations have set up sponsorship programs to help students who leave the country for educational purposes.

¹⁴CULTURAL HERITAGE

Maldivian cultural traditions reflect their ancient ties to southern India and Sri Lanka, as well as their contact with Arabic and African peoples who settled on their shores. The popular film industry in India, based in Mumbai and known as Bollywood, has also influenced Maldivian culture. North Indian dances, such as kathak, are widely enjoyed. Many elderly Maldivians enjoy Hindi songs from the 1950s and 1960s.

A local form of music and dance is known as bodu beru. The term translates as "big drum" and refers to an instrument made from the trunk of a coconut tree that has been hollowed out. Men will play the drum while others sing and dance. Any celebration is likely to feature the bodu beru, but the drum also is brought out for everyday entertainment. The bodu beru is said to have originated in the northern atolls in the 11th century, and some scholars trace the drum to African settlers in Maldives. The dance and music practice begins with a slow, rhythmic beating of the drum. The beat gradually gets faster and louder. Along with the bodu beru are other instruments including the bulbul, which resembles an accordion, and a form of music that is said to have Arabic roots known as thaara.

Culturally, Maldivians also have a rich tradition in calligraphy and stone-carving. Many art pieces reflect these works, including tombstones in older cemeteries, stonework at mosques, and verses from the Quran that are on display at the country's Islamic Center.

¹⁵WORK

Most Maldivians work in tourism and the industry makes up nearly one-third of the gross domestic product of Maldives. Fishing, agriculture, and manufacturing also employ Maldivians. It is not unusual for families to send one or more members to resort islands to work and earn income to support the rest of the family.

Maldivians who remain on their home islands tend to work in fishing or subsistence farming.

¹⁶SPORTS

The deep blue waters of the Indian Ocean that surround Maldives and its year-round tropical climate have made swimming a favorite sport. Most Maldivian men are excellent swimmers and many free-dive long distances for pleasure. Islamic codes discourage women from revealing their bodies. However, many women enjoy the ocean waters by swimming fully clothed.

Maldivian men also enjoy playing soccer and volleyball. Early evening matches take place frequently on the non-resort islands. Women enjoy the game of bashi, which is similar to softball but is played with a tennis ball and racquets.

[17] ENTERTAINMENT AND RECREATION

Watching Hindi films from India and listening to Hindi songs is a favorite pastime among Maldivians, particularly those of older generations. Younger people enjoy playing sports such as football and tennis, and making day trips to resort islands. Evening walks along the beaches and marinas are extremely popular as well.

Nearly all Maldivians engage in fishing, either for work or pleasure. Night fishing is a particularly unique form of entertainment in the archipelago. Maldivians will anchor a boat to a reef just before sunset, prepare their fishing lines, and drop them into the water. Through the evening, they will sit under the stars quietly, relaxing and feeling the gentle rock of sea waves. The hope is to catch a red snapper, but many find the experience of being out on the water satisfying enough.

[18] FOLK ART, CRAFTS, AND HOBBIES

Maldivians are known for weaving, ceramics-making, wood-carving and painting. The rise of tourism has helped revive many traditional crafts, and beautiful, bright-colored, intricate reed mats are a favorite souvenir item for visitors. Vases made from local woods and painted in bright colors also have found a tourist following, as have large pots and jars.

[19] SOCIAL PROBLEMS

A rapidly increasing population, overcrowding, and the threat of rising sea levels produced by global warming are major problems that face Maldives. The tiny island-nation's birth rate has long been one of the highest in the Asia Pacific region. As a result, more than 50% of the local resident population in the state capitol is under the age of 15, according to a report on the Maldives prepared by the United Nations' Ministry of Planning, Human Resources, and the Environment for the Asia Pacific region. The report also notes that housing in the capital is so tight that many dwellings are literally jammed together side-by-side along the one-kilometer (0.6-mile) length of the island. The high rate of births and a correspondingly high number of infant deaths have made issues of malnutrition and poverty serious concerns among Maldivians. The government has taken steps in recent years to launch a population control program and is developing an information campaign that is aimed at educating Maldivians on the uses of contraception and on the importance of reducing the size of families.

The low elevation of Maldives makes it quite vulnerable to rising sea levels. Former president Mamoun Abdul Gayoom warned of the threat in 1992, stating that scientists had predicted that the archipelago could disappear altogether within the next century if steps were not taken to reduce global warming. When the 2004 Indian Ocean tsunami occurred, ocean waters submerged the islands for several minutes. Only nine islands did not experience flooding. Fifty-seven islands experience serious damage, and fourteen islands were completely evacuated. Six islands were destroyed forever. The tsunami left more than 100 people dead, and displaced 12,000 others from their homes. Damage estimates exceeded $300 million. Although the economy has since rebounded, the experience of seeing islands that are no more than three feet in elevation submerged by waves that were reached fourteen feet illustrated the threat that a rising sea level poses for Maldivians.

[20] GENDER ISSUES

Maldives had one of the world's highest divorce rates until recently, when the government instituted laws that required the person requesting a divorce to pay child support to the other. Males typically had requested divorce, but the financial obligation has lessened that likelihood.

The change in divorce laws has been accompanied by a general improvement in the status of women. Women used to marry as early as age 14. Now, they wait until their early 20s. Males used to engage widely in the practice of polygamy. Today, even though Maldivian laws allow men to have up to four wives, most have only one.

More than 25% of Maldivian women work outside the home. Some work for the government and while others work in the tourism industry. In more rural areas, women tend crops and make handcrafts. Maldivian laws allow both men and women to inherit property.

[21] BIBLIOGRAPHY

Adney, M., and W. K. Carr. "The Maldives." In J. M. Ostheimer, ed. *The Politics of the Western Indian Ocean Islands,* 1975.

Anderson, R. C., and A. Hafiz. *The State of the Maldivian Tuna stock: Analysis of Catch and Effort Data and Estimation of Maximum Sustainable Yield,* 1985.

———. "An Appropriate Management Policy for the Tuna fishery in the Maldives." *Asian Fisheries Science* 2: 163–175, 1989.

———. "Artisanal Fisheries, Tourism and Development: Economic Analysis of the Maldives and Fishing-Boat Mechanisation." Ph. D. Thesis, University of Newcastle, New South Wales, Australia, 1988.

Ash, J.S. *Vertebrate Pest Management in the Maldives (Bat and Crow Control).* Food and Agriculture Organization of the United Nations (FAO), Rome, 1984.

Bell, H. C. P. *The Maldive Islands, An Account of the Physical Features, History, Inhabitants, Productions and Trade.* Colombo 1983.

Cole, R. V. "The Island States of the Indian Ocean: A View from the South Pacific." *Pacific Economic Bulletin* 1 (2): 41–46, 1986

Doń Hiyala āi Alifulu. *Abdullah Sādigu, Muli.* Malé: Novelty Press, 1996.

———. "Environmental Management for Sustainable Economic Development in Island Economies: The Maldivian Experience." In K. C. Roy, H. C. Blomqvist, and Hossain Iftekhar, eds., *Development That Lasts,* 1997.

Geiger, Wilhelm. *Maldivian Linguistic Studies.* Reprint 1919 edn. Malé: Novelty Press, 1986.

Government of Republic of Maldives. Official Website, www.maldives-info.com

Hamilton, Jon. "Maldives Builds Barriers to Global Warming," National Public Radio Jan. 28, 2008. http://www.npr.org/templates/story/story.php?storyId=18425626 (retrieved Jan. 22, 2009).

Haq, Mahbub ul and Khadija Haq. *Human Development in South Asia.* Oxford: Oxford University Press, 1988.

Maniku, H. A. *The Republic of Maldives,* 1980.

———. "Marine Areas as Tourist Attractions in the Southern Indian Ocean." In M. L. Miller, and J. Auyong, eds., *Proceedings of the 1990 Congress on Coastal and Marine Tourism*, 1990.

Ministry of Planning, Human Resources and Environment. *Statistical Year Book of Maldives*, 1998.

———. "Problems Faced by Indian Ocean Island Economies: The Case of the Maldives." In R. Gabbay, R. N. Gosh, and M. A. B. Siddique eds., *Economics of Small Island Nations*, 1996.

Sathiendrakumar, S. *Development of Resources of the Sea for Regional Cooperation and National Development*, 1983.

———, C. A. Tisdell. "Tourism and the Development of the Maldives" *Massey Journal of Asian and Pacific Business* 1 (1): 27–34, 1985.

———. "Fishery Resources and Policies in the Maldives: Trends and Issues for an Island Developing Country." *Marine Policy* 10 (4): 279–293, 1986.

———. "Maldives—Ethnography." http://www.maldives-ethnography.com/ (retrieved Jan. 13, 2009).

———. "The Maldives.com." http://www.themaldives.com/Maldives/Maldives_people.htm (retrieved Jan. 13, 2009).

———. "Maldives—The Sunny Side." http://www.visitmaldives.com/Maldives/culture.php (retrieved Jan. 13, 2009).

———. "Migration from Traditional Rural Communities and Outside Employment: A Study of Maldivian Fishing Villages." *South East Asian Economic Review* 8 (2): 121–63, 1987.

———. "Optimal Economic Fishery Effort in the Maldivian Tuna Fishery: An appropriate Model." *Marine Resource Economics* 4 (1): 15–44, 1987.

———. "The Maldives: Development and Socio-Economic Tensions." *South East Asian Economic Review* 9 (2): 125–162, 1988.

———. "Economic Importance of Tourism for Small Indian Ocean and Pacific States." In C. A. Tisdell, C. J. Aislabie, and P. J. Stanton, eds., *Economics of Tourism: Case Studies and Analysis*, 1988.

———. "International Tourism and the Economic Development of the Maldives." *Annals of Tourism Research* 16 (2): 254–264, 1989.

———. "Determinants of Relative Wealth in Maldivian Fishing Villages." *Asian Profile* 17 (2): 155–168, 1989.

———. "International Tourism and the Economic Importance of an Archipelago: The Case of the Maldives." In J. L. Kaminarides, Briguglio, and H. Hoogendonk, eds., *The Economic Development of Small Countries: Problems, Strategies and Policies*, 1989.

———. "Technological Change and Income Distribution: Findings from Maldivian Fishing Villages." *Journal of Economics and International Relations* 3 (3): 217–240, 1990.

———. "Towards and Appropriate Effort-Based Fishery Model for the Tuna Fishery of Maldives." *Indian Journal of Fisheries* 34 (4): 433–454, 1987.

Webb, P.C. *People and Environment of Maldives*. Malé: Novelty Press Pvt. Ltd, Republic of Maldives, 1988.

World Bank. *The Maldives: An Introductory Economic Report*, 1980.

———. Fishery: Sector Policy Paper, 1982.

Xavier Romero-Frias, *The Maldive Islanders, A Study of the Popular Culture of an Ancient Ocean Kingdom*. Barcelona, 1999.

———. "Republic of Maldives." Culture Grams. 2008. http://online.culturegrams.com.ezproxy.spl.org:2048/secure/world/accessible_report.php?cid=216 (retrieved Jan. 13, 2009).

———. "Culture of the Maldives." http://www.nationmaster.com/encyclopedia/Culture-of-the-Maldives (retrieved Jan. 13, 2009).

———"Maldives." *CIA World Factbook*. https://www.cia.gov/library/publications/the-world-factbook/geos/mv.html (retrieved Jan. 13, 2009).

Rasheed, Khilath. "The Truth About Cats and Folklore," Haveeru News Service, 19 November 1998, http://www.maldivesculture.com/fandit04.html (retrieved Jan. 15, 2009).

"Maldivian Folklore," http://www.nationmaster.com/encyclopedia/Maldivian-Folklore (retrieved Jan. 15, 2009).

———. "Maldives: Social Policy and Population Section," United Nations Economic and Social Commission for Asia and the Pacific. http://www.unescap.org/esid/psis/population/popin/profiles/maldives.asp (retrieved Jan. 22, 2009).

—by M. Njoroge

MALIANS

PRONUNCIATION: MAHL-ee-uhns
LOCATION: Mali
POPULATION: 12–13 million
LANGUAGE: French (official); national languages: Bamana, Bobo, Bozo, Dogon, Fulfulde, Hassaniyya, Khassonke, Maninka, Minyanka, Senufo, Soninke (or Sarakolle), Songhai (or Sonrhai), and Tamasheq.
RELIGION: Islam, Christianity, indigenous beliefs
RELATED ARTICLES: Vol. 1: Bamana; Dyula; Malinke; Songhay; Tuaregs

¹ INTRODUCTION

Mali has a very long and rich history. Although economic indicators place the country among the poorest in the world today, the empires of Ghana, Mali (see **Malinke**), and Songhai (see **Songhay**) developed and flourished in different parts of its territory long before the arrival of Europeans. The Mali Empire had the most enduring influence on various peoples of the region and has given the country its name. In addition to the early empires, other states of variable size existed at different points in time.

The area of contemporary Mali captured the European imagination ever since the medieval trans-Saharan gold trade and Emperor Musa I's famous pilgrimage to Mecca in 1324–25. Europeans began to explore the territory in 1795 in search of new markets and raw materials, followed by territorial conquest in the latter part of the 19th century. Advancing from their colony of Senegal in the west, French troops created a post at Bamako in 1883 and from there pushed north and eastward. In spite of resistance from the leaders of then-existing states and from autonomous villages and nomads, the French had consolidated their conquest into the colony of "Soudan Français" by the turn of the century. Administered from Bamako, the name was changed to Haut-Sénégal-Niger from 1900–1920 and the boundaries were altered several times during the period of French colonial rule. Following the struggle for independence and a short-lived federation with Senegal (known as the Mali Federation), the colony became the Republic of Mali on 22 September 1960.

The first government under President Modibo Keita had a socialist orientation. It was overthrown by a group of military officers in 1968 that made Moussa Traoré the new president. Traoré was able to maintain himself in power until 1991 when he was removed by some of his officers after ordering the army to put down demonstrations with brutal force. A transitional government was formed and elections were held within a year. Alpha Oumar Konaré became the new president in 1992. He was reelected for a second five-year term in 1997. His successor Amadou Toumani Touré also was elected for a second term (2007–2012).

² LOCATION AND HOMELAND

Located in the interior of West Africa, the Republic of Mali shares borders with seven countries: Algeria in the north; Mauritania and Senegal in the west; Guinea and Côte d'Ivoire in the south; and Burkina Faso and Niger in the east. In 2008 the country's population was estimated at more than 12 mil-

lion with over one million living in the Bamako metropolitan area. Over 2 million Malians are said to live and work elsewhere in Africa, Europe, North America, and other parts of the world. Although the territory of the republic extends over 1.24 million sq km (478,767 sq mi), a large part of it is covered by the Sahara Desert and receives less than 30 cm (12 in) of rain a year. As a result, most of the population is concentrated in the southern half of the country. The Niger, one of the major rivers in Africa, traverses Mali for 1,700 km (1,050 mi) of its course. It flows in a northeasterly direction, joined by the Bani River in the city of Mopti to form a vast interior delta before making a wide bend to continue southeastward into the neighboring Republic of Niger. Mali is divided into eight administrative regions, each headed by a governor, with capitals at Kayes, Koulikoro, Sikasso, Segou, Mopti, Timbuktu, Gao, and Kidal, respectively. The national capital of Bamako is a separate administrative district. In early 1991 groups of Tuareg people in the northern desert regions began a rebellion to protest their marginalization in the national power structure and the distribution of resources. Following extended negotiations, the Konaré government brought about a political solution but isolated incidents of violence continue to occur from time to time.

³ LANGUAGE

The official language of Mali is French but national languages remain the preferred mode of communication. The Bamana language has become the lingua franca and is mutually intelligible with Maninka. Bobo, Bozo, Dogon (several dialects), Fulfulde, Hassaniyya, Khassonke, Minyanka, Senufo, Soninke, Songhai, and Tamasheq have variable numbers of speakers and dominate in different parts of the country. Most television programs are in French, but many radio stations broadcast news and other programs in the different national languages.

Tamasheq has a script (*tifinagh*) dating back to the early centuries of the common era. A Guinean Maninka speaker created N'ko, an alphabet for Bamana/Maninka, in the late 1940s. Starting in 1967 a newly created national linguistic institute began developing writing conventions for Maninka/Bamana, Fulfulde, Songhai, and Tamasheq. By 1972 the first newspaper was published in the Bamana language. N'ko has gained some proponents but most Malians who are literate in any of the national languages use the orthographies developed by the national linguistic institute.

⁴ FOLKLORE

For many Malians, the ancestors who actively resisted French colonization (e.g., Babemba Traoré of Sikasso) hold the status of national heroes. Otherwise, heroes and myths vary from one ethnic group to another. Sunjata Keita occupies a special place as the founder of the empire that gave the country its name; the recitation of his epic to musical accompaniment can arouse strong emotions among the Maninka people in the southern parts of the country. Only specially trained *griots* (praise-singers and oral historians) from certain families are permitted to perform the epic. All of Mali's ethnic groups have a rich store of proverbs, riddles, and tales that communicate and transmit cultural norms and moral values.

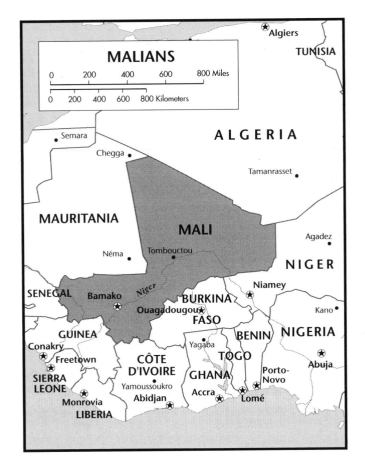

MALIANS

5 RELIGION

About 90% of Malians identify as Muslims. Trans-Saharan traders first introduced Islam to their local hosts and members of the political elite. Islam spread gradually among different populations beginning in the 11th century but it did not become a majority religion until the 20th century. The ways in which Islam is practiced across Mali today reflects the historical legacy of different Muslim leaders and movements, transregional connections, the recent influx of funds from Arab countries as well as the use of broadcast media in the dissemination of Islamic knowledge.

Christians constitute less than 2% of the population. The overwhelming majority are Catholics because Christianity was introduced by Catholic missionaries during French colonialism. Protestant Christian churches have thus far had only limited success in their search for converts. The remainder of the population continues to follow indigenous religious practices which may involve sacrifices to the ancestors and to community spirits, divination, spirit possession, and membership in initiation societies.

6 MAJOR HOLIDAYS

Public offices and some private businesses (e.g., banks) are closed on Sundays. Offices close at midday on Friday to allow the faithful to participate in Friday prayer at the mosque. Muslim holidays, as well as Christmas and Easter, are officially recognized. The two most important Islamic holidays are *'Id al-fitr*, at the end of the holy month of Ramadan, and *'Id al-adha*

(also known as *Tabaski*), on the tenth day of the last month in the Muslim calendar. Each lasts three days and is celebrated with public prayers, new clothes for family members, festive meals and visiting with family and friends. Families commemorate Abraham's sacrifice by slaughtering a sheep on Tabaski.

Secular holidays include September 22, Independence Day (see above), and March 26, Democracy Day. The latter memorializes the end of the three-day uprising that brought down the Traoré regime.

7 RITES OF PASSAGE

Special ceremonies mark birth, marriage, and death throughout the country. The way they are celebrated varies somewhat between ethnic groups, urban and rural areas, and according to religious affiliation and economic status. However, they commonly bring together the extended family and larger social networks, with men and women congregating in different parts of the home. In urban areas, women relatives and friends come to the name giving ceremony with a gift of cloth or soap for the mother of the baby. The mother of a bride also receives cloth from her relatives and friends on behalf of her daughter. Men give money to a bridegroom on his wedding day to help him defray expenses, since it is the husband and his family who are responsible for the wedding festivities. When someone dies, male and female relatives, neighbors, and friends visit the bereaved family to offer condolences as soon as they receive the news. Among Muslims, only men accompany the body to the cemetery.

Most of Mali's ethnic groups practiced circumcision for boys and excision for girls. In the past, the highly ritualized procedure took place during the teenage years, but it is now often done much earlier. Many urban parents currently have their infant boys circumcised in the hospital shortly after birth, and an increasing number no longer excise girls. Women's groups have been engaging in educational campaigns to discourage excision nationwide.

8 INTERPERSONAL RELATIONS

Maintaining personal dignity, one's own and that of others, is extremely important and requires proper greeting and hospitality. Upon entering a household, a visitor initiates a short greeting. If the visitor is a stranger or someone who visits only irregularly, the host responds with a longer greeting, inquiring about the person's well-being and that of his or her relatives; the visitor then does the same in turn. Young people visiting a friend show their respect by greeting the head of household and/or the friend's mother. A visitor who arrives at meal time is invited to share the food. Greetings may be exchanged without physical contact, or by taking the interlocutor's right hand. Shaking hands is common among coworkers in offices. Late afternoon, before sundown, is the preferred time for paying social calls.

Young women and men usually socialize in groups, either same- or mixed-sex. Dating occurs more often in the company of others than as a couple. Although many young people in urban areas now choose their spouses themselves, a young man must still send a family representative to the family of the woman he wishes to marry. The woman's family must give their consent and stipulate the gift exchanges to take place before the wedding can be celebrated.

⁹ LIVING CONDITIONS

Successive governments elected since 1992 have sought to improve the basic infrastructure of the country. Nonetheless, life remains difficult for the majority of Malians. Those with an income must support not only their nuclear families, but also aged relatives and members of the extended family who are unemployed. Households rarely encompass only a nuclear family, and even well-to-do Malians have numerous obligations toward less fortunate relatives. The most commonly owned consumer goods are transistor radios, cell phones, and motor bikes or bicycles. In Bamako, car ownership has increased significantly since the 1990s. A growing number of households with access to electricity own television sets and, to a lesser extent, VCRs. Many urban families aspire to a living room furnished with a couch, table, chairs, and a china cabinet, but the interiors of most rural and urban homes are more modest. Given the climate, much of daily life takes place in the courtyard or in the shade of the veranda. A substantial part of income is spent on food, clothing, and health care. The majority of physicians practice in urban areas while nurses and midwives are the primary healthcare providers in rural areas. Aspirin and malaria medication are readily available and relatively inexpensive, but the cost of prescription drugs is high. For this reason, and because some herbal remedies are very effective, people may resort to indigenous pharmacopeia or seek out a healer before going to a clinic.

¹⁰ FAMILY LIFE

Malian law allows men to have more than one wife. A substantial number have two wives but only a small percentage has three or four, as permitted by Islam. Each wife is entitled to her own house or apartment. Women in polygamous households take turns preparing family meals. Many urban households with a regular income employ live-in domestic servants, generally young unmarried women from the rural areas. Household size and composition vary between rural and urban areas and, though more restricted in the latter, are usually not limited to a man and his wife (or wives) and their children. Visitors are also common for varying lengths of time.

Women work in all sectors of the rural and urban economy; only a minority is not involved in income-generating activities. Even women designated as "housewife" in the national census frequently engage in activities that range from small trade in cooked food to craft production, market gardening, and rain-fed agriculture. Women, like men, dispose of their own income, though spouses have different responsibilities for the maintenance of the family.

¹¹ CLOTHING

Traditional dress varies for Mali's different ethnic groups, though what is considered "traditional" has also changed over time. Conversion to Islam and integration into a commodity economy has brought about greater uniformity in clothing styles throughout the country. For married women to be well-dressed means wearing an ample, full-length tunic (called *boubou*) combined with a matching wraparound skirt (*pagne*) and headdress. Men wear the *boubou* over matching pants and a loose-fitting shirt. Type and quality of material, design details, and embroidery create distinctions and signal a person's means. Unique colors are often achieved through hand dyeing. Women complement their attire with gold jewelry, especially on festive occasions. Some men wear the *jellabiya* common in the Middle East. A minority of Malian women cover themselves in a black *burka* when they leave the home and a growing number express their piety by wearing a thin veil over their clothing since the end of the 1990s, particularly in the urban areas.

Teenage girls and young women in their twenties dress in wraparound or narrow tailored skirts and matching tops made of colorful cotton prints. The tops are done in a variety of styles with innovative details which change with the fashions. A small number of teenage girls in urban areas wear pants, mainly when they go out in the evening.

When working, many men wear Western-style pants and shirts or short (waist- or hip-length) tunics. Women put on wraparound skirts and tunics or tailored tops made of less expensive cottons while working at home. Imported second-hand clothing from Europe or North America, especially blouses, shirts, T-shirts, and (for men) pants, is also common during manual labor. Young people often have good second-hand clothing refitted and restyled for regular everyday wear.

¹² FOOD

Traditional foods are regionally specific. The food and eating habits discussed here are those of the capital city. They show some uniformity in spite of the population's ethnic diversity. The two staples throughout most of the country are boiled rice and a stiff porridge or a couscous made of millet. Millet is the more traditional food, but rice is preferred and has almost replaced millet for those who can afford it daily. Both are served with a sauce which may include fresh vegetables, fish, meat, or chicken. Those who are able return home at midday for their main meal and then eat something lighter, or some leftover food, in the evening. Others make do with a snack (e.g., some fried plantain or a skewer of beef with French bread) until the early evening. A light meal may be a cream of rice, liquid enough to be eaten like a soup. Salad is also gaining in popularity among those born since the mid-1950s. A typical breakfast food is gruel made with millet flour, tamarind, and sugar or, for variety, small leavened pancakes made with millet. French bread and coffee with milk and sugar are popular with many in the cities, but too expensive for the vast majority.

Western-style kitchens are rare, and most cooking is done on a brazier in the courtyard or in a detached kitchen house. Food is served in bowls, and family members gather around a common bowl and eat with their hands or with a spoon. Children are taught at an early age to wash their hands before eating, to eat with their right hand, and to wash again after eating. In large families, women and men generally eat separately.

¹³ EDUCATION

Estimates of the percentage of children enrolled in formal education range from 30–50%. This includes children in *madrasas* but not in Quranic schools because the Malian state does not recognize Quranic schools as formal education. Created in the 1940s, madrasas are private Islamic schools where Arabic is the primary language of instruction for religious and secular subjects and French is taught for several hours a week beginning in the third grade. About 30-40% of all school-going children today are said to be in madrasas.

Public schools consist of two main types: schools whose entire curriculum is in French and bi-lingual schools where a national language is the medium of instruction during the first four years. Mother tongue instruction in the Bamana language began on an experimental basis in a few schools in 1979. It was expanded gradually and other languages were added over time. By 2006, 2550 schools across Mali hosted bi-lingual programs in one of eleven national languages. In spite of this increase, the percentage of children in bi-lingual programs compared to the classical French programs has actually declined (less than 10% in 2005) due to demographic growth and the expansion of schooling.

Many new madrasas and secular schools (funded by the state or by local communities) were created after the democratic opening in 1991. Universal primary education however remains a challenge since about 50% of Mali's population is under the age of 15. Many parents cannot afford to send or keep their children in school even where schools exist. Enrollment varies across regions. Bamako has the highest enrollment rates in primary and secondary education. The national university, created in 1996, is located in Bamako. Numerous private institutions provide professional and some university-level education.

¹⁴ CULTURAL HERITAGE

The old towns of Djenne and Timbuktu and the tomb of Askia Mohamed in Gao are world heritage sites. The Ahmed Baba Center and the Kati Foundation in Timbuktu house rich collections of Arabic manuscripts from the period when the city was a flourishing center of Islamic scholarship (13th to 16th centuries).

Music, theater, dance, and oral literature particular to the different cultural traditions of the country continue to be practiced in rural villages as well as in urban neighborhoods. They also evolve as they address new themes and incorporate new technologies. Musical performances are a regular feature on Malian television. Successive governments have made the promotion and development of Mali's cultural heritage an integral aspect of national politics since independence. Beginning in the 1960s, youths in the various regions were encouraged to develop theater, music, or dance performances and the best groups were selected to represent their region at a biennial festival in Bamako. Since the late 1990s, regional festivals (e.g. in the north of Mali) are also organized through local initiatives. The National Institute of Arts, a professional secondary school in Bamako, has long promoted the cultural heritage through training in several artistic genres and professions (e.g. music, theatre, jewelry making, etc.). A Conservatory of the Arts and Media was recently created to provide advanced training in the plastic arts, theater, dance, and multi-media. It is directed by the internationally acclaimed painter Abdoulaye Konaté. The National Museum has a permanent arts and crafts collection from different periods and cultural traditions and also hosts excellent temporary exhibits.

The male and female Malian musicians who have become household names on the world music scene are too numerous to mention. The films of Souleymane Cissé and Cheik Oumar Cissoko and the photography of Seydou Keita and Malick Sidibé are internationally recognized. Mali has also produced a number of literary figures writing in French such as Amadou Hampaté Ba, Massa Makan Diabaté, Moussa Konaté, Ibrahima Ly, Yambo Ouologuem, and Fily Dabo Sissoko, to name only a few.

¹⁵ WORK

The majority of Malians are self-employed, making a living in agriculture, herding, fishing, trade, craft production, small-scale enterprises, and services. Profit margins are generally small. Most of the salaried positions are in the civil service or in international organizations. Beginning in the 1980s, structural adjustment policies imposed by the World Bank and the International Monetary Fund compelled the government to reduce the civil service and thus to hire fewer secondary school and higher-education graduates. This has resulted in greater unemployment and underemployment because the private formal sector, though growing, is still limited. Many Malians, single men as well as entire families, emigrate in search of work and better opportunities on a short- or long-term basis.

¹⁶ SPORTS

Soccer is by far the most popular sport and is played recreationally as well as in national and international competitions. Mali hosted the Africa Cup in 2002. Basketball is played by some male and female teams. Athletics has gained wider attention through the Grand Prix de Bamako since Mali began hosting the Pan African Athletics meeting in 2000.

¹⁷ ENTERTAINMENT AND RECREATION

Private radio stations have mushroomed since the 1990s and people of all ages tune in for their favorite programs. Many urban residents relax in the evening by watching Brazilian or North American soap operas or other programs on television, often in the company of neighbors or friends. Young people enjoy listening to Malian, other African, and international popular music. Concerts by well-known performers draw large crowds. While rural youths dance mostly at local festivals, urban youths also frequent discotheques and other dance events on weekends. Socializing with relatives, friends, and neighbors remains the most popular pastime for young and old, men and women, in urban and rural areas. In the cities, many men belong to a *grin*, a circle of friends with whom they meet regularly to talk or play cards while brewing a strong sweet tea. The importance of movies as a form of entertainment has diminished in recent years and a number of theaters have closed.

¹⁸ FOLK ART, CRAFTS, AND HOBBIES

Folk arts and crafts are alive, and some flourish, as a stroll through the open-air markets of Bamako will reveal. Different regions and ethnic groups specialize and excel in particular products: Fulbe men in the Mopti region, for example, weave wool blankets with a variety of geometric designs, Tuareg women in the north of Mali make dyed leather goods (pillow covers, bags, knife sheaths, etc.), and women from Kayes are known for their indigo dyed cloth. Although the bulk of wool blankets and leather goods are now intended for the tourist market, they and other products are also made for home consumption. These include gold and silver jewelry, pottery (e.g., water jars), spoons and ladles made of squashes, and a range of mats and basketry. Hand woven cotton cloth in various colors and patterns is still sewn into blankets for use during the winter months but its production for women's wrappers and men's tunics has declined considerably. The tie-dyed damask cloth produced by urban women in innovative designs and colors, especially in Bamako, is prized for elegant wear not only in Mali but also in neighboring countries.

¹⁹ SOCIAL PROBLEMS

From 1960 to the overthrow of the Traoré government in 1991, political prisoners were frequently banished to the salt mines of the Sahara desert. Since the democratic opening of 1991, local human rights activists and the dynamic press keep the spotlight on the government and don't hesitate to discuss social, political, and economic problems openly. Most social problems result from the inability of many Malians to find employment and/or to earn an adequate income. Theft, prostitution, and homelessness are most prevalent in the cities. Drug use exists in some youth circles but is discouraged by the government and by Islam. Alcoholism is not widespread.

Malaria diminishes the quality of life and economic productivity of many individuals during the rainy season and, in the south of the country, at other times of the year as well. Lack of refrigeration often leads to gastrointestinal problems. Respiratory illnesses, parasites, and infections of various kinds are also common among children and adults. In 2003 HIV/AIDS prevalence in adults was estimated at 1.9%. Internationally funded initiatives seek to mobilize youths in the fight against HIV/AIDS and sexually transmissible diseases.

²⁰ GENDER ISSUES

Women's and men's rights and responsibilities within the family, and their contributions to the household economy, vary in accordance with age, marital status, position within the household, as well as between ethnic groups and between urban and rural areas. Male and female legislators have worked for years to revise the national family law code to bring about greater equality between men and women in the areas of marital status, parental rights, ownership of land and inheritance, wages and pensions, employment laws, and education. Opposition from conservative groups has led to repeated compromises and has delayed passage.

In several regions of the country a majority of girls are married before the age of eighteen. As with excision, women's associations carry out educational campaigns with strong financial support from international donors.

Awa Keita (b. 1912), a trained midwife who lived and worked in different parts of the country, was active in the struggle for independence and in the organization of the women's branch of the USRDA nationalist party. In spite of this example, only small numbers of women have sought political office. The major political parties have attempted to change this pattern by setting quotas for female representation to encourage women to run for elective office.

²¹ BIBLIOGRAPHY

Agence de coopération culturelle et technique. *L'artisanat créateur au Mali*. Paris: Dessain et Tolra, 1977.

Bouwman, Dinie and Anneke Breedveld, eds. "Education in the Mande World." *Mande Studies* 8, 2006.

Konaré, Alpha Oumar, and Adam Ba. *Grandes Dates du Mali*. Bamako: Editions Imprimeries du Mali, 1983.

Maliweb. www.maliweb.net/ (June 2008).

—by M. Grosz-Ngaté

MALINKE

PRONUNCIATION: mah-LING-kay
ALTERNATE NAMES: Mandinka, Maninka, Manding, Mandingo, Mandin, Mande
LOCATION: Territory covering The Gambia, Senegal, Mali, Guinea Bissau, Guinea, Sierra Leone, Liberia, and Côte d'Ivoire (Ivory Coast)
POPULATION: 7.75 million
LANGUAGE: Variations of Mande languages
RELIGION: Islam
RELATED ARTICLES: Vol. 1: Gambians; Guineans; Ivoirians; Malians; Senegalese

¹ INTRODUCTION

The name Malinke is just one of many similar names used for a large group of closely related peoples in West Africa. They are also commonly referred to as Mandinka, Maninka, Manding, Mandingo, Mandin, and Mande. The areas that they occupy are among the earliest places of Neolithic agricultural settlements in sub-Saharan Africa, dating as far back as 7,000 years.

The Malinke have the distinction of being heirs to the great Mali Empire, a medieval merchant empire that flourished from the 13th to the 16th centuries and greatly influenced the course of West African history. Much of the northern region of Africa, of which the Malinke territories were a part, was incorporated into the world of Islam in the 11th century, and most of the West African chieftains adopted the Islamic religion. One of the famous kings of the Mali Empire, Kankan Musa (r.1312–37), made a pilgrimage to Mecca in 1324 with a tremendous entourage of camels laden with gold, and some 60,000 men, including 500 slaves carrying golden staffs. The renowned city of Islamic teaching, Timbuctu, was also part of the vast and prosperous Mali Empire. The empire declined in the 15th century and was gradually absorbed and usurped by the Songhai Kingdom, which extended to the 17th century.

As early as 1444, Portuguese traders had enslaved the first Malinke people, and in the next three and a half centuries, thousands of Malinke and other peoples were transported by Portuguese, British, French, and Dutch merchants to the Caribbean and the Americas to work as slaves on plantations.

Interesting descriptions of the areas inhabited by the Malinke were gathered in the late 18th century by Scottish explorer Mungo Park, who led two expeditions exploring the Gambia and Niger Rivers. During the first expedition, between 1795 and 1797, he was imprisoned by an Arab chieftain for four months before escaping, and later lay ill in a Malinke town for seven months. Park wrote a book about this expedition, called *Travels in the Interior Districts of Africa* (1797). Park was drowned during an attack by natives on the Niger River in 1806.

During the 19th century the kingdoms of the Malinke peoples were subjugated by the British, French, and Portuguese and were incorporated into their colonial systems. It would take over a century for them to gradually gain autonomy in independent African nations whose boundaries crossed their tribal territories.

The Malinke people gained some popular attention when Alex Haley published his best-selling book, *Roots* (1974), later made into a television series. The story of Haley's ances-

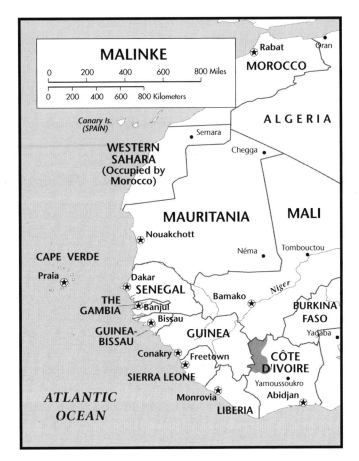

MALINKE

0 200 400 600 800 Miles

0 200 400 600 800 Kilometers

MOROCCO
Rabat
Oran
ALGERIA
Canary Is.
(SPAIN)
Semara
WESTERN
SAHARA
(Occupied by
Morocco)
Chegga
MAURITANIA
MALI
Nouakchott
Néma
Tombouctou
CAPE VERDE
Praia
Niger
Dakar
SENEGAL
Bamako
THE
GAMBIA
Banjul
BURKINA
FASO
Bissau
Yagaba
GUINEA-
BISSAU
GUINEA
Conakry
Freetown
CÔTE
D'IVOIRE
SIERRA LEONE
Yamoussoukro
Abidjan
ATLANTIC
OCEAN
Monrovia
LIBERIA

² LOCATION AND HOMELAND

Today there are more than 7.75 million Malinke distributed over several African nations within a wide arc that extends 1,300 km (800 mi). It starts at the mouth of the Gambia River in the northwest and circles around in a bow form, ending in Côte d'Ivoire (Ivory Coast) in the southeast. The territory includes areas in the nations of The Gambia, Senegal, Mali, Guinea Bissau, Guinea, Sierra Leone, Liberia, Ghana, Burkina Faso, and Côte d'Ivoire. There are numerous other African ethnic groups sharing these areas. Of the 7.75 million Malinke scattered throughout West Africa, there are 2.8 million in Guinea; 1.1 million in Mali; 1 million in the Ivory Coast; 1 million in Senegal; 600,000 in The Gambia; 400,000 in Sierra Leone; 400,000 in Burkina Faso; 200,000 in Guinea-Bissau; 100,000 in Liberia; and 100,000 in Ghana. They do not form a majority group in any of the above countries. In The Gambia they represent approximately 39% of the country's total population, in Guinea 32%, and in Guinea-Bissau 14%.

³ LANGUAGE

The Malinke peoples speak slight variations of the broad Mande branch of the Niger-Congo family of languages. The term "Mande" frequently refers to a group of closely related languages spoken by the Malinke and other West African peoples, such as the Bambara, the Soninke, and the Dyula. The Mandinka language, sometimes referred to as Mandingo, is a Mande language spoken by millions of Mandinka people in Mali, Senegal, The Gambia, Guinea, Ivory Coast, Burkina Faso, Sierra Leone, Liberia, Guinea-Bissau, and Chad; it is the main language of The Gambia. It belongs to the Manding branch of Mande, and is thus fairly similar to Bambara and Maninka or Malinke. It is a tonal language with two tones: low and high.

⁴ FOLKLORE

Details of the early days of the Mali Empire and the lifestyles of the people have been kept alive for centuries through the epic poem, "Sonjara" (or "Sundiata"; also "Sunjata"), which has been sung and resung through many generations by the *griots*, bards or praise-singers of West Africa. In over 3,000 lines of poetry in the oral tradition, it tells the story of Sonjara, a legendary leader who, after countless obstacles and trials, unites the Malinke clans and chiefdoms at the beginning of the 13th century. As a young child he was hexed and made into a cripple by his father's jealous second wife, who wanted her own son to be king. He finally learns to walk and decides to become a hunter, giving up his claim to the throne and starting on a long exile with his mother and siblings. After many adventures, a delegation from Mali pleads with him to come back and save them from an evil sorcerer-king, Sumanguru, who has put calabashes (gourds) over the mouths of their heroes. Sonjara organizes an army to return and regain his rightful throne. With help from his sister, who seduces the evil sorcerer-king to discover his vulnerable points and, after long and bloody battles, he triumphs over Sumanguru, liberating and uniting the surrounding chiefdoms. "Sonjara" is now considered one of the famous epics of world history, and it is still being performed by griots for the Malinke.

tral family and the book's main character, Kunta Kinte of the Mandinka (Malinke) people, personalized the terrible plight of African slaves and their families who were sold into slavery. Indeed, a great many slaves were taken from the areas around the present countries of The Gambia and Senegal, particularly in the 16th century. By the mid-18th century, when Kunta Kinte was captured into slavery, regions to the south mostly supplied the slave trade.

The Malinke were not only victims of the slave trade, but they were also perpetrators of the trade themselves, having had a long history of owning and maintaining slaves. The explorer Mungo Park, during his first journey through the area of Senegal and The Gambia, estimated that three-quarters of the population were hereditary slaves. There were two distinct kinds of slaves to be found: those that had been captured in battle or purchased; and those that had been born into the slave families of their village. The first had no rights and were treated like objects to be bought and sold. The second kind had a number of rights and privileges and could sometimes even buy their freedom. These hereditary slaves might be sold out of the village as punishment for a crime. Mungo Park documented how some free people, during a severe drought, would voluntarily give themselves as slaves to relatively wealthy Malinke farmers in order to save themselves from starvation.

The indigenous slave trade persisted into the 19th century, somewhat beyond the time that the British, French, and American slave trade had been declared illegal. Even today the lowest caste in the Malinke system of social structure comprises descendants of former slaves.

⁵ RELIGION

The majority of the Malinke are Muslim and have adapted the tenets of Islam into their native beliefs, resulting in a wide range of syncretic variations. Most Malinke villages have a mosque, often a large cylindrical structure with a thatched roof that contains a hole through which the call to prayer can be shouted; some village mosques have a minaret, and most mosques are enclosed by a palisade fence. Women sit separate from the men, both in the mosque and during outside religious services. Those villagers who have made a pilgrimage to Mecca, or even descendants of those who have made the journey, are highly respected. They may have the word for the sacred pilgrimage, *Hadj*, as part of their name.

The principal religious leader is the elected *imam*, an elder who leads prayers at the mosques and has great religious knowledge. The other Islamic clerics who play a major role as healers and religious counselors are the *marabouts*. They are respected as preservers of morality through oral tradition and as teachers of the Quran. These specialists have many talents, being able to foretell the future, interpret natural signs, and make herbal concoctions for curing illnesses. They are experts at preventing and healing ailments or injuries inflicted by evil spirits or by mortals.

Prevention and cure is frequently done by means of *gri-gris*, or charms. The most common ones are written charms. The marabout copies selected lines in Arabic script from a master copy—either from the Quran or from a book with medicinal messages. These lines written on a piece of paper comprise a charm that can be folded in any shape—rectangle, triangle, square—and taken to the leatherworker to be covered in a leather pouch with a string and worn around the neck, waist, or arm. Charms can be obtained for protection from illness, from bullets or weapons, for help in finding employment, or even for making oneself attractive to the opposite sex. Another type of charm is the water charm, in which some lines from the master copy are written in washable ink onto a writing board. The ink is washed into a bowl. The recipient can drink a bit of the solution every day or rinse the body with it, for example, to help gain success in school.

A marabout can also provide a blessed string to be placed on the wrist of an infant hours after birth to protect it from evil spirits, or on the tails of cattle if there is fear of an epidemic caused by evil spirits. A personal blessing of the marabout is considered helpful for healing: he will spit lightly on the forehead of a patient and press the area with the palm of his hand. Children in particular may be seen with several charms around their neck, waist, or wrist. The common use of charms is an indication that the Malinke are fearful of many evil spirits, which can bring death or misfortune.

⁶ MAJOR HOLIDAYS

The Malinke look forward to the important Islamic holidays. The favorite is Tabaski, which usually falls in the spring or summer, the day being determined according to the Islamic lunar calendar. Tabaski commemorates the moment when Abraham was about to sacrifice his son Isaac in obedience to God's command, when God interceded and a ram was substituted. The Malinke start saving months ahead of time for the celebration to purchase new clothes and to have an abundant supply of food. The most expensive item is the ram or sheep to be slaughtered at the precise moment determined by the lunar calendar. It is prestigious to have a very large and fat ram to slaughter. Households that can only afford a goat or chicken are rather embarrassed. On this day people attend the mosque, and there is much eating (especially roasted mutton) and visiting of friends. Other religious holidays include the Feast of Ramadan celebrated at the end of the annual 30-day Muslim fast, and Muhammad's birthday.

⁷ RITES OF PASSAGE

A week after the birth of an infant, the Malinke hold a name-giving ceremony. A marabout leads prayers during a ceremony, shaves the infant's head, and announces the name of the child for the first time. If the parents can afford it, a goat or sheep will be killed, and the meat will be served along with balls of dough blessed by the marabout.

Puberty rites and circumcision are very significant in the lives of the Malinke, both male and female. Children are teased about the status of being uncircumcised, and from an early age they are curious as well as fearful. It is the most important rite of passage, for one cannot attain adulthood or marry without it. For boys the rite is held about once every five years and includes novices from 6 to 13 years old, who may be in a group of 30 to 45 boys. There are variations in the ceremony, but the following is typical. A circumcision lodge is built with millet stalks after the harvest in December or January. At dawn the novice is carried to the place of circumcision on the shoulders of an "older brother" or guardian who has already been circumcised. The village men proceed to the lodge. Each boy is circumcised, after waiting reflectively, by a circumciser or elder; the boy sits at the edge of a hole with his legs around it, and the foreskin is buried in the hole. Either indigenous herbs or Western ointment may be used to help heal the wound. Just after the circumcision the guardians race back to the village to spread the news, waving branches in the leaf dance.

In the evening the novices, draped in white clothing with hoods, enter the lodge to begin a period of six to eight weeks of seclusion. They carry large square charms to ward off evil spirits. They undergo an education in a fearful atmosphere by the lodge chief and guardians who teach them to act as a collective group. The frightening sounds of a bull-roarer (a flat board whirled around on a string) are heard, and they are threatened that evil demons will be called in. They learn circumcision songs that reflect the values of society, for example, respect for elders. The novices undergo four stages of education, including a feast prepared by their mothers. When they return home with a new status there will be a polite distance between mother and son. The boys who were circumcised in one ceremony form an age-set, which is given a name; they will have a close bond for life.

The girls' circumcision is organized and convened by the "circumcision queen," a village woman leader who is a respected midwife and supervises rituals concerning women. Girls are circumcised in smaller groups, and the ceremonies occur more frequently. The girls are carried on the backs of their "older sisters," their guardians, just as mothers carry infants on their backs. They are blindfolded and taken to a symbolic women's tree used to make women's tools or mortars and pestles. Each novice in turn sits on the edge of a hole, supported by an elder woman behind her. The clitoridectomy is done by an elder woman specialist. Boiled bandages and ointments are applied, and the girls stay secluded for ten days to two weeks. During this time they are taught Malinke values and how to work together as a group. The stages of seclusion are similar to those of the boys. In recent years there is pressure to have circumcision in clinics. In general, however, the older generation is very reluctant to let go of these traditional rituals, and circumcision is still an important prerequisite to marriage.

Marriage ties are important for creating and cementing bonds between families. Marriage for a Malinke girl may begin with her betrothal at birth to a boy who may be 12 years old or less. The preferred marriage partner is the matrilateral cross-cousin: the boy is betrothed to his mother's brother's daughter. Prior to marriage, several steps in the payment of a bride-price by the suitor to the parents of the prospective bride are made, taking from three to seven years. The installments include money, kola nuts (bitter, mildly hallucinogenic nuts), salt, and some livestock. Although the girl can sleep intermittently with her future husband, she cannot go to live in his compound until the full payment is made, amounting to what is a large sum in Malinke economy. Additional gifts are made to the bride's mother-in-law before the actual marriage ceremony can take place.

The typical Malinke wedding, called a "bride transfer," takes place on a Thursday or Friday—the two holiest days of the week. The bride is dressed in dark blue with a white smock, a blue turban, and a dark blue shawl over her head with just the eyes showing. She wears anklets and bracelets of silver beads and ties a silver coin in her hair. The "circumcision queen" comes to the bride's house and performs a dance. The bride walks behind the queen with her hands on the queen's hips; this is called "carrying the bride." The two are followed by a throng of women, symbolically weeping because the bride will be leaving her parents' home. The bride goes to her husband's house and sits on his bed. A period of seclusion lasting up to three days begins, a period in which the bride is considered very vulnerable to an evil spirit. The seclusion ends when the husband unveils the wife. The village women give gifts of cooking utensils and hold a dance.

The Malinke practice polygyny (plural wives), and Islam permits men to take up to four wives. Only prosperous men can afford several wives due to the expensive bride-price and the fact that all wives should be provided for equally.

The final rite of passage, death, is not seen as a natural event for the Malinke. Their word "to die" also means "to kill," and death is seen to be caused by some evil force. At the same time, the person is believed to rise again to one of three regions in an afterlife: heaven, hell, or purgatory (somewhere in between). The corpse is ritually bathed and the water collected so it cannot cause sickness. The men conduct the funeral while the women gather nearby. A senior marabout gives the eulogy and the imam says the final prayers. Men carry the body on a mat to the burial place with the women wailing. It is buried on its right side, head facing east, feet to the north. A fence is built around the grave to protect it from animals; sticks are put over the hole to provide a "breathing space." The corpse is said to be interviewed by the angel Malika during a 45-day judgment period. In that time three mortuary ceremonies are held at which oil cakes and kola nuts are distributed to those attending.

8 INTERPERSONAL RELATIONS

When the Malinke encounter a family member or friend, the greetings they have for one another are very important, as they are for other West Africans. An extensive ritual exchange of rather formal greeting questions ensues, that can take up to a minute. They might say, "Peace be with you.," "Is your life peaceful?," "How is everything going?," "Are your family members in good health?," "How is your father?," or "Is the weather treating your crops well?" The questions go back and forth and may end with, "Thanks be to Allah." Even if one is not feeling well or if things are not going well, the answers are usually positive. It is considered very bad manners not to engage in the lengthy greeting exchange.

The Malinke people in general are very warm and hospitable. If a guest drops by at mealtime, he or she will surely be invited to share the meal. Giving gifts and sharing are very important values in the Malinke culture. Richer people especially are expected to be generous. The idea is that those who have been blessed by Allah should be willing to share some of their wealth. If not forthcoming with generosity, a person might be asked outright to give something.

9 LIVING CONDITIONS

The Malinke who live in the cities have adapted to an urban lifestyle. Most, however, still live in traditional villages of anywhere from a few hundred to a few thousand people. The villages are rather compact, consisting of groups of compounds enclosed by millet-stalk fences. A compound contains several cylindrical houses built of sun-baked bricks or wattle and daub, with a thatched roof; there will also be a granary and a separate cylindrical kitchen with low half-walls and a thatched roof. Behind each house in a traditional compound is a small enclosure containing a pit latrine. This enclosure is also used as a private place for bathing with a bucket of water.

As the residence pattern after marriage is patrilocal, those living in the compound will be the brothers of a family with their wives and unmarried children. If a man has more than one wife, each will have her own house in the compound. The houses are grouped around a center courtyard that may contain a well. Much activity will be going on in the courtyard: children playing, women engaged in activities, such as washing clothes, shelling peanuts, or cooking (a very lengthy and laborious task). The houses, which may have a couple of small windows, are very sparsely furnished; they may just have a bed consisting of a frame with thin poles across the width, covered by a mat; a small table; and a chair or two. Possessions may include a transistor radio and a suitcase with diverse mementos and valuables. Most of the living and socializing goes on outside in the courtyard, where the beds may be placed to sit on, or to sleep on when it is too warm inside.

An average village may have a small shop selling a few items. The most popular local consumer goods are refined sugar, tea, kola nuts, salt, cooking oil, tobacco, cigarettes, matches, and batteries. For transportation, a bicycle, an occasional motorbike, an ox cart, or a horse cart are the means used by those who can afford these items. More frequently, villagers walk to a road where there is a bus or perhaps a "collective taxi," or they simply walk to their destination. Women do not have much opportunity to leave their villages because travel for women is discouraged by the Malinke culture.

10 FAMILY LIFE

The Malinke consider large families to be important. Children are one's wealth in an agrarian society. A large compound with brothers and their plural wives will always be bustling with family members of several generations and children of many ages. Young girls who are old enough to carry an infant will usually be seen with one strapped to their back or carrying one on their hip. Infants are coddled and indulged, never lacking attention. Mothers carry their infants on their backs wherever they go and breastfeed them whenever they cry. Young children have certain chores to do, but in general they lead a wholesome and carefree life with plenty of playmates around.

For men and women there is a division of agricultural labor. The men do the plowing, sowing, planting, and a major part of the harvesting work. Some also engage in hunting and fishing. Women do weeding and tend vegetable plots. Women are always busy with some kind of work, while it is common to see men sitting under a tree in the village square, chatting with other men and having a smoke and some tea that the women have brought them. The women are responsible for cooking, which involves many labor-intensive steps. They gather the firewood and bring it back on their heads in large bundles. They draw water at the well. They pound the millet, sorghum, or corn for hours with a mortar and pestle and then sift it to prepare the staple food of couscous. Cooking the meal involves hours of squatting in intense heat, tending earthenware pots propped on three stones around an open wood fire. Usually the women of a compound share the many tasks of cooking and take turns being responsible for meals. The women also wash the clothes and do much maintenance and cleaning work in the compound. While tending the children they are usually doing some income-generating activity, such as shelling peanuts.

The male head of the household is responsible for food procurement for his family, for buying clothes, and for providing agricultural tools and seeds for planting. The household heads have the authority to make all important decisions, although women wield a significant amount of power behind the scenes.

The social organization of the Malinke is based on an ancient caste system into which members are born. A Malinke can never change the caste-status into which he or she is born. There is rarely intercaste marriage. In an average village, however, the difference in wealth or status among the castes is barely visible. There is more of a feeling of egalitarianism, and all people have an agrarian lifestyle, cultivating crops and tending small herds of livestock. The size of the family is often more of an indication of wealth; small families with few children and few extended family members are thought of as poor and unfortunate. The caste system is comprised of nobles at the top, artisans and griots in the middle, and the descendants of slaves at the bottom. It is an elder from among the nobles who serves as headman or chief. All castes may provide marabouts, but certain other functions are caste-specific.

The artisans are divided into two main occupations: blacksmiths and leatherworkers. The blacksmiths are considered to be the most important of the middle caste. They make iron tools and implements, such as plow points and axe heads, as well as wooden furniture, mortars, and pestles. Some Malinke smiths have gained excellent reputations as sculptors and artists in iron objects or woodcarvings. They are usually the bicycle repairmen of the village as well. Smiths have a reputation for truthfulness and hospitality. They have the important function of male circumciser and chief of the lodge in circumcision ceremonies. There are many leatherworkers who are just farmers and do not do much work in leather. Some, however, have a good additional income from making the leather pouches or cases to cover the gri-gri charms.

The griots are the traditional bards or storytellers, providing entertainment and singing songs that keep alive the oral tradition of the people. Some just chant praise and recite honorific names and parables from the Quran. Others recite rhymed phrases accompanied by a drummer. They are paid for their skills at various ceremonies. Many griots are musicians who know how to play the kora, a stringed instrument made from half a large gourd covered with leather as a resonator. Some griots play the balaphon, a wooden xylophone with a row of gourd resonators. They teach all these skills to their children from an early age. Often the musicians will migrate from village to village to market their talents.

In addition to the castes, the Malinke have groupings in age-sets consisting of men or women who were circumcised at the same time and who maintain a strong egalitarian bond throughout life. Sometimes particular age-sets are called on to perform community tasks. The male age-sets pass through three age-grades, which are an important aspect of social control. The "boys" are those from about 10 to 20 years of age, who are the focus of enculturation, learning the proper norms and values of the Malinke culture. The "young men" include those from about 20 to 40 years old who are either unmarried or who have just formed their own nuclear family unit; they are responsible for carrying out decisions made in village meetings. The "elders" are those over 40 years old who are heads of extended family household units; they are the most influential in making decisions and settling disputes.

Malinke villages have secular leaders and religious leaders, whose roles sometimes overlap. The secular leader is the chief, who is typically a descendant of the noble caste and the village founders. The chief presides over a council of elder men who may convene to settle disputes, for example, if there is a theft or a question of someone's livestock damaging crops, or if a decision must be made about the return of the bride-price if an abused wife goes back to live in her father's compound.

The imam is the principal religious leader who may serve several small villages. Unlike the chief, the imam is elected; the position is open to elders with Quranic wisdom, who are not descendants of slaves. His main duty is to lead prayers at the mosque. Sometimes the chief is also a marabout, an Islamic healer and counselor, who can rival the imam in performing religious duties.

Many Malinke villages have an additional influential person who could be said to be a leader: the kanda. A kanda is a self-made man, who with his large family, strong personality, organizational abilities, and hard work has amassed considerable wealth. He has no formal power, and he does not refer to himself as a kanda for fear of jealousy and alienation. He wields a great deal of authority at meetings and when important decisions must be made. Because of the deep respect for elders, both men and women, it can be said that they are also village leaders. Their status grows as they age, and younger people are instilled with the value of respecting their elders.

In addition to the council of elder men who settle disputes, the Malinke have a fascinating means of social control—through the powerful demon-spirit called a kangkurao, portrayed by a mask-wearer who covers his body with blood-red bark, making an awesome and frightful figure. The kangkurao must be summoned by the chief, the imam, or the circumcision lodge chief, who gives the demon-spirit a benevolent mission to carry out. The spirit figure can demand that people participate in public works, such as digging a well or weeding for fire prevention; he can enforce taboos against eating fruit until it is ripe; and he can discipline novices at circumcision ceremonies. Moreover, he can exact fines for those who do not obey. Even though the Islamic religion prohibits graven images, the kangkurao has survived as part of the Malinke tradition.

¹¹ CLOTHING

Malinke who live today in urban centers, especially the men, may have adopted Western-style clothes. Villagers, on the other hand, take pride in their traditional clothing, which is important to them. In fact, one of the obligations of a husband is to give each wife the cloth for at least two new outfits every year.

Women generally wear a loose, scoop-necked smock over a long skirt made by a wrap-around piece of cloth. They often tie a matching piece of cloth around their head in an informal turban, each woman's turban having its own special flair. They use brightly colored cotton prints with splashy, large designs; some also wear tie-dyed, wood-block, or batik prints. The traditional casual dress for men is made with the same bright prints fashioned in an outfit that resembles pajamas.

For formal occasions men and women may wear the *grand boubou*. For women this is a loose dress that extends to ground level and may be trimmed in lace or embroidery. For men it is a long robe-like garment covering long pants and a shirt. Many middle-aged or elder men wear knit caps. Shoes are leather or rubber thongs.

¹² FOOD

Traditional Malinke are cultivators who grow varieties of millet, sorghum, rice (in the swampy areas), and corn as staple crops. As cash crops they grow peanuts and cotton and, to supplement their diet and gain a bit of income at weekly markets, grow diverse vegetables in garden plots. Some villages have a bakery where small loaves of French-style bread are baked.

The wealthier Malinke own some livestock—cattle, goats, chickens, and perhaps a horse for plowing. The cattle are used for milk and for the prestige of owning them; they are rarely slaughtered. There is little meat in the diet. Those who live near rivers or lakes may supplement their meals with fish.

A typical breakfast might consist of corn porridge eaten with a spoon made of a small, elongated calabash (gourd) split in half. The midday and evening meals may consist of rice or couscous with sauce and/or vegetables. Couscous can be made of pounded and steamed millet, sorghum, or cornmeal. A substantial quantity of rice or couscous is placed in a plastic or enamel basin around which those sharing the meal sit. Small bowls of sauce—often peanut sauce—or vegetable mixtures are distributed over the rice or couscous. Those sharing the meal take portions of it with the right hand, forming a bite-sized ball.

Tea-time is an important break for the Malinke. Tea is made by filling a small pot with dried tea leaves and covering these with boiling water. The brewed tea is extremely strong and is served with several small spoons of sugar in tiny glasses. After the first round of tea, the pot is filled with boiling water a second and third time, thus the second and third rounds of tea are a bit diminished in strength.

¹³ EDUCATION

Many villages today have a government school and a Quranic school for learning to recite verses from the Quran. The educational models of the government schools, as well as the medium of instruction, are based on those of the ex-colonial masters, either French or British. As the nations where the Malinke are found today have many tribal peoples in addition to the Malinke, it is likely that the teachers posted to the school will be of a different ethnic group and will not speak the Malinke language.

It is difficult for a child to start first grade in a school that teaches only in French or English, languages totally different from his or her native Malinke. Poor attendance and high drop-out rates are common in the village schools. There are few instructional materials, and the teaching methods are very formal: rote recitation, "chalk and talk," and copying exercises. As the Islamic parents do not think it is as important for their daughters to get an education as it is for their sons, the enrollment of boys is much higher than that of girls. Only a small percentage of the village pupils can pass the state examination at the end of sixth grade in order to go on to high school. The countries in which the Malinke are found have generally low literacy rates, around 40%, with literacy for males much higher than for females.

¹⁴ CULTURAL HERITAGE

Much of the cultural heritage of the Malinke is embedded in the great Mali merchant empire of the 13th to the 16th centuries and the Islamic religion that was adopted by the chieftains. There was a flourishing trade in gold, and many ornate ornaments, jewelry, and staffs of gold date from that period, documenting a wealthy and proud past. Additionally, the cultural heritage has been immortalized in the famous epic poem "Sonjara," sung by *griots* (minstrels) since the 13th century (*see* Folklore).

¹⁵ WORK

Farming is a respected occupation, and all members of society are given farming tasks. The children, too, guard the fields against wild boar, monkeys, and birds. The Malinke use natural fertilizer, allowing livestock to graze on the fields lying fallow. Children are often seen tending the livestock.

¹⁶ SPORTS

The Malinke of today have some traditional sports in their school curriculum that were introduced with the French model of education. Many of the village schools are too poor to have good quality balls or much sports equipment. Boys might be seen playing soccer with a homemade ball. They enjoy listening to soccer matches, both national and international, on the radio or watching these on television in town; many Malinke men and boys can recite the names of international soccer stars.

¹⁷ ENTERTAINMENT AND RECREATION

In addition to the storytelling and music provided by the griots, the Malinke like to listen to the radio, a typical possession in most households. If they live in a village with electricity, a television set is a prized item. It is common for large groups of villagers to gather in the compound of the television's owner, who will position his set on a high platform outside so large numbers of people can watch.

"Woaley" is a board game similar to backgammon. It is a major pastime for the Malinke as well as other West Africans. The board is in the form of a rectangle with twelve indentations to hold beans and two larger indentations at the ends to hold the captured beans. Both spectators and players of all ages enjoy woaley matches. (The game is referred to by many other names as well.)

[18] FOLK ART, CRAFTS, AND HOBBIES

Some of the most important art of the Malinke is the oral art, songs, and epic poems sung by the griots playing a kora musical instrument. In former times it was common for the blacksmiths to forge ornamental oil lamps from iron and large iron door locks, as well as fanciful iron figures of spirits or animals to crown the staffs; the blacksmiths also carved wooden figures and masks. These artistic endeavors are less common today.

Present day hobbies of Malinke young men may include collecting cassette tapes of their favorite singers, which could be reggae singers from Jamaica or American rock stars. Something that young women enjoy doing and might consider a hobby is braiding each other's hair, making decorative rows or braiding in long strands of synthetic hair.

[19] SOCIAL PROBLEMS

As the Malinke people are socialized with a strong sense of responsibility to their family and lineage, many of the kinds of social problems that might be prevalent in an industrialized society are not encountered. AIDS and the spread of venereal diseases by men who have brought these back from urban areas is a problem in some places. Since the society is Muslim, alcoholism is not found. At the same time, malnutrition and a lack of understanding of its causes is a subject that needs attention. From a Western perspective, the situation of women, including fewer opportunities for education, fewer rights, and having to share a husband with co-wives, may be seen as a social problem.

[20] GENDER ISSUES

Malinke society is patrilineal (male-dominated) and the smallest social unit is the family. The oldest male serves as the head of the lineage. A "minor lineage" consists of a man and his immediate family. A "major lineage" consists of households of relatives and their families. The majority of the Malinke men are farmers. The men do all of the fieldwork by hand with no help from machinery or fertilizers. The staple crops native to this area are rice, millet, sorghum, and peanuts. There are also many men who raise livestock. Cattle are rare and are used mainly to show prestige or used as a bridal dowry. Only men are allowed to hold positions of high respect in a Malinke village. Among the Malinke, men do the heavy farm work, hunt, and fish. They also hold leadership positions, such as village elders and *imams*. The women help with the farming, as well as cooking, cleaning, and caring for the children.

Traditionally, parents arranged their daughters' marriages while the girls were still infants. Today, marriages are still arranged, but not as early. The groom is required to work for the bride's family both before and after the wedding. He must also pay the girl's family a "bride price." Polygamy is commonly practiced, but the men rarely have more than three wives.

Malinke believe the crowning glory of any woman is the ability to produce children, especially sons. The first wife has authority over any subsequent wives. The husband has complete control over his wives and is responsible for feeding and clothing them. He also helps the wives' parents when necessary. Wives are expected to live together in harmony, at least superficially. They share work responsibilities of the compound, cooking, laundry, etc.

While farming is the predominant profession among the Malinke, men also work as tailors, butchers, taxi drivers, woodworkers, metal workers, soldiers, nurses, and extension workers for aid agencies. However, most women, probably 95%, remain in the home as wives and mothers.

[21] BIBLIOGRAPHY

Bird, Charles S. "Oral Art in the Mande." In *Papers on the Manding*, edited by Carleton T. Hodge. Bloomington, IN: Indiana University Press, 1971.

Conrad, David, and Barbara Frank. *Status and Identity in West Africa*. Bloomington, IN: Indiana University Press, 1995.

Dalby, David. "Introduction: Distribution and Nomenclature of the Manding People and Their Language." In *Papers on the Manding*, edited by Carleton T. Hodge. Bloomington, IN: Indiana University Press, 1971.

De Bruijin, Mirjam, and Han Van Dijk. "Fulbe Mobility: Migration and Travel into Mande." *Mande Studies*, 1: 41–62, 1999.

Haley, Alex. *Roots*. Garden City, NY: Doubleday, 1976.

Hodge, Carleton T., ed. *Papers on the Manding*. Bloomington, IN: Indiana University Press, 1971.

Johnson, John William. *The Epic of Son-Jara. A West African Tradition*. Text by Fa-Digi Sisoko. Bloomington, IN: Indiana University Press, 1992.

Keita, Mamady. *A Life for the Djembe: Traditional Rhythms of the Malinke*. San Diego: Tam Tam Mandingue, 2004.

McCall, Daniel R. "The Cultural Map and Time-Profile of the Mande Speaking Peoples." In *Papers on the Manding*, edited by Carleton T. Hodge. Bloomington, IN: Indiana University Press, 1971.

McNaughton, Patrick R. *The Mande Blacksmiths: Knowledge, Power, and Art in West Africa*. Bloomington, IN: Indiana University Press, 1988.

Nwanunobi, C. Onyeka. *Malinke*. New York: Rosen Publishing Group, 1996.

Schaffer, Matt, and Christine Cooper. *Mandinko: The Ethnography of a West African Holy Land*. Prospect Heights, IL: Waveland Press, 1980.

Weil, Peter M. "Political Structure and Process Among the Gambia Mandinka: The Village Parapolitical System." In *Papers on the Manding*, edited by Carleton T. Hodge. Bloomington, IN: Indiana University Press, pp. 249-272, 1971.

———. "The Masked Figure and Social Control: The Mandinka Case." *Africa* 41, no. 4 (1971): 279—293.

—revised by M. Njoroge

MAURITANIANS

PRONUNCIATION: mawr-uh-TAY-nee-uhns
LOCATION: Mauritania
POPULATION: 3.3 million (2007 est.)
LANGUAGE: Hassaniyya Arabic; French; Azayr; Fulfulde; Mande-kan; Wolof
RELIGION: Islam (Sunni Muslim)
RELATED ARTICLES: Vol. 1: Wolof

¹ INTRODUCTION

Mauritania is located in the western Sahara region of Africa, which also includes Algeria, Mali, and Morocco. Archaeological evidence, oral history, and legends indicate that the western Sahara supported a flourishing culture during the millennia preceding Christianity. There is archaeological evidence of copper mining and refining in west-central Mauritania dating back to 500 bc to 1000 bc. An early Berber group called the Bafour inhabited the area that is now known as Mauritania. The Bafour engaged in fishing, hunting, and rural livestock herding. The ancestors of two modern-day ethnic groups—the Toucouleur and the Wolof black Africans—engaged in valley cultivation. Changes in Mauritania's climate and the desertification of the Sahara caused these early Mauritanians to move southward.

Waves of immigrants began to flow into Mauritania from both the north and south during the 3rd century ad. The first group to immigrate to the country were the Berbers of North Africa. Berbers first settled in Mauritania during the 3rd and 4th centuries; a second wave of immigrants settled there during the 7th and 8th centuries. Some indigenous Mauritanians became vassals to the Berbers; others migrated to the south.

Between the 8th and 10th centuries, a loose association of states known as the Sanhadja Confederation served as a decentralized political system linking the major Berber groups. The Sanhadja Confederation was controlled by the politically dominant Berber group, the Lemtuna. During this time, caravan trade routes linked Mauritania with neighboring peoples in North Africa, the empire of Ghana (which included all of present-day southeastern Mauritania in its territory), and the empire of Mali. Gold, ivory, slaves, salt, copper, and cloth were carried by caravan. Important towns developed along the trade routes, becoming commercial and political centers.

By the 11th century ad, Berber and Arab traders had spread the Islamic religion throughout the western Sahara. Early in that century, the Sanhadja Confederation broke up, and a group known as the Almoravids conquered the entire region of the western Sahara. The group was established around 1041 when 'Abdallah ibn Yassin, a Sanhadja theologian, and his followers built a religious center known as a *ribat*. The men of the ribat were called *marabouts*, or *murabitun*, and they became known as the Almoravids. In 1042, the Almoravids launched a war to establish a purer form of Islam in the western Sahara region. The Almoravid empire spread from Spain to Senegal and replaced Ghana's hegemony over southeastern Mauritania. The Almoravids ruled Mauritania until the 12th century.

Between the 12th and 17th centuries, black Africans from Ghana, Mali, and Songhai immigrated to Mauritania. By the late 17th century, a wave of Yemeni Arabs had penetrated Mau-

ritania from the north, and a Yemeni group known as the Bani Hassan dominated the area. As the Arabs moved southward, the Berbers and blacks migrated further south as well. The Berbers tried to fight Arab domination during the unsuccessful Thirty Years' War of 1644–74. When they failed to achieve liberation from the Arab forces, the Berbers became vassals to the Arabs.

By the late 17th century, Mauritanian society comprised four social groups. Three of these—the Arabs, the Berbers, and the black slaves—spoke Hassaniyya Arabic and became known as the *Maures*. The fourth social group was composed of free black Africans who settled in the Senegal River basin in the south.

Early European interest in Mauritania was limited. In the mid-15th century, about 1,000 slaves per year were exported to Europe. The Dutch and French purchased gum arabic from producers in southern Mauritania during the second half of the 16th century. Interest became more intense in the mid-19th century, when French forces briefly occupied two of Mauritania's southern regions—Brakna and Trarza. Early in the 20th century, French forces occupied and set up a colonial administration in Mauritania. France ruled Mauritania indirectly through its existing institutions and made little attempt to develop the region's economy. After World War II (1939–45), France granted some administrative and political freedoms to Mauritania, touching off disputes between the Maures (Arabs and Berbers) and the black Africans. Some Arabs and Berbers wanted to unite with Morocco to the north, whereas many southern (non-Maure) black Africans wanted to join with Senegal and Mali.

Mauritania became fully independent on 28 November 1960. The nation's first president, Moktar Ould Daddah, ruled until a coup ousted him from power in 1978. Divisions between the Maures and the non-Maure black Africans continued after independence, as the non-Maure blacks resented Maure domination of the Mauritanian political system and armed forces.

By 1975, Mauritania had become embroiled in a military conflict over the Western Sahara—territory then known as the Spanish Sahara—with the Polisario guerrillas of the Sahrawi Arab Democratic Republic (SADR). The Polisario is a group seeking national self-determination for the people of the Western Sahara, Mauritania's neighbor to the northwest. It is the military wing of the SADR, the government in exile of the Western Sahara. Mauritania occupied a southern province in the Western Sahara, partly to prevent Morocco (which also had claims to the country) from occupying the entire territory. In 1976, Spain relinquished control of the Western Sahara, dividing the territory between Morocco and Mauritania. The Polisario guerrillas then waged a war against Morocco, and Mauritania allied itself with Morocco against them. The result was a costly war and resentment of the ruling Maures among black Mauritanians.

Rising political dissension led to a military coup in July 1978 that made Colonel Mustafa Ould Salek the prime minister. Salek was replaced in April 1979 by Colonel Ahmed Ould Bouceif and Colonel Muhammad Khouna Ould Haidalla. Bouceif died soon afterward in an airplane crash, and Haidalla became Mauritania's prime minister. Haidalla ended Mauritania's military involvement in the Western Sahara and gave diplomatic recognition to the SADR. In 1984, Haidalla was replaced in yet another coup by Colonel Ma'ouya Ould Sidi Ahmad Taya, who established a military government. Taya began to reform the political system, holding local elections and releasing some political prisoners. In the area of foreign relations, Taya strengthened relations with the Soviet Union and China and with the wealthy Middle Eastern states. His objectives were to gain access to trade and financial assistance and to rid Mauritania of its dependence on the West. In May 1987, Taya named three women to cabinet-level positions in the government. One was appointed minister of mines and industries; another became associate director of the presidential cabinet; and a third was named general secretary of the health and social affairs ministry. In July 1991, Mauritania drafted a new constitution, which, importantly, legalized a multiparty system in place of the former one-party system. As soon as the restrictions were lifted, 16 political parties were formed. The constitution stresses equality and individual freedoms (article 10). It makes Islam the state religion (article 5) and decrees that the president must be a Muslim (article 23).

A bloodless coup in 2005 ended Taya's 21-year autocratic rule. A council of military leaders took control of the country, promising democratic reforms. The 2007 elections, deemed free and fair by observers from both the United States and the European Union, brought to power Sidi Ould Sheikh Abdullahi, a former finance minister in the Taya government. He won 52.8% of the vote. Abdullahi campaigned on promises to redress Mauritania's serious problems of human trafficking and slavery. Although slavery was explicitly outlawed in 1981, many black Maures continue to serve their former masters as household servants and farmhands. In 2008, Human Rights Watch reported that slavery continued to be a serious problem.

Mauritania's government comprises three branches: executive, legislative, and judicial. The president, who is elected to a five-year term, heads the executive branch. The prime minister (Zeine Ould Zeidane since 2007) is appointed by the president. The legislative branch has two houses: a National Assembly consisting of 95 members who are elected by the people to five-year terms, and a Senate consisting of 56 members who are elected by municipal councilors to six-year terms. The judicial branch safeguards individual freedoms and ensures enforcement of the laws of the country.

2 LOCATION AND HOMELAND

Mauritania is located in Africa at the intersection of North Africa (a region known as *the Maghrib*) and West Africa. Its neighbors to the north are Morocco and Algeria; to the northwest lies the Western Sahara; to the east and southeast lies Mali; and to the southwest lies Senegal. The Atlantic Ocean borders Mauritania to the west.

Mauritania's official name is the Islamic Republic of Mauritania. Its capital is Nouakchott. The country is roughly 1.5 times the size of Texas. It spans an area of 1,031,000 sq km (398,069 sq mi), about two-thirds of which is desert, with an occasional oasis. The topography is generally flat, arid plains, and only 400 sq km (150 sq mi) of the area is water. There is very little rain in the northern 75% of the country, which is desert or semidesert, and in the far south, the yearly rainfall averages 40–60 cm (16–24 in). Most of this falls between the months of July and September.

About 40% of the country is covered with sand. Some of the sand sits in fixed dunes; other dunes are carried about by the wind. Mauritania has four geographic zones: the Saharan, the

Sahelian, the Senegal River valley, and the coastal zone. The Saharan zone covers the northern two-thirds of the country. Temperatures in this zone fluctuate widely between the morning and afternoon. It has very little vegetation. The Sahelian zone, south of the Saharan zone, extends to within 30 km (20 mi) of the Senegal River to the south. Temperatures here have much smaller daily variations. More vegetation grows in the Sahelian zone, including grasslands, acacia trees, and date palm trees. The Senegal River valley is a belt of land extending north of the Senegal River. It is vital to Mauritania's agricultural production, though it has suffered much desertification during severe and prolonged droughts since the 1960s and into the 21st century. Nevertheless, it experiences more rainfall than the rest of the country, and the river floods annually. The coastal zone is made up of the western section of the country along the Atlantic coast. It has minimal rainfall and moderate temperatures.

The census of 2007 determined that Mauritania had a population of about 3.3 million people. The annual population growth rate is almost 2.9%. The number of Mauritanians who can be considered urban dwellers is difficult to calculate because of the country's nomadic culture and sporadic industry. Among Mauritanian urban migrants, by far the most live in the capital city of Nouakchott and in Nouadhibou. The remainder live on farms or in small towns. Almost half of the population, more than 45%, is under the age of 15.

The Maures, descendants of both the Arabs and Berbers, are the largest ethnic group in Mauritania. They live mainly in the northern and central regions. Over the centuries, there has been much intermarriage between those of Arab-Berber origin and the black African population. The Maures are thus a group that includes both blacks and whites. The other major ethnic groups are racially black African; these are the Bambara, Fulbe, Soninke, Toucouleur, and Wolof groups. Black Mauritanians are traditionally farmers, livestock herders, and fishers and live mainly in the south. According to government figures, Maures constitute 70% of the population. This figure is disputed by black Africans, who argue that the Maures manipulate the figures to maintain dominance over the blacks.

Mauritania's largest city is the capital, Nouakchott, now home to thousands of former farmers and livestock herders who lost their farms and herds after drought and desertification began to plague the country in the 1970s. These Mauritanians flocked to Nouakchott and other cities in search of new jobs. The result was overcrowded living conditions and difficulty finding enough jobs for the influx of migrants. In 1960, Nouakchott had 5,000 inhabitants. By 1985, the number had reached 500,000. In 2005, the population was reported to be between 900,000 and 1.1 million. The discrepancy can be attributed to the migratory nature of Mauritanian culture and traditions.

3 LANGUAGE

Since 1968, Mauritania's official language has been Hassaniyya Arabic, which is spoken mainly by the Maures. The study of Hassaniyya in secondary schools was made compulsory in 1966. Hassaniyya is a largely Arabic language with many Berber loan words, and it reflects the both Arab and Berber ancestry of the Maures. Many people in the larger cities and villages speak French, which is also an official language. Mauritania's other official languages are Arabic, Poular, Soninke, and Wolof. These have many similarities, and most are rooted in the Niger-Congo language family.

Common boys' names are *Ahmad, Hamadi, Muhammad,* and *'Uthman.* Common girls' names are *Fatima, Bana, Hadia,* and *Safiya.*

4 FOLKLORE

It is common in Mauritania to believe in divination and supernatural powers associated with holy men who lead Islamic Sufi brotherhoods (mystical associations). These religious leaders are venerated among West Africans and North Africans and are considered well educated. They are called *marabouts,* or *murabitun,* and it is believed that their *baraka,* or divine grace, allows them to perform miracles. They make and administer amulets and talismans. These are believed to have mystical powers that give them protection from illness and injury.

5 RELIGION

Most Mauritanians are Sunni Muslims. The region's inhabitants have adhered to Islam since the 9th century ad. Mauritania's Constitution Charter of 1991 declared Islam to be the state religion and requires that the president be a Muslim.

In Mauritania, as in much of West Africa, Islamic Sufi brotherhoods known as *tariqas* gained importance around the 13th century. Sufism is a religious movement that stresses mysticism and the needs of the human spirit. The brotherhoods transcended ethnic and tribal lines, thus helping to develop a broad national identity going beyond that of individual clans and ethnic groups. Mauritania has two major and several minor brotherhoods. The major brotherhoods are the Qadiriyya and Tijaniyya orders. The Qadiriyya brotherhood stresses Islamic learning, humility, generosity, and respect for one's neighbors. The Tijaniyya brotherhood places less stress on learning. It is a missionary order that denounces theft, lying, cheating, and killing and emphasizes continual reflection on God.

6 MAJOR HOLIDAYS

Mauritania's major national holiday is Independence Day (November 28). It is celebrated with a military exhibition in which soldiers, tanks, and citizens parade in front of a stage on which the president and his entourage sit. The president delivers a speech to the nation addressing political and economic developments. The secular New Year (as opposed to the New Year on the Islamic calendar) is celebrated among the younger generation. They organize parties and have a New Year's Eve countdown, though without the traditional champagne, as Islamic countries forbid the consumption of alcohol.

Two major Islamic holidays are observed in Mauritania. One is *Eid al-Fitr,* which comes at the end of the holy month of fasting called Ramadan. During Ramadan, Muslims refrain from eating, drinking, smoking, or having sexual relations during the daytime in order to reflect on God and on the plight of the unfortunate who do not have enough food. At the end of the month, Muslims celebrate for three days. The other major Muslim holiday is *Eid al-Adha,* which commemorates the willingness of the Prophet Abraham (Ibrahim in Arabic) and his son to obey God's command in all things, even as Abraham was ready to sacrifice his son. The holiday signals the end of the Muslim pilgrimage to Mecca, or *hajj,* which every Muslim must undertake at least once during his or her lifetime. Traditionally, Islamic holidays are celebrated by wearing new clothes and cooking grilled meat. Girls color their hands with henna.

7 RITES OF PASSAGE

Every Mauritanian is expected to marry and have children. A wedding ceremony consists of an *'aqd,* the Islamic contractual commitment in which the bride and groom pledge themselves to the marriage. This ceremony is followed by a party. The next step in the wedding is the *marwah* party, which is a reception to see the bride off to her new family. The marwah is bigger, noisier, and has more entertainment and dancing than the 'aqd party.

8 INTERPERSONAL RELATIONS

Like most Arabs, Mauritanians are known to be friendly people. Even in the capital city of Nouakchott, which suffers from poverty and overpopulation as a result of urbanization, people are friendly. Elders, even outside one's family, are respected by the young. This practice, known as *essahwa,* requires the young to respect social customs in the presence of an elderly person. For example, a young Mauritanian would not smoke in front of an elderly Mauritanian. Also, the young must be careful to use appropriate language (no swearing), to avoid displays of affection (e.g., kissing) with an intimate friend, and to avoid talking too loudly in the presence of the elderly.

⁹ LIVING CONDITIONS

Mauritanians, for the most part, are very poor. Those who are wealthy have incomes comparable to those of middle-class Europeans. The unemployment rate is 24%. The per capita gross national product in 2007 was estimated at $1,800, although income derived from barter is not reflected in this estimate. The capital, though a desperately poor city by most measures, has modern appliances such as mobile phones, televisions with DVD players, and Internet cafés. Estimates suggest that the country has about 100,000 Internet users; its domain is .mr. There were two satellite television providers as of 2008. The national telecommunications company was privatized in 2001. Mobile phone penetration was 35 per 100 persons in 2008.

In the desert valleys of the countryside, known as the *badiya,* people live in tents made of cotton. These are light-colored on the outside so that they do not absorb sunlight and have brightly colored fabrics draping the inside of the tent walls. The floor of the tent is sandy, but it is covered with large woven mats known as *hasira*s. Furniture in the tents is made of wood and leather, and it can be folded to be transported on camels through the desert. Because they have no plumbing, desert dwellers get their water from an outside well. Containers made of animal skins, called *guerbas,* are used to carry water from the well to the tent. Cooking is done over an outdoor fire.

In the southern regions, homes are built of cement. They are rectangular with flat roofs and small windows. City homes are furnished with carpets, mattresses, and floor pillows. The villages have public faucets, from which people fill large buckets or tubs with water to carry back to their homes. There, the water is poured into a clay pot to keep it cool and clean. Stoves fueled by gas tanks are used for cooking in the villages.

The drought that has afflicted Mauritania since the 1970s has forced the northern population to migrate southward. The result has been a major housing crisis in the towns of southern Mauritania. Shantytowns, known as *kebe*s, were erected around the towns and along the major streets. The migrants set up homes of wood and scrap metal, sun-dried bricks, or tents. In the capital of Nouakchott, more than half of the population lived in shantytowns and slums in the early years of the 21st century.

Health care and medical facilities do not meet the needs of the population, especially in rural areas. In 2005, the World Health Organization (WHO) reported a life expectancy among Mauritanians of 55 for males and 60 for females. In all, 125 Mauritanian children per 1,000 can expect to die before the age of five. In 2004, total expenditures on health care totaled 2.9% of gross domestic product. In that year, the WHO also reported that that were 0.11 physicians for every 1,000 people. Many diseases are common, such as measles, tuberculosis, and cholera in the north and malaria and schistosomiasis in the south. Hepatitis, bacterial and protozoal diarrhea, and Rift Valley fever also are problems. It is reported that child malnutrition is a major problem. For example, in rural areas, 38% of children under five suffer to such an extent their development is stunted. The figure for urban areas, 30.2%, is hardly better. In 2008, HIV/AIDS prevalence was low at 0.6%.

Mauritania has two major airports—at Nouakchott and Nouadhibou—that are capable of handling international air traffic. In 2008, the country also had 25 smaller airports (8 with paved runways, 17 without) for internal domestic flights between Mauritania's cities. Nouakchott and Nouadhibou are also major seaports. Although some roads are paved, most are not, especially in the desert, where roads consist simply of tracks in the sand.

¹⁰ FAMILY LIFE

Mauritania's traditional social unit is the family and its descent, or lineage, group. A family's lineage is traced back five or six generations. The lineage serves as a basis of socialization for the young, with elder members of the lineage guiding younger members to conform to social norms. A group of related lineages that maintain social ties is known as a clan. The smallest unit within the clan is the extended family, which consists of related males with their wives, sons, and unmarried daughters. Marriage within the clan is preferred. First cousins are traditional marriage partners.

There is great emphasis on homemaking skills for girls, and so most daughters are given training in raising a family and taking care of the house. Often, girls are educated at home instead of at school. Mothers are expected to prepare their daughters for their future careers as homemakers, and fathers are expected to provide well for their daughters so that they can grow up to be healthy and physically attractive. Thin girls are not considered beautiful, and preteen girls are encouraged to eat well, and especially to drink milk, in order to ensure their physical beauty. Traditionally, girls became engaged or married by the time they were 8 or 10 years of age, but today many girls wait until they graduate from high school or college.

Mauritanian men are permitted to marry more than one wife. Though some choose to do so, most do not. Often, however, they marry in succession, divorcing one wife and then marrying a second. In 2008, the country had a very high fertility rate of 5.78.

¹¹ CLOTHING

Mauritanian attire is influenced by the desert heat and Islamic practice. Islam dictates that women should cover all the body except the hands and face, and men should cover the area from the navel to the knees. Both men and women in Mauritania often wear attire that covers the entire body, commonly with the face, hands, feet, and arms showing. Women wear a *malaffa,* which is a long cloak wrapped loosely around the body from head to toe. The men wear a *dar'a,* which is a long, loose robe worn over baggy pants known as *sirwal.* Some men wear head coverings, predominantly turbans or *hawli,* for protection from the winter cold and summer heat. Typical office attire for men is Western-style pants and shirts. Southern women wear dresses or skirts and blouses. They also wear long robes called *boubous.*

¹² FOOD

Lunch is the largest meal of the day in Mauritania. Commonly, villagers eat a spicy fish and vegetable stew with rice for lunch. Another popular Mauritanian lunch that is common in the northern desert is spicy rice mixed with *tishtar,* or small pieces of dried meat. A common dish served at dinnertime is *couscous;* it is semolina wheat sprinkled with oil and water and rolled into tiny grains. The grains are then steamed and ready for use in a favorite recipe. The couscous can be mixed with a number of sauces and vegetables. In some parts of Mauritania, couscous is known as *lachiri.*

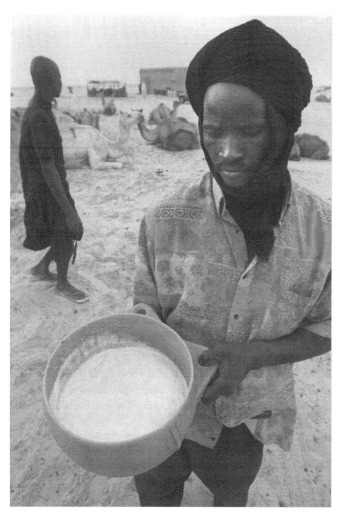

Babi, a camel milker near the Mauritanian capital of Nouakchott, shows the milk collected from a camel, which will be made into camel cheese. Camel cheese exports would put cash into the hands of this nation's nomads if international regulations could be overcome. (AP Images/Ben Curtis)

After washing their hands, members of the family gather around a large platter of food placed on the floor. They scoop up small portions of food from the platter with either their hands or utensils. Each person eats only from his or her side of the platter. Many households use a central serving platter but provide diners with individual plates. In some households, men and women eat separately.

A favorite drink is *zrig,* a cool beverage made from goat's milk, water, and sugar. Despite the heat of the desert, tea is consumed throughout the country. Mauritanians drink imported green tea (from China). It is made with fresh mint and served in small glasses a few times per day. Alcoholic beverages are forbidden in Islam, and in 1986 the government banned their import, purchase, and consumption.

13 EDUCATION

It is not mandatory that children attend school, and attendance is far from universal. Only 35% of young children attend elementary schools, while even fewer older children—only 8% to 19%—attend secondary school. Though girls often attend elementary school (25% of girls under the age of 11 attended elementary school in 2003), once this education is complete, it is common for girls to stay home. The French colonial administration established public schools, mainly in the Senegal River valley, where black Africans constituted most of the population. Black Africans thus came to have a primarily secular education. After independence from colonial rule, the Mauritanian government also stressed secular education. Elementary school lasts for six years, followed by two cycles of secondary school. The lower secondary cycle lasts for four years, and the upper secondary cycle lasts for three years.

Schools that provide Islamic education are common throughout the country. These traditional schools are often centered around a learned Islamic leader known as a *marabout.* Parents encourage their children to learn from these men. Boys generally attend religious schools for seven years, and girls attend for two years. Though emphasis is placed on religious learning—that is, memorizing passages from the Quran—language, arithmetic, logic, and other subjects are also taught.

Mauritania has one major secular university, one Islamic institute of higher education, and some vocational institutes. The Mauritania Institute for Scientific Research (founded in 1974) and the Advanced Center for Technical Education (founded in 1980) are perhaps the nation's oldest. According to the nation's 2005 census, the literacy rate was 52%, though this figure is believed to be inflated.

Arabic is taught in all schools. Other local ethnic languages are also taught in elementary schools. French is taught throughout the public school system.

14 CULTURAL HERITAGE

Much of the literary work of Mauritanian writers focuses on Islamic and legal affairs. Islamic jurists pen elaborate discussions of Islamic norms. In addition to the focus on religion, there is also a love of literature and poetry. Stories and poems are passed down through the generations in musical form, recited by storytellers known as *ighyuwn.* As the ighyuwn tells his tale, he is accompanied by a drum, by the music of the Mauritanian guitar *(tidinit),* or by women playing a harplike instrument *(ardin).* The stories told are often short fables. Poetry is sung by minstrels and ballad singers. At social events, poetry praising the host or the guests is commonly sung.

15 WORK

Until a devastating drought struck Mauritania beginning in the 1970s, 80% to 90% of Mauritanians led a nomadic or seminomadic lifestyle, raising cattle, sheep, and goats. Tens of thousands of animals have died in the drought, which encroaches on previously fertile land by about 6.5 km (4 mi) per year. By the early 21st century, about 85% of herders had moved to the cities to find other employment.

The largest employer of Mauritanians outside the public sector is the mining industry. Iron and copper ores, both discovered in the 1950s, together accounted for 40% of the nation's exports in 2007. Another major employer is the fishing and fish-processing industry; the country's national waters are some of the richest in the world. Unfortunately, although some Mauritanians are employed by the fishing companies, Koreans, Japanese, and Russians have attained major fishing rights off the Atlantic coast, depriving Mauritanians of income that could improve the economy.

[16] SPORTS

Football (called soccer in the United States) is by far the most popular sport in Mauritania. In 2008, the national team was ranked one-hundred-fourteenth in the world by FIFA (International Federation of Association Football).

[17] ENTERTAINMENT AND RECREATION

Because of the desert heat during the afternoon, desert dwellers rest after lunch, waiting for the sun to descend. In the evenings, families gather outside the tent, sitting on a light mat called a *hasira*.

Children are creative and make many of their toys, such as cars and airplanes made of wire and tin cans. They also play games requiring no toys. One of these games is a variation of tug-of-war known as *ligum*.

[18] FOLK ART, CRAFTS, AND HOBBIES

The products of skilled craftspeople and artisans are valued among the elite in Mauritanian society. They are known for their woodwork, jewelry, leatherwork, pottery, weaving, tailoring, and ironwork. Handwoven rugs and handcrafted silver and gold jewelry and cutlery are popular with tourists.

[19] SOCIAL PROBLEMS

One of the major problems facing Mauritania is the extent of desertification of the land. By 2006, more than 90% of once-arable land had become desert. Other major problems are low standards of health care and shortages of medical equipment and professionals. Infectious diseases such as malaria are prevalent.

A political problem has arisen as a result of the low social status accorded to non-Maure black Africans in Mauritania. The Maures, who comprise both black and white members, dominate the political and social system, government bureaucracy, education, and land ownership. They openly discriminate against the non-Maure black Africans. The non-Maure black population has been a source of slaves, a problem that continued into the early 21st century. Maure domination of the country has spurred opposition among some black groups. The requirement that all secondary school students learn Arabic has also created dissent among the black Africans. The Toucouleur, also called the Halpularen, are the largest black African ethnic group in Mauritania, and it has challenged the domination of the Maures. The Toucouleur lead an illegal antigovernment organization based south of Mauritania, in Senegal—the African Liberation Forces of Mauritania, or the Forces de Libération Africaine de Mauritanie (FLAM). Antigovernment activities by the FLAM have, according to the government, included attempts to overthrow the government. The government has executed some FLAM members for these activities, resulting in demonstrations against racism and violent clashes between supporters and opponents of the government. Following the 2005 coup, a FLAM splinter group renounced violence for political ends and engaged in tentative political negotiations with the government of President Abdullahi. As of 2008, few outstanding issues had been resolved.

[20] GENDER ISSUES

Of the total Mauritanian workforce, the United Nations has calculated that 44% are female and, of these women, 53% work in agriculture. Human slavery and the trafficking of women remain serious concerns.

In response to these issues, the government enacted several laws and policies regarding the rights of women and children. The United Nations reports that in the early 21st century, the president issued decrees that changed domestic laws to bring them into line with international norms. The minimum age for marriage, for example, was raised to 18—high for a Muslim country. In 2003, the country implemented the Act on the Suppression of Trafficking in Persons, prohibiting all forms of sexual exploitation and human trafficking. Additionally, Mauritania initiated reforms to increase female access to education beginning in 2002.

[21] BIBLIOGRAPHY

Handloff, Robert E., ed. *Mauritania: A Country Study*. Washington, DC: Federal Research Division, Library of Congress, 1990.

Miles, William F. S., ed. *Political Islam in West Africa: State-Society Relations Transformed*. Boulder, CO: Lynne Rienner, 2007.

Weekes, Richard. *Muslim Peoples: A World Ethnographic Survey*. Westport, CT: Greenwood Press, 1978.

—revised by J. Henry

MOROCCANS

PRONUNCIATION: muh-RAHK-uhns
LOCATION: Morocco
POPULATION: 33.7 million (2007)
LANGUAGE: Arabic; French; English; Berber; Spanish
RELIGION: Islam; Christianity; Judaism

¹ INTRODUCTION

Morocco is located in an area called the Maghrib, a region in the western part of North Africa that borders the Mediterranean Sea. (Maghrib is the Arabic word referring to the direction of the sunset.) Morocco is known as *al-Maghrib al-Aqsa*, the furthest west, or simply *al-Maghrib*, a fitting name for this country that is located at the extreme western corner of North Africa. Morocco is ruled by a king who claims direct descent from the Prophet Muhammad, the 7th-century messenger of Islam.

Morocco has endured a series of foreign intrusions throughout its history. The inhabitants of Morocco were called *Barbari* by the Romans—a broad, derogatory term for peoples outside the purview of the Roman Empire—and in time, they came to be called Berbers. During the Punic Wars between Rome and Carthage (located in present-day Tunisia) in the 2nd and 3rd centuries bc, the Berbers sided with the Carthaginians. In 149 bc, the Carthaginians were defeated, and the Romans began to settle in North Africa. The Roman emperor Claudius divided the empire's possessions in ad 42 and established a series of provinces across the northern coast of Africa, naming what is now known as Morocco *Mauretania Tingitana*. Roman control of the region was never extensive, and the Berber tribes periodically rebelled against the invaders. As a result, Rome abandoned most of Mauretania Tingitana in the period ad 286–304, though it retained control of strategic locations in the north to oversee the Strait of Gibraltar.

In ad 429, the German king Gaiseric, backed by 80,000 Vandals (a German tribe), invaded North Africa from Spain. The Vandals' influence in North Africa was relatively short-lived. Like the Romans, they found that they could not suppress the Berber uprisings and either abandoned the region or were absorbed by the remaining Roman elites. The Byzantine emperor Justinian sent his army to North Africa in 533 and, for a time, regained at least tenuous control over Morocco.

The next invaders were Arab Muslims. Beginning in ad 662, the Arabs, led by Uqba bin Nafi, were by far the most influential conquerors of Morocco. At the time, many Berbers were Jewish, animist, or polytheistic in their religion, and there was strong resistance on the part of the Berber tribes to the new invaders. Eventually, however, the majority of Berbers adopted the Islamic religion. The ruling Arab view of Islam at the time was that Islam was primarily a religion for Arabs, and therefore non-Arab converts were treated as second-class citizens—a practice that fostered tensions between the Arabs and the Berbers. The tensions persisted until 786, when the Arab Moulay Idris, a self-proclaimed descendent of the Prophet Muhammad, followed by his son, Idris II, established a dynasty that would control large sections of the Maghrib for nearly 200 years.

Following the decline of the Isdrisids, Morocco was ruled for almost 500 years by dynasties of Berber origin. The first of these were the Almoravids, who spread Islam further north into southern Spain. Under the Almoravids, Andalusian culture, art, and architecture were brought from Spain to Morocco, marking the beginning of a cross-cultural flowering that would continue until the late 15th century. By 1140, another tribal dynasty, the Almohads, had seized control of Morocco. Under the Almohad caliph 'Abd al-Mu'min, the country became a center of learning, and under Almohad patronage, the study of philosophy, mathematics, and Islamic law, as well as Islamic mysticism (known as Sufism), flourished.

Spain, Portugal, England, and France all had a strong interest in their neighbor to the south, and during the 15th century, each set out to control various coastal areas of Morocco. By this time, small Christian communities from Europe had settled in Morocco. Direct descent from the Prophet Muhammad became the chief source of political authority, replacing the tribal systems that had dominated Moroccan political leadership for centuries. The Sa'adi rulers brought great unity and prosperity to Morocco. They were succeeded in the middle of the 17th century by the 'Alawis, who, despite substantial colonial interference from the European states, continue to rule Morocco as of 2008.

By the 19th century, Europeans had gained many concessions from the 'Alawi rulers and virtually controlled Morocco, though they stopped short of political governance. This changed during the early 20th century, when Spain gained control of a northern strip of Morocco, which it would hold until 1956. In 1912, France established a protectorate over the rest of Morocco. The 'Alawi sultan, Moulay Hafid, authorized the protectorate by signing the Treaty of Fez, which gave France the power to establish civil order in Morocco. The result went beyond mere civil authority—France took over Morocco's foreign and economic policy as well. The European presence expanded in Morocco, and by the mid-1930s, 200,000 Europeans, 75% of them French, were living in Morocco. They built new towns and roads, expanded the existing railroads, modernized agriculture, and built ports.

Anti-French Moroccan nationalism began to grow in the 1920s and strengthened during World War II (1939–45). During the war, the Vichy government that supplanted the French government insisted on the persecution of Jews in Morocco. The Moroccans were unwilling to cooperate in this persecution, and tensions mounted between the colonial French rulers and the Moroccans. Moroccans fought on the side of the Allied powers during the war, and Morocco was liberated by Allied troops in 1942. When Sultan Muhammad V met with the Allied powers at Casablanca in 1943, he expressed his desire for independence from France, but it would be more than a decade before this desire was realized.

In 1947, a national campaign for self-government was launched, and in 1949, Sultan Muhammad V gave the campaign his official backing. In 1953, the sultan was deposed by the French, with some Berber assistance. He was exiled to Madagascar, an action that precipitated a number of anti-French disturbances in Morocco. In 1955, Berbers killed every French person in the town of Oued Zem. In the aftermath of the violence, the French restored Sultan Muhammad V to power. Independence was finally granted to Morocco on 2 March 1956. In the same year, the northern territory under Spanish rule was granted independence as well. In 1957, the sultan adopted the title of king and named his son, Hasan, crown prince. The prince became King Hasan II after his father's death in 1961. Hasan II survived attempted coups in the early 1970s and confronted, in the course of his reign, a number of critical economic and political challenges, notably the emergence of an increasingly influential Islamist movement.

In 1971, Hasan II began a battle to establish sovereignty over the resource-rich Western Sahara, a territory then known as the Spanish Sahara, to Morocco's south. He encountered resistance from Algeria and Libya. In April 1976, an agreement was reached whereby Morocco would retain a section of the disputed territory. Mauritania would control another section, and the remainder of the Spanish Sahara would become independent under the name Western Sahara. Mauritania later relinquished its claim, and Morocco annexed the freed territory. Conflict between Morocco and the Algerian-backed Popular Front for the Liberation of the Sahara and the Rio de Oro (Polisario) continued throughout the 1980s. A cease-fire was brokered in 1991, although sporadic fighting continued. For many years, the international community has sought a resolution to this long-running dispute, but with little success. Formal talks between Morocco and the Polisario resumed in 2007 and continued as of March 2008.

Muhammad VI took the throne upon his father's death in 1999. The early years of his reign were characterized by cautious liberalization—politically, economically, and socially. Generally enjoying broad popular support, Muhammad VI became part of new generation of Arab leaders attempting to maintain a viable balance between tradition and modernization, continuity and change.

The king is head of state and, by virtue of his descent from the Prophet Muhammad, he is known as *amir al-mu'minin,* or "Commander of the Faithful." The king appoints a cabinet, known as the Council of Ministers. He also appoints a prime minister as head of the government. A *Majlis al-Nuab,* or Council of Representatives, is made up of legislators elected by the people. The council is referred to as the Parliament, but it legislates only criminal, civil, and commercial matters and can be disbanded by royal decree.

² LOCATION AND HOMELAND

Morocco, a country divided into 43 provinces, has an area of 446,550 sq km (172,368 sq mi) covering the northwest corner of Africa. It lies 13 km (8 mi) to the south of Spain, separated by the Strait of Gibraltar. The Mediterranean Sea separates Morocco from Europe. Morocco is bordered on the west by the Atlantic Ocean, on the east and southeast by Algeria, and on the south by the Western Sahara. The Moroccan coastline is more than 1,600 km (1,000 mi) long, allowing for a thriving fishing industry (mackerels, anchovies, and sardines) and a tourism industry that features beach resorts on the Atlantic and Mediterranean coasts. The population of Morocco was estimated to be 33,757,175 in 2007.

The Moroccan landscape consists of mountains, rivers, desert, and plains. It has four major mountain ranges. In the north, bordering the Mediterranean Sea, are the Rif Mountains. While the Rif themselves rise only to 2,100 m (6,890 ft), their cliffs drop off sharply to the sea and thus make access by modern transportation difficult. The Rif area has few coastal towns or beaches. South of the Rif are three ranges that make

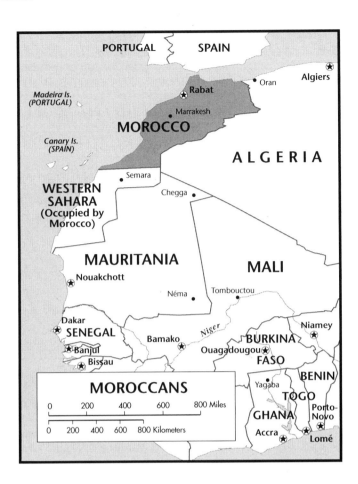

up the Atlas Mountains. From north to south, these are the Middle Atlas, which rise only to 3,000 m (9,850 ft); the High Atlas, rising to more than 4,000 m (13,130 ft); and the Anti-Atlas, rising only to 2,400 m (7,880 ft). Morocco's highest mountain is Mount Toubkal in the High Atlas range. Mount Toubkal is 4,165 m (13,670 ft).

The northwestern part of the Sahara covers Morocco from the foothills of the Anti-Atlas Mountains to the east. Most of the habitation consists of small groups of people living in the oases.

Morocco's rivers are not navigable, but they are a significant source of irrigation and provide water for 20% of the arable land. Three rivers rise in the Middle Atlas and empty into the Atlantic Ocean. These are the Sebou, Morocco's largest river; the Bou Regreg; and the Oum al-Rabi'. The Moulouya also rises in the Middle Atlas and flows northward into the Mediterranean. To the south are the Tensift, the Sous, and the Dra'a rivers, which flow into the Atlantic Ocean, and the Ziz and Rheris rivers, which flow into the desert.

Several flat, featureless plains lie between the mountain ranges and between the Atlantic coast and the mountains. A variety of crops are cultivated, some of which are processed for export. The most fertile region lies between the Atlas Mountains and the Atlantic Ocean. Here, oranges, figs, olives, almonds, barley, and wheat are grown in abundance. The west-central plain boasts the largest phosphate reserves in the world, and Morocco is responsible for nearly 20% of the world's phosphate extraction.

Morocco has a variety of weather patterns. The desert is hot and dry, cooling off precipitously during winter nights. The coastal plains and coastline enjoy a Mediterranean climate, with mild temperatures attributable to the proximity of the sea. In the low mountain elevations, summers are hot and dry, and winters are cold and rainy. In the higher mountain elevations, summer days are hot and nights are cool. Winters are cold there, and snow is common.

³ LANGUAGE

Both Arabic and French are taught in Moroccan schools. English is also taught in some schools. Modern Standard Arabic is the official state language, and it is used in most forms of public discourse. Moroccans speak their own dialect of Arabic, which displays slight regional variations. This dialect is increasingly used in formal contexts such as advertising and public awareness campaigns. Some of the more common Arabic words used in Morocco are religious in nature. When pledging to do something, a Moroccan Muslim often says *insha' Allah,* or "if God wills it." Prior to any action, a Muslim will often say *bismillah,* or "in the name of God." Common female Arabic names are *Fatima, 'Aisha,* and *Khadija.* Common male Arabic names are *Muhammad* (and variants such as *Ahmed* or *Hamid*), *Hasan,* and *'Ali.* All of these are also the names of famous people in Islamic history.

Educated Moroccans are expected to speak French, and French vocabulary words have entered the Moroccan language as a result of years of French colonization. French is commonly used in business transactions and in hotels and resort areas where foreigners congregate. Fluency in French helps Moroccans to climb the social ladder. Spanish is spoken in the northern region of Morocco, which was formerly under Spanish rule.

Berber, among the oldest languages in Africa, is spoken almost exclusively by the Berbers, although some Berber words have made their way into Moroccan Arabic. Berbers speak three distinct dialects: Tarifit in the north, Tamazight in the Middle Atlas region, and Tashelhit in the south. Approximately 55% of Berbers speak both their native dialect and Arabic. In 2001, the Royal Institute of Amazigh (Berber) Culture was founded, and Berber was recognized as an official language. On 11 February 2003, King Muhammad VI declared that Tifinagh would be the official alphabet of written Berber. The language has since been used in computers and word processing programs.

Titles of respect are often attached to names. Thus, an older woman may be referred to as *Lalla,* which is comparable to "Ma'am." A man may be referred to as *Sidi,* or *Si* for short, which is comparable to "Mr." A more respectful title, reserved for men of high political status, is *Moulay.* A man who has undergone the pilgrimage to Mecca is called *Hajj,* and a woman who has done so is called *Hajja.*

⁴ FOLKLORE

Morocco has many legends based on the exploits of Muslim leaders who acted as mediators in disputes between families and tribal groups. These leaders often came from religious backgrounds and were considered well educated. These holy men, or *murabitin* in Arabic, are somewhat analogous to the Christian saints, and they were believed to possess *baraka,* or divine grace, which allowed them to perform miracles. Their burial sites, small domed structures surrounded by a walled courtyard, are often sites of pilgrimage. Many people visit the murabitin to ask for intercession and hope that they will receive blessings and favors from the popular saints. The burial sites have also become unofficial centers for the collection of alms for the needy. The murabitin are more commonly found in the countryside than in the urban areas.

Some Moroccans believe in spiritual beings called *jinn*— often translated in English as "genies"—who are said to assume the guise of animals so as not to be recognized. They are thought to frequent public baths and other areas associated with water. To ward off these spirits and to prevent them from meddling in human affairs, Moroccans wear verses from the Quran on an amulet. They also wear the "hand of Fatima," a charm in the shape of the right hand that protects against the evil eye. In the years following the 2003 terrorist bombings in Casablanca, the hand of Fatima was used as a symbol for anti-terrorism campaigns.

Often, women in the Moroccan countryside believe in (and might practice) *sihr,* or witchcraft. Sihr is administered orally, usually as a potion mixed with food or drink, with the intention of influencing the behavior of another person. This might involve casting a spell to make someone fall in love or administering a curse to take revenge on someone for hurtful behavior. The victim of such a curse might seek the advice of a religious teacher to undo the spell.

Most folklore in Muslim countries tells stories of important figures in religious history, many of which are found in or derived from material found in the Quran or in later forms of Islamic literature.

⁵ RELIGION

The overwhelming majority (99%) of Moroccans are Sunni Muslim, about 69,000 are Christian (mainly Roman Catholic), and a minority of 6,000–7,000 are Jewish. Islam is the state religion, and although many Moroccans do not outwardly practice all of the pillars of Islam, most profess adherence to the religion. The Malaki school of Islamic law, or *Shari'a,* has traditionally predominated in Morocco. Sufism has historically been an important dimension of Moroccan Islam, and Sufi groups continue to play an important role in both official and popular forms of the religion. The Hassan II Mosque in Casablanca is the second largest mosque in the world (second only to the Great Mosque in Mecca) and can accommodate 25,000 inside and a further 80,000 in its courtyard.

⁶ MAJOR HOLIDAYS

Moroccans commemorate both secular and Muslim religious holidays. One major Muslim holiday is *Eid al-Fitr,* which comes at the end of the month of fasting called Ramadan. During Ramadan, Muslims refrain from eating, drinking, or having sexual relations during the daytime in order to reflect on God and on the plight of the less fortunate. At the end of the month, Muslims celebrate for three days. The other major Muslim holiday is *Eid al-Adha,* which commemorates the willingness of the Prophet Abraham, as well as his son, to obey God. This holiday signals the end of the Muslim pilgrimage to Mecca, or *hajj,* which every Muslim is obliged to undertake at least once during his or her lifetime. Traditionally, each family slaughters a lamb to feast on during Eid al-Adha. Today, because of the high cost of purchasing a sheep, it is not uncommon for poorer families to pool their resources and purchase an animal to share.

Secular holidays include King Hassan II's Coronation Day (March 3), Labor Day (May 1), Independence Day (November 18), and New Year's Day (January 1). Festivals are also held to commemorate anniversaries of the birth or death of saints.

7 RITES OF PASSAGE

Marriage is the norm in Moroccan society. Weddings are conducted over a period of several days, during which the families of the bride and groom might hold separate parties. These are elaborate affairs featuring food, music, and dancing. Child-bearing is expected of every wife. When the newborn baby is seven days old, a celebration known as the *subu'* is held. It is common for a lamb to be roasted for the party, and guests bring gifts for the baby and the mother. Circumcision of males is an obligation within Islam. In Morocco, it is usually undertaken while the boy is young, before his sixth birthday.

Upon the death of a relative or a neighbor, the deceased is buried within 24 hours, and family and friends gather together to mourn for a period of three days. This involves ritual recitations from the Quran. Close friends prepare food for the bereaved family during the mourning period. Another mourning period occurs on the fortieth day after the death. Again, friends and relatives gather together to recite the Quran in memory of the deceased. At this time a large meal, known as *sadaqa,* is offered to guests who join in the mourning.

8 INTERPERSONAL RELATIONS

Moroccans shake with the right hand during greetings and farewells, and they will often touch the hand to the heart to show respect or affection. Close friends of the same sex commonly hug and exchange kisses on the cheek. It is appropriate for persons of the opposite sex to simply shake hands without intimate physical contact. Some very religious women prefer not to shake hands with men, believing that any physical contact is inappropriate. In the home, men and women often sit and converse in separate sections of the room or house. A common greeting among Moroccans is the phrase *al-salamu 'alaykum,* which means, "May peace be upon you." The response is *wa 'alaykum al-salam,* or "May peace be upon you also." During greetings, Moroccans often exchange a great number of pleasantries and inquiries about one another's families before beginning the conversation.

Homes are shelters against public intrusion, and windows are usually shaded to preserve a family's privacy. Family members are generally courteous to one another, and guests in a Moroccan home characteristically receive gracious attention and respect. Though a Moroccan will show the utmost hospitality to a guest in his or her home, the street or marketplace is a public space in which no such courtesies are necessary. Thus, in public, each person hopes to advance his or her own interests and therefore may show little regard for the interests of others.

Boys and girls are typically kept apart until they are old enough to understand sexuality. Intermingling of the sexes outside marriage is generally considered inappropriate, and perhaps even shameful. Premarital sex is strictly forbidden, and a girl who loses her virginity outside marriage is stigmatized and brings great shame to her family's reputation. Moroccan men are free to socialize outside the home; the café is

Moroccan women have more freedom in the cities, while more restrictions are placed on rural women. (Cory Langley)

a common gathering place. Women are rarely (never, in rural areas) seen at cafés. Homosexuality is illegal in Morocco.

9 LIVING CONDITIONS

A majority of Moroccans live in urban areas, most of which comprise a precolonial district, or *medina,* and a colonial or postcolonial area, sometimes called the *ville nouvelle.* The medina is usually surrounded by high, thick walls that enclose houses ranging in age from medieval to modern. Many Moroccans live in *bidonvilles,* shantytowns that are erected on the periphery of urban areas. Originally built as temporary settlements for migrant workers, these bidonvilles, in many cases, have become permanent slums with little infrastructure and few public services, if any. The range and quality of the public services available in Moroccan homes varies widely. Houses in the north are frequently white, whereas those in the south are often reddish brown. In the newer, postcolonial towns, houses are built with Western amenities. These may be either single-family detached dwellings or rows of townhouses attached at the sides or rear. Many homes, especially in the city of Marrakech, feature an open courtyard surrounded by several stories of rooms. Most rooftops are flat, and they are used for washing and hanging out laundry, as well as a variety of social purposes. In areas of high elevation, such as in the mountainous Middle Atlas village of Ifrane, roofs are slanted to allow the snow to slide off.

Moroccans generally have access to clean water and to cooking and heating fuel. Cooking stoves range from a common three-burner cooking top to full ovens and ranges. These may be fueled by bottled propane or butane gas. The majority of residential toilets are porcelain-covered holes in the ground. Modern homes have Western-style toilets with seats. Most homes also have electricity, with at least one outlet per room. Some homes, though by no means most, have central heating and telephones. Nearly half of all Moroccans own cellular phones, and approximately 6 million people are connected to the Internet.

Streets are well maintained, and most cities are connected by two-lane roads. As of 2007, there were 507 km (315 mi) of new, multilane expressways, or *autoroutes,* linking the major cities. At present, there are autoroutes linking Casablanca to Al-Jadida, Tangier, Marrakech, and Fes. Those connecting Tangier to Ceuta in the north, and Agadir to Marrakech in the south, were still under construction as of 2008. Railroads built during the era of French colonization continue to operate today. Approximately 1,907 km (1,185 mi) of rail runs east to west and north to south, connecting most of Morocco's major cities and connecting Morocco with Algeria. Cities that cannot be reached by train are serviced by buses, which offer extensive coverage. The country has four major seaports and more than a dozen smaller ones. Morocco is linked to the rest of the world by its seven international airports. There are more than 50 civil airports as well.

Moroccans' median age is 24.3 years; approximately 31% of the population is under the age of 14. Casablanca is the most populous city, with more than 3 million inhabitants. The next most populated city is the capital, Rabat, with approximately 1.7 million people. Morocco's population growth rate is 1.528%, and its life expectancy is 68 years for males and 73 for females. Morocco has an infant mortality of 39 deaths per 1,000 live births.

10 FAMILY LIFE

The family is central to the vast majority of Moroccans' lives. Children live with their families until they marry or go away to school. After a Moroccan man is married, it is common for the husband to bring his wife to his family's home, where they live together with the extended family. The elderly are highly respected, and when they are too old to take care of themselves, they are cared for by their families. Both men and women may play a strong role in decision making, but females are taught early on that they are expected to take care of the home and their siblings. Women generally have more freedom in the cities, whereas more restrictions are placed on rural women.

Marriage is expected of every Moroccan, both men and women. For many women, marriage and childbearing are the ultimate goals in life. Ideally, most women seek to be married before their mid-20s, and most men before they turn 30. Though not all marriages are arranged, parents have great influence over the spousal choices made by their children. Marriage is thus a family decision, not merely an individual one. Generally, the family seeks to make sure that the prospective spouse will bring prosperity and virtue to the family, so that the family's good name and reputation are enhanced. Divorce is seen in a very negative light, but it is not forbidden. Both men and women can initiate divorce proceedings.

11 CLOTHING

The national attire of the Moroccans is a one-piece, floor-length, hooded garment known as a *jellaba*. It is commonly worn by men and women of every social class, both urban and rural. The wealthy often have their jellabas tailor made, whereas many simply purchase them from a ready-to-wear rack. Western attire is often worn under the jellaba. Western-style—often very fashionable—attire for women and suits and slacks for men are also common, especially in cities. Religious or conservative women cover their hair in public. Berber women wear long, colorful dresses, often covering their heads with straw hats. They often have tattoos on their forehead, cheek, or neck; this custom is slowly fading away, however. Rural men often wear turbans, and a knitted skullcap is common attire for men going to a mosque. The maroon-colored fez, once a ubiquitous sign of respect and wealth, is declining in popularity, especially among younger men. In cold weather, many men cover their jellabas with a hooded cloak called a *burnus.*

12 FOOD

Moroccans generally eat three meals per day. Breakfast consists of bread, olive oil, butter, and preserves. It may also include eggs, croissants, a pancake-like food known as *baghrir,* and a number of other pastries and breads. Coffee or tea usually accompanies the meal. Lunch, the largest meal of the day, is a time-consuming affair. Dinner may be a light or a heavy meal, with soup and bread being common. Moroccans are avid tea drinkers. Sweet green tea flavored with mint is served all day long. Coffee, usually with much milk and sugar, is also very popular. Moroccans, being Muslim, are prohibited from consuming pork and alcoholic beverages. The latter, however, are served in bars and cafés throughout the country. Despite the Islamic prohibition, Morocco produces its own domestic wines.

Moroccans eat at a low, round table, and they are often served from one platter. Bread is commonly served with every meal; it is used to scoop up food. Berbers bake bread virtually every day. Morocco's national dish is *couscous.* This is steamed semolina wheat formed into tiny granular particles that are combined with other ingredients to make a main course. Couscous can be accompanied by meat, such as lamb or chicken, or mixed with a variety of vegetables. It is generally served on Friday, the Muslim day of rest. Another favorite Moroccan dish is *tajin,* which is a stew of vegetables and meat baked in an earthenware pot. *Harira,* Moroccan soup, is made in many different styles, each often associated with a particular ritual. For example, during Eid al-Fitr, it consists of semolina flavored with anise. After a woman gives birth, she is given harira flavored with wild mint and thyme. Harira is also consumed to break the fast during the month of Ramadan.

13 EDUCATION

Public schools are free and, since 1963, compulsory for children between the ages of 7 and 13. The Moroccan government spends approximately 20% of its budget on education. As of 2005, 85% of girls and 90% of boys attended primary school. Participation in education is markedly higher in urban areas. In 2004, an average of 52.3% of adults were literate—65.7% of men and 39.6% of women. Although the country's schools teach Arabic-language curricula, public schools are modeled on the French system. French is taught in all public schools from the

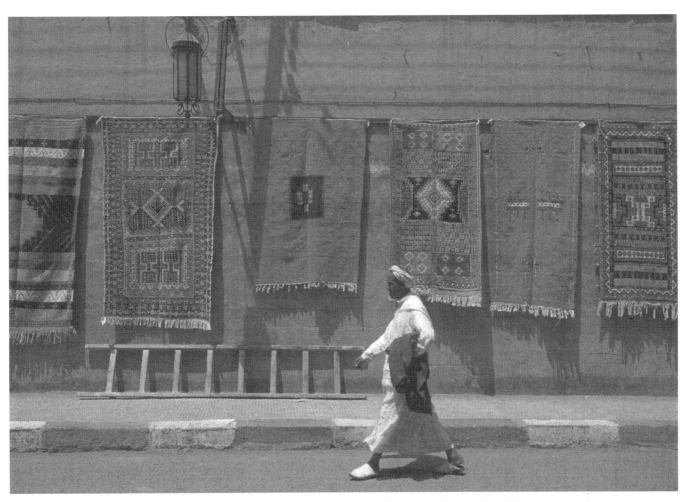

A man walks past Berber carpets on display in Marrakesh, Morocco. (Tim Graham/Getty Images)

third grade through the completion of secondary school. English is taught in public schools at the secondary level. Morocco has many institutions of higher learning, the largest and most prestigious of which is Muhammad V University in Rabat. An English-language university—Al-Akhawayn—opened in the Middle Atlas region in 1995. Private American schools in Casablanca, Rabat, and Tangier offer courses in English from elementary through secondary school. Private French schools are found in every city. The school year is similar to that in Western countries: Classes begin in September and end in June.

14 CULTURAL HERITAGE

Moroccans enjoy rhythmic music and dancing. Though most music on the radio and television is traditional Arab entertainment, an increasing amount of Western music is being broadcast, with a great variety of music channels now available by satellite on television. Traditional Arabic music is dominated by string instruments, such as the *rebec, lotar, 'ud,* and *kamanja.* Hand-held drums of different shapes and sizes are played at parties. It is common to see girls and women dancing at informal gatherings. Sometimes, dancers enter a trance-like state that may culminate in fainting. *Gnawa* music, which is of Berber, Arab, or African origin, is very popular; it features a

three-stringed bass-like instrument called the *gimbri* with percussion accompaniment.

Much dancing and musical entertainment takes place at festivals held in honor of local saints. The festivals often feature horsemen, wearing white robes and white turbans, who gallop toward the audience and then fire their guns into the air.

15 WORK

Morocco's upper class is made up primarily of wealthy merchants and wholesalers or of descendants of the Prophet Muhammad, known as the *Sherfa.* The latter group includes the royal family. The middle class is made up of educated professionals such as university professors, civil servants, doctors, lawyers, and high school teachers. The less educated tend to fall into a lower socioeconomic status. These Moroccans are employed predominantly in factories and farms. In 2007, the urban unemployment rate was 15%. In 2005, a plan was initiated to reduce poverty and unemployment in Morocco's slums. Many of the unemployed take odd jobs as they become available, find work as day laborers, or beg on the streets. Many Moroccans also seek employment outside Morocco and join the emigrant workforce, or *mujahirin.* Most of these people find work in France, Belgium, Canada, Italy, Libya, and the Netherlands. The remittances they send to their families in Morocco are a significant source of foreign currency in the country.

The service sector accounts for nearly half of Morocco's gross domestic product. As of 2003, 45% of Moroccans worked in the service sector, 40% in agriculture, and 15% in the industrial sector. Many of Morocco's industries are centered around the city of Casablanca. Berbers in particular engage in small-scale livestock farming, most commonly sheep and goats. Farming methods are not highly developed, although modern equipment and irrigation technology are increasingly being used. The plains of Morocco are cultivated with barley, corn, wheat, tobacco, citrus fruits, olives, tomatoes, and other fruits and vegetables. Though some of these crops are processed for export, Morocco's chief source of export income is phosphate mining and processing. Morocco has the largest phosphate reserves in the world. Other minerals in the country, though not fully exploited, are iron ore, coal, cobalt, copper, lead, manganese, and zinc. The presence there of key resources is one reason for the ongoing conflict over the status of neighboring Western Sahara. Fishing and tourism are also key sources of revenue.

¹⁶ SPORTS

Football (known as soccer in the United States) is popular in Morocco, as it is throughout the Middle East and North Africa. It is both a spectator sport viewed on television and a field sport engaged in by men and boys throughout the country.

¹⁷ ENTERTAINMENT AND RECREATION

Moroccan men spend much of their leisure time socializing at outdoor cafés. Women in rural areas do not go to cafés, although women in urban areas have begun to frequent them. Most socialization among women is done in the home or on the rooftop. There, they might knit, crotchet, or embroider in the company of other women. Women also socialize in public baths. Large cinemas and shopping malls are increasingly found in Morocco's cities, and they are frequented by both men and women.

Morocco has several television stations, with programming in both Arabic and French. Arabic programs come predominantly from Egypt. Satellite transmission has brought a wide range of programming to the country, with tens of thousands of channels to choose from. Even the relatively poor may have access to satellite channels.

¹⁸ FOLK ART, CRAFTS, AND HOBBIES

Moroccan crafts include rugs, pottery, woodworking, textiles and leatherwork. Rugs and carpets are often woven by hand using a loom; the work is frequently done by women. These rugs have intricate patterns and can take months to complete. Handbags and clothing are crafted from animal skins, which are first prepared and dyed at a leather tannery. Tattooing is an art learned by many women, especially Berbers. Henna, a nonpermanent natural dye that tints the skin a reddish-orange color, is often used to adorn the hands and feet in very detailed, ornate patterns. The construction of the Hassan II Mosque in Casablanca utilized skilled craftsmen from throughout Morocco and features a rich variety of indigenous Moroccan styles and techniques.

¹⁹ SOCIAL PROBLEMS

The government uses strong tactics against people and groups it considers threats to internal security. Members of political opposition movements have thus become targets of arrest campaigns. Morocco has many political prisoners, drawing criticism from human rights organizations. These include both left-wing and Islamist activists, such as members of movements known as the Islamic Youth, the *mujahideen,* and Justice and Charity (al-'Adl wa al-Ihsan). International attention prompted the government to release 2,163 political prisoners between June 1989 and April 1990, despite denial of their existence. A 2003 Human Rights Watch report criticized article 489 of the Moroccan penal code, which criminalizes consensual homosexual acts.

Many claim that Morocco's most pressing problem is the lack of socioeconomic opportunities available to the population. Several riots have taken place to protest the rising cost of food and education. Unemployment is widespread, particularly in rural areas. The current unemployment rate is about 15%, but underemployment is much more prevalent. The government discourages people from moving from the countryside to the urban areas in search of job opportunities. These and other socioeconomic concerns have prompted increased numbers of young Moroccan men to join Islamist movements such as al-Qaeda and other groups operating in Iraq and Central Asia.

Crime is common in Morocco, but very little of it is violent. Thefts and burglary are perhaps the most common crimes. Though hard drugs are a rarity, hashish and marijuana are common but illegal.

In the past, the Moroccan government has spent a large proportion of its foreign reserves fighting a war against the Western Sahara's independence movement, the Popular Front for the Liberation of the Sahara and the Rio de Oro (Polisario).

²⁰ GENDER ISSUES

Morocco has historically been a patriarchal society. Since the 1980s, however, women have begun to play a more prominent role in Moroccan public life. In the early years of that decade, approximately 20% of families had female heads as a result of rising divorce rates. By 1990, women constituted more than one-third of the workforce, working as judges, doctors, teachers, and university professors. In 1992, Morocco's constitution was amended to place greater emphasis on the equality of men and women in the political sphere and on human rights generally.

In the late 1990s, the Moroccan government began to draw up the Plan for Action to Integrate Women into Development, a document that proposed changes to the Moroccan *mudawwanah,* or family code, in order to improve women's legal rights, health, economic development, and education. The plan met with strong resistance from conservative and Islamist groups. On 12 March 2000, organized marches took place in both Rabat and Casablanca. In Rabat, the Moroccan March 2000 for Women demonstrated support for the objectives contained in the Plan for Action and called for banning polygamy, raising the legal marriage age for women from 14 to 18, and improving women's legal rights in cases of divorce. The Casablanca march, in which Islamist groups were the dominant actors, demonstrated in direct response to the Rabat march and in support of more traditional, Islamic roles for women. Accurate numbers for the marches are not available, but large numbers of both women and men participated in both demonstrations.

In January 2004, the mudawwanah was reformed to ensure equality between men and women, particularly in family roles. The reforms abolished the principle of wifely obedience to one's husband, raised the legal marriage age for women to 18, granted wives the right to request a divorce and the right to property in the case of a divorce, granted women the right to retain child custody in the event of remarriage, and included several important items safeguarding the rights of children. Despite these advances, in 2007, the World Economic Forum's *Global Gender Gap Report,* which measures inequality between men and women in terms of economic participation, educational attainment, political empowerment, and health and survival, ranked Morocco one-hundred-twenty-eighth out of 132 countries studied.

21 BIBLIOGRAPHY

Cabré, Yolanda Aixelà. "The Mudawanna and Koranic Law from a Gender Perspective: The Substantial Changes in the Moroccan Family Code of 2004." In *Language and Intercultural Communication* 7, no. 2 (2007): 133–43.

Diouri, Abdelhai. "Of Leaven Foods: Ramadan in Morocco." In *Culinary Cultures of the Middle East,* edited by Sami Zubaida and Richard Tapper. London: I. B. Tauris, 1994.

Eliot, Andrea. "Where Boys Grow Up to Be Jihadis." In *New York Times,* November 25, 2007.

Ennaji, Moha. *Multilingualism, Cultural Identity, and Education in Morocco.* New York: Springer Science, 2005.

Freeman, Amy. "Re-Locating Moroccan Women's Identities in a Transnational World: The 'Woman Question' in Question." In *Gender, Place and Culture* 11, no. 1 (March 2004): 17–41.

Ghanmi, Lamine. "Western Sahara Talks to Resume." In *International Herald Tribune,* January 4, 2008.

Hargraves, Orin. *Culture Shock! Morocco: A Guide to Customs and Etiquette.* Portland, OR: Graphic Arts Center, 1995.

Hausmann, Ricardo, et al. *The Global Gender Gap Report 2007.* Geneva, Switzerland: World Economic Forum, 2007.

"Morocco." In *The Middle East and North Africa, 1997,* 43rd ed. London: Europa, 1997.

Nelson, Harold D., ed. *Morocco: A Country Study.* Washington, DC: American University, 1985.

Park, Thomas K. *Historical Dictionary of Morocco.* Lanham, MD: Scarecrow Press, 1996.

Pennell, C. R. *Morocco: From Empire to Independence.* Oxford, UK: Oneworld, 2003.

Wilkins, Frances. *Morocco.* New York: Chelsea House, 1987.

—revised by J. Henry

MOSSI

PRONUNCIATION: MOH-say
ALTERNATE NAMES: Moose, Moshi, Mosi
LOCATION: Burkina Faso, Côte d'Ivoire
POPULATION: 5 to 6 million in Burkina Faso, 1.2 million in Côte d'Ivoire
LANGUAGE: Moré
RELIGION: traditional religion (3 main components: creator, fertility spirits, ancestors)
RELATED ARTICLES: Vol. 1: Burkinabe; Ivoirians

1 INTRODUCTION

The Mossi make up the largest ethnic group in Burkina Faso. Because of extensive migration to more prosperous neighboring countries, Mossi also are the second-largest ethnic group in Côte d'Ivoire (Ivory Coast). The Mossi occupied the interior lands within the *"boucle de Niger"* ("great loop of the Niger River") and thus controlled trade between the empires along the great Niger River and the forest kingdoms to their south. The three Mossi kingdoms were known for their resistance to Islam in a region where all other kingdoms and empires were Muslim, at least in their ruling elites, after about the 10th century. Mossi culture nonetheless shows Muslim influences.

The Mossi's story of their origins involves the conquest of native farming peoples by immigrant cavalry soldiers from the northeast, toward what is now northern Nigeria. From the beginning, the Mossi people moved, and their idea of society included people moving in, out, and around.

Mossi migration increased notably after the French conquest of the Mossi in 1896–97; the Mossi were one of the last peoples in Africa to be brought under colonial rule. Like the other colonial powers, the French wanted their colonies to generate money for their European homeland. In less than 10 years after the first conquest, the French demanded that the Mossi pay taxes in French francs. Traditional Mossi taxes to chiefs and kings had been paid in goods, and cowrie shells had served as money. By making the Mossi pay in French money, the colonial government required them to grow, dig, make, or do something the French were willing to pay for. As little was grown or mined in Mossi country that the French wanted to buy, many Mossi were forced to migrate to the Ivory Coast (then a French colony) and the neighboring British Gold Coast (now Ghana) to earn money there. The demand for labor on the mainly African-owned coffee and cocoa farms in the coastal forest in those countries coincided with the dry season in the savanna of Burkina Faso, so Mossi men could migrate south between growing seasons and bring money back to their families. Mossi men also traveled widely as traders and as soldiers in the French army.

The Mossi were organized into three kingdoms, Tenkodogo, Wagadugu, and Yatenga, along with a number of buffer states around their edges. All of them together are sometimes described as "the Mossi empire," but there has never been a time when all the Mossi were unified under one ruler. Each kingdom was ruled by a king, with a court of officials who were responsible for various functions, such as defense, and who governed different areas of the kingdom. Within such areas, groups of up to 20 villages were ruled by a district chief, and

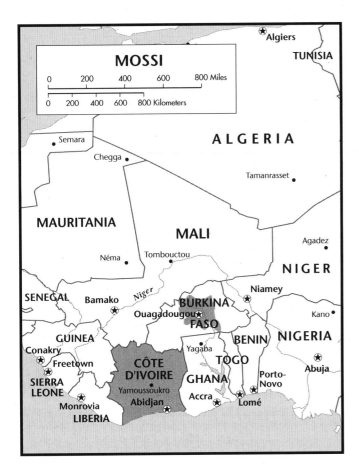

² LOCATION AND HOMELAND

The Mossi homeland is the central portion of Burkina Faso, known until 1984 as Upper Volta for its location on the three branches of what in Ghana becomes the Volta River.

Because the Mossi were the dominant people in the region before and during colonial rule, their population statistics in relation to the modern nation have been affected by political factors. In 1962, the French counted 10% of the population and estimated from that sample survey that 48% of the total population was Mossi. However, there has been suspicion that the number 48% was picked by the French so that the Mossi, who already were most of the leaders of the new country, would not have an outright majority as the Republic of Upper Volta became independent. The following censuses of 1975 and 1985 did not publish national totals for the country's ethnic groups, in order to avoid ethnic conflict. Therefore, estimating the Mossi population is a matter of dividing the national population roughly in half. In 1995, the estimated national population of Burkina Faso was 10,422,828, of whom some 5 to 6 million would be Mossi.

Burkina Faso is roughly the size of Colorado, with the Mossi area in the center running from Tenkodogo in the southeast to Ouayagouya in the northwest. The national capital, Ouagadougou, is also the capital of the largest and strongest Mossi kingdom, which has the same name. The importance of Ouagadougou as a kingdom was emphasized by the fact that its *Naba* was the only one whose title was not just the name of the kingdom, district, or village attached to the word *Naba,* but was *Mogho* (or *Moro*) *Naba,* meaning "ruler of the world." The country is mainly savanna, or grassland, with scattered trees; unfarmed land is brush and trees. The extreme north of the country is part of the true Sahel, the transition zone between the Sahara desert and the savanna grasslands. The few rivers and streams are seasonal, with only scattered pools keeping water through the dry season; most water used by the Mossi is drawn from wells.

As the economies of Ghana and the Ivory Coast improved, and as transportation became easier, more and more of the Mossi did not merely migrate seasonally to work as farm laborers, but settled and became farmers or city or town dwellers. As a result, there is a network of Mossi across all three countries, greatly expanding opportunities for relatives back home. The Mossi are the second-largest ethnic group in the Ivory Coast; they were the majority of the 1.2 million Burkinabe counted in the 1988 census.

³ LANGUAGE

The Mossi language is Moré. It is a language of the Gur group within the larger Niger-Congo language family. Like many African languages, Moré uses tones (differences in pitch) as well as individual sounds to distinguish meanings; also, like many African and African-influenced languages, it indicates both tense and "aspect." That is, a verb indicates both whether an action is in the past, the present, or the future, and also whether it is an ongoing action or one happening only at one particular time. Mossi speech, both in everyday use and in formal political contexts, is rich in proverbs.

A person's name is not a random choice by his or her parents, but it also reflects circumstances of birth. Names can refer to events that happened during pregnancy or just before or during childbirth. A baby might be named *Gyelle* if his or

---

each village had its own chief. There is one word for all these rulers—kings, district chiefs, and village chiefs: *Naba.* A Naba is a man who has been properly installed as ruler by the community and thereby has been granted the *nam, which is* the religious power to rule other people. A person who seized power without being properly chosen and without the correct rituals of installation would not be regarded as a real ruler by the Mossi. The fact that the political system of the Mossi was so closely connected to their religion was the main reason that their rulers resisted conversion to Islam at the time when their counterparts to the east and west across the savanna were accepting Islam. Even when individual kings converted, as happened once or twice, the society as a whole did not. Not until the French conquest showed that divine protection of the traditional system was not absolutely guaranteed did Mossi people in any numbers convert to Islam or to Christianity.

Nabas were chosen by the court officials from among the sons of the previous Naba. While in principle the oldest son should succeed his father, the ministers tried to ensure that the new Naba was capable of ruling well. In the case of kings, who had many wives, the number of eligible sons might be large. One of the ways that the Mossi states expanded their territory was that sons who were not chosen to succeed their fathers founded new political units on the edges of the Mossi area, conquering (or persuading) local peoples who had the same general way of life, but lacked kingdoms, to become Mossi.

Exactly when the Mossi states were founded is still debated, but a Mossi raid on Timbuktu in 1329 is recorded in Arabic histories written in that city.

her mother accidentally broke an egg while she was pregnant. Many names refer to sacred places or forces whose protection was sought for the birth or the baby.

As with many other West African peoples, there are Mossi names indicating the day of the week when a person was born: *Arzuma* (boy) or *Zuma* (girl) signifies a child born on Friday, whereas *Hado* was born on Sunday and *Larba* on Wednesday.

Being born during a festival may also be reflected in a person's name. Festivals have one or more names associated with them, which are given to a baby born at that time; often the name is the same name as that of the event: *Basga*, for example, or *Tengande*. Such events might reflect Muslim rather than traditional Mossi holidays. *Lokre* is a name for someone born at the end of the fasting month of Ramadan, while *Kibsa* names one born during the festival of Tabaski forty days later, when Muslims sacrifice a ram in honor of the biblical patriarch Abraham.

In much of Africa, high rates of infant mortality meant that twins (who were each usually smaller than other babies, and therefore weaker) were less likely to survive; twins therefore have a special religious significance (sometimes seen as a blessing, sometimes as the opposite, but almost always different) and have special names. For the Mossi, there are special names for twins, *Raogo* ("boy") and *Poko* ("girl"), with diminutive forms for a "younger" twin of the same gender, the younger being the *first* one born and therefore in the uterus for a shorter time. There are even special names for the second, third, and fourth children born after a set of twins.

Children who are born in Muslim or Christian families, or persons who convert to those religions, have names common to Muslims and Christians everywhere in the world, which are Arabic forms of Quranic and Biblical names for Muslims (Adama, Aminata, Binta, Azara, Fatimata, Issa, Issaka, Karim, Mariam, Moussa, Ousman, Saidou), and French forms of Biblical names and (for Roman Catholics) saints' names (Abel, Daniel, Elisabeth, Etienne, Jean, Marie, Moise, Pascal, Pauline, Philippe, Pierre).

4 FOLKLORE

While there have always been some Mossi who were Muslim and literate in Arabic, in general there were no written records in Mossi society. Specialist praise singers, usually called *griots* across the West African savanna, were the keepers of royal traditions and genealogies, but the entire society relied upon folktales and proverbs to concentrate wisdom and experience and to pass them on to succeeding generations.

The Mossi's account of their founding is handed down through an oral tradition that nicely exemplifies important and necessary elements for such an origin myth. Long ago (over 40 generations), a king of the Dagomba, Mamprusi, and Nankana peoples in what is now northern Ghana, Naba Nedega, had a daughter whom he would not allow to marry because he valued her warrior skills so highly. Therefore, Princess Nyennega took a horse and fled north into what is now Mossi country, where she married a local man. Their son was named *Ouedraogo* ("stallion") and after growing up with his maternal grandfather, he returned with Dagomba cavalry and conquered Tenkodogo and its indigenous people, his father's ethnic group, the Bisa. The Mossi people came from the intermarriage of Ouedraogo and his cavalry with Bisa women. To this day the royal families of the two largest Mossi kingdoms,

Ouagadougou and Yatenga, are named *Ouedraogo*. There is a statue of Princess Nyennega on horseback in the city of Ouagadougou to commemorate the story.

The tale of Princess Nyennega and Ouedraogo highlights several important points that illustrate how such stories serve as the basis for organized society. Princess Nyennega is a woman, who marries a man she finds in what becomes Mossi country. This is important for two reasons. First, like most African peoples, Mossi do not believe land can be bought or sold; it is in trust from the ancestors to the living, who must maintain it for generations still to come. Land is owned by the family that originally "domesticated" it by clearing uninhabited wilderness. Secondly, Mossi, like about two-thirds of peoples in the world, trace family membership and family names through the lineage of fathers and their fathers.

For the Mossi to be legitimate owners of their land, then, they had to have a story tracing their ancestry back to the original inhabitants of the land, even though the kingdoms were founded by members of a cavalry (the dominant military technology of the West African savanna until this century) who were immigrants. By making the founding cavalry leader a son of a local man and an immigrant princess, the Mossi validate their claim to their kingdoms. That founder's name, and its perpetuation in the name of the royal clan, underlines the importance of horse soldiers in creating kingdoms where people previously had lived only in extended families.

5 RELIGION

The Mossi are like many African peoples in having traditionally had a religion with three main components. There is a belief in an all-powerful creator, *Wende*, usually discussed as *Wennam*, "God's power." *Nam* is the power ritually granted to a *naba* to rule over humans. While Wende is all-powerful, he is also very distant and not concerned with the daily lives of people. More important in day-to-day religion are generalized spirits of rain and the earth, which govern fertility and crops, and the role of ancestors in the lives of their descendents.

The fertility spirits are worshiped as needed, by sacrifices of sheep or goats, or more often of chickens or guinea fowl, and of eggs by the poorest people, at sacred spots in the landscape, such as an outcropping of rocks or a notable baobab tree. Offerings of millet beer and millet flour in water also accompany prayers at such times when a whole village may gather, for example, to seek rain in time of drought.

The most immediate part of religion, however, is the part played by ancestors. Families are traced in the male line from founding ancestors through the living to future generations. The ancestors watch over their descendents, punishing them or rewarding them for their behavior. The cycle of rituals is mostly concerned with them. A household has a shrine, an inverted pottery bowl, with sacred plants and objects under it, which is honored once a year at the time of the harvest festival, when sacrifices and offerings are made to this shrine and to graves of male ancestors (which are located near where their houses stood); these offerings are like those given to the earth spirits.

6 MAJOR HOLIDAYS

The *Basega* festival comes in December, after the millet crop has been harvested. It is a festival of thanksgiving, thanking the ancestors for their part in bringing in a successful harvest and asking their aid with the coming year's crops. It is a family-based ritual even though it takes place in a political context. That is, a family cannot sacrifice to its ancestors until the day when their district chief sacrifices to his, and the chief cannot do so until the king has done so. While the king's *Basega* is a very large and impressive ceremony (with the luxury of bulls being sacrificed), witnessed by many of his subjects who partake in feasts he offers, strictly speaking he is sacrificing to his ancestors for his harvest, not for the whole kingdom's. Sacrifices and food offerings are also made on special occasions, such as the threshing of a family's millet.

The Muslim community pays formal respects to the king at his *Basega* but celebrates its own holidays, as do the Christians. Most Mossi Christians are Roman Catholic; the first African Cardinal in that Church was a Mossi. About one percent of Mossi are Evangelical Christians, members of the Assemblies of God Church.

While most Mossi are not formally educated—because the nation's poverty limits the number of schools, and children are needed for farming, herding, and household work—those children who do attend school have frequent holidays, since the schools and the government observe secular holidays as well as Muslim and Christian ones. The anniversary of the date marking full independence from France, 5 August 1960, has long been a holiday, as has December 11, the anniversary of the proclamation of the Republic in 1958. Since the revolution of 1983, its anniversary, August 4, has been the official national day. National holidays are celebrated with parades and, in towns and cities, bicycle races.

Besides the national and religious holidays, the need to mobilize people for special tasks makes some days special events in a given community. Until modern times, the Mossi used horses (for the rulers and the rich) and donkeys for transporting goods and people but not for pulling plows. Farming was, and mainly still is, done with short-handled iron hoes. Tasks, such as preparing fields for planting, weeding them, harvesting millet, and threshing it, as well as house-building jobs, such as making a thatched roof and lifting it onto an adobe (mudbrick) hut, requires more labor than an individual household can supply. So, for such occasions, the family whose fields are being hoed or whose millet is being threshed summons neighbors and relatives (more or less the same people), prepares millet beer and food and hires drummers to provide a rhythm for working. People gather, work for intervals, take breaks for food and conversations, and work some more. People have a good time, the work gets done, usually in a morning, and in return the family being helped owes similar labor to the people who have helped them. These are not formally holidays, but they are special days.

On a more regular cycle, and one going beyond individual villages, there is market day. In Mossi society almost everyone is a farmer, but some people are also merchants in a cycle of markets. Because buyers want as many choices as possible, and a merchant can be in only one place at a time, each region of Mossi country has an organized market system. Each day is a market day somewhere within a walkable distance, but only one place has a market on a particular day. Each market recurs every third day. When a market falls on a Friday, the Muslim Sabbath, which happens every 21 days, it is especially large and draws people from greater distances. This is so even though most Mossi are not Muslim.

7 RITES OF PASSAGE

From birth until death (and, indeed, after death, in the ceremonies honoring ancestors), major transitions in a person's life are marked with formal rites of passage. In much of Africa, the number three is associated with males and four with females. A Mossi baby is formally presented to the community three days after birth for a boy and after four days for a girl. At that time, the baby's name is announced, and the child is formally welcomed into its lineage and becomes a bearer of the family name.

In the past, children at one or two years of age were given distinctive facial scars, but since children who are marked in this way may not be enrolled in school due to modern laws against the practice, markings have been eliminated.

Before puberty, both boys and girls, in separate groups, are circumcised. Boys go in groups of 15 to 30 to bush camps, where they stay for 90 to 100 days. This allows time for them to recover from the operation, to form a group that will be closely linked for the rest of their lives, and, not least, to be instructed by older men in what they need to learn to become members of society. Full adulthood is marked by marriage.

In a society with few or no written records, the cumulative experience of elders is crucial to everyone's life; for example, an elder might recognize a particular kind of crop blight that no younger person has ever seen before and could be the only one who would know what to do about it, or, at least, what to expect as a result. The great respect shown by all African societies toward elders is in part a recognition of this all-important store of wisdom they hold for the community and is at the same time, and for related reasons, a consequence of the fact that the elders are "almost ancestors" and will soon make the transition from living members of the community to (deceased) spiritual guardians of the community.

Therefore, Mossi funerals are important family and religious events. A funeral is different from a burial, although both are rituals. In a tropical country, burial must occur very soon after death. Men are buried at the edge of their home, just west of the patio area outside the walled family compound. Women are buried in fields; while they are buried in their husband's village, the burial ritual is done by members of their own family, symbolizing their continued membership in it even though they have borne children for, and lived among, their husband's family.

The funeral occurs ordinarily up to a year after a burial and may be very much later. It is the ritual that confirms the transition of the dead person to the ancestors. The next of kin is responsible for the funeral—the eldest son for his father's, for example. If the son were working in another country, in an extreme case a funeral might be held 20 or 30 years after the burial.

8 INTERPERSONAL RELATIONS

Mossi greetings are very elaborate, more so than in most African societies. The persons greeting each other shake hands while each asks how the other is. The questions extend to how each other's wives are, and their children, and their cows, and sheep, and so on. A full Mossi greeting of an honored elder can take half an hour. While the greeting is taking place, the person who is of lower status shows respect to the other by placing himself or herself in a lower position in relation to the other. If a commoner is formally greeting a chief, he will lie down in front of him and symbolically throw dirt onto his head to show how much lower he is in status.

If two people of equal status meet, however, each tries to respect the other by slowly dropping from a standing posture to a crouching one. Since each person is simultaneously trying to show respect to the other one, two people start out standing shaking hands and finish up, still shaking hands, each crouched low and sitting on their heels.

When visiting a household, a guest stands outside the walls of the compound and claps his or her hands to announce his or her arrival. The head of the household then comes out of the walled compound to greet the visitor. Only a close friend or relative would go into the walled compound.

⁹ LIVING CONDITIONS

The Mossi live in villages of extended families. The village boundaries may be streams or other natural features, but in general the village is a social unit more than a geographical one. This is because houses are 75 to 100 yards apart and surrounded by fields, so that when the main crop, millet, is fully grown to 10 to 12 feet in height, the houses are invisible to each other. Where one village stops and another begins may not be obvious from the landscape.

The traditional Mossi house is a number of round adobe huts with conical thatched roofs, all surrounded with an adobe wall. The household might include a man, his younger brothers, and their married sons. Each of them, and each wife, would have their own hut, and there would be other huts for kitchens, storage, and the sheep, goats, and chickens. There would also be granaries for storing the threshed millet. Houses face west, and the notion of the house is wider than just the walled compound; it includes a patio-like area of pounded, swept dirt with an awning, where people rest during the day and guests are greeted.

As the modern economy has involved increasingly greater numbers of Mossi, the rural standard of living has changed. Corrugated-aluminum roofs are sometimes seen; they are something of a status symbol although they are hotter and are noisier during rainstorms than the traditional thatched straw. Bicycles are common for transportation, with better-off people owning motorbikes. Transistor radios are also common. Radio programming includes "personal notices" programs that allow people in separate parts of the country to pass messages to each other. Vans have replaced trucks as the main form of long-distance transportation in Mossi country. Most people, even in cities, cannot afford an automobile.

Malaria remains a chronic health problem among the Mossi; the cost of importing malaria-suppressing drugs is so high that most people cannot afford them. The fact that most people are infected with malarial parasites makes them less able to fight off other diseases. Measles is a major health problem for children, for whom it is often fatal. Again, the cost of foreign-made vaccines and the staff and transportation to administer them means that this entirely preventable disease continues as a serious health problem.

The impact on the Mossi of the great Sahelian drought of the 1970s was compounded by the fact that some of the potentially most fertile land, along the larger rivers with year-round water, was uninhabitable due to onchocerciasis, or river blindness. This disease, whose parasite is transmitted by the bite of the black fly, can eventually result in blindness. In the 1970s and 1980s, the world's largest public-health project attempted to eliminate this disease and allow people to resettle from crowded parts of the country into potentially fertile lands that had become infested. This has been done by suppressing the black flies that carry the parasite. But, since the flies can only be suppressed, not wiped out, the new, mostly Mossi, villages will be kept habitable only through regular helicopter spraying of the rivers for the foreseeable future.

¹⁰ FAMILY LIFE

As noted above, traditional Mossi villages are groups of households surrounded by fields, where men related to each other through their fathers live with their wives and children. Because the incest taboo means that a man must marry a woman from another family, women ordinarily live in a village other than the one where they grew up, in a household of closely related men and the women from various other families who have married in. This makes life harder for women, who are outsiders in the household. While many Mossi men have only one wife, there are two reasons wives often want their husbands to have an additional wife or wives: the sheer drudgery of household work makes it useful to have another wife to help, and another wife is equally a stranger and someone to talk to when a husband is surrounded by his relatives for support and advice.

Marriage is ordinarily arranged between families. The idea that the family is a continuous set of kin from ancestors to as-yet-unborn descendants gives the whole lineage a stake in making sure there are children to carry on the family. Since the wives who will bear the children have to come from other families, the whole family is involved in arranging the marriage. Because the reproductive power of the woman is taken away to bear children for a different family, her own family is compensated upon the marriage by payments from her husband and his kin. Traditionally, this "bridewealth" was in the form of cattle and trade goods, but in the modern world there is a wider range of possibilities for payment.

Paying bridewealth is sometimes labeled "bride price" by writers describing societies, such as the Mossi, that practice it, but it does not mean "buying" a wife, any more than the European or Asian custom of dowry meant "buying" a husband. It does underline, though, the fact that marriage in many, if not most, societies is not based upon romantic attraction between two individuals, but instead is a much more complex relationship involving families' need to perpetuate themselves and individuals' need for both male and female skills and roles to make a household economy work. (For example, Mossi men weave cloth, but the women spin the cotton thread from which it is woven.)

In the modern era, with more Western-style education, more ways of earning a living than farming, and, especially, easier long-distance transportation, it is less rare for men and women who have fallen in love to elope if they cannot convince their families to agree to the marriage. It has never been true that all marriages were arranged.

The importance of complementary roles in the daily household routine extends to more than husbands and wives. Children have important roles to play in watching the family's sheep and goats, and in helping to haul water and gather fire-

A Mossi man from Yakko, Burkina Faso, wearing traditional clothing. It is increasingly common for men to wear shirts and trousers, whether of Islamic or European style. (David Johnson)

wood for cooking, both of which are major tasks. There is so much work to be done in the kitchen, for example, that if a household does not have a preadolescent girl to help with the cooking, it will foster one from another part of the extended family. Major modern improvements in rural life have been the digging of deeper, cement-lined, year-round wells to ease water hauling, and the acquisition of gasoline-powered mills to grind millet seeds into flour, previously done by hand with a grindstone.

It seems that household sizes are getting smaller in modern Mossi society as more people pursue more varied ways of earning a living and become more involved in a money economy, in which they are more interested in spending their cash on their own children and are less involved in the joint farming of a larger household. But, it is certainly not unusual for households to have more than one wife, or more than one set of husbands and wives. The high infant mortality rate and the lack of social security payments for most people still place a premium on having lots of children to ensure that some will survive to help in making a living and to support their parents in their old age. The infant mortality rate has dropped in the last 30 or so years from roughly 50% to an estimated 11%.

Within the walled compound of the Mossi house, each wife has her own hut for herself and her children and prepares meals for herself and for them, with her husband joining each in rotation if he has more than one wife.

Pets are not usual in Mossi society. Dogs are used for hunting and as watchdogs but are not treated with the affection and pampering that Europeans and Americans usually give them. A rural household will have chickens and guinea fowl, sheep and goats, and sometimes pigeons, as household animals, but they are raised for food, for market, and for sacrifices, and are not pets.

Wealthier Mossi may own cattle, but these are not kept at home. Instead, they are cared for by Fulani herders who live in the unfarmed lands among the Mossi. The Fulani, who live all across the West African savanna, are herders rather than farmers. For the Mossi, having cattle with the Fulani means both that the animals are in the care of specialists and that a man's wealth in the form of cattle may be kept hidden from government tax collectors and from his own relatives. Only in the last 20 or so years have some Mossi begun to use oxen or donkeys to pull plows, and donkey-drawn carts were also introduced only in the modern era.

Horses were the basis of the Mossi kingdoms and chieftaincies because cavalry was the basis of military power, even after guns began to be traded in from the Ashanti states to the south. The lack of wheeled transportation for hay made it difficult to concentrate horses, and the lack of pastures to keep them in have meant that horses were, and are, status symbols whose cost in care and feeding limits their possession to chiefs and other nobles and a few especially well-off commoners.

11 CLOTHING

The Mossi grow cotton and weave it into cloth. The traditional loom wove a long strip of plain or patterned cloth about six inches wide. Strips were sewn together to make cloth for clothes or blankets. In pre-colonial times the Mossi exported large "wheels" of cotton strips, carried on donkeys, to other West African peoples. The French greatly encouraged the growing of cotton as a cash crop, as does the Burkinabe government.

While traditional strip-woven cloth is still available, and is still worn, most everyday clothing is made from factory-woven cotton cloth in one-by-two-meter panels. Such cloth is manufactured in Burkina Faso and is also imported.

Women wear a long skirt made of a cloth panel wrapped around the waist. It is now common to wear a top as well, but this is a recent change in rural areas. It is increasingly common for men to wear shirts and trousers, whether of Islamic or European style. Wealthy men and chiefs wore, and wear, richly embroidered robes in the Muslim-influenced style of the savanna. Modern sewing machines have made the embroidery easier to do, but it is still a luxury.

In the last 30 years or so, a major trade in used American clothing has reached into even rural Mossi markets, so that the everyday working outfit of a farmer is likely to be a strip-woven shirt and a pair of cutoff blue-jean shorts. Rubber shoes and sandals have been added to the leather ones Mossi have traditionally worn.

12 FOOD

The staple of the Mossi diet is millet, along with its relative, sorghum. These crops require less rain, and less regular rain, than wheat. Millet is ground into flour and made into porridge by boiling in water. The result, a loaf-like bowl of somewhat doughy food, is called *sagabo* in Moré and *tô* in West African French. One eats it by breaking off a piece with the right hand

and dipping it into a sauce made of vegetables, spices, herbs, and, sometimes, meat. The sauce supplies the protein and most of the flavor. Sorghum is used to brew a cider-like beer that is drunk from calabashes, half-gourds, by all except Muslims and Protestant Christians.

Rice was domesticated in West Africa and has long been a luxury food for the Mossi; it is served for weddings and other special occasions. It is cooked to a very soft consistency and formed into balls the size of baseballs and is eaten in the same way as the millet porridge.

Corn (maize) is a recently introduced crop that is grown widely; since it depletes soil nutrients faster than millet and is less tolerant of irregular rain, millet remains the staple food.

Peanuts, also native to West Africa, are widely grown; they are eaten boiled, roasted, and ground into sauces.

The extended families to which people belong are grouped into larger clans. Except for chiefs' families, who must be able to show exactly how a claim to a position is justified, most families do not keep detailed genealogies, but just maintain enough sense of kinship to share lineage land, and in the wider community, to know who is an eligible marriage partner and who is not. Members of clans often cannot state exactly how they are related, but they will share a family name and a claim of common descent from some distant, usually heroic, ancestor. Each clan's story of its origin frequently includes an account of how its ancestor was saved at some point of danger by an animal, which then has a special relationship to the clan's members. One clan would not eat crocodile meat because a crocodile was said to have helped hide its ancestor from his enemies; but Mossi in other clans could, and would, eat that animal. Food taboos, then, tend to vary from clan to clan. Some families will eat dog meat, for example, and others will not.

In a farming society where most families do not have electricity, people rise early and go to bed soon after dark. Breakfast may be leftover millet porridge, or, today, French-style bread and coffee. The main meal is in the evening. Food is taken out to those family members working in the fields. Meat is enough of a luxury that it is usually added to sauces in small amounts; grilled meat is for special celebrations.

13 EDUCATION

In traditional Mossi society, most education came from living with, watching, and helping more experienced people older than oneself. The circumcision camps provided a few months of group instruction to boys. There have always been some Muslims among the Mossi, and especially among those who were long-distance traders for whom Islam was a key link to traders in other places. For them, there were Koranic schools where Arabic and the Koran were taught. On the other hand, even though most Mossi did not go to school, they often spoke other African languages besides their own, especially Fulbe (Fulfulbe), the Fulani language.

Modern education is becoming available, but it is not universally offered anywhere. Thirty years ago only 7% of Mossi children attended school. As of 1990, only 18% of the population over age 15 could read and write; they comprised 28% of men and 9% of women. Such education is given in French, the national language of Burkina Faso. The government has established standards for writing the Mossi language, but little beyond Christian religious texts and some agricultural information is written in it.

The rather small number of schools in existence during the French colonial period meant that independence brought job opportunities for Mossi and other Burkinabe who had even an elementary education. As more schools have reached more students, however, the limited number of jobs in one of the world's poorest countries has meant that today's students do not qualify for jobs that their parents or older siblings might have gotten in the past with the same educational qualifications.

14 CULTURAL HERITAGE

Music has been important to Mossi society for entertainment and also for work, in setting rhythms for tasks such as hoeing and threshing. The main instruments are drums. Some drums are large calabashes with leather drumheads and are played with the hands. There are also wooden drums played with sticks, whose pitch can be changed while it is played by a change in arm pressure on the strings tying the head to the drum. There are also flutes and stringed instruments. Drums are made and played only by members of a specific clan, which is also the only Mossi clan that makes pottery.

Some, but not all, Mossi, have traditions of masked dancing for rituals such as funerals. More secular dancing occurs at celebrations and festivals.

The Mossi have a rich literature of proverbs and folktales. Proverbs are not merely a means of transmitting traditional wisdom, but in political debate they provide a way to make the discussion less a contest between rivals and more a weighing of the collective wisdom and experience of the whole society.

15 WORK

Besides the drummers and potters just mentioned, ironworking among the Mossi (as in many African societies) has been restricted to only one clan, whose members were both feared and needed because of their skill. Smelting iron requires mining; and digging in the earth, the source of fertility, is considered supernaturally dangerous. Mossi smiths no longer smelt iron from ore, but work imported and recycled iron into hoes, knives, and axes.

Traditionally, Mossi were farmers, some of whom were part-time traders or soldiers (although wars tended to halt during the farming season), with a few specialist artisans and the chiefs and their courts who governed. Modern Mossi, of course, have all the occupations of a modern nation open to them, and have gone into all of them, but most are still farmers. Farming is nowadays a mix of subsistence farming and cash crops; cotton is grown, but so is the millet needed for city dwellers. Some farmers grow vegetables or fruit for urban markets and for export, and they increasingly use modern technologies, such as fertilizers and insecticides, as well as animal- or tractor-drawn plows.

16 SPORTS

Traditional Mossi society had little leisure time. There were games like *warri*, in which stone or seed counters are moved in pits on a board or in the dirt in a game of strategy aimed at capturing the opponent's pieces. Military training required practice with swords, spears, and bows and arrows.

As part of modern Burkina Faso, the Mossi participate in soccer and bicycle racing, the two major national sports. Towns and cities have bicycle races on most holidays. Basketball has a

Mossi using traditional cultivating methods with oxen near Toma, Burkina Faso. Only recently have more modern occupations been integrated into the farming tradition. (David Johnson)

small presence and a national team, but reaches few Mossi or other Burkinabe.

¹⁷ ENTERTAINMENT AND RECREATION

Aside from music, dance, and conversation, there were not many forms of entertainment or recreation in traditional Mossi society. Griots recited genealogies and traditions at weddings and other events. Radio is important to modern Mossi both for entertainment and for communication in a society with few telephones and relatively few people able to read or write letters.

Television is barely a factor in Mossi life. In 1992 (the most recent available figures), there were only two television stations in the country, one each in Ouagadougou and in Bobo-Dioulasso, the county's second-largest city, to the west of Mossi country. There were only some 41,500 TV sets in this country of some 10 million persons, and the TV stations broadcast only two hours a day during the week and five hours each on Saturday and Sunday.

Movies are important, although theaters are limited to the larger towns and cities. Relatively few movies are made in Africa, or in African languages, so that the movies people see are often from foreign cultures and in foreign languages (Films from India, for example, are widely viewed in Africa.). This is changing, however, and Burkinabe and Mossi filmmakers are playing a major role. The main film festival in Africa is FES-

PACO, the Festival Panafricain du Cinéma d'Ouagadougou. Mossi filmmakers, such as Gaston Kaboré and Idrissa Ouédraogo, are making feature-length films that are seen increasingly in Europe and North America, but also, because they are in Moré, are fully accessible to the Mossi themselves. As videotape makes it easier to bypass theaters, more and more Mossi will be able to participate in this modern expression of their culture.

¹⁸ FOLK ART, CRAFTS, AND HOBBIES

Pottery is limited to the one clan of potters and drummers. For those Mossi communities that have masked dancing, the carving and painting of masks is a major art form; Mossi masks are in most major collections of African art. Unlike some other peoples sharing the same general culture and related languages, the Mossi do not paint designs on houses. Metal earrings and jewelry are produced. Hats, bags, and cushions are made from dyed leather. Cowrie shells from the Indian Ocean were once used as money by the Mossi and are still used as decorations for clothing and hats. Venetian glass trade beads have been worn by Mossi for centuries. Children often make toy cars and airplanes from wire; these are now sometimes seen in American museums and shops. Some craft techniques, such as batik dying of cloth, have recently been introduced into Mossi culture to produce craft items for export or for sale to the relatively few tourists who visit Burkina.

¹⁹ SOCIAL PROBLEMS

The Mossi share the social problems that many African societies and peoples face in dealing with very rapid social change in some areas, and not enough change, not fast enough in others.

As more Mossi live in Ouagadougou and other cities and large towns and earn their living in an increasing variety of ways, traditional gender and family roles come under pressure. A man is supposed to grow his family's millet, but urban wage-earners cannot. So far, urban life for the Mossi is less dangerous than urban life in many other parts of the world. Ouagadougou is hundreds of years old, so cities as such are not new to the Mossi. At the same time, some of the most powerful films by Mossi filmmakers have dealt with the pressures of urban life and the pressures of traditional life upon women and young people.

Burkina Faso was long noted in modern Africa as having more political freedom than most countries, even (paradoxically) when there was a military government. African governments face the task of meeting many demands with few resources, which can result in few tangible accomplishments; in turn this can make way for the military to seize power in the name of honesty and efficiency. Burkina has the distinction of twice having the army seize power, without injuring anyone, and then eventually returning the government to civilian rule. When younger officers led by Thomas Sankara seized power in 1983, however, there were casualties in the fighting and from execution of political rivals. Sankara made a strong effort to break the country out of its dependence on foreign aid, but in 1987 he himself was killed by his associates, who continue to rule the country. Burkina has multiparty elections, but they have been extensively boycotted by parties that argue that the government is manipulating the political system.

Alcohol and drugs are not major problems. While there is a brewery in the country, and there have been complaints of French army veterans drinking their pensions instead of investing in development, the cost of commercially-produced alcohol is too expensive for many Mossi to consume in quantity. The traditional millet beer is alcoholic but is an established part of both traditional society and household organization and is therefore a culturally controlled substance. Kola nuts, rich in caffeine and the basic ingredient in cola drinks, are widely chewed and are a routine gift to a host, three or four (according to gender) being offered. They are imported from Ghana to the south. They are the preferred stimulant for Muslims, who do not drink alcohol.

²⁰ GENDER ISSUES

As in most African countries, traditional practices have kept women in a subordinate position. In the traditional setting a woman is considered to be property that can be inherited upon the death of her husband. As such, traditional law does not recognize inheritance rights for women. Women suffer from frequent domestic sexual abuse and violence, and no specific laws have been put in place to protect women. Abusive husbands go free as there are no legal channels to investigate or prosecute such individuals. Another problem for girls is that they are married early in life. It is estimated that about 52% of women are married before the age of 18.

However, female excision (commonly known as female genital mutilation) was abolished in 1996. A committee known as The National Committee for the Fight Against Excision was also established in 1996 to work toward complete eradication of this practice in Burkina Faso. Estimates indicate that up to 70% of girls and women had undergone the procedure before it was abolished in 1996. Since then, incidences of excision have declined by about 40%, and more than 400 people have been sentenced for performing the practice.

Women are responsible for subsistence agriculture, and few are involved in the more lucrative private sector. Women hold only about 11.7% of the seats in parliament and form about 25% of the government workforce. Many of the women in government earn low wages as they generally hold low paying jobs. In terms of human rights, excessive poverty has seen many Mossi living deplorable lives with no access to basic human rights. Child labor, child trafficking, violence, and discrimination against women and children are quite rampant in the country. People are also arrested without charge or trial and excessive force is often used against civilians with official impunity.

²¹ BIBLIOGRAPHY

Cordell, Dennis D., Joel W. Gregory, and Victor Piché. *Hoe & Wage: A Social History of a Circular Migration System in West Africa.* Boulder, Colo.: Westview Press, 1996.

Decalo, Samuel. *Burkina Faso.* World Bibliographical Series, vol. 169. Oxford, England; Santa Barbara, Calif.: Clio Press, 1994.

Guirma, Frederic. *Princess of the Full Moon.* New York: Macmillan, 1970.

———. *Tales of Mogho: African Stories from Upper Volta.* New York: Macmillan, 1971.

McFarland, Daniel Miles. *Historical Dictionary of Upper Volta (Haute Volta.)* Metuchen, N.J.: Scarecrow Press, 1978.

McMillan, Della E. *Sahel Visions: Planned Settlement and River Blindness Control in Burkina Faso.* Tucson: University of Arizona Press, 1995.

Skinner, Elliott P. *African Urban Life: The Transformation of Ouagadougou.* Princeton, N.J.: Princeton University Press, 1974.

———. *The Mossi of Burkina Faso: Chiefs, Politicians, and Soldiers.* Prospect Heights, Ill.: Waveland Press, 1989.

—revised by Ezekiel Kalipeni)

MOZAMBICANS

PRONUNCIATION: mo-zam-BEE-kuhns
LOCATION: Mozambique
POPULATION: 20.9 million
LANGUAGE: Portuguese (official); 33 African languages; English (trade)
RELIGION: traditional African religions; Islam; Christianity
RELATED ARTICLES: Vol. 1: Chewa; Swahili

¹ INTRODUCTION

As is the case with the vast majority of African countries, the boundaries of Mozambique resulted from the European "scramble for Africa" and are not reflective of a single distinct cultural group. Mozambicans are a people in transition, still recovering from two recent traumatic experiences. First, from 1962 until 1975 the country experienced guerrilla warfare led primarily by the Mozambique Liberation Front (FRELIMO) in opposition to Portuguese colonial rule; this eventually led to independence from the colonial power on 25 June 1975. From 1975 until the early 1990s, however, guerrilla forces continued to war in Mozambique as FRELIMO was challenged by the Mozambican National Resistance (RENAMO).

FRELIMO formed in 1962, and under the leadership of Eduardo Mondlane initiated an armed campaign against the Portuguese. When Mondlane was killed in an explosion in 1969, Samora Machel led FRELIMO and was appointed the first president of Mozambique after independence in 1975. Machel died in an air crash in 1986 and was succeeded by Joaquium Chissano. Since the ascendancy of Joaquium Chissano to the presidency, three multi-party general elections have been held. The ruling FRELIMO party has won each time. Just before the third election, Chissano voluntarily stepped down after almost two decades in power. Guebuza led FRELIMO to its third victory in February 2005. FRELIMO pursued Marxist-Leninist policies, envisioning a socialist country in Mozambique that would avoid the capitalist abuses of the colonial system. However, in recent years the FRELIMO government began to adopt free market enterprise with support from the International Monetary Fund (IMF) and the World Bank. A progressive constitution is in place, which guarantees press freedom, gender equality and basic human rights.

Following independence from Portugal, the FRELIMO government of Mozambique supported the anti-apartheid movement in South Africa. RENAMO was formed from neighboring Rhodesia (which became Zimbabwe in 1980) to discourage Mozambican support of the Zimbabwe nationalist movement. After Zimbabwe's independence in 1980, South Africa continued to support RENAMO's terrorism of Mozambique in order to distract FRELIMO from supporting anti-apartheid forces in South Africa. The cause of the plane crash that killed President Machel was never determined, and the Mozambique government believed that South African involvement caused the crash. A General Peace Agreement was signed between RENAMO and FRELIMO on 4 October 1992, and a general cease-fire began. In 1994 Joaquium Chissano was democratically elected president of Mozambique.

The long-term war economy in Mozambique has meant that normal activities, like going to school, were not common until recently, and that cultural identity in Mozambique is in transition. During the war years, many Mozambicans could not distinguish between RENAMO and FRELIMO forces; many could not identify the president of the country; and many did not realize that the world referred to them as Mozambicans. Part of FRELIMO's socialist strategy was to minimize ethnic and racial distinctions after independence, but most people in Mozambique continue to identify more with local and/or traditional African groups than with their nationality. The 10 major ethnic groups currently found in Mozambique include the Macua-Lomwe, Ajao, Nguni, Tonga, Chope, Shona, Maconde, Maravi, Chicunda, and the Nyungwe.

Historically, the area of present-day Mozambique was populated by the Yao, Tumbuka, Batonga, and Makua peoples. The first inhabitants of the area were Bushmanoide hunters and gatherers, ancestors of the Khoisan peoples who are presently found in South Africa, Botswana, and Namibia. Around ad 1–4, Bantu-speaking farmers and ironworkers migrated from the north into the plateau and coastal areas of present-day Mozambique. The Zanj migrated east of Lake Nyasa by the 7th century. Islamic chiefs came to the Pemba/Zanzibar coast by the 9th century, and coastal trading forts were held by Arabs as far south as the island of Mozambique. Tsonga and Ronga (later known as Zulu) were in the south of the country from the 15th century, and at about the same time Caranga (also known as Shona) peoples moved to the north.

Since peace officially came to Mozambique in 1992, civil strife and natural disasters have continued to plague the country. The aftermath of nearly 30 years of war has been intensified by recurrent drought in the hinterlands; severe drought and floods in the central and southern provinces; cyclones in the coastal areas; and desertification and pollution of surface and coastal waters due to increased migration to urban and coastal areas. Mozambique remains one of Africa's poorest countries. Indeed, many sources name Mozambique as the world's poorest country.

² LOCATION AND HOMELAND

Mozambique is located in southern Africa between South Africa and Tanzania. Malawi, Swaziland, Zambia, and Zimbabwe all border Mozambique to the west, and the country's eastern coastline is separated from the island country of Madagascar by the Mozambique Channel. The country is slightly less than twice the size of California, with a total area of 303,037 sq mi. The climate is tropical to subtropical, and most of the country is coastal lowlands. Uplands in the center of the country rise to high plateaus in the northwest and mountains in the west. Mozambique is divided into 10 provinces. The capital, Maputo (formerly known as Lourenco Marques), has an estimated population of 2 million. The second and third largest cities are Nampula in the far north and the port city of Beira in central Zambezi Province.

With a population of nearly 20.9 million, Mozambique also has an estimated 100,000 refugees from the earlier years of civil war living in Malawi, Zimbabwe, and South Africa. By the end of 1994, 1.6 million refugees had returned to Mozambique. One million Mozambican refugees were in Malawi in 1991. In 1990, it was estimated that 3 million Mozambicans had been displaced by the war. Of the current population, 99% are indigenous ethnic groups such as Shangaan, Chokwe, Manyika,

Sena and Makua; 0.06% are European; 0.2% are Euro-African; and 0.08% are Indians from India.

³ LANGUAGE

The official language adopted by FRELIMO is Portuguese, though only an estimated 30,000 people in Mozambique speak the language, and 27% of those speak it as a second language. The *Ethnologue* lists 33 languages spoken in Mozambique. Those with more than one million speakers include Makhuwa-Makhuwana (2.7 million speakers), Makhuwa-Metto (1.5 million speakers), and Lomwe (1.3 million speakers). Makhuwa-Shirima, Chopi, and Chwabo follow in popularity. In urban centers, particularly in Maputo, English is becoming popular because many neighboring countries use English as their official language.

⁴ FOLKLORE

The various ethnicities of Mozambique contribute to a rich and important presence of myths and legends in the country. Traditional African religions generally place great emphasis on the importance of ancestors. The long dependence on the use of oral tradition to pass histories from one generation to the next has resulted in a wealth of folk traditions and stories. One such legend from the Maconde people demonstrates the importance of folklore to present-day Mozambicans. The Maconde believe that they descended from one man who lived alone in the forest like a wild pig. The man wanted a family, so he carved a wife and eventually had children. The first two children were born near the river and both died. The third was born on the plateau and survived. This was taken as a sign that the Maconde should live on high ground. The Maconde, who are world-renowned for their wood carvings, believed that their carving abilities proved they could control the world of nature and communicate with ancestors and spirits. The Maconde word for woodcarving, *machinamu*, also means ancestors and carvers. They have traditionally produced human figures for family worship as well as masks for initiation ceremonies.

⁵ RELIGION

As indicated by the variety of ethnicities found and languages spoken in Mozambique, an array of religions are practiced. Roughly 60% of Mozambicans practice traditional African religions, 30% are Christian, and 10% are Muslim. Most traditional African religions believe in one supreme being who acts through spirits and ancestors. Traditional religions are not necessarily viewed as incompatible with "imported" religions such as Christianity and Islam. Many Mozambican Christians continue to practice the witchcraft, sorcery, spells, and magic associated with traditional religions. RENAMO used the traditional beliefs of Mozambicans to gain the respect of peasants and to influence soldiers. RENAMO commanders were often Ndua-speakers, among whom *espiritistas* (spirit mediums), *curandeiros* (healers), or *feiticeiros* (witch doctors) enjoyed great influence. Such mediums were believed to give fighters courage, and many practiced rites to make warriors "invisible" or "bulletproof." While the Ndaus constitute less than 2% of the Mozambique population, they were well known for their use of magic.

At first, FRELIMO tried to ignore traditional African religion and discounted curandeiros and chiefs, preferring to emphasize "scientific socialism." FRELIMO soon relaxed the

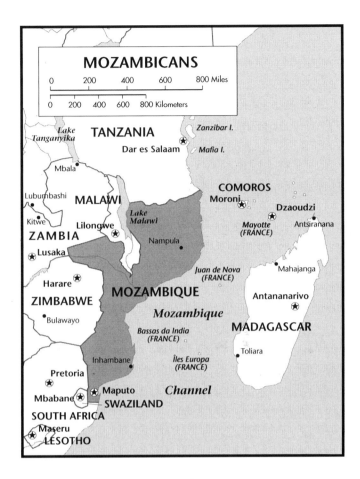

party's anti-religious policies, however, and traditional beliefs influenced peace as well. Spirit mediums were believed to have created "neutral zones" by harnessing supernatural powers. Both sides in the fighting respected such areas.

⁶ MAJOR HOLIDAYS

In addition to the national holiday, Independence Day (June 25), many major religious holidays are celebrated in Mozambique. The Portuguese Catholic influence is very heavy among the 30% Christian population, and consequently, holidays such as Christmas and Easter are celebrated much as they are in Western cultures. Similarly, the Muslim population observes Islamic holy days.

During wartime, Independence Day was often marked by increased caution by the general public, as RENAMO often chose the holiday as a time to increase attacks.

⁷ RITES OF PASSAGE

As with most traditional African societies, rites of passage are very important to the peoples of Mozambique. Such practices, however, vary from one ethnic group to another. The Tsua, a sub-group of the Tonga, practice circumcision of boys aged 10 through 12, while the Shona (also called Caranga) do not practice initiation or circumcision for boys. The Maconde practice initiation ceremonies that integrate young people into the adult world through links with ancestors and supernatural beings. Circumcision is an important part of the Maconde

Mozambican families taking the ferry to Catembe Island for a day on the beach. (Jason Laure)

passage from boyhood to manhood, and the Maconde rites of passage ceremonies include the use of masks.

8 INTERPERSONAL RELATIONS

As with rites of passage and religious practice, customs concerning greetings, visiting, body language, and dating vary from one ethnic group to another. Portuguese and English greetings are common in urban areas.

9 LIVING CONDITIONS

Life under civil war was devastating, and Mozambique has not yet truly emerged from the heavy influence of its more than 30-year struggle. The influence of colonialism also remains in many aspects of life, including housing. "Cement town" describes European-style settlements once occupied by colonists, and "cane towns" are the African settlements that surround them. Mozambican homes are often constructed of cane and mud. In the cities, high-rise apartments are crowded, with 20 people sometimes living in three-room apartments. Electricity and plumbing are often unreliable in the cities and are nonexistent in rural areas.

In 1995 there were only 3.8 radios per 100 inhabitants and in 2000 there were 0.5 television receivers per 100 inhabitants. Two television broadcasting organizations—the national state television network and another private organization—offer two television channels with an average of nine hours of programming per day. The city of Maputo contains 64% of tele-

communications lines. In 1995, 69 of the 142 administrative districts in the country had no lines at all. Mozambicans have a very low awareness of computer communications, though e-mail was introduced in 1995 at Centro de Informatica Universidade Eduardo Mondlane (CIUEM). Most Internet users, however, are members of international organizations located in the country.

The war left nearly half of the country's primary healthcare network destroyed. Today, children continue to die of preventable diseases like measles and malnutrition. An estimated one million land mines remain in the country. Since 1995 in the Maputo province alone, scores of people have stepped on landmines—many of whom were children. The current death rate is 18.97 per 1,000, and life expectancy at birth is 41.6 years.

During the war years, airplanes provided the only safe transportation mode in Mozambique. RENAMO forces destroyed railways and attacked automobiles on roadways, even those autos protected by government convoys. Many roads still have not been repaired since the war ended, nor have industries necessary for automobile maintenance been developed. Most taxis now found in Mozambique cities are many years old and in disrepair.

10 FAMILY LIFE

While Western cultures generally place equal importance on descent and kinship through both the mother's and father's side of the family (bilineal), most African cultures emphasize one more heavily than the other. In matrilineal groups, for example, not only is the family tree traced through the mother's side of the family, but property passes from one generation to the next based on matrilineal descent. Kinship ties are more important in African societies than in Western societies, in part because land ownership is usually exercised by the extended family group rather than individuals.

Both matrilineal (the Maconde and the Macua-Lomwe, for example) and patrilinial descendant groups exist in Mozambique, although men usually have a decided advantage in terms of decision-making. Men generally control issues related to ownership and access to land. Polygamy is practiced in some areas, although economic pressures have reduced the number of families with multiple spouses. Families in Mozambique continue to practice subsistence farming as a means of survival. Men traditionally perform the initial plowing or hoeing to prepare the land for planting, but women maintain the farm and are responsible for most of the harvesting. Women are also responsible for the traditional roles of taking care of children, food preparation, and home making. During the war years, women were called on to do more than their traditional responsibilities, and as a new social structure emerges in Mozambique, the roles of women are expected to change and to become less subordinate.

Children are also expected to help with farming, and most children do not attend school past the primary years. The usual pets such as dogs and rabbits are popular in Mozambique.

11 CLOTHING

During the war, *deslacados*, people dislocated by the war, often had no clothes and covered themselves with tree bark. Clothing became a precious commodity and was often more valued than currency in many areas. In Maputo, guards were posted at clotheslines, and a shirt cost as much as a laborer could earn in a month. Western-style clothing is common, but traditional clothing such as *capulanas* and head scarves are still in use. *Capulanas* are squares of colorful cloth that can be worn as a wraparound skirt or on the upper body, where they double as baby slings.

12 FOOD

In parts of Mozambique meat is scare, but pork and wild pig are favorite dishes and are usually prepared in a marinade. One marinade consists of Madeira (a type of wine) and wine vinegar, salt, pepper, garlic, cloves, red peppers, and bay leaf. Following as much as eight hours of marinating, the meat is fried. Just before serving it on a bed of rice, the meat is laced with orange juice and more wine. The Portuguese influence can be found in Mozambique cuisine in the use of spicy sauces such as *piri-piri*. *Piri-piri* is a sauce made of lemon juice, olive oil, red pepper, salt, and garlic. Products of the fishing industry, especially prawns and shellfish, are popular in the coastal region. The mainstay, however, in Mozambique as well as other parts of southern Africa, is maize. Mealie pie, for example, is a cornmeal mash that is a southern African staple. Many Mozambicans during the war depended on food from relief agencies, some scavenged for wild berries, nuts, and caterpillars, and many others starved.

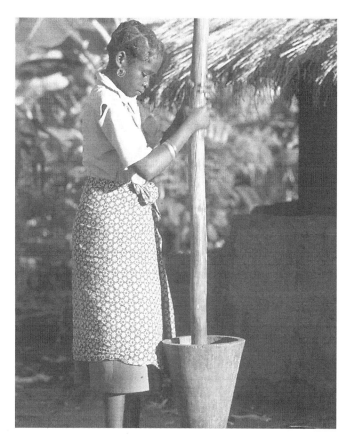

A young woman grinds grain in Nampula, Mozambique. Maize is the principal grain for Mozambicans and many other peoples living in southern Africa. Mozambican families continue to practice subsistence agriculture as a means of survival. (Corel Corporation)

13 EDUCATION

By 1989, 52% of first-level primary schools in Mozambique had been destroyed or forced to close by RENAMO. War had so disrupted education that most students in Zambezia Province in 1988 were in the first grade, and *deslocados* were often too hungry to attend school. Teachers, also hungry, were targeted for attack by RENAMO.

A 1995 estimate qualified 33% of Mozambicans over the age of 15 as literate. In 1975, 97% were illiterate. A very small percentage of primary school students continue to secondary school, and the country has limited capacity for professional and academic education. Primary education is free of charge, and 40% of primary school age children enroll. Secondary education is not free. Based on 1992 statistics, of the 1.2 million enrolled in the first five-year phase of primary education, only 100,000 continue with the second, two-year phase. Of that 100,000, only 50,000 continue for secondary, professional, technical, or university education. The 1992 higher education enrollment in the country was 4,600.

During the war, school was often conducted under trees, without books or supplies. Many schools were destroyed during the war years. Mozambique has a very small educated population from which to draw teachers, and families often cannot afford the loss of labor in subsistence farming for children to attend school.

In recent years, the government has made efforts to decentralize its political and economic structures and improve social services. Schools have increased their enrollments dramatically. The net school attendance rate, only 43% in 1991, shot up to 71% in 2004, according to the *UNDP Human Development Report 2006*. However, the quality of education remains a challenge. Most classrooms are overcrowded with about 70 children to just one teacher, almost half of whom are unqualified. Repetition rates are high, reaching 21% in 2004. The proportion of girl pupils attending school remains lower than that of boys and literacy rates for men in 2006 were 67% compared with 38% for women.

14 CULTURAL HERITAGE

Mozambicans practice various forms of music, dance, and storytelling. As in most of Africa, African art is used to communicate spiritual messages, historical information, and other truths to society. Thus, cultural heritage plays an important role among the various ethnic groups in Mozambique. Various groups are known for different aspects of their cultural heritage. The Chope, for example, who were believed to have come from the Vilankulu, are masters of the African piano, the *mbila*. The Maconde are world renowned for their wood carvings.

Many writers and artists are natives of Mozambique, including the poet Albuquerque Freire; short-story writer and journalist Luis Bernardo Honwana (also known as Augusto Manuel); and poet and painter Malagatana Gowenha Valente. Poet and artist Rui de Noronha is considered to be the "father of modern Mozambican writers," and Noemia Carolina Abranches de Sousa (also known as Vera Micaia) is considered to be the first Mozambican woman writer. Much Mozambique literature, like other African literature written in Portuguese, is anticolonial and promotes traditional African themes.

15 WORK

Most Mozambicans rely on *machambas,* family garden plots, for survival. As much as 80%–90% of the population practice some agricultural activity, primarily subsistence farming. During the war, people sometimes had to walk one to two hours to farm their plots during the day, then return to settlements that were guarded against RENAMO bandits at night. The need for and demands of subsistence farming undermined FRELIMO's attempts to establish communal farms and villages in Mozambique following independence. The annual per capita income for Mozambicans is $90 per year, and unemployment registers at about 21%.

16 SPORTS

Soccer is the most popular organized spectator sport in Mozambique. One of the leading soccer players for Portugal in the 1960s, in fact, was Eusobio from Mozambique. Many other Western sports are played by children and adults, particularly in the urban centers.

17 ENTERTAINMENT AND RECREATION

In Mozambique's urban centers, theater and television are popular. FRELIMO tried to promote rural village theater, but the effort was disrupted during the war years and has not been reestablished. Children enjoy playing games such as hopscotch and hide-and-seek.

18 FOLK ART, CRAFTS, AND HOBBIES

As previously noted, the various ethnic groups have rich cultural heritages that contribute to the art of Mozambique. For example, the Maconde, a matrilineal ethnic group of the Mueda Plateau in North of Pemba Province, are well known for their wood carvings. The carvings now reflect more recent styles. In the Shetani style, the carvings are tall and gracefully curved with stylized and abstracted faces and symbols, and most are carved in heavy ebony. "Shetani" is a Swahili word meaning "devil." The carvings are used to translate a spirit or group of spirits. The Ujamaa-style carvings are totem-type structures showing lifelike people and faces, huts, and everyday articles like pots and agricultural tools. These carvings are representative of family. The Maconde are also known for their water pots as well as masks used in initiation ceremonies.

19 SOCIAL PROBLEMS

A vast array of social problems obviously afflict a country so recently traumatized by war. While Mozambique adopted a democratic constitution in 1990, human rights violations continue to be reported, including a pattern of abusive behavior by security forces and an ineffective judicial system. Mozambique is facing continuing uncertainty as a result of the war years, and the transition to better economic conditions, improved health care and education, and the guarantee of human rights will take time.

20 GENDER ISSUES

The Mozambican constitution enshrines gender equality and legislation has been passed to support women's rights. Unlike in other African countries, women are well represented in parliament. As of 2008 30% of members of parliament (MPs) were women, as was the prime minister and the foreign minister. But in the home women often have little negotiating power. They continue to be subservient to men. Despite the government's efforts to eliminate gender disparities in access to education, the proportion of girls attending school is significantly lower than for boys. In secondary schools only 40.7% of the students are girls. In terms of human rights, Mozambique's constitution and legal framework establish safeguards for all citizens' civil rights and liberties, but the treatment of individuals who are arrested or detained remains a concern. In addition, prison conditions are substandard, and trafficking of children and women has increased.

Homosexuality is illegal in Mozambique. Laws covering homosexual activity criminalize male homosexuality with a penalty of up to three years imprisonment in a "re-education institution" where hard labor is used to alter the prisoners "aberrant behavior." However, the decision in South Africa to legalize same-sex marriages has had an impact on the way Mozambique looks at homosexuality. Following South Africa's decision, homosexuality got a very positive discussion in the national press in Mozambique.

21 BIBLIOGRAPHY

Azevedo, Mario. *Historical Dictionary of Mozambique*. London: Scarecrow Press, 1991.

Dillon, Diane, and Leo Dillon. *The African Cookbook*. New York: Carol Publishing Group, 1993.

Finnegan, William. *A Complicated War: The Harrowing of Mozambique.* Berkeley: University of California Press, 1992.

Newitt, Malyn. *A History of Mozambique.* London: Hurst & Co., 1995.

Oppong, J. and Kalipeni, E. "The Geography of Landmines and Implications for Health and Disease in Africa: A Political Ecology Approach." In *Africa Today* 52, No. 1 (2005): 3-25.

—revised by E. Kalipeni

NAMIBIANS

PRONUNCIATION: nuh-MIB-ee-uhns
LOCATION: Namibia
POPULATION: 2.2 million
LANGUAGE: Afrikaans (most widely used); English (official); Diriku; Herero; Kwangali; Kwanyama; Lozi; Mbukushu; Nama; Ndonga; Tswana; Juǀ'hoan; Subiya; Zemba and also German
RELIGION: Christianity (80–90%); indigenous beliefs (10–20%); Muslim and Hindu also occur

¹ INTRODUCTION

German Chancellor Otto von Bismarck proclaimed South West Africa (now Namibia) a German protectorate in 1884. The conquest of German South West Africa by South African forces during World War I resulted in its subsequent administration by that country, from 1917 to 1990, under a League of Nations mandate. A war (1966–1989) between the occupying South African forces and the SWAPO (South-West African People's Organization) liberation movement finally led to the implementation of United Nations Resolution 435 on 1 April 1989. This made provision for free and fair elections, which resulted in SWAPO coming to power. On 21 March 1990, Dr. Sam Nujoma was instated as the country's first president. Namibia has been governed by SWAPO since independence and in November 2004 Hifíkepunye Pohamba was elected to replace Nujoma as president.

The last African country to become independent, Namibia is not as well known as some of its neighbors, but is truly a land of remarkable contrasts. Situated along the southwestern coast of the African continent it has a land surface of 824 269 square kilometers, nearly four times the size of Great Britain. Situated south of Angola, north of South Africa, and west of Botswana, Namibia has 1,500 kilometers of Atlantic coastline. The cold waters off this coast ensure that deep-sea fishing represents Namibia's third largest industry and export. The Atlantic also spits diamonds onto the sands of the coastal Namib Desert, which earn Namibia, along with smaller quantities of gold, copper, uranium and other metals, over one billion dollars per year.

Namibia was furthermore the first country in the world to incorporate the protection of the environment into its constitution and some 14% of the land is protected, including virtually the entire Namib Desert coastal strip.

² HOMELAND

Despite its size, Namibia is one of the most sparsely populated countries in Africa with its estimated population of about 2.2 million people. The north-central part of the country is the most densely populated area with an average population density of 26 people per square kilometer, more than 10 times the national average.

Namibia boasts three distinct environments—the Namib Desert in the east, the more populous Central Plateau, and the Kalahari Desert in the west, famous for the San people (known as Bushmen) and majestic wildlife. The defining term for all three regions is *dry*. Namibia averages less than 28 cm (11 in) of rain per year, and most of that falls on the central Plateau,

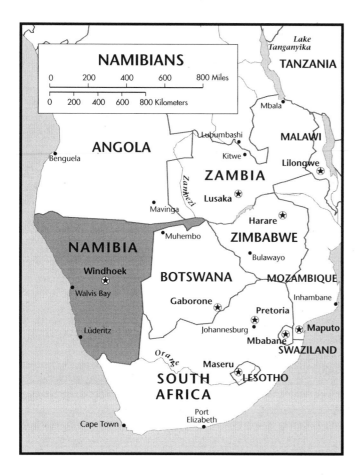

supporting cattle, goat and sheep herding, and marginal subsistence agriculture. The borders are formed by the Kunene and Okavango rivers in the north and by the Orange in the south. Interior rivers become dry washes, called *oshana*, in the dry season, and most irrigation is provided by bore-holes. A severe drought in 1992 turned a precarious situation into a disaster, sending 30,000 farmers to live as squatters in the cities as their crops and animals died.

To the west, the icy Atlantic Ocean pounds the Namib desert shore with relentless fury, throwing up all manner of flotsam, including numerous shipwrecks. It is called the Skeleton Coast for obvious reasons.

In many ways Namibia is a startling country. It contains the world's second largest canyon, the highest dunes, the oldest desert, the largest existing meteorite, and the smallest antelope. Vast areas of the country are true wilderness, which is home to an array of wild animals.

For nearly two decades since independence, Namibia has enjoyed peace and stability. Economic development has recently been due to its productive mining, fishing, tourism, and agricultural industries.

Though for such a vast country, the population is small, yet it is home to a rich diversity of people. The ancestors of the San (Bushmen) arrived in Namibia 2,000 years ago as hunter-gatherers. They were followed by Bantu-speakers after AD 1500 and several other groups joined them subsequently.

The largest population group, the Ovambo, comprise some 50% of Namibians. Other significant communities are: the Kavango (9%); Herero (7%); Damara (7%); Whites (6.6%); Nama

(5%); Caprivian (4%); Bushmen (3%); Baster (2%); Tswana (0.5%); and so-called Coloreds.

The *Ovambo* are mainly found in the northern-most area of Namibia, previously known as Ovamboland. They comprise subgroups with different dialects: the Kwanyama (divided by an indiscriminate international border drawn by the colonial Portuguese and Germans between Angola and Namibia); the Ndonga; Kwambi; Ngandjera; Kwaluudhi; Mbalanthu; Nkohonkadhi; and the Eunda. The Ovambo are agriculturalists and cattle breeders and plant mahango, a kind of millet, their preferred staple diet.

The large *Kavango* community, a riverine people, lives along the banks of the Kavango River in northeast Namibia. They practice agriculture along the narrow strip of soil along the river. Cattle and goats are kept for their milk, meat, and hides. Funnel-shaped fishing baskets are used in the river and the men are renowned wood carvers.

The *Herero* people moved south into Namibia during the 16th century, probably from an area west of Lake Tanganyika. Some (the Ovahimba) stayed behind in Kaokoland in north western Namibia, and a large group moved on to settle in the central and southwestern regions but mainly in the district of Okahandja. The Herero are known for their vast herds of cattle. The Himba, who stayed behind, faced long spells of drought, which forced them to live off the land, collecting wild fruit and digging for roots. Because of this the proud southern Herero regarded them as inferior, thus calling them "Tjimba" from "ondjimba-ndjimba," meaning aardvark, or someone who digs food out of the ground. The Himba are characterized by their traditional loin cloth and the fact that they smear their bodies with red ochre mixed with animal fat.

Most of the *Damara* people live in the northwestern regions of the country but others are found widely across Namibia working in towns, on commercial farms, in mines, and at the coast. They are unrelated to any of the other communities and are believed to have their origin in northwestern Africa from where they migrated south long before the other migrations of African people to the southern parts of the continent. They were originally hunter-gatherers but due to domination and enslavement by the Nama and Herero, they lost their language and cultural traditions. When pursued by the dominant peoples they used to flee into inhospitable mountains and hence became known as "Bergdamara" or Mountain Damara.

The large *white* community is the result of the arrival of people of European descent in different stages. Explorers, hunters, adventurers, prospectors, and traders first travelled north from South Africa. The first missionaries from the Berlin Missionary Society settled in 1806. Soldiers (German) and administrative personnel arrived during the Herero Nama conflict and Boers/Afrikaners came to the country particularly as a result of the Anglo-Boer (South African) War of 1899–1902. The discovery of diamonds attracted more Europeans and after the First World War new white settlers increasingly bought property in Namibia.

A Khoekhoen ("Khoi") people, having initially moved south, and some of the *Nama* later migrated from South Africa back to Namibia. Originally nomadic pastoralists, the Nama still today keep stock. They are found in scattered communities all over Namibia, e.g. the Topnaars at Sesfontein in Kaokoland, the Bondelswarts at Warmbad, the Fransmanne, Kopers, Veldskoendraers, GootDoden, Swartboois, Witboois, etc. There are 15 distinct such communities.

The *Caprivians* are hunters and fishermen but they also till the soil, keep stock, and gather food. They live along the rivers of the Caprivi Strip in the far northeastern corner of Namibia. Two communities are distinguished, the Fwe in the west and the Subia in the east.

Essentially gatherers of food who also hunt for game, the *Bushmen (San)* are some of the earliest inhabitants of Namibia. One of the smallest communities in the country, they have become increasingly sedentary. Thus, the largest of their communities, the !Kung, are found in Okavango; the Mbarakwengo, or River Bushmen, are found along the eastern Kavango River region, the Heikom around the Etosha National Park, the Naro east of the towns of Grootfontein and Gobabis and in neighboring Botswana, and the very small, near-extinct Auni, in the lower Nossob district.

The progenitors of the *Baster* ("Bastard") people were the early Dutch and other European men, who intermarried at the Cape in South Africa with local Khoekhoen and San (Bushmen), and later also Malays, brought there by the Dutch from the East Indies. Having first gathered around mission stations in South Africa, some eventually moved north to Namibia in 1868 and reached Rehoboth in 1870 where they settled. They adopted the language, Afrikaans, and culture of their forefathers and this included particularly the observance of Christian beliefs.

A relatively small community of *Tswana* people lives on the Namibian side of the border of Botswana ("Land of the Tswana") to the east. Botswana is however where most of the Tswana live and the Namibian Tswana share affinities, including kinship relations, with them.

The small *Colored* community of Namibia also stems from early mixed marriages at the Cape (hence "colored" or mixed), and their antecedents moved from there due to discrimination denying them full participation in social and economic activities of the then South Africa. Afrikaans is their native language, and they are found centered mainly in the larger Namibian towns.

³ LANGUAGE

Although only 7% of the population speaks English as a mother tongue, it is the official language. Afrikaans is the most common language and the languages of Ovambo (Kwanyama, Ndonga, Kwambi, Ngandjera, etc.), together referred to as Oshivambo, are the most widely spoken. The languages of the San (Bushmen) and Khoekhoen (Nama) are characterized by click sounds. The other Namibian languages were earlier referred to in Section 2. "Hello" in some of these languages is: *Hallo*—Afrikaans; *Nawa*—Ovambo; *Matisa*—Damara; *Koree*—Herero; and *Mazwara*—Okavango.

⁴ FOLKLORE

Through oral tradition most of the Namibian communities have their legends and beliefs handed down over generations. Likewise certain customs are still practiced by people in rural areas, given that Namibia is a country with a population that is still 68% rural.

Many Namibian folk heroes achieved their status through stories of more recent battles. One 19th century Ovambo sub chief, named Madume Ndemufayo, fought the Angolan Por-

tuguese from the north and the Germans from the south, only to be captured and killed by the Germans. His exploits were passed on through oral tradition, as indigenous languages had never been written. The Herero, too, have their stories of resistance and military exploits. Many Herero feel, in fact, that they are not given the same recognition in national lore and policy as the earliest victims and resisters of the Germans. The 1904 German-Herero War ultimately resulted in genocide: over 75% of the Herero population was massacred or banished to die in the Kalahari.

⁵ RELIGION

Namibians describe themselves as very spiritual. European missionaries saw early success here, and today 90% are Christians, mostly Lutheran. While it is common for Africans to incorporate traditional beliefs and practices into their religious life, less than 20% of Namibians claim to do so. Western churches hold great influence in Namibia, which may account for some traditional practices like polygyny (marrying more than one wife) not being accommodated in the country's legal code.

⁶ MAJOR HOLIDAYS

Two important Namibian holidays fall on August 26. This day was first established in the 19th century as Red Day by the Herero in remembrance of their fallen chiefs and is still marked by the wearing of dark red costumes. After independence, August 26 also became Heroes Day, an official holiday celebrating SWAPO's first armed battle with the South African military. Many Herero feel that the honor of Red Day is being challenged by Namibia's ruling party government. Independence Day, March 21, bears the characteristics of Independence Days celebrated throughout the world: military parades, speeches by politicians, plenty of food, alcohol, and reverie.

⁷ RITES OF PASSAGE

Much of Namibian ritual life involves cattle. Cattle have provided the economic cornerstone for most of Namibia's ethnic groups for centuries. A gift is presented by a man to his future father-in-law before marriage can be sanctioned, in the case of the Ovambo this is an ox or *oyonda*. Cows in general play a particularly important role in funerary ritual. The passage from life to death for a man of an Ovambo household is a case in point: His body must remain in the house for at least one day before burial, during which time all his pets must be killed. Traditional Ovambo compounds, called *kraals*, have gates that regulate the comings and goings of both cattle and humans. But at death, the owner may not pass through this gate, or the cattle will die and the kraal will come to ruin. A new hole is cut for him to pass through. A bull is slaughtered, cooked without oil or flavoring of any kind, and a portion is eaten by everyone in the village. Then the kraal and all its contents must be moved at least 15 meters (50 feet). The cattle are not permitted to rest on the same earth that witnessed the death of their owner.

⁸ INTERPERSONAL RELATIONS

Namibia is one of the most peaceful nations in Africa. Due both to its increasing prosperity and the friendly demeanor of its inhabitants, the people generally go about their ways.

The average Namibian household has five to seven members. One-third of all dwellings have electricity, and slightly fewer have plumbing. Those that do not have plumbing typically have lime-pit outhouses. In the rural areas, children can walk miles to school, and the donkey is often the best form of transportation. (Cory Langley)

Namibia is ruled by a multiparty parliament with a democratic constitution. The government's policy of national reconciliation and unity embraces the concepts of tolerance and respect for each other.

The friendly way people, even strangers, greet each other seems to bear witness to this. The sparsely populated and rural nature of much of the country probably has much to do with this and also with the various ways different communities show respect. Among some groups, women and youth bend at the knees as a sign of respect to older men. When greeting or agreeing, Caprivians clap their hands. Basters may kiss close friends and relatives on the lips. But, the handshake is the most common form of personal introduction.

⁹ LIVING CONDITIONS

The Namibian economy is heavily dependent on the extraction and processing of mineral for export, yet this sector only employs about 3% of the population while nearly half of the population depends on subsistence agriculture for its livelihood. Namibia normally imports about 50% of its cereal requirements and in times of drought food shortages are a major problem in the rural areas. A high per capita gross domestic product (GDP—estimated at $5,200 in 2007), relative to the region, hides one of the world's most unequal income distributions. The United Nations Development Program's (UNDP)

2005 Human Development Report for example, indicated that 34.9% of the population lives on $1.00 per day and 55.8% lives on $2.00 per day.

Life expectancy is 43.1 years (2007 estimate); the infant mortality rate is 47 deaths per 1,000 live births (birth rate: 34.17/1,000 population—or 23.19/1,000, 2008 estimate); and the literacy rate has been variously put at 65% (Namibia Tourism Board, 2008) and 85.4% (Namibia Facts and Figures, 2001 census, counting literacy as those aged 15 and over being able to read and write). Some of the estimates are now beginning to take into account the effects of excess mortality due to AIDS. The adult prevalence rate for HIV/AIDS was 21.3% in 2003, the number of people living with HIV/AIDS was 210,000 in 2001, and HIV/AIDS deaths totaled 16,000 in 2003.

Although medical services in Namibia are of a relatively high standard, the availability of most services is restricted to the main towns.

¹⁰ FAMILY LIFE

Africa has been thrust into modern life more suddenly than any other continent, and Namibia is no exception. As a result, family life has changed drastically and sometimes painfully. One of the most obvious changes regards the role of women in society. Polygyny had been the traditional ideal for men in many ethnic groups and the practice is still significant, al-

Namibian men mining diamonds. Namibia is among the world's leading producers of gem-quality diamonds, and the mining industry is the largest private sector area of employment. (Jason Laure)

though not accommodated in legislation. Virginity before marriage had been the traditional ideal for women and errant women could even be banished. Today, one-third of all girls by the age of 18 have had at least one child, while 21 is the average age for first conception, and 25 is the average age for marriage among women. A related trend is the number of households run by women. In Ovamboland, a matrilineal society where men had always been the heads of households and the only owners of property, 45% of all households are headed by women, many of whom are single parents to their children. Namibian women have legal access to birth control, as well as rights to demand child support for their children. More and more women are exercising these rights. Modern birth control is used by 25% of all women, far more than in most of Africa.

Despite women's gains in reproductive choice, their rights to family property are still precarious. In most Namibian cultures, when a man dies his property often accrues to his parents and siblings.

¹¹ CLOTHING

Most Namibian city-dwellers dress in modern fashions, as in the West. Several examples of customary dress stand out, however. Herero women, both rural and urban, have adopted the German Victorian fashions of the 19th century colonists, wearing long petticoated gowns, shawls, and adding extravagant headdresses. The Himba, as was mentioned, a cattle-herding

people from the extreme northwest, whose traditional culture has not changed extensively, typically wear leather thongs or skirts, smearing their bodies with ochre—a reddish pigment extracted from iron ore. The women wear elaborate braids and copper or leather bands around their necks, making them appear elongated.

¹² FOOD

Fish is Namibia's largest non-mineral export, yet Namibians do not eat much fish as most of them are not a coastal people. Canned pilchards and dried horse mackerel are available in the towns, but are not a traditional staple. Ostrich farming has become big business in Namibia, but nearly all ostrich meat is exported to northern Europe. Beef, mutton, milk products, millet, sorghum, peanuts, pumpkins, and melons are common subsistence crops. Mealie, a dish similar to hominy grits, is the most common and inexpensive staple grain. While game hunting was traditionally practiced all over Namibia, it tended to take a back seat to livestock raising, and often marked special occasions. Today, private game parks abound to serve the Western tourist interested in hunting.

¹³ EDUCATION

Namibia's adult literacy rate has been improving rapidly over the last number of years (see *Section 9: Living Conditions*, above). Namibia also has one of the most highly skilled bureaucratic classes on the continent. One reason for this is the policy of reconciliation that the SWAPO government adopted in order to keep the white, educated business owners and civil servants in the country after independence. As of 1993, 20% of the population had never been to school, and only 1% went on to university. Those that do get a higher education can go to the university in Windhoek, though some go to South Africa or Germany. In addition, several ministries have internal training colleges to better prepare their new class of African civil servants for work.

14 CULTURAL HERITAGE

The Namibian government has established a team of cultural preservationists to encourage the continuation or resuscitation of cultural traditions and heritage. The job of this group of performers, artists, historians, and researchers is to record and then bring to life the cultural heritage of Namibia's people before it is irrevocably lost. Given the largely rural population of Namibia and the remote dispersal of many communities, there is still a significant adherence to such practices.

15 WORK

Namibians have a strong work ethic. While the state provides pension and social security plans, many elderly people expect to feed themselves from their own agricultural labor until they are physically unable to do so. Urban government workers can invest in savings plans or the local stock market. Still, two-thirds of all Namibians are rural dwellers, and most of them describe themselves as subsistence farmers or herders. The government is currently trying to convince some communities to abandon their conception of cattle as the highest form of saved wealth and to turn their skills toward commercial ranching and beef export. Among some traditionalists this is inconceivable, because selling off the herd for mere cash is like selling the legacy of the ancestors. Namibians consider themselves very self-reliant and in many of the outlying areas this is what they became accustomed to over generations.

16 SPORTS

As everywhere in Africa, soccer, or football as it is known in Namibia, is the national sport with the most passionate followers. Even Himba children grow up playing it, maybe making do with a ball made of twine. Track and field, called "athletics" locally, is becoming more popular, especially with the silver medal win of compatriot Frankie Fredricks in the 100- and 200-meter dash at the 1996 Olympic Games in Atlanta. Schools and clubs in towns have well-supported rugby teams and Namibia has fielded a national team at the Rugby World Cup. Most Namibians get their physical exercise through daily chores. Many rural children must walk or run five kilometers a day to school and hoeing and harvesting is the lot of most adults.

17 ENTERTAINMENT AND RECREATION

American popular culture is so pervasive globally, it is almost unavoidable. Most popular music tends to come from South Africa, with its rich history of local performers. Namibia has produced a number of popular performers but more often than not they seek the more lucrative market to the south, in South Africa. Pockets of more traditional music are found in the more remote rural areas.

18 FOLK ART, CRAFTS, AND HOBBIES

Traditional arts and crafts in Namibia cater to daily living. Wood carving, despite the relative dearth of trees, has a long history, and beautiful utensils, knife handles and sheaths, masks, musical drums, beer strainers, and sleeping mats continue to be made and sold. Baskets for holding everything from fish to grain to water are made out of the palm leaf, or out of reeds along the northern rivers.

19 SOCIAL PROBLEMS

Unemployment reached 35% in urban areas after the 1992 drought but by 2006 the unemployment rate was 5.3%. After independence, the government did not nationalize all industries nor did it confiscate land and equipment from the white ruling class. As a result the economy remained stable by 2008. The international investment community has more confidence in Namibia than it does in many African countries that have experienced undisciplined governments and crumbling infrastructures. Interpersonal and intergroup relations are positive, and the Namibian economy is growing steadily and significantly—which all augers well for the future.

20 GENDER ISSUES

The constitution of Namibia, underpinned by appropriate legislation, provides for the protection of individual rights. In the urban centers and other public domains there is also an increasing awareness and recognition of the position of women and their rights as citizens of Namibia. However, in many of the rural areas (see *Section 2: Homeland* and *Section 10: Family Life*, above) women still function in patriarchal societies where the males as husbands or leaders hold sway in terms of authority and privilege. This even applies to the matrilineal Ovambo, bilineal Herero, and the bilateral/cognatic San-Bushmen—all kinship systems where a certain acknowledgement or emphasis is accorded to females.

21 BIBLIOGRAPHY

Bruwer, J.P. van S. Bruwer. *South West Africa: The Disputed Land*. Bloemfontein: Nasionale Boekhandel, 1966.

De Jongh, M. ed. "S.W.A. or Namibia? An Anthropological Survey." An *Ethnos Publication*, Vol. VI, 1975.

———. "South West Africa. An Anthropological Survey." An *Ethnos Publication* Vol. VII, 1977.

Hahn, C.H.L. and Vedder, H. *The Native Tribes of South West Africa*. Cape Town: Cape Times Ltd, 1928.

Kaela, Laurent C.W. *The Question of Namibia*. Houndmills: UK: Macmillan Press; New York: St. Martin's Press, 1996.

Leys, Colin. *Namibia's Liberation Struggle: The Two-Edged Sword*. London: J. Curry; Athens: Ohio University Press, 1995.

Malan, J.S. *Peoples of Namibia*. Wingate Park: Rhino Publishers, 1995.

Pendleton, Wade C. *Katutura: A Place Where We Stay. Life in a Post-Apartheid Township in Namibia*. Athens: Ohio University Center for International Studies, 1996.

—revised by M. de Jongh

NDEBELE

PRONUNCIATION: nn-deh-BEH leh
ALTERNATE NAMES: Amandebele; Ndzundza; Manala
LOCATION: The Mpumalanga and the Northern provinces of South Africa
POPULATION: 403,700
LANGUAGE: Ndebele (IsiNdebele); Sepedi; Afrikaans; English
RELIGION: Christianity; African Christianity

¹ INTRODUCTION

The Ndebele of South Africa refer to themselves as "Amandebele," or "Ndzundza" and "Manala"—denoting two main sections or tribal groupings. Early writers used the term "Transvaal Ndebele" to distinguish them from the "Zimbabwean Ndebele" (or "Matebele"). On geographical grounds, the Transvaal Ndebele was subdivided into the "Southern" (Ndzundza and Manala sections) and "Northern" Ndebele. Oral tradition points to a possible common origin for both the Southern and Northern groups, although the latter, as the numerically smaller group, became absorbed into their Northern-Sotho-speaking neighbors.

After a succession struggle, the Ndzundza section migrated to KwaSimkhulu ("Place of Large Fields"), approximately 260 km (160 mi) east of the present Pretoria, in the Mpumalanga province. The numerically smaller Manala section occupied settlements such as Ezotshaneni, KoNonduna, and Embilaneni, which include the present eastern suburbs of Pretoria in the Gauteng Province.

The Ndzundza chieftaincy is believed to have extended its boundaries along the Steelpoort (Indubazi) river catchment area between the 1600s and early 1800s. Several of these settlement sites (KwaSimkhulu, KwaMaza, and Esikhunjini) are known through oral history and are currently under archaeological investigation.

Both the Ndzundza and Manala chiefdoms were almost annihilated by the armies of Mzilikazi's Matebele (Zimbabwean Ndebele) around 1820. The Manala in particular suffered serious losses, while the Ndzundza recovered significantly under the legendary Mabhoko during the 1840s. He revolutionized Ndzundza settlement patterns by building a number of impenetrable stone fortresses and renamed the tribal capital: KoNomtjharhelo (later popularly known as Mapoch's Caves). The Ndzundza developed into a significant regional political and military force during the middle 1800s. During the colonial era, white settlers derogatively referred to the Ndzundza-Ndebele as "Mapoggers" after their ruler Mabhoko, called Mapog or Mapoch by whites.

The Ndzundza-Ndebele soon had to face the threat of these white colonials, against whom they fought in 1849, 1863, and finally in 1883 during the lengthy Mapoch War against the ZAR forces. The latter's tactic of besiegement forced the famine-stricken Ndzundza to capitulate. They lost their independence, their land was expropriated, the leaders were imprisoned (Chief Nyabela to life imprisonment), and the Ndebele were displaced and indentured as laborers for a five-year (1883–1888) period among white farmers. (The Manala chiefdom was not involved in the war and had previously (1873) settled on land provided by the Berlin Mission some 32 km (20 mi) north of Preto-

ria, at a place the Manala named KoMjekejeke, also known as Wallmannsthal.)

Chief Nyabela Mahlangu of the Ndzundza was released in 1903 after the Anglo-Boer War (1899–1902) and died soon afterwards. His successor tried fruitlessly in 1916 and 1918 to regain the tribal land. Instead, the royal house and a growing number of followers privately bought land in 1922, around which the Ndzundza-Ndebele reassembled. They have never gained permission to reoccupy their original land.

Within the framework of the bantustan or homeland system in South Africa, the Ndebele (both Manala and Ndzundza) were only during the late 1970s allowed to settle in a homeland called KwaNdebele.

² LOCATION AND HOMELAND

The majority of Ndebele live in the Mpumalanga and the Limpopo provinces) of South Africa between 24°53' to 25°43' south latitude and 28°22' to 29°50' east longitude, and approximately 65 km to 130 km (40–80 mi) northeast of Pretoria, South Africa. The total area amounts to 350,000 hectares (865,000 acres), including the Moutse and Nebo areas. Temperatures range from a high of 36°C (97°F) in the northern parts to a low of –5°C (23°F) in the south. Rainfall in the north averages 5 cm (2 in) per year and 8 cm (3 in) per year in the south. Almost two-thirds of the entire former KwaNdebele lies within a vegetational zone known as Mixed Bushveld (Savanna-type) in the north. The southern parts fall within the Bankenveld (False Grassland-type) zone.

Population figures are based on the 1991 census figures for the former KwaNdebele homeland (now part of Mpumalanga Province), updated for the April 1994 general elections. The total population for the area was estimated at more than 403,700 people. A minority of labor tenants and farm workers outside the former homeland are not included.

³ LANGUAGE

The Ndebele language, called IsiNdebele by its users, is one of nine official languages recognized by the interim South African constitution. It forms part of the Nguni language group (including Zulu, Swazi, and Xhosa), which comprises 43% of mother-tongue languages in South Africa. It is estimated that Ndebele comprises 1.55% of African languages in South Africa. Mother-tongue speakers seldom distinguish between the dialects of IsiNdzundza and IsiNala. A written orthography was only recently published, in 1982. Most Ndebele are fluent in the neighboring Northern Sotho language called Sepedi, as well as in Afrikaans (mostly elderly people) and English (the younger generation).

IsiNdebele, like other Nguni-type languages, contains a variety of click sounds. The Ndebele have also absorbed a proportionate amount of Afrikaans words in their vocabulary. These assimilated terms were probably adopted during the period of indenture on Afrikaner-owned farms. The everyday greeting term is, "Lotjani!" ("Good day"), followed by "Kunjani?" ("How are you?"), etc. The departing person will end the conversation with: "Salani kuhleke!" ("Goodbye to all of you!")

⁴ FOLKLORE

Among a rich collection of oral traditions, many relate and explain the founding history of the various clans or family names (called *izibongo*), most of all that of the ruling Mahlangu clan among the Ndzundza. Praise poetry, as recited by praise poets (iimbongi), relates heroic escapes from captors, battle field tactics, treachery and revenge, and the introduction of new customs, by past rulers (i.e. circumcision by Mahlangu).

The most well known oral tradition concerns the founder of the Ndebele, a chief called Musi who lived at KwaMnyamane ("Place of the Black Hills") near Pretoria. Musi had five sons and there was a succession struggle between Musi's two eldest sons, which shows remarkable similarity to the Jacob and Esau myth in the Bible. While the eldest son Manala was on a hunting trip he was betrayed by his younger brother Ndzundza (the clever one), who disguised himself as Manala and received the royal regalia from his aged and blind father Musi. When Manala pledged revenge in pursuit of the already fleeing Ndzundza and his followers, the other three sons migrated northwards and one of them, Kekana, became the founder of the Northern Ndebele, among others.

Many past events and experiences, and even recent events, are handed down through generations via the media of song and dance. During the 1986–87 unrest in the former homeland, Ndebele women protested, through female initiation rituals and songs of protest, the atrocities committed by the infamous Imbokodo vigilante movement who terrorized the area. One such song mourned the death of a popular community leader (Somakatha), and another celebrated the death of the notorious vigilante leader (Maqhawe).

Even contemporary heroes of the struggle against apartheid are remembered: Prince James Mahlangu, leader of the comrades movement against the Imbokodo vigilantes in 1986–87;

and Umkhonto Wesizwe (MK) African National Congress (ANC) military-wing-martyr Solomon Mahlangu, who was reburied in Mamelodi in Pretoria and honored with a memorial that was unveiled by Nelson Mandela.

⁵ RELIGION

Traditionally, there is the belief in a creator god, Zimu, and in ancestral spirits (abezimu). Disgruntled ancestral spirits cause illness, misfortune, and death. The royal ancestral spirits are annually honored, while individuals may consult the family ancestral spirits before and during important rituals and even before the annual school examinations. Traditional practitioners (iinyanga and izangoma) act as mediators between the past and present world and are still frequently consulted. Sorcerers (abathakathi or abaloyi) are believed to use familiars such as the well-known "baboon" midget utikoloshe, especially in cases of jealousy towards achievers in the community in general. Both women and men become healers after a prolonged period of internship with existing practitioners.

Nineteenth-century missionary activities by the Berlin Mission did little to change traditional Ndebele religion, especially among the Ndzundza. Although the Manala lived on the Wallmannsthal mission station from 1873 on, they were in frequent conflict with local missionaries. Recent Christian and African Christian church influences spread rapidly, and most Ndebele are now members of these churches: ZCC (Zion Christian Church), a variety of (African) Apostolic churches, Roman Catholic, etc.

⁶ MAJOR HOLIDAYS

Apart from national holidays, the two Ndebele royal houses (of Ndzundza and Manala) honor their past heroes with celebrations at the respective historical settlements and graves. Since 1969 the Ndzundza have celebrated Nyabela day on December 19 at KoNomtjharhelo (Mabhoko's caves), where they were forced to surrender during the 1883 war. The site has been declared a national monument and a statue of Nyabela was erected from funds contributed by the Ndzundza community. Several Manala-Ndebele chiefs (e.g., Silamba, Libangeni) are buried at the KoMjekejeke historical site at Wallmannsthal where the tribe holds their annual celebrations on Silamba day.

In recent years, apart from paying tribute to past heroes with praise poetry, song, dance, and music during these events, Ndebele politicians have used the occasions for political rallying and to air grievances on issues such as land restitution and better governance within the Mpumalanga Province.

⁷ RITES OF PASSAGE

Initiation at puberty dominates ritual life in Ndebele society. Girls' initiation (iqhude or ukuthombisa) is organized on an individual basis within the homestead. It entails the isolation of a girl in an existing house in the homestead, which is prepared by her mother after the girl's second or third menstruation. The week-long period of isolation ends over the weekend when often more than 200 relatives, friends, and neighbors attend the coming-out ritual. The occasion is marked by the slaughtering of cattle and goats, cooking and drinking of traditional beer (unotlhabalala), song and dance, and the large-scale presentation of gifts (clothing and toiletries) to the initiate's mother and father. In return, the initiate's mother presents large quantities of bread and jam to attendants. The notion of reciprocity is prominent. During the girls' initiation, female activities (including song, dance, and the display of traditional costumes) dominate those of men who are spatially isolated from the courtyard in front of the homestead.

Male initiation (*ingoma* or *ukuwela*), which includes circumcision, is a collective and quadrennial ritual that lasts two months during the winter (April to June). The notion of cyclical regimentation is prominent as initiates receive a regimental name, with which Ndebele men identify themselves for life, from the paramount (chief). The Ndzundza-Ndebele have a system of 15 such names that run over a period of approximately 60 years, and the cycle repeats itself in strict chronological order. The Manala-Ndebele have 13 names.

The numerical dimension of Ndebele male initiation is unparalleled in South Africa. During the 2006 initiation, some 13,000 young men were initiated. The ritual is controlled, officiated, and administered by the royal house. It is decentralized over a wide area within the former KwaNdebele, in rural as well as urban (township) areas. Regional headmen are assigned to supervise the entire ritual process over the two-month period that involves nine sectional rituals at lodges in the field and the homestead.

8 INTERPERSONAL RELATIONS

Three institutions pervade Ndebele daily life. Firstly, there is the lineage segment or family (the *ikoro*), which consists of three to four generations and is of functional value, especially in ritual and socioeconomic reciprocity. Secondly, this lineage is composed of various residential units (homesteads) called imizi. The third important unit is an economic one, the household, which may be composed of a man, his wife and children (including children of an unmarried daughter), wives and children of his sons, and his father's widowed sisters.

A Ndebele woman has a lifelong obligation to observe the custom of *ukuhlonipha* or "respect" for her father-in-law. The custom implies the physical avoidance of her father-in-law. While he has unlimited freedom of movement in and around the homestead, she will at all costs enter and exit the homestead bearing in mind her father-in-law's whereabouts in an effort to avoid him. In the event of accidental contact, she will turn her back on him and cover her face. She will furthermore never mention his first name.

Space in and around the Ndebele homestead is gender-specific. There is an abstract division between front (male) and back (female), and inside the house between left (female, *incabafazi*) and right (male, *incamadoda*). Male visitors on arrival at the homestead occupy the front courtyard (*isirhodlo*), while women visitors proceed to the "domestic" back courtyard (*isibuya*). During meals this spatial separation is maintained. Even in modern Western-style houses, men dine in the lounge/TV room while women eat in the kitchen.

9 LIVING CONDITIONS

Living conditions for rural and urban Ndebele are integrally part of the past and current political and economic conditions in South Africa. The Ndebele is probably numerically the single largest community that has never been allowed to reclaim the land they lost in 1883. When they were drawn into apartheid's homeland dispensation, the land they received was alien to them in more than one respect: it was far away from ances-

tors, climatologically harsh, and without infrastructure (e.g., transport).

Apart from a few examples in KwaNdebele and on White-owned farms, the three-generational homestead (*umuzi*) has almost disappeared. This type consists of a number of houses (*izindlu*) representing various households centered around a cattle enclosure (*isibaya*). Other structures in the homestead include the boys' hut (*ilawu*), various smaller huts for girls behind each house, and granaries. Each house complex is separated from the other by an enclosure wall called *isirhodlo*.

Pre-colonial Ndebele structures were of the thatched beehive dome-type. Since the late 1800s, they have adopted a cone-on-cylinder type of structure consisting of mud walls and a thatched roof, while simultaneously reverting to a linear outlay that has replaced the circular center cattle pattern. The present settlement pattern consists of a single house built on a square stand and occasionally providing for two or more extra buildings, as well as cattle and goat enclosures. A wide range of modern building material and house designs have been introduced.

10 FAMILY LIFE

Ndebele society is structured into approximately 80 patrilineal clans (*izibongo*), each subdivided into a variety of subclans or patrilineages (*iinanazelo*). Each clan associates itself with a totem animal or object. Members of the same clan do not marry, and certain clans, such as the Nduli's and the Giyana's, will not intermarry because there is a saying, "Long ago, we were brothers!"

Polygyny (more than one wife) has almost disappeared. Bride-wealth (*ikhazi*) consists of cattle and/or money. Marital negotiations between the two sets of families are an extended process. These include the presentation in installments of six to eight heads of cattle, the last installment often given long after the birth of the first child. Fathers demand more bride-wealth for educated daughters. Nowadays wealthy women with children often marry very late or stay single.

Weddings often involve a customary as well as a Christian ceremony. The married couple settles at the husband's village for a few years, and the new bride (*umakhothi*) is involved in cooking and the rearing of other small children of various households in the homestead. The taking of a substitute wife (*umngenandlu* or *ihlanzi*), in cases of infertility, was still common in the 1960s. In case of divorce, witchcraft accusation, and even infidelity, a woman is forced to return to her natal homestead.

11 CLOTHING

Western-style dress is the norm among most South Africans. Traditional Ndebele attire such as beaded aprons and blankets, and beaded arm bands and anklets for women are worn during ritual performances as indicated in Rites of Passage above.

12 FOOD

The rural staple diet consists of maize, bread, vegetables, and, to a lesser extent, meat. Considering the climate and low rainfall in the rural area, very little maize is self-produced but is rather bought at stores, as is chicken, and if people can afford it, red meat. The only time when there is a relative abundance of meat is during rituals when cattle and goats are slaughtered. During the summer rain season (September to March), many container gourds called *amarhabha*, which are then sealed and stored away to ferment for three to four days. The opening of the containers is often publicly announced to boast the skills of the manufacturer, usually an old woman and her younger team.

¹³ EDUCATION

Like most other Black South Africans, the Ndebele, in particular those in the former homeland, still suffer from the consequences of the Bantu education system. During the homeland period, teachers were grossly underqualified, classrooms were overcrowded, and text books were in perpetually short supply. Although school buildings and equipment were never damaged or destroyed, as was the case elsewhere in South Africa during the unrest periods (1976, 1986–87), the area experienced frequent school boycotts, student and teacher stayaways, and strikes. Another concern of parents during the late 1970s was the complete absence of mother-tongue education and the lack of Ndebele-speaking teachers. Teaching in IsiNdebele could only be gradually introduced after 1982.

The adult literacy rate in the area is low. The majority of female and male students have become early school drop-outs, mainly due to economic circumstances. It appears as if the tide is turning as many early dropouts, after spending some time earning a salary, are now reregistering either as full-time or part-time students. In the early 21st century, the education system is still hampered by lack of resources such as classrooms, textbooks, and qualified teachers.

¹⁴ CULTURAL HERITAGE

Communal singing and dancing in Ndebele society is either related to tribal ritual activities (initiation, divination, and weddings) or of the congregational type practiced during church services. Women in particular are active participants in tribal singing and dancing since traditional costumes play an integral part. Musical instruments are limited, although a plastic tube *(iphalaphala)*, replacing the antelope horn, and anklet rattles *(amahlwayi)* are used during the dance.

A royal praise poet *(imbongi)* always accompanies the paramount and guests on arrival at the royal capital. When the paramount attends official meetings outside the royal capital, he is always presented to his audience by this same poet. The poet, dressed in traditional costume, asks guests to rise, shouting, "Bayede!" "Ngwenyama!" and "Ndabezitha!" As the paramount enters the room, the imbongi recites the royal praises, which could last for half an hour if he wishes, depending on the historical depth of the recital.

Most Ndebele love listening to music of their choice on the regional Radio Ndebele (SABC) service that broadcasts from Pretoria. Young people attend discos at night, or the occasional music concert in the area. African jazz (Soweto String Quartet), local African bands (Mendoza and Ladysmith Black Mambazo), reggae (Lucky Dube), and Lionel Ritchie are among the favorites. Ndebele are particularly fond of local heroines such as Nothembi Mkhwebane.

¹⁵ WORK

The majority of Ndebele are daily, weekly, or monthly migrants to urban Johannesburg and Pretoria, where most women are employed in the domestic sector and men in the building and

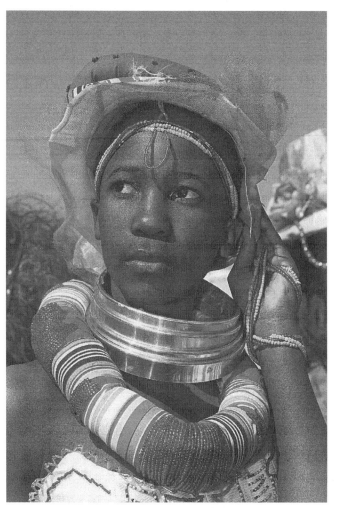

South African model Nonkululeko Sibisi dressed in a traditional Ndebele outfit for a fashion competition at the annual Canon Gold Cup horse race in Durban, South Africa. The high-profile event attracts socialites, racing enthusiasts, and celebrities, who dress up to watch the race. (Rajesh Jantilal/AFP/Getty Images)

Ndebele women seem to be able to produce their own vegetables *(umrorho)*, such as two indigenous types of spinach *(imbuyane* and *irude)*, and tomatoes. Spinach is often dehydrated, stored, and consumed during the winter months. Other popular vegetables include cabbage and pumpkin.

Maize porridge *(umratha)* accounts for more than 80% of the daily diet and is consumed during midmorning and during the evenings. Occasionally soft porridge *(umdogo)* is eaten with sour milk *(amasi)* during the day. Breakfast, in particular for school children, consists of sliced bread, often without any spread, and tea. Dinner as the main meal mostly consists of porridge, a piece of cooked chicken, tomato sauce, and spinach or cabbage.

A delicacy that is often consumed during rituals is "Ndebele beer" or *unotlhabalala*. No social event is regarded as complete without this drink of which the main components are mealie (corn) and sorghum sprouts. Sprouts are ground with a grinding stone *(imbokodo)*, cooked, sieved, and filtered, mixed with maize flour, and cooked again before being poured into large related industries. There are few employment opportunities inside their home area.

Elderly women engage in hawking fresh produce near shopping centers and taxi stands. Likewise, men in the former bantustan have few job opportunities, mostly in the heavily competitive taxi industry; low-income industries such as vehicle repairs; and private enterprise, including selling liquor privately or running a bar lounge and opening *spaza* shops (small-scale general stores) at home. Economically, rural Ndebele depend heavily on the resources of urban kin to support the household.

Most male urban Ndebele employees have over the past four decades carved a niche for themselves in the building industry, a skill it is believed they obtained during the arduous years of indenture and labor tenancy on farms. Many of these building artisans are private contractors—bricklayers, plumbers, electricians, pavers, and painters—especially in the Pretoria region, and are in great demand.

Many Ndebele women are domestic servants, and in certain suburbs in Pretoria they tend to "ethnically monopolize" the area. Others choose self employment and become street vendors in fresh produce or sell hot food (*vetkoek,* meat and maize porridge). The latter category cook food on paraffin or gas stoves, or on wood (referred to as *imbawula*) in open parking areas, on street corners, or alongside taxi ranks.

16 SPORTS

The sport of netball, introduced by the schools, is popular among girls, while soccer tops the list in terms of popularity among men and women. Bets are taken before most important matches in the South African Professional Soccer League itinerary. No particular club is favored, although the Orlando Pirates (Bucs), Kaizer Chiefs (Amakosi), and the Pretoria-based club Mamelodi Sundowns (Brazilians) are among the most popular.

The most- talked-about Ndebele sports star is the 1996 Atlanta Olympic gold medalist in the marathon, Josiah Tungwane. Special honor was bestowed upon him when the late Paramount Mayisha presented him with a special Ndebele *iporiyana* (ritual cloth for males).

17 ENTERTAINMENT AND RECREATION

A variety of traditional games such as *umadlwandlwana* (freely translated as "to play house") and *unomkhetwa* are still popular pastimes for children. *Unomkhwetwa* usually involves two players who try to outdo each other by tossing a collection of stones up in the air and catching it without losing any stones, almost like juggling.

18 FOLK ART, CRAFTS, AND HOBBIES

If anyone around the globe remembers the name Ndebele, it would most probably be in connection with the mural art and beadwork that has made them internationally famous, especially since the late 1950s. Mural painting (*ukugwala*) is done by women and their daughters and entails the multicolored application of acrylic paint on entire outer and inner courtyard and house walls. Earlier paints were manufactured and mixed from natural materials such as clay, plant pulp, ash, and cow dung. Since the 1950s, mural patterns show clear urban and Western influences. Consumer goods such as razor blades; urban architectural features, including gables and lamp posts; and symbols of modern transportation such as airplanes and license plates act as inspiration for women artists.

Beadwork (*ukupothela*) also proliferated during the 1950s and shows similarity to murals in color and design. Ndebele beadwork is essentially part of female ceremonial costume. Beads are sewn on goatskins, canvas, and nowadays even cardboard, and worn as aprons. Beaded necklaces and arm and neck rings form part of the outfit, which is worn during rituals such as initiations and weddings.

As Ndebele beadwork became one of the most popular curio art commodities, women also started to bead glass bottles, gourds, animal horns, etc. The recent prolific trading in Ndebele beadwork concentrates on "antique'" garments as pieces of art. Some women are privately commissioned to apply their painting to canvas, shopping center walls, and even cars. The first artist who won international fame was Esther Mahlangu (from KwaNdebele) who painted murals and canvasses in Paris, Japan, Australia, and Washington D.C. Others started to follow in her footsteps and apply their mural art on an international level e.g. by painting shopping center surfaces, automobiles, and aircraft carriers.

19 SOCIAL PROBLEMS

Except for the 1800s, the Ndebele as a political entity were not involved in any major regional conflicts, especially since 1883 when they lost their independence and had their land expropriated. In 1986, almost a century later, they experienced violent internal (and regional) conflict when a minority vigilante movement called Imbokodo ("Grinding Stone") took over the local police and security system and terrorized the entire former homeland. In a surprising move, the whole population called on the royal house of Paramount Mabhoko for moral support, and within weeks the youth rid the area of that infamous organization. Human rights abuses relating to that period are heard by the national Truth and Reconciliation Committee.

Probably the most challenging problem for the Ndebele leadership at present is how to define and negotiate the former homeland's residents' needs in terms of the provincial dispensation. Large-scale discontent has emerged among the rank-and-file Ndebele on the authoritarian and ethnically chauvinist way in which the new Mpumalanga Provincial government in Nelspruit is handling the well-being of the residents in the area. There is widespread discontent with the lack of resources in the region, in particular hospitals and clinics, schools, electricity and pure water reticulation.

20 GENDER ISSUES

Ndebele society is a patriarchal one with male dominance in most socio-economic and socio-cultural sectors. Rural Ndebele women have found it difficult to cope with notions such as gender equality, which is regularly advocated in the South African Constitution and the Gender Commission. However, there were a few landmark events in the recent past that gave them a foothold on regional and national level. During the 1986 unrest it was the female vote that helped with the toppling of the Imbokodo vigilante regime in the homeland. Before that election (in 1988) Ndebele women did not have the franchise. They obtained this on the eve of election with an urgent court interdict, successfully brought by themselves. Ever since the 1970s Ndebele women use the female initiation ritual (the iqhude) to mock and demean male dominance when they perform the so-termed "traffic cop" performance. During this rite they dress in traffic cop attire and "fine" male taxi drivers who transport participating female guests to these rituals. Although this is performed only over weekends, Ndebele argue that this opportunity empowers them to take control of the dominant male order.

21 BIBLIOGRAPHY

Courtney-Clarke, Margaret. *Ndebele; The Art of an African Tribe.* Cape Town: Struik, 1986.

Delius, Peter. "The Ndzundza-Ndebele. Indenture and the Making of Ethnic Identity." In *Holding Their Ground,* edited by Phil Bonner, Isabel Hofmeyr, Debora James, and Tom Lodge. Johannesburg: Ravan Press, 1989.

James, Debora. "A Question of Ethnicity: Ndzundza Ndebele in a Lebowa Village." *Journal of Southern African Studies* 16, no. 1 (1990).

Kuper, Adam. "Fourie and the Southern Transvaal Ndebele." *African Studies* 37, no. 1 (1976).

Levy, Di. "Ndebele Beadwork." In *Catalogue: Ten Years of Collecting (1979-1989),* edited by David Hammond-Tooke and Anitra Nettleton. Johannesburg: Wits University Press, 1989.

McCaul, Colleen. *Satellite in Revolt. Kwandebele-an Economic and Political Profile.* Johannesburg: South African Institute of Race Relations, 1987.

Schneider, Elizabeth, A. "Ndebele Mural Art." *African Arts* 18, no. 3 (1985).

Van Vuuren, Chris J. "Historical Land and Contemporary Ritual: The Innovation of Oral Tradition in Understanding Ndzundza-Ndebele Ethnicity." In *Oral Tradition and Innovation,* edited by Edgar Sienaert, Nigel Bell, and Meg Lewis. New Wine in Old Bottles, 1991.

———. "Ndebele." In *Encyclopedia of World Cultures.* Volume 9, edited by John Middleton and Amal Rassam. Boston: GK Hall, 1995.

———. "Ndebele Praise Poetry (iibongo) and the History of the Land." *Southern African Journal for Folklore Studies* 17, 1 (2007).

—by C. Van Vuuren

NIGERIANS

PRONUNCIATION: nigh-JIR-ee-uhns
LOCATION: Nigeria
POPULATION: 138.2 million
LANGUAGE: English; English Creole; Bantu; and Chadic languages
RELIGION: Traditional African religion; Islam; Christianity
RELATED ARTICLES: Vol. 1: Fulani; Hausa; Igbo; Ijo; Yoruba

1 INTRODUCTION

Beginning in ad 600, the territory that is now Nigeria witnessed the steady rise and decline of city-states, kingdoms, and empires. While states like Bornu became wealthy through interstate trade, others such as the Niger Delta states increased their power by slave trading. By 1862, the British had annexed Lagos, and they took control of the palm oil plantations of the Niger Delta in the 1880s. Following a series of struggles with individual states and with the French, the British united the colony of Nigeria and established a capital at Lagos in 1914. For the next half-century the British ruled the colony indirectly through local potentates and chiefs, strengthening regional differences and, after independence, encouraging regional rivalries. The most serious conflict occurred from 1967–70, when the Igbo fought unsuccessfully to secede as the Republic of Biafra. More than one million died in the war, with many dying from famine, illness, and starvation.

Since independence in 1960, Nigeria has weathered a series of military coups. A succession of military and civilian governments have tried, not very effectively, to control corruption, nepotism, and regional favoritism in public affairs. Moshood Abiola, a southerner, won the democratic presidential election in 1993, but General Sani Abacha seized power. Pro-democracy strikes and regional strife followed. However, despite its domestic instability, Nigeria has demonstrated that it is the political and economic giant of West Africa. Nigeria led the Liberian peacekeeping effort in the 1990s, and in May 1997 sent troops to Sierra Leone to restore order following a military coup. Nigeria is the dominating member of the West African Economic Community (ECOWAS).

A major challenge for Nigeria has been to unite a diverse group of peoples and to balance political rule with economic and social development among three major groups: the Hausa-Fulani in the north, the Yoruba in the west, and the Igbo in the east. To hedge against ethnic rivalry and regional divisions, Nigeria experimented with federalism and expanded its number of states from 18 to 39. A change in electoral rules also required that national leaders win a minimum number of votes from each state. Since 1992, the capital has moved from Lagos to the more centrally located Abuja, which, like Washington, D.C., is a federal district.

A new constitution, adopted and made effective in May 1999, launched a new period of multi-party elections. Despite being marred by serious voting irregularities, violence and protests, the 1999 and 2003 presidential elections provided a measure of consensus among Nigerians for civilian rule—the longest period without military interference since independence. In the general elections of April 2007 Umaru Musa Yar'adua of the People's Democratic Party (PDP) succeeded President

Obasanjo. Although these elections also were criticized as seriously flawed, they marked the first civilian-to-civilian transfer of power in the country's history. The PDP kept its majority in the legislature winning 70 seats, and 75% of state governorships. Yar'adua has surprised many observers by exerting his independence from Obasanjo, dispelling predictions that he would be Obasanjo's rubber stamp.

2 LOCATION AND HOMELAND

Nigeria is the most populous country in Africa and is the sixth most populous in the world (138.2 million est. 2008). Indeed, one in five Africans is Nigerian. At current growth rates, the population should reach nearly 191 million in 2015. It is also one of the world's most ethnically diverse countries, with more than 250 distinct groups. The largest of these is the Hausa and Fulani (29%), followed by the Yoruba (21%), the Igbo/Ibo (18.0%) and the Ijaw (10%). The Kanuri, Ibibio and lesser groups account for the remainder. Nigeria is very densely populated in the Niger Delta, where there are more than 1,000 persons per square mile. Four-fifths of the country has fewer than 200 persons per square mile.

Nigeria shares borders with Benin, Niger, Chad, and Cameroon. From the Gulf of Guinea in the south, a series of plateaus and plains cover much of the country. To the east, the Gotel and the Mandara Mountains form a common border with Cameroon. With the equator just to the south, the climate becomes tropical in the central regions and arid in the north.

3 LANGUAGE

English is the official language, but English Creole is the lingua franca (common language). Besides these, many Bantu and Chadic languages are spoken in the regions.

4 FOLKLORE

Proverbs, chants, folk stories, and riddles are popular folkloric forms. Because of Nigeria's long and diverse past and its oral traditions, folklore constitutes an area for much research. In one unusual example, the people of the Ijo village of Toro Arua perform the *Ozidi* saga. Performances occur only once in a generation. Therefore, all village members attend. The saga tells the story of the mythological history of the people of this community. Lasting more than eight days, each morning a sacrifice to the water spirits is made to ask for their blessing. A poetic narrator, an orchestra of drums, a choir of singers, male and female dancers, and actors portray the heroes and foes of the community. The event reminds adults and instructs youth about their glorious past and their distinguished ancestral heritage.

5 RELIGION

Nigerians widely hold on to their traditional African religious beliefs in addition to subscribing to various branches of Islam and Christianity. The state maintains neutrality in religious issues, and the constitution guarantees freedom of worship. Islam is most firmly rooted in the north, where it was first a religion of rulers and courtiers in the 11th century ad. Muslims now constitute about 50% of the population with Christians comprising roughly the other half, thanks to strong missionary campaigns in the 19th century. Currently, Protestants outnumber Catholics by about two to one. Of note are the African

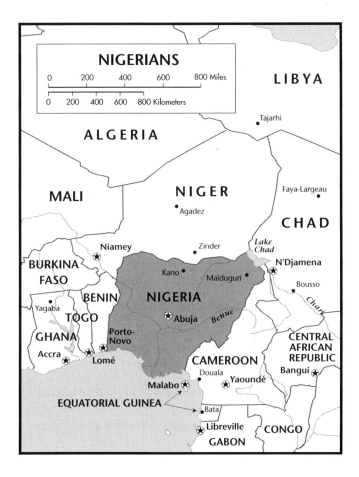

church movements and breakaway groups rooted in the 1920s and 1930s that established African versions of Christianity. About 11% of the population belongs to these distinctly African Christian churches.

Very much alive is traditional religion, which operates on three levels. Most ethnic groups have names for a supreme being whom they believe created the universe. The Yorubas call him Olorun (Lord of Heaven), the Hausas, Ubangiji (God), and the Efiks of Calabar, Abasi Ibom (The Great God). Lesser gods and deities are more accessible and act as intermediaries between people and the Creator. They possess special powers. People build shrines, make sacrifices, and offer prayers and libations to them. At the lowest levels are spirits of the dead, both good and evil, that have not yet found their rest. They may do the wishes and desires of persons who properly handle them. Sacred objects represent the lesser gods and spirits, and care must be taken not to offend them or the deities with which they are associated. Traditional religion has influenced Nigerian crafts, art, music, dance, agriculture, and language.

6 MAJOR HOLIDAYS

Secular holidays include National Day (October 1). Muslim and Christian holidays include *Tabaski* (commemorating Abraham's sacrifice) and the end of Ramadan and Easter and Good Friday.

Beside these non-indigenous holidays, Nigerians celebrate many cultural festivals throughout the year, such as the Argungu Fish and Cultural Festival on the banks of the Sokoto

Woman winnowing grain in Gumel, Nigeria. About 43% of Nigerians work in agriculture. (Corel Corporation)

River. During this celebration, hundreds of fishermen jump into the river at once, scaring the fish into the air and into their nets. Their yellow calabashes bob around on the water waiting to be filled with the catch.

7 RITES OF PASSAGE

Nigerians typically celebrate rites of passage with music, dance, and ceremony. These life-defining moments are critical for the individual within his or her community, and therefore are borne by all members of the community. At his or her naming ceremony a child becomes a member of the community; at initiation, an adolescent assumes the responsibilities of adulthood; a woman moves to her husband's family after marriage; an elder is bequeathed a title for lifelong service; and eventually, a community member joins the spirit world.

Nevertheless, modernity and urbanization are breaking down customary rituals. In a 1993 documentary film on initiation rites for girls (*Monday's Girls*), urban pressures and the weight of custom collide in the delta region. Here, Waikiriki girls participate in a five-week coming-of-age ceremony (*Iria*), which transforms them into marriageable women. A city girl who has returned to the village for the ceremony contrasts with the other girls. She and her cohorts are secluded in a house and "fattened up" for the ceremony. They are pampered and must do no work. Elderly women shear their hair, teach them how to be mothers and take care of their husbands. The old women paint the initiate's bodies before the young women appear in public with uncovered breasts to be scrutinized by the elders.

This act serves to verify the initiate's purity. Throughout, the city girl resists the process, allowing just a shock of her hair to be cut, and refusing to appear in public uncovered. She argues that she does not need anyone to teach her how to treat a husband. In the end, she greatly offends her father and disgraces her family. The other girls, though bored with their confinement toward the end, seem happy to have fulfilled this traditional rite.

8 INTERPERSONAL RELATIONS

Nigerians often use English in greeting strangers because of their linguistic diversity. In the Igbo language, *Isalachi*, and in Hausa *Yayadei*, mean "good morning." As elsewhere in Africa, two men may hold hands and stand near each other when talking because their sense of personal space is closer than that of Americans.

In most parts of sub-Saharan Africa, passing an object with the left hand or with only one hand is impolite. Nigeria is the same. Children especially must learn to offer and accept objects with both hands. Some Nigerians consider waving an insult, particularly close to the face.

9 LIVING CONDITIONS

Despite being Africa's largest oil-producer (2.44 million barrels a day), half of all Nigerians live below the poverty line. The infant mortality rate is high even for Africa at 94 for every 1,000 live births, and life expectancy is under 50 years of age. The HIV/AIDS prevalence rate is also high for West Africa at 5.4% and the number of people living with HIV/AIDS is 3.6 million (est. 2003). In terms of living standards and quality of life, Nigeria ranks near the bottom—158th out of 177 countries worldwide on the Human Development Index.

Depending on region and disposable income, Nigerians build simple rectangular or cylindrical houses of reed, mud brick, or cinder block. In urban areas, the federal and state governments have sometimes helped low-income people get affordable homes. Migrants often live in crowded conditions with several families sharing a few rooms, common cooking areas, and latrines. Lower- to middle-level income workers can afford small- to medium-sized houses with at least a standpipe in the courtyard, if not indoor plumbing. Middle- to upper-level groups have Western-style furniture, refrigerators, television sets, and motorcycles or cars. A small, very rich elite live in mansions and drive Mercedes.

Except urban squatter areas, conditions are generally more rudimentary in rural areas than in urban. About 70% of Nigerians live in villages and without indoor plumbing and electricity. Only half of all families have access to a potable water source, which means that many people—mostly women and children—have to walk great distances to draw water suitable for drinking. They may go further to scavenge wood for cooking in northern arid regions. Men and women often alternate bathing periods at a local stream or river. Laundering of clothes takes place near bathing sites so that long trips are reduced. Like many sub-Saharan people, Nigerians must cope with tropical and infectious diseases. Lack of window screens, refrigeration, mosquito nets, and hygienic water storage contribute to health problems.

One benefit of Nigeria's oil revenues is the extensive network of roads and rail lines. The major railways run from coastal port cities such as Lagos and Port Harcourt to terminals upcountry as far as Nguru and Maiduguri. Many trunk roads are paved, and several interstate highways connect commercial centers and medium-sized towns. Nigeria even has toll plazas, and a four-lane expressway links Lagos with Ibadan. Secondary and tertiary roads may be bumpy, rocky, and unimproved. Vehicle life on these roads is usually shortened considerably, but Nigerians are good mechanics. Though car bodies may rattle and shake, every mile is squeezed out of them.

10 FAMILY LIFE

Typically Nigerian families live together in compounds where nuclear families share the same hut. The father and husband are generally the dominant heads of the household. Family members deeply respect their elders, and the mark of a well-reared child is quiet and respectful behavior in the presence of adults.

Nigerians practice polygyny, and under Islamic law, a Muslim man can have up to four wives if he can support them. Typically the groom will pay a bride-price to the family of his bride. In the cities one sees Western-style dating, but this is rare in the villages. Because weddings are expensive, many couples may live together without social stigma until they can afford to give a proper wedding feast.

Nigerian women hold distinction in international circles as leaders in academia and business. They spearheaded a national feminist movement that gained momentum in 1982. Traditionally, non-Muslim women have had independent economic status and have made their mark in interregional trade. Despite these advances, Nigerians still regard single women as an oddity, and men consider them sexually available. Abortion is legal only when the mother's life is threatened or in cases of rape or incest.

11 CLOTHING

Western-style garments, makeup, hats, bags, shoes, and other accessories—symbols of the Western-educated elite—are increasingly replacing traditional apparel, especially in the cities. In the past, men dressed to show their acquired prestige. Women wore necklaces, earrings, bracelets, toe rings, finger rings and hair ornaments made from stone beads, ivory, leather, seeds, mother-of pearl, iron, the teeth and claws of animals, and the vertebrae of snakes. Vestiges of the past are seen in rural areas, where many women and men wear long loose robes of either white or bright colors. Women often wear scarves or turbans. The Igbo traditional dress is a *danshiki*, a long loose-fitting top. Formerly Igbo women added pieces of cloth to show their status in marriage and number of children. Colors were also used to symbolize cultural status, royalty, or bloodline.

Nowadays special dress is losing its traditional functions. Men dress for status rather than prestige. Cheaper European cotton thread and commercial dyes have replaced the aesthetically superior hand-woven cloths. European makeup and cheap costume jewelry, too, are supplanting traditional cosmetics and ornaments. The former elaborate traditional hairdressing is losing its symbolic meanings.

12 FOOD

Nigerians rise early, and therefore may eat several times a day. Early breakfast begins at 5:00 am and late dinner comes at 9:00 pm. Breakfast may consist of rice and mango or fried plan-

Vestiges of the past are seen in rural areas, where many women and men wear long loose robes of either white or bright colors. Women often wear scarves or turbans. Western-style garments are increasingly replacing traditional apparel, especially in the cities. (Jason Laure)

tains. At around 11:00 people might eat *efo* (stew) or *moyinmoyin*, bean pudding made with steamed black-eyed peas.

Nigerians generally like their food hot and spicy. Therefore, cooks do not spare hot red peppers either in the dishes themselves or alongside as a relish. Typically, stews or sauces are made from greens or fish, and if one's means allow, from meat or chicken. These are eaten with rice or yams. Cassava and corn are popular too, and various flours, such as yam and cassava, may be mixed and cooked into a steaming ball of fufu. Nigerians in the coastal regions drink palm wine and locally brewed beer. Muslims are great tea drinkers. In the cities, coffee houses and pubs are very popular.

13 EDUCATION

The Nigerian formal educational system is patterned after the British public school system. At the age of six or seven, children begin primary school. Muslim children learn Arabic and religious teachings in informal Quranic schools, or private Quranic schools licensed by the government. Others in rural areas receive basic farming instruction and other skills through an apprenticeship system. Some preschool, special education, adult education, and classes for the gifted and talented exist, too.

Nigeria has one of Africa's most developed systems of higher education. At least 25 institutes of higher learning, including several universities, exist. The largest of these is Ahmada Bello University in Zaria. Despite high school enrollments, many Nigerian children leave early because of economic hardship. A significant portion of the population still views advanced education as unnecessary for girls. This attitude is reflected in literacy rates—in 2005 the overall literacy rate was 69%, but only 44% of girls and women could read and write. The literacy trend for girls however, is positive; more than 60% of girls aged 15–19 are now literate.

14 CULTURAL HERITAGE

Nigerians have a long history of music, traditional dancing, visual art, and oral literature. Modern drama, opera, cinema, films, and written literature build on Nigeria's cultural heritage. Historically, culture has flourished in these various forms; it dates back 2,000 years in Nok figurines, Ife terra cottas and bronzes, Benin ivories, and Igbo Ukwu objects. The Yoruba are famous artists, making magnificent masks such as the ones used at the Ogen Festival. Sculptures served to comfort the bereaved. Benin bronzes depicted individuals and events at court and glorified the king, immortalized the dead, and served to worship the royal ancestors. The Yoruba traditionally sculpted wooden verandah posts, ceremonial masks, twin figures for the cult of the twins, and bowls and trays for Ifa divination. The Igbo make exquisite carvings of masks and the elephant spirit headdresses.

To many Nigerians, culture is synonymous with dance because traditional dancing at festivals combines music, artistic masks, costuming, body painting, drama, poetry, and storytelling. Much can be said of Nigerian dance and music because they are essential to the celebration of events connected with every aspect of life. People often celebrate child-naming, marriage, burial, house warming, chieftaincy installations, and harvesting with music and dance. At initiations, priests and initiates perform dramatic dances, and deities are represented by elaborate costumes and masquerades that conceal the identity of the wearer.

Nigerian authors are gaining international recognition for modern written works. Chinua Achebe's *Things Fall Apart* and *A Man of the People,* harsh critiques of colonial days and contemporary Nigerian politics and society, now make regular appearances in American college classrooms.

15 WORK

Because the petroleum industry has provided easy money, Nigeria has a relatively undiversified economy and undeveloped labor force of over 50 million workers. Most people remain in subsistence agriculture (nearly 70%). In the cities, people do whatever it takes to survive. They carry water, sell food on the street, wash clothes, peddle household items, haul lumber, and engage in prostitution. Many sleep where they work until they can afford to rent a room or share an apartment. Lagos has the world's sixth largest population (over 20 million) and draws thousands of migrants daily to its slums in search of work.

One of the more enterprising developments in recent times is Nigeria's burgeoning film industry, dubbed "Nollywood." Nollywood employs more than 20,000 workers and continues to grow. Its digital home video films are distributed around the world and are readily available in the United States.

16 SPORTS

Nigerians enjoy several sports. Traditionally Nigerians have wrestled, performed archery, organized foot and horse races, and developed acrobatic displays. Soccer now tops the list of modern competitive sports. Schools at all levels, business, and industry organize matches throughout the country, which has been described as "football mad." Some 62 league clubs exist. Nigerians competed internationally in World Cup competition most recently in 2002. During the playoffs, people crowded in front of TV sets stacked on top of each other on sidewalks to view their Super Eagles. In professional boxing, Nigeria has produced at least three world champions. Other sports include table tennis, tennis, basketball, polo (especially in the north), cricket, and swimming.

17 ENTERTAINMENT AND RECREATION

Home visiting is popular, and now many middle-class people have home entertainment centers with sound systems and television. As a measure of television's popularity, the government estimates that some 40 million Nigerians watch it on about 40 stations. Over the past decade, the Nigerian home videos have become very popular. Western dating customs in the towns make these forms of recreation even more popular. For music and dancing, the older generation may still appreciate high life bands, but younger people prefer Afro-Beat and Juju music—styles that originated in the Lagos area.

18 FOLK ART, CRAFTS, AND HOBBIES

Nigerian folk arts and crafts range from ivory carvings to body painting to painting of the interior and exterior walls in decorative motifs. Many arts and crafts traditionally owe their inspiration to religion and royalty. Colonial repression of indigenous religion and its artful expression led to its degeneration. Nowadays commercial motives have taken over as artists supply the tourist market.

Given the plentiful grasses on the northern plains, craftspeople there make colorful and durable baskets, fans, tables, and floor mats. Wood carving has flourished in Benin and Awka. Carvers make figures for shrines, portraits, masks, and spirit representations of natural features such as fields, forests, streams, water, fire, and thunder. The thorn of the wild cotton tree serves to make delicate, but decorative sculptures giving the effect of dresses, caps or head ties, and shoes. Some of these works have become collectors' items. Artists also cast sculptures in bronze and brass, produce glass and metal work, and make quality leatherwork and calabash carvings in Kano and Oyo. Nigerian pottery has a long tradition and ranks among the most artistic in the world. Cloth weaving in the town of Akwete also has caught the fancy of many women. The designs are both colorful and imaginative, and the pieces are unusually wide, about 1,200 mm.

19 SOCIAL PROBLEMS

Nigeria suffers a plethora of social ills. Corruption has left the country more than $37 billion in debt (2006). Dubbed as the "resource curse," oil has fueled greed and nepotism and turned the country into a showcase of embezzlement, fraud, and bribery. In the oil-rich delta region, gangs kidnap oil workers, abduct officials, and takeover oil installations. Bunkering—illegal tapping into oil pipelines—drains 10% or more of oil production and has killed thousands of people in explosions and fires. Gang clashes in Port Harcourt resulted in at least 10 deaths in 2007.

Nigeria also has been a staging point for drug trafficking to Europe and the United States. Political instability, crime and lack of rule of law continue to plague the country. Government occasionally shuts down independent newspapers, and it harasses opposition journalists. In an internationally acclaimed case in 1995 the government hung human rights leader Ken Saro-Wiwa and eight other activists in a trial that observers widely denounced as based on trumped-up charges. Many high-level officials and wealthy individuals are known to be involved in racketeering and scams of various types.

20 GENDER ISSUES

As elsewhere on the continent, women do not enjoy the same rights and privileges as men and are subject to lower pay, unequal inheritance rights, and other societal discrimination. Polygamy is legal and one out of five girls and women undergoes female genital mutilation. The law permits husbands to chastise their wives, but owing to weak enforcement, domestic violence, rape, trafficking and other crimes against women and girls often go unpunished. In addition to raising children and keeping house, women in rural areas walk several miles a day to hoe fields, gather firewood, fetch water, and do the marketing. In some areas women are considered part of their husbands "property" to be inherited along with his other possessions. In 12 of the northern states, women's rights are subject to Shariah Law, which affects both Muslim and non-Muslim women. For example, in Zamfara women are obliged to take separate transportation and use separate health care facilities. Of the more than 500 high-level political posts in the country, women hold 6 cabinet, 9 senatorial, and 27 representative positions.

21 BIBLIOGRAPHY

Achebe, Chinua Albert. *A Man of the People.* London: Heinemann, 1966.

———. *Things Fall Apart.* London: Heinemann, 1958.

Africa South of the Sahara 2007. "Nigeria." London: Europa Publishers, 2008.

Biobaku, Saburi O., ed. *The Living Culture of Nigeria.* Lagos: Thomas Nelson, 1976.

Eades, Jeremy Seymour. *The Yoruba Today.* New York: Cambridge University Press, 1980.

Federal Republic of Nigeria, Federal Ministry of Information. *Nigeria 1991: Official Handbook.* Lagos: Emaconprint Ltd., 1991.

Metz, Helen Chapin, ed. *Nigeria: A Country Study.* Washington, D.C.: U.S. Government Printing Office, 1992.

Onwurah, Ngozi. *Monday's Girls.* Produced by Lloyd Gardiner. BBC, 1993.

Packer, George. "The MegaCity." *The New Yorker*, 13 November 2006.

—by R. Groelsema

NIGERIENS

PRONUNCIATION: nee-zher-YEN
LOCATION: Niger
POPULATION: 13.3 million
LANGUAGE: Hausa; Zarma; Songhay; Fulfulde; Tamasheq; Kanuri; Arabic, Tubu; Gourmantche; French
RELIGION: Islam; small numbers of Catholics and Protestants; indigenous religious practices
RELATED ARTICLES: Vol. 1: Fulani; Hausa; Songhay; Tuaregs

1 INTRODUCTION

Niger was one of the world's least known countries until the severe drought of the 1970s brought the terrible predicament of Sahelian rural populations to the attention of Europe and North America. Today, still, a commonly made assumption is that "Niger" is simply a misspelled term for "Nigeria," the powerful, oil-producing southern neighbor of this thinly populated Sahelian nation. A landlocked, drought-ridden country in the heart of West Africa, Niger is composed of a variety of ethnically diverse populations who, despite their shared Sahelian traits, struggle to survive as a nation and to find common values and goals. Though this former French colony is presently situated in one of the globe's harshest ecological regions, it was not always so. When early inhabitants established themselves in the area 60,000 years ago, the northern territories of what is now the Republic of Niger were blessed with relatively abundant rainfall, and extensive human settlements were founded. People first relied on agriculture, and later engaged in cattle herding, besides developing complex stone tools.

As ecological conditions changed and the northern regions became drier, people were forced to relocate south and to develop mixed economies based on agriculture, farming, and long-distance trade. By the 7th century ad, the Western area was controlled by the powerful Songhay state, while the eastern regions were under the influence of the Kanem-Bornu Empire. As the authority of these states gradually waned in the 16th century, the Hausa states emerged as significant political and economic centers, thanks to their location at one of the terminus of trans-Saharan trade routes.

Meanwhile, the pastoralist Tuareg, always quick to impose their domination on sedentary communities whenever possible, were making incursions into southern territories and were becoming increasingly involved in trade and agriculture. By the 19th century, the dominant Hausa power in the eastern regions was Damagaram. Most of the central Hausa states were tributaries of the Sokoto caliphate, whose holy war against the un-Islamic practices of its neighbors had resulted in the creation of a vast Fulani empire. The French conquest of Niger culminated in the creation of the colony of Niger in 1922, after the Tuareg resistance was crushed.

Niger was granted independence from France in 1960. Except for a brief boom in the 1970s, however, the end of colonial rule has not translated into prosperity for this already economically marginal West African nation. Niger was governed by a single party civilian regime until 1974, when then-President Hamani Diori was ousted in a military coup led by Col. Seyni Kountché. Kountché's death in 1987 marked the beginning of a 12-year period in which power frequently changed hands

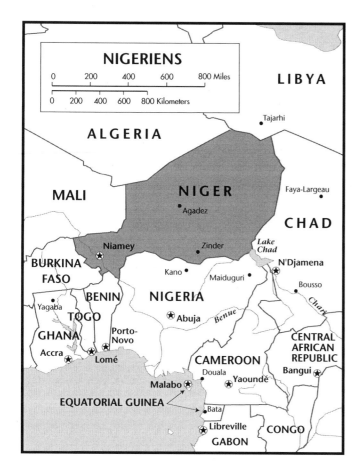

NIGERIENS

between civilian and military governments. From 1990–1995 there was an armed rebellion by Tuareg peoples from northern Niger, who sought an autonomous desert region and greater control over the country's uranium revenues. In 1999 Mamadou Tandja was elected president in a democratic election. He was reelected in 2004. In May 2007 a second Tuareg rebellion began.

² LOCATION AND HOMELAND

The territory of Niger, two-thirds of which is located in the central Sahara, lies between 11°37' and 23°23'n. Surrounded by Algeria and Libya to the north, Chad to the east, Nigeria and Benin to the south, and Burkina Faso and Mali to the west, Niger is primarily desert. The southern part of the country, where the vast majority of the population lives, is semi-arid Sahel and receives between six and twenty inches of rain per year. In the Sahelian region, most people grow millet, sorghum, peanuts and peppers or herd cattle, goats, sheep or camels. Niger is a predominately rural country, and villages generally incorporate people of different ethnic identities. Over the last 50 years, dwindling resources and opportunities in the rural areas have forced many to migrate to the cities. Niamey, the capital, has thus grown with the influx of migrants from all parts of the country.

³ LANGUAGE

To downplay ethnic differences and prevent divisiveness, the people of Niger are usually classified according to ethno-lin-

guistic categories. Though over 30 distinct groups and 21 languages have been identified, the population is nevertheless divided into five major groups:

the Hausa, who speak Hausa, constitute the largest group, with over 56% of the total population;

the Zarma/Songhay/Dendi, who speak Zarma or closely related Songhay, make up about 21% of the population;

the Fulani or Peul, who speak Fulfulde, are 8.5% of the population;

the Tuareg, who speak Tamasheq, represent 9.3 % of the population;

the Kanuri, who speak Kanuri, make up 4.7% of the population;

Arabs, Tubus, or Gourmantches, unrelated groups who speak Arab, Tubu, and Gourmantche, make up the remaining 1.2% of the total population.

Many Nigeriens speak more than one language. For instance, in Niamey, the capital, most native Zarma speakers also speak Hausa, which has become the lingua franca (common language) of Niger. Nigeriens who have attended Western-style schools (approximately one-third of the population) also speak French, the primary language of government and education.

⁴ FOLKLORE

The people of Niger believe they are surrounded by spiritual forces that regularly intervene, for better or for worse, in the lives of humans. In the pre-colonial era, some of these spirits protected communities from enemy attacks and were regularly propitiated to ensure the prosperity of one's land or herd. Today, spirits allegedly grant health, fame, protection, or fortune to those who obey their requests for sacrificial offerings or who become their mediums. Among the Zarma-Songhay, the Hausa, the Fulani, and the Tuareg, for instance, some individuals are chosen by the spirits to become their human vessels. A family strife, declining prosperity, or lengthy illnesses that cannot be cured by Western medicine, Islamic medicine, or herbal remedies alone may be diagnosed as being caused by spirits who are reminding their victims of their powers.

Among Hausa-speaking populations, a myth explains the presence of these powerful, but invisible, creatures as follows. Adamu, the first man, and Hawa, the first woman, had given birth to 50 sets of twins. One day, the supreme being and their creator told them that he wanted to see the children. Afraid that he would keep them for himself, the cunning Hawa told her husband they would hide the more beautiful siblings of each 50 pair of twins in a cave, and only show the supreme being the remaining ones. Seeing how they had deceived him, the omniscient god decided he would punish Adamu and Hawa by making the hidden twins invisible forever. The spirits who plague humans and are dependent on them for subsistence are nothing but the descendants of the beautiful twins condemned by God to remain invisible.

Witchcraft, experienced and expressed in various forms, is also thought to be a major cause of pain, illness, and misfortune. Mothers, for instance, cover their young children's bodies with amulets in the hope of warding off the nefarious influence of human agents as much as the destructive powers of spiritual forces.

⁵ RELIGION

Islam first came to Niger through traders involved in trans-Saharan commerce in the 9th century. For nearly 1,000 years, Islam was primarily a religion of the governing elite, traders, and the educated. Widespread conversation to Islam began in the 19th century. Today, 95% of the Nigerien population is said to be Muslim, though in many cases being a follower of the prophet Muhammad is not antithetical to the propitiation of spirits or the use of divination. Thus, anyone may enlist the help of the spirits to pass an exam, to ensure one's safe return from a trip, or to protect oneself from jealous kin. Wherever it has taken roots in Niger, Islam has been influenced by local beliefs and practices. Today, children are given Muslim names, while most men (especially in the rural areas) wear Muslim flowing gowns and pray conspicuously five times a day.

Of late, reformist religious groups such as *Izala*, an anti-Sufi movement, have made numerous converts among the youth by preaching against an Islam that they see as tainted by local traditions. Izala members advocate frugality and Islamic education for all, challenge the authority of elders, and condemn the use of amulets.

During the colonial period, Christian missions were established throughout Niger. Today, they are still active but Catholics and Protestants make up less than 5% of Niger's population.

⁶ MAJOR HOLIDAYS

In Niger, a variety of Christian, Muslim and national holidays are celebrated. Legal holidays include January 1 (New Year's Day), April 24 (Concord Day, commemorating the coup that ousted Hamani Diori in 1974), May 1 (Labor Day), August 3 (Independence Day), December 18 (Republic Day), and December 25 (Christmas Day). Most Nigeriens celebrate also celebrate Muslim holidays, which fall on a different day each year because they are determined by the lunar calendar. Muslim holidays include *Tabaski* (a feast commemorating the sacrifices of Abraham), *Mouloud* (the prophet Muhammad 's birthday), and *Eid al-Fitr* (a feast marking the end of Ramadan, a holy month of fasting). Nigeriens celebrate the *Tabaski* by slaughtering a ram, which they cook on an open fire and eat with friends and family. During *Eid al-Fitr* and *Mouloud*, people wear new clothes, enjoy feasts of meat, rice, and fruit, and men go to the mosque to pray.

⁷ RITES OF PASSAGE

When a Nigerien woman delivers her first child, she becomes an adult by virtue of having demonstrated that she is capable of giving life. Among the Tuareg, the new mother's coming of age is celebrated by a blessing of the mother's tent and a lively display of wrestling by the wealthiest and most prestigious women. On the sixth day after her baby's birth, female relatives perform the *kishakish* ritual, during which the newborn is brought out of the tent for the first time and later given a name. The Tuareg naming ceremony bears similarities to rituals performed among the Hausa and other populations of Niger. A ram is usually killed and the baby's head is shaved to signify the change of status.

Membership into the spirit possession troupe usually requires the holding of an initiation ritual, during which the medium's new status is officially recognized.

Marriage, especially to a first spouse, involves an important change of status for both men and women (in Hausa, for instance, there is no word for a woman who had reached adulthood but has never been married). But "tying the knot" involves more than anything the union between two lineages, and this is why it is so important to know the background of the person one marries.

Death, since the advent of Islam, no longer involves specific rituals intended to separate, once and for all, the dead from the living. Burial is a simple affair. The deceased is buried immediately after death. Kin, friends, and neighbors come to offer their condolences to the grieving family, but in most cases tears should not be part of the picture. Restraint and dignity are expected of everyone; women who visit a grieving mother, for example, should chat as if nothing special was going on so as to distract the mourner from her pain.

⁸ INTERPERSONAL RELATIONS

Nigeriens are warm and friendly, but, because of the influence of Islam on local life, there exists a strong segregation between the sexes. Muslim women are, by and large, constrained by their domestic duties, while men have access to more public spaces such as the market or the court. What goes on between men and women in public or in private varies, of course, with education, social status, and ethnic identity. Younger women are more daring, and they usually have a say in the choice of a husband. They must remain modest, and once married, it is improper for a Muslim wife to look at her husband directly in the eye or to confront him.

Proper behavior is characterized by restraint and modesty to such an extent that it is considered inappropriate, for instance, to complain about pain or to advertise one's hunger. Greetings, in Hausa for instance, involve asking about one's health, the health of one's children, and whether one has had a good night, morning, etc. To the question *Ina kwana?* ("how was the night?"), it is appropriate to answer *Lahiya lau* ("fine") even if one is at death's door.

Nigeriens are highly hospitable people who always have food available for guests and visitors. Generosity is valued regardless of one's degree of wealth. Among the Hausa, it is, in fact, primarily by redistributing one's wealth that one achieves prestige, visibility, and respectability.

⁹ LIVING CONDITIONS

Niger remains a very impoverished country struggling to become, with the aid of international partners, a stronger and more self-sufficient nation. Most rural communities have no electricity, and in many villages women still draw water daily from the communal well. With the spread of conservative Islam, an increasing number of wives are living in seclusion, which means that their mobility during the day is severely curtailed. Men who seclude their wives usually pay another woman to bring water to the household, while they themselves purchase the necessary ingredients for the family meals.

While free healthcare is available in towns and cities, most people in rural areas do not have access to a hospital or dispensary. Malnutrition among young children is prevalent, which

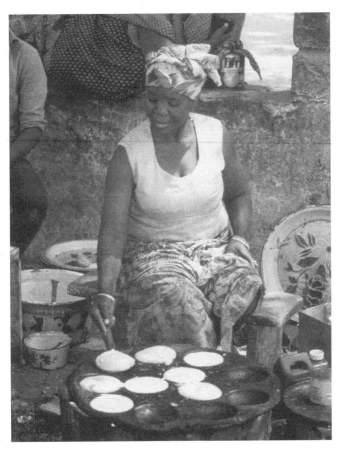

A Nigerien woman baking. In Niger, where drought is a constant
threat to human survival, the staple food is millet.
(Cory Langley)

explains the high rate of child mortality. In Niger, one third of children born do not reach the age of five.

Nigeriens travel a great deal to visit relatives or to search for seasonal work. While they may walk or ride a horse to visit a nearby village, they often use bush-taxis to cover large distances.

¹⁰ FAMILY LIFE

The concept of family among sedentary populations usually includes a host of extended kin who may or may not live in the same household. This has long meant that members of extended families pooled their resources together under the authority of the head of the household. Under the post-colonial pressures of increasingly individualist modes of farming, the extended family has splintered. Young men have become largely responsible for raising the money for bride-price and for paying taxes—expenses that had traditionally been the responsibility of the household head.

Women spend most of the day taking care of the children and preparing meals. According to Islam, men can marry up to four wives at a time; there is no limit to how many they can marry in their lifetime, as long as they keep divorcing their previous wives. Women who are divorced usually go back to their parents' homes until they remarry. Tension and competition between co-wives is not infrequent, but husbands are en-

couraged by Islam to minimize jealousy by not privileging one wife at the expense of another.

Among the Hausa, relations of avoidance prevent a woman from publicly showing her affection for the first two or three children she gives birth to. She cannot utter their names, nor can she call her husband by his name, tease him, or contradict him. A good wife should be humble and obedient. Grandparents, on the other hand, enjoy a joking relationship with their grandchildren, which means that they can be affectionate towards them, tease them, or be teased by them.

¹¹ CLOTHING

Through the style, lavishness, and color of their clothes, Nigeriens communicate a great deal about their ethnicity, religious identity, and educational and social status. While most Zarma, Songhay, and Hausa women wear gay, cotton, custom-made blouses with flounces, pleats, elaborate collars, and short-sleeves together with wrappers of the same fabric, women among the Tuareg or Fulani wear dark indigo-dyed clothes. In urban areas, professional women may wear Western clothes, but many are pressured by reformist Muslims to give up their revealing garments in favor of the more modest local attire that often includes a type of head-covering. While many women wear a small scarf or even a large veil that shrouds their shoulders, female Izala members are covered from head to ankle by a voluminous tent-like veil, the *hijabi*, whose bright color matches the rest of their outfit.

For many Nigerien men, the flowing, sleeveless gown of heavy brocade that is worn over a matching shirt and drawstring pants has become the garment of choice. Despite its cumbersomeness, it gives respectability to its wearer by advertising his or her Islamic status. When they do not wear a turban, men often sport an embroidered rimless hat. Among the Tuareg, it is not the women but the men who cover their faces with a veil. Among Bororo Fulani, men make up their faces and compete in beauty pageants, during which women designate the most handsome participants. Educated civil servants characteristically wear tight-fitting European pants and tailored shirts in dull colors and go hatless.

¹² FOOD

In Niger, where drought is a constant threat to human survival, the staple food is millet. Millet is the main ingredient in the traditional midday meal of *fura*, a porridge of water, spices, sometimes milk or sugar, and cooked flour. Pastoral Tuareg, who rely heavily on the consumption of dates, add crushed dates to their fura. Millet can be consumed during the evening meal as a thick paste having the consistency of polenta, onto which is spooned a spicy sauce that may contain tomato paste, onion, okra, sorel, squash, pumpkin, eggplant, or meat. Along the Niger River, the Songhay prepare a thick paste of corn with a sauce made of baobab leaves, to which is added meat or smoked fish. When they do not eat millet or sorghum, Nigeriens enjoy beans or rice. For breakfast, they usually eat the leftovers of the previous meal, though in town, coffee and bread are becoming increasingly appreciated by those who can afford the expense. All enjoy snacks made of skewered meat, grilled tripe, fried bean meal beignets, or ground peanut cakes. The mango season brings ample supplies of these sweet delicacies to rural communities that have otherwise little opportu-

Nigeriens with their camels. (Cory Langley)

nity to sample fruits. During the cricket season, women fry the insects for snacks.

Observant Muslims do not eat pork or consume alcohol; they eat only meat that has been slaughtered by a Muslim man in the proper Muslim fashion.

13 EDUCATION

In Niger, where schooling is free but compulsory between the ages of 7 and 15, students can attend a Western-style school where all instruction is in French, or they can acquire an Islamic education in Arabic. Only a small minority of Nigeriens are literate and can read either in French or Arabic. Even fewer finish secondary school to later pursue a higher education. An increasing number of children are attending Quranic schools thanks to the renewed Islamic fervor the country has been experiencing. There, they first learn by rote the entire Quran before moving on to the second stage of learning, which consists of understanding and interpreting each of the verses they have memorized.

In French private or public schools, the curriculum as established by the Ministry of National Education is designed to impart strictly secular knowledge. Local languages such as Hausa or Zarma are banished from the curriculum, and all instruction is in French. Children learn French grammar, math, science, civics, history, geography, drawing, music, and physical education.

Many parents believe that government schools are dangerous places because their children will forget their traditions and will be lost to their parents. Pious Muslims may send their sons, but keep their daughters home for fear of sexual promiscuity.

14 CULTURAL HERITAGE

The history and tradition of Nigerien people is often evoked at social gatherings and celebrations by the *griots*, bards (most often male) who are simultaneously praise-singers, messengers, and historians. Men sing in Tuareg society, while in Hausa society women often use the medium of song to express themselves, whether they sing lullabies to their babies, work songs, or verses mocking their husbands.

Nigeriens are very fond of listening to and reciting tales that explore traditional themes and values of the local culture and history, such as marital relations, virtue, generosity, or religious piety. Storytelling, like the recitation of song poems, praise-singing, or theater plays, is an important form of entertainment among children and adults alike. Today, the stories are often told by women, while men concentrate more on Islamic narratives and poems.

The Nigerien theater, in its present form, was introduced by French colonial administrators through schools and cultural associations. Nearly all comic, the plays, which reflect and promote popular concerns and aspirations, are improvised from a scenic outline arranged from a chosen theme. Performed in schools, village cultural centers, and on national radio and television, plays enjoy a wide popularity and are often performed in Hausa (the most widely understood language in Niger).

Nigerien writers and poets are not well-known outside of Niger, except perhaps for Boubou Hama, the former president of the National Assembly, whose wonderfully rich autobiography, *Kotia Nima*, received the main literary prize of Sub-Saharan Africa in 1970.

15 WORK

A majority of Nigeriens remain farmers. They grow millet, sorghum, and beans as primary crops, but almost all of them are involved in secondary occupations such as petty trade, smithing, dyeing, tailoring, etc. Land is unfortunately becoming an increasingly scarce resource as parcels divided up between male children keep getting smaller. One-sixth of the work force is engaged in livestock production. Tuareg and Fulani, who were traditionally pastoralists, are progressively abandoning a precarious existence to settle in urban or semi-urban areas. Employed civil servants who are fortunate enough to receive a monthly salary are often faced with the predicament of having to support more relatives than their meager resources can bear.

16 SPORTS

Traditional wrestling has been promoted by the government as an activity that is distinctly part of the cultural heritage of Nigeriens. Wrestling tournaments draw large crowds. Each city now has a wrestling arena where people can come to follow the careers of their champions. Soccer is a popular source of entertainment for young boys and men. Given the fondness of Hausa and other Nigeriens for horses, horse races are also events that attract numerous onlookers.

Among pastoral Fulani, young men regularly engage in *soro*, a competitive game in which a man violently hits his partner with a large stick on the chest. The receiver pretends not to be hurt and simply smiles at the audience to demonstrate his control over pain.

17 ENTERTAINMENT AND RECREATION

Spirit possession ceremonies are public performances that can draw large crowds of onlookers in search of entertainment. Despite the Muslim prohibition on dancing and mixed-sex gatherings, many men and women enjoy stomping their feet to the sounds of the drums (calabashes) and the one-stringed violin during these events. The birth of a child is an occasion to rejoice and eat food. Wedding celebrations in urban areas also involve an evening of dancing to the sound of African pop music.

Though it remains a luxury that only salaried workers or wealthy traders can afford, television is becoming increasingly popular among Nigeriens. Parents and children enjoy American televisions series when they are not watching a Nigerian or Indian video at the house of a neighbor who is charging entrance fees to increase his earnings. In some rural communities, villagers can watch television even though they have no electricity. Thanks to solar-powered batteries, some neighborhoods share a television that is turned on every night after the evening meal.

Hausa and Hindu melodramas or karate films are popular among the younger generation who, in urban areas, can watch their idols on the big screen in open air cinemas. In the rural areas, market days are occasions to meet friends or relatives and catch up on the latest news. The market is often the place to hear gossip, to learn about new fashions, or to discuss marriage plans.

18 FOLK ART, CRAFTS, AND HOBBIES

Nigeriens are skilled craftsmen. Zarma women, for instance, are deft potters, known for their large earthenware water jars decorated with white geometrical motifs. Songhay pottery is decorated with ochre, black, or white triangular motifs. Hausa earthenware jars have a characteristically large opening.

Tuareg and Hausa craftsmen are famous for their elaborate leather work—beautiful boots, colorful sandals, and multi-pocketed bags in goatskin. Tuareg men manufacture leather boxes with intricate geometrical designs, as well as horse and camel saddles, sword sheaths, and multi-colored, fringed cushions and pouches.

Hand-woven, multi-colored cotton blankets made of thin bands that are sown together are part of women's most treasured possessions. Hausa women, for instance, keep their blankets in trunks and only display them on the day that their newborn child is given a name. The embroidery that enlivens the collars of the large Islamic robes worn by so many Nigerien men is also a local craft.

Smithing is a traditional activity among the Tuareg, who manufacture a wide range of jewelry: Agadez or Iférouane silver crosses, rings, wrist and ankle bracelets made of braided silver or copper strands, necklaces made of beads or agate set in silver, amulets, and locks worn around the neck. Fulani women wear numerous large silver earrings and heavy brass anklets.

The people of Niger enjoy music, whether they listen to Islamic chanting on the radio or attend a formal musical event honoring local authorities. They listen with great pleasure to the griots, the professional bards whose praise-singing is accompanied by drumming from a whole series of instruments, including the *ganga*, a medium size drum, and the *kalangu*, an hourglass drum held under the armpit. On formal occasions, one may hear the sound of the *algaïta*, a reed instrument that requires of its player an elaborate breathing technique. Among the Tuareg, three women are needed to play the *tinde*, a type of drum that is often accompanied by a flute (*tassinsack*). Tuareg men enjoy singing about their exploits as warriors or lovers while women perform instrumental music.

19 SOCIAL PROBLEMS

When Niger gained its independence in 1960, only 5% of the population lived in cities. Since the 1984–85 drought that displaced so many pastoralists, Niamey, the capital, has expanded by over 10% every year. This dramatic urbanization has introduced a variety of social ills that the successive regimes have failed to address seriously. There has been, for instance, a significant increase in violent crime, juvenile delinquency, and alcoholism. Drug use among workers is reportedly on the increase. Growing numbers of partially educated youths who cannot find work in the public or industrial sector either remain unemployed or are absorbed by the informal sector in petty trade, hustling, and smuggling when they do not turn to crime. Another drought and locust infestation in 2005 led to food shortages for as many as 2.5 million Nigeriens.

Infanticide, rape of young girls, forced early marriage, and teenage prostitution are becoming increasingly common. Faced with Niamey's demographic explosion, the state has been unable to supply the most basic services. This is why postal service, sewage system, and water supply are nonexistent in many neighborhoods of the capital.

[20] GENDER ISSUES

Because of the influence of Islam on local life, there exists a strong segregation between the sexes. Muslim women are, by and large, constrained by their domestic duties, while men have access to more public spaces such as the market or the court. What goes on between men and women in public or in private varies, of course, with education, social status, and ethnic identity. Younger women are more daring, and they usually have a say in the choice of a husband. They must nonetheless remain modest. Once married, it is improper for a Muslim wife to look at her husband directly in the eye or to confront him.

Gender strongly affects access to education in Niger. While 43% of men are literate, only 15% of women can read and write. Many women are unable to attend school because of responsibilities within the home and early marriage (often between the ages of 14 and 20). The average Nigerien woman will have between seven and eight children in her lifetime, one of the highest fertility rates in the world.

[21] BIBLIOGRAPHY

Alidou, Ousseina. *Engaging Modernity: Muslim Women and the Politics of Agency in Postcolonial Niger.* Madison: University of Wisconsin Press, 2005.

Charlick, Robert B. *Niger: Personal Rule and Survival in the Sahel.* San Francisco: Westview Press, 1991.

Coles, Catherine, and Beverly Mack, ed. *Hausa Women in the Twentieth Century.* Madison: University of Wisconsin Press, 1991.

Cooper, Barbara M. *Evangelical Christians in the Muslim Sahel.* Bloomington, Indiana University Press, 2006

Masquelier, Adeline. "Identity, Alterity and Ambiguity in a Nigerien Community: Competing Definitions of 'True' Islam." In *Postcolonial Identities in Africa.* Ed. Richard Werbner. London: Zed Books, 1996.

"Mediating Threads: Clothing and the Texture of Spirit/Medium Relations in *Bori*." In *Clothing and Difference: Embodied Identities in Colonial and Post-Colonial Africa.* Ed. Anne A. Hendrickson. Raleigh-Durham: Duke University Press, 1996.

Miles, William. "Islam and Development in the Western Sahel: Engine or Break?" *Journal Institute of Muslim Minority Affairs* 7, no. 2 (1986): 439–463.

Stoller, Paul. *Embodying Colonial Memories: Spirit Possession, Power, and the Hauka in West Africa.* New York: Routledge, 1995.

Worley, Barbara. "Where All the Women are Strong." *Natural History* 101, no. 11 (1992): 54–63.

—revised by C. Breedlove

NUER

PRONUNCIATION: NOO-uhr
LOCATION: Southern Sudan
POPULATION: 4 million
LANGUAGE: Nuer
RELIGION: Traditional faith (worship of Kuoth); Christianity
RELATED ARTICLES: Vol. 1: Dinka; Shilluk; Sudanese

[1] INTRODUCTION

To generations of anthropology students, the Nuer of southern Sudan have been one of the best-known peoples in Africa, thanks to the pioneering cultural studies of British social anthropologist E. E. Evans-Pritchard.

Early in the 20th century, the Nuer were estimated to number about half a million. They occupied the swampy flood plain known as the Sudd region along the White Nile. These farmer-herders lived by raising cattle and cultivating crops, moving away from their permanent settlements in the dry season after the rains had tapered off and the floods had receded in order to take advantage of grazing in low-lying areas near rivers and streams. Fishing, hunting, and the gathering of wild fruits rounded out their diet.

When the British conquered Sudan and eventually brought the Nuer people under their control, they were surprised that the Nuer could have high population densities and broad, stable networks of social organization without any formal political organization or leadership. To account for this complexity of this relatively egalitarian organization based on kinship relations, as well as the legendary military successes the Nuer enjoyed, the famous British anthropologist E. E. Evans-Pritchard developed the concept of "segmentary lineages." These kinship groups, which traced descent in the male line, could mobilize in opposition to similar-level opponents in any social conflict among the Nuer or between them and outsiders. Thus, even without a centralized political leader, they could effectively unite against enemies, making them a formidable military foe. The theory of segmentary opposition and studies of the Nuer have fascinated anthropologists and their students ever since.

Thus the fame of the Nuer stems from their early notoriety as one of the most courageous and steadfast peoples of Africa in their resistance to colonial conquest and imperial domination. British and Egyptian forces conquered Sudan in 1898, and most Nuer communities had nominally submitted to British rule before the outbreak of World War I, but non-cooperation and resistance remained widespread. It was not until the 1920s that systematic efforts were made to extend effective British presence into some areas of Nuerland. The last large-scale armed uprising was not put down until the end of the 1920s, when Royal Air Force planes were deployed in an "experiment in the pacification of primitive peoples" to fire-bomb Nuer villages and the earthen mounds dedicated to their prophets. The invaders also strafed the fleeing people and confiscate their cattle.

Once armed resistance was finally crushed, the British colonizers had the difficult task of subjecting the proudly independent Nuer people to the principles of "indirect rule" and regularizing administration and taxation in spite of the lack of native institutions and structures for political control. The

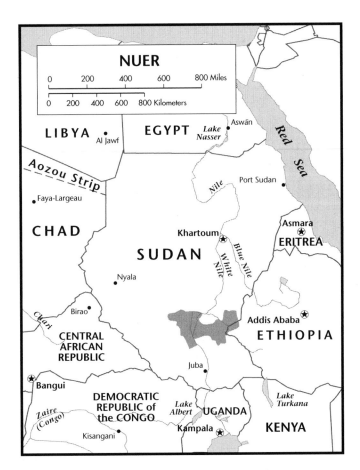

NUER

British never truly accomplished this task; neither did the series of Sudanese governments that followed. In fact, by the time of Sudanese independence in 1956, civil war had broken out in the southern region, eventually pulling the entire Nuer area into armed conflicts that continue into the late 1990s, with only one short relatively peaceful period from 1972 to 1983. The Khartoum government brutally suppressed the African ethnic groups in an attempt to control the oil and water on their land.

The civil war between the Sudan People's Liberation Movement/Army (SPLM/A) led by the late General Garang and the Government of the Sudan (GoS) raged from 1983 to 9 January 2005 when a Comprehensive Peace agreement was signed between the two parties. The war claimed millions of lives, forced many into exile and wasted livelihoods of millions of people, destroyed the physical infrastructure, hampered the economic base and caused the disintegration of social fabrics. This in turn has had a serious impact on traditional value systems, norms, and adaptation mechanisms. The treaty granted Southern Sudan a semi-autonomous status within the larger Sudan. Nevertheless, many Nuer still feel that they have been shortchanged in the composition of the Government of National Unity (GONU), headed by President Al Bashir and Salva Kiir Mayardit. They allege the government is dominated by the Dinka tribe and therefore misrepresents the Sudanese reality.

² LOCATION AND HOMELAND

Nuerland is located in the southern Sudan between 7° and 10° north and 29° and 34° east. The main channel of the Nile River divides the country into western and eastern regions. The vast majority of the Nuer today live in their traditional homeland, located in the east Upper Nile Province around the junction of the Nile River with the Bahr el Ghazal and Sobat Rivers, and extending up the Sobat across the Ethiopian border. Nuer are geographically located in the heartland of the Upper Nile towards the Eastern Region of Jonglei state in Southern Sudan. They are bordered by the Gawaar of Ayod from the West, Dinka of Bor from the South West, Murle from the South, Anyuak from the East, Jikany of Nasir from the North East, Dinka of Ngok, and Luach from the North.

The region receives heavy rains—about 50 to 100 cm (20 to 40 in) per year—which falls almost entirely from May through October, with average daily maximum temperatures about 30° to 32°C (86° to 90°F). Dry winds blow from the north from November until April, bringing clear, sunny skies, with March and April being very hot months with high temperatures in the range of 38°C (100°F). The Nuer homeland is very flat, causing slow drainage and widespread flooding during the rainy season. Those same lands offer lush grazing for cattle during the dry season. The landscape also includes a few trees, such as small groves of thorny acacias and lalob trees, a very large shade tree, and a few palm trees.

While most Nuer still live in their home area, many have migrated to urban areas at various times to take advantage of job opportunities. During the civil wars in the period since 1955, and especially since 1983, thousands of Nuer have also fled north to the national capital, Khartoum, to other cities, or even to other countries to seek refuge from the fighting. Since the 1960s, thousands of rural Nuer have lived outside Sudan, particularly in western Ethiopia along the upper stretches of the Sobat river.

It is difficult to assess how life has changed in the traditional territories of the Nuer along the upper Nile and Sobat rivers because of the disruption of life in the region. However, in the time since the end of the colonial period, many Nuer have come to live outside their homeland, particularly in the cities of the north, where they have led very different lives. Taxes imposed by the British, as well as measures restricting Nuer raids on other groups for cattle, led to the first significant migrations of Nuer in search of work for pay. Most migrants intended to return home after a brief period, with enough money to buy a herd large enough to support a family in the traditional way of life; but the dislocations of the civil war and a devastating flood in 1964 that destroyed many herds have made returning increasingly difficult for many Nuer.

In seeking wage employment in the north, the Nuer men looked for work that they considered in keeping with their proud heritage as brave warriors. Much of the work available was in domestic service and other menial work that Dinka and other refugees from neighboring southern communities accepted, but which most Nuer rejected as demeaning. Instead, many Nuer found their way into construction labor, where they became the core labor of the labor force in many northern cities and on construction crews for irrigation dams and other structures. Women eventually began to accompany the men, and whole families would live on construction sites in shelters built from available scrap material. This reduced the living costs of the workers, but it created problems because the conditions were not compatible with the standards of female modesty and seclusion common among Muslim northerners.

³ LANGUAGE

The Nuer call themselves *Naath*, which means "human beings." The Nuer, Dinka, and Atwot (Atuot) are sometimes considered one ethnic group. The Nuer language is a Nilotic language closely related to the speech of the Dinka and Atwot. The language is uniform with no definable dialects.

To the ears of English speakers, the Nuer language sounds airy, light, melodic, and breathy, with few hard consonants. It has several consonants that are not usually found at the beginning of English words, such as the sound *ng* (as in *sing*) or *ny* (as the Spanish *ñ* in *señor* or French *gn* in *Boulogne*. For example, most common names for Nuer women and girls begin with the latter sound: *Nyayoi, Nyawec* (the *c* at the end is pronounced *ch*). Because of these unusual sounds, the written form of the language developed by missionaries in the 1930s and 1940s includes several letters not used in writing European languages.

To identify a person, the given name is followed by the name of the father, since the Nuer consider kinship through the father's line very important. So if a man named Cuol names his son Gatkuoth and his daughter Nyaruol, they would be called Gatkuoth Cuol and Nyaruol Cuol. A child is usually named by the father or another member of the father's family and may have another name that the relatives on the mother's side use. Women do not change their names when they marry, but after a woman has a child (named *Wei*, for example), other women might often call her "mother-of-Wei." People also have nicknames and ceremonial names. Among male friends of their own age groups, for example, boys and men are often called by the name of the bull they received at initiation or the name of their current favorite bull in their herd.

Most Nuer cannot read their language, but oral language is well developed. Nuer enjoy verbal wit, and are known as brilliant conversationalists. Major forms of entertainment include joking, creating and reciting poetry, and composing and performing original songs for one another. Sample Nuer expressions include *wut pany* ("a real man"), *male magua!* ("big hello!"), *jin athin?* ("Are you there?"="How are you?"), and *nyang* ("crocodile").

⁴ FOLKLORE

Nuer honor the memory of their famous prophets, known as *guk*, who are believed to be possessed by one of the sky spirits or lesser divinities. One such prophet was a man named Ngundeng, who died in 1906. He was said to be able to cure illnesses and infertility. During his lifetime he and his followers constructed a large earthen pyramid, approximately 12 m (40 ft) high, made of earth, ashes and cattle camp debris; they surrounded it with over a hundred upright elephant tusks. It was built in honor of the sky god Deng and for the glory of the prophet Ngundeng; people came from miles around to help with the building and later to sacrifice cattle there. The monument was blown up by the British in 1928. The songs and prophecies of Ngundeng and other prophets are passed down the generations through oral tradition and are still influential today. It is believed that the spirit that possesses a prophet later possesses one of his descendants.

⁵ RELIGION

The Nuer religion involves belief in a divine creator or high god, *Kuoth, who sustains life and health, and in many lesser spirits*. The Nuer honor both the high god and the spirits (or lesser divinities) through observance of moral rules (including observation of kinship duties and other social obligations) and sacrifices. The two kinds of leaders in the Nuer religious system are prophets, who are believed to be earthly representatives of some of the lesser divinities/spirits of the air, and "earth priests," also known as "leopard-skin chiefs." The latter name for these leaders comes from their traditional mark of office, a leopard skin cape, and their recognized leadership role; but they are not really political leaders, as the term "chief" seems to imply. Instead, they are considered sacred people who can intercede with spirits, conduct sacrifices to help cure illnesses that are believed to be spiritually based, and serve as intermediaries between feuding families, as when revenge is sought after a murder. There are still some active Nuer prophets today, including Wutnyang Gatakek (whose name means "man of crocodile, son of reputation"), a young man who encourages his followers to work hard, become self-reliant, and not succumb to the tendency to blame other ethnic groups for their problems (a practice known as "tribalism"). He does not consider his spiritual leadership to be in conflict with Christianity, and he encourages Christians to continue to follow their religion.

During periods of epidemics or even individual health crises, oracles are sought out to identify the offended spirits and determine the proper recourse. Frequently an offering is presented or an animal is sacrificed in order to appease or drive away the evil spirit. The Nuer pray for health and well-being, offering sacrifices to Kuoth so he will answer their petitions. There is no organized religious hierarchy or system, but many individuals serve as diviners and healers.

The Nuer own the Bieh State, a name which originated from the emerging days of Ngun-Deng Bong, the well known great prophet of Nuer. Bieh in the Nuer language means shrine of Nyun-Deng. It is a Holy place where Nuer people including the non-Nuer from all walks of life come periodically to Bieh for worship.

The Nuer do not believe in a place of after life for the spirit, and their religious concepts deal with concerns of this life. However, they do believe the spirits of the dead can affect their current life, with the more recently deceased having more influence. The Nuer honor and appease the spirits of their ancestors. Cattle are sacrificed to god and the spirits. As among the neighboring Dinka, religious thought and practice is a dialogue with Kuoth. The Nuer pray for health and well-being to Kuoth, offering sacrifices of cattle in hopeful expectation that their sentiments may be realized. Whereas many individuals become diviners and healers (*tiet*), there is no organized cult or hierarchy of religious functionaries. In most cases, other available medical resources are resorted to when spiritual healing does not bring about the desired outcome. Like other Nilotic peoples, the Nuer regard long-deceased ancestors with respect and veneration, but are concerned in their earthly lives with the power of the recently deceased to cause misfortune. Cattle play an important part in Nuer religion and ritual. Cows are dedicated to the ghosts of the owner's lineages and any personal spirits that may have possessed them at any time. The Nuer believe they establish contact with these ancestor ghosts and spirits by rubbing ashes along the backs of oxen or cows dedicated to them, through the sacrifice of cattle. No important Nuer ceremony of any kind is complete without such a sacrifice. There is also a widespread belief in the concept of the "evil eye," where a malevolent person possessing supernatural powers can cast a spell on someone just by gazing upon them.

Although Christian missionaries had worked in some Nuer areas for several decades, relatively few rural Nuer had converted before 1964, the year when all foreign church workers were expelled by the government. In the period of peace (1972–83), however, many new Christian congregations were formed and many Nuer, particularly in the east, converted to Christianity. The majority of Sudan's people, living in central and northern Sudan, are Muslims, and although some southerners have converted to Islam, recent reports suggest that the Nuer prefer their traditional faith or Christianity. The government of Sudan, especially in the period after Islamic Law was declared in 1983, tried to pressure the non-Muslim peoples of the south to convert to Islam. Since the Islamic-led government has more respect for Christianity than for traditional African religions like the Nuer religion, many Nuer have preferred to become Christians. This has made for many interesting social dilemmas among the Nuer. For example, when Christian and non-Christian Nuer socialize together, as when an animal is sacrificed for religious reasons and later eaten, they try to avoid conflict over beliefs by not referring to the major Divinity or by asserting that "Divinity is one"; that is, they express the belief that there is only one god, even if different people use different names and worship differently.

⁶ MAJOR HOLIDAYS

Until recently, most Nuer did not use dates to calculate the passage of time. Even during the 1970s, most Nuer did not know in what year they were born or how old they were. A woman might tell you her daughter was born "the year of the measles epidemic" or the year of a flood when they had had to eat a lot of *lalob* fruit. So instead of specific dates for annual holidays, people hold rituals and celebrations whenever they seem appropriate. For example, if a group of boys is ready to be initiated, it can be done at any time of the year, although it is most likely to take place at the end of the rainy season, after harvest, when people have the time and plenty of food has been stored.

⁷ RITES OF PASSAGE

A woman in childbirth is attended to by another woman, usually a close relative, who must herself be a mother. People are careful to protect the mother and newborn child from any spiritual danger by making sure that pregnant women or their husbands do not enter the house.

The Nuer nomenclature is rather complex. In some groups the child is named along the male lineage, but traced either through the mother or father's ancestry. A similar system gives the child the last name of the paternal grandfather's first name, the middle name being the father's first name, and the first or given name selected by the father. Christian children often have Biblical names and Sudanese names, used interchangeably. First names, when used, are commonly preceded by a title, like "Mr."

Among the Nuer, puberty is seen as the passage into adulthood and its responsibilities and is a marked occasion for both sexes. The Nuer do not circumcise either boys or girls, but they do practice certain other body modification rituals related to life transitions. For girls, passage from childhood to adulthood is marked by the first menstruation, at which time the mother prepares her for motherhood and home management.

For males, there is a complicated set of rituals which an entire village age-set progresses through, culminating in ritualized tattooings or scarifications across the forehead. In the past, nearly all boys (and, at least in some areas, girls, too) had their four lower incisors removed at about the age of eight. Aesthetically, this permanent loss of teeth was accompanied by efforts to force the top front teeth outward a little, so that the beautiful white teeth would be more visible in the smiling face. This "orthodontia" was for the purpose of making the children look more beautiful. More recently some families have refused to continue these practices.

Between the ages of 9 and 13, Nuer boys seek permission from their fathers to undergo a manhood initiation ritual. In the past, the boys were much older, about 14 to 16 during the 1930s and about 16 to 18 a century ago. They wait until a group grows to between 5 and 15 boys for mass initiation. The ritual requires extensive preparation of food, and the boys must be healthy and well fed prior to the ritual. On the chosen day, the boys' heads are shaved and anointed. The climax of the ritual is a ceremony in which the boys lie down in a row. Each in turn is cut with a knife by the scarifier, who makes six horizontal lines across the entire forehead and above the ears, all the way down to the bone. Although it is extremely painful, the boys try to show courage and remain silent. Parents and friends gather to watch. Loss of blood is a risk, and the wounds are sometimes cauterized to stop the bleeding.

After the cutting, the young men stay secluded together in a house while the scars are healing, lying for a time on their backs to keep the forehead upward. They can have unmarried people, nursing mothers, and old people as visitors, and they have nothing to do but eat porridge and milk, sleep, and play. Once they are considered healed (after some weeks), the young men are released and lead a procession to the river to bathe. They then return home and declare themselves men, and they and their families and guests celebrate with feasting, games, singing, and dancing. Traditionally the father of each initiate presents him with a spear, a fishing spear, and a bull from which he takes his "bull name." After this initiation, boys can begin to be sexually active and marry and they take on adult work roles. Those initiated in the same period of years have a very special friendship throughout life.

Some young men today do not want to undergo this ritual, under the influence of education and Christianity. Those who do not undergo the full manhood initiation are being called "bull boys," indicating that people know they are grown up, but do not recognize them as fully adult men who have proven their courage and been scarred like other Nuer.

The next significant transition rite is marriage. This usually follows a period of courtship when visits, poetry recitations, and other intimate exchanges give a couple a chance to decide whether they love each other. Incest is a taboo. If the parents agree to the marriage, the man's family must supply an agreed-upon number of cattle to the bride's family as a brideprice payment. In the old days when cattle were plentiful, the payment might be as many as 40 cows, but today marriages require fewer cattle due to the difficulties of civil war and migration. Some other valuables, such as money, can be substituted for some of the cows.

When a person dies, the corpse is laid to rest in a fetal position on a cowhide in a grave about four feet deep, then covered with another cowhide and buried. Families mourn for a few months, during which time close relatives do not wear ornaments. They then hold a ceremony in which one or two cattle are killed (both to honor the dead and to provide meat for a feast), purification rites are performed, lengthy speeches are made, prayers are offered, and people wash themselves and the possessions of the deceased and shave their heads. (Since almost everyone wears their hair short for cleanliness, it is not unusual for both men and women to shave their heads.) After these ceremonies people again wear ornaments.

8 INTERPERSONAL RELATIONS

Nuer place great value on behaving in a respectful way toward others, offering greetings to strangers and friends alike, and offering hospitality to travelers. It is not considered necessary to offer every visitor a meal, especially if there is no woman around at the moment (since men are not expected to cook for guests), but offering something to drink is important.

Wit, joking, and animated conversation are common among friends and as part of courtship. People generally show respect for their elders. Although men are in a social position somewhat superior to that of women, women have much personal freedom and make most of their own decisions about work, possessions, and interpersonal relations. Relative age is of great importance in interpersonal relationships, determining not only the terms of address but also the manner of acting with others. For example, men of the same "age set" will call each other "brother" and will act informally with one another. Alternatively, someone older than you is accorded utmost respect, and is referred to as "uncle" or "aunt," or even "father" or "mother" if related by blood.

The sharing of food forms a common bond among people. Leaders who extend hospitality and do not rely excessively on others are admired. Relatives are always expected to share food with each other. Newlyweds do not eat together until after the birth of their first child, when their two families are then considered more solidly related.

9 LIVING CONDITIONS

In rural areas, Nuer build round, one-room houses out of poles, which are plastered with an adobe-like mixture of mud and dung that dries into solid brown walls. The tall, pointed roofs are thatched with straw. Sometimes the doorways are built very small, so that one has to crouch or even crawl to enter, making it easier to barricade the door at night as protection against wild animals. Similar construction methods are used for the large cattle barns. During the rainy season, the cattle sleep inside, and many of the young men sleep in the rafters of the barns. Since there are many insects—flies by day and mosquitoes by night—smoky fires are lit near the cattle at night; both people (especially children) and animals are often smeared with ashes to keep some of the insects off. While people may look rather strange when newly covered, this is the only insect repellent available in the villages.

Villages do not have electricity or running water, so people must draw water from wells, rivers, or pools, and they make good use of natural light, rising early, and enjoying the warmth and glow of fires at night. Furniture is simple—mats, cowhides, logs for benches, and simple stools and headrests are common; and some people have wood-frame rope beds. For containers, pottery, aluminum pots, and bottles, as well as gourds and baskets, are ordinarily used.

The Nuer homeland is not hospitable for horses, camels, and donkeys, which are commonly ridden in other parts of Sudan, since they develop hoof problems during the rainy season. When people want to travel, they either walk or get a ride on top of the load carried by one of the large open trucks that travel the bumpy, rutted dirt roads of the region. During the rainy season, the roads cannot be used. Dugout canoes or rafts are used on the rivers.

The Nuer experience numerous difficulties in accessing medical care, although to different degrees depending on background factors like educational level exposure to biomedical care in Sudan. They routinely share over-the-counter medications or borrow prescription medicines from others to treat similar symptoms. This is a result of coping with chronic shortages of medicine and severely limited care facilities in Sudan, and of course it circumscribes expensive medical costs.

Herbal preventive and curative measures are particularly relied upon where there is no access to clinics. There are multiple herbal and traditional remedies used by Sudanese. For example, a widely used cure for migraine headaches is a certain chalky compound (clay, mixed with certain leaves and water), which is rubbed over the head. To relieve the symptoms of malaria, there is a certain root chewed like a stick. One common form is called *visi ri*, a bitter shrub that bends its shoot to follow the sun.

10 FAMILY LIFE

Each married woman has her own house where she and her young children live. The Nuer practice polygyny, so husbands can marry more than one wife if they can afford to. Husbands sleep in the houses of their wives (if they have more than one wife, they go to whichever they wish) or in the cattle barns with other men. Several married women's houses in an extended family may surround large family courtyards, or people can live separately. Houses are usually built near the fields where crops are grown, and often there are some good shade trees and a thicket or forest nearby which can provide firewood and other wild products.

Young children usually work with their parents, gradually learning skills such as milking, gardening, herding, spreading cow dung to dry for fuel, and caring for younger siblings. Fathers and mothers as well as grandparents and other relatives enjoy playing with children. The Nuer prefer to have large families with several children, but poor health conditions and the war have made it difficult for many of their children to survive. It is probably rare today for a mother to have more than three or four surviving children.

Families often have scrawny short-haired dogs that eat scraps and help protect the homestead. They usually do not receive much attention. In contrast, the cattle, although they are the main economic assets of a family, are treated in some ways like pets. People often try to make their cattle beautiful, as by working on their horns as they grow so as to give them interesting shapes, or by brushing the coats of the cattle or decorating their horns with tassels and beads. Sometimes people compose songs or poetry praising their beautiful cattle.

At the domestic level, a woman may, with luck, give birth to six children during her childbearing years. Co-wives do not necessarily reside in proximity. And when they do, the domestic unit can easily number more than a dozen individuals.

11 CLOTHING

The Nuer homeland is a hot climate, and for much of the year people do not need to wear much. Thirty years ago, a simple leather skirt or loincloth was all that a person needed while in his or her own village, although women usually had at least one good dress and both men and women wore capes or blankets tied over one shoulder when they traveled away from home. Currently, men and boys prefer to wear loose-fitting cotton shirts and shorts, while women and girls prefer colorful cotton dresses with perhaps a cape or a head scarf in addition.

Body decoration has always been important to the Nuer. Not only do they remove the lower front teeth, as noted above, but they also make decorative scars on the body in dotted patterns, especially on women's torsos, faces, and other parts of the body. Earrings are popular with both men and women, and the Nuer were doing multiple piercings of the ear long before it became popular in the West. Some people like to stretch the ear piercing with progressively larger plugs, working their way up to film canisters. One style is to loop stiff black giraffe hairs through ear piercings to make macramé-like decorations. Lip piercings decorated with metal ornaments are popular with some girls. For men especially, hair dyeing (especially orange) and patterned head shaving are popular, as is hair sculpture, with some arrangements made to look like cattle horns. Beautiful white beads are made from broken ostrich eggshells (found in ostrich nests), and these are made into stunning white necklaces and waistbands. Some people are skilled at fashioning ivory bracelets that both men and women like to wear on the wrists or upper arms. Ivory is not so common any more as the elephants have become scarce and cannot be hunted, so bone, cowrie shells, and imported plastic and glass ornaments have become more commonly used as jewelry.

Since Nuer have very dark skin, there is no tradition of tattooing, but people often mark their bodies in patterns made with temporary colorings (especially chalky white) for celebrations.

12 FOOD

The commonest daily foods for the Nuer are dairy products, especially milk for the young and soured milk, like yogurt, for adults. Liquid butter is also made from milk that is soured in long-necked gourds and shaken for an hour or so to separate out the fat. Since there are no refrigerators to chill the butter, it remains liquid and is used for cooking or poured onto cooked foods. Grains such as corn and sorghum are cooked and eaten with large spoons like hot cereal, with milk, yogurt, or butter. Apart from cow's milk, a soft porridge made from fermented sorghum, mixed with a sour fruit, is commonly used as a weaning food (as well as a food for the infirm or elderly). In the general diet, sorghum, prepared in many different ways, is the most common starch.

The Nuer do not eat meat very often; they prefer to keep their cattle alive, but on a special occasion one of the cattle may be sacrificed and then eaten. When a cow is killed, the meat is often shared with relatives and neighbors, and some of the extra meat is hung out to dry, like beef jerky, to preserve it for future use. Men and older boys normally carry spears with them when they walk around the countryside, in case they have a chance to hunt an antelope, gazelle, or other animal. If they are lucky, this can mean a delicious meat meal without anyone having to give up a cow.

Fish are eaten often during the dry season when the herds are taken to pasturelands near the rivers or pools left in low places as the floods recede. River fish trapped in pools are easy to catch as the waters dry up, so that even very young children can catch them by throwing fishing spears in shallow water. Boys 8 to 10 years old can bring home dinner for the whole family while they are out playing in the water on a hot day. At times when fish are plentiful, people can catch more than they need and sun-dry the extras to sell or save for later in the year. Drying gives fish a sour, tangy, flavor that is an acquired taste.

Various vegetables—squash, tomatoes, chili peppers—are grown and cooked, generally in pots on outdoor fires. Vegetables and greens, both wild and cultivated, make up a large proportion of the traditional diet, with meats including freshwater fish, and chicken (although chickens are generally more valued for egg production).

Another very nourishing food that is an acquired taste is cooked cow blood. A small amount of blood can be taken from the neck of a healthy animal without harming it. When cooked, it becomes solid, like the blood sausage eaten by some Europeans, and eating it is somewhat like eating a hunk of bologna.

Wild fruits and nuts are favorite snacks. The most popular food is wild honey, but it is hard to find. A favorite of older people during the dry season—when there is not much work to do and plenty of grain has been harvested—is homemade beer. It looks more like a thin porridge and is very cool and filling, but only mildly alcoholic. Most younger people seem to consider beer drinking in the shade of a tree a rather boring way to spend an afternoon, and since they take pride in being healthier, stronger, and less decadent than their elders, they do not drink beer. Similarly, the pipe tobacco that is raised seems to be smoked mainly by older married men and women.

13 EDUCATION

Most Nuer children today still do not have the opportunity to attend school, since the few rural schools that once existed were destroyed or disrupted by the civil war. However, concerted efforts are being made by both the Government of Southern Sudan and the international community ever since the signing of the Peace Agreement in 2005, to improve the education sector as part of the reconstruction program. Many Nuer are still returning home from refugee status. As refugees go back home they have to reconstruct their individual and family lives and it is common for children to try to support themselves by selling things in the streets or looking for jobs.

Long before the civil war, some missionary schools taught children to read their own language; they also learned English, the language of their colonial power (Britain), and then Arabic. Thus among the educated Nuer in the older generation, many are able to speak, read, and write three languages. But the vast majority of Nuer men and women, although they speak Nuer and often also Arabic, are illiterate.

However most of the Nuer who were able to secure asylum in North America, Western Europe, Australia, and Kenya, for instance, have been able to access education in special programs.

For instance some of the Nuer refugees in Kenya were allowed to attend the same classrooms as other Kenyan children.

¹⁴ CULTURAL HERITAGE

Nuer music consists mainly of singing. People sing songs they have composed, sometimes accompanying themselves on a simple instrument like the so-called African thumb piano (a small, hollow wooden box with metal tines of different lengths that give different pitches when they are twanged). The *rababa*, a rural Sudanese stringed instrument, is also often used, in a homemade form made from simple materials: a gallon can, wooden rods, and wires for strings. Whistles and bells are also used in music and dance, but the human voice is the most popular musical instrument. Some songs are widely known and sung in unison, but most are solos. The Nuer do not sing in harmony. Some songs are very rhythmic, and others are more pensive and chantlike. Dancing is usually accompanied by singing and is mostly done for fun.

Written literature is rare, since a system for writing the Nuer language was not developed until the 1930s. But oral literature is well developed, with songs and poetic prophecies passed down through memorization from generation to generation.

¹⁵ WORK

Nuer who live in the rural areas must know how to do many types of work just to survive, for they have only themselves to rely on. Children and young men and women herd the cattle. Adult men are responsible for many other tasks and decisions involved in caring for the cattle, as well as slaughtering and butchering. Women and children usually milk the cattle and goats, and women make dairy products. Both men and women grow crops, cultivating with hoes, and children help them. Women process grain, cook food, and brew beer. All adults participate in various aspects of building and repairing houses. Men hunt with spears and sometimes find honey, and everyone gathers wild fruits or nuts when they find them.

For Nuer men living in cities—as many do for at least part of their lives—the most common type of work for pay has been in the construction industry. Often the whole family may live at a construction site for a few months while Nuer workers put the wooden frames, bricks, and mortar of a high-rise building into place. The goal of this urban work is often to save money for buying more cattle when the family returns home.

¹⁶ SPORTS

The popularity of soccer has spread to many areas, but children usually do not have real soccer balls and have to improvise with whatever they can find.

¹⁷ ENTERTAINMENT AND RECREATION

Children and young teenagers often play with small objects they have made from mud, which contains much clay. Because they are cattle herders, Nuer children often form the mud into cows and bulls. In the last several years, with their experience of war, many children have begun to mold rifles with the mud. Given the warm climate, squirt guns would probably be popular, but there are few plastic or other manufactured toys. In addition to the objects made from mud, there are carved wooden animals and rag dolls.

Older teenagers enjoy singing and dancing, especially around the evening campfires. In one particularly athletic dance style, young men repeatedly leap rhythmically straight up into the air as high as they can, trying to make their movements seem nonchalant and effortless. Girls and boys dance as individuals in a group or with partners. Young men and women sometimes sing personal songs to try to attract many dance partners of the opposite sex. In some areas, a popular dance style for young men is a mock duel, in which one dancer "accidentally" leaps backwards and bumps into a young woman whose attention he is trying to get.

People make themselves as attractive as possible for dances, often decorating themselves with flamboyantly colored leggings and beads and carrying special dance rods, flashlights, or other fancy portable trade goods, even including books. One popular type of dance skirt for women and girls is made with twisted grass ropes that hang from the waist to just above the knees and may be decorated with cattle tails or small bells. For dancing, men and boys wear tight shorts, especially ones with pockets, and go shirtless. Sometimes dancers use simple body paints that imitates cattle markings, and they may even decorate a cow or two for a special occasion.

Nuer also enjoy games, including the two-player game of distributing small stones or mud tokens in rows of pits hollowed in the ground, and attempting to win more pieces than the opponent. This game, which is played in many parts of Sudan and other parts of Africa, can be played by people from different cultures who cannot understand each other's language.

¹⁸ FOLK ART, CRAFTS, AND HOBBIES

The Nuer in rural areas have always been fairly self-sufficient, making and decorating many of their own household items. The carved headrest is probably the most common piece of furniture for the Nuer, something that is light and easy to carry when they hike to the cattle camps but which makes it much more comfortable to lie on a mat or cowhide on the ground. Some people are very skilled at making decorated pottery and the bowls for pipes, while others make aesthetically pleasing and highly functional baskets. Smiths process scrap metals into beautiful spoons shaped like the old-fashioned cattle-horn spoons, make spear heads, decorate pipe stems with brass, and fashion bracelets.

¹⁹ SOCIAL PROBLEMS

The ongoing post-war resettlement and reconstruction is the main challenge facing the contemporary Nuer people. Many had lost their homes or had to escape the fighting by moving to other countries or to cities. Some had been captured by neighboring hostile groups and forced to work or become part of their captors' families. Others had undergone military training at an early age, deepening the "culture of violence" that has led to small arms proliferation in Nuerland. Others have been psychologically scarred by the tragedies of war and displacement threatens to displace some of their more positive traditional values. Cultural erosion which condemns the immorality in Nuer ancestral life is now being replaced with the culture of unjust banditry and other similar activities. For the Nuer living in cities, poverty, sickness, and insecurity are daily problems. For all of these Nuer, a peaceful and just implementation of the January 2005 Peace Agreement are a major part of their hope for the future.

[20] GENDER ISSUES

Nuer domestic groups are based on the ideals of patrilateral descent. Each Nuer village typically contained a patrilineage segment, some of the in-laws of the "ruling" males and an adopted Dinka lineage. The male elders are the "bulls" of the village. People named hamlets or villages after the numerically dominant patrilineal group.

During marriage, cattle and women are—and have always been—the central objects of reproductive exchange and hallmarks of the distinctive Nuer culture. This is seen in the transfer of cattle at the bride wealth exchange, which is considered crucial for the reproduction and survival of the agnatic line. Through the second half of the 20th century, the range of exchangeable objects expanded to include weapons and cash. For instance, bridewealth negotiations were traditionally settled with what Hutchinson refers to as "cattle of girls" (i.e., cattle collectively acquired through the agnatic line's exchange of daughters).

Women, as expected by the society, take pride in the number of children they bear.

Polygyny and wife inheritance are practiced. A man may marry additional wives depending on his economic ability. Widows usually remarry one of their husband's close relatives (such as a brother), without any additional bride wealth. Co-wives, however, do not necessarily reside in proximity; the bride is relocated in the husband's natal family following her intermarriages. Patrilateral residence at marriage further consolidates the patrilineal structure of Nuer communities.

Childrearing is traditionally the responsibility of all the women in the village; while the father takes considerable pleasure in his children, discipline is the responsibility of the mother.

[21] BIBLIOGRAPHY

Burton, J. W. "Nuer." *Encyclopedia of World Cultures*. Boston: G.K. Hall and Co., Vol. IX, 1995.

Carisle, R. *The Illustrated Encyclopedia of Mankind*. N.Y.: Marshall Cavendish, 1990.

Crazzolara, J.P. *Outlines of a Nuer Grammar*. St. Gabriel, Modling bei Wien, Oesterreich: Verlag der Internationalen Zeitschrift "Anthropos", 1933.

Deborah, S. *Emma's War*. New York: Pantheon Books, 2004.

Evans-Pritchard, E. E. *Kinship and Marriage Among the Nuer*. Oxford: Oxford University Press, 1951.

———. *The Nuer: A Description of the Modes of Livelihood and Political Institutions of a Nilotic People*. Oxford: Oxford University Press, 1940.

———. *Nuer Religion*. Oxford: Oxford University Press, 1956.

Frank, W. J. *Nuer Noun Morphology*. Buffalo, NY: SUNY: Unpublished M.A. Thesis, 1999.

Holtzman, J. *Nuer Journeys, Nuer Lives: Sudanese Refugees in Minnesota*. Boston: Allyn and Bacon, 2000.

———. *Nuer Journeys, Nuer Lives*. Boston: Pearson Education, Inc., 2007.

Huffman, R. *Nuer Customs and Folklore*. London: Franks Cass & Co. Ltd., 1931.

Hutchinson, S. *Nuer Dilemmas: Coping with Money, War, and the State*. Berkeley: University of California Press, 1996.

Johnson, D. H. *Nuer Prophets: A History of Prophecy from the Upper Nile in the Nineteenth and Twentieth Centuries*. Oxford: Oxford University Press, 1994.

Kulan, G. and Gatluak, P. *Nuer-English Dictionary*. Nairobi: Sudan Literature Centre, 1999.

Malakal Language Conference. *Rudiments of Nuer Grammar: Decisions of Malakal Language Conference Held at Malakal, Sudan in February, 1944*. Yambio, Sudan: 1950.

Rejaf Language Conference. *Report of Proceedings Held at Rejaf, Mongalla Province, Sudan, 9th to 14th April, 1929*. London: Sudan Government, 1928.

Sanderson, L. *Education, Religion & Politics in Southern Sudan 1899–1964*. London: Ithaca Press, 1981.

Shandy, D. *Nuer-American Passages: Globalizing Sudanese Migration*. Gainesville: University Press of Florida, 2007.

Vandevort, E. *A Leopard Tamed: The Story of an African Pastor, his People, and his Problems*. New York: Harper & Row, 1968.

Yigezu, M. "The Nuer Vowel System." *Journal of African Languages and Linguistics*, Vol. 16, pp. 157-70, 1995.

—revised by M. Njoroge

NYAMWEZI

PRONUNCIATION: nyahm-WAY-zee
ALTERNATE NAMES: Wanyamwezi
LOCATION: Unyamwezi (Tanzania: Provinces of Tabora and Shinyunga, Northwest central, between Lake Victoria and Lake Rukwa)
POPULATION: 1.5 million
LANGUAGE: Kinyamwezi; Nyamwesi; Kiswahili (Tanzania's national language); English; languages of neighboring ethnic groups
RELIGION: spirituality shaped by traditional beliefs; Islam; and Christianity
RELATED ARTICLES: Vol. 1: Tanzanians

¹ INTRODUCTION

The Nyamwezi people, or the Wanyamwezi, live in the East African country of Tanzania. (The country of Tanzania was created when Tanganyika and the island of Zanzibar formed a union in 1964. Before German colonial occupation in the late 1890s there was no geographical entity known as Tanganyika.) They are the second largest of over 120 ethnic groups in Tanzania. Their home area, Unyamwezi, which means "the place of the Wanyamwezi," is located in the western plateau area of the Tanzanian provinces of Tabora and Shinyanga, south of Lake Victoria and east of Lake Tanganyika. While this is considered the traditional homeland of the Wanyamwezi, many Wanyamwezi work in the commercial and agricultural centers of Tanzania.

In trying to understand Nyamwezi culture, it is important to remember that it is not static or insulated from broader political and economic changes that have affected the larger Tanzanian society. Nyamwezi society and culture have been dynamic, constantly evolving to meet the changing environment. Over the years, Nyamwezi culture has both influenced and been influenced by the cultures of neighboring African societies as well as the national Tanzanian culture. Islam and Christianity have also had a great impact on modern Nyamwezi cultural practices. According to oral tradition, the Nyamwezi are thought to have settled in west central Tanzania (their present location) sometime in the 1600s. The earliest evidence comes from the Galahansa and confirms their presence there in the late 1600s.

The notion held by many Europeans during the colonial era, that the Nyamwezi were an ethnically uniform tribe ruled by a chief, did not fit the realities of Nyamwezi life. Even though the Wanyamwezi shared a common language and culture, they did not see themselves as one people and they were never united into one political entity that corresponded with the boundaries of their cultural group. The Wanyamwezi speak three distinct dialects of their Kinyamwezi language and are made up of four distinct subgroups, the Wagalaganza, the Sagala, the Kahama, and the Iguluibi. Each group claims to descend from its own special ancestor. The largest group, the Wagalaganza, consisted of thirty states in the 1860s. Culturally and linguistically, there is very little that separates the Wanyamwezi from their neighbors, including the Wasukuma, who are the largest ethnic group in Tanzania (more than 5 million or 13% of the population). Before the onset of colonial rule, all people who

were part of the present day Sukuma, Sumbwa, and Nyamwezi ethnic groups were called Nyamwezi by outsiders to the region.

The term *Nyamwezi* probably meant either "people of the moon" or "path of the moon," most likely referring to their location in the Western part of Tanzania. In the Nyamwezi language, *Sukuma* means "north," and the Wasukuma were those who lived north of Unyamwezi. Perhaps the best way to characterize Nyamwezi identity before colonialism would be as an ethnic category, meaning that the people shared a common language and culture without a sense of self-identification.

The Wanyamwezi are believed to have migrated during the 16th and 17th centuries from various parts of east and central Africa to their homeland in western Tanzania. The first Nyamwezi settlers formed small communities that grew into larger kingdoms ruled by a *mtemi*, or king. Prior to the 1860s, Nyamwezi states tended to be small, usually numbering a few thousand persons. They had no standing armies and depended on the men of the society to defend their country from raids or to raid neighboring states. These raids and counter raids were aimed at capturing grain, cattle, and other goods or avenging a wrong done by one state or ruler to another. Prior to the 1860s, it was unusual for one state to use military power to impose its authority over another. However, in the years leading up to the 1860s Nyamwezi societies began to undergo important changes.

The Wanyamwezi were well-known traders in the pre-colonial era and played an important role in developing the region's trade. They pioneered caravan routes throughout east and central Africa, while Nyamwezi trading settlements spread throughout central Tanzania. It is the Nyamwezi who are said to have established the caravan routes to the coast that were later used by Swahili and Arab traders and European explorers, including Dr. David Livingstone, Henry Morton Stanley, Richard Burton, and John Hanning Speke. In the years leading up to the 1860s, trade with the coastal areas became increasingly important. As trade developed with the coast, one of the Nyamwezi states, Unyanyembe, became a prosperous trading center. Unyanyembe used its wealth to become the most powerful state in Unyamwezi. Soon after the rise of Unyanyembe, a rival state under the leadership of the famous mtemi Mirambo challenged Unyanyembe's control over the caravan routes. Unlike Unyanyembe, which used its control over trade to increase its military power, Mirambo was a great military tactician who used force to enhance his country's trading position. Mirambo can be thought of as a Nyamwezi nationalist with the vision of a unified Nyamwezi people. However, Mirambo was unable to conquer Unyanyembe and failed to build a united Nyamwezi nation-state. After Mirambo's death in 1884, Urambo split into a number of smaller kingdoms.

The onset of colonial rule brought many important changes for Nyamwezi society. For the first time the Wanyamwezi, along with the 140 other African ethnic groups in Tanzania, were united under one government. The German colonial occupation of Tanzania was very brutal. During the 1880s and 1890s Germany conducted a series of military operations throughout Tanzania with the aim of establishing a colony. Vicious reprisal raids against African areas that resisted German authority characterized German military campaigns. Often the Germans depended on local allies in their wars and raids. The first German military expedition arrived in Unyamwezi in

1890. Although it did not spark an immediate confrontation, it planted the seeds for a future German military conquest of Unyamwezi. Its commander, Emin Pasha, allied himself with the opponents of the mtemi Isike of Unyanyembe.

In 1892, another German expedition reached Unyanyembe and, acting on reports from Pasha and Isike's enemies, launched a series of attacks on Isike's headquarters, *Isiunula* (the "impregnable" fort). Isike's fortress proved to be well named, as the European attackers were defeated three times by Isike's troops. Later, in December of 1892, the Germans sent their best military officer, Lieutenant Tom von Prince, to fight Isike. Prince formed alliances with the son of Mirambo, Katukamoto, who ruled what was left of Urambo, and Bibi Nyaso, an internal opponent of Isike from Unyanyembe.

Using German African troops and the forces of Isike's enemies, Prince was able to capture Isiunula. Rather than being captured by the Germans, Isike unsuccessfully tried to commit suicide by blowing himself up with his ammunition dump. After the Germans stormed the fort, they hanged his nearly lifeless body from the closest tree and shot his young son. The Germans then made Bibi Nyaso the mtemi of Unyanyembe. The killing of Isike, however, did not bring Unyamwezi fully under German control; for two years after the attack on Isiunula, Isike's chief minister, Swetu, led a guerrilla war against the Germans. Swetu was eventually forced to retreat from Unyanyembe, bringing an end to Nyamwezi armed resistance to German colonial rule. Ironically, Mirambo's son, Katukamoto, who used the Germans to defeat his rival Isike, was later imprisoned by his onetime ally in 1898. The Germans then broke up the remaining parts of Urambo and appointed their own mtemi to rule it.

In many respects the European colonialists in Tanzania used the "take us to your king" approach to rule Tanzania, and where no king existed the Europeans created one. For example, in nearby Usandawe, Mtoro, the leader of a Nyamwezi trading settlement, was appointed chief of the Sandawe people. The Wasandawe had no supreme leader or king and authority was dispersed throughout society. These types of African societies were difficult for Europeans to understand and to incorporate into their colonial administration. In Usandawe, the Germans mistakenly thought that the Wanyamwezi settlers were an immigrant ruling class, much as the Germans saw themselves in Tanzania. However, the Nyamwezi trading center was more of an enclave that the Wasandawe tolerated but did not particularly like.

When the Germans appointed Mtoro the headman of the Wasandawe, the Wasandawe showed their displeasure by expelling the Wanyamwezi settlers from their territory and taking their cattle. In response, the Germans launched two punitive expeditions against the Wasandawe. The first force killed 800 Wasandawe without suffering any casualties, and the second confiscated over 1,000 head of cattle, most of which were given to the displaced Wanyamwezi settlers. Under German protection the Wanyamwezi returned to their settlement. But when the German soldiers left Usandawe, they were attacked by the Wasandawe, who also raided the Wanyamwezi settlers. The Germans responded by launching a bloody war against the Wasandawe that finally established their authority in the area.

Colonial rule in Unyamwezi and throughout Tanzania was based on physical violence and a racial hierarchy in which Africans were segregated into a rural and urban underclass.

Nyamwezi *watemi* (watemi is the plural of mtemi) were made responsible to German colonial authorities. Nyamwezi leaders who did not suit the Germans were removed. The Germans forced watemi to collect taxes and to supply men to labor on European plantations or public-works projects such as roads and railroads. These activities often made African leaders who cooperated with the Germans unpopular with their people, for the conditions for African laborers were very harsh, including whippings, beatings, and the withholding of food and wages. However, African leaders who resisted the Germans faced the threat of being deposed, arrested, or exiled, or possibly of exposing their societies to brutal retaliatory raids by the Germans. The goal of the Germans was to reduce the authority of the *watemi* and to administer Unyamwezi directly through German colonial officials.

German rule was deeply resented. One of the notable acts of resistance to colonial rule was the Maji-Maji rebellion, which engulfed Tanzania from 1905 to 1907. A prophet named Kinjikitile, who called on the African people to take up arms to expel the Germans, inspired the rebellion. Specially trained assistants who traveled throughout Tanzania spread Kinjikitile's message. While historians believe that many Wanyamwezi supported Kinjikitile, Unyamwezi did not erupt in violence against the colonialists, as did the southern and coastal regions.

After World War I, Britain replaced the defeated Germany in Tanzania. Britain inherited Tanzania as a League of Nations Trust Territory. As such, Tanzania was to be administered to the benefit of the African inhabitants, but in practice, British administration of the territory was characterized by racial segregation.

While the Germans aspired to administer Tanzania directly without going through traditional or indigenous leaders, the British strove to create a system of local government, called "indirect rule," which incorporated "tribal" units of government into the colonial administration. Like the Germans, British colonial authorities believed that all Africans belonged to a tribe, just as all Europeans belonged to a nation. They viewed the tribe as a cultural and political unit with a common language, a single social system, established customary law, hereditary membership, and a chief. But the realities of African social structures often did not match European conceptions, and African societies were restructured, and sometimes invented, by colonial authorities. In Unyamwezi, the British followed a policy of amalgamating smaller Nyamwezi states into larger ones to create larger administrative units. For example, the British subordinated a number of smaller Nyamwezi states into Unyanyembe. They also replaced the ruling line of Bibi Nyaso as *mtemi* of Unyanyembe with a descendant of Isike, in order to avenge Bibi Nyaso's collaboration with the Germans. Under British rule, Africans were denied the right to participate in politics or public administration outside of "tribal" government.

Conflicts between chiefs and Arab traders lasted through the last half of the 19th century. Chiefs such as Isike and Mirambo, no longer being purely ritual, had found that the arrival of firearms enabled them to establish standing armies and a new state organization. It was firearms and trade that transformed the region, for trade generated the wealth needed to obtain firearms. Chiefs were normally ritual figures who had no very rigid rules of succession. They lived very restricted lives, with the most significant duties being carried out by headmen. They were strangled when they became seriously ill (as probably happened to Mirambo while dying of cancer) for the well being of the state and its continuation was identified with chief and his subordinate administrators. A hierarchy of territorial offices came into being. There were sub-chiefs, assistant chiefs, headmen elders, ritual officials, etc., as each dynasty seized power from another. Greater Nyamwezi had become a war zone.

Colonialism brought about a fundamental change in the way the Wanyamwezi perceived themselves. Many Wanyamwezi, fighting against the racism associated with colonial rule, which portrayed Africans as primitive, culturally backward, and unfit for independence, directed their energies into promoting their cultural traditions, writing histories, and developing feelings of Nyamwezi identity. While a shared language and culture, which provided the foundation for building an ethnic group, had existed in Unyamwezi since the early 1800s, it was not until the onset of the colonial era that the Wanyamwezi began to see themselves as one people. In the towns, the Wanyamwezi formed ethnic associations to help their members find work, organize and conduct funerals, write letters for the illiterate, and help in other ways in times of need. One of the first Nyamwezi urban associations was "The New Wanyamwezi Association," formed in 1936 in Dar es Salaam. The organization reflected the loose sense of Nyamwezi identity and was open to all people from the western plateau, including the Sukuma and Sumbwa.

Many Wanyamwezi, like Tanzanians of other ethnic groups, played important roles in the struggle for independence. The brother of the chief of Unyanyembe, Abdallah Fundikira, was an early leader of the Tanzania National African Union (TANU), the political party that spearheaded the fight for Tanzanian independence. Many Wanyamwezi became labor leaders after workers gained the right to form labor unions during the midst of the independence struggle in the 1950s.

While numerous traditional leaders including Abdallah Fundikira supported TANU, many others did not and sided with colonial authorities. After independence the role of traditional leaders in local government was abolished by TANU, which was interested in developing a national culture that helped people to identify with the new nation, rather than promoting sub-national identities.

Tanzania like many modern African states embraces a democratic system of Government with multiparty competitive elections and a free-market economy. The Wanyamwezi participate actively in the political process of Tanzania. A number of Wanyamwezi have emerged as leaders of the opposition parties and have played important roles in the ruling party, CCM (Chama cha Mapinduzi/Party of the Revolution, formerly known as TANU).

2 LOCATION AND HOMELAND

The Nyamwezi make up about 4% of the Tanzanian population and number around 1,500,000. They live in the northwest central area of the country, between Lake Victoria and Lake Rukwa. Unyamwezi is located in a high plateau area with elevations ranging from about 900 to 1,375 meters (about 3,000 to 4,500 feet). Much of the land is covered by dry woodland with strings of ridges and numerous granite outcroppings. Most of Unyamwezi is not considered prime agricultural land. Water

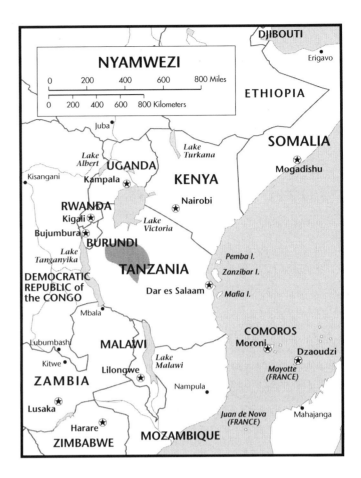

is often scarce. From April to October, very little rain falls and the rivers often dry up. The rainy season lasts from October to April and is characterized by wide variations in yearly rainfall. Unlike some of the more fertile agricultural regions, which have two growing seasons, Unyamwezi has only one. The major city in Unyamwezi is Tabora, a famous pre-colonial trading center and former colonial administrative center. Tanzanians of various ethnic groups live in Unyamwezi. Many Wasukuma, Wasumbwa, and Watusi live throughout Unyamwezi, and even in some rural areas, non-Wanyamwezi may make up as much as 73% of the population. Many small shop owners in the rural areas are Arabs, as there are many people in Tabora. There are also a number of Asian Tanzanians, whose ancestors came from India and Pakistan, living in the larger commercial centers of Unyamwezi. About 30% of the Nyamwezi live and work outside Unyamwezi, mainly in neighboring areas and in the coastal regions.

3 LANGUAGE

Historically, there have been five tribal groups, all referring to themselves as Wanyamwezi to outsiders: Kimbu, Nyamwezi, Sukuma, and Sumbwa, who were never united. All groups normally merged have broadly similar cultures, although it is an oversimplification to view them as a single group. The Nyamwezi have close cultural ties with the Sukuma people. Their homeland is called Unyamwezi, and they speak the language Kinyamwezi, although many also speak Swahili or English. Many Wanyamwezi can speak at least three languages. Most are also fluent in Kiswahili, Tanzania's national language. Many Wanyamwezi are also able to speak English and the languages of neighboring ethnic groups, such as Kisukuma, the language of the Sukuma people.

Kiswahili has borrowed many words from Kinyamwezi, and vice versa. For example, the Kiswahili term for the president's residence is *Ikulu*, which is the Kinyamwezi word for the mtemi's residence. Kinyamwezi has about 84% lexical similarity with Sukuma, 61% with Sumbwa, and 56% with Nilamba.

⁴ FOLKLORE

One of the most important historical figures for the Wanyamwezi is the mtemi Mirambo. Mirambo was the mtemi of a small state in Unyamwezi called Uyowa. By the time of his death, he had created a central African empire that incorporated the greater part of Unyamwezi. Mirambo was a brilliant military tactician, known for his fierceness in battle. Ironically, the inspiration for the innovations that made Mirambo's army a powerful fighting force came from an early battlefield defeat. After failing to conquer a neighboring state, Mirambo decided to reorganize his army. Mirambo asked a neighboring chief to train his army in Ngoni fighting techniques, which were based on the style of warfare pioneered by Shaka Zulu of South Africa. It was said that Mirambo acquired his name, which means "corpses" in Kinyamwezi, from his Ngoni allies who marveled at the large number of people he killed in battle. Mirambo was so feared throughout Unyamwezi that mothers would stop their children from crying by telling them, *"Hulikaga, Limilambo likwiza"* ("Be quiet, Mirambo is coming").

Mirambo created a standing army called *rugaruga*, which was organized into regiments of similar-aged soldiers. Soldiers between 20 and 30 years of age formed the backbone of the *rugaruga*. They were not allowed to have wives, children, or houses and lived with Mirambo inside his fortress capital, Iselemagazi. These young *rugaruga* were used on campaigns to conquer other states and to raid for cattle, slaves, and property. The young *rugaruga* wore red cloth often decorated with feathers or human hair said to have been shaved off their fallen victims. The *rugaruga* were armed with pistols, muzzle-loading rifles, spears, bows and arrows, and shields. Before battle, Mirambo's soldiers would eat meat specially prepared by ritual experts and smoke *bhangi* (Indian hemp, or marijuana). Older, more experienced soldiers were mainly used for defensive purposes and organized into units called *sinhu*. They were allowed to marry and have their own houses. A special king's guard, wearing black uniforms and turbans, was created to protect Mirambo during battle.

After reorganizing his army, Mirambo conquered and raided the other Nyamwezi states as well as nearby non-Nyamwezi states. Success on the battlefield led to a rapid expansion of Mirambo's *rugaruga*, which grew from a few hundred in the 1860s to 10,000 by the 1880s. The fear of Mirambo's *rugaruga* led many states to voluntarily accept Urambo rule. Leaders who aligned their states with Urambo were allowed to continue as leaders of their territory, but those who fought against Urambo were killed

Mirambo used military force to take control of the caravan routes leading west to Lake Tanzania, over which ivory and slaves passed, as well as the caravan routes heading north to Lake Victoria and the markets in Buganda, Bunyoro and the other large kingdoms in the lakes region. Mirambo's kingdom grew in size and power to the point of rivaling Unyanyembe, the dominant Nyamwezi state of the time. Urambo blocked Unyanyembe's access to important markets to the west and north. Feeling their position threatened by Mirambo, the merchants in Tabora and the leaders of Unyanyembe invited dissidents from Urambo to train their army in Mirambo's military tactics. The growing tension between Urambo and Unyanyembe caused Mirambo to close the caravan routes to traders from Unyanyembe. Hostilities broke into open warfare in 1871, when Unyanyembe attacked Urambo. After reaching far into Mirambo's territory, Unyanyembe's army was successfully ambushed by Mirambo's forces. Mirambo then attacked Tabora. Mirambo was unable to conquer Unyanyembe, however.

Mirambo's war with Unyanyembe interrupted trade and angered the large Arab and Indian commercial houses on the coast. In an effort to defeat Mirambo militarily, the Sultan of Zanzibar sent three thousand troops to help Unyanyembe. However, the Tabora Arabs refused to cooperate with the leader of the troops, and the troops were withdrawn. On the coast, the Sultan enforced sanctions against Mirambo, especially with regard to firearms and gunpowder. To evade sanctions, Mirambo entered into blood brotherhoods with European missionaries, traders, and explorers and asked them to trade his goods on the coast. Mirambo died in 1884 while on a campaign against the Nyamwezi state of Ukune. After Mirambo's death, the component states of Urambo reasserted their independence and his empire broke up.

The historical importance of Mirambo lies in the fact that he was a brilliant military leader and diplomat who was able to deal with Europeans from a position of strength and use Europeans to further his own interests. The example of Mirambo challenged the basic assumptions on which European colonial rule in Africa was built.

In honor of the important historical role played by Mirambo, his grave was made a national monument by the government after independence. A major street in the nation's capital, Dar es Salaam, and the military garrison at Tabora were also named after him. One of Mirambo's war songs, *"Ohoo Chuma chabela mitwe"* ("Iron has broken heads"), was adopted by Julius Nyerere, Tanzania's first president, who changed the words and used it to inspire the young nation. However, one major difference existed between Mirambo and the nationalist movement. While Mirambo was dedicated to creating a great Nyamwezi kingdom through the force of arms, the nationalist movement was geared toward creating an independent Tanzania through peaceful means. The violence associated with Mirambo has lessened to some extent, his suitability as a hero for modern Tanzania.

⁵ RELIGION

Traditional beliefs, Islam, and Christianity have shaped Nyamwezi spirituality. Most follow a traditional religion, despite conversion attempts by Islam and Christianity. They believe in a powerful god called Likube (High God), Limatunda (Creator), Limi (the Sun) and Liwelolo (the Universe), but ancestor worship is a more frequent daily practice. Traditional Nyamwezi spirituality centers on the connection between the living and their ancestors. Ancestors are seen as upholding the tradition, law, and values of society. The spirits of the ancestors are believed to be capable of intervening into the affairs of the living, either to show their pleasure or, more commonly, to show their anger. Not honoring one's ancestors is a sign of disrespect for Nyamwezi culture and tradition and is bound to lead to adverse consequences, usually sickness.

Offerings of sheep or goats are made to ancestors, and the help of Likube is invoked beforehand. Spirits also play an active role in Nyamwezi religious life, with mfumu, witchdoctors, or diviners, playing the role of counselor and medical practitioner. Bulogi (witchcraft) is a powerful force in Nyamwezi culture, with cults forming around (for example) possession by certain types of spirit. The Baswezi society recruits people possessed by the Swezi spirit.

With the main exceptions of the villages around Tabora and of areas around some Christian missions, neither Islam nor Christianity has flourished strongly among villagers. Religion in the area, like society itself, is accretive rather than exclusive.

Beliefs in a High God are widely held but involve no special cult. Ancestor worship is the main element in the religious complex. Chiefs' ancestors are thought to influence the lives of the inhabitants of their domains, but ordinary ancestors only affect their own descendants. Belief in witchcraft is widespread and strong.

In addition to the High God and the ancestors, some nonancestral spirits are believed to influence some people's lives. Spirit-possession societies, such as the Baswezi, deal with such attacks and recruit the victims into membership. As a link between belief and action, the diviner (mfumu) is a key figure in religious life; diviners interpret the belief system for individuals and groups. They decide which forces are active and help people to deal with them. Although it is not strictly an hereditary art, people often take up divination when a misfortune is diagnosed as having been induced by a diviner ancestor who wishes them to do so. There are often several diviners in a village, but only one or two are likely to attract a wide clientele. All diviners, like their neighbors, engage in farming and participate fully in village life.

Divination takes many forms, the most common being chicken divination, in which a young fowl is killed and readings are taken from its wings and other features. Sacrifices and libations, along with initiation into a spirit-possession or other society, may result from a divinatory séance. Divination and subsequent rituals may divide people, especially if witchcraft is diagnosed, but in many contexts the system allows villagers to express their solidarity with each other without loss of individual identity. In addition to ritual focused upon individuals and attended by their kin and neighbors, there is some public ceremonial at village and wider levels. Chiefly rituals are still sometimes performed, and there are ceremonies to cleanse a village of pollution when a member dies.

Likewise, the inability to live socially with family and friends is liable to cause the ancestors to intervene. Relations with the ancestors and respect for Nyamwezi traditions are maintained through ritual activity such as animal sacrifices and other ceremonies. These activities are overseen by diviners, who act as spiritual advisers for the Wanyamwezi, interpreting events and determining which spirits are involved and what rituals should be followed to restore balance in people's lives. Both men and women can become diviners, many of whom are self-taught, having worked through their own serious spiritual difficulties.

During pre-colonial times, spirituality underscored the mtemi's power. The mtemi was seen as the embodiment of the law of the ancestors on earth. He was mediator in the relationship between the living and their ancestors and had an important ceremonial role. Each inhabitant of a Nyamwezi country was seen as the child of his or her own ancestors and a child of the royal ancestors. The mtemi would oversee royal spiritual ceremonies directed toward the former watemi, societal heroes, and legendary diviners. The relationship between a community and its ancestors was very important. Breaks in this relationship could lead to ancestors' showing their displeasure with the mtemi or society through some calamity such as drought or military defeat.

Nyamwezi spirituality fulfills two needs. First, it is practical in that rituals are designed to help people diagnose the source of their problems and offer solutions. For example, diviners will tell people the cause of their sickness and what ceremonies to perform to restore a balance in their lives. Secondly, Nyamwezi spirituality centers on giving a moral meaning to people's problems. It focuses on how people can live at peace with themselves and with those around them.

Although Nyamwezi religion emphasizes living in harmony with one's ancestors and community, witchcraft is a serious problem in Unyamwezi. It offers an outlet to built-up social tensions that are found in the intense interpersonal relations that develop in rural village society. Some people have moved from their homes to escape the power of witches, who are believed to be able to poison and bring misfortune to their victims.

The traditional Nyamwezi belief system has influenced the way many Wanyamwezi interpret Islam and Christianity. While many rural Wanyamwezi are not practicing Christians or Muslims, they do believe in one overarching god. However, unlike Christianity or Islam, which provide their followers with a personal religious code to be followed, Nyamwezi spirituality emphasizes personal spiritual development and the creation of personal behavioral taboos so that the individual can live in harmony with the community and ancestors. While many Wanyamwezi follow traditional practices in regard to healing, this does not preclude going to doctors or hospitals. Rather than competing with Christianity, Islam, and modern medicine, traditional Nyamwezi beliefs and diviners supplement the newer religions and practices.

⁶ MAJOR HOLIDAYS

The major holidays in Tanzania are Union Day (April 26), which celebrates the creation of the union between mainland Tanzania and the Islands of Zanzibar; May day/Workers Day (May 1); Independence Day (December 9); and New Year's Day (January 1). Major religious holidays are Christmas, Good Friday, Easter, Id ul-Fitr (end of Ramadan), Id ul-Haj (Festival of Sacrifice), Islamic New Year, and the Prophet Muhammad's Birthday. Secular holidays such as Independence Day are characterized by military parades and speeches by the country's leaders, while religious holidays are usually celebrated by attendance at the mosque or church and visits with family and friends. Feasts on these days often feature pilau, a spicy rice dish.

⁷ RITES OF PASSAGE

For the Wanyamwezi, the first major rite of passage is birth. It should be noted that with the introduction of Western medical practices and new values, many of the practices surrounding birth have changed. Traditionally, newborn babies were secluded until their umbilical cords fell off. When the child was brought out of seclusion, he or she was presented to the village and given a name by the midwife. The child would often be named after her grandfather or grandmother. If the pregnancy had been difficult, the child was usually named Maganga, Misambwa, or Kalamata. If the mother or father had died before the child was born, the child would be called Mulekwa or Kalekwa, meaning "the one who is left behind." For baby boys, their father would make them a small bow and arrow as a symbol of strength. The male child, together with his bow, was then taken before the male village elders. After a feast, the elders one by one would shell a peanut near the child's ear in a ceremony called *bupatula matwi,* so that the child would be alert and attentive when he grew up. If the child was a girl she would be brought before a group of women elders.

Traditionally, twins, babies born with teeth, and those born legs first were considered a bad omen for their parents and the community. It was thought that if they lived, the parents would die and the community would experience disasters. Usually these children were killed and elaborate ceremonies involving the mtemi were needed to counter the effects of their birth. Not surprisingly, many of the early converts to Christianity in Unyamwezi were these outcast children and their families. Today, these practices are against the law, and new societal norms and practices have been adopted.

In precolonial times (and even today), long journeys were considered a rite of passage into manhood. Another rite of passage is the requirement that a man be capable of establishing his own household, meaning that he must be economically independent before he can get married.

Marriage is a very important Nyamwezi institution. As in the United States, the majority of marriages end in divorce. Nyamwezi men usually marry for the first time in their late teens or early twenties; women tend to marry at a slightly younger age. Polygyny is practiced in Nyamwezi society, but in many respects polygynous marriages tend to be unstable than single-partner marriages. The courtship process typically involves a young man's search for a suitable young woman to marry. With one or two male friends, he visits her home and discusses the possibility of marriage. Usually this process goes on for a number of weeks. If, after consulting with her female elders, the young woman agrees, bride wealth negotiations begin. Male neighbors of the groom and bride, acting on instructions of the couple's fathers, meet at the bride's house to discuss bride wealth. Often negotiations are carried out for several days before an agreement can be reached. Typical payments consist of livestock for the bride's paternal grandfather and maternal uncle. Other payments might also be required. Much, but not all, of the bride wealth would be returned in case of divorce. After the bride wealth is agreed upon, the groom's father holds a large feast, during which a delegation from the bride's family comes to collect the cattle and other goods. After the bride wealth has been paid, a wedding ceremony, usually lasting one to three days, is held; and amidst much feasting, dancing, and singing, the bride and groom receive blessings in public from their parents and relatives. Many of these traditional practices have been incorporated into Christian weddings, while Muslim weddings tend to mirror those found at the coast.

The last important rite of passage is death. After a person dies, close relatives have their heads shaved in mourning. The bereaved parents and spouse go into a period of seclusion.

When it is time for the actual burial, all the men in the village come together to help; the women and children must hide themselves until the body is buried. A special ritual is then performed to purify the village, followed by a divination to determine the cause of death. Finally, a ceremony is held to mark the end of mourning. Traditionally, witches and people with diseases such as leprosy would not be buried, and their bodies would be left in the bush. This practice is no longer followed. Funerals are important rituals for bereaved families and their kin and neighbors. Neighbors dig the grave and take news of the death to relatives of the deceased who live outside the village. The dead become ancestors who may continue to affect the lives of their descendants and demand appeasement. The idea that the dead live on in their descendants is expressed in terms of shared identity between alternate generations

8 INTERPERSONAL RELATIONS

Greetings are very important in Nyamwezi society. Greetings last for several minutes, and it would be considered rude just to pass a friend on the street and say, "Hi" as in the United States. As a form of respect, younger people usually initiate greetings with their elders; then the elder will take the lead in the ensuing conversation, inquiring how the person is doing, how work or studies are going, and whether the relatives are well. One greets very important people by bowing, clapping one's hands, and averting one's gaze before a handshake. Greetings among close friends are less formal and often incorporate some teasing and joking. Greeting is always accompanied by a handshake, as is leave-taking. After the greetings, it is considered impolite to "get straight to the point," and the matter to be discussed is usually approached gradually in an indirect manner.

Visiting relatives and friends is a favorite activity on the weekends, on holidays, or after work. Hospitality is taken very seriously. It is customary for the visitor to be given some refreshments, usually soda, tea, coffee, or traditional beer, and a snack. If the person comes at mealtime, he or she will be invited to join the family for the meal. It is customary to cook more food than is usually eaten by the family, in case guests arrive. If an important visitor comes or someone comes from a long journey, it is customary to slaughter a chicken and have a large feast in the person's honor. At parties or celebrations, it is the responsibility of the host to provide guests with a good meal, beverages, and entertainment. As some celebrations last all night, the host is often responsible for providing sleeping accommodations.

9 LIVING CONDITIONS

Tanzania is one of the poorest countries in the world. Within Tanzania the most prosperous area is Dar es Salaam, the capital, while the poorest region is the southern coast. Unyamwezi falls between these two extremes. Although Tanzania is one of the poorest countries, its quality of life indicators such as literacy rates, life expectancy, and access to safe drinking water tend to be comparable with countries that have higher income levels.

Most people in Unyamwezi live in houses made of mud bricks with either thatched grass or corrugated iron roofs with dirt floors. Most houses do not have electricity or indoor plumbing. Since rural incomes are very low, most people have few material possessions; these consist mainly of radios, bicycles, lanterns, secondhand clothes, shoes, and household goods.

One of the main problems affecting the Wanyamwezi is malaria. The disease is endemic in most parts of Tanzania, including Unyamwezi, and it is about as common as the flu is in North America. The disease, while not usually fatal for healthy adults, can be fatal for people in a weakened condition or for the very old or very young. Another major health problem in Unyamwezi is the tsetse fly. It is slightly larger than a housefly and has a stinging bite. The tsetse fly is a carrier of two diseases, which adversely affect humans. One disease, sleeping sickness, is lethal to humans. The other is lethal to cattle and is called trypanosomiasis. Tsetse flies thrive in areas where there are abundant wild animals, which are immune to the diseases that strike humans and their livestock.

Diviners and other local experts provide herbal and other forms of treatment for illness. Shops sell some Western medicines, including aspirin and liniments. Village dispensaries and state and mission hospitals also provide Western medicine. People commonly use both Western and indigenous treatments rather than trusting wholly in either.

Transportation is a major problem in Tanzania. Most roads are in terrible shape and filled with potholes, making long-distance travel very difficult. Currently a major project to repair the roads in Tanzania is under way, which has eased some of the difficulties in road transportation. Tabora, the main city in Unyamwezi, is at the crossroads of the central railway line and is easily reached from Kigoma on Lake Tanganyika, Mwanza on Lake Victoria, and Dar es Salaam. There is also an airport in Tabora, but the cost of tickets keeps most people from flying.

10 FAMILY LIFE

Most families are made up of a mother, a father, and their children. Families often take care of relatives' children. Men have traditionally controlled most of the power within a household. For example, only men are able to inherit property. This pattern is changing, as the government has stressed equal rights for women. Within the household women are responsible for many of the daily chores, such as weeding crops and cooking, while the men are responsible for work such as building the house and clearing the fields. Children help their parents watch the fields to keep birds from eating the millet and sorghum. Girls also help their mothers with household work, while boys help with herding the livestock. It is not unusual for school enrollment rates in rural areas to fall during harvest and planting times as children help their parents with agricultural work.

Historically, villages were normally not kinship units and people found their relatives spread over wide areas. Spouses generally came from outside the Tembes and sons commonly moved away from their father's homestead. The core members of a domestic group consisted of the husband, his wife or wives, and any children who still lived with them. Sometimes relatives, such as a mother, younger unmarried brothers or sisters, and their children could be found together. The sexes usually ate separately. In general men did the heavy work, while women did the recurring tasks and much of the everyday agricultural work.

Ideally every adult person should be married, and every married woman should have her own household and bring her own household utensils. The husband is said to technically own his wife's hut, fields, and most of the household's food,

but a wise husband usually listened to the wife's advice. There was little ranking between co-wives, although seniority in terms of who was first married was at times recognized. Jealously and sorcery were common, much depending on how well co-wives got along. Unlike the Wagogo, divorce was common, a large majority of persons experiencing at least one divorce by the time they were 50 years of age, which included the return of bride wealth minus the number and sex of the children born. Divorce was most often accomplished by the separation of either party. Chiefdom courts found certain reasons to automatically justify divorce: a woman's desertion, being struck by a wife, the wife's adultery, sexual refusal of the wife, and having an abortion, were all adequate reasons. Grounds for a husband to claim divorce were failure of the wife to carry out household duties, visiting a doctor without permission, and possible infertility. A wife could divorce if the husband deserted for a period of time without supporting her; if the husband seriously injured her by, for example, breaking a limb, but not simply beating her; the husband's impotence or perversions; or if her husband generally failed to maintain her and her children properly. A husband's adultery would not be one of the grounds.

It was customary for the younger brother of her former husband to inherit a widow, (a kind of "widows and orphans" security system), although it was not done against her will. Among some, inheritance of a widow by her husband's sister's son was particularly favored.

11 CLOTHING

Wanyamwezi traditionally wore clothing made of bark cloth, but as trade grew in the 18th century, imported textiles became popular. Many women wear *khangas*, printed cloth adorned with Swahili sayings and vitenge, printed cloth with brightly colored and ornate designs. Dresses based on Arab, European, and Indian styles are also popular. Men wear trousers and shirts, and on special occasions Muslim men wear flowing white robes called *Kanzus*.

12 FOOD

A favorite food is *ugali*, a stiff porridge made from corn, millet, or sorghum meal and served with beef, chicken, and vegetables. Cassava, rice, bread, peanuts, spinach, cassava leaves and other vegetables are also eaten. Snacks often consist of fruits. When available, the meat from wild game is a special treat. Ugali a porridge made from hominy and served with meat and vegetables. Beer made from fermented corn, sorghum, or millet was also common. Goats were used for ancestor sacrifices, but the economic value of goats and sheep lay in their meat and skins. By tradition five goats or sheep equated one bull; two bulls were worth one cow. Their year is divided into two seasons, wet and dry, with considerable variation depending on time and place.

13 EDUCATION

Before the European colonial occupation of Unyamwezi, children were educated by their elders. They would learn how to farm, hunt, cook, herd cattle, and do other work from their parents. Stories told by parents or grandparents after the evening meal were an important way in which children were socialized into Nyamwezi society. Typically stories began with a call and response, in which the story teller would tease the listeners as follows:

Listeners: Story!

Storyteller: A Story.

Listeners: There once was what?

Storyteller: Someone.

Listeners: Go on!

Storyteller: You know who.

Listeners: Go on!

Many children's stories in the United States are based on African folktales. For example, one Nyamwezi story closely resembles the tale of "Br'er Rabbit." It tells of some farmers who decided to catch a hare that was eating their crops by using a wood carving covered with glue. When the rabbit came to the field and saw the wood carving he tried to talk to it. When the carving did not respond the rabbit resorted to violence, kicking and punching the carving and becoming stuck in its glue. When the farmers returned to kill the rabbit he pleaded with them not to beat him to death on the sand. When the farmers tried to do this, the soft sand broke the rabbit's fall and he was able to run away.

Proverbs are another important way in which Nyamwezi culture is passed on from generation to generation. One Nyamwezi proverb states that "Hoes that are together don't stop scraping each other." What this proverb means is that when people live together, disagreements are going to occur. Unlike American society, where people place a high value on their privacy and are socialized to mind their own business, Nyamwezi culture stresses the importance of outside intervention in a conflict. When quarrels erupt it is expected that neighbors, friends, family members, and elders will help to calm the situation. After a disagreement it is customary for the people involved to tell their sides of the story to mediators and for a consensus to be reached on who is at fault. The guilty party is then asked to refrain from the same behavior in the future, and the parties shake hands to show they have made up.

While informal education is still important for teaching societal values, formal education plays an important role in equipping the Wanyamwezi with the basic skills needed for life in modern Tanzanian society. After independence the leaders decided to devote most of the educational resources to providing free elementary education for all Tanzanian children. Until about 1980, this policy was very successful in improving elementary attendance rates: from 45% before independence to around 90% by 1980. However, enrollment rates have dropped in recent years in response to deteriorating economic conditions and the poor quality of some elementary schools. Very few Tanzanian children (around 5%) have a chance to go to high school, and only a very small percentage of high school graduates are accepted for university studies. Until 1994, all students who finished high school were required to attend National Youth Service. However, economic difficulties have caused the suspension of this program.

Education is very important for most Tanzanian families. But their appreciation of education is mixed with practicality. The low quality of some elementary schools, rising costs associated with education, strong competition for the few spots available in secondary schools, and the difficulties many secondary and university graduates have in finding jobs have caused some parents and students, especially in poorer families, to question the usefulness of elementary school.

14 CULTURAL HERITAGE

The Wanyamwezi have a rich cultural heritage. Perhaps the most important part of their heritage is their emphasis on harmonious and balanced social relations. Nyamwezi society has historically been open and placed a high value on tolerance. This has allowed many people from outside Unyamwezi to live peacefully in the area and has allowed the Wanyamwezi to live throughout Tanzania. One of the unique institutions governing the relations among different ethnic groups in Tanzania is *utani*, or what is often called a joking relationship. Utani involves a special bond that allows people from different ethnic groups to verbally abuse each other without taking offense. Usually these joking relationships also entail an exchange of services and mutual aid, such as helping with funerals or helping visitors with directions or getting settled. Utani allows people arriving from a distant place or coming as strangers into a community to seek and receive help. Historians speculate that utani developed as a way to manage previously hostile and sometimes violent relationships between people of different ethnic groups. In addition to creating a positive and peaceful relationship between groups whose relationships could otherwise be marked by tension, hostility, and unpredictability, utani provides amusement and elevates the insult to a high art form.

For the Wanyamwezi, music and dance are an important part of their cultural heritage and play an important part in wedding festivities and other ceremonies.

Hunting is also an important part of Nyamwezi culture, and many men belong to secret societies of hunters with special rituals to help them track various types of animals.

It had always been part or the Nyamwezi system for the chief to receive tribute, bring success and prosperity to the people, and play an active role in ceremonies. All land was said to have belonged to the chief and he had the right to expel witches and undesirables; abuse was checked by the general need to maintain a large population; and while no one had the right to sell land in a chiefdom, the people had considerable security in their rights to the land. Permission to clear land was not needed, but care was taken so as not to conflict with others in the area. If there was a shortage of land in an area to be inherited, a headman could insist upon other holdings. Water was free to all.

Representational art is not strongly developed; it has mainly ritual functions. Music and dancing are the main art forms, and drums are the main instruments, although the nailpiano (a box with metal prongs that twang at different pitches) and other instruments are also found. Traditional songs are sung at weddings and at dances, but new songs are also composed by dance leaders. Male dance teams are the most common, but some female and mixed teams perform. Ritual and other societies have their own dance styles. Transistor radios are now widespread. Local and visiting jazz and other bands play in the towns.

15 WORK

In the precolonial era the Wanyamwezi were known for their trading activities. From the beginning of the 19th century, Nyamwezi long-distance trading caravans dominated the central routes through Tanzania, stretching from Mrima coast ports such as Bagamoyo and Saadani to Ujiji on Lake Tanganyika. Despite the inroads of Omani Arab and Swahili trading enterprises from the middle of the century, the Nyamwezi maintained a position of strength. In the second half of the 19th century, market relations emerged as the dominant form of economic organization along the central routes, although the market for many commodities was clearly fractured by transport difficulties, and non-market relations frequently substituted for weakly developed commercial institutions and tools. Most caravan porters in 19th century Tanzania were free wage workers, and nearly all were clearly migrant or itinerant laborers. The development of a labor market for caravan porters was an early and significant stage in the transition to capitalism, which began in a period of violence and political upheaval. The argument that porters were mostly wage laborers rests on evidence that their labor was bought and sold according to fluctuating labor market conditions. Market conditions in the second half of the 19th century shows a broadly rising demand for porters, a demand that could only be met if caravan operators offered adequate wages and observed the customs established within porter work culture. Thus, market conditions along the central routes contributed to the development of a free wage labor, characterized by a unique labor culture The Wanyamwezi acted as middlemen for bringing goods plentiful in one area to areas where they were scarce. For example, salt was a scarce commodity throughout mainland Tanzania. However, high-quality salt was produced nearby at Uvinza, so the Wanyamwezi traded it for iron goods in neighboring Usumbwa and Usukuma. The Wanyamwezi would trade the salt and iron for cattle and skins from the Wagogo, who lived in central Tanzania (around the present day city of Dodoma). They would also trade grain, honey, bark cloth, and other forest products for cattle from the Wasukuma, Wahaya, and Waha. Nyamwezi traders traveled as far as present-day Zambia and southern Democratic Republic of the Congo and pioneered trade routes to the coast in the late 1700s. By the 1800s large Nyamwezi caravans consisting of thousands of people would head to the coast carrying ivory to trade for cloth, beads, firearms, ammunition, and gunpowder. From the early 1800s to the Civil War, the United States was one of eastern Africa's major trading partners, with ships from Salem, Massachusetts, trading American-produced cloth (called *marakani*) for ivory to make billiard balls and piano keys and gum copal, which was used in making varnish.

While the Wanyamwezi had a reputation for trade before the colonial era, they gained a reputation as laborers during the European occupation. The transformation of the Wanyamwezi from traders to workers had its origins in the years preceding the colonial occupation. Shortly after Nyamwezi caravans began to bring ivory to the coast, Arab and Swahili caravans launched from the ports of Bagamoyo, Pangani, Tanga, Sadani, and Dar es Salaam went into the interior and established trading centers. With support from the State of Zanzibar, coastal traders increasingly displaced their Wanyamwezi counterparts. Many Wanyamwezi porters were forced to work on contract or as slaves on coastal caravans.

After the Germans took power in Tanzania they used physical coercion and taxation to force the Wanyamwezi into migrant labor while at the same time discouraging them from earning money through cash-crop production. As early as the 1890s, labor recruiters spread throughout the western plateau, trying to gain workers. Many Wanyamwezi went to work on European-owned plantations in order to pay their taxes. As work conditions on the plantations were very bad, characterized by flogging, poor housing, hunger, and disease, there were chronic shortages of labor. Areas of labor migration for the Wanyamwezi have included sisal plantations near Tanga, the clove plantations of Pemba, and more recently the cotton-growing areas of Usukuma. The Wanyamwezi became the backbone of mainland Tanzania's labor force, being employed in great numbers to construct and work on the railways; work on the docks in Mombasa, Kisumu, Tanga and Dar es Salaam; work on Kenyan farms and in the Kenyan police; work for British safari firms; and even work in South African gold mines.

Since independence, a number of Wanyamwezi have become politicians, civil servants, teachers, businesspeople, and professionals such as doctors, lawyers, and accountants. While many Wanyamwezi have become involved in the various aspects of the modern economy, most are agriculturalists relying on traditional farming techniques.

While trade and wage labor were important activities for the Wanyamwezi, the backbone of Nyamwezi society has been agriculture. Many Wanyamwezi men would farm for half the year and engage in trade for the other half. As in the past, most of the farming is done manually although some tractors and animals are now used. Since the Wanyamwezi live in areas where rainfall is often unreliable, they long ago developed techniques, such as ridging their fields, to conserve water. The major crops are sorghum, millet, maize (corn), rice, sweet potatoes, cassava, peanuts, beans, chickpeas, gourds, sunflowers, pumpkins, cotton, and tobacco.

Elephant hunters have historically been one of the most prestigious occupations among the Nyamwezi, since the elephant hunters could get very rich from ivory trade. The elephant hunters were organized in a guild, which only accepted those who could pass the apprenticeship and the tests that were associated with it. Hunting had a wide variety of forms. Guild members often used lethal poison, and when they used it, in a German sergeant's words, "it worked slowly but surely."

The guild members believed they possessed powerful hunting medicine acquired through rigorous apprenticeships, tracking game in all types of terrain and moving swiftly and silently through thorny underbrush. The elephant hunting lead to a decrease in elephant population, which combined with the increased trade in slaves, lead to large changes in the social and economic conditions.

In addition to agriculture, crafts were a part-time occupation and were not hereditary. Regionally traded products of importance were drums, ladles, stools, storage boxes for grain, and snuffboxes of horn. Iron and cloth were very important in regional networks, but the cloth industry in particular was ailing in 1857 because of severe competition from India, and over the next 60 years almost disappeared. Ironwork came from localized settlements whose products were then traded over wide areas: bows, arrows, spears, the payment of fines, and the extremely valuable hoes for bride wealth were all produced with considerable ritual by the smiths; and depending on the place that was blamed, for the heavy deforestation to obtain charcoal.

16 SPORTS

By far the most popular sport is soccer. The Tanzanian landscape is dotted with soccer fields, and children and teenagers enjoy playing the game, often in bare feet with homemade soccer balls. On weekends many people enjoy listening to soccer games on the radio. For those who can go to the stadium, Simba and Young Africans of Dar es Salaam are the most popular teams to watch. Many Wanyamwezi also support their local team, Mirambo, based in Tabora and named for the great precolonial leader Mirambo.

17 ENTERTAINMENT AND RECREATION

Besides soccer, many people like to play cards or play a board game called *bao*. *Bao*, sometimes called African chess, is a very complex game in which good players need to plan many turns in advance to capture their opponents' markers, or pieces. One plays by placing one's markers (usually large round seeds) into carved-out depressions on a large wooden board. More affluent families enjoy watching videos, especially action films, musicals, and Indian films—which usually combine a musical, an action film, and a love story into one movie. Perhaps the most important form of relaxation in Unyamwezi, especially in the rural areas, is visiting friends after work or on the weekends and drinking traditional homemade beer.

18 FOLK ART, CRAFTS, AND HOBBIES

A hobby for many children is making their own toys. Children in Unyamwezi have done this for many years. In the 1870s, children made toy guns and used ashes for gunpowder. More modern toys consist of wire cars with wheels cut out of old pieces of rubber from tires or flip-flops. Children also make their own soccer balls out of string tied around old plastic bags or socks.

Important crafts in Unyamwezi include iron-working, basket making, and making traditional stools. Some skills are closely guarded secrets that are passed down within a family or a close-knit secret society. For example, in the case of iron-working, most blacksmiths are non-Wanyamwezi, outsiders, whose work is cloaked in magic and spirits. In the case of stool making, this skill is more widely spread through Unyamwezi and is not particularly associated with any immigrant community or guild.

For adults, beer brewing is an important hobby. There are many types of traditional beer brewed by people in Unyamwezi. One of the more popular is called Kangala and is made from fermented corn bran. After the beer has been prepared, a process that takes several days, the brewer will have a party with much singing and dancing. Traditional beer is an important part of Nyamwezi life. It is used in numerous ceremonies, including weddings, funerals, feasts, and holidays. It is said that next to water, traditional beer is the most popular drink in Unyamwezi.

19 SOCIAL PROBLEMS

The most pressing problem facing the Wanyamwezi, as with most Tanzanians, is poverty. Malnutrition, along with lack of clean water, health care, and medicine allow opportunistic diseases to take their toll. As in most countries, poor people are often put at a severe disadvantage in dealing with more afflu-

ent groups and in protecting their rights and advocating their interests within official channels.

Tanzania was ruled from 1965 to 1992 by a one-party state that tended to restrict political rights and individual liberties. The implementation of a radical new societal development plan called ujamaa, or African socialism, in the 1960s and 1970s led to numerous economic problems including a shortage of basic goods, corruption, high rates of inflation, declining production, and a deterioration of the nation's physical infrastructure. However, these problems need to be considered within the context of a ruling regime that seemed committed to building a new egalitarian society and promoting a national culture that has so far avoided much of the ethnic animosity that has characterized numerous other multiethnic societies.

Malnutrition, the lack of clean water, and insufficient health care allow diseases to take their toll. As in most countries, poor people are often at a severe disadvantage in protecting their rights and advocating their interests through the official channels of government.

20 GENDER ISSUES

In traditional Nyamwezi society the roles of men and women were different. Women had an extremely important economic role as the food producers and in some cases held high political office. It is also suggested that at the village level, perceptions about correct gender roles have not changed greatly, and there is a willingness to accept women in authority, which is an indication of changing times and attitudes.

There is a strong gender division of labor. In general, men do shorter, heavy tasks, and women do more repetitive chores. Cattle are mainly men's concern, as are iron working and machine sewing. Only men hunt. Pottery is women's work. Some urgent tasks, such as harvesting, are done by both sexes. Most diviners are men. The state has been keen to draw women into politics, but only moderate progress has been made.

21 BIBLIOGRAPHY

Abrahams, R. G. *The Nyamwezi Today*. Cambridge: Cambridge University Press, 1981.

———.*The Political Organization of Unyamwezi*. Cambridge: Cambridge University Press, 1967.

Beier, Ulli, *The Origin of Life and Death: African Creation Myths*. London 1966.

Bennett, Norman Robert. *Mirambo of Tanzania Ca. 1840–1884*. Oxford: Oxford University Press, 1971.

Blohm, Wilhelm. *Die Nyamwezi, Land und Wirtschaft*. Hamburg: Friederichsen, De Gruyter & Co.,1931.

Chenya, Fr. Hendricks. "Chiefs of Busumabu." *Lumuli*, 9 (1958), 3.

———. "Our Chiefdoms." *Lumuli*, 4 April 1962.

———. "Our Villages." *Lumuli*, 15 March 1963.

Cohen, D.W. "A Survey of Interlacustrine Chronology," *Journal of African History*, 11, 2 177-201. (1970).

Collinson, J.D.H. *Witchcraft and Sorcery amongst the Wanyamwezi*. Ph.D. dissertation, Oxford University, 1974.

Cory, Hans. *The Ntemi: The Traditional Rites in Connection with the Burial, Election, Enthronement and Magic Powers of a Sukuma Chief*. London: Macmillan, 1951.

———. *Sukuma Law and Custom*. London, New York: Oxford University Press, 1953.

———. "Sukuma Twin Ceremonies-Mabasa." *Tanganyika Notes and Records,* 17 (1944), 34-44.

———. "The Buyeye: A Secret Society of Snake Charmers in Sukumaland, Tanganyika Territory." *Africa,* 16, 3 (1946), 160–178.

———. The Indigenous Political System of the Sukuma and Proposals for Political Reform, *Eastern Africa Studies,* 2 (1954)

———. "Religious Beliefs and Practices of the Sukuma/Nyamwezi Tribal Group." *Tanganyika Notes and Records,* 54, 1960.

Cotter, Fr. G. *Sukuma Proverbs.* Nairobi: Beezee Secretarial Services. 1970?

Iliffe, John. *A Modern History of Tanganyika.* Cambridge: Cambridge University Press, 1979.

Kabeya, J. B. *King Mirambo.* Dar es Salaam: Tanzania Literature Bureau, 1976.

Maganga, C., and T. C. Schadeberg. *Kinyamwezi: Grammar, Texts, and Vocabulary.* Cologne, Germany: Rudiger, Koppe Verlag, 1992.

Tcherkezoff, S. *Dual Classification Reconsidered: Nyamwezi Sacred Kingship and Other Examples.* Cambridge: Cambridge University Press, 1987.

Unomah, A. C. *Mirambo of Tanzania.* London, England: Heineman Educational Books, 1977.

World Bank. *Tanzania AIDS Assessment and Planning Study.* Washington, D.C.: World Bank, 1992.

———. *World Development Report.* Oxford: Oxford University Press, 1996.

—revised by M. Njoroge

OROMOS

PRONUNCIATION: Oro-moo-s
LOCATION: Oromia in the Ethiopian Empire; Kenya; Somalia
POPULATION: 40 million
LANGUAGE: Afaan Oromoo
RELIGION: Waaqeeffannaa (original Oromo religion); Islam; Christianity
RELATED ARTICLES: Vol. 1: Ethiopians

[1] INTRODUCTION

Although Oromos have their own unique culture, history, language, and civilization, they are culturally related to Afars, Somalis, Sidamas, Agaws, Bilens, Bejas, Kunamas, and others. Oromos are best known for their former egalitarian social system known as *Gada,* and their military organization that enabled them to emerge as one of the strongest ethnonations in the Horn of Africa between the 12th and mid-19th centuries. Gada was a form of constitutional government; it was also a social system. Politically it was practiced through the election of political leaders; corrupt or dictatorial leaders would be removed from power through *buqisu,* or recall before their official tenure. Oromo women had a parallel institution known as *Siqqee.* This institution promoted gender equality in Oromo society.

Gada closely connected social and political structures. Male Oromos were organized according to age and generation for both social and political activities. The Gada government was based on democratic principles: the *Abba Boku* was an elected "chairman" who presided over the assembly, and the *Abba Dula* (the defense minister) was one of the leading figures in the government. The Abba Boku presided over the assembly and proclaimed the laws, and the Abba Dula was the leader of the army. A council known as *Shanee* or *Salgee* and retired Gada officials also assisted the Abba Boku in running the government. Gada laws were passed by the *Chaffee* (assembly) and implemented by officials. This assembly is called Gumi Gayo, and held every eight years.

All Gada officials were elected for eight years by universal adult male suffrage; the main criteria for election to office included bravery, knowledge, honesty, demonstrated ability, and courage. The Gada government worked on local, regional, and central levels. The political philosophy of the Gada system was manifested in three main principles of checks and balances created to avoid subordination and exploitation: periodic succession of eight years, balanced opposition between different sectors, and power sharing between higher and lower political organs. The Gada government was based on popular democracy and equal representation for adult males. This government had independent executive, legislative, and judicial branches for balancing and checking the power of political leaders to avoid corruption and misuse of power. Some elements of Gada are still practiced in southern and other regions of Oromia.

The Gada system was the pillar of Oromo culture and civilization, and it helped Oromos develop democratic political, economic, social, and religious institutions for many centuries. The Gada political system and military organization enabled Oromos to defend themselves against enemies who were competing with them for land, water, and power for many

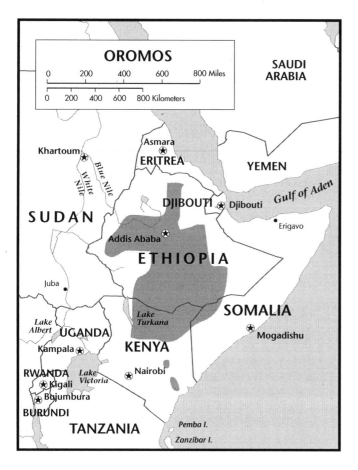

OROMOS

al resources including barley, wheat, sorghum, xxafii (a grain), maize, coffee, oil seeds, *chat*, oranges, and cattle are abundant in Oromia. Oromia is also rich in gold, silver, platinum, marble, uranium, nickel, natural gas, and other minerals. It has several large and small rivers that are necessary for agriculture and to produce hydroelectric power. Today the resources of Oromia are exploited by the Tigrayan-led Ethiopian government and its domestic and international supporters. The nominal state of Oromia is still a colony of Ethiopia. There are millions of Oromo refugees in Africa, the Middle East, North America, Australia, Europe and other parts of the world. Particularly, the number of Oromo refugees has increased since 1992, when the Tigrayan government started its terrorism and genocidal massacres.

³ LANGUAGE

The Oromo language is called Afaan Oromoo. Afaan Oromoo has more than 65 million speakers; ethno-national groups such as the Sidama, Berta, Adare, Annuak, Koma, Kulo, Kaficho, and Guraghe speak the Oromo language in addition to their respective languages. Afaan Oromoo is the third-most widely spread language next to Arabic and Hausa in Africa; it is the second-most widely spoken indigenous language in Africa south of the Sahara.

Despite the attempt by successive Ethiopian regimes to destroy the Oromoo language, it has continued to exist and flourish in rural areas. Until recently Oromos were denied the right to develop their language, literature, and alphabet. It was a crime to try to write in this language for almost a century. With the development of the Oromo national movement, Oromo intellectuals adopted the Latin script for this language in the early 1970s. The OLF adopted this script and began to introduce literacy in Afaan Oromoo. Today millions of Oromos write and read in their language although the Tigrayan-led Ethiopian government banned independent Oromo institutions and organizations that are committed to develop this language. Every Oromo word has historical or contextual meanings.

⁴ FOLKLORE

Oromos believe that Waaqa Tokkicha (the one God) created the world and them. They call this Supreme Being Waaqa Guuracha (the Black God). Most Oromos still believe that it was this God that created heaven and earth and other living and nonliving things. Waaqa created *ayaana* (spiritual connection) to connect itself to its creatures. The Oromo idea of creation starts with the element of water, since it was the only element that existed before other elements.

Oromos believed that Waaqa created the sky and earth from water; he also created dry land out of water, and *bakkalcha* (star) to provide light. With the rise of *bakkalcha, ayaana* emerged. With this star, sunlight also appeared. The movement of this sunlight created day and night. Using the light of *bakkalcha,* Waaqa created all other stars, animals, plants, and other creatures that live on the land, in air, and in water. When an Oromo dies, he or she will become spirit. There are still Oromos who believe in the existence of ancestral spirits with whom they attempt to establish contact through ceremonies. These ancestral spirits appear to relatives in the form of flying animals. Original Oromo religion does not recognize the existence of hell and heaven. If a person commits sin by disturbing

centuries. Today Oromos are engaged in a national liberation movement under the leadership of the Oromo Liberation Front (OLF) to achieve their national self-determination and to restore Oromo democracy. Most Oromos support this liberation organization and its army, the Oromo Liberation Army. There are many Oromo organizations in North America, Europe, the Middle East, Australia, and Africa that support the Oromo national movement. Oromos are struggling for self-determination and the opportunity to reinvent an Oromian state that will reflect the Gada system of popular and representative democracy.

² LOCATION AND HOMELAND

Oromos call their nation and country Oromia. They have been living in the Horn of Africa for all of their known history. They are one of the largest ethnonations in Africa with a population estimated at about 40 million people. Oromia is located mainly within the Ethiopian Empire and covers an area of 600,000 sq km (232,000 sq mi). The 3.5 million-year-old fossilized human skeleton known as "Lucy," or "Chaltu" in Oromo, was found in Oromia. Oromos also live in Kenya and Somalia. During the last decades of the 19th century, Oromos were colonized and mainly incorporated to Ethiopia and lost their independent institutional and cultural development. Great Britain, France, and Italy supported the Ethiopian colonization of Oromos. Oromia is considered the richest region of the Horn of Africa because of its agricultural and natural resources. It is considered by many to be the "bread basket" of the Horn. Agriculturthe balance of nature or mistreating others, the society imposes appropriate punishment while the person is alive.

Oromo heroes and heroines are those individuals who excelled in doing something for the benefit of the community. Thinkers who invented the Gada system, *raagas* (prophets), military leaders, etc., are considered Oromo heroes and heroines. Currently, those individuals who are contributing to the Oromo national movement politically, militarily, intellectually, and in other ways are considered heroes and heroines.

5 RELIGION

Oromos recognize the existence of a Supreme Being or Creator that they call Waaqa. They have three major religions: original Oromo religion (Waaqeeffannqa), Islam, and Christianity. The original Oromo religion considers the organization of human, spiritual, and physical worlds to be interconnected phenomena whose existence and functions are regulated by their creator, God or Waaqa. Waaqa acts in the person's life through each person's *ayaana* (spiritual connection). There are three Oromo concepts that explain the organization and interconnection of human, spiritual, and physical worlds: *ayaana*, *uuma* (nature), and *saffu* (the ethical and moral code).

Uuma includes everything created by Waaqa, including *ayaana*. *Saffu* is a moral and ethical code that Oromos use to differentiate bad from good and wrong from right. The Oromo religious institution is called the *qallu*; the *qallu* is the center of the Oromo religious view. *Qallu* leaders traditionally played important religious roles in Oromo society. The Ethiopian colonizing structure suppressed the Oromo system of thought and worldview by eliminating Oromo cultural experts such as the *raagas* (Oromo prophets), the *ayaantus* (time reckoners), and oral historians. Today Islam and Christianity play important religious roles in Oromo society. In some Oromo regions, Orthodox Christianity was imposed on the Oromos by the Ethiopian colonizing structure; in other areas, Oromos accepted Protestant Christianity to resist Orthodox Christianity. Some Oromos accepted Islam to resist Ethiopian colonialism and Orthodox Christianity. Islam was imposed on other Oromos by Turko-Egyptian colonialism. However, some Oromos have continued to practice their original religion. Both Christianity and Islam have been greatly influenced by the original Oromo religion.

6 MAJOR HOLIDAYS

Oromo original holidays, such as *Ireecha* or *buuta,* and Islamic and Christian holidays are celebrated in Oromo society. Recently Oromos have started to celebrate an Oromo national day to remember Oromo heroines and heroes who have sacrificed their lives to liberate their people from Ethiopian colonialism.

7 RITES OF PASSAGE

Since children are seen as assets, most Oromo families are large. The birth of a child is celebrated because each newborn child will become a potential worker. Marriage is also celebrated since it is the time at which boys and girls enter the stage of adulthood in the society. Death is also an important event that brings members of the community together to say goodbye to the deceased member.

Traditionally Oromos had five gada-grades; the names of these grades varied from place to place. In one area, these grades were *dabalee* (ages 1–8), *rogge* (ages 8–16), *follee* (ages

16–24), *qondaala* (ages 24–32), and *dorri* (ages 32–40). There were rites of passages when males passed from one gada-grade to another. These rites of passages were called *buuta* or *errecha*. Between the ages of 1 and 8, Oromo male children did not participate in politics and had less responsibility. When they were between 8 and 16 years old, they were not allowed to take full responsibility and marry. Between ages 16 and 24, they took on the responsibilities of hard work, learning war tactics, politics, law and management, culture and history, and hunting big animals.

When young men reached between 24 and 32 years of age, they served as soldiers and prepared to take over the responsibilities of leadership, of peace and war. Those males between 32 and 40 years old played important roles and shared their knowledge with the *qondaala* group, and carried out their leadership responsibilities. Nowadays those who can afford it send their children to school. These children also complete their teenage years in school. Children and teenagers engage in agricultural and other activities to survive. Young boys and girls marry and start the life-cycle of adulthood.

8 INTERPERSONAL RELATIONS

Oromos are friendly people, and they express their feelings openly. Oromos greet one another when they meet by shaking hands; they talk to one another warmly. *"Asahama?"*—*"Atam?"*—*"Fayaadha?"*—and *"Matinkee atam?"* ("How are you?"—"Are you healthy?" and "Is your family o.k.?") are common greeting phrases or questions. The respondent answers, *"Ani fayaadha"* ("I am fine"), *"Matinkos nagaadha"* ("My family is o.k."), *"Ati fayaadha"* ("What about you, are you fine?").

When people visit Oromo families, it is customary to be provided with something to drink or eat. It is expected that visitors will eat or drink what they are offered. Individuals can drop by and visit friends or relatives without informing them in advance.

Dating is an important interpersonal relation between a boy and a girl. Usually a young boy initiates this kind of relationship by expressing his love for a girl whom he wants to date. When a girl agrees that she loves him, too, they start dating each other. Premarital sex is not expected, but kissing and dancing are acceptable. Parents are not usually informed of a dating relationship. Dating may or may not lead to marriage. Having girlfriends and boyfriends provides social status and respect among peers.

9 LIVING CONDITIONS

Since Oromos are colonial subjects, their resources are mainly extracted by Ethiopian elites and their supporters. The majority of Oromos are rural people who lack social amenities, such as school and health services. They do not have basic services such as clean water, electricity, appropriate housing, transportation facilities, clinics, and hospitals. Electricity that is produced by Oromian rivers is mainly used by Amhara and Tigrayans.

Sometimes the Oromo people do not have enough food to eat because of the exploitation by the Ethiopian government. Since Oromos have been denied education by successive Ethiopian regimes, the size of the Oromo middle class is very small. The living condition of this class is better than that of the Oromo majority. Members of this class mainly live in urban areas.

Currently, because of the military conflict between the Oromo Liberation Army and the Ethiopian government militia, Oromo peasants are constantly harassed, murdered, or imprisoned by the government. The Ethiopian government robs their properties, claiming that they are harboring guerrilla fighters. Because of poverty, war, lack of modern agricultural technology, lack of education, and exploitation, the living standard of the Oromo people is very low. They live in overcrowded huts; most huts house large, extended families consisting of parents and grandparents, brothers and their wives, unmarried brothers and sisters, and other relatives. Oromos use human labor and animals such as donkeys and horses for transportation in rural areas. They use cars, wagons, buses, and trucks for transportation in cities. Oromos are probably one of the most impoverished societies in the world.

10 FAMILY LIFE

The basic unit of a household is the family. There are neighborhoods and communities that are important social networks connected to the extended family. A man, as head of the family, has authority over his wife (or wives) and unmarried sons and daughters. An Oromo man in general has one wife, but because of religious conversion to Islam and other cultural borrowing, some Oromo men marry more than one wife (a practice known as polygamy). Divorce is discouraged in Oromo society. Recently, Oromo women have begun to resist polygamy. Because of patriarchy and sexism, Oromo women are subordinate to men. Despite the fact that there are Oromo women fighters and military leaders who are engaged in the liberation struggle, the status of Oromo women is not yet changed.

11 CLOTHING

Some Oromo men wear *wooya* (toga-like robes), and some women wear *wandabiti* (skirts). Some Oromo men and women wear garments of leather or animal skin robes, and some women wear *qollo* and *sadetta* (women's cloth made of cotton). Oromo men and women also wear different kinds of modern garments made in different parts of the world. In cash-producing areas and cities, Oromos wear modern Western-style clothes. Oromos have special clothes for special days. They call clothes they wear on holidays or other important days' *kittii*, and clothes that they wear on working days *lago*.

12 FOOD

The main foods of Oromos are animal products including *foon* (meat), *anaan* (milk), *baadu* (cheese), *dhadha* (butter), and cereals eaten as *marqa* (porridge) and *bideena* (bread). Oromos drink coffee, *dhadhi* (honey-wine), and *faarso* (beer). There are Oromos who chew *chat* (a stimulant leaf).

The special dish of Oromos is called *itoo* (made with meat or chicken, spices, hot pepper, etc.) and *bideena* (made from xxafi or millet). Sometimes mar*q*a or *qincee* (made from barley) is eaten for breakfast. All members of the family eat together. *Ancootee* (root food) is special food in some parts of western Oromia. Members of the family sit on stools, eat off wooden platters or dishes, use wooden spoons or other spoons for liquid foods, and use washed hands for nonliquid foods. The majority of Oromos eat twice, in the morning and at night. Muslim Oromos do not eat pork for religious reasons.

13 EDUCATION

Literacy is very low in Oromo society, probably less than 5%. Oromos mainly depend on family and community education to transmit knowledge to the younger generation since they do not have control over modern education. Older family and community members have a social responsibility to teach children about Oromo culture, history, tradition, values, etc. When some children go to colonial school to learn what the colonial government wants to teach them, oral historians and cultural experts make sure that these children properly learn about Oromo society.

Although their numbers are very limited, there are three kinds of schools in Oromia: missionary, *madarasa* (Islamic), and government schools. Islamic schools teach through sixth grade, and the other schools teach until twelfth grade. Oromos do not have control over these schools; hence, Oromo culture and values are constantly attacked by these schools. Despite all these problems, Oromo parents have very high expectations for education. If they can afford it, they do not hesitate to send their children to school.

14 CULTURAL HERITAGE

Respect and social equality are expected among members of the Oromo community. These values are expressed in *geerarsa* or *mirisa* (singing), storytelling, poems, proverbs, etc. *Geerarsa* is used to praise good behavior and discourage behavior that is not approved by the community. Respect for elders, social responsibility for the community and individuals, helping others, bravery, hard work, and work excellence are all appreciated. Historical and cultural knowledge is admired. Oromos can count their family trees through 10 generations or more.

Oromo cultural heritages are expressed through *mirisa, weedu,* and different cultural activities. There are different kinds of *weedu,* such as *weedu fuudha* (marriage song), *weedu lola* (war song), and *weedu hoji* (work song). Oromo women have their own song called *helee* that they use to express their love for their country, children, husbands, etc. Young boys sing to call girls to marriage ceremonies by singing *hurmiso*. Men do *dhichisa* (a men's dance to celebrate the marriage ceremony) and girls do *shagayoo* (singing and dancing) during marriage ceremonies. There are prayer songs called *shubisu* and *deedisu*.

15 WORK

Oromos are mainly farmers and pastoralists. Young educated Oromos move to cities to look for job opportunities and other social amenities. There are also merchants in Oromo society, although their number is very small. There are also weavers, goldsmiths, potters, and woodworkers.

16 SPORTS

Hunting and military skills were important sports in pre-colonial Oromia. Oromo men used to hunt large animals for a test of manhood; they also used products of the game, such as hides, ivory, and horns. Hunting was seen as a school of warfare for young Oromos; it helped them learn how to handle their weapons and prepare themselves for difficult conditions.

Popular sports played by children and young adults in Oromo society include *gugssa* (horseback riding), *qillee* (field hockey), *darboo* (throwing spears), *waldhaansso* (wrestling), *utaalu* (jumping), and swimming. Oromo society has pro-

Oromo women binding straw. (The Image Works)

duced athletes who have competed and won in international sports events. Wami Biratu, an Oromo soldier serving in the Ethiopian colonial army, was the first Oromo athlete to participate in the Olympic Games, in 1956, and he became a source of inspiration for other Oromo athletes.

Ababa Biqila, another Oromo soldier, won the 1960 Rome Olympic Marathon and set a new world record by running barefoot. Another Oromo soldier, Mamo Wolde, became the 1968 Olympic Marathon Champion. Other Oromo soldiers had also succeeded in international competitions, including Mohammed Kedir, 10,000-meter bronze medalist, and Kebede Balcha, Bakala Daballe, Daraje Nadhi, Wadajo Bulti, Eshetu Tura, Adunya Lama, and Challa Urgeesa who were international cross-country champions. Their Oromo coach, Nugussie Roba, won three consecutive international cross-country titles.

In 1988, Ababa Makonnen, Ababa Biqila's nephew, won the Tokyo Marathon, and Wadajo Bulti and Kabada Balcha came in second and third. Daraje Nadhi and Kalacha Mataferia won first and second place, respectively, in the World Cup marathon in 1989. In 1992, Daraartu Tullu, an Oromo woman, won the gold medal for her victory in the 10,000-meter race in the Barcelona Olympic Games. In 1996, another Oromo woman, Fatuma Roba, became a women's marathon gold-medalist; she was the first from Africa to win this kind of victory, and she was the fastest marathon runner in the world. The successes of these Oromo athletes demonstrate the rich cultural heritage of athleticism in Oromo society. Unfortunately, the victories of these athletes went to Ethiopia, not Oromia.

¹⁷ ENTERTAINMENT AND RECREATION

Oromos come together and enjoy themselves during ceremonies such as weddings, holidays, and harvest festivals. During these events they eat, drink, sing, dance, talk, etc. Jumping, running, swimming, wrestling, and other sports activities are used for recreation by boys and young adults. Oromo adults like to come together and sit and chat during weekends, after work, and on holidays.

¹⁸ FOLK ART, CRAFTS, AND HOBBIES

There are Oromos who specialize in making musical instruments such as the *kirar* (five-stringed bowl-lyre), *masanqo* (one-stringed fiddle), drums, etc. Iron tools, such as swords, spears, hoes, axes, and knives, have been important for farming, fighting, and hunting. Woodworking has been known for a long time in this society; carpenters make such objects as platters, stools, spades, tables, plows, bows and arrows, wooden forks, honey barrels, etc.

Similarly, goldwork has been practiced in some parts of Oromia. Goldsmiths specialize in making earrings, necklaces, and other gold objects. There are Oromos who specialize in making other utensils from horn, pottery, and leather. Mugs, spoons, and containers for honey-wine are made from horn. Basins, dishes, water jars, and vessels are made from pottery. Various kinds of milk vessels are made from leather. There are Oromos who specialize in making clothes.

19 SOCIAL PROBLEMS

Oromo human and civil rights have been violated by successive Ethiopian governments and their supporters. Oromos do not have control over their lives, lands, other properties, or their country. They do not have a voice in the government, and they are not allowed to support independent Oromo political organizations. Oromos have been systematically harassed, murdered, or imprisoned for sympathizing with the Oromo national movement, particularly the OLF. Oromos are not administered by the rule of law. Today the Tigrayan-led government engages in state terrorism and gross human rights violations because of two major reasons. The first reason is to destroy the Oromo national movement led by the OLF. The second reason is to loot the resources of the Oromo people and in order to enrich the Tigrayan elites and develop Tigray.

Today thousands of Oromos are kept in secret concentration camps and jails just for being Oromo or trying to determine their destiny as a people. Some Oromo activists or suspected activists are killed by Ethiopian soldiers, and their bodies are thrown on the streets to terrorize the Oromo people and to prevent them from supporting the Oromo national movement. Human rights organizations such as Africa Watch, Oromia Support Group, and Amnesty International have witnessed many human rights abuses inflicted on Oromos.

20 GENDER ISSUES

Before the colonization of Oromo society by Abyssinia/Ethiopia, the Oromo people had their own government and institutions such as Gada and Siqqee. These intuitions defended the interest of Oromo women on some level. The Ethiopian colonial system suppressed or destroyed both the Gada system and the Siqqee institutions and undermined the role and power of Oromo women in society. The emergence of class and gender stratification in some regions of Oromia also undermined the role of Oromo women in those regions.

The Habasha (Ethiopian) colonial government targeted Oromo women by cutting their breasts, raping, terrorizing, torturing and killing them. All of these crimes against humanity have been committed on Oromo women to commit genocide on Oromo society. Currently, the agents of the Meles regime are frequently raping Oromo women and young girls in an attempt to demoralize and destroy the Oromo people. The soldiers and officials of the Meles government have collected young Oromo girls and women into concentration camps and gang raped them in front of their relatives, fathers, and husbands to humiliate them and the Oromo people.

Because of Ethiopian colonialism and an oppressive cultural system, almost all Oromo women are part of the most impoverished sector of Oromo society. Today, the Oromo people in general and Oromo women in particular are exposed to state-terrorism and other forms of violence and poverty. They do not have personal and economic security. Since Oromo resources such as land are owned by the Tigrayan government, Oromo women cannot produce enough food and cash crops to feed their children. The Ethiopian government controls and owns most of Oromo economic recourses, including the land.

In Oromo society, the remaining economic resources are mainly in the hands of Oromo men. As a result, Oromo women are denied access to education, business, health services and other opportunities. In addition, Oromo families usually use their meager economic resources to educate Oromo boys while limiting Oromo girls to engage in agricultural and domestic activities. The three forms of oppression—national, class and gender—are combined to force Oromo women to the bottom of Oromo society. Generally speaking, Oromo women have been also oppressed because of gender norms even by their parents, brothers, husbands and communities. Religious beliefs also do not promote equality of gender in Oromo society.

Oromo culture does not promote gender equality despite the claim of Gada democracy and the legacy of Siqqee institution. There are several ways in which the inferior position of women is expressed in Oromo society. Oromo families are happier when baby boys are born than when girls are born. Jeylan W. Hussein notes that "after a child is born the midwives declare the sex of the child, usually by ululating five times for the baby son and four times for a baby daughter." This cultural practice demonstrates how society values boys more than girls. In addition, most Oromo families and communities send only boys to school. Consequently, there are only a few educated Oromo women today in Oromo society.

One way of maintaining the norms of gender inequality in Oromo society is proverb (mammakissa). For instance, let us consider the meaning of the following proverb: "Beerti qoonqoo tolchiti malee dubbi hintolchitu." Those who use this proverb limit the role of Oromo women to cooking and deny their capacity to engage in other roles such as education and administration. Another proverb says, "Beeraafi harreen ba'aa hin dhadhaban" (Women and donkeys do not complain about burden). This proverb claims that women should do difficult tasks without complaining in their society, such as cooking, fetching water, and rearing children. Some proverbs reflect that women are ignorant and are not capable of comprehending much. "Dhalaan akkuma harmaati ayyliin rarraati" (Women's hearts sway just like their breasts). Feminine body parts and brains are attacked by this kind of proverb to humiliate women and maintain gender stratification.

Oromo culture prepares women to be subservient to men. It victimizes them culturally, politically and psychologically. For example, one proverb states the following: "Niiti fii farda abbatu leenjifata" (The owner domesticates his horse and his wife). First of all this proverb reduces the status of a wife to that of a horse. This automatically violates her human rights. Second, if a husband treats his wife and his horse equally, the wife is not a free human being. Of course, there are proverbs that demonstrate Oromo women are very important in society. One of them is, "Dudaaf dubartin ka'u" (A man who has a strong and intelligent wife is successful in life). Yet, women have to work day and night to earn such praise. These oppressive gender values in Oromo culture have limited the development of the vision and potential of Oromo women as the Ethiopian colonial system has negatively affected both men and women. Both Islam and Christian beliefs enforce these oppressive values. Islam allows a man to be married to more than one wife. There are non-Muslim Oromo who get married to many wives. Such practices oppress Oromo women.

Today in the 21st century, very few Oromo women are formally educated because of the denial of access to education both by the Ethiopian colonial system and Oromo cultural values. Almost all Oromo women are also denied economic opportunities, liberties, and social power. As the most oppressed and exploited sector of Oromo society, Oromo women struggle daily for the survival of their families and children by focusing on basic necessities such as food and shelter. Most of them suffer from absolute poverty, malnutrition, disease, and other social disabilities. Moreover, they do not have security and protection in their own communities because of the violence of the Ethiopian government that targets Oromo women to destroy the foundation of Oromo society.

In addition, they do not have adequate knowledge, skills, and time to organize themselves to represent their interest in society by being involved in decision-making processes on the political level. These conditions have also limited the involvement of women in the Oromo national struggle both in Oromia and the Diaspora. Since the population of Oromo women is equal to or more than Oromo men, without their vision and full participation, to think about the liberation of the Oromo people is an illusion. Therefore, the realization of the potential of Oromo women is required to fully mobilize the Oromo nation to struggle for liberation, freedom, economic development, and democratic governance and national security.

Although a serious attention is not given for the liberation of Oromo women from gender oppression by Oromo nationalists and Oromo liberation organizations, it is impossible to liberate the Oromo nation without the total mobilization of Oromo girls and women. The mobilization of Oromo girls and women requires to include their interest in the Oromo national struggle and to involve them in the decision-making process at all levels. While struggling against Ethiopian colonialism, it is very important to fight against gender inequality and the aspects of Oromo cultural values that degrade women. Furthermore, Oromo women need to organize themselves in order to fully participate in the ongoing Oromo national struggle and social revolution to liberate themselves from all forms oppression and exploitation.

21 BIBLIOGRAPHY

Amnesty International. *Ethiopia: Accountability Past and Present: Human Rights in Transition.* Amnesty International report, April 1995.

Bartles, Lambert. *Oromo Religion.* Berlin: Dietrich Reiner Verlag, 1990.

Bulcha, Mekuria. "Darartu Tullu: An Interview with Africa's New Olympic Star." *The Oromo Commentary* 2, no. 2 (1992): 31–33.

Demie, Feyisa. "The Oromo Population and the Politics of Numbers in Ethiopia." *The Oromo Commentary* 6, no. 1 (1996): 21–27.

Huntingford, G. W. B. *The Galla of Ethiopia: The Kingdom of Kafa and Janjero.* London: International African Institute, 1955.

Hussein, J.W. "A cultural representation of women in the Oromo society." *African Study Monographs,* 25(3): 103-147, 2004.

Jalata, Asafa. *Oromia & Ethiopia: State Formation and Ethnonational Conflict, 1868–1992.* Boulder, CO and London: Lynne Rienner Publishers, 2005 [1993].

———. "The Struggle for Knowledge: The Case of Emergent Oromo Studies." *The African Studies Review* 39, no. 2 (September 1996): 1–29.

Legesse, Asmarom. *Gada: Three Approaches to the Study of African Society,* New York: Free Press, 1973.

Megerssa, Gemetchu. "Knowledge, Identity and the Colonizing Structure: The Case of the Oromo in East and Northeast Africa." Ph.D. dissertation, University of London School of Oriental and African Studies, 1993.

Tufa, Jimma. "Sport in the Oromo Society." *The Oromo Commentary* 2, no. 1 (1992): 27–30.

—by A. Jalata and Z. Kalil

RWANDANS

PRONUNCIATION: ruh-WAHN-duhns
LOCATION: Rwanda
POPULATION: 9 million
LANGUAGE: Kinyarwanda; French; Swahili; English
RELIGION: Catholicism (60%); Protestantism (20–30%); Islam (5%); small numbers of Baha'is
RELATED ARTICLES: Vol. 1: Hutu; Tutsi

¹ INTRODUCTION

Since 1994, the country of Rwanda has become infamous for political upheaval and ethnic strife. This unfortunate image has obscured the fact that Rwanda in better times is a very pleasant country to live in or to visit, and its people are quite industrious. Rwanda is one of the few ancient African kingdoms to have survived colonialism as a viable political entity. However, it underwent profound changes during the colonial era that continue to have negative repercussions. The population is composed of three ethnic groups: the Hutu (approximately 85–90% of the total population), the Tutsi (10–15%), and the Twa (less than 1%). The two most numerous groups, the Hutu and the Tutsi, have often been pitted against one another in what appears to be an ancient tribalistic struggle, but really is a direct result of the way Rwanda was governed under colonialism (1895–1960).

When German colonialists first established contact with the Rwandan king in the 1890s and later signed a treaty with him that turned Rwanda into a colony, the Germans thought that, because the king was Tutsi, the entire Tutsi group was racially superior and more intelligent than the Hutu group. As a result, a small number of Rwandan Tutsi benefited from German colonial rule and became native chiefs. Later, when the Germans lost World War I (1914–1917), Rwanda came under Belgian colonial control. The Belgians did little to change the pattern in ethnic relations that had emerged under the Germans. A small number of Tutsi (though not the entire group) continued to benefit disproportionately from the colonial system. Naturally, this did much to foster resentment among the much more numerous Hutu. Despite these conflicts, the Hutu, Tutsi, and Twa have spoken the same language, Kinyarwanda, for the past 500 or more years and have shared many cultural characteristics.

During the 1950s it began to appear that many Tutsi favored independence from Belgium (possibly inspired by anti-colonialist leaders in the neighboring Belgian Congo, such as the alleged "communist," Patrice Lumumba). The Belgians, therefore, decided to change directions and favor the Hutu. Towards the end of the decade, Belgian colonial administrators began replacing Tutsi chiefs with Hutu ones, and encouraged the Hutu's animosity towards the Tutsi. Claiming that they were acting in the interests of Rwanda's majority and thus being "democratic," the Belgians were actually creating a new system of ethnic favoritism. Events took a violent turn in 1959 after several Hutu political leaders were slain by Tutsi. Shortly afterward, large numbers of Hutu began to attack, kill, and/or drive Tutsi from their homes. Tens of thousands of Tutsi were slain, and many more fled to neighboring countries as refugees. In UN-monitored elections in 1962, Hutu political parties won an overwhelming majority, and the Tutsi monarchy was abolished.

For the next three decades, Rwandan Tutsi were treated as second-class citizens. In 1990, however, a rebel group—the Rwandan Patriotic Front, composed largely, though not entirely, of Tutsi refugees—invaded Rwanda from Uganda. Fighting raged on and off for the next four years. The Rwandan government resorted increasingly to racist anti-Tutsi propaganda to assure its shaky support among Hutu. Finally, after the Rwandan president was killed in a mysterious rocket attack on his plane in April 1994, a genocide against Rwandan Tutsi was launched in which up to 1 million people were killed. Victims of this carnage were mostly Tutsi, although perhaps thousands of Hutu opponents of the regime also perished. In July 1994, the rebel group (the Rwandan Patriotic Front) defeated the former government's army. Since then, Rwanda has been governed by a group dominated by Tutsi, but in which there are several Hutu who occupy important positions. Many Rwandan Hutu, however, mistrust the present Rwandan Patriotic Front (RPF) government.

Unity and reconciliation between Rwandan citizens is a high political priority for the present government, who vows to break completely with the past 100 years of Rwandan history and to construct a society in which ethnicity no longer plays a part. The government's national reconciliation discourse is based on a view that ethnicity in Rwanda was invented and politicized by colonial occupation. Consequently, in today's public discourse, all references to Hutu, Tutsi and Twa have been banned and replaced with the all-inclusive Rwandans. The Rwandan population is urged to reconcile with each other and to live with each other peacefully.

The local juridical court (known as Gacaca, which is translated as "justice on the grass") and the solidarity camps (known as Ingando) are some of the initiatives that the government has taken in order to reach unity and reconciliation among its citizens. The International Criminal Tribunal for Rwanda, located in Tanzania, has concentrated on bringing the ringleaders of the genocide to account. However, tens of thousands of other genocide suspects still await trial in Rwanda's crowded prisons. Given Rwanda's shortage of judges and lawyers, the government has turned to the Gacaca, a traditional system of justice, in order to escape impunity (freedom from punishment). Over 250,000 community members have been trained to serve in Gacaca courts all over Rwanda. Gacaca hearings are held outdoors every week, and most villagers take part. The tribunals first identify victims, then suspects—and finally hold trials. Local residents give testimony on behalf of and against the suspects, who are tried in the communities where they are accused of committing crimes, and many of those who are tried become prisoners.

Ingando are civic education camps that the government runs to plant seeds of reconciliation. Rwandan citizens from diverse walk of life, including students, church leaders, ex-soldiers, ex-combatants, genocidaires (perpetrators of the genocide), and others, are encouraged or required to attend Ingando. The camps include lectures on the government program, Rwandan history, and unity and reconciliation. In spite of the governmental efforts to unite the Rwandans, many people still feel insecure and suspicion remains strong between different groups. Retribution and false accusations at the Gacaca courts constitute some of the fears. Witnesses also feel insecure, as many of them have been attacked and even killed in connection with Gacaca. Coming to terms with the ethnic divisions of the past remains a major challenge.

2 LOCATION AND HOMELAND

Rwanda is a tiny country about the size of the US state of Massachusetts. It is located in the Great Lakes region of Central Africa. To Rwanda's west lies one of Africa's largest countries, the Democratic Republic of the Congo (formerly Zaire), while to the east is Tanzania. Uganda is the country directly to the north, while Burundi is located to the south. Despite the country's proximity to the equator (about 2°s), high altitude keeps the climate temperate. Most Rwandans live at altitudes between 1,500 m (5,000 ft) and 2,100 m (7,000 ft) above sea level. Rwanda usually receives a fair amount of rain (about 100–150 cm or 40–60 in), but there are occasional droughts. During a typical year, there is one long rainy season (March to May), one long dry season (June to September), another wet season (October to December), and a short dry season (January and February), but these seasons are seldom regular.

Rwanda is Africa's most densely populated country and the population has increased with almost 2 million people since the genocide in 1994, currently reaching a total population of approximately 9 million people. Approximately 89% of Rwanda's population lives in rural areas and gains its livelihood from agriculture, but there are several cities. Kigali, the capital, is the largest city, with a population of about 800,000 people.

In 1994 over 3 million refugees, virtually all Hutu, scattered across the region, residing in refugee camps in Tanzania, the Democratic Republic of the Congo (DRC), and Burundi. These refugees fled Rwanda in the late spring and summer of 1994 as the Rwandan Patriotic Front (RPF) gradually took control of the country. Some fled the country out of fear that the largely Tutsi RPF would take reprisals against them. Others fled simply because they were forced to do so by soldiers of the former Rwandan government's army and its allied militias. During the last months of 1996, the RPF invaded the DRC and destroyed refugee camps; thousands of Hutus were killed during those attacks while most others had to re-enter Rwanda, and began to return in large numbers. A high percentage of Tutsi, who fled to neighboring countries during the 1960s, have also returned to Rwanda since the RPF came to power. The government of Rwanda has encouraged all Rwandans who fled the country to come back. In 2007, 50,000 Rwandans still remained in exile, while all the rest had returned. Most of the returnees are re-integrated and accepted back into their communities. The majority of Rwandans who remain in exile do so due to disagreements with the present government, or out of fear of facing genocide charges upon their return.

3 LANGUAGE

All Rwandans speak Kinyarwanda, a Bantu language, that is rather difficult for most foreigners to master. One of its major sources of difficulty for Europeans and Americans is its vowel system. Vowels can differ in length and tone, and such changes entirely alter the meaning of a word or phrase. Another difficulty in Kinyarwanda is the fact that there are 20 different noun classes. English has only two basic noun classes: singular and plural.

Many educated Rwandans also speak French, the country's second official language and the language used by the Bel-

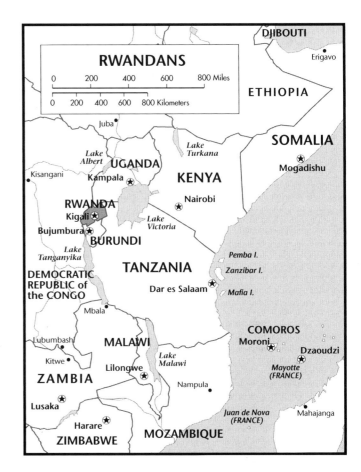

gian colonialists. Rwandans may also speak Swahili, which is something of a lingua franca (common language) in East and Central Africa. Finally, English is becoming increasingly common, especially in urban areas. This is partly because the new group of leaders in Rwanda (affiliated with the Rwandan Patriotic Front) were raised in English-speaking Uganda. But it is also because many people in recent years have decided to learn English at courses taught in Kigali and other cities.

4 FOLKLORE

Rwandan culture is rich in oral traditions, including legends, stories, and poetry. In fact, Rwandan art is much more devoted to literature, poetry, music, and dance than it is to painting or sculpture. Much of Rwandan folklore from the 19th and early 20th centuries had to do with Rwandan sacred kingship. Until 1931, the Rwandan king was non-Christian and was believed by many of his subjects to have sacred powers. Ritual specialists associated with the king possessed special knowledge of Rwandan history and ritual. Much of this enormous body of knowledge was kept in their memories in the form of poetry. Occasionally, the specialists were called upon to recite their allotted portions of the sacred texts.

In the early 20th century, Belgian colonial authorities and Catholic missionaries succeeded in deposing the non-Christian Rwandan king and replaced him with his Christian son. By the 1940s and 1950s, it became apparent that the sacred knowledge possessed by the ritual specialists would soon die with them, as they were growing old and no new specialists were being trained. In order to prevent this, Rwandan and European scholars set about recording and transcribing the sacred and historical texts. For this reason there is a record of traditional Rwandan ritual, poetry, history, and literature that far surpasses most other sub-Saharan African societies. The rituals that were associated with Rwandan sacred kingship included rainmaking rituals, rituals to stop the rain in the event of flooding, rituals to assure that the cattle reproduced in abundance, rituals to assure that the bees produced honey in abundance, and rituals to assure victory in battle.

Where ordinary people were concerned, Rwandan culture was also quite rich in stories and legends for the moral instruction of children, or simply for entertainment and distraction. Many of these stories, or variants of them, are still recounted to this day.

5 RELIGION

Catholic and other Christian missionaries have extensively evangelized Rwanda since the colonial era. For that reason, about 60% of Rwandans today are Catholic, and another 20–30% are Protestants of various denominations. The number of Muslims has increased in recent years. Many that have converted to Islam are said to have done so because of mistrust towards the Christian church, as some Catholic and Protestant religious leaders played an active role in the genocide, while Muslims stayed neutral in the conflict. Still, the Muslims make up less than 5% of the population in Rwanda. In a few Rwandan cities such as the capital of Kigali, the Baha'i faith is gaining a foothold.

It is difficult to determine with precision how many Rwandans follow a traditional religion. Often Rwandans will follow both traditional religious practices and some form of Christianity at the same time. They see no contradiction in doing this, for they feel that Imaana (the supreme being) can only be reached through intermediaries. Whether these intermediaries are Christian or traditional in origin is of little importance. According to Rwandan conceptions, Imaana is both a benevolent, creative spirit responsible for all life, and at the same time a distant and indifferent god. The most common means of communicating with Imaana is through the spirits of deceased family members *(abazimu),* or through more important deities that are like "super" ancestors. Two of the most common deities of this latter sort are Ryangombe, who is quite commonly venerated in southern and central Rwanda, and Nyabingi, a goddess who is venerated in northern Rwanda. In both cases, people who venerate either Ryangombe or Nyabingi claim that these spirits are intermediaries to Imaana, not ultimate sources of power and beneficence.

With regard to ancestors, many Rwandans (Christian or not) believe that after death one's spirit joins other ancestral spirits. Usually these spirits are thought to exert a protective influence upon the living, as long as the living remember to honor the ancestors with occasional sacrifices. An ancestral spirit might afflict a living person with illness, if the living person "forgets" the ancestor, i.e., neglects to offer the occasional small sacrifice in the ancestor's honor. Ancestral spirits might also afflict one of their descendants because the latter has wronged another member of the extended family.

6 MAJOR HOLIDAYS

Rwandans today go by the Christian calendar and observe the major Christian holy days such as Christmas and Easter. Other Roman Catholic festivals are also observed, such as Ascension Day and All Saints' Day. National holidays also include Independence Day on the first of July, which marks independence from the Belgian colonizers, and Liberation Day the fourth of July, which marks the end of genocide. Liberation Day is celebrated throughout the country with music, dance and recitals. Moreover, the country observes a national day of mourning each year on April 7, the day on which the genocide started. Each year a new site is chosen from which bodies from the genocide are exhumed and given a formal burial. The president leads the ceremony, which is broadcast on state television and radio. The day is also commemorated all over the country at lower administrative levels. National television and radio channels devote their broadcasts to the theme of genocide. The month of April more generally is considered to be a month of mourning and parties or celebrations of any kind are discouraged.

Most of the traditional Rwandan festivals are no longer officially observed, with the exception of *Umuganura,* a harvest ritual that is celebrated in August.

7 RITES OF PASSAGE

Rwandans mark major transitions in life by performing rituals that demonstrate to the community that an individual has changed her or his social status. These include birth, marriage, the joining of the cult of Ryangombe or Nyabingi, blood-brotherhood, and death. For those Rwandans who practice the traditional religions (the cult of Ryangombe, or the cult of Nyabingi), becoming a member of the cult also requires the performance of a rite of passage. For those Rwandans who are members of Christian sects, baptism and confirmation serve as rites of passage.

Birth is the first important rite of passage. When a woman gives birth to a child, she and the child are supposed to be kept in seclusion, traditionally for eight days, though today it is usually only for four days. Care is taken during this time to properly dispose of the umbilical cord and the placenta, which are usually buried near the house. On the day that the woman and her child leave their seclusion, friends and family members visit the household and share in a celebration. Many people bring gifts to the new mother and father. The parents of the new mother bring a gift to their daughter's husband, and a quantity of sorghum porridge to their daughter. It is also on this day that the baby is presented to the public for the first time, and that the child's name is announced.

In contrast to many other sub-Saharan African peoples, Rwandans do not celebrate any type of initiation at puberty for either boys or girls. After puberty, marriage is the most important rite of passage. Females marry by about age 18 and males by age 22 or later. Marriage is extremely important for Rwandans because a person is not considered fully adult until she or he has been married and had at least one child. Marriage is actually a series of rites of passage, beginning with the betrothal and continuing with the wedding and with the birth of each child. At each of these stages, gifts are exchanged between the families of the wife and the husband. The most important of these gifts is the bride-wealth cow that the husband gives his wife's father. Later, when this cow gives birth to a female calf, the calf will be given to the husband. It is extremely important to have children in Rwandan culture because dying without leaving descendants means that no one will honor the deceased's spirit.

A funeral ceremony is the final rite of passage for a Rwandan. Although most Rwandans have a Christian funeral through their respective churches, many Rwandans also practice traditional rituals at this time. Because death is said to be "hot," it is not rare for a traditional ritualist to come to the home of a deceased person to "cool' the house and to aid the deceased's spirit in its transition to an ancestral spirit. It is also common to sacrifice a cow or bull as part of this ritual.

8 INTERPERSONAL RELATIONS

Under most circumstances, Rwandans are polite, warm, and helpful. Greetings are a central part of social etiquette. In rural areas, it is important to greet everyone that one passes in the fields and on pathways. Although this etiquette is not closely observed in large cities like Kigali, where one passes many people on the street, even in an urban environment it is considered rude not to acknowledge someone with whom one has some acquaintance. For certain people, a heartier form of greeting is in order. Here, the two parties "embrace" one another. In this type of greeting, the left hand reaches out to gently clasp the other person's hip, while the right hand reaches upward to touch the other person's shoulder.

To be a socially acceptable person, one must visit one's friends and relatives, as well as accept the visits of others. Rwandans spend much of their time visiting one another. This helps to maintain good social relations with others. Someone who rarely visits others is considered antisocial and would probably arouse the suspicions of his neighbors and relatives. Although Rwandans do not always offer a guest something to eat, it would be considered a breach of etiquette if the guest were not offered something to drink. Drinking is the foremost social activity among Rwandans, and drinks range from very mildly alcoholic to moderately so. The two most common forms of alcoholic beverage are a drink made from sorghum, and one made from fermented plantains. Whenever a visitor arrives, the good Rwandan host attempts to find him or her something to drink. If a guest is present at one's home while others are drinking and is not offered something to drink, it is considered an insult.

It would be wrong to assume, however, that all people are equal when it comes to social occasions where drinking or eating is involved. It is here that we see Rwanda's ethnic differences at work. When Tutsi and Hutu eat or drink together, they will often share the same cooking and drinking vessels. They may, for example, pass a calabash (gourd container) with a wooden straw in it from one person to another. Each person drinks in turn, pressing his or her lips to the straw. When Twa are present, though, they are not allowed to drink or eat from the same vessels. They will be served something to drink or eat, but their drinking and eating utensils will be separate from those of the others present.

9 LIVING CONDITIONS

Living conditions vary immensely between social classes and between urban and rural Rwandans. Affluent Rwandans who live in cities enjoy the amenities of running water, indoor plumbing, electricity, and phone service. Their houses resemble those one would find in an affluent American suburb, and are usually made of brick and concrete. But the majority of urban Rwandans live more simply. Many have small mud-walled houses with corrugated iron roofs. Although some may have electricity in their dwellings, most have neither electricity, running water, nor indoor plumbing.

In rural areas, a variety of house types exist. One may occasionally find brick houses with tile roofs, but only wealthy rural notables occupy this type of house. More frequently, one finds houses of wattle-and-daub construction. The traditional shape of a house is circular, but since colonial times many Rwandans have built rectangular houses. The roofs of such houses are usually constructed from corrugated iron, but it is not uncommon to find thatched-roof houses as well. These houses almost never have indoor plumbing, electricity, or running water. To obtain water, one must usually walk some distance to a spring or stream, a difficult and time-consuming chore that men leave to women and children. A few years ago, many rural Rwandans had to travel a long way to access a phone. Today village phones, that are found in many areas where no telecommunication service previously existed, allow people to make phone calls near their homes. Thanks to an improved health care system, access to health care has also improved for the rural population. Approximately 85% of all Rwandans live within 10 km of a primary health care facility. However, medical care remains an economical barrier to many people, and geographic distance and mountain terrain still constrain access to health care for many rural Rwandans. Rwanda is characterized by what is known as a "dispersed settlement pattern." This means that individual homesteads are spread out all over the countryside, rather than being gathered together in hamlets or villages. When Rwandans speak of their local area, they talk about which hillside they come from, rather than which village.

10 FAMILY LIFE

The term for family in Kinyarwanda, *inzu*, can mean either "family," "household," or "house." This unit consists of a husband, a wife or wives (a small percentage—perhaps 10%—of Rwandan men have more than one wife), and their children. When a man has more than one wife, each one will have a "house" within the fenced-in enclosure that encircles the whole homestead. Sometimes other persons who are related to the man of the house by blood, adoption, or marriage will live within this unit as well, but this is not common.

People from several related inzus who trace their descendance from a common male ancestor about five or six generations back comprise another kinship unit known as an *umuryango*. Usually the eldest or most influential male is considered the head of this unit. As descent through males is most important where one's social identity is concerned, Rwandan society is said to be patrilineal. The umuryango often controls a portion of land that it divides and allocates to its individual adult male members. Today, however, as a result of colonialism, much of Rwanda's land is owned by individuals as private property and can be bought and sold without seeking the approval of an umuryango.

When Rwandans marry, they must marry outside of their *umuryango*. A young man who is interested in marrying a particular young woman makes this wish known to his father. The father will then visit the young woman's father, bringing sorghum and plantain-beer as a gift, and the two fathers will

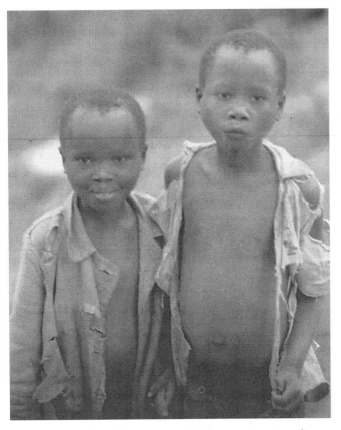

Rwandan children begin primary school at age seven. According to Rwandan law, all children are guaranteed at least a sixth-grade education. (Jason Laure)

discuss the issue. Very often, several visits will be necessary, which becomes costly for the prospective bridegroom's father as he must bring beer each time. Moreover, the bridegroom and his father will have to pay at least one bride-wealth cow to the bride's father in order for the marriage to take place. It is this payment of the bride-wealth cow that legitimizes any children that result from the marriage.

11 CLOTHING

In precolonial and early colonial times, Rwandans wore clothing made from animal skins and from pounded bark-cloth. Today this type of clothing is seen only in museums. Today Rwandans wear clothing that is the same as that worn by people in Western countries. The only difference is that the clothing Rwandans wear is second-hand. Only some Rwandans can afford to buy new clothing made by tailors in Rwanda. Rwandans began wearing European clothing during the colonial era. Today there is an active import trade in used clothing. In the cities men often wear shirt and pants. Rwandan women often wear dresses and scarves made from the printed cloth, but in the last ten years urban women and girls have increasingly started to use pants.

12 FOOD

The diet of the average Rwandan is high in starches, low in protein, and quite low in fat. The two most common foodstuffs are starchy plantains and beans. Often the two are boiled together.

Perhaps the next most common foodstuff is sorghum grain, which may be consumed as a cereal beverage, a porridge, or as sorghum meal. Sorghum and plantains are also used to prepare native Rwandan beers. Other commonly consumed vegetable foodstuffs include white potatoes, sweet potatoes, manioc, and maize (corn). Cabbage and carrots are also eaten occasionally. In certain areas of Rwanda, avocados are seasonally available, as are mangoes and pineapples.

Most Rwandans rarely eat meat, although the wealthy may consume it daily. The most commonly eaten meat is goat, which is usually barbecued over a charcoal burner. Beef is the most desired meat, but it is usually available only when a rural Rwandan has sacrificed a bull or cow on a ceremonial occasion. Urban Rwandans may consume beef more frequently. Cattle are valued for their prestige value and for their milk. Rwandans who can regularly drink milk count themselves as very fortunate. Mutton is also eaten, but most Tutsi, and many Hutu, spurn it because sheep are deemed to be peaceful animals whose presence is calming to cattle. In the past, only Twa ate mutton. When a sheep died, it was skinned. The skin was used to hold a baby on its mother's back, while the meat was given to Twa to eat. Today, though, many Rwandans eat mutton. Another new item in today's diet that was rarely eaten in the past is fish. Tilapia and catfish have become much more common as fish farming expands.

Only urban Rwandans eat three times a day. Rwandan farmers usually wake early, have something to drink, and work in the fields until about midday, at which time they eat something that they have brought with them. Often they cook the food right in the field. At the end of the day, after returning home, they eat again.

13 EDUCATION

Rwandan children begin primary school at age six. According to Rwandan law, all children are guaranteed at least a sixth-grade education. In reality, this does not always occur because parents sometimes cannot afford the cost of school uniforms, school supplies, and other minor expenses that even a primary student needs, and some families need their children's support in the household or to generate income. After the sixth grade, attendance at a secondary school is dependent upon selection. Before 1994, admission to secondary school was supposedly based on grades and test results, but it was often a political matter. Until the change of government in 1994, Tutsi stood much less chance of being admitted to secondary school than did Hutu, and virtually no Twa attended secondary school. Today the selection is based on the national exam taken at the end of primary school. The transition to secondary school is however very low. The reason for this low transition rate include poor performance in primary examinations, high fees charged in secondary schools, and long distance to existing schools, especially in rural areas.

Kinyarwanda is taught in all schools in the lower grades, while French and English are used for instruction in secondary school. Education in Rwanda seeks to inculcate a culture of nationhood marked by tolerance, social cohesion, and conflict resolution, and to stem the spread of HIV/AIDS. Challenges met are how to include orphans and children from child-headed households into education, and how to teach about the modern history of Rwanda and the genocide, a subject that still remains excluded from the curriculum.

Rwandans gather to watch dancers. Ritual occasions such as weddings include traditional music and dance, but there is also likely to be modern popular music as well. (Cynthia Bassett)

Higher education is mainly provided by universities and specialized institutes. Beyond secondary school, it is possible to attend a university in Rwanda, to attend nursing school, or even to attend medical school. There are also many post-secondary institutions that offer a wide range of courses such as finance, management, computer studies, statistics, economics and secretarial studies. There are also a number of teacher training colleges. Rwandan students who complete secondary school are required to attend Ingando (see Introduction) before they commence their university studies.

Although the literacy rate in Rwanda is only 49%, with a high rate of illiteracy in the countryside, many other Rwandans are quite well educated. Some have also had the opportunity to study in Europe or the US. Because of the number of educated people in Rwanda, international organizations have little trouble filling positions that require a college education or better. In recent years, educated Rwandans have been experiencing difficulty in obtaining employment.

High educational attainment is respected in Rwanda, and families make sacrifices to educate their children. Although every family strives to educate all its children, this is rarely financially possible. Because of the great expense of education, some children are favored over others. For those who receive the privilege of an education, it is expected that they will financially assist their other siblings and their parents in old age.

¹⁴ CULTURAL HERITAGE

Rwandans have a rich musical culture. Special dance groups known as *intore* perform dances that once had ritual significance in the context of war and sacred kingship. Dancers in the intore groups wear flowing headdresses made from dried grasses and carry small shields on their left arm. Variations of these dance styles are also perfomed by ordinary people at festive occasions such as weddings and other rites of passage. Several traditional musical instruments are played in Rwanda, and many among the Twa people are renowned as highly proficient musicians. Rwandans also possess a rich oral literature.

¹⁵ WORK

Rwandans are very industrious. In rural areas, men try to find paid employment wherever and whenever possible. They usually participate in some farming tasks as well. Women tend to farm the family land rather than work in wage-labor employment. In urban areas, though, many women have salaried jobs. In recent years, the number of women with salaried jobs has increased as the educational opportunities for women have improved.

¹⁶ SPORTS

The most popular sport in Rwanda is soccer. Numerous soccer clubs exist, competing in organized leagues. Rwandans attend soccer matches in droves, especially when the national team is playing. If they cannot attend an important match in person, they listen to it on the radio. The sport has become so popular that from a very tender age boys can be seen kicking and running after a "ball" that is merely a spherical bundle of rolled-up banana leaves. Often young girls join in these games as well, and there are even a few soccer clubs for adult women in cities like Kigali. Perhaps the next-most-popular sport after soccer is running, an activity that also inspires competitive interest from a very young age. Very few Rwandans swim. Those that live near lakes may swim recreationally but do not engage in the activity as a sport. Finally, there are a few urban, affluent Rwandans who have taken up tennis.

17 ENTERTAINMENT AND RECREATION

Ritual occasions such as weddings serve an important recreational function. Although a good portion of a wedding ceremony is likely to consist of speeches made by both the groom's and the bride's sides of the family, food and Rwandan beers will also be served. Later, when the speeches have ended, there will be music and dancing. Some of this will consist of traditional music and dance, but there is also likely to be modern popular music as well. Although the custom of formally inviting people to weddings and other ceremonies is becoming more common, no one who shows up is turned away from a festival. In fact, a large crowd at such an occasion reflects positively on the prestige of the host.

Rwanda has had a national radio station for almost 30 years, and a number of private radio stations have arisen in recent years. In the past 15 years, a television station has also been operative. Virtually everyone in the country owns and listens to a radio. In urban areas, TV ownership is increasing but is still mostly confined to the more affluent. Watching videos on VCRs has also become so popular that video rental stores now exist in large cities. Popular music, particularly American rock music, has had tremendous success in Rwanda. In urban discotheques, one can hear American rock, Caribbean reggae, and Zairian and Kenyan pop music. American dances and clothing fashions are quite popular, but these are always given something of a Rwandan "twist."

18 FOLK ART, CRAFTS, AND HOBBIES

Rwandans are known for their basket- and mat-weaving. Woven into these everyday utensils are elaborate geometric designs. One can also see these same designs painted on the large cooking vessels made by Twa potters. Occasionally these same motifs can be observed on the interior walls of traditional Rwandan houses, but today this is quite rare. In former times, Rwandans did not engage in woodcarving, sculpture, or artistic painting, but in recent years, these have become important craft activities. In cities, one can find many Rwandan artists who sell paintings, woodcarvings, and ceramic sculptures.

19 SOCIAL PROBLEMS

After the genocide of the Tutsi in 1994, and the following massacres of Hutus by the RPF army, reconciliation among Rwandans is a great challenge. Many initiatives have been taken by the Rwandan government to bring Hutu and Tutsi along the road to reconciliation, but genocide still leaves its mark for the most part of society.

The genocide has left a profound sense of injustice, fear and distress among Rwandans. The survivors of the genocide

have complained that they have not received appropriate compensation for their suffering. A large part of the Hutu population also consider themselves to be victims of the war, refugee camps or post-genocide revenge killings, but feel that they are being silenced and disregarded in the recovering process, rendering distrust towards the government. This situation has engendered resentment and frustration among the population, as well as suspiciousness between the groups.

Truth telling and fulfillment of justice through Gacaca (see Introduction) helps reconciliation for some Rwandans, but also means fear for a lot of people. Internal immediate conflicts are centered on Gacaca; genocide suspects, witnesses, and survivors have been assaulted, threatened and even killed in connection to the trials. In July 2006 the Gacaca commenced the trials of over 700,000 people accused of genocide, and during 2007 close to 100,000 people were held in Rwanda's overpopulated prisons, most of them accused of participation in the genocide. Groups of Hutus have left the country rather than to face the Gacaca courts, some out of fear of false accusations, which has already imprisoned several innocent Hutus and caused anger among them and their families. In spite of the government's work to obtain unity and reconciliation, and the will of many citizens to do so, mistrust prevails in many places, and fear of the other group still exists. Security is generally a pressing problem for survivors.

Rwanda is, even by African standards, a very poor country. Food security is a problem for a large part of the population, and the growing economic disparities between urban and rural population has created tension in the country. Since the era of colonialism, some Rwandans have improved their economic condition significantly. Others, particularly those involved in agriculture, have not yet seen their circumstances improved. Having a family member in prison is a heavy burden for an impoverished Rwandan household to carry, since the absence of labor is detrimental to agriculture, reducing productivity and hence food availability. Survivors left without family or relatives are also unable to cultivate land effectively. Further, AIDS is keeping many adults out of work and unable to support their already vulnerable households. AIDS has also left thousands of children orphaned, and when combined with the large number of Rwandan children who lost their parents in the genocide, this has resulted in one of the world's largest orphan populations (1.26 million). These children are extremely vulnerable to further neglect, abuse, and exploitation, and many are left to fend for themselves and their younger siblings.

20 GENDER ISSUES

Gender relations have changed in Rwanda since 1994. After the genocide, many women found themselves without a husband or male relatives to provide for them and were forced to handle tasks that they previously had not been considered suitable for. Furthermore, a strong political commitment to include women in the reconstruction of a country that was in shambles, has enabled women to enter the political arena. Rwanda's new constitution, adopted in 2003, mandates a 30% quota for women in parliament and in government. Additionally, political parties have promoted female candidates, which resulted in the world's highest ranking of women parliamentarians, 49 %, in the elections in 2003. However, the commendable achievements in parliament and other decision-making positions have not yet translated into any major differences for the vast majority of women in Rwanda. At a grassroots level, women's unpaid household work, feelings of inferiority, lack of experience in politico-administrative activities, and the high level of illiteracy, are barriers to their political participation.

Female-headed households constitute more than a third of all the households in Rwanda (which is largely a legacy of the genocide as it left many women widowed, and many men in prison). Those households are generally more affected by poverty than households led by men. Moreover, Rwanda is a patriarchal society that influences women's social position and gender relations in practice: Boys are sent to school rather than girls, and women remain in inferior positions to men and their social roles are foremost as mothers and wives.

21 BIBLIOGRAPHY

Buckley-Zistel, S. "Remembering to Forget: Chosen Amnesia as a Strategy for Local Coexistence in Post-Genocide Rwanda." In *Africa* Vol. 76 No. 2, 2006.

"Country Profile: Rwanda." In *The Economist Intelligence Unit,* The Economist Intelligence Unit, 2007.

D'Hertefelt, M., and A. Coupez. *La royaute sacrée de l'ancien Rwanda.* Teruven, Belgium: Musée Royale d'Afrique Centrale, 1954.

Handloff, R., ed. *Rwanda: A Country Study.* Washington, D.C.: Government Printing Office, 1990.

Kubai, A. "Walking a Tightrope: Christians and Muslims in Post-genocide Rwanda," In *Islam and Christian-Muslim Relations,* Vol.18 No. 2, 2007.

Lewis, R. *Ruanda-Urundi.* London: Oxford University Press, 1963.

Mamdani, M. *When Victims Become Killers: Colonialism, Nativism and the Genocide in Rwanda.* New Jersey: Princeton University Press, 2001

Maquet, J. *Le système des relations sociales dans le Ruanda ancien.* Teruven, Belgium: Musée Royale d'Afrique Centrale, 1954.

Meyerstein, A. "Between Law and Culture: Rwanda's Gacaca and Post-Colonial Legacy," In *Law and Social Inquiry,* Vol. 32, No. 2, 2007.

Mgbako, C. "Ingando Solidarity Camps: Reconciliation and Political Indoctrination in Post-Genocide Rwanda," In *Harvard Human Rights Journal,* Vol 18, 2005.

Newbury, C. *The Cohesion of Oppression.* New York: Columbia University Press, 1995.

Obura, A. *Never again: Educational reconstruction in Rwanda.* Paris: International Institute for Educational Planning, 2003.

Prunier, G. *The Rwanda Crisis: History of a Genocide.* New York: Columbia University Press, 1995.

"Republic of Rwanda." In *Amnesty International Report,* London: Amnesty International, 2007.

Reyntjens, Filip. "Post-1994 Politics in Rwanda: Problematising 'Liberation' and 'Democratisation,'" *Third World Quarterly,* Vol. 27, No. 6, 2006.

Taylor, C. *Milk, Honey and Money.* Washington: Smithsonian Institution Press, 1992.

—revised by A. Berglund

SAN

ALTERNATE NAMES: Khoi-San, Kung, Khwe, Juwasi, Basarwa, Bushmen
LOCATION: Botswana, Northern South Africa, Namibia
POPULATION: 100,000
LANGUAGE: Khoisan
RELIGION: San Religion

1 INTRODUCTION

The San trace their roots to the Kalahari Desert region of southern Africa. Several ethnic groups who historically survived through a hunter-gatherer lifestyle comprise the San people. The language of these groups is similar in origin. At one point in history, the San were known as "Bushmen," a term that most scholars today regard as racist. Controversy still surrounds the naming of these peoples. Other terms such as Khwe and Basarwa also have been used to describe these groups. The term San has been the preferred term by anthropologists since the 1970s, although the term Khoi-San also is commonly used. The Khoi (Hottentots) differ from the San in that they are taller and made their living through agriculture instead of foraging.

It is believed that San have lived in the area of the Kalahari Desert for thousands of years; they may be the first humans to have occupied this region before the appearance of the Nguni and other black peoples. Historians and anthropologists attribute the presence of the San in the Kalahari to animated paintings that appear on on rocks, walls, and caves in areas as distant as Namaqualand, the Drakensberg, and the Southern Cape. These forms of painting are considered the oldest in Africa. Many San subgroups continue today to live nomadic lives among more sedentary peoples such as the Bantu. There are many different San peoples, who lack a collective name but are variously referred to as "Bushmen," "San," "Basarwa" (in Botswana), and so on. The individual groups identify by names such as Juhoansi and Kung, and most call themselves "Bushmen" when referring to themselves collectively.

As hunter-gatherers, San initially subsisted on animals they caught, as well as honey, roots, and fruits they would gather. What they ate and where they resided was dependant traditionally on the seasons and the movement of animals indigenous to the Kalahari. Many scholars regard their traditional way of life as being in harmony with nature. The San would take care to use only what they needed and would not overhunt or take too many plants. Their bodies are characterized as short and slight in build. Their hands and feet are small, and their yellow-brown skin would wrinkle early in life. Some San groups most likely kept cattle and sheep.

Two languages spoken by the San—Khoe and Zhu I õasi—contain words referring to agricultural terms that date back 2,000 years. Further development of an agriculturalist way of life appears to have occurred 500 years later with the arrival of Bantu-speaking peoples to the region. The Bantu planted sorghum and millet, kept goats, and practiced metallurgy. Some linguistic evidence suggests that San peoples sold or traded cattle with Nguni and Sotho-Tswana Bantu speakers. These patterns suggest that while foraging remained important to the San people, it was combined with herding and farming over time.

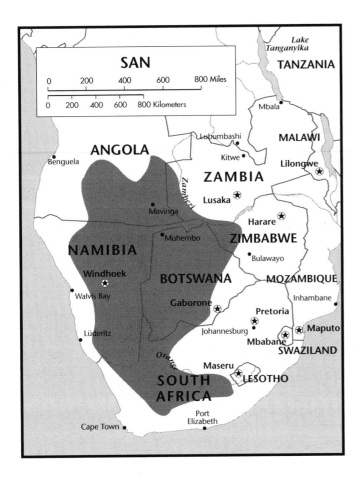

The arrival of white colonists to the San's traditional hunting grounds in the 17th century changed the San way of life. While some San joined the white society in subservient roles, others migrated to the west and north in search of lands where they could continue their traditional way of life. Today the San live primarily in the northwestern Cape, the Kalahari, Namibia, and Botswana. While a few San, mainly those who continue to live in the desert, still practice their traditional way of life, the people as a whole are considerably less nomadic.

Most San groups maintain a practice of hereditary leadership. This tradition is seen in the term for "chief," which is I xaiha and comes from a root word for "wealth." The authority of these leaders is limited today, although some individuals who possess such leadership positions will be elected to state-created offices, such as heads of village development committees. Holders of such positions tend to be older and respected among their people.

Since the mid-1990s the central government of Botswana has promoted a relocation policy aimed at moving the San out of their ancestral land on the Central Kalahari Game Reserve into newly created settlements. Although the government categorically denies that relocation has been forced, a 2006 court ruling confirmed that the removal was unconstitutional and residents were forcibly removed. Opponents to the relocation policy claim that the government's intent is to clear the area—an area the size of Denmark—for the lucrative tourist trade and for diamond mining. As of the mid-2000s, many San were

poised to return to the Central Kalahari Game Reserve, one of Africa's largest protected nature reserves.

Similarly, the San group as a whole has little voice in the national political process and none of the tribal groups is recognized in the constitution of Botswana. Over the generations, the Bushmen of South Africa have continued to be absorbed into the African population, particularly the Griqua sub-group, which are an Afrikaan-speaking people of predominantly Khoisan. Today, less than 5% of the approximately 100,000 San live as hunter-gatherers. Their cultural heritage is in danger of disappearing.

²LOCATION AND HOMELAND

The San peoples occupy highly diverse geophysical regions that share a number of features: seasonal rains, falling mainly as localized thunderstorms during the hot months, October to May; high variation in average annual rainfall—around 45 centimeters (18 inches) in Ngamiland (some 50% higher in Angola and 50% lower in central Botswana); summer temperatures that often exceed 37°C (99°F); and cool winters, with night temperatures as low as –4°C (25°F) in Botswana and Namibia. The Zhu I õasi live in northwestern Botswana, in a semi-arid savanna region known as Ngamiland and in surrounding regions of Namibia. The Xu group live in more tropical open woodlands in southern Angola that receive considerably more precipitation. Axoe occupy the banks of the Okavango River, in the Caprivi Strip of Namibia while the Hai I I om reside in north-central Namibia, between the Cunene River and the Etosha Pan. The Nharo live in the Ghansi District of Botswana, an area known for its limestone. The G I wi, G I I ana, and Koõ live in central Botswana and Namibia in areas that are sandy and receive little rainfall. The I I Anikhoe live in a flood plain created by the Okavango Delta; the Deti live along the Boteti River. Several other peoples who are called San in the ethnographic literature speak Khoe languages and live in the hill, mopane (a type of tree)forest, and salt-pan environments of eastern Botswana.

Because the San groups are so diverse, estimating the population is difficult. In 1980, it was estimated that about 30,000 San-speaking peoples lived in Botswana, about 12,000 in Namibia, and about 8,000 in Angola—representing about 3% of the population of Botswana, 1.2% of that of Namibia, and 0.1% of Angola's people. As of 2008 the entire San population was estimated at about 100,000. That year, regions with significant San populations include Botswana (55,000), Namibia (27,000) and South Africa (10,000).

The Zhu I õasi, who previously had a low birthrate and often waited years between births to conceive, now have one of the highest recorded birthrates in the world. In 1980, 6.7 live births were recorded for every 1,000 women of childbearing age. However, the infant mortality rate for the Zhu I õasi is comparatively low among Africans; in 1980, it stood at 85 per 1,000 births. Life expectancy has been improving since the 1960s when it was 45 years for Zhu I õasi. Now, demographers estimate that children who live to age 5 have a good chance of living into their 70s. Health ministry surveys done in Botswana suggest the Zhu I õasi statistics are similar for other San groups.

³LANGUAGE

The term "San" as an ethnographic term refers to both the contemporary and the pre-colonial southern African peoples who speak, or spoke, languages containing click consonants and who traditionally practiced a hunter-gatherer or forager way of life. They speak numerous dialects of a group of languages known for the characteristic "clicks" that can be heard in their pronunciation, all of which incorporate "click" sounds represented in writing by symbols such as ! or /.

Thus, San-speaking peoples do not constitute an ethnic group in the usual sense. The most widely known are those who call themselves "Zhu I õasi" (Kung or Juwasi in most ethnographies), although the other peoples mentioned above have also been extensively described; about 10 other groups have been well studied by linguists.

San languages are considered part of the Khoisan language family. Among the San languages are three sets. The first set is the Northern Khoisan Group. It consists of speakers of Zhu I oasi, Xu, and Au I I ei and was common to the area around Lake Ngami. This language today has few living speakers, and is distinct from other Khoisan languages in its grammar, syntax, and vocabulary. The second set is known as the Central Khoisan Group. It includes speakers of G I wi, G I I ana, Kxoe, Nharo, and I I Anikhoe, plus several other dialects, Deti, Buga, Tshukhoe, and Kwa, among them. It is closely related to Nama (also known historically as Hottentots), and Hai I I om, a dialect of Nama. The languages within the Central Khoisan Group are generally quite similar to each other, though differences in vocabulary and sentence structure develop in regions that are further from the central area. The final group of languages is known as Southern Khoisan, and consists of languages spoken along the southern Kalahari area. The primary languages in this area are Koõ and Tsassi. All of the Khoisan languages are known for containing mostly mono- and bisyllabic words. They also are tonal in nature, and contain click consonants. In writing, symbols such as ! and ¦ typically designate a click consonant, although Bantu orthography is starting to replace that practice by using c for ¦ and q for !. The use of letters in place of symbols is occurring more frequently in eastern Botswana, and some of the Khoisan languages are being replaced altogether by Setswana. That replacement marks a further erosion of San culture.

⁴FOLKLORE

San stories grow out of an oral tradition in which dramas about natural phenomena, dancing, drumming, poetry, death, and struggles between justice and mercy provide insight into how the ancient San people lived. In one story, retained as part of an online collection of oral narratives, the sun and moon spar. Ultimately, however, the sun spares the backbone of the moon so that it may grow again. Other works capture feelings of sadness that come from separating from a friend, or a loss of community because of migration and a desire to return home.

⁵RELIGION

San religions are polytheistic. Many gods are worshiped; however, San people do acknowledge that one god is supreme. Religious rituals show respect for deities, wives and children of deities, and spirits of those who have died. Some San also refrain from tilling soil, believing that such an agricultural practice would violate the world order established by god. San stories incorporate the role of gods in day-to-day life, with deities often serving as educators about good moral behavior. How gods are viewed varies with the different San peoples. The Zhu I õasi and the Koõ, for instance, regard the supreme god as playing the role of creator as well as administrator of earthly events. Lesser gods in many San groups are ancestors from their communities.

Many San practice a communal dance as a healing ritual for their community. The dance is believed to transform spiritual energy into medicine. During the dance, many participants go into a trance, and spiritual energy is called on to heal physical and psychological illnesses. Religious practitioners in San communities tend to be healers or shaman who will visit the world of spirits in order to create rain, ward off evil, and cure illness. Many San use blood, fat, and sweat from the eland (an African antelope) to generate spiritual energy, and images of the eland today often are made from the actual blood of the animal. The dancing that the San practice often involve performing in a circle around an animal carcass. As men and older women move their bodies in trance, young women clap and sing. The dancing occurs for hours, and leads often to an altered state of consciousness and hallucinations on the part of the shaman. The dances occur during occasional ceremonies or when the community is in crisis.

⁶MAJOR HOLIDAYS

No major holidays exist in indigenous San culture. San who have converted to Christianity or moved to more urban areas generally observe the same holidays as the dominant communities of those locales.

⁷RITES OF PASSAGE

The main ceremonies among San peoples are dance performances; these are usually attended by members of an extended family, but may include other relatives. The first menstruation of girls and the arrival of adolescence for boys traditionally were celebrated with dances initiating the youngsters into adulthood.

In the past, scar marks would be applied to the face, back, and chest of men and to the thighs of women to mark important life events, but these rituals are rarely performed today. Female genital mutilation also has not been recorded among the San people. Zhu I õasi, Nharo, and G I wi girls have a brief initiation at first menstruation, and Tshukhoe boys are circumcised.

Most San marriages are monogamous, although polygamous relationships are permitted for wealthier men. San parents generally arrange marriages of their children, in consultation with elders within their kinship groups. Some San groups—including the Zhu I õasi and Khoe—will allow cousins to marry. For others, the choice of more distant relatives as marital mates is preferred. If a child is not quickly born to a newly married couple, divorce is likely to occur.

The San treat death as a movement into a new spiritual realm. The Zhu I õasi understand death as a source of food for the supreme god. In this belief, humans are caused to die so the deity can eat. Some relatives of a newly deceased individual will believe that the god would try and cause the early deaths of survivors out of a desire to eat them, as well. The worry of early death fades as time passes.

8 INTERPERSONAL RELATIONS

The San organize their households and their communities on the basis of kinship ties. The Zhu I õasi, for instance, make use of what they call *hxaro* networks that link persons who are related through common great-grandparents. Sometimes, these networks create communal living arrangements. At other times, they create a sense of family among nomadic communities that span distances of 200 kilometers (125 miles) or more. Other San groups, including the Nharo and Khoe groups, have similar exchange networks. In the hxaro networks, marriages are arranged and certain familial obligations are imparted to participants. Gifts—called *kamasi* in Zhu I õasi and *kamane* in Nharo—are given in separate exchanges. San peoples also create social networks based on individuals who might not be related by blood but are of a similar age, as well as name groups, which often were based on identification with particular clans.

San groups maintain order through the use of ridicule, verbal abuse, dispersal, and divination. These practices have replaced executions and murders that were communally sanctioned in the past. The communities use informal hearings to resolve minor disputes. More serious cases are referred to local and district courts.

San children often live in huts built next to those of their parents. Parents and elders teach children proper forms of behavior at an early age. As a result, children tend to be well behaved and are taught to play with each other and to treat members of the opposite sex with respect and kindness. The wisdom and knowledge about the past that elderly San possess also is greatly valued by the community.

9 LIVING CONDITIONS

The Kalahari Desert makes living conditions for the San harsh. San shelters are made of sticks that are arranged in a circular form. Mats woven from reeds cover the sticks on top and along the sides. The idea behind such simple dwellings was to keep them simple and fast to take apart and re-assemble for when the San group was ready to move to a new locale. Such mat-covered huts are still used in Namaqualand.

Today, most San peoples live in or near villages that have small shops that provide for their needs. Groups in the central Kalahari, western Ngamiland, and at cattle posts, however, still rely on trades and itinerant visitors for goods. These groups often will travel several dozen kilometers by foot, donkey, or horseback for necessary supplies.

10 FAMILY LIFE

Each family resides in its own hut. As children reach adolescence, they often will move out of their parent's hut and built a separate dwelling nearby. If a family is polygynous, each wife will typically have her own hut. The extended family network remains important in San life and often families will live together in a homestead, where houses will be built close together and open up into a common area. Use of certain lands is often based on inherited rights that are based on past practices. However, to continue use of a particular area of land, one must reside on that area and participate in family affairs regularly. The current leader of a landholding group is generally regarded as the "owner" of the land and can grant permission to nonresidents to use the land. Permission generally is granted to family members but not to others.

A dozen homesteads, each one with a set of households for extended members, will make up a San settlement. Larger settlements often consist of 200 to 300 individuals. The homesteads typically will be located near seasonal rain pools where hunting and foraging of plants can take place, wells can be built, and livestock can be maintained. At times, many San groups, each speaking a different language, may reside in a single settlement, particularly in Ngamiland. Although homesteads are compactly built, a settlement may be more dispersed, with homesteads scattered apart by 2–3 kilometers (1–2 miles). Often, clients of a family or domestic help will live in huts adjacent to the families that employ them.

Both the arrangement of huts within homesteads and the collecting of homesteads into settlements reflects the interdependence that the San people regarded traditional as crucial to their survival. As foragers of food and hunters of meat, working in small groups who could quickly take down and build up an encampment was a means of living with little but always having enough. Rules based on names and age were frequently used to dispel confusion over relationships among family members. In recent years, many San have begun to settle into larger groups around water sources, and many have also settled into the communities of their neighbors.

11 CLOTHING

Traditional San clothing consists of a cloak known as a *kaross*, which is used to carry foods and supplies such as firewood, and loin cloths, sandals, and short aprons made of animal skin. All of the clothing is designed in a way that makes it easy to move quickly and carry basic household needs.

12 FOOD

Households within a San homestead may move apart during the winter when food supplies dwindle. The traditional San diet includes wild melons, roots, and berries that women gather. Men will use a bow and arrow to hunt wild animals. Arrowheads are covered with a poison made from an insect. San men are known for having great stamina. They are willing to follow an animal herd for days until they are close enough to use their bow and arrow to kill. A kill results in a feast. Families build a fire, and sing and dance in a trance-like ritual.

During hard times, women will chew on a tree bark that acts as a contraceptive to reduce the potential of having more children. San peoples also will eat snakes, lizards, and scorpions when necessary. They store water in ostrich shells, which they bury deep into the desert sands until the time comes to tap them for drinking.

13 EDUCATION

Traditional San education occurred within families, with elders teaching children proper behavior. Today, many San children face challenges in learning how to balance a rapidly modernizing world against their community's traditional way of life.

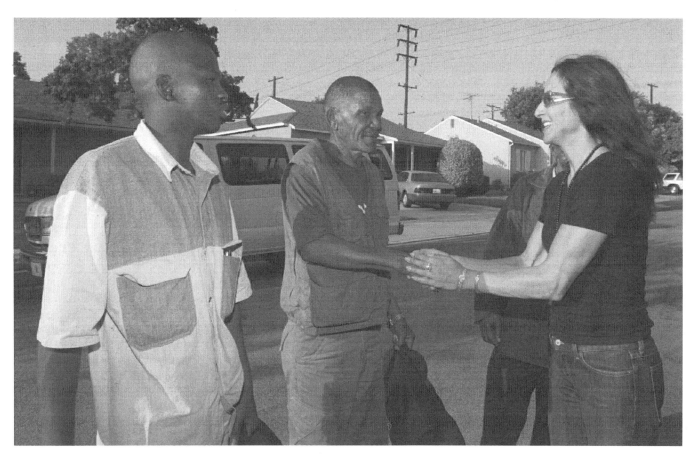

Jumanda Gakelebone looks on while Roy Sesana is greeted by Kim Langbecker. The San (Bushmen) were locked in a legal battle over Botswana's Central Kalahari Game Reserve and came to the United States for a month-long journey. (AP Images/Nick Ut)

*14 CULTURAL HERITAGE

In 2006 archaeologists reported evidence of rituals practiced by the San around 70,000 years ago—the oldest indications of human rituals ever found. The ancient artwork and artifacts were discovered in the Kalahari Desert in Botswana in a cave that the San have traditionally used for rites associated with the python, an animal that plays a major role in their creation stories.

The long and rich cultural heritage that the San add to southern Africa has been exploited in recent years in an effort to promote tourism. Stereotypical depictions of the "Bushman hunter" that were first popularized in Western films such as "The Gods Must Be Crazy" have led to interest in developing more awareness and knowledge of San culture. However, the San people have drawn little benefit from these efforts. They suffer much poverty, social marginalization, and general indifference on the part of other Africans. A cultural center, known as !Khwa ttu, was established north of Cape Town in 2006 in an effort to change the San situation. The center is run by San communities who use it to promote education of their people and entrepreneurship opportunities for members of their communities. The center also creates a place for scholars to help the San themselves learn more about their cultural background and past.

The center continues a legacy of San traditions. The community, for instance, has long valued modesty and egalitarianism.

Although elders within families and kinship groups do command some authority, there is economic or political differentiation among the San people themselves. The community has long valued cooperation between others. Material goods are usually shared communally. In many ways, that egalitarianism fits with the mobile nature of the San people. There is no point is accumulating wealth or material goods because the groups are always prepared to move when necessity arises. If they are burdened with material goods, that mobility is threatened.

15 WORK

Traditionally the San have had a strong work ethic. Many continue that practice today and balance farming with traditional practices of hunting and foraging along with jobs in industry and trade. Other traditional work practices that the San engaged in included pottery making and metallurgy.

The hunter-gatherer nature of the San way of life continues to some extent. In the 1970s, for instance, hunting provided less than 20% of the diet of the Zhu I õasi and plants that were gathered by women contributed about 80% of the calories that were consumed by those who owned no livestock. San communities also fish along rivers, and hunt large antelope as well as giraffe. As communities have begun to rely more on farming, many families also create small products for sale or for trade, such as iron for arrow points and spears, metal containers, glass beads, tobacco, sugar, coffee, and tea. Many San women also brew and sell beer.

Although some San men began working in South African gold and diamond mines in the late 19th and early 20th centuries, those opportunities are no longer available to San speakers.

16 SPORTS

Few San people engage in games or sports activities in the Western sense.

17 ENTERTAINMENT AND RECREATION

Leisure activities include conversations, music, and gathering for ritual communal dances.

18 FOLK ART, CRAFTS, AND HOBBIES

San peoples are known for beads that they make from the ostrich eggshells. Many also create glass beadwork from glass beads obtained through trade. Three San artists (two Zhu I õasi and one Nharo) have gained recognition as watercolorists, and San rock paintings remain famous as one of the world's oldest art forms.

19 SOCIAL PROBLEMS

The San have suffered displacement periodically over the centuries. Bantu tribes invaded their homelands around 500 AD and white colonists began fighting for control of the rich resources in southern Africa beginning in the 17th century. These invasions have caused the San to suffer discrimination, eviction from ancestral lands, murder, and oppression. Today, many San groups are perceived as backward and primitive, and face pressure to assimilate with more urban communities or to live more like sedentary agriculturalists. Governmental policies that restrict their movement and limit land-use rights continue to be implemented into the early twenty-first century.

Alcoholism and related social problems are said to be widespread and men have been imprisoned for unauthorized hunting.

20 GENDER ISSUES

Although traditional responsibilities were gender based, the status of San women is relatively equal to that of San men. While men retain control over hunting, women determine when and where to gather traditional foods. Men tend to gain power and influence when they bring meat to their settlements. However, it is women who retain control over the daily life of the settlement when men go on hunting trips, often for days at a time.

21 BIBLIOGRAPHY

Barnard, Alan. *Hunters and Herders: A Comparative Ethnography of the Khoisan Peoples.* Cambridge: Cambridge University Press, 1991.

Blundell, Geoffrey. "San Ethnography." In *Timeline of Art History.* New York: The Metropolitan Museum of Art, 2000.

_____. "Bushmen." http://www.humanistictexts.org/san. htm (retrieved January 11, 2009).

Denbow, James. "Prehistoric Herders and Foragers of the Kalahari: The Evidence for 1500 Years of Interaction." In *Past and Present in Hunter Gatherer Studies,* edited by Carmel Schrire, 175-193. Orlando, FL: Academic Press, 1984.

Guenther, Mathias. *Tricksters and Trancers: Bushman Religion and Society.* Bloomington: Indiana University Press, 1999.

Hollmann, Jeremy C, ed. *Customs and Beliefs of the Xam Bushmen.* Johannesburg: Wits University Press, 2004.

Howell, Nancy. *Demography of the Dobe Kung.* New York: Academic Press, 1979.

Lee, Richard. *The Kung San: Men, Women, and Work in a Foraging Society.* Cambridge: Cambridge University Press, 1979.

Lee, Richard and Irvin DeVore. *Kalahari Hunter-Gatherers: Studies of the Kung San & Their Neighbors.* Universe, 1999.

Lewis-Williams, J. David, ed. *Stories That Float from Afar: Ancestral Folklore of the San of Southern Africa.* Cape Town: David Philip, 2000.

_____. "The Remarkable Khoi and San People of the Past," Encounter South Africa. http://www.encounter.co.za/article/49.html (retrieved January 11, 2009).

_____. "San." http://encarta.msn.com/encyclopedia_761561208/San_(people).html (retrieved January 11, 2009).

_____. "San Cultural Center Opens in South Africa," Cultural Survival, 15 June 2006. http://www.culturalsurvival.org/print/3068 (retrieved January 11, 2009).

_____. "San Information," (1998). Arts & Life in Africa Online. http://www.uiowa.edu/~africart/toc/people/San.html (retrieved January 11, 2009).

_____. "San Speaking Peoples." World Culture Encyclopedia. http://www.everyculture.com/Africa-Middle-East/San-Speaking-Peoples (retrieved January 11, 2009).

Shostak, Marjorie. *Nisa: The Life and Words of a Kung Woman.* New York: Vintage Books, 1983.

Silberbauer, George. *Hunter and Habitat in the Central Kalahari Desert.* Cambridge: Cambridge University Press, 1981.

Vossen, Rainer, and Klaus Keuthmann, eds. (1986). *Contemporary Studies on Khoisan: In Honor of Oswin Köhler on the Occasion of his 75th Birthday.* Hamburg: Helmut Buske, 1986.

_____. "What is a Trance Dance?" Art of Africa. http://www.theartofafrica.co.za/serv/trancedance.jsp (retrieved January 11, 2009).

Wilmsen, Edwin (1989). *Land Filled with Flies: A Political Economy of the Kalahan.* Chicago: University of Chicago Press, 1989.

———. "Almost Outcasts: Paradigmatic History of San-Speaking Peoples and Current Attempts at Reconstruction." *Current Anthropology* 31:489-524, 1990.

_____. "World's Oldest Ritual Discovered: Worshipped the Python 70,000 Years Ago," Science Daily, 30 November 2006. http://www.sciencedaily.com/releases/2006/11/061130081347.htm (retrieved January 11, 2009).

—by M. Njoroge

SÃO TOMÉANS

LOCATION: São Tomé & Príncipe
POPULATION: 206,178
LANGUAGE: Portuguese, Angolar, Príncipense, São Toménse,
Creole dialects
RELIGION: Christian (80% Roman Catholic, 15% Protestant,
3% Muslim)

¹INTRODUCTION

São Toméans live on the islands of São Tomé and Príncipe off
the Atlantic coast west of Equatorial Guinea and south of Cameroon and Nigeria. São Tomé is the Portuguese word for St.
Thomas. Portuguese explorers stumbled upon São Tomé in the
1470s. The first wave of Portuguese settlers came to the island
in the 1480s. It consisted of several thousand Jewish children
forcibly taken from their parents and converted to Christianity. There were also exiled undesirables in Portuguese society,
known as *degradados*, who were banished there, such as convicts and prostitutes. The new settlers soon brought African
slaves to the islands to work on sugar plantations.

By decree of the king of Portugal, Jewish settlers and other degradados were allowed to marry slave women in order
to increase the population of the island. Their offspring were
promised freedom from slavery. The population increased dramatically, creating a large free African and mixed-race population. A new cultural entity was born from the intermixing and
intermarriages between the Portuguese settlers and the African slaves. As such São Toméans are culturally a Luso-African
creole people who trace their descent from Portuguese settlers
and African slaves.

São Tomé and Príncipe remained a Portuguese colony until its independence in 1975. The Movement for the Liberation
of São Tomé and Príncipe (MLSTP) took power from the Portuguese in 1975 and ruled the islands as a single-party state
until in the elections of 1990 when the MLSTP was defeated
in multi-party elections. During the post-independence era,
there has been a substantial immigration of new arrivals from
Angola, Mozambique and Cape Verde.

Today, six different ethnic groups of São Toméans can be
identified based on whom they descended from. The first group
is the Mestico. These are mixed-blood descendants of African
slaves brought to the islands from Benin, Gabon, and Congo
during the early years of settlement. They are also known as
"filhos da terra" or "sons of the land." The second group is the
Angolares, who are said to be descended from Angolan slaves
who survived a 1540 shipwreck near the islands. Today, their
main livelihood is fishing. The Forros form the third group
and are descended from freed slaves after the abolishment of
slavery. The fourth group is known by the name "Servicais."
These are contract laborers from Angola, Mozambique, and
Cape Verde who have come to the island to make a living and
hope to return home. Tongas, forming the fifth grouping, are
the children of contract laborers who are born on the islands.
The final group is the Europeans, largely of Portuguese origin.
The São Toméans are thus made up of peoples with many different ethnic backgrounds.

²LOCATION AND HOMELAND

The islands of São Tomé and Príncipe are located in central Africa about 200 miles west of the coast of Gabon and Equatorial
Guinea and south of Nigeria and Cameroon. They are located
right on the equator in the Gulf of Guinea. They are two tiny
volcanic islands with an area of about 400 square miles. The
topography is mountainous with tropical climatic conditions
and two distinct wet and dry seasons.

The mountainous topography of São Tomé rises to about
2,000 m (6,640 ft). This geography results in swift streams ra-
diating down the mountains through lush forest and cropland
on their way to the sea. Along the coastal areas the climate is
hot and humid with average temperatures of up to 27°C (80°F).
Given their tropical climate, the islands experience ample
amounts of rainfall ranging from 101 cm to 508 cm (40 in to
200 in) per year, with the rainy season lasting from October
through May. The volcanic soils are rich for the production of
plantation crops such as sugar.

³LANGUAGE

Portuguese is the official language and the language of education. However, there are several other dialects that are simply
known as Luso-African creole spoken by Africans with quite
a substantial number of words from Portuguese. São Tomeans
refer to their creole language by different names, the most popular of which is Forro. Apart from Portuguese, there are three
main creole dialects that are spoken by São Toméans on the
two islands, namely Angolar, Príncipense, and São Toménse.
All three trace their origin from Kwa and Western Bantu languages. Angolar is spoken on the southern tip of São Tomé and
has its origin in Kimbundu of Angola, Kongo, Bini, and Nd-
ingi. Príncipense is the creole spoken on the island of Príncipe,
while São Toménse is the creole spoken on São Tomé.

⁴FOLKLORE

Among the São Toméans, poetry has become a major vehicle
for narrating historical events. Poetry and stories tell of the
discovery of the islands by Portuguese explorers, early Portuguese settlements, and the slave trade that saw large numbers
of Africans arriving on the islands to boost the islands' population. There is also a well developed set of plays and performances, all of which are designed to convey the rich history
of the various ethnic groups that arrived on the islands in the
15th century. For example, masked performers in colorful attire accompanied by drums, flutes, and dancers entertain the
audience with Portuguese historical plays.

⁵RELIGION

São Toméans are largely Christians, with the majority being
Roman Catholics (80%). Protestant and evangelical churches
account for 15% of the population and 3% are Muslim, with
the rest having no religion or practicing some indigenous African traditional religion. Many of the African population still
retain their beliefs in ancestral spirits that can be traced back
to the homelands they were uprooted from during the slave
trade era. It is, therefore, not surprising that while believing
in Christianity, São Toméans of African descent also practice
rituals that are not sanctioned by the Church. For example, the
Forro ethnic group practice a communal ritual called *djambi*
in which an entire neighborhood or village gathers to drum,

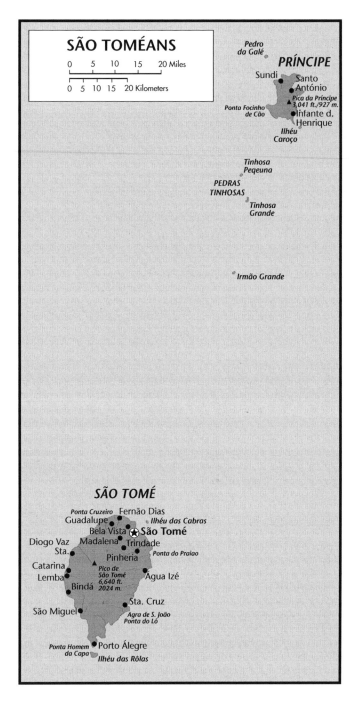

SÃO TOMÉANS

0   5   10   15   20 Miles

0 5 10 15 20 Kilometers

PRÍNCIPE

Pedro
da Galé

Sundi

Santo
António

Pica da Príncipe
3,041 ft./927 m.

Ponta Focinho
de Cão

Infante d.
Henrique

Ilhéu
Caroço

Tinhosa
Peqeuna

PEDRAS
TINHOSAS

Tinhosa
Grande

Irmão Grande

SÃO TOMÉ

Ponta Cruzeiro   Fernão Dias
Guadalupe   Ilhéu das Cabras
        Bela Vista   São Tomé
Diogo Vaz   Madalena   Trindade
Sta.
            Pinheria
Catarina   Ponta do Praiao
Lemba   Pico de
                São Tomé
                6,640 ft.   Água Izé
Bindá   2024 m.

São Miguel   Sta. Cruz
            Agra de S. João
            Ponta do Ló

Ponta Homem   Porto Álegre
da Capa   Ilhéu das Rôlas

dance, and witness spirit possession. Traditional medicine men are also readily available to provide divination, healing, and protection from evil spirits.

⁶MAJOR HOLIDAYS

São Toméans celebrate a number of public and religious holidays throughout the year. The most important ones are New Year's Day on January 1, Martyrs' Day on February 3, Labor Day on May 1, Independence Day on July 12, Armed Forces Day on September 6, Agricultural Reform Day on September

30, All Saints Day on November 1, and Christmas Day on December 25.

⁷RITES OF PASSAGE

Rites of passage among São Toméans are largely determined by membership in the Roman Catholic Church. Soon after birth, the newborn is baptized as the first rite of passage. As one gets older, he or she goes through the Catholic Church rites of first Communion, confirmation, and so on. Children also attend the modern school system.

Some African traditions have survived the test of time as rites of passage. For example, the Forros believe that the spirits of the dead are never disconnected from the world of the living. They thus follow a strict form of funeral rites, similar to that practiced by Africans on the coastal zones of Equatorial Guinea and Gabon. Once a death occurs, all adults except pregnant women are expected to participate in ceremonies of singing and dancing. A goat or a chicken is often sacrificed with the blood poured on the dead. At the cemetery, the corpse is buried in the grave in the fetal position to signify that it will rise and be reborn. Thus, the dead are considered to be part and parcel of society, necessitating the offering of sacrifices to placate the spirits of the dead until they are reborn.

⁸INTERPERSONAL RELATIONS

Similar to other ethnic groups in Africa, São Toméans value good conduct. Age brings with it seniority and, therefore, respect from the community. Older men and women are considered to be the keepers of wisdom and are treated with great respect and deference. Men and women with many children and/or grandchildren are treated with great respect. When greeting each other, it is courteous for one to inquire about the health of an individual and his family.

⁹LIVING CONDITIONS

Poverty is one of the major problems affecting the living conditions of São Toméans. Many live in abject poverty, but the rich oil finds off the waters of these two islands have great potential to raise wealth and, therefore, improve living conditions. However, corruption is another obstacle in translating the new-found wealth into something that benefits all.

Houses are typically made out of local materials, with brick or cinderblock walls and iron sheets as roofs. For the poor, the walls of houses are constructed either of mud or planks made from timber with the roofs covered by galvanized iron sheets. The poor live in shanty towns with few amenities and dilapidated buildings. Wealthy families live in modern houses or in old colonial bungalows. Run-down old colonial bungalows are often occupied by the poor.

Life expectancy in São Tomé is 63 years up from 56 years in 1970, a decent increase at a time when many countries in Sub-Saharan Africa are experiencing declining life expectancies because of the HIV/AIDS epidemic. Almost all children receive vaccinations for tuberculosis, polio, measles, DPT, and Hepatitis B.

¹⁰FAMILY LIFE

Given that almost 95% of São Toméans identify themselves as Christians, marriages are conducted in the Christian tradition and are supposed to be monogamous. Polygamy is not an accepted norm, although it is practiced in rural areas to a lesser extent. In spite of this, many men and women have several partners concurrently or over the course of their lives. Poor women often have visiting relationships with several men. This affords them a little income to subsist on and take care of their children.

In rural areas, women are responsible for taking care of the household chores, such as farming, gathering wood and water, preparing food, and raising the children. Fertility rates in rural areas are quite high, with a total fertility rate of over four children per woman. In the city, women live better lives in comparison to their rural counterparts. They have fewer children and may compete for male-dominated jobs.

¹¹CLOTHING

São Toméan dress is similar to Western forms of clothing. Men will normally wear pants, shirts, suits, neckties, shoes, and so on, depending on the occasion. Women also generally dress in Western fashions. Some women may dress in traditional garb, consisting of a blouse and a loin cloth that they wrap around their waists to below the knees. Boys and girls prefer to wear the omnipresent jeans and T-shirts. São Toméans will go to great lengths to wear colorful and descent clothing during religious ceremonies and holiday celebrations or festivals.

¹²FOOD

Given their location surrounded by the Atlantic Ocean, the main source of protein is fish. The fish is taken with carbohydrate rich tropical root crops, such as yams and cassava, as well as plantains and bananas. Tropical fruits, such as mangoes, guava, papaya, and citrus trees, are widespread and quite abundant. The favored national dish among the São Toméans is stew with traditional palm oil.

Spices are used to add taste and color to dishes. There is also a diversity of vegetables that are used in fixing delicious São Tomé dishes. Goat, lamb, beef, chicken, and wild monkey form the main meat dishes that are taken with rice, spices, raisins, almonds, and honey. One of the classic ways of preparing chicken is to stew it in a peanut and tomato sauce. Another tasty São Toméan meat dish is chicken marinated in an onion-mustard mixture. The Portuguese influence in food preparation can be seen during important occasions, such as weddings, baptisms, and funerals, when São Toméans prepare lavish tables with a large array of dishes for all to admire. For the wealthy families, the dishes may be served with bottled beverages and wines, while the poor have locally made palm wine and cane alcohol.

Most food needs to be imported. Many of the people are subsistence farmers, producing inadequate amounts for their families. As a result, a small proportion of the population suffers from malnutrition. Food insecurity is a direct result of the plantation system of agriculture that was introduced during the colonial era and continues to this very day, where cash crops, such as coffee and cocoa, take precedence over food production.

¹³EDUCATION

Education is patterned after the Portuguese system of primary school, secondary school, and university, with Portuguese as the language of instruction. Although primary school is universal and compulsory, data shows that only 78% of chil-

dren are enrolled in school. One of the major challenges of the country's educational system is regional inequality between urban and rural areas. Urban schools enjoy higher standards of education in comparison to rural schools. For rural residents, secondary education is nonexistent. Some rural residents send their children to live with relatives in urban areas so they may continue their education. The country also faces a major challenge to rehabilitate its crumbling educational infrastructure.

Despite these difficulties, the country has a 79% literacy rate, one of the highest on the continent. Gender-parity in educational attainment is also near equal. The girls-to-boys ratio was 0.92 in 2000. Over 68% of children finish elementary school, but there is a high drop-out rate at the secondary level, due to their unavailability in rural areas. Up until 1996, there were no institutions of higher education on the islands. The only way for a high school graduate to receive university education was to go abroad, something many could not afford. However, since 1996 the Ministry of Education has established two institutions of higher learning in São Tomé and Príncipe. The first one, created in 1994, is private and the second one, established in 1997, is public.

¹⁴CULTURAL HERITAGE

Centuries of Portuguese colonialism makes the country a homogeneous cultural entity. The government has attempted to stress the country's African heritage with little success. Language, family structure, and religion are basically Portuguese. However, many African elements have been adopted in the cooking, customs, beliefs, and dress of the common people. The poorer individuals speak creole, a language that traces its origin from several Bantu languages, but with many Portuguese words.

São Tomé is a party to the World Heritage Convention, whose main aim is to preserve historic sites. For example, in the framework of the Slave Route Project, the country has participated in the implementation of the Tourism of Memory program. Storytelling reflects this heritage, with many of the stories recounting the slave trade experience. Poetry is the most highly developed form of literary expression, with historical events as the main subject. Folktales and short stories are also part of the cultural heritage of São Toméans.

The mixture of Portuguese and African heritage is clearly illustrated in dance and music. During festivals, masked dancers in colorful attire are accompanied by drums and flutes to entertain the audience. Drama is often conducted to portray Portuguese historical events. The young people prefer to dance to imported music, such as the samba from Brazil and popular music from the United States and the Democratic Republic of the Congo.

¹⁵WORK

Subsistence agriculture and fishing are the main activities for the majority of the people on the islands. Subsistence crops grown for local consumption include root crops, vegetables, plantains, and bananas. Industries are virtually nonexistent, except for a few processing plants for food, beverages, and soap. The timber industry through logging has contributed to the economy, but it has resulted in deforestation of pristine tropical rainforests. The two islands of São Tomé and Príncipe are endowed with natural beauty and a relatively safe environment. This could propel the country into a tourist haven, but it still remains to be realized due to unreliable air transportation to the islands. The international community is also unaware of the existence of these two islands, as there is rarely any news about them, much less travel brochures. There has been some investment in hotels and other tourist facilities in recent years.

The country is heavily dependent on an export-oriented plantation economy of cash crops, such as cocoa and coffee. In turn it imports rice, beans, and salt fish to feed the plantation workers. Cocoa is the major export, accounting for over 90% of foreign exchange earnings. Other export crops grown on the plantations include coffee, coconuts, and palm kernels.

Recently the country has run into some fortune. Billions of barrels of oil are believed to be present off its shores. Should the oil reserves come to fruition, São Tomé's economy will certainly go through massive transformation overnight. Drilling of the oil reserves is under way and commercial production is expected to begin within a few years.

[16] SPORTS

Soccer is the most popular sport in São Tomé. Although the country has a national soccer team, it has not been active in international sports and has recently been removed from the FIFA World Rankings list. There are several other popular sporting activities, such as basketball, handball, volleyball, and track.

[17] ENTERTAINMENT AND RECREATION

There are two television stations in São Tomé and Príncipe to provide entertainment to its citizens. Wealthy families may have access to a satellite dish that connects them to what is happening throughout the world.

[18] FOLK ART, CRAFTS, AND HOBBIES

Crafts are an area of interest for the government, which is trying to adapt local production to the demands of the international market. Many of the paintings by local artists depict important historical folk scenes. These paintings can be viewed at the Francisco Tenreiro Cultural Center or the National Museum.

[19] SOCIAL PROBLEMS

Among the major challenges facing São Toméans in the 21st century are poverty, food insecurity, and the prevalence of malaria. Poverty is the major cause of petty theft on the islands. Consumer goods are also in short supply. Malaria remains one of the biggest health problems, although initiatives begun in 2000 have helped reduce the number of cases. There have also been recurrences of cholera.

[20] GENDER ISSUES

In terms of education, São Tomé has achieved gender equality in primary school education. Nevertheless, women are still under-represented in the job and the political sectors. Although the country had a female prime minister, women are rarely represented in politics, with only 4 out of 55 deputies being women in the parliament in 2008. Data also shows that the labor participation rate was 39% for women against 80% for men. Traditional beliefs and a high rate of teenage pregnancies often reduce women's educational and economic opportunities.

Within the family, women exercise some control over their resources. Women are able to own businesses that are run independently of the husband or other male relatives. Some women have been able to accumulate a large amount of cash through the selling of produce and fish at markets. This cash is managed by the women independent of the men.

[21] BIBLIOGRAPHY

Becker, Kathleen. *São Tomé e Príncipe*. Chalfont St. Peter: Bradt Travel Guides, 2008.

Burness, Donald. *Ossoboi: Essays on the Literature of São Tomé e Príncipe*. Trenton, NJ: Africa World Press, 2005.

Chabal, Patrick, and Birmingham, David. *A History of Postcolonial Lusophone Africa*. Bloomington: Indiana University Press, 2002.

Cohn, Paul D. *São Tomé*. Bozeman, MT: Burns-Cole Publishers, 2005.

Eyzaguirre, Pablo B. "The Ecology of Swidden Agriculture and Agrarian History in São Tomé." *Cahiers d'Etudes Africaines* 26, no. 101–102, (1986): 113–129.

———. "The Independence of São Tomé e Príncipe and Agrarian Reform." *Journal of Modern African Studies* 27, no 4 (1989): 671–678.

———. "São Tomé e Príncipe." In John Middleton (Ed.), *The Encyclopedia of Africa South of the Sahara*. New York: C. Scribner's Sons, 1997.

———. "Culture of São Tomé and Príncipe." Online resource at http://www.everyculture.com/Sa-Th/S-o-Tom-e-Pr-ncipe.html.

Hodges, Tony, and Newitt, M. D. D. *São Tomé and Príncipe: From Plantation Colony to Microstate*. Boulder, Colo: Westview Press, 1988.

Seibert, Gerhard. *Comrades, Clients and Cousins: Colonialism, Socialism and Democratization in Sao Tome and Principe*. Leiden: Brill, 2006.

———. "Essays on the Literature of São Tomé E Príncipe." *Lusotopie* 14, no. 2 (2007): 195-200.

Weszkalnys, Gisa. "Hope &; Oil: Expectations in Sao Tome E Principe." *Review of African Political Economy* 35, no. 3 (2008): 473-482.

—revised by E. Kalipeni

i

SENEGALESE

PRONUNCIATION: sen-uh-guh-LEEZ
LOCATION: Senegal
POPULATION: 12.8 million
LANGUAGE: French; Wolof; 38 African languages
RELIGION: Islam (Sunni, with traditional aspects); Roman
  Catholicism
RELATED ARTICLES: Vol. 1: Fulani; Malinke

¹ INTRODUCTION

Senegal has a rich precolonial history with a rare degree of unity. The lands now comprising Senegal once were part of three successive empires: Ghana, of which the Tekrour King was a vassal; Mali, which brought Muslim culture and letters, peace, and trade to the region until AD 1350; and Songhai, which reached its apex nearly 200 years later. In the 11th century, the Fulani and Tukulor ethnic groups converted to Islam and later waged jihads (religious wars) over a period of 225 years. Senegalese culture strongly reflects influences from these Islamic rulers and conquerors.

In 1444, Portuguese sailors became the first Europeans to visit the Senegalese coast. The French later founded the Senegal colony in 1637, making it the oldest and longest-lasting French colony in Africa. The slave trade, which flourished from the 1600s until 1848, devastated this area. Today one sees remnants of this tragic epoch in the island fortress of Gorée off the coast from the capital, Dakar. Gorée had served as one of West Africa's main slavery depots.

As the French advanced their territorial claims eastward, Wolof states resisted them in the 1880s, but eventually succumbed to superior military force. In 1889, an agreement with the British created The Gambia, a country along the valley of the navigable Gambia River that is almost entirely surrounded by Senegal. The location of The Gambia has had the negative effect of cutting off the southern Senegalese province of Casamance. Dakar acquired added importance when the French made it the capital of their West African territories in 1902. Under Léopold Senghor, who was a member of the Académie Francaise and a French parliamentarian, Senegal declared its independence in 1960. Senegal formed confederate governments twice, first with Mali (1958–60), and then with Gambia (1982–89).

In 1975 Senegal became one of Africa's first countries to allow a political opposition. For 40 years, however, a de facto government ruling party—the Socialist Party—dominated the competition. Then in 2000 President Abdoulaye Wade was elected, marking one of Africa's first civilian transfers of power to an opposition party. Wade was reelected in February 2007, but 12 opposition parties boycotted the June 2007 legislative polls alleging fraud. The boycott gave 131 of 150 seats in Parliament to the ruling coalition, SOPI, and in the 100-member Senate (a new legislative body), the opposition gained virtually no seats. In May 2008 press reports circulated that Wade (in his second and last term) was considering tampering with the two, five-year term limit rule, something other African leaders have done to prolong their hold on power.

Senegal has had mostly peaceful relations with its neighbors, although a brief border conflict (1989–90) with Mauri-

tania to the north resulted in the expulsion of nationals from both sides. However, the most serious threat to stability has been the low-level insurgency in the southern region of Casamance where rebels have been fighting a secessionist war with the government since 1984.

² LOCATION AND HOMELAND

Located at the westernmost point of Africa, Senegal has a total area of 196,713 sq km (75,951 sq mi), making it smaller than the US state of South Dakota. Senegal shares borders with Mauritania, Mali, Guinea, Guinea-Bissau, and The Gambia. Much of Senegal is very arid with scattered trees and scrub covering low, rolling plains that become foothills in the southeast that reach an altitude of 581 m (1,906 ft). Four main rivers run east to west to the Atlantic Ocean. Three of these—the Saloum, Gambia, and Casamance—form large estuaries inland. The Casamance runs through a marshy basin before reaching the ocean.

The climate varies greatly from north to south, but rains fall throughout the country from December to April. Hot, dry, Harmattan winds blow from the Sahara Desert during the summer. Natural resources include phosphates, iron ore, manganese, salt, and oil. However, seasonal flooding, overgrazing, and deforestation contribute to environmental erosion and desertification.

In 2008, estimates placed Senegal's population at 12.8 million, growing at a rate of 2.6%. Senegalese are members of more than 20 ethnic groups, which for the most part have managed to live harmoniously together. The largest is Wolof (43%), followed by Fulani (24%), Serer (15%), and lesser groups including Toucouleur, Diola, Malinke, and Soninke. Large numbers of Lebanese traders live in the cities.

³ LANGUAGE

French is the official language of Senegal, but most people speak Wolof. Besides French and Wolof, people speak the language of their ethnic group, such as Pulaar, Serer, and 38 different African languages.

⁴ FOLKLORE

In Senegalese society, the most accomplished storytellers are professional African bards, or *griots*. In a way, they are like the European minstrel of the Middle Ages. They are Africa's renaissance women and men, combining the historian, poet, musician, and entertainer all into one person. They must be familiar with history, know many people, and talk about them diplomatically, but honestly and critically. Griots use props, flutes, harps, and break into song as they perform. No ceremony or celebration of consequence is held without them.

Senegal's well-known modern statesman, Léopold Senghor, was also an accomplished poet. He was Senegal's first president and the founder of the negritude movement, a revival of the African cultural past. A poet, academic, and politician of great influence, Senghor left a lasting imprint on Senegal, Africa, and the African diaspora. Someday griots will recount his accomplishments much as they do the deeds of past heroes. Senegal's modern griot is Sembene Ousman, whose stories and films in French, Wolof, and Diola chronicle politics and social life in Senegal and France (see Cultural Heritage).

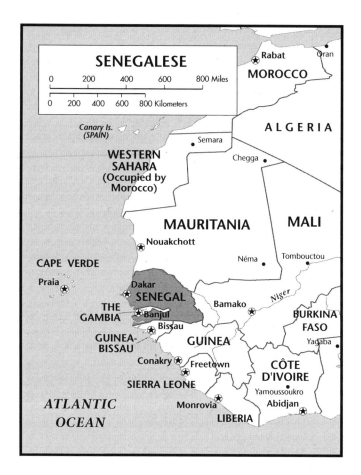

5 RELIGION

The Senegalese are overwhelmingly Muslim. More than 90% of the population belongs to the Sunni branch of Islam. Less than 10% is Christian, mainly Roman Catholic. Religious practice is highly tolerant, and clashes between members of different faiths for religious reasons are virtually unknown.

Marabouts play a unique role in Senegalese society. In orthodox Muslim communities, marabouts are teachers of the faith, and where indigenous beliefs mix with Islam, they are also diviners and fetishers. In Senegal, they became intermediaries between Allah and the faithful. Under the French, they assumed leadership of administrative units (*cantons*), replacing traditional ethnic chiefs. Their political influence remains strong, particularly in determining the outcomes of elections in the hinterlands.

As in many colonized cultures, people overlay their traditional beliefs with the imposed religion, such as Islam. The Wolof typically wear protective amulets or *gris-gris* to overpower evil spirits. Whereas the small leather pouches once contained herbs and medicines, they now hold verses of the Quran. The Bassari in the east and the Diolas to the south retain their animist beliefs more than the other groups.

6 MAJOR HOLIDAYS

Independence Day is April 4. Muslims celebrate the end of the holy month of Ramadan by feasting for three days. Catholics celebrate Easter and Christmas. Each region has its own secular and traditional folk feasts according to its own calendar. In

Casamance, Oussouye hosts an annual royal feast day, which occurs at the end of the agricultural season and before the beginning of the school year. It is announced in Dakar, and people from the region, as well as others who just want to see the spectacle, come. The highlight of the feast is a fight featuring young women, one of whom may be chosen by the king to spend the night in the sacred woods in the heart of the forest.

7 RITES OF PASSAGE

Most Senegalese today follow Islamic custom in their rites of passage, including baptism, circumcision, marriage, and death. Each passage marks a part of the cycle culminating in passage to the spirit world. To this end, people and communities constantly celebrate life events. Griots are an integral part of these occasions.

In ancient times, Senegalese peoples celebrated the arrival of puberty with initiation rites. The minority populations in the south still organize rites of initiation, lasting from one to three months during the long school vacations. The purpose of initiation is to build courage and endurance, communicate traditional and practical knowledge of life, and transfer responsibility to a younger generation. Some of the knowledge is known only to males, and therefore cannot be shared with females or with the uninitiated. The initiation begins with circumcision, binding the boys by blood. Elders initiate boys of the same age, dividing them into age sets or groups. These sets become "fraternities" for life. Members have both the duty to help each other and the right to reprimand each other for improper behavior. Girls pass through similar processes, and many also are circumcised. However, for girls, this practice is increasingly questioned for reasons of health and sexual fulfillment.

Initiation rites often mark occasions of great community celebration. The Bassari, for example, bring down sacred masks from the mountains that represent supernatural powers. Dancers wearing these masks engage the newly circumcised adolescents in a mock battle, which becomes dance, song, and feasting.

8 INTERPERSONAL RELATIONS

Greeting is an extremely important custom and can last for several minutes. Indeed, it is quite possible that if you do not greet someone and inquire after their health, family, and well-being, he or she will not talk to you. The French custom where men and women kiss three times on the cheeks is common in Dakar and in towns but much less so in villages. Friends and strangers typically greet each other by offering a handshake with the right hand, sometimes touching the left hand to the right arm. However, men and women do not shake each other's hands. A common Wolof exchange (with 5–10 additional inquiries) would be as follows, with praise for Allah interspersed throughout the greetings:

"*Nanga def?*" (How does it go?)
"*Mangi fii rekk.*" (I am here only.)
"*Nunga Fe.*" (They are there.)
"*Mbaa sa yaram jamm.*" (I hope your body is at peace.)
"*Jamm rekk.*" (Peace only.)
"*Alhumdullilah.*" (Praise be to Allah.)

As in many African societies, Senegalese give much respect to age and status. It would be impolite to make eye contact

Senegalese fishermen. Senegal's national dish is Tiebou Dienn, a type of fish stew. (Carolyn Fischer)

with an elder, a person of higher status, or someone of the opposite sex. Traditional girls and women normally would curtsy to elders out of respect. In Muslim society, the right hand is used to pass and to take objects. Pointing is considered rude, but people may point with their tongues.

People are accustomed to visiting each other unannounced. They never consider impromptu visits to be rude or an inconvenience. Senegalese do not permit a visitor to leave without sharing a meal, having tea, or spending the night. The Senegalese refer to this hospitality as *Terranga*.

⁹ LIVING CONDITIONS

The government continues to make reforms to the economy, although jobs are hard to find leaving many young Senegalese to migrate out of Senegal in search of employment and a better life elsewhere. In 2006–07 Dakar experienced regular power outages, and urban centers around the country continued to struggle with inadequate water supply, poor sanitation, and environmental degradation. In general, high population growth outstrips the capacity of the government to provide basic services. Inflation and a high cost of living, especially in Dakar, also made life difficult for the average family.

Nonetheless, living conditions for the middle- and upper-middle class have reached very comfortable levels in some Dakar neighborhoods. In addition, many affluent Dakarois have beach houses on the *petite cote* (outside Dakar), and a mix of Senegalese and foreigners—mostly French—are buying condo-

miniums in resort areas on the coast. Their lifestyles, however, are not reflective of average living conditions. Most people in urban and peri-urban areas live in small, cramped cinder-block housing, which may have indoor plumbing, but might also depend on outdoor kitchens, standpipes, and latrines. In rural areas, many houses are made of local materials such as mud brick, millet stalks, or reeds, and roofs of thatch. Dirt floors are common, but are swept daily. As families acquire the means, they build more durable structures of concrete and galvanized iron. Partially finished houses are a common sight because people build them in stages as money comes in.

In arid rural areas, women and girls do the washing at wells. Few people have access to streams and rivers and still fewer to plumbing. A daily chore for women and girls is going to the well, which is traditionally hand-dug, to fetch water for the family. The well is often at the center of the village and serves as a social gathering place. The huge plastic tubs are filled with water and carried on top of the head to some sort of holding tank (or old oil drum) in the family compound. In the cities, people have access to indoor plumbing or may share a communal faucet.

Senegal has one of the best paved road networks in Africa, but it still only has four miles of expressway (in Dakar), and about 2,500 miles of paved roads overall. The most common form of transportation is by bush taxi—French Peugeot 504s—which take up to seven passengers just about anywhere in the country. Colorful pickup trucks painted with designs and inscriptions, outfitted with truck caps and wooden plank benches, are also available. These carry as many as 14 to 24 passengers. Their roof racks hold suitcases, packages, and small livestock.

¹⁰ FAMILY LIFE

Traditional Senegalese live in compounds with their extended families. Nuclear families live in their own huts. The elders are highly respected. Besides hauling water, women gather firewood and cook the meals. Few women work outside the home, unless it is to cultivate family gardens and fields, or to sell goods at the market. Men increasingly leave their villages and homes during the dry season to look for work in the cities.

Western ideas take root more easily where traditional family influences are absent or less prevalent. This is noticeable in Dakar where more girls and women speak French, and where women hold political offices, practice law or medicine, and teach. As society changes, so also must laws. Senegal permits a couple to adopt an optional prenuptial agreement limiting the number of wives a husband will take during his marriage either to one or two. Divorce is consensual. Women have the right to initiate a divorce process, though in practice they seldom do.

¹¹ CLOTHING

In Senegalese society, personal appearance is very important. Most urban men and women wear Western-style clothing. Men typically wear shirts and trousers and wear suits for dress occasions. Women wear dresses. One rarely sees women in jeans or pants. Similarly, shorts are reserved for children, unless they are worn for sports. In more traditional settings, people wear *boubous*, loose-fitting cotton tunics with large openings under the arm. Men wear cotton trousers underneath, while women wear sarongs. With much imagination, women tie matching headscarves or turbans to complement their boubous. For men, footwear includes open or closed and pointed leather sandals, according to the occasion. Women have a greater variety of footwear including colorful, decorated sandals. Depending on the purpose of the boubou, it may be elaborately embroidered and could cost $200 to $300.

¹² FOOD

Senegal's staple foods include rice, corn, millet, sorghum, peanuts, and beans. These foods are typically found throughout Africa at this latitude. Milk and sugar also form an important part of the diet for some people and certain ethnic groups. The Senegalese generally eat three meals a day, with the main meal at about 1:00 pm, and the evening meal served late. In traditional households, men, women, and children usually eat separately. It is not polite to make eye contact while eating. Senegalese eat from a communal platter or large bowl with the right hand, as is the Muslim custom. Muslim adults, and children aged 12 and older, do not eat or drink from sunrise to sunset during the holy month of Ramadan.

Senegal is famous for its national dish, *Tiébou Dienn* (pronounced "Cheb-oo Jen"). The dish can be made as simply or as elaborately as desired. Basically, it is a fish stew cooked in cilantro, scallions, garlic, pepper, onions, tomato paste, bouillon cubes, and oil. The stew is mixed with squash, sweet potatoes, okra, tamarind, and different kinds of peppers. People eat this on rice, which has been cooked in the fish broth. The Wolof people are also known for their *Mbaxal-u-Saloum,* a spicy tomato, peanut, and dried fish sauce with rice. Another popular dish is *Menue*, cornmeal mush, served with *baloumbum,* a peanut sauce.

Meat is a sign of wealth, as is oil. Special occasions usually require a meat dish, but one might also serve Yassa chicken. The chicken is marinated in a sauce of red vinegar, lemon juice, red chili peppers, bouillon cubes, and soy sauce, and then grilled over charcoal. It is served with heaps of sliced browned onions over cooked rice, on a platter placed on a cloth spread on the ground. Guests sit or squat around the tray, after having washed their hands and removed their shoes. Using their right hands, they gather a morsel of chicken, sauce, and rice from the part of the tray in front of them, squeeze it gently into a compact ball, and eat.

¹³ EDUCATION

Senegalese place a high value on education, but the cost of living, school fees, and the need for children to help with family income deter most children from attending beyond the primary level. Literacy is about 40%, and only about 29% of women and girls can read and write in French. Many girls leave school to wed. Parents of means send their children away to live with relatives in a town where schools are better organized and commuting is easier. In addition to formal schooling, the majority of children attend Quranic (Muslim) schools in the afternoons or evenings where they learn Arabic and memorize portions of the Quran. Technical schools offer training in dyeing, hotel management, secretarial work, and other trades.

In the mandatory formal system, primary school begins with a two-year initiation class called *Ceci*. At the end of four more years, pupils take a high-school qualifying exam. In the French system, classes begin with Class Six, counting down to Class One. A final year follows, which prepares the student for the state baccalaureate exam. But few students reach this level, and an even smaller percentage of high school graduates continues at the University of Dakar, which in Africa is quite prestigious. Before independence, Africans from all over French West Africa came to study public administration at the famous William Ponty school.

¹⁴ CULTURAL HERITAGE

Senegal has one of the richest bodies of written and film literature in all of Africa. Leopold Senghor was a leading poet and philosopher and the author of the *négritude* movement. Similar to the Harlem Renaissance school in the United States, négritude aimed to restore dignity and pride to African peoples through a revival of their cultural past. Senegalese filmmakers such as Sembene Ousman and Safi Faye are internationally famous.

Literature and film notwithstanding, the title of Senegal's national anthem offers a clue to Senegalese musical culture: "Pluck your Koras, Strike the Balafons." The traditional *kora,* a stringed calabash (gourd) instrument, symbolizes the bard tradition in the country. A unique percussion sound is made with a small drum held under the arm, which can be pressed against the body to produce different pitches. The goatskin drumhead is hit by a wooden stick with a curved end.

Senegalese musicians have adapted traditional music by using electric and acoustic guitars, keyboards, and a variety of drums. Several Senegalese rap groups in Dakar have evolved

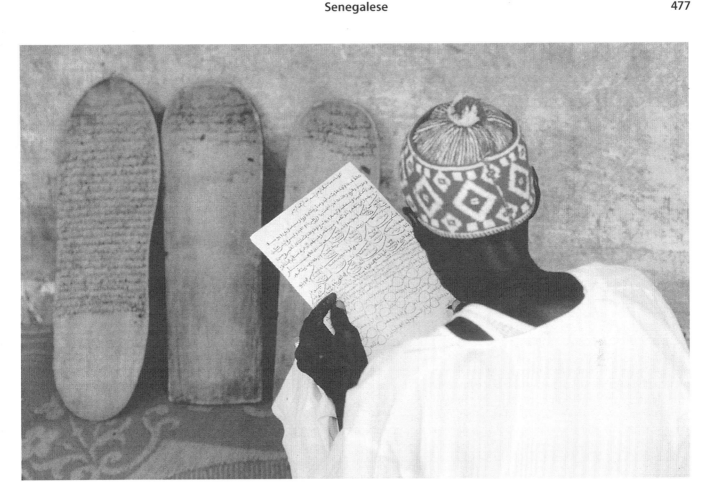

Some 90% of Senegalese belong to the Sunni branch of Islam. The remaining 10% are Roman Catholic. (David Johnson)

from the special blend of Western and African musical traditions. In particular, *griots* (bards) perform traditional Senegalese rap songs to tell stories about society, much like ancient griots narrated the lives of ancient kings.

One of the best known Senegalese performers is Youssou N'Dour. N'Dour is a leader in popular world music, and sings in English, French, Fulani, and Serer, besides his native Wolof. He has collaborated with Paul Simon *(Graceland)*, Peter Gabriel *(So)*, Neneh Cherry, and Branford Marsalis.

15 WORK

Rural Senegalese typically work in subsistence agriculture or grow cash crops for export such as peanuts and cotton. Senegal is well known for its peanut production in the Kaolack region. Senegal has a small industrial sector (less than 10%), and because of its long dry season, limited amounts of arable land (27%). About one in four people works in the service sector, but half of the workforce is un- or underemployed. Tourism is important, accounting for about 60% of the gross domestic product. Most urban dwellers work in the informal sector as petty traders and small service providers. They peddle clothing, watches, and electronic goods; polish and repair shoes, tailor shirts, cut hair, and sell goods at market. In downtown areas, it is typical to be approached constantly by peddlers. Motorists caught in traffic can buy anything from apples to brooms from roadside hawkers.

16 SPORTS

Soccer, basketball, track and field, and jogging all are popular sports in Senegal. The national soccer team, the Lions, has produced some world-class players, reaching the World Cup quarter-finals in 2002. Senegal is also known for its traditional wrestling—*Laamb* in Wolof. It is renowned especially among the Serer people. In ancient times, wrestlers competed before the king and queen in village squares. Singers, dancers, and storytellers embellished the match. Wrestlers wore amulets to ward off evil spirits and black magic from their opponents. Nowadays, the tradition remains strong. As in former times, *griots* (bards) praise the victors in song and dance. Drumming, dancing, singing, and a *marabout's juju* (religious leader's fetish magic) are vital to the competition.

17 ENTERTAINMENT AND RECREATION

Dakar offers a variety of recreation from television to movies, to DVD rentals, night clubs, and sporting events. Foreign and national films are enjoyed, especially in the towns where technology is more advanced. Dakar popular music is enjoyed and danced to widely throughout the country by teenagers, and adults, too. Some 20 FM stations have emerged since the 1990s, with several Dakar stations playing hip-hop music. The Internet also has blossomed, and Internet cafés are now popular meeting spots in every town around the country.

The more traditional pastimes such as socializing and visiting people in their homes remain popular as well. Older men enjoy playing checkers. *Griots* (bards) entertain at ceremonies such as baptisms and marriages. Cultural events such as folk ballets, theater productions, or local dance troupes also provide recreational outlets. However, in many rural areas, *marabouts* (religious leaders) frown upon dancing and sometimes do not allow drumming or dancing in their villages.

18 FOLK ART, CRAFTS, AND HOBBIES

Each region of Senegal has its own traditional crafts. Senegal's many tourists have given a boost to folk art and crafts cottage industry. One finds jewelry, baskets, pottery, handwoven fabrics, glass paintings, and woodcarvings. Handcrafted jewelry includes gold, silver, and bronze. Bead and amber necklaces, which Fulani women traditionally wore, are also popular. Tourist items such as handbags, clothing, and footwear are made from locally printed fabrics and leather. Craftspeople fashion animal skins, such as iguana and crocodile, into belts and shoes.

Although tourists are attracted to the decorative quality of the *kora* (traditional gourd instrument), Senegalese artisans build professional instruments to meet local demand. Their exquisite koras are made from huge calabashes (gourds), through which a 1.5-m (5-ft) wooden pole is set. The strings are stretched from the calabash (the sound chamber) to the pole on which they are tied. The musician faces the instrument, grasps two wooden pegs that serve as handles, and plucks the strings mainly with the thumbs. The calabashes have eye-catching decorations of brass and silver buttons and traditional designs. A hole about 12 cm (5 in) across in the side of the calabash serves to project the sound, and also makes a convenient "hat" into which tips can be placed.

19 SOCIAL PROBLEMS

Senegal's most basic social problems are related to its economic constraints. The widespread use of marijuana among young men and migration to Europe are indications of the severity of the problem. Some villages are populated only by women, children, and old men. Another indication is the never-ending secessionist struggle in Casamance. On the one hand, Casamance has been the country's most distant and neglected province, but on the other is unable to develop as long as rebels and splinter groups kill civilians, commit robberies and harass local populations Government forces now fight not only against rebels of the Movement of Democratic Forces of the Casamance (MFDC), but also with the Movement of the Liberation of the People of the Casamance and with Atika, another separatist movement led by Salif Sadio.

Senegal does not incarcerate as many of its citizens as does the United States, but its jails hold twice the number of prisoners they were designed to hold. Because of corruption and weak law enforcement, traders administer mob justice on thieves, and there are reports of domestic violence, child abuse, child marriage, child trafficking, abusive child labor and male and female infanticide. While these practices may get reported to the authorities, the police often do nothing and the courts fail to prosecute perpetrators.

20 GENDER ISSUES

Women face discrimination, especially in rural areas where traditional customs and polygynous relationships are the norm. Indeed, one in two marriages in the hinterlands are po-

lygynous, and unless agreed to beforehand, husbands do not need to notify or seek consent of their wives to enter into subsequent marriages. Even though the law proscribes marriages for girls under 16, it is not uncommon in rural areas for girls 13–15 years old to be married as they represent a means of income via the brideprice. Female genital mutilation (FMG) is also widespread, despite efforts by government officially to eradicate it. Programs implemented by NGOs such as TOSTAN to create more awareness of the health risks associated with it, have reduced the incidence of FMG, but the practice remains deeply ingrained in the culture. Since the man is the head of the household, women cannot take legal responsibility for children, and women have difficulty inheriting and purchasing property. In addition to running the household, they also do 85% of the agricultural work.

21 BIBLIOGRAPHY

Colvin, Lucie Gallistel, ed. *Historical Dictionary of Senegal.* African Historical Dictionaries, no. 23. Metuchen, NJ and London: Scarecrow Press, 1981.

Delcourt, Jean. *Naissance et Croissance de Dakar.* Dakar: Editions Clairafrique, 1985.

Dilly, Roy, and Jerry Eades, ed. *Senegal.* World Bibliographical Series, vol. 166. Oxford: Clio Press, 1994.

Diop, Abdoulaye-Bara. *La Société Wolof: Tradition et Changement.* Paris: Editions Karthala, 1981.

Faye, Louis Diene. *Mort et Naissance: Le Monde Sereer.* Dakar: Les Nouvelles Editions Africaines, 1983.

Gellar, Sheldon. *Democracy in Senegal: Tocquevillian Analytics in Africa.* Melbourne: Palgrave Macmillan, 2006.

Gritzner, Janet H. and Charles F. Gritzner. *Senegal.* London: Chelsea House Publications, 2005.

Kane, Katherine. *The Gambia and Senegal.* Footscray: Lonely Planet Publications, 2006.

"Senegal." In *Africa South of the Sahara 2007*, London: Europa Publishers, 2008.

—by R. Groelsema

SEYCHELLOIS

PRONUNCIATION: say-shel-WAH
LOCATION: Seychelles Islands
POPULATION: 82,247
LANGUAGE: Creole, English, and French (official languages);
Gurijati; Chinese; other European and Oriental languages
RELIGION: Christianity (Roman Catholicism)

¹ INTRODUCTION

The Seychelles Islands take their name from the Viconte Moreau de Seychelles, controller-general of finance in the reign of Louis XV of France. A French possession until 1814, the Seychelles then became a dependent of Mauritius under the British and then a British crown colony in 1903. Early European settlers cut down and sold the hardwood trees of the islands, altering the original ecology and replacing it with a plantation economy. After the abolition of slavery in 1834, Africans worked mainly as sharecroppers, traders, fisherfolk, artisans, and wage laborers. Seychelles gained its independence from Britain in 1976.

From 1977 to 1993, Seychelles was an authoritarian, one-party socialist state. The country's 1979 constitution failed to provide for basic human rights, including them instead in a preamble as a goal of the Seychellois people. France-Albert René took power in a coup in 1977, and intimidated dissidents and opponents by threatening indefinite imprisonment, exile, or confiscation of the property of his political opponents. Police brutality, though not widespread, occurred as a result of René's unchecked power. In June 1993, Seychellois voted for a new constitution, and in July 1993 they voted in the country's first free and fair multiparty elections since the coup. René emerged victorious and was re-elected in 2001. He later surprised many observers when he stepped down in favor of his vice president, James Michel, in 2004. In July 2006 Michel outpolled Wavel Ramkalawan and was elected to a five-year term. His government continues to maintain control over public sector jobs and contracts.

² LOCATION AND HOMELAND

The Republic of Seychelles is one of the world's smallest nations in size and population. It has a total land area of only 444 sq km (171 sq mi), about two-and-a-half times the size of Washington, D.C. The population measures only 82,247 (2008 estimate). The exact number of islands is unknown but has been estimated at 115, of which about 41 are granitic and the remainder coralline. The republic also includes numerous rocks and small cays. Hills up to 940 m (3,084 ft) high characterize the granite islands, with some narrow coastal plains. The granitic islands are of striking scenic beauty. Coral reefs are found on the east coast, but the coral islands are without fresh water. The tropical climate varies little, rainfall is balanced throughout the year, and temperature is tempered by monsoon ocean breezes.

Mahé, the main island, is the largest at 25 km (15.5 mi) long and 8 km (5 mi) wide, with an area of about 148 sq km (57 sq mi). About 90% of all Seychellois live on Mahé. It contains the capital and only city, Victoria, and the only port, with a population somewhat over 25,000 people (2008 estimate). Vic-

toria lies approximately 1,600 km (1,000 mi) east of Mombasa, Kenya; 2,750 km (1,700 mi) southwest of Bombay; 1,700 km (1,060 mi) north of Mauritius; and 885 km (550 mi) northeast of Madagascar. The only other important islands by virtue of size and population are Praslin and La Digue, situated about 50 km (30 mi) to the northeast of Mahé. The population of the outer coralline group is only about 500 people, mainly composed of plantation workers gathering coconuts for copra. To restrict population growth on Mahé, the government has encouraged people to move to Praslin and other islands where water is available. The population growth rate nationally is only 0.43%.

Most of the population is a relatively homogeneous mixture of African, European, Indian, and Chinese. The majority is Black, having Black African ancestors who arrived on the islands in the 18 and 19th centuries. Chinese were attracted to the islands by small trade. Then British and French colonials came. The Malabards from Maurice Islands and India arrived after the abolition of slavery. Over time, the groups have intermarried, creating an assortment of racial characteristics and numerous shades of complexion. The blending is such that it is impossible to define a typical Seychellois.

³ LANGUAGE

Seychellois have three official languages: Creole, English, and French. Ninety-six per cent of the population speaks Creole; 45%, English; 37%, French; 0.5%, Gurijati; 0.4%, Chinese; 0.9%, other Oriental languages; and 0.6%, other European languages. Creole was adopted as the first official language in 1981. English is the second official language, and French is the third. The government has emphasized Creole to facilitate reading among primary school pupils and to help establish a distinct culture and heritage. Opponents of the René government thought it a mistake to formalize Creole, which according to them had no standardized spelling system. They regarded it as a great advantage for Seychellois to be bilingual in French and English.

Creole in Seychelles developed from dialects of southwest France spoken by the original settlers. It consists basically of a French vocabulary with a few Malagasy, Bantu, English, and Hindi words and has a mixture of Bantu and French syntax. Very little Seychelles Creole literature exists. The development of an orthography (spelling system) of the language was completed in 1981. The government-backed Kreol Institute promotes the use of Creole by developing a dictionary, sponsoring literary competitions, giving instruction in translation, and preparing course materials to teach Creole to foreigners.

The great majority of younger Seychellois read English, which is the language of government and commerce. It is the language of the People's Assembly, although speakers may also use Creole or French. The principal newspapers carry articles in all three languages. Seychellois Radio and Television Broadcasting both offer programs in Creole, English, and French. Although discouraged by the René regime as a colonialist language, French continues to carry prestige. It is the language of the Roman Catholic Church, and it is used by older people in correspondence. Some 40% of television transmissions are in French—beamed by satellite to an earth station provided by the French government—and most Seychellois can speak and understand the language.

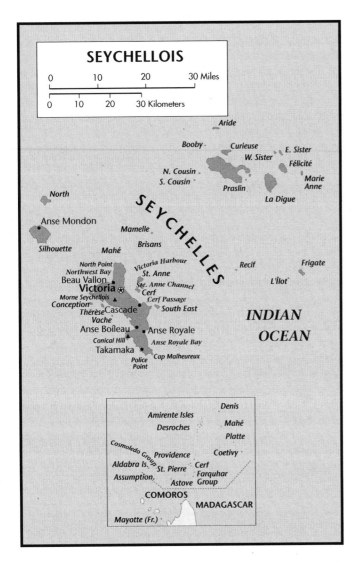

SEYCHELLOIS

the performance to give the desired tone. As in the past, drinks of palm-wine and sugarcane liquor lubricate the performance. The dance is still very personal in some outer islands, and performers often use satire and well-intentioned social critiques to entertain and to teach people of all ages.

5 RELIGION

Almost all the inhabitants of Seychelles are Christian, and more than 90% are Roman Catholic. Seychelles comprises a single diocese, directly responsible to the Holy See. British efforts to establish Protestantism during the 19th century were not very effective. Sunday masses are well attended, and religious holidays are celebrated throughout the archipelago, as both religious and as social events. Practicing Catholicism, similarly to speaking French, confers a certain social status by its association with French culture.

About 7% of the population of Seychelles are Anglican, most coming from families converted by missionaries in the late 19th and early 20th centuries. Evangelical Protestant churches are active and growing, among them Pentecostals and Seventh-Day Adventists. Some 3% of the population are adherents of other faiths, including Hinduism, Buddhism, and Islam. A small group of Indian Muslims do not mix with the other groups. No restrictions are imposed on religious worship by any of the faiths.

Similar to other Africans, many Seychellois reconcile their Christian beliefs with traditional religious practices, such as magic, witchcraft, and sorcery. It is common for Christians, despite the disapproval of Church authorities, to consult a local seer known as a *bonhomme de bois* or a *bonne femme de bois* for fortunetelling. People want to influence the course of events in their love life, a court case, or a job interview. They may also wish to obtain protective amulets or charms, known as *gris-gris,* or to cause harm to enemies.

6 MAJOR HOLIDAYS

The Seychellois have 10 public holidays, some of which reflect the strong Roman Catholic background of the Seychelles: New Year's Day, January 1; January 2; Good Friday; Easter Sunday; the Fête Dieu (Corpus Christi); Assumption Day, August 15; All Saints' Day, November 1; the Day of the Immaculate Conception, December 8; Christmas Day, December 25; and the Queen of England's official birthday. Families often take advantage of public holidays to picnic at the beach and swim. On these occasions, they may also find entertainment in the coconut groves, where local musicians and dancers put on a *moutia*-style performance (see "Folklore").

7 RITES OF PASSAGE

Weddings and funerals are occasions for lavish spending. A family might spend half a year's income on a child's wedding because such displays confer status on the family. The guests may stay to party all night. Sometimes both families foot the bills, but sorting out who pays what and how much is tricky and often creates ill feelings when the accounts come due.

Funerals also make social statements about wealth and status. On Mahé, the Catholic Church offers three basic categories. The full treatment consists of bell-ringing three times, singing, organ music, and a sermon. The loud tolling should make the death known to everyone. The middle category involves ringing the bells twice, and everything is much less

4 FOLKLORE

Seychellois folklore is as rich as its people's cultural heritage. Accomplished storytellers and singers teach people their culture and social mores through fables, songs, and proverbs. The Creole proverbs are interesting also for the way they demonstrate linguistic derivation. For example, "Sak vid pa kapab debout" (One doesn't work on an empty stomach) translated literally reads "an empty bag will not stand up on its own."

Storytelling becomes more dramatic at night in the light of a bonfire or under a full moon. Moon shadows from the palm trees, and moonlight glinting from the palm fronds, create a natural theatrical atmosphere for the *moutia* performance. The *moutia* began as African slave dancing and improvisational storytelling, which provided a form of release after a long day of laboring for French colonial masters. Two men opened with dialogues on the hard labors of the day. Women then joined in the dance, to much singing and chanting. The pure form has rarely been seen by outsiders, but contemporary performances have become popularized. They still involve dancing with typical African rhythms and hip movements and musicians playing drums from hollowed-out coconut trunks covered with goatskins. The drums are heated by a palm frond fire before

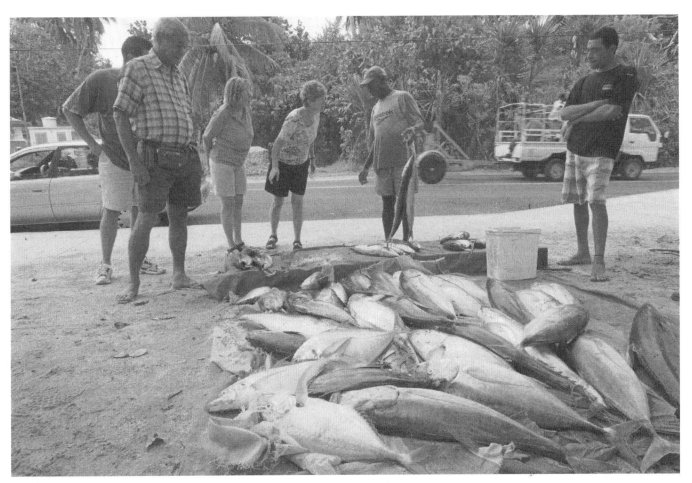

A fisherman displays his catch to visitors at a roadside on the main island of Mahé in the Seychelles. Most visitors to the area spend time on this island for its beaches, larger hotels, and water sports facilities. (AP Images/Sayyid Azim)

showy. The lowest category provides only a single bell rung 11 times, but it is free. Islanders might not attend such a funeral, however, for fear of losing status.

⁸ INTERPERSONAL RELATIONS

Seychellois are extremely sociable as a rule and often gather in the evening to enjoy each other's company. While older people may share a game of cards or checkers, younger people prefer playing the guitar and singing together on the veranda. Western-style dating is fairly common in Victoria, but in the outer islands traditional forms of recreation usually bring couples together with other young people.

Officially no racism exists in the islands, but Seychellois associate higher social status with lighter skin shades. This norm derives from the formerly dominant Europeans who monopolized wealth and public authority. Thus property, plantation, and business owners, and higher civil servants—mainly Whites or near Whites—are called Grand Blancs. Some 20 planter families, for example, trace their heritage back to French settlers. Under the socialist government, they lost the power and social prestige they once had. The working-class White who works for the grand blanc bears the humorous label, *Blanc Coco* (white chocolate). *Blanc Rouille* or "Rusted White" refers to a plantation owner who has inherited a big fortune but is lazy, without education, and needs an educated Black Seychellois to do the accounting. Whites whose cleanliness is doubtful are called *Blanc Pourri* (Rotten White). Lower-class landless people, mostly of African origin, are at the bottom of the status ladder and are called *Rouge* (Red) or *Noir* (Black), depending on the darkness of their skin.

Thus, skin color figures importantly in social relationships and in career opportunity. A Grand Blanc generally marries into a family of Whites and near Whites, but so might a person of darker skin color if he or she has the wealth. Since higher-paying prestige jobs usually go to near-White or light-skinned people before those of darker complexion, marrying someone with lighter skin also brings its economic rewards. It is said, jokingly, that after giving birth, a Seychellois mother asks first what the color of her child is and second whether it is a boy or girl.

⁹ LIVING CONDITIONS

Health and nutritional conditions are remarkably good in the Seychelles Islands, approaching those of a developed country. Seychelles ranks 36th out of 177 countries on the Human Development Index with the average life expectancy at birth in 2008 at 72.6 years overall. Many factors account for long life expectancy, including a healthy climate; the absence of infec-

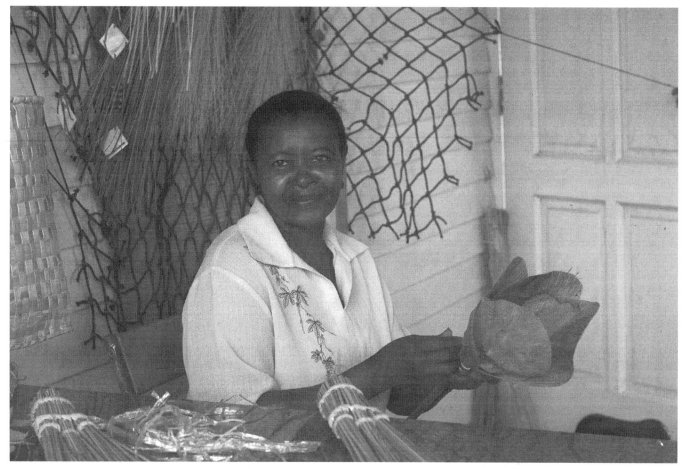

A woman makes palm flowers to sell as souvenirs from the Seychelles. (Alison Wright/National Geographic/Getty Images)

tious diseases such as malaria, yellow fever, sleeping sickness, and cholera; and the availability of free medical and hospital services to all Seychellois. Improvements in prenatal and post-natal care since the late 1970s have brought the infant mortality rate down from more than 50 deaths per 1,000 live births in 1978 to an estimated 14.4 deaths per 1,000 live births in 2008, a rate comparable to that of Western Europe. Some 90% of protein in the diet is derived from fish, which along with lentils, rice, and fruits, gives most people a reasonably nutritious diet. Nevertheless, poverty, limited education, poor housing, polluted water, and unbalanced diets adversely affect the health of children. Hookworms and tapeworms have become serious health threats to barefoot children, or to people who eat improperly cooked pork.

Traditional houses rise on stilts above the ground. The main room is used for eating and sleeping. The kitchen is separate to maintain cleanliness. Woven coconut leaves make naturally cool walls and roofs, although galvanized iron is gradually replacing them for roofing.

Buses and cars are the main form of ground transportation in Seychelles. No trains exist. People depend on a government ferry service, which links Mahé, Praslin, and La Digue. The airlines, serviced by 15 airports—six of them with unpaved runways, provide access to the outer islands.

¹⁰ FAMILY LIFE

A unique feature of the Seychellois social and family system is the prevalence of sexual relationships without formal marriage. Most family units take the form of de facto unions known as living *en menage*. One result of this practice is that nearly three-fourths of all children born in the islands are born out of wedlock, but many are nonetheless legally acknowledged by their fathers.

The institutionalization of *en menage* unions as an alternative to legal marriage can be attributed to several factors. The expense of socially required wedding festivities, trousseaus, and household furnishings can exceed a year's income for a laborer. An extreme difference in economic status of partners, a mother's wish to retain the earning potential of her son, or a previous marriage by one partner may be impediments to marriage. The difficulty and expense of divorce also tend to discourage a legal relationship. Although frowned upon by the Church and civil authorities, *en menage* unions are generally stable and carry little stigma for either partner or for their children. Among women of higher status, prevailing standards of social respectability require that they be married to the men with whom they are living. Sexual fidelity is not as likely to be demanded of husbands, who often enter into liaisons with lower-class women.

The pig is a common sight around the Seychellois homestead, much like dogs or chickens. Outside town, 45% to 50%

of homes keep at least one pig—veritable "piggy banks." Pigs are fattened up for sale at peak condition and are usually sold when the family needs cash.

11 CLOTHING

Dressing well is important for Seychellois, particularly to go to Mass and to special functions. Generally, whether formal or informal, clothing in the Seychelles is similar to that in the United States. For everyday use, people dress comfortably depending on their work. Women go to market in cotton smocks and sandals, wearing locally made straw hats for sun protection. They may also wear African sarongs. These are dressy when going out. Men wear hats too and loose-fitting, short-sleeved shirts and trousers. In the island environment, both men and women wear shorts when dressing casually. Some uniformed public servants, such as traffic police, also wear shorts.

12 FOOD

The Seychellois are splendid cooks and offer a wide variety of cooking styles, such as English, French, Chinese, and Indian. The diversity of all these cooking styles is combined to create Creole cuisine. Creole cooking is rich, hot, and spicy—a blend of fruit, fish, fresh vegetables, and spices. The basic ingredients include pork, chicken, fish, octopus, or shellfish. Coconut milk makes a good sauce for seafood meals. Seychellois cuisine includes crab, beef, lentil, and onion soups and a whole range of shellfish, fish, poultry, and meat dishes. People also enjoy salads and fruit desserts of mango, papaya, breadfruit, and pineapple.

Seychellois consume an average of 80 kg (176 lb) of fish a year. It is served in many ways: grilled on firewood, curried, in bullions, and as steak. Turtle meat was once easily found and is called "Seychelles beef."

Typically, people eat three meals a day. Breakfast may include eggs and bacon, while lunch is the heaviest meal of the day and usually includes rice. The high consumption of rice means that much rice must be imported. The government subsidizes rice imports, but wines and imported fruits and drinks are expensive and out of reach for most budgets. Locally made alcoholic beverages include palm-wine (calou) and bacca, a powerful sugarcane liquor regulated by the government. People drink bacca on ceremonial occasions.

13 EDUCATION

Seychelles has a high literacy rate: more than 92% of school-aged children read and write. Although many older Seychellois did not learn to read or write in their childhood, thanks to adult education classes, 85% were literate by 1991. Until the mid-1800s, schooling in the islands was mainly informal. Both the Roman Catholic and Anglican churches opened mission schools in 1851. The missions continued to operate the schools (the teachers were monks and nuns from abroad) after the government took charge in 1944. After a technical college opened in 1970, a supply of locally trained teachers became available, and many new schools were established. In 1979, the government introduced free and compulsory primary education for children between 6 and 15 years of age. In 1980, the government initiated a program of educational reform based on the British comprehensive system. Since 1981, a system of free education has been in effect, requiring attendance by all children

in grades one to nine, beginning at age 5. Some 90% of all children also attend nursery school at age 4.

Children first learn to read and write in Creole. Beginning in grade three, English becomes the teaching language in certain subjects. In grade six, pupils begin learning French. After completing six years of primary school and three years of secondary school, students who wish to continue their education attend a National Youth Service (NYS) program. The NYS is a Seychellois hybrid of scouting and 4-H. Students live at an NYS village and wear special brown and beige uniforms. In addition to academic instruction, the students receive practical training in gardening, cooking, housekeeping, and livestock-raising. One of the purposes of this program is to reduce youth unemployment. Students produce much of their own food, cook their own meals, and do their own laundry. They learn the principles of self-government by holding group sessions and serving on committees.

After completing their NYS program, students may attend Seychelles Polytechnic, a technical trade school. The largest number of students are enrolled in teacher training, business studies, humanities and sciences, and hotels and tourism. Since no opportunities for higher education are available on the islands, students study abroad through British, US, and French scholarship programs.

14 CULTURAL HERITAGE

The diversity of peoples has made Seychellois culture unique. African, European, and Asian influences are present in Seychellois music, dance, literature, and visual art. African rhythms are apparent in the moutia or séga dance performances, which include body-shaking and hip movements found on the continent. The sokoué dance resembles masked African dancing. Dancers portray birds, animals, and trees under the camouflage of coconut leaves and straw. The contredanse is a French import, with origins in the court of Louis XIV. The earliest French colonists introduced it to the islands. It synthesizes waltzing and polka, and is enjoyed at parties and weddings. Traditionally, Seychellois performed their music with drums, violins, accordions, and the triangle. Nowadays, the acoustic guitar typically accompanies these instruments.

Seychellois life is also told through poetry. Poems tell of the good old days, legends, superstitions, nature, and community. Seychelles' most celebrated poet is Antoine Abe.

15 WORK

Seychelles' economy is built upon tourism, fishing and offshore business and financial services. With a per capita gross domestic product (GDP) over more than $18,000 in 2007, Seychelles ranked in the upper-middle income group of countries. However, given Seychelles' dependence on imports and the consequent high cost of living, the minimum wage of $290/month (2007) did not provide a living wage. To make ends meet, many households kept a home garden and a family pig (see "Family Life").

Most jobs on the islands are created by tourism. Up to 180,000 annual visitors—the vast majority of whom are tourists—provide employment in services, hotel construction and other tourist industry activities. Thirty percent of the population is directly employed by this sector.

An unusual profession on the islands is calou (palm-wine) tapping. The government has licensed several thousand palm trees for this purpose. A tapper may rent a tree from its owner for tapping, or may collect the sap for the owner or tree-renter. The tapper must climb the tree twice daily and collect the juice, which flows from a tap, which pierces the growing tip of the palm. The sap is collected in a bamboo or plastic receptacle. A palm cannot produce coconuts and *calou* simultaneously. Constant tapping, however, can kill a tree.

16 SPORTS

Seychellois play a variety of sports. The most popular participant and spectator sport is soccer, but basketball is also popular. Leisure sports such as diving, sailing, windsurfing, and waterskiing are mainly enjoyed by tourists.

17 ENTERTAINMENT AND RECREATION

Seychellois have moved into the age of modern communications and world culture through television, cell phones, and the Internet. The government reported that Seychellois had 13,000 television sets in 1994. The government television station reaches between 75% and 80% of the population via three relay stations. Videos, DVDs, and movies are popular, too. More than one-third of the population uses the Internet for news, entertainment, and messaging.

Traditional forms of recreation revolve around socializing, music and dancing. Families and friends enjoy a Sunday afternoon at the beach and gathering on their verandas in the evening for friendly games of checkers and cards. Seychellois also are fond of singing and often perform informally at night when visiting with friends. At parties they may dance the whole night through. They are quite uninhibited in this respect. Thousands of people listen to Sechellois music on the radio throughout the day. Two young performers, Patrick Victor and David Filoé, have transformed the traditional *moutia* and *séga* dances in their contemporary music.

18 FOLK ART, CRAFTS, AND HOBBIES

Seychellois artisans have transformed traditional folk art and crafts into livelihoods. Seychellois are accomplished painters, drawing inspiration from the mountains, coves, palms, sun-streaked skies, and workers in the islands. Sculptors and carvers fashion chalices of teak, cigar, and jewelry boxes, and board games such as dominoes and backgammon. Jewelers make coral and shell bracelets, necklaces, and earrings. Batik-dyed cloth is becoming fashionable and is in high demand by tourists. Artisans use natural motifs such as birds and fish in their original designs.

19 SOCIAL PROBLEMS

Although close to being an island paradise, the archipelago is not without its social problems. Since the 1970s, Seychelles has struggled with patronage, corruption, and human rights violations. Since the early 1990s, the record has improved—partly because the government has relaxed its attitude toward dissident and opposition groups. However, other social problems are emerging. Juvenile delinquency, associated with boredom and isolation, is a growing problem. Many adults suffer from alcoholism, and an alarming number of young people are beginning to use marijuana and heroin. Venereal diseases are widespread, and efforts to contain them have been ineffective. Wife-beating remains a problem, and reports indicate that a significant number of girls under 15, usually from low-income families, are being raped and sexually abused. The police have not prosecuted these cases vigorously.

In addition, the financial benefits of Seychelles' tourist industry come with costs. After 11 September 2001, the number of tourists dropped sharply serving as a reminder to the country that its major industry was vulnerable to terrorist threats and outside shocks. Moreover, thousands of visitors stress the country's fragile eco-system, and along with indigenous population pressures, have an adverse impact on the environment. Further, efforts to accommodate tourists have increased illegal drug use and encouraged prostitution.

20 GENDER ISSUES

In principle, women enjoy the same legal, political, economic, and social rights as men. Women form nearly half of the enrollment at the prestigious Seychelles Polytechnic. In 2008 two women held cabinet posts, and there were 10 women in the 34-seat national assembly, seven of whom were directly elected and three of whom were chosen by proportional representation.

Female assertiveness is due partly to an essentially matriarchal society. Mothers are dominant in the household, controlling most daily expenditures and looking after the interests of the children. Men are breadwinners, but their domestic role is relatively peripheral. Older women can usually count on financial support from family members living at home, or from contributions of grown children. Family size is relatively small by African standards, largely because about one-third of all Seychellois women of reproductive age use some form of contraception (1980).

Nevertheless, women are not exempt from exploitation and they do suffer discrimination. In 2007 the police registered more than 50 rape cases, four sexual assaults, and there were reports of domestic violence and female prostitution.

21 BIBLIOGRAPHY

Africa South of the Sahara 2007. "Seychelles." London: Europa Publishers, 2008.

Alexander, Douglas. *Holiday in Seychelles: A Guide to the Islands.* New York: Purnell, 1972.

Bennett, George. *Seychelles.* Denver, CO: Clio Press, 1993.

Desiles, Clarisse. *A La Reunion, A l'Ile Maurice, Aux Seychelles.* Poitiers, France: Offset-Aubin, 1976.

Franda, Marcus. *The Seychelles Unquiet Islands.* Boulder, CO: Westview Press, 1982.

Groelsema, Robert J. "Seychelles: Ramkalawan and SNP Gain Ground on SPPF" *Africa Contemporary Record*, vol. 28, (2001–02), New York: Holmes and Meier, 2005.

Mancham, R. James. *Paradise Raped: Life, Love and Power in the Seychelles.* London: Methuen, 1983.

Tartter, Jean R. "Seychelles." In *Indian Ocean: Five Island Countries*, edited by Helen Chapin Metz. Washington, DC: Headquarters Department of the Army, 1994.

Touboul, Richard. *Les Seychelles Aujourd'hui.* Paris: Les Editions Jeune Afrique, 1979.

U.S. Department of State. "Seychelles Country Report on Human Rights Practices for 2007." Washington, DC: Government Printing Office, 2008.

—by R. Groelsema

SHAMBAA

PRONUNCIATION: shahm-BAH
ALTERNATE NAMES: Shambala (Bantu people)
LOCATION: Shambaai (West Usambara mountain range—northeastern Tanzania)
POPULATION: 664,000
LANGUAGE: Shambala, Swahili
RELIGION: Traditional Shambaa beliefs (healing the land and the body), Mufika (ancestor worship), Christianity, Islam

¹ INTRODUCTION

The Shambaa, also referred to as the Shambala, are a Bantu people found mainly on the West Usambara mountain range in Tanzania. Their language is Shambala. The homeland of the Shambaa is called Shambaai (or Shambalai). Other Bantu ethnic groups in the area include the Bondei, the Zigua, the Nguu, and the Pare.

The Shambaa were traditionally ruled by kings. The Shambaa kingdom was made up of several descent groups with a common origin, but the kingdom was governed by a single descent group. The survival of the whole descent group and its steady increase in size were crucial. The king ruled over several chiefdoms. Growth of the kingdom led to growth in the number of chiefdoms. The chiefs were appointed by the king and received tribute from their chiefdoms as representatives of the king. All the wealth of the land was regarded as the king's. This gave him control over his subjects and the right to demand tribute from them. The king, in return, was expected to bring rain and food to his territory.

Peasants and slaves were the king's subjects. Peasants lived in village groups under a patriarchal system. The nuclear family's well-being was important for the whole village. The peasants were free to go about their daily work on the farm and homesteads. They paid tribute to the king in the form of food, livestock, and labor. Slaves lived in the king's household, where he was free to deal with them as he pleased. At times they were sold to the coastal slave traders or even killed at the king's command.

The system of chiefdoms no longer exists in Tanzania; it was abolished soon after independence. The country is now divided into regions, which are further subdivided into districts. A district commissioner (DC) is in charge of each district. Regional commissioners are appointed by the president to govern the regions.

² LOCATION AND HOMELAND

The Usambara range is located in Tanga province in northeastern Tanzania, south of the border with Kenya. The range rises out of a plain. Shambaai is divided into two administrative districts, Lushoto and Korogwe. Muheza and Handeni are the neighboring districts.

In 2001 the Shambaa population was estimated to number 664,000 persons. Most of the people in Lushoto are Shambaa, with some Pare and Ma'a speakers as well. Korogwe is shared by the Shambaa with the Zigua and Bondei from neighboring Handeni and Muheza districts. The Shambaa are also found in the neighboring districts of Same in the northwest and Muheza

in the southeast. Across the border in Kenya to the north live the Kamba, and to the east live the Wataita and the Wataveta.

The Shambaa are located in the mountain area accessible from the plains. This is an area of abundant rainfall, with thriving banana plants. The Shambaa regard the *nyika* (plains) as a dangerous place of disease and death, preferring instead the mountain area. Thus, the population density is high in the mountain area, where the villages are located near each other with nearly all arable land cultivated. Overpopulation is considered a problem as it affects traditional farming practices. Some Shambaa people have now moved to the *nyika* and to urban areas, such as Dar es Salaam and Tanga.

³ LANGUAGE

Shambala is the main language spoken by the Shambaa; it has three main dialect areas. Mlalo forms the center for the northern area, Korogwe for the southern area, and Lushoto for the central area. Despite these differences in dialect, the Shambaa can understand one another's speech. Shambala is mutually understandable also with the Bondei, Zigua, and Nguu languages. Lexical similarity is 75% with Bondei, 68% with Ngulu and Zigula. While Shambala is the first language of most Shambaa, it is used mainly for oral communication. Only a few people can write in Shambala at this time.

The Shambaa also speak Swahili, the national language of Tanzania, which is now having an influence on the development of Shambala, especially its vocabulary. Young people prefer to speak Swahili, and they use Swahili words in Shambala. Swahili was initially spread to Shambaai by the coastal people. Other factors affecting Shambala and its use are urbanization, the mobility of speakers, ethnicity, and intermarriage between peoples. Many Shambala speakers can switch easily from one dialect to another and to Swahili.

Shambaa children are taught Swahili in primary school. It is used in business, communications, and other places of employment. Instruction in secondary schools and universities is in English.

⁴ FOLKLORE

The story of Mbegha (or Mbega) is the most famous of Shambaa myths. There are more than 26 versions of this myth. Mbegha was a hunter from Ngulu Hills to the south of Shambaai. He was forced to leave his homeland after a dispute with his kinsmen over his share of an inheritance. Mbegha fled to Kilindi, where he became a blood brother to the chief's son. The chief's son died accidentally while hunting with Mbegha. This caused Mbegha to flee again, into the bush, to escape punishment from the chief. He lived in caves and camps, hunting wild animals. After crossing the Pangani River, Mbegha arrived on the southern escarpment of the Usambaras. The Ziai people saw the smoke of his campfire and approached him. Upon learning that Mbegha was a skilled pig hunter, they asked him to rid their village of pigs. He was invited to live in Bumbuli, where he grew famous as an arbitrator, hunter, and storyteller. The grateful villagers gave Mbegha a wife. Mbegha also helped the people of Vugha and was known as a lion slayer after killing a lion on the way to their village. He was made the chief of Vugha. Mbegha's son Buge grew to be the chief of Bumbuli. When Mbegha died, Buge succeeded him as king of Shambaai.

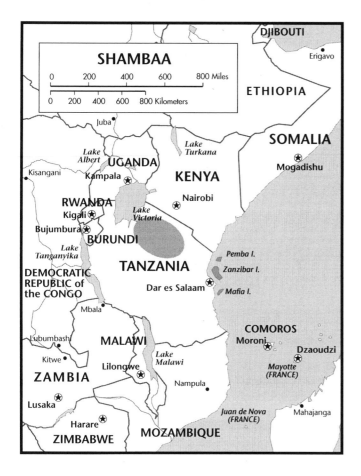

⁵ RELIGION

Traditional Shambaa beliefs center on healing the land and the body. Rainmakers were important people in the society, for they were believed to have the power to prevent or cause rainfall.

Mufika (ancestor worship) was important since the Shambaa believed that ignoring one's ancestors, especially one's deceased father, was sure to lead to misfortune. A traditional medicine man was called in to perform the rites of ancestor worship, at which women were not allowed to be present. Even today, *waghanga* (local healers) are called in to treat illness.

The Protestant and Catholic faiths are both well established in Shambaai. The Christian influence in Shambaai was spread by missionaries through education and preaching. The missionaries learned Shambala in order to be able to communicate freely with the Shambaa; religious texts, including the New Testament and the Book of Psalms, were translated into Shambala. Congregations in all areas of Shambaai used these texts. Christianity was more influential in the northern area of Shambaai. It has brought changes to traditional Shambaa beliefs and practices, which have been weakened and adapted to the newer Christian beliefs.

Islam was spread in Shambaai by the Zigua, mainly in the trading towns.

⁶ MAJOR HOLIDAYS

The Shambaa observe both secular and religious holidays. The main government holidays now celebrated are New Year's Day,

Union Day (April 26), Workers Day (May 1), Peasants Day (August 8), and Independence Day (December 9). Government holidays are public rest days when offices and shops remain closed. Nationwide public rallies are held in the urban areas, with military parades and speeches by government officials. Villagers generally continue with their farm work during these holidays.

Both Christian and Muslim holidays are celebrated with public observances. The major Christian holidays are Easter weekend and Christmas. The major Muslim holidays are Id-el-Fitre, Id-el-Hajji, and Maulid. Religious holidays are a very special time for family gatherings. Urban dwellers visit their families in rural areas. Special dishes cooked at this time include roast meat, *chapatis* (flat bread), and *pilau*.

⁷ RITES OF PASSAGE

The Shambaa consider it very important to have children. Before the birth of his children, the father is expected to complete all his marriage rituals and bride payments. Failure to do so will mean that his children will belong to their mother's clan. When his wife is pregnant, the husband gives his father-in-law a female goat. After the birth of his child, another goat is sent to the in-laws. A cow is sent after the second child is born. The children are then regarded as the husband's. A goat is also given to the in-laws with every subsequent birth. It is the custom for the pregnant wife to leave her home and go back to her father's house to give birth. The new father does not see his child until later when he visits his wife at his in-laws' home. Traditionally, a baby may be killed by the father for various reasons, including having deformities, cutting its upper incisors first, or having been conceived in adultery.

Traditionally, the Shambaa held initiation ceremonies for both young women and young men. Initiation for boys began with the *ngwaliko wa kava*, in which a boy was circumcised when he reached the age of three or four years and a *kungwi* (mentor) was chosen for him. After circumcision, a boy was considered a *wai* (initiate) until all ceremonies were complete; then he was regarded as an adult. At puberty, the initiate undergoes the *gao* ceremony, in which he is instructed in acceptable behavior.

Now, circumcision takes place in health facilities for sanitary reasons. The initiation ceremony has been shortened but is still required before the young man takes on adult responsibilities. Young women are not circumcised, but they also go through a *gao* ceremony of instruction that is required before a young woman can marry or become a mother. It is scandalous for a young woman to get pregnant before the *gao* ceremony. In the past, a baby so conceived before the ceremony would have been killed by its grandfather.

The final rite of passage for the Shambaa is death. A man keeps a banana garden near his homestead to serve as his burial place. After a man dies, his wealth (mainly livestock) is divided among his wives and their children, with the first wife's elder son receiving the largest share. Each child inherits wealth from his or her mother. Girls may inherit household items, ornaments, and clothes from their mother and sisters. Boys inherit the land and livestock given to their mother when she married their father.

8 INTERPERSONAL RELATIONS

Greetings are important in Shambaa culture. When people meet for the first time, they exchange the particular greeting required for that time of day. In the morning one may say *onga mahundo* ("Good morning"), and may receive the reply *ni vedi. Hangize wako* ("Fine and yours"). *Onga mshi* is an afternoon or evening greeting. *Ikaa wedi* is said to wish someone well when leaving. Greetings may be prolonged, for it is customary to inquire after a person's family, health, and even work, and people exchange them before conducting any business, no matter how urgent or important. Younger people are expected to show respect and deference to their elders while greeting and conversing with them and to help them with their work without being asked.

Some taboos have developed from required polite behavior. These include pointing at someone, which may suggest a curse, and sitting with one's head between one's hands, which may make people think one is in mourning when no one has died.

Traditionally, men and women were socially segregated, and this has formed the basis for all their relationships. Couples do not eat together at home. Mothers usually eat with their children while the father eats alone. Persons of opposite sexes do not show any affection publicly through bodily contact; this is considered highly inappropriate. Male companions and female companions may hold hands out of friendship in public without fear of having the action misinterpreted. At social gatherings, women keep to themselves in their own clusters while eating and drinking, as do the men in theirs. This practice of segregation has extended to official gatherings and even to churches.

A person may drop in at any time for a visit and usually arrives with a gift for the host. If the person arrives at mealtime, he or she is expected to join in the meal. Refusal to eat may be considered an insult and distrust of one's host. The Shambaa normally cook an extra share so as to have food for any visitor who may drop in. Visits are normally made in the late afternoon or evening hours, when it is cooler and most of the farm work has been completed.

9 LIVING CONDITIONS

The Shambaa live in large villages consisting of peoples of several lineages, or family groups. Villages are usually located on upper hillsides. Banana groves separate the homesteads and protect against famine. A traditional Shambaa house is round, with thatched roof and sides. Traditionally, when household members would go out to work on their farms, they would tie a rope to the front door to show visitors and passersby that no one was at home. There are also rectangular houses in Shambaai, with walls of wattle and mud and thatched roofs, modeled on what is called a Swahili design. Now, these houses commonly have cement walls and corrugated metal roofs.

Compared to most rural regions in Tanzania, the infrastructure network in Shambaai is better developed. Some major roads are blacktopped or all-season dirt roads. A major road-repair program is under way. Buses transport villagers to and from Tanga town, Dar es Salaam, and other regional centers. There is a railway line linking Dar es Salaam and Moshi and passing through the Korogwe district, providing a valuable link for passengers and products. Some people own small trucks and provide rides to villagers for a small fare.

The Shambaa child mortality rate has fallen, thanks to improved access to Mother and Child Health (MCH) services, which provide health education and immunization. Health centers and dispensaries are available in the rural areas, with larger hospital facilities available in the cities.

10 FAMILY LIFE

Polygamy was widely practiced by the Shambaa. A man married as many women as he could support. He also fathered as many children as possible. It was the father's duty to defend the family from all harm, including illness and hunger. Under the influence of Christianity, Christian marriages are now often monogamous.

Survival skills and material goods were handed down from father to son. The son's well-being, his family and prosperity, all depended on his father's pleasure. Incurring the father's displeasure was dreaded as it could lead to a curse *(ute)*. It was believed that the curse could cause the son to lose all his possessions, wander about like a fool, and even die. A father had considerable authority while alive and was believed to retain some control as a ghost even after his death. Thus, all the sons are believed to share a common fate through their dependence on their father, both alive and as an ancestral ghost. The ghosts' influence over the daughters and their descendants ceased when the daughter died.

A father was required to pay the bridewealth for his sons' first wives. He was also required to pay the medicine man when any of his family members fell ill. He also provided his son with an additional garden when the son married for the first time. A Shambaa man cannot marry within his own lineage or marry a cousin from an outside lineage. He is often expected to marry within his neighborhood. Women are free to accept or reject a marriage proposal. It is the responsibility of the husband to allocate a garden to each wife as a source of food for her and her children. The children help their mother in her garden when they are old enough to do so. The garden is the sons' inheritance. For more affluent Shambaa, expectations for providing for wives and children were much higher. For example, a king provided each wife with chiefdom for her children to rule.

The wife was responsible for the daily farm work. A husband was responsible for increasing his *mai* (wealth). Wealth was increased mainly through acquisition of more livestock in the form of goats, cattle, and sheep. Cattle were kept mainly for bridal payments and ceremonial purposes. A person increased his status and standing in the community by lending out his livestock. This enabled the person to build a network of supporters who could help in times of need. Those who were lent cattle used the milk and were sometimes allowed to keep the offspring to build up their own herds.

An adult son was given his own farm by his father. The son could buy livestock from the sale of his harvest, but he was still dependent on his father for bridewealth.

Traditionally Shambaa families have kept dogs as watchdogs and cats as rodent catchers. Today some animals may be kept as pets, especially in urban areas. Other animals are kept for food, transportation, or farmwork.

11 CLOTHING

The Shambaa dress code has been greatly influenced by the coastal people, who are mainly Muslim and who have been influenced, in turn, by their religion and by Arab traders.

Men wear *khanzus* (long, flowing white robes) and a small cap, or *barghashia,* on their heads. Women use lengths of colorful cloth as wrappers for the body; these are called *kangas* and *kitenges*. A wrapper may be worn over a dress or used to carry a baby on the back or hip. Young women after puberty are required to wrap a *kanga* around their waist when working or leaving the homestead. Married women cover their heads and clothes with two pieces of *kanga*. Women purchase these colorful pieces of cloth from the marketplace or shops and may also take them to tailors to have them sewn into dresses and skirts. Men may also have tailors sew trousers and shirts for them. Shambaa men may be seen wearing shirts and trousers especially in the urban areas; however, for ceremonies and important events they put on *khanzus*.

Traditionally, women do not wear short clothes in public. Short skirts with shorts may be worn for sporting events and in military camps. Secondhand clothing *(mitumba)* may be bought in the marketplace and is generally worn by the poorer people.

12 FOOD

The Shambaa plant many different food crops adapted to the climate of the area, including tubers, medicinal plants, tobacco, beans, and bananas. Banana plants are better suited to the Shambaai than to the *nyika* and used to be the main food crop of the Shambaa. This has changed with the introduction of maize and cassava to the area. Cassava is drought-resistant and is grown as a safeguard against famine. Maize is grown in both *nyika* and Shambaai in different planting and harvesting seasons. Many farmers plant maize during both seasons and are kept busy all year.

The Shambaa diet is composed of starchy foods, such as rice, maize, and sweet potatoes, usually accompanied by beans, meat, and vegetables. Dairy products are available, and sour milk is often drunk for breakfast. Meat consumption is on the increase.

13 EDUCATION

Traditionally, Shambaa children have received instruction from their parents. Youths receive further instruction during the *gao* ceremonies in the form of songs and stories. During this time the young men are taught the tribal norms and proper sexual conduct by a *shefaya* (ritual leader), the youths' mentors *(makungwi),* and other village adults. Young women are taught their responsibilities and proper conduct by women elders.

The Christian missionaries were the first to offer the Shambaa formal education. When the missionaries arrived, those Shambaa who were able to obtain some education rose in status in their local areas. Generally young men were sent to these schools while girls were kept at home. Those girls who went to school often dropped out earlier to get married because parents thought that it was a waste of money to educate daughters who would move to other households when they married.

The Shambaa, like other Tanzanian people, are encouraged to obtain at least primary-level education. Since 1971, the government has required that all children seven years of age and older attend primary schools for at least seven years. Primary education has been provided free for all Tanzanians, but in the early 1990s the government reinstated school fees. Four years of secondary education are required before a student can continue to high school, after passing the national Ordinary Level examinations. High school is for two years; then the student sits for the Advanced Level examinations before applying for university admission. Alternative trade and business schools provide instruction for those students unable to continue with formal education and wishing to acquire skills. Parents now have to pay more for their children's education since the government is no longer able to provide fully subsidized education. Older people, especially in the rural areas, are involved in adult literacy programs.

14 CULTURAL HERITAGE

The Shambaa have a rich cultural heritage of songs and dances. Songs are used to instruct younger people on their history and expected behavior as adult members of the tribe. Drums were used to transmit messages of approaching danger as well as important news, such as the death of a king. Storytelling by the elder generation is a popular evening pastime with children. Storytelling serves to maintain oral history. Traditional dances are still popular, especially at wedding celebrations.

The Shambaa have shown a liking for the various types of music they have encountered through interaction with other cultures. Swahili songs produced by various Tanzanian bands may be heard frequently over the airwaves in public places. The Shambaa enjoy listening to *taarab* (ballads), a tradition introduced to the coastal people by the Arabs. *Kwasa kwasa* and other west and central African music and dance forms are also gaining popularity and may be heard during various celebrations. The younger generation of Shambaa prefers to listen and dance to Western music, including reggae, pop, and hip hop.

15 WORK

Traditionally, for the Shambaa work centered on the farm and was divided between men and women. The whole household was responsible for the production of subsistence food crops. Farmwork and crop yields were divided between a husband and his wives. Men were responsible for planting and tilling on the farms while women were in charge of weeding and harvesting their own farms.

With the ever-diminishing size of the land holdings and declining yields and soil erosion, the Shambaa men are increasingly forced to seek outside employment. The Shambaa have been forced to change their farming patterns because of their increased population density. Women are usually left in the homestead to tend to the farm and children while the husband seeks employment in the urban areas and on plantations, visiting his family periodically.

Educated Shambaa have better chances of finding jobs in the cities as clerks, teachers, and administrators. Previously, all Tanzanians were guaranteed employment, on completion of postsecondary education, in the civil service or parastatals (government-owned companies). Now both men and women in the urban areas compete for jobs in the private sector, for the government is no longer able to hire everyone.

16 SPORTS

Like other Tanzanian children, the Shambaa children first come into contact with sports at school. Primary-school children are encouraged to participate in interschool competitions leading to interregional level and national level championships. Popular sports at school are soccer for boys and netball for girls. All children participate in athletics. At secondary schools Shambaa youth may be introduced to other sports, such as basketball, table tennis, and volleyball.

Soccer is the most popular sport in Tanzania. The national soccer league broadcasts games, which are greatly enjoyed by the Shambaa. There is a friendly rivalry between the supporters of the two major soccer teams in the league, Simba and Yanga. On weekends, standard and makeshift soccer fields are crowded with spectators and players.

17 ENTERTAINMENT AND RECREATION

Radio broadcasts by the state-owned radio station have been the major source of entertainment. Many households have transistor radios, and people enjoy listening to music, radio plays, and sports programs. The government uses the radio station to transmit major broadcasts and matches. Shambaa men gather around a radio in public meeting places, usually with a local brew in hand. Recently the government has allowed private TV and radio stations to operate, increasing the choice and quality of programs. Many people now own television and video sets, and they may tune in to broadcasting stations in Dar es Salaam, Zanzibar, and Kenya. Television ownership has led to the opening of many video lending libraries in Tanga, where action movies are the most popular.

18 FOLK ART, CRAFTS, AND HOBBIES

The Shambaa are mainly agriculturists and prefer tilling the land to craftwork. They have been fortunate to be able to obtain their ornaments and tools through trade. There were blacksmiths forging iron tools and weapons. Toymaking was a favorite pastime for children who adapted pieces of wood into objects like small spears and cooking utensils. Children still make their own toys, especially boxcars and cloth dolls, as manufactured toys are expensive.

19 SOCIAL PROBLEMS

The greatest problem facing the Shambaa today is the gradual loss of cultural identity. Interest in the norms and culture of the Shambaa is declining in the younger generation. They now prefer to adopt a national identity of being simply Tanzanian as opposed to being a Shambaa first. This decline in cultural identity may be attributed to exposure to new religions espousing the unity of humankind and formal education leading the Shambaa to accept Western culture. The use of Swahili as a national language has led to a preference for it in daily use in Shambaai. Tribal intermarriages are on the increase, no longer seen as objectionable. The Shambaa are trying to reverse the erosion by recording their cultural values and history. Younger people in the urban areas are encouraged to regularly visit Shambaai, where they may learn their traditions and converse in Shambala.

Another serious problem facing the Shambaa is a shortage of land. The reasons for this are population increase and stability among the tribes. Formerly the Shambaa could obtain new land by clearing the forests and engaging in warfare against neighboring tribes. Under colonial administration, the land to the north of Shambaai was declared a forest reserve and unavailable for cultivation. Plantation estates were also created around Shambaai for growing of sisal, further limiting land availability. This decrease in arable land in Shambaai has led to soil depletion since the land is not left to fallow. Soil erosion is also on the increase on the mountain slopes, further compounding the problem. The government is trying to introduce better crop types and farming practices into the area through its research center at Amani, Tanga. The Shambaa cannot rely on work in the sisal plantation estates, for the crop has declined sharply in value on the world market since the late 1960s. Younger people are seeking employment farther and farther from Shambaai.

Like all Tanzanians, the Shambaa face the problem of poverty. Tanzania has been experiencing economic problems since the late 1980s. By the early 1990s the government was no longer able to sustain its social services, especially in education and health. By 2002, 80% of the population was engaged in agriculture, and 36% of the population lived below the poverty line.

20 GENDER ISSUES

Shambaa culture is predominantly patrilineal, with the men controlling most aspects of the society. Although Christianity has brought about a monogamous influence on the modern Shambaa family, polygyny was widely practiced by the Shambaa, depending on how many wives and children the husband could raise and support.

Labor among the Shambaa was also slightly divisible by gender. While the men were responsible for planting and tilling the fields, weeding and harvesting was left to the women.

The husband was responsible for increasing his *mai* (wealth) by tightly controlling the lending of his livestock, a practice that would eventually help to increase his wealth and social status. However, now women are usually left in the homestead to tend the farm and children while the husbands seek wage employment in the urban areas and on plantations.

Whereas there was little control over what men should wear, women's dressing and even sexuality was largely tied to social taboos and customs such as women should wear clothes that cover their full-length bodies and married women in particular were to cover their heads as a sign of subjugation.

In terms of educational opportunities, while the boys were sent to school, the girl-child was left at home to be trained on house-bound tasks and eventually get married off.

21 BIBLIOGRAPHY

Avorgbedor, Daniel K., ed. *The Interrelatedness of Music, Religion, and Ritual in African Performance Practice*. Lewiston, NY: E. Mellen Press, 2003.

Besha, Ruth M. "A Study of Tense and Aspect in Shambala." *Language Studies in East Africa* 10. Berlin: Reimer, 1989.

———. "A Classified Vocabulary of the Shambala Language with Outline Grammar." *Bantu Vocabulary Series* 10. Tokyo: ILCAA, 1993.

Feierman, Steven. *The Shambaa Kingdom: A History*. Madison: University of Wisconsin Press, 1974.

———. *Peasant Intellectuals*. Madison: University of Wisconsin Press, 1990.

Maddox, Gregory H., and James L. Giblin, eds. *In Search of a Nation: Histories of Authority and Dissidence in Tanzania.* Oxford: James Currey; Dar Es Salaam: Kapsel Educational Publications; Athens: Ohio University Press, 2005.

Pelt, P. *Bantu Customs in Mainland Tanzania.* Tabora: TMP Book Department, 1971.

Winans, Edgar V. *Shambala, the Constitution of a Traditional State.* Berkeley: University of California Press, 1962.

World Bank. *1995 World Development Report.* New York: Oxford University Press, 1995

—revised by M. Njoroge

SHILLUK

PRONUNCIATION: shil-UK
LOCATION: Sudan
POPULATION: about 150,000
LANGUAGE: Shilluk
RELIGION: Animism; indigenous beliefs
RELATED ARTICLES: Vol. 1: Dinka; Nuer; Sudanese

¹ INTRODUCTION

The Shilluk have long occupied a region along the White Nile in the modern Sudan. It is estimated that Prenilotes may have been present in the area from the 4th millennium BC. Arab travelers to the central Sudan in the 9th century AD recorded Prenilotic Barea and Kunama peoples in this area. During the Funj Sultanates from 1504 to 1821, it appears that slave raiders attacked Shilluk lands. Regional disturbances during the Funj Sultanates probably led to some southward migration of the Shilluk in the 16th century and to a more concentrated village pattern. Perhaps reflecting this time, the Shilluk mythology records that Nyakang (Nyikang) was the first *reth* or king to unify the Shilluk people in a proto-state formation.

The area was first reached by Europeans in the 18th century. The Ottoman slave raids of the early 19th century victimized the Shilluk. Ottoman administration reached them in 1867. Mahdist rule (1884–98) was generally resisted by the Shilluk as they were set upon by zealous and slave-raiding Arabs from the north. The Shilluk region was again inaccessible to Europeans at this time. It was not until the early 20th century that serious ethnographic and historical attention began to be paid to the Shilluk. Even then, the interest was focused on the concerns of the British colonial administration and missionaries who were in the Shilluk region. A new census is planned but not yet conducted.

² LOCATION AND HOMELAND

The Shilluk are concentrated along the western banks and islands of the White Nile, especially between the Renk-Malakal reach, as well as being located on the lower section of the Sobat River. In other terms, they live between 9° and 14° degrees north latitude, about 640 km (400 mi) south of Khartoum, the modern national capital of the Sudan. Malakal, the present provincial capital, is in the southern portion of Shilluk land, but on the east bank of the Nile.

The precise ancestral homeland of the Prenilotic Shilluk is unknown but is likely to be in the present vicinity of Shilluk concentration. Perhaps it was they who replaced the aboriginal hunting and gathering population. The Shilluk and Nilotic people are remarkably tall (179 cm or 5 ft 10 in on average) and lean and may be distinguished from other neighboring Africans for this reason. Blood samples of the Shilluk and other Nilotics show Rh-allele frequencies which are notably different from all their neighbors. Even though malaria is now present in Shilluk lands, they also have a very low frequency of sickle cell alleles. These facts add up to a picture of long-term isolation.

The ecosystem is mainly grasslands, swampy river banks, and islands, but some trees appear in places. There are something like 150 compacted hamlets (*myer*) constituting the Shilluk domain. They are divided into the Ger (northern) and Luak (southern) royal districts. Each of these has its own supreme chief and royal settlement at Golbany and Kwom, just north and south of the central capital at Fashoda (also known as Ko-dok) on the western bank. The royal heads of Ger and Luak must concur about the appointment of a new reth.

At Fashoda the reth usually makes his royal residence with his royal children, courtiers, bodyguards, and retainers (bang reth), and his wives. It is here that he receives the council of lineage elders, while he sits on his royal stool-throne. Fashoda was also the site of an historic meeting in 1898 of the military forces of the French (under Major Marchand) and the English (under General Kitchener) in determining the European partition of the Sudan. The French withdrew; the Sudan became an Anglo-Egyptian colony.

Neighboring the Shilluk to the east are the related Anuak people; to the immediate south are the Nuer and the vast Sudd papyrus swamplands which blocked exploration for millennia. In the 19th century the region supported large elephant herds, which have since been decimated for their ivory. Further to the southwest are large populations of Dinka. West of the Shilluk are diverse sedentary peoples of the Nuba mountains. To the northwest the Shilluk meet various nomadic Arab peoples from whom they must sometimes defend themselves.

³ LANGUAGE

The Shilluk belong to the Eastern subfamily of the Sudanic linguistic stock. The Sudanic languages have only a few loan words from the Semitic languages to the north or Cushitic languages to the east. Within the Sudanic stock, the Shilluk are further identified with the Nilotic language speakers, which also include the Anuak and Meban peoples, who are collectively considered as Prenilotes. The Shilluk preceded, but are related to, other Nilotic groups, like the Nuer and Dinka, whose languages are understood by many Shilluk. The Shilluk are also self-known as the "Chollo." Gender, number, and case can be noted in the Shilluk language.

⁴ FOLKLORE

As with most animist or polytheist religious systems, the sacred and secular worlds of the Shilluk are linked. Spiritual forces abound in animals, elements, and places, and the folklore of the Shilluk serves to integrate the people with this worldview through storytelling, origin myths, sacrifices, and invocations. For example, the great creator, Jo-uk, is tied through four supernatural generations to Nyakang, the founder of the Shilluk rethship.

The father of Nyakang, U-kwa, has many folkloric expressions. He lived along the Nile, where he was attracted to women with half-crocodile bodies who lived in the water. Tempted by these women, U-kwa captured two of them (Nik-ki-yah and Ung-wahd). Their cries quickly drew their father (U-dil-jil), whose presence had been unknown. The father's left side was human, while his right side was a green crocodile. After some debate and negotiation, U-kwa married the women and from his wife Nik-ki-yah he had his son Nik-kang (likewise half-man and half-crocodile). From a third wife, U-kwa had three more sons, one of whom was Du-wad, who became Nyakang's rival as reth. The conflict escalated and was only resolved when Nyakang and his brothers, Omoi and Jew, created a new kingdom at the mouth of the Sobat River. There, Nyakang created

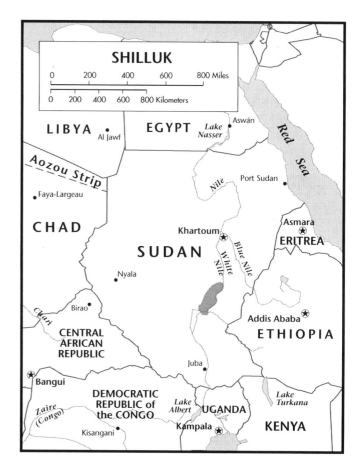

men and women from hippopotamuses, crocodiles, and wild animals to populate his kingdom. The animal ancestors died and the Shilluk people were thereby born.

Nevertheless, Nik-ki-yah lives forever, usually as a crocodile, and she is sometimes offered a goat as a sacrifice. Occasionally, in trials-by-ordeal, suspected people are forced into the river to be judged by Nik-ki-yah. Fear of crocodiles quickly has them confessing.

⁵ RELIGION

The complex animist religious beliefs of the Shilluk are held most devoutly. The most important spiritual force is that of Nyakang. Special annual sacrifices are made to Nyakang at the start of the rainy season. In addition to this ancestral spirit of all Shilluk, there is also the universal Shilluk creator god, Jo-uk, with whom deceased persons will reside eternally, if they are well-behaved during their lifetime. According to Shilluk origin myths, it was from the Nile that Jo-uk created D'ung Adduk (White Cow). In turn, D'ung Adduk gave birth to a son, Kola, whom she nursed. Kola had a son named U-mah-ra, whose son was Wad-maul, whose son was U-kwa, who was the father of Nyakang, ancestor of all reths. A few Shilluk have turned to Islam and Christianity, but traditional beliefs are still strongly held. As more Shilluk are educated more are turning toward Christian faiths.

6 MAJOR HOLIDAYS

The Western concept of "holiday" is not really inherent to Shilluk life, but some note may be given to Sudanese national holidays such as Independence Day on 1 January. Those who are Muslim or Christian might follow those religious celebrations. For the Shilluk, the chief "holidays" would be the installation of a new reth, a marriage festivity, collective fishing and harvesting, and especially the celebration of Nyakang at the start of the rainy season, which involves the slaughtering of animals, dancing, and drinking fermented sorghum (merisa). Most villages have a shrine to Nyakang where amulets and charms may be placed to invoke ancestral spirits, often by a tree.

The election of a reth is considered the most significant event in Shilluk life. This integrates the society with its traditions, provides for political leadership and continuity, and presents the greatest opportunity for public oratory and group confirmation. A notable amount of the literature on the Shilluk is focused on the transfer of rethships.

The first stage in the appointment of a reth begins with a mock battle without real spears. This "battle" between the northern and southern Shilluk groups is mediated by a messenger who carries scornful retorts between the two "competing" groups. An effigy of the reth is symbolically paraded with an ostrich-feather fan shade which is placed on the royal stool. When the effigy is restored to its shrine, the new reth will be infused with the spirit of Nyakang, and he can then assume the official responsibilities by sitting on the royal stool.

The bipartite or moiety structure of the Shilluk is based on a model of segmentary opposition, similar to a modern monarchy with a bicameral parliament. The chiefs of each component settlement group (podh) of the Ger and Luak districts are consulted at a lower level. Typically a reth's son does not inherit from his father, although the work of Evans-Pritchard presents the opposing view that he usually does. In any case, a new reth is found from a prince (nyireth) or close relative, or from a different natal village, often during an interregnum struggle. The ritual conflict preceding the appointment and purification of the reth is a central feature of Shilluk society.

Some early reports state that regicide was practiced by royal wives or close kinfolk when a reth was deemed to be too ill, old, or ineffective to continue in office. Evans-Pritchard (1962: 76, 82–83) considers that the reports of institutional regicide were a fiction but that violent ends for reths certainly did occur amidst the precarious balance in Shilluk political life. In any case, the persistent discussion of regicide, whether symbolic or real, is not only a warning to seated reths but is also a symbolic expression that the spirit of Nyakang is no longer at ease and needs transfer, since the spirit of Nyakang resides eternally with the reth, and the reth himself is mortal.

As the reth gains his position through the council of lineage elders (jal dwong pac), it seems evident that the council can also determine that a prince (nyireth) of the royal clan (kwareth) is justified in recognizing a failed rethship, and that regicide is appropriate so that intraethnic struggles can be avoided and the continuity of the Shilluk people thereby ensured. A certain measure of rotation between the royal lineages (kwareth) of the north and south also assists in reaching this political equilibrium.

Clearly the reth will be eternally nervous about his position and he will make public efforts to be responsive to the lineage elders. Alternatively he will make special provisions to be protected by armed attendants and to be aloof and reserved. The formal, mock battle between village groups symbolizes the actual power struggles for this prestigious appointment.

The Celebration of the January 2005 Comprehensive Peace Accord is observed nationally.

7 RITES OF PASSAGE

Unlike many Sudanese Arabs, few Shilluk girls are subject to female circumcision as a rite of prepubesence. The practice of removing the lower incisor teeth is common for Shilluk youths, as well as ethnic scarification which consists of making a series of raised bumps across the forehead just above the eyebrows. Other decorative scars are also known. The umbilicus of baby boys is buried to the right of the front door while Shilluk girls have their umbilicus buried to the left. Other gender-differentiated customs are seen with Shilluk boys who have noted puberty rites of passage while Shilluk girls have few special rites and are rarely subject to female circumcision. Likewise dancing, clothing, decoration and child names are gender specific.

The death of commoners is followed by burial in the ground, unlike other Nilotes who may use water burial. Upon the death of the reth, the corpse is walled in his royal house, which thereby becomes his temporary tomb. Later his bones are collected for interment in the hamlet of his birth.
Male or female commoners are washed and shaved at death and wrapped in a shroud. The body is rested on its right side with the head facing easterly. Post-mortem memorial services take place first at graveside, a few months later, and for higher status person a commemoration can take place a year or more later.

8 INTERPERSONAL RELATIONS

The interpersonal relations of Shilluk people are guided by kinship, social hierarchy, and gender. They follow a form of matrilineal descent, unlike their Arab neighbors to the north. The Shilluk follow a descriptive type of cousin terminology which implies specific role relationships within the kinship network. Lineage membership is a critical feature of interpersonal relations. Within lineage groups, solidarity is maintained by age-grade cohorts, which are common in societies requiring military defense for the nation and the reth. The position of the reth is also distinguished by deferential behavior, sociolinguistic markers, a hippo-hide whip and staffs, use of royal antelope skins for dress, ritual stepping over color-selected bulls, and the exclusion of children from the royal compound. The well-being of the bang reth (the reth's retainers) rests upon their unquestioned loyalty, which is rewarded by the reth through provision of food and security.

Aside from the royal personnel (bang reth) surrounding the reth at Fashoda, the Shilluk have a second class of people who are high-ranking but without legitimate access to the rethship. An additional group of nobility are known, but these are the Shilluk who had access to authority in the past and are no longer associated with the reth. The largest group of Shilluk are commoners (colo) who belong to various lineages but are not high-ranking whatsoever and are expected to show deference to those who are. Last in the traditional hierarchy are slaves who have entered Shilluk society as war captives, for punishment, by purchase, or as refugees from famine and disorder.

The reth and the council of lineage elders are responsible for maintaining order in Shilluk society. If conflicts arise within lineages, the elder or his council intervenes; if there are conflicts between lineages, such as raiding, adultery, or theft, the reth intervenes and, under his almost absolute authority, he can apply various punishments such as confiscation of property or enslavement with use of his royal bodyguard. Adultery with the daughter of a reth is punished by death. The reth also controls trade in ivory, giraffe tails, and slaves. Toniolo and Hill (1975: 251) estimate that in 1876, two-thirds of the slaves in the northern Sudanese town of Wad Medani were of Shilluk, Dinka, and "Fertit" origin.

9 LIVING CONDITIONS

The Shilluk live in hamlets of compact villages made of round houses (tukls) of wattle and daub construction and with conical thatched roofs. The house of the lineage-head, especially if he is the reth, might be placed on a higher elevation indicative of higher status. Electricity, piped water, and other conveniences were not present until modern times in the provincial capital. Many Shilluk have moved from rural areas to Malakal, the largest regional center.

10 FAMILY LIFE

Shilluk marriage is a primary institution which requires the use of a considerable quantity of livestock to collect the bride-wealth payments for completing the marriage contract. Unlike Arabs, Shilluk usually avoid marrying first cousins, and they practice lineage exogamy. However, like Arabs, the Shilluk do allow for polygyny, in particular a man marrying sets of sisters (sororal marriage). Postmarital life follows a pattern of matri-patrilocal (sometimes avunculocal) residence in a compound of houses. If the household is polygynous, then additional houses are built to accommodate the other family members with their mothers.

11 CLOTHING

Today most Shilluk men wear Western clothing or Arab jellabiyas, but traditional attire is still seen. For women, traditional clothing was either animal-hide wraps, skirts (rahat), or aprons. Women's hair was usually shaven. Males were traditionally naked, but a reth or his noblemen could wear a toga-like garment. For men and women, armlets, breastplates, bracelets, beads, bells, necklaces, and body-painting were common. For men, hair sculpture (especially in a popular flared helmet shape, protected at night by a headrest) and ostrich feathers in the hair were widespread. For those young men with military functions, their dress would not be complete without their narrow hide-shields, clubs, spears with broad leaf-shaped points, drums, and leopard skins.

12 FOOD

The Shilluk are predominantly sedentary farmers of the fertile banks and islands in the White Nile. Their economy is based on the Sudanic food complex of millet (durra) or sorghum, but other foods such as corn, melons, okra, sesame, and beans are also known. The durra is fermented to make an alcoholic drink (merisa). As farmers they are endowed with livestock including sheep, goats, and especially cattle which play important roles in religion and kinship. However, cattle for the Shilluk are not nearly as significant as they are for the neighboring Nuer and Dinka. Shilluk men are in charge of milking the cows, and

they do not use fresh cattle blood, unlike the Dinka and Nuer. Because the Shilluk are riverfolk, their foods are diversified by hunting and fishing. Antelope-hunting on royal island preserves is restricted.

13 EDUCATION

Only under British colonialism and under post-independence Sudanese governments did the Shilluk receive a formal secular or missionary education. Traditional education was structured around acquiring the skills of an agricultural and military population. On the other hand, the transmission of oral history was very important, especially in maintaining the lineage system from which political leadership emerged for the council of elders and the reth.

14 CULTURAL HERITAGE

The population of the Shilluk has not been properly counted for years, but early in the post-colonial period there were at least 110,000 Shilluk-speakers who shared a common cultural heritage. The Shilluk's unique office of the reth and the role of Nyakang bond them closely together in their villages and region. The Shilluk traditions of the royal throne, semi-divine kingship, dynastic rule, social hierarchies, sororal marriage, oppositional division of the kingdom, the use of a water purification ritual, and origin myths are noted to be held in common with ancient Egyptians. The degree to which this may be true, and the direction of cultural borrowing, is not determined with precision, but the hypothesis that these two ancient Nile valley populations are related remains an important subject for research.

15 WORK

For the traditional Shilluk, work is assigned by gender, age-grade, and lineage rank. The reth, ranking princes, and lineage elders do very little physical work, while females are heavily engaged in domestic tasks, food production, and child care. Young males have cultivating, fishing, herding, and hunting tasks. Dugout canoes (2.5–6m or 8–20 ft long) and small reed floats (ambatch) are made for fishing and local transport.

16 SPORTS

Some modern Shilluk play soccer.

17 ENTERTAINMENT AND RECREATION

Traditional recreation was usually aimed at improving military and hunting skills, such as at the mock battles that surrounded the election of a new reth. Songs, poetry, and call-and-response dancing are popular. Among the popular dances are a mock threat "war dance" with infantry spear charges; an amusing hyena dance-play in which hunters stalk and "kill" an enacted hyena threatening sleeping children; and a lion dance in which masked dancers appear with lion heads and are pursued by hunters until wounded and killed.

18 FOLK ART, CRAFTS, AND HOBBIES

Like other Nilotes, the Shilluk entertain themselves with public and private discourse which can include folklore. Expressions of folk arts are in jewelry, clay sculpture, hairstyling, and hide-tanning.

[19] SOCIAL PROBLEMS

The gravest structural challenge within traditional Shilluk society is the interregnum between reths. This potentially conflictful time can sometimes spill over into violence. Meanwhile, relations between Dinka and Nuer can involve mutual cattle-raiding which can evolve into wider conflicts. During the current war in the southern Sudan, these ethnic groups sometimes spend as much time quarreling among themselves as against their perceived common enemies in the Afro-Arab northern Sudan.

Among the greatest present social problems are regional development and security, as well as the prejudicial attitude of some northern Sudanese towards southerners. Many post-colonial governments in Khartoum have pursued military rather than political solutions for national integration, and the Shilluk have long occupied a main river route connecting these conflicting regions. The economic development of the Shilluk and their survival from famine, relocation, and military operations have been major concerns.

[20] GENDER ISSUES

Traditionally Shilluk culture was markedly patriarchal and paternalistic as the ruling positions were dominated by men, although it is reputed that in the mid-17th century one reth, Abudok nya Bwoc, was a woman. Also, in such cases woman-to-woman marriage was rare but possible. However, at present after many years of regional civil war between Arab northerners and southern Nilotics there have were many instances of gender violence such as rape and assault. Generally the Shilluk managed to be somewhat less involved in the main battlefields and contests for power, with some important exceptions in contests for political and military leadership.

As a result of the historic Comprehensive Peace Accord of 2005, the southern Shilluk women were more empowered to address gender roles and improved the position of women in general and address some specific matters in education and in HIV/AIDS education. Thus traditional social values are intact, but are being negotiated more substantially than previously. The prominent Shilluk national leaders such as Pagan Amum Okech, Lam Akol Ajawin, and Peter Adwok Nyaba are also oriented to progressive and more secular models of cultural transformation that have helped to improve the position of Shilluk women.

[21] BIBLIOGRAPHY

Dugmore, A. Radclyffe. *The Vast Sudan*. New York: Frederick A. Stokes Co., 1924.

Evans-Pritchard, E. E., "The Divine Kingship of the Shilluk of the Nilotic Sudan" [based on his Frazer lecture in 1948]. In *Essays in Social Anthropology,* Glencoe, NY: Free Press, 1962.

Giffen, J. Kelly. *The Anglo-Egyptian Sudan*. London: F. H. Revell, 1905.

Grotanelli, V. L. "Pre-Niloti." In *Annales Lateranensi,* 12 (1948): 282–326.

Howell, P. P. "The Shilluk Settlement." In *Sudan Notes and Records,* 24 (1941): 47–67.

Howell, P. P., and W. P. G. Thomson. "The Death of a Reth of the Shilluk and the Installation of His Successor." In *Sudan Notes and Records,* (1946).

Murdock, George P. *Africa, Its Peoples and Their Culture History.* New York: McGraw-Hill, 1959.

Pumphrey, M. E. C. "The Shilluk Tribe." In *Sudan Notes and Records,* 24 (1941): 1–45.

Roberts, D. F., E. W. Ikin, and A. E. Mourant. "Blood Groups of the Northern Nilotes." In *Annnals of Human Genetics* 20 (1955): 135–154.

Roberts, D. F., and D. R. Bainbridge. "Nilotic Physique. " In *American Journal of Physical Anthropology,* 21 (1963): 341–70.

Roberts, Edward, ed. *The Shilluk*. In *Disappearing World* videotape series. Granada, 1976.

Toniolo, Elias, and Richard Hill, ed. *The Opening of the Nile Basin, 1842–1881.* New York: Barnes and Noble, 1975.

—by R. Lobban, Jr.

SOMALIS

PRONUNCIATION: suh-MAH-leez
ALTERNATE NAMES: Somalians
LOCATION: Somalia
POPULATION: More than 7 million
LANGUAGE: Maxaad tiri; Arabic
RELIGION: Islam (Sunni)
RELATED ARTICLES: Vol. 1: Swahili

¹ INTRODUCTION

Somalia was much in the news during the last two decades. Many people have therefore gained their knowledge of the country and the Somali people from brief television images of pick-up trucks fitted with large caliber weapons, American marines hitting the beach, tomahawk missile attacks on suspected terrorist enclaves, street fighting among different factions in Mogadishu and starving people in rural areas. This image of a country and people in distress does not convey the richness and complexity of Somali life and culture, a culture that stretches back hundreds of years with roots in Arabia and both North and sub-Saharan Africa.

Somalia, unlike the majority of nation-states in Africa, has only one ethnic group. That group does have, however, significant divisions based on membership in various clan-families. What unites the Somalis is a common language, a reliance on animal husbandry, a shared Islamic heritage, the long-term inhabitancy of the Horn of Africa, and a belief that all Somali speakers, whether they live within the boundaries of Somalia or not, are descended from a common ancestor. Thus, in addition to the approximately 7-8 million Somalis who inhabit Somalia proper, the Somali-speakers who live within the northern province of Kenya, the Ogaden region of eastern Ethiopia, and the country of Djibouti are all considered to be part of one Somali nation.

² LOCATION AND HOMELAND

Somalia is located in eastern Africa on what is commonly termed the Horn of Africa. The Horn extends into the Indian Ocean to the east, and the Gulf of Aden to the north. As a result, Somalia has a coastline extending almost 3,200 km (2,000 mi). To the west, Somalia is bounded by Ethiopia; to the southwest, by Kenya; and to the northwest, by Djibouti. The total area of the country is about 647,500 sq km (250,000 sq mi). Two long, sandy coastal plains dominate the coastal areas of the country. The interior is characterized by a series of moderate mountain ranges in the north, and a large rugged plateau in the south. The major rivers in Somalia are the Jubba furthest south, and the Shabeelle in the south-central area. The climate can be described as ranging from semiarid to arid, with average rainfall being less than 28 cm (11 in) per year. Animal husbandry is the most common subsistence activity in Somalia, with the major animals kept being camels, cattle, sheep, and goats. Agriculture is possible between the country's two major rivers, with sorghum, maize (corn), and a variety of legumes being raised.

In the late 19th century, the northern half of Somalia became a British protectorate. The southern half of Somalia was an Italian colony until 1960 when it was united with the north-ern half to become an independent republic. However, independence did not unite all Somali people. A unification that would bring Somalis living in Kenya, Ethiopia, and Djibouti into an expanded nation-state has remained a political goal for the last half century.

³ LANGUAGE

The language spoken by the vast majority of the Somali people is referred to as Maxaad tiri, but various dialects are spoken by members of the major clans within the country. Maxaad tiri and Arabic are official languages in Somalia, and many older people in the south also speak Italian. Government officials in the cities often speak English. Names for both males and females follow the Islamic pattern of a given first name followed by one's father's name, then one's father's father's name, father's father's father's name, and so forth. It is therefore common for a Somali to have names stretching back 15 generations. Somalis take extreme pride in their patrilineal ancestry. The perpetuation of family names, and the ability to recite each of them, is an important way of maintaining a connection with these ancestors.

⁴ FOLKLORE

Ceremonial feasts among the Somali people always include the telling of heroic tales of ancestors, as well as stories of more recent events in the lives of the storytellers themselves. As patrilineal ancestors are held in such high esteem by the Somalis, much of their folklore revolves around these family "heroes" who have aggrandized the wealth or status of the clan through fighting or clever economic actions.

⁵ RELIGION

The official state religion of Somalia is Islam, and almost 100% of the Somali population is Sunni Muslim. Although the Somali follow the practices associated with Islam—praying five times a day, not eating pork products, abstaining from alcohol, and males having up to four wives at one time—they are not as traditional as many Muslims. Women do not practice *purdah,* or seclusion. They do not wear veils or cover their entire bodies when outside the home. They are full participants in subsistence activities in the rural areas, and they frequently own shops and work in a variety of occupations in urban areas, as well. (See section on Gender issues for more detail.)

As is common in many parts of the Islamic world, Somalis incorporate a belief in a spirit world into their religious system. These spirits, or *jinns,* can be good or evil and can affect the lives of individuals, families, and even large kinship groups. It is therefore necessary to placate them, and sometimes to metaphorically fight them, in order to avoid and overcome illness, loss of property, marital problems, infertility, and even death. There are specialists who "fight" *jinns* through prayer, ceremonies resembling exorcisms, and the ritual killing of animals. In addition to providing remedies for a variety of misfortunes, these ceremonies serve as important mechanisms for both enhancing clan solidarity and linking different kinship groups.

⁶ MAJOR HOLIDAYS

Holidays in Somalia are associated with Islam. Ramadan is a month-long fast during which Muslims, in order to exhibit their beliefs, do not eat or drink during daylight hours. Rama-

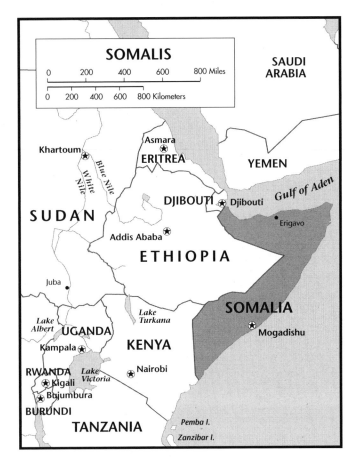

SOMALIS

SAUDI ARABIA

YEMEN

Khartoum

Asmara
ERITREA

DJIBOUTI Djibouti   Gulf of Aden

• Erigavo

SUDAN

Addis Ababa

ETHIOPIA

Juba

SOMALIA

Lake
Turkana

Lake
Albert   UGANDA

KENYA

Mogadishu

Kampala

RWANDA   Lake
Victoria
Kigali   Nairobi
Bujumbura

BURUNDI

TANZANIA   Pemba I.
Zanzibar I.

dan ends with the feast of Id Al-Atah. This is also the first day of the month of Haaj during which believers are expected, at least once in their lives, to make a pilgrimage to Mecca. Muhammad's birthday, Mowluud, is also a holy day among the Somalis and is celebrated with feasting.

7 RITES OF PASSAGE

Life events among the Somali are celebrated by feasting. The type and number of animals killed, and the particular individuals invited to the feast, depend on the wealth of the family involved and the nature of the event. The feasting is both an announcement that an important event has occurred, and a validation of the role of the family in the life of the clan. Birth is always an important event. Although boys are more highly valued among the Somali than girls, one or more sheep or goats will be killed to celebrate the birth of either. Death also results in feasting. The type and number of animals killed varies directly with the status of the deceased: a goat for a young child, to one or more camels for the death of an old, wealthy male.

Marriage is viewed by Somalis as a bond between two kinship groups, rather than only between two individuals, and is marked by a series of exchanges and ceremonies. The opening exchange is termed fad and usually consists of a relatively small amount of sorghum, a sheep, or a goat that the potential groom's patrilineal kin group presents to the kin group of the family of the potential bride. If the fad is accepted, then negotiations over the much larger bride-price (meher) can begin.

The *meher is* gathered by the groom's patrilineal kinfolk and can consist of camels, cattle, sheep, and goats. These animals are given to the family of the bride and are further distributed to close kin of the bride's father. The bride's family prepares the items necessary for family life: the *aqal* (a portable house), a bed, cooking utensils, mats, ropes, and skins. These are given to the married couple. The groom's family is responsible for slaughtering a camel and/or cow, which is consumed by the two immediate families. The bride's family will slaughter one or more animals to feed all the other guests.

8 INTERPERSONAL RELATIONS

Contrary to their depiction on television over the last two decades as rampaging killers, the vast majority of Somalis are extremely friendly, warm, and peaceable. There is a strong tradition of hospitality that obligates individuals to welcome close kinfolk, clan members, and even strangers with tea and food. Because of the continual movement of people and animals throughout a large territory, and the precariousness of the arid environment, this type of hospitality is not uncommon among pastoralists, but the Somalis take special pride in providing it. The most common greetings are "Maalin wanaagsan" (Good day) and "Nabad myah?" (How are you?). For men, these greetings are followed by an extended shaking of hands, which is usually repeated with the same person even after a short absence. Women are less formal when greeting each other, and men and women who are not closely related by blood never shake hands or express other forms of intimacy.

There is nothing that could be construed as dating in the rural areas of Somalia. Even in urban areas, the contact between unmarried men and women is limited. Marriage is closely controlled by older men, and premarital sex is strongly forbidden. Unmarried men in their 20s will display their virility and prowess to women of marriageable age by dancing as a group, but older men do all they can to keep the young men far away from the unmarried women.

Although chronological age is not the sole marker of elder status, there is a general level of respect given to "older" men, especially when age is combined with success in other areas of Somali life. In particular, wealthy older men are accorded great respect, since wealth can only be gained by making wise decisions about animals, labor allocations, and marriages. It is expected that these older men use their status to increase the wellbeing of their immediate patrilineal kin and their clan.

9 LIVING CONDITIONS

It is necessary to differentiate between the inhabitants of rural and urban areas when discussing the living conditions in Somalia. The vast majority (90%) of the Somali people live in small villages scattered throughout the rural areas of the country. Few of them have electricity, clean running water, paved roads, or public services. There are two types of housing utilized by people in the rural areas: *mundals* and *aqals*. Mundals are permanent structures made of a mud and dung mixture spread over a wooden frame and then topped with a thatched roof. These houses are occupied by a husband and wife, with their children. An *aqal* is a mobile house made of wooden sticks and hides, which can be transported on the back of a camel from one location to another. Every married woman owns an aqal and is responsible for erecting and dismantling it as animal camps are moved.

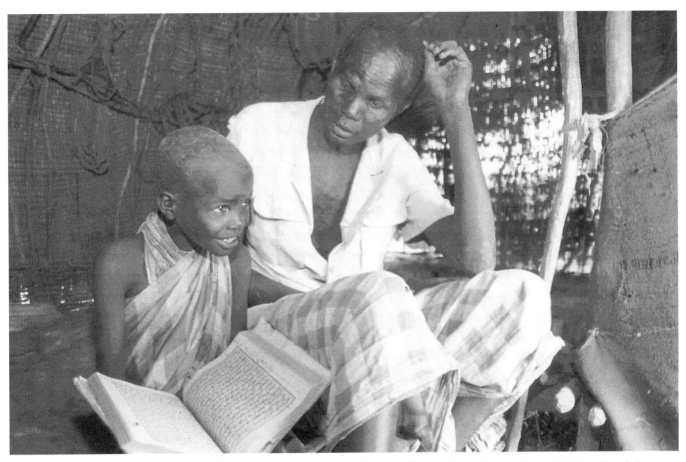

Somali family structure is based on patrilineal descent. Men belong to the clan of their fathers and trace relationship through male lines back to the beginning of the clan, with the inheritance transferred from father to son. (AP Images)

The approximately 10% of the Somali population who live in cities experience a life much different from those who live in the rural areas. Before the civil war began, the residents of Mogadishu, Baidoa, Hargeysa, Kismayu, Berbera, and Marka had access to electricity, running water, paved roads, hospitals, and large markets. Most urban dwellers lived in single-family houses and in the 1990s worked as shopkeepers, traders, or craftspeople, or for the government. Conditions brought about by continued civil-strife in several urban centers, especially Mogadishu and Baidoa, have made it impossible for normal life to function.

10 FAMILY LIFE

Since wealth is equated with the number of animals a man has, the goal for most men is to have more than one wife, and as many children as possible, in order to care for more animals. As Muslims, men are allowed as many as 4 wives at one time. It is not unusual for older wealthy men to have 3 or 4 wives. However, divorce is easy and common, and therefore some men may have had 10 or more wives during their lifetime. Likewise, many women will have been married to more than one man because of divorce or the death of a husband. Men do not usually marry until they are in their late 20s and have been able to accumulate some camels and cattle. Women, on the other hand, marry for the first time at 13 or 14 years of age.

After marriage, women live in the village or animal camp of their husband.

Family structure is based on patrilineal descent. Men belong to the clan of their fathers and trace relationship through male lines back to the beginning of the clan, with inheritance *(wahaad)* from father to son. There are six major patrilineally based "clan-families" in Somalia. The Daarood, the largest, live in an area from the tip of the Horn westward into Ethiopia. The Hawiyya are found primarily in the central plains and eastern coastal regions, and the Dir inhabit the most northern area of Somalia into Djibouti. The Isxaaq occupy the area between the Dir and Daarood in the northern plains. The Digil live along the southern coast between the Jubba and Shabeelle rivers; and the Rahanwiin inhabit the fertile area north of the Digil.

11 CLOTHING

Clothing worn by Somalis is greatly influenced by the hot and dry climate of the Horn. Consequently, men have traditionally worn a long piece of lightweight cloth *(mawhees)* as a wrap-around skirt. A lightweight shirt is usually worn, and most men also use a long piece of cloth as a shawl at night when the temperature can drop to near freezing, and as a turban during the heat of the day when temperatures can reach above 38°C (100°F).

Somali women dressed in traditional costumes perform at Mogadishu. Women traditionally wear dresses that cover their entire body from shoulders to ankles. It is also customary for women to wear shawls which they can use to cover their heads when in the presence of nonfamily males. (Jason Laure)

Even though women do not keep *purdah* (seclusion), they still traditionally wear a dress that covers their entire body from shoulders to ankles. It is also customary for women to wear a shawl that they can use to cover their heads when in the presence of nonfamily males. This layering of clothing allows women to remove their shawl when indoors or when outside in the heat of the day, and yet have appropriate covering for modesty purposes and when temperatures fall.

Prior to puberty, young girls usually wear a simple dress made of a lightweight fabric. Young boys wear shorts and, most recently, imported tee-shirts with a variety of logos of American and European sports teams. Unmarried males in their late teens and early 20s are responsible for herding their family's camels and often spend months far away from their homes. They wear the traditional mawhees, but are almost always shirtless in order to show off their physiques. To further accentuate their virility, these young men cover their torsos and cake their hair with *ghee*—aged butterfat. This form of attire is worn to attract females and is abandoned immediately after marriage.

12 FOOD

Given that the main economic activity among Somalis is the raising of animals, it is not surprising that the most desired food is meat. Although camel, cattle, goat, sheep, and even chickens are killed and eaten, camel meat is the most desired. Even though animals are plentiful and meat is the most desired food, it would be a mistake to think that meat is eaten every day. In rural areas, animals are generally only killed and meat eaten on special occasions. In urban areas, meat is available at markets, but once again it is not eaten daily. Instead, grains and vegetables are the everyday staple.

Sorghum, a grain crop widely grown in sub-Saharan Africa, is the most common food. Maize (corn), both locally grown and imported, began to be available in the 1970s in the urban areas of the country, as did imported rice. All the grains are cooked as a porridge and are traditionally eaten from a common bowl. Following Islamic practice, the porridge is eaten using only the right hand, without utensils. When meat is eaten, it is cooked separately from the porridge and then placed on top of the cooked grain. It is common, especially in rural areas, for men and women to eat separately.

Food delicacies include camel's hump, sheep's tail, goat's liver, and camel's milk. Camel's hump and sheep's tail (which are primarily fat stored by the animal in order to be reabsorbed during the dry season) and goat's liver are fried, and are only served on special occasions. Camel's milk is drunk more frequently, especially by unmarried males who are responsible for herding these animals. Although these traditional foods are available in markets, urban dwellers have access to a much wider range of foods, including specialty foods imported from overseas.

13 EDUCATION

Although during the 1970s and 1980s education for all children was a high priority for the government of Somalia, few children in rural areas attended school. Even fewer of those who did completed more than the primary grades. Children in urban areas had a greater opportunity for education, and college attendance was increasing. However, the continuing civil strife has destroyed the educational infrastructure, and almost all government-run schools have been closed since the mid-1990s. The only schooling that exists today for the majority of children are Koran schools taught by Sheikhs, Muslim holy men. These schools are usually attended only by boys and emphasize the memorization of important portions of the Koran. However, since the factional fighting began, many of these schools have expanded their curriculum in order to provide a broader education.

14 CULTURAL HERITAGE

At feasts, usually associated with rites of passage, men recall past events affecting their animals and lives, tell heroic tales of patrilineal ancestors, and recite passages from the Koran. This feasting and storytelling promotes unity among members of a particular subclan, the larger clan family, and ultimately the entire Somali nation. Dancing, accompanied by singing, is usually only performed by unmarried males in their 20s. These sexually charged "dances" often involve the young men proving their bravery by slashing their arms and legs with large knives. Although leaving dramatic scars on their bodies, this expression of virility in most cases does not permanently harm the participants. Although "frowned upon" by married men, who themselves usually have numerous scars on their arms and legs, these ceremonies are an important activity.

15 WORK

Somalis practice a clear division of labor based on gender. Men and boys tend to the animals, and women and girls prepare meals and undertake other domestic tasks. Boys as young as 6 or 7 years old are responsible for the care of sheep and goats, which are kept close to the village or animal camp. Teenage boys and men care for the cattle, which are moved further from home in search of feed and therefore require more skill to handle. Camels are herded by young men in their late teens and 20s. The camels and their herders are often away from their homes for months at a time in search of grazing and water. Thus, the ability for these males to make decisions and protect this valuable asset is an important rite of passage. In rural areas, older men function as resource managers as they constantly adjust their labor force comprised of their wives and children to maximize production of animals and, in the southern part of the country, grain.

Women are primarily responsible for child-rearing, food preparation, and all other domestic tasks. Although at first glance these domestic roles appear far less dramatic, and perhaps even less important, than the care of the herds, without the completion of these tasks males would be unable to successfully care for the herd animals. One particularly important task undertaken by women is the preparation for moving the household from animal camp to animal camp. This involves dismantling the family's *aqal* (portable house), packing it and all other domestic items on a camel, trekking to the next camp site and reassembling the aqal, reestablishing the homestead, and preparing the evening meal, all in less than 10 hours. In areas where domestic crops can be grown, women undertake an even greater work role, as they, and their children, are largely responsible for tending, weeding, and harvesting the crops. In urban areas, it is very common for women to own and run small shops selling a wide-range of products.

16 SPORTS

Soccer is the most popular and widely played sport in Somalia. However, its play is primarily restricted to the cities and larger towns and is not that prevalent in the villages. This is because children assume important roles within the pastoral society at an early age and particularly boys have little time for organized sport. Boys and girls play games, but the responsibilities assumed by children at an early age restrict the free time necessary for the organization and play of games.

17 ENTERTAINMENT AND RECREATION

Most entertainment among rural Somalis is in the form of ceremonies associated with major life transitions: birth, puberty, marriage, and death. For these ceremonies, animals are killed and the meat distributed to all who are in attendance. Most patrilineal kinfolk will be invited to these ceremonies, as well as relatives through marriage and other members of a village or animal camp. The main object is to reinforce kinship and other relationships through feasting and talking. Storytelling, recitation of ancestral names, and recounting the accomplishments of kinfolk and ancestors is a form of entertainment that has been lost in Western society, but which provides hours of pleasure for the pastoral Somalis.

Television is nonexistent in Somalia, although before the civil war the government did provide a radio service. Many urban and rural Somalis listen regularly to BBC broadcasts on the radio and are consequently well-informed about world events. Movie theaters also operated in all major cities and towns before the outbreak of widespread fighting. Most movies shown were either produced in India or were adventure movies from Hollywood.

18 FOLK ART, CRAFTS, AND HOBBIES

The Somali have little activity that could be described as folk art or crafts, but this does not mean that they make few objects. Quite the contrary, the Somali are quite proficient in crafts, producing fine wooden utensils, leather goods, woven mats and ropes, knife blades, and arrow points. However, each of these products has a definite utilitarian function, rather than being a remnant of a previous folk art or craft. Just as there are religious specialists and healers, there are people who specialize in, for example, ironworking or woodcarving. Much of the craft work, however, is undertaken by ordinary inhabitants of villages who have need of a woven rope or a carved knife handle. Perhaps in the future these utilitarian crafts will become a folk art, but until then, these are skills that are necessary for the functioning of Somali society.

[19] SOCIAL PROBLEMS

Because of the continuing civil strife, there has been a complete breakdown of civil government since the early 1990s, resulting in the cessation of most public services in many of the areas of the country. This civil strife is the culmination of a movement to depose General Muhammad Siad Barre, who seized power in a military coup in 1969 and ruled as a virtual dictator until 1991.Unfortunately, the united clans that drove Barre from the country could not agree on a governmental structure. Fighting among them began in late 1991 and in some form or another, has been going on ever since. During the fighting, agriculture and livestock-raising has been disrupted, and well over one-half million people died of starvation and at least another 100,000, mostly in Mogadishu and surrounding areas, died in the fighting. The United Nations and a variety of non-governmental relief organizations (NGOs) have launched relief efforts over the last two decades, but the lack of a central government has resulted in little actual help for the people who need it most. The lack of a central government that could control the various clan factions, eliminate fighting and provide basic services for the population resulted in the rise of the Union of Islamic Courts (UIC) in 2005. By 2006, the UIC had gained control of Mogadishu and much of southern Somalia and, through the imposition of Sharia courts (the application of traditional Islamic justice), had brought relative peace to much of Mogadishu and the south. However, splinter groups of the UIC, especially a group of young Islamist fighters known as al-Shabab, made alliances with other world-wide radical Islamists resulting, in 2006, with the United States placing the UIC on its list of "foreign terrorist organizations." In response to this action, Ethiopian troops invaded Somalia in late 2006 to aid Somalia's government in its fight against the UIC. Since Ethiopia is the traditional enemy of the Somali peoples, this action resulted in the formation of the Alliance for the Liberation of Somalia (ALS) in late 2006 to launch both military and diplomatic actions to force the Ethiopians out of the country. In 2007 the African Union sent the first troops to Mogadishu in an attempt to reestablish civil order, but these efforts have had little positive impact. As of early 2008 over 250,000 Somali had been displaced from urban centers and were living in squalid refugee camps in rural areas of the country.

[20] GENDER ISSUES

Gender issues among the Somali are largely dependent on the local interpretation of Islamic law and traditional practice. Although traditionally Somali women have had more rights and independence of actions than in many other Islamic countries, the rise of more fundamentalist factions has resulted in purdah being imposed, depending on which faction is in control, in Mogadishu and other urban areas.

Since traditionally marriage functions to unite kin groupings, most marriages are arranged by older males within the clan with neither groom nor bride having input in the marriage choice. Men dominate marriages and can easily initiate and be granted divorce, while women have only limited ability to initiate divorce. It is very common for men to not only have more than one wife at any given time, but to marry and divorce frequently. Women can remarry after divorce, but most frequently these marriages are less desirable. Because they have lost the ability to provide children to the clan of a potential husband, post-menopausal women have the most difficulty remarrying.

Within marriages, men dominate almost all economic matters and it is difficult, but not impossible, for women to own and control animals and land independent of their husbands. Children are members of their father's clan with the result that mothers, although having normal maternal responsibilities, have little say in the most important matters impacting their children, e.g., marriage partner and inheritance. This does not mean that children do not feel strong affection towards their mothers and it is not unusual for sons to support their mothers once widowed or divorced, but the patrilineal bond dominates all kin relationships. It is not an exaggeration to term traditional Somali society as patriarchal.

[21] BIBLIOGRAPHY

Cassanelli, L. V. *The Shaping of Somali Society.* Philadelphia: The University of Pennsylvania Press, 1982.

Helander, B. "Disability as Incurable Illness: Health, Process and Personhood in Southern Somalia." In *Disability and Culture,* edited by B. Ingstad and S. R. Whyte. Berkeley: University of California Press, 1995.

Korn, Fadumo. *Born in the Big Rains: A Memoir of Somalia and Survival.* New York: Feminist Press at the City University of New York, 2006.

Lewis, I. M. *A Pastoral Democracy.* London: Oxford University Press, 1961.

Massey, G., A. P. Glascock, et al. *Socio-Economic Baseline Study of the Bay Region.* Laramie: University of Wyoming, 1984.

Mburu, Nene. *Bandits on the Border: The Last Frontier in the Search for Somali Unity.* Trenton, NJ: Red Sea Press, 2005.

Mohamoud, Abdullah A. *State Collapse and Post-Conflict Development in Africa: The Case of Somalia (1960-2001).* West Lafayette, IN: Purdue University Press, 2006.

—by A. P. Glascock

SONGHAY

PRONUNCIATION: song-HIGH
LOCATION: Eastern Mali, western Niger, northern Benin
POPULATION: 3.5 million
LANGUAGE: Dialects of Songhay; French
RELIGION: Islam combined with indigenous beliefs
RELATED ARTICLES: Vol. 1: Beninese; Malians; Nigeriens

¹ INTRODUCTION

The Songhay have one of the most glorious histories of any African people. Known throughout West Africa as great and fearless warriors, the Songhay established one of the three great medieval West African Empires in 1463. The first Songhay king, Sonni Ali Ber, who spent much of his 30-year reign engaged in war, extended the boundaries of the Songhay state far beyond its ancestral lands, which extended some 100 km (62 mi) from each bank of the upper bend of the Niger River in what is today eastern Mali and western Niger. His successor, Askia Mohammed Touré, who founded a new dynasty, the Askiad, ruled from the Songhay capital at Gao, still a town today along the banks of the upper Niger River in Mali. Askia Mohammed made Songhay a great empire by extending its control throughout much of West Africa.

The political skill of Askia Mohammed's sons, who succeeded him, paled in comparison to that of their father, who set up elaborate and efficient bureaucracies to govern the empire. During his sons' reigns, however, corruption weakened the structures of imperial bureaucracy and treachery compromised imperial power. Toward the end of the 16th century, imperial Songhay was little more than an empty shell. In 1591 a small column of Moroccan soldiers crossed the Sahara and routed the excessively large Songhay army at the battle of Tondibia. The Moroccans installed a pasha (civil and military official) and controlled the northern sectors of Songhay. The Songhay nobles, all descendants of Askia Mohammed, fled southward to present-day Niger, where they continued their much diminished imperial rule. In time, the southern empire splintered into independent principalities that were mutually hostile. These principalities remained independent until 1899 when they were subjected to French colonial authority, which continued until the founding of the Republic of Niger in 1960. In the first three governments of the Republic of Niger, Songhay played central political roles. Compared to other ethnic groups in the Republic of Niger, they have a disproportionately large representation in the officer corps of Niger's army.

² LOCATION AND HOMELAND

The Songhay-speaking peoples live near the Niger River in eastern Mali, western Niger, and northern Benin. Key towns in Songhay country include Gao and Timbuktu in Mali, and Ayoru, Tillaberi, Niamey, and Tera in Niger. Songhay country is situated in the semiarid Sahel, which consists of flat rocky plains broken by rocky mesas in the south, and sandy dunes in the north.

The vast majority of Songhay are agriculturalists who grow millet and sorghum in sandy fields or cultivate rice in the shallows of the Niger River. This region features one of the harshest climates in the world. From October to May it does not rain. The dry period consists of two seasons: cool and hot. The cool season is dry, windy, and dusty with daytime temperatures rising well above 27°c (80°F) and nighttime temperatures often plummeting below 10°c (50°F). By February, however, the daytime readings reach 38°c (100°F) or more. By April and May, afternoon temperatures sometimes exceed 46°c (115°F). At night, the mercury drops only to 30°c (85°F) or so. The rains come in late May or early June and break the heat. The rainy season lasts from June through September.

Songhay-speaking peoples have a more than 100-year history of migration from Niger and Mali to the Guinea Coast countries of Nigeria, Benin, Togo, Ghana, and Ivory Coast. More recently Songhay traders have traveled to France as well as to the United States, where Songhay traders live and work in New York City. The vast majority of Songhay people, however, remain in Mali and Niger. Into the 21st century, in the US, most Songhay immigrants live in New York City, mostly in Harlem and the South Bronx and in a vibrant community in Greensboro, North Carolina.

³ LANGUAGE

Songhay is a language spoken by 3 million people in the Republics of Mali, Niger, and Benin. There are several dialects of Songhay. In Timbuktu, Songhay people speak *kwaara cini* (literally, "town talk"). The Songhay spoken between Gao and Tillaberi along the Niger River is called *issa cini* (literally, "river talk"). By contrast, people living in far western Niger in such towns as Tera, Dargol, and Wanzerbe are said to speak Songhay. Peoples living east of the Niger River from Tillaberi south to the town of Say speak the Zarma dialect. People living along the Niger River near the Niger-Benin border speak Dendi, yet another Songhay dialect. Because Mali, Niger, and Benin are all French-speaking nations, many Songhay people living in these states are conversant in French.

As in many African languages, greetings are important in Songhay. The first greeting is: "*Manti ni kaani,*" "How did you sleep?" One usually replies, "*Baani sami, walla,*" meaning, "I slept (implied) well, in health." The greetings in the morning focus upon work and the health of people in one's compound. The midday greetings ask after one's afternoon. Late afternoon greetings reference questions of health. In the dusk greeting, people exchange salutations of peace and health. At bedtime, one says: "*Iri me kaani baani,*" which means "May we both sleep in health and peace."

⁴ FOLKLORE

Songhay trace their origins to the 8th century AD and the coming of Aliman Dia to the Niger River. Aliman Dia possessed iron weapons and with these he subdued the resident peoples, *sorko* (fishers) and *gow* (hunters). Aliaman Dia brought these peoples together and founded the first Songhay dynasty, the Dia. Descendants of Aliaman Dia governed Songhay until the 15th century when a dynasty, the Sonni, succeeded them.

The ancestor of the *sorko*, Faran Maka Bote, like Aliman Dia, is a Songhay culture hero. Faran Maka Bote's father, Nisili Bote, was a fisherman. His mother, Maka, was a river spirit. Faran grew to be a giant with vast magical powers. As an adult he battled a river spirit, Zinkibaru, for the control of the river spirits, which meant control of the Niger River. Faran won this battle and became master of the Niger River. But his confidence soon surpassed his capacities. Dongo, the deity of lightning and thunder, demonstrated his displeasure with Faran by

SONGHAY

the path of Songhay sorcerers, descendants of the Songhay king, Sonni Ali Ber. There is the path of *sorkotarey*, which is followed by praise-singers to the spirits, descendants of Faran Maka Bote. Healers descended from slaves, called *horso*, follow the path of their ancestors *(horsotarey)*, practicing magic passed down from generation to generation. *Cerkowtarey* is the path of witches, who precipitate illness, misfortune, and death in Songhay villages. They are said to fly in the night and to be able to transform their appearance. Death results when witches steal and eat their victims' souls. There is also the path of *zimatarey* that is followed by spirit-possession priests, who work with the *sorko* to stage spirit-possession ceremonies. Except for witches, who receive their powers through ingesting their mothers' milk if their mothers are witches, these specialists must serve long apprenticeships to master the knowledge of history, plants, words, and practices. Along their paths, apprentices become vulnerable to the powers and rivalries of the spirit world, which the Songhay call "the world of war."

For most Songhay, whose contact with the spirit world may well be frightening but is generally infrequent, the path of Islam is well followed. They pray five times a day, avoid alcohol and pork, honor and respect their elders, give to the poor, observe the one-month fast of Ramadan, and try to the best of their ability to make the exceedingly expensive pilgrimage to Mecca. If they submit to these practices, they believe that they will ascend to heaven. These beliefs, however, do not preclude beliefs about the spirit world.

6 MAJOR HOLIDAYS

Songhay people, like other groups in the Republic of Niger, celebrate Nigerien Independence Day, and other state-related holidays. They also celebrate such major Islamic holidays as Muhammad's birthday, the end of the Ramadan fast, and *tabaski*, which commemorates Abraham's biblical sacrifice of a ram. For *tabaski*, people slaughter one or two sheep and roast them in their compound. They feast on the roasted mutton and offer raw and cooked meat to needier people who knock on their door seeking an offering.

7 RITES OF PASSAGE

Like all peoples throughout the world, the Songhay perform rituals to underscore the major events of the life-cycle. Most of these rituals follow Islamic prescriptions, though some practices related to birth, puberty, marriage, divorce, and death predate Islam in sub-Saharan Africa. Birth, for example, is seen as a time of danger for both mothers and their children. During pregnancy, most Songhay women avoid certain foods. During and immediately following childbirth, men are kept from the mother and child. Mother and child are presented to family and neighbors for the first time at the *bon chebe* (literally, "showing the head"), at which the child is named. As children mature, they are educated by their fathers and mothers. Young boys learn to farm millet and sorghum, cultivate rice, fish, and hunt; young girls learn cooking, child care, and other domestic chores. In the past, young Songhay practiced a pre-Islamic female initiation called the *gosi*, during which young girls were ritually purified for marriage. This practice did not involve female genital mutilation. Young boys once underwent circumcision at a relatively late age. Circumcision specialists *(guunu)* would travel from village to village and circumcise

burning villages and killing people. He summoned Faran and demanded that the giant pay his humble respects to Dongo by offering music, praise-poems, and animal sacrifices. Dongo told Faran that if he organized festivals, Dongo would descend into the bodies of dancers and help the people along the Niger River. This event marked the first Songhay possession ceremony. These ceremonies are still performed today. One of the most important members of a Songhay possession troupe, moreover, is the *sorko*, praise-singer to the spirits and direct descendant of Faran Make Bote. In this way, myth in the Songhay world is connected to ongoing social and religious practices.

5 RELIGION

Although almost all Songhay are practicing Muslims, Islamic practices have not excluded pre-Islamic beliefs. Songhay see life as a series of paths (the life path or paths; in the Songhay language, the *fonda* or *fondey*) that constitute life in the world. Like paths in the Songhay bush, the metaphoric paths of life end when they meet two new paths that fork off in different directions. At these crossroads, points of potential danger where the spirit and social worlds meet, people are vulnerable to misfortune, sickness, and possibly death. Because life is seen as the continuous negotiation of dangerous crossroads, Songhay people regularly consult diviners, who read shells that indicate what precautions a person must take to move forward on her or his path.

The paths of Songhay religious specialists are steeped with learning and fraught with difficulties. There is *sohancitarey*, scores of boys in one afternoon. These days, circumcisions are performed on toddlers by physicians in hospital settings.

In adolescence, Songhay often forge life-long friendships. Groups of friends will work together and attend social events like drumming ceremonies or dances organized by the *samaryia*, which is a village-level young people's organization. Eventually women and men are ready to marry. In the recent past, there were many cousin marriages among the Songhay, especially among families of nobles, descendants of Askia Mohammed Touré. Young men and women were encouraged to marry the children of their father's siblings. Nowadays, cousin marriages are less frequent.

Once the groom asks the bride's father for permission to marry the latter's daughter, he is expected to pay his future father-in-law a bride-price, which today is a fixed sum of money. He is also expected to give his future wife many gifts: cloth, blankets, perfume, and soap. He will also give his in-laws gifts of rice, meat, and kola nuts. The significant expense of marriage makes it difficult for young men to afford to marry, which is why most Songhay grooms are significantly older than their wives. The marriage ceremony is marked by the presentation of gifts and the sanctification of an Islamic contract (*kitubi*) that binds husband to wife. Drummers play music and people eat and dance in the bride's compound.

Divorce, which is quite common among the Songhay, is not marked by ceremony. Men initiate formal divorce by consulting a Muslim cleric and proclaiming, "I divorce thee" three times. If there are children in the marriage, they live with the father after two years of age. This practice, too, follows Muslim law. Since there is no joint property held between husband and wife, divorces are easy to obtain and free of property disputes. Women informally initiate divorce by leaving their husbands, who then proclaim their divorce in the wife's absence.

Adulthood among the Songhay is spent working and raising families. As people age, they have fewer responsibilities. When they become elders, they spend much of their time conversing with their friends and imparting wisdom to the younger generations. When Songhay die, they are buried quickly and without fanfare. Mourning lasts for 40 days, during which the family receives regular visits from relatives and friends. During these visits people honor the person who died by talking about his or her life, his or her likes and dislikes, and perhaps his or her peculiar expressions.

8 INTERPERSONAL RELATIONS

Generosity, grace, and modesty are key ingredients of ideal Songhay interpersonal relations. One is supposed to direct one's social energies towards the other and the group. Self-absorption is looked down upon. The Songhay are, like many peoples in the West African Sahel, known for their generosity. When strangers arrive they are housed, well fed, and treated with great dignity—even if the hosts are poor. Such is the hallmark of Songhay graciousness, which may have developed in response to the harsh ecological and economic conditions in which they live.

Songhay are also modest people. If they are wealthy in comparison with their neighbors, they do not flaunt their material success. Dress is also modest. Men wear long flowing robes (*boubous*) over loose-fitting cotton trousers and shirts. Women wear long wrap-around skirts (*pagnes*) and tops. In both cases, people dress for comfort and avoid wearing clothes that show off their bodies. Young men are supposed to be respectful of young women, who in turn are supposed to be shy around young men. This code is expressed in body language. Boys do make eye contact with girls. Girls, however, will often look at the ground when talking in public to boys. Whenever young men and women become involved with one another, they do so in private. Their public behavior maintains a socially sanctioned modesty.

9 LIVING CONDITIONS

Songhay people in rural areas live mostly in small villages, which are usually near a water source—a series of wells, a pond, or the Niger River. Families live within walled or fenced compounds, which usually consist of a main house for the husband, and smaller houses for each of his wives and their children. The houses are usually made of mud bricks and have thatched roofs. More traditional homes are circular huts with thatched roofs. New houses may be made of cement and feature tin roofs. Homes offer Songhay protection from heat, wind, and rain. Most social activity, however, is conducted out of doors in the compound, where food is prepared and eaten, and where people visit one another in the evenings.

Songhay who live in such urban areas as Niamey, the capital of the Republic of Niger, also live in compounds. Space in urban areas is, of course, limited, which means that people live in crowded conditions that tend to be less sanitary than in the countryside. In the Songhay Diaspora in France and in New York, families live in small apartments in neighborhoods in which other West African immigrants have settled. In New York City Songhay men and women live in Harlem, the South Bronx, and in Brooklyn.

10 FAMILY LIFE

Songhay families tend to be large. In rural areas, brothers live with their father, mothers, wives, and children in large communal compounds. In some cases, more than 100 people might live in a rural compound. In urban areas, families are a bit more scattered and smaller in size. In the family, women play central roles. They fetch water, buy and prepare food, clean the house and compound, and look after the children. As a woman ages, she expects younger wives (if the marriage is polygamous), daughters-in-law, or daughters to perform domestic chores. Men work in the fields and are often away from the family compound. When they return, women give them bathing water and feed them.

Men and women lead fairly separate lives. They do different kinds of work. They eat separately. They often talk exclusively to other people of their own gender. When a marriage occurs, a woman's primary allegiance is to her blood kin, for it is from them that she will inherit wealth. If husbands are abusive, the wife's brothers will often intervene to end the abuse. If a woman earns money, she will keep it for herself or share it with her blood kin. She rarely gives her husband money, for it is his responsibility to feed, clothe, and otherwise care for his wife. In the Diaspora, Songhay husbands spend long periods of time away from their wives and families. They meet their familial obligations by wiring money to their families in Niger.

11 CLOTHING

Rural as well as urban Songhay men today wear a combination of traditional and Western clothing. More often than not,

A Songhai bride from Mali adorns her hair with silver coins and gold filigree ornaments containg blessings. The remarkable hairstyles of the Songhai woman are reminders of the sophisticated Songhai Empire that held sway for 600 years until the end of the sixteenth century. (Carol Beckwith/Angela Fisher/Getty Images)

they wear tailored suits consisting of trousers and a loose-fitting shirt that they wear untucked. Younger men might wear used jeans and tee-shirts they buy at local or regional markets. There are some men, however, who prefer to wear traditional garb, which includes a damask cotton three-piece outfit, consisting of matching drawstring trousers, long-sleeved loose-fitting shirt with an open neck, and long billowy robe *(boubou)* with a deep chest pocket. These robes are sometimes covered with elaborate designs brocaded in silver and gold thread. The only Songhay women who wear Western fashions belong to the upper classes of Nigerien society. Most Songhay women rarely, if ever, wear Western clothing.

¹² FOOD

The staple of the Songhay diet is millet, a highly nutritious grain that Westerners use principally as bird seed. Millet is consumed in three ways: as a pancake *(haini maasa)*, as porridge *(doonu)*, or as a paste *(howru)*. No matter how it is consumed, the millet must first be pounded or milled into flour.

Millet flour can then be mixed with water to make a pancake batter, which is then fried on a griddle. This food is usually eaten at breakfast. Porridge, which is eaten at the noon meal, is mixture of millet flour that has been shaped into a doughy ball, milk, water, and sugar. Millet paste is made by mixing millet flour in a pot of boiling water until the mixture stiffens. This paste, which is consumed at the evening meal, is topped by a variety of usually meatless sauces made from okra, baobab leaf, or peanuts. Songhay season their sauces with ginger *(tofunua)*, hot pepper *(tonka)*, onion flour with sesame *(gebu)*, sorrel paste *(maari bi)*, and a variety of other ingredients that have no English-language equivalents.

Food is served in porcelain bowls that Songhay buy at markets. In rural areas, bowls are fashioned from large gourds and are decorated. Men and women eat separately. Food is served in a common bowl from which people eat with their right hands. The left hand, which people use to clean themselves, is considered impure.

¹³ EDUCATION

Education takes two forms among the Songhay: informal and formal. Mothers and fathers informally educate their children in matters of subsistence: farming, fishing, hunting, building huts and houses, cooking, weaving, and sewing. Even though thousands of Songhay children attend elementary school, illiteracy is common. In remote areas, some Songhay parents see formal schooling as a loss, for it often means that semieducated sons and daughters leave the countryside for towns and cities. Elementary school students must pass screening examinations to attend middle schools. Middle school students must pass the *brevet*, another screening exam, to advance to the *lycée*, or high school. After four years of high school, students must pass a baccalaureate exam in order to qualify for university education. In Niger there is one university, Université de Niamey; several normal schools, which train primary school teachers; and several advanced education centers where bureaucrats and technocrats acquire their respective training.

¹⁴ CULTURAL HERITAGE

The Songhay are proud of their imperial past and celebrate it with song, dance, and epic poetry. Singing, dancing, and praise-songs, performed by *griots* (both male and female), are central to the celebration of births, marriages, and secular and religious holidays. Epic poetry is also performed on secular and religious holidays. It recounts the heroic feats of cultural heroes like Sonni Ali Ber and Askia Mohammed Touré, the greatest of the Songhay kings. Poetry performances are frequently broadcast on national radio.

¹⁵ WORK

The principal activity of most Songhay men has been millet and rice farming. Since the tasks associated with farming do not consume an entire year, many Songhay men have developed secondary occupations: trading, transport, or tailoring. More than a few Songhay men spend the nonplanting season working for wages in Niamey, the capital of Niger, or in faraway coastal cities like Abidjan, Lome, or Lagos. Except in upper-class families, Songhay women remain wedded to domestic activities. In some cases, divorced women sell cooked foods or trade in cloth to make their way in the world. A small percentage of Songhay women work as civil servants for the government of Niger. In the Diaspora, Songhay men in New York City work as street vendors, import-export businessmen, security guards, factory laborers and gas station attendants.

16 SPORTS

Soccer is the major sport among Songhay boys and young men. No matter the size of the village, there is a space where young boys and men regularly play soccer. Larger villages support soccer clubs and teams that compete against other villages. The national team recruits its players from these local soccer clubs and competes against teams from other African nations. Boys and men also race horses both informally and formally. During secular holidays, villages sponsor horse races and present the winners with prizes.

Wrestling is the other major sport. The idea is not to pin one's opponent but merely to throw him to the ground. There are wrestling competitions in most larger villages as well as a prestigious national competition. Songhay girls are not encouraged to participate in sports, although those who attend school are required to take physical education and engage in intramural competition.

17 ENTERTAINMENT AND RECREATION

Such religious rituals as spirit-possession ceremonies are also occasions for group entertainment. When a spirit-possession ceremony is staged, vendors come to sell cigarettes, cooked foods, and candy to the audience. In many Songhay towns there is a local theater, in which young people stage plays about the social conflicts of growing up in a changing society. Sometimes these local theater troupes perform on national radio. Towns also sponsor local singing and dance groups, as well as gatherings for young people where they can dance and socialize.

Television has become an important medium of entertainment in many of the larger Songhay towns. Most people cannot afford electricity, let alone a television set. But neighborhood chiefs, who own televisions, will invite their neighbors into their compound for evenings of television viewing.

18 FOLK ART, CRAFTS, AND HOBBIES

Songhay are well known for weaving blankets and mats. The elaborate cotton blankets woven by men in the town of Tera (*terabeba*) are highly prized throughout the Sahel. Women living along the Niger River weave palm frond mats that feature geometric designs.

19 SOCIAL PROBLEMS

There are two great social problems facing the Songhay. The first is the ever-present prospect of drought and famine. Songhay live in the Sahel, which throughout its history has been prone to drought and famine. In the past 35 years there have been many devastating droughts and famines that have prompted the widespread migration of rural Songhay to towns and cities. In any given year, even the slightest disruption of the cycle of rains can precipitate grain shortages, hunger, and famine.

The second principal social problem involves politics. At present the Republic of Niger is politically unstable. The first three governments of the Republic of Niger were led by Songhay-speaking peoples, which led to charges of ethnic favoritism from the other ethnic groups (Hausa, Fulani, Kanuri, and Tuareg) that constituted the majority of the population. Thirty years ago, the issue of tribalism was important. Today, the power and relevance of the state has diminished, especially in rural areas. While in the past people might have charged the government with ethnic favoritism toward the Songhay, people in the present must concentrate their energies on making their way in a politically and socially uncertain world. In the Diaspora, the principal social problem is the separation of families, which sometimes precipitates divorce. This same separation sometimes results in new marriages in the host country, meaning that some Songhay men have two families: one in Niger and one in a new home like New York City

20 GENDER ISSUES

Gender is central to the flow of social relations. In rural Songhay villages, men and women have relatively distinct identities. These identities have been shaped by patterns of work and social obligation as well as by the influence of Islam. In general, women run household economies and, for the most part, participate directly in child-rearing. The man's domain is usually outside of the home—in the fields or at the market. These "roles" shift somewhat in urban areas in which women engage in economic activities outside the home. Indeed, some urban Songhay women are educated and have civil service positions. These women hire others to cook, clean, and look after their young children. The same can be said of Songhay women who live in places like Paris or New York City. Sometimes, the expanded roles that Songhay women enjoy in urban or diasporic communities precipitate domestic tension in the household.

21 BIBLIOGRAPHY

Charlick, Robert. *Niger: Personal Rule and Survival in the Sahel.* Boulder, CO: Westview Press, 1991.

Fugelstad, Finn. *A History of Niger, 1850–1960.* London: Cambridge University Press, 1983.

Stoller, Paul. *Embodying Colonial Memories: Spirit Possession, Power, and the Hauka in West Africa.* New York: Routledge, 1995.

———. *Fusion of the Worlds: An Ethnography of Possession Among the Songhay.* Chicago: University of Chicago Press, 1989; paperback edition, 1997.

———. *Money Has No Smell: The Africanization of New York City.* Chicago: The University of Chicago Press. 2002.

———. *The Power of the Between: An Anthropological Odyssey.* Chicago: The University of Chicago Press. 2008.

Stoller, Paul, and Cheryl Olkes. *In Sorcery's Shadow: A Memoir of Apprenticeship Among the Songhay of Niger.* Chicago: University of Chicago Press, 1987.

—by P. Stoller

SOTHO

PRONUNCIATION: SOO-too
LOCATION: Lesotho, South Africa
POPULATION: 8.2 million in South Africa, 2.1 million in Lesotho
LANGUAGE: Sotho language (Sesotho or Sepedi)
RELIGION: Traditional beliefs (supreme being Modimo), Christianity

¹ INTRODUCTION

The Sotho people are an ethnic group living in Lesotho and South Africa. There are two major branches, the southern Sotho and the northern Sotho (also called the Pedi). Southern Sotho people make up about 99% of the population of Lesotho. The southern Sotho and the northern Sotho taken together are the second largest ethnic group in South Africa. Speakers of southern Sotho make up about 8% of the South African population while speakers of northern Sotho make up about 9.5%. Culturally and linguistically, both groups are also closely related to the Tswana people of Botswana.

Sotho society was traditionally organized in villages ruled by chiefs. The economy was based on the rearing of cattle and the cultivation of grains such as sorghum. In the early nineteenth century, several kingdoms developed as a result of a series of wars, the *difaqane*, which engulfed much of southern Africa. During this period, southern Sotho people as well as other ethnic groups sought refuge in the mountainous terrain of Lesotho. A local chief named Moshoeshoe emerged as a skillful diplomat and military leader who was able to keep his country from falling into the hands of Zulu and, later, white (Afrikaner) forces. After Moshoeshoe's death in 1870, this independence was weakened, and white (English) authorities from the Cape Colony tried to administer Lesotho as a conquered territory. The people resisted this attempt at control, however, leading to the Gun War of 1880-1881 in which the Cape Colony was defeated.

The northern Sotho suffered much devastation at the hands of African armies during the *difaqane*, but several chiefdoms were able to recover. After 1845, the Pedi also had to contend with an influx of white Afrikaner settlers, some of whom seized Pedi children and forced them to work as slaves whom they euphemistically labeled "servants" (*inboekseling*). The Pedi ruler Sekwati and, later, his son Sekhukhune, successfully resisted Afrikaner encroachment on their territory for a number of years, but the Pedi were finally conquered by a combined force of British, Afrikaner, and Swazi men in 1879. Thus the northern Sotho lost their independence and fell under the political control of white authorities. All of the land of the northern Sotho was fragmented and turned into the African "reserve" of Sekhukhuniland. Under apartheid, Sekhukhuniland and some surrounding lands occupied by other African peoples were made into the Bantustan of Lebowa. There were forced relocations of Sotho people to Lebowa, QwaQwa, and several other Bantustans, causing great hardship. These structures were disbanded with the end of apartheid.

In 1884, Lesotho became a British protectorate. Unlike the Pedi kingdom, therefore, Lesotho was not incorporated into South Africa. However, rich agricultural land once claimed by Moshoeshoe (territory which included much of the South African Free State) was lost to Afrikaner control. Lesotho became an independent country in 1966, although because it was surrounded by apartheid South Africa, it was never completely free. The nation has also had trouble in establishing a democracy of its own. The first democratic elections after independence were voided by the government of Leabua Jonathan. Jonathan ruled Lesotho from 1970 until he was overthrown in a coup in 1986. Military rule came to an end in 1991, but the transition to democracy has been difficult. In 1998 and 1999 violence erupted in many parts of the country as a result of disputed election results. For several months during this period, the country was occupied by South African and other African forces who maintained they were there as invited peacekeepers. This period saw the destruction of much valuable property, particularly in urban areas. Although there are many opposition parties, the Lesotho Congress for Democracy (LCD) has held power since this time.

² LOCATION AND HOMELAND

According to 2008 estimates, there were about 8 million people who identified themselves as southern or northern Sotho in South Africa. In Lesotho there were about 2.1 million southern Sotho.

The home of most of the southern Sotho is in Lesotho and in South Africa's Free State Province. There are also many Sotho who live in South Africa's major cities. Lesotho is a mountainous country that is completely landlocked within the borders of South Africa. It has an area of about 30,350 sq km (about 11,700 sq mi). The Free State is a highland plain, called a *highveld* in South Africa, bordering Lesotho to the west. The eastern section of Lesotho is also a highveld, punctuated by plateaus similar to those found in the American Southwest. The Maloti and Drakensberg mountains are in the central and western parts of the country. The Drakensberg Mountains form sharp cliffs that drop off dramatically to South Africa's KwaZulu/Natal Province. The climate of South Africa in general is temperate, but the mountains make for cold winters. In fact, winter snows are not uncommon in the Lesotho highlands.

The region considered a traditional home by many rural Pedi is between the Olifants and Steelpoort rivers in South Africa's Limpopo Province. It is bounded by the Leolo Mountains on the east and by dry plains to the west. This region and neighboring areas are also home to other ethnic groups, including the Lovedu, Tsonga, Ndebele, Venda, Zulu, and Afrikaners. Northern areas of South Africa are much warmer than Lesotho.

Although many people of northern Sotho background considered the territory that became Lebowa their homeland, this Bantustan was to a large extent an artificial creation. In the 1970s and 1980s, ethnic tensions developed as a result of the apartheid state's attempt to define peoples in terms of a simplistic notion of homeland and tribe. Other peoples defined by the apartheid state as southern Sotho were forced to move to the impoverished "homelands" of Bophuthatswana and QwaQwa. Conflict generally has intensified in rural areas because the lands of northern and southern Sotho people have been heavily eroded, overpopulated, and overgrazed for many years.

³ LANGUAGE

The Sotho language, or Sesotho, is a Bantu language closely related to Setswana. Bantu languages are characterized by a system of organizing nouns by prefixes. For example, the "se" prefix is used in front of all languages while "ba" is used with nouns for people. To be polite it is most appropriate even in English to speak of the Sotho people as "Basotho" or, when referring to one person, as "Mosotho." As in the South African languages Zulu and Xhosa, Sotho discourse is rich in proverbs, idioms, and special forms of address reserved for elders and in-laws.

The division between southern and northern Sotho people is based on the dialectal differences between the two groups. The southern form of Sotho is spoken in Lesotho, and the northern form is spoken by many in South Africa's Limpopo Province. The northern form is called Sepedi. Southern Sotho utilizes click consonants in some words (although not so many as in Zulu and Xhosa), while Sepedi and Setswana do not have clicks. Currently, southern Sotho has two spelling systems, one in use in Lesotho and another in South Africa. For example, in Lesotho a common greeting is *Khotso, le phela joang?* (literally, "Peace, how are you?). In South Africa, the word *joang* (how) is written *jwang*, and *khotso* is written *kgotso*.

Names in Sotho generally have meanings that express the values of the parents or of the community. Common personal names include *Lehlohonolo* (Good Fortune), *Mpho* (Gift), and *MmaThabo* (Mother of Joy). Names may also be given to refer to events. For example, a girl born during a rainstorm might be called *Puleng,* meaning "in the rain." Individuals may also be named after clan heroes. Surnames are taken from relatives on the father's side of the family.

In recent years, African languages have been undergoing rapid change due to the influence of European languages. There is also influence from multicultural urban slang. As a result, many Sotho speakers today readily mix words and phrases from other languages into their speech.

⁴ FOLKLORE

According to one Sotho tradition, the first human being emerged from a sea of reeds at a place called Ntswanatsatsi. However, little is known or said about the events of this person's life.

Sotho has a rich tradition of folktales (*ditsomo* or *dinonwane*) and praise poems (*diboko*). These are told in dramatic and creative ways that may include audience participation. Folktales are adventure stories that occur in realistic and magical settings. One of the best known of the folktales is about a boy named Sankatana who saves the world from a giant monster.

Praise poems traditionally describe the heroic real-life adventures of ancestors or political leaders. Here is the opening verse of a long poem in praise of King Moshoeshoe:

"You who are fond of praising the ancestors,
Your praises are poor when you leave out the warrior,
When you leave out Thesele, the son of Mokhachane;
For it's he who's the warrior of the wars,
Thesele is brave and strong,
That is Moshoeshoe-Moshaila."

Such traditional forms of creative expression continue but they have also been incorporated into contemporary

music and art. One young performer notable for incorporating Sotho praise poetry into modern poetic and musical forms is Lesogo Rampolokeng. Modern or "urban" legends also circulate informally today about unusual events and circumstances that are said to have occurred recently.

⁵ RELIGION

The supreme being that the Sotho believe in is most commonly referred to as Modimo. Modimo is approached through ancestral intermediaries, the *balimo,* who are honored at ritual feasts. The ancestral spirits can bring sickness and misfortune to those who forget them or treat them disrespectfully. Among the North Sotho Kgakga clan, a drum cult centered around the figure of the paramount chief (king), who was venerated as a rainmaker and ensurer of fertility. Like some other South African peoples, the Sotho have traditionally believed that the evils of our world are the result of the malevolent actions of sorcerers and witches.

Today, Christianity in one form or another is professed by the majority of Sotho-speaking people, with rates as high as or more than 90% in many areas. In Lesotho Catholics make up about 45% of the population, with the largest Protestant group, the Lesotho Evangelical Church, representing about 26%.

In recent years, independent South African denominations founded by charismatic African preachers have been growing in popularity. The independent churches combine elements of African traditional religion with the doctrines of Christianity. They also place a strong emphasis on healing and the Holy Spirit. One of the largest of these churches in South Africa, the Zion Christian Church (ZCC), was founded by two brothers of Pedi background. This church has been very successful in attracting followers from all over South Africa, Swaziland, and Lesotho. Each spring the ZCC hosts an Easter ceremony that attracts tens of thousands of people to the church's rural headquarters at Moria City, in the Limpopo Province.

6 MAJOR HOLIDAYS

The major holidays among the Sotho of South Africa are the same as those of South Africa as a whole. These include the Christian holidays, plus Workers' Day (May 1), the Day of Reconciliation (December 16), Heritage Day (September 24), Youth Day (June 16), and Human Rights Day (March 21). Another important holiday recognizes April 27 as the day black South Africans first voted in a genuine national election.

Lesotho has a number of holidays that recognize its own history. These holidays include Moshoeshoe's Day (March 12) and Independence Day (October 4). Moshoeshoe's Day is marked by games and races for the nation's young people. Independence Day is celebrated by state ceremonies that often include performances by traditional dance groups.

7 RITES OF PASSAGE

Women give birth with the assistance of female birth attendants. Traditionally, relatives and friends soaked the father with water when his firstborn child was a girl. If the firstborn was a boy, the father was beaten with a stick. Among other things, this suggested that while the life of males is occupied by warfare, that of females is occupied by domestic duties such as fetching water. For two or three months after the birth, the child was kept secluded with the mother in a specially marked hut. The seclusion could be temporarily broken when the baby was brought outside to be introduced to the first rain. These traditions continue in modified form today, although they are practiced to different degrees in different areas.

There are elaborate rites of initiation into adulthood for boys and girls in Sotho tradition. For boys, initiation involves a lengthy stay in a lodge in a secluded area away from the village.

The lodge may be very large and house dozens of initiates (bashemane). During seclusion, the boys are circumcised, but they are also taught appropriate male conduct in marriage, special initiation traditions, code words and signs, and praise songs. In Lesotho, the end of initiation is marked by a community festival during which the new initiates (makolwane) sing the praises they have composed. In traditional belief, a man who has not been initiated is not considered a full adult. Changing elements of the initiation are particularly evident at the time of the makolwane. Here new elements of fashion may show up in the way the young men ornament themselves, particularly with eye wear and jewelry. Today some urban or Westernized youths may chose not to undergo the ritual but they are still looked down upon by traditionalists.

Initiation for girls (bale) also involves seclusion, but the ritual huts of the bale are generally located near the village. Bale wear masks and goat-skin skirts, and they smear their bodies with a chalky white substance. They sometimes may be seen as a group near the homes of relatives, singing, dancing, and making requests for presents. Among some clans, the girls are subjected to tests of pain and endurance. After the period of seclusion, the initiates, now called litswejane, wear cowhide skirts and anoint themselves with red ocher. Initiation for girls does not involve any surgical operation. Today initiation seems less popular for girls than it is for boys although this may vary by local area.

When someone dies, the whole community takes part in the burial. Speeches are made at the graveside by friends and relatives, and the adult men take turns shoveling soil into the grave. Afterward, all those in attendance go as a group to wash their hands. There may also be a funeral feast.

8 INTERPERSONAL RELATIONS

In Sesotho, the words for father (ntate) and mother (mme) are used commonly as address forms of respect for one's elders. Politeness, good manners, and willingness to serve are values very strongly encouraged in children. The general attitude toward childhood is well summarized by the proverb Lefura la ngwana ke ho rungwa, which roughly translates as "Children benefit from serving their elders."

The standard greetings in Sotho reflect this attitude of respect towards age. When saying hello to an elder, one should always end with ntate (my father) or mme (my mother). Words for brother (abuti) and sister (ausi) are used when one talks to people of the same age. A child who answers an adult's question with a simple "Yes" is considered impolite. To be polite, the child needs to add "my father" or "my mother."

Good hospitality and generosity are expected of normal people. Even those who have very little will often share their food with visitors. Of course, those who share also expect the favor to be returned when it is their turn to visit.

Dating was not part of traditional Sotho life. Marriages were arranged between families, and a girl could be betrothed in childhood. Nowadays, most people pick their mates.

Traditionally, interpersonal relations were overseen by village headmen and chiefs. Today, although some are unsure of its place in the contemporary world, a modified system of chieftaincy continues. For example, 22 seats in the national senate of Lesotho are reserved for the country's principle hereditary chiefs.

9 LIVING CONDITIONS

Rural areas in South Africa and Lesotho are marked by high rates of poverty and inadequate access to health care. Diarrheal diseases and malnutrition are not infrequent. Malaria is also found in the low-lying regions of Limpopo Province. In recent years many people have moved to urban areas in search of employment. This has led to the development of urban shantytowns with little or no sewer, water, or electrical services. A number of development projects to improve these conditions are underway, but they are hampered by needs that are greater than resources.

There is a brighter side to this picture, however. Those with access to land and employment can enjoy a reasonable standard of living. Lesotho's capital city, Maseru, and most of South Africa's cities and towns, for example, include a well-developed service infrastructure. Sotho people enjoy going from shop to shop to get the best prices for consumer goods. In South Africa and Lesotho there are also a growing number of vendors who sell their goods in informal markets.

Many South Africans identify the Sotho of Lesotho with the brightly colored blankets that they often wear instead of coats. These blankets have designs picturing everything from airplanes to crowns to geometric patterns. Although these are appropriately identified with the Sotho, there is no tradition of local manufacture. The blankets are store-bought. (Jason Laure)

The most common forms of transportation for black people in southern Africa are buses, trains, and "taxis." "Taxis" are minivans that carry many individual riders at one time. Most such taxis are used for short distances in urban areas, but they are also used as a faster alternative to the long-distance routes of buses. Personal cars and trucks are also not uncommon, although in recent years high rates of inflation and skyrocketing oil prices have driven prices up considerably.

¹⁰ FAMILY LIFE

In Sotho tradition, the man was considered the head of the household. Women were defined as farmers and bearers of children. Family duties were also organized into distinct domains based on gender for all Sotho, but the Pedi maintained a stricter separation of living space into male and female areas. Polygynous marriages were not uncommon among the elite, but they were rare among commoners. Marriages were arranged by transfer of *bohadi* (bridewealth) from the family of the groom to the family of the bride. Upon marriage, a woman was expected to leave her family to live with the family of her husband.

The Sotho have clans, many of which bear animal names, such as the *Koena* (crocodile). These clans stress descent through the male line, but there is considerable flexibility in defining clan membership. A unique feature of Sotho kinship was that a person was allowed to marry a cousin (*ngwana wa rangoane*) who was a member of the same clan.

Family life for many rural Sotho has been disrupted for generations by migrant labor. Today, many Sotho men continue to live in all-male housing units provided by the gold-mining companies they work for. With the end of apartheid, some of the families previously separated by the old labor laws are leading new lives together in urban areas.

¹¹ CLOTHING

Much about Sotho apparel is the same as the apparel of people in Europe and the United States. However, the most acceptable form of clothing for a woman is still the dress, and her hair is expected to be covered with a scarf, head cloth, or hat. The *mokorotlo*, a conical hat topped with a complicated form, is the national symbol. A handicrafts shop located prominently in Lesotho's capital is shaped in the form of this hat. Many South Africans identify the Sotho of Lesotho with the brightly colored blankets that they often wear instead of coats. These blankets have designs picturing everything from airplanes to crowns to geometric patterns. Although these are appropriately identified with the Sotho, there is no tradition of local manufacture. The blankets are store-bought.

¹² FOOD

Sotho people share many food traditions with the other peoples of South Africa. Staple foods are corn (maize), eaten in the form of a thick paste, and bread. Beef, chicken, and mutton are popular meats, while milk is often drunk in soured form. The South African form of sorghum beer, brewed at home or store-bought, is more nutritious than Western beer.

Eggs were traditionally taboo for women, and a newly wedded wife was not allowed to eat certain types of meat.

The major mealtimes are breakfast and dinner (in the evening). Children may go without lunch, although there are some school lunch programs.

Sotho people enjoy food and drink from other cultural traditions, but typically retain a fondness for beef and mutton. Sotho-style food is not spiced with pepper or curries, but some today may use such spices as they are readily available in many areas.

¹³ EDUCATION

The first Western-style schools for Sotho-speakers were begun by missionaries. Religious institutions and missionaries continue to play a major role in education in Lesotho today. Many of Lesotho's high schools are boarding schools affiliated with churches. Discipline can be strict at these schools, but students may participate in entertainment such as school concerts, dances, and movies. In Lesotho, only a minority of students manage to graduate from high school because school fees are high and the work is very demanding. To graduate, one must pass the Cambridge Overseas Examination. Today, Lesotho claims an adult literacy rate in the Sotho language of nearly 85%.

Under apartheid, Africans' access to education in South Africa was restricted, and many of the best schools were closed. As a result, adult literacy rates dropped, in some areas to as low as 30%. Today, the goal is free education for everyone 7 to 17 years of age. Literacy and education are now seen as keys to success and are highly valued by most people in Lesotho and South Africa.

¹⁴ CULTURAL HERITAGE

Sotho traditional music places a strong emphasis on group singing, chanting, and hand clapping as an accompaniment to dance. Instruments used included drums, rattles, whistles, and handmade stringed instruments. One instrument, the *lesiba*, is made from a pole, a string, and a feather. When it is blown, the feather acts as a reed, producing a deep, resonant sound.

Dance groups are regularly featured during public celebrations. *Mokgibo* is a dance done by women who perform by moving their heads and shoulders in unison to the music while all sitting down on their knees and lower legs. *Mohobelo* is a men's line dance that is characterized by rhythmic marching and high stepping kicks.

Generations of mine labor have led to a distinct migrant-worker subculture in Lesotho. This subculture includes song and dance traditions. Some types of mine dances have synchronized high-kicking steps. One song tradition, *difela*, has lyrics relating the travels, loves, and viewpoints of the migrant workers. Other popular music in Sotho includes dance tunes played by small groups on drums, accordions, and guitars.

Sotho written literature was established in the nineteenth century by converts to Christianity. One of the first novels in a South African language was *Chaka*, written in southern Sotho by Thomas Mofolo in the early years of the 20th century. It is still read today and has been translated into a number of languages. Oliver Kgadime "O.K" Matsepe is considered by many to be the "Sepedi Shakespeare." He wrote 14 books including the 1954 novel *Sebatakgomo*.

¹⁵ WORK

Wage labor for many rural Sotho has meant leaving home to find employment in the city. In Lesotho, a term of mine work was once considered a kind of rite of passage that marked one as a man, but increasingly in the 20th-century such work became necessary for supporting a family. However, as South Africans increasingly look to their own citizens for the country's labor, there have been increasing ethnic tensions. By 2003, the number of mine workers from Lesotho was said to be fewer than 60,000 compared to a high of more than 125,000 a decade earlier. This also remains a dangerous business. In 2006, some 200 miners were killed in various mining accidents.

In South Africa, Sotho people under white rule were most frequently hired as miners and farm laborers. Women also worked as farm laborers, but work in domestic service was more highly valued. For those with high school and college educations, the greatest opportunities were in health care, education, and government administration. Today, the Sotho seek degrees in all fields.

South Africa's migrant-labor system has dramatically altered Sotho social life. Besides putting strains on the family, migrant labor has led to the development of new social groups. For example, associations of young men called *Marussia* formed with values that combined urban and rural attitudes. Critics see the "Russians" as no better than the criminal gangs based on home ties.

In recent years Lesotho experienced a rapid growth in garment manufacture. However, this has suffered a serious downturn since 2005 due to the lifting of international quotas on China and the declining value of the American dollar.

¹⁶ SPORTS

Many of the games popular among Sotho children are found worldwide. These include skipping rope, racing, swimming, playing catch, dodgeball, and hopscotch. Boys also enjoy wrestling and fighting with sticks. A common pastime for rural boys is making clay animals, especially cattle. Young boys and girls enjoy playing make-believe house (*mantlwantlwaneng*). The most popular traditional game among young men and old men is a game of strategy called *morabaraba*. This is similar to the game played elsewhere in Africa known as mancala.

Today, the most popular sport in Lesotho and South Africa is soccer. This is played informally by neighbors as well as by amateur and professional teams. In South Africa, there are many professional teams as well as teams associated with schools and businesses. In Lesotho, every district has several amateur teams. In the schools, there are also organized races and field events.

¹⁷ ENTERTAINMENT AND RECREATION

Contemporary people enjoy modern entertainment in the form of movies, plays, music, and television. Most of the movies are imported from foreign countries, but there is a growing South African film industry as well. Director Teboho

Mahlatsi's 2006 short film set in Lesotho, *Meogho and the Stick Fighter*, received international critical acclaim. Televisions and videocassette recorders are becoming widespread, although listening to the radio is most common due to the lower cost. South Africa broadcasts some shows in Sotho as well as other African languages, with soap operas being the most popular shows. Music videos of popular South African musical groups are also seen. In rural areas, however, there can be little to do for entertainment.

South Africa has a well-developed music industry. Recorded music includes many forms, from choral music and the songs of migrant workers to pop tunes, jazz, and reggae. Since 1999, a large annual music festival has been held annually in the town of Morija, Lesotho. Some popular musicians and groups of recent decades include Puseletso Seema, Tau ea Linare, Ray Phiri, Stimela, and Amatso Makaota, Tau ya Matsega.

18 FOLK ART, CRAFTS, AND HOBBIES

Traditions of folk art include beadwork, sewing, pottery making, house decoration, and weaving. Functional items such as sleeping mats, baskets, and beer strainers continue to be woven by hand from grass materials. Folk craft traditions have been revived and modified in response to the tourist trade. Popular items include tapestries and woven hats such as the *mokorotlo*, the national hat.

19 SOCIAL PROBLEMS

Many of the social problems faced by Sotho people today stem to some degree from the apartheid past. They include high rates of poverty, malnutrition, crime, and broken homes. Competition for scarce resources in South Africa has also led to conflict with other ethnic groups. Recently, illegal immigrants in South African shantytowns, most of them from Zimbabwe, have been subjected to violent attacks. In Lesotho, the end of apartheid has not meant the end of dependence on the wages of migrants.

The Sotho community also has internal divisions that have led to social problems. Significant differences exist in the values and aspirations of the young and old, the rural and urban, the highly educated and illiterate, and men and women. In addition, there is potential for conflict between the old systems of rule through chiefs and the military, and the new forms of participatory democracy.

20 GENDER ISSUES

Sotho culture historically assumed that female status was subordinate to that of males. A woman was considered a junior member of society in that when she married, responsibilities for her were transferred from the father to the husband. Upon divorce, custom also indicated that children should remain with the husband's family.

Economic circumstances have contributed to changes in women's status and behavior. Because of the migrant labor system, many rural women were left in practice as household heads. Harsh economic conditions have also forced many women to fend for themselves. This also led to changes in sexual practices. Long periods of separation between husbands and wives led to problems of adultery and prostitution. Some men and women also engaged in homosexual practices, although the idea of a gay identity has not been widely accepted.

Because young men traditionally were expected to spend most of the day tending livestock, girls often had greater opportunity to receive schooling. Consequently, unlike in many countries of the world, in Lesotho women have a higher rate of literacy than men. This is estimated by the government to be about 75% for men and 95% for women.

Today, both the South African government and the Lesotho government have policies promoting gender equality.

21 BIBLIOGRAPHY

Ashton, Hugh. *The Basuto.* London: Oxford University Press, 1952.

Cobbe, Jim. "Lesotho: Will the Enclave Empty?" *Country Profile.* Washington: Migration Policy Institute, 2004.

Coplan, David. *In Township Tonight: South Africa's Black City Music and Theater.* London: Longman, 1985.

Coplan, David. *In the Time of Cannibals: The Word Music of South Africa's Basotho Migrants.* Chicago: University of Chicago Press, 1995.

Damane, M., and P. B. Sanders. *Lithoko: Sotho Praise-Poems.* Oxford: Clarendon Press, 1974.

Delius, Peter. *The Land Belongs to Us: The Pedi Polity in the Nineteenth-century Transvaal.* Berkeley: University of California Press, 1984.

Hammond-Tooke, W. D. *Boundaries and Belief: The Structure of a Sotho Worldview.* Johannesburg: Witwatersrand University Press, 1981.

Hofmeyer, Isabel. *"We spend our years as a tale that is told": Oral Historical Narrative in a South African Chiefdom.* Portsmouth, NH: Heinemann, 1994.

"Lesotho." In *The Statesman's Yearbook 1996-1997,* edited by Brian Hunter. New York: Macmillan, 1996.

Mofolo, Thomas. *Chaka.* London: Heinemann, 1981.

Monig, H. O. *The Pedi.* Pretoria: J. L.van Shaik, 1988.

Murray, Colin. *Families Divided: The Impact of Migrant Labour in Lesotho.* Cambridge: Cambridge University Press, 1981.

National Union of Mineworkers. www.num.org.za (October 2008).

Pitje, G. M. "Traditional Systems of Male Rducation among Pedi and Cognate Tribes." *African Studies,* vol. 9, no 2, 1950: 53–76.

Statistics South Africa. www.statssa.gov.za (October 2008).

—by R. Shanafelt

SUDANESE

PRONUNCIATION: soo-duh-NEEZ
LOCATION: Sudan
POPULATION: 40 million
LANGUAGE: Arabic; many distinct indigenous languages; English
RELIGION: Islam; Christianity; indigenous beliefs
RELATED ARTICLES: Vol. 1: Azande; Dinka; Fulani; Nuer

¹ INTRODUCTION

The history of the Sudan, "Land of the Blacks," has been predominantly one of invasion and conquest. The earliest known events date back to 750 BC when Piankhy, king of Napata in northern Sudan, invaded Egypt and founded the 25th dynasty. A century later, his successors were forced back to Napata, and in c. 590 BC moved their capital south to Merowe, on the confluence of the Nile and Atbara rivers. The kingdom of Merowe was to be a major political power in the region for over 900 years. Remains of Meroitic culture can still be seen in the small pyramids beneath which their kings were buried. The culture was obviously influenced by Egypt, but also reflected contact with the wider classical world. A society of farmers and herders, its long prosperity was due primarily to trade and to ample supplies of iron ore. The art of ironworking may well have developed locally and spread from Merowe to other parts of Africa.

In AD 350 the kingdom of Merowe was destroyed, probably by invading armies from Ethiopia. The center of power then shifted to the Christian kingdoms of Nubia, which persisted till the late 14th century. In 1504, the remains of the Nubian forces were defeated by a powerful group known as the Funj, who had moved into the area from farther south. From their capital town, Sennar, on the Blue Nile, the Funj dynasty (also known as the Black Sultanate) ruled a vast area for over 300 years.

By 1820, the Funj dynasty was in decline and put up little resistance to the invading army of Muhammad 'Ali, viceroy of Egypt (then a province of the Ottoman Empire), who was seeking to control the trade in gold and slaves. For the next 60 years, the region was ruled by the Turkish-Egyptian administration in Cairo. During this period, Khartoum was developed as a capital, and much of the administrative infrastructure of modern Sudan was laid: the telegraph and rail systems, commercial agriculture, and international trade.

Turkish-Egyptian rule was already weakened by 1881 when Muhammad Ahmed, a holy man living on Aba Island on the White Nile, declared himself to be the *Mahdi* (Promised One) sent by God to return Islam to its original ideals. People from many different tribes rallied to his support as he declared a *jihad* (holy war) and successfully repulsed an Anglo-Egyptian force sent to restrain him. In 1884, General Charles Gordon was sent from Cairo to Khartoum to assist in the withdrawal of the Egyptian forces. Gordon was killed when the Mahdi's forces captured the capital. For the next 14 years (the *Mahdiya*), the Sudan was an independent Islamic state. It was led (after the Mahdi's untimely death in 1885) by the *Khalifa* Abdullahi. However by 1898, the region was again caught up in European politics. An Anglo-Egyptian army led by General

Herbert Kitchener routed the Khalifa's brave but poorly armed troops at ʻKerari (also known as the Battle of Omdurman). Though the pretext for the invasion was to avenge the death of Gordon, the real motive was to strengthen British interests in this part of the world. It ushered in the period of joint Anglo-Egyptian rule in the Sudan known as the Condominium (1898–1956), in which real power rested with the British. The present boundaries of Sudan were only finalized in the early years of the Condominium, by agreements between the British and other European nations trying to establish their interests in the region. They largely disregarded local tribal, cultural, and linguistic boundaries and the history of slavery in central Africa. Herein lay the causes of much contemporary political upheaval and distress. The Sudan has been sharply divided between north and south, as people from the south and west have struggled to either secede or gain some autonomy, from those powerful northern elites who inherited power from the colonial state. In the process, the divisions are over-simplified between Arab and African, or Muslim and non-Muslim. The reality remains far more complex.

In the half century since independence (1956), three periods of parliamentary rule (1956–8, 1964–9, 1986–9), have alternated with three of army rule (1958–64, 1969–86, 1989–present). The longest period of stability and prosperity was during the administration of Jaafar Nimeri (1969–85). In the first 10 years of his presidency, Sudan's economy boomed, as oil was discovered in the southwestern region. Nimeri even succeeded in bringing peace to the south. By the early 1980s, however, Sudan faced recession, drought, and political instability caused partly by large numbers of refugees from neighboring countries. Nimeri himself became increasingly unpopular, and when he introduced a severe form of the *Shariah* (Islamic law), opposition to him quickly mounted. He was ousted in a peaceful coup in 1985, but after a brief period (1986–9) of democratic rule under Sadiq al-Mahdi (grandson of the Mahdi), the army once again seized power under General Omar al-Bashir, supported by the powerful National Islamic Front (NIF). The country has since become increasingly isolated from the west, both politically and economically, despite a shift towards civilian rule in 2001 and the cessation of the so-called "second" civil war (1983–2005) with the signing of the Comprehensive Peace Agreement (CPA) between the government of President al-Bashir and the Sudan People's Liberation Movement (SPLM). The halting of hostilities led to the renewal of oil production in southwestern Sudan, and to a general economic recovery in the country as a whole.

Meanwhile in 2003 civil war erupted in the west, in Darfur, when opposition groups there sought similar government concessions, and government-supported militias (called *janjawid*) attacked "rebel" villages. In the intervening years, thousands of innocent bystanders have been killed, displaced or subject to terrible trauma and violation.

² LOCATION AND HOMELAND

The Republic of the Sudan (generally known simply as Sudan) is the largest country in Africa, encompassing nearly 2.6 million sq km (1 million sq mi) and stretching over 2,000 km (1,250 mi) from north to south, slightly more than a quarter the size of the US. It shares common boundaries with nine countries: Egypt, Libya, Chad, Central African Republic, the Democratic Republic of the Congo, Uganda, Kenya, Eritrea, and Ethiopia.

Its landscapes range from rocky desert in the north (almost a quarter of its total area), through savanna with increasing vegetation, to the mountainous rain land along the Uganda border in the south. Its most important physical feature is the Nile River, which traverses the whole length of the country. The Blue Nile (rising in Ethiopia) meets the White Nile (from Uganda) in the capital city of Khartoum, and they wind jointly north through a series of cataracts or falls to Lake Nubia (the "Aswan Dam"), the largest artificial lake in the world.

Sudan has an estimated population of approximately 40 million, with a new government census planned for 2008. The population includes a large number (almost 600) of distinct ethnic or tribal groups. The country remains predominantly rural, but towns have expanded rapidly since Sudan gained its independence from Britain in 1956.

As a result of the long civil wars, and opposition to political realities, there is now a very large Sudanese diaspora, scattered from the US to Australia, with large concentrations (of southern Sudanese) resident in neighboring Kenya and Uganda, and (largely of northern Sudanese) throughout the Middle East.

³ LANGUAGE

Arabic is the official language of Sudan, although many other languages continue to be used in the home. At independence, it was estimated that 100 distinct languages were spoken in the Sudan. Today, all educated people speak the local or colloquial form of Arabic—the language of government, schools, and of most northern Sudanese. This is reflected in the preponderance of Arabic names: Muhammad, Abdullah, and 'Ali for men, for example, and Fatima, Aisha, or Muna for women.

In the south and west, English is spoken alongside the variety of indigenous languages, of which Dinka [see **Dinka**] is the most widespread. Common southern names such as Deng (Dinka) or Shull (Shilluk), sometimes coupled with Christian names, such as Maria Deng, reveal the bearer's ethnic as well as religious background.

⁴ FOLKLORE

The Sudanese have a rich and varied folklore that embodies much of their indigenous wisdom. It continues to be passed on orally, at least in the countryside, and is passing into the lyrics of popular music and culture, now widely enjoyed on television and radio. Certain older women are renowned for their storytelling, embroidering often brief tales with elaborate gestures and colorful description. Many of the stories reflect the rural way of life, the society and culture to which the Sudanese belong, and center on human rather than animal or supernatural themes. A favorite character in Muslim Sudan is Fatima the Beautiful, who outwits a variety of male relatives and rivals in a series of amazing feats. She usually ends up marrying the man of her choice, and often vindicates her whole family as well. A supernatural figure who figures large in warning stories told to small children is Umm Ba'ula, the mother of bogeys, who carries a large basket in which she carries away disobedient children.

⁵ RELIGION

The majority of Sudan's population (70%) is Sunni Muslim. Islam was introduced to the northern Sudan by Arab traders as early as the 7th century AD. For many centuries Islam coexisted with an earlier branch of Christianity (which had spread

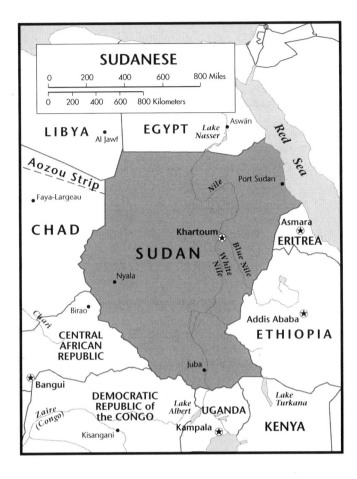

here from Alexandria), though Islam ultimately absorbed it. From the beginning, Islam was spread largely by traders and wandering holy men (*faki*, pl. *fugara*) who preached a more mystical *(Sufi)* form of Islam. Many of these established a way (*tariga*, also called Brotherhood) that their followers observed. These Brotherhoods continue to be very important in the practice of Sudanese Islam, particularly the *Qadriyya* (the oldest Brotherhood), the *Sammaniya*, and the *Khatmiyya* (a more modern organization that grew out of 18th century reformist movements). Sufi practices also exert a considerable influence on popular culture, as the religious songs (*madih*) of the much beloved late Sammaniya Shaikh al-Bura'i attests.

Sudan is now an Islamist state, run by the National Congress Party (NCP), which replaced the National Islamic Front (NIF) and which in turn grew out of the Sudanese Muslim Brotherhood. This reformist movement reached Sudan from Egypt in the 1950s and became popular particularly with the emerging intellectual class. Other reformist trends known as Salafism (*al-salafiyya*) further contribute to the dynamic and diverse Islamic landscape of Sudan, with groups like the *Ansar al-Sunna al-Muhammadiyya* also seeking to purify existing Islamic practices.

However, many peoples, particularly in southern and western Sudan, are not Muslim. Some (5%) are Christian, as various denominations of missionaries have been active outside the Sudanese Islamic areas since the mid-19th century. Many (25%) also continue to practice indigenous beliefs, particularly those concerned with various types of spirits. Such beliefs also infuse the practices of both Islam and Christianity in the

Sudan. One of the most widespread is known as *zar*, which is found throughout northern Africa.

6 MAJOR HOLIDAYS

The major holidays in the Sudan are religious holidays. In Muslim areas, the celebrations at the end of the fasting month of Ramadan and to mark God's sparing of Ishmael (the *Eid* of Sacrifice) are most important, marked with special foods, new clothes, and family visits. The birthday of the Prophet (the *Moulid*) is also celebrated over several days, an occasion for the various Brotherhoods to perform their ritual prayers and recite their historical narratives.

In Christian areas, the major holidays are also religious events. Christmas is particularly important, celebrated with special church services, as well as new clothes and traditional foods.

The day independence was gained from Britain is officially recognized on January 1 but has little significance in everyday life for the Sudanese.

7 RITES OF PASSAGE

"To the house, wealth, and children" is the customary congratulations given to newlyweds. Children are greatly desired and a birth is a significant event. An expectant mother tries to return to her parent's home to give birth, and is attended by some of her closest friends and the local midwife. After the birth, she and the baby may remain confined for 40 days, at the end of which a party is held to name the child and introduce it to outsiders.

The major rite of passage for most children in northern Sudan is circumcision, which is routinely performed on many girls and all boys between the ages of 4 and 8. The child is referred to as the bride or bridegroom, and much of the formal ritual of a marriage ceremony is foreshadowed in the practices that surround the operation and party. The use of brightly colored silk sheets (*jirtiq*), of cosmetics and perfumes, and the sacrifice of a sheep, as well as the foods served to guests, all anticipate rituals to be repeated with greater drama in the marriage ceremony.

After a child has been circumcised, gender segregation becomes marked. Young girls help their mothers and aunts, and care for younger siblings. Young boys begin to spend more time with their peers outside the home and away from the company of women. For boys, adolescence is often a time of irresponsibility and freedom, while adolescent girls are expected to carry out a large share of the domestic chores and at the same time observe strict rules of modesty, thus protecting both their own honor and the honor of their family.

In much of southern Sudan, initiation into age-sets (rather than circumcision) was formerly essential for entry into adult status. Ceremonies of initiation differed from tribe to tribe and for males and females, though they were less common for girls than boys [see **Dinka** and **Nuer**].

Marriage is the major event, of religious and social importance, in every Sudanese's life, celebrated with great ritual even in poor neighborhoods. It is at least partly arranged, seen as an alliance between families rather than simply between two individuals. In the Muslim North, marriage with a close relative is common: for a girl, usually with her *wad amm*, the son of her father's brother, a member of her own lineage. The legal basis of the marriage is the marriage contract, based on the *Shariah* (Muslim law) and drawn up by a learned man together with (male) representatives of the bride and groom. In southern Sudan, marriages were arranged differently [see **Dinka** and **Nuer**]. The unwritten contract was traditionally arranged between male elders of both families, sometimes without the knowledge of either the bride or the groom. This revolved around the payment of bride-wealth—special cattle were reserved for this type of exchange, though by the early 1980s a small proportion might be paid in cash.

Payment of bride-wealth by the groom's family to the bride's family remains an essential part of the marriage process. In the north, it includes gifts and money for the bride's family to help finance the wedding, as well as gifts for the bride herself, particularly gold, which is the basis of the bride's own formal assets. With the rise in overseas employment, there has been a great inflation in bride-price and consequent delay in the time of marriage. Many men find they have to postpone marriage until they can save what are often exorbitant sums. Increasing numbers of women remain unmarried or have to accept a polygynous marriage. In much of the south, the old marriage currency in cattle has broken down because of the long wars, and weddings tend to be briefer and cheaper.

Formal religion surrounds many of the rites associated with death and burial. Because of the heat, the deceased is buried quickly, usually the same day. Formal mourning lasts for several days, during which all acquaintances of the family are expected to visit to offer condolences.

8 INTERPERSONAL RELATIONS

The Sudanese are intensely social people, caring about family and neighbors in a very personal way. Although much social interaction is highly formalized, it is accompanied by great warmth. Visits from guests, for however long a period, are regarded as an honor to the host and his whole family, and take priority over other arrangements. Such visits should also be returned before too long, and need not be scheduled ahead of time. Refreshments are served to guests immediately—a cup of water to relieve them after their journey, followed by hot sweet tea and later by coffee and food, if the visit seems prolonged.

Greetings are warm and often effusive. Accompanied by handshaking, the Arabic greeting *"Izeyik"* is exchanged, followed by inquiries about each other's health, *"Qwayseen?"* (Are you well?), to which the standard reply is to thank God— *"Al-humdulilah."* For older people especially, this is then an opportunity to proclaim their devoutness through a lengthy exchange of Quranic verses. Throughout the exchange, each person underscores their pleasure in meeting. When one person indicates they want to take their leave, the other urges them to stay a little longer. Finally, goodbyes are exchanged: *"Maasalam!"* followed by *"Al-iy-selimik,"* which may also be accompanied by warm handshakes.

People are more relaxed with friends of the same sex. Friendship is especially valued, and it is not uncommon to see two young men walking hand in hand, or with their arms draped across each others' shoulders.

The concept of "dating," as in the Western world, is still quite rare, at least in Muslim Sudan. Until the successful completion of the marriage ceremonies, bride and groom and their families are concerned to protect their honor. Thus, meetings between unrelated men and women are closely monitored and efforts are made in the work place to segregate men and women, at least publicly. However young people now are given some input into their choice of marriage partner, in which class and education levels are becoming as important as family connections.

⁹ LIVING CONDITIONS

Early European visitors to Sudan found it a difficult and unhealthy place. They succumbed frequently to such tropical diseases as malaria, bilharzia, cholera, and dysentery, diseases that continue to plague many Sudanese. Health issues are further exacerbated by contemporary economic problems, food shortages caused by drought, and political instability. In addition, many disorders not known to Western physicians are recognized locally, such as those caused by the Evil Eye, by spirits, or by sorcery. For such conditions, the advice of local healers continues to be sought.

Although Sudan is regarded as one of the poorest countries in the world, its people have long found ways to accommodate their harsh environment. In the rural areas of the north, even without electricity and air conditioners the mud-baked flat-roofed houses remain cool in the hottest temperatures. In the south, the conical grass huts provide warmth and safety from heavy rains and more variable climates. In the towns and cities, there is a wider range of buildings and standards of living. In first-class districts occupied by senior officials, wealthy merchants, and families supported by expatriate relatives, European-style villas, cooled by air-conditioners and flaunting satellite technology, are surrounded by elegant lawns. In contrast, on the outskirts of towns and cities, squatter settlements of make-shift huts and lean-tos (rakuba) provide temporary homes for new migrants and their families, but offer little shelter from the heat, cold, or discomfort.

Markets have long been important centers in this region, and they continue to reflect the many faces of the Sudan. Goods imported from Libya or China are sold alongside craft articles produced locally, and foods and crops grown in the surrounding countryside. Bargaining is expected, and indeed the social ties developed through such trade are regarded as essential aspects of the economic transaction.

There is a wide range of public transportation within the Sudan, although few people own cars. Within settled communities, public cars (often small trucks with specially constructed passenger areas on the back) provide an effective network around town for a small fee. In recent years, large numbers of motorized rickshaws have been imported from India and provide a slightly more expensive, but more private option. Between communities, the more affluent travel by bus (which between major cities is now air-conditioned), though most people settle for a place on the back of a truck, which is often part of a commercial fleet of such vehicles. Train service connects the capital, Khartoum, with other major cities. Since compartments are usually packed, enterprising passengers also crowd onto the roof. Finally, many individual men own their own donkey, bicycle, or (occasionally) horse and cart (caro).

¹⁰ FAMILY LIFE

In Sudanese life, the family is highly valued and much protected. Large families are universally desired. Children are looked on with incomparable pride, welcomed as the only reliable insurance against old age, as well as their parents' natural heirs and assistants in business. For a woman, childbearing brings

esteem. Also, if her husband dies, she is secure in the knowledge that, at least under Islamic law she and her children will inherit favorably.

Women's roles are primarily those of homemaker and mother. In Muslim families, after the birth of her first son, a woman is henceforth known as Umm 'Ali, "Mother of 'Ali," for example, a practice known as teknonymy. This emphasis on male offspring and the male line is found throughout the country, as families are overwhelmingly patrilineal and patriarchal in nature.

While nuclear families are becoming common, extended families are still found and are often polygynous (more than one wife). Polygyny is acceptable in Islam as well as in Southern tribes [see **Dinka** and **Nuer**], and cuts across urban/rural and social differences. The levirate, whereby a man may marry his deceased brother's widow, is still practiced. This is believed to safeguard the welfare of a widow, for whom her husband's family, specifically her brother-in-law, is regarded as responsible. Among non-Muslim Sudanese, relationships between wives and their children are structured more according to seniority and age. Here children of a levirate union are regarded as belonging to the deceased man, a situation possible because of the cultural separation of concepts of physical and social parenthood. The sororate, whereby a man marries his deceased wife's sister, is found only when the dead woman has borne no children. So-called "ghost marriages" are also common among Nilotic peoples. Should a man die without children, his relatives are obliged to take a "ghost-wife" for him. The children she bears are his descendants. Finally, a Nuer or Dinka woman who is infertile may become, in effect, a social man. She may "marry" a wife who produces children for her.

With the imposition of the Shariah (Islamic law), it seems probable that ethnic variations in family forms will slowly disappear. Patrilineal, patriarchal families, with increasing limitations on women's roles and intolerance for alternative social practices, have been the trend since the early 1990s.

Attempts to control the birth rate in Sudan are slowly making progress. Modern contraception is expensive (in financial and social terms), and there has been a lack of investment in terms of training sensitive fieldworkers to determine individual and family needs, but the high costs of living, coupled with expanding education opportunities for women, is resulting in somewhat smaller families. The fertility rate in 2007 was 4.69 children born to one woman.

¹¹ CLOTHING

Western-style clothing (long trousers, with a shirt) is commonly worn by Sudanese men in professional workplaces. However, elsewhere Muslim Sudanese prefer traditional dress: long pastel-colored robes (jalabiya), with a skullcap (tagia) and length of cloth ('imma) covering their head. Laborers wear baggy pants (sirwal) covered by a thigh length tunic (ragi).

Women in public today are bound to wear Islamic dress. For much of the 20th century, this was simply a 9-m (30-ft) length of material (tob) wound round the body, leaving the wearer looking elegant and distinctive. Today some women choose instead to wear an Islamic shawl (hijab) folded tightly over their head, a loose long-sleeved shirt, and a long, plain skirt, a style of dress found throughout the Muslim world. Many women also wear the abayah, a black overcoat more common in the

Middle East. In the privacy of their own homes, women simply wear light dresses.

12 FOOD

For most Sudanese, the staple food is *durra*, sorghum, which is grown locally and used to make breads (both leavened and flat) and porridges. These are then eaten with various types of stew, beans, lentils, and salads. Sheep is the favorite meat, though beef and chicken are also consumed. Meat may be fried, stewed, or (occasionally) roasted. For desserts, seasonal fruit is sliced and served fresh, though *créme caramelle,* jelly, and sugared rice are also common. Meals are eaten communally and by hand from a round tray on which the various bowls of food are surrounded by breads used for dipping. After the Quranic injunction, only the right hand should be used for eating; and great care is taken before and after the meal to ensure its cleanliness. Meals are segregated by gender, younger children usually eating with the women or with each other.

Water is the preferred drink, generally protected in a large clay pot (*zir*) that keeps it cool. Favorite beverages for guests are tea and coffee. Both are served very sweet and often mixed with spices (known as medicine, *dowa*, but commonly either cinnamon or cardamom). Tea is served in small glasses, and coffee (roasted and ground fresh, and very strong) is served in thimble-like cups. Another delicious drink is made from freshly squeezed limes, and during the month of fasting either this or a sweet and nutritious drink made from sorghum (known as *abrit*) are commonly used to break the fast. Several types of homemade cakes, such as *ligimat* (a type of doughnut) or *cak* (which resembles shortcake) are served to guests or simply enjoyed for breakfast or supper.

Sudanese eat two, sometimes three meals a day. Sweet tea with milk (or water) is drunk when they awake in the morning, and breakfast is eaten several hours later, usually necessitating a break from work. Lunch, the main meal of the day, is served in mid-afternoon, after work or school is over. A light supper, not unlike breakfast, is sometimes eaten in the evening.

In the past two decades there has been a steady deterioration of the average daily diet, as traditional staples (beans, fruit, meat) become too expensive for poorer families, who are forced to rely on cheaper, less nutritious foods such as macaroni and sugar.

13 EDUCATION

Quranic schooling, based on memorizing the Quran, has a long history in the Sudan and remains popular. More secular forms of formal education go back only to the early years of the 20th century and are still not universal. Adult literacy (measured probably in terms of secular education) is now 61%, and there is intense competition among children for the limited places in schools, particularly higher education. For the most part, parents are anxious for both sons and daughters to receive formal education, seeing this as a path to a more successful future. Unfortunately, their expectations are not always realized, and opportunities for both higher education and jobs in the modern sector are still limited.

Occupations for women are especially limited. Until recently, high school diplomas were seen primarily as their path to a good marriage. Though this began to change as more women entered the professions (medicine, law, education), women generally have fewer opportunities for employment and advancement than men.

14 CULTURAL HERITAGE

The cultural heritage of contemporary Sudanese is particularly evident in their music. Singing, drumming, and dancing are popular, spontaneous activities for children, and are indispensable for any major celebration. Elaborate wedding parties include a group to sing and play, and a microphone to make sure the whole community can share in the festivities. Western, Arab, and Indian, as well as African performers have become popular through film, television, and radio. Their influence is evident in the dynamic and distinctive musical forms of Sudan. The best-known Sudanese singers today include Muhammad Wurdi, Gabli, and Muhammad el Amin, poets as well as musicians.

The favorite instrument of the Sudanese is the drum, and small children learn very early how to pound out a rhythm and to dance. For all ceremonies, the *daluka* (baked mud and cowhide drum) is used to accompany singing and dancing. Another favorite instrument is the *rababa*, a type of violin that points to an Arab link, as does the classical *lud*, used on more formal occasions.

In Muslim Sudan, men and women dance separately and have different dancing styles. Men use their arms more and take wider, firmer steps, while women remain stationary and stretch their necks, their feet, and their chests, at the same time demonstrating control of their bodies. Elsewhere, such distinctions are less apparent, and there are other popular styles of dancing such as the "Stomp Dancing" of the Nuba Mountains and further south.

Story telling has long been a popular and admired art form that underlies a rich tradition in poetry and fiction. Sudan's greatest novelist in Arabic is Tayeb Salih (b.1929). His novel *Season of Migration to the North* (1967), which draws on his country's colonial experience, set in a typical village context, has been translated into many languages. His short story "The Wedding of Zein" has been made into a film by that name. Popular Sudanese writers in English include Leila Aboulela (b.1964), author of several novels including *The Translator* and *Minaret,* and Jamal Mahjoub (b. 1960) whose novels include *The Drift Latitudes* and *Travelling with Djinns.* Both draw on their own multi-cultural backgrounds in tales that are wideranging in time and space.

15 WORK

Despite massive migration to urban areas since independence, many Sudanese continue to work in agriculture. This includes pastoralism (dependence on large herds, particularly camels and cattle) and cultivation: both subsistence cultivation (where the staple crop is sorghum, mixed with vegetables, peanuts, and beans) and commercialized agriculture, particularly on irrigated agricultural schemes. The largest and oldest of these is the Gezira Scheme, between the Blue and White Niles, which produces the bulk of the country's major export crop, long-staple cotton. This has served as the model for other agricultural schemes set up since independence, in which tenant farmers grow export crops under the management of the state-owned company, as well as foods for their own use. These schemes have been less than successful, partly because there appears to be insufficient incentives to farmers to collaborate

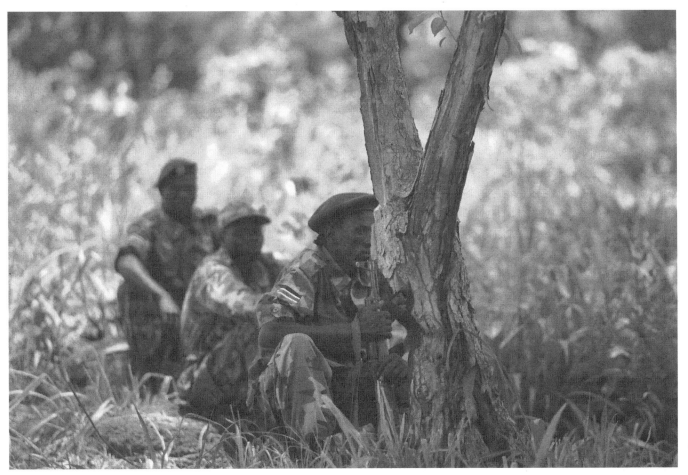

South Sudanese army personnel keep vigil at Rikwangba near Garamba forest on April 10, 2008. The site was to host a peace agreement to be signed by elusive rebel leader Joseph Kony, Uganda's top rebel leader of the Lord's Resistance Army (LRA). Kony requested further consultations before signing a peace agreement to end one of Africa's longest conflicts.
(AFP Photo/Tonu Karumba/Getty Images)

with the company, and because deteriorating political and economic situations pushed many farmers into joining the exodus to seek alternative work in towns or outside the country, especially to the oil-rich Arab states. Labor migration throughout the Middle East, and to Europe and North America, has had a considerable impact on the Sudanese economy and overseas remittances are a major source of income.

Agricultural work in Muslim areas is also subject to gender segregation. In poorer families, females usually carry out tedious tasks such as picking cotton while males perform the heavier work of clearing the land, digging irrigation ditches, and planting. In families more comfortably situated, women are expected to work only inside the home, while men do the outside jobs, including marketing.

Family work is also very demanding in the Sudan. This includes not only taking care of the family and household, but also demonstrating concern for the wider family and community by a tireless round of visiting, caring for the sick, attending neighborhood ceremonies such as weddings, thanksgivings, and funerals; and providing labor and cash to support these ceremonies.

¹⁶ SPORTS

Sudan, like many African countries, has a love affair with soccer. Most small boys learn to play, even if they have to use a wooden ball, and identify with one of the leading national football teams. Among the educated, tennis and (to a lesser extent) volleyball are played in some of the clubs that continue to serve as reminders of the colonial past. Sudanese regularly compete against other African countries in most major sports but have yet to develop the resources for Olympic competition.

¹⁷ ENTERTAINMENT AND RECREATION

Television is popular throughout the country. Even in rural areas, the men's club usually owns a set that village children are able to watch. Among the most popular programs are the nightly soap operas *(musalsal),* often acquired from Egypt or Lebanon, though Sudan has begun to produce its own. Islamic programs are also widely enjoyed.

Open-air cinemas are found in all the towns and larger villages and are attended by mainly male audiences. They tend to show some of the worst exports from the East (especially India) and West (Italian gangster movies are popular). Most people, however, prefer to spend their spare time visiting with friends and family, attending neighbor celebrations such as weddings or homecomings, or simply chatting quietly in the shelter of the night. Again this is largely divided by gender: men frequently gather in one of the men's clubs after supper, while women visit with their neighbors at home.

18 FOLK ART, CRAFTS, AND HOBBIES

Various traditions reinforce the importance of large families and community closeness among Sudanese. Before marriage, a girl learns from her friends and relatives how to perform traditional dances and to use specific homemade cosmetics (incense, oils, smoke-baths, henna decoration, perfumes) that are believed to enhance sensuality and are very much a part of marital relationships. Throughout the country, people employ charms or amulets to stimulate fertility, as well as to decorate themselves.

The most elaborate folk craft is basketry. Some of the finest baskets come from the west of the country, from Darfur, in the form of large round food covers, used to protect the food tray from insects and dust. Even more common is the manufacture of rope beds and stools, staple items of furniture that appear to have changed little since Pharaonic times, and that are still widely used.

19 SOCIAL PROBLEMS

The 2005 peace agreement (CPA) between North and South has so far withstood the death of the former Southern leader Colonel John Garang and escalating hostilities in western Sudan. Peace and security remain elusive in much of southern Sudan, however, and provisions for a referendum for the south in 2011 make fragmentation of the present state seem likely. Meanwhile more than 2 million people have been displaced and at least 200,000 people have died as a result of the violence in Darfur, which in 2008 showed no sign of abating, despite the presence of African Union troops in the region. Indeed many innocent bystanders have lost their liberty and even their lives in the violence.

Ongoing environmental issues also present serious problems. Changing climatic patterns, including the inexorable movement of *al-Sahara* (the desert), declining forest and woodland, expanding urbanization and increasing pollution are all taking their toll on human life. Within the congested squatter settlements in the towns particularly, new and old diseases add to human difficulties: malaria and tuberculosis, diabetes and bilharzia, various gastro-intestinal and respiratory problems. Despite a much expanded medical profession, not everybody can afford help. The cost of living has risen so dramatically that even former staple food items have become luxuries that few can afford. The benefits of oil revenues have yet to trickle down to the poorer in society.

In addition, the massive relocations of people to larger villages, to towns (especially to the greater Khartoum area) and even outside the country, have led to breakdowns in many Sudanese families. The elderly are no longer automatically surrounded by their caring children, while the young may not have the support of their parents. The immediate future for the Sudanese, therefore, does not look bright, but most remain optimistic that better times lie ahead.

20 GENDER ISSUES

Many gender issues in Sudan today are part of a larger complex of problems associated with war, violence, and poverty that affects society as a whole, though particularly those in the south and west. Women in Darfur have suffered disproportionately in recent years, from displacement, violence, rape, sickness, and hunger, as their male relatives have been killed or fled. A peace settlement, a return to their homes, and some measure of stability is desperately needed by women of all ages.

Women's roles have also been targeted by the reforms of the Islamist government. Their dress, their public appearance, and their occupations have all been variously subject to political scrutiny and censure. Invariably it is poor women and non-Muslims in particular who suffer most as Sudanese society is variously redefined by those in power.

Female circumcision (including excision and infibulations, and known locally as *fironi,* pharaonic circumcision) has long been practiced in Muslim Sudan, alongside male circumcision. In the past decade there are clear signs that this is now a contested tradition; many parents are either giving up the practice for their daughters or are preferring more moderate forms of cutting. It remains to be seen how far this trend will become lasting.

21 BIBLIOGRAPHY

Abusharaf, Rogaia Mustafa. *Wanderings: Sudanese Migrants and Exiles in North America.* Ithaca: Cornell University Press, 2002.

De Waal, Alex and Flint, Julie. *Darfur: A Short History of a Long War.* London: Zed Books, 2005.

Deng, F. M. *Tradition and Modernization: A Challenge for Law among the Dinka of the Sudan.* New Haven, Conn.: Yale University Press, 1987.

Gruenbaum, E. *The Female Circumcision Controversy: An Anthropological Perspective.* Philadelphia: University of Pennsylvania Press, 2001.

Holt, P. and M. Daly. *History of Sudan.* London: Pearson Educational Group, 2000.

Hutchinson, S. *Nuer Dilemmas: Coping with Money, War and the State.* Berkeley: California University Press, 1996.

Kenyon, Susan M. *Five Women of Sennar. Culture and Change in Central Sudan.* 2nd edition. Long Grove, IL: Waveland Press, 2004.

Lesch, Ann M. *The Sudan—Contested National Identities.* Bloomington: Indiana University Press, 1998.

Warburg, Gabriel. *Islam, Sectarianism and Politics in Sudan since the Mahdiyya.* Madison: University of Wisconsin Press, 2003.

—by S. M. Kenyon

SWAHILI

PRONUNCIATION: swah-HEE-lee
LOCATION: Eastern Africa from southern Somalia to northern Mozambique
POPULATION: 772, 642
LANGUAGE: KiSwahili
RELIGION: Islam (Sunni Muslim); spirit cults
RELATED ARTICLES: Vol. 1: Kenyans; Tanzanians

¹ INTRODUCTION

For at least a thousand years, Swahili people, who call themselves Waswahili, have occupied a narrow strip of coastal land extending from the north coast of Kenya to Dar es Salaam, the capital of Tanzania, and also several nearby Indian Ocean islands (e.g., Zanzibar, Lamu, Pate). Legends claim that Swahili people migrated from a place in northeast Africa called Shungwaya; however, archeological studies and epic poems locate the earliest settlements on Kenya's north coast. Over the past few hundred years, the coastal area has been the site of extraordinary movements of people and goods and has been conquered and colonized several times: by Portuguese who captured Mombasa in the 16th century, by Middle Eastern Arabs who ran a slave trade in the 19th century, and by British colonizers in the 20th century. Thus, Swahili people are accustomed to living with strangers in their midst, and they have frequently acted as "middlemen" in trade relations. In addition, they have incorporated many people and practices into their vibrant social world.

Waswahili are all Muslims. They became Muslim through the influence of people coming from the north and also from across the Indian Ocean. They have forged extensive economic, political, and social ties with Middle Eastern Muslims. Since at least the 18th century, Muslim men from Oman and Saudi Arabia have married Swahili women. Waswahili are known for bringing people into their ethnic group, including slaves brought from the interior of Africa in the 19th century and members of nearby ethnic groups (e.g., Giriama). Scholars have long debated whether, given their tendency to embrace new people, Waswahili even constitute an ethnic group, like the Zulu or the Ashanti, but Swahili people themselves have no doubts that they are a culturally distinct group of Muslims with a mixed African and Arab ancestry.

In the early 19th century the Sultan of Oman moved his capital to the island of Zanzibar and, from there, governed the coastal region. Swahili people competed with Arabs for political and economic power, yet they were a strong community by the end of the last century. During the colonial period and since independence in the early 1960s, Swahili people have been a minority Muslim population in the secular states of Kenya and Tanzania.

² LOCATION AND HOMELAND

Given the shifting nature of Swahili ethnicity, it is difficult to substantiate the general belief that Swahili people number about a half a million.

The deep harbors along the coast have long sustained a profitable fishing and shipping economy. The extensive coral reef several miles off the coast keeps these waters calm. The lush coastal plain provides a fertile environment for growing coconut palms, fruit trees, spices, and mangrove in swamp areas. Today, Swahili people live primarily in the urban areas of Lamu, Malindi, Mombasa, Tanga (mainland Tanzania), the island of Zanzibar, and Dar es Salaam.

Hundreds of Swahili people left for the Middle East after the Zanzibar Revolution in 1964. Over the past several decades, thousands have migrated to the Middle East, Europe, and North America largely for economic reasons.

³ LANGUAGE

Kiswahili, the Swahili language, is widely spoken across East Africa. For most Kenyans and Tanzanians, Kiswahili is learned as a second language. Swahili people speak Kiswahili as their "mother tongue," and it reflects their mixed origins and complex history. The language includes many words borrowed from Arabic (and other languages), yet its grammar and syntax place it in the Bantu language family, which has roots on the African continent. Like many Kenyans, Swahili people also use English in their daily interactions, particularly in schools, government offices, and the tourist industry.

As in other Bantu languages, all Kiswahili nouns are organized into classes. A noun's class governs the formation of plurals and the agreement among subjects, verbs, and adjectives. The "person" class includes *mtu* (person) and *mwalimu* (teacher). The "n" class includes many words that begin with the letter "n," such as *ndoa* (marriage) and also many borrowed words, for example, *televisheni* and *komputa*. Kwanzaa, the African American holiday, incorporates many Kiswahili terms from the "u" class of abstract nouns, including *ujamaa* (pulling together) and *umoja* (unity).

Most names are Arabic in origin and indicate a person's Muslim identity by linking him or her with a prophet or with a Muslim ideal. Common names for girls are Amina and Fatuma; for boys, Mohammed and Moussa. A person's first name is followed by their father's name: Mohammed bin (son of) Moussa or Amina binti (daughter of) Moussa. Clan names added to these reflect the relations among larger groups of people. Shortened forms of standard names (e.g., Tuma for Fatuma) are popular as nicknames.

Kiswahili has a wide population of speakers with records of as many as 50 million. Currently, it is the official language in Tanzania. In Kenya and Uganda, it is a national language, since official communication and the medium of instruction in the two countries is English. The language is also spoken in the Democratic Republic of Congo, Rwanda, Burundi, Somalia and South Africa.

⁴ FOLKLORE

Myths and heroes are generally from Islamic sources. For example, many people tell short, moralistic tales based on the Prophet Mohammed's life.

⁵ RELIGION

Being Swahili is inextricably connected to being Muslim. Excavations of mosques provide evidence that Islam flourished from at least the 12th century. Swahili Muslims recognize the five pillars of faith that are basic to Islamic practice worldwide: 1) belief in Allah as the Supreme Being and in Mohammed as the most important prophet; 2) praying five times a day; 3) fasting during the month of Ramadan; 4) giving charity; and

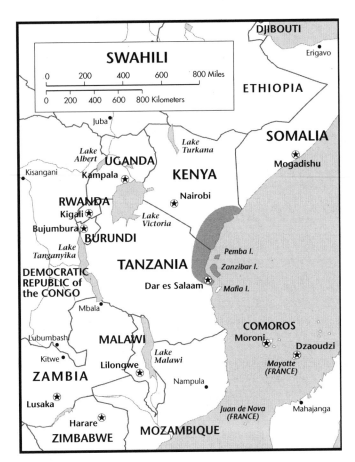

SWAHILI

| 0 | 200 | 400 | 600 | 800 Miles |
| 0 | 200 | 400 | 600 | 800 Kilometers |

DJIBOUTI
Erigavo
ETHIOPIA
SOMALIA
Mogadishu
Juba
Lake Turkana
UGANDA
KENYA
Kisangani
Kampala
Nairobi
RWANDA
Kigali
Lake Victoria
Bujumbura
BURUNDI
Lake Tanganyika
Pemba I.
Zanzibar I.
TANZANIA
DEMOCRATIC REPUBLIC of the CONGO
Dar es Salaam
Mafia I.
Mbala
COMOROS
Moroni
Lubumbashi
MALAWI
Dzaoudzi
Kitwe
Lake Malawi
Mayotte (FRANCE)
Lilongwe
Nampula
ZAMBIA
Lusaka
Juan de Nova (FRANCE)
Mahajanga
Harare
ZIMBABWE
MOZAMBIQUE

5) making a pilgrimage (Hajj) to Mecca, if feasible. For Swahili people, Islam encompasses more than just spiritual beliefs and practices; Islam is a way of life. The times for prayer organize each day, and Muslims pray at home or at mosques. On Friday, the holiest day of the week, men pray together. Both men and women attend religious lectures on Fridays and other days.

Like most African Muslims, Swahili people claim allegiance to the Sunni sect of Islam, yet their practices are distinctive in several ways. Some communities revere local religious figures from times past, paying them homage as "saints" on special holy days. Islam includes the belief in spirits (*jini*, singular; *majini*, plural). These beings are capable of possessing individuals for good or evil purposes. Those who are afflicted by bad spirits and, as well, people skilled in controlling them, participate in groups where, through prayers, trance, and ceremonies, spirits are called forth to account for their acts. Dangerous spirits can be driven away by a skillful practitioner of Islamic spiritual medicine. Such local practices are criticized as old fashioned by some who promote either more "modern" religion or a purer version of Islam. Although some young men in the cities are involved in political parties organized to promote Muslim causes, the influence of fundamentalism is low compared with other African contexts (e.g., Algeria, Sudan).

⁶ MAJOR HOLIDAYS

Along with all other Kenyans, Swahili people celebrate the nation's secular public holidays, including Jamhuri Day and Madaraka Day, which mark the steps toward Kenya's Independence in the early 1960s.

For Muslims, the most important holidays are religious. Idd il Fitr marks the end of the month of Ramadan. Idd il Hajj celebrates the yearly pilgrimage to Mecca. Each Idd is celebrated by praying at a mosque or at home, visiting relatives and neighbors, eating special foods and sweets, and, on Idd il Hajj, slaughtering a goat and sharing the meat with family and neighbors. During the month of Ramadan, Swahili Muslims fast from sunrise to sunset. Even though Swahili people endure the hardships of going without food, water, or cigarettes for about 14 hours each day, Ramadan is a very festive time. After breaking the fast at the end of each day by eating a date and drinking strong coffee, families enjoy a meal of many different delicious foods. Then the evening and most of the night is spent visiting friends, watching videos, praying, playing cards, or, as Idd nears, going shopping at the stores, which stay open late. The last meal is eaten shortly before dawn. Maulidi, or the Prophet's Birthday, is widely celebrated by Muslims; however, the largest celebration in all of East Africa is hosted by the island of Lamu. Thousands of Swahili and other Muslims come for the occasion that lasts several days and includes large gatherings for prayers at the main mosque and many cultural events. Older men dazzle the crowds with the subtle beauty of their "cane dance," which they perform by holding canes as they sway slowly from side to side. Young people wander the island, and groups of religious school students march in a parade.

⁷ RITES OF PASSAGE

Prior to giving birth most women return to their parents' homes to receive help from their female relatives. Once the newborn is washed, a relative whispers *Allahu Akbar* ("God is Great") into each ear to call him or her into the Muslim faith. Seven days after birth, males are circumcised in a ceremony attended by family members. Newborns wear a string around the waist with charms, and black ink is painted on the forehead to ward off bad spirits. A new mother rests at her parents' home for 40 days after giving birth. As she regains her strength, relatives help her to care for the new baby.

There are no specific rites of passage for children or teens. Birthday parties are increasingly popular, and these celebrations include eating cake, disco dancing, and opening presents. Ceremonies associated with secular and religious school, such as graduations, are occasions for marking a young person's educational progress. For example, most religious and secular schools hold yearly performances where students recite lectures and poems.

Marriage marks a person's transition to adulthood. Marriages are usually arranged by parents who try to find a kind, responsible, and appealing spouse for their child. A young woman cannot get married without her father's permission, and at the same time she has the right to refuse someone chosen for her. Prior to the wedding, a female relative or family friend counsels the bride about her duties as a wife. Weddings can include several days of separate celebrations for men and women, such as dancing and drumming, musical performances, viewing the bride in all her finery, and eating lavish meals. Only men attend the actual marriage vows, which take place in a mosque. A male relative represents the bride. One of the women's events, attended by only close relatives, is a purification rite during which the bride's skin and hair are beautified with herbs.

Muslims are buried within 24 hours of dying. They are wrapped in a white cloth and carried to the graveyard by men who offer prayers. The female relatives of the deceased stay at the house wailing to express their sorrow. Women friends and family gather to comfort the bereaved and to pray. Relatives sponsor remembrance prayers forty days after the burial and again after one year.

⁸ INTERPERSONAL RELATIONS

Swahili people are as likely to greet one another with the Arabic greeting *"Asalaam Aleikhum"* as they are to say *"Jambo,"* which is the common Kiswahili greeting in East Africa. People who know each other exchange a string of greetings enquiring about the health of family members and the latest news. Greetings can reflect the time of day (*"Habari za asubuhi?"*— "What's new this morning?") or the length of time since a previous encounter (*"Habari tangu jana?"*—"What's new since yesterday?"). Upon entering a Swahili house, a guest greets everyone present, shaking each person's hand. From a very young age children are taught to greet an elder with respect by kissing his or her hand. Friends who have not seen each other for a long time grasp hands warmly and kiss on both cheeks.

Swahili people greatly value modest behavior. To guard against romantic relationships developing outside of marriage, men and women are not permitted to mix freely. Most people pursue their daily activities with others of the same gender. Close relatives interact across gender lines, although women are encouraged to congregate at home, while men spend time in public places.

As in many parts of Africa and the Middle East, the right hand is considered "clean" and the left "dirty." Accordingly, most gestures between people—shaking hands, eating communally, or even handing something to someone—are done with the right hand. A polite way to accept a gift is to place the left hand under the upturned right palm. To indicate that something (e.g., a bus, a room, a cup) is full (of people, water, etc.) the left fist is clapped against the right palm striking the base of the thumb in several quick movements. It is considered rude to call someone over by using the index finger. Instead, the right hand is extended and the straight fingers bent to the palm in a sharp inward gesture repeated several times.

Because coastal culture is marked by frequent coming and going, visiting is a well-established custom. Visitors call out *"Hodi!"* to announce their arrival, and the response *"Karibu!"* welcomes them in. Many women either go visiting or receive visitors daily, usually in the late afternoon. Friends and relatives coming from far away are welcomed to spend the night.

Because marriages are usually arranged by family members, dating between men and women of any age is frowned on and generally non-existent. Also, gender segregation makes it difficult for people of the opposite sex to meet openly. But young people (and some older ones too) do manage to meet each other in school, at social events like weddings or parades, or even when traveling on the bus. They routinely succeed in striking up friendships and sometimes fall in love. Secret phone calls to boyfriends or girlfriends are a favorite pastime of young people brave enough to risk severe reprimands from disapproving parents.

⁹ LIVING CONDITIONS

Swahili people suffer the diseases of developing countries, such as malaria, yellow fever, and polio, and, because they eat a diet high in fat, they also experience the diseases of industrialized countries, such as cancer, high blood pressure, and diabetes. Most people have access to rudimentary medical care in government and private hospitals, although treatment is sometimes expensive. Traditional Swahili medicine includes herbal remedies, massage, and bloodletting. Also, some practitioners treat emotional troubles through prayer, protective charms, or exorcising evil spirits.

As the longtime middlemen in a mercantile economy, Swahili people are avid consumers who, depending on their means, seek out new products. Radios, TVs, VCRs, watches, and cameras are obtained from relatives or friends returning from travel outside Kenya where such goods are cheaper. Women save to buy imported clothes and jewelry for themselves and their children. Teens have limited cash, but they try to keep up with the latest fashions, such as running shoes and track suits for boys and beaded veils from the Middle East for girls.

Houses vary depending on a family's means and the type of town in which they reside. "Stone towns," like Lamu and Mombasa, are characterized by large stone houses, some divided into apartments. Some Swahili people living in "country towns" still occupy houses made of hardened mud and stones, although these are less common than houses of stone or coral.

Most homes have electricity, indoor plumbing, several bedrooms, and a living room furnished with a couch and chairs. Access to water is critical for Muslims who must wash before prayers.

In comparison with many people in Kenya, Swahili people enjoy a relatively high standard of living. They are firmly in the cash economy, even though they are more likely to have limited commercial ventures rather than big businesses. Some own their own property.

Travel among the coastal towns is an important part of Swahili life, and many Swahili men work in the transportation industry. Buses, vans, and a small number of private cars are the main means of transport.

¹⁰ FAMILY LIFE

In family matters, Swahili women are the partners of men, yet their partnership is unequal. Under Islam, husbands and fathers have authority in the home; they can make decisions for wives and daughters and compel them to behave properly to preserve the family's honor. But, Swahili women also wield considerable power in the daily life of the family, as they take charge of meals, marriage arrangements, and holiday celebrations.

The average number of children in each family has declined from 10–14 early in the 20th century to 5–8 at mid-century to 3–4 for young couples today. Women who have been educated and/or work outside the home tend to limit births. Entrusting a friend or relative to raise one's child is a common practice that draws the parents and caregivers closer together. Residents of an individual household might include many people beyond the immediate family, such as grandparents, nieces and nephews, and in-laws.

Marriages are generally arranged by family members, with preference made for marrying cousins. Most newlyweds are not well acquainted with one another; however, Waswahili believe that love grows as the marriage endures. Men are permitted to marry up to four wives, but the expectation that they must support each one equally means that most marriages are monogamous. Divorce is frequent, especially among young people who decide that the arranged choice is not working and among older couples if the husband marries another wife.

Arab heritage emphasizes relations through the father's family (patrilineal descent) as the primary form of kinship, but Swahili people also recognize close ties through their mother's relatives. Each Swahili family also identifies with a clan.

Cats live in many Swahili households, and, although children sometimes play with them, they are valued less as pets than for their service in warding off mice. Dogs are thought of as dirty and not allowed near homes.

11 CLOTHING

In the early 20th century in Swahili fishing villages, women wore brightly colored cotton cloths (*kanga* or *leso*) wrapped around their waists and upper bodies and draped over their shoulders and heads. Some women adorned themselves with plug earrings of up to an inch in diameter. Family status determined how a woman veiled. For example, wealthy women in Zanzibar Town walked unseen behind a cloth enclosure carried by servants. Men wore a striped cloth (*kikoi*) wrapped around the waist and hanging to the knees. As a mark of being Muslim some men sported small white caps with elaborate tan embroidery. Both men and women wore leather sandals, and wealthy families used wooden platform shoes when they entered the bathroom. Islam forbids men to wear precious metals, but women own gold necklaces, earrings, and bracelets. Gold, which many women receive at the time of marriage, is both an adornment and an investment that they might cash in if times become financially tough.

Clothing reflects a Swahili family's status and also an individual's personal style. Dressing well and dressing modestly are both highly valued. Women wear "Western style" dresses in many colors, patterns, and fabrics. At home, a woman might wrap a kanga around her waist, like an apron. Outside the house, she wears a long, wide, black, floor-length cloak with an attached veil, called a *buibui*. She pulls the veil tight against her cheeks and secures the fabric under her chin, leaving her face exposed. Women veil to show that they are proper Muslims from respectable families. Men wear Western-style trousers and shirts. On Fridays, or other religious occasions, they wear long, white caftans. Shorts are worn only by children.

12 FOOD

Swahili cuisine, which is highly spiced, has African, Middle Eastern, and Indian influences. Rice, the staple, is cooked with coconut milk and served with tomato-based meat, bean, or vegetable stews. Meals incorporate locally-available vegetables (eggplant, okra, and spinach), fruits (mangoes, coconuts, pineapples), and spices (cloves, cardamom, hot pepper). Fish—fried, grilled, or stewed in coconut sauce—is also central to the diet. Sweet tea with milk is served several times a day. It is prepared by placing loose, black tea (2 teaspoons) in a small saucepan with milk (1 cup) and water (1 cup). Bring to a boil, reduce heat and cook for about five minutes, stirring frequently. Bring to a boil again and cook longer if a creamier tea is desired. Stir in sugar (at least 2 teaspoons) and a pinch each of powdered ginger and powdered cardamom. Strain to serve.

Rice cooked with meat and spices (*pilau*) and served with a tart tomato and onion salad is a favorite dish for special occasions. Chicken and goat meat are popular for holiday meals. Special sweets include moist, rice flour cake flavored with coconut and *kaimati*, which resemble doughnut holes, and are soaked in rose water syrup. When Kenya's first president, Jomo Kenyatta, tasted *kaimati* for the first time, he enjoyed them so much that he asked the joking question: "Can I get the seeds that Waswahili use to grow these?"

Although increasingly people eat at tables, they often spread straw mats on the floor and sit around a large, metal tray on which is piled the rice to be shared. They pass bowls of stew, vegetables and fruit and eat either with their right hand or a spoon. Before the meal begins, food is protected from insects by brightly painted straw covers. Several utensils are needed to process coconut, which is a frequent addition to rice and stews. First, the coconut is cracked in half with a sharp blow from an iron bar. Then, the cook grates each half on a serrated blade attached to a low stool. The gratings are placed in a long straw tube, which is then soaked in water to release a thick white milk.

Waswahili, like all Muslims, are prohibited from eating pork or drinking alcohol. The members of one clan from northern Kenya observe a taboo on eating fish.

Guests are always offered something to eat or drink, and it is polite to accept. Gifts of meat or special sweets are routinely exchanged among neighbors and relatives. Even children are encouraged to share food.

A light breakfast of tea and bread is eaten early in the morning. Many people have more tea and snacks mid-morning, and the main meal is eaten in the early afternoon. Supper includes tea and leftovers or light fare, such as an omelette.

13 EDUCATION

Through Islam, literacy came to the East African coast much earlier than to most other parts of the continent. Knowing how to read the Koran is religiously important, thus Swahili people have a high rate of literacy. Some people are literate in Arabic as well as Kiswahili. Those who have been to secular school are literate in English as well.

Many adults over fifty have had no secular education. Some adults in their forties had limited primary education, and only a very small number, mostly men, went on to secondary schools. Adults in their thirties tend to have at least several years of primary education. Young people today tend to finish primary school, and some go on to secondary school. Most Swahili young people attend religious school at least several times a week where they learn to read Arabic and to recite passages from the Koran.

Most parents, particularly those in urban areas, recognize the value of education in preparing their children for employment. Families vary as to whether they believe that girls should be educated as extensively as boys. The availability of single sex schools can affect this decision.

14 CULTURAL HERITAGE

Taarab music, which has distinctly Arabic origins, is performed at weddings and concerts. Band members play keyboards, flutes, brass instruments, and drums to accompany singers. Many of the Kiswahili lyrics are double entendres that hint at romantic love.

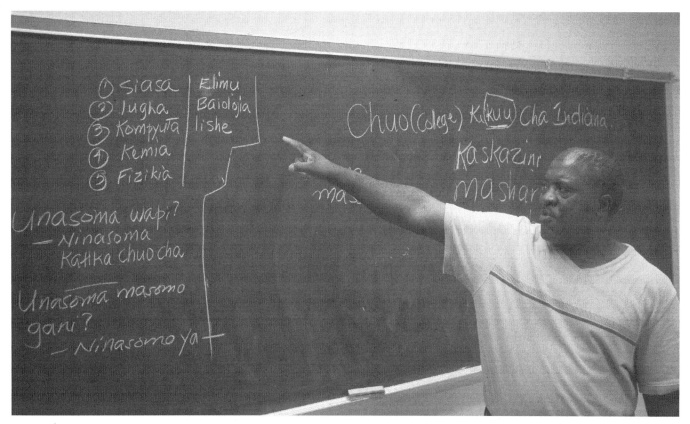

University of Kansas teacher Leonce Rushubirwa, from the United Republic of Tanzania in East Africa, helps students learn the African language of Swahili at the University of Indiana. About 80 students enrolled in a seven-week course at the Summer Cooperative African Language Institute. The goal of the course was to increase the number of competent African language speakers in the United States. (AP Images/Herald-Times, Jeremy Hogan)

Several women's dance groups perform at weddings for all-female audiences. They dance *chakacha*, which resembles belly dancing, and also *lelemama*, a very subtle dance with tiny hand movements. These groups used to engage in competitions, and they wore elaborate costumes, including military uniforms.

Kiswahili oral literature includes songs, sayings, stories, and riddles. The main written form is poetry. Kiswahili poems, which include long epics, prayers, and meditations on many subjects, conform to a complex rhyme and meter.

15 WORK

Some Swahili still fish, farm, and trade as they did in previous generations. But the difficult local economy has meant that many people are unemployed or dependent on the unpredictable tourist industry. Educated men and women enter the civil service and work in offices, shops, and schools. Although husbands are obligated to provide for their families, many wives earn money for their families through cooking food, sewing, or trading from their homes.

16 SPORTS

Few adults play sports. Many boys join soccer teams and play in hotly contested competitions. Soccer matches involving Kenyan regional teams or local boys' clubs provide rare, though exciting entertainment, mostly for men. In school, girls play

sports such as netball and track. Children are sometimes taken to swim at the ocean.

17 ENTERTAINMENT AND RECREATION

Weddings and holiday celebrations are the most important forms of entertainment. The main guests at weddings are adults; however, young people enjoy weddings too, especially the musical concerts at night. Groups of young women, using their veils as camouflage, watch the wedding festivities from the sidelines. Traveling to and from weddings, people sing songs and celebrate with vigor.

There are only a few theaters in the urban areas, and young men are the most likely to attend films. Watching videos is a favorite pastime, especially for women and young people. Although not every household has a television and VCR, people tend to know friends or relatives with whom they can watch videos, such as action films from Japan, romances from India, Islamic epics, and detective stories from the United States. If a video contains love scenes, an adult might fast-forward to protect the modesty of those present. Local and foreign soap operas, news, and sports are also popular. Young people enjoy music tapes and music videos from the United States, Europe, India, and the Middle East. Several local bands are also popular, although men are much more likely than women to see them perform. On the weekends, young people sometimes go to discos, and women enjoy walking on the beach or going for a picnic.

[18] FOLK ART, CRAFTS, AND HOBBIES

Artisans on the island of Lamu are famous for their intricately carved wooden furniture and doors. They also construct miniature, painted replicas of the boats (*dhows*) used for fishing. Young boys play with these at the shore. Women use brown colored henna to paint complex flower designs on their hands and feet (up to the knees) as preparation for attending a wedding. The color, which stains the skin and nails, lasts for several weeks.

[19] SOCIAL PROBLEMS

Waswahili view the declining economy and erosion of their culture by tourism as significant social problems. Tourists who walk around in immodest clothing (e.g., shorts and bikinis), drink alcohol in public, and encourage loose behavior among young people have threatened the proper Islamic life that many Swahili people struggle to maintain.

Waswahili face some discrimination by Kenyans who have resented their connection to the slave trade and their ties to Middle Eastern wealth. Their role in Kenyan politics, though marginal, is increasing as Kenya moves forward in multiparty democracy.

Although some individuals drink alcohol, even to excess, the Islamic prohibition mentioned above guards against widespread alcoholism. A more worrisome problem is the growing prevalence of drug use (marijuana) among young men, which is condemned as anti-social. However, chewing *miraa*, a plant grown locally that contains a mild stimulant, is regarded as an acceptable social activity in which participants share stories and jokes as well as the bubble gum that must be chewed to hide miraa's bitter taste.

[20] GENDER ISSUES

Although Swahili culture is generally a heavily patriarchal system, women did once play vital roles both socially and politically. There is recorded evidence that show that Swahili women held high political positions, some of the women ruled as queens while others as chiefs. Even while male rulers predominated, some women occupied positions of authority, such as Asha Binti Muhammad, Chief of Ngumi in AD 1686; Mwana Mkishi, the first ruler of Mombasa around AD 1500; Queen of Pemba in AD 1686; and other queens such as Mwana Fatuma binti Darhash, Mwana Aisha and Mwana Mize binti Mnaba. After the 17th century, however, tilted political positions remained the exclusive domain of men.

In the traditional Swahili society, women fully participated in familial and public festivities. They were not excluded from attending mosques alongside men and even went through literacy programs just like their male counterparts. Women became literate and studied formal Islamic sciences. They even enjoyed the rights to property and inheritance just as men did. However, Swahili women slowly lost control of economic resources and were increasingly denied access to education. Despite the strides made in education in East Africa, Swahili women still occupy subordinate roles to men in religious, economic, and political spheres.

[21] BIBLIOGRAPHY

Abdulaziz, Mohamed. *Muyaka: 19th Century Swahili Popular Poetry.* Nairobi: Kenya Literature Bureau, 1979.

Allen, James de Vere. *Swahili Origins.* London: James Currey, 1993.

Askew, Kelly. *Performing the Nation: Swahili Music and Cultural Politics in Tanzania.* Chicago: University of Chicago Press, 2002.

Bakari, Mtoro bin Mwinyi *The Customs of the Swahili People.* Berkeley: University of California Press, 1981.

Caplan, Pat."But, the Coast, of Course, Is Quite Different': Academic and Local Ideas about the East African Littoral," *Journal of East African Studies,* 1 (2): 305-320, 2007

———. *African Voices, African Lives. Personal Narratives from a Swahili Village.* London: Routledge, 1997.

Eastman, Carol. "Who Are the Waswahili?" *Africa* 41(3): 228236, 1971.

Fair, Laura. *Pastimes and Politics: Culture, Community, and Identity in Post-Abolition Zanzibar, 1890-1945.* Oxford: James Currey, 2001.

Fuglesang, Minou. *Veils and Videos: Female Youth Culture on the Kenyan Coast.* Stockholm: Stockholm Studies in Social Anthropology, 1994.

Glassman, Jonathan, "Sorting out the Tribes: The creation of Racial Identities in Colonial Zanzibar's Newspaper Wars," Journal of African History 41 (2000), pages 395-428.

Hirsch, Susan F. *Pronouncing and Persevering: Gender and the Discourses of Disputing in Coastal Kenyan Islamic Courts.* Chicago: University of Chicago Press, forthcoming.

Horton, Mark. "The Swahili Corridor." *Scientific American* 257:8693.

Knappert, Jan. *Four Centuries of Swahili Verse: A Literary History and Anthology.* London: Heinemann, 1979.

Matsuoka, Atsuko and John Sorenson, Ghosts and Shadows: Construction of Identity and Community in an African Diaspora. Toronto, Buffalo, London: University of Toronto Press, 2001.

Mazrui, Alamin M. and Ibrahim Noor Shariff. *The Swahili: Idiom and Identity of an African People.* Trenton: Africa World Press, 1994.

Middleton, John. *The World of the Swahili: An African Mercantile Civilization.* New Haven: Yale University Press, 1992.

Mirza, Sarah and Margaret Strobel (ed.). *Three Swahili Women: Life Histories From Mombasa, Kenya.* Bloomington: Indiana University Press. Nurse, Derek and Thomas Spear, 1989.

Porter, Mary. *Swahili Identity in Post-Colonial Kenya: The Reproduction of Gender in Educational Discourses.* Seattle: University of Washington. Ph.D. Dissertation, 1992.

Strobel, Margaret. *Muslim Women in Mombasa 18901975.* New Haven: Yale University Press, 1979.

The Swahili: Reconstructing the History and Language of an African Society. Philadelphia: University of Pennsylvania Press, 1985.

Swartz, Marc J. *The Way the World Is: Cultural Processes and Social Relations among the Mombasa Swahili.* Berkeley: University of California Press, 1991.

Willis, Justin. *Mombasa, the Swahili, and the Making of the Mijikenda.* Oxford: Clarendon Press, 1993.

—revised by M. Njoroge

SWAZIS

PRONUNCIATION: SWAH-zeez
LOCATION: Swaziland
POPULATION: 1,100,000 (2006)
LANGUAGE: SiSwati
RELIGION: Christianity (various sects), traditional religious beliefs, and Islam

¹ INTRODUCTION

Swazi history dates back to the late 16th century when the first Swazi king, Ngwane II, settled southeast of modern-day Swaziland. His grandson, Sobhuza I, established a permanent capital and drew the resident Nguni and Sotho people within a centralized political system. During the mid-19th century, Sobhuza's heir, Mswati II, from whom the Swazis derive their name, expanded the Swazi nation to an area much larger than modern Swaziland. Mswati established contact with the British, who later made Swaziland a protectorate following the Anglo-Boer War of 1899–1902. Swaziland became independent in 1968.

Today, Swaziland's government is headed by a dual monarchy, consisting of Mswati III, the hereditary king and head of state who is titled *Ingwenyama* (Lion), and the queen mother who is titled *Indlovukati* (Lady Elephant). This traditional structure operates parallel to a "modern" (post-European contact) structure, consisting of the administrative head of government, i.e., the prime minister, and statutory bodies including a cabinet and a bicameral parliament, which enacts legislation subject to approval by the king. Swaziland did not have a Constitution after 1973; a Constitutional Review Commission (CRC) submitted proposals for a new Constitution to the King, and it was adopted in 2006.

² LOCATION AND HOMELAND

The Swazi reside primarily in Swaziland, a small landlocked country of 17,363 sq km (6,704 sq mi) which is perched on the edge of the southern African escarpment. It is bounded on three sides by South Africa and on the fourth side by Mozambique, both countries also housing many ethnic Swazis. Four distinctive topographic steps largely determine the characteristics of its natural environment: the highveld, middleveld, lowveld, and the Lubombo mountain range.

Swazi identity is based on allegiance to the dual monarchy, and ethnic Swazis living in the Republic of South Africa and Mozambique are not under its effective political control. In 2006, the World Bank estimated the total number of Swazis at about 1.1 million people. The population is growing at a rate of 2.9% per year, and nearly half (44.4%) of all Swazis are 14 years of age or younger. Swaziland is one of the few African countries with a homogeneous (sharing common descent) population. Most Swazis live in rural homesteads, but in the middleveld, where nearly one-half of the Swazi population resides, rural homesteads are interspersed with densely populated settlements around employment centers. The two major cities are Mbabane and Manzini.

³ LANGUAGE

"Swazi" refers to the nation, tribe, or ethnic group. The language spoken is referred to as "siSwati." SiSwati speakers are found in Swaziland, South Africa, and Mozambique. SiSwati is a tonal Bantu language of the Nguni group, closely related to Zulu and, more distantly, to Xhosa. It is spoken in Swaziland and in the Eastern Transvaal province of the Republic of South Africa. Little has been published in SiSwati.

⁴ FOLKLORE

Swazi oral historical tradition is arguably the richest still existing in southern Africa. The reason largely lies in the fact that the Swazis' political structure was not disrupted following colonial rule to the same degree as were the structures of other southern African kingdoms. Elder Swazis still recount rich histories of their forebears—numerous conquering kings and chiefs—dating back several centuries. The first king, Ngwane II, who led his followers from their home on the east coast and moved inland, is commemorated in one of many royal praise-songs, "Nkosi Dlamini—You scourged the Lebombo in your flight."

⁵ RELIGION

Adherents of traditional Swazi religion believe in an aloof supreme being known as *Mkhulumnqande*, who created the earth but who is not worshipped and is not associated with the ancestral spirits *(emadloti)*. He demands no sacrifices. Swazis believe that ancestral spirits are ranked, as are humans. Men play important roles in traditional religious life, offering sacrifices for the spirits, but women, acting as diviners, also communicate with spirits. The Queen Mother serves as custodian of rain "medicines." Among the Swazi, spirits take many forms, sometimes possessing people and influencing their welfare, primarily their health.

The Methodists established the first Christian mission in Swaziland. Currently, many Christian sects are present in the country, ranging from the more eclectic Catholics to the more rigid Afrikaner Calvinists. Although the statistical breakdown of adherents to different religions varies in different accounts, it is probably reasonable to state that the population is approximately 35% Protestant, 25% Roman Catholic, 30% Zionist (indigenous Christianity), and 10% Islamic or other beliefs. The majority of Swazis are registered as Christian, but it should be noted that most Swazis also follow traditional beliefs. Moreover, as the statistics above indicate, a significant number of Christian converts belong to Zionist churches, which practice a flexible dogma and great tolerance of custom.

⁶ MAJOR HOLIDAYS

The annual ritual of kingship, the *Incwala,* is a traditional national holiday that is rich in Swazi symbolism and only understandable in terms of the social organization and major values of Swazi life. The central figure is the king, who alone can authorize its performance. The *Incwala* reflects the growth of the king, and his subjects play parts determined by their status, primarily rank and gender. Before this ceremony (which is sometimes described as a "first fruits ceremony" or a "ritual of rebellion") can be performed during a three-week period each year, considerable organizational and preparatory activities must be undertaken. For example, water and sacred plants are

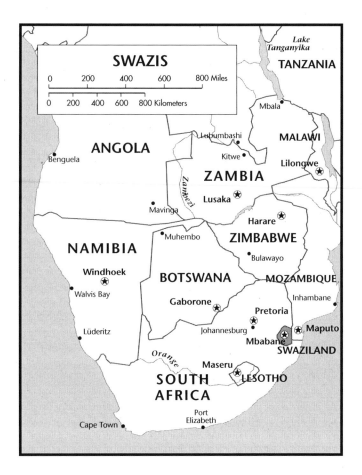

about manhood and service to the king. A girl, upon having her first menstruation, is isolated in a hut for several days and instructed by her mother about observances and taboos. The Swazi have not circumcised males since King Mswati's reign in the mid-19th century, but both boys and girls traditionally had their ears cut (ukusika tindlebe).

Following puberty, a girl's and boy's families begin marriage negotiations. A man and his family acquire rights to children by transferring to the woman's family bride-wealth (lobola) valuables such as cattle and nowadays some cash. A new bride thereafter goes to live with her husband and in-laws. In contemporary Swaziland, a couple may contract one of several forms of marriage: a customary marriage, which may take the form of a "love" marriage, an arranged marriage (ukwendzisa), or a bride-capture marriage (the third form is uncommon and may not involve the exchange of bride-wealth), or a Christian marriage. In the past, a preferred form of customary marriage was the sororate, in which a woman married her sister's husband, thereby becoming the subsidiary wife (inhlanti). A customary marriage ceremony, particularly for high-ranking couples, tends to involve numerous and protracted ritual exchanges between the families (sometimes lasting decades), and brings into play singing, dancing, wailing, gift-giving, and feasting. In recent years, greater numbers of individuals have opted to elope or remain single.

Following death, the corpse of a deceased person undergoes a mortuary ritual that varies according to the deceased's status and his or her relationship with different categories of mourners. The more important a deceased person was the more elaborate are the funerary rites given his or her corpse—especially true in the case of a deceased king. The closer the blood or marital ties were between a deceased person and a mourner, the more elaborate is the mourner's ritualized display of grief. A widow may be expected to continue her husband's lineage through the levirate (ngena), in which she marries a brother or another male relative of her deceased husband; however, this practice is not practiced as frequently as in the past. Many Swazis believe that the spirit of a deceased person can manifest itself in illness and in various omens, occasionally materializing in the form of a snake.

8 INTERPERSONAL RELATIONS

The Swazi, who like the Zulu were once feared as fierce warriors, display a multiplicity of traits in their daily interactions. They can be generous to a hungry stranger or receptive to a jovial comrade, but they can also be proud and arrogant to the unfortunate stranger who transgresses the rules of social propriety. In particular, the Swazi demand strict adherence to rules concerned with kingship and the associated sociopolitical hierarchy: forms of greetings; body language; and gestures. According to custom, youth must show deference to their elders, women to men, and low-ranking persons to high-ranking persons. People demonstrate respect by lowering their eyes, kneeling, and moving quietly.

An interesting symbolic representation of interpersonal relations among Swazis was once found—and to some extent is still found—in beads. In the past, a newborn baby was welcomed into the world with white "luck" beads placed around its waist, wrists, and/or ankles. An adult wore beads to designate his or her social status (i.e., commoner or royalty) and love or marital status. Regarding the latter, a young woman

collected at distant points to strengthen and purify the king. Thereafter, the oldest warrior regiment opens the Incwala. Sacred songs that are concerned with the important events of kingship (a king's marriage to his main ritual wife, the return of ancestral cattle from the royal grave, and the burial of kings) as well as dances are performed. Themes of fertility and potency predominate. Celebrants are adorned in striking clothing, including feathers of special birds and skins of wild animals. The Incwala symbolizes the unity of the state and attempts to reinforce it: it dramatizes power struggles between the king and the princes, or between the aristocrats and commoners, with the Swazi king ultimately triumphing. Other national royal rituals include the Reed Dance and rainmaking rites, while local rituals include funerals, marriages, and initiations.

A contemporary national holiday is Independence Day, which has been celebrated since the country's independence from Britain on 6 September 1968.

7 RITES OF PASSAGE

During childhood, young Swazi boys play and run errands around rural homesteads until they are old enough to accompany their age-mates to the fields with the cattle herds. Young Swazi girls play and help their mothers with minor domestic chores and child care. Fathers may play a small role in child rearing—especially if they are employed at distant locations within Swaziland or in South Africa.

At puberty, a boy is tended by a traditional healer and eventually joins his age (warrior) regiment (libutfo), where he learns

Swazis participating in the Umhlanga (Reed Dance) in celebration of the Harvest Festival. (Jason Laure)

gave beadwork to her sweetheart as a token of love. In a sense, beadwork served as her "courting letter," with different bead patterns representing different stages in the courtship. Within the beadwork pattern were symbols that represented letters and words that communicated ideas. In "reading" a beadwork love message, groups of girls noted the meaning of the bead color, its position in the pattern, the background on which it was fitted, and the sex or social status of the recipient.

⁹ LIVING CONDITIONS

Everyday concerns of Swazis relate to housing, transport, and the acquisition of basic household necessities. Many consumer items are available—particularly to people who reside in urban areas and receive an income through wage labor. In urban areas people have better access to public transport, medical services, and jobs, and they are also better situated to receive electricity and piped water. Most people buy manufactured blankets, clothing, and cookware; many people buy "prestige" items such as battery-operated radios; and a few people are able to purchase cars or trucks for transport. Most people satisfy their food requirements through their own or relatives' labors in agriculture and animal husbandry, although nearly all people purchase processed foods such as bread, sugar, and tea. Most Swazis construct their own homes from rocks, logs, clay, and thatch; those persons with sufficient funds hire builders and buy corrugated iron roofs, glass windows, and solid wood doors.

A special concern of Swazis relates to health and general well-being. Swazis direct their health concerns to both Western-influenced, biomedical practitioners and traditional practitioners. Many Swazis believe that traditional practitioners, who serve a much larger segment of the population, identify and correct the imbalances between the human and spirit worlds that lead to misfortunes and illnesses. These practitioners are of three types: herbalists or *tinyanga* (about 50%), diviner-mediums or *tangoma* (about 40%), and Christian faith-healers (about 10%). Men are usually tinyanga, and women are usually tangoma. Most Swazis believe that serious diseases do not simply happen; rather, they are created and sent mystically by a person of ill-will. Swazis differentiate between conditions or diseases that are "African" and conditions or diseases that are foreign; they emphasize that a condition, such as madness caused by sorcery, is best treated by traditional medicine and practitioners, while a disease, such as cholera, is best treated by Western medicine and biomedical practitioners. In the current context of the AIDS pandemic, both biomedical and traditional practitioners are treating patients; importantly, the two types of practitioners are often working cooperatively in treating patients.

¹⁰ FAMILY LIFE

In rural areas, the ordinary Swazi resides in a homestead, *umuti*, which is headed by a male homestead head, *umnumzana*, who is assisted by his wife (or main wife in a polygamous mar-

Swazi nuclear families typically are large by American standards, with six children or more. (Cory Langley)

riage). The head determines resource allocation such as land distribution, makes major decisions regarding both production (plowing and types of crops grown) and economic expenditures, and mobilizes homestead labor. Homestead residents have access as individuals to arable land, and as community members to communal pasturage.

Within a complex homestead are households; each household *(indlu)* generally consists of one nuclear family (a man, his wife, and their children) whose members share agricultural tasks and eat from one kitchen. Sometimes a wife has an attached co-wife, *inhlanti,* who, along with her children, forms part of the same "house." A married son and his wife (wives) and dependents may form another house within the wider "house" of his mother.

Many Swazi homesteads have few or no chairs or beds, and people therefore sit and sleep on grass mats. If a homestead lacks a stove, women or girls will cook on an open fire in a hut or in the yard. Women's and men's utensils and tools may be limited and homemade. Homestead residents are resourceful in accomplishing tasks: for example, some women clean their earthen floors by smearing moistened cow dung over them—a process which leaves them smooth and sweet-smelling.

11 CLOTHING

Swazis wear either traditional or modern-day clothing in both towns and rural areas and for both everyday and ceremonial purposes. Men's traditional clothing consists of a colorful cloth "skirt" covered by an *emajobo* (hide apron), further

adorned by various ornamental items on ceremonial occasions: the *ligcebesha* (neckband), *umgaco* (ties), *sagibo* (walking stick), *siphandle* (limb ornaments), and in the case of royals, the *ligwalagwala* (red feathers). Women's traditional clothing consists of the *ilihhiya* (cloth). Married women cover their upper torso and sometimes wear traditional "beehive" hairstyles, whereas single women sometimes wear only beads over their upper torso—particularly at special ceremonies, such as the Reed Dance performed in honor of the Queen Mother.

12 FOOD

Swazis cultivate maize, sorghum, beans, groundnuts, and sweet potatoes for consumption. They also raise cattle, the traditional basis of wealth and status within their society, as well as smaller livestock. Mealie-meal (ground maize) serves as the primary food and is accompanied by cultivated or wild vegetables and meat—chicken on ordinary occasions and beef on festive occasions. Sometimes traditional Swazi beer is brewed.

Most people eat a breakfast consisting of tea, bread, and/or sour-milk porridge; a lunch consisting of bread or leftovers; and a dinner consisting of porridge, vegetables, and meat. Although most people eat from metal, plastic, or ceramic dishware, some people follow customary practice, thereby drinking beer from a black clay pot and eating meat from a carved, wooden bowl. Many people enjoy sharing food from the same plate or bowl with their friends and age-mates; each person scoops out food with his or her fingers.

13 EDUCATION

In the past, Swazi children were educated within their families and age-groups. Both boys and girls were taught domestic and agricultural tasks, and boys were instructed in warfare. Today, intertribal warfare no longer exists, but male members of the warrior age-classes *(emabutfo)* continue to learn how to perform ritual functions.

In contemporary Swaziland, children receive a secular education under the auspices of the Ministry of Education. Many children attend mission schools which convey Christian values. Schoolchildren do their lessons from siSwati textbooks in the lower grades and English textbooks in the higher grades. SiSwati literary tradition is not highly developed as the language was not put into writing until the 20th century.

Only those children whose families can afford to pay their annual school fees receive a formal education. Mothers often assume primary responsibility for earning the money to educate their children; they prepare and sell crops, handicrafts, and other goods to pay the school fees and purchase uniforms. Children who complete school are expected to assist with the education of their younger siblings and to care for their parents in old age.

The ongoing AIDS pandemic has created many orphans—most of whom lack sufficient funds to pay for their education. When the government allocated money in 2003 to pay the school fees of orphans, the impoverished parents of other children complained about favoritism. In any case, the money proved to be vastly inadequate to assist all orphaned children. By 2006, UNICEF estimated that 80,000 children had been orphaned by AIDS in Swaziland.

¹⁴ CULTURAL HERITAGE

Swazis have inherited a rich tradition of music and dance. Their ceremonial music has been unaffected by Western influence and retains a distinctive individual style which sets it apart from that of related ethnic groups. Nonetheless, the *siBhaca* recreational dance music has been adopted from the Xhosa-speaking people of South Africa.

Swazi women sing together as they work in groups on tasks such as digging or weeding, and men sing together as they pay tribute to their chiefs or past and present kings. Celebrants also perform special songs at weddings, royal rituals, coming-of-age ceremonies, and national Independence Day festivities. Swazi praise-poets have long been known throughout southern Africa. They compose praise-poems for kings, chiefs, and prominent persons.

Swazi specialists craft musical instruments to accompany popular singing and dancing activities: among those instruments used either in the past or present are the *luvene* (hunting horn), *impalampala* (kudu bull horn), *ligubhu* and *makhweyane* (a calabash attached to a wooden bow), and *livenge* (a wind instrument made from a plant). Some people play drums and European instruments.

¹⁵ WORK

Swazis divide work tasks according to sex, age, and pedigree. Men construct house frames and cattle *kraals* (corrals), plow, tend and milk cattle, sew skins, and cut shields; some men are particularly accomplished at warfare, animal husbandry, hunting, and governing. Women hoe, plant and harvest crops, tend small livestock, thatch, plait ropes, weave mats and baskets, grind grain, brew beer, cook foods, and care for children; some women also specialize in pot- and mat-making. Age is important in determining who will perform tasks associated with ritual performances. Rank is important in determining who will summon people for work parties in district and national enterprises and who will supervise the workers. Nowadays, some men migrate within Swaziland and to South Africa in search of work and income.

In contemporary Swaziland, people derive income from various agricultural and commercial activities. The country's main export crop is sugar, based on irrigated cane. Several other cash crops, including maize, rice, vegetables, cotton, tobacco, citrus fruits, and pineapples, are traded both within and outside the country. Swaziland's mineral wealth, which consists of iron ore, coal, diamonds, and asbestos, is mined for export. Meat and meat products are also exported. The industrial estate at Matsapha produces processed agricultural and forestry products, garments, textiles, and many light manufactured goods. According to government statistics from 2000, 63,598 people were employed in the private sector, and 28,554 people were employed in the public sector. As of 2004, the national unemployment rate was 31%.

¹⁶ SPORTS

Soccer (i.e., football) is popular throughout the country and is played by boys and men. In rural areas, both boys and girls play games with various sorts of balls which are often homemade from twine or rubber.

¹⁷ ENTERTAINMENT AND RECREATION

In the past, various ritual ceremonies, including weddings and funerals, provided the main opportunities for people within and across communities to gather and enjoy themselves. Feasts were held and traditional dances were performed. Some elder Swazis currently lament that young men no longer know the traditional warrior dance, the *umgubho*.

Nowadays, with family members living and working in distant locations, and with the advent of technological innovations, the occasions and forms of entertainment have changed. In urban areas, where electricity is more readily available, some households have televisions. In rural areas, many households have battery-operated radios and people enjoy musical, news, and sports programs. Rural Swazi children, as in many parts of Africa, usually do not have sufficient money to buy manufactured toys; nonetheless, they are adept at creating toys out of discarded items, such as tires, tin cans, wires, and maize cobs. Boys build intricate, moveable toy cars from rubber and metal scraps, and girls fashion dolls from maize cobs.

¹⁸ FOLK ART, CRAFTS, AND HOBBIES

In the past, smithing, a task assigned to men, was a prestigious activity that produced iron hoes, knives, and various kinds of spears as weapons of war. Today, smithing is less important, but pottery-making and woodcarving continue. Pottery-making, using the coil technique, is a task assigned to women. Basket-weaving is also done by women. Woodcarving, a task performed by both men and women, results in functional, unornamented implements and utensils, such as meat dishes and spoons. Schools are encouraging the production of masks or sculptured figures for the tourist trade.

¹⁹ SOCIAL PROBLEMS

In present-day Swaziland, various social and economic changes, including altered sex roles, increased job competition, labor migration, and the growth of an educated elite class, have produced new problems. These problems include, for example, an increase in crime and alcoholism—particularly in the outskirts of urban areas. Some Swazis complain that they are no longer able to deal effectively with their problems because traditional "witchfinding" is legally prohibited, thus freeing perceived social miscreants to behave as they please.

Some Swazis argue that a significant social-political problem concerns the hierarchical ranking system, headed by the King and the royal family. In recent years, this system has been challenged by disaffected new elites who have achieved status through the acquisition of an education and wealth but who do not have hereditary position.

Most Swazis, as well as outside observers, argue that the country's most significant social problem concerns a health issue, the HIV prevalence rate, which at 38.8% of the country's adult population (2003 estimate), is the highest in the world. In 2007, life expectancy was less than 33 years. As indicated above, huge numbers of children who were orphaned by AIDS are not well cared for and face an uncertain future.

²⁰ GENDER ISSUES

Swazi society is patriarchal, with men continuing to hold positions of power in both the private and public sectors. Before Swaziland's new constitution was adopted in 2006, women had the legal status of minors and were unable to own property or open a bank account without the permission of a male relative or husband. Some observers have linked Swazi women's low status to their high HIV infection rates as well as to the high rates of sexual violence against them (a survey in 2007 indicated that one in three Swazi women experienced some form of sexual violence before turning 18). In addition, some observers attribute the high rate of sexual violence against Swazi women and girls to the belief by some HIV-positive men that sleeping with a virgin girl can prevent AIDS. It remains to be seen whether the new constitution, together with new legislation and policy—particularly as concern land and property rights—will eventually improve women's status in practice.

[21] BIBLIOGRAPHY

Beidelman, T. O. "Swazi Royal Ritual." *Africa*, vol. 36, no. 4, 1966: 373–405.

Daly, J. "AIDS in Swaziland: The Battle from Within." African Studies Review, vol. 44, no.1, 2001: 21-35.

Green, E. C. "The Integration of Modern and Traditional Health Sectors in Swaziland." In *Anthropological Praxis,* edited by R. Wulff and S. Fiske. Boulder, CO: Westview Press, 1987.

Kuper, Hilda. *An African Aristocracy: Rank among the Swazi.* London: Oxford University Press, for the International African Institute, 1947.

———. *The Swazi: A South African Kingdom.* New York: Holt, Rinehart and Winston, 1963.

Marwick, Brian Allan. *The Swazi: An Ethnographic Account of the Swaziland Protectorate.* Cambridge: Cambridge University Press, 1940.

Ngubane, Harriet. "The Swazi Homestead." In *The Swazi Rural Homestead,* edited by Fion de Vletter. Social Science Research Unit, University of Swaziland, 1983.

Nhlapo, Ronald Thandabantu. *Marriage and Divorce in Swazi Law and Custom.* Mbabane, Swaziland: Websters, 1992.

Rose, Laurel L. *The Politics of Harmony: Land Dispute Strategies in Swaziland.* Cambridge: Cambridge University Press, 1992.

———. "Women's Strategies for Customary Land Access in Swaziland and Malawi: A Comparative Study." *Africa Today,* vol. 49, no. 2, 2002: 122-149.

Twala, Regina G. "Beads as Regulating the Social Life of the Zulu and Swazi." *African Studies*, vol. 10, 1951: 113–23.

Zigira, Christopher Amherst Byuma. *Religion, Culture and Gender: A Study of Women's Search for Gender Equality in Swaziland.* Ph.D. dissertation, University of South Africa, 2000.

—by L. Rose

TANZANIANS

PRONUNCIATION: tan-zuh-NEE-uhns
LOCATION: Tanzania
POPULATION: 39.3 million
LANGUAGE: Swahili; English; Arabic; 130 indigenous languages
RELIGION: Islam; Christianity; indigenous beliefs
RELATED ARTICLES: Vol. 1: Chagga; Luo; Maasai; Nyamwezi

[1] INTRODUCTION

The United Republic of Tanzania, or *Jamhuri ya Mwungano wa Tanzania,* includes the mainland of Tanganyika, Zanzibar, and some offshore islands. Zanzibar and the coast have a long history of lucrative trading, which Arabs, Europeans, and Africans each have attempted to control. In 1840 the Sultan of Omani established his capital in Zanzibar. From there the caravan trade brought the Swahili language and Islam into the hinterlands as far as what is now the eastern part of the Democratic Republic of the Congo. In 1885, the Germans gained control and made Tanzania a protectorate, incorporating it into German East Africa along with Burundi and Rwanda. Dispossessed of its colonies after World War I, Germany ceded control to the British, who ruled until 1946 under a League of Nations mandate. The UN made Tanzania a trust territory under British rule after 1946.

Anti-colonial sentiment grew as the British administration favored white settlers and immigrant farmers. In 1929 Tanzanians formed the Tanganyika African Association. Julius Nyerere transformed it into the Tanganyika African National Union in 1954. Nyerere's party won 70 of 71 seats in the national assembly in 1960, and he became prime minister in May 1961. On 9 December 1961, Tanzania gained its full independence.

After independence, Tanzania embarked on an ambitious, large-scale project of national self-reliance. Led by Nyerere, the teacher *(mwalimu),* the government promoted *ujamaa* (family villages), whose aim was to bring scattered families together in village cooperatives. Simultaneously, under the Arusha Declaration of 1967, Nyerere's single-party government nationalized banks, industry, schools, and transport. The main goal was to promote an African-based form of development, where villages work together and people reach decisions through discussion and consensus.

Although *ujamaa* made it easier to organize rural development, it did not achieve the lofty economic goals envisioned. In the 1980s Tanzania joined many African countries undergoing structural adjustment and poverty reduction programs with the World Bank and the International Monetary Fund. Disillusioned with his program's lack of success, Nyerere became one of Africa's first presidents to resign on his own accord in 1985. His vice-president, Mwinyi, replaced him. After serving two terms, Mwinyi was succeeded by Benjamin Mkapa, and in 2005, Jakaya Kikwete was elected president. Because of its extensive patronage networks, the ruling party has never been seriously threatened at the polls.

Post-independent Tanzania has had to make nation-building a top priority. Nyerere insisted that Swahili be the common unifying language for Tanzania, and unique electoral and representational rules kept Zanzibar and the mainland under one

Republic. For example, Zanzibar elects a president who is head of government for matters internal to Zanzibar, and while the National Assembly enacts laws that apply to the entire Republic and also only to the mainland, Zanzibar has its own House of Representatives that enacts laws pertaining solely to Zanzibar.

² LOCATION AND HOMELAND

Tanzania covers 942,804 sq km (364,017 sq mi), about twice the size of the US state of California. Tanzania borders Mozambique, Malawi, Zambia, the Democratic Republic of the Congo, Burundi, Rwanda, Uganda, and Kenya. The mainland has 1,374 km (854 mi) of coastline on the Indian Ocean. Tanzania's climate and topography relief have much variety. The highest point in Africa is at the summit of Mt. Kilimanjaro 5,883 m (or 19,300 ft above sea level) and the lowest point is at the floor of Lake Tanganyika 361 m (or 1,184 ft below sea level). Temperatures range from tropical to temperate and vary with elevation. Rainfall for much of the country comes from December to May, but the central third of the country is semiarid. Sporadic rainfall makes agricultural and livestock production unpredictable.

Tanzania's physical and climatic variation is rivaled by its ethnic and cultural diversity. Its peoples belong to more than 120 ethnic groups, none of which exceeds 10% of the population. The Sukuma and the Nyamwezi are the largest, together making up about 21% of the population. Many Indians and Pakistanis live in the urban centers.

At 39,300,000 people in 2008, Tanzania is one of Africa's most populous countries, but its growth rate has slowed from 4.3% in 1995 to 2.07% in 2008. Despite its size, the population remains quite rural. On the fertile slopes of Mt. Kilimanjaro, population densities reach 250 persons per sq km (402 persons per sq mi). The coastal city of Dar es Salaam had 2.5 million residents as of the 2002 census.

³ LANGUAGE

Tanzania, like most African countries, is composed of numerous ethnic groups each with its own language, culture, and traditions. Thanks to this diversity, the country has over 130 living languages, but successfully adopted a single African language—Swahili—for purposes of national unity. As a trade language, Swahili (or Kiswahili) belonged to no single ethnic group. It became the language of instruction in secondary education and in some university courses. It also became popular in literature. Unlike Congolese, who sing their national anthem in French, or Kenyans, who sing theirs in English, Tanzanians sing "Mungu ibariki Africa," ("God Bless Africa") in Swahili.

Swahili originated on the coast and became the lingua franca (common language) for much of East Africa, including Kenya, Uganda, and the eastern part of the Democratic Republic of the Congo. Though Swahili is a Bantu language in its origin and structure, it draws its vocabulary from a diversity of sources, such as English, Arabic, and other Bantu languages. The media use Swahili in television, radio, and newspapers. English is also the official primary language of administration, commerce, and higher education. Arabic is widely spoken on Zanzibar Island.

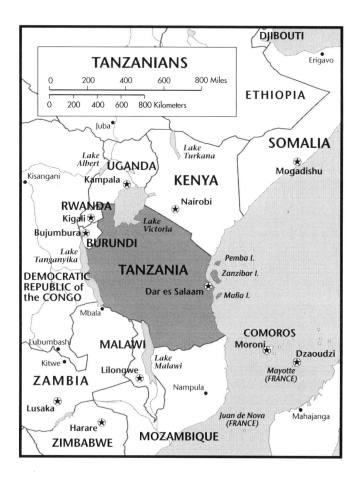

⁴ FOLKLORE

In many Tanzanian ethnic groups, heroes are illustrious ancestors who distinguished themselves in valor, intelligence, and generosity. Younger generations become aware of these ancestors through storytelling and wedding ceremonies. In the Bahaya group, for example, the groom must research his family history and choose an ancestor whose reputation will be recalled during the marriage ceremony. It is understood that the young man will be expected to measure up to this role model. By contrast, experts in ceremonial rituals in the Masai tribe believe themselves to be descended from a boy with magical powers. According to legend, Masai warriors found the young child naked and seemingly abandoned on a mountaintop, and they decided to adopt him. They observed that he had the power to make springs gush forth, grass to grow, and pools of water to appear. Even in times of famine, his cattle were always well fed and fat.

While Tanzanian folklore largely revolves around figures associated with individual ethnic groups, as time passes it becomes more likely that characters will emerge from a national stage. It will be interesting in this respect to observe how Tanzania's first president, Julius Nyerere, will be extolled and mythologized in national folklore by future generations.

⁵ RELIGION

As a potentially divisive issue, religion has assumed great importance in Tanzania. Approximately 30-40% of the population identifies itself as Muslim with an equal percentage subscribing to Christianity. Zanzibar is 99% Muslim. The remainder practices indigenous religion, although an overlay of indigenous beliefs characterizes much of the country. Islamic Law may apply to Muslims in cases of domestic issues and the president of Zanzibar appoints a Mufti, who is a public servant, to settle disputes and register Islamic groups on the archipelago. Christians include Roman Catholics, Protestants, Pentacostals, Seventh-day Adventists and others, while the vast majority of Muslims (more than 80%) are Sunni.

Though relations between Muslims and Christians have generally been peaceful, at times they have been tense and occasionally violent, owing to perceptions on both sides that government favors one faith over the other in hires, public benefits, and law enforcement. Tanzania therefore has had to balance relations carefully between the two major faiths. For example, in 2005 according to an unwritten rule of Tanzanian politics requiring alternating power between the two faiths, the ruling party nominated Jakaya Kikwete, a Muslim to succeed President Mkapa, who is Catholic. In 2007 Christian groups accused President Kikwete of favoring Muslims in his political appointments.

Indigenous religion usually blends the Muslim/Christian notion of a high god with African belief in lesser, intermediate gods. For example, children usually have a Christian or Muslim name, and in addition will be named for an ancestor whose name reflects a relationship with the spirit world. One such name in a local language means "demigod," that is, a spirit of an intermediate level who intercedes with the high god. As is common in Africa, many people resort to diviners to detect the cause of misfortune, and in case of sickness, they consult traditional healers.

6 MAJOR HOLIDAYS

In the spirit of impartiality, Tanzanians celebrate eight religious holidays—four Christian and four Muslim. Among them are Christmas, Easter, the prophet Muhammad's birthday, and the beginning and end of Ramadan. As a rule, Christian and Muslim friends invite each other to celebrate their religious holidays. On Christmas and Muhammad's birthday, children receive gifts of clothing, and everybody hopes to wear something new.

Tanzanians remember President Mwinyi for restoring several holidays in the country. Should a holiday fall on a weekend, it is moved to the following Monday. Tuesday is then declared a holiday as well to allow for a long break. Among the secular holidays are Zanzibar Revolution Day; *Nane Nane* (formerly *Saba Saba*—Farmer's Day, in August); Independence Day (9 December 1961); and Union Day (26 April 1964), which commemorates the unification of Zanzibar and the mainland.

People celebrate holidays differently depending on their occupation and location. In the village, secular holidays may offer an occasion simply to tend the fields as on most any other day. If the holiday falls on a long weekend, city people take advantage to travel to their home villages, if possible. Huge parades or party events at the stadium usually take place in the cities. On Labor Day (May 1) for example, office colleagues gather at their place of work to be ferried to government rallies at the stadium. Everyone with a radio at home just turns it on for the day, since the president may have a proclamation to make regarding pay raises or promotions. Shops close on all holidays, but hotels, restaurants, and nightclubs are open for party-goers.

7 RITES OF PASSAGE

Tanzanians of all ethnic backgrounds participate in rites of passage. The form and content of the rites vary according to tribal group and religious faith, but they remain important as symbolic markers of growing up, assuming responsibility, exercising leadership, protecting loved ones, and commitment to a particular faith or worldview.

To the extent that people practice traditional ways, their rites reflect the accumulated wisdom of previous generations. In the example of the Masai, all of life is seen as a conquest. Young boys leave home early to watch the calves, then the cows and other cattle. Their mission is to learn to conquer fear. They soon are left on their own, protecting their herds from lions and other wild beasts. Children of both sexes voluntarily undergo body piercing and tattooing. Incisions are made with needles and knives. Large holes in the upper ear cartilage are first made with a hot iron. Then marvelous ornamental earrings adorn the ears of young girls.

Circumcision or excision follows. This most important rite decides the self-control and bravery of the child in becoming an adult. Flinching during the ceremony would bring dishonor and humiliation to the family. On the other hand, the successful male initiate receives gifts of cattle, and the female feels prepared to undergo whatever pain childbearing entails. From this level, both males and females must prove themselves productive and cooperative members of Masai society.

8 INTERPERSONAL RELATIONS

People place much importance on greetings because they denote politeness, respect, and relationship in Tanzania. Therefore, greetings are usually more complex than a casual "Hi" or a simple wave of the hand, as is common in Western cultures. The type of greeting offered may depend on someone's status. A special greeting used only between married men suggests their elder status. Similarly, a younger brother uses a particular form of greeting to address his older brother. A generic but common Swahili greeting among friends is *"Ujambo, habari gani?"* ("Good morning, what is your news?").

Dating and marriage in Tanzania differ considerably from European and American customs. Western-style dating is uncommon, especially in the rural areas. In the village, young people choose their spouses but their families help arrange the marriage. For example, in Kagera Province on Lake Victoria, young men ask for the hands of their fiancées indirectly through designated representatives. The envoy generally is a family relative but might be a professional marriage intermediary. In any case, the ambassador must be articulate and eloquent and must be the first to visit the father of the fiancée on the day of the request. Since Africans begin their day early, it would be unsafe to arrive later than 6:00 am. The envoy then prostrates himself before the father and creatively implores the hand of the daughter for his master. The process usually takes several visits and many cases of beer. In rural areas, the finest local brew makes its appearance, and customarily is first refused as unfit for consumption. The repartee over the quality of the drink and the qualifications of the taster goes on until the fiancée's family "gives in" and agrees to the marriage. Women dance and ululate (hoot or howl) to announce the joyous conclusion. Members of clans sharing the same totem (such as a certain animal) may not marry.

9 LIVING CONDITIONS

Living conditions qualify as among the most difficult in the world. The Human Development Index, which offers a broad comparison of well-being and standard of living worldwide, ranks Tanzania 159th out of 177 countries (2005). This low score reflects extremely low purchasing power (GDP per capita of $744/year), and weak economic growth due in part to the impact of HIV/AIDS on working aged people. Because the majority of Tanzanians live on less than $2 a day, there is no discretionary income to purchase extras.

Social indicators are alarming. Life expectancy at birth is 51 years, the infant mortality rate is 70 for every 1,000 live births, and the HIV/AIDS prevalence rate is nearly 9%. As children grow, malnutrition and tropical diseases such as malaria, schistosomiasis, and sleeping sickness cause illness and fatalities. Preventable diseases thrive in open sewers and latrines and uncovered garbage piles. In the villages, many people draw their water from contaminated streams, lakes, and pools. While conditions have improved in some towns, urban migration has outpaced government capacity to plan for and provide basic services. Given lack of zoning and building code enforcement, houses tend to be poorly ventilated and overcrowded, thereby contributing to ill health and low productivity.

10 FAMILY LIFE

As in most of Africa, families tend to be large and extended, but socially cohesive. Cousins are considered brothers and sisters, and nieces and nephews as children. In towns and cities, nuclear families may absorb relatives for long periods, and given the absence of social safety nets, grandparents live with their adult children in the same household. In polygynous households mothers usually live separately with their children and in the village they occupy their own huts within the same compound. The women and girls perform the household chores, while all who work outside the home are expected to help cover family expenses. Although family members may go their own ways early in the day, they typically return home to eat an evening meal together. Among some ethnic groups, women and men eat separately.

Family members have special relationships that bind them intergenerationally. Grandchildren refer to their grandmothers as *bibi yangu* (my wife) while grandmothers refer to their grandsons as *bwana yangu* (my husband). Grandmothers may tease their actual husbands by calling their grandsons *banda*, "rivals" of their husbands' affection.

11 CLOTHING

In rural regions, Muslim men usually wear a long embroidered cotton gown, or *kanzu,* with a matching skull cap. Muslim women often wear a *kanga* consisting of two or three pieces of brightly colored fabric wrapped around them and covering their head. On the island of Zanzibar and along the mainland coast, Muslim women wear *buibui,* a black veiled shawl, and *chador* (veils), which allow them to go out while avoiding male scrutiny of their physical beauty. Few women wear more jewelry than the Masai, who adorn themselves with elaborate beaded earrings, necklace bands, rings, and headbands.

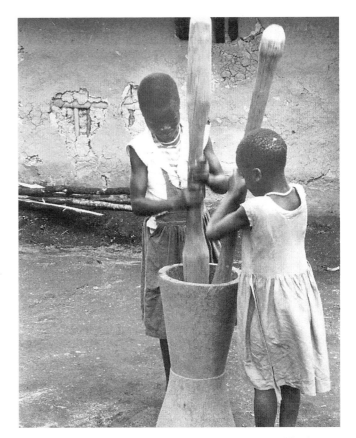

The typical family meal in rural Tanzania is prepared by the mother with help from her daughters. The most popular staple is ugali, a stiff dough made of cassava flour, cornmeal, millet, or sorghum. (International Labour Office)

In urban areas, Western-style clothing is common. Men wear suits and ties on formal occasions; otherwise, they wear shirts and trousers. Women wear dresses. Shorts, miniskirts, and revealing clothing, considered indecent, are avoided.

12 FOOD

The typical family meal in rural Tanzania is prepared by the mother with help from her daughters. They may cook it on a wood or charcoal fire in the open courtyard, or in a special kitchen either attached to the house or separate from it. People usually have two main meals a day, although tea is drunk throughout the day while socializing and visiting.

The most popular staple is *ugali,* a stiff dough made of cassava flour, cornmeal, millet, or sorghum. The coastal people prefer rice as a staple, while plantains are consumed daily in the north. Ugali is eaten with a stew of fish, vegetables, or meat from a communal bowl, using the right hand. People pass a basin of water for hand washing before and after meals.

Tastes in food vary greatly, but Tanzanians generally are fond of goat meat, chicken, and lamb. *Pilau* is a delicious dish of rice spiced with curry, cinnamon, cumin, hot peppers, and cloves. *Vitumbua* are sweet fried breads eaten between meals or accompanying tea. For breakfast, masala-spiced milk tea and freshly baked French-style bread are popular. The milk is brought to a boil, and then tea, masala, and sugar are add-

A Tanzanian loads bananas onto his bicycle. About 90% of Tanzanians make their living in agriculture, though only 5% of the land is arable. Many people are subsistence farmers, meaning that small field plots of 2 hectares (5 acres) or less are cultivated.
(Cory Langley)

ed. The Masai diet is exceptional in that it consists of only six foods: meat, milk, blood, animal fat, tree bark, and honey.

While the marriage laws have made it more common for families to eat together, eating customs vary according to ethnic group and religious beliefs. In some groups, taboos forbid fathers-in-law from sitting to eat at the same table with their daughters-in-law. Taboos may also prohibit men from entering the kitchen. Women in some tribes abstain from eating eggs or chicken. In Muslim households, men and women usually eat separately. During the holy month of Ramadan, Muslims do not eat or drink from sunrise to sunset.

13 EDUCATION

Former President Nyerere, an educator by profession, placed great importance on learning for all Tanzanians. Nyerere's self-reliance and *ujamaa* (family village) programs promoted literacy in the Swahili language, increasing the literacy rate to over 70% (extremely high for Africa). Literacy programs also aimed to raise consciousness about hygiene, agriculture, crafts, basic math, and personal achievement.

School completion rates are high (for Africa). About 56% of school-eligible children graduate from primary school, and about 33% from secondary (high) school. Completion rates for boys and girls are the same, reflecting Tanzania's egalitarian approach to education. Although in principle schooling is

free, parents often pay for books, uniforms, and school lunches in addition to basic fees, especially beyond form two (second year of high school) where day students typically pay $15 and boarding school children $61 a year in fees. Extra-curricular activities such as art, music, and sports receive much less attention than in Europe or the U.S. and schools mostly concentrate on basic academic preparation.

To enter secondary school, students are required to pass an exam. Languages specific to ethnic groups are taught in the earlier years of schooling, then progressively Swahili and English are introduced in the educational system. The National University of Dar es Salaam has an international reputation and once belonged to the prestigious East African system, which included the Universities of Makerere (in Kampala, Uganda) and Nairobi.

14 CULTURAL HERITAGE

Tanzania has a rich oral and written literature in Swahili. Film is less developed, but filmmaker Flora M'mbugu-Schelling's prize-winning films in Swahili portray significant social issues facing Tanzanian women. Tanzania's major music contribution is its Swahili, Arab-influenced classical music tradition. Many accomplished composers and musicians produce this unique blend of African-Arab-Indian sound.

In art, Tanzanians produce many fine pieces of jewelry and carved ivory, some for the tourist trade. Artists excel most, however, in refined wood sculpture. African art is much preoccupied with the human figure and with its moral and spiritual concerns. In particular, the Makonde people of the southeast are famous woodcarvers of statuettes and masks, which sell internationally. One of their pieces, probably produced for the European market, depicts a "tree of life" carved from ebony. The carver has surrounded an ancestor with present and past generations of people, one on top of the next, supporting each other throughout time. The motif shows the influence of traditional African thought in a modern sculpture.

15 WORK

Most Tanzanians are subsistence farmers, meaning that small field plots of two hectares (five acres) or less are cultivated with traditional African hoes, without the benefit of irrigation. Some of these farmers, and others—employed by large companies—produce crops for export. The slopes of Mt. Kilimanjaro and Mt. Meru are extremely fertile coffee, tea, and pyrethrum (used in making insecticides) areas. Along with sisal, cotton, tobacco, cashews, fruits, and cloves (Zanzibar), they account for more than 50% of the gross domestic product.

Tanzania also has 23 export processing zones with economic free zones that provide employment in light manufacturing and assembly. More traditional industry consists of the processing of sugar, beer, cigarettes, sisal twine, and light consumer goods. Some diamond and gold mining exists as well.

Wages in the informal sector tend toward survival, but also are low in the formal sector. In 2006 the minimum wage for hotel workers was $55 per month, while workers in the mining sector made $300 per month. To pay for school fees and health care, many Tanzanians engage in side businesses such as tailoring and cooking and they send their children into the streets to peddle wares. Government employees are covered by the 40 hour per week work law, but the vast majority of people work at least 50 hours a week. Officially 35% of children ages 5–14 are in the work force, but in reality this number is far higher.

16 SPORTS

Few adults actively play sports, but men follow national African and professional European soccer teams religiously on television and radio. In rural areas it is common to see boys playing soccer on the village pitch near the school or the village square. Basketball, boxing, and running are popular, and though not as successful as Ethiopia and Kenya, Tanzania has produced several world-class long-distance runners. Although many westerners think of big game hunting on the Serengeti plains as sport, trophy hunting is reserved for foreign tourists and the locals depend on game for food and livelihood.

17 ENTERTAINMENT AND RECREATION

The daily grind of hauling water, tending herds, gathering firewood, cooking meals, caring for children, and mending huts leaves little time for leisure for most Tanzanians. Yet people find time in the evenings for the things they love, especially music and dancing, storytelling, and socializing. In cities and towns, people socialize at coffee houses and make home visits—typically unannounced. These visits are an important social custom and at the same time provide people with a low-cost form of entertainment. On the coast, people play *mbao*, a board game that uses small stones. Women dance the *chakacha* at celebrations and marriages. Tanzanians are fond of action-packed martial arts and kung fu films. Movies made in India are also popular. In addition to AM and FM radio, many urban Tanzanians now get entertainment and news at Internet cafes.

18 FOLK ART, CRAFTS, AND HOBBIES

Tanzanians produce many arts and crafts of high quality. The Zaramo on the outskirts of Dar es Salaam produce conventional figures of Masai warriors, elderly men, nude women, and carved walking sticks. They carve these using only hand tools. Meerschaum pipe-carving is also one of Tanzania's international trademarks. Besides the tourist market, the Nyamwezi (in former times) carved thrones for their chiefs. The Masai make shields with intricate geometric designs. Zanzibar doorways with their geometric patterns offer a glimpse of the island's Arabic history and tradition.

19 SOCIAL PROBLEMS

Many social ills are linked to poverty, weak law and order, discrimination, and cultural beliefs such as witchcraft. The scarcity of good jobs means that husbands look for work in South Africa, girls are vulnerable to early marriage and prostitution, and children often are forced to work in conditions of servitude. Men who have worked as migrants often return home with the AIDS virus and infect their partners. Corruption on grand and petty levels undermines economic growth. Nearly 20% of the national budget is lost each year to corruption, and because of corrupt and ineffective police, people turn to street justice. In 2006 a mob burned a man who was caught stealing two chickens.

Discrimination hurts marginalized members of society such as the handicapped. Albinos are deliberately killed for their body parts, which are trafficked for their presumed powers of witchcraft. Older women are subject to accusations of witchcraft and there is low tolerance for homosexuals. Tanzania has welcomed some 600,000 refugees from Congo and Burundi, but their presence has placed additional stress on land and has caused resentment owing to differential treatment from international aid agencies. The negative impact of HIV/AIDS cannot be overstated. The disease afflicts some 3.5 million persons. The absorption of more than 2 million AIDS orphans by family and relatives has strained family life and persons living with AIDS face societal discrimination in hiring and services.

20 GENDER ISSUES

Women do most of the work, have fewer privileges under the law, and as many as 25% report physical and sexual violence since the age of 15. Wife beating is considered acceptable. Though illegal, as many as 15% of girls are subjected to female genital mutilation (FGM) often performed by *Ngaribas*, traditional practitioners. A concerted movement led by Tanzanian and international nongovernmental organizations (NGOs) to end FGM has successfully reduced the practice from 18% to 15% during the period from 1995–2005.

In spite of these issues, Tanzanian women enjoy greater social status than in many neighboring countries. After the 2005 elections, women occupied 91 of 320 parliamentary seats (nearly reaching the 30% constitutional guarantee), 7 ministerial and 10 deputy ministerial posts including Finance, Foreign Affairs, and Justice. Seven women serve as justices on the High Court and one on the Union Court of Appeal. Also, many women engage in trade and keep their earnings for themselves and their children. Girls must be at least 15 years old to marry, wives must register their official approval before their husbands take a second-wife, and Muslim husbands can no longer simply declare "I divorce thee" three times before a divorce occurs. Although many women are not aware of their rights, they have recourse to a marriage reconciliation board, and they are entitled to inheritance when their husbands die.

[21] BIBLIOGRAPHY

Africa South of the Sahara 2007. "Tanzania." London: Europa Publishers, 2008.

Berger-Levrault. *Les Maasai: Guerriers de la Savane.* Collection Explorer. Paris: Berger-Levrault, 1984.

Da Silva, Ladis. *Through a Doorway in Zanzibar: An Ethnological Study of the Peoples of East Africa.* Scarborough, Ontario: Celaz Print Shop, 1994.

Goodall Institute. *Forty Years at Gombe: A Tribute to Four Decades of Wildlife Research, Education and Conservation.* New York: Stewart, Tabori and Chang, 2000.

Kaplan, Irving, ed. *Tanzania: A Country Study.* Washington, DC: The American University, 1978.

Ndembwike, John. *Tanzania: The Land and its People.* Elizabeth Town, PA: Continental Press, 2006.

Ofcansky, Thomas P. and Rodger Yeager. *The Historical Dictionary of Tanzania.* Second Edition. Lanham, MD: Scarecrow Press, 1997.

—by R. Groelsema

TIGRAY

PRONUNCIATION: TIH-gray
ALTERNATE NAMES: Tigre, Tigrai, or Tigrinya
LOCATION: Tigray state (Ethiopia), Eritrea
POPULATION: 4.3 million in Ethiopia, 2.3 million in Eritrea
LANGUAGE: Tigriñña, Amharic
RELIGION: Christianity
RELATED ARTICLES: Vol. 1: Eritreans; Ethiopians

[1] INTRODUCTION

The Tigray (Tigre, Tigrai, or Tigrinya) have a history that goes back before the time of Jesus Christ. Over the past two thousand years, all the Ethiopian emperors have been either Tigray or Amharas (the ethnic group in Ethiopia most closely identified with the Tigray). According to Tigrayan, as well as Amharan, history, the Axumite empire, which later became the Ethiopian empire, was founded by Menilik, the son of King Solomon of Israel, and Queen Sheba (or Saba). According to this history, it was Menilik's men who captured the Ark of the Covenant from the Israelites and brought it to Axum (also spelled *Aksum*) in what is now the Tigray region in Ethiopia, where it remains to this day.

The seat of the Ethiopian empire has moved over the centuries. It has been located in a Tigriñña-speaking area (also spelled Tigrinya); in other times it has been in an Amharic-speaking area. In the 4th century, a Syrian named Fromentius was brought to Axum as a scribe in the royal court because he was literate in Greek. The court at Axum, like other courts of the ancient world, maintained an orientation toward Greek culture. Fromentius's influence went far beyond that of a scribe. He was a Christian, and his conversion of the court spread this religion to most of the Tigriñña, and later to the Amhara-speaking areas. After the collapse of the Mediterranean worlds of the Greeks and the Romans, the Ethiopian empire had less contact with outside centers of culture. During the Middle Ages in Europe, the Ethiopian empire was known as the home of legendary Christian ruler, Prester John of the Indies.

Between 1884 and 1891, Italy attempted to conquer Ethiopia, in an effort to become a colonial power but lost at the battle of Aduwa (a town near Axum). Emperor Yohannes did, however, cede the region that is now the heart of Eritrea to Italy as part of a strategy of solidifying Christian power in the south. In 1936, Italy added the remainder of Ethiopia to its holdings. With the expulsion of Italy in 1941, Eritrea was officially made a province of Ethiopia. A struggle for Eritrean independence from Ethiopia began in the 1960s and finally succeeded in 1991. Today Tigriñña is the dominant language of the Tigray region of Ethiopia. Tigriñña and Arabic dominate in neighboring Eritrea.

The Tigray and the Amhara (as co-inheritors of the Ethiopian empire) have represented the political elite of the country, except during a brief period of Italian colonial rule (1936–1942). Until the Empire ended with the Marxist revolution and Haile Selassie's death in 1974, all emperors were either Amharas or Tigrays. In the post-empire period, many Tigray became part of the Eritrean Liberation Front and Tigrayan People's Liberation Front, which for a time became the most powerful antigovernment force. Since the ouster of the socialist government of Mengistu Haile Mariyam in 1991, Tigray have dominated the Ethiopian government.

2 LOCATION AND HOMELAND

Today, Tigriñña speakers number about 6.6 million and are concentrated in Tigray state (Ethiopia) and in Eritrea. The regions of Ethiopia and Eritrea where most Tigriñña speakers live are high plateau, separated from the Red Sea by an escarpment (cliff-like ridge) and a desert. In good years, rainfall on the plateau is adequate for the plow agriculture engaged in by the majority of Tigray. However, when rainfall is low, the region is subject to disastrous droughts. Approximately 80 per cent of the Tigray live in a rural setting. It is these Tigray who are discussed here.

A significant number of Tigray still live in the Sudan, where they moved as refugees from the Ethiopian civil war and the Ertirean war of independence. Tigriñña speakers live in many urban centers of the United States and Europe, notably Washington, D.C. and Minneapolis.

3 LANGUAGE

Tigriñña, the language spoken in Tigray, is from the Semitic family of languages, and is related to Arabic, Hebrew, and Aramaic (the language spoken by Jesus Christ). To the north of the Tigriñña speakers live people who speak the closely related language known as Tigre. Amharic, the official language of Ethiopia, is so closely related to Tigriñña that most Tigray have little difficulty communicating in Amharic. Tigriñña, Amharic, and the liturgical language Gi-iz are written with the same script. Many of the letters used in writing these languages derive from ancient Greek. Many young men learn to read and write while studying to become deacons and priests. Between World War II and 1991, public schools taught Amharic and English. After 1991 public schools put an emphasis on local languages. Only a minority of rural Tigray attend school.

Most Tigray names have specific meanings. Some examples appear in the accompanying table. Generally, people refer to one another by their first names. If one wished to distinguish between several people with that name, one would add the person's father's name. Abraha, for example, becomes Abraha Gebre Giyorgis, meaning, Abraha is the child of Gebre Giyorgis. If a further distinction must be made, the grandfather's name could be added, for example, Abraha-Gebre Giyorgis-Welede Mariyam. Men's and women's names follow the same rules, with the exception that wives are often given new names by their mothers-in-law when they first come to live with the husband's family. This applies only to the first name; distinguishing names (father's, father's father's, etc.) remain the same.

Some examples of Tigriñña names include:

NAME	MEANING
Abraha	the dawn
Atsbaha	the sunset
Gebre Giyorgis	granted by Saint George
Gebre Yesus	granted by Jesus
Gebre Selassie	granted by the Holy Trinity
Gidey	my share
Mitslal Muz	shadow as sweet as the banana
Haile Mariyam	the power of Mary
Welede Mariyam	child of Mary
Zenabu	rains

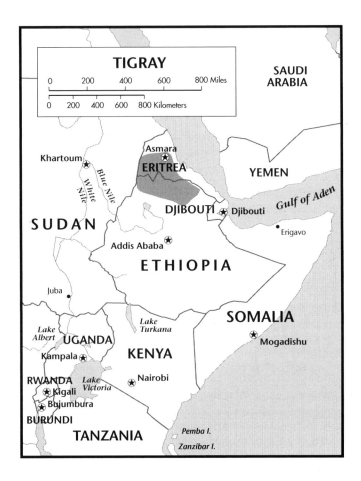

Most names represent things of high and positive value. In this context, a few names would appear to be strange. For example, a name such as Gidey (my share) is often given to a child if the family's earlier children have died. By naming a child Gidey, one could be seen as saying: "God, you have already taken your share: let this child be *my share.*"

4 FOLKLORE

Most Tigray place a high value on verbal skills. Poetry, folktales, riddles, and puns are central to entertainment. A person who has returned from studying at a monastery and can display a facility with *qene,* the art of "poetic combat," is much sought after for public gatherings. One indicator of the value placed on verbal skills is that the heroic figures of folklore are often known for the cleverness of the poetic couplets they composed. At a wedding, a qene expert might give a greeting that on the surface complemented the guests, but by a small change in pronunciation state that they are sitting on a royal dunghill. Riddles are an endless source of pleasure. This value on verbal cleverness is also seen in royal figures and saints. The Ethiopian saint Tekle Haymanot ("sower of the faith") is depicted as having verbally outwitted the devil. Another Ethiopian saint represents a contrasting heroic quality. Gebre Memfis Qudus ("granted by the holy spirit") gained sainthood by showing extraordinary compassion. The future saint was a monk who wandered among the wild animals. During one of Ethiopia's droughts he came upon a bird that was dying of thirst. The monk was so moved by the bird's plight that a tear formed under his eye. He allowed the bird to drink the tear. This bird was actually the Holy Spirit. These two heroic figures, Tekle Haymanot and Gebre Menfis Qudus, express two virtues—one of the mind, the other of the heart—highly prized by the Tigray.

5 RELIGION

Many people think of Christianity in Africa as a European import that arrived with colonialism, but this is not the case with the Tigray (or with the Amhara). The empire centered in Axum and Adowa was part of the Mediterranean world in which Christianity grew. Fromentius's 4th-century arrival in Axum was roughly contemporary with St. Patrick's arrival in Ireland and predated the arrival of Christianity in most of Europe by hundreds of years. Many Tigrayan churches were cut into cliffs or from single blocks of stone, as they were in houses of religion in Turkey and in parts of Greece, where Christianity had existed from its earliest years.

The church is a central feature of communities and of each family's daily life. Each community has a church with a patron saint. There is a close relationship between the community of worship and the community of citizenship. Until recent years, a town meeting was held just beyond the walls of the churchyard after Sunday mass. Members of the community moved from worship directly to the discussion of such topics of community governance as when to repair a village road or how to collect the taxes. Today's administrative structure retains the sense of community participation, but separates administrative and legislative meetings from the church.

Tigray, like members of other culture groups, often justify action on the basis of long-standing practice of belief. An example of a traditional Tigray explanation of an individual's symptoms of illness would be that he or she was possessed by a *zar* spirit. Another traditional belief is that some people—*Budda* and *Tebib*—have the capacity to unknowingly cause another person to have misfortune when they feel envy toward that person. Such beliefs are comparable to the "evil eye" in many Mediterranean cultures.

6 MAJOR HOLIDAYS

As in much of the rest of Ethiopia, most Tigray holidays are associated with the church calendar (Easter, Epiphany, etc.). The secular holidays include Ethiopian or Eritrean national holidays. The Ethiopian calendar runs on a different cycle from that originating in Europe. New Years entails a major holiday but comes on what in our calendar is September 11. There is also a difference in the calendar year and the clock. The Ethiopian millennium celebration fell in the European calendar year 2007. The sun rises at about 12 o'clock.

7 RITES OF PASSAGE

Births are attended by female friends and neighbors, and are private affairs. The infant is recognized as a member of the community in a naming ceremony held 40 days after birth for boys, and 80 days after birth for girls. Should a baby die after the naming ceremony, a funeral is required in recognition that a person has died; death in early infancy prior to the naming is not marked with a funeral.

Mothers have primary responsibility for children under age seven, who stay close to home. Boys older than seven begin accompanying their fathers to the fields. About the age of 12, children reach the "age of reason" and take on more responsi-

bility, such as helping care for younger brothers and sisters and for herding farm animals. Also at about this age, children are baptized and enter the community of religion.

Adolescence is a time when boys begin to prepare for a career. For most rural Tigray, this career will be secondary to farming. Boys often begin studying with a biblical master, known as *diakonin* or *deftera* (deacons), who have been ordained by the Bishop (*Abuna*). Many of these young men hope to become priests (*qashi*) or deacons themselves. Orthodox deacons and priests are not prohibited from marriage, so a priest is often also a husband and farmer.

Studying the Bible is not simply part of religious training; it is also a stepping stone to other forms of career advancement. Students learn to read and write Ethiopian script, traditionally a necessity for most political offices. The path through religious study toward literacy is becoming less important with the increased availability of government schools. Boys who are serious about becoming priests often become mendicants (religious beggars), and go door-to-door asking for food. Because religious roles are not available to women until late in life, religious study is not an avenue to literacy for girls. For boys, studying, begging, and becoming a deacon are also steps toward careers such as medicine. Most diagnosis of illness and prescription of cures is done by *deftera* (deacons or diviners) who have left formal religious work. Whether Bible students or not, adolescence is a time for young people to develop a reputation for competence, and to show that they are prepared to become good heads of households (for women, *ba-altigeza*, and men, *ba-algeza*). Young women demonstrate culinary skills and take care of their younger brothers and sisters. Young men are expected to accumulate a sum of money.

With adulthood come new responsibilities. One of the signs of adulthood is community citizenship, that is, attendance at village meetings after church on Sunday mornings. Other signs are marriage or becoming a deacon.

The death of a person requires a funeral. Funerals, with ceremonies in both the village and the church, normally take place before the sun sets on the day following death.

8 INTERPERSONAL RELATIONS

Tigriñña uses an elaborate system of greetings to indicate honor, the closeness of the relationship, and gender. There are ten personal pronouns people use to address one another. The choice of greeting is important in establishing and maintaining good relations. When meeting a stranger whom one judges may deserve some special respect, one might decide to address him with *khamihaduru* ("How are you, my honored equal?"). After learning that a stranger is due a great deal of respect, one might address him with *khamihadirom* ("How are you, my honored superior?").

The body language employed by Tigray is even more elaborate than the terms they use to address one another. Between any two people, there is always relative rank, referred to as a *azazi-tazazi* ("servant-master") relationship. Every person is *azazi* (servant) in some relationships, but *tazazi* (master) in others. This relative rank is expressed in both greetings and body language. One may express deference by lowering the eyes when meeting a superior's gaze. Both men and women move to lower seats, stand back to allow others to pass at doorways, or bow to show respect to others. Draping of the toga is an important part of social interaction. The socially successful person is adept at switching the arrangement of the cloth rapidly to go from indifference to respect when moving from one person to another in a social gathering. Used European clothing has replaced the toga for many rural Tigray, requiring a corresponding replacement of clothing's communication with other body language.

When a Tigray man or woman arrives at someone's house, he or she does not knock on the door to signify he or she has arrived at someone's house; rather, he clears his throat. On hearing this signal, the occupants of the house will come out to greet the arriving guest and invite him in. Guests are usually offered coffee. The way the coffee, *buna*, is served also expresses the relative status of relationships. If the host wishes to be polite, he or she will offer the first cup of coffee to the guest with the greatest *khibri* (honor). The guest is likely to refuse the offer, expressing humility, and the sentiment that the host is even more worthy, and should therefore drink the first cup. Similar interactions take place between the next most important guest and the host, and so forth, until all have been offered coffee. Finally, the most honored person will give in and accept the cup of coffee, signally that all guests can be served, in order, giving a clear picture of the honor each is accorded.

When *sewwa* (beer) is served, quite a different social dimension is expressed—for the moment, all present are equal members of a community, and the host makes sure that all glasses are always full. While coffee is used to reinforce the differences among people, beer is used to emphasize commonality.

For rural Tigray, there is no dating in the Western sense. Expressions of romantic interest between two people are not indicated by the couple going out together. Instead, parents of both create an agreement for a union between the two households, and a marriage takes place. Parents generally take the interests of their child into account. If a person becomes divorced, he or she may date prior to entering into a second marriage.

9 LIVING CONDITIONS

There are still few Western-trained physicians and life expectancy is low in Tigray. An increase in government clinics has not eliminated this problem. Chronic, parasitic diseases, such as malaria and schistosomiasis, are a problem in some regions. Many children die from communicable diseases such as measles and chicken pox. However, heart disease and lung cancer are rare, and people in their 50s are at the peak of their careers. By age 70 most people have retired from active farming.

In rural areas the main prestige items purchased are mules, often as status symbols for display to people outside the community. Generally speaking, status symbols have little importance. Within a community, people know one another well, and only deeds can add to a person's reputation.

A Tigray house provides shelter and contributes to the occupant's reputation in the community. A young couple's first house is usually a *gujji*, a practical, unimpressive house that the couple builds for itself. A gujji is a hut of wattle and daub—rods interwoven with twigs or branches—with a thatched roof. If the couple is successful, their next house will be more elaborate, with masonry walls and domed roofs supported by heavy wooden beams. Increasingly houses are roofed with sheetmetal. A very powerful family may later add stone walls around the yard.

Guests often bring stones with them as gifts of respect, to be added to the walls. One may view the walls as a concrete demonstration of one's friends' esteem.

Even the most elaborate rural houses have neither electricity nor running water. Candles or oil lamps provide light in the evening. The masonry walls and domed roofs provide good insulation and are comfortable in both cold and hot seasons. Fires for cooking and heating are fueled by wood or dried cow dung.

An average household in a farming community produces and consumes goods valued in hundreds of dollars per year; even small purchases by Western standards, such as soft drinks, represent substantial expenditures for rural Tigray.

Trucks and buses provide nearly all the road transportation, but many places people wish to go are not accessible by roads. Thus, many people travel by foot and carry loads on donkeys, mules, and camels. (Camels and mules also carry salt tablets from salt beds below sea-level in the Danakil depression up to the 8,000 ft plateaus of Tigray, where they are loaded onto trucks for transport to other parts of Ethiopia.)

10 FAMILY LIFE

The people living in a Tigrayan household are a family. They are generally related to each other and have a moral responsibility for one another. A rural Tigray household can also be seen as an agricultural firm, consuming directly most of what it produces, but selling some to get cash to buy items like spices and needles. To function efficiently, each family farm needs all jobs to be filled, and relies on every member to perform her or his job effectively. If a family is large, a son or daughter may go to live with an aunt or an uncle to help operate that household's farm.

Tigray women and men both bring property into the marriage; should there be a divorce each takes out what she or he brought in, and either party may call for the divorce. Typically, domestic goods, pots and pans, etc., are claimed by the wife. Farming tools, plows, etc., are claimed by the husband. In the case of divorce, younger children tend to stay with their mother. Older children stay with their same sex parent. When a household has both a wife and a husband, the husband is expected to represent the household's views to the outside world. The wife will speak for the household if her husband is not available. When a household is headed by a single woman, she is the spokeswoman. Though women occasionally hold political office, most offices are held by men.

Women are responsible for food preparation and the care of small children. The husband is responsible for plowing, planting, and the care of animals. Older girls work beside their mothers, older boys beside their fathers. Men may help around the house, and woman may help in farming, especially in weeding and at the harvest. In the case of divorce or death of a spouse, the surviving spouse will hire the help he or she needs to keep the farm and household in operation.

Households vary widely in size, from one member (widow or widower) to twenty (extended over two or three generations). The average family has a husband, wife, and four children.

For most couples, the first marriage is arranged by a contract between the parents of the bride and the groom. After a divorce, second marriages involve contracts between the new husband and new wife. Except for priests and deacons, couples typically do not go through a church marriage until later in life.

Tigray households go through changes as the occupants mature. A household is usually established by a new couple, with children added soon afterward. When young adults are old enough to marry, they may bring a spouse to live within the parental household. Whether the new couple joins the wife's or the husband's family's household is a matter of choice. In this manner, powerful families often add several subfamilies—the families of their married children. Most young couples leave their parents' household as soon as they can afford to farm on their own.

Families often keep dogs and occasionally keep a cat. However, these animals are generally regarded as working animals—watchdogs and mousers—and not companions.

¹¹ CLOTHING

Traditional Tigray clothing is white, which is regarded as Christian, with little adornment. For dressy occasions and church, women express piety—reverence for religious obligations—by wearing ankle-length dresses with long sleeves made of fine material. Men wear a form of jodhpur—ankle-length pants that are tight from the knee to the ankle and baggy in the upper legs and hips. A fitted, long-sleeved shirt covers the upper body. The shirt extends to just above the knee for laymen and to just below the knee for priests and deacons. Both men and women wear a *gabbi* or kutta (toga) draped around the shoulders; it can be draped in a complex set of patterns to express a person's relationship to others.

Until recently, everyday clothing was similar to dress clothes. Men wore a variety of shirts and pants under their togas. For women, everyday clothing was simply less fancy than church clothes. For many Tigrays, used clothing imported from Europe has replaced traditional clothing for day-to-day wear.

¹² FOOD

Probably the most important fact about food in Tigray is that there is not enough of it. Households must make up for food deficits with government subsidies. In Tigray, bread is one of the main foods. Two of the more common varieties are a thin, pancake-like bread preferred by most people, and a dense, disk-shaped loaf of baked whole wheat bread known as *khambasha*. Pancakes are 30 to 45 cm (12 to 18 in) in diameter, and are made from many kinds of cereal grains (wheat, barley, etc.). The favorite pancake is made from a grain called *taff* that does not grow in all regions. Where taff cannot be grown, *khambasha* is the everyday food. A variety of *tsebhi* (spicy stew) is eaten with the bread. Families and guests normally eat from a *messob* (shared food basket), with each person breaking off pieces of bread from the side nearest them and dipping it into tsebhi (stew) in the center of the basket.

Special occasion foods are similar to those eaten everyday, but use higher-quality ingredients. Festive breads are made of whiter flour, and stews are more likely to include meat. *Mies*, a honey wine or mead may replace *sewwa* (barley beer).

Eating utensils, such as silverware, are not used at most meals. One uses the right hand to tear off a piece of injera (pancake) or bread and dips it into the stew (or sauce), much like eating "dip." On festive occasions like weddings, where a large piece of meat (sometimes uncooked) is served to each guest,

a knife is provided. Cups have a variety of shapes and meaning. One of the first investments a new couple makes is a set of *finjal*, small coffee cups resembling those used to serve tea in Chinese restaurants. Beer glasses come in three basic varieties: cow horn, unglazed pottery, and glass or plastic. The *mies* (honey wine) should be served in a *berile* (special glass flask) with a long narrow neck. A Tigray saying is "*Mies* served without a *berile* is just beer."

In Tigray, using the left hand to touch food that others will have contact with is regarded as very bad manners. The same relationship between left and right can be seen in many settings. For example, sitting on the right side of someone important is better than having to sit on the left. The right side of the church, as viewed from the altar, is holier than the left.

Some foods—pork, shellfish, and rabbit—are believed to be unfit for Christian Tigray to eat. (Most are also considered non-kosher or prohibited foods by Jews.) The justification for these food prohibitions is found in the Christian Old Testament book of Leviticus. During the 40 days of Lent, plus a 14 day cleansing period before it, observant Tigray Christians do not eat animal products, including meat, milk, cheese, butter, or eggs.

The first meal of the day is eaten shortly after rising and usually consists of leftovers from the night before. On most days, both the midday meal and afternoon dinner consist of pancakes or bread and stew (or a sauce). When people are in the fields plowing, herding, winnowing, or weeding, they bring lunch in an *agelgil* (leather covered lunch basket). Snacks generally consist of toasted grains, and are eaten as one eats popcorn.

¹³ EDUCATION

Traditionally, boys learn to read Tigriñña, Gi-iz, and Amharic as Bible students. Today, some rural boys, and a few girls, attend public schools, with a percentage of them completing high school. Children living in town are much more likely to go to school than their rural counterparts. In larger towns, such as Makelle, Aduwa, or Aksum, public education is available through high school. There are universities in Addis Ababa and Makelle in Ethiopia and in Asmara in Eritrea.

Many rural parents encourage Bible study for literacy and the career opportunities it provides. Rural parents see advantages (in terms of a non-farming career) and some disadvantages to sending their children to school in town: although the student receives an education, he or she may not return to the family farm, and thus may not support their parents in old age.

¹⁴ CULTURAL HERITAGE

There are two main categories of music: church music and praise songs. Deacons sing and accompany the song with drums and a tsinatsil (sistrum, a rattle-like instrument) as part of the mass. Praise singers form a kind of caste—families of praise singers intermarry with other families of praise singers. Singers accompany themselves with a one-stringed instrument that is a little like a violin. Hosts often hire singers to entertain at parties, such as weddings. Guests give tips to the singers to sing, often humorously, about their friends.

Deacons dance as part of some church holidays. Women dance as entertainment on a few secular occasions. Rural men and women do not dance together in public.

Passages from the "Book of Psalms" are frequently brought into discussions of people's behavior. Many priests and deacons carry the psalms called a *dawit* (for King David) in a leather pouch.

Qene is an admired form of poetry known for its use of double meanings, beautiful language, and cleverness. A couplet should have a surface meaning and a deeper one. *Qene* is described as being like "wax and gold," an analogy that refers to the process of casting gold objects in wax molds pressed into sand. In *qene,* the listener "hears the wax" and must use thought to find the gold inside. Tigray kings and princes are often remembered for their *qene* compositions.

15 WORK

Until recently, most rural Tigray considered farming to be the most honorable work. Today's food shortages have made many parents rethink this proposition. Trade and government employment are seen as providing better opportunities. Those who make their living as blacksmiths, weavers, potters, or musicians are looked upon with some disfavor and suspicion. Most families farm, including those of priests and deacons. Farmers need plow animals in the Tigray region. The plow used is similar to those of Egypt further north, with a main shaft made from olive wood for strength. The plow shear is tipped with steel provided by blacksmiths. Because all farmers need plow animals, most are considered herders as well. People who can't afford animals must form partnerships with wealthier households. Since the 1974 revolution, Tigray farming has gone through several land redistributions, aimed at equalizing wealth. Nevertheless, shortages of oxen for plowing means that some households must form alliances with others who are better off than themselves.

The calculations that go into food production in the Tigray environment are complex and daunting. Nearly all parts of Tigray are subject to drought. Rainfall varies in timing and intensity. Different soil types perform differently. Tigray select from 17 varieties of cereal crops. Each household must choose the right seeds to maximize the amount of food and to minimize the chances of having too little food in years when rain is too heavy, too light, too early, or too late for any given field. An aggressive a choice of mixes of seed might lead to wealth for the household or starvation if the rains and the seeds are a bad match that year. A conservative set of choices may lead to the household not getting ahead. The calculations are comparable to what is required to manage a stock portfolio and is taken at least as serious by Tigrayan farmers.

Men are responsible for crops and women for the house and young children. Both help in the other's domain, and household decisions are made by mutual discussion. Teenage boys do much of the herding and help with plowing. Teenage girls work alongside their mothers.

16 SPORTS

A sport that seems to be unique to the Tigray and Amhara is a kind of cross-country field hockey. Those who are serious about the game grow their own hockey sticks, by training saplings to grow with the proper curve. When the sapling reaches the right stage of growth, they cut the tree and shape it into a hockey stick. The game is played running across the countryside, over cattle-yard fences, and through creeks. Hockey is associated with Easter.

A young Tigray girl in the Tigray state in Ethiopia. Tigray women wear their hair in braids and have tattoos on their faces and arms. (Travel Ink/Getty Images)

The game played most by the Tigray is *Timkhats,* sometimes described as chess. In the center of neighborhoods, men play it all year round, and boys play it while watching the herds. *Timkhats* is played on a grid usually scratched in the ground. Two players take turns placing markers on intersections of the grid in what might be thought of as a three-dimensional tick-tack-toe game. The rules are similar to those of the German game, *die müller.* Spectators offer advice on, and criticism of, the players' moves.

While *Timkhats* is the most common spectator sport when measured in hours spent by the most people, soccer is the sport that captures people's passions as they cheer for their favorite school teams and town teams.

17 ENTERTAINMENT AND RECREATION

While film, television, and to a large extent radio, are more a part of life in town than in rural areas, storytelling and riddles are part of the popular culture in both.

18 FOLK ART, CRAFTS, AND HOBBIES

Some of the most spectacular Tigray art is associated with the church. Tigray churches are famous for their architecture, with many cut into solid stone. The churches that are built of masonry are large and incorporate design features of the Parthenon in Athens, Greece. Icon painting—the creation of images of sacred people—is another art form associated with the church. Some deacons who have studied at *debri* (monasteries) return as icon painters. Icons are purchased by individuals and used to reinforce a relationship with a particular saint.

The major non-religious art forms are architecture and basketry. Masonry houses are meant to reflect the personality of the owner, and include details such as decorative borders below the roof line. Basketry, including the beautiful *messob* (shared-food baskets) that are the centerpieces of entertaining, are produced by women after their children have left home. Families specializing in weaving produce embroidered dresses. Some artisans and craftspeople—such as weavers, musicians, blacksmiths, and leather workers—are expected to marry within their group.

19 SOCIAL PROBLEMS

Since the 1970s, Tigray and Eritrea have experienced powerful social upheaval. In these two areas of greatest Tigray concentration, people have experienced a civil war, a struggle for independence, and a number of famines. Many observers believe that the human rights situation, after improving, has taken a downturn. Many challenges remain for the governments and people of Eritrea and Ethiopia.

Probably the most important social problems are associated with Tigray's food deficit and un- and underemployment. The government's attempt to combat these problems has taken two forms—relief efforts and public works—much of it in the form of terracing to improve the region's agricultural output.

Each government interprets civil rights in its own way, and government policy has gone through much transformation as it evolved from the imperial rule of Haile Selassie (1936–74), the Marxist-oriented government of Mengistu (1974–91), to the current, more democratic government. In 2008, Melles Zenawi, a Tigray, is the president

HIV-AIDS has become a significant public health issue, particularly in road towns.

Alcoholism is not widespread among rural Tigray. The *sewwa* (beer) brewed by each household is very low in alcohol content. *Mies* (honey wine) is somewhat higher in alcohol content, but is reserved for special occasions, such as weddings or entertaining political figures. *Araqi* (anise flavored brandy) is occasionally drunk to symbolize the finalizing of agreements, such as wedding contracts.

20 GENDER ISSUES

Under both traditional law and current law, men and women have equal rights. Under the pre-Mengistu land tenure systems rights to land were counted equally through male and female ancestral claims. On a mother's death, all of her children (male and female) had equal claim on shares of her land. The same was true in the event of a father's death. In other words, each household's holding were a mix of claims through combinations of male and female ancestors. Similarly, after a divorce each spouse kept his or her own land. Movable community property was divided equally. Nevertheless, in practice divorce often created more of a problem for women than for men. For practical reasons of sharing herding duties new households were often set up near the husband's parents. Thus a woman was more likely to have to move after a divorce.

In public life, men are usually the spokesmen for their households. As a matter of etiquette, a man will act as host. In the husband's absence, the wife will act as host. A woman and her husband are equally "owners" of the household. A woman will represent her household, before an adult son will. Ownership counts more than gender in representing the household.

There are two major settings in which men and women are seated separately. In church, men sit on the right half of the church and women on the left, from the perspective of the altar. In a community meeting people sit in three groupings. Married men, representing their households sit as a group. Female household heads sit in another. Adult men who have not yet established a household sit in yet another.

Male and female roles are quite separate. As mentioned in the Section 15, above, men have responsibility for agricultural production and women have responsibility for food preparation and childcare. While each may help in the other's domain, the responsibilities are defined.

21 BIBLIOGRAPHY

Bauer, Dan. *Household and Society in Ethiopia: An Economic and Social Analysis of Tigray Social Principles and Household Organization.* East Lansing, MI: African Studies Center, Michigan State University, 1985.

———. "The Sacred and the Secret: Order and Chaos in Tigray Medicine and Politics." In William Arena and Ivan Karp, eds. *Creativity of Power: Cosmology and Action in African Societies.* Washington, DC: Smithsonian Institution Press, 1989.

Gerster, Georg. *Churches in Stone: Early Christian Art in Ethiopia.* New York: Phaidon, 1970.

Levine, Donald N. *Wax and Gold: Tradition and Innovation in Ethiopia Culture.* Chicago: University of Chicago Press, 1972.

McCann, James. *From Poverty to Famine in Northeast Ethiopia: a Rural History 1900–1935.* Philadelphia: University of Pennsylvania Press, 1987.

———. *People of the Plow: An Agricultural History of Ethiopia.* Madison: University of Wisconsin Press *1995.*

—by D. F. Bauer

TONGA

PRONUNCIATION: TAWNG-guh
LOCATION: southern Zambia
POPULATION: 1,500,000
LANGUAGE: Chitonga
RELIGION: Christianity combined with indigenous religious beliefs
RELATED ARTICLES: Vol. 1: Bemba; Chewa; Zambians

1 INTRODUCTION

The Tonga live in southern Zambia in a corridor along the Zambezi River. The name "Tonga" is apparently a Shona term which means "independent," a reference to the fact that the Tonga people were a people without chiefs before the era of colonization. While many other ethnic groups in southern Africa had developed centralized forms of political organization, the Tonga recognized no political leaders as chiefs and preferred to live in dispersed homesteads rather than in villages. The Tonga belong to the Bantu group of peoples, and evidence seems to indicate that they are descendants of the earlier Iron Age Bantu peoples who migrated to the southern parts of Zambia during the 15th and 16th centuries from the Congo area. Due to the fact that the Tonga were a chiefless society, many scholars argue that this reduced their power and influence in comparison to the Bemba and Chewa. Indeed, upon the arrival of colonial rule, the colonial administration appointed individuals of influence as local chiefs whom the Tonga jokingly referred to as "Government Chiefs."

Although the Tonga are generally known as a chiefless society, there were some important people within Tonga society that wielded influence, such as the *Sikatongo,* a priest who made sure that the spirits took care of the people and made the crops grow. He could also cause rain, cure all diseases, and protect the people from all kinds of calamity. In every neighborhood (a grouping of several villages), there was also a man called the *Ulanyika,* the owner of the land. The *Ulanyika* was usually the first person to settle and live in the neighborhood. He commanded some influence in his neighborhood, and hunters gave him parts of every animal they killed within the surroundings of the neighborhood. Like all the peoples of Zambia, the Tonga came under British colonial rule at the end of the 19th century. Zambia gained independence in 1979 under the leadership of Dr. Kenneth Kaunda, who ruled Zambia until 1991 when he lost the presidency to Frederick Chiluba. After a two-term stint of five years each as president of Zambia, Chiluba was succeeded by President Levy Mwanawasa in 2001. Mwanawasa attempted to steer Zambia away from corruption that had become well entrenched during Chiluba's rule.

2 LOCATION AND HOMELAND

The Tonga are concentrated in southern Zambia along the Kafue and the middle Zambezi rivers. Most of the Tonga area has low-quality soil and erratic rainfall, which makes it less significant for agricultural purposes. The area is sparsely populated, except in the Gwembe Valley region of the middle Zambezi and areas along the Kafue River and the line of rail on the plateau. Most of the Tonga region is a plateau of high altitude ranging from 900 m to 1,500 m (3,000–5,000 ft) above sea level. Some areas of the plateau provide favorable environments for agricultural and pastoral living. The agricultural cycle is centered around a single rainy season which begins in November and ends in April. While on average the region gets about 65 cm to 90 cm (25–35 in) of rainfall per year, there have also been years of drought and years of flooding, with rainfall as low as 25 cm (10 in) and as high as 125 cm (50 in). In terms of population, the Tonga account for 15% of Zambia's total population, currently estimated at 11.5 million people.

3 LANGUAGE

Linguistically, the Tonga people are part of the Bantu language family. The Tonga language is known as Chitonga and has a substantial number of words that are similar in many respects to other Bantu languages such as Bemba, Chichewa, and Luyana. For example, "to write" in all three languages is *kulemba;* a chicken is known as *a'nkoko* in Bemba, *nkuku* in Luyana, *nkhuku* in Chichewa, and *inkuku* in Tonga; a traditional doctor in all four languages is called *ng'anga.*

4 FOLKLORE

The Tonga have no written history prior to their encounter with the British explorer David Livingstone in the early 1850s. Nevertheless, like many other peoples in Africa, they have a rich tradition of oral history and folklore. In almost all the villages, elders are the reservoirs of mythical stories. The stories, usually featuring animal characters, are narrated around a fire at night. They convey certain traditional principles, values and customs, and the origins of the Tonga people. One of the stories deals with the beginning of Tonga society. Contrary to popular belief that the Tonga are a chiefless society, local tradition suggests that there was once a powerful chief in the town of Monze before the arrival of the British. According to oral tradition, the first Monze chief descended from heaven and called the Tonga people, including those living outside of Tongaland proper, to join him and settle in his chiefdom centered around the present-day town of Monze. The chief was liked by most people because he had powers to heal, to cause rain, and to maintain peace by frustrating enemies through his communication with the ancestral spirits.

5 RELIGION

In traditional Tonga society, there is a well-developed cult of the "shades" or *muzimu.* It is believed that at death each person leaves a shade or spirit, a muzimu. The muzimu commutes between the spirit world and the world of humans. Usually the muzimu is integrated into society by selecting an individual within the lineage to inherit the muzimu at a special ritual. Witchcraft is also central to traditional beliefs in that there are some bad people and spirits in society who can cause great bodily harm to an individual through sorcery. However, many of the Tonga people have been converted to Christianity because of early mission influence and European settlement in Tongaland. Initially, there were only a few converts because the missionaries demanded complete renunciation of traditional beliefs such as polygamy, bride-wealth, ancestor worship, and witchcraft. Today, there are a substantial number of people who practice both Christianity and indigenous religious beliefs. Converts to Christianity merely add a new religion, while retaining their traditional beliefs.

Chewa. In the traditional setting, as a girl approached puberty she was trained for her future role as a man's wife. Usually, there was a period of seclusion during which a short ceremony was observed to mark the girl's maturity, and she was given a new name to signify her adult status.

In terms of marriage, the prospective husband had to pay bride-wealth to the family of the girl, usually in the form of cattle. A man could pay two cattle or some clothing to marry a girl. Although the Tonga are a matrilineal society, the preferred form of residence is patrilocal; in other words, the husband goes to the wife's village, gives presents, and brings the wife back to his village where they set up their own household. Polygamy was encouraged, but this practice is on the wane because of the influence of Christianity and a modern economic system. Highly educated individuals feel that polygamy is uneconomic.

When a child is born it is given an ancestral as a well as a Christian name, in the case of those who are Christians. A special naming ceremony may be held at which beer-drinking and dancing occur. In the old days, every baby was believed to be protected by one of its ancestral spirits. It was therefore necessary for the parents to give the baby the name of the right ancestor, which was divined by saying all the names of the ancestors to the baby until he or she cried. Whatever name the parents had spoken when the baby cried was that of the protecting ancestor, whose name the baby was then given.

Although the Tonga no longer have specific initiation ceremonies for boys and girls, there is a strong belief that children must be taught and trained for adult life, and that growing up is not a simple process of maturation. Throughout the process of growing up, children are taught proper manners by older people, including older children. During their teenage years, boys and girls are encouraged to do their separate chores according to sex roles; for example, girls' chores are to draw water from wells and fetch firewood, while boys hunt small game and fish. This is not to imply that these are always mutually exclusive tasks; there are instances when boys carry out girls' chores, and vice versa.

When death strikes, there are special rituals to be performed during burial and soon after burial to make sure that the "shade" or spirit of the dead person is reintegrated into society and does not cause harm to anybody. Devout Christians follow church dogma and sing Christian hymns and prayers at funerals.

8 INTERPERSONAL RELATIONS

Girls and boys who have not reached puberty are encouraged to play together. Since there is no specific instruction given on sexual matters, children are expected to acquire such information by casual observation and through experimentation on their own. People talk freely in the presence of children about sexual matters such as menstruation, pregnancy, and childbirth. In the village setting, children are even allowed to be present at childbirth during labor but are excused when the baby is about to be born. Most parents feel that sexual play between children of the same age is not a matter for concern. However, an older man and/or woman is not expected to have sexual liaisons with a girl or boy below the age of puberty since it is believed to be detrimental to the health of both parties.

When a boy who has reached puberty decides to marry, he can find his own mate, but he must inform his uncles and par-

6 MAJOR HOLIDAYS

The major national holiday in Zambia is Independence Day on 24 October. Zambia obtained its independence from Great Britain in 1964 on 24 October. During this day every year there are celebrations arranged in major urban areas and throughout the country. There is much drinking, dancing, and singing. In the afternoon, people congregate in stadiums to watch a game of soccer between major leagues, or to see the national team play a friendly match with a national team from a nearby country such as Malawi. In addition to Independence Day, Zambia also observes several other holidays (both secular and religious) which include: January 1, New Year's Day; Second Monday in March, Youth Day; March or April, Good Friday and Easter Monday; May 1, Labor Day; May 25, African Freedom Day; First Monday in July, Heroes' Day; First Tuesday in July, Unity Day; First Monday in August, Farmers' Day; December 25, Christmas Day; and December 26, Boxing Day.

7 RITES OF PASSAGE

Throughout Zambia today the law states that an individual becomes an adult at the age of 18. At this age an individual is allowed to vote and to drive a car. In most cases, no special ceremonies are performed to show that one has achieved adult status. In the past, most Zambian peoples had special initiation ceremonies and education for children as they attained puberty. The Tonga were no exception in this regard. However, the Tonga did not have an elaborate initiation ceremony such as *Chisungu* among the Bemba and *Chinamwali* among the ents to negotiate with the parents of the girl since bride-wealth must be paid. Cross-cousins of the same generation and age are in a joking relationship and may be addressed by spousal terms such as "my wife" or "my husband" and may cajole and harass each other without any recriminations. Boys sleep in the same room as their parents until age seven, when they move into their own hut. However, girls may continue to sleep in the same room as their parents until they reach puberty, or they may be allowed to sleep in the hut of an older woman, preferably a widow.

Generally, married women are expected to respect and cook for their husbands, and men are expected to take care of their wives. For example, when in the presence of men, a woman is expected to observe certain aspects of traditional female etiquette such as downcast eyes and servility. Women are also expected to dress modestly since any view of knees or thighs is thought to be an irresistible provocation. However, in urban areas many women have sought to retain their social autonomy and resist male dominance in numerous ways, such as staying single and earning a wage through a regular job or some type of home-based employment such as brewing beer.

⁹ LIVING CONDITIONS

The different circumstances of Tonga society such as short lineages, dispersed homesteads, the lack of chiefs, and their location along the line of rail from Zimbabwe to the copperbelt on soils suitable for agricultural production made it easy for the Tonga to participate fully in commercial agriculture during the colonial era. Due to the availability of a colonial market, the Tonga responded by intensifying and dramatically increasing their agricultural production. The Tonga were one of the few peoples to adopt agricultural innovations, such as ox-drawn plows and the use of fertilizer and hybrid seed, earlier on during the colonial period. Thus a relatively wealthy group of commercialized farmers among the Tonga emerged, and most Tonga chose to participate in agricultural activities rather than to migrate to the urban centers and the mines in the copperbelt. There also developed a series of smaller urban centers such as Monze, Livingstone, Makoli, Zimba, Kalomo, Mazabuka, etc., along the line of rail, which spawned a local urban elite in Tongaland. Today these urban Tonga consider themselves part of modern Zambia, the wealthy elite with modern consumption patterns such as a modern home and occasionally a car.

In rural areas, people live in isolated homesteads or villages with a few huts. In most cases, houses, granaries, and cattle *kraals* (corrals) are temporary structures which can be easily abandoned within a short period of 5 to 10 years. New sites can then be cleared and new structures raised. With the advent of commercial farming and a cash economy, some houses are of modern appearance, durable and nicely decorated. Roofing materials for such houses are corrugated iron sheets. Some of the Tonga live in small urban areas along the line of rail that passes through their territory. These are part of the sub-elite; they may own a well-stocked shop with modern goods such as sugar, tea, clothing, milk, etc. Just like in other parts of Zambia, tropical diseases such as malaria, bilharzia, intestinal worms, etc., are quite common among the Tonga.

¹⁰ FAMILY LIFE

Similar to many African societies, "family" among the Tonga refers to the wider extended unit rather than the nuclear family of wife, husband, and children. The extended family unit, much like a lineage or clan, cooperates in many ventures, such as farming and provision of food. In times of trouble, such as famine and drought, the extended family serves as a social safety net with members coming to each other's rescue. In most instances, a village may be a large extended-family unit composed of members that can trace descent from a common ancestress.

Marriage is a negotiation process between two families rather than an affair of two individuals. Marriage involves the transfer of bride-wealth from the groom's family to the bride's family. As noted earlier, although the Tonga follow the matrilineal system of kinship arrangement, the preferred form of residence is patrilocal where, after the payment of bride-wealth, the wife moves to the husband's village. In the traditional setting, bride-wealth is not considered a form of "buying" a wife; rather, it has three main functions. The first function is to serve as a legitimizing symbol of a marriage, much like a marriage certificate in the West. Secondly, it functions as insurance for the continued survival of the union. Both families have a vested interest in the survival of the marriage since, if divorce should occur and the wife is in the wrong, all the bride-wealth would have to be returned; or, in cases where the husband is at fault, his extended family would lose the bride-wealth after the breakup. The third function, common among patrilineal societies, is that bride-wealth serves as a mechanism to transfer any offspring from the union to the father's lineage so that in times of divorce all the children remain with the father. Bride-wealth apparently does not serve this function among the Tonga since children remain with the mother's lineage but are free to choose either to live with the father or the mother after divorce.

Bearing as many children as possible is the most important undertaking in a Tonga marriage since children are valued for their labor and social security in old age. While divorce is quite common among societies without bride-wealth, marriages in societies that pay bride-wealth are relatively stable. There is a general feeling these days that modern, urban life has brought increasing instability to the family and that the divorce rate is much higher than it used to be. As more girls spend more time in school, coupled with the breakdown of traditional morals in urban areas, many women are opting to be single, to break away from the shackles of traditionalism that put women in an inferior position, and to exercise their own autonomy. Polygamy, although still practiced in rural areas, is not as common as it used to be and is generally a thing of the past. However, there is a contemporary practice in urban areas where men keep mistresses or "girlfriends" outside the home, something which could easily be interpreted as men informally exercising their right to many wives. This kind of practice, however, only serves to increase the proliferation of sexually transmitted diseases such as HIV/AIDS.

¹¹ CLOTHING

Clothing among the Tonga is used to differentiate the sexes. As soon as the children begin to run about, girls are given a dress or a skirt, while boys are given a shirt and a pair of shorts. Children are taught that boys and girls wear different types of clothes, girls in dresses and boys in shorts and shirts; thus, dress marks the beginning of sex identification. But women in urban areas do wear pants and shirts just like their male counterparts, although the majority of women still prefer traditional women's clothing.

12 FOOD

Most of the area in which the Tonga live is rural, and the majority follow a subsistence way of life, growing maize as the main staple. Other traditional staple crops are millet and sorghum. The diet consists of *inshima* (thick porridge), taken together with a relish in the form of either meat and gravy or vegetables such as beans and pumpkin leaves. Typically a group of relatives eat from the same dish, using their fingers to break off a piece of *inshima* from the common dish and dip it in gravy before eating it. This diet is taken twice a day during the slack season, i.e., for lunch and dinner, and once a day during the agricultural season since the women are busy tending the field and have very little time to cook.

13 EDUCATION

Most parents send their children to a nearby primary school. Boys and girls begin their day by helping out with household chores, such as taking the cattle for a short grazing trip and/or going to draw water for the parents, in the morning before going to school. At school they learn a few basic subjects such as English, biology, and arithmetic. After 8 years of primary school, it is possible to be selected to attend a secondary school with forms 1 through 4, modeled on the British Ordinary Level General Certificate of Education. The subjects may include mathematics, chemistry, physics, and biology, among others. The few lucky students who do extremely well in government exams are selected to attend the university, or different types of colleges.

In 1976, the government of Zambia made education free in the hopes that it would be accessible to the great majority of people. The end result has been a dramatic increase in literacy rates at the national level from a low of 10% at the time of independence in 1964 to 70% at present. Some parents, especially those living in urban areas, value education quite highly and have great aspirations for their children. This is not the case for people in rural areas where children's labor, rather than their education, is more critical to daily living.

14 CULTURAL HERITAGE

Music, dance, and literature are part and parcel of Tonga daily life. Stories that impart much-needed knowledge and principles to the young are narrated by grandfathers and grandmothers during the early hours of the evening around a fire. Each story might have several lessons for both the young and the old. The lessons could be as varied as how to act in a clever way, how to be imaginative, how to demonstrate intelligence to win the hand of a beautiful girl, the virtue of perseverance in bringing success, and appropriate behavior in certain situations. Drumming, singing, and dancing at beer parties, funerals, and naming ceremonies are a daily activity among the Tonga. At beer parties, men and women dance together in the open.

15 WORK

Urban elites in the few urban areas of Tongaland mostly find jobs in the government bureaucracy. Some find jobs as teachers, nurses, office clerks, or laborers on the railway. (During the colonial era, most of these positions were taken up by Europeans and Asians.) Others engage in petty trading such as selling fish, salt, sugar, and other basic commodities in open markets. But the majority of the Tonga people remain subsistence farmers who basically produce enough for the family and a little surplus to sell for money. Some of the local farmers who have adopted Western farming techniques have become relatively wealthy and are in a special class of their own. Livestock, such as cattle and goats, are another preoccupation for the Tonga. Such livestock provide a nutritious diet but are considered mainly to be a repository of wealth. Livestock such as cattle are also important in paying bride-wealth in times of marriage.

16 SPORTS

Even in the most remote parts of Tongaland, soccer (locally called football) is the favored sport for boys and young men. There is usually a makeshift soccer field in each village and whenever a ball is available, boys will play soccer continuously until they are very tired. School-going girls like to play netball, a game somewhat like basketball. In well-equipped secondary schools, boys and girls play games with which students in the West are familiar, such as tennis, badminton, and gymnastics. In rural areas, boys and girls will normally devise different games and play together when they have free time from household chores.

17 ENTERTAINMENT AND RECREATION

The most popular game among boys and girls that have not reached puberty is playing "house," especially during the slack season when agricultural work is completed. Children build themselves ramshackle playhouses at the edge of the village and pretend they are adults, with girls taking the sex-roles of women, and boys the roles of men. Girls do the cooking and boys come to eat the food. This is part of growing up and socialization within the traditional setting.

Although game is rare, men still like to go out for hunting and fishing in the nearby woodlands and rivers, such as the Kafue and the Zambezi and the numerous tributaries of these rivers.

18 FOLK ART, CRAFTS, AND HOBBIES

Pottery, carvings, basketry, and mats are crafted by older men and women among the Tonga for use in their daily lives. For example, pots are made in different sizes to be used for drawing water, cooking, brewing beer, and storing grain and other foods.

19 SOCIAL PROBLEMS

At the time when Zambians were demanding independence from British colonial rule, one of the most prominent politicians in Zambia was Harry Nkumbula, a school teacher from Tongaland. He opposed colonial rule alongside prominent leaders such as Simon Kapwepwe and Kenneth Kaunda, both from the Bemba-speaking group. In time, Nkumbula lost favor with Kenneth Kaunda and Simon Kapwepwe and was sidelined in the new independent Zambia. Naturally, the Tonga were not pleased and Nkumbula continued to draw support from his ethnic group, which became a stronghold of anti-Kaunda sentiments. Although the government of Kaunda did not punish the Tonga openly, few of them were invited to join the national political establishment. Despite the ethnic animosities between the Tonga and the post-independence government leadership, however, human rights in Zambia have generally been better than in other African dictatorships.

20 GENDER ISSUES

In Zambia, like in many African countries, the participation of women in government and other gainful economic activities is still extremely low. For example, in the 2006 poll, elected women candidates accounted for less than 15%, despite women constituting the majority of voters. Girls are also marginalized in the educational system, with 11% of girls aged 15 to 24 illiterate compared with 8% of boys. However, the Zambian government is slowly moving in the right direction in as far as gender issues are concerned in the sense that a National Gender Policy and a bill on gender-based violence have been approved. These efforts will somewhat assist in helping to empower women and bridge the gender gap.

In traditional Tonga society a man is considered to be the head of the household/family. This is a role assigned to men who are viewed as natural leaders and decision makers at the household level, even in cases where men may not be knowledgeable. When a wife makes a decision within the home she is supposed to keep such a deviation from the norm secret. The low position of women in Tonga society is in contradiction to their matrilineal traditions in which women are supposed to command the high ground. The mix of patrilineal and matrilineal traits among the Tonga has resulted in women being subject to the disadvantages of each system without the benefits of either.

Although human rights in Zambia are enshrined in the constitution, and the Mwanawasa government has been credited with respecting the rule of law with regard to human rights, Zambia has a poor human rights record. It has been reported that the security forces routinely carry out unlawful killings, torture, beatings, and abuse of criminal suspects and detainees. Prison conditions are often very poor and life-threatening. Rallies by the political opposition have often been obstructed and violence against women and/or homosexual groups is quite common. As a matter of fact the first ever homosexual association to be formed in Zambia in 1998 (the Lesbians, Gays, Bisexual, and Transgender Association—LEGATRA) was immediately banned by the government soon after its formation.

21 BIBLIOGRAPHY

Aldridge, Sally. *The Peoples of Zambia*. London: Heinemann Educational Books, 1978.

Clark, Sam, Elizabeth Colson, James Lee, et al. "Ten Thousand Tonga: A Longitudinal Anthropological Study from Southern Zambia, 1956-1991." Population Studies 49(1) (1995): 91-109.

Colson, Elizabeth. *Marriage and the Family among the Plateau Tonga of Northern Rhodesia*. Manchester: Manchester University Press, 1958.

———. "Land Law and Land Holding among the Valley Tonga of Zambia." *Journal of Anthropological Research* 42 (fall 1986): 261–68.

———. *Social Organization of the Gwembe Tonga*. Manchester: Manchester University Press, 1960.

Irin News. "Zambia: Humanitarian Country Profile." February 2007.

Kaplan, Irving. *Zambia: A Country Study*. Washington, DC: The American University, 1984.

Lancaster, Chet and Ken Vickery. *The Tonga-Speaking People of Zambia and Zimbabwe: Essays in Honor of Elizabeth Colson*. Lanham MD: University Press of America, 2007.

O'Brien, Dan. "Chiefs of Rain—Chiefs of Ruling: A Reinterpretation of Pre-Colonial Tonga (Zambia) Social and Political Structure." *Africa* 53, no. 4 (1983): 23–42.

Saha, Santosh C. *History of the Tonga Chiefs and Their People in the Monze District of Zambia*. New York: Peter Lang, 1994.

Vickery, Kenneth P. *Black and White in Southern Zambia: The Tonga Plateau Economy and British Imperialism, 1890–1939*. New York: Greenwood Press, 1986.

—by E. Kalipeni

TUAREGS

PRONUNCIATION: TWAH-regs
LOCATION: Saharan and Sahelian Africa (mostly Niger, Mali, Algeria, Libya, and Burkina Faso)
POPULATION: Approximately 1.2 million
LANGUAGE: Tamacheq
RELIGION: Islam, combined with traditional beliefs and practices
RELATED ARTICLES: Vol. 1: Algerians; Burkinabe; Libyans; Malians; Nigeriens

¹ INTRODUCTION

The Tuareg, a seminomadic, Islamic African people, are best-known for their men's practice of veiling the face with a blue, indigo-dyed cloth. Hence, early travel accounts often referred to them as "the Blue Men" of the Sahara Desert, the region where many Tuareg live. Tuareg are believed to be descendants of the North African Berbers and to have originated in the Fezzan region of Libya. They later expanded into regions bordering the Sahara and assimilated settled farming peoples from regions south of the Sahara into their traditionally stratified, hierarchical society. Tuareg traded with these populations and also, in the past, raided them for slaves, absorbing the slaves into their families. Therefore, today Tuareg display diverse physical and cultural traits, ranging from North African Arabic influences to influences from Africa south of the Sahara.

The Tuareg came to prominence as livestock-breeders and caravanners in the Saharan and Sahelian regions at the beginning of the 14th century, when trade routes to the lucrative salt, gold, ivory, and slave markets in North Africa, Europe, and the Middle East sprang up across their territory. As early as the 17th century AD, there were extensive migrations of pastoral nomadic Berbers, including the two important groups related to contemporary Tuareg: Lemta and Zarawa. Invasions of Beni Hilal and Beni Sulaym Arabs into Tuareg Tripolitania and Fezzan pushed Tuareg southwards to the Air Mountains, located in contemporary Niger Republic. Among these was a group of seven clans, allegedly descending from daughters of the same mother. There are "matrilineal" or female-based forms of inheritance and descent, which trace property and family ties through women, and many myths and rituals emphasize founding female ancestors. These institutions counterbalance more recent "patrilineal" institutions introduced by Islam, which emphasize male-based family ties and inheritance of property from father to son.

By the late 19th century, most trade from the Saharan interior had been diverted to the coast of Africa by the ocean routes. European explorers and military expeditions in the Sahara and along the Niger River led to French domination and incorporation of the region into French West Africa. By the early 20th century, the French had brought the Tuareg under their colonial domination, abolished slavery, and deprived Tuareg of their rights to tariff collection and protection services for trans-Saharan camel caravans.

Since the early 1990s, Tuaregs in Niger and Mali have sought either autonomous desert states or independence. In both countries, Tuaregs have been disappointed with the responses of national governments to serious droughts in the 1970s and 1980s, when many Tuaregs lost all or most of their animals. In Niger, Tuaregs also sought a greater portion of uranium revenues, as uranium comes from the historic Tuareg homeland in the Air Mountains. Peace accords were signed in both countries in 1995, but sporadic fighting began again in 2007.

² LOCATION AND HOMELAND

Most Tuareg today live in the contemporary nation-states of Niger, Mali, Algeria, Libya, and Burkina Faso, where they are ethnic minorities. For example, Tuaregs constitute about 8% of the population of Niger. The total population of Tamacheq-speakers who identify themselves culturally as Tuareg has been estimated to be about 1 million. The Saharan and Sahelian regions of southern Algeria, western Libya, eastern Mali, and northern Niger where most Tuaregs live includes flat desert plains; rugged savanna and desert-edge borderlands, where agriculture is possible only with daily irrigation; and volcanic mountains. The major mountain ranges are the Hoggar Mountains in Algeria, and the Air Mountains in Niger. Climatic features include extreme temperatures (up to 55°C or 130°F in the hot season), aridity and erratic rainfall (often less than 25 cm or 10 in of rainfall each year). Many herds of animals were decimated in the droughts of 1967–73 and 1984–85. During the brief cold season, there are high winds and sandstorms. Recently, many Tuareg have migrated to rural and urban areas farther south, due to natural disasters of drought and famine, and political tensions with the central state governments of Mali and Niger.

³ LANGUAGE

There are numerous dialects of Tamacheq, the major language, which is part of the Berber language family. A written script called Tifinagh is used in poetry and love messages and also appears in Saharan rock art and on some jewelry and musical instruments. Many contemporary Tamacheq-speakers also speak Songhay, Hausa, and French, and read Arabic.

Significant in Tuareg identity are names referring to the pre-colonial social categories based on descent and inherited occupational specialties, which remain important in rural communities. For example, *imajeghen* (nobles) refers to those Tuareg of aristocratic origin. *Imghad* refers to those of tributary origins, similar to the European category "vassal," who in the past raided for nobles. *Inaden* refers to the smiths/artisans. *Iklan* and *ighawalen* refer, respectively, to peoples of various degrees of servile and client or "serf"-like origins, who in the past worked for and paid rent to nobles. In principle, individuals are supposed to marry within their own social category, but this practice has been breaking down for some time, particularly in the towns.

⁴ FOLKLORE

There are many proverbs, riddles, myths, and folk tales among the Tuareg. These are usually recited orally, by smiths/artisans and women in the evening at home. Animal tales depicting human moral dilemmas are used to socialize children. They feature the jackal, hyena, and rabbit—animal characters widespread in African folklore. Many Tuareg groups recognize mythical female founding ancestors such as Tagurmat, who fought a battle on Mount Bagzan in the Air region, and whose twin daughters allegedly founded the herbal healing profession. Other stories depict mythical Berber queens and ancestors such as Tin Hinan in the Hoggar Mountain region of southern Algeria; and Kahena, who allegedly fought the Arab invaders. Another popular figure in myth and folk tales is Aligouran, said to be the author of messages and drawings on rocks throughout the Sahara. Aligouran is portrayed in a series of tales about the adventures of an uncle and his nephew. Other heroes are Boulkhou, an early Islamic scholar who built the first mosque and sank the first well in the Air Mountain area; and Kaousan, leader of the 1917 Tuareg revolt against the French. Many stories are about spirits, called *jinn,* who are believed to trick humans traveling alone in the desert.

5 RELIGION

Most Tuareg are Muslims, but religious practices generally incorporate pre-Islamic beliefs in jinns, spirits that mediate interactions between humans and the natural world, as well. Most spirits are considered evil, the cause of many illnesses that require healing by special exorcism rituals featuring drumming and songs. Some Tuareg perform divination and fortune-telling with cowrie shells, lizards, mirrors, and the Quran. Also, smiths/artisans play important roles in many Tuareg rites of passage, alongside Islamic scholars.

Islam most likely came from the west and spread into the Air Mountain region in the 7th century AD. Tuareg initially resisted Islam and earned a reputation among North African Arabs for being lax about Islamic practices. For example, local tradition did not require female chastity before marriage. Today most Tuareg women freely go about unveiled in public, and women may independently inherit property and initiate divorce. Islamic scholars, popularly called *marabouts,* are believed to possess a special power of blessing, called *al baraka.* They educate children in Quranic verses, officiate at rites of passage and Muslim holidays, and practice psychosocial counseling and, in rural areas, Quranic law.

6 MAJOR HOLIDAYS

Important holidays the Tuareg celebrate include Muslim holy days, as well as secular state holidays. Tabaski commemorates the story (from the Bible as well as the Quran) of Abraham's sacrifice of a ram in place of his son. Each household slaughters a goat or ram, feasts on its meat, and prays at the prayer ground. Tuareg celebrate Ganni (also called Mouloud in the Muslim world), the Prophet Muhammad's birthday, by special sacred and secular songs and camel races. The end of the month-long Ramadan fast, during which Tuareg neither eat nor drink from sunrise to sundown, is celebrated by animal sacrifice, feasting, prayer, and evening dancing festivals.

7 RITES OF PASSAGE

Principal rites of passage are namedays, weddings, and memorial/funeral feasts. In addition, there is a ritual marking men's first face-veiling. Namedays are held one week following a baby's birth. On the evening before the official nameday, elderly female relatives take the baby in a procession around the mother's tent and give him or her a secret Tamacheq name. The next day, while a smith woman shaves the baby's hair in order to sever the baby's ties to the spirit world, the *marabout* (Islamic scholar) and the father give the baby his or her official Arabic name from the Quran at the mosque. The marabout pronounces the baby's official Quranic name at the same mo-

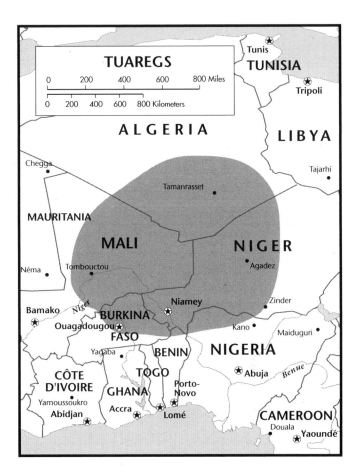

ment as he cuts the throat of a ram. There follow feasts, camel-races, and evening dancing festivals.

Weddings are very elaborate. They last for seven days, during which the groom's side of the family arrive in the camp or village of the bride on gaily decorated camels and donkeys, and elderly female relatives of the bride construct her nuptial tent. At weddings, there are camel-races and evening festivals featuring songs and dances. These are accompanied by a drum called a *tende,* constructed from a mortar covered with a goatskin and struck with the hands; and a calabash (gourd) floating in water, struck with a baton. These musical instruments are symbolically associated with romantic love, and their music is opposed to the sacred music and prayer identified with Islam. The wedding festivals provide an opportunity for youths of diverse social backgrounds to initiate romantic relationships outside of official marriage.

Mortuary rites are simpler than namedays and weddings. Burial takes place as soon as possible after death and is quickly concluded with a graveside prayer led by an Islamic scholar. Burial is followed by *iwichken* or condolences, when relatives and friends gather at the home of the deceased, and an Islamic scholar offers a prayer and blessing. Guests consume a memorial feast, consisting of foods similar to those at namedays and weddings. Sometimes, these memorial feasts are repeated at intervals following death, offered as alms in the name of the deceased. According to Tuareg belief, the soul *(iman)* is more personalized than spirits. It is seen as residing within the living individual, except during sleep when it may rise and travel about. The souls of the deceased are free to roam, but usually

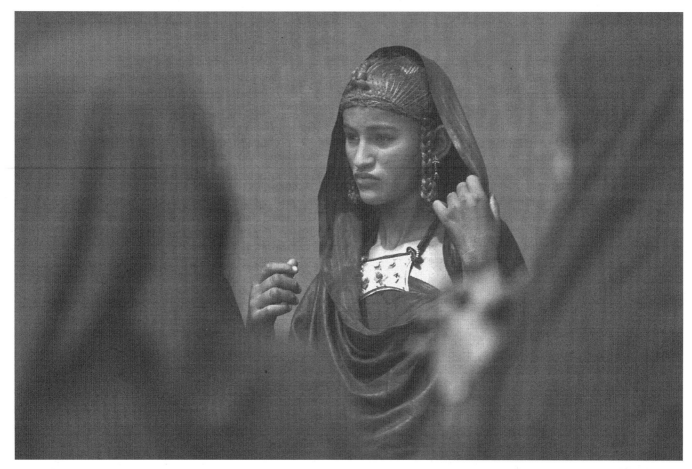

A Tuareg woman, hands colored by the traditional indigo dye, performs a dance in Tombouctou, Mali. (AP Images/Ben Curtis)

do so near graves. Tuareg make offerings of date-wine at tombs of important Islamic scholars, in order to obtain the special *al baraka* blessing.

Tuareg men begin to wear the face-veil at approximately 18 years of age. This marks their adult male status and signifies that they are ready to marry. The first veiling is performed in a special ritual by an Islamic scholar, who recites verses from the Quran as he wraps the veil around the young man's head.

8 INTERPERSONAL RELATIONS

As in many African societies, greetings among the Tuareg are extremely important and elaborate. Upon encountering someone, it is considered highly impolite not to greet her or him. In the Air regional dialect, *"Oy ik?"* signifies "How are you?" (directed to a man). This is followed by *"Mani eghiwan?"* signifying, "How is your family?" and additional greetings such as *"Mani echeghel?"* ("How is your work?") and sometimes *"Mani edaz?"* ("How is your fatigue?"). The usual polite response to these questions is *"Alkher ghas,"* or "In health only." In addition, there are many nonverbal greetings, for example, extending and withdrawing the right hand (associated with religious purity) several times. Other hand signals are used at festivals to indirectly express romantic interest. Visiting is frequent in both rural and urban communities. Gift exchange between women is important as a sign of friendship.

9 LIVING CONDITIONS

Since independence and the establishment of nation-states in the region in the early 1960s, Tuareg have continued to lose economic strength and power. They resisted French and, later, central-state schools and taxes, believing them to be strategies to force them to settle down so that they could be more easily controlled. As a result, Tuareg tend to be underrepresented today in urban jobs in the new economies of their nations, as well as in central governments in the region. These governments have imposed restrictions on trade with neighboring countries to protect national economic interests. Droughts and decreasing value of livestock and salt—their last remaining export commodity—have weakened a once strong and diverse local economy. Geographic barriers, economic crises, and political tensions have had an impact upon health care. Health care among Tuareg today includes traditional herbal, Quranic, and other ritual therapies, as well as Western-style biomedical clinics. However, traditional medicine is more prevalent in rural areas because many rural Tuareg, especially women, tend to be suspicious or shy of medical personnel who are of outside origins. Thus, although many rural residents desire some biomedical remedies such as antibiotics, they rely more upon traditional specialists and remedies. These include Quranic scholars who cure with verses from the Quran and psychotherapy; female herbalists who cure with leaves, roots, barks, and holistic techniques of verbal incantations and laying on of hands; and curers called *boka* who work with perfumes and incense.

¹⁰ FAMILY LIFE

In rural communities, each tent or compound corresponds to the nuclear household. Each compound is named for the married woman, who owns the nomadic tent. This tent was built by elderly female relatives and provided as dowry upon the woman's marriage. She may eject her husband from the tent upon divorce. Compounds in less-nomadic communities contain diverse residential structures. These may include several tents, a few conical grass buildings, and sometimes, among the more well-to-do in settled oases, an adobe house, built and owned by men. Thus, there are significant changes in property-balance occurring between men and women upon the increasing settlement of nomads.

Most camel-herding is still done by men. Although women may inherit and own camels, they tend to own and herd more goats, sheep, and donkeys. Caravan trade is exclusively done by men. Women may, however, indirectly participate in caravan trade by sending their camel(s) with a male relative, who brings goods back to them. Men plant and irrigate gardens. Women harvest crops. Although women may own gardens and date-palms, they leave the gardening to male relatives.

Islam has had long-term effects upon the family, the role of women, and property. Unless the deceased indicates otherwise before death with a witness in writing, Quranic patrilineal inheritance prevails: two-thirds of the property goes to the sons; one-third, to the daughters. Alternative inheritance forms from pre-Islamic institutions include inheritance called "living milk herds," animals reserved for sisters, daughters, and nieces; and various pre-inheritance gifts. Clan membership allegiance is through the mother and social class affiliation through the father. Political office in most groups goes from father to son. There are relaxed relationships featuring joking and horseplay with cousins and extremely reserved relationships featuring distance and respect with in-laws. Cultural ideals are marriage within one's own social category (noble, tributary, smith, and former slave) and close-cousin marriage. In the towns, both these patterns are breaking down. In rural areas, these rules remain strong, but many individuals marry close relatives only to please their mother, and later divorce, subsequently marrying nonrelatives. Some prosperous gardeners, chiefs, and Islamic scholars practice polygynous marriage to several women at the same time.

¹¹ CLOTHING

The Tuareg men's face-veil has several levels of meaning. It is, first of all, a symbol of male gender role identity and conveys important cultural values of respect and reserve. It also protects from evil spirits believed to enter through bodily openings. Furthermore, it has aesthetic importance; it is considered attractive and can be worn in diverse styles. In addition to personal preference, the style of the veil depends upon the social situation. The face-veil is worn highest (covering the nose and mouth) in order to express respect and reserve in the presence of important chiefs, older persons, and parents-in-law. Tuareg women do not wear a face-veil, but rather a head-scarf that covers the hair. A woman begins to wear this after her wedding to convey her new social status as a married woman. Other features of Tuareg dress include men's long Islamic robes in rural

areas; women's wrapper-skirts and "bolero"-style embroidered blouses; and in the towns, more varied dress, including West African tie-dyed cottons and, among more cosmopolitan Tuareg, European styles.

¹² FOOD

On oases, crops include millet, barley, wheat, corn, onions, tomatoes, and dates. Millet, spices, and other foods are also obtained through caravan trade. Almost 95% of the daily rural diet consists of cereal, with the added protein from animal products (milk and cheese), as well as a few seasonal fruits such as dates, mangoes and melon. Dried and pounded vegetables are added to sauces. Meat is consumed primarily on holidays and at rites of passage. A very sweet, thick, and richly blended beverage called *eghajira* is also consumed on these special occasions, as well as when traveling. It consists of pounded millet, dates, and goat cheese, mixed with water and eaten with a ladle. In towns, the diet is slightly more varied but, nonetheless, still consists of mostly nonmeat protein. Along the River Niger, some fish (both dried and fresh) are consumed.

¹³ EDUCATION

Until recently, many Tuareg, particularly nobles, resisted secular schools established by French and, later, central-state governments, because the schools are associated with forced settling of nomads and taxation. Nowadays, however, more Tuareg recognize the importance of education. Many rural residents achieve at least a primary school education, and some continue on to junior high school and high school levels in towns. Very few Tuareg are represented at universities. Quranic schools are important and respected. Much traditional education also consists of apprenticeship in adult tasks with older relatives.

¹⁴ CULTURAL HERITAGE

In Tuareg culture, there is great appreciation of the visual and oral arts. The large body of music, poetry, and song are of central importance during courtship, rites of passage, and festivals. Men and women of diverse social origins who dance and perform vocal and instrumental music are admired for their musical creativity. But distinctive musical styles, dances, and instruments are associated with the various social categories. *Marabouts* (Islamic scholars), men, and older women perform sacred liturgical music on Muslim holidays. Youths perform more secular music on such instruments as the *anzad* and the *tende*. The *anzad*, a bowed, one-stringed lute, was traditionally played by noble women, and the *tende* drum was historically played by smiths and former slaves.

¹⁵ WORK

Traditionally, occupations corresponded to social origins. Nobles controlled the caravan trade, owned most of the camels, and remained more nomadic, coming into oases to collect a proportion of the harvest from their client and servile peoples. Tributary groups raided and traded for nobles and had rights to the products and offspring of nobles' animals in their care. Peoples of varying degrees of client and servile status performed domestic and herding labor for nobles. Smiths manufactured jewelry and household tools and performed praise-songs at noble patron families' weddings. They also served as important oral historians and political go-betweens and assisted in noble marriage negotiations.

Because of natural disasters and political tensions, it is now increasingly difficult to make a living solely off nomadic herding. Thus, there is now less correspondence between social origins, occupation, and wealth. For example, many nobles have become impoverished from loss of herds. Most rural Tuareg today combine different occupations, practicing herding, oasis gardening, caravan trading, and migrant labor. Other contemporary careers include tourist art, in which many smiths are active, and house-guarding in the towns. In towns, there are a few business entrepreneurs and teachers.

[16] SPORTS

Soccer is extremely popular among young people. Traditional wrestling has been actively promoted by the governments of Niger and Mali, and wrestling arenas exist in most major towns. Tournaments are generally held at least once a year. Finally, camel races occur at major festivals and celebrations and are considered an important expression of Tuareg cultural heritage.

[17] ENTERTAINMENT AND RECREATION

In the towns, television, films, parades, and culture centers offer diversion. Movies from Nigeria, India, and China are popular. In the countryside, most residents make their own entertainment. Children make their own dolls and other toys; and adults dance, sing, and play musical instruments at festivals. In addition, people of all ages play board games with stones and date pits, which approximately resemble Western board games such as chess.

[18] FOLK ART, CRAFTS, AND HOBBIES

Visual arts consist primarily of metalworking (silver jewelry), woodworking (delicately decorated spoons and ladles and carved camel-saddles), and dyed and embroidered leather, all of which are specialties of smiths, who formerly manufactured these products solely for their noble patrons. In rural areas, nobles still commission smiths to make these products, but in urban areas many smiths now sell jewelry and leatherwork to non-Tuareg such as African civil servants and European tourists, as nobles experience greater economic difficulty in supporting smiths.

[19] SOCIAL PROBLEMS

Development programs involving the Tuareg from the 1940s into the 1970s failed miserably because they worked against the traditional pastoral herding production systems. During the 1984–85 drought, some Tuareg men, who called themselves *ishumer* (a Tamacheq variant of the French verb *chomer*, which means "to be unemployed") left for Libya, where they received military training and arms support. In the early 1990s, they returned to their homes and demanded regional autonomy in a separatist rebellion from 1990–1995. Since that time, there has been continued sporadic fighting in some regions of Mali and Niger. Some Tuareg have been forced into political exile and refugee camps.

[20] GENDER ISSUES

Tuareg women are known for their independence and ability to freely circulate in public spaces before marriage. In spite of the fact that the vast majority of Tuaregs are Muslims, Tuareg women do not veil. Women also exert significant influence over political and economic matters. Men are normally chiefs, but chieftaincy passes through maternal bloodlines. Inheritance of property is also matrilineal, and it is not uncommon to find women engaged in large-scale trade.

Within the household, women are generally responsible for collecting water, preparing meals, and caring for children. Many Tuareg women also have herds of goats and donkeys. They are also permitted to own camels, though camel herding is generally left to men. Women usually do not participate in long-distance caravan trades with men, and thus are left responsible for their households when men are traveling.

[21] BIBLIOGRAPHY

Baier, Stephen and Paul E. Lovejoy. "The Tuareg of the Central Sudan: Gradations in Servility at the Desert Edge (Niger and Nigeria)," in *Slavery in Africa: Historical and Anthropological Perspectives*, Suzanne Miers and Igor Kopytoff, eds. Madison: University of Wisconsin, 1977.

Childs, Larry, and Celina Chelala. "Drought, Rebellion, and Social Change in Northern Mali: The Challenges Facing Tamacheq Herders." *Cultural Survival Quarterly* (Winter 1994): 16–20.

de Foucault, Fraternité Charles. *Initiation a la Langue des touaregs de l'Air.* Niamey and Agadez, Niger: Petites Soeurs de Charles de Foucault, Service Culturel de l'Ambassade de France, 1968.

Giuffrida, Alessandra, "Clerics, Rebels and Refugees: Mobility Strategies and Networks among the Kel Antessar," *Journal of North African Studies* 10:3-4 (September 2005): 529-543.

Murphy, Robert. "Social Distance and the Veil." *American Anthropologist* 69 (1964):163–170.

Nicolaisen, Johannes. *Ecology and Culture of the Pastoral Tuareg.* Copenhagen: National Museum, 1963.

Norris, H. T. *The Tuareg: Their Islamic Legacy and Its Diffusion into the Sahel.* Wilts, England: Aris and Phillips, 1975.

Rasmussen, Susan. *Spirit Possession and Personhood among the Kel Ewey Tuareg.* Cambridge: Cambridge University Press, 1995.

Salifou, André. *La question touarègue au Niger.* Paris: Karthala, 1993.

US Department of State. "Niger: Background Notes, 1–3." Washington, DC: Bureau of Public Affairs, 1987.

—revised by C. Breedlove

TUNISIANS

PRONUNCIATION: too-NEE-zhuhns
LOCATION: Western North Africa (the Maghrib)
POPULATION: 10.25 million
LANGUAGE: Arabic; French
RELIGION: Islam (Sunni Muslim)

¹ INTRODUCTION

Tunisia is one of the countries forming the *Maghrib,* the term used to describe the western part of North Africa. Modern Tunisia's name can be traced back to the ancient settlement of Tunis, which by the 13th century had developed into Tunisia's capital. Tunisia was known to the Roman and Arab conquerors as *Africa (Ifriqiyyah),* and later *Africa* came to be used for the entire continent. Tunisia is the most westernized state in North Africa and maintains strong ties with France, the colonizing power from 1881 to 1956. Until recently, Tunisia's modern development was considered a model for other nations emerging from European colonialism.

Tunisia's history dates back to Neolithic times (the Stone Age). Anthropologists have found evidence indicating that the coastal area was populated by hunters and fishermen as well as farmers. While south of the Atlas mountains, Tunisia is now primarily desert, until 4000 BC, the region was a vast savannah with giant buffalo, elephants, rhinoceros, and hippopotamus. Neolithic civilization, which is characterized by animal domestication and agriculture, developed in the area between 6000 and 2000 BC.

The various nomadic peoples who eventually settled in the area came to be called Berbers. The Phoenician, Roman, Greek, Byzantine, and Arab conquerors all attempted to defeat or assimilate the Berbers into their cultures, with varying degrees of success. Phoenician traders arrived in the area around 900 BC and established the city of Carthage around 800 BC. From there, the Phoenicians established towns along the coast. These became centers for trade with areas as far away as Lebanon. The Berbers were either enslaved by the Phoenicians or forced to pay tribute. By the 4th century BC, the Berbers formed the largest part of the Phoenician slave army and eventually revolted as the power of Carthage weakened. In time, several Berber kingdoms were created that vied with each other for power until the arrival of the Romans in AD 24.

The Roman conquest was disastrous for the Berbers. Tribes were forced to become settled or leave the area. For this reason, the Berbers continuously resisted Roman rule. The Romans began their occupation by controlling the coastal lands and cultivating the area. It is estimated that the Roman province of Africa produced 1 million tons of cereals each year for the Roman Empire along with fruits, figs, grapes, beans, and olive oil.

Along with the Roman presence, Judaism and Christianity began appearing among the Berbers. Many Jews who had been expelled from Palestine by the Romans settled in the area, and some Berber tribes converted to Judaism. Christianity arrived in the 2nd century AD and was especially attractive to slaves. By the end of the 4th century, much of the settled areas had become Christian.

In AD 429, the German king Gaiseric, along with 80,000 Vandals (a German tribe), invaded North Africa from Spain, eventually weakening Roman control. With the weakening of Rome, Berber tribes began to return to their old lands. Meanwhile, the Byzantine emperor Justinian sent his army to North Africa in AD 533 and within a year conquered the German forces, although the Byzantines never established as firm a hold on the area as had the Romans.

The most influential conquest in the area was the invasion of Arab Muslims between AD 642 and AD 669. In AD 670, the Arabs established the town of al-Qayrawan south of Tunis as a rival to the Byzantine influence of the more northern areas. The largely Christian Berber tribes in Tunisia converted to Islam, and in AD 711 the Muslims established firmer control in the region.

The ruling Arab view of Islam at the time was that Islam was primarily a religion for Arabs and Arabs subsequently treated non-Arab converts as second-class citizens. Many political trends developed among Muslims in the Arabian Peninsula, however, that rejected the Arabism of the ruling Umayyad dynasty in favor of strict equality for all Muslims. Followers of this movement, called Kharijites, spread to North Africa, and many Berbers became attracted to their message of Islamic equality and strict piety. They eventually rebelled against the Arab caliphate's control of the area and established a number of kingdoms.

In AD 750, the Abbasids—who had succeeded the Umayyad dynasty—spread their rule to the area and appointed Ibrahim ibn al-Aghlab as governor in al-Qayrawan. The Aghlabi dynasty was a perfect example of what has been called the Judeo-Islamic culture of the Muslim world. A thriving Jewish community with a long intellectual tradition existed in Muslim Spain and North Africa, and there was a great deal of interaction between the two communities.

Al-Qayrawan became a great center of learning, attracting students from all over the Muslim world. In the 10th century, Constantius Africanus, a Christian from Carthage, went to Italy and introduced the advanced Islamic learning to Europe. The works of the ancient Greeks, which had been translated long ago by the Arabs and studied as major texts, were now translated into Latin, thus reintroducing the Greek works to Europe.

To the west of Aghlabi lands, the Kharijites, under Abd al-Rahman ibn Rustum, established a Rustumid kingdom from AD 761 to AD 909. The leaders were elected by the leading citizens of the town and gained a reputation for honesty and justice. There was much support for scholarship, astronomy, astrology, theology, and law. By the end of the 9th century, Ismaili Muslims (Shia Muslims who followed a more esoteric and mystical interpretation of Islam) led a revolt against the established Sunni rulers in Tunisia and the rest of North Africa. In AD 909 the Ismaili forces established the Fatimid Dynasty in North Africa, first at al-Qayrawan and later in Cairo, Egypt.

The Fatimids were more interested in the lands to the East and left Tunisia and neighboring Algeria to Berber rule. However, considering the conflicting loyalties of the different tribes, conflict became inevitable. In the 11th century, the Fatimids sent Arab bedouins to North Africa to assist their forces against other Berbers. Eventually, the influx of Arabs promoted the Arabization of the entire area.

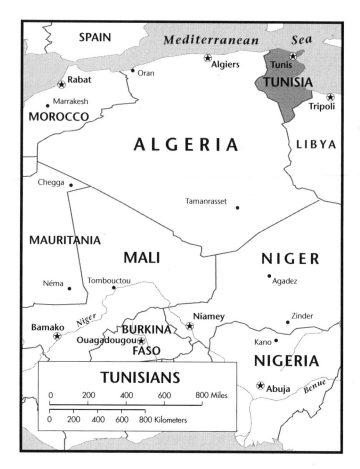

SPAIN

Mediterranean Sea

• Oran
Algiers

Tunis
TUNISIA

★ Rabat
• Marrakesh
MOROCCO

Tripoli

A L G E R I A

LIBYA

• Chegga

• Tamanrasset

MAURITANIA

MALI

NIGER

• Néma
• Tombouctou

• Agadez

Niger

Niamey
• Zinder

Bamako
BURKINA
Ouagadougou
FASO

Kano
NIGERIA

TUNISIANS

★ Abuja
Benue

0   200   400   600   800 Miles

0   200   400   600   800 Kilometers

Tunisia quickly attempted to modernize its government institutions and build a modern army. Tunisia took huge loans from French banks in order to pay for the reforms. Mustafa Khaznader, the prime minister and treasurer at the time, unscrupulously cooperated with French banks to build up a large personal fortune while allowing France to charge extortionately high interest rates for its loans. This provided France with a lever to further its colonialist goals in Tunisia.

Eventually, as Turkish power weakened worldwide, Europe began imposing reforms on Turkey as well as Tunisia designed to make the economic environment more favorable for European exploitation. Meanwhile, the Tunisian government's policies of assuming huge loans from an obliging France, as well as famines and the plague, finally led to its bankruptcy. In 1868, Tunisia was forced to give up control over its financial affairs to a commission of French, British, and Italian bankers called the International Financial Commission (IFC). The Europeans restructured Tunisia's economy to provide payments to the European banks. Lands, for example, were confiscated from Tunisians and sold to Europeans.

In 1878 at the Congress of Berlin, Britain and France secretly agreed to allow each other the "right" to take over certain Ottoman territories. Britain took Cyprus, and France was given Tunisia. France, however, had to wait until 1881 for an excuse to invade Tunisia from Algeria. Using the pretense that tribesmen from Tunisia had raided in Algeria, France sent more than 40,000 troops to take over Tunis. In the south, a tribal leader named Ali ben Khalifa, with the help of Ottomans in Libya, held out until 1883.

France established what it called a "protectorate" in Tunisia, creating a model to be followed by a number of European countries thereafter. The leaders in the country were allowed to remain in power and personally profit from the occupation as long as they provided legitimacy for France's presence.

Unlike the brutal occupation in Algeria, the colonization of Tunisia was a more gradual affair. Parallel institutions were created for Europeans and Muslims. French corporations moved in to take over the best land. The previous inhabitants of these areas were then hired as low-wage earners for the French corporations.

As in most occupied Muslim territories, a new nationalist class composed of Western-educated leaders developed in Tunisia. At first, they carefully asked for more rights and greater equality with the Europeans, never challenging the French occupation of the country. This made them more popular with the elite Tunisians, who also had been educated in the West, than with the overwhelming majority of Tunisians, who led a much tougher existence under occupation. In order to broaden their appeal, the nationalists, who called themselves the "Young Tunisians," also began advocating the rights of Tunisian workers.

During World War I (1914–18), more than 60,000 Tunisians joined the French army to fight in Europe, expecting more rights upon their return. They were sorely disappointed, however, thereby increasing support for the nationalists. As the Young Tunisians became more popular and organized themselves into political parties, they were able to exert greater political influence on Tunisians, through newspapers and direct petitions to the government. The French began to take tougher action against them and on 9 April 1938, the French killed

Nevertheless, independent kingdoms did manage to establish themselves in the area. The greatest of these were the Almoravids, the Almohads, the Hafsids, and the Zayanids. These kingdoms were all led by Muslim leaders who greatly encouraged learning and the arts.

Meanwhile, the Catholics of Spain were involved in reconquering southern Spain from Muslim control. Spain had become a cosmopolitan and pluralistic center of learning under Muslim rule. The Spanish conquest in 1492, however, fundamentally changed the character of the area. The new rulers forced all Muslims and Jews to convert to Christianity. Many fled to North Africa, and a sizable community of Jews settled in Algeria, Tunisia, and Morocco. Tunis changed hands a number of times until 1574, when Muslim troops loyal to the Ottoman Empire (based in present-day Turkey), finally established rule over Tunis.

The Ottoman empire controlled Tunisia through appointed governors, or Beys, for the next 250 years. However, by the beginning of the 1800s, real power was in the hands of the Beys, who had established the Husayn dynasty. In 1830, France invaded neighboring Algeria on a self-proclaimed "civilizing mission." In June of that year, 34,000 French soldiers invaded Algiers, and after a three-week battle, took the city. Then, in 1835, the Ottomans re-established direct rule in Libya. In light of the brutality of the French invasion and subsequent annexation of Algeria by France, a direct threat to Tunisia's west, and increased Ottoman power in Libya, to the east, the Tunisian leaders instituted a number of policies thought to be favorable to Europe.

122 rioting Tunisians and many prominent nationalists were arrested.

During World War II (1939–45), the Muslims joined the French forces in opposing the Nazi invasion. Once France was quickly defeated by Hitler's forces, the local French government in Tunisia also joined Hitler's forces and allied with Mussolini's Italy.

As the Germans took over the area, they freed Arab nationalist leaders, including Habib Bourguiba of Tunisia. Germany tried to court favor with the nationalists, urging them to provide support for the fascists. Despite their profound distrust of French leaders, the nationalists unanimously refused to issue any statements of support for Germany.

Coordinated attacks by American and Free French forces from the west and British forces from the east eventually defeated the German and Italian armies in North Africa, with heavy fighting on Tunisian soil. Tunisians once again had high expectations that they would be granted independence as a reward for their steadfast support of the Allies. Bourguiba even had a personal correspondence with U.S. President Franklin D. Roosevelt, expressing his admiration of American democracy and urging American support for self-determination in Tunisia. The Allies, however, were more interested in maintaining the status quo, fearing instability if independence were granted to any colonies. The French leaders were reinstated in Tunisia, and the nationalists were once again imprisoned.

By 1952, Tunisian resistance turned violent, and many civilians—European and Arab—were killed. By 1954, the French decided to negotiate an agreement in Tunisia while exerting most of their military efforts in Algeria. Internal autonomy was provided to Tunisians for the first time since the protectorate. By 1956, Tunisia was officially independent and in 1957, the monarchy was abolished and Habib Bourguiba became the country's first president. Although France maintained military forces in Tunisia along with a large settler presence, the nationalists' gradual approach to independence was in stark contrast to the bitter war in neighboring Algeria.

After independence, Tunisia became a one-party socialist state ruled by Bourguiba's Neo-Destour (the New Constitution) Party. French law was maintained on many civil issues at the expense of Muslim sensibilities. For example, a part of the *Al Zaytuna* mosque, the center for Muslim scholarship, was incorporated into the University of Tunis, but the rest of the center was simply closed down. Tunisia announced a policy of non-alignment, allying with neither the Soviet Union nor the United States, although in practice Tunisia continued to have very close relations with France and, in recent years, with the United States.

Bourguiba personally led Tunisia to adopt Western laws and practices in public and private spheres. Polygamy, or the practice of marrying more than one wife, was outlawed. Women were provided with social rights similar to men. In order to increase productivity, Bourguiba even encouraged Muslims to stop fasting during the Muslim month of Ramadan as required by Islam.

However, Bourguiba did not extend his Westernizing policies to politics. Under his strong one-party rule, all dissension was effectively quashed, and opposition to his policies was viewed as sedition. By the 1970s, the strong-arm tactics of the government and the lack of political freedom led to a series of strikes and demonstrations by students and unions. These were also encouraged by rising unemployment and lower standards of living resulting from the government's economic policies. By 1977 the army was called in to fight demonstrators and strikers for the first time since independence, and in 1978, 150 Tunisians were killed in clashes with security forces.

Opposition parties, some in exile and some in Tunisia, began to form. One of the most influential was the Islamic Tendency Movement (MTI). The MTI wanted to promote economic reform along with the increased "Islamization" of the state. Eventually, the government began taking stronger action against MTI activists, finally arresting their leader, Rachid al-Gannouchi, and thus causing further disturbances. The aging Bourguiba had become increasingly authoritarian and erratic in his behavior, and attempted to have the head of the MTI executed. The United States and France both intervened, fearing civil unrest if the order were carried out. Although Bourguiba at first acquiesced, he once again attempted to have Gannouchi executed and was finally deposed by his prime minister, Zine al-'Abidine Ben 'Ali, a 51-year-old former army general trained in the United States. Gannouchi was subsequently exiled from Tunisia. In 2008 Ben 'Ali remained in charge of Tunisia as president.

Ben 'Ali stabilized the situation by calling for political pluralism and respect for human rights. In strong contrast to the secular Bourguiba, Ben 'Ali publicly acknowledged Tunisia's Arab Islamic heritage. However, within a couple of years this atmosphere of trust and openness was gone and most of the leadership of the MTI (which had changed its name to *Al Nahda*) were either imprisoned or in exile. Ben 'Ali refused to support U.S. intervention in the first Gulf War in 1991. This move angered the United States and the European Union (EU) but was popular with Tunisians.

After introducing a highly restricted form of political pluralism, Ben 'Ali went on to win three landslide election victories, gaining over 98% of the vote. Facing constitutional term limits, he engineered a constitutional change that cleared the way for him to continue to run for the presidency indefinitely. Economically, his rule has been relatively successful, with Tunisia among the most liberalized economies in Africa and the Middle East. Unlike its neighbor Algeria, which has experienced varying degrees of civil war between secularist and Islamist factions since the 1990s, Tunisia has remained a reliable, relatively secular ally of Western power in the region.

² LOCATION AND HOMELAND

Tunisia has a population of 10.25 million, 24% of whom are under the age of 14. Some 300,000 Tunisians live abroad, many in France. Half the population in Tunisia lives in urban areas, with the remainder in rural areas. Unlike in other North African states, the Berber and Arab populations in Tunisia are completely intermixed, and all speak Arabic.

The country is located on the northern border of the continent of Africa. Tunisia, Algeria, Morocco, and Tripolitania (in northwest Libya) together form the region of the Maghrib. The Mediterranean Sea borders Tunisia on the north and east. The country has three gulfs: Tunis, Hammamet, and Gabes. Tunisia has an area of about 164,000 sq km (63,320 sq mi) and a coastline of about 1,600 km (994 mi). To the west, Tunisia shares a border with Algeria; to the south and east, it borders Libya. Northern Tunisia is relatively fertile and mountainous.

The Dorsale mountain chain, Tunisia's branch of the Atlas Mountains, extends from the northeast to the southwest. The Mejerda River, which lies north of the mountains, rises in Algeria and drains into the Gulf of Tunis. The far south includes part of the Saharan desert.

³ LANGUAGE

Arabic is the national language of Tunisia. Arabic arrived with the Arab conquests of the 7th and 8th centuries, before which Berber dialects were the chief spoken languages. Berber is today used by very few Tunisians, mainly in the south of the country.

Arabic, a highly evolved Semitic language related to Hebrew and Aramaic, is spoken by almost everyone. Written Arabic is in the form of classical Arabic or a simpler version called "modern standard," which is taught in schools throughout the Arab world and is originally based on the Quran. This Arabic is used in the media, government, and literature throughout the Arab world, tying the Arab world together culturally. Tunisians also speak a North African dialectical Arabic that includes a number of slang terms, many from French. The Tunisian dialect also includes many Berber words, including the names for plants and geographic areas.

When the French occupied Tunisia, they emphasized the use of French. After independence, the new Tunisian government implemented a policy of reintroducing Arabic while maintaining the use of French. Today, French is used orally as well as in the sciences and the military and is important in education, international trade and government. About 60% of television programs are in Arabic and 40% are in French, and some of the major newspapers are printed in French. However, while most Tunisians have some knowledge of French, only an educated minority can speak it fluently.

Common women's names in Tunisia are *Leila, Hayat, Wasila,* and *Mariam.* Common men's names are *Muhammad, Habib, Moncif,* and *`Ali.*

⁴ FOLKLORE

The Maghrib, including Tunisia, has many legends based on the exploits of Muslim leaders who acted as arbiters in disputes between families and tribal groups. These leaders often came from highly religious backgrounds and were considered well learned. They are called *marabouts* (holy men), and they were believed to have *baraka* (divine grace), which allowed them to perform miracles. Despite the fact that in Islam only God can bestow baraka, some marabouts have become saints in the popular mind, with sacred powers of their own and many Tunisians make pilgrimages to the tombs of these saints to ask for intercession. These tombs also act as focal points for local communities and as sites for yearly festivals, occasions for the reestablishment and confirmation of group solidarity. Many such tombs are located at or near particular landscape features, at natural springs, in forests, caves, or on hilltops, for example, suggesting links to more ancient religious beliefs. Before independence, Tunisian marabouts were very influential, but their popularity has dwindled since.

Many other folk beliefs have also lost popularity since independence, primarily because Bourguiba, the first president, encouraged modernization and discouraged superstition. Some Tunisians believe in evil spirits called *jinn,* who are said to assume the guise of animals so as not to be recognized. To ward off these evil spirits, Tunisians wear verses from the Quran on an amulet. They may also wear the *khomsa* ("hand of Fatima"), a charm in the shape of the right hand that protects against the evil eye.

Most folklore in Muslim countries tells stories of important figures in religious history. One such story, which is also cause for annual commemoration throughout the Islamic world, is that of *al-Isra' wa al-Mi`raj.* According to legend, on the 26th day of the Islamic month of Rajab, the Prophet Muhammad traveled at night from Mecca, Saudi Arabia (then Hijaz) to Jerusalem. From Jerusalem, he rode his wondrous horse, al-Burak, on a nocturnal visit to heaven.

⁵ RELIGION

The overwhelming majority (98%) of Tunisians are Muslims. Most Tunisians belong to the *Maliki Sunni* school of Islam, introduced by the Arab invasions in the 7th and 8th centuries. There are still remnants, however, of the Muslim *Kharijite* influence in the south, which espouses a stricter egalitarianism. *Sufi* Islam, which stresses the mystical nature of the divine and which was closely connected to the monarchy, has lost much of its former influence. There are also small Jewish and Christian minorities.

Islam teaches that God (Allah) regularly sent guidance to humans in the form of prophets, and Islam accepts the earlier Semitic prophets, including Abraham, Moses, and Jesus. Muslims believe that Muhammad was the last in the line of prophets sent with the message that there is only one God. Muslims also believe in heaven and hell, the Day of Judgment, and angels. The Quran is the holy book of Muslims, and it teaches that, to get to heaven, men and women must believe in God and do good works by struggling in God's way. Belief and action are tightly bound together in Muslim literature.

The Islamic religion has five pillars: (1) Muslims must pray five times a day; (2) Muslims must give alms, or *zakat,* to the poor; (3) Muslims must fast during the month of Ramadan; (4) Muslims must make the pilgrimage, or *hajj,* to Mecca; and (5) each Muslim must recite the *shahada —ashhadu an la illah ila Allah wa ashhadu in Muhammadu rasul Allah—*which means "I witness that there is no god but Allah and that Muhammad is the prophet of Allah."

Most Tunisians use the Quran, *Hadith* (oral traditions relating to the words and deeds of the prophet Muhammad) and a form of *Shariah* (Islamic law) to define and regulate their behavior, social relations, and daily rituals. The practice and belief of Islam varies, with the urban middle and upper classes generally being more open to the adoption of non-Muslim practices such as Western forms of dress (like the bikini), public socializing between the sexes, and the consumption of alcohol.

As in many other parts of the Muslim world, personal piety became highly politicized in the last decades of the 20th century. Many political parties have been created in opposition to authoritarian governments in the region, using Islamic symbols to promote their legitimacy and support within society. In Tunisia, where political parties based on such factors as religion, language, region or ethnicity are illegal, the main Islamist opposition group, *Al Nahdah* ("The Renaissance"), has been banned and its leaders imprisoned or exiled. The government has also responded by increasing harassment of Muslims who

Tunisians parade with camels during the reenactment of a Bedouin traditional wedding at the 36th Sahara Festival of Douz in southern Tunisia. The festival showcases cultural traditions, including dance, poetry, and crafts. (AP Images/Hassene Dridi)

exhibit outward signs of piety either in their dress or behavior under the assumption that certain kinds of religious behavior, attendance at a particular mosque for example, is an indication of political opposition. This has not only begun to fracture society between the more "secular" and the more "religious", but has also led to rising apathy and discontent towards civil society in general.

6 MAJOR HOLIDAYS

Tunisia commemorates secular and Muslim religious holidays. One major Muslim holiday is *Eid al-Fitr,* which comes at the end of the month of fasting called Ramadan. During Ramadan, Muslims refrain from eating, drinking, or sexual relations during the daytime in order to reflect on God and on the plight of the unfortunate. In Tunisia, perhaps more so than any other Muslim nation except Turkey, the practice of fasting is quietly discouraged by the government, although the holiday at its end, *Eid al-Fitr,* is still celebrated for three days. The other major Muslim holiday is *Eid al-Adha,* which commemorates the willingness of the prophet Abraham and his son to obey God's command in all things, even when Abraham was about to sacrifice his son. Eid al-Adha signals the end of the Muslim pilgrimage to Mecca, or *hajj,* which every Muslim must attempt to undertake at least once during his or her lifetime. Religious holidays are celebrated by going to the mosque for communal

prayers and then coming home to large meals with family and visiting relatives. Islamic practice says that a part of the meat slaughtered for the feast is given to relatives and to the poor. More Sufi Islamic holidays such as the Birthday of the Prophet Muhammed and the Feast of *Ashura,* commemorating the martyrdom of the Prophet's grandson at the Battle of Kerbala, usually involve communal visits to tombs and shrines.

Secular holidays include the Proclamation of the Republic Day (25 July); socialist May Day (or Labor Day, 1 May), which commemorates worker solidarity around the world; Independence Day (20 March); Martyrs' Day (9 April); to commemorate a French massacre of 122 Tunisians in 1938; and a holiday to mark the final evacuation of French troops in 1963 (15 October). There is also Constitution Day (1 June), Women's Day (13 August), and a holiday to mark the assumption of the presidency by Ben 'Ali (7 November).

7 RITES OF PASSAGE

The main rites of passage are regulated by Islamic traditions. The birth of a child in Tunisia is a much-celebrated event. Immediately after she delivers a baby, a new mother is fed a creamy mixture of nuts, sesame seeds, honey, and butter, known as *zareer.* On the seventh day after the birth, guests visiting the mother and baby are given the same sweet desert in celebration of the birth. On the seventh day, it is also customary to slaughter a lamb and have a dinner party with friends and family who bring gifts for the newborn child.

Male circumcision is carried out an almost all Tunisian prepubescent males. The boys are dressed up in formal clothes, taken to the local hospital where the operation is quickly carried out. They are then taken home where they are visited by extended family, congratulated and presented with gifts.

Engagement can be a long and difficult process, with much negotiation over finances, etiquette and gifts. Marriage, almost universal in Tunisia, can be arranged through the extended family or according to individual choice, generally depending on the socioeconomic status of the family. Cousins are preferred, as they are seen to hold equal social status, a particularly important factor for girls. Mothers in Tunisia often search for brides for their sons in the *hammmam* (public bathhouse). On marriage, the bride is taken to the newly prepared house of the groom, who then enters and consummates the union. The newlyweds are usually left alone for several days before they reappear in public society.

Pilgrimage to Mecca, a duty for all Muslims, is the most important midlife rite of passage both for men and women. The extended family is usually closely involved in helping to prepare for and fund this costly journey. Much prayer and celebration surrounds the pilgrimage, and the returnees are addressed as *hajj* (men) or *hajja* (women), terms of real respect within the community.

Death is considered a natural transition and the soul is believed to live on. Mourners are encouraged to bury a loved one as soon as possible after death. The corpse is washed and wrapped in a shroud. It is then carried by a group of mourners dressed in red to the family tomb. There the body is laid on its left side facing Mecca. Condolences are given for three days after a death, and it is understood that the mourning period is over after the third day.

8 INTERPERSONAL RELATIONS

While Tunisian society is relatively egalitarian, traditional manners still inform behavior and women are expected to dress and behave with modesty in public. In public, many women will wear a *sifsari* (a long plain cloth garment with head covering) over their normal clothes. Men, too, are expected to show respect to women and each other. For example, a man should not smoke when in the company of his father. Brothers might choose to frequent different cafés so as not to inhibit each other's relaxation.

Upon greeting, men shake hands with other men and with women. Two men who have not seen each other for a long time may kiss on the cheeks. Women may either shake hands with other women or kiss each other on the cheeks. Men and women, however, cannot kiss one another in public, and it is considered improper for unmarried men and women to kiss. In formal settings, it is common to greet one another using titles, mainly French—*Monsieur, Madame, Mademoiselle, Docteur,* and *Professeur.* The Arabic word for Mr. is *sayyid,* Mrs. is *sayyida,* and Miss is *anisa.*

Boys and girls attend separate classes until they enter college, and there is little dating until a man and a woman are ready for marriage. Male-female relations are governed by the Islamic code of modesty, and men and women avoid public displays of affection.

As Muslims, Tunisians eat and shake hands with the right hand. Tunisians enjoy bathing in the *hammams,* or public bathhouses, which they visit to socialize. These have separate hours for men and women, except in some resort towns where *hammams* are unisex for the benefit of tourists. Cafés are popular hangouts for men in the evenings. Here they smoke *chichas* (water pipes) and play cards. Both men and women smoke, but women hesitate to do so in public.

9 LIVING CONDITIONS

The government has actively promoted housing development and the vast majority of Tunisian families own their own homes. Most of the main Tunisian cities contain a traditional Islamic core, colonial and postcolonial suburbs, and slum areas. The Islamic urban center is comprised of the mosque as communal political locus, the market for exchange, and the public baths for health, informal networking, and relaxation.

Tunisian homes differ from region to region, although most are built stone, adobe, or concrete because of a scarcity of lumber. Most homes have white walls and blue doors. In Tunis, the capital, it is common to find luxury homes and modern apartment buildings. Tunis is crowded, as are the other Tunisian cities, because of a growing middle class, and because former country folk have moved into urban areas. In urban areas, homes sit directly adjacent to the roads; there are no front yards and very few windows. The front doors of houses open directly onto streets. Most single-family homes are small, and it is common for neighboring walls to touch each other. Many houses are built to two or three stories to make up for the small size of the foundation. The flat rooftops are commonly used as outdoor living space. As of the early 21st century, most houses had water, electricity, sewerage, and other public services.

Surrounding the capital, many families live in *gourbis,* which are permanent tents set up for those who had once tended flocks of animals but have now settled into a sedentary life. Rural families often live isolated on their farmland and access to sufficient water was increasingly a problem in the late 20th and early 21 century. In southern Tunisia, Berber dwellings are carved out of rocks, and in Matmata homes are built more than 6 m (20 ft) underground in enormous craters that have a central courtyard. Since these homes are built out of the mud and stones that are excavated for the construction, they tend to be cool in the summer and warm in the winter. Scenes from the 1977 movie *Star Wars* were filmed there.

Tunisian cities are connected by railroads and highways, 80% of which are metalled. Tunis has a modern tram system. Railroads reach most urban centers and the mines in the southwest, and provide a link to neighboring Algeria. Tunis, Bizerte, Sfax Gabes and Sousse are all major ports. Tunisia has five international airports, with the largest located in Tunis.

The Tunisian telephone system has been automated since the mid-1980s and international calls can be placed directly from homes. However, as of 2006, there were six times as many cellular phones as land lines. The telecommunications market has been deregulated and Internet access is rising rapidly, though it is subject to government censorship.

Upon the evacuation of the French forces, Tunisia's modern health care system virtually collapsed as the vast majority of doctors, who were of European origin, left the country. Since independence, Tunisia has made great improvements in health care, although much remains to be done. In 2003, the government spent over 7% of its budget on health care. A pyramid-like health care system was created in which the government constructed many local clinics and small hospitals that would refer more serious cases to larger regional hospitals, which, in turn, would refer the most serious cases to specialized hospitals in large cities. More than 80% of all health care provided is free. Even for those who must pay, the cost is subsidized. The greatest problem with the health care system is the concentration of facilities in Tunis. About 60% of all the country's doctors practice in the capital, leaving rural areas and other cities understaffed.

More traditional forms of health care also play a role in Tunisian society. The public baths, *hammam*, important for a variety of rituals, including engagements, weddings and pregnancy, is also a locus for medicine and healing. An innovative program of health care, and one that has received international praise, is based on the traditional postpartum visit to the hammam by the mother, about 40 days after giving birth. A group of Tunisian doctors adapted this custom so that postpartum women are provided with a comprehensive range of health care services for both themselves and their newborn child, and the program has been adopted nationally.

In parts of the center and south of the country especially, traditional ideas of health persist. In the practice of *Tasfih*, for example, pre-menstrual girls receive seven small cuts to the knee, recite ritual language, and eat raisins soaked in the blood from the knee to encourage chastity as they enter pubescence. Just before marriage, a similar ritual is then carried out to allow conjugal relations.

10 FAMILY LIFE

Before the French occupation, Tunisian family life was very traditional and based heavily on kinship ties. Tunisians lived with their extended families in tightly knit communities. A mother and father would live with their children in one home, and the father's parents would usually also live with them. As the male children married, they would bring their wives to the family as well. If a daughter became divorced or widowed, she too would live with the family. Children were raised by the entire extended family, and the people in a town paid close attention to all children in case they needed anything. Marriages were conducted by negotiation between the families of the bride and the groom.

A combination of the French occupation and the country's attempt to industrialize since independence have gone a long way to break down these traditional family structures. In the cities as well as rural areas, the nuclear family started to predominate. For example, by 2004 the average family consisted of only four members, and more than 11% of family heads were women, a consequence of widowhood, divorce, single parenting, and males emigrating to work abroad.

The role of women has changed most noticeably. Women had traditionally been segregated in public life; their primary responsibilities were raising children and taking care of the home and the husband. Although this remains the popular view even among the Westernized elite, the Tunisian government has passed a number of laws giving women social rights similar to those of men.

Society, however, has found it difficult to keep up with the law. Although educated men began seeking out educated women to marry, in part because they could have careers and bring home an additional income, the traditional expectations of women as keepers of the home and family have persisted. This has created unrealistic demands on women, who must essentially have two careers—one at home and one in the public sector. These clashes of expectations have contributed to a remarkably high divorce rate for a Muslim country—nearly 50%. Because of increased economic uncertainty, many families have begun to return to more traditional frameworks. Many marriages are still conducted within extended families, and some women have left their public careers to work at home.

11 CLOTHING

Two trends in clothing are visible in Tunisia. Many Tunisians dress in Western-style clothing; Western suits for men and dresses for women are common. Traditional dress, however, also remains common, particularly in the villages and among the elderly. Tunisian men often were a *chehia* on their heads. This is a type of fez the shape and color of which vary depending on the part of Tunisia the wearer is from. The hat is made of brown or red felt and either rounded or flat-topped. The fez was made almost exclusively in Tunisia in the 19th century and exported throughout the Ottoman domains. Traditionally, men wear a *jalabiyya* (a long dress-like garment) and baggy pants.

Traditionally, women wear a *sifsari* (a long outer garment with loose folds and head covering) over Western-style dress. The sifsari is a practical garment, keeping women warm in the winter and protecting them from dusty winds in the summer. Country women wear a *mellia* (a large, loose head covering) draped across the head and shoulders. Berber women commonly use *kohl* (black eyeliner). Some tattoo their faces with ochre and blue designs, mainly on the forehead, cheeks, and chin. It is not strange to find women walking side-by-side in Tunis, one dressed in traditional *sifsari* and the other in a skirt and blouse. Since 1956 Bourguiba's secularization of Tunisian society and Ben 'Ali's strict clampdown on Islamism have resulted in the government officially discouraging the wearing of the *hijab* (Muslim veil) by women. As in Turkey, female government employees are banned from wearing hijab and risk losing their jobs by doing so.

12 FOOD

The most popular dish in Tunisia, as in all the Maghrib, is *kusksi* (couscous). This consists of semolina wheat sprinkled with oil and water and rolled into tiny grains. The grains are then steamed and ready for use in favorite recipes. Couscous can be mixed with a number of sauces (e.g., tomato sauce), and then combined with a stew of meat and/or vegetables. It is served regularly for lunch and dinner. Lamb cutlets, seafood, and shish kebabs are also common foods.

A very popular Tunisian salad is *chakachouka*, made of tomatoes, onions, peppers, and hard-boiled eggs. *Mechouia* (literally, "the grilled") is a main course that combines grilled tomatoes, peppers, and onions with olive oil, tuna fish, sliced hard-boiled eggs, lemon juice, and capers. Tunisian food is often cooked and/or served with *harissa*, a hot red sauce made from chili peppers, spices, garlic, olive oil, and tomatoes.

Tunisians cook a variety of *tajines,* stews that are cooked in conical *tajine* earthenware dishes. Spinach tajine consists of beans, beef, onions, tomato sauce, pepper, spinach, and egg—all combined and baked in an oven. Other varieties of tajine make use of everything from chicken to prunes and honey. Reflecting the influence of the French colonial days, Franco-Tunisienne cuisine is common, especially in tourist restaurants and hotels. Seafood, especially lobster, is a prominent menu item. Tunisians commonly drink strong Turkish coffee and sweet mint tea. Pork and alcohol are both forbidden by Islamic religious code. However, alcohol is widely available and consumed, much of it produced by Tunisian companies.

13 EDUCATION

One of the government's major reforms after independence was to emphasize education for children. The government adopted the French system, creating three levels of education. First, there is a six-year primary-level cycle that all students must attend. The secondary level includes a three-year comprehensive cycle. The third level includes a four-year cycle of specialized academic or technical education similar to the American university system. Students who do not go to the third level may enroll in three-year vocational cycles that teach students various technical trades. Women are considered the primary teachers of children and thus are encouraged to get an education. In agricultural areas, however, women's education takes second place to working in fields and caring for the home. Almost half of urban students are girls and nearly 40% of all university students are women, but the percentages are far lower in rural areas.

All schooling, even at the university level, is free. This includes books, school supplies, uniforms, and meals. University students in Tunisia and abroad receive stipends equal to those of a factory worker in Tunisia. However, in many cases, Tunisian students must supplement this with private funding. Classes are taught in French and Arabic, with an increasing emphasis on the latter. In the 1990s and early 2000s, English language materials were being used more frequently in Tunisian schools.

Literacy rates in Tunisia are evidence of the success of its education program. At independence, the nation had a literacy rate of only 30%. As of 2004, at least three quarters of the population over the age of 15 was considered literate, although rates for women stood at just 65% compared to over 80% for men.

14 CULTURAL HERITAGE

Malouf is a uniquely Tunisian form of music, played on lutes, guitars, violins, and drums. It is thought that this music originated in North Africa and was exported to Spain in the 8th century. There it was influenced by Iberian folk songs and reexported to Tunisia in the 17th century when Jews and Muslims were expelled from Spain. Today's *malouf* music is sad. Players sing along with the highly rhythmic music, and members of the audience often cry as they listen.

Tunisian literature, more in Arabic than French, has thrived. Such writers and poets as Tahar Haddad, Ali Douagi, and Aboul Kacem Chabbi have built international reputations for their work. There are increasing numbers of women writers and poets, such as Amina Sa'id and Hayat ben al-Shaykh. However, many, such as the poet Tahar Bekri, have chosen to remain outside the country owing to the lack of political freedom, thus limiting their Tunisian audience, especially if they write in French.

Tunisian film, a major focus of interest for Bourguiba, has earned a respectable international reputation. In the 1960s and 1970s, Omar Khilfi's films on anticolonial resistance, for example, were very successful and he became one of the most prolific directors in North African cinema. In the late 1970s and 1980s, a new generation of directors appeared, such as Selma Baccar, Ferid Boughedir, and Nourid Bouzid (a former political detainee). This generation focused more on sociopolitical critique, issues of gender, and comedy. The 1990s saw the rise of more women directors, including Moufida Tlatli, with a focus on women, the growing Islamism in Tunisia, and the effects of globalization on Tunisian society.

15 WORK

Slightly more than half of Tunisia's population works in agriculture. Since independence, a major focus has been on expanding industrial production. This has meant a broadening of types of employment for Tunisians. Many work at oil fields, in electricity production, in cement production, and in mineral mining (especially phosphates). Investments in the food industry have produced jobs in flour milling, sugar refining, vegetable canning, and water bottling, among others. One of the major employment sectors is tourism, and students attend tourism schools and institutes of hotel management to cater to the large pool of tourists who visit Tunisia in the summer months.

Traditionally men go out to work while women are expected to work at home, processing foods or spinning wool, for example. Some women work as agricultural wage labor, where they are paid half the men's rate. Many urban women also work, in factories, offices and as professionals, but they are still expected to fulfill the more traditional duties of the housewife. While child labor is relatively uncommon, unemployment levels in Tunisia are relatively high, officially about 14% in 2007, though unofficial rates are probably considerably higher.

Although poverty has declined significantly, from an estimated 40% in 1970 to 4% in 2000, rural poverty is four to five times the urban rate and the rural population remains vulnerable to economic downturn. There is considerable rural-to-urban migration in the search for work, and there are an estimated 400,000 Tunisians working overseas, particularly in the Persian Gulf countries.

16 SPORTS

Tunisia's national sport is soccer ("football"), which is both a spectator sport and played in the streets and open fields. Soccer in Tunisia is highly developed, with most towns fielding their own teams. Teams are organized into a three-tier league system. The Tunisian national team has qualified for the FIFA World Cup four times, and in 2004 it won the African Nations Cup.

Athletics is also becoming a major sport among both men and women, and Tunisian teams often win medals, particularly for long distance events. In the northern mountains, horse riding and hunting wild boar are popular. The development of tourism as a major industry has introduced and popularized such sports as scuba diving, windsurfing, and golf. Camel races are another spectator sport and are the focus of festivals, such as the International Festival of the Sahara, which began in 1910 and is held in Douz each November.

[17] ENTERTAINMENT AND RECREATION

Tunisians hold many festivals throughout the year. Camel races are held at the International Festival of the Sahara, which is held in Douz each November. Parades are held at the festival in Nefta each April. Classical music and theatre performances are held at a festival in Dougga held each summer. In 1997 Dougga was named a UN World Heritage site. A falconry festival is held in el-Hawaria in June. Theater performances are held at the Roman theatre during the Carthage festival in July and August. The Carthage film festival is held biennially in October.

Tunisians seeking recreation often turn to water activities. They socialize while bathing in the *hammam* (public bathhouse), and they flock to the beaches that line the coast of the Mediterranean Sea. Tunisians are also increasingly subscribing to satellite television and the Internet. There is a well-developed, though government-censored, press, reflecting the high rates of literacy.

[18] FOLK ART, CRAFTS, AND HOBBIES

Craftsmanship is an ancient tradition in Tunisia. Craftsmen make goods out of olive wood, copper, textiles, leather, wrought iron, glass, and ceramics. Pottery is made for everyday use, and molded pots are made in rural areas. Blankets, rugs, and grass mats are woven in rural areas. Hand-woven rugs and carpets are particularly popular, especially with tourists. Knotted carpets follow traditional decorative designs; Berber rugs *(mergoums)* are brightly colored and have geometric designs. Jewelry is also handmade. A very popular design is the shape of a hand, known as the *khomsa,* or the "hand of Fatima." This is made of either gold or silver and found on earrings and pendants.

[19] SOCIAL PROBLEMS

The greatest problems facing Tunisia today stem from continued economic stagnation and a lack of political freedom. The growing Tunisian middle class (80% of the population) is pushing for greater participation in society, for greater political freedom and pluralism, and for an expanded and more independent civil society, currently dominated by huge government funded organizations. Although Tunisia is a highly secular society and the government has banned Islamist groups, the failure of the government to positively address economic and political complaints has contributed to the growth of a religious conservatism among both urban and rural dwellers. Monitoring and controlling this has led to an expansion of the security services and a deteriorating human rights record, and in the winter of 2006–2007, security forces engaged in armed clashes with Islamist terror cells on the outskirts of Tunis.

While college studies have been emphasized as part of the nation's education drive, this has resulted in an excess of graduates who cannot find appropriate jobs, particularly in nonscientific fields such as languages and social sciences. Unemployment and social problems related to it are expected to increase, as many educated Tunisians are unable to find suitable work. The labor market was already tight in the 1990s; it will be hard-pressed to meet the demands of the next two decades. In the past, many Tunisians emigrated to France and Italy in search of work. However, the immigration policies of European countries, in response to their own economic and political conditions, have become stricter. Laws to further limit immigration to European nations were expected to be passed, which will certainly increase social pressures in Tunisia.

[20] GENDER ISSUES

Gender issues in Tunisia are dominated by the Code of Personal Status (CPS) or *majalla* of 1956, a key part of Bourguiba's program of secularization and modernization. The CPS, revolutionary for its time, regulated marriage, divorce, custody, and inheritance and profoundly changed family law and the legal status of women by significantly expanding their rights and responsibilities. For example, polygamy and forced marriage were criminalized, a minimum age for marriage for women was established, and a man's right to divorce through simple repudiation was abolished. The result of this was that women were generally considered by law to be equal to men in terms of inheritance, ownership of property, custody of children, and divorce.

Since its passage, the CPS has been almost updated frequently, to increase separated and divorced women's control over their minor children, establish a fund to support divorced women and their dependent families, and to allow women to marry non-Muslims, for example. The CPS therefore lies at the core of the Arab world's most gender-progressive society.

Tunisian society is characterized by high divorce rates, around 50%, and female-headed households are common. Contraception is widely available and socially accepted. Abortion for the first trimester is fully legal (the only Arab country where this is the case). In addition, there are a number of increasingly powerful women's political, economic, and social organizations. Tunisia's statistics for school and higher education enrollment, life expectancy, and reproductive health are all at the high end for both Africa and the Middle East. There are significant numbers of women in politics, business, and the professions: almost half of all doctors and secondary school teachers, a third of lawyers and journalists, and a quarter of all judges are women.

In practice, women in Tunisia still face discrimination on individual and collective levels. Many working women are expected to fulfill their duties as housewives and recent research has found that sexual harassment remains ubiquitous. On the other hand, the incidence of rural teenage girls being employed as domestics or for agricultural labor is declining, mainly due to effective law enforcement.

Homosexuality is illegal in Tunisia and there is no formal lobbying focus for gay or transgender rights.

[21] BIBLIOGRAPHY

Leaman, Oliver. Ed. *Companion Encyclopedia of Middle Eastern and North African Film.* London: Routledge. 2001.

Memmi, Albert. *The Colonizer and the Colonized.* Boston: Beacon Press, 1965.

Murphy, Emma C. *Economic and Political Change in Tunisia: From Bourguiba to Ben Ali.* London: Palgrave Macmillan. 1999.

Perkins, Kenneth J. *A History of Modern Tunisia.* Cambridge: Cambridge University Press, 2004.

Sherif-Trask, Bahira. Ed. *Greenwood Encyclopedia of Women's Issues Worldwide: The Middle East and North Africa.* London: Greenwood Press, 2003.

Spencer, William. *The Land and People of Tunisia*. New York: J.B. Lippincott Company, 1967.

Tunisia: Country Profile. World Health Organization Regional Office for the Eastern Mediterranean. Cairo: WHO, 2005.

Fareed, Hassan. *Tunisia: Understanding Successful Socioeconomic Development*. New York: World Bank, 2005.

Voll, John Obert. *Islam: Continuity and Change in the Modern World*. Boulder, CO: Westview Press, 1982.

Walden, Hilaire. *North African Cooking: Exotic Delights from Morocco, Tunisia, Algeria, and Egypt*. Edison, NJ: Chartwell Books, 1995.

Zartman, I. William. *Man, State, and Society in the Contemporary Maghrib*. New York: Praeger, 1973.

—revised by J. Henry

TUTSI

PRONUNCIATION: TOOT-see
LOCATION: Rwanda, Burundi, northeastern Democratic Republic of Congo (formerly Zaire)
POPULATION: Approximately 3–4 million
LANGUAGE: Kinyarwanda, Kirundi, Swahili, French, English
RELIGION: Christianity (with aspects of traditional belief)
RELATED ARTICLES: Vol. 1: Burundians; Rwandans

¹ INTRODUCTION

Tutsi refers to the people who live in the densely populated African countries of Rwanda, Burundi, and in border areas of neighboring countries. In Uganda Tutsis are commonly known as *Bafumbira*; in the Democratic Republic of Congo (DRC) as *Banyamulenge*. The Tutsi share many cultural traditions with the Twa and the Hutu. In fact, Tutsi, Twa, and Hutu are not only culturally similar; they also share the same language and culture.

During the period of colonial rule in Rwanda and Burundi, Tutsi and Hutu labels became associated with rigid stereotypes, although it is quite difficult to say exactly what the labels mean today. Both Tutsi and Hutu have been victims of violence that can be accurately described as genocide.

The Tutsi are said to be people of Nilotic (region of the Nile River) origin who were traditionally cattle-herding pastoralists, living the life of herders. They are said to differ physically from the Bantu farmers and Twa hunters who inhabited the region before the Tutsi arrived.

The Tutsi label is also used to refer to members of a high-ranking social category, similar to a caste. This is because in Rwanda and Burundi Tutsi came to form the majority of an aristocratic elite, even though they were a minority of the population in both countries. To further complicate things, some believe that the Tutsi and Hutu were not always ethnically different, but that they became two separate groups as a reflection of their different ways of life. Whatever their origins, people known as Tutsi came to rule others called Hutu. Lowest in this status system were the Twa, who were descended from pygmy people.

There are important divisions within the Tutsi category that complicate this picture even more. For example, in Burundi the highest status Tutsi were the *ganwa* (princes) and the people of the *Tutsi-Banyaruguru* (royal family). Lower status Tutsi, the *Tutsi-Hima,* were looked down upon by the royals.

With such complexities, it has not been difficult to distort what is known of the past for crass political purposes. For example, some have overemphasized ethnic divisions in order to foster ethnic and racial hatred. On the other hand, some have downplayed Tutsi-Hutu distinctions in order to maintain that that there has been no systematic domination of one group over another. In reality, the true history of the Tutsi-Hutu divide is incompletely understood, although it certainly has had much to do with kingship, the changes brought by colonialism, and contemporary struggles for power.

Through many periods of history, the rule of the *mwamis* (Tutsi kings) was autocratic, but it was not always unpopular. Historically, the *mwami* was strongest in central Rwanda. In Burundi the Tutsi king relied more on Hutu support. Hutu leaders were able to rise to positions of power and influence within the court.

Social relations in Rwanda and Burundi were modified by European rule—Germans from the 1890s until World War I and Belgians from World War I until 1962. During most of this period, the Tutsi were treated with favor by the Europeans, but the Hutu were encouraged to attempt to end Tutsi domination by the Belgians toward the end of their rule.

The first major social upheaval began in Rwanda in the wake of a Hutu-led campaign for independence from Belgian rule in 1959. Hutu leaders seized power and abolished the monarchy, and some Tutsi fled to neighboring countries. During this period, and again in 1962 and 1963, thousands of Tutsi civilians were killed.

In Burundi, there was a more peaceful transition to independence in 1962. Initially, the king served as an intermediary between Tutsi and Hutu sides, but the monarchy was abolished by Tutsi leaders following a failed Hutu coup attempt in 1965. Law and order broke down altogether after Hutu forces invaded the country from Tanzania in 1972. This was followed by another coup that brought the Tutsi-Hima into power. After repulsing the Hutu invasion, they implemented widespread repression. All those identified as educated Hutu, even down to the level of elementary school students, were systematically hunted down. More than 100,000 people were killed in a campaign of what has been called "selective genocide."

The Tutsi-Hutu divisions in Rwanda and Burundi thus became more rigid and violent as a result of colonial rule and the independence process. The end result of the colonial period was that opposite sides controlled each country. In Rwanda, the Hutu became associated with the power of the state. In Burundi, the state came to be controlled by a branch of the Tutsi. Efforts to end Tutsi domination in Burundi were crushed in 1988; five years later, in 1993, there was another period of genocidal violence. This was followed by a long period of conflict between the Tutsi dominated army and Hutu rebels that did not abate until a peace deal was reached in 2003. (Even then the conflict has not entirely been settled.) In Rwanda, Hutu domination ended only after the army of the RPF (Rwandan People's Front) succeeded in overthrowing the government in the wake of the genocide of 1994. Since then, thousands of Tutsi refugees have returned to the country.

Former RPF commander Paul Kagame has been the dominant leader in Rwanda since 1994. In 2003 he won election as president. In Burundi, a former Hutu rebel leader and college professor, Pierre Nkurunziza, was elected president in 2005.

2 LOCATION AND HOMELAND

Rwanda and Burundi are mountainous countries in east-central Africa. Burundi shares a northern border with Rwanda. Rwanda's northern border is with Uganda. Both countries are bounded by the Democratic Republic of Congo (formerly Zaire) to the west and Tanzania to the east, but much of western Burundi is bounded by Lake Tanganyika. The combined total area of Rwanda and Burundi together is approximately 20,900 sq mi (54,100 sq km). This is roughly comparable to the combined size of Maryland and New Jersey.

Tutsi also live in northeastern Democratic Republic of the Congo, particularly in the Mulenge region of the South Kivu province where they have lived for many generations. However, because of Congo's recent civil war, many have had to flee as

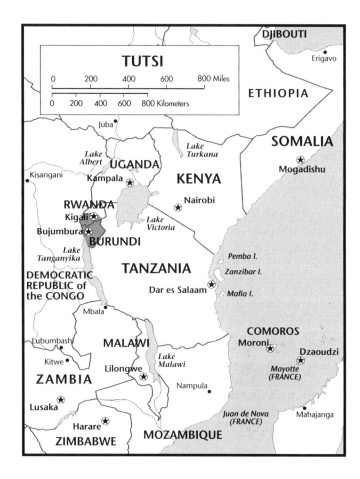

refugees from the Mulenge region. Congolese Tutsi are commonly referred to as *Banyamulenge*.

Population densities in the region are among the highest in Africa. In 1994, there were an estimated 208 people per sq km (220 per sq mi) in Burundi. In 1993, there were an estimated 280 people per sq km in Rwanda. Today these figures are even higher. Despite the years of genocide and poor health care, the combined population of all groups in Rwanda and Burundi was approximately 19 million in 2008. Of these, more than one half are young adults and children.

3 LANGUAGE

The Hutu, Tutsi, and Twa of Rwanda and Burundi all speak a Central Bantu language. This language is called Kinyarwanda in Rwanda, and Kirundi in Burundi; the two are dialects rather than distinct languages. Banyamulenge may be most at home speaking Congolese languages as well as French and the East African trade language, Swahili.

As with Bantu languages in general, Kinyarwanda/Kirundi is characterized by a system of noun classes identified by prefixes. These prefixes differentiate singular from plural, and group nouns into like categories. Thus, a word such as *Banyamulenge* ("Ba-nya-mulenge") can be broken down into parts. The prefixes "banya" refer to people; Mulenge is the name of a region. Altogether, the word means "people of Mulenge." Bantu prefixes are often omitted in English. For example, *Kinyarwanda* may be referred to as Rwanda in English, or *Kirundi* as Rundi. Many Tutsi from the region also speak Swahili.

As a result of its colonial history, Rwandese and Burundians have long received their formal schooling in French. Another implication of this is that many people in the two countries have French first names. However, since the change in government in Rwanda in 1994, English has become increasingly important there.

African personal names have meanings that reflect important cultural values. They may be derived from events, borrowed from praise poetry, or reflect attitudes about religion, kingship, or cattle. For example, the name *Ndagijimana* means "God is my herder." *Hakizumwami* is a name that means "only the king can save." *Muvunanyambo* means "the defender of noble cows." Greetings may also reflect the traditional value placed on cattle. For example, a common greeting is "amasho," literally meaning "may you be rich in cattle."

Traditionally, the ability to express oneself well orally was highly valued. Aristocrats were expected to maintain a dignified style in speaking, and demonstrated their high status by calculated use of silence. Cattle terms were used to refer to the best and most precious aspects of social life. For example, the king of Rwanda was referred to as "the bull of the herd."

4 FOLKLORE

Verbal arts include praise poetry, proverbs, folktales, riddles, and myths. Traditionally, these were vibrant parts of everyday life. Tutsi elite typically knew the names of their ancestors to at least six generations, and many believed they were descendants of a mythical founding king named Gihanga.

Among the Tutsi, the most elaborate praises were reserved for the king, but cattle were named individuals worthy of praise and poetry as well. Herders commonly entertained themselves by singing the praises of their cattle during their daily rounds to the pastures.

One popular folktale tells the story of a greedy man named Sebgugugu. Sebgugugu is a poor man who is helped by God. God provides food for him and his family in a number of miraculous ways, but each time the greedy Sebgugugu wants more. Through his greed, Sebgugugu finally loses everything.

5 RELIGION

Most people in modern-day Rwanda and Burundi are Christians, particularly Catholics. In the wake of the 1994 genocide, many Tutsi have converted to Islam. In traditional thought, the Creator is somewhat remote, although his power is manifest in the king. The word for creator, *Imaana*, means both God and "God's power to ensure prosperity and fertility." The king had special access to this power, and he demonstrated this to the people through his sacred fire, the royal drums, and the royal agricultural rites. For this reason, he was thought to be responsible for the nation's fate. Ancestral spirits, called *abazima*, also act as intermediaries between God and the human world. However, the *abazima* may also hold grudges against the living and bring misfortune to those who do not respect them. To protect against the *abazima*, offerings are made, and diviners are consulted to interpret their wishes. Special ceremonies are held to pay respect to the most powerful of the *abazima*.

6 MAJOR HOLIDAYS

National holidays include Independence Days, May Day, New Year's Day, and the major Christian holidays. Rwanda has several new holidays. These include February 1 (National Heroes Day); April 7 (Genocide Memorial Day); July 4 (National Liberation Day); and 1st of October (Patriotism Day). Other traditional holidays, such as the annual holidays connected with the *mwami*, are no longer observed. The elaborate royal rituals associated with these holidays included specially trained dancers and the use of giant sacred drums. Some of these practices have been preserved in the form of professional entertainment.

7 RITES OF PASSAGE

Rites of passage for Tutsi and Hutu are very similar. The first ritual of life passage, the naming ceremony, takes place seven days after a child's birth.

Marriage is legitimated by the transfer of *bridewealth,* a kind of compensation for the loss of the woman's labor. Bridewealth is paid by the family of the groom to the family of the bride. For most Tutsi, bridewealth consisted traditionally of a cow and other gifts. In central Rwanda, however, the prestige of the Tutsi elite was such that they were often exempt from bridewealth payment. The traditional marriage ceremony itself is complex, and the details vary from region to region. These customs may or may not be practiced today by people most influenced by European culture. Except for marriage, there is no formal initiation process to celebrate the change from adolescence to adulthood.

Death is marked by prayers, speeches, purification rituals, and restrictions on many everyday activities. Close family members are expected to refrain from sexual relations and to avoid physical exertion during the period of mourning, at the end of which the family hosts a ritual feast.

8 INTERPERSONAL RELATIONS

Social life in traditional Rwanda and Burundi was dictated by status distinctions. Signs of social status are indicated by posture, body language, and style of speech. The ideal for a person of elite status is to act with dignity, emotional restraint, and decorum. This ideal was called *kwitonda*.

There are separate greetings for morning, afternoon, and evening. In the early decades of the twentieth century, people of the same age greeted each other in an elaborate ritual that included sung greetings, stylized embraces, and formalized gestures. Subordinates showed deference to their social superiors by kneeling in their presence.

A system of cattle exchange helped to keep harmony among the factions of society. In this system wealthy elites (often Tutsi) lent cattle to herdsmen (often Hutu) in exchange for their labor, loyalty, and political support. This was called *buhake* in Rwanda and *bugabire* in Burundi.

Traditionally, romantic relationships between young men and women were expected to occur within the caste group, and marriages were usually arranged. In the late twentieth century, socializing in group activities was more common than individual dating, although Western-style dating and socializing at nightclubs is practiced by some in urban areas.

9 LIVING CONDITIONS

The average life expectancy in Rwanda and Burundi is very low by world standards. However, in the past Rwanda and Burundi have been healthy and prosperous places, benefitting from the high elevation that offered protection from malarial mosquitoes. More recently, there are not only the problems of extreme political violence but also of inadequate nutrition, health care, and diseases such as bacterial diarrhea, hepatitis A, and typhoid fever. It is also estimated that about 5% of adults are suffering from AIDS. Infant mortality is also very high.

Despite a high population density, the majority of the population remains rural. Houses were traditionally bee-hived shaped huts of wood, reeds, and straw, surrounded by a high hedge that served as a fence. The hut interiors of wealthy Tutsi were often elaborately decorated with screens that functioned as room dividers. Modern Tutsi are using the money they make from the sale of agricultural products to buy Western-style housing material to build rectangular houses, with corrugated iron or tile roofing.

For rural people, the chief source of income comes through the sale of agricultural products such as coffee and tea.

Transportation infrastructure in the region is not well developed. Roads are often unpaved, and there is no railway. In Rwanda, an aggressive plan of economic development has been promoted by President Kagame.

10 FAMILY LIFE

The basic unit of society is the household. These were not organized in villages but remained distinct as separate homesteads built on hills spread across the landscape. The concept of house, or *inzu*, is so important that it refers not only to a physical home but also to one's family and ancestral line.

Tutsi and Hutu families are organized patrilineally (through the fathers) into lineages and clans. Polygyny (a man having more than one wife) was permitted but the goal was to have a large family. Although love matches were not unknown, and elopements occurred, marriage in Rwanda and Burundi was traditionally about maintaining power and relationships between families. In modern times, however, marriage is more often a matter of personal choice.

Legitimate marriages between Tutsi and Hutu did occur, but they were rare. Twa men and women were looked down upon by both Hutu and Tutsi and were not generally considered acceptable mates. People from mixed Tutsi-Hutu families were also targeted in the 1994 Rwandan genocide.

11 CLOTHING

Tutsi men and women wore gowns and robes imported from the African coast before the arrival of the Europeans. A common form of dress was a wrap around skirt and top piece tied at the shoulder, not unlike a Roman toga. A woman's ceremonial dress included a plain white robe, with perhaps a few geometric designs, and a number of white headbands. On most occasions today, however, Western-style clothing is worn. Women wear dresses, headscarves, and the printed clothes that are popular throughout East Africa. Men wear pants and shirts.

In the past, Tutsi women wore numerous copper bracelets and anklets. These were often so heavy that the elite women were unable to do much work. In fact, this very inability to do agricultural labor helped distinguish them from the ordinary women who had to work in the fields.

12 FOOD

Milk, butter, and meat are the most highly valued foods traditionally. Because of the social and religious value of cattle, however, people do not often butcher a cow without some ritual justification. While goat meat and goat milk may be consumed as well, these foods were taboo. The ideal for the elite Tutsi was a pure diet of milk products, supplemented by beer made from fermented plantains or sorghum grain. Meal times are flexible, often revolving around work obligations.

Today the most common foods are beans, corn, cassava, peas, plantains, and sweet potatoes. Tropical fruits are also popular.

13 EDUCATION

Literacy rates have been at times lower than 50% in Rwanda and Burundi in the vernacular (native language), and lower in French, but seem to be improving. Rwanda currently reports a literacy rate of about 70%. In Burundi, literate Hutu were persecuted in 1972, but education began to be encouraged again in the 1980s. There are teacher-training schools and at least one university in both countries.

In Rwanda, educational structures were disrupted by the 1994 political violence. Prior to 1994, the Rwandese school system was moving toward an emphasis on education in French but there is now a new emphasis on English, with a goal of trilingual education. The government also has the goal of providing free primary and secondary school education for all.

14 CULTURAL HERITAGE

The kings of Rwanda and Burundi maintained elaborate dance and drum ensembles that were associated with royal power. On ritual occasions in Burundi two dozen tall, footed drums were arranged in a semicircle around a central drum. The musicians moved in a circle around the drums, each taking a turn beating the central drum. This style of drumming has survived the demise of the kingship. Since the 1960s the Royal Drummers of Burundi have toured the world giving performances. They have also recorded albums and collaborated with Western musicians.

In Rwanda some young men, children of nobility, were singled out for special training. Known as *intore,* these students received the best education in rhetoric and warfare and served as the king's elite dance troupe. Their dances involved leaping and rhythmic stomping of the feet. Today they perform for tourists at the national museum.

Music, dancing, and drumming are all important in rural life. People compose many kinds of popular songs—hunting songs, lullabies, and *ibicuba* (songs praising cattle). In some areas, there were traveling minstrels who sang the news, accompanying themselves with a seven-string zither. A special dance was also part of the rituals of courtship. These days people also enjoy modern entertainment by way of television, movies, and recorded music. Some of today's musicians have developed new forms of music that combine elements of traditional and modern elements.

Many of the details of the cultural heritage of Rwanda were described in French by the renowned Rwandan scholar-priest Alexis Kagame. One example of his work is *La poésie dynastique au Rwanda* (The dynastic poetry of Rwanda), which was published in 1951. More recently, a number of individual Tutsi survivors of the genocide have published autobiographies and Rwandans who have gained experience working on such movies as *Hotel Rwanda* have begun to produce their own films.

15 WORK

People of Tutsi background who cultivated the soil were often considered poor and could lose their status as nobles. In this

Jeanette Nyirabaganwa, a Tutsi, in a coffee warehouse that she runs for the Maraba Coffee cooperative in Butare, Rwanda. Most of her family was murdered in the Rwandan genocide of 1994, where about 1 million Tutsis were killed by Hutus. Nyirabaganwa now employs many of those suspected of the killings on her coffee and sorghum plantation.
(Melanie Stetson Freeman/The Christian Science Monitor/Getty Images)

way some Tutsi "became" Hutu. On the other hand, an especially high status was reserved for the *abashumba* pastoralists. These were a special class of herders whose job it was to take care of the king's prize cattle (*inyambo*).

Today Tutsi as well as Hutu are farmers. In addition to growing food crops, they also produce cash crops, especially coffee and tea.

16 SPORTS

The main spectator sport in Burundi is soccer. Many people also enjoy playing the game informally.

17 ENTERTAINMENT AND RECREATION

There are movie theaters that show contemporary European and American films in the capital cities. People also enjoy television, video, and a variety of modern musical forms. Contemporary musicians from Tutsi backgrounds who have developed international reputations include Jean-Paul Samputu and Cornelius Nyungura, popularly known as "Corneille" (Crow).

A popular game for young people and adults is *igisoro*, played with a wooden board that has rows of hollowed-out places for holding beads or stones that are used as counters. The object of the game is to line up one's pieces in rows in such a way as to capture as many counters as possible. This is very similar to the game is known as mancala played in other parts of Africa.

18 FOLK ART, CRAFTS, AND HOBBIES

Both Rwanda and Burundi have traditions of basketwork, pottery, woodwork, metal work, and jewelry making. Items carved from wood included drums, quivers, shields, and stools, but wood carving was not highly developed. Metal objects included copper bracelets and rings, and iron spear points. Traditionally, Tutsi women were noted for their expertise in weaving, especially for their intricately woven screens with geometric designs used in the houses of the wealthy as room dividers and decorations. Recently, handicrafts are being produce for the international market. Most notable among them are the "peace baskets" woven by Rwandan women and marketed by a major American department store.

A national ballet was established to promote folk dance traditions in Rwanda during the rule of Juvénal Habyarimana (1973-1994). At its height it had more than 200 members. However, its reputation was tarnished when its founding director was implicated in the genocide.

¹⁹ SOCIAL PROBLEMS

Sporadically since the early 1960s, the peoples of Rwanda and Burundi have experienced some of the worst violence in the history of Africa. In Burundi, massive genocide was carried out against Hutu by Tutsi in 1972 and in 1993. Perhaps 100,000 died in the first case, and at least that many died in the latter case. In Rwanda, the roles of killer and victims have been reversed. In 1962, Hutu people massacred thousands of people they defined as Tutsi. Thirty-two years later, Hutu leaders directed the killing of an estimated 800,000 people, most of them Tutsi. Labeling this violence simply as Hutu versus Tutsi is an oversimplification, however. In practice the killings were not merely ethnic but also political. For example, in some regions, there was also major Hutu-on-Hutu violence that appears to have been related to local disputes. In addition, the United Nations and the major world powers have not acted effectively to stop the genocides.

The effects of the 1994 Rwandan genocide spilled over into neighboring Congo after defeated Hutu soldiers fled there, while an influx of civilian refugees into Burundi contributed to that country's pre-existing instability. In 1996 a military conflict began in the DRC between *Banyamulenge* (ethnic Tutsi) and the remnants of the Hutu military who had fled to the refugee camps there in the wake of their defeat in Rwanda.

After the Hutu soldiers were routed, most the Hutu civilian refugee population was able to return to Rwanda. Nonetheless, the incursion of armed Rwandans into the DRC helped spark a violent civil war that ultimately led to the death of several million Congolese.

In Rwanda, the government has made some dramatic attempts at Hutu-Tutsi reconciliation. Most prominent among these was implementation of the *gacaca court* system under which low level actors in the 1994 genocide were offered the opportunity for amnesty. In this system local communities conducted public proceedings and the mass of perpetrators who acted under the auspices of higher authorities were given the opportunity to confess. Critics complain, however, that attempts at political reconciliation are hampered by practices in government that discourage open dissent.

²⁰ GENDER ISSUES

Traditionally women were socialized to seek fulfillment as wives and mothers. They were expected to be subordinate to their husbands and did not have full rights of property and inheritance. Historically, a major exception to this occurred in central Rwanda under the administration of Mwami Rwabugiri (1865–1895). During this time some Tutsi women were able to acquire land. Some even could go to war or become war chiefs.

More recently, moves toward gender equality have been promoted. Both Burundi and Rwanda now require that a significant percentage of its elected representatives be women. In Rwanda, the government has enacted legislation to support women's economic rights. While once women were discouraged by many from obtaining education, today dropout rates for females have fallen and their rate of college attendance has increased dramatically. The gap between males and females in literacy rates appears also to be narrowing. Nearly 50% of the parliament is composed of women representatives; and half of national judges are women. For such accomplishments, President Kagame received the "African Gender Award" from the Pan-African Center for Gender, Peace, and Development in 2007.

Violence against women remains a problem in the area. In the lead up to the 1994 genocide in Rwanda, propaganda was particularly directed against Tutsi women, and they were frequently raped before being killed. As a consequence of the ongoing civil conflict in Burundi, women continue to be subjected to high rates of violence there.

Homosexuality is rarely openly acknowledged by Tutsi or Hutu. This is also something that many people find sinful according to the doctrines of the Catholic church. Homosexual acts are illegal in Burundi. In 2007, the government of Rwanda began considering a provision to the penal code that that would also penalize homosexual behavior.

²¹ BIBLIOGRAPHY

Adekunle, Julius O. *Culture and Customs of Rwanda*. Westport, CT: Greenwood Press, 2007.

Albert, Ethel M. "Rhetoric, Logic, and Poetics in Burundi." In *American Anthropologist*, 66(6), 1964: pp. 35–54.

"Anthology of World Music: Africa—Music From Rwanda." Audio CD. Rounder Select, 1999.

Celis, G. "The Decorative Arts in Rwanda and Burundi." In *African Arts*. 4 (1), 1970: pp. 41–42.

Cook, G. C. "Lactase Deficiency: A Probable Ethnological Marker in East Africa." *Man*. 4 (2), 1969: pp. 265–267.

Cooke, Peter. "Burundi." In *The New Grove Dictionary of Music and Musicians*. Edited by Stanley Sadie. Washington, DC: MacMillan, 1980.

Dallaire, Roméo. *Shake Hands with the Devil: The Failure of Humanity in Rwanda*. New York: De Capo Press, 2004.

d'Hertefelt, Marcel. "The Rwanda of Rwanda". In *Peoples of Africa*. Edited by J. L. Gibbs, pp. 403–440. New York: Holt, Rinehart, and Winston, 1965.

Gansemans, J. "Rwanda." In *The New Grove Dictionary of Music and Musicians*. Edited by Stanley Sadie. Washington, DC: MacMillan, 1980.

George, Usha. *Rwanda: A Cultural Profile*. AMNI Centre: University of Toronto Press, 2001.

"Ghosts of Rwanda." Frontline documentary. PBS Home Video, 2005.

Hatzfeld, Jean. *Life Laid Bare: The Survivors in Rwanda Speak*. New York: Other Press, 2007.

Hiernaux, Jean. "Human Biological Diversity in Central Africa." *Man* 1(3), 1966: pp. 287–306.

Hunter, B., ed. "Burundi," In *The Stateman's Yearbook 1996-1997*. New York: Macmillan, 1996.

———. "Rwanda." In *The Stateman's Yearbook 1996–1997*. New York: Macmillan, 1996.

Keogh, P., et al. "The Social Impact of HIV Infection on Women in Kigali, Rwanda." *Social Science and Medicine*. 38 (8), 1994: pp. 1047–54.

Kimenyi, A. *Kinyarwanda and Kirundi Names: A Semiological Analysis of Bantu Onomastics*. Lewiston, NY: The Edwin Mellon, 1989.

Lemarchand, Rene. *Burundi: Ethnocide as Discourse and Practice*. New York: Cambridge University Press, 1994.

Lemarchand, Rene. *Rwanda and Burundi*. London: Pall Mall, 1970.

Malkki, Liisa H. *Purity and Exile: Violence, Memory, and National Cosmology among Hutu Refugees in Tanzania.* Chicago: University of Chicago Press, 1995.

Maquet, Jacques J. "The Kingdom of Ruanda." In *African Worlds: Studies in the Cosmological Ideas and Social Values of African Peoples.* Edited by Daryl Forde. London: Oxford University Press, 1954.

Overdulve, C. M. *Apprendre la langue Rwanda.* The Hague: Mouton, 1975.

Ramkisson, Indra. *Burundi: A Cultural Profile.* AMNI Centre: University of Toronto Press, 2001.

Taylor, C. (1988). "The Concept of Flow in Rwandan Popular Medicine." *Social Science and Medicine.* 27(12): pp. 1346–1348.

Werner, Alice. *Myths and Legends of the Bantu.* London: Frank Cass, 1968.

—by R. Shanafelt

TWA

ALTERNATE NAMES: BATWA, MBUTI (BAMBUTI), BAKA, AKA
LOCATION: Congo-Brazzaville (Republic of the Congo), Democratic Republic of the Congo, Rwanda, Uganda, Zambia
POPULATION: About 100,000
LANGUAGES: Kinyarwanda, Kirundi, Rukiga, Balese, Bira, Mangbetu
RELIGION: Indigenous (traditional) religions (90%), Christianity (10%)

¹ INTRODUCTION

The Twa people of the Great Lakes Region in Africa are a pygmy minority strewn across several countries, including Cameroon, Congo-Brazzaville, Democratic Republic of the Congo, Rwanda, Burundi, Tanzania, and Uganda. It should be noted at the outset that the term "pygmy" is considered derogatory by many scholars as it perpetuates the discrimination of this group of people due to their characteristic small stature. The total population of the Twa and other similar groups is estimated to be anywhere from 82,000 to 126,000 people. The Twa, also known as the Batwa, are one of many ethnic groups, such as the BaKola, Aka, BaBongo, BaMbuti, Mbuti (Bambuti), Baka, and Aka. They are often referred to as the forest people, the original inhabitants of this region. They are traditionally a hunter and gatherer group, surviving on what the rainforests provide. However, as forests continue to dwindle due to deforestation, their livelihoods and way of life have become ever precarious, and many are undergoing a lifestyle change. They are no longer able to hunt or gather from the bounty of the tropical rainforest, but are reduced to a precarious lifestyle of subsistence agriculture. Those still found deep in the tropical rainforest continue to practice their culture and lifestyle as they have done for thousands of years.

The arrival of the Bantu peoples in the region brought the subjugation of the Twa. The Bantu people began arriving in the area from their original homeland (eastern Nigeria and Cameroon) between the 12th to the 15th century. Two such groups in present day Rwanda and Burundi were the Tutsi, a Bantu-speaking Nilotic people, and the Hutu, a Bantu group. The Tutsi soon became the ruling group that dominated both the Hutu and the Twa. The Tutsi created a highly centralized kingdom, presided over by Tutsi kings who came from one ruling clan. In pre-colonial times, the relationship between the ordinary Hutu, Tutsi, and Twa was one of mutual benefit through the exchange of labor and the goods they traded. However, during the colonial era, the Tutsi were more favored by the colonizing powers, particularly the Belgians. Coupled with the hierarchical nature of Rwandan traditional society with the Tutsi at the top, the colonial policies laid the foundation for present day upheavals and genocide in this region.

It is estimated that during the 1994 Rwandan genocide, over 30% of the Twa lost their lives. Today, the Twa play a marginal role in Rwandan and Burundian politics and are often ignored in discussions about the conflict between the Hutus and Tutsis. Many have been pushed away from the remaining patches of tropical rainforest and forcibly settled in areas where they have to abandon their way of hunter/gatherer life. They are currently undergoing untold hardship as they try to adopt new ways of making a living, such as agriculture and raising livestock. Massive deforestation of their habitats, because of agriculture, logging and other development by their Bantu and Tutsi counterparts, has deprived the Twa of the natural resources essential for the cultural survival of this endangered and marginalized group.

2 LOCATION AND HOMELAND

The homeland of the Twa and associated groups is generally the tropical rainforest of central Africa around the Great Lakes of Eastern Africa. The Twa are scattered in a number of countries in this region, which include Cameroon, Gabon, Congo-Brazzaville, Democratic Republic of the Congo, Rwanda, Tanzania, Uganda, and Zambia. The rainforest homeland of the Twa people is tropical and experiences large amounts of rainfall, ranging from 127 to 203 cm (50 to 80 in). The forest, which experiences a short dry season for about a month or two, is a moist and humid region with many rivers and lakes. Not all Twa are restricted to the tropical rainforest, some are found in the savannah environments of southern Africa where they might have migrated out of the rainforest alongside the great migration of the Bantu people.

Around the Great Lakes region of eastern and central Africa the Twa people resided in high altitude mountain forests around Lakes Kivu, Albert, and Tanganyika. The tropical rainforest offers an excellent habitat for the semi nomadic and hunter-gatherer way of finding food that the Twa have survived on for generations. However, because of massive deforestation, as a result of logging and agriculture, their traditional homeland is under siege and many find themselves landless, poor, deprived of their traditional hunting and gathering grounds, and despised by other groups in the region because of their small stature.

3 LANGUAGE

There is no such thing as a language for the Twa people. The Twa speak several different languages, depending on the country or region in which they find themselves. For example, in Rwanda they speak Kinyarwanda, in Burundi they speak Kirundi, and in Uganda they speak Rukiga. This is not to say that they never had a language of their own. Some still speak their original languages, such as Balese, Bira, and Mangbetu among the Bambuti in the Democratic Republic of the Congo. For some of them, interaction with other groups has resulted in their languages being diluted and/or disappearing altogether. Thus, interaction with the new groups that moved into their homeland has resulted in the dilution and, in many cases, the death of their languages and the modification of their rituals. Kinyarwanda, Kirundi, and Rukiga are part of the Bantu group or the Niger-Congo group of languages. Lukiga/Rukiga has a noun class system in which prefixes on nouns mark membership of one of the noun genders. Examples here include the following: *mu* - person (singular), e.g. *mukiga* = inhabitant of Bakiga land; *bu* - land, e.g. *Bukiga* = land of the Bakiga; *lu/ru* - language, e.g. *Lukiga/Rukiga* = language of the Bakiga; *ba* - people, e.g. Bakiga = The Bakiga people; *ki* - customs or traditions, e.g. *kikiga*, denotes religious tradition common to the Bakiga people. This is also true of languages such as Kinyarwanda and Kirundi.

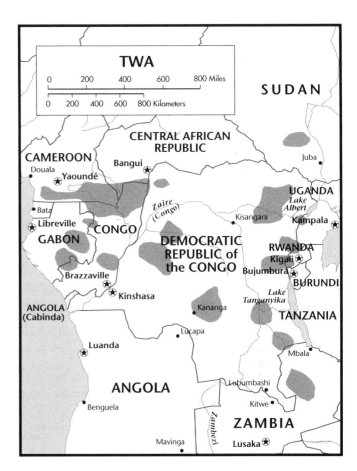

4 FOLKLORE

The Twa have a well-developed and sophisticated folklore with legends, stories, and poetry. Their folklore has important lessons about their forest environments, movements, and their history and origin. For example, one of the legends narrates the origins of the Mbuti group of the Twa. It notes that Mutwa was a native of African tropical rainforests. He occupied the current Itwari and Bwindi forests in the Democratic Republic of Congo and western Uganda respectively. In the DRC he was known locally as Mumbuti (singular) and Bambuti (plural), while in Uganda he was Mutwa (singular) and Batwa (plural). He was a nomadic hunter and gatherer. In most cases, Mutwa lived in solitude. Therefore, when he died no one else was there to witness the death or burial. The legend goes on to narrate burial customs and taboos, the use of spears for hunting, and the glorious life in the forest. In short, this legend refers to the Twa as singular, denoting their lifestyle of roaming in small bands as individuals and their way of hunting and gathering what the environment provides, i.e. honey, animals, fruits, and other edible plants from time immemorial.

Another famous folklore legend narrated by Turnbull (1961) concerns the singing of the "Bird" with the "Most Beautiful Song." Turbull writes:

> "This bird was found by a young boy who heard such a Beautiful Song that he had to go and see who was singing. When he found the Bird he brought it back to the camp to feed it. His father was annoyed at having to give food to the Bird, but the son pleaded and the Bird was

fed. The next day the Bird sang again; it sang the Most Beautiful Song in the Forest, and again the boy went to it and brought it back to feed it. This time the father was even more angered, but once again he gave in and fed the Bird. The third day (most Pygmy stories repeat themselves at least three times) the same thing happened. But this time the father took the Bird from his son and told his son to go away. When his son had left, the father killed the Bird, the Bird with the Most Beautiful Song in the Forest, and with the Bird he killed the Song, and with the Song he killed himself and he dropped dead, completely dead, dead for ever."

This legend tells of the importance of singing among the Twa in their forest homeland. Indeed, during the early hours of the night, the Twa sit by the fire outside their camp in their small bands and tell riddles and legends. Some sing, mimicking the various beautiful animal sounds in the forest. Central to the folklore of the Twa people are the many animals found in their environment. Many of these animals take on characteristics of men, for example, the ever-wise turtle and the cunning trickster hare. Thus, animals are used to tell entertaining stories designed to teach about human behavior and relationships.

⁵ RELIGION

Only a small portion (about 10%) of the Twa people has been converted to Christianity. The majority continue to adhere to indigenous beliefs in many gods. The most important deity of the Twa people is the god of the hunt, Khonvoum. He wields a bow made from two snakes that together appear to humans as a rainbow. His second in command is the god of thunder, through which he contacts mortal man. The Twa believe that man was forged from clay by Khonvoum, who forged different races and peoples from different types of clay, e.g. black people from black clay, white people from white clay, and the Twa from red clay. Khonvoum was also generous to the Twa by providing them with a forest rich of resources and animals for them to hunt. There are, of course other gods, such as Tore who is the god of the forest, as well as the god associated with death, as he decreed it on humans after his mother had died. Many of these gods appear as animals, such as the elephant, the chameleon, the leopard, and reptiles. This is keeping with the fact that the life of the Twa is part and parcel of the forest, their great provider, something to keep in awe, a sacred place bequeathed to them by their benevolent pantheon of gods.

⁶ MAJOR HOLIDAYS

For the Twa people, there are very few holidays and, when celebrated, they are often impromptu. They celebrate a few traditional holiday events, such as the rite of passage for young boys, the end of Nkumbi (the honey feast dance), and other ceremonial activities. These traditional festivities are in keeping with their lifestyle of hunting and gathering. However, the few Twa that have been settled and live sedentary lives may be involved in national holidays, such as Independence Day or Christmas for Christians.

⁷ RITES OF PASSAGE

In traditional Twa society, there were and still are rites of passage for boys and girls. The girls' initiation is called the *elima*. The *elima* initiation ceremony signifies the coming of age of girls. This is done during the first menstruation of the girl. She is immediately secluded into a hut with her friends who have also celebrated the coming of maturity. The girls are taught the duties of motherhood by an older and wiser woman in the community. There is much singing and dancing by both older women and girls. The *elima* is considered a great joyous occasion celebrated over days or weeks.

Boys undergo the *nkumbi* initiation ceremony. The *nkumbi* is the village circumcision school, which is done in partnership with the Bantu villages near the forests. The Twa and the Bantu have long interacted with each other, trading goods and resources from the forest. It was during these interactions that the Twa adopted some of the customs of the village Bantu and vice versa. One such custom is the *nkumbi* ceremony that is celebrated jointly. It happens after every four years. Boys from both the Bantu village and the nomadic Twas are secluded and undergo circumcision and initiation into manhood together. However, the relationship is still unequal, with the village boys in a more dominant position than the Twa, who are considered to be in a subservient position of their more powerful Bantu partners. Nevertheless, the joint initiation and circumcision ceremony is evidence of the symbiotic relationship between these two groups, in that one group provides material goods the other group does not have. In this way the two groups take care of each other. However, some initiation rituals are kept a total secret among the Twa. For example, the rite of initiation and the Spirit of the Forest is the preserve of Twa men only, who are revered as the holders of initiation knowledge. They are never supposed to talk about or reveal the secrets of this initiation to anyone, including their own women.

Another important ritual occurs when an important person in the Twa society dies. This is referred to as the *molimo* ritual that is celebrated with much noise. The Twa believe that they are the children of the forest and the forest is their caretaker and protector. They believe that when one dies, the forest must have gone to sleep and needs to be woken up, hence the noisy *molimo* celebration. The *molimo* is actually a trumpet made of wood or bamboo that is played by the men during the death ritual. When not in use, it is hidden away in the forest. The ritual is conducted at night around the campfire, and only men are allowed to be present. The *molimo* is also said to be a dangerous animal from the forest, not to be seen by women and children, who are hurriedly sent off into the huts. The men surround the *molimo* as it bellows out its forest noises and songs. There is much dancing and feasting by the men as they awaken the forest to come and protect them from death and other calamities.

⁸ INTERPERSONAL RELATIONS

The Twa have what might be considered an egalitarian society in which no one has authority over another. It has been suggested that egalitarianism was one of several central characteristics of nomadic hunting and gathering societies, since mobility precluded the accumulation of material possessions for any one single member in the band. Furthermore, clear evidence exists concerning the sexual division of labor among Twa. Females are primarily assigned the food-gathering chore as they have developed a keen sense for and the greatest familiarity with nutritive plants, such as wild fruits and vegetables. Hunting activities are the realm of men. The Twa do not see themselves as living a solitary or poor life, constantly at the mercy of the environment. They consider themselves to be living in a forest paradise on this earth.

Women continue to play a major role in community decision-making. Women are free to access forest resources anytime they wish. The Twa people have great respect for each other. Children learn this aspect of life early on, because anyone in a band can and is allowed to discipline any child. Children are also free to wander around into other peoples huts at will and are generally cared for by anyone in the band. Night is a time for socializing around a campfire. People come together to tell stories, legends, and riddles and sometimes to settle disputes between members of the camp.

The Twa are also a gregarious people that like to live in small groups or bands. However, from time to time, individuals or families will travel to visit other camps in the forest, where they might stay for substantial periods of time, to socialize and look for prospective wives or husbands. There is also a symbiotic relationship between the Twa of the forest and their Bantu neighbors, with whom they have interacted for generations. Although many consider the relationship between the Twa and their sedentary Bantu neighbors as unequal in favor of the Bantu villagers, others have argued that this is an interdependent relationship in which there is a flow of commodities either away. It is seen as a mutually beneficial relationship and, in some cases both groups, share some rituals such as the joint initiation of boys.

9 LIVING CONDITIONS

The Twa people live simple but rewarding lives. Their huts, often built by women, are made of branches and leaves. The Twa consider the forest to be their father and mother, a benevolent force that provides all their material needs. Hunting is one of the most important activities, as it is the main way of providing food and sustaining the group. Their material possessions are simple, geared towards the hunting and gathering way of life. The most prized possessions of the Twa are spears, bows and arrows, nets for hunting, and pots for cooking. They have developed an excellent trading relationship with the sedentary Bantu groups around them, with whom they trade forest products for important items, such as metal tips for their weapons. The huts are simple and temporary and can be abandoned anytime the group desires to move on. Women construct the huts from tree branches, covered with large leaves to ward off the constant dripping of the rain. The Twa sleep on leaves and sometimes mats woven from reeds. They usually live in a camp for up to one to five months, until they have exhausted the food resources around the camp and it is necessary to move on to a new environment. Thus, material comfort and wealth are not a significant aspect of Twa society. The forest provides the necessities for survival.

10 FAMILY LIFE

The Twa live in small camps of about 30 to 100 individuals. They learn to depend on each other and share everything they collect from the forest. Children are raised by the entire group, calling all women mother. In terms of family and marriage, the Twa used to practice monogamy, but this may have changed slightly with the influence of their Bantu neighbors, who practice polygamy. In terms of kinship and descent, the Twa follow the patrilineal system in which children belong to the father, particularly male children. A typical Twa family consists of a husband, a wife, and their children. Marriages can be arranged or two individuals can fall in love and marry each other. However, as in many other ethnic groups, marriage is the affair of extended families; it joins two groups, rather than simply the husband and wife. As a patrilineal society, when a marriage ends in divorce, male children stay with the father or return to the father's band when they grow up.

11 CLOTHING

The Twa's clothing is simple, consisting of a loincloth for men either made from bark cloth or fabric. Bark cloth is made from the layer underneath the bark of selected species of trees. The bark is beaten until it is thin and soft to wear. The Mbuti and Efe groups of the Twa in the Ituri rainforest in northeast DRC and southwest Uganda are best known for their bark cloths. Today, cotton fabrics and western forms of clothing are quite common for both men and women.

12 FOOD

The forest provides all the food the Twa need. Hunting is one of the most important activities of Twa men. Skilled hunters who specialize in hunting big game, such as elephants, are highly respected in Twa society. Other hunted animals include wild pigs, the giant forest hog, antelopes, and monkeys. While men are hunters, women gather products from the forest, such as wild yams, berries, fruits, roots, leaves, cola nuts, mushrooms, and other edible plants, as well as small animals such as larvae, snails, ants, termites, caterpillars, and reptiles.

Men and women also get involved in fishing activities, using various techniques such as traps, dams made of branches and trees, and nets for fishing from canoes. The most popular fishing technique by women is dam fishing. During the dry season, when the water level is low, areas of the river can be drained to catch the fish in the mud. The collection of honey, one of the most prized treats among the Twa, is left to men, as sometimes they have to climb 15 m (50 ft) to collect it from the trunks of huge forest trees.

Food is prepared in various ways. Meat is cooked in earthenware pots, children help to pound cassava or manioc with a pestle and mortar, vegetables are minced before cooking, and palm oil is processed and used in cooking food. Some Twa have adopted the agricultural lifestyle, farming crops of yams, legumes, beans, squash, sweet potatoes, peanuts, plantains, cassava, and maize. Sometimes these foods are obtained by trading with their agricultural neighbors. The Twa also practice certain food taboos. For example, a group may not hunt or eat an animal that is used as a totem for that band.

13 EDUCATION

The Twa who have been settled and now follow a sedentary way of life send their children to schools, especially in parts of Rwanda and Burundi. However, many Twa have resisted Western forms of education, preferring to teach their children in the ways of their life and traditions. From as early as three years old, boys are taught to use the bow for hunting and to climb trees to collect honey. Quite often, young boys accompany older men on their hunts. The boys carry the hunting nets, arrows, and bows for the older men. Girls are initiated into the tasks of a woman, which include gathering forest products for food, cooking, and fishing.

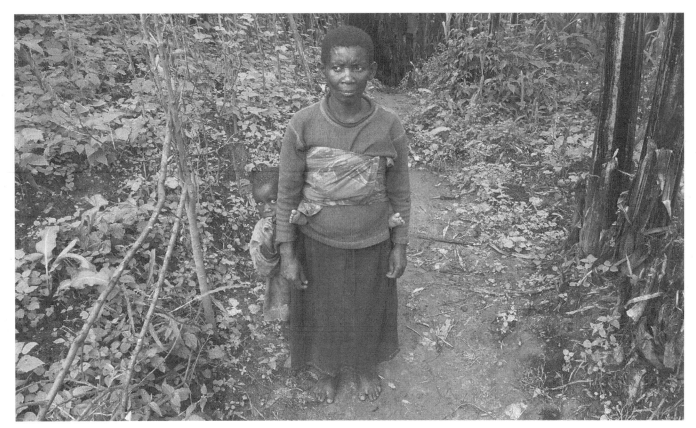

A Rwandan Twa pigmy woman poses with her son in the village of Bweyeye in southwestern Rwanda. Twa pygmies are being forced into greater poverty due to conservation rules that threaten their traditional way of life. (Jose Cendon/AFP/Getty Images)

¹⁴ CULTURAL HERITAGE

The Twa people are renowned for their musical skills. As children of the forest, they mimic the many sounds they hear in the forest in their songs and dance. Twa culture is dominated by music and dances; from almost all life events, from healing to initiation rituals, from traditional tales to group games, from hunting songs to entertainment moments, music is ever present. Birth, initiation, and death are all marked by rituals where music and dance play a very important role.

When night falls, it is time to sit around a campfire and tell stories and folktales about legendary ancestors and forest spirits. While some may think there is little to talk about concerning the cultural heritage of the Twa, they have nevertheless perfected a way of living that promotes egalitarianism and teaches all members to do their part for the good of the entire community. Perhaps this aspect of their culture is their greatest legacy. Community and family come first and the individual is but a part of the whole.

¹⁵ WORK

The most important work for the Twa is hunting and gathering. For the Twa deep in the forest, they hunt and gather just enough for them to survive. However, for the Twa who are in contact with the Bantu or African villagers, they hunt and gather a little more to trade for commodities they need from the villagers. They hunt and gather from the forest meat, honey, and fruits to exchange for plantains, maize, beans, cloth, and iron tools. Recently, money has found its way into Twa society.

As such, both men and women offer their labor to the villagers to help them cultivate their fields in exchange for cash. They are also asking for cash even for the forest products they bring to the villagers instead of simple bartering.

Although there is some division of labor by gender among the Twa, certain activities are a communal affair. For example, men, women, and children can all get involved in a hunt if nets are used. In such instances, women will make noises and beat the bushes to herd the animals towards the net, while the men wait by the net to trap the animals that come their way. Some activities, such as foraging, are done by both men and women, while others such as cooking, cleaning, building huts, and obtaining water are reserved for women. For small game, such as monkeys and antelope, men may hunt alone using poison-tipped arrows.

¹⁶ SPORTS

As in every society, Twa children are quite playful. Children play games that teach them important hunting and gathering skills, as well as group cooperation. Children and adults play games together where hunting skills are imparted into the children through mock hunts. For the adults, women and men may compete in a tug-of-war to see who is the strongest. The game is designed to teach the members of a band their interdependence on each other.

[17] ENTERTAINMENT AND RECREATION

Entertainment among the Twa comes in the form of feasting and dancing, especially after a successful hunt during which the giant forest hog or an elephant has been brought down. This would imply lots of meat and feasting for the group. There are celebrations, such as the honey festival, where there is much singing and dancing. In the shadow of the full moon at night, children, men and, women sit around a campfire for entertaining storytelling, riddles, or dancing.

[18] FOLK ART, CRAFTS, AND HOBBIES

The Twa are skilled in fashioning many of the implements they need for hunting and gathering, such as bows and arrows. They also make their own nets from forest vines for hunting, and weave baskets and mats from reeds and grasses. They have excellent skills for making bark cloth that they fashion into loincloths.

Given that music plays a central role in the daily life of the Twa, they have developed an impressive array of musical instruments. Some of the instruments are obtained from the Bantu villagers, such as the cylindrical drums, the arched harp, and rattles. Others are traditional to the Twa, such as the musical bow (made and played exclusively by women) and flutes.

[19] SOCIAL PROBLEMS

One of the major problems facing the Twa today is their disappearing homeland, due to clearing of forests for agriculture purposes by the Bantu groups. Forested areas have receded as agriculture has expanded on the rich volcanic soils in the Rwanda, Burundi, Uganda, and DRC regions. By the 1980s, much of all the available land, apart from areas reserved for wildlife conservation and environmental protection, was under cultivation, particularly in Rwanda and Burundi. Pressures on the forests intensified through production of export crops such as tea, quinine, and coffee.

Thus, the forest environments for the Twa hunting and gathering activities have decreased resulting in their becoming a landless and endangered group. Their traditional forest-based culture that includes their religion and rituals as well as their language is in grave jeopardy. Some Twa have adapted themselves to new forms of livelihoods such as making pottery, basketry, and metalworking. Others have attached themselves to powerful and rich individuals in a subservient position and have become singers, dancers, messengers, guards, warriors, and hunters for these individuals. But, many continue to remain poor and landless with their food supply threatened. The ongoing civil unrest in the great lakes region has also affected them adversely.

In short, recent activities in the region, including logging, mining, road building, and commerce have brought the Twa into greater contacts with the modern world that threatens to erode their values, beliefs, and way of life. In addition to the loss of their tropical rainforest homeland, the Twa are despised and exploited by their Bantu neighbors, who often regard them to be subhuman. Recently, HIV/AIDS has been introduced into the Twa society, as many Bantu believe that sexual intercourse with a Twa can cure diseases such as AIDS. For those who have moved to live in towns and cities, commercial sex work for Twa women is on the increase putting them at an even greater risk for HIV infection. For the Twa still in the forests, there have reports of soldiers in the Congo hunting and eating them in order to absorb their forest powers. These factors have caused untold hardships for a people used to living in harmony with their environment, and their culture could be obliterated in the near future.

[20] GENDER ISSUES

As an egalitarian society, men and women have equal power and women are often involved in making important decisions, such as where to move the camp or where and when to go hunt or forage for food. Although some chores are left for women alone (e.g. cooking, cleaning, and fixing huts), women and men often go out hunting or fishing together.

There are of course some gender issues among Twa society that affect women unfairly. For example, the custom of sister exchange as a common form of marriage implies the bartering of women, rather than marriage through love. However, it needs to be emphasized that monogamy is the norm for Twa marriages and bride wealth does not exist in Twa society. Polygamous unions are increasing, although these are also rare in Twa society. In short, gender equality is an aspect of Twa society.

[21] BIBLIOGRAPHY

Ballard, Chris. "Strange Alliance: Pygmies in the Colonial Imaginary." *World Archaeology* 38, no 1(2006): 133–151.

Cavalli-Sforza, Luigi L. *African Pygmies*. Orlando, Florida: Academic Press, 1986.

Campagnoli, Mauro. "Pygmies of Central Africa with Photos and Ethnographic Notes." http://www.pygmies.info/.

Gilbert, Elizabeth L. *Tribes of the Great Rift Valley*. New York: Abrams, 2007.

Green, Jeffrey. "Edwardian England's Forest Pygmies." *History Today* 45 (1995): 33–39.

Hewlett, Barry S. "Cultural diversity among African pygmies." In *Cultural Diversity Among Twentieth-Century Foragers*, edited by Susan Kent. Cambridge, England: Cambridge University Press, 1996.

Jackson, Dorothy. "Central Africa: Nowhere to Go; Land Loss and Cultural Degradation; The Twa of the Great Lakes." *WRM* Bulletin no 87 (October 2004). http://www.wrm.org.uy/bulletin/87/CentralAfrica.html.

Jackson, Dorothy, and Katrina Payne. *Twa Women, Twa Rights in the Great Lakes Region of Africa*. London: Minority Rights Group International, 2003.

Klieman, Kairn A. "The Pygmies Were Our Compass," *Bantu and Batwa in the History of West Central Africa, Early Times to c.1900 C. E.* Portsmouth, NH: Heinemann, 2003.

Lewis, Jerome. *The Batwa Pygmies of the Great Lakes Region*. London: Minority Rights Group International, 2000.

Minority Rights Group International. *Uganda: The Marginalization of Minorities; the Batwa in Uganda*. Minority Rights Group International, 2001.

Salopek, Paul. "SPECIAL AFRICA ISSUE—Who Rules the Forest?" *National Geographic* 208, no. 3 (2005): 74.

Turnbull, Colin M. *The Forest People*. New York: Simon & Schuster, 1968.

Turnbull, Colin M. *The Mbuti Pygmies: Change and Adaptation*. New York: Holt, Rinehart, and Winston, 1983.

—revised by E. Kalipeni

UGANDANS

PRONUNCIATION: yoo-GAN-duhns
LOCATION: Uganda
POPULATION: 26,404,543 million
LANGUAGE: English (official); various tribal languages
RELIGION: Christianity; Islam; indigenous beliefs
RELATED ARTICLES: Vol. 1: Baganda; Banyankole

¹ INTRODUCTION

Uganda's present ethnic history is largely a result of two population movements that occurred in the first 500 years of the 2nd millennium AD. The first movement by cattle herders, known as Hima, into exclusively agricultural areas contributed to the development of centralized kingdoms in the west-central portion of the country. The second movement of Nilotic speakers into the northern and eastern areas also stimulated the further development of centralized kingdoms to the south by contributing ruling clans to them. These migrations contributed to the political and ethnic divisions that were present at the arrival of the British in the latter half of the 19th century and that can still be seen today.

Until 1967, Uganda had a number of tightly centralized kingdoms such as Butoro, Buganda, Bunyoro, Bunyankole, and Busoga in its southern and western areas. These kingdoms were sometimes internally divided between cattle owners, who were considered to be royal, and farmers, who were subservient to them. In Bunyoro, these groups are called Huma and Iru; and in Ankole, Hima and Iru, respectively. In Rwanda and Burundi, countries to the west of Uganda, these still warring groups are called Tutsi and Hutu. Northern Uganda was made up of Nilotic-speaking peoples (of the plains, and of the rivers and lakes) who did not develop kingdoms, although they had contributed leaders through conquest of the ancestors of the southern kingdoms. At the time of Uganda's independence in 1962, a sharp linguistic and cultural divide still existed between northern and southern regions of the country. A relatively more socialistic, egalitarian philosophy was preferred in the north. In the south, however, existing class differences were more compatible with capitalism.

The British established Uganda as a protectorate and worked with the Baganda from 1900 onward to establish their control over the other ethnic groups. Asians of Indian or Pakistani descent had been brought over to work as laborers on the Uganda railroad, which extended from Mombasa on the coast of Kenya to Kampala, Uganda. The British developed cotton as a cash crop in Uganda in the early 20th century. The Asians remained in Uganda as brokers in this and other emerging business enterprises. In the 1920s, for example, sugarcane was established in Uganda through plantations and processing plants run by Asian entrepreneurs. By this time, three-fourths of the cotton gins in Uganda were owned by Asians. Much later, coffee emerged as the most important export of Uganda. Europeans, particularly the British, were important in government, church, education, and banking, but their population in Uganda was quite small in comparison to the neighboring colony of Kenya, which attracted a large white settler community.

Uganda, which Winston Churchill once called "the pearl of Africa," had a promising future at the time of independence. A favorable environment with fertile soil and regular rainfall, as well as a talented, multiethnic population contributed to this optimism. Nevertheless, ethnic divisions proved insurmountable. In 1967, Prime Minister Milton Obote from the north declared kingdoms illegal and tried to impose on the nation his "Common Man's Charter," a socialist doctrine. Sir Edward Mutesa, the Kabaka (King) of Buganda, and the first president of the Republic of Uganda, was overthrown by Obote, who then declared himself the president. In 1971, Obote was overthrown by his army commander, Idi Amin. This led to a repressive reign of terror against all Ugandans. The Asian community was ordered out of the country in 1972, and their businesses were given away to Ugandans without respect to their qualifications. The economy was soon in ruins. Milton Obote returned to power after a combined force of Tanzanian soldiers and Ugandan exiles drove Amin from the country. Obote became president again in 1980, although it was claimed that the elections had been rigged. An ensuing guerrilla war ended in 1986, with Yoweri Museveni becoming president. Uganda currently is experiencing a rejuvenated economy and political system under its present government, which has maintained an open style of leadership receptive to the participation of all ethnic groups.

² LOCATION AND HOMELAND

Uganda is located in East Africa astride the equator between Kenya and the Democratic Republic of the Congo. Its area is not large, being about the size of the state of Oregon. Uganda is landlocked but has several large inland waterways, including Lake Victoria with its inland water ports at Jinja and Port Bell. Its climate is tropical with two rainy seasons; however, the northeast is semiarid. The country is primarily plateau with its capital city of Kampala about 1,200 km (4,000 ft) above sea level. Its population is about 20 million people. The Africans belong to about 40 ethnic groups, of which the Baganda, the Karamojong, the Iteso, and the Lango are the largest groups. There also are a small number of Europeans, Asians, and Arabs. A republic with a one-party political system, Uganda has a president as chief of state. The current president is Lt. General Yoweri Kaguta Museveni.

³ LANGUAGE

The official, national language of Uganda is English. Bantu languages are spoken by the greatest number of speakers in the nation, concentrated in the southern and western areas of the country. Nilotic languages predominate in the northern regions. The northwest area includes Moru Madi-speakers. The eastern border of Uganda, which is shared with Kenya, has both Bantu languages, such as Lusamyia, and Nilotic languages, such as Teso. Kiswahili, a Bantu language, is spoken widely throughout eastern Kenya.

Luganda, another Bantu language, is the mother tongue of the Baganda, who are the largest ethnic group in Uganda, comprising 17% of the population. Luganda spread throughout Uganda, particularly in the southern, eastern, and western regions, during the late 19th and early 20th centuries as a language of domination. This was supported by the British, who worked through Baganda chiefs as a form of indirect rule over other Ugandan ethnic groups. For this reason, Luganda, to this day, is understood in various sections of the country. There is also a well-developed indigenous literature in Luganda in the form of histories, stories, folk tales and songs, political documents, plays, and newspapers.

Ugandans are typically comfortable in more than one language. Luganda, English, and Kiswahili, for example, are commonly used languages in Kampala. In other regions of the country, children learn English in addition to their own ethnic language. Nevertheless, even among the most highly-educated Ugandans, there is a strong preference for the mother tongue at home and in social situations. For this reason, perhaps, there is a strong tendency for individuals to marry those that speak a common ethnic language, or to remain within either the Bantu or Nilotic language families.

4 FOLKLORE

All the ethnic groups of Uganda have a rich oral tradition made up of tales, legends, stories, proverbs, and riddles. Folk heroes include, for example, those thought responsible for introducing kingship into a society, such as the legendary Kintu, the first *Kabaka* (king) of the Baganda, or the first *Bito* ruler of the Bunyoro, King Isingoma Mpuga Rukidi. Morality tales were common throughout Uganda. Some Ankole tales include one about a wise woman and her selfish husband, which teaches faithfulness to one's wives during hard times; one about a pig and a hyena, which preaches against self-indulgence; and the wisdom of the hare, which demonstrates the advantages of being quick-witted and friendly against all odds.

Proverbs and riddles are perhaps the most significant mechanisms for teaching values to the young, while at the same time providing entertainment. The importance of parenting, for instance, can be seen in the following proverbs from the Baganda:

I will never move from this village, but for the sake of children he does.

He who does a good service to one's child, does better than one who merely says he loves you.

An only child is like a drop of rain in the dry season.

My luck is in that child of mine if the child is rich.

A skillful hunting dog may nevertheless produce weaklings.

A chicken's feet do not kill its young.

That which becomes bad at the outset of its growth is almost impossible to straighten at a later stage.

Collective riddling games are a popular evening entertainment in rural villages. Among the Baganda, these games involve men and women of all ages. A person who solves a riddle is given a village to rule as its "chief." Some examples of riddles are:

Pass one side, and I also pass the other side, so that we meet in the middle? (a belt)

He built a house with only one pole standing? (a mushroom)

He goes on dancing as he walks? (a caterpillar)

He built a house with two entrances? (a nose)

He has three legs? (an old man walking with his stick)

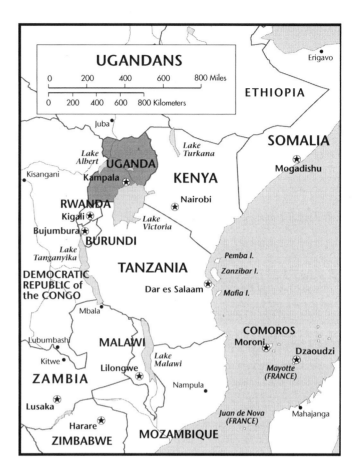

5 RELIGION

About two-thirds of Ugandans are Christian, evenly divided between Protestants and Roman Catholics. The remaining third are about evenly divided between Muslims and those practicing indigenous, African religion. Religious holidays are celebrated in Uganda, especially Christmas and Easter for Christians, and Ramadan for Muslims. Each of the major religious denominations is associated with its own hill in Kampala, reflecting the practice of major institutions being situated on a hill in 19th century Uganda. Thus, there is a hill for the university, for the national hospital, and for the Catholic, the Anglican, and the Muslim houses of worship. Of international interest is the shrine near Kampala dedicated to the Uganda martyrs who are recognized as saints in the Roman Catholic tradition. These Christian martyrs were executed in the 19th century for refusing to renounce their religion at a time when Christians, traditionalists, and Muslims were competing for converts and influence in the emerging, but hostile, religious plurality of the day.

Indigenous supernatural ideas, such as belief in witchcraft, the evil eye, and night dancers, are still widespread. Among some groups, such as the Samia, amulets are worn to protect children from the evil eye of a jealous woman, which is thought to cause them sickness or death. Witches found in most societies also cause misfortune to people of all ages. A widely feared person throughout Uganda is the night dancer. He is a community member by day, who is thought to roam about at night eating dead bodies while floating along the ground with fire between his hands. People generally avoid traveling alone at night for fear of these *Basezi*. Ancestors are highly respected and feared. They communicate with the living through dreams to warn them of impending dangers and to advise them on family matters. Children are advised to report their dreams to their elders soon after arising in the morning. Among the Lango, ancestor spirits *(Tipu)* are thought to cause illness, barrenness, impotence, and quarrels among the living, which may result in the division of kinfolk into new communities.

Most societies in Uganda believe that there is a high god who is the supreme creator. Among the Baganda, for instance, their supreme god was called *Katonda*. He was also known by other names that suggested his power, such as *Mukama* (the Master), *Lugaba* (the Giver), and *Liisoddene* (the Great Eye). *Were*, the high god of the Samia, is associated with the sun and was venerated each morning with its rising. Today, such beliefs have merged with Christianity and Islam. The older pantheon of lesser deities, each with their oracle priest and priestesses and special temples, has given way to churches and mosques. Nevertheless, Ugandans remain a very religious people with a deep-seated spirituality.

⁶ MAJOR HOLIDAYS

There is a single national holiday, celebrated on October 9, which commemorates the day in 1962 when Uganda achieved its independence from the United Kingdom.

⁷ RITES OF PASSAGE

The ethnic groups in Uganda recognize developmental stages in the life-cycle. Birth is generally received with a great deal of joy, as children are warmly welcomed into the community. Infancy is considered to be an important period in the child's development. For this reason, ceremonies such as those related to the milestone of sitting up alone and also obtaining one's clan name, often occur during the first years of life. Among the Baganda, for example, an infant is seated on a mat along with others who are to receive their clan names. Prior to this time, the infant has been regularly encouraged to sit by being placed in a hole in the ground or in a washbasin with cloths around the waist and buttocks for support. When the infant succeeds in sitting alone for the first time, there is a brief ceremony, and it is proclaimed, "now you are a man," or "now you are a woman," accordingly. Among the Lango, *Kwer* ceremonies are held throughout childhood to recognize changes in the status of a mother that are associated with the maturation of her child. Ceremonies involve exchanges of food and the drinking of beer by adult relatives of the child. Such celebrations occur, for example, shortly after childbirth when the mother spends several days in seclusion; after a mother has given birth to several children; after her oldest child is about 8 years old; when the oldest child is sick; and when the oldest child is about 12 years of age.

Childhood varies depending on whether the child comes from a wealthy or a poor family, or lives in the city of Kampala or in a small, rural village. Many young children walk upwards of 16 km (10 mi) daily to school. Since schools require fees, family members often need to pool their resources in order to send children (or, in some cases, only the most promising child) to school. This child, if successful, is expected to help other family members in turn. Boys and girls generally have household tasks to do. Girls 7 to 9 years old can be seen caring for their younger siblings while the mother is working in the home or garden. During this time, the child caretaker will carry the infant on her back, sing lullabies, play, and otherwise amuse the baby. In rural areas, young boys typically are expected to care for livestock. Children from wealthy parents, by contrast, have fewer work responsibilities and more leisure time in that they live in homes with servants. They are also afforded opportunities for travel, better schooling, and luxury material goods, such as computers, TVs, and videos.

The teenage years are devoted to education, work, and courtship. Girls in rural areas are increasingly likely to become pregnant prior to marriage, especially if there is little prospect for education or gainful employment later in life. Although parents frown on teenage pregnancy, the infant is usually welcomed by the infant's maternal grandparents and may be raised as their own child. Abortions are discouraged in Uganda, given the high value placed on children.

Among many of the Nilotic societies, an age-group system is important. For the Karamojong, all males are formally initiated into an age-set that provides an established ranking. For example, all males are in one of two fixed generations, so that all the sons of one generation are in the same group, regardless of their ages. Therefore, the junior generation contains members who are still too young to be initiated. Should a male child be born before all members of the preceding generation have been initiated, he must wait to be named and publicly recognized. About every 25 years, a new generation is publicly established through a series of rituals officiated over by grandfathers of the new group. A final ceremony of inclusion occurs for a man with the ritual slaying of an ox that is then eaten in a communal feast. When a new generation is allowed to begin, some men are middle aged while others are quite young during this first year of initiation. Initiations are held about every 3 years with the average age being about 19. The name of a new group is chosen by the senior men. Common names are buffalo, jackal, leopard, topi, and snake. The age-set system functions most notably during rituals and determines participation, seating, and distribution order of meat. Authority is strictly along age-set lines in matters of discipline and community morality.

Pubescent girls were traditionally secluded and formally instructed by elder women (such as one's *Ssenga*, or father's sister), in societies that have patrilineal descent in sexual matters, domestic skills, and other expectations for married life. While the age-set system for boys is still evident in some communities, the seclusion of girls and associated sexual and domestic instruction has largely disappeared. Instead, girls learn about these matters through advice columns in daily newspapers and magazines and peer gossip in secondary schools. Traditionalists sometimes bemoan the fact that sex education is nowhere to be seen in the contemporary school system and dominant Christian ideology. Teenage pregnancies are thought to be one consequence of this change.

Adult life is concerned with work, family, religion, and community and national service of various forms. Death is a significant social event in all ethnic groups, where visiting and rituals are obligatory. Absenteeism from work for attendance at funerals is frequent and excused. Christian or Muslim burial is now commonplace. Ugandans widely believe that spiritual life continues after death, in accordance with Christian or Islamic concepts. Belief in the continued involvement of dead ancestors in family life is not uncommon. In some societies, infants are named after ancestors so that a person can live on as long as his or her name is remembered. This form of reincarnation was seen by some demographers to be a deterrent to family planning efforts, given that to limit one's offspring is in a very real sense limiting one's opportunity to be reincarnated. Exposure to newer religions has caused some practices to decline, although many still persist from indigenous religions.

⁸ INTERPERSONAL RELATIONS

Ugandans on the whole are deeply imbedded in the social life of their communities, be these villages, schools, neighborhoods, clubs, churches, mosques, age-sets, clans, homesteads, or extended families. There are, of course, individual exceptions to this generalization, especially among those who are highly educated and who have the opportunity to travel. Ugandans enjoy looking "smart" (attractive) and are exceptionally fashionable. Women from Uganda have a favorable reputation in neighboring countries for their beauty and charm. Women from western Uganda, for example, traditionally went into seclusion prior to marriage and spent an extended period of time drinking milk in order to gain a good amount of weight prior to marriage. Today, plumpness is still considered desirable. Thus, eating disorders, such as bulimia and anorexia nervosa, are virtually nonexistent in a culture where thinness is not valued. Obesity, nevertheless, is also extremely rare since Ugandans remain quite physically active, given that most do not own cars and, therefore, travel on foot.

Sociability is best symbolized through a pattern of ritualized greetings that vary according to time of day, a person's age, social status, and length of time since an encounter. Each ethnic group tends to have its own characteristic greeting pattern and vocabulary. Not to greet someone is considered to be a serious impropriety. The following is an example of a Kiganda greeting:

Mawulire ki? (What is the news?)
Tetugalaba. (We have none.)
Mmm or Eee.
Mpoza mmwe? (Perhaps you have?)
Naffe tetugalaba or Nedda. (We have none either.)
Mmm or Eee.

Dating occurs prior to marriage in a variety of social contexts. Young people meet at funerals, weddings, churches, and school socials. Nightclubs are a popular place for dancing, with friends or on a date. Love songs are popular with people of all ages. Some post-independence songs heard on jukeboxes in bars, and on the radio contain clever phrases that are admired in courtship. The following are some examples of songs in Luganda by Baganda composers. The song, *"Nassuna,"* by E. Kawalya contains the lyric: "Your photograph which I have is now like my mirror. I always look at it. Great are the parents who gave birth to you." Another song, *"Nakiganda,"* by C. Ssebaduka states: "I have been waiting for you, Nakiganda, my love. Why are you late? I placed my chair by the road so that I could watch you come. . . . Your picture you gave me. . . I took it and showed it to my parents." It goes on to explain that if the gentleman did not marry Nakiganda it must be, according to his father, due to someone "bewitching" him. A third, popular song also mentions parents in the context of love and romance precisely because marriage throughout Uganda involves large,

extended families and is not simply a matter of two individuals falling in love. The song, *"Ntonga,"* by D. Mugula laments, "Really, Ntonga, I beg you and your parents not to listen to those who may want to come between our friendship. . . Here is some sugar for your parents, for what harm did they do in giving birth to a beauty like yourself?"

⁹ LIVING CONDITIONS

President Museveni's rule has had to contend with severe political and economic devastation brought about by the previous Obote and Amin regimes. Nevertheless, Uganda is in the process of making a comeback. Tourism is being revived, with an emphasis on conservation and ecology. Agriculture remains the basic livelihood, with about 90% of the population continuing to reside in rural areas. Important subsistence crops include millet, corn, cassava, and plantains. Beef, poultry, and milk are also significant, especially among pastoral populations where agriculture is less significant than cattle as a means of livelihood. Coffee remains the largest export, earning over 75% of foreign currency. Recently, flowers such as roses are being cultivated for export to European countries. Fishing along the northern and western shores of Lake Victoria is important for communities located in these areas.

Population densities are highest in the south and southeastern areas, sometimes exceeding 116 persons per sq km (300 persons per sq mi). Other regions of Uganda are sparsely populated. Kampala, the capital city, and its environs have about 0.5 million people. It is the administrative, commercial, and cultural center of the country. This city is a transportation hub with a network of good, paved roads connecting Kampala with smaller towns in rural areas throughout the country. The taxi market is an impressive sight, with hundreds of "speed taxis" coming and going with travelers to and from the city. Outdoor markets with foodstuffs, household items, second-hand clothing, and various other items are densely crowded. Automobiles are seen commonly in Kampala, but in rural areas the bicycle is the most important conveyance, especially for transporting items to and from the marketplace.

Homes in rural areas are frequently made of wattle and daub and have thatched or corrugated-iron roofs. Affluent residents of rural areas may, however, have elaborate homes. This is particularly true for those who have gained wealth through commercial farming and livestock maintenance. Urban homes are typically of concrete with corrugated-iron or tile roofs, and have glass windows. In the suburbs of Kampala, multilevel and ranch homes are very plush, with servant quarters, swimming pools, and elaborate gardens. Urban gardens of produce and flowers are also a common feature of the city landscape.

Uganda's population suffers from malaria and HIV/AIDS, known locally as "slim disease." Despite efforts at eradication, malaria-infested mosquitoes are present throughout the country. Southern Uganda has a particularly high rate of HIV/AIDS infection, and virtually every family there has lost loved ones to the disease. The government has maintained an active policy of public education. The daily newspaper, *The New Vision*, carries a regular column known as "AIDS Corner," which is meant to educate the public. Infant mortality rates are also high due to poverty, malnutrition, diarrhea, and measles. The infant mortality rate is 112 deaths per 1,000 live births.

Ugandan life is concerned with work, family, religion, and community and national service of various forms.
(Paul Joynson-Hicks)

¹⁰ FAMILY LIFE

Marriage and family life are primary pursuits of most Ugandans, whatever their ethnic group or religion. The extended family concept continues to be the ideal, although individualism and the nuclear family have made inroads due to European and Christian influences on the nation's culture. Monogamy (one husband and one wife at a time) is now the national ideal, even though polygyny (one husband and several wives at a time) is sometimes encountered. Polygyny is functional in situations in which marriage is very much a negotiation between large, extended families. Polygyny became a mechanism for large, extended families to increase the number of children in their community—not a bad idea in a rural, subsistence economy based on human labor. Ideals of love and affection were maintained in both monogamous and polygynous marriage situations.

The importance of extended family ties in marriage can be illustrated by the Banyankole people's complex traditional marriage customs. When a man decided he wanted to marry, he visited the girl's parents and informed them. If they agreed to the marriage, he returned with some of his relatives and, over pots of beer, discussed with his prospective father-in-law and his brothers the amount of the marriage fee. Routinely, goats, for example, were divided as follows: seven for the bride's father, three for an elder brother of his, two for his mother's brother, one for the father's sister, and one for a younger brother of the father. The bridegroom would go to his own family members to raise the fee needed for his marriage. After these fees had been paid, the bridegroom kissed both palms of his father-in-law's hands and returned home. His home was a portion of his own father's large compound. When the bride arrived in her new home for the first time, she entered the room of her father- and mother-in-law. She sat first on her father-in-law's lap and then on her mother-in-law's lap, to symbolize that she was now like a daughter who would bear children for the family. After this ceremony, future contact with her father-in-law was taboo. Emphasis on large, extended families and bride-fees seen in the context of reciprocal exchange often made for strong, lifelong relations between brothers and sisters because wealth brought into the family on the occasion of a girl's marriage often provided the means for the brother to obtain a bride for himself.

Nowadays, Ugandans typically continue to have some form of marriage fee, maintain allegiances to their extended families and clans, and generally marry outside of them (a custom known as exogamy). Children of these unions usually belong to the clans of their fathers and take their clan names from his group. Some common clans in Uganda are elephant, bushbuck, rat, fish, lion, mushroom, civet cat, and many other plants and animals. People are not supposed to eat the plant or animal associated with their clan names. In some societies, such as the Lango or the Karamojong, women join the clans of their husbands; but, in other groups, such as the Baganda, they do not.

Traditional marriage ceremonies, rituals, and practices persist in varying degrees depending on ethnic group and location, as well as on degree of conformity to Christian or Muslim ideals. Most women, regardless of their educational level, desire to have children. Family planning, when it is used, has the function of attempting to space children, rather than to reduce their number or to avoid having them at all.

¹¹ CLOTHING

Most Ugandans wear Western-style clothing. Young people are especially attracted to American clothing styles, such as jeans and slacks. The most prominent indigenous form of clothing is found in southern Uganda among the Baganda. The woman typically wears a *busuuti* (a floor-length, brightly colored cloth dress with short puffed sleeves, a square neckline fastened by two buttons, and a sash placed just below the waist atop the hips). Baganda men frequently wear a *kanzu* (long white robe). For special occasions, a western style suit jacket is worn over the kanzu. In western Uganda, Bahima women wear full, broad cotton dresses, with a floor-length shawl used to cover their bodies while seated, and to cover their heads and shoulders while standing. Northern societies such as the Karamojong wear cowskins, and signify social status (e.g., warrior, married person, elder) by items of adornment, such as feather plumes and large coiled, copper necklaces, and armlets.

¹² FOOD

Ugandan stores, supermarkets, and open-air markets make available a wide choice of foods from local and international sources. Each region of the country tends to have its own local foods and traditions, which have endured since pre-colonial times. Among pastoral groups, such as the Karamojong, there is a strong emphasis on cattle that provide meat and milk (sometimes eaten in curdled form, or mixed with blood drawn from the neck of an ox). Cattle are also a source of many other necessities, such as clothing and blankets. Containers are made from the horns and hoofs. Cattle urine is mixed with mud as a base for the floor of huts, since water is scarce. Dung is used for fertilizer in those communities where grain is grown. Millet and sorghum are common grains available to communities throughout northern regions, where rainfall is not sufficient for root crops such as cassava, manioc, and sweet potatoes. Root crops and plantains are staples in southern and eastern Uganda where rain is plentiful year-round. In western Uganda, the Banyankole are internally divided into the Bahima, who are pastoralists having very long-horned cows; and the Bairu, who grow grains such as millet and sorghum.

Kampala is supplied daily with large amounts of plantains (*matooke*). Matooke is the staple of the Baganda, the largest ethnic group in Uganda and in the city of Kampala. Matooke is served with various sauces that may be composed of peanuts, green leaves, mushrooms, tomatoes, meat, fish, white ants, and/or grasshoppers. Before eating, a bowl of boiled water and soap are passed around so that each person can wash his or her hands. Banana leaves are used to cover the steamed plantain while cooking and during serving. Matooke is eaten by taking the right hand and forming a small portion of the matooke into a ladle, which is then dipped in the sauces. The combination of a staple with a sauce is common throughout Uganda, as is eating with the right hand, although cutlery is available when desired.

Drinks include a wide variety of bottled beers and soft drinks. In rural areas, traditional beer fermented from maize (corn), bananas, millet, sorghum, or pineapples is sometimes available. Metal cooking pots and pans, dishes, and glassware are now commonplace in rural areas, although traditional gourds and ceramic containers are also prevalent. Throughout the country, agriculture is the special domain of women, who are responsible for the farming of staple foods. They also exercise much control over the foods that they grow and prepare in the kitchen, which is also considered to be a woman's domain. Men tend to be responsible for cash crops such as coffee and tea.

Chocolate bars and other sweet candies are not generally eaten as treats by children in rural areas. Instead, children enjoy picking sugarcane and chewing it for its sweet juices. Fruits, such as mangoes and small sweet bananas, are also favorite treats. These preferences make for strong gums and teeth. Thus, dental problems are rare, a fact also attributed to the custom of cleaning each tooth separately with a stick. Dental problems are becoming more of a problem, however, among young people today who have more exposure to processed sweets.

¹³ EDUCATION

The Obote and Amin years witnessed deterioration in the educational standard of the country. Makerere University College, which began as a secondary school in the 1920s, became a university in 1950 (known then as the University College of East Africa). It drew students from Kenya, Tanganyika (now Tanzania), and Zanzibar, as well as Uganda. In 1961, it became Makerere University College and continued throughout the 1960s to educate a large number of East Africans in a wide variety of fields including medicine. What was a distinguished university and faculty was decimated by the interventionist policies of Amin, who drove into exile or killed faculty and students

Success in school is seen as the means to a better livelihood for the individual who is, in turn, expected to help his extended family. For this reason, Ugandan students are typically very hardworking and achievement-oriented. (AP Images)

alike. The vice-chancellor of Makerere "disappeared," never to be seen again. Prior to 1970, an excellent secondary school system was also in place, and included very prestigious schools such as Kings College Budu, Kisubi, and Gyaza Girls among others. The school system was modeled after the British system, having primary, secondary (Cambridge certificate—O level), higher (A levels), and three years of university education.

The present government is in the process of rebuilding the nation's school system. There are many challenges. For example, in the total population aged 15 and over, about half are illiterate. Literacy is higher among males than females. This sex imbalance is due in part to a policy of favoritism shown by the British during the protectorate years for the education of boys. Another problem interrupting the education of girls is a high rate of pregnancy among schoolgirls, usually requiring that they leave school. Poverty is another factor contributing to illiteracy, given that schooling can be expensive. For those with means, the boarding school is a popular concept, as are single-sex institutions.

Parental expectations are high concerning education. Success in school is seen as the means to a better livelihood for the individual who is, in turn, expected to help his extended family. For this reason, Ugandan students are typically very hardworking and achievement-oriented. They can be found working and studying in all professions and vocations both in Uganda and abroad.

[14] CULTURAL HERITAGE

The expressive arts embodied in music and dance remain a significant part of Uganda's cultural heritage. Dance forms vary somewhat by ethnic group, but everywhere people of all ages participate in dance and song in the course of routine rituals, family celebrations, and community events. Among the Karamojong and their neighbors, dance is especially significant during times of courtship, when young people dance late into the night outside in the open air. They dance by jumping up and down, facing members of the opposite sex, in accompaniment to hand-clapping and singing. Musical instruments are not present in these lively interactions.

Many Baganda households contain at least a small cowhide drum for regular use in singing and dancing. During the kingship, there were 93 royal drums called *mujaguzo* that varied in size, each with its own name and specific drumbeat. Other musical instruments included string instruments, such as fiddles and harps, and woodwind instruments such as flutes and fifes. Baganda dancers are skilled in their ability to swiftly move their hips to the alternating beats of drums playing simultaneously.

Among the Banyankole, pots are used as a percussion instrument. These are ordinary water pots filled with different levels of water, whose mouths are beaten by sticks to which small bundles of weeds are attached. Men and women accompany the rhythms, which sound not unlike drums, by singing, dancing, and beating their hands on their bodies. A familiar dance routine in imitation of cows is done. The dancer jumps up and down while holding the arms overhead, in imitation of a cow's horns, while producing a hissing sound with the mouth.

Modern nightclub and disco dancing are also part of the teenage scene, particularly in urban areas. Nevertheless, visits to rural areas to see relatives or friends may engage young people in traditional dances. In some areas, during large celebrations, such as a wedding or a funeral, many older people gather around the drum or water pot for music, while the young people prefer international music from the radio or CDs and audio cassettes played on a boom box.

Before the devastation of Uganda's economic and intellectual life, Uganda was in the process of developing an extremely rich literary tradition in English, especially in association with Makerere University. The Baganda also had developed a robust vernacular literature in Luganda that included novels, short stories, essays, historical writings, songs, plays, and poems. Perhaps the most famous Ugandan writer from the pre-Amin years was Okot p'Bitek, an essayist, poet, and social critic who once headed the Uganda National Theatre and was professor of creative writing at Makerere. Although he died in 1982, his work is still read throughout East Africa, as well as internationally. His best known work, "Song of Lawino," depicts the circumstances of modernization in his native Acholi land through the eyes of a woman who laments her husband's blind preference for women who wear modern makeup, speak English, know all of the modern dances and customs, and who look down on traditional women, such as herself.

[15] WORK

During the Amin years, the economy in Uganda lost virtually all of its expatriate and Asian populations, who were significantly involved in the modern sector of banking, commercial activities, and industry. Nevertheless, Uganda has maintained (up to the present) a strong subsistence agricultural base, so that recovery from the Amin years has the advantage of a plentiful food supply and a population that is overwhelmingly agrarian and rural in lifestyle. Most urban-dwellers in Kampala maintain continued access to nearby agricultural areas. These abound within short distances of the city and provide a reliable, inexpensive source of local food on a year-round basis.

Small-scale economic opportunities, involving tailoring, shop keeping, hair care, repair work of various sorts, carpentry, and the marketing of food and other household necessities, employ numerous Ugandans in Kampala and throughout the country's smaller towns and villages. The professions, including teaching, law, and medicine, are growing and employ many supportive staff, such as secretaries, receptionists, and computer personnel. Comparatively poor people can be seen operating small all-purpose stands, with huts that are folded up and taken down at closing time. Cigarettes, matches, candy, soft drinks, biscuits, cookies, and bread are available here for sale to people who may have missed a chance to visit stores during regular hours.

The leisure-time industry is quite lively, encompassing restaurants, bars, and nightclubs that together employ many thousands of Ugandans. A somewhat unique and striking aspect of this industry is the uniformed barmaid found in bars throughout the country, even in remote rural areas. Tourism, involving safaris to game parks to see mountain gorillas, tree-climbing lions, crocodiles, and elephants, is once again on the upswing as well.

[16] SPORTS

Soccer is the most popular sport, with a national league and hotly contested playoffs. Cricket and rugby are also quite popular sports enjoyed by many spectators. Boxing is another competitive sport for which there is a national trophy awarded for the best in each division. Uganda sends competitors abroad to international events such as the Olympics and has in the past won medals for excellence in track-and-field.

[17] ENTERTAINMENT AND RECREATION

Most Ugandans own radios and enjoy listening to the variety of educational programs, plays, stories, news, and music offered. There are 10 stations, broadcasting in English and the major ethnic languages. There is a national television station that includes programs from the United States and England, in addition to its local subject matter. The American CNN provides an entertainment and news link to worldwide news. Television is available in most affluent homes and in hotels.

Individuals and families enjoy visiting restaurants and clubs where they can watch traditional dancing, whose performances are regularly available in Kampala. Popular theater is also a very significant means of entertainment in Uganda. Plays have a long-standing tradition often containing themes of concern to the population at large such as politics, social change, and health and family matters. Recently, plays have been used in Kampala and throughout the country to promote knowledge about health matters, especially those concerning HIV/AIDS and its prevention. The significance of public plays for educational purposes cannot be underestimated in a country in which about half of the country's population is illiterate.

[18] FOLK ART, CRAFTS, AND HOBBIES

Rural Ugandan women can often be seen sitting on the ground outside their homes weaving beautiful and colorful straw mats. Tightly woven coiled baskets are also prevalent. Wooden milk pots and bowls are carved and decorated. Elaborate and simple pipes for smoking are popular in remote areas. In general, much of Ugandans' everyday artistic endeavors involve useful objects that are part of their everyday existence.

Basketry is a highly developed art form in Uganda. Common fibers used to weave are banana palm, raffia, papyrus, and sisal. Weaving is used for house walls, fences, roofs, baskets, mats, traps, and receptacles for drink and food. Table mats and cushions are also common uses today. Bark-cloth was once a widespread craft used for many purposes, including clothing. Today, remnants of bark-cloth can be seen in its use as decoration on place mats and greeting cards, as well as in the making of blankets and shrouds. Another art form using cloth is batik, a type of cloth painting that can be hung on walls for decoration. The revival of the tourist industry currently underway is likely to stimulate the production of arts and crafts for foreign consumption.

[19] SOCIAL PROBLEMS

Uganda suffers from one of the highest HIV/AIDS infection rates in the world. It has one of the best public awareness programs associated with HIV/AIDS anywhere. Many families have experienced the loss of loved ones to this disease, resulting in a large number of orphans. Another problem is the flow of refugees coming to Uganda from neighboring nations suffering from political turmoil. Hundreds of thousands of southern Sudanese have fled to Uganda in recent years, due to religious conflict in the Sudan. Regularly, refugees from Rwanda fleeing from ethnic conflict enter Uganda's western border. Many Banyarwanda are now citizens of Uganda, having fled there in the 1960s. Despite one of the most highly publicized terrorist regimes in modern times under Idi Amin, Uganda by all accounts is now well on the way to democracy, although it is still under one-party rule. Ugandans, on the whole, are very optimistic about their future.

[20] GENDER ISSUES

In spite of the significant social and economic responsibilities that women shouldered in the traditional Ugandan societies, their roles were still subordinate to those of men. From their infancy, women would be taught to accede to the wishes of the men in their lives, including fathers, brothers, and husbands. Women were expected to demonstrate their subordination to men in public. For instance, among the Baganda, women would kneel while conversing with a man.

The responsibilities of childcare and subsistence farming rested in the hands of women. In religious circles, women also were allowed a dominant role. For example, Alice Lakwena, a religious Ugandan woman, led a revolt against Ugandan political establishment dominated by men. In a few areas, women owned property and large tracts of land for cash crop farming. In Uganda societies, there seems to be a clear-cut gender-based division of labor. The kitchen in most societies is a woman's domain, while taking care of cattle is a man's domain. Boys over the age of 12 were forbidden from going to the kitchen.

In the family circles, men have the overall authority. Women and older girls share the domestic chores while men and older boys may help digging in the farms or taking care of the livestock. Defending the society as well as making societal decisions was a man's duty. Women depend so much on men that they rarely have influence on matters related to their families or society in general. They are tied to male relationships for their sustenance and survival of their children.

The political violence that characterized Uganda in 1970s and 1980s during the rule of Idi Amin Dada affected women more negatively than it did men. Women faced a lot of hardships at home especially because they had very limited economic opportunities. It was, perhaps, these challenges that inspired them to be involved in the political struggle that led to the fall of Idi Amin and ushered in the reign of the current president. Ugandan government has promised to do away with all forms of discrimination against women and there are many women in the parliament due to affirmative action.

[21] BIBLIOGRAPHY

Abid, Syed, ed. *Uganda Women in Development,* 1990.

Allen, Tim. "Understanding Alice: Uganda's Holy Spirit Movement in Context." *Africa* 61 (3): 37–39, 1991.

Antrobus, P. "The Empowerment of Women." *Women and International Development* 1 (2): 189–207, 1989.

Bernt Hansen, Holger, and Michael Twaddle eds. Uganda Now: Between Decay and Development, 1988.

Dicklich, Susan. "Indigenous NGOs and Political Participation." In Holger Bernt Hansen and Michael Twaddle, eds. *Developing Uganda,* 145–158, 1998.

Gender Relations, Livelihood, Security and Reproductive Health among Women in Ikafe Settlement, Uganda. www.library.qur.nl/wda/dissertation/dis3837 (September 2008)

Gertzel, Cherry. "Uganda's Continuing Search for Peace." Current History 89 (547): 205–228, 231–232, 1990.

Hansen, Holger Bernt, and Michael Twaddle, ed. *Uganda Now: Between Decay and Development.* London: James Currey, Ltd., 1988.

Ingham, Kenneth. *The Making of Modern Uganda,* 1983.

Kilbride, Philip L., and Janet C. Kilbride. *Changing Family Life in East Africa: Women and Children at Risk.* University Park: The Pennsylvania State University Press, 1990.

Kabwegyere, T. B. *The Politics of State Formation and Destruction in Uganda,* 3rd ed. 1995.

Khadiagala, G. M. "State Collapse and Reconstruction in Uganda." In William I. Zartman, ed. *Collapsed States,* 1995.

Masculinity in Urban Uganda in the Age of AIDS. allacademic.com/meta/p_mla_apa_research citation/1/0/2/8/3/p102836 (September 2008)

Nsibambi, Apolo R. "The Restoration of Traditional Rulers." In Holger Bernt Hansen and Michael Twaddle, eds. *From Chaos to Order: The Politics of Constitution-Making in Uganda,* 1996.

Southall, Aidan W. "Social Disorganization in Uganda: Before, During, and After Amin." *Journal of Modern Africa Studies* 18 (4): 627–656, 1980.

Tindigarukayo, Jimmy, K. "Uganda, 1979–85: Leadership in Transition." *Journal of Modern African Studies* 26 (4): 607–22, 1988.

Van Zwanenburg, R. M. A, and Anne King. *An Economic History of Kenya and Uganda, 1800–1970,* 1975.

Watson, Catherine. "Uganda's Women: A Ray of Hope." *Africa Report* 33 (6): 32–35, 1988.

Welbourn, F. B. *Religion and Politics in Uganda, 1952–1962,* 1965.

World Bank. *Uganda: Towards Stabilization and Economic Recovery,* 1988.

—revised by M. Njoroge

WOLOF

PRONUNCIATION: WOE-loff
LOCATION: Senegal
POPULATION: About 5 million
LANGUAGE: Wolof
RELIGION: Islam (Sunni Muslim); Roman Catholic; small percentage of Protestants
RELATED ARTICLES: Vol. 1: Mauritanians; Senegalese

¹ INTRODUCTION

The Wolof form the majority ethnic group in Senegal and are influential culturally and politically in Senegalese life. Apart from oral narratives, information about their pre-colonial origins is sketchy and incomplete. The earliest Portuguese explorers in the 15th century observed that the Wolof and Sereer groups were well established along the Senegalese coast at that time. The Wolof had probably occupied that area for centuries and over time assimilated smaller neighboring groups. An alternative theory holds that several groups including the Soose, Sereer, and Pulaar joined to constitute the Wolof.

From the 1600s to the mid-1800s, slave trading caused much dislocation, though it did not deplete the Wolof to the same degree as other West African peoples. A reminder of this tragic epoch is the island fortress of Gorée, off the coast of Dakar, which served as one of West Africa's main slavery depots.

The French founded the Senegal colony in 1637, making it the oldest French colony in Africa and the longest-lived. As the French advanced their territorial claims eastward, the Wolof states resisted in the 1880s, but eventually succumbed to superior military force. Dakar acquired added importance when the French made it the capital of their West African territories in 1902. Colonization favored the Wolof and in just seventy years, from 1900 to 1970, the group nearly quadrupled its population to 1.4 million.

Since the first political reforms in 1946, the Wolof have played a leading role politically, culturally, and economically in Senegal. Despite the country's weak economy—or perhaps because of it—the Wolof have built a reputation for international commerce and trading. Wolof businesspeople are found throughout Africa, Europe, even on the streets of New York City and Washington, D.C. In Senegal, their key challenges are similar to those of their fellow citizens in neighboring countries: cope with stagnating economies, create living wage job opportunities, build adequate housing and provide basic services to meet rapid population growth and relentless urbanization.

² LOCATION AND HOMELAND

The Wolof presently occupy the westernmost point of Africa, between the Senegal River to the north and the Jurbel region about 300 km (185 mi) south. From the Atlantic Ocean on the west, the Wolof extend to the Ferlo desert, some 300 km (185 mi) east. In pre-colonial times, this territory included the kingdoms of Waalo, Jolof, Kajoor, and Baol. Today, this area remains approximately the same as the group's ancestral homeland. Neighboring minorities include the Maures and the Tuculor, the Sereer and the Peul—some of whose members have lived for centuries within the Wolof area.

In Senegal, the Wolof account for nearly 40% of some 13 million people (estimate 2008), followed by the Fulani (15%), Serer (15%), Toucouleur (9%), Dyula (9%), Malinke (9%), and others (3%). In Mauritania they account for about 7% of the population. Though they are a minority in The Gambia, they nonetheless comprise about 50% of the population of Banjul, the coastal capital city of The Gambia.

Physically, their homeland is flat and desert-like, covered by dunes and sandy plains. These are easily traversed in the dry season when vegetation is sparse and thin. The vegetation consists mainly of bushes, acacia, ficus, and baobab trees, and clay soils favor the cultivation of millet. Where the Senegal river overflows its banks, farmers grow sorghum, potatoes, and beans. There is a short rainy season lasting three months from July to September, but cyclical droughts and increasing deforestation add to the insecurity of crop farming.

³ LANGUAGE

Wolof is Senegal's dominant language. Practically all Senegalese understand Wolof, and the vast majority of non-Wolof speak it as a second language. Senegalese radio and television broadcast both in French and Wolof. Wolof is also spoken in Mauritania and Mali, and in The Gambia, although in a different form. Given the large number of emigrés, one finds Wolof speakers in France, and on the streets of West Harlem in New York City. Some 7 million people worldwide speak one or more of the six dialects of Wolof (which belongs to the Niger-Congo and Atlantic-Congo family of languages). One growing concern is that the language, especially among Dakar youth, is becoming 'polluted' by French. It is rare in Dakar to hear a complete Wolof sentence without one or several French words mixed in.

⁴ FOLKLORE

As elsewhere in Africa, orality characterizes Wolof folklore. In Wolof and Senegalese society, the most accomplished storytellers are African bards, or *griots*. They are similar to the European minstrel of the Middle Ages, combining the functions of historian, poet, and musician. They must be familiar with history, have many acquaintances, and speak about them diplomatically, but honestly. *Griots* use props, play flutes and harps, and break into song as they perform. Because they are archivists and entertainers in one, no ceremony or celebration of consequence is held without them.

The Wolof consider Lat Dior Diop, the Damel (king) of Kayor, to be a hero and liberator from French occupation in the 19th century. He opposed the building of railroads because he believed they would allow the French to control the entire region. In Senegalese schools, children learn that he was shot by the French and died in battle. Ironically, according to legend, after Diop's death, his horse stood on railroad tracks until hit by a train.

⁵ RELIGION

An overwhelming majority of the Wolof are Muslim, belonging to the Malikite branch of the Sunni group. The remaining 10% are Roman Catholic. Less than 1% is Protestant. There has been some syncretism of traditional, Muslim, and Christian beliefs. The Wolof typically wear protective amulets or "grisgris" to overpower evil spirits. The small leather pouches once contained herbs and medicines, but they now hold verses of the Koran.

The Wolof depend on *marabous*, teachers of the faith, who also exercise much political and economic influence. People give a portion of their salaries to the marabous, to build mosques and make charitable donations.

⁶ MAJOR HOLIDAYS

The Wolof celebrate Muslim as well as Christian holidays and also secular holidays, such as Senegalese Independence Day (April 4). Four of the Muslim holidays are determined by the lunar calendar. The most popular of these is Tabaski, or the "feast of the lamb." This feast commemorates Allah's provision of a lamb for Abraham to sacrifice in the wilderness in the place of his son Isaac. In the morning prayers are offered at the mosque, and then a lamb is slaughtered. People get together with family to partake of a large meal and then visit their friends later in the day. Typically, children receive new clothing and money, and families often go into debt for the occasion.

⁷ RITES OF PASSAGE

The most important Wolof rites of passage are naming ceremonies, circumcisions, marriages and funerals. Much significance is attached to names. Parents carefully choose a name for their children, usually the name of a family member or friend who has influenced them and who will provide a model for their child. The decision may take up to a year and is revealed during a naming ceremony.

At age seven to eight, boys are taken from their homes and circumcised in the bush, where they wear white gowns and caps. When they return, they are looked after by a big brother, or *Selbe*, until they are fully healed. The *Selbe* educates them about Wolof heroes and legends. They also visit friends and family and receive gifts from them. After this rite, the community regards them as men.

Marriages give much reason to celebrate as they unite two families and symbolize readiness for children. Weddings are festive and typically involve civil, religious, and traditional ceremonies before they are complete. The reception is held at the home of the groom where the bride will come to live. In order to gain the consent of the bride, the groom's parents bring gifts to her parents. Once the bride has given her consent to marriage, her parents distribute cola nuts to family and friends as a way of announcing the marriage.

At death, according to Islamic custom, funerals are held at home the same or the following day. In the city, where regulations are stricter, the corpse may be taken to a funeral home. A 40-day mourning period follows, during which people visit the family of the deceased and offer gifts of money.

⁸ INTERPERSONAL RELATIONS

Greetings can last 10–15 minutes. One who does not take time to inquire after another person's health, well being, and family may be snubbed altogether. The French custom of kissing three times on the cheeks is common in Dakar and in the towns. Handshaking is the preferred traditional greeting, but men and women do not shake each others' hands. A common Wolof exchange is illustrated below, although 5 to 10 additional inquiries would be routine. Praise for Allah is interspersed throughout the greetings:

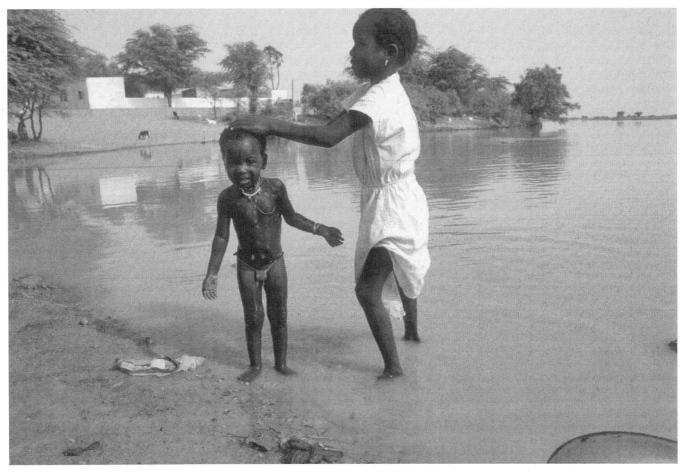

A Wolof girl helps bathe her little sister. (The Image Works)

"Nanga def?" (How does it go?).

"Mangi fii rekk." (I am here only).

"Nunga Fe" (They are there).

"Mbaa sa yaram jamm" (I hope your body is at peace).

"Jamm rekk" (Peace only).

"Alhumdullilah" (Praise be to Allah).

As in many African societies, Wolof respect both age and status. It is considered impolite for a woman to look a man directly in the eye. Women and girls traditionally curtsy to their elders. As in other Muslim societies, only the right hand must be used to shake hands, or to pass and receive objects, because the left hand—used for personal cleansing—is thought unclean. Pointing is considered rude, although people do point with their tongues.

Wolof are accustomed to visiting each other unannounced, even as late as midnight. Impromptu visits are not considered rude or inconvenient, though customs are changing owing to the cell phone culture. A visitor must share a meal, have tea, or spend the night. This traditional hospitality is called *Terranga.*

9 LIVING CONDITIONS

Living conditions vary greatly from the city to the countryside. In Dakar, St. Louis, and Diourbel, most homes have electricity and indoor plumbing, although the water supply—and sometimes electricity too—are unpredictable. Houses are made of concrete with tin roofs. People who can afford it cook with bottled gas; however, most people use charcoal. Jobs, adequate housing, and coping with inflation pose major challenges for city dwellers. The cost of living in Dakar is relatively high.

Health care is available from the state for a nominal fee, though people must pay for their medicine. Many Wolof prefer to consult traditional healers first. While their spells have no known scientific basis, their other treatments involve the use of local herbs, bark, and roots that do indeed have medicinal properties.

Outside the cities, life is rustic. People live in huts made of millet stalks and thatched roofs. They sleep on traditional beds of wooden sticks with one end raised and draw water from wells or rivers. With no electricity, the only modern appliances to be found in some villages are radios—and yes, cell phones. In the absence of paved roads, the countryside is honeycombed with sand tracks. Trucks follow these or make new "roads," going almost anywhere they please in the dry season.

10 FAMILY LIFE

The nuclear family is the pillar of Wolof life. Whatever misfortune may befall them, family members are there to support each other. The man of the family may officially make the decisions, but the wife and mother runs the household. She takes care of the children, does the marketing and cooking, draws water, and finds firewood. Mothers nurse their children for about one year. A Wolof father blames the mother if the children make mistakes ("Look what your son did!"), but enjoys taking credit for a child's accomplishments. A typical family has as many as ten or eleven children. In polygynous households, wives occupy separate rooms or dwellings, but they live together as co-mères. The first wife exercises seniority over her co-mères, but all join in the child-raising communally.

Traditionally, when a child comes of age, the mother looks for an appropriate spouse of equal or higher social status. For example, members of the *Guer* (noble) caste generally do not marry into the *Griot* (artist) caste. Similarly members of the *Griot* caste do not marry *Jam* (serfs), whose ancestors were servants. The father waits for the mother's selection of a prospective spouse and then usually approves it.

Wolof do not keep pets, fearing that their prayer mats and other furnishings will be ruined if dogs bring dirt and fleas into the house and that friends might be discouraged from visiting. Cats are not well liked either, except to catch mice. However, people keep lambs because they believe that the "evil eye" will be deflected on the lamb instead of the family.

11 CLOTHING

In Wolof society, personal appearance is important. In town, men typically wear shirts and trousers and suits for special occasions; women wear dresses. It is becoming common to see teenage girls in jeans and T-shirts, but only children wear shorts in public. In traditional settings, people wear *boubous*, loose-fitting cotton tunics with large openings under the arms. Men wear cotton trousers underneath, while women wear sarongs, as well as matching headscarves or turbans that complement the *boubous*. Some *boubous* are elaborately embroidered and may cost as much as two to three hundred dollars. Men wear open leather sandals, or closed, pointed ones; women's sandals may be colorfully decorated.

The wearing of tattoos is gaining popularity among urban youth, and ear piercing is traditional for girls. It is becoming popular with boys as well. White teeth are a sign of beauty, and teenage girls pierce their gums with needles to whiten them. Girls braid their hair, especially in the country.

12 FOOD

The Wolof usually eat three meals a day. Townspeople with the means to afford them drink cacao and eat French bread with butter or mayonnaise, jam, and processed cheese imported from France. The traditional breakfast consists of a paste-like dough made of millet with milk poured over it *(lakh),* or *sombee* (boiled rice covered with curdled milk, sugar, and raisins).

Wolof are famous for *Tiébou Dienn* (cheb-oo-jen), a dish that can be made as simply or elaborately as desired. Essentially, it is a fish stew cooked in cilantro, scallions, garlic, pepper, onions, tomato paste, bouillon cubes, and oil. The stew is mixed with squash, sweet potatoes, okra, tamarind, and different kinds of peppers. It is eaten with rice that has been cooked in the fish broth. The Wolof people also are known for their *Mbaxal-u-Saloum*, a spicy tomato, peanut, and dried-fish sauce with rice. Another popular dish, *Mafé*, is made with peanut sauce, meat, and potatoes, sweet potatoes, or cassava, with a bit of dried fish to flavor it. The favorite drink of the Wolof is *bissap*, which is red and tastes somewhat like cranberry juice. It is considered a purgative, or a digestive drink.

People eat together on a large floor mat. They kneel on one knee and eat the food directly in front of them, using only their right hands. After finishing their portions, they wait for their neighbors to push some food their way. The goal is to get to the center of the food tray.

At night, Dakar residents enjoy going out to a *Dibiterie* (or Dibi) for the traditional mutton cooked over a wood fire and covered with a spicy sauce. A meal is completed with the evening tea ritual, *ataya* (the Arabic word for green Chinese tea). Three servings are poured into small glasses, each round sweeter than the last.

13 EDUCATION

Only 30% of Wolof read and write in French, and only about one woman in five is literate. School is mandatory and based on the French system, but attendance is not enforced. At the age of four or five, the majority of children attend Koranic schools, where some continue until they have memorized the entire Koran. In the cities, however, this practice is dying out.

Six years of primary school begin with a two-year preparatory program. At the end of four more years, pupils take a high-school qualifying exam. In the French secondary education system, classes progress from Class Six to Class One. A final year follows, in which the student prepares for the state baccalaureate exam. Few people reach this level, so holding a high-school diploma confers considerable prestige on its holder. A small percentage of high-school graduates continue at the University of Dakar. Those who can afford it prefer studying abroad in France or other French-speaking countries like Belgium, Switzerland, and Morocco.

14 CULTURAL HERITAGE

Senegal is a leader in West African film and literature. Its internationally known filmmakers include Djibril Mambeti Diop, who is a Wolof. Another Wolof, Alioune Diop, founded *Presence Africaine*, the foremost African publishing house in Europe. He was also a prolific writer.

Wolof are accomplished musicians and have pioneered modern forms of traditional *griot* music. Modern *griot* "rap" performed in the Wolof language narrates stories about society, much like ancient *griots* narrated the lives of ancient kings. The internationally acclaimed singer Youssou N'dour performs in his native Wolof and in several other languages, including English, and has recorded CDs as well. Traditional Wolof instruments include a small drum (*tama*), held under the arm, which can be pressed against the body to produce different pitches. The goat-skin drum head is hit by a wooden stick with a curved end. The Wolof have skillfully adapted such instruments for pop music.

15 WORK

Many Wolof farm and keep herds. Although Wolof generally do not fish, a Wolof-speaking people, the Lebu, are fisherfolk on the coast of Senegal. If the Wolof have an international reputation, it is mainly for their tailoring, wood carving, and business acumen. They have traded with Arabs for centuries and specialize in import-export trading. According to a popular Wolof joke, when Neil Armstrong landed on the moon, a Wolof tapped him on the shoulder and asked, "*Gorgui* (sir), would you like to buy this product?"

¹⁶ SPORTS

The Wolof participate in soccer, basketball, track and field, and jogging. Their traditional sport, however, is similar to ancient Greco-Roman wrestling. Called *Laamb*, it has been played for centuries. Each year, champions are crowned and praised in traditional songs. Two forms exist. In the first, wrestlers strike each other with their bare hands, whereas in the second this form of physical contact is not permitted. A wrestler loses the match when his back touches the ground.

In addition to its physical dimension, *Laamb* also has a spiritual dimension. Like promoters in American boxing, Wolof wrestlers count on *marabous* or "Juju Men" to organize pre-match rituals. Even the most technically proficient wrestlers would not dare enter the ring without participating in these rites. The wrestlers dance around the ring with drummers and singers. They wear amulets on their arms, legs, and waist to protect them from the witchcraft of their rivals. Spectators enjoy this aspect of the sport as much as they do the fight. In ancient times, matches were organized in the village squares and provided occasions for storytelling by *griots*.

¹⁷ ENTERTAINMENT AND RECREATION

City folk have access to videos, video games, radio and (satellite) television, but it is cheaper and more enjoyable for many people to create their own fun. For example, in Dakar, as the day cools down late in the afternoon, *griots* play drums in the streets, often accompanied by very suggestive dancing. The *griot* can speed up the beat to dizzying levels.

Young people enjoy nightclubs. In Dakar, some clubs are very elaborate, with moving dance floors, electronically controlled backdrops, and special effects including smoke, mirrors, and sophisticated light shows. *M'balax* is the Senegalese pop music. Rap, reggae, Caribbean zouk, macossa from Cameroon, and sukous from the Democratic Republic of the Congo are also popular with the younger set.

Older people find enjoyment in quieter pursuits, such as socializing at home, in the mosques or playing checkers at a local coffee house. For excitement, they go to wrestling matches, traditional dug-out canoe racing, and horse racing on weekends (although betting is frowned on). Cap-Vert, as the Dakar peninsula was so named by Portuguese explorers, is surrounded by water on three sides. It has excellent beaches, like N'Gor, offering respite from the heat as well as people-watching entertainment on the weekends.

¹⁸ FOLK ART, CRAFTS, AND HOBBIES

The Wolof *Laobé* are known for their woodcarvings. They fashion statues, figurines, and masks, mainly for the tourist market. Wolof are also fine tailors, and the *Teug* caste specializes in jewelry. Men prefer silver bracelets and rings, while women wear gold necklaces, chains, and rings. Some Wolof are traditional weavers. Hobbies may be practical, such as gardening, or instructive, such as storytelling.

¹⁹ SOCIAL PROBLEMS

Wolof society is undergoing rapid change from a rural to an urban style of living, which places stress on social structures, family relationships, and traditional values. Many Wolof villages have been depopulated as men migrate to the cities hoping to find work, especially white-collar jobs. Children and young people often find it difficult to adjust—a factor in the rising abuse of alcohol and drugs by the Wolof.

Unemployment is also a major problem. Poverty and idleness have led to an increase in burglary, prostitution, mugging, drug trafficking, and even human trafficking. Pickpockets are common in downtown Dakar. Beggars frequently knock on doors for food, and people often cook extra food, in preparation for these visits. Nevertheless, serious crimes such as murder and armed robbery are still very rare. Handicapped people are generally, but not always, cared for by their families.

²⁰ GENDER ISSUES

Women face discrimination, especially in rural areas where traditional customs and polygynous relationships are the norm. Indeed, one in two marriages in the hinterlands is polygynous and, unless agreed to beforehand, husbands do not need to notify or seek consent of their wives to enter into subsequent marriages. Even though the law proscribes marriages for girls under 16, it is not uncommon in rural areas for girls 13-15 years old to be married as they represent a means of income via the brideprice. Female genital mutilation (FMG) is also widespread, despite efforts by government officially to eradicate it. Programs implemented by NGOs, such as TOSTAN, to create more awareness of the associated health risks have reduced the incidence of FMG, but the practice remains deeply ingrained in the culture. Since the man is the head of the household, women cannot take legal responsibility for children, and women have difficulty inheriting and purchasing property. In addition to running the household, they also do 85% of the agricultural work.

²¹ BIBLIOGRAPHY

Clark, Andrew F. and Lucie Colvin Phillips. *Historical Dictionary of Senegal.* Second sub-edition. Lanham, MD: Scarecrow Press, 1994.

Delcourt, Jean. *Naissance et Croissance de Dakar.* Dakar: Editions Clairafrique, 1985.

Dilly, Roy, and Jerry Eades, eds. *Senegal.* World Bibliographical Series, Vol. 166. Oxford, England: Clio Press, 1994.

Diop, Samba. *The Oral History and Literature of the Wolof People of Waalo, Northern Senegal: The Master of the Word (Griot in the Wolof Tradition).* Ceredigion, UK. and Lewiston, NY: Edwin Mellen Press, 1995.

Gellar, Sheldon. *Democracy in Senegal: Tocquevillian Analytics in Africa.* Melbourne: Palgrave Macmillan, 2006.

Gritzner, Janet H. and Charles F. Gritzner. *Senegal.* London: Chelsea House Publications, 2005.

Kane, Katherine. *The Gambia and Senegal.* Footscray: Lonely Planet Publications, 2006.

Perry, Donna. "Wolof Women, Economic Liberalization and the Crisis of Masculinity in Rural Senegal." *Ethnology.* June 22, 2005.

"Senegal." In *Africa South of the Sahara 2007.* London: Europa Publishers, 2008.

—by R. J. Groelsema and Y. Fal

XHOSA

PRONUNCIATION: KOH-suh ("X" represents a click sound)
LOCATION: South Africa (southeastern and urban areas)
POPULATION: 8 million
LANGUAGE: Xhosa (Bantu)
RELIGION: traditional beliefs (supreme being *uThixo* or *uQamata*), Christianity

¹ INTRODUCTION

The word Xhosa refers to a people and a language of South Africa. The Xhosa-speaking people are divided into a number of subgroups with their own distinct but related heritages. One of these subgroups is sometimes rather confusingly called Xhosa as well, while other subgroup names are Bhaca, Bomvana, Gcaleka, Mfengu, Mpondo, Mpondomise, Xesibe, and Thembu (Tembu). Unless otherwise stated, this article includes all these subgroups, and refers to all Xhosa-speaking people.

The Xhosa, among all the Bantu-speaking peoples of South Africa, penetrated furthest south towards the Cape of Good Hope. Well before the arrival of Dutch in the 1650s, the Xhosa had settled the southeastern area of South Africa. In this territory, they interacted with the foraging and pastoral people who were in South Africa first, the Khoi and the San.

The Europeans who came to stay in South Africa first settled in and around Cape Town. As the years passed, this limited region was not enough for some of the settlers. A subculture of *trekboers* (white pastoralists) moved away from the Cape, increasing the territory of white control. This expansion was first at the expense of the Khoi and San, but later Xhosa land was taken too. A series of wars between *trekboers* and Xhosa began in the 1770s. Later, in the nineteenth century, the British became the new colonizing force in the Cape. They directed the armies that were to vanquish the Xhosa. Sustained military resistance to the Cape forces ended in 1853, although warfare continued for another 25 years until at least 1878.

Christian missionaries established their first outposts among the Xhosa in the 1820s, but met with little success. Only after the Xhosa population had been traumatized by European invasion, drought, and disease did Xhosa convert to Christianity in substantial numbers. Most of the initial conversions began in the 1850s following the failure of a prophetic movement known as the Cattle Killing. Some 20,000 people died of hunger and disease after killing their cattle to fulfill the Cattle Killing prophecy. Without other recourse and in despair, many Xhosa sought help from the missionaries. Others were forced to flee the territory, taking menial positions working for whites.

In the aftermath of the Cattle Killing, a cultural division developed between mission-educated "school" people and traditionalists, who were called "Reds" after their practice of anointing themselves with red ocher. School people saw themselves as enlightened by Christianity and civilized by Western education, while red people saw themselves as being true to proper Xhosa traditions and the ways of their ancestors.

In addition to land lost to white annexation, legislative acts such as the Glen Grey Act of 1894 reduced Xhosa ability to control their own political affairs. Political authority was allocated to white magistrates, and landholdings were privatized.

Over time, Xhosa people became increasingly impoverished and had no other option except to become migrant laborers. In the late 1990s, Xhosa make up a large percentage of the workers in South Africa's gold mines.

Under apartheid, the South African government created separate regions that were described as *Bantustans* (homelands) for black people of African descent. Two regions—Transkei and Ciskei—were set aside for Xhosa people. Although these regions were proclaimed independent countries by the apartheid government, they were not recognized as such outside South Africa. Apartheid policy denied South African citizenship to many Xhosa, and thousands of people were forcibly relocated to remote areas in Transkei and Ciskei. Rural areas became even more impoverished, although a few urban centers such as Umtata did achieve some economic growth. After apartheid ended, these areas became part of the Eastern Cape province. In fact, only one of the six districts of the Eastern Cape was not formerly a part of Transkei or Ciskei

² LOCATION AND HOMELAND

Before the arrival of the Europeans in the late 1600s, Xhosa-speaking people occupied much of eastern South Africa, extending from the Fish River to regions inhabited by Zulu-speakers south of the modern city of Durban. This territory includes well-watered rolling hills near scenic coastal areas as well as harsh and dry regions further inland. Many Xhosa-speaking people live in Cape Town (*iKapa*), East London (*eMonti*), and Port Elizabeth (*iBhayi*). They can be found in lesser numbers in most of South Africa's major metropolitan areas. As of 2007, there were about 8 million Xhosa, making up approximately 17.5% of South Africa's population. Others may speak Xhosa as a second language without necessarily identifying themselves as a Xhosa person.

³ LANGUAGE

The Xhosa language, properly referred to as *isiXhosa*, is a Bantu language closely related to Zulu, Swazi, and Ndebele. There are also a number of dialects that are frequently associated with clans predominant in certain areas. "Thembu," for example, may refer to people of a particular clan as well as a particular dialect. It is often suggested that the dialect of the Mpondo is most distinctive. As with other South African languages, Xhosa is characterized by respectful forms of address for elders and in-laws. The language is also rich in idioms. To have *isandla esishushu* ("a warm hand"), for example, is to be generous.

The historically close relationship between the Xhosa and other peoples is evident in the language. For example, Xhosa contains many words with click consonants that have been borrowed from Khoi or San words. The "X" in Xhosa represents a type of click made by the tongue on the side of the mouth. This consonant sounds something like the clicking sound English-speaking horseback riders make to encourage their horses. English speakers who have not mastered clicks often pronounce Xhosa as "Ko-Sa." There are other consonants used in the written language to represent clicks as well, including "c," "gc," and "nq." Modern Xhosa speakers also borrow words liberally from English and Afrikaans.

Names in Xhosa often express the values or opinions of the community. Common personal names include *Thamsanqa* ("good fortune") and *Nomsa* ("mother of kindness"). Names

XHOSA

0   200   400   600   800 Miles

0   200   400   600   800 Kilometers

may also make reference to topical events, or be coined from English words. Adults are often referred to by their *isiduko* (clan or lineage) names. In the case of women, clan names are preceded by a prefix meaning "mother of." For example, a woman of the Thembu clan might be called *MamThembu*. Women are also named by reference to their children, real or intended; *NoLindiwe* is a polite name for Lindiwe's mother.

⁴ FOLKLORE

Stories and legends provide accounts of the Xhosa ancestral heroes. According to one oral tradition, the first person on Earth was a great leader called Xhosa. Another tradition stresses the essential unity of the Xhosa-speaking people by proclaiming that all the Xhosa subgroups are descendants of one ancestor, Tshawe. Historians have suggested that Xhosa and Tshawe were probably the first Xhosa kings or paramount (supreme) chiefs, although the time of their reigns cannot be precisely dated. Madzikane, a hero among the Xhosa-speaking Bhaca, was a contemporary of the famous Zulu leader Shaka in the early 19th century.

Xhosa tradition is rich in creative verbal expression. In the hands of masters, *intsomi* (folktales), proverbs, and *isibongo* (praise poems) are told in dramatic and creative ways. Folktales relate the adventures of both animal protagonists and human characters. These are related in ways that make them both theatrical and musical performances. Praise poems traditionally relate the heroic adventures of ancestors or political leaders. Folk themes are also incorporated into the modern

storytelling art produced on television and other media. One prominent artist named Gcina Mhlope tells stories in this way to promote literacy and education in general.

⁵ RELIGION

The supreme being among the Xhosa is called *uThixo* or *uQamata*. As in the religions of many other Bantu peoples, God is only rarely involved in everyday life, but may be approached through ancestral intermediaries who are honored through ritual sacrifices. Ancestors commonly make their wishes known to the living in dreams.

Xhosa religious practice is distinguished by elaborate and lengthy rituals, initiations, and feasts. Modern rituals typically pertain to matters of illness and psychological well-being. A common spiritual affliction is a demand from ancestors to undergo *ukutwasa* ("initiation") into *amagqira,* a cult of healers. An individual may experience physical ailments until he or she agrees to undergo the initiation process, which may take many months and is very expensive.

Christianity in one form or another is accepted by most Xhosa-speaking people today, although historically there was a division between traditionalists who rejected Western belief and those who embraced Western education and the message of missionaries. Among Xhosa-speaking Christians, this division may still be observed—traditionalists are more likely to belong to independent denominations, rather than to one of the denominations that were brought to South Africa by the missionaries. In South Africa, the independent denominations combine the Christian creed with acceptance of the ancestors and other traditional beliefs and practices. These denominations make up a slight majority of today's Xhosa Christians. Statistics gathered in recent years in the Xhosa heartland of the Eastern Cape suggest that the most popular internationally known Christian denominations are Methodist (19%), Catholic (7%), Anglican (6%), and Presbyterian (5%). Varieties of independent churches known as "Zionist" are followed by approximately 13% of Xhosa while those known as "Apostolic" make up about 9%. Another 9% of Xhosa do not identify with any religion.

⁶ MAJOR HOLIDAYS

Xhosa observe the same holidays as other groups of South Africa. These include the Christian holidays, Workers' Day (or May Day, May 1), the Day of Reconciliation (December 16), and Heritage Day (September 24). During the apartheid era, two unofficial holidays were observed to honor black people killed in the fight for equality and political representation: June 16th, a national day of remembrance for students who were killed by police in Soweto on that day in 1976; and March 21, a holiday honoring protestors who were killed by authorities during a demonstration in Sharpeville in 1960. Both days are recognized with a day of rest, meetings, and prayer. Another important holiday recognizes April 27, the date of the first national election in which black South Africans could vote.

⁷ RITES OF PASSAGE

After giving birth, a mother is expected to remain secluded in her house for at least ten days. In the past, this seclusion lasted longer, frequently until the child's umbilical cord dropped off and the navel area healed. In Xhosa tradition, the afterbirth and umbilical cord were buried or burned to protect the baby from sorcery.

At the end of the period of seclusion, a goat was sacrificed. The meat was distributed in a prescribed way, and the baby anointed with the meat juice. Those who no longer practice the traditional rituals may still invite friends and relatives to a special dinner to mark the end of the mother's seclusion. On this occasion, guests bring presents or money for the baby and mother.

Initiation for males in the form of circumcision is practiced among most Xhosa groups, except among the Mpondo, Bhaca, and Xesibe. The *abakweta* ("initiates-in-training") live in special huts isolated from villages or towns for several weeks. Like soldiers inducted into the army, they have their heads shaved and wear special clothing. They wear a loincloth and a blanket for warmth, and their bodies are smeared from head to toe with a white clay. They are expected to observe numerous taboos and to act deferentially to their adult male leaders. Traditionally, the initiation was complete when young *amakrwala* ("graduates") performed dances wearing special grass and reed costumes. Different stages in the initiation process were marked by the sacrifice of a goat. The actual physical operation of circumcision has considerable health risk because the surgeon typically have not received medical training. Risks include infection, gangrene, and even death. Recently in some areas, formally trained physicians have been working in the Eastern Cape to lessen these risks.

The ritual of female circumcision is considerably shorter, although there are similarities with the boys' ceremonies. The *intonjane* ("girl to be initiated") is secluded for about a week behind a screen set up at the rear of her home. During this period, there are dances, and ritual sacrifices of animals. The initiate must hide herself from view and observe food restrictions, but there is no actual surgical operation.

A traditional marriage agreement is finalized by the parents of the bride and groom and formalized by the transfer of *lobolo* ("bridewealth") from the groom's family to the bride's family. When the agreement was settled, traditionally the family of the bride walked in procession to the home of the family of the groom, driving a sacrificial ox before them. The traditional full marriage ceremony took place over several days and involved a number of ritual sacrifices and dances. The bride and her female attendants were led out of their hut, their faces, heads, and bodies completely covered by hoods and blankets. In a ceremony that took place inside the family's cattle enclosure, the women's coverings were removed at a dramatic moment. These days such ceremonies may be combined with Western church weddings or they may be abandoned all together.

Funeral ceremonies are important community rituals. Friends, relatives, and neighbors gather at the house of the deceased, bearing gifts of money and food. Prior to the burial, a *inkonzo yomlindo* ("wake") is often held, during which a large gathering of people sing hymns and pray through the night.

8 INTERPERSONAL RELATIONS

Xhosa have traditionally used greetings to show respect and good intentions to others. In rural areas, greetings between strangers frequently extend into conversations about travel intentions, health, and personal well being. In greeting, a distinction is made between addressing an individual and a group. *Molo* ("hello") is used when greeting one person, and

molweni when greeting two or more. On departing, one makes the same distinction: *Hamba kakuhle* ("Go well") for one person and *Hambani kakuhle* for two or more.

In interacting with others, it is crucial to show respect (*ukuhlonipha*). In order not to be rude, youths are expected to keep quiet when elders are speaking and to lower their eyes when being addressed. Hospitality is highly valued, and people are expected to share with visitors what they can. Socializing over tea and snacks is a common form of interaction practiced throughout English-speaking southern Africa.

In Xhosa tradition, one commonly found a girlfriend or boyfriend by attending dances. One popular type of dance, called *umtshotsho* or *intlombe*, could last all night. On some occasions, unmarried lovers were allowed to sleep together provided they observed certain restraints. A form of external intercourse called *ukumetsha* was permitted, but full intercourse was taboo. For Westernized Xhosa, romances often begin at school, church, or through mutual acquaintances. Dating activities include attending the cinema as well as going to dances, sporting events, concerts, and so forth.

9 LIVING CONDITIONS

During the early period of white rule in South Africa, Xhosa communities were severely neglected in terms of social services. In fact, rural areas were deliberately impoverished so as to encourage Xhosa to seek wage labor employment. In the later years of apartheid, some attempts were made to address major health concerns in these areas, but most government money continued to be set aside for social services that benefited whites. As the Xhosa population in rural areas expanded through natural increase and forced removals, rural lands became increasingly overcrowded and eroded. In the twentieth-century, many men and women migrated to urban shantytowns such as those that exist on the outskirts of Cape Town. Poverty and ill health are still widespread in both rural and urban communities. Tuberculosis, malnutrition, hypertension, and diarrheal diseases are common health problems. Since 1994, however, the post apartheid government has expanded health and nutritional aid to the black population.

Housing, standards of living, and creature comforts vary considerably among Xhosa-speakers. Xhosa people make up some of the poorest and some of the wealthiest of black South Africans. Poor people live in round thatched-roof huts, labor compounds, or single-room shacks without running water or electricity. Other Xhosa people are among an elite who live in quiet suburban neighborhoods, in large comfortable houses on par with any to be found in Europe or the United States. In South Africa, a person can acquire all the creature comforts that money can buy, provided that one has the money to buy them.

The most common forms of transportation for black people in South Africa are buses, commuter trains, and "taxis." "Taxis" are actually minivans that carry many individual riders at a time. Most such taxis are for short distances in urban areas, but they are also used as a faster alternative to the long-distance routes of buses. Personal cars and trucks are also not uncommon, although in recent years high rates of inflation and increasing fuel costs have driven up prices considerably.

¹⁰ FAMILY LIFE

The traditional Xhosa family was patriarchal. Men were considered the heads of their households; women and children were expected to defer to men's authority. Polygynous marriages were permitted where the husband had the means to pay the *lobolo* (bridewealth) for each and to maintain them properly. Women were expected to leave their families to live with the family of her husband. The elaborate marriage ceremony discussed previously helped ease a woman's transition to the new home. In addition, her acceptance into the family was confirmed when she was given a ritual offering of milk.

In urban areas, traditional restrictions on sexual expression have been hard to enforce. Consequently, there have been higher rates of unmarried pregnancies than existed in the past. The migrant labor system has also put great strains on the traditional family, with some men establishing two distinct families—one at the place of work and the other at the rural home. With the end of apartheid, some of the families previously separated by the labor laws are beginning new lives in urban areas. Some of these families live under crowded and difficult conditions in shanty towns and migrant labor compounds.

¹¹ CLOTHING

Many Xhosa men and women dress similarly to people in Europe and the United States. However, pants for women have only recently become acceptable. Also, as a result of missionary influence, it has become customary for a woman to cover her hair with a scarf or hat. As a head covering, many rural women fold scarves or other clothes into elaborate turban shapes. These coverings (*imithwalo*), plus the continued practice of anointing the body and face with white or ocher-colored mixtures, gives a distinctive appearance that marks them as Xhosa. Other signs of Xhosa identity in dress include intricately sewn designs on blankets that are worn by both men and women as shawls or capes.

¹² FOOD

Xhosa people share many food traditions with the other peoples of South Africa. Staple foods are corn (maize) and bread. Beef, mutton, and goat are popular meats. Milk is often drunk in its sour form, while sorghum beer, which is also sour in taste, continues to be popular.

One particular food popularly identified with the Xhosa is *umngqusho*. This is a dish that combines hominy corn with beans and spices. Xhosa also regularly eat the soft porridge made of corn meal flour that is widespread in Africa. Eggs were traditionally taboo for women, while a newly wedded wife was not allowed to eat certain types of meat. Men were not supposed to drink milk in any village where they might later take a wife.

The major mealtimes are breakfast and dinner. Children may go without lunch, although school lunch programs have been established recently by the government. As with other South African peoples, food preferences change with the time. For example, a variety of American or British-style fast-food services are available in urban areas throughout the country. Fine locally produced wines are also popular.

¹³ EDUCATION

The first Western-style schools for Xhosa-speakers were begun by missionaries. Many of these schools were remarkably successful. One of the most famous of the missionary institutions, the University of Fort Hare, boasts Nelson Mandela and a number of other famous African leaders as former students. Unfortunately, however, an indirect consequence of the mission-school heritage was that public education for Africans was not considered a matter of national concern.

Under apartheid, African access to education was restricted and many of the best mission schools were shutdown. As a result, adult literacy rates dropped, in some areas to as low as 30%. Today, the goal is free education for all those aged seven to seventeen. Literacy and education are now seen as keys to success and are highly valued by most people.

¹⁴ CULTURAL HERITAGE

Xhosa traditional music places a strong emphasis on group singing and handclapping as accompaniment to dance. Drums, while used occasionally, were not as fundamental a part of musical expression as they were for many other African peoples. Other instruments used included rattles, whistles, flutes, mouth harps, and stringed-instruments constructed with a bow and resonator.

Xhosa people also have specific styles in the material arts. They have distinctive forms of beadwork, pottery making, body decoration, basketry, and, as mentioned above, headwear. Many Xhosa-speaking artists today see themselves as employing their traditions creatively in the context of the world's entire art scene.

Missionaries introduced the Xhosa to Western choral singing. Among the most successful of the Xhosa hymns is the South African national anthem, *Nkosi Sikele' iAfrika* (God Bless Africa), written by a school teacher named Enoch Sontonga in 1897, with additional verses by S.E. K Mqhayi.

Xhosa written literature was established in the nineteenth century with the publication of the first Xhosa newspapers, novels, and plays. S.E. K. Mqhayi (1875-1945) is considered by many to be the Xhosa national poet. His work *USamson*, published in 1907, is arguably the first Xhosa novel. Other early writers include Tiyo Soga, A.C. Jordan, I. Bud-Mbelle, and John Tengo Jabavu.

Today there are many individuals of Xhosa background working in literature and the arts. Among them are Fatima Dike, John Kani, Zakes Mda, Gcina Mhlope, and Sindiwe Magona.

¹⁵ WORK

Wage labor for many rural Xhosa has meant leaving home to find employment in the city. Under white rule, Xhosa men were most frequently hired as miners and farm laborers. Women also worked as farm laborers, but work in domestic service was more valued. For those with high school and college educations, the greatest opportunities were in health care, education, and government administration. Today, Xhosa seek degrees in all fields.

South Africa's migrant labor system has dramatically altered Xhosa social life. Besides putting strain on the family, migrant labor has led to the development of new social groups. For example, associations of young men called *iindlavini* were formed. *Iindlavini* are typically young men with some schooling who have spent time working in the mines. They adopted some of the ways of the city while developing their own particular traditions as well. Changes in international economic conditions greatly affect Xhosa peoples. For example, when gold prices declined in recent years, many Xhosa lost their jobs. These workers and the people who depend on their wages suffered considerably.

16 SPORTS

Many of the games popular among Xhosa children are found worldwide. These include skipping rope, racing, swimming, playing hopscotch, and so forth. Boys also enjoy wrestling and stick fighting.

The most popular sport in South Africa is soccer. There are many professional teams as well as teams associated with schools and companies. In school, there are also organized competitions in athletics, what Americans call "track and field."

17 ENTERTAINMENT AND RECREATION

Popular entertainments include attending movies, plays, and musical performances. Televisions and videocassette recorders are also popular. Most of the movies are imported foreign films, but a South African film industry is developing. A Xhosa version of Georges Bizet's Carmen (*U-Carmen eKhayelitsha*) set in a Cape Town won top honors in the 2005 Berlin Film Festival. Plays are often broadcast over TV and radio. Television broadcasts also include programs in Xhosa, with Xhosa "soap operas" a regular feature. Music videos can be seen as well.

South Africa has a well-established music industry. The most popular musicians are typically those that perform dance tunes, although religious choirs are also popular. One of the most famous of South Africa's musicians, Miriam Makeba, is of South African background. By listening to her version of the "click" song, one can get a good sense of how clicks operate in the language, but she is also known for her contributions to world music. Today there are many other Xhosa musicians whose work is globally oriented and multicultural. Among them are the classically trained composer Bongani Ndodona-Breen and the late pop musician Brenda Fassie. Xhosa-speaker Thandiswa Mazwai is also known as one of the founders of the South African pop music form known as kwaito.

18 FOLK ART, CRAFTS, AND HOBBIES

Folk craft traditions include beadwork, sewing, pottery making, house decoration, and weaving. Hand-woven materials were generally functional items such as sleeping mats, baskets, and strainers. Xhosa ceremonial clothing is often elaborately decorated with fine embroidery work and intricate geometric designs.

Xhosa-speaking artists today may see themselves as employing their traditions creatively in the context of the world's entire art scene. Thus, they incorporate traditional forms into modern works of art.

19 SOCIAL PROBLEMS

Most of the social problems found among Xhosa people today stem directly or indirectly from the apartheid past. These include high rates of poverty, disease, fractured families, mal-

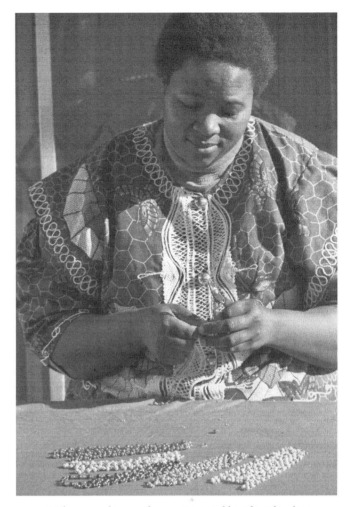

A Xhosa-speaking worker creates a necklace from beads at Umtha Beads, a craft business run by David and Cheryl Milligan. The couple started the business after David was laid off work as companies restructured in the new South Africa. (The Image Works)

nutrition, and crime. Poverty and social dislocation may also tempt people to form gangs and to abuse drugs and alcohol. Competition for scarce resources has also led to conflict with other South African groups such as the Sotho, the Zulu, and people of mixed-race. The high numbers of refugees and illegal immigrants who have come to South Africa from other African countries in recent years has also led to tension. There are divisions within the Xhosa community as well—between men and women, young and old, rural and urban, and highly educated and illiterate—which may lead to tensions if not resolved in the post-apartheid era. One of the biggest challenges for South Africa as a whole is to meet rising expectations for education, employment, and improved standards of living.

South Africa as a whole has suffered considerably from HIV/AIDS. Recent estimates suggest that nearly 700,000 people in the Eastern Cape are HIV positive with some 5.4 million South Africans suffering from the condition. These are some of the highest rates in the world. Deaths from AIDS and AIDS-related diseases have also led to a high proportion of orphans and poorly cared-for young people. On a more positive note, the numbers who are receiving appropriate treatment has increased dramatically since 2006.

20 GENDER ISSUES

Xhosa society was in the past fairly typical of patriarchically organized societies. Women were expected to seek primarily fulfillment as wives and mothers. Under apartheid family bonds were strained under the system of migrant labor upon which many rural people depended. During this time, women in effect became household heads when their husbands' were away at their jobs. Families were further impoverished during the period of forced settlement in the Bantustans. These conditions also fostered high rates of gender violence, including domestic abuse and rape. The forced separation of husband and wives under apartheid led to other problems as well, such as adultery and prostitution. Also, some men and women engaged in homosexual behaviors, although the idea of a gay identity has not been widely accepted.

The South African government has made improving conditions of gender inequality an important part of its educational and economic development strategy. In terms of education, roughly the same proportions of males and females attend school and graduate, but they do not always achieve parity in employment and promotion opportunities. To correct this within the government, one goal is to have 50% of the managers in public service be women.

21 BIBLIOGRAPHY

Dase, Gcinikhaya, Sizwe Sotewu, and John Steele. "Cultural Heritage in the Work of Two Xhosa-speaking Ceramic Artists." *African Arts*, vol. 40, no. 3, 2007: 64-77.

Hammond-Tooke, W. D. *Bhaca Society*. Cape Town: Oxford University Press, 1962.

Mayer, Philip. *Townsmen or Tribesmen: Conservativism and the Process of Urbanization in a South African City*. Cape Town: Oxford University Press, 1971.

Mda, Jakes. *The Heart of Redness: A Novel*. New York: Picador, 2003.

Ngonini, Xola A. "Anxious Communities: The Decline of Mine Migration in the Eastern Cape." *Development Southern Africa*, vol. 24, no. 1, 2007: 173–185.

Opland, Jeff. "The First Xhosa Novel." *Research in African Literatures*, vol. 38, no. 4, 2007: 87-110.

Pauw, B. A. *The Second Generation; A Study of the Family among Urbanized Bantu in East London*. Capetown: Oxford University Press, 1963.

Peires, J. B. *The House of Phalo: A History of The Xhosa People in the Days of Their Independence*. Berkeley, Calif.: University of California Press, 1982.

Peltzer, Karl., Ayanda Nqeketo, George Petros, and Xolo Kanta. "Traditional Circumcision During Manhood Initiation Rituals in the Eastern Cape, South Africa." In *BMC Public Health*, vol. 8, no. 64, 2008.

Ramphela, Mamphela. *A Bed Called Home: Life in the Migrant Labour Hostels of Cape Town*. Athens, Ohio: Ohio University Press, 1993.

Rycroft, David K. "Nguni Music." In *The New Grove Dictionary of Music*. Edited by Stanley Sadie. Washington, D.C.: MacMillan, 1980.

Soga, J. H. *The Ama-Xhosa: Life and Customs*. Lovedale: Lovedale Press, 1931.

Statistics South Africa. www.statssa.gov.za. (May 2008).

Switzer, Les. *Power and Resistance in an African Society: The Ciskei Xhosa and the Making of South Africa*. Madison: University of Wisconsin Press, 1993.

West, Martin. *Abantu: An Introduction to the Black People of South Africa*. Cape Town: Struik, 1976.

Wilson, Monica Hunter. *Reaction to Conquest: Effects of Contact with Europeans on the Pondo of South Africa*. London: Oxford University Press, 1961.

Zenani, Nongenile. *The World and the Word: Tales and Observations from the Xhosa Oral Tradition*. Collected and edited by Harold Scheub. Madison: University of Wisconsin Press, 1992.

—by R. Shanafelt

YORUBA

PRONUNCIATION: YAWR-uh-buh
LOCATION: West Africa (primarily Nigeria; also Benin and Togo)
POPULATION: 19,327,000
LANGUAGE: Yoruba
RELIGION: Ancestral religion, Islam, Christianity
RELATED ARTICLES: Vol. 1: Beninese; Nigerians

¹ INTRODUCTION

The Yoruba are one of the largest and most important ethnic groups south of the Sahara desert. Their tradition of urban life is unique among African ethnic groups. The Yoruba rank among the leaders in economics, government, religion, and artistic achievement in West Africa. Within Nigeria, where they dominate the Western part of the country, the Yoruba are one of the three largest and most important ethnic groups. The Yoruba people are not a single group, but are a series of diverse people bound together by common language, dress, ritual, political system, mythology, and history.

There has been much speculation about the origins of the Yoruba people. Based on their beautifully cast brass sculptures from Ife, one opinion held that Yoruba culture had been introduced by Etruscans who reached West Africa by way of the "lost continent" of Atlantis. Others suggested that the Yoruba may have come from Egypt. Many educated Yoruba people accept this view, which is also supported by theories relating to similarities in the languages of the two people.

However, archeological evidence has not supported any of these claims. It is now recognized that Ife was the early center of an important glass-making industry and the home of native brass casting. Archeologists have also uncovered a town wall of about 8.8 km (5.5 mi) in circumference surrounding the city that was probably built between AD 950 and 1400. A later town wall of about 12.8 km (8 mi) in circumference from the middle of the 19th century was also discovered. This evidence seems to indicate that Ife was an important artistic and religious center by around AD 1000. As far as the origins of the Yoruba are concerned, all that archeology can point to is some stylistic similarities between pottery in Ife and in Northern Nigeria, dating to a period between 900 BC and AD 200. This indicates that they probably migrated southward from the savanna into the tropical forest area after that time.

The Yoruba are divided among over fifty kingdoms. Yoruba mythology holds that ultimately all Yoruba people descended from a hero called Odua or Oduduwa, and the Yoruba kings validate their right to rule by claiming direct descent from him through one of his sixteen sons. Today there are over fifty "kings" who claim to be descendants of the sons or grandsons of Odua and to have migrated directly from Ife. It is not possible to determine how many kingdoms there were before warring began between them in the last century, but they probably numbered over twenty. Yoruba country was torn by warfare for decades. One of the most damaging effects of the centuries-long warfare was the enslavement of many Yoruba people and their transport to the Americas. In 1893, the Governor of Lagos brought the Yoruba kingdoms in Nigeria under the Protectorate of Great Britain, and peace was achieved. Until 1960 Nigeria was a British colony and the Yoruba were British subjects. On 1 October 1960 Nigeria became an independent nation with the political structure of a federation of states.

² LOCATION AND HOMELAND

The Yoruba people live in West Africa, primarily in the country of Nigeria, but with some scattered groups in Benin and Togo. According to the 1963 census, out of a total Yoruba population of 5.3 million, 4.1 million lived in the five states of Oyo, Ibadan, Abeokuta, Ijebu, and Ondo. These states are primarily Yoruba, with the percentages of Yoruba in the population ranging from 89.2% for Ondo state to 97.7% in Ibadan State. These states have a combined area of 75,370 sq km (29,100 sq mi), giving an average population density of 58 per sq km (150 per sq mi), but ranging from a low of 31 per sq km (81 per sq mi) in Oyo state to a high of 141 per sq km (365 per sq mi) in Ibadan State.

Most of the other Yoruba are found in the Federal Territory, in Ilorin and Kabba Provinces in Northern Nigeria, in Benin, and in Togo. In Nigeria, the Itsekiri of Warri are a Yoruba-speaking offshoot who have been strongly influenced by Benin culture. Yoruba traders are also found in nearly all the major market towns of West Africa. Descendants of Yoruba slaves, some of whom can still speak the Yoruba language, are found in Sierra Leone where they are known as Aku, in Cuba where they are known as Lucumi, and in Brazil where they are known as Nago. During the four centuries of the slave trade when their territory was known as Slave Coast, uncounted numbers of Yoruba were carried to the Americas where their descendants preserved Yoruba traditions. In several parts of the Caribbean and South America, Yoruba religion has combined with Christianity, resulting in Yoruba deities being identified with Catholic saints.

The Yoruba homeland in West Africa stretches from a savanna region on the north to a region of tropical rain forests on the south. Lagos, the present federal capital of Nigeria, is located at the southern end of this area. It is this range of climate, together with the intensity of cultivation in the savanna area, that determines a very sharp division between regions and in the occupations and living situation of the Yoruba in the two areas.

³ LANGUAGE

The Yoruba language belongs to the Niger-Congo branch of the Congo-Kordofanian language family that includes most West African languages. While there are many dialects within Yoruba, Yoruba-speaking people can all understand each other.

Yoruba is a tonal language; the same combination of vowels and consonants has different meanings depending on the pitch of the vowels. For example, the same word, *aro*, can mean cymbal, indigo dye, lamentation, and granary, depending on intonation. *Pele o* is "Hello;" *Bawo ni?* is "How are you?;" and, *Dada ni* is "Fine, thank you."

⁴ FOLKLORE

The most important myths of the Yoruba are related to their origins. Yoruba believe that, not only did they originate at the city of Ife, but the earth and the first human beings were created there as well. According to this myth, the deities originally lived in the sky, below which there was only primeval water. Olorun, the Sky God, gave to Orishala, the God of Whiteness,

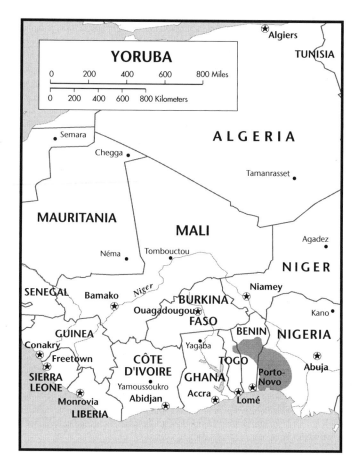

YORUBA

a chain, a bit of earth in a snail shell, and a five-toed chicken, and told him to go down and create the earth. However, as he approached the gate of heaven, he saw some deities having a party and he stopped to greet them. They offered him palm wine, and he drank too much and fell asleep, drunk. Odua, his younger brother, had overheard Olorun's instructions, and when he saw Orishala sleeping, he took the materials and went to the edge of heaven, accompanied by Chameleon. He let down the chain, and they climbed down it. Odua threw the piece of earth on the water and placed the five-toed chicken upon it. The chicken began to scratch the earth, spreading it in all directions, and as far as the ends of the earth. After Chameleon had tested the firmness of the earth, Odua stepped on it at Idio where he made his home and where his sacred grove in Ife is located today.

When Orishala awoke and found that the work had been completed, he put a taboo on wine that his worshippers observe today. He came down to earth and claimed it as his own. He insisted that he was the owner of the earth because he had made it. The two brothers began to fight, and the other deities who followed them to earth took sides with them. When Olorun heard of the fighting, he called Orishala and Odua to appear before him and told them to stop fighting. To Odua, the Creator of the Earth, he gave the right to own the earth and rule over it. To Orishala he gave a special title and the power to mold human bodies; he thus became the Creator of Mankind.

Yoruba mythology goes on to explain that when Odua grew old he became blind. He sent each of his sixteen sons in turn to the ocean for salt water that had been prescribed as a remedy.

Each returned unsuccessfully, bringing only fresh water, until Obokun, the youngest finally succeeded. Odua washed his eyes in the salt water and could see again. In gratitude, he gave Obokun a sword. Obokun took it and cut some of the beaded fringes from Odua's crown; because of this, he was not permitted to wear a crown to cover his face, as the other Yoruba kings do. Obokun went to the city of Ilesha where he became king, and the other sons founded kingdoms of their own.

5 RELIGION

In the last census the number of Yoruba who said that they adhere to their ancestral religion, rather than being Christians or Muslims, varied from 20% of the population in Oyo to only 6% in Ijebu. However, most people continue to participate in the annual festivals of their town, though Muslims are probably somewhat more rigid than Christians in the non-observance of certain rites. The rest are divided about evenly between Muslims and Christians.

Yoruba traditional religion holds that there are 401 deities. Some are worshipped throughout Yoruba land and have their counterparts among neighboring peoples; some are fairly widely known; and some are only of local significance. Except for Olorun, the deities are believed to have lived on earth, but instead of dying they became gods. The worshipers of a deity are referred to as his "children." An individual usually worships the deity of his father and some of his mother. Many deities are identified with a particular clan. After marriage, women return home for the annual festival of their own deity but they assist in the performance of the annual festival of their husband's deity. The priests of Yoruba cults usually hold no political office; they do not sit among the chiefs. They are usually men of little wealth; their prestige in the community is often low, but their sacred powers are feared.

There are three gods who are available to all. Olorun is the high god, the Creator, but no shrines exist to him, and there is no organized priesthood. He is invoked in blessings or in thanks, and one may call on him with prayers or by pouring water on kola nuts on the ground. Eshu is the youngest and cleverest of the deities and is the divine messenger who delivers sacrifices prescribed by the diviners to Olorun, after these are placed at his shrine. Regardless of what deity they worship, everyone prays frequently to Eshu. Ifa is the God of Divination and a close friend of Eshu. He is often spoken of as a scribe or clerk and is described as a learned man or scholar. Olorun gave him the power to speak for the gods and communicate with human beings through divination. Most importantly, he is the one who transmits and interprets the wishes of Olorun to mankind and who prescribes the sacrifices that Eshu carries to him. Whatever personal deities they may worship, all believers in the Yoruba religion turn to Ifa in time of trouble.

Other gods include Odua, the creator of the earth; Orishala, the god of whiteness; Ogun, the god of iron; Oranmiyan, the son of Ogun and Odua; Shango, the god of thunder; Shopona, the god of smallpox; and a number of river gods and goddesses. Cults to these deities are maintained by families or clans whose members participate in the annual festivals.

6 MAJOR HOLIDAYS

In addition to local town festivals (usually dedicated to individual deities), Yoruba may also celebrate the following holidays, depending on whether they are Christians or Muslims:

(Muslim holidays vary according to the lunar calendar): New Year's Day, January; *Idul Adha* ("Feast of Sacrifice") June or July;

Easter (March or April); *Maulid an-Nabi* ("Muhammad's birthday") September or October; Ramadan (March–April), followed by a 3 day feast; Nigerian Independence Day (October); *Idul Fitr* (March–April); Christmas (December).

7 RITES OF PASSAGE

A newborn infant is sprinkled with water to make it cry. No word may be spoken until the infant cries, in the belief that silence will prevent the infant from becoming impotent or barren. No one younger than the mother should be present. The infant then is taken to the back yard where the umbilical cord is bound tightly with thread and then cut, using either a knife from the midrib of a leaf of the bamboo palm, or a piece of glass. The placenta is buried in the back yard. On the burial spot, the child is bathed with a loofah sponge and rubbed with palm oil. The child is held by the feet and given three shakes to make it strong and brave. After a specified number of days, a naming ceremony is held and attended by relatives who bring gifts of small amounts of money. Circumcision (boys) and clitoridectomy (girls) are usually performed in the first month and scarification of the face (the cutting of the facial marks) follows about two months later. Christians and Muslims are giving up scarification, but circumcision and clitoridectomy is still done.

Many children are given special names according to the circumstances of their birth. For example, the first-born twin, who is considered younger because he was sent ahead by the other, is called Taiwo, meaning that he came to inspect the world. The second-born or senior twin is called Kehinde, meaning that he arrived afterwards. There are special names for the first, second, third, and fourth children born after twins, for children born with the umbilical cord around their neck, for children born in an unruptured caul (membrane surrounding the fetus), for children born face down, for children born with six fingers, and for other circumstances of birth. Many Yoruba names begin with the name of the deity that the individual worships, for example, *Fagbemi* means "Ifa helps me."

In the past, men past adolescence were divided into a system of age-graded associations. These groups were formed at three-year intervals and continued until the death of all their members. Membership was automatic and universal. The age grades designated a young man's public duties in the town. The youngest grade, 0–9 years, did no work. The next grade weeded the roads, and the two highest grades provided the warriors. At the age of 45, a man became an elder and was exempt from manual public work. This system is now becoming obsolete, as all children attend school.

Girls were generally engaged before puberty in former times, often by age five. This is no longer the practice, although a man still must negotiate through an intermediary with the girl's father (usually before the girl reaches puberty) to arrange a marriage and cannot approach either the girl or her parents directly to propose marriage. If the parents approve of the young man, they consult a diviner. If he is approved by the diviner, the suitor is told to visit the family and to bring the first installment of the bridewealth (payment to the bride's family) to seal the engagement. This process is known as "becoming in-laws." The second installment, known as "love money" can

be given at any time before the third year after puberty when the girl becomes marriageable. The final installment is made just before marriage and is known as "wife money." When the girl reaches marriageable age her family notifies her suitor that it is time for her to have her body decorated with scarified designs. The groom then sends six calabashes (gourd-like fruit, hollowed out and used as a carrier) of water, six bundles of firewood, and the necessary leaves, oils, and other materials. Weddings are frequently performed in the season after the heavy rains. The night begins at the bride's house after dark with a feast to which the groom also contributes yams. The bride then is taken to the groom's house by women from his house after she has been blessed by her mother and her father. In the groom's house she is taken to the main chamber where she is washed from foot to knee with an infusion of leaves meant to bring her many children. For a period of 84 days, the bride then makes ritual visits to her parents' home, returning to her husband's compound after nightfall. For eight days, starting with the wedding night she spends two nights and two days each in her husband's and in her parents' compounds alternately, returning on the ninth day to make a sacrifice to the God of Divination in her husband's home.

Burials are performed by the adult men of the clan of the deceased, but those who can trace actual relationship to the deceased, including a man's brothers and sons, do not join them. The men divide themselves into two groups: one digging the grave and the other bathing the corpse. The body is laid out in the house and laid on fine cloths placed on a bed and covered with still finer cloth. Relatives and friends are notified of the death as soon as possible and they come to console the immediate family and to pay their respects to the departed. The grave is dug in the floor of the room where the deceased lived. Interment in the past was delayed as many as eight days, during which time there was feasting. Now it follows as soon as the grave has been dug. After the burial there is a period of feasting, lasting as long as eight or ten nights if the children can afford it. These funeral ceremonies may be postponed up to a year if the children do not have the resources to do it at once. Many of the rituals associated with burial are intended to insure that the deceased will be reborn again.

8 INTERPERSONAL RELATIONS

Kinship is the most important relationship for the Yoruba. This is where an individual gets his identity and where his primary loyalties lie. Not all ties are based on kinship, however. Friendship may or may not cut across kinship lines. A best friend is referred to as "friend not-see-not-sleep," meaning one does not go to sleep without having seen his best friend. Through experience one learns whose advice he can rely upon and whom he can trust not to reveal confidences. In times of trouble Yoruba turn to the best friend even before turning to the mother. The Yoruba shares his last wishes with the best friend—what is to be done at his burial, how he wishes his property to be divided—and the best friend shares this information with his family at his death.

The second institution that is not based on kinship is the club or association that may grow out of childhood associations. When his clan is performing a religious festival, or when he is sacrificing to his ancestral guardian soul, a child may invite his playmates and their friends to come to eat with him; and, he may be invited by them in return. If this continues,

Yoruba girls in Lagos, Nigeria. Every Yoruba is born into a patrilineal clan whose members are descended from a remote common ancestor. The clan and sub-clan completely overshadow the immediate family in importance. (Jason Laure)

they choose a name for the club and invite an elder man and an elder woman to serve as advisors. The members of clubs will consequently be more or less the same age. A man can invite the members of his club to his feast when he is performing a festival and to accompany him as he travels around town accompanied by a drummer on that day. A man's social position is judged by the number of his followers on such occasions. Clubs hold monthly meetings, with the members serving as hosts in turn.

9 LIVING CONDITIONS

The Yoruba people have lived in towns as long as their history has been recorded. These towns consist of dense aggregates of buildings housing 30 persons to the hectare (75 persons to the acre) in the built-up areas. The traditional compounds in these aggregates are vast structures of rectangular courtyards, each with a single entrance. Around each courtyard is an open or a semi-enclosed porch where the women sit, weave, and cook; behind this are the rooms of each adult. Today, the old compounds are rapidly being replaced by modern bungalows made of cement blocks with corrugated iron roofs.

Most Yoruba towns, even small ones, have adequate basic services, including electricity, running water, and paved roads. The major Yoruba cities, such as Ibadan and Abeokuta, have modern central areas that include banks, government buildings, churches, and hospitals. There is public transportation connecting all settlements, mostly by mini-buses and taxis. The more affluent people own cars.

Traditional medicine continues to play an important role in the health care of people, alongside modern Western health services. Among the Yoruba both practices flourish. Since Nigeria became independent, the general health of the population has improved with the expansion of the public health network. In the late 1980s, an increase in vaccination against major childhood diseases was carried out under the government's health policy. Nevertheless, many problems remain, and chronic diseases, such as malaria and guinea worm, still resist efforts at eradication.

10 FAMILY LIFE

Whether urban or rural, the Yoruba live in large residential groups, called compounds. The members of the compounds consist of patrilineally related men and their wives and children. After marriage, a bride comes to live in one of the many rooms in the compound of the groom's father. Every Yoruba is born into a patrilineal clan whose members are descended from a remote common ancestor. An individual accepts all members of his own clan as blood relatives, even if he does not know in what way they are actually related. Both sons and daughters are born into the clan of their father.

Clan members are spoken of as "children of the house" with males distinguished as "sons of the house" from the females or "daughters of the house." The females live in the compound of their birth until they marry, when they go to live with their husbands. The males constitute the nucleus of the compound, being born, married, and buried in it. The wives of the male clan members are known as "the wives of the house." Except for their own children, they are not related by blood to the rest of the compound members.

The clan and the sub-clan are each headed by its eldest male member, known as the *Bale* or "father of the house," a term that also refers to a husband as the head of his own family. No one except a male member of the clan can hold this position, and it follows according to strict seniority. The *Bale* serves as the principal judge of the compound, presiding when disputes are brought before him. A husband is responsible for settling quarrels within his own family; but if he is unsuccessful or if an argument involves members of two different families within the compound, it is referred to the *Bale*. The *Bale* is also responsible for assigning living quarters within the compound, administering clan farmlands assigned to the compound, sacrificing to the founder whose name the compound bears, and making medicines and atonements to keep its inhabitants in good health and at peace.

The hierarchy within the clan, based on seniority, runs from the eldest *Bale* of its several compounds down to the youngest child, and is very important in regulating conduct between the members. Each person is "elder" to all others born or married into the clan after him. The reciprocal obligations involve authority on the one hand, and deference and respect on the other. Males are seated and served according to their relative seniority, and elders can take larger and choicer portions of what is served.

In terms of seniority or age, the male members of the compound are divided into three groups: the elders, the adult males who are economically independent, and the young men and boys who are still economically dependent on their fathers. The elders, the adult males, and wives of the compound hold separate monthly or bimonthly meetings to discuss the affairs of the compound, the allocation of clan farm land, and the collection of taxes.

The clan and sub-clan completely overshadow the immediate family in importance. The immediate family, consisting of a man, his wives, and their children is of less significance and is known only by a descriptive name referring to the dwelling that it occupies, "house that of mine," to distinguish it from the compound.

The sub-family, consisting of a wife and her children within the polygynous family (husband with two or more wives), is an important unit of everyday life. They have a room in the husband's house to themselves, and they share possessions in common. Each mother cooks for her own children only, and ties of close affection bind a mother and her children. A man is expected to treat each wife equally and not according to the number of her children, but the mothers compete to gain additional favors for their own children. The father is distant and authoritarian, often seeing little of his children. When they are young, children of co-wives play together on the best terms, but as they grow older and property rights become important, they usually grow apart because of quarrels over possessions. When the father dies, his personal property is divided into approximately equal shares according to the number of children each wife has. It is the children, not the wives, who inherit, and the eldest son of each wife takes one share in the name of all the children of his mother. He may keep and use this inheritance as he sees fit, but he is held responsible for the economic welfare of the others.

¹¹ CLOTHING

Western-style dress is the style of clothing worn in urban areas. Traditional clothing, which is still worn on important occasions and in rural areas, is very colorful and elaborate. Women wear a head tie made of a rectangular piece of cloth tied about the head in a number of distinctive ways. Women carry babies or young children on their backs by tying another rectangular cloth around their waists. A third such cloth may be worn over the shoulder as a shawl, on top of a loose-fitting, short-sleeved blouse. A larger rectangular cloth serves as a wrap-around skirt.

Men wear tailored cloth hats, gowns, and trousers of several different patterns. A popular form of gown is shaped like a poncho; it reaches to the fingertips, but is worn folded back on the shoulders. Trousers are usually very loose and baggy. All the cloth from which traditional clothing is made is hand woven and often decorated with elaborate embroidery.

Facial and body scarification (making small, superficial incisions or punctures in the skin) are both symbols of clan affiliation and a means of beautification. Hair styles, referred to as hairdress, are important forms of decoration for women. The most common hairstyles are composed of parallel, tightly braided stripes running from the forehead to the back of the head. From there, they are wound in a row of tiny queues, from the back of the head to the forehead, from the top of the head downward and ending in a circle of tiny queues on the top of the head where they form a small topknot.

¹² FOOD

The Yoruba diet consists of starchy tubers, grains, and plantains, supplemented by vegetable oils, wild and cultivated fruits and vegetables, meat, and fish. Although yams are the staple food, they are both expensive and there is prestige associated with serving them. Therefore, they are reserved for social occasions. The daily family diet relies on cassava, taro, maize, beans, and plantains. One of the most popular foods is *foo-foo*, similar to a dumpling, but made of cassava. Rice is now widely grown all over Nigeria, and the Yoruba use it for ceremonial or important meals. In the past, meat was also reserved for ceremonies and special occasions. The predominance of starch in the diet is indicated by the fact that of 56 food recipes recorded in Ife, 47 describe different ways of preparing yams, maize, plantains, cassava, and taro. Six are stews, which may or may not contain meat or fish; they are made of vegetable oil and are highly seasoned with salt and chili pepper. Of the remaining three, two are based on melon seeds and one is simply toasted peanuts.

The following recipes are very popular and are usually served together:

Pounded Yam

White yams, preferably round and fat in shape with long, thorn-like hairs

1. Scrub yams, peel, and cut into chunks or slices. Place in a pot with water to cover. Cover and cook until the yams can

be pierced easily with a fork.

2. Pound the yams in a mortar, one piece at a time, until it forms a mass that pulls away from the sides of the mortar and is elastic to the touch. (This cannot be done with electric mixers, because the pounded yams will be very stiff.)

Pounded yam is served with soups and stews of many types at main meals.

Variation: Boil some ripe plantain with the yam and pound it with the yam.

Chicken and Okra Soup

Ingredients:
1 medium chicken
1 small onion, chopped
18 large okra
3 grams (1 teaspoon) dry ground red pepper
40 grams (1.4 ounces) dry crayfish, ground
2 medium fresh tomatoes
6 grams (2 teaspoons) tomato paste
Pinch of salt
1.5 grams (½ teaspoon) potash

1. Clean and cut the chicken into pieces, breaking the bones. Place in a pot with salt and pepper, cover with water and boil until tender. Drain, reserving the broth.

2. Grate the okra coarsely. Combine with remaining ingredients and boil for 5 minutes. Add the chicken to the okra mixture and continue to cook for 5 minutes more. Serve with the pounded yam.

13 EDUCATION

When Nigeria gained independence from Britain in 1960, its new parliamentary government set a priority on education, and universal primary education soon became the norm in southern Nigeria where the Yoruba live. Secondary school (high school) education also became widespread. The Yoruba were much involved in these efforts since education had a long tradition among them. The first university in Nigeria—established in 1947–48 and originally called University College, Ibadan—was located in a Yoruba city. (After independence, it was renamed the University of Ibadan.) The majority of students at Ibadan are Yoruba.

As a consequence of the priority on education, the literacy rate among people under 30 is high, even though the older generations may still be illiterate.

14 CULTURAL HERITAGE

The Yoruba cultural heritage includes verbal arts, such as praise names, praise poems, tongue twisters, hundreds of prose narratives and riddles, and thousands of proverbs. Whether the principal characters are humans or animals, the folktales all have a moral or lesson. Myths and legends impart information that is believed to be true about Yoruba heritage.

An evening session of telling folktales is usually preceded by a riddling contest among the children. Riddles sharpen the wits and train the memory of children. Adults share proverbs that express Yoruba morals, ethics, and social approval and disapproval.

There are songs of both ridicule and praise, as well as lullabies, religious songs, war songs, and work songs. These usually follow a "call and response" pattern between a leader and chorus. Rhythm is provided by drums, iron gongs, cymbals, rattles, and hand clapping. Other instruments include long brass trumpets, ivory trumpets, whistles, stringed instruments, and metallophones. Perhaps the most interesting musical instrument is the "talking drum."

15 WORK

Traditional Yoruba economy was based on hoe farming, craft specialization, and trade. About 75% of the Yoruba men are farmers, producing food crops for their domestic needs. Farming is considered men's work, and men only do clearing or hoeing fields. Wives can help their husbands with planting yams or harvesting corn, beans, or cotton. Wives also help at the market selling farm produce. A common practice was for several men to have a labor exchange, where they work together an equal number of days or hoeing the same number of heaps on each farmer's land. Alternatively, a man might invite his relatives, his friends, or the members of his club to a working bee during busy periods. Wealthier farmers could hire laborers.

Since the 1920s cocoa has been an important cash crop in the Yoruba economy. This caused a shift in emphasis to wage labor, doing away with much of the traditional forms of exchange labor.

The Yoruba enjoy trading and huge markets with over a thousand sellers are common. In addition, Yoruba long distance traders can be found as far away as Accra in Ghana and Bamako in Mali. Trade in foodstuffs and in cloth is confined to women; meat selling and produce buying is the province of men.

A farmer can become prosperous by working hard, by enjoying good health and by being blessed with many sons. Today only a few men have enough capital to establish large cocoa farms worked by hired labor. But, by trading an astute man can become very rich. In the past there were noted traders; today the produce buyers, the building contractors and the truck owners are a town's wealthiest men, enjoying the highest prestige. In the past this wealth was often spent on luxuries—houses, clothing, and the acquisition of wives. Today modern houses and cars are in vogue and every man hopes to send his children, especially his sons, to be educated at a university. The new, educated generation is moving away from farming and its members are looking for white collar jobs.

16 SPORTS

See the following section entitled "Entertainment and Recreation."

17 ENTERTAINMENT AND RECREATION

In addition to rituals, dances, and traditional music, modern forms of entertainment include television, going to the movies, and discos. Many urban households own television sets. The more religious households prohibit family members, especially women, from going to see films. Among urban teenagers, American youth culture is popular. Most young people listen to rap and rock music.

18 FOLK ARTS, CRAFTS AND HOBBIES

The Yoruba engage in both visual and verbal art forms. Visual arts include weaving, embroidering, pottery making, woodcarving, leather and bead working, and metalworking. The Yoruba are considered among the most prolific of the art-producing people of Africa.

Both men and women weave, using different types of looms. Women weave on a vertical "mat loom," producing a cloth about 60 cm (2 ft) wide and 213 cm (7 ft) long. Men weave on the horizontal narrow-band treadle loom that produces a strip of cloth only 3 to 4 in (7.5 to 10 cm) wide, but as long as may be needed. The long strips are cut to the desired length and sewn together to make clothing. Patterns are named often after the clubs that ordered them. Cloth is woven from wild silk and from locally grown cotton.

Men also do embroidery, particularly on large gowns worn by men and on men's caps. Men are also the tailors and dressmakers. Floor mats, mat bags for storing clothing, baskets, and strainers are also made by the men.

Women are the potters. In addition to palm oil lamps, they make over twenty kinds of pots and dishes for cooking, eating, and carrying and storing liquids. Most everyday pottery is brown or black without decoration. Pottery used for rituals is decorated with red, white, or blue designs. Gourds or calabashes (a gourd-like fruit) are also used for drinking, serving food, and for carrying palm wine sacrifices and goods to sell in the market. Some are also used as containers for the ingredients of medicines. Some calabashes are decorated with carved designs.

Woodcarving accounts for the greatest variety of decorated and sculptural forms. The woodcarvers, all of whom are men, carve "art," that is, both sculpture and geometrical designs. Those who carve masks and figurines are distinguished from those who simply carve wood into mortars, pestles, and utilitarian bowls. Some Yoruba woodcarvers also work in bone, ivory, and stone.

Blacksmiths work both in iron and brass to create utilitarian and decorative objects. The brass Ife heads of the period before contact with outsiders are considered among the finest art works of the world.

19 SOCIAL PROBLEMS

There are vast differences in wealth among Yoruba social classes. Differences in income and lifestyle are related to the person's occupation. In some rural areas, farmers barely manage to feed their families. Many traditional urban occupations, such as water carriers, hawkers, and sweepers, also do not provide adequate wages to support a family. Lower-skilled workers are employed in house construction and crafts, or as clerks, all at very low incomes. The oil boom and provisions of schooling in the 1970s and 1980s resulted in the growth of a sizable middle class, most of whom adopted a Western lifestyle. The social elites include traditional chiefs and wealthy business and government leaders. The elite lifestyle is characterized by conspicuous consumption of material goods.

Nigeria is party to several international human rights treaties, but the current government's human rights record is poor. Military rule deprives many citizens of their rights through detention without trial, physical assault, torture, and harassment. An active human rights group, the Civil Liberties Organization (CLO), was founded by a group of lawyers led by Olisa Agbakobe, a Yoruba. It is one of several organizations critical of the government's violations of civil rights.

The crime rate in Nigeria is high, particularly in Lagos, Ibadan, Abeokuta, and other urban areas. More than half the offenses are property crimes. Worsening economic conditions and an infective police and military heightened the incidence of crime in the 1980s

Drug-related crime has emerged as a major problem, and young people are using both marijuana and cocaine in increasing numbers.

20 GENDER ISSUES

Gender relations among the Yoruba are complex. A lot of gender constructs are portrayed in their myths, which form both their social and religious practices. Some of the Yoruba gods, like Osun, were females and there were female priestesses too, thus illustrating the pivotal role that women played in Yoruba religious and spiritual matters.

As in many other societies, there were specific expectations for females and males. Such expectations were determined by the people's living experiences. For example, women were expected to be peaceful and fruitful; thus, female principles were generally regarded as symbols of coolness, whereas male principles were construed as representing toughness and virility. Consequently, men were portrayed as rough and violent while women were portrayed as peaceful. Hence, some years that are difficult are called "Male Years" (ako odun) while those that are fruitful and peaceful are referred to as "Female Years" (abo odun). In Yoruba culture, a woman who acts like a man is ridiculed and so is a man who behaves like a woman.

The people's social expectations as recorded in wise sayings and proverbs further portray social expectations. For example the Yoruba proverb Ogbo-ogbon lagbalagba-a fi nsa fun eranla (It is with dissembling that a venerable man flees from a wild beast). This proverb encourages men to confront danger with bravery and not to run away. Such would be the social expectation.

In Yoruba culture, the gender constructs stress complementary relations between women and women. Thus, they do not necessarily translate to issues of oppression and domination of women by men. This complementary nature of Yoruba gender relations is deeply ingrained in the socio-religious domains and the either gender is vital for a smooth coexistence and harmonious living experience in the society. In fact neither gender fully dominates a particular domain, be it private or public. All the same, either gender can enjoy prominence in a specific area like religious rituals, while the other may be prominent in settling disputes and reconciliation. For example, while women take care of the children and are in charge of the daily running of the homes, men are the providers of resources, such as yams, and defenders of the community against any imminent attacks. Thus, both females and males manifest cooperation in the running of the affairs of the community.

21 BIBLIOGRAPHY

Amina Mama, "Women's Studies and Studies of Women in Africa during the 1990s," *Feminist Knowledge: Review Essays*, GWS Africa.

Bascom, William. *The Yoruba of Southwestern Nigeria*. New York: Holt, Rinehart and Winston, 1969.

Diedre Badejo and Osun Seegesi. *The Elegant Deity of Wealth, Power, and Femininity.* Trenton, NJ: Africa World Press, 1996.

Kokole, Omari H. ed. *The Global African: A Portrait of Ali A. Mazrui.* Trenton, NJ: Africa World Press, 1998.

Lloyd, P. C. "The Yoruba of Nigeria." In *Peoples of Africa*, edited by James L. Gibbs, Jr. New York: Holt, Rinehart and Winston, Inc., 1965.

Olajubu, Oyeronke. "Seeing Through a Woman's eye: Yoruba Traditions and Gender Relations." *Journal of Feminist Studies in Religion.* Indiana University Press, 2004.

Oyeronke Oyewumi. *The Invention of Women: Making an African Sense of Western Gender Discourses.* Minneapolis: University of Minnesota Press, 1997.

Peel, J. D. Y. "Gender in Yoruba Religious Change," *Journal of Religion in Africa* 32, 2002, pp. 136-66.

———. *Religious Encounter and the Making of the Yoruba.* Bloomington: Indiana University Press, 2000).

Turner, James. "Universal Education and Nation-Building in Africa." *Journal of Black Studies* 2, no. l: 3–27.

United Nations. *Demographic Indicators of Countries: Estimates and Projections as Assessed in 1982.* New York: United Nations, 1985.

Warne, R. "Gender," in *Guide to the Study of Religion*, ed. Willi Braun and Russell T. McCutcheon London: Cossell, 2000, pp. 140–54.

—revised by M. Njoroge

ZAMBIANS

PRONUNCIATION: ZAM-bee-uhns
LOCATION: Zambia
POPULATION: 11 million
LANGUAGE: English; Bemba; Nyanja; Tonga; Lozi; Lunda, Luvali and Kaonde
RELIGION: Christianity; Christianity with traditional African beliefs; Hindu; Islam; traditional African beliefs
RELATED ARTICLES: Vol. 1: Bemba; Chewa; Tonga

¹ INTRODUCTION

Although the 70 recognized ethnic groups who now reside in Zambia have distinct migration histories, different languages, and varying social, economic, and political organizations, they share a common colonial and post-colonial history. Zambia is a butterfly-shaped, landlocked country in southern Africa whose political boundaries are the result of European colonization of the region. The distinct groups who were living within the arbitrarily drawn boundaries at the time were first referred to as "Northern Rhodesians" under British domination. They became "Zambians" in the post-independence era.

For at least the past 500 years, the people of Zambia have been characterized by a high degree of migration. This migration, including urban to rural, rural to urban, and rural to rural, continues today. History and archeological evidence reveal that by 1500 much of modern Zambia was already occupied by Bantu-speaking horticulturalists who are the ancestors of many of the present day Zambians, particularly the Bisa and the Ila people. The Ngoni and the Kololo arrived in the region in 1855. Both groups came from South Africa as a result of the wars sparked by Chaka. The Ngoni and Kololo found the Tonga people already residing in the south, and the Chewa and Nsenga groups in the east. The Chewa and Nsenga had migrated earlier from the territory that would later be called Malawi. The Lozis trace their history to the Lunda people, and the Bemba trace their roots to the Luba people.

Prior to the arrival of the British, the nation's ethnic groups lived in relative isolation from one another. The first Europeans in the area were the Portuguese in the 16th century. David Livingstone traveled through the region in the 1850s and "discovered" Victoria Falls in 1855. He is credited with bringing British attention to the area. In 1889, the British South Africa Company (BSAC), under the leadership of Cecil Rhodes, received permits to trade and establish a government in what would become Northern Rhodesia. The BSAC maintained economic and political control of the region until 1924, when the British crown took over administration of the country by means of indirect colonial rule.

Kalomo, now a small district capital, was the first Capital of Northern Rhodesia, until 1911 when the capital shifted to the town of Livingstone. Livingstone remained the capital of Northern Rhodesia until 1935. Lusaka became the administrative center at that time. Between 1929 and 1939, four large copper mines in the north-central part of the country opened. Northern Rhodesia became a supplier of copper to the world market.

Along with many African countries, Zambia won its independence in 1964. It was a multiparty state until 1972, when it became a "one-party participatory democracy." The freedom-fighter leader Kenneth Kaunda was president of Zambia from 1964 to 1991. President Kaunda's greatest strength as a leader was his ability to unite the various ethnic groups of Zambia under his "humanism" platform of "One Zambia, One Nation." The first decade after independence was marked by the government's proclaimed commitment to socialism, and its investment in social welfare programs. This was the decade of prosperity when copper prices and people's spirits were high.

The historical importance of copper and the subsequent growth of the mining industry in Zambia, led to the rapid growth of Zambia's towns. From the end of World War II to the late 1960s, Zambia's urban areas, especially the Copperbelt and Lusaka, grew at phenomenal rates. Zambia soon became the most urbanized and industrialized of Africa's countries. In 1980, 43% of Zambians lived in town, compared to roughly half that for the rest of Africa. Currently it is estimated that 36% of Zambians live in urban areas.

Compared to Zambia's relative prosperity of the 1960s, overall economic growth rates throughout Africa have declined since the mid-1970s. Throughout the continent, economic troubles have increased due to a decrease in agricultural production and a continued, albeit slower, growth of the urban areas. Zambia's problems were compounded by the sudden drop in the world market price of copper in the mid-1970s. At that time, copper accounted for 94% of Zambia's export earnings. Over reliance by the government on copper revenues had resulted in little economic diversification in general, and tremendous neglect of the agricultural sector in particular. Subsidies on maize (corn) meal, which the urban population had come to rely on, compounded the agricultural sector's problems. The combination of all of these factors in Zambia led to what observers have called "the greatest—and most rapid—economic decline" among all the nations of sub-Saharan Africa.

In the wake of economic problems in the 1970s and 1980s, President Kaunda's government made several attempts at economic reform, all of which failed. In an attempt to revamp the economy, the 1980s saw the implementation of the Structural Adjustment Program (SAP). This approach, however, failed to achieve its intentions, as it left some 73% of the people in the country living in poverty. Throughout the 1980s, support for the government continued to erode. In October 1991, for the first time in decades, Zambia held multiparty elections. Long-time president Kaunda was voted out of power and President Chiluba, of the Movement for Multiparty Democracy (MMD), was voted in. In an effort to redress the economic recession, the MMD adopted the Economic Recovery Program (ERP). As of 2004, 67% of the population was still living in poverty.

President Chiluba's objectives were to diversify the economy, increasing the country's food supply and thereby reducing food imports. Because copper was the primary export and foreign currency earner, the agricultural sector has long been ignored. Only 7% of the land area is under cultivation, with corn, sorghum, and cassava being the primary subsistence crops. The agricultural system is still largely unreliable, as it is dependent on rainfall. In 2001, at the end of his second term, per the constitution, President Chiluba stepped down. Elections were held and the MMD maintained the presidency, with Levy Mwanawasa as the new president. President Mwanawasa provided a level of stability and continuity, which, combined with increasing commodity prices, led to investment and growth. In 2006

Zambia issued its Fifth National Development Plan, which has a vision for Zambia in 2030 to be a prosperous and stable middle income country. According to the United Nations' Millennium Development Goals, Zambia appears to be on the path toward achieving that vision.

² LOCATION AND HOMELAND

Zambia is a landlocked country of south-central Africa, with an area of 751,000 sq km (290,000 sq mi). Zambia is bordered on the south by Zimbabwe and Namibia, on the southeast by Mozambique, on the east by Malawi, on the northeast by Tanzania, on the north and west by the Democratic Republic of the Congo, and on the west by Angola. Zambia is dominated by a tropical savanna climate. Most of the country has a single rainy season. Zambia has four great rivers: the Zambezi, Kafue, and Luangwa in the south and east of the country; and the Luapula in the north. The rivers offer a valuable resource potential in the form of hydroelectric power. Zambia has a wealth of mineral resources, including copper, lead, zinc, and coal. The earth is characterized as red and powdery and not very fertile. The country was very rich in game before the advent of widespread poaching. Now many species are threatened.

Thirty-six percent of Zambia's 11 million people live in urban areas, with a trend indicating that urban to rural migration is growing. Most of the people are of Bantu origin (including Bemba, Tonga, Lozi, and Lunda). Some 98% of the population is African, with less than 2% being European and Asian.

³ LANGUAGE

The official language of Zambia is English, which also serves as the lingua franca (common language), but there are seven national languages. Bemba is largely spoken on the Copperbelt, where the majority of the labor force are Bemba. The Bemba people were largely recruited to mine copper because of their proximity to the Copperbelt. Nyanja is another commonly spoken language which comes from the Chewa and Nsenga people of Malawi, and now also from people of the eastern province of Zambia. Nyanja can be heard most commonly in the capital city of Lusaka because of the large eastern-province population that was recruited to work there by the British. The other national languages are Tonga, spoken largely in the south of the country, Lozi, spoken in the west of the country, with its origins in Botswana, and three languages are found in the northwest of the country: Lunda, Luvale and Kaonde.

⁴ FOLKLORE

Zambians have an active tradition of oral history and have passed proverbs, fables, riddles, and creation myths down through many generations. Even today, parables are in active use in conversation.

⁵ RELIGION

Some 72% of Zambia's population report that they are Christian or combine Christianity with traditional African religions. The remainder practice African beliefs, or are Hindu or Muslim. Zambia was officially declared a Christian Nation by President Chiluba, who was himself a born-again Christian. However, there is religious harmony in the country.

⁶ MAJOR HOLIDAYS

Official holidays include New Year's Day (January 1); Youth Day, March 12, Easter weekend (late March or early April); Labor Day (May 1); African Freedom Day (May 25); Heroes and Unity Day (the first Monday and Tuesday in July); Farmers Day (the first Monday in August); Independence Day (October 24), and Christmas and Boxing Day (December 25 and 26).

⁷ RITES OF PASSAGE

Initiation ceremonies for boys are practiced among a number of Zambia's tribal groups. These rituals commonly involve circumcision in the north western part of the country, as well as instruction in hunting and in the group's culture and folklore throughout the country. At puberty, girls are also instructed in the ways of their culture, and receive instruction in sex, marriage, and child rearing, as well.

Both traditional arranged marriages and modern marriages are accompanied by the *lobola,* or bride-price, a payment by the man to his fiancé's family. Many Zambians have church weddings., however traditional marriages are also very common.

Zambia is governed by both statutory law as well as customary law. These are sometimes in conflict with each other, such as in the case of property inheritance. Statutory law allows for the wife to inherit at least 20% the property of her deceased husband, while with customary law all property belongs to the family of the deceased husband. Many women have found it difficult to access their lawful right to property, due to the strong influence of customary law and the poor enforcement of statutory law.

Upon the death of a spouse, in-laws may require that a widow or widower undergo sexual cleansing (an act of intercourse with a member of the deceased family, often a brother or other close relative). In some areas it is said that this takes place to rid the widow or widower of the ghost of the deceased spouse. In the age of HIV and AIDS there was a lot of concern that this was increasing the transmission of HIV, therefore, many traditional leaders have outlawed the practice in their areas.

The funeral of a relative, even a distant relative, is considered an event of great importance that one must attend to show respect for the dead. However, in the era of HIV and AIDS, funeral traditions have been modified to ease the high cost of a funeral, as people were finding themselves overwhelmed with the higher than normal rate of mortality. Fortunately the introduction of HIV treatment has begun to slow this higher death rate.

⁸ INTERPERSONAL RELATIONS

In formal situations, Zambians address each other by their last names, prefaced by the terms for "Mr.," "Mrs.," or "Miss" in their local languages. Different greetings are used in different parts of the country. *Mulibwanji* ("How are you?") is common in the Lusaka area; *Mwapoleni* ("Welcome") is generally used in the Copperbelt region; and *Mwabonwa* ("Welcome") is a standard greeting in the southern part of the country. In most parts of Zambia, people commonly greet each other with a handshake, using the left hand to support the right, a gesture traditionally considered a sign of respect. People in the Luapula, Western, and North-Western provinces frequently use a greeting that involves clapping and squeezing thumbs. People often kneel in the presence of their elders or those who are their social superiors. Zambians, like many other Africans, often avoid eye contact out of politeness. It is considered unacceptable for men and women to touch when greeting each other.

⁹ LIVING CONDITIONS

Zambia's towns are bustling centers with a host of problems that are common to cities in general. Most of Zambia's urban residents live in poverty in low-cost, high-density housing areas, out of sight of the relatively few elite who reside in the few low-density, previously European sections of town. In the decade following independence, the population of Zambia's cities doubled in size. In those years the city represented opportunity and privilege. There was food on the table, transportation in the streets, and goods in the shops. Economic opportunities drew people from every province of Zambia, with the largest populations arriving in Lusaka from the Eastern Province (Chewa and Ngoni), and arriving on the Copperbelt from the Central Province (Bemba). The growing discontent in Zambia's large towns, as a result of the economic decline that began in Zambia in the mid-1970s, caused many Zambians to take up the challenge of leaving town and trying to make a living growing food. Recent renewed prosperity can be seen in the urban centers, especially Lusaka, where there is a housing boom, with a lot of new construction and high rents.

Average life expectancy in Zambia has dropped to under 40 years. This is largely due to HIV and AIDS and the opportunistic infections associated with it, such as tuberculosis

A Zambian woman and her sons grinding millet into flour. (Jason Laure)

and various cancers. The country also has a high rate of infant mortality—85 deaths out of every 1,000 live births, due to malnutrition, diarrhea, and childhood illnesses such as measles. Malaria is also a major cause of death in all age groups, but recent innovations in the use of insecticide-treated bednets, and household spraying are beginning to pay off with a reduction in the incidence of malaria.. The country has over 1,200 health facilities with 12 major medical centers, concentrated in urban areas, and smaller health centers throughout the country. Free medical care is provided for those who cannot afford to pay for it.

In rural areas, buses are the main mode of transportation. With the recent economic prosperity, more and more Zambians own cars and traffic is becoming a problem in some urban areas. Taxis are also available to urban-dwellers.

10 FAMILY LIFE

Urban and rural studies of Zambia, as well as census data, indicate that relationships between the sexes are difficult and tenuous. As heads of households, men assume authority within the home. The cultural double standards of condoning polygyny (having more than one wife) and men's extramarital affairs while expecting complete fidelity from women, causes friction in many urban households and contributes to the spread of HIV. What is more, men are not obliged to share their resources within the household, and their access to resources is greater than women's. Certain themes about relations between women and men recur in the Zambian literature. Customary practices continue to shape gender and generational relation-

ships in conflict with, or accommodation to, ongoing social and economic changes.

Regardless of whether descent is traced matrilineally (through the mother's line) or patrilineally (through the father's line), cultural norms and assumptions support male authority and power. A woman's access to productive resources is very often mediated through a man: her father, husband, uncle, or brother. Bride-wealth continues to be transferred at marriage—from the groom's household to the bride's. Kinship and family systems often influence the manner in which women are able to act as full participants in all kinds of relationships. In general, women's access to and rights over property and people are still much more circumscribed than men's.

11 CLOTHING

With the decline of the economy, and the growth of the world trade economy, there has been a tremendous growth in the second-hand clothing industry, or what Zambians call *salaula*. The term *salaula* means to "rummage through a pile." In this case, the term refers to the bundled used clothing that arrives via Tanzania and South Africa from the industrialized north, including the United States, Canada, Denmark, and the United Kingdom. During the colonial era, and in the decade following independence, Zambians could afford to produce their own textiles and wear tailor-made clothing. With the decline in the economy, they have been forced to purchase the first world's second-hand clothing from local traders, who purchase the large bundles and sell pieces individually. Zambians have a keen sense of style, nonetheless, and have been characterized by visitors and researchers in the past as being very stylish and particular about appearances.

There is little form of traditional dress, except in the western part of Zambia. The Lozi people appear to have been influenced by Victorian culture and women wear a dress made with local style *chitengi* cloth, but in a design with a long skirt and many petticoats. The men wear outfits more reminiscent of what one would consider traditional dress, with skins forming the man's short skirt, and a red beret on the head.

In other regions of Zambia, women commonly wrap a *chitengi* around their waist as a skirt. In many areas, men and women have adopted some of the more West African style of tailoring, using chitengi cloth. In both cases, these are not traditional to Zambia.

12 FOOD

The most important dietary staple is a dough or porridge called *nshima* generally made from cornmeal, but in some areas from cassava, or millet. It is typically eaten in combination with foods such as meat stew, vegetables, or a relish made from fish or chicken. Sweet potatoes and peanuts are commonly eaten in rural areas. Families that can afford it eat hot meals at both lunchtime and dinnertime, and a breakfast of porridge or bread and tea. However, in rural areas, especially during the seasonal period before the harvest, many families can only eat one meal a day. Beer is a popular beverage, both commercial and traditional brews, and alcohol abuse is a big problem.

13 EDUCATION

Education in Zambia continues to be modeled on the British system, where children begin in kindergarten and progress through the grades to high school. In an effort to provide basic education to all Zambian, public school is free, up to grade eight, but there are costs, such as the Parent-Teacher Association (PTA) fees and uniforms which can make education too expensive for some Zambians. As a result, illiteracy is high, totaling 27% (higher for women). Only 20% of Zambians have a secondary education, and only 2% are college graduates. Recently, with the increase in orphans and children made vulnerable due to HIV and AIDS, there has been a dramatic increase in open community schools, which do not require uniforms, but they also receive little support from the government and the standards can be quite low. In an effort to redress this, there is now a distance education radio program to support the community schools and to standardize the learning among those students.

14 CULTURAL HERITAGE

Dance, accompanied by drumming, xylophone, or thumb piano, plays an important cultural role in Zambia. Dances are generally done in two lines, with men in one and women in the other. Dances, which are traditionally associated with the casting out of evil spirits, are performed to celebrate personal milestones (such as an initiation) as well as major communal events. In addition to their own traditional forms of music, Zambians enjoy contemporary music and music from neighboring African countries. To support the arts in Zambia, the National Arts Council introduced an annual national arts awards ceremony, the Ngoma Awards, which recognize Zambian talent in all areas of the arts.

15 WORK

If work is defined as wage-earning, than the history of work in Zambia has largely been characterized by high levels of rural to urban migration. When the British arrived, the people residing in Zambia were farmers and/or cattle-herders. The people (primarily men) were recruited by the British to work in the cities for cash, either working in the mines or as domestic servants. For rural entrepreneurs and farmers, access to labor is varied and often influenced by gender- and age-related access to resources. Men are more often wage-earners and homeowners than are women, and they have greater access to cash than women do. Women often find work or are able to recruit workers through personal networks. The 1980 census reports that men are more economically active in the urban areas, while women are more active in rural settings. The census defines the working population as those engaged in agriculture, forestry, hunting, fishing, or production and other related occupations. Subsistence farming, which is not included under the category "work," was dominated by females, with 69% of all women engaging in subsistence farming compared to 44% of all men.

The Bemba are best known for their slash-and-burn cultivation practices, called *citimene*. The Bemba farm in the central region of Zambia where the soil fertility is low. The ashes left from cutting, piling, and burning the brush fertilize the soil, enabling farmers to grow grains (mainly). After a few years when the soil is depleted, the farmer will move on and repeat the citimene process. The MMD government has placed a high priority on increasing land productivity through foreign investment, and encouraging a largely unemployed urban sector to "go back to the land."

16 SPORTS

Soccer is the leading sport in Zambia, which entered a soccer team in the 1988 Summer Olympic Games in South Korea. Also popular are boxing, track and field, basketball and cricket. Golf is considered a game of the elite. The most popular sport among young women is a version of basketball called "netball."

17 ENTERTAINMENT AND RECREATION

In the rural areas of Zambia, the primary forms of recreation are drinking and traditional dancing. Urban-dwellers participate in social clubs, church activities, and volunteer groups. Other leisure-time pursuits include dancing at discos, and amateur drama (*ifisela*), as well as a variety of sports. Television is available to people living in the cities and larger towns.

18 FOLK ART, CRAFTS, AND HOBBIES

The people of the Northwestern Province of Zambia are known for their masks, which are made of bark and mud, with fierce faces painted on them in red, black, and white. A traditional art among Zambian men is the carving of wood sculptures, sometimes decorated with costumes made of beads. Zambian crafts include sleeping masks, various types of beadwork, and the weaving of baskets and *chitenges*, the national costume, which consist of brightly dyed cloth wrapped around the body. Some of the designs on Zambian pottery are thousands of years old.

Recently there has been an increase in the production of modern art in Zambia. This includes painting, sculpture in

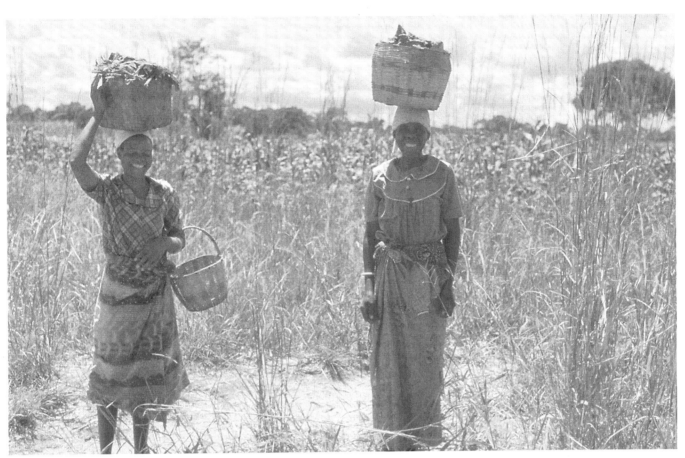

Kinship and family systems often influence the manner in which Zambian women are able to act as full participants in all kinds of relationships. In general, women's access to and rights over property and people are still much more circumscribed than men's.
(Cory Langley)

wood and stone, lithography, and multi-media installations. Famous Zambian artists include the naive painter, Stephen Kapata, and sculptor Friday Tembo.

[19] SOCIAL PROBLEMS

Poverty, crime, unemployment, rapid inflation, lack of health care and education opportunities, and housing shortages as well as a mushrooming informal economy are causing a growing discontent among residents of Zambia's towns. Pressure on the land, resulting in environmental degradation including deforestation and soil erosion, is a more immediate concern. Estimates indicate that of the 24 million hectares (over 59 million acres) of arable land in the country, only 6% is utilized. Land is currently being distributed to encourage development and investment .

[20] GENDER ISSUES

Zambian women have a relatively low socioeconomic and political status. They face multiple forms of discrimination and abuses, including gender-based violence and insecure property rights. For example, in a survey in 2001, more than half of the ever-married women reported being beaten or abused by their husbands.

On the positive side, the government has enacted laws to protect women and their rights. The government has established specialized units of the police to handle cases of domestic violence and in 2006 a cabinet minister was appointed for gender and development. Zambia has also ratified many regional and international treaties that require the government to eliminate violence and discrimination against women and to guarantee their rights to health, physical security, non-discrimination and life. One such international agreement was the ratification of the UN's Millennium Development Goals, which include national targets on gender equality and the empowerment of women. There are many civil society organizations that provide services and support to women, especially those who experience violence.

[21] BIBLIOGRAPHY

Amis, P. "Key Themes in Contemporary African Urbanization." In *Housing Africa's Urban Poor*, edited by Amis and Lloyd. Manchester: Manchester University Press, 1990.

Bates, R., and P. Collier. "The Politics and Economics of Policy Reform in Zambia." In *Political and Economic Interactions in Economic Policy Reforms*, edited by Bates and Krueger. London: Basil Blackwell, 1993.

Burdette, M. *Zambia: Between Two Worlds*. Boulder, CO: Westview Press, 1988.

Gann, L. H. *A History of Northern Rhodesia: Early Days to 1953*. London: Chatto and Windens, 1964.

Hall, R. *Zambia*. London: Praeger, Inc., 1965.

Kapland, I. *Area Handbook for Zambia.* Washington, DC: Foreign Area Studies of the American University, 1974.

Moyo, S. *The Southern African Environment: Profiles of the SADC Conference.* London: Earthscan Publications, 1993.

Mvunga, M. *The Colonial Foundations of Zambia's Land Tenure System.* Lusaka: National Educational Company of Zambia, Ltd., 1980.

Republic of Zambia. *2005 Population and Housing Census of 2000 Zambia.* Lusaka: CSO, 2005.

———. *Living Conditions Monitoring Survey.* Lusaka: CSO, 1998.

———. *Zambia Demographic and Health Survey 2001–2002.* Lusaka: CSO, 2002.

Roberts, A. *A History of Zambia.* New York: Africana Publishing Co., 1976.

—by L. Ashbaugh; revised by E. Serlemitsos

ZIMBABWEANS

PRONUNCIATION: zim-BAHB-wee-uhns
ALTERNATE NAMES: (Formerly) Rhodesians
LOCATION: Zimbabwe
POPULATION: 12.5 million
LANGUAGE: ChiShona; isiNdebele; English
RELIGION: Indigenous beliefs; Christianity; Islam
RELATED ARTICLES: Vol. 1: Ndebele

¹ INTRODUCTION

Internationally, particularly in the West, Zimbabwe (formerly Rhodesia) has been known for its rich tradition of stone sculpture and natural tourist attractions such as the Great Zimbabwe and Victoria Falls. Zimbabwe has a total area of about 400,000 sq km (150,000 sq mi). Before its colonization by Britain in 1896, the country was ruled by various autonomous ethnic kingdoms. The earliest people to inhabit the country were the San, sometimes referred to as the Qoisan or Khoisan (erroneously called "Bushmen"—this is a derogatory label). Their presence in the country can be deduced from the rock paintings scattered all over the country. After the San, the Shona arrived, who built stone walls in the region; the best-known of these are the Great Zimbabwe and Khami Ruins. Some of the well-known pre-colonial Shona kingdoms were the Great Zimbabwe, Munhumutapa, Torwa, Barwe, and the Rozvi.

Zimbabwe has been in a state of economic crisis since the early 2000s. The roots of the crisis date back to the mid-1960s and the era of African independence. In 1965, Ian Smith, the leader of Southern Rhodesia, declared unilateral independence from Britain, but imposed white minority rule, through the Unilateral Declaration of Independence (UDI). The UDI resulted in international backlash, including sanctions, and a guerrilla war, which lasted until 1979. More than 36,000 people died in the war and at least 15 million people were displaced. A peace deal was negotiated between Ian Smith's government, Robert Mugabe's Zimbabwe African National Union (ZANU) and Joshua Nkomo's Zimbabwe African People's Union (ZAPU).

Elections were held in 1980 and Mugabe became prime minister. In 1988, the ZANU and ZAPU parties merged into ZANU-PF, effectively creating a one-party state. In 1990, Mugabe's attempt to create a de jure one-party state failed, but despite that, in 1996, Mugabe succeeded in winning reelection on a platform of land reform. By 2000, Mugabe backed war veterans as they forcibly seized many of the white-owned farms. This led to shortages of commodities and a crippling of the economy.

The economic and political crisis has continued. Inflation is spiraling out of control. In January 2008, inflation was pegged at over 100,000%—the world's highest. Chronic food shortages, the collapse of basic services, compounded with over 20% HIV prevalence and corruption have led Zimbabwe to the brink of disaster. It remains to be seen if international pressure or negotiation will bring Zimbabwe back, or if collapse and chaos are inevitable.

2 LOCATION AND HOMELAND

Zimbabwe is situated in Southern Africa; it is one of South Africa's northern neighbors. It is located between 14° to 23°s and 25° to 33°e. By 2003, the country's population was estimated at 12.5 million—some 98% are African, and 2% are European, Asian, and mixed-race (sometimes referred to as "colored"). The geographic distribution of the population reflects the racial, ethnic, and economic make-up of the country. The rich farm land with favorable climatic conditions is inhabited and cultivated by the former colonial Europeans (whites), while Africans (blacks) cultivate poorer, overcrowded land. The industries in urban centers are controlled by the former colonial Europeans, Asians, and people of mixed race more than by Africans. Among Africans, those who live and work in the city are better-off economically than those who live in the countryside.

3 LANGUAGE

The African population of Zimbabwe is made up of at least 13 ethnic groups who speak different languages. Some of these ethnic groups are the Tonga, Kalanga, Nambya, Ndebele (who migrated from present-day South Africa), Shona (who migrated from present day northeast Africa), Shangani, Sotho, San (Abathwa), Dema, Shangwe, amaFengu, Sena, and Lemba. Two ethnic groups that have received much academic study and international visibility are the Shona and Ndebele. The Shona people make up over 70% of the country's population, while the Ndebele people make up less than 20%.

While these ethnic population groups have distinct cultures and languages, most people in the country speak at least two languages, including one of the three official languages: chiShona, isiNdebele, and English. All the indigenous languages fall within the so-called Bantu group of languages. Most of them are tonal languages.

These African groups also share some cultural practices pertaining to their social organization, folklore, religion, and historical experiences such as colonialism, pastoral economies, and the war of national liberation against British colonialism. Ironically, it was colonialism that provided the context within which most of the integration between the various ethnic groups occurred, particularly the educational, religious, and political systems. Even today, the education system has provided one of the means of developing a national culture that cuts across ethnic and racial boundaries.

4 FOLKLORE

Each ethnic group has its own historical heroes or heroines, legends, and myths that recount their origins, traditions, and history. Some of the heroes such as Mbuya Nehanda, Kaguvi, and Lobengula have become national symbols.

5 RELIGION

Historical processes have resulted in changes that have altered indigenous African life. Most families live in two worlds—the African and the European (or Western), and in their daily lives, they blend these two. Thus, while ancestral worship is the most dominant religious practice, Christianity and Islam have a stronghold in Zimbabwe.

Every ethnic group has its particular language, folklore, history, religion, cultural practices, cultural heritage, and folk

arts. All indigenous Zimbabweans practice some form of ancestral religion, and more than 75% of the population are also Christian or Muslim.

Some of the indigenous practices such as rites of passage, interpersonal relationships, family life, clothing, food, work, sports, and other forms of entertainment have borrowed some elements from European culture. Most of these changes are fostered by the education system. In essence, there is no longer what could be regarded as purely indigenous practices. However, some of the practices are heavily embedded in indigenous culture.

6 MAJOR HOLIDAYS

The various racial and ethnic groups of Zimbabwe share a number of holidays. There are about 12 public holidays observed nationally, as well as those observed by the various religious groups such as Muslims and Christians. There are no indigenous holidays observed nationally, but families may have special days in the year during which they remember their deceased relatives. The most important national holidays are Independence Day, April 18; Workers' Day, May 1; Africa Day, May 25; Heroes Day, August 11; and Defense Forces' Day, August 12. These are generally celebrated under the supervision of the state. Government officials, including the president of the country, usually address the nation, especially on Independence, Heroes', and Defense Forces' days. These celebrations are accompanied by poetry, music and dance, and plenty of food and drink. Workers' Day is run by trade unions.

Easter and Christmas holidays are Christian holidays celebrated by Zimbabwean Christians. For most people, these holidays are an opportunity for rest or travel. They provide urban workers with the opportunity to visit their families in the communal lands (in the country).

7 RITES OF PASSAGE

While most Zimbabweans still practice their indigenous culture, that culture has been significantly eroded by Christianity and European colonization. Most of the traditional practices and beliefs associated with rites of passage are being replaced with Western ones such as baptism and birthday parties. The public celebration of rites of passage associated with birth and puberty has almost ceased, except among a very few ethnic groups such as the amaFengu (a subgroup of the amaXhosa people of South Africa). The amaFengu practice public adolescent male circumcision, to announce boys' graduation to manhood. There is one minor ethnic group, the Remba, who still practice infibulation, an extreme form of female genital mutilation. Marriage and death are still conducted in a manner that is very close to tradition. Marriage has remained a symbol of one's graduation into adulthood, while death and burial mark one's passage into the world of the "living dead," that is, ancestors.

8 INTERPERSONAL RELATIONS

Interpersonal relations in Zimbabwe are characterized by a combination of African and European cultural practices. These practices vary according to ethnic group, although different ethnic groups borrow some practices from one another. Each ethnic group has its particular greetings and visiting customs. In some groups, elders have to initiate greetings, while in others someone younger should initiate them. Some shake hands and some do not. Bowing one's head, and bending one's knees are other customs followed by some groups but not others. Whenever one visits another person's homestead, the visitor has to humble himself or herself before the hostess or host. Gesturing, including eye and facial expressions, are also an important aspect of greetings and interpersonal relations.

Another important aspect of interpersonal relations that has been affected by Western culture is dating. Any form of dating in Zimbabwe always has a mediator. Most people do not usually date a stranger, for obvious reasons. Dating a complete stranger is regarded as one of the recipes for disharmony in a relationship. Another explanation has to do with incest. People who do not know each other's family histories risk being involved in an incestuous relationship. However, these beliefs are changing because most young people meet and date in schools, colleges, and universities with no prior knowledge of each other's family background.

9 LIVING CONDITIONS

Not all Zimbabweans enjoy the same living conditions, particularly health facilities, housing, and transportation. Rural parts of the country are the worst, and cities enjoy most of the best conditions. However, the current economic crisis has heavily impacted both rural and urban areas. Most rural families do not have tap water. Transportation has become challenging in all parts of the country due to both fuel shortages and poor upkeep of the road system. Many parts of the country no longer have regular transport. The same is true for health facilities.

The whole country does not have adequate health facilities, but the rural population is hardest hit. Many communities do not always have access to a fully trained nurse let alone a doctor. Medicines are always inadequate. Some of the most common diseases are malaria, bilharzia, sexually transmitted diseases, tetanus, cholera, polio, and typhoid, and this is all compounded by the high HIV prevalence.

In both the city and the country, there are also local differences in the standard of living. In the city, the differences are based on race, gender, and class. People of European origin, Asians, people of mixed race, and elite blacks enjoy a better standard of living. In cities, women are the worst off because of the employment discrimination and related sexist practices that keep them from accessing resources such as land, credit, and housing.

10 FAMILY LIFE

Marriage and the family are the cornerstones of Zimbabwean society, regardless of ethnic group and race. Besides being an important rite of passage, marriage is regarded as a sacred practice. It is through marriage that the living are connected with their ancestors. It is within the family that gender roles are defined. Most ethnic groups have patriarchal families, in which women play a subordinate role. They are expected to serve their husbands, work for them, and bear them children. However, women have particular rights, and access to a form of power that is not usually expressed publicly. Families are usually headed by men, although there are a growing number of single-parent families headed by women. A typical family is made up of a husband and wife and at least two children. Traditional families are big, including five or more children, grandparents and children of relations. There are also what are known as extended families, composed of a father, a mother, and their son or sons with their own families.

Some men have more than one wife. It is not uncommon to find a man with 10 wives. One of the most common features of a Zimbabwean family, especially in the rural parts of the country, are animals. Most animals are not reared merely as pets but to serve other purposes. For instance, cats are kept in houses in order to kill pests such as mice and rats, and dogs are used to guard homes and for hunting.

11 CLOTHING

Most Zimbabweans do not wear traditional clothing as part of their everyday dress. European dress is the most dominant form of clothing in the country. There are very few people who wear traditional clothes on a regular basis. Traditional dress comprises a headdress, wraparound cloth, and ornamentation such as earrings, necklaces, and bracelets. This dress is usually seen during ceremonial and state occasions such as Independence Day and Heroes' Day.

12 FOOD

Zimbabwe's staple food is called *sadza*, made out of cornmeal and eaten with any relish, the most common being either greens or meat (particularly beef and chicken). Other traditional foods are milk, wild fruits, rice, green maize (corn on the cob), cucumbers, peanuts, beans, and home-brewed beer. While most of the utensils used are Western, some traditional utensils are still in use. Some of these are calabashes (gourds) that are used to store and cool water and milk; and clay pots

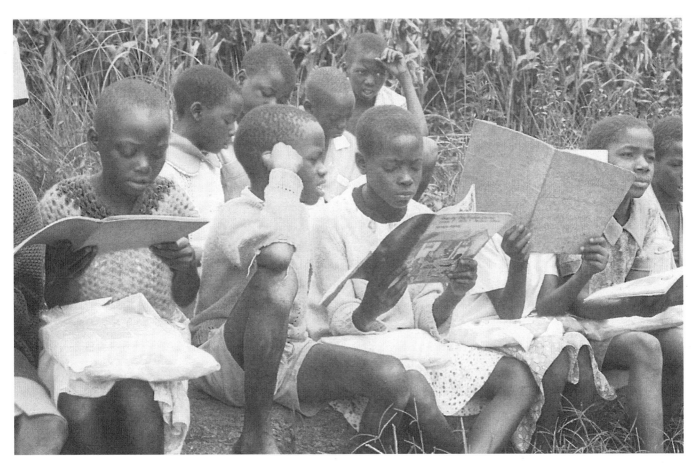

Education is regarded as an asset in a family since it is perceived as a passport to a good job. Zimbabwean parents invest a lot of money in the education of their children as a form of future investment, because children are supposed to look after their elderly parents. (Jason Laure)

used for cooking special foods such as meat, and for storing milk. Wooden plates and spoons are still in use alongside Western ones. Since colonization, Zimbabweans have adopted some of the European food or the foods introduced by Europeans, especially sugar, bread, and tea. Most families usually have a minimum of three meals: breakfast, lunch, and dinner. Nowadays, for breakfast people may eat porridge made out of cornmeal or oatmeal, cereal, or bread and tea. Leftovers from the previous day may be eaten for breakfast, too. For lunch, people usually have sadza with an accompanying relish, or any available heavy food. A similar meal might be eaten for dinner. However, foreign foods such as macaroni and cheese and mashed potatoes are now part of the staple diet. In cities, people can get meals from restaurants or take-out food places. Some of the fast-food places are Chicken Inn and Kentucky Fried Chicken.

There are taboos associated with certain types of foods. These taboos depend on a number of factors: family name, age, sex, and context. In some cultures, certain food is eaten only when it is in season. For instance, the amaNdebele discourage the eating of corn on the cob outside its season. Most ethnic groups also discourage the consumption of an animal, plant, or any other form of food that bears their family name. For instance, if one's family name is Nkomo (cattle: cow or oxen), one is not supposed to eat beef. Young children are discouraged from eating eggs. When a woman is menstruating, she is

not supposed to drink milk because it is believed that doing so might harm cows and their calves.

¹³ EDUCATION

Zimbabwe has traditionally been one of the very fortunate countries in Southern Africa to have basic education facilities, especially for young people. While there are some people who cannot read or write, historically most people have at least three years of elementary education. Education has been regarded as an asset in a family since it is perceived as a passport to a good job. Thus, parents traditionally spend a lot of money on the education of their children as some form of future investment, because children are supposed to look after their elderly parents. After independence, especially in the late 1980s, the country invested many resources in education. This resulted in huge numbers of students graduating from four years of secondary school education. There was also an increase in the number of students with six years of secondary school education, the requirement for university enrollment. On average, the highest level of education is four years of high school. However, there have been growing numbers of people with a college education. Recently, the economic chaos has also had an impact on the education system. Many of the private schools have closed and the quality of public education has plummeted.

The national adult literacy rate increased from about 62% in 1982 to about 90% by 2004. The adult literacy rate is higher in urban areas than in rural areas. In both rural and urban areas, there are more literate males than females, and more males than females attain higher education levels. Attendance is mandatory for primary levels. Primary education is 7 years; secondary school, 6 years; college, about 2 to 3 years; and university at least 3 years to 7 for medical school.

University or college education gives one's family pride and happiness. However, the education system reflects the cultural and economic practices of Zimbabwean society. Most Africans in the country believe in educating sons rather than daughters because when daughters marry, they take family resources to another family.

14 CULTURAL HERITAGE

Zimbabwe has a very rich tradition of the arts, including music, dance, fine art and crafts, and literature. Traditionally, Africans transmitted knowledge through the arts, especially through music and dance. Music and dance were, and to some extent are still, part of ceremonial celebrations and rites of passage. Other media continue to be used as forms of communication, such as praise songs (an equivalent of poems), stories and proverbs.

15 WORK

Traditionally, work is defined along gender lines. Most domestic work such as cooking, brewing, and housekeeping is performed by women, while men work outside the home tending cattle, hunting and cultivating land. However, women also participate in agricultural work, by performing tasks that are defined as "light," such as planting and cultivation. These roles are changing, however. Men help with some of the roles that were previously set aside for women, and women and girls now herd and milk cattle. In the early days of colonization, some families did not allow women to engage in waged employment in the city, mines, or commercial farms. The colonial state also did not allow the employment of women, especially black women, in wage-labor. However, despite these constraints, women found their way into cities to seek work. The independence government introduced legislation that abolished labor discrimination against women. As a result, the number of women in waged labor, such as factories, corporate, and government positions, increased. There is still a lot to be done, however, for women and the disabled to improve their opportunities.

16 SPORTS

The country's national sport is soccer. The Zimbabwe national soccer team is one of the rising soccer powerhouses in Southern Africa, if not in all of Africa. The team participates in the African Cup and World Cup competitions quite regularly. There are a handful of Zimbabweans who play on European soccer teams, especially in Britain, Germany, and Belgium. Other sports are track-and-field, golf, cricket, rugby, wrestling, boxing, netball (women's), tennis, and horse-racing. Sports in Zimbabwe are organized and funded along racial lines. Soccer, boxing, wrestling, and track-and-field are popular among Africans, while Europeans prefer golf, cricket, rugby, tennis, and horse-racing. However, people from either race cross over to other sports that are not common in their community.

Before colonization, people played indigenous games such as hide-and-seek, and engaged in various hobbies for amusement. Boys, while herding cattle, ran races or mounted small bulls, and played a type of stone game called *intsoro* or *tsoro*. Girls also had their own games such as *nhoda*, another kind of stone game. Today, most of the sports and games played are a mixture of indigenous and foreign ones. This has come about through the influence of schools and the mass media.

17 ENTERTAINMENT AND RECREATION

Traditional forms of entertainment such as drinking, singing, and dancing have persisted in contemporary society. Traditional ceremonies, state functions, and rites of passage also serve as entertainment. Race, class, and geographical location shape one's form of entertainment or recreation. Europeans (whites) have their own forms of entertainment such as going to movies, horseracing and riding, bird watching, stamp collecting, boating, watching plays, flying kites, and going to concerts. The concerts that whites and Asians go to are usually different from those that Africans attend.

Children have their own forms of entertainment and hobbies that are developed through the school system and the mass media, especially radio and television. They watch a lot of television and listen to Top 40 radio. Most of the television programs, videotapes, and films come from the United Kingdom and the United States. Children in Zimbabwe also play video and computer games. Zimbabwe is one of the dumping grounds of cheap and old popular culture products from the United States and the United Kingdom, such as TV shows like *Dallas* and *Falcon Crest,* professional wrestling, and soccer games. As a result, young people dress and try to imitate the lifestyles of musicians and actors from these two countries, especially African American performers. They also listen to local and regional pop artists, especially those from South Africa and the Democratic Republic of the Congo. Some of the local well-known musicians are Oliver Mutukuzi, Dorothy Masuka, Thomas Mapfumo, Lovemore Majaivana, Bhundu Boys, and Andy Brown and Storm. Two internationally known films have come from Zimbabwe: *Neria,* a story about a woman whose property is about to be taken away from her by the relatives of her deceased husband; and *Jit,* a serious comedy centered on a young man who is torn between Western life and his ancestors.

18 FOLK ART, CRAFTS, AND HOBBIES

Zimbabwe is well known for its folk arts, particularly stone sculpture and woodcarving. Stone sculpture is a Shona tradition, while mat making and related arts and crafts are popular among the Ndebele, Kalanga, and Nambya people. Among the most-practiced arts in the past were house-decorating, beadwork, tie-dyeing material, mat- and basket-making, and iron-smelting. Pre-colonial Zimbabweans made weapons, hoes, and other tools for domestic use, such as knives from iron. Wild cotton and wild bark were used to weave mats, dresses, beehives, food containers, and water coolers. Baskets, storage containers, chairs, fish traps, carpets, and sleeping mats were and are made from cane, reed, grass, sisal, and related materials, both for domestic use and for sale.

Some of the traditional arts and crafts have continued to be used and adapted to the present. This can be seen in urban toys such as wire bicycles, hats, pieces of sculpture sold at airports, and related crafts, as well as popular culture such as music. Some dances and crafts are now used to attract and entertain tourists at places such as Victoria Falls.

19 SOCIAL PROBLEMS

Despite the long strides that Zimbabwe has made in terms of building a democratic society, since the 2000s, these gains have been undermined. Soon after independence in the early 1980s, there was a lot of political instability and violation of human rights in the southwestern part of the country known as Matebeleland, where the government claimed there was some rebel political activity (dissident activity). In an attempt to deal with the situation, government forces killed many civilians and violated other human rights in the region. This continued until 1988. It is estimated that more than 5,000 people were killed. Opposition is a political right in Zimbabwe, but it is not tolerated by the current government. Most opposition parties have found themselves having to give up because the state blocks their access to the government-controlled mass media and other resources that any political party requires. Most minority parties cannot access state funding because of existing legislation. As of 2008 the political crisis had shed light on more human rights abuses and raised concerns that the abuses could escalate. In 2005 the government undertook mass evictions and the demolition of many informal structures, known as Operation Murambatsvina. The United Nations reported that this operation deprived over 700,000 Zimbabweans of their homes or their livelihoods, or both. It has been suggested that this operation was conducted to punish those who were not supportive of the ruling party. There are concerns that more repressive laws are being introduced to suppress criticism of government policies. For example, in 2005 the parliament passed the Constitutional Amendment Act, giving government the power to expropriate property without the possibility of judicial appeal and to invalidate passports for those considered a threat to national security. Concerns have been expressed that while much of the international community has expressed outrage over these developments, the African leaders have been more conservative in their response, opting for "quiet diplomacy."

Another area of human rights concern is the treatment of women. It is a well-known fact that Zimbabwe had become one of the countries in the world with a very progressive legal system as far as human and women's rights are concerned. However, this legal system has not been backed with action. The current government continues to harass and detain women as prostitutes, and has taken away some of the gains that women had made since independence. Some of the laws that empowered women, such as the Legal Age of Majority Act that gave women the right to marry whomever they wanted independent of parental approval are likely to be repealed.

Economic and social problems are intertwined. Since the late 1980s, the country has seen growing unemployment, especially among high school graduates. Coupled with the effects of the war of national liberation and consistent drought cycles, this has resulted in more social problems such as crime, drug and alcohol abuse, disease, and a depressed health system.

20 GENDER ISSUES

The constitution says that "every person in Zimbabwe" has fundamental human rights, regardless of race/color, tribe, place of origin, political or religious opinion, or gender, how-

ever, domestic violence and discrimination against women remains a problem.

Women are underrepresented in government and politics. In the year 2000 only 20 of the 150 members of parliament were women. While women may legally participate in politics without legal restriction, traditionally husbands, particularly in rural communities, direct women to vote according to the husband's preferences.

Violence against women, especially wife beating, is common. In 1998 more than 60% of the murder cases tried in the Harare High Court were due to domestic violence. There has been increased media reporting on sexual violence against women, but it has been noted that some High Court Judges impose lenient sentences in such cases.

The health status of women is worse than men. Women are more likely to be infected with HIV than men, due to both biological and cultural reasons. While women normally carry a heavier burden of care-giving, this has been intensified as a result of the high prevalence of HIV. While fertility is relatively low, with only 3.34 children per woman, maternal mortality is very high, with almost 600 per 100,000 live births resulting in the death of the mother.

Despite the efforts of government and an active civil society supporting the empowerment of women, women remain disadvantaged in society. Widespread illiteracy, economic dependency, social norms and traditional practices reinforce discrimination. Girls are less educated than boys, more likely to marry at a young age and to a person not of their choosing. They are also less likely to have their own land, formal employment, or to achieve economic independence. Furthermore, tradition does not respect decision making among women.

21 BIBLIOGRAPHY

Bourdillon, M. F. C. *The Shona Peoples: An Ethnography of the Contemporary Shona, with Special Reference to Their Religions.* Gweru: Mambo Press, 1976.

Bozongwana, W. *Ndebele Religion and Customs.* Gweru: Mambo Press, 1983.

Central Statistical Office. *Census 1992: Zimbabwe National Report.* Harare: Central Statistical Office, 1994.

Diary Notebook: Southern African Women Artists. Harare: Zimbabwe Women In Contemporary Culture Trust, 1995.

Dube, Caleb. *Ndebele Oral Art: Its Development within the Socioeconomic Context.* Harare: University of Zimbabwe, 1987.

Hamutyinei, M. A., and A. B. Plangger. *Shumo-Shumo: Shona Proverbial Lore and Wisdom.* Gweru: Mambo Press, 1974.

Human Rights Watch. Human Rights Watch World Report, 2006.

International Crisis Group. CrisisWatch, 2008.

Kuper, Hilda, A. J. B. Hughes, and J. van Velsen. *The Shona and Ndebele of Southern Rhodesia.* London: International African Institute, 1954.

McCrea, Barbara, and Tony Pinchuck. *Zimbabwe and Botswana: The Rough Guide.* Kent: Harrap Columbus, 1990.

Spectrum Guide to Zimbabwe. Derbyshire: Moorland Publishing Co., Ltd, 1991.

—revised by E. Serlemitsos

ZULU

PRONUNCIATION: ZOO-loo
LOCATION: KwaZulu-Natal Province of South Africa, urban areas
POPULATION: 23.8% of South Africa's 47.4 million people are Zulu-speakers
LANGUAGE: IsiZulu (mother tongue)
RELIGION: Traditional beliefs, Christianity, and syncretic religions

¹ INTRODUCTION

For many people, the Zulu are the best-known African people. Their military exploits led to the rise of a great kingdom that was feared for a long time over much of the African continent. They have a royal line that can be traced back to Shaka, the king of the Zulu during the 19th century. Shaka built his kingdom from small tribes that resided in what is today the South African province of KwaZulu-Natal. The Zulu are the descendants of Nguni-speaking people. Their written history can be traced back to the 14th century, when they migrated southward from the east to settle in what is now South Africa. Archaeological excavations on early Iron Age sites indicate that people ancestral to the Nguni-speaking peoples of KwaZulu were settled there from about 1500. At that time, all the Nguni tribes of the area were autonomous; however, some were more powerful than others.

In the early 19th century a young prince, Shaka, from the Zulu tribe came onto the scene and welded most of the Nguni tribes into the powerful Zulu Kingdom. Shaka ruled from 1816 until he was assassinated by his brothers in 1828. During his reign, Shaka recruited young men from all over the kingdom and trained them in his own novel warrior tactics. After defeating competing armies and assimilating their people, Shaka established his Zulu nation. Within twelve years, he had forged one of the mightiest empires the African continent has ever known. Few leaders in history have accomplished so much so quickly. However, during the late 1800s, British troops invaded Zulu territory and divided the Zulu land into 13 chiefdoms. In 1906, a section of the Zulus under chief Bambatha attempted a rebellion against the British, but they were defeated by a better-equipped British force.

The Zulu never regained their independence. Throughout the mid-1900s they were dominated by different white governments, first the British and later on the Afrikaner. In the period leading up to South Africa's first democratic election in 1994 and continuing into the 21st century, the Zulu endeavored to regain a measure of political autonomy via the Inkatha Freedom Party. They have been unsuccessful, however, both with the National Party government and the African Nationalist Congress-dominated government. As of 2008, the president of the majority ANC party was Jacob Zuma, who is Zulu by birth.

² LOCATION AND HOMELAND

Approximately 75% of the Zulu-speaking people live in KwaZulu-Natal Province of South Africa, while the remaining 25% are scattered throughout the other South African provinces. KwaZulu-Natal is situated between 27° to 31°s and 29° to 31°e.

It borders on Mozambique in the north, Eastern Cape province of South Africa in the south, the Indian Ocean in the east, and Lesotho in the west. The provincial capital is Pietermaritzburg. KwaZulu-Natal constitutes 92,180 square kilometers (35,590 square miles), which is 7.6% of the total area of South Africa. It is a semi-fertile region with a flat coastal plain, highlands to the west, and numerous rivers and streams. The subtropical climate brings lots of sunshine and brief, intense rain showers.

Some 23.8% of South Africa's total population of 47.4 million are Zulu-speaking. While many Zulu still live in traditionally orientated rural communities, others have migrated to urban areas. However, links between urban and rural residents remain strong. A mixture of traditional and Western ways of life is clearly evident in the lives of almost all Zulu people. With urbanization, rural people have been affected directly and indirectly by modernization. Normal daily life for a 21st century Zulu is difficult to distinguish from that of other black people in South Africa.

³ LANGUAGE

The dominant language in South Africa is isiZulu, known commonly as Zulu. In KwaZulu-Natal, the most frequently spoken languages are Zulu and English. Zulu as a paralanguage is idiomatic and proverbial and is characterized by many clicks. The daily life of a Zulu person can be captured in the naming system of people, buildings, organizations or associations, events, etc. Every name has a meaning and may relate to the past, the present, or the future. For example, the name "Welile" means literally "a person who has crossed something" (the river). Figuratively, it means a person who has overcome obstacles.

The Zulu language is characterized by words that pertain to the details of life, making distinctions that are difficult for others to comprehend. It is also characterized by *hlonipha* (respect) terms. Addressing those who are older than oneself, especially elderly and senior people, by their first names is viewed as disrespectful. Therefore, terms like *baba* (father) and *mama* (mother) are used not only to address one's own parents, but also other senior men and women of the community.

⁴ FOLKLORE

The belief in ancestral spirits (*amadlozi* or *abaphansi*) has always been strong. These are the spirits of the dead. The Zulu people recognize the existence of a supreme being. God is known as uMvelinqangi (One Who Came First) or uNkulunkulu, because he appeared first. This supreme being is far removed from the lives of the people and has never been seen by anyone. No ceremonies are, therefore, ever performed for uMvelinqangi, and his influence on the lives of the people is not direct. Zulu people believe that the intermediaries between uMvelinqangi and the people on earth are the spirits of the dead. The deceased heads of families are supposed to return after death to watch over the destinies of those who remain behind. The spirits, in turn, act as mediators with uMvelinqangi. Death is believed to bring one nearer to that mysterious supernatural personage. Because the ancestral spirits are believed to watch over those left behind, those alive have to ensure that they do not offend them. The ancestral spirits are believed to be offended when people break away from accepted customs. This belief has contributed to the conservatism for which some Zulus are known.

Zulus believe in a long life that continues after death. Getting old is seen more as a blessing than an unfortunate or unwanted phenomenon. This is based on the myth that long ago people did not die but rather lived for years. According to this myth, the Creator did not think that people should die and spoke to a chameleon, saying, "Chameleon, I am sending you to the people. Go and tell them that they are not to die." Although the chameleon was very slow, the Creator did not mind. He waited for the reply. However, after walking a long distance, the chameleon saw wild berries and decided to stop and eat them. The chameleon convinced itself that the Creator would not find out. Unfortunately, the Creator saw the chameleon and became very angry. Now the Creator called the lizard, which came swiftly. Angry, the Creator told the lizard to go and tell the people that they were to die. The lizard sped off, passed the chameleon on the way, and delivered the message to the people. After a long time, the chameleon appeared, breathing heavily, and delivered its message. The people were very angry and said to it, "Why did you waste time? We have already received the lizard's message!" Thus, growing old among the Zulu is seen as a special privilege, signifying that the Creator is overriding the lizard's message. Elderly people are believed to be sacred and are thus always respected.

⁵ RELIGION

Ancestral spirits are important in Zulu religious life. Offerings and sacrifices are made to the ancestors for protection, good health, and happiness. Grave sites are sacred because that is where the dead (who in turn will become ancestral spirits) are buried. Ancestral spirits come back to the world in the form of dreams, illnesses, and sometimes snakes.

The Zulu also believe in the use of magic. Anything that is beyond their understanding, such as bad luck and illness, is considered to be sent by an angry spirit, either from an ancestor or someone bewitching them. When this happens, the help of a diviner or herbalist is sought. He or she, in turn, will communicate with the ancestors or use natural herbs and prayers to get rid of the problem. Kinship members are prohibited from practicing magic or bewitching each other.

Under colonialism, many Zulu converted to Christianity. Although there are a large number of Christian converts, ancestral beliefs have far from disappeared. Instead, there has been a tendency to syncretize traditional beliefs and Christianity. This kind of religion is very common, especially among urbanites. Besides these two types of religions, there is a third type: fervent Christians who view ancestral belief as outdated and sinful.

⁶ MAJOR HOLIDAYS

In addition to recognizing the national holidays of the Republic of South Africa, the Zulu people celebrate Shaka's Day every year in September. This holiday is marked by celebrations and the slaughtering of cattle to commemorate the founder of the Zulu Kingdom. On this festive day, Zulu people wear their full traditional attire (clothing and weapons) and gather at Shaka's tombstone, kwaDukuza in the village of Stanger, KwaZulu-Natal province. This is a very colorful day attended by both national and international dignitaries who represent their governments. *Izimbongi* (praise-poets) sing the praises of all the Zulu kings, from Shaka to Zwelithini, whose reign began in

1968. Zwelithini remained traditional king of the Zulu as of 2008.

⁷ RITES OF PASSAGE

Life among the Zulu is seen as a cycle that starts at birth, continues through puberty and marriage, and finally ends in death. All these stages are celebrated and marked by the slaughtering of sacrificial animals to ancestors. The first two stages are particularly celebrated. To Zulu traditionalists, childlessness and giving birth to girls only, are the greatest of all misfortunes, and no marriage is permanent until a child, especially a boy, is born. In olden days, relatives of a childless woman used to send her sister to the woman's husband to beget a new generation. When a child is born, the older women take great care in handling the umbilical cord and the afterbirth, which are buried near the birthplace. The new mother and her child are secluded for a time, usually until the navel string of the child falls off. During this period, the mother is believed to be polluted (unclean) and weak, and thus a possible source of evil influences. After a period of a month, a ritual ceremony is performed, to "introduce" the baby to its ancestors.

The next in the cycle of rites of passage is usually *umemulo* (the puberty ceremony), which entails a transition to full adulthood. This ceremony, which nowadays is performed only for girls, involves separation from other people for a period to mark the changing status from youth to adulthood. This is followed by "reincorporation," which is characterized by the ritual killing of animals, dancing, and feasting. After the cer-

Zulus celebrate Shaka's Day every year in September. This holiday is marked by celebrations and slaughtering cattle to commemorate the founder of the Zulu Kingdom. On this big day, Zulu people wear their full traditional attire. (Jason Laure)

emony, the girl is declared ready for marriage. The courting days now begin and the girl may take the first step by sending a "love letter" to a young man who appeals to her.

Zulu "love letters" are made of beads. Different colors have different meanings, and certain combinations carry particular messages. White beads are the symbol of love; black symbolizes darkness, doubt, or unhappiness; green represents weak or jealous feelings; pink signifies poverty; yellow symbolizes wealth; red signifies hurt and sorrow; and blue beads represent a happy dove that can fly over hills and rivers. Hence, a string of white and pink beads would express a young woman's love and her concern that the young man might not have the means to take care of her when they are married.

Dating for Zulu people occurs when a young man visits or writes a letter to a woman telling her how much he loves her. Sometimes the man may not be known to the woman. Once a woman decides that she loves this man, she can tell him so. It is only after they have both agreed that they love each other that they may be seen together in public. They usually hide their relationship from the parents, who should become aware of it only when the man informs them that he wants to marry their daughter.

Death and burial are not a family matter but involve the whole community. This is a time of unity and solidarity. Burial rites among the Zulu have a twofold purpose: first, to separate the deceased as painlessly as possible from the living; and second, to usher him or her into a marginal waiting period. After

death, the spirit of the deceased person is believed to wander about, in the veld or near the grave, until the *ukubuyisa* ceremony is performed, whereby the spirit of the dead person is integrated into the world of the ancestors. The *ukubuyisa* ceremony is only performed for men. A special beast is set aside by the members of the household to be slaughtered. The animal should be large enough to satisfy the deceased. A small, lean one might annoy him. On the appointed day and time, all men assemble in the cattle *kraal* (corral) where the beast is to be slaughtered. One of the oldest male relatives of the deceased recites the *izibongo* (praise-poems) of the deceased and also those of his fathers and forefathers. As he recites the praises of the dead, he implores the spirit of the departed one to return and look after his children still remaining on earth. The beast is then slaughtered.

8 INTERPERSONAL RELATIONS

In contrast to their reputation as fierce warriors, on a personal level the Zulu are very warm and amicable people. *Ubuntu* (literally, humanness, good moral nature, good disposition) shapes the everyday life of the Zulu people. This comes from a notion that a human being is the highest of all the species in the world. There are hundreds of proverbs written about ubuntu, relating to the treatment of people, good and bad behavior, pride, ingratitude, bad manners, moral degeneracy, conceit, cruelty, obstinacy, pretense, helping others, etc. Very often a Zulu will be heard remarking, "*Wo, akumuntu lowo.*

Akazi ukuthi lithatha osemsamo limbeke emnyango" ("Oh, that is no person, he/she does not know that it [lightning] takes the one at the back and throws him/her in front"). This saying is an apt warning to people who, because they find themselves in easy and comfortable circumstances, tend to ignore and ill-treat those who are less fortunate. Just as the action of lightning is unpredictable, so is the future. In other words, "He who is scorned today may hold the whip in his hand tomorrow."

"Sawubona" is usually enough of a greeting for strangers, but a formal greeting is more appropriate for those who are familiar. The formal greeting includes a three-times handshake, while asking about the well-being of the person and his or her relations *("Ninjani?")*. It is considered bad manners to greet people while they are involved in conversation. In these situations, raising the right hand is usually more appropriate. Taking leave involves the standard *"Sala /Nisale kahle"* ("Remain well"), with the other person responding, *"Uhambe /Nihambe kahle"* ("Go well"). It is customary for juniors and the young to initiate the greetings when they meet their seniors and their elders.

It is considered rude and pompous to refuse an offer, especially of food. A straight answer like, "No, thank you" is received like a slap in the face. An excuse of any sort will be more appropriate. It is also considered "inhumane" and an embarrassment to the host not to offer a visitor something to eat. Elders and seniors are always considered in the right and women are supposed to take an inferior or subservient position. Not following this traditional hierarchy would be considered "lack of respect". However, some of the *hlonipha* (respect code) behavior is losing ground with modernization.

9 LIVING CONDITIONS

In South Africa, living conditions cannot be divorced from local politics, and conditions for the Zulu are similar to those of other black people. As of the early 21st century, they can be categorized into two groups, namely the rural and the urban Zulu. Most of the rural areas do not have adequate basic services such as electricity, clean water, formal housing, transport, hospitals, or clinics. Urban Zulu live in the so-called black townships of South Africa and the areas fringing industrial cities. Their living conditions are, at least, better than those in rural areas. Urban Zulu constitute the middle class and their lifestyle is usually no different from that of other Western urbanites. Since the education available in rural black schools is inferior, the people in these areas are not equipped to migrate and seek a better life in the urban areas, where living conditions are better. Even if they migrate, most of them end up in the poor areas fringing cities. Democratization and modernization has brought far-reaching changes and Zulu-speakers are to be found making their mark in every walk of South African life–as star athletes, politicians, academics, and business people.

In the rural areas of KwaZulu-Natal, a typical Zulu homestead will be circular and fenced. The houses themselves are thatched-roof rondavels. Most households comprise extended families: brothers with their wives, unmarried sisters, children, parents, and grandparents all staying together in the same homestead.

10 FAMILY LIFE

Although the Zulu are aware of their immediate family, the term "family" *(umndeni)* includes all the people staying in a homestead and who are related to each other, either by blood, marriage, or adoption. As a sign of respect, parents and seniors are not called by their first names; instead, kinship names are used. The Zulu believe that first names are not important because changing such names is very easy, whereas patriclan names never change. To the question, "Who are you?" the answer given is one's surname rather than the first name.

The Zulu family is patriarchal, with a man not only being the head of the family but also the figure of authority. It is not unusual for young men to have as many girlfriends as they wish. If they can afford it, they can take more than one wife when they decide to get married. In the past, for a man to pass by a woman on the street without showing interest was viewed as an insult. Women were not supposed to go out and work, since it was a man's responsibility to care for and support them. However, the status of Zulu women is slowly improving with more women receiving education.

Marriage is exogamous. Marriage to any person belonging to one's father's, mother's, father's mother's, and mother's mother's clan is prohibited. If it happens, the *ukudabula* (literally, cutting of the blood relationship) ritual is performed. Once a man decides that he wants to marry his girlfriend, his clan group sends an *umkhongi* (a go-between) with *lobolo* to the girl's family to open negotiations. To an outsider, lobolo can be mistakenly viewed as a business transaction, but to the Zulu it is part of the gifts that pass to and fro between the "contracting" families. Modern lobolo is usually in monetary form and, on average, totals about $4,000. To show that this is not an economic exchange of women, the bride's parents also reciprocate with endless gifts. Only children born after lobolo has been handed over will be regarded as legitimate.

11 CLOTHING

The everyday clothing of a modern Zulu is no different from that of any modern urbanite. Traditional clothing, however, is very colorful. Men, women, and children wear beads as accessories. Men wear a garment, *amabheshu,* made of goat or cattle skin. It looks like a waist apron, worn at the back. They decorate their heads with feathers and fur. The men also wear frilly goatskin bands on their arms and legs. Women wear *isidwaba,* a traditional Zulu black skirt made of goat or cattle skin. If a woman is not married, she may wear only strings of beads to cover the top part of the body. If she is married, she will wear a tee-shirt. Only on special occasions, such as Shaka's Day and cultural gatherings, do Zulu wear their traditional clothes.

12 FOOD

Since the rural Zulu economy is based on cattle and agriculture, the main staple diet consists of cow and agricultural products. This includes barbecued and boiled meat; *amasi* (curdled milk), mixed with dry, ground corn or dry, cooked mealie-meal (corn flour); *amadumbe* (yams); vegetables; and fruits. The Zulu traditional beer is not only a staple food but a considerable source of nutrition. It is made from grain which is soaked, allowed to sprout, then dried, ground, boiled, fermented, and finally strained. The result is a whitish, not altogether homogeneous, beverage. Besides the nourishment it provides, it is socially and ritually important and is drunk on all important occasions.

The everyday staple food of the Zulu today is soft porridge, made of mealie-meal, with bread and tea for breakfast; leftovers or any available light meal for lunch; and for supper, which is the main meal, any curry and *uphuthu* (made by boiling mealie-meal in salted water for about 20 minutes). The Zulu uphuthu differs from that of the Sotho-speaking people of South Africa in the sense that the latter is like a hard porridge while the former is coarse.

On average two meals are prepared each day—breakfast, after which adults and children leave the household, and supper when everyone is back from school and work. During lunch time, people eat whatever is available. If there are no leftovers, lunch may consist of bread alone. In South Africa, bread has become a basic food for most black households because it is relatively inexpensive and easy to prepare.

Many traditional utensils are still used in the modern Zulu kitchen, but the main one is the calabash (a decorated gourd). It is used to store Zulu traditional beer. The kitchen and the preparation of food is women's domain. The preparation of beer is also a woman's duty.

The Zulu follow many food taboos. A newly widowed woman cannot prepare food until cleansing rites are performed. In the past, unmarried women were not allowed to eat eggs and chicken so that they would not embarrass their parents once they were married by stealing their in-laws' chickens and eggs. Sour milk was reserved for clan members only and not for outsiders.

Drinking and eating from the same plate was and still is a sign of friendship. It is customary for children to eat from the same dish, usually a big basin. This derives from a "share what you have" belief that is part of *ubuntu* (humane) philosophy.

13 EDUCATION

Illiteracy is high among most black South Africans. However, by the mid-2000s education in South Africa in general, and that of Zulu children in particular, was slowly improving. In the past, children had gone to school only if their parents could afford to send them. Schooling started at 7 years of age and continued until about 24 years of age. It is, however, difficult to estimate the actual number of years of schooling. Since education was not compulsory, pupils could take their time to finish matric (high school) and no teacher could tell them that they were too old to be in school. Passing matriculation was and still is regarded as a high achievement by the whole community. In daily conversation, people will talk about so-and-so having "finished schooling." After finishing matric, those parents who can afford it usually send their children to college. Although the literacy rate for South Africa as a whole is 86.4%, the literacy rate for the largely rural Zulu people is the lowest in the country. The traditional professions for Zulus who seek higher education were teaching and nursing, but other professions are increasingly being pursued by some students. Once the children achieve these levels, the parents feel that they have done their part and thus can "retire" and wait for their children to take care of them. The University of Zululand was exclusively for Zulu people until 1994, and few Zulu students enrolled elsewhere. But students now enroll wherever their career plans, financial resources, and practical considerations allow them to go.

Raising and educating a child is one part of the family cycle among the Zulu. Parents spend all they have to raise and educate their children and, in turn, the children take care of their parents and their own children when they start working. This becomes a necessary cycle, and a person who breaks it is viewed as a community outcast and one who has forgotten about his or her roots. Consequently, education is regarded as a personal achievement and also an achievement by the whole community.

14 CULTURAL HERITAGE

The Zulu are fond of singing as well as dancing. These cultural activities promote unity, especially when the occasion calls for a great degree of harmony within the group, e.g., in the anxious moments of happiness and sorrow, and at all the transitional ceremonies such as births, weddings, and deaths. All the dances are accompanied by thunderous drums, the men are dressed as warriors, and they dance waving their clubs and thrusting their cowhide shields forward.

The tradition and folklore of the Zulu are transmitted through storytelling, praise-poems, and proverbs. These explain Zulu history and teach moral lessons. Praise-poems (poems recited about the kings and the high achievers in life) have become part of popular culture in South Africa.

15 WORK

In the past, it was only able-bodied men who were supposed to work. Before the 1970s, especially in rural areas, when a young boy was capable of sending a written letter and receiving a reply, he was considered ready to go and look for work. He might seek employment in the big cities or go to work in the gold mines in Johannesburg. Being able to read and write was once a kind of rite of passage. However, that has changed with parents and children striving to pass matriculation before entering the workforce.

In the mind of the Zulu, work should benefit either one's parents or children and siblings. The first paycheck (or at least a large portion of the first paycheck) is usually given to parents in return for blessings.

16 SPORTS

Soccer, called football in South Africa, is very popular with both young boys and men. Children learn the game by watching their older brothers play. Whenever boys are together and not engaged in some household or school activity, they play soccer. Having a ball (of any kind) means a game of soccer for a group of local boys. They have their own rules and usually everyone is familiar with them. In rural areas, where living standards are poor, the stake for a game can be two to five dollars. Whoever wins gets the money. The spectators are usually friends of the players. Adult soccer is played like any other soccer (football) in the world. Young boys, especially those who live next to big rivers, also compete in swimming.

Girls, if they are not at school, are expected to assist their mothers in the house. However, they can play games once they have finished their chores. Games change with every generation, but one of the popular games played by girls, especially in rural KwaZulu is *masishayana/maphakathi*. Two girls stand opposite each other, usually not too far apart. Another girl stands between them, facing the one who is holding a tennis ball. The idea of this game is to try to hit the girl standing in the middle with the tennis ball, while she tries to avoid being hit. If the ball hits her or touches her clothes, she is out. Being able to avoid being hit ten times earns the girl a point. Having the most points means winning a game and becoming the best player in your circle of friends. One sport that both girls and boys participate in is athletics (track and field), which is an organized school sport.

¹⁷ ENTERTAINMENT AND RECREATION

Ritual ceremonies, including transitional ceremonies, serve as part of the entertainment and recreation for the whole community. A formal invitation to any occasion where food will be served, like weddings and birthday parties, is not part of Zulu custom. They believe that food should be shared; thus, uninvited arrival at a celebration is not frowned upon but is considered an honor by the host. During these celebrations, singing and dancing will be enjoyed.

From a young age boys engage in stick fighting and as they grow older and more proficient this activity becomes an intensely competitive and macho pastime.

Television is very popular in urban Zulu households. Those who can afford to go to the movies do so. However, since electricity in rural areas is often not available, owning a television set is a luxury for rural Zulu. For urban teenagers, American youth culture, especially clothing and music, is very popular. Among the adults, *stokvels* (voluntary or common-interest associations) not only function as financial assistance associations, but also as occupational, friendship, and recreational associations.

¹⁸ FOLK ART, CRAFTS, AND HOBBIES

The Zulu, especially those from rural areas, are known for their weaving, craft-making, pottery, and beadwork. Women and children weave mats for everyday use, beer sieves, and baskets for domestic purposes. They also make calabashes (decorated gourds that serve as storage vessels). Men and boys carve various household objects and ornaments from wood and bone, such as headrests, trays, scrapers, household utensils, chairs, etc. Beadmaking is mainly women's work, because beads are believed to be a unique way of sending messages without being direct.

¹⁹ SOCIAL PROBLEMS

The Zulu terms *ubuntu* and *hlonipha* summarize everything about human rights. However, if these factors are studied thoroughly, it becomes evident that some individuals in Zulu society, particularly women and children, enjoy fewer human rights than others. KwaZulu-Natal has a history of struggle between the two political parties, the African National Congress and the Inkatha Freedom Party. People have been known to be killed, not only in fights between these groupings, but also between other factions.

Alcoholism and drugs are not serious social problems, especially among rural Zulu. The level of alcoholism and drug abuse is not high. *Dagga*, the most common drug, was smoked traditionally like a cigarette; it can be and is still grown like any other plant. However, with Christianization and since colonialism, dagga is forbidden and illegal. The use of alcohol is very low among rural females. Culturally, a woman who drinks alcohol and smokes cigarettes is regarded as lacking morals.

However, modern Zulu women in urban areas do smoke and drink alcohol.

South Africa no longer conventionally issues birth rate, health, mortality rate, and other statistics by community or race, but the HIV/AIDS rates are much higher for certain sections of the nation, such as the colored townships (townships where black South Africans live). For South Africa as a whole, the HIV/AIDS adult prevalence rate was 21.5% according to a 2003 estimate. This translates to about 5.3 million people who are living with HIV/AIDS. An estimated 370,000 people died from HIV/AIDS in 2003. However, the statistics for Kwazulu-Natal, where the Zulu people predominantly live, have consistently the highest among all South Africa's provinces.

²⁰ GENDER ISSUES

South Africa's constitution, in Act 108 of 1996, defines individual rights and protections. Equal rights for all citizens are guaranteed in Chapter 2 [9(3)], which specifically indicates that "The State may not unfairly discriminate directly or indirectly against anyone on one or more grounds, including race, gender …. etc". But the reality is that a significant percentage of the Zulu-speaking people still live in rural-traditional contexts. Elder/senior males are still considered to be always in the right and must be shown respect; females are regarded as inferior; women are not supposed to go out to work, as work is regarded as a man's responsibility; polygyny is still practiced; a woman can become a regent but does not succeed to become a chief or king (contrary to both the constitution and legislation); women, like children, do not generally enjoy full human rights.

However, with migration, urbanization, modernization, and democratization, change has taken place. Even in the rural areas where Zulu tradition still thrives there are minor signs of improved conditions for Zulu women.

²¹ BIBLIOGRAPHY

Bryant, A. T. *The Zulu People*. Pietermaritzburg: Shuter & Shooter, 1949.

———. *Zulu Medicine and Medicine-Men*. Cape Town: C. Struik, 1970.

Guy, Jeff. *Remembering the Rebellion: The Zulu Uprising of 1906*. Scottsville, South Africa: University of KwaZulu-Natal Press, 2006.

Hammond-Tooke, W. D. (ed). *The Bantu-speaking Peoples of Southern Africa*. London: Routledge & Kegan Paul, 1974.

Haskins, J., et al. *From Afar to Zulu*. New York: Walker and Company, 1995.

Krige, E.J. *The Social System of the Zulus*. Pietermaritzburg: Shuter & Shooter, 1965.

Lock, Ron. *Zulu Vanquished: The Destruction of the Zulu Kingdom*. Mechanicsburg, PA: Stackpole Books, 2005.

West, M. *Abantu*. Cape Town: C. Struik Publishers, 1976.

— revised by M. de Jongh

GLOSSARY

a capella: singing without musical accompaniment.

aboriginal: the first inhabitants of a country. A species of animals or plants which originated within a given area.

acupuncture: ancient practice of treating disease or relieving pain by inserting needles into pressure points on the body. The Chinese are associated with this medical treatment.

adobe: a clay from which bricks are made for use in making houses.

adult literacy: the capacity of adults to read and write.

agglutinative tongue: a language in which the suffixes and prefixes to words retain a certain independence of one another and of the stem to which they are added. Turkish is an example of an agglutinative tongue.

agrarian economy: an economy where agriculture is the dominant form of economic activity.

active volcano: a large rock mass formed by the expulsion of molten rock, or lava, which periodically erupts.

acute accent: a mark (´) used to denote accentual stress of a single sound.

agglutinative tongue: a language in which the suffixes and prefixes to words retain a certain independence of one another and of the stem to which they are added. Turkish is an example of an agglutinative tongue.

agrarian economy: an economy where agriculture is the dominant form of economic activity.

agrarian society: a society where agriculture dominates the day-to-day activities of the population.

All Saints' Day: a Christian holiday on 1 November (a public holiday in many countries). Saints and martyrs who have no special festival are commemorated. In the Middle Ages, it was known as All Hallows' Day; the evening of the previous day, October 31, was called All Hallow Even, from which the secular holiday Halloween is derived.

All Souls' Day: a Christian holiday. This day, 2 November, is dedicated to prayer for the repose of the souls of the dead.

allies: groups or persons who are united in a common purpose. Typically used to describe nations that have joined together to fight a common enemy in war.

Altaic language family: a family of languages spoken by people in portions of northern and eastern Europe, and nearly the whole of northern and central Asia, together with some other regions, and divided into five branches, the Ugrian or Finno-Hungarian, Samoyed, Turkish, Mongolian, and Tungus.

altoplano: refers to the high plains of South American mountain ranges on the Pacific coast.

Amerindian: a contraction of the two words, American Indian. It describes native peoples of North, South, or Central America.

Amerindian language group: the language groups of the American Indians.

Amish: Anabaptist Protestants originally from Germany. Settled in Pennsylvania and the American Midwest.

Anabaptist: Christian sect that was founded in Switzerland during the 16th century. Rejected infant baptism as invalid.

ancestor worship: the worship of one's ancestors.

Anglican: pertaining to or connected with the Church of England.

animism: the belief that natural objects and phenomena have souls or innate spiritual powers.

anthropologist: one who studies the characteristics, customs, and development of mankind.

anti-miscegenation laws: prohibition of marriage or sexual relations between men and women of different races.

anti-Semitism: agitation, persecution, or discrimination (physical, emotional, economic, political, or otherwise) directed against the Jews.

apartheid: the past governmental policy in the Republic of South Africa of separating the races in society.

appliqué: a trimming made from one cloth and sewn onto another cloth.

aquaculture: the culture or "farming" of aquatic plants or animals.

arable land: land which can be cultivated by plowing, as distinguished from grassland, woodland, common pasture, and wasteland.

archipelago: any body of water having many islands, or the islands themselves collectively.

arctic climate: cold, frigid weather similar to that experienced at or near the North Pole.

arid: dry; without moisture; parched with heat.

aristocracy: a small minority that controls the government of a nation, typically on the basis of inherited wealth. Political power is restricted to its members. Also may referred to any privileged elite of a country.

artifacts: objects or tools that date back to an ancient period of human history.

Ash Wednesday: a Christian holiday. The first day of Lent, observed 46 days before Easter, is so called from the practice of placing ashes on the forehead of the worshipper as a sign of penitence. In the Roman Catholic Church, these ashes are obtained from burning palm branches used in the previous year's Palm Sunday observation. (Palm Sunday commemorates the entry of Jesus into Jerusalem a week before Easter Sunday, and it begins Holy Week.) On Ash Wednesday, the ashes are placed on the forehead of the communicant during Mass. The recipient is told, "Remember that you are dust, and unto dust you shall return" or "Turn away from sin and be faithful to the Gospel."

Ashura: a Muslim holiday. This fast day was instituted by Muhammad as the equivalent of the Jewish Yom Kippur but later became voluntary when Ramadan replaced it as a holiday of penance. It also commemorates Noah's leaving the ark on Mt. Ararat after the waters of the Great Flood had subsided. In Iran, the martyrdom of Husayn, grandson of Muhammad, is commemorated with passion plays on this day.

assembly: in government, a body of legislators that meets together regularly.

Assumption: a Christian holiday. This holiday, observed on 15 August in many countries, celebrates the Roman Catholic and Eastern Orthodox dogma that, following Mary's death, her body was taken into heaven and reunited with her soul.

atheist: a person who denies the existence of God, or of a supreme intelligent being.

atherosclerosis: a disease of the arteries. Characterized by blockages that prevent blood flow from the heart to the brain and other parts of the body.

atoll: a coral island, consisting of a strip or ring of coral surrounding a central lagoon. Such islands are common in the Pacific Ocean and are often very picturesque.

aurora borealis: the northern lights, consisting of bands of light across the night sky seen in northern geographical locations.

Australoid: pertains to the type of aborigines of Australia.

Austronesian language: a family of languages which includes Indonesian, Melanesian, Polynesian, and Micronesian sub-families.

B

Babushka: a head scarf worn by women.

Baltic States: the three formerly communist countries of Estonia, Latvia, and Lithuania that border on the Baltic Sea.

Bantu language group: a name applied to the south African family of tongues. The most marked peculiarity of these languages is their prevailing use of prefixes instead of suffixes in derivation and inflection. Some employ clicks and clucks as alphabetic elements.

baptism: any ceremonial bathing intended as a sign of purification, dedication, etc. Baptisms are performed by immersion of the person in water, or by sprinkling the water on the person.

Baptist: a member of a Protestant denomination which practices adult baptism by immersion.

barren land: unproductive land, partly or entirely treeless.

barter: Trade in which merchandise is exchanged directly for other merchandise or services without use of money.

bilingual: able to speak two languages. Also used to describe anything that contains or is expressed in two languages, such as directions written in both English and Spanish.

boat people: a term used to describe individuals (refugees) who attempt to flee their country by boat.

Bolshevik Revolution: pertaining to the Russian revolution of 1917. Russian communists overthrew Tsar Nicholas II and ended the feudal Russian empire.

borscht: cold beet soup, topped with sour cream.

Brahman: a member of the sacred caste among the Hindus. There are many subdivisions of the caste, often remaining in isolation from one another.

bratwurst: seasoned fresh German sausage. Made from pork or veal.

bride price: the price paid to the family of the bride by the young man who seeks to marry her.

bride wealth: the money or property or livestock a bride brings to her marriage. *See* **dowry**.

Buddhism: the religious system common in India and eastern Asia. Founded by and based upon the teachings of Gautama Buddha, Buddhism asserts that suffering is an inescapable part of life. Deliverance can only be achieved through the practice of charity, temperance, justice, honesty, and truth.

bureaucracy: a system of government which is characterized by division into bureaus of administration with their own divisional heads. Also refers to the institutional inflexibility and red tape of such a system.

bush country: a large area of land which is wild with low, bushlike vegetation.

Byzantine Empire: an empire centered in the city of Byzantium, now Istanbul in present-day Turkey.

C

Cajun: name given to Canadians who emigrated to Louisiana from Acadia, the old name for Nova Scotia. Contraction of the name Accadian.

Calvinist: a follower of the theological system of John Calvin.

Candlemas: a Christian holiday. A national holiday on 2 February in Liechtenstein, this observation is now called the Presentation of the Lord, commemorating the presentation of the infant Jesus in the Temple at Jerusalem. Before a 1969 Vatican reform, it commemorated the Purification of Mary 40 days after giving birth to a male child in accordance with a Jewish practice of the time.

capital punishment: the ultimate act of punishment for a crime; the death penalty.

capitalism: an economic system in which goods and services and the means to produce and sell them are privately owned, and prices and wages are determined by market forces.

cash crop: a crop that is grown to be sold, rather than kept for private use.

caste system: one of the artificial divisions or social classes into which the Hindus are rigidly separated according to the religious law of Brahmanism. The privileges and disabilities of a caste are passed on to each succeeding generation.

Caucasian: the "white" race of human beings, as determined by genealogy and physical features.

Caucasoid: belonging to the racial group characterized by light skin pigmentation. Commonly called the "white race," although it can refer to peoples of darker skin color.

celibate: a person who voluntarily abstains from marriage. In some religious practices, the person will often take a vow of abstention from sexual intercourse as well.

censorship: the practice of withholding certain items of news that may cast a country in an unfavorable light or give away secrets to the enemy.

census: an official counting of the inhabitants of a state or country with details of sex and age, family, occupation, possessions, etc.

Central Powers: in World War I, Germany and Austria-Hungary, and their allies, Turkey and Bulgaria.

centrally planned economy: an economic system in which all aspects are supervised and regulated by the government.

cerebrovascular: pertains to the brain and the blood vessels leading to and from the brain.

chancellery: the office of an embassy or consulate.

chaperone: an older married person, usually female, who supervises the activities of young, unmarried couples.

chattel: refers to the movable personal property of an individual or group. It cannot refer to real estate or buildings.

cholera: an acute infectious disease characterized by severe diarrhea, vomiting, and often, death.

Christianity: the religion founded by Jesus Christ.

Christmas: a Christian holiday. The annual commemoration of the nativity of Jesus is held on 25 December. A midnight Mass ushers in this joyous celebration in many Roman

Catholic churches. The custom of distributing gifts to children on Christmas Eve derives from a Dutch custom originally observed on the evening before St. Nicholas' Day (6 December). The day after Christmas—often called Boxing Day, for the boxed gifts customarily given—is a public holiday in many countries.

Church of England: the national and established church in England. The Church of England claims continuity with the branch of the Catholic Church which existed in England before the Reformation. Under Henry VIII, the spiritual supremacy and jurisdiction of the Pope were abolished, and the sovereign was declared head of the church.

chaplet: a wreath or garland of flowers placed on a woman's head.

cistern: a natural or artificial receptacle or reservoir for holding water or other fluids.

city-state: an independent state consisting of a city and its surrounding territory.

civil law: the law developed by a nation or state for the conduct of daily life of its own people.

civil rights: the privileges of all individuals to be treated as equals under the laws of their country; specifically, the rights given by certain amendments to the U.S. Constitution.

civil unrest: the feeling of uneasiness due to an unstable political climate or actions taken as a result of it.

civil war: a war between groups of citizens of the same country who have different opinions or agendas. The Civil War of the United States was the conflict between the states of the North and South from 1861 to 1865.

coca: a shrub native to South America, the leaves of which produce alkaloids which are used in the production of cocaine.

cohabitation: living together as husband and wife without being legally married.

cold war: refers to conflict over ideological differences that is carried on by words and diplomatic actions, not by military action. The term is usually used to refer to the tension that existed between the United States and the USSR from the 1950s until the breakup of the USSR in 1991.

collard greens: a hearty, leafy green vegetable. Popular part of southern American and West Indian cuisine.

collective farm: a large farm formed from many small farms and supervised by the government; usually found in communist countries.

collective farming: the system of farming on a collective where all workers share in the income of the farm.

colloquial: belonging to the language of common or familiar conversation, or ordinary, everyday speech; often especially applied to common words and phrases which are not used in formal speech.

colonial period: in the United States, the period of time when the original thirteen colonies were being formed.

colonist: any member of a colony or one who helps settle a new colony.

colony: a group of people who settle in a new area far from their original country, but still under the jurisdiction of that country. Also refers to the newly settled area itself.

commerce: the trading of goods (buying and selling), especially on a large scale, between cities, states, and countries.

commodity: any items, such as goods or services, that are bought or sold, or agricultural products that are traded or marketed.

common law: a legal system based on custom and legal precedent. The basic system of law of the United States.

common law spouse: a husband or wife in a marriage that, although not legally formalized through a religious or state-sanctioned ceremony, is legally acknowledged based on the agreement of the two people to consider themselves married.

communicable disease: referring to infectious or contagious diseases.

communion: 1. The act of partaking of the sacrament of the Eucharist; the celebration of the Lord's Supper. 2. A body of Christians who have one common faith, but not necessarily ecclesiastical union; a religious denomination. 3. Union in religious worship, or in doctrine and discipline.

communism: a form of government whose system requires common ownership of property for the use of all citizens. All profits are to be equally distributed and prices on goods and services are usually set by the state. Also, communism refers directly to the official doctrine of the former USSR.

compulsory education: the mandatory requirement for children to attend school until they have reached a certain age or grade level.

condolence: expression of sympathy.

Condomblé: American name for the Yoruba pantheon of 401 gods and goddesses.

Confucianism: the ethical system taught by the Chinese philosopher Confucius. It was enlarged upon by his contemporary Mencius so that political systems would be tested with the same ethical standards. (*See* **Taoism**)

constitution: the written laws and basic rights of citizens of a country or members of an organized group.

consumer goods: items that are bought to satisfy personal needs or wants of individuals.

Coptic Christians: members of the Coptic Church of Egypt, formerly of Ethiopia.

Corpus Christi: a Christian holiday. This holiday in honor of the Eucharist is observed on the Thursday or Sunday after Trinity Sunday, which is the Sunday after Pentecost. In the Roman Catholic and Eastern Orthodox Churches, the Eucharist is a sacrament in which the consecrated bread and wine become the body and blood of Jesus Christ, a belief stemming from New Testament accounts of the Last Supper.

corrugated steel: galvanized metal with furrows that give added strength. This metal is often used as roofing materials on houses in tropical countries because of its strength.

coup d'état: a sudden, violent overthrow of a government or its leader.

covert action: secret, concealed activities carried out without public knowledge.

cricket (sport): a game played by two teams with a ball and bat, with two wickets being defended by a batsman.

criminal law: the branch of law that deals primarily with crimes and their punishments.

crown colony: a colony established by a commonwealth over which the monarch has some control, as in colonies established by the British Commonwealth.

Crowning of Our Lady of Altagracia: a Christian holiday in honor of Mary, this day is celebrated in the Dominican Republic on 15 August with a pilgrimage to her shrine. (Altagracia Day, 21 January, is also a holiday in the Dominican Republic.)

Crusades: military expeditions by European Christian armies in the 11th, 12th, and 13th centuries to win land controlled by the Muslims in the Middle East.

cuisine: a particular style of preparing food, especially when referring to the cooking of a particular country or ethnic group.

cultivable land: land that can be prepared for the production of crops.

cursive script: a style of writing in which the letters are joined together in a flowing manner.

Cushitic language group: a group of Hamitic languages which are spoken in Ethiopia and other areas of eastern Africa.

cyclone: any atmospheric movement, general or local, in which the wind blows spirally around and in towards a center. In the northern hemisphere, the cyclonic movement is usually counter-clockwise, and in the southern hemisphere, it is clockwise.

Cyrillic alphabet: an alphabet adopted by the Slavic people and invented by Cyril and Methodius in the 9th century as an alphabet that was easier for the copyist to write. The Russian alphabet is a slight modification of it.

D

Day of Our Lady of Mercy (Las Mercedes): a Christian holiday in honor of Mary, this observance on 24 September is a holiday in the Dominican Republic.

Day of Santa Rosa of Lima: a Christian holiday. The feast day in honor of the first native-born saint of the New World, declared patron saint of South America by Pope Clement X in 1671, is 23 August, but in Peru, she is commemorated by a national holiday on 30 August.

Day of St. Peter and St. Paul: a Christian holiday. This observance, on 29 June, commemorates the martyrdom of the two apostles traditionally believed to have been executed in Rome on the same day (c. AD 67) during the persecution of Christians ordered by Emperor Nero.

deforestation: the removal of a forest ecosystem.

deity: a being with the attributes, nature, and essence of a god; a divinity.

delta: triangular-shaped deposits of soil formed at the mouths of large rivers.

democracy: a form of government in which the power lies in the hands of the people, who can govern directly, or indirectly by electing representatives.

demography: that department of anthropology which relates to vital and social statistics and their application to the comparative study of races and nations.

desegregation: the act of removing restrictions on people of a particular race that keep them separate from other groups, socially, economically, and, sometimes, physically.

détente: the official lessening of tension between countries in conflict.

developed countries: countries which have a high standard of living and a well-developed industrial base.

diacritics: as in diacritical marks, a dot, line, or other mark added or put adjacent to a letter or sign in order to give it a different sound or to indicate some particular accent, tone, stress, or emphasis. An example of diacritical marks would be those used in dictionaries to aid in pronunciation of words.

dialect: One of a number of related forms of speech regarded as descending from a common origin. The speech pattern of a locality or social class as distinguished from the generally accepted literary language.

dictatorship: a form of government in which all the power is retained by an absolute leader or tyrant. There are no rights granted to the people to elect their own representatives.

direct descendant: the offspring in an unbroken line of ancestors.

divine origin: having originated directly, or by direct descendant, from a divine being.

dogma: a principle, maxim, or tenet held as being firmly established.

domicile: a place of residence of an individual or family; a place of habitual abode.

dowry: the sum of the property or money that a bride brings to her groom at their marriage.

druid: a member of a Celtic religion practiced in ancient Britain, Ireland, and France.

Druze: a member of a religious sect of Syria, living chiefly in the mountain regions of Lebanon.

ducal: Referring to a duke or a dukedom.

dysentery: painful inflammation of the large intestine.

E

Easter: the chief Christian holiday is Easter, the annual celebration of the resurrection of Jesus Christ. Like Passover, the Jewish feast from which it is derived, the date of observation is linked to the phases of the moon. Since the Christian calendar is a solar one rather than a lunar one, the date of Easter changes from year to year. Easter is celebrated on the first Sunday after the first full moon following the spring equinox; in the Gregorian calendar, it can occur as early as 22 March or as late as 25 April. The Easter date determines the date of many other Roman Catholic holidays, such as Ash Wednesday, Ascension, and Pentecost.

Easter Monday: a Christian holiday. The day after Easter is a public holiday in many countries.

empire: a group of territories ruled by one sovereign, or supreme ruler.

Epiphany of Our Lord: a Christian holiday. Traditionally observed on 6 January but now observable on the Sunday falling between 2 January and 7 January, this feast commemorates the adoration of the Magi, who journeyed to the place of Jesus' birth. In the Orthodox churches, however, it is the feast celebrating Jesus' baptism.

episcopal: belonging to or vested in bishops or prelates; characteristic of or pertaining to a bishop or bishops.

equestrian culture: a culture that depends on horses for its livelihood. Mastery of the horse is an essential part of the culture's identity.

escarpment: a steep cliff formed from a geological fault or erosion.

ethnographic: referring to the division of anthropology which studies primitive cultures.

ethnolinguistic group: a classification of related languages based on common ethnic origin.

exodus: the departure or migration of a large body of people or animals from one country or region to another.

extinction: dying out of a species of animals or a culture of people.

F

fauna: referring to species of animals found in a specific region.

Feast of Our Lady of Angels: a Christian holiday. This feast, on 2 August, is celebrated as a national holiday in Costa Rica in honor of the Virgin Mary. Pilgrimage is made to the basilica in Cartago, which houses a black stone statue of the Virgin.

fetishism: the practice of worshipping a material object which one believes has mysterious powers residing in it or is the representation of a deity to which worship may be paid and from which supernatural aid is expected.

feudal society: In medieval times, an economic and social structure in which persons could hold land given to them by a lord (nobleman) in return for service to that lord.

Finno-Ugric language group: a subfamily of languages spoken in northeastern Europe, including Finnish, Hungarian (Ugric, Magyar), Estonian, Lapp, and others.

flora: referring to native plant life in a specific region.

folk religion: a religion with origins and traditions among the common people of a nation or region; relevant to their particular lifestyle.

folk tale: an oral story that is passed from generation to generation. Folktales are cultural records of the history and progress of different ethnic groups.

free-market economy: an economic system that relies on the market, as opposed to government planners, to set the prices for wages and products.

fundamentalist: a person who holds religious beliefs based on the complete acceptance of the words of the Bible or other holy scripture as the truth. For instance, a fundamentalist would believe the story of creation exactly as it is told in the Bible and would reject the idea of evolution.

G

gastroenteritis: inflammation of the stomach and small intestines.

geometric pattern: a design of circles, triangles, or lines on cloth.

geriatrics: the study and treatment of diseases of old age.

Germanic language group: a large branch of the Indo-European family of languages including German itself, the Scandinavian languages, Dutch, Yiddish, Modern English, Modern Scottish, Afrikaans and others. The group also includes extinct languages such as Gothic, Old High German, Old Saxon, Old English, Middle English and the like.

glottal stop: a sound formed in speech by a brief but complete closure of the glottis, the opening between the vocal cords. It is a typical sound in certain British dialects.

godparent: a male or female adult who is asked by the parents of a newborn child to assume responsibility for the care and rearing of the child in the event of the death of the parents. Godparents sometimes contribute school tuition, gifts on birthdays and holidays, as well as take an active part in the child's life.

Good Friday: a Christian holiday. The day after Holy Thursday, it is devoted to remembrance of the crucifixion of Jesus and is given to penance and prayer.

Greek Catholic: a person who is a member of an Orthodox Eastern Church.

Greek Orthodox: the official church of Greece, a self-governing branch of the Orthodox Eastern Church.

H

haiku: a form of Japanese poetry, consisting of three lines. Each line has a specific measurement of syllables.

Hanukkah: a Jewish holiday. The Festival of Lights, corresponding roughly to the winter solstice, is celebrated over an eight-day period beginning on 25 Kislev, the third month. Also known as the Feast of Dedication and Feast of the Maccabees, Hanukkah commemorates the rededication of the Temple at Jerusalem in 164 BC. According to tradition, the one ritually pure container of olive oil, sufficient to illuminate the Temple for one day, miraculously burned for eight days, until new oil could be prepared. A feature of the Hanukkah celebration is the lighting in each Jewish home of an eight-branched candelabrum, the menorah. This festival, though not a public holiday in Israel, is widely observed with the lighting of giant menorahs in public places.

harem: in a Muslim household, refers to the women (wives, concubines, and servants in ancient times) who live there and also to the area of the home they live in.

harmattan: an intensely dry, dusty wind felt along the coast of Africa between Cape Verde and Cape Lopez. It prevails at intervals during the months of December, January, and February.

Hinduism: the religion professed by a large part of the inhabitants of India. It is a development of the ancient Brahmanism, influenced by Buddhistic and other elements. Its forms are varied and numerous.

Holi: a Hindu holiday. A festival lasting 3 to 10 days, Holi closes the old year with processions and merriment. It terminates on the full moon of Phalguna, the last month, corresponding to February or March.

Holocaust: the mass slaughter of European civilians, the vast majority Jews, by the Nazis during World War II.

Holy (Maundy) Thursday: a Christian holiday. The Thursday preceding Easter commemorates the Last Supper, the betrayal of Jesus by Judas Iscariot, and the arrest and arraignment of Jesus. In Rome, the pope customarily performs a ceremony in remembrance of Jesus' washing of his apostles' feet (John 13:5–20).

Holy Roman Empire: a kingdom consisting of a loose union of German and Italian territories that existed from around the ninth century until 1806.

Holy Saturday: a Christian holiday. This day commemorates the time during which Jesus was buried and, like Good Friday, is given to solemn prayer.

homeland: a region or area set aside to be a state for a people of a particular national, cultural, or racial origin.

homogeneous: of the same kind or nature, often used in reference to a whole.

homophonic: music that has a single part with no harmonies.

Horn of Africa: the Horn of Africa comprises Djibouti, Eritrea, Ethiopia, Somalia, and Sudan.

human rights issues: any matters involving people's basic rights which are in question or thought to be abused.

humanist: a person who centers on human needs and values, and stresses dignity of the individual.

hydrology: the science of dealing with the earth's waters and their distribution above and below ground.

I

Id al-Adha: a Muslim holiday. The Great Festival, or Sacrificial Feast, celebrates the end of the special pilgrimage season, or Hajj, to Mecca and Medina, an obligation for Muslims once in their lifetime if physically and economically feasible. The slaughter of animals pays tribute to Abraham's obedience to God in offering his son to the Lord for sacrifice; a portion of the meat is supposed to be donated to the poor. The feast begins on 10 Dhu'l-Hijja and continues to 13 Dhu'l-Hijja (14 Dhu'l-Hijja in a leap year). In Malaysia and Singapore, this festival is celebrated as Hari Raya Haji; in Indonesia, Lebaran Haji; in Turkey, Kurban Bayrami.

Id al-Fitr: a Muslim holiday. The Little Festival, or Breaking-Fast-Festival, which begins just after Ramadan, on 1 Shawwal, the 10th month, is the occasion for three or four days of feasting. In Malaysia and Singapore, this festival is called Hari Raya Puasa; in Turkey, Seker Bayrami.

Iemanja: Brazilian name for Yoruba river goddess, Yemoja. Represented as a mermaid.

Immaculate Conception: a Christian holiday. This day, 8 December, celebrates the Roman Catholic dogma asserting that Mary's conception, as the future mother of God, was uniquely free from original sin. In Paraguay, it is observed as the Day of Our Lady of Caacupé.

incursion: a sudden or brief invasion or raid.

indigenous: born or originating in a particular place or country; native to a particular region or area.

indigent: person without any means of economic support.

indigo: a blue dye that is extracted from plants.

Indo-Aryan language group: the group that includes the languages of India; within a branch of the Indo-European language family.

Indo-European language family: the large family of languages that includes those of India, much of Europe, and southwestern Asia.

indulgence: a Catholic blessing given for a person's soul after death.

infant mortality: infant deaths.

infant mortality rate: the number of deaths of children less than one year old per 1,000 live births in a given year.

infanticide: the act of murdering a baby.

infidel: one who is without faith, or unbelieving; particularly, one who rejects the distinctive doctrines of a particular religion, while perhaps remaining an adherent to another religion.

inflective: refers to a language in which differences in tone and pitch give meaning to words and indicate grammatical constructions.

interferon: a drug used in the treatment of cancer in Mexico.

Inuit: an indigenous people of northwestern Canada. They are sometimes mistakenly called Eskimos.

Islam: the religious system of Mohammed, practiced by Muslims and based on a belief in Allah as the supreme being and Mohammed as his prophet. The term also refers to those nations in which it is the primary religion.

isthmus: a narrow strip of land with connecting large bodies of water on either side.

J

Jehovah's Witness: a member of a Christian sect that believes that the end of the world is near and that God should establish a theocracy on earth.

Judaism: the religious system of the Jews, based on the Old Testament as revealed to Moses and characterized by a belief in one God and adherence to the laws of scripture and rabbinic traditions.

Judeo-Christian: the dominant traditional religious makeup of the United States and other countries based on the worship of the Old and New Testaments of the Bible.

Juneteenth: an African American holiday that celebrates the freeing of slaves in America. It is thought to coincide with the surrender of the Confederacy to the Union armies.

Junkanoo: a holiday celebrated around December in the Caribbean and South America. It also has been observed in the United States in Alabama. The holiday has West African origins. Also known as John Canoe and Yancanu.

K

kale: Another hearty, green leafy vegetable that is sometimes mixed with spinach and collard greens to vary the flavor of these vegetables.

khan: a title given Genghis Khan and his successors who ruled over Turkey and Mongolia in the Middle Ages.

kielbasa: seasoned Polish sausage. Made from beef or pork.

L

lagoon: a shallow body of water connected to a larger body of water. It is sometimes separated from the larger body by reefs.

lama: a celebrated priest or ecclesiastic belonging to that variety of Buddhism known as Lamaism. The Dalai-Lama and the tesho- or bogdo-lama are regarded as supreme pontiffs.

land reforms: steps taken to create a fair distribution of farm land, especially by governmental action.

latke: potato pancake.

Leeward Islands: northern islands of the Lesser Antilles in the Caribbean that stretch from Puerto Rico southward.

leprosy: an infectious disease of the skin or nerves which can cause ulcers of the skin, loss of feeling, or loss of fingers and toes.

life expectancy: an individual's expected lifespan, calculated as an average.

lingua franca: Originally, a mixed language or jargon of Mediterranean ports, consisting of Italian mixed with Arabic, Turkish, Greek, French, and Spanish. Nowadays, the phrase is used to denote any hybrid tongue used similarly in other parts of the world; an international dialect.

linguist: a person skilled in the use of languages.

linguistic group: a group of related languages.

literacy: the ability to read and write.

lox: kosher smoked salmon.

Lutheran: of or pertaining to Martin Luther (1483–1546), the reformer, to the Evangelical Protestant Church of Germany which bears his name, or to the doctrines taught by Luther or held by the Evangelical Lutheran Church.

M

macron: a horizontal mark placed over a vowel to indicate its pronunciation as long.

maize: another name (Spanish or British) for corn or the color of ripe corn.

Malayo-Polynesian language group: also referred to as the Austronesian language group, which includes the Indonesian, Polynesian, Melanesian, and Micronesian subfamilies.

mangrove: a kind of evergreen shrub growing along tropical coasts.

marimba: a type of xylophone found in Central and South America.

massif: a central mountain-mass or the dominant part of a range of mountains. A part of a range which appears, from the position of the depression by which it is more or less isolated, to form an independent whole.

matriarchy: a society in which women are recognized as the leaders of the family or tribe.

matrifocal: a society in which women are the focus of activity or attention.

matrilineal (descent): descending from, or tracing descent through, the maternal line.

Mayan language family: the languages of the Central American Indians, further divided into two subgroups: the Maya and the Huastek.

Mecca (Mekkah): a city in Saudi Arabia; a destination of pilgrims in the Islamic world.

Mennonite: a member of the Christian denomination which originated in Friesland, Holland in the early part of the 16th century and upholds the doctrine of which Menno Simons (1492–1559) was the chief exponent.

mestizo: the offspring of a person of mixed blood; especially, a person of mixed Spanish and American Indian parentage.

metamorphosis: referring to the shamanic practice of changing from a person to an animal.

Methodist: a member of the Christian denomination founded by John Wesley (1703–1791). The name was first applied to Wesley and his companions on account of their methodical habits in study and in religious life.

millennium: any one-thousand-year period, but also refers to a real or imagined period of peace and happiness.

missionary: a person sent by ecclesiastical authority to work to spread his religious faith in a community where his church has no self-supporting organization.

Mohammed (or Muhammed or Mahomet): an Arabian prophet, known as the "Prophet of Allah" who founded the religion of Islam in 622, and wrote The Koran, the scripture of Islam. Also commonly spelled Muhammed, especially by Islamic people.

Mongol: one of an Asiatic race chiefly resident in Mongolia, a region north of China proper and south of Siberia.

Mongoloid: having physical characteristics like those of the typical Mongols (Chinese, Japanese, Turks, Eskimos, etc.).

monogamy: the practice of marrying one spouse.

monolingual: speaking one language only.

monsoon: a wind occurring in the alternation of the trade-winds in India and the north Indian Ocean. They occur between April and October when the regular northeast trade-winds are reversed and, with occasional interruptions, the wind blows at almost a steady gale from the southwest. In some areas, as in China, the change of the monsoons is followed with storms and much rain.

Moors: one of the Arab tribes that conquered Spain in the 8th century.

Mormon: an adherent of the religious body the Church of Jesus Christ of Latter-day Saints founded in 1830 by Joseph Smith.

Moslem: a follower of Mohammed (spelled Muhammed by many Islamic people), in the religion of Islam.

mosque: a Mohammedan place of worship and the ecclesiastical organization with which it is connected.

mother tongue: a tongue or language to which other languages owe their origin. One's native language.

Motown: nickname for Detroit. A contraction of Motor City Town.

mujahideen or **mujahedeen:** *see* **mujahidin.**

mujahidin: rebel fighters in Islamic countries, especially those supporting the cause of Islam.

mulatto: one who is the offspring of parents of whom one is white and the other is black.

multicultural: awareness of the effect and existence of more than one cultural viewpoint within one's value system and world view.

multilingual: having the ability to speak several languages. Also used to describe anything that contains or is expressed in several languages, such as directions written in English, Spanish, and French.

mummify: ancient method used to preserve the dead. Associated with ancient Egyptian culture.

Muslim: same as Moslem.

Muslim New Year: a Muslim holiday. Although in some countries 1 Muharram, which is the first month of the Islamic year, is observed as a holiday, in other places the new year is observed on Sha'ban, the eighth month of the year. This practice apparently stems from pagan Arab times. Shab-i-Bharat, a national holiday in Bangladesh on this day, is held by many to be the occasion when God ordains all actions in the coming year.

N

native tongue: one's natural language. The language that is indigenous to an area.

Nobel Laureate: a person awarded a prize for lifetime achievement in literature, sciences, economics, or peace. Prize founded by Swedish industrialist Alfred Nobel, inventor of dynamite.

nomad: a wanderer; member of a tribe of people who have no fixed place or abode, but move about from place to place depending on the availability of food sources.

novena: a series of prayers in honor of a saint for a specific reason.

O

obsidian: a black, shiny volcanic rock, resembling glass.

official language: the language in which the business of a country and its government is conducted.

Ottoman Empire: a Turkish empire founded by Osman I in about 1603, that variously controlled large areas of land around the Mediterranean, Black, and Caspian Seas until it was dissolved in 1918.

outback region: the rural interior region of the continent of Australia. It is sparsely populated, mainly by aboriginal peoples.

overgrazing: allowing animals to graze in an area to the point that the ground vegetation is damaged or destroyed.

P

pagan: a person who worships more than one diety. Sometimes refers to non-Christians.

pagoda: in the Far East, a sacred tower, usually pyramidal in outline, richly carved, painted, or otherwise adorned, and of several stories. They can be, but are not always, connected to a temple.

Paleoasiatic languages: languages that date back to a prehistoric or unwritten era in linguistic history.

parochial: an institution supported by a church or parish.

parody: dance or song ridiculing a serious subject in a silly manner. Usually focuses on the person or people who dominate another cultural group.

Parsi: one of the descendants of those Persians who settled in India about the end of the seventh century in order to escape Mohammedan persecution, and who still retain their ancient religion. Also Parsee.

Passover (Pesach): a Jewish holiday. Pesach, lasting seven days in Israel and eight outside it, begins on 15 Nisan, at roughly the spring equinox, and recalls the exodus of the Hebrews from Egypt and their delivery from bondage. The chief festival of Judaism, Pesach begins with a ceremonial family meal, or seder, at which special foods (including unleavened bread, or matzoh) are eaten and the Passover story (Haggadah) is read.

pastoralist: a nomadic people who move with their herds of sheep or cattle, searching for pasture and water.

patois: a dialect peculiar to a district or locality, in use especially among the peasantry or uneducated classes; hence, a rustic, provincial, or barbarous form of speech.

patriarchal system: a social system in which the head of the family or tribe is the father or oldest male. Kinship is determined and traced through the male members of the tribe.

patrilineal (descent): Descending from, or tracing descent through, the paternal line.

patrilocal: a society in which men take the larger role in activities and receive greater attention.

peccary: a pig-like animal native to North and South America and the Caribbean Islands. Noted for its musky smell, sharp tusks, and gray color.

pentatonic: music consisting of a five tone scale.

Pentecost Monday (Whitmonday): a Christian holiday. This public holiday observed in many countries occurs the day after Pentecost (derived from the ancient Greek pentekostos, "fiftieth"), or Whitsunday, which commemorates the descent of the Holy Spirit upon Jesus' apostles on the seventh Sunday after Easter and is derived from the Jewish feast of Shavuot. It was an important occasion for baptism in the early church, and the name "Whitsunday" originated from the white robes worn by the newly baptized.

Pentecostal: having to do with Pentecost, a Christian holiday celebrated the seventh Sunday after Easter, marking the day that the Holy Spirit descended upon the Apostles.

peyote: the tops of the small spineless mescal cactus. Native to the southwestern United States and northern Mexico.

phoneme: slightly different sounds in a language that are heard as the same by a native speaker.

pierogie: a Polish dumpling made from pastry dough. It contains various fillings, such as meat and potatoes.

pilgrimage: a journey to a sacred place in order to perform some religious vow or duty, or to obtain some spiritual or miraculous benefit.

polygamy: the practice of having two or more spouses at the same time.

polygyny: the practice of having two or more wives and/or mistresses.

polyphonic: combining a number of harmonic sounds. Music that has more than one sound.

polytheism: belief and worship of many gods.

post traumatic stress disorder: psychological disorder that accompanies violent or tragic experiences. Known as shell-shock during World War I.

Prayer Day: a Christian holiday. This Danish public holiday is observed on the fourth Friday after Easter.

Presbyterian: of or pertaining to ecclesiastical government by elders or by presbyteries.

Prophet Muhammed: *see* **Mohammed**.

proselytizing: inducing or persuading someone to become the adherent of some religion, doctrine, sect, or party. To convert.

Protestant: a member or an adherent of one of those Christian bodies which descended from the Reformation of the sixteenth century. Originally applied to those who opposed or protested the Roman Catholic Church.

province: an administrative territory of a country.

Purim: a Jewish holiday. This holiday, celebrated on 14 Adar (Adar Sheni in a leap year), commemorates the delivery of the Jews from potential annihilation at the hands of Haman, viceroy of Persia, as described in the Book of Esther, which is read from a scroll (megillah). The day, though not a public holiday in Israel, is widely marked by charity, exchange of edible gifts, and feasting.

R

rabbi: a Jewish religious leader; head of a congregation.

racial integration: to remove all restrictions and barriers preventing complete access to society to persons of all races.

racially homogeneous: composed of persons all of the same race.

rain forest: a tropical vegetation in the equatorial region of the world which consists of a dense growth of a wide variety of broadleaf evergreen trees and vines.

Raksha Bandhan: a Hindu holiday. During this festival, which usually falls in August, bracelets of colored thread and tinsel are tied by women to the wrists of their menfolk, thus binding the men to guard and protect them during the year. It is celebrated on the full moon of Sravana.

Ramadan: a Muslim holiday. The first day of Ramadan (the ninth month) is a public holiday in many countries, although the religious festival does not officially begin until the new moon is sighted from the Naval Observatory in Cairo, Egypt. The entire month commemorates the period in which the Prophet received divine revelation and is observed by a strict fast from sunrise to sundown. This observance is one of Islam's five main duties for believers.

Rastafarian: a member of a Jamaican cult begun in 1930 as a semi-religious, semi-political movement. Rastafarians are usually lower class men who are anti-white and advocate the return of blacks to Africa.

refugee: one who flees to a refuge, shelter or place of safety. One who in times of persecution or political commotion flees to a foreign country for safety.

respiratory: pertaining to the lungs and other breathing passages.

Roman alphabet: the alphabet of the ancient Romans from which the alphabets of most modern western European languages, including English, are derived.

Roman Catholic Church: the designation of the church of which the pope or bishop of Rome is the head, and which holds him, as the successor of St. Peter and heir of his spiritual authority, privileges, and gifts, as its supreme ruler, pastor, and teacher.

Romance language: the group of languages derived from Latin: French, Spanish, Italian, Portuguese and other related languages.

Rosh Hashanah: a Jewish holiday. The Jewish New Year is celebrated on 1 Tishri, the first month. In synagogues, the sounding of the shofar (ram's horn) heralds the new year. Rosh Hashanah begins the observance of the Ten Penitential Days, which culminate in Yom Kippur. Orthodox and Conservative Jews outside Israel celebrate 2 Tishri, the next day, as well.

runic music: music that is ancient, obscure, and mystical.

Russian Orthodox: the arm of the Orthodox Eastern Church which was the official church of czarist Russia.

S

Sacred Heart: a Christian holiday. The Friday of the week after Corpus Christi is a holiday in Colombia. The object of devotion is the divine person of Jesus, whose heart is the symbol of his love for mankind.

Samaritans: a native or an inhabitant of Samaria; specifically, one of a race settled in the cities of Samaria by the king of Assyria after the removal of the Israelites from the country.

samba: a Brazilian dance and musical tradition based on two beats to the measure.

sambo: indicates a person of visible African ancestry. Familiar form of address for an uncle from the Foulah language of West Africa.

Santer'a: Christian religion with West African origins. It merges Christian saints with Yoruban dieties.

savanna: a treeless or near treeless plain of a tropical or subtropical region dominated by drought-resistant grasses.

schistosomiasis: a tropical disease that is chronic and characterized by disorders of the liver, urinary bladder, lungs, or central nervous system.

sect: a religious denomination or group, often a dissenting one with extreme views.

self-determination: the desire of a culture to control its economic and social development.

Semitic tongue: an important family of languages distinguished by triliteral verbal roots and vowel inflections.

Seventh-day Adventist: one who believes in the second coming of Christ to establish a personal reign upon the earth. They observe the seventh day of the week as the Sabbath and believe in the existence of the spirit of prophecy among them.

shaman: holy man or woman said to have the power to heal diseases. Also thought to have magical powers.

shamanism: a religion centered on a belief in good and evil spirits that can be influenced only by shamans.

Shavuot: a Jewish holiday. This festival, on 6 Sivan, celebrates the presentation of the Ten Commandments to Moses on Mt. Sinai and the offering of the first harvest fruits at the temple in Jerusalem. The precursor of the Christian Pentecost, Shavuot takes place on the 50th day after the first day of Passover.

Shia Muslim: member of one of two great sects of Islam. Shia Muslims believe that Ali and the Imams are the rightful successors of Mohammed (also commonly spelled Muhammed). They also believe that the last recognized Imam will return as a messiah. Also known as Shiites. (*Also see* **Sunni Muslim**.)

Shiites: *see* **Shia Muslim**.

Shintoism: the system of nature- and hero-worship which forms the indigenous religion of Japan.

Shivarati (Mahashivarati): a Hindu holiday. Dedicated to the god Shiva, this holiday is observed on the 13th day of the dark half of Magha, corresponding to January or February.

Shrove Monday and Shrove Tuesday: a Christian holiday. These two days occur just prior to the beginning of Lent (a term which derives from the Middle English lente, "spring"), the Christian season of penitence that ends with Easter Sunday. These are days of Carnival, public holidays of feasting, and merriment in many lands. Shrove Tuesday is also known as Mardi Gras.

shunning: Amish practice of not interacting in any way with a person who has been cast out by the church and the community.

sierra: a chain of hills or mountains.

Sikh: a member of a politico-religious community of India, founded as a sect around 1500 and based on the principles of monotheism and human brotherhood.

Sino-Tibetan language family: the family of languages spoken in Eastern Asia, including China, Thailand, Tibet, and Burma.

slash-and-burn agriculture: a hasty and sometimes temporary way of clearing land to make it available for agriculture by cutting down trees and burning them.

slave trade: the transportation of black Africans beginning in the 1700s to other countries to be sold as slaves-people owned as property and compelled to work for their owners at no pay.

Slavic languages: a major subgroup of the Indo-European language family. It is further subdivided into West Slavic (including Polish, Czech, Slovak and Sorbian), South Slavic (including Bulgarian, Serbo-Croatian, Slovene, and Old Church Slavonic), and East Slavic (including Russian Ukrainian and Byelorussian).

Society of Friends: a religious sect founded about 1650 whose members shun military service and believe in plain dress, behavior and worship. Also referred to as the Quaker religion by those outside it.

Solemnity of Mary, Mother of God: a Christian holiday. Observed on 1 January, this celebration was, before a 1969 Vatican reform, the Feast of the Circumcision of Our Lord Jesus Christ.

sorghum: a type of tropical grass that is grown for grain, syrup, and livestock feed.

St. Agatha's Day: a Christian holiday. Celebrated on 5 February, it is the feast day of the patron saint of San Marino. St. Agatha is also the patron saint of nurses, firefighters, and jewelers.

St. Dévôte Day: a Christian holiday. Observed on 27 January in Monaco in honor of the principality's patron saint, this day celebrates her safe landing after a perilous voyage, thanks to a dove who directed her ship to the Monaco shore.

St. James's Day: a Christian holiday. Observed on 25 July, this day commemorates St. James the Greater, one of Jesus' 12 apostles. St. James is the patron saint of Spain.

St. Joseph's Day: a Christian holiday. The feast day in honor of Mary's husband is observed on 19 March as a public holiday in several countries.

St. Patrick's Day: a Christian holiday. This holiday, observed on 17 March, is celebrated in Ireland to honor its patron saint.

St. Stephen's Day: a Christian holiday. The feast day in honor of the first martyred Christian saint is 26 December, the day after Christmas. St. Stephen is the patron saint of Hungary.

steppe: a level tract of land more or less devoid of trees. It is a name given to certain parts of European and Asiatic Russia, of which the most characteristic feature is the absence of forests.

stigmatize: branding someone as a disgrace because of his or her behavior.

straits: a narrow passage of water connecting two bodies of water.

stroganoff: Russian beef stew. Sauce made from sour cream and wine.

subcontinent: a landmass of great size, but smaller than any of the continents; a large subdivision of a continent.

subsistence farming: farming that provides the minimum food goods necessary for the continuation of the farm family.

Sudanic language group: a related group of languages spoken in various areas of northern Africa, including Yoruba, Mandingo and Tshi.

Sufi: a Mohammedan mystic who believes (a) that God alone exists, and all visible and invisible beings are mere emanations from Him; (b) that, as God is the real author of all the acts of mankind, man is not a free agent, and there can be no real difference between good and evil; (c) that, as the soul existed before the body, and is confined within the latter as in a cage, death should be the chief object of desire, for only then does the soul return to the bosom of the divinity; and (d) that religions are matters of indifference, though some are more advantageous than others, and Sufism is the only true philosophy.

Sukkot: a Jewish holiday. This ancient Jewish harvest festival, which begins on 15 Tishri, recalls the period in which harvesters left their homes to dwell in the fields in sukkot, or booths—small outdoor shelters of boards, leaves, and branches—in order to facilitate gathering the crops before the seasonal rains began. In religious terms, it commemorates the 40 years of wandering in the desert by the ancient Hebrews after their exodus from Egypt. The 8th day of Sukkot (and the 22d day of Tishri) is Shmini Azeret/Simhat Torah, a joyous holiday in which the annual cycle of reading the Torah (the Five Books of Moses) is completed and begun anew. Outside of Israel, Simhat Torah and the beginning of a new reading cycle are celebrated on the next day, 23 Tishri.

sultan: a king of a Muslim state.

Sunni Muslim: Member of one of two major sects of the religion of Islam. Sunni Muslims adhere to strict orthodox traditions and believe that the four caliphs are the rightful successors to Mohammed, founder of Islam. (Mohammed is commonly spelled Muhammed, especially by Islamic people.) (*Also see* **Shia Muslim**.)

surname: a person's last name. Generally different from his or her first name.

T

taboo: a system, practice, or act whereby persons, things, places, actions, or words are placed under ban, curse, or prohibition, or set apart as sacred or privileged in some specific manner.

taiga: a coniferous forest in the far northern areas of Canada, Alaska, and Eurasia.

Taoism: the doctrine of Lao-Tzu, an ancient Chinese philosopher (about 500 BC) as laid down by him in the Tao-te-ching.

Thaipusam: a Hindu holiday. A holiday in Malaysia, Thaipusam honors Subrimaya, son of Shiva and an important deity in southern India. The three-day festival is held in the month of Magha according to when Pusam, a section of the lunar zodiac, is on the ascendant.

Tibeto-Burman language group: a subgroup of the Sino-Tibetan language family which includes Tibetan and Burmese.

Tishah b'Av: a Jewish holiday. This holiday, which takes place on 9 Av, commemorates the destruction of the First Temple by the Babylonians (Chaldeans) in 586 BC and of the Second Temple by the Romans in AD 70. It is observed by fasting.

toboggan: a kind of sled without runners or a steering mechanism.

topography: an accurate drawing representing the surface of a region on maps and charts.

toucan: a brightly colored, fruit-eating bird of tropical America with a distinctive beak.

trachoma: contagious, viral infection of the cornea. Causes scarring in the eye.

tribal society: a society based on tribal consciousness and loyalties.

tribal system: a social community in which people are organized into groups or clans descended from common ancestors and sharing customs and languages.

tsetse fly: any of the several African insects which can transmit a variety of parasitic organisms through its bite. Some of these organisms can prove fatal to both human and animal victims.

tundra: a nearly level treeless area whose climate and vegetation are more characteristically arctic due to its northern position. Although the region attains seasonal temperatures warm enough to allow a thin layer of soil on the surface to unthaw enough to support the growth of various species of plants, the subsoil is permanently frozen.

tutelary: a god or spirit who acts a guardian that watches over a person or group of people.

typhoon: a violent hurricane occurring in the China Sea or Philippine region, principally between the months of July and October.

U

unemployment rate: the overall unemployment rate is the percentage of the work force (both employed and unemployed) who claim to be unemployed. The natural unemployment rate is the lowest level at which unemployment in an economy can be maintained and still reflect a balance of the labor market and the product market.

untouchables: in 19th century India, members of the lowest caste in the caste system, a hereditary social class system.

They were considered unworthy to touch members of higher castes.

urban center: a city.

USSR: an abbreviation of Union of Soviet Socialist Republics.

V

veldt: in South Africa, an unforested or thinly forested tract of land or region, a grassland.

Vesak: this last full moon day of Visakha highlights a three-day celebration of the birth, enlightenment, and death of the Buddha. It falls in April or May.

voodoo: a belief system which is based on sorcery and other primitive rites and the power of charms and fetishes, originating in Africa.

W

wadi(s): the channel of a watercourse which is dry except in the rainy season. Also called wady.

Windward Islands

Windward Islands: a southern group of islands stretching south to Trinidad. Part of the Lesser Antilles, but does not include Barbados.

Y

Yom Kippur: a Jewish holiday. The Day of Atonement, spent in fasting, penitence, and prayer, is the most solemn day in Judaism. It takes place on 10 Tishri.

yucca: a plant native to Mexico, Central and South America, and the southwestern United States. Can grow to the 12 feet in height.

yurt: a framework tent of stretched felt or skins. Associated with Siberia and Mongolia.

Z

Zoroastrianism: the system of religious doctrine taught by Zoroaster and his followers in the Avesta; the religion prevalent in Persia until its overthrow by the Muslims in the 7th century.

INDEX

The "v" accompanied by a numeral that precedes the colon in these index citations designates the volume number for *Worldmark Encyclopedia of Cultures and Daily Life, Second Edition.* Thus, v1 references are found in the Africa volume; v2 in Americas, v3 in Asia & Oceania, v4 in Asia and Oceania continued, and v5 in Europe. Page numbers follow the colon.